I0200160

TEXAS RANGER BIOGRAPHIES

RANGERS
Photo by
Jim Alexander
El Paso
9-24-18
Sergent J.C. Perkins.
A.J. Robertson
Edd. Hollebeke
J.D. McClelland.
S.R. Ikard.
Texas

Charles H. Harris III,
Frances E. Harris, and
Louis R. Sadler

University of New Mexico Press
Albuquerque

Printed in the United States of America

Library of Congress Cataloging-in-Publication Data

Harris, Charles H. (Charles Houston)
Texas Ranger biographies : those who served 1910–1921 /
Charles H. Harris III, Frances E. Harris, and Louis R. Sadler.
p. cm.
Includes bibliographical references.
ISBN 978-0-8263-4748-0 (cloth : alk. paper)
1. Texas Rangers—Biography. 2. Texas Rangers—History—20th century.
3. Law enforcement—Texas—History—20th century. 4. Frontier and
pioneer life—Texas. 5. Texas—History—1846–1950.
I. Harris, Frances E., 1940– II. Sadler, Louis R. III. Title.
F391.H283 2009
976.4'05—dc22

2009024361

Cover design: Mina Yamashita
Interior design and composition: Robyn Mundy
Typeset in Clearface 9.5/13
Display type set in Centaur

To Donaly E. Brice

ARCHIVIST EXTRAORDINAIRE

FOREWORD

EACH YEAR THOUSANDS of persons contact the Texas Ranger Hall of Fame and Museum in Waco to research the Texas Ranger service of specific individuals. Such are the history and deeds of this unique law enforcement agency that any personal link or heritage is considered prestigious. Having a Texas Ranger ancestor in the West is like having a Mayflower ancestor in the East.

Of these patrons, many are determined genealogists who arrive with briefcases full of research, clues and family folklore. Casual visitors to the museum will drop in to the Research Center and ask whether their great-great-granddad truly was a Texas Ranger. Texas Rangers, working "cold cases," seek information and the files of Rangers who worked crimes decades ago and are now "out of the system."

And then there are the more interesting contacts. Law enforcement officers from Britain have called asking if a "bloke purporting to be a retired Texas Ranger" making the rounds of the local pubs really was one? Enthusiastic fans of *Walker: Texas Ranger* and *Lonesome Dove* have asked, in all earnestness, to see the biographical files of their favorite *fictional characters*.

One of the most common first questions these researchers pose is "can we see the list of all Rangers?" Unfortunately, there is no single, comprehensive roll of all Texas Rangers, and compiling a complete list is likely impossible for a variety of reasons.

During the three centuries in which the Texas Rangers have served, many early records were destroyed by fires and floods or discarded by clerks, administrators and Rangers to make room for more recent files. Reconstructing the enlistment rolls of the Texas Rangers is an ongoing process, and every month the Research Center staff adds "new" Rangers to the biographical files as records surface or invaluable research—such as this work—is released.

Today there are two state-sanctioned archives that work closely to collect, preserve and make available the historical record of the Texas Rangers service: the Texas State Library and Archives in Austin and the Texas Ranger Research Center in Waco.

The Texas State Library and Archives in Austin (TSLA) is the primary historical archives of the State of Texas. Their massive holdings cover all of state government, including the largest holdings of official Texas Ranger state records. Each year the dedicated TSLA staff makes heroic progress in organizing this material, compiling finding aids and electronically posting enlistment rolls, pension records and related documents for reference. However, this record is not complete. Some records were never forwarded to the TSLA and its predecessors and there are other "unofficial" categories of Texas Ranger documents that are not within the primary focus of the TSLA.

The second archive of Ranger history is the Texas Ranger Research Center (TRRC) in Waco, a division of the Texas Ranger Hall of Fame and Museum. It was established in the 1970s with the goals of becoming the nexus of research into the Texas Rangers and augmenting the holdings of the TSLA. The staff strives to make researchers aware of the array of records and resources related to the Texas Rangers and to guide them in their research.

While the TSLA is charged with the formidable task of serving all of state government, the TRRC has the luxury of focusing solely upon the Texas Rangers. In recognition of its service, in 1997 the State Legislature conferred upon the TRRC the designation of official state repository for Ranger records and memorabilia, making it an official adjunct to the Texas State Library and Archives.

The TRRC actively collects copies of scattered Texas Ranger official records that have escaped the TSLA including items such as personal copies of Rangers' commissions, discharges, pension awards and various company reports. The staff also avidly collects a wide spectrum of items that are not categorized as state records: scrapbooks, personal photographs, mementos, deaccessioned case files and personal correspondence. It has an active program, funded by the Texas Ranger Association Foundation, to record and transcribe oral histories from retired Texas Rangers. And it encourages new research through an on-line magazine *The Texas Ranger Dispatch* and an on-line electronic library.

As Charles and Frances Harris and Louis Sadler have found, research into the Texas Rangers can be mind-numbingly complex. The amorphousness of the service during times of crisis and lapses in its official records lead to many animated discussions among scholars, avocational historians and descendents of Texas Rangers.

As the authors of this book note, only recently have devotees of Ranger history begun to examine issues such as ethnic and cultural diversity, who was or who was not a Texas Ranger and the "official" founding date of the Texas Rangers. This book adds valuable information, but the findings are not likely to gain universal acceptance. Ethnic heritage and classification of service are two examples of these discussions.

Until recently, popular folklore held that enlistment in the early Texas Rangers—and the command of Texas Ranger units—was restricted to Southerners of Anglo-European descent. In reality, issues of mutual defense, survival and political expediency often made allies and countrymen of racially and culturally disparate groups—at least in the short term.

Hispanic Texans, it has been revealed, have Ranger roots in all eras of the Texas Ranger service, beginning with Stephen F. Austin's pre-revolutionary Texas Rangers of the 1820s up to the current Chief of the Texas Rangers, Senior Captain Antonio Leal. Misconceptions about this abound, and news reporters and feature writers continue to contact the Hall of Fame asking how recently the first Hispanic was appointed a Texas Ranger.

Claims that Texas Rangers were "blood enemies" of all Native Americans are equally dispelled by the historical record. Apaches, Delawares, Cherokees and others served the Republic of Texas individually and in companies of tribally-mixed Indian Rangers. So effective and tenacious were these native contingents that Sam Houston personally eulogized Chief Castro—a fallen Lipan Apache Texas Ranger captain. On at least one occasion the TRRC staff has confirmed that the "family rumor" of a visitor of Native ancestry was true—his ancestor was an officer in the Texas Rangers.

William Jesse "Bill" McDonald, the best known of the pre-1910 Ranger captains, was a transitional figure between the Frontier Battalion and the Rangers of the Mexican Revolution. *Photo courtesy of the Texas State Library.*

The history of African-Americans in the early Texas Rangers is indistinct and intriguing. The first discernable involvement began in the 1870s with what would now be called "civilian contractors"—teamsters and cooks. Reconstruction politics and biases prevented them from being full-fledged Texas Rangers; however, we know from reports, photographs and reminiscences that they fought alongside and were respectfully depicted in company photographs alongside "white" Rangers. We suspect that persons of African-American ancestry served as Rangers long before the modern era, but the research remains to be done.

Deciding who was, or was not, a Texas Ranger before the incorporation of the Rangers into the Texas Department of Public Safety in 1935 can be vexing and spark animated disagreements. The TRRC strives to base its findings on criteria including mission, chain-of-command, structure, funding source, authority and whether "regular" Texas Ranger companies were operating at the time. This is little consolation, however, to someone who fervently wants their ancestor to have been a Texas Ranger—or in some cases the *first* Texas Ranger.

In the early nineteenth century Rangers were more likely to be called "spies" and "mounted gunmen" than Rangers, terms having about the same meaning as modern military Long Range Reconnaissance Patrol units. Debates still rage about whether Texas Rangers existed before the term "Texas Ranger" was in common use, and whether Ranger service under Stephen F. Austin during the Mexican era truly constitutes Texas Ranger service.

The Civil War added confusion that persists to this day. Each year researchers contact the TRRC concerning Ranger ancestors who served in units such as Terry's Texas Rangers (actually known as the 8th Texas Cavalry). Such was the effect of the name "Rangers" that more than two dozen Confederate cavalry units adopted "Ranger" as part of their nickname or name. When the staff explains that they were Confederate soldiers, and not State Texas Rangers, the disappointment can be palpable.

During the Mexican Revolutionary period, and the furor surrounding the revelation of the Plan de San Diego, the state made provisions for mass "Ranger" enlistments. This work will likely reopen debate regarding categories of Special Rangers (railroad detectives, oil field security and cattle detectives) and the massive recruitment of Loyalty Rangers. The authors approach the debate with a liberal interpretation, assigning "real Ranger" status based on the utilization of the term Ranger. Others will point to assigned missions, payroll and structure.

No matter what the eventual resolution of these questions is, stimulating research, analysis and debate is the essence of scholarship. The Harrises and Sadler have made an invaluable contribution to Texas Ranger scholarship with their previous work and this landmark addition.

Byron A. Johnson, Director
Texas Ranger Hall of Fame and Museum

PREFACE

THE MEXICAN REVOLUTION of 1910–1920 was the world's first great social revolution of the twentieth century. Its significance extends beyond Mexico, and part of its impact had an important effect on Texas. For example, the Revolution was launched from San Antonio on November 20, 1910, by the exiled Francisco I. Madero, who enlisted the support of Hispanics throughout the Southwest. Against all odds, by June 1911, Madero overthrew the iron-fisted dictator General Porfirio Díaz, who had controlled Mexico since 1876. A grateful nation elected Madero as president, but his tenure proved brief and ineffectual. The well-meaning Madero was overthrown and murdered by a military coup in February 1913, a coup that elevated General Victoriano Huerta as the new strongman of Mexico. To Huerta's dismay, many Mexicans considered him a usurper who had shot his way into power, and Madero's image was that of a martyr. Armed opposition to Huerta flared up in the state of Morelos, led by General Emliano Zapata, crusader for land reform. But the main anti-Huerta movement developed in the northern tier of Mexican states, led by the governor of the state of Coahuila, Venustiano Carranza, who not only organized the Constitutionalist army but would dominate the Revolution between 1913 and 1920.

Supporting Carranza were talented amateur generals such as Francisco "Pancho" Villa and Alvaro Obregón, who developed into formidable military figures. Constitutionalist armies began to achieve victory on the battlefield. They were aided by the United States, which refused to accord diplomatic recognition to Huerta as the legitimate president of Mexico. Any Mexican ruler found it essential to receive American diplomatic recognition; otherwise the United States retained the option of supporting his enemies. This is exactly what happened to Huerta—the United States demonstrated its opposition by seizing the port city of Veracruz, interdicting Huerta's lifeline to Europe. The Constitutionalists systematically demolished Huerta's forces, and by August 1914, he fled into European exile. There then erupted a savage struggle among the winners, a round of civil war pitting Carranza and his principal general, Obregón, against Villa and Zapata. Although Villa had the initial advantage, his Division of the North being the most powerful army in Mexico, Obregón succeeded in defeating Villa's hitherto-invincible forces. Villa was reduced to being a regional figure, as was Zapata. But Villa still proved capable of causing considerable trouble, as when he raided Columbus, New Mexico, on March 9, 1916, provoking a new military intervention by the United States in the form of General John J. Pershing and the Punitive Expedition. Although these developments embarrassed Carranza, the self-styled First Chief of the Constitutionalist movement, he continued to function as the de facto president of Mexico. Formally elected to that post under a radical new constitution promulgated in 1917, Carranza was barred from seeking reelection when his term ended in 1920. By then the Carranza regime had assassinated Zapata, and Obregón had developed presidential ambitions.

When Obregón declared his candidacy, Carranza tried to imprison him and, failing that, tried to impose a puppet president, hoping to remain the power behind the scenes. But in May 1920, Obregón's supporters swept him into power in a rebellion that toppled Carranza with ridiculous ease and resulted in his murder. And while an interim regime prepared Obregón's formal election, Pancho Villa cut an advantageous deal with the government, agreeing to retire in return for a large hacienda and a cash subvention. Thus when Obregón became president he began the process of reconstructing Mexico after a decade of ruinous civil war. Ironically, he used some of the same techniques that Porfirio Díaz had used prior to the Revolution.

The Revolution was not only organized in Texas, but the state remained a hotbed of revolutionary activity throughout the decade. Access to the United States was what enabled revolutionists in the northern tier of Mexican states to emerge as the ultimate winners. And since Texas covers half of the entire border, much of the revolutionary intrigue took place there: Mexican factions organized juntas, recruited cannon fodder, raised money, smuggled arms and ammunition, marketed loot and, if defeated, fled to Texas to regroup. The revolutionary decade had another effect in Texas—it greatly inflamed ethnic tensions. Not only were Anglos outraged by armed raids into Texas, but the loyalty of the predominantly-Hispanic population along the border was suspect.

Tensions increased significantly as of 1915 when the Plan de San Diego surfaced in South Texas. This was the most bizarre irredentist conspiracy in American history. The Plan called for nothing less than the execution of all Anglo males over sixteen years of age and, among other things, the creation of a Hispanic republic composed of Texas, New Mexico, Arizona, Colorado, and California. The result was something verging on a race war, with raids into Texas and a score of Anglos and some three hundred Hispanics killed, most of the latter summarily executed. The Rangers' role in these events is the most controversial episode in the organization's history. While the authorship of the Plan is still obscure, the available evidence shows that Venustiano Carranza used the turmoil to obtain diplomatic recognition from the United States. Carranza promised to end the raids (which his regime was secretly sponsoring); they ended within a week of his receiving recognition on October 19, 1915. The surviving Plan de San Diego militants remained in Mexico under the Carranza regime's protection, in case they were again needed. They were. Carranza revived the Plan in 1916 as a ploy to force the United States to withdraw the Punitive Expedition from Mexico. A series of Plan de San Diego raids struck the border between Laredo and Brownsville. The implied message was, of course, that if the Punitive Expedition were withdrawn the raids would cease. But this time Carranza overreached himself; in response to a raid near Brownsville, American troops crossed into Mexico in hot pursuit, and on June 18, 1916, President Wilson mobilized the entire National Guard of the United States and rushed some 128,000 guardsmen to the border. The United States and Mexico were on the verge of full-scale war. Happily, the differences between the countries were addressed by diplomacy rather than by conflict.

The Texas Rangers played a unique role in American history. They were of course a state constabulary, but they also helped to defend the United States border, and in 1911 received a federal subsidy to do so. The decade of the Mexican Revolution was a turning point in the history of the Texas State Ranger Force, as the organization was named from 1901 to 1935, when it was incorporated into the Department of Public Safety. Basically, the Mexican Revolution saved the Texas Rangers. As of 1910, there was growing support for abolishing the Rangers. Their traditional role of fighting Indians, Mexicans, and outlaws had pretty much ended, and they were performing functions that were carried out by sheriffs and other types of peace officers. Moreover, since the Rangers were under the direct control of the governor, there was the perception that they were the governor's personal police and were used for political purposes. Oftentimes citizens resented the presence of the Rangers as an infringement on their rights. This was especially true at elections, when one faction viewed the Rangers as peacekeepers and the other saw them as intimidators.

The Mexican Revolution ushered in a new era. Because of turmoil on the border, the Rangers were now *needed*. The Anglo citizenry clamored for Rangers to protect them not just from raids but also to prevent any Hispanic uprising. The size of the Texas Ranger force waxed and waned in direct proportion to events in Mexico. The Rangers reached their height during World War I. Faced with an unstable, hostile, and pro-German Mexico on its southern border, the Texas legislature authorized expanding the Rangers to a thousand men. These wartime Ranger companies were deactivated when the war was over, and once again the Rangers endured repeated budget cuts from a legislature that praised their achievements but hated to spend money on the organization. Nevertheless, the Mexican Revolution had gotten the Texas State Ranger Force twenty-five more years of existence as a separate entity. We have dealt with the revolutionary decade in considerable detail in *The Texas Rangers and the Mexican Revolution: The Bloodiest Decade, 1910–1920* (Albuquerque: University of New Mexico Press, 2004).

For the period before 1935, a critical—and controversial—question is: Just who was a "real" Texas Ranger? It has been argued, for example, that Captain Leander McNelly, whose exploits along the Rio Grande in 1877 are a conspicuous part of Ranger lore, was not a Texas Ranger because he wasn't a member of the Frontier Battalion, the official name of the Rangers from 1874 to 1901. McNelly commanded another unit, which the legislature called "special state troops."[1] Yet those championing the claim that McNelly was a Ranger, notably Walter Prescott Webb, argue that because McNelly considered himself a Ranger, acted like a Ranger, and people thought of him as a Ranger, he was a "real Ranger." Here then is a case of a man who was not a Ranger but is considered a "real Ranger." Conversely, there is the case of a Ranger commander who is not considered a "real Ranger." Lieutenant John B. Tays in 1877 surrendered his men to a mob of Mexicans. Webb rationalized this inglorious episode by asserting that Tays wasn't a "real Ranger." This argument is as specious as alleging that if a commissioned army officer proved to be a coward he wasn't a "real officer."

In the twentieth century, a major source of Ranger pride is Frank Hamer's role in the ambush that killed the notorious Bonnie and Clyde in 1934. But at the time, Hamer wasn't a "real Ranger." He had been, but he'd resigned his commission and was working for the Texas Prison System. More recently, the Rangers tout the exploit of Ranger Ramiro Martínez, who killed mass murderer Charles Whitman in the tower of the University of Texas. But Martínez wasn't a Ranger at the time; he was an Austin policeman. If the Rangers take credit for what Rangers did before and after their Ranger service, the organization must also take credit for the actions of people such as ex-Captain Carroll Bates, who was convicted of bootlegging in 1929 and sent to federal prison.

When dealing with the period 1901–1935, it is advisable not to treat the Rangers in terms of clear-cut categories. The most conspicuous were the Regular Rangers, paid by the State of Texas and assigned to Ranger companies. The Regulars by statute had the powers of a sheriff but had jurisdiction throughout the state. They took a notarized oath of office and enlisted for a two-year tour of duty. Their commissions were signed by the adjutant general and by a responsible captain who attested to the veracity of the information on their application. Some would argue that the only "real Rangers" were the Regulars, perhaps reflecting a presentist point of view: because the Rangers today are a small and elite organization, they must always have been, and the restrictions placed on Special Rangers since 1935 must have always applied. However, an analysis of the thousands of service records between 1901 and 1935 reveals that this restrictive definition just doesn't hold up. The problem is that sometimes Regular commissions didn't conform to the above criteria. To cite only a few examples: During the first two decades of the twentieth century, Special Ranger commissions were issued as a matter of course to the Texas and Southwestern Cattle Raisers' Association's brand inspectors. In 1918, some of these inspectors were reclassified as Regular Rangers in order to avoid the draft, but they weren't paid by the state and continued to work for the Cattle Raisers. And sometimes people received Regular Ranger commissions with the notation "without pay" or "without compensation," another instance of the above criteria not obtaining. Furthermore, some recipients of Regular Ranger commissions never served in a company. A former adjutant general, W. D. Cope, was commissioned as a Regular Ranger but was never assigned to a company, and he most certainly didn't spend his time chasing outlaws. Clifford Beckham was a lawyer and investigator, likewise not assigned to any company. Neither was A. T. Bullard, who was a labor foreman, nor Hume Graves, an investigator, nor Pat McGee, a "federal employee," nor Sewall Myer, a lawyer, nor (gasp!) Lucille Phelps, a secretary. Another anomaly was Regular Ranger Lee Shannon, who served between June and December 1923, and was paid directly by the governor. As these few examples indicate, there are many exceptions to the above restrictive definition of Regular Rangers.

Turning to the second broad category, the Special Rangers, the same caveat applies. There were two main incentives for people to become Specials: the prestige associated with the Rangers and being able lawfully to bear arms. Special Rangers received exactly the same warrant of authority as did Regulars, but with the wording about compensation crossed out and the term of enlistment usually being only one year. But here again, some received a two-year commission. It has been suggested that some clerk just reached into a drawer and used the same forms and procedures as for Regular Rangers. This of course begs the question as to why prior to 1935 Special Rangers had the same statutory powers as did Regulars. In the Adjutant General's Correspondence in the Texas State Archives there is considerable correspondence over the years in which adjutants general are writing to or about Special Rangers, and they don't seem to consider them mere clerical expedients. Theoretically, Special Rangers weren't paid by the state and weren't assigned to a Ranger company. One wonders what the difference was between a Regular Ranger commissioned "without compensation" and not assigned to a company and a Special Ranger who was likewise not paid by the state nor assigned to a company. The category of Special Rangers included, as we've seen, brand inspectors, as well as railroad policemen and detectives, hundreds of whom are listed as Railroad Rangers. For example, when a major railroad strike occurred in 1922, with significant disturbances in Denison, the governor commissioned some 450 men as Special Rangers.[2] Constituting yet another exception to the rule, many of them were in fact enlisted in Regular companies, although most served for only the short period of labor disturbance. Men continued to be commissioned as Railroad Rangers into 1935. Speaking of companies, for years a number of Special Rangers who didn't happen to work for a railroad were assigned to a company, Company C. But the vast majority of Special Rangers were unassigned. And if Special Rangers weren't "real Rangers," then the Ranger career of Frank Hamer, for one, was considerably curtailed, for he held Special Ranger commissions in 1915–1917, 1925–1927, and 1946–1955. There was another type of Special Ranger in 1918–1919, the Loyalty Rangers. Under the Hobby Loyalty Act of 1918, three Specials per county were to be commissioned to combat subversion and disloyalty. As with other types of Specials, they received exactly the same warrant of authority as did the Regulars.

There was a more discreditable aspect to the Special Rangers, however. A number of commissions were issued for frivolous or publicity reasons, sometimes to persons who didn't even live in Texas. Among the recipients were the humorist Will Rogers, the country singer Jimmie Rodgers, and the movie actor Tom Mix, in appreciation for his help in organizing the first Texas prison rodeo. A particularly egregious example of this practice was the commission for Ranger Captain Jerry Gray's twelve-year-old son Jerry Cope Gray. In addition, hundreds of Special commissions went to political hacks, especially during the gubernatorial administrations of James and Miriam Ferguson. Members of the public could hardly be blamed for the perception that Special Ranger commissions were something on the order of Kentucky Colonel certificates.

Who, then, were "real Rangers" during the life of the Texas State Ranger Force? It seems that the definition has to be one that is valid not just in some instances or in most instances but in all instances and does not involve semantics or mental gymnastics in attempting to explain away the exceptions, anomalies, and contradictions. We believe that a "real Ranger" during that time was one who held a Texas Ranger commission, of whatever type.

The Regular Rangers were thus but the tip of a considerable law enforcement pyramid. What is striking in this connection is the phenomenal number of Rangers who were related to other Rangers or to other types of peace officers. Especially in South Texas there were virtual law enforcement clans. As Maud Gilliland noted in her groundbreaking study *Wilson County Texas Rangers 1837–1977*,[3] in Wilson County the Carnes, Shely, Hamer, Brady, Craighead, Webb, Wright, Tumlinson, and West families produced dozens of Rangers; the hamlet of Fairview (now a ghost town) had twenty-two residents who became Rangers, which is truly extraordinary.

Perhaps the best illustration of the familial relationships is the infamous San Benito ambush. On the night of July 31, 1910, a party of four lawmen was shot up by Mexican outlaws near San Benito, Texas. Cameron County Deputy Sheriff Benny Lawrence and Ranger Quirl Bailey Carnes were killed, Ranger Pat Craighead and Deputy Sheriff Earl West were seriously wounded. Ranger Quirl Bailey Carnes's brother was Ranger Herff Carnes, later a mounted Customs inspector. Their brother Alfred Burton Carnes was sheriff of Wilson County from 1918 to 1938. Their nephew Tom Carnes would join the Border Patrol, nephew Bob Carnes would become an FBI agent, nephew Don Carnes was Wilson County sheriff from 1953 to 1960, and nephew Don Gilliland was a Ranger in 1922–1923. Ranger Pat Craighead had been a Wilson County deputy sheriff before enlisting in the Rangers. His brother Charles A. Craighead was a Ranger and later a policeman and mounted Customs inspector. Their father John S. Craighead was Wilson County sheriff from 1894 to 1898. Pat Craighead served as Jim Hogg County sheriff from 1916 to 1921. Deputy Sheriff Earl West became a Special Ranger in 1918. His father Milton Crockett West was a Special Ranger in 1918–1919. His brother Paul More West was a Ranger in 1915. His brother Milton H. West was a Regular Ranger in 1911–1912 and a Special Ranger in 1927–1928.

There has been a pronounced tendency by historians of the Texas Rangers to focus on a literal handful of men who acquired formidable reputations—usually exaggerated—while ignoring the ninety-nine percent of Rangers who served in virtual anonymity as members of what is arguably the most famous law enforcement organization in the world. As a result, some studies of the Texas State Ranger Force for the period 1901–1935 have at best been skewed while others have been blatantly incorrect both in fact and interpretation. The principal reason has been the unwillingness or inability of writers to conduct the breadth of research necessary to understand what the Rangers did and did not do and more importantly, who they were. This reference book is designed to rescue from the trash heap of history those who also served.

While we make no claims to intellectual omnipotence on the subject of the Rangers, we have attempted comprehensively to examine all of the available sources, many of which have been underutilized by historians. The basic source is the mass of documentation in the Adjutant General's Correspondence, which includes the Ranger records, located in the Archives and Information Services Division of the Texas State Library, Austin, Texas. Using these data as a base, we compiled dossiers on the 1,782 men who served from 1910 through 1921. In *The Texas Rangers and the Mexican Revolution* we included a fifty-eight-page appendix naming them, their dates of service, and the type of commission they held.

Besides the Adjutant General's Correspondence we examined the papers of the Texas governors at the Texas State Library and the Center for American History (CAH) at the University of Texas at Austin. The Rangers did not operate in a vacuum; they were very much affected by politics, but this political dimension to their history had not been thoroughly examined. And at the Center for American History we used the Walter Prescott Webb transcripts. As is well known, Webb conducted extensive research before publishing in 1935 his classic history, *The Texas Rangers: A Century of Frontier Defense*.[4] Webb went camping with the Rangers, received a commission as a Special Ranger, packed a gun, and was given virtual carte blanche in the Ranger records. He copied hundreds of pages of documents, some of which today no longer exist in the Ranger records at the Texas State Library; therefore, Webb's transcripts are invaluable. In addition, at the CAH we examined the Emanuel A. "Dogie" Wright Papers and the Roy Wilkinson Aldrich Papers, both of which were quite valuable. It should be noted that there is a small Roy Aldrich collection at the Archives of the Big Bend at Sul Ross State University in Alpine, Texas. There is also a quantity of Texas Ranger documents at the Texas National Guard headquarters at Camp Mabry in Austin that should be utilized for any research project related to the Mexican Revolution. The Texas Ranger Hall of Fame and Museum at Waco is a treasure house of Ranger material, including the valuable Manuel T. "Lone Wolf" Gonzaullas Papers that contain a large and unique photographic collection, and the Hall of Fame's vertical files on individual Rangers.

While it has been customary in writing histories of the Texas Rangers to rely principally on Ranger records, ironically one of the best sources for the period of the Mexican Revolution is the "Old Mex 232" documents of the Federal Bureau of Investigation. Comprising twenty-four reels of microfilm, this massive collection of approximately eighty thousand pages of previously classified records is invaluable.[5] This body of documents is extremely difficult to use, both because a significant percentage of the papers are poorly microfilmed and oftentimes because one page of a document is in one reel and the remaining pages in another. As a result we were forced to copy frame by frame from the microfilm and then reassemble the pages chronologically.

The value of these FBI reports is best illustrated by an incident that we describe in *The Texas Rangers and the Mexican Revolution*. The only extant copy of the Monthly Return (MR) for Company A for May 1916 is found in the "Old Mex 232" FBI documents. What is extraordinarily important about this specific document is that it deals with the disappearance of two prominent

Plan de San Diego militants who vanished in May 1916, while in Rangers' custody. Because the two were federal prisoners, the federal Bureau of Investigation was keenly interested to learn their fate. But when a Bureau agent contacted the Rangers he was met with a wall of denial and indifference. He finally enlisted the help of Texas Assistant Attorney General (and future Chief Justice of the Texas Supreme Court) C. M. Cureton. They examined a copy of Company A's Monthly Return and Cureton stated, "This means they killed them." The federal agent filed the copy of the Monthly Return with his report, and it is preserved in the "Old Mex 232" microfilm. There is not a copy to be found in the Texas Ranger files at the Texas State Library or, for that matter, anywhere else. Only the FBI has a copy. This is but one example of the significant documentation bearing on the Rangers in the FBI's archive.

If the FBI's records are invaluable, the Federal Records Center in Fort Worth has an equally important collection of federal court case and U.S. commissioners' files with numerous references to Ranger activities, especially in the Western and Southern Districts of Texas. An often-neglected source is the enormous archive of the U.S. Department of State (243 reels of microfilm) relating to the Internal Affairs of Mexico, 1910–1929, which contains many documents relating to the Rangers during the Mexican Revolution.

Unfortunately, Mexican sources have been virtually ignored by historians of the Texas Rangers.[6] This has led to some fundamental misinterpretations. Whereas the Plan de San Diego has been treated as an Hispanic struggle for liberation, Mexican sources clearly demonstrate that the Carranza regime manipulated the militants for its own ends and controlled the raids into Texas. The evidence is in the microfilmed archive of General Pablo González at the Nettie Lee Benson Latin American Collection at the University of Texas at Austin and in President Venustiano Carranza's archive at the Centro de Estudios de Historia de México, Departamento Cultural de Condumex, in Mexico City. It is thus advisable to examine more than just Ranger records when writing about this venerable Texas law enforcement organization.

Historians are at a particular disadvantage in dealing with the records on individual Rangers because record keeping was not the Rangers' strong suit. Instead of recording an individual's birth date, they merely noted how many years and months old he was when he enlisted. Moreover, most men were listed by their initials rather than their full names. And even when their names were recorded, there were errors. For example, there are two separate service records for Ranger Art Robertson. One identifies him as "Art Robinson" because that was what his captain thought his name was. The other correctly lists him as "Art Robertson."

We have combined printed sources and online services in compiling the biographical sketches in this reference book. In a very few cases it was impossible to learn more about an individual than what was on his service record. We give a man's name, date and place of birth, physical description, his residence and occupation each time he enlisted, his career as a Ranger, and any pertinent remarks. In addition, we list whatever information we have about his immediate family and any law enforcement relatives (not all of whom necessarily served between 1910 and 1921). Further to illustrate the familial connections, we include several genealogical charts, in which the names of Rangers are capitalized and those of other types of peace officers are underlined.

The bibliography is somewhat unusual. For reasons of space, sources are denoted in numbers and letters. The numbers are assigned to published works in our files, while the letters refer to sources on the Internet. Given the thousands of names that are mentioned, inevitably there will be errors. Anyone who has ever used the various Census files is aware that a lot of enumerators could have used substantial additional instruction in penmanship and spelling. We welcome corrections, additions, or suggestions. Please direct your comments to Frances E. Harris, c/o Department of History, MSC 3H, PO Box 30001, New Mexico State University, Las Cruces, New Mexico 88003-0008.

Notes

1. See Robert Draper, "The Twilight of the Texas Rangers," *Texas Monthly*, (February 1994): 76–83, 107, 108, 110, 112–13, 118.
2. He used Article 6755, Title 116, *Complete Texas Statutes, 1920*.
3. Brownsville: Springman-King Co., 1977.
4. Boston & New York: Houghton Mifflin Co. 2nd ed. Austin: University of Texas Press, 1965.
5. Records of the Federal Bureau of Investigation, Record Group 65, microcopy, no number, National Archives and Records Service, College Park, Maryland.
6. To cite only some examples: Walter P. Webb, *The Texas Rangers*; Charles M. Robinson III, *The Men Who Wear the Star: The Story of the Texas Rangers* (New York: Random House, 2000); Robert Utley, *Lone Star Justice: The First Century of the Texas Rangers* (New York: Oxford University Press, 2002); and *Lone Star Lawmen: The Second Century of the Texas Rangers* (New York: Oxford University Press, 2007).

ACKNOWLEDGMENTS

THIS BOOK IS a byproduct of a book we wrote in 2004—*The Texas Rangers and the Mexican Revolution: The Bloodiest Decade, 1910–1920*. We view *Texas Ranger Biographies: Those Who Served 1910–1921* as a companion volume. When we wrote *The Texas Rangers and the Mexican Revolution*, we included a fifty-eight-page appendix that identified all of the Rangers who served during the 1910–1920 decade, their dates of service and what kind of Ranger they were: Regular Ranger, Special Ranger or Loyalty Ranger.

Unfortunately space was not available to enable us to publish all of the information we had obtained from the Texas Ranger Service Records or from Ranger company Monthly Returns and a variety of other archival sources. However, it dawned upon us that we had the foundation for a major biographical study of what is unquestionably the most famous law enforcement organization in the world—the Texas Rangers—during the most crucial decade in their existence. This volume is the result of our quest to provide a full-blown biographical study of the Rangers.

Our indebtedness to institutions and individuals who directly and indirectly assisted our efforts is substantial. First among these are the Weatherhead Foundation, New York City, for its generous financial support of our research and the Arts and Sciences Research Center at New Mexico State University for its support of our initial efforts to obtain funding.

In Austin, Texas, the Lorenzo de Zavala Texas State Library (TSL) provided a haven for two non-Texas based historians over almost a third of a century. Former Director David Gracey, former Archivist Michael Dabrishus and Archival Technician Eddie Williams (now retired) were enormously helpful. Most recently Archivist Donaly Brice could not have been more helpful in steering us through the archival maze. Photo Archivist John Anderson combed the TSL Archives for photographs for this volume.

Second only to the TSL, the Texas Ranger Hall of Fame and Museum in Waco provided both documents and photos. Director Byron Johnson wrote the Foreword for this volume and with good grace agreed and disagreed with us on a variety of Ranger topics. Assistant Director Christina Stopka and Librarian Christy Smith fielded numerous questions, copied dozens of photographs and made us feel most welcome. Before she left the museum, Librarian Judy Shofner did the same. Bobby Nieman, the managing editor of the Ranger Hall of Fame's excellent online publication *Texas Ranger Dispatch* has over a period of years been a fount of information about Ranger history. We hope he likes this volume.

At the Dolph Briscoe Center for American History at the University of Texas at Austin, a number of archivists and technicians alike expedited our acquisition of both documents and photographs from their collections. We thank them all. At the J. Evetts Haley History Center and the Nita Stewart Haley Memorial Library in Midland, Texas, Archivist Jim Bradshaw made us welcome in their excellent facility. We are indebted to our friend Chuck Bailey for his sage advice.

Without our colleague and former student Mark Milliorn we simply could not have brought this volume to print. Our indebtedness to him is enormous.

The genealogical charts of prominent Ranger families were ably produced by Michael Harris, who happens to be a grandson of Charles and Frances Harris. Michael is an undergraduate at New Mexico State University.

We thank Ray Sadler's better half Betty Sadler for her constant support and especially for advice on questions of grammar and style.

On a number of occasions we have had to go to the well when stumped on arcane historical problems. Invariably our old friend Bill Beezley at the University of Arizona has the answer. For information on gunfighters and Western badmen, our friends Bob Alexander and Allen Hatley have no peer and that is the reason we call on them with some frequency.

At the University of New Mexico Press, Editor-in-Chief Clark Whitehorn, Managing Editor Maya Allen-Gallegos, Senior Book Designer Mina Yamashita, Assistant Editor Elizabeth Albright, Designer Robyn Mundy, and Production Editor Elise M. McHugh did an excellent job in bringing this manuscript to publication. We thank them all.

Finally, beginning with Department Head Jeff Brown, our colleagues in the History Department at New Mexico State University are undoubtedly ecstatic that they will no longer have to hear more than they ever wanted to about the Texas Rangers.

Charles H. Harris III
Frances E. Harris
Louis R. Sadler
Department of History
New Mexico State University
Las Cruces, New Mexico

ABBOTT, BENJAMIN PRESTON. Born Nov. 3, 1873, Oconee County, South Carolina. Ht. 6 ft., blue eyes, dark hair, light complexion, married. Rancher, Bovina, Parmer County, Texas. LOYALTY RANGER June 6, 1918–Feb. 23, 1919. REMARKS: Died 1957, Clovis, Curry County, New Mexico. FAMILY: Parents, John Benjamin Abbott (b. 1839, SC) and Elizabeth Patience Carpenter (b. 1842, SC); siblings, A. C. (b. 1867, SC), S. C. (b. 1869, SC); spouse, Mae Elizabeth Messenger (b. 1894, IA), married Sept. 4, 1913, Congregational Church, Friona, Parmer County; son, John Benjamin (b. 1916, TX). *SR; A1a, d, f, g; A3a; A4a, b, g.*

ABERNATHY, ROBERT HENRY. Born Oct. 27, 1880, Dallas, Dallas County, Texas. Tall, gray eyes, brown hair, married. Barber, Edna, Jackson County, Texas. LOYALTY RANGER July 29, 1918–Feb. 24, 1919. REMARKS: In 1920 was a barber in Yoakum, DeWitt County, Texas. Died Sept. 16, 1929, DeWitt County, Texas. FAMILY: Parents, Joseph Abernathy (b. 1849, NC) and Sophia S. (b. 1855, MS); siblings, Anna S. (b. 1877, TN), Brownie (b. 1884, TX); spouse, Emma (b. 1881, TX), married about 1907; children, Agnes (b. 1908, TX), Joseph Luther (b. 1912, TX). *SR; A1d, e, f; A2b; A3a.*

ABNEY, GLENN MAURICE. Born Dec. 12, 1887, Austin, Travis County, Texas. Ht. 5 ft. 11 in., brown eyes, black hair, fair complexion. Constable, deputy sheriff, San Patricio County, Texas. REGULAR RANGER Sept. 19, 1917–Feb. 28, 1918 (private, Co. A). Resigned. Farmer, Hidalgo County, Texas. SPECIAL RANGER Mar. 1, 1918–Jan. 15, 1919. REMARKS: Living in Donna, Hidalgo County in 1920; was a gravel pit contractor in Hidalgo County in 1930; died Nov. 20, 1944, Hidalgo County, Texas. FAMILY: Spouse, Ruth Marie "Myrta" Rickey (b. 1899, IA), married about 1920; sons, Glenn M., Jr. (b. 1921, TX) and William H. (b. 1922, TX). *SR; 471; Hunter to AG, Dec 17, 1917, AGC; Abney and Hester to Hanson, Nov 7, 1918, WC; A1f; g; A3a; A4b; C.*

ACKER, PHILIP HENDRIX. Born Jan. 30, 1885, Caseyville, Union County, Kentucky. Ht. 6 ft., dark eyes, dark hair, dark complexion, married. Farmer, Dimmit, Castro County, Texas. LOYALTY RANGER July 27, 1918–Feb. 1919. REMARKS: Lived in Indiana in 1910. Died Nov. 4, 1969, Castro County, Texas. FAMILY: Parents, Philip Acker (b. 1833, Germany) and Mary Catherine Oberhausen (b. 1859, IN); siblings, Margaret Catherine (b. 1883, KY), John (b. 1887, KY), Anna Louise (b. 1889, KY), Jacob (b. 1892, KY), Valentine (b. 1894, KY), Andrew (b. 1897, KY); spouse, Gertrude Ann Behrens (b. 1890, NE), married Apr. 20, 1915, Holy Family Catholic Church, Castro County; children, Clara K. (b. 1917, TX), Herman P. (b. 1918, TX), Alice M. (b. 1919, TX). *SR; A1d, e, f, g; A2a, b; A3a; A4a, b; B1.*

ACOSTA, DIONICIO. Born Oct. 9, 1893, Rock Ranch near Floresville, Wilson County, Texas. Ht. 5 ft. 10 in., blue eyes, black hair, light complexion. Deputy sheriff, Wilson County, Texas. REGULAR RANGER Dec. 21, 1917–Mar. 31, 1919 (private, Co. D, K). Resigned. REMARKS: Constable,

Floresville, Wilson County. Chief deputy sheriff, Wilson County, 1925–1937; was chief deputy under Sheriff Burt Carnes. Died Mar. 3, 1946, Wilson County, Texas (name spelled "Deonicio" in Death Index). LAW ENFORCEMENT RELATIVES: Son, Adolph, was chief deputy (1953–1960) under Sheriff Don Carnes, Burt Carnes's son. FAMILY: Parents, Victor Acosta (b. 1865, TX) and Trinidad (b. 1875, TX); sisters, Engracia (b. 1895, TX), Carmen (b. 1897), Francisca (b. 1899, TX); spouse, Mary (b. 1898, TX); children, Adolfo (b. 1921, TX), Trinidad (b. 1928, TX). *SR; 471; 470:83; 1000: iii, 126; A1d, g; C.*

ADAMS, CHARLES D. Born Jan. 1884, Pearsall, Frio County, Texas. Ht. 6 ft. 4 in., gray eyes, brown hair, light complexion, married. Rancher, Crestonia, Duval County, Texas. SPECIAL RANGER Apr. 29, 1918–Jan. 15, 1919. REMARKS: Was a farmer in Webb County, Texas, in 1930. LAW ENFORCEMENT RELATIVES: Ranger Thomas J. Adams, brother. FAMILY: Parents, Abner DeWitt Adams (b. 1850, TX) and Catherine Hannah Stutsman (b. 1852, MO); siblings, William Abslum (b. 1873, TX), Thomas J. (b. 1874, TX), Hannah Catherine "Kitty" (b. 1877, TX), Sarah Jeanette (b. 1879, TX), John Quincy (b. 1882, TX), Cordelia (b. 1886, TX), Pearle (b. 1889, TX), Jessie (b. 1892, TX); spouse, Ida Emma (b. 1895, TX); children, Emma Lu (b. 1918, TX), Katy B. (b. 1919, TX), Vivian (b. 1922, TX), Charles, Jr., (b. 1925, TX). *SR; A1d, f, g; A3a; A4b.*

ADAMS, COLUMBUS WILLIAM. Born May 20, 1872, Greene, Lincoln County, Missouri. Ht. 5 ft. 10 in., blue eyes, dark hair, dark complexion, married. Rancher, Comstock, Val Verde County, Texas. SPECIAL RANGER Dec. 3, 1917–Jan. 15, 1919 (Co. A Volunteers). REMARKS: Lived in Hookerville, Burleson County, Texas as a young boy. By 1910 was a stockman in Val Verde County. In 1930 was a rancher living in Sutton County, Texas. Died Jan. 5, 1952, Sonora, Sutton County, Texas. FAMILY: Parents David Quince Adams or David General Adams (b. 1838, VA) and Serena E. Estes (b. 1841, KY); siblings, Francis Marion (b. 1859, KY), Wiley Bailey (b. 1861, KY or MO), Emaline Malinda (b. 1863, KY or MO), Alzada (b. 1864, KY or MO), Sarah Alice (b. 1866, KY or MO), Linesa Rebecca (b. 1868, KY or MO), Thomas Boone (b. 1870, MO), Louisa E. (b. 1874, MO), Malinda Frances (b. 1876, TX), David Quincy (b. 1878, TX), Mattison Estes (b. 1881, TX), Serena (b. 1883, TX), spouse #1, Sereptirie Josie Vina McNutt (b. 1876, TX), married about 1895; children, Myrtle (b. 1896, TX), Harmon (b. 1898, TX), Estes (b. 1900, TX), Serena (b. 1902, TX), Ulice (b. 1905, TX), Elba (b. 1907, TX), George (b. 1910, TX), Leo (b. 1914, TX); spouse #2, Dovie Franks. *SR; A1b, e, f, g; A4a, b; C.*

ADAMS, EUGENE OLAN. Born Feb. 17, 1885, Bosque County, Texas. Ht. 5 ft. 11 in., gray eyes, brown hair, fair complexion, married. Merchant, Cross Plains, Callahan County, Texas. SPECIAL RANGER June 7, 1917–Dec. 1917 (attached to Co. C). REMARKS: Was a U.S. mail carrier in Callahan County in 1918; was a trucking contractor in Cross Plains in 1930. Died Sept. 10, 1976, Big Spring, Howard County, Texas. FAMILY: Parents, William C. Adams (b. 1863, LA) and Laura B. (b. 1866, TX); siblings, Charles (b. 1883, TX), Mary Beulah (b. 1887, TX), Chesley (b. 1889, TX), Myrtle (b. 1890, TX), Jessie M. (b. 1892, TX), Katie B. (b. 1894, TX), Willie D. (b. 1899, TX), Edwin Glenn (b. 1901, TX), Gladys P. (b. 1903, TX); spouse, Loria or Toria (b. 1885, TX), married about 1905; children, Olan (b. 1906, TX), Arlton C. (b. 1909, TX), Bonnie W. (1913, TX), Athlee E. (b. 1914, TX), Billie M. (b. 1918, TX). *SR; A1d, e, f, g; A2a, b; A3a.*

ADAMS, HAROLD WILLIAM. Born Dec. 25, 1896, New Braunfels, Comal County, Texas. Ht. 5 ft. 11 in., blue eyes, brown hair, fair complexion. Bookkeeper, Comal County. REGULAR RANGER Jan. 16, 1918–Dec. 23, 1920 (private, Co. K; transferred to Co. D, June 20, 1919). Resigned. REMARKS: Was a bank cashier in Comal County in 1930. Died July 22, 1966, New Braunfels, Comal County, Texas. LAW ENFORCEMENT RELATIVES: Comal County sheriff (1908–1920) William Adams, father. FAMILY: Parents, Harold William Adams (b. 1866, TX) and Adele Louise "Hulda" Habermann (b. 1873, TX); brothers, Herbert (b. 1895, TX), Marvin (b. 1899, TX), Donald (b. 1902, TX); spouse, Leonie Zipp (b. 1901, TX), married about 1922; daughters, Marilyn June (b. 1923, TX), Jane (b. 1937, TX). *SR; 471; 1503:124; A1d, f, g; A2a, b, e; A3c; A4a.*

ADAMS, ROY HODGE. Born Jan. 30, 1889, Hallettsville, Lavaca County, Texas. Ht. 6 ft. ¼ in., brown eyes, light hair, light complexion. Salesman. REGULAR RANGER Sept. 1, 1909–Jan. 8, 1911 (private, Co. C; transferred to Co. B,

Oct. 9, 1910). Discharged for disorderly conduct in Brownsville on Jan. 5, 1911. REMARKS: Lived in Travis County, Texas, in 1910. Secret agent for Mexican government in San Antonio, Bexar County, Texas, Mar.–May 1911, and in Del Rio, Apr. 1913. Webb County, Texas, deputy sheriff, 1913. Deputy collector U.S Internal Revenue Service, Corpus Christi (in charge of Fifth Division of Texas—20 counties in South Texas), 1915–1917. First lieutenant, Infantry, assistant intelligence officer at Camp Travis, 1917–1919. Discharged from Army on Aug. 24, 1919. On Aug. 23, 1919, Adams applied to reenlist in the Rangers, was sent the relevant forms and reportedly joined Captain Stevens's Company B at El Paso, but this is not reflected in his service record. In 1930 was a narcotics agent for the government in San Antonio, Bexar County, Texas. Died Mar. 6, 1971, Webb County, Texas. FAMILY: Parents, Will G. Adams (b. 1859, TX) and Annie (b. 1859, TX); brother, Guy (b. 1875, TX); spouse, Mae Bell (b. 1890, TX), married about 1908; son, Roy, Jr. (b. 1913, TX). *SR; 471; Co B, MR, Jan 1911; Ellsworth to Secretary of State, May 6, 1911, 812.00/1717, RDS; LWT, Aug 17, Sept 7, 1913, Jan 17, Feb 14, 1915; 344:169–172; BDH, Feb 22, 1917; Adams to Harley, Aug 23, 1919, AGC; Harley to Armistead, Aug 29, 1919, AGC; Armistead to Harley, Aug 22, 1919, AGC; Cope to Adams, Aug 27, 1919, AGC; LWT, Aug 31, 1919; A1d, e, g; A2a, b; A3a, c.*

ADAMS, THOMAS JOURDAN "TOM." Born July 14, 1874, Goliad, Goliad County, Texas. Ht. 6 ft. 3 in., brown eyes, brown hair, dark complexion, married. Ranch foreman, Hebbronville, Jim Hogg County, Texas. SPECIAL RANGER May 3, 1918–Jan. 15, 1919. REMARKS: Died Apr. 22, 1942, Jim Hogg County, Texas. LAW ENFORCEMENT RELATIVES: Ranger Charles D. Adams, brother. FAMILY: Parents, Abner DeWitt Adams (b. 1850, TX) and Catherine Hannah Stutsman (b. 1852, MO); siblings, William Abslum (b. 1873, TX), Hannah Catherine "Kitty" (b. 1877, TX), Sarah Jeanette (b. 1879, TX), John Quincy (b. 1882, TX), Charles D. (b. 1884, TX), Cordelia (b. 1886, TX), Pearle (b. 1889, TX), Jessie (b. 1892, TX); spouse, Martha Little (b. 1879, TX), married Apr. 15, 1895, Frio County; sons, Dee (b. 1896, TX), Daniel Robert (b. 1897, TX), Ramzy Lee (1899, TX). *SR; A1b, d, e; A3a; A4a, b; C.*

ADDISON, AMOS KENT. Born Apr. 1872, Louisiana. Ht. 6 ft. 3 ½ in., brown eyes, black hair, dark complexion, married. Superintendent for protection, Freeport Sulfur Co., Freeport, Brazoria County, Texas. SPECIAL RANGER July 22, 1918–Jan. 15, 1919. REMARKS: Applied on Jan. 18, 1919, for reappointment. Had worked as a prison guard in Burleson County, Texas in 1900 and in Huntsville, Walker County, Texas in 1910. In 1930 was a detective for a sulfur company in Brazoria County. Died June 22, 1957, Brazoria County, Texas. FAMILY: Parents, William Addison (b. 1828, LA) and Jane (b. 1838, LA); siblings, John (b. 1847, LA), Augusta (b. 1862, LA), Ashford (b. 1866, LA), Mary (b. 1868, LA), Hallie (b. 1875, LA), Emet (b. 1878, LA); spouse #1, Ula (b. 1879, TX), married about 1897; children, Emmit (b. 1898, TX), Kent (b. 1899, TX), Hannah (b. 1902, TX), Bert (b. 1904, TX), Murray (b. 1907, TX), May (b. 1909, TX); spouse #2, Carrie C. (b. 1890, TX). *SR; A1b, d, e, g; A2b.*

AKENS, JOHN SILAS. Born Feb. 16, 1871, Sand Mountain, Morgan County, Alabama. Ht. 5 ft. 10 in., brown eyes, dark hair, sandy complexion, married. Farmer, Hawley, Jones County, Texas. SPECIAL RANGER July 4, 1917–Dec. 1917 (attached to Co. C). REMARKS: Died Aug. 12, 1956, Abilene, Taylor County, Texas; buried in Midway Cemetery, Hawley. FAMILY: Parents, John W. Akens (b. 1832, NC) and Nancy J. Daniel (b. 1835, AL); siblings, Caroline (b. 1860, AL), Eliza (b. 1866, IL), Mary (b. 1867, IL), Alice (b. 1872, AL), Ellen (b. 1874, AL), Martha (b. 1876, AL), David (b. 1880, GA); spouse, Sarah Elizabeth "Lizzie" Horn (b. 1876, AL), married July 11, 1895 in Texas; children, Loice or Louise (b. 1897, TX), Thomas "Tom" (b. 1898, TX), Totsy (b. 1900, TX), Exie (b. 1901, TX), Trixie M. (b. 1903, TX), Womberson H. "Dub" (b. 1906, TX), William (b. 1907, TX). *SR; A1b, e, f, g; A2b; A4b.*

ALBIN, GEORGE LEWIS. Born Nov. 10, 1864, Comanche, Comanche County, Texas. Ht. 5 ft. 8 in., blue-gray eyes, dark brown hair, medium complexion, married. Livestock inspector, Baird, Callahan County, Texas. SPECIAL RANGER May 28, 1917–Dec. 1917 (attached to Co. C). REMARKS: Had been a cattle dealer in Comanche County. In 1930 was a night watchman for the city of Baird. Died Feb. 27, 1956, Fort Worth, Tarrant County, Texas. FAMILY: Parents, Harrison Wiley Albin (b. 1818, IL) and Eliza N. Williams (b. 1822, GA); siblings, Melissa A. (b. 1841), Martha Ann (b. 1842), Jasper Joshua (b. 1845, MS), John F. (b. 1847, MS), Durcella E. or Lucella (b. 1849, AL), Sarah

Francis (b. 1851, AL), Josephus Warren (b. 1853, AL), Isaac S. (b. 1856, AL), Harrison Payton (b. 1860, TX), Susan A. (b. 1863, TX), Louise M. "Lula" (b. 1868, TX); spouse #1, Jennie Bird Patterson (b. 1864), married Sept. 16, 1885; children, Jefferson Davis (b. 1887, TX), Sam O. (b. 1889), Isla Elizabeth (b. 1892, TX), Louis Brown (b. 1894, TX); spouse #2, Ora Elizabeth Toalson (b. 1874, TX), married Nov. 16, 1899; children, Hilda (b. 1903, TX), Leah (b. 1905, TX), Grady Lewis (b. 1907, TX). *SR; A1a, b, e, g; A2b; A4a, b, g.*

ALDERMAN, STANBERRY. (Some sources spell his name as Stanbery or Stanbury.) Born Sept. 22, 1883, McConnelsville, Morgan County, Ohio. Ht. 5 ft. 9 ½ in., gray eyes, brown hair, fair complexion, married. Superintendent of the Western Telephone Co., Big Spring, Howard County, Texas. LOYALTY RANGER June 5, 1918–Feb. 1919. REMARKS: In 1920 was an oil company bookkeeper in Big Spring. In 1930 was living in Dallas, Dallas County, Texas. FAMILY: Parents, Charles Leslie Alderman (b. 1863, OH) and Elizabeth M. Stanbury (b. 1862, OH); siblings, Blanche M. (b. 1888, OH), Justice Reynolds (b. 1895, OH), Maydell (b. 1900, OH); spouse, Roberta (b. 1884, GA); son, Robert S. (b. 1917, TX). *SR; A1d, f, g; A4a; B1.*

ALDRICH, ROY WILKINSON. Born Sept. 17, 1869, Quincy, Adams County, Illinois. No Service Record. No physical description, married. Real estate broker in Corpus Christi, Nueces County, Texas and San Antonio, Bexar County, Texas, 1907–1915. REGULAR RANGER Mar. 26, 1915–Oct. 31, 1947 (private, Co. A; promoted to sergeant, Co. A, Jan. 1, 1916; in 1917 transferred to Co. D as sergeant; promoted to captain, Co. H, Dec. 1, 1917; became Quartermaster captain, June 20, 1919; fired by the AG as Ranger Quartermaster, 1931; recommissioned as captain, 1933; captain, unassigned, Nov. 9, 1938; private, unassigned, Sept. 1, 1939; private, Headquarters Detachment, Jan. 20, 1941). Retired. REMARKS: Spent his childhood in Golden City, Missouri and his youth in Arizona, Idaho, and Oklahoma Territory. In Spanish-American War was a second lieutenant in Second Missouri Volunteer Infantry regiment; served on Mindanao during Philippine Insurrection; served in British Army remount service in South Africa during the Boer War. Was sheriff of Kiowa County, Oklahoma Territory, 1903–1907. Interested in history and natural history; was an avid collector of artifacts and books. Sul Ross State University (Alpine, Brewster County, Texas) acquired his 10,000-volume library in 1958; his papers are at Sul Ross and the Center for American History at the University of Texas at Austin (Travis County, Texas). In Ranger Force, served longer than any other Texas Ranger. Died Jan 29, 1955, Austin, Travis County, Texas. LAW ENFORCEMENT RELATIVES: Ranger J. W. Aldrich, brother. FAMILY: Parents, Joseph W. Aldrich (b. 1844, IL) and Georgie (b. 1845, OH); brother Jules (b. 1872, IL); spouse, Delia Dunlap (b. 1888, IA), married about 1905. *471; 522:15–16; Hobby to Harley, May 19, 1919, WC; 319:130, 157–158, 194–199; biography: 552; 172:I, 98; A1b, e; A2b; A4b.*

Ranger Captain Roy Wilkinson Aldrich. *Photo courtesy Texas Ranger Hall of Fame and Museum.*

ALLBRIGHT, JAMES JACOB. Born May 25, 1873, Martindale, Caldwell County, Texas. Ht. 5 ft. 8 ¾ in., gray eyes, dark hair, fair complexion. State employee—State of Texas Markets and Warehouse Department, Austin County, Texas. SPECIAL RANGER Mar. 30, 1918–Jan. 15, 1919. REMARKS: In 1920 was a cotton seed trader in Willis, Austin County. In 1930 was a farmer in Fort Bend County, Texas. A James Jacob Allbright died Nov. 15, 1939, Wharton County, Texas. FAMILY: Parents, William Nelson Allbright (b. 1840, GA) and Elizabeth Fredonia Murff (1851, TX); siblings, Margaret, May (b. 1874), William Nelson (b. 1878, TX), Bonnie Elmer (b. 1880), John Ireland (b. 1883); spouse Mary Guyler (b. 1890, TX); children, Guyler (b. 1912, TX), James J., Jr. (b. 1915, TX), Marion (b. 1919, TX), William Nelson (b. 1925, TX). *SR; A1e, f, g; A3a; A4a, b; C.*

ALLDAY, WILLIAM DAVID. Born Aug. 4, 1876, Milam County, Texas. Ht. 5 ft. 11 ½ in., blue eyes, light hair, dark complexion. Farmer, Milam County. REGULAR RANGER Aug. 6, 1910–Sept. 30, 1910 (private, Co. C). Resigned to accept a more lucrative job. FAMILY: Parents, David Allday (b. 1831, GA) and Sarah L Taylor (1845, MS); siblings, James S. (b. 1866, TX), Emma (b. 1868, TX), Peter McClem (b. 1870, TX), John M. (b. 1872, TX), Janett L. "Janie" (b. 1878, TX), Roxie A. (b. 1883, TX), Charles (b. 1888, TX). *SR; 471; AS, Oct 1, 1910; A1b, d, e; A3c; A4b, g.*

ALLEE, ALONZO WILLIAM. Born May 1878, Goliad, Goliad County, Texas. Ht. 5 ft. 9 ¾ in., gray eyes, sandy brown hair, fair complexion, married. Stockman. SPECIAL RANGER July 10, 1916–Apr. 21, 1917. Resigned. REMARKS: Stockman in LaSalle County, Texas in 1910. In 1912, killed two Hispanic ranchers. Died 1918, Crystal City, Zavala County, Texas. LAW ENFORCEMENT RELATIVES: Ranger Alfred Young Allee, father; Ranger Captain Alfred Young Allee, son; Ranger Alfred Young Allee, Jr., grandson. FAMILY: Parents, Alfred Allee (b. 1855, TX) and Helen Eliza Bruton (b. 1861, TX); sister, Julia Ella (b. 1880, TX); spouse, Lela Belle Kellogg (b. 1882, TX); children, Elbert Joe (b. 1904, TX), Margaret (b. 1905, TX), Alfred (b. 1907, TX), Ruby (b. 1909, TX); Julia (b. 1911, TX), Warren (b. 1916, TX). *SR; 471; LWT, Aug 8, 25, Nov 10, 17, Dec 15, 1912, Jan 19, April 20, May 4, 18, June 29, 1913; 470:139; 1500; 172:I, 107; A1b, e, g; A4a, b, g.*

ALLEN, CALVIN JOSEPH. Born Dec. 1859, Nuecestown, Nueces County, Texas. Ht. 6 ft. 2 ½ in., blue eyes, brown hair, fair complexion, married. Stockman, Calallen, Nueces County, Texas. LOYALTY RANGER July 15, 1918–Feb. 1919. REMARKS: In 1910 was a ranch foreman in Nueces County. Died Feb. 10, 1922, Nueces County, Texas. FAMILY: Parents, Henry Davis Allen (b. 1833, TX) and Nancy Jane Selman (b. 1829, AL); siblings, John Bunyon (b. 1855, TX), Henry Davis (b. 1857, TX), Alice Belzora (b. 1861, TX), Margaret Rebecca "Maggie" (b. 1863, TX), Nathan Gray (b. 1867, TX); spouse, Mary Ann Ball (b. 1862, TX), married about 1881, Nuecestown; children, Frank C. (b. 1882, TX), Lula Mary (b. 1884, TX). *SR; A1aa, a, b, d, e, f; A4a, e; C.*

ALLEN, SAMUEL MILTON "SAM." Born Aug. 1, 1881, El Buey, Harris County, Texas. Ht. 6 ft., dark eyes, black hair, dark complexion, married. Cattleman, Houston, Harris County, Texas. SPECIAL RANGER Dec. 5, 1917–Jan. 15, 1919. REMARKS: In 1918 was a stockman, living in Pasadena, Harris County. In 1930 was a stockman and rancher living in Houston. A Samuel M. Allen died Dec. 21, 1943, in Harris County, Texas. FAMILY: Parents, Sam E. Allen (b. 1848, TX) and Rosie L. (b. 1858, TX); sisters, Lula (b. 1879, TX), Clara D. (b. 1883, TX); spouse #1, Jennie (as of Sept. 1918); spouse #2, Bessie C. (b. 1893, TX), married about 1922. *SR; A1d, g; A3a; C.*

ALLEN, WILBUR PRICE. Born Sept. 26, 1879, La Grange, Fayette County, Texas. Ht. 5 ft. 6 in., gray eyes, brown hair, fair complexion, married. Rancher, Hebbronville, Jim Hogg County, Texas. SPECIAL RANGER May 6, 1918–Feb. 1919 (rank: "High Private"). Cattleman (owned Jesus Maria and La Josephina ranches, Jim Hogg County, Texas—residence: La Josephina) and lawyer (partner in firm of Allen and Allen, Austin, Travis County, Texas). SPECIAL RANGER Aug. 30, 1919–unknown. REMARKS: In 1900 attended school in Austin while living with his uncle, George W. Allen, an attorney. FAMILY: Spouse, Josephine (b. 1887, TX); children, Florence C. (b. 1907, TX), John H. (b. 1909, TX), Wilbur (b. 1911, TX). *SR; Allen to Harley, Feb 18, 1919, AGC; A1d, e, f; A3a.*

ALLEY, POWELL GRANBERRY. Born Jan. 12, 1869, Grimes County, Texas. No physical description, married. Peace officer, Houston, Harris County, Texas. REGULAR

RANGER Dec. 13, 1917–Mar. 15, 1919 (private, Co. M). Honorably discharged because Co. M was disbanded on March 10, 1919. Applied, apparently unsuccessfully, for reenlistment on June 24, 1919. REMARKS: In 1900 was a salesman in Montgomery County, Texas. In 1920 was a railroad car repairer in Del Rio, Val Verde County, Texas. Died Feb. 29, 1948, Harris County, Texas. LAW ENFORCEMENT RELATIVES: Ranger William T. Alley, brother. FAMILY: Parents, William Thomas Alley (b. 1842, VA) and Tabitha Jane Kelley (b. 1852, TX); siblings William Thomas (b. 1872, TX), Robert Allen (b. 1875, TX), Maurice (b. 1878, TX), Emmett Marvin (b. 1881, TX); spouse, Minnie Madeley (b. 1882, TX), married 1899, Montgomery County; children, Ada Jane (b. 1900, TX), Jake (b. 1902, TX), Minnie (b. 1904, TX), Powell (b. 1906, TX), Herbert Douglas (b. 1908, TX). *SR; 471; Special Orders No. 21, March 10, 1919, WC; Alley to Harley, June 24, 1919, AGC; A1b, d, e, f; A4a, b, g; C.*

ALLEY, ROBERT FRANK. Born Mar. 6, 1879, Gonzales County, Texas. Tall, medium build, light brown eyes, black hair, married. Stock farmer, Hale Center, Hale County, Texas. SPECIAL RANGER June 13, 1918–Jan. 15, 1919. REMARKS: Had been an overseer on a stock farm as early as 1910. In 1930 was still farming in Hale County. Died Oct. 16, 1955, Lubbock County, Texas; buried in Hale Center. FAMILY: Parents, Alexander Wellington Alley (b. 1855, TX) and Mary Kate Fritz (b. 1860, KY); sister, Anna (b. 1877, TX); spouse, Mary Leona "Mayme" Lamkin (b. 1878, TX); daughters, Mary Margaret (b. 1904, TX), Anne Caroline (B. 1908, TX). *SR; A1b, e, f, g; A3a; A4b; C.*

ALLEY, WILLIAM THOMAS. Born Aug. 3, 1872, Anderson, Grimes County, Texas. Ht. 6 ft. 6 in., brown eyes, dark red hair, red complexion. Peace officer, Del Rio, Val Verde County, Texas. REGULAR RANGER Mar. 15–Mar. 20, 1921 (private, Co. C). Discharged. REMARKS: Served for six days. In 1920 was deputy sheriff in Grimes County. Died Sept. 11, 1941 in Navasota, Grimes County, Texas. LAW ENFORCEMENT RELATIVES: Ranger Powell Alley, brother. FAMILY: Parents, William Thomas Alley (b. 1842, VA) and Tabitha Jane Kelley (b. 1852, TX); siblings Powell (b. 1869, TX), Robert Allen (b. 1875, TX), Maurice (b. 1878, TX), Emmett Marvin (b. 1881, TX). *SR; 471; A1b, f; A4a; C.*

ALLISON, WILLIAM DAVIS "DAVE." (Listed in Ranger Service Records as ALLISON, DAVID WILLIAM.) Born Jan. 21, 1861, Cincinnati, Ohio. Ht. 5 ft. 9 in., blue eyes, gray hair, light complexion, married. Sheriff, Midland County, Texas 1888–1898. SPECIAL RANGER 1892–1895. REGULAR RANGER Oct. 1, 1899–Dec. 18, 1899 (private, Co. D). Honorably discharged. SPECIAL RANGER Dec. 28, 1899–unknown. REGULAR RANGER Oct. 19, 1901–Dec. 20, 1902 (private, Co. D; promoted to sergeant, Feb. 7, 1902). Resigned—honorably discharged. Brand Inspector, Cattle Raisers' Association of Texas, Sierra Blanca, Hudspeth County, Texas. SPECIAL RANGER Apr. 21, 1917–Dec. 24, 1917 (attached to Co. C). Evidently resigned. SPECIAL RANGER Jan. 19, 1918–Jan. 15, 1919. REMARKS: Had been sheriff, Midland County, Texas, Nov. 6, 1888–Nov. 8, 1898. Was an Arizona Ranger, 1903–1906. Was city marshal, Roswell, Chaves County, New Mexico, 1911; constable, Sierra Blanca, 1915. In 1920 lived in Post, Garza County, Texas. Was brand inspector for Cattle Raisers' Association of Texas until his death, Apr. 1, 1923, in Seminole, Grimes County, Texas. Allison and fellow brand inspector H. R. Roberson were murdered in Seminole by rustlers. Allison was buried in Roswell. FAMILY: Parents, Dr. John Pryor Allison (b. 1832, AL) and Mary Waters Clive (b. 1837, VA); siblings, Ellen C. (b. 1859, MS), George Clive (b. 1865, MS), Patricia Winston (b. 1868, TX), Luke Pryor, John, Paul Clifton (b. 1875, TX), Clara Belle; spouse, Lena Lee Johnston (b. 1870, TX), married Feb. 21, 1889, Midland, Texas; daughter, Hazel (b. 1889, TX). *SR; 471; Allison to Harley, Dec 30, 1917, AGC; 319:379–380; 1020; biography: 1501; 1503:373; A1aa, a, d, f; A4b.*

ALLMAN, AMBRUS FOSTER. (First name also spelled AMBROS.) Born June 16, 1882, Jacksonville, Duval County, Florida. Ht. 5 ft. 10 ½ in., blue eyes, brown hair, ruddy complexion. Farmer. REGULAR RANGER May 26, 1916–Aug. 15, 1916 (private, Co. D). REMARKS: As of Sept. 1918 was a restaurant operator in Waco, McLennan County, Texas. In 1920 was a bus driver living in Marlin, Falls County, Texas; still living in Marlin in 1930. Died Oct. 29, 1966, Falls County, Texas. FAMILY: Mother, Mary (b. 1842, MS); spouse, Eula (b. 1883, GA). *SR; 471; A1e, f; A2a, b; A3a.*

A

ALSOBROOK, WILLIAM M. Born Aug. 23, 1883, near Paris, Lamar County, Texas. Ht. 5 ft. 9 in., gray eyes, black hair, dark complexion. Constable, Precinct 1, Clarksville, Red River County, Texas, 1913–1917. LOYALTY RANGER June 1, 1918–Feb. 1919. Farmer, Clarksville. REGULAR RANGER June 16, 1919–Dec. 9, 1919 (private, Co. D, Co. I). Accidentally shot Dec. 8, 1919, at Crestonia, Duval County, Texas; died Dec. 9, 1919, at Laredo, Webb County, Texas. REMARKS: Had become popular in Jim Hogg County, Texas and probably would have been the next sheriff. FAMILY: Parents, James G. "Jim" Alsobrook (b. 1859, TX) and Frances Fern "Fannie" White (b. 1859, TX); siblings, Sims (b. 1880, TX), Clyde (b. 1887, TX). *SR; 471; LWT, Dec 14, 1919; A1d, e; A2b; A3a; A4b.*

AMES, LAFAYETTE. Born July 25, 1874, Holmes County, Mississippi. Ht. 5 ft. 8 in., blue eyes, brown hair, light complexion, widower. Salesman, Strawn, Palo Pinto County, Texas. LOYALTY RANGER June 7, 1918–Feb. 1919. REMARKS: Had been deputy sheriff, city marshal. In 1930 was a farmer in Palo Pinto County. Died Nov. 17, 1968, Palo Pinto County, Texas. FAMILY: Mother, Sarah Frances (b. 1855, MS); spouse #1, Emma (b. 1879, TN); children, Bessie (b. 1899, TX), Robert (b. 1900, TX), Stella (b. 1904, TX); spouse #2, Edna (b. 1894, TX), married about 1920; children, Sarah Beth (b. 1923, TX), John Edward (b. 1925, TX). *SR; A1b, d, f, g; A2b; A3a.*

AMONETT, WILLIAM LUCIENE. Born Apr. 1872, White County, Arkansas. Ht. 5 ft. 8 ¾ in., brown eyes, dark hair, ruddy complexion. Cattleman, El Paso, El Paso County, Texas. SPECIAL RANGER Mar. 11, 1918–Jan. 15, 1919. REMARKS: Had been a saloon keeper in Roswell, Chaves County, New Mexico. In 1918 was secretary, Panhandle and Southwestern Cattleraisers' Association. Was cashier and board member, Sierra Blanca State Bank, Hudspeth County, Texas, 1919. In 1930 was a real estate salesman in El Paso, El Paso County. FAMILY: Parents, William S. Amonett (b. 1838, TN) and Matilda (b. 1845, AL or LA); siblings, Elijah (b. 1868, AR), Leonora "Nora" (b. 1870, AR), Talala (b. 1877, TX), Albert (b. 1878, TX); spouse, Mary E. (b. 1883, KS), married about 1900; son, W. L., Jr. (b. 1917, TX). *SR; Hudspeth to Hobby, Jan 25, 1918, AGC; A1a, b, d, e, f, g.*

ANDERS, JOSEPH LEE. Born Jan. 1871, Bainbridge, Georgia. Ht. 5 ft. 8 in., dark eyes, gray hair, fair complexion. Merchant, Austin, Travis County, Texas. REGULAR RANGER July 19, 1909–Mar. 1910 (private, sergeant, Co. C). Resigned to become chief deputy sheriff, Hempstead, Waller County, Texas. REGULAR RANGER Mar. 16, 1910–Sept. 30, 1910 (private, Co. C; promoted to sergeant, Apr. 1, 1910). Resigned to become one of Mayor H. B. Rice's special police officers, Houston, Harris County, Texas. REGULAR RANGER Aug. 29, 1911–Dec. 31, 1911 (private, Co. A). Resigned to become a Houston special police officer again. REGULAR RANGER Sept. 6, 1913–Jan. 31, 1915 (private, Co. B). Discharged. Peace officer, Houston. REGULAR RANGER July 30, 1915–Mar. 31, 1916 (private, Co. D). Resigned. Wells Fargo guard (also held policeman's commission), Houston. SPECIAL RANGER July 22, 1916–Sept. 29, 1916. Peace officer, Houston. REGULAR RANGER Sept. 30, 1916–Feb. 15, 1921 (sergeant, Co. D, promoted to captain of Co. D., Aug. 20, 1918; was transferred as captain to Co. E, Jan. 1, 1921). Discharged—Co. E was disbanded on Feb. 15, 1921. REMARKS: Before enlisting in Rangers had been a convict guard for seven years. A Joe Lee Anders died Jan. 27, 1930, Harris County, Texas. FAMILY: Parents, William H. Anders (b. 1841, GA) and Ana or Santeppo (b. 1842, GA); siblings, William A. (b. 1870, GA), Ada A. (b. 1875, GA), James G. (b. 1878, GA). *SR; 471; Co. C, MR, Jan–Dec, 1910, AGC; AS, Mar 16, April 1, Oct 1, 1910; Co. A, MR, Aug–Dec 1911, AGC; Hughes to AG, Dec 24, 1911, WC; AG to Rice, Jan 28, 1915, AGC; Taft to Hutchings, July 19, 1916, AGC; Hobby to Harley, May 19, 1919, WC; AA, July 22, 1920; A1a, b; A2b.*

ANDERSON, HERBERT HAMILTON. (Some documents list name as HUBERT.) Born Sept. 27, 1882, Selma, Guadalupe County, Texas. Ht. 6 ft. 2 in., gray eyes, brown hair, light complexion, married. Auto and garage business, Anson, Jones County, Texas. SPECIAL RANGER May 31, 1917–Dec. 1917 (attached to Co. C). REMARKS: Had been a blacksmith in Anson. In 1930 was a bookkeeper in a cotton office in Abilene, Taylor County, Texas. Died Nov. 20, 1965, Wichita County, Texas. FAMILY: Parents, Hugh Allen Anderson (b. 1846) and Mary Ellen Hamilton (b. 1847, TX); siblings, Bertha Catherine (b. 1869, TX), Kent Haile (b. 1871, TX), Leila (b. 1874, TX), Julia (b. 1876, TX), Esther (b. 1878, TX), Laura (b. 1880, TX); spouse Rosa Ann Haynes

(b. 1885, AL), married Feb. 13, 1905; son, Hugh Allen (b. 1906, TX). *SR; Dodson to Ferguson, May 18, 1917, AGC; Cunningham to Ferguson, May 18, 1917, AGC; A1e, f, g; A2a, b; A3a; A4b.*

ANDERSON, JOHN W. Born 1872, Gonzales County, Texas. Ht. 6 ft. 3 in., dark eyes, dark hair, dark complexion, married. REGULAR RANGER, served two years (before 1906) under Captain Brooks (private, Co. A). Wood superintendent at a lumber mill, Westville, Trinity County, Texas. SPECIAL RANGER June 20, 1918–Jan. 15, 1919. REMARKS: Deputy sheriff, Trinity County, 1915–1920. In 1930 was "Quarter Boss" at a sawmill in Trinity County. LAW ENFORCEMENT RELATIVES: Ranger Samuel R. Anderson, brother. FAMILY: Parents, Balam Anderson (b. 1835, TN) and Jane (b. 1847, MS); siblings, Sarah E. "Betsy" (b. 1864, TX), Lenora or Molly (b. 1866, TX), Lee, (b. 1868, TX), Samuel R. (b. 1870, TX), James M. (b. 1874, TX), Martha J. (b. 1876, TX), Balis (b. 1878, TX), Margaret (b. 1880, TX); spouse, Callie (b. 1876, TX), married about 1898; sons McKay (b. 1899, TX), John (b. 1899, TX). *SR; 471; Phillips to Ferguson, June 4, 1915, AGC; A1a, b, e, f, g.*

ANDERSON, OTTIS ALLEN. Born Jan. 25, 1896, Oakville, Live Oak County, Texas. Ht. 5 ft. 11 in., brown eyes, dark hair, dark complexion. Truck driver, Kingsville, Kleberg County, Texas. SPECIAL RANGER June 20, 1918–Jan. 15, 1919. REMARKS: WWI draft registration form stated he was born in Beeville, Bee County, Texas. In 1917, lived in Cleburne, Johnson County, Texas, working on a dairy farm. In 1920 was a herder on "Little Pasture" in Kleberg County; in 1930 was an auto mechanic in Houston, Harris County, Texas. Died Nov. 3, 1979, Houston, Harris County, Texas. FAMILY: Parents, Thomas F. Anderson (b. 1861, TX) and Sonia J. (b. 1863, TX); siblings, Earnest L. (b. 1892, TX), Lillie J. (b. 1894, TX), Alexander J. (b. 1898, TX); spouse, Stella (b. 1905, TX); stepdaughter, Margaret McGrew (b. 1926, TX). *SR; A1d, f, g; A2a, b; A3a.*

ANDERSON, SAMUEL R. Born May 1870, Gonzales County, Texas. Ht. 6 ft. 1 in., blue eyes, dark hair, light complexion, married. Rancher, Asherton, Dimmit County, Texas. SPECIAL RANGER July 13, 1918–Jan. 15, 1919. REMARKS: Had been a Webb County deputy sheriff for one year and a deputy game warden for two years. In 1930 was a cattle ranch manager in Carrizo Springs, Dimmit County. LAW ENFORCEMENT RELATIVES: Ranger John W. Anderson, brother. FAMILY: Parents, Balam Anderson (b. 1835, TN) and Jane (b. 1847, MS); siblings, Sarah E. "Betsy" (b. 1864, TX), Lenora or Molly (b. 1866, TX), Lee (b. 1868, TX), John W. (b. 1872, TX), James M. (b. 1874, TX), Martha J. (b. 1876, TX), Balis (b. 1878, TX), Margaret (b. 1880, TX); spouse #1, Marrey (b. 1872, Germany), married about 1908; spouse #2, Mina (b. 1888, TX). *SR; A1a, b, d, e, g.*

ANDREWS, WALKER WILLIAM. (Ranger Service Record name is WALTER WILLIAM ANDREWS.) Born Dec. 12, 1891, Rockdale, Milam County, Texas. Ht. 6 ft. 1 in., brown eyes, dark hair, dark complexion. Cowboy, Marathon, Brewster County, Texas. REGULAR RANGER Aug. 22, 1919–Dec. 15, 1921 (private, Co. E). RAILROAD RANGER Oct. 7, 1922–Dec. 15, 1922 (Headquarters Co.). Discharged. REMARKS: Died Dec. 12, 1969, Kerrville, Kerr County, Texas; was a widower at the time of his death. FAMILY: Parents, James N. Andrews (b. 1850, AL) and Nancy V. (b. 1854, AL); siblings, Alice E. (b. 1879, TX), Laura H. (b. 1884, TX), Wallis J. (b. 1886, TX), George M. (b. 1889, TX), Emmett T. (b. 1896, TX). *SR; 471; A1d; A2a, b.*

ANGLIN, EVERETT W. Born Feb. 1884, Smiley, Gonzales County, Texas. Ht. 6 ft., blue eyes, brown hair, fair complexion, married. REGULAR RANGER 1905 (private, Co. A). City marshal, McAllen, Hidalgo County, Texas. LOYALTY RANGER June 18, 1918–Feb. 1919. REMARKS: As a young man lived in Alpine, Brewster County, Texas, and punched cattle in the Big Bend. In 1910 was deputy sheriff living in Mercedes, Hidalgo County. Mounted Customs inspector, Brownsville, Cameron County, Texas, 1910–1912. Deputy U.S. marshal for the Southern District of Texas, 1913. Mounted Customs inspector, 1914. Deputy sheriff, Harlingen, Cameron County, 1914, 1917. City marshal, McAllen, 1915–1919. As of Sept. 1918 was captain, Troop G, 2nd Cavalry, Texas National Guard, McAllen. Partner in Anglin and Dixon Garage, McAllen, 1918–1919. In 1920 was a real estate agent in McAllen. In 1926 opened a real estate office in Harlingen: Anglin Brothers and Berley. In 1930 was living in Crystal City, Zavala County, Texas working as a real estate agent. Was sheriff, Zavala County, Jan. 1, 1931–Jan. 1, 1941. LAW ENFORCEMENT RELATIVES: Ranger Captain William M. Hanson, distant cousin (Anglin's mother was Hanson's cousin). FAMILY: Spouse #1, Eva (b. 1884, LA), married about 1906; spouse #2, Mary (b. 1888, IN), married about 1925; stepson, Robert E. Melburg (b. 1915, TX). *SR; 471; Vann to Hanson, April 3, 1918, AGC; Assistant AG to Hanson, April 25, 1918, AGC; BDH, May 14, 15, Sept 12, 1913, Dec 3, 1914, May 10, 1916; LWT May 10, 1914; BDH, June 4, Sept 6, 1917; AA, Oct 2, 1919; 1503:561; 1508; A1e, f, g; A3a.*

APEL, HIRAM WESLEY. Born Aug. 5, 1860, Mineola, Wood County, Texas. Ht. 6 ft., dark eyes, dark hair, dark complexion, married. Farmer, Mineola. SPECIAL RANGER June 1, 1918–Jan. 15, 1919. REMARKS: Was sheriff of Wood County, 1898–1902 and Nov. 7, 1916–Nov. 2, 1920. In 1910 was detective for the railroad in Wood County. In 1920 and 1930 was a farm manager in Mineola. Died May 8, 1931, Dallas County, Texas; buried in Concord Cemetery, Wood County. FAMILY: Parents, William M. Apel (b. 1823, Germany) and Melissa Elizabeth Reich (b. 1838, IN); siblings, John Ulrich (b. 1859), Mary Moriah (b. 1862), William Houston (b. 1865, TX), Gertrude C. (b. 1867, TX), J. McFarland (b. 1869, TX), Godfried Charles (b. 1871, TX), Martha Elizabeth (b. 1875, TX), Sarah Habile (b. 1878, TX), Benjamin Franklin (b. 1880, TX); spouse, Elizabeth S. "Lizzie" Hall (b. 1859, AL), married in 1879; children, Lilly I. (b. 1881, TX), Eva E. (b. 1884, TX), Robert Wesley (b. 1890, TX), Evelyne N. (b. 1892, TX), Corinne (b. 1895, TX), Pauline A. (b. 1898, TX). *SR; 1503:554; A1b, d, e, f, g; A4a, b, g; C.*

APODACA, ANTONIO J. Born Sept. 26, 1892, Belen, El Paso County, Texas. Ht. 5 ft. 11 in., brown hair, black eyes, dark complexion, married. Boilermaker, Ysleta, El Paso County. REGULAR RANGER Aug. 18, 1919–unknown; was still a Ranger at Ysleta as of Jan. 1920 (private, Co. B). REMARKS: Was PFC in Army, served one year in France during WWI. His World War I draft registration document was filed in Tucson, Pima County, Arizona where he was a boilermaker for the SP Company. In 1930 was farming in El Paso County. Died Mar. 2, 1943; buried in Fort Bliss National Cemetery, El Paso. FAMILY: Parents, Francisco Apodaca (b. 1857, TX) and Jesusita (b. 1862, Mexico); siblings, Gregorio (b. 1888, TX), Benigna (b. 1890, TX), Catalina (b. 1895, TX); spouse, Mary Ellen (b. 1896, CA); children, Jessie (b. 1916, AZ), Mary E. (b. 1922, TX), Antonio (b. 1925, TX). *SR; 471; Aldrich to Apodaca, Feb 25, 1920, AGC; A1d, f, g; A3a, c.*

APPLEBY, JOHN ARTHUR. Born Aug. 5, 1875, Bellville, Austin County, Texas. Ht. 5 ft. 8 in, brown eyes, dark hair, fair complexion, married. Railroad brakeman, Bexar County, Texas. SPECIAL RANGER July 25, 1916–Oct. 1, 1918. Discharged. REMARKS: In 1918 was a conductor for the I&GN Railroad in San Antonio, Bexar County. Died May 2, 1919, Bexar County, Texas. FAMILY: Spouse #1, Lula R. (b. 1870, TX), married about 1902; children, Vernon W. (b. 1903, TX), Goldie L. (b. 1907, TX), Arline L. (b. 1908, TX); spouse #2, Olga Foerster (b. 1892, TX), married sometime before Sept. 1918; son, Robert F. (b. 1919, TX). *SR; A1e, f; A3a; C.*

APPLING, JOHN LOWELL. Born Apr. 20, 1871, Fayette County, Alabama. No physical description, married. Rural mail carrier, Louise, Wharton County, Texas. SPECIAL RANGER June 8, 1918–Jan. 15, 1919. REMARKS: Had been a merchant in a general store in Wharton County. In 1920 was a cotton farmer in Wharton County. Died May 6, 1922, El Campo, Wharton County, Texas. FAMILY: Parents, Samuel Burwell Appling (b. 1823, AL) and Rebecca M. Whiteside (b. 1836, AL); siblings, Jessee (b. 1859, AL), twins Johnathan Mortimore and Samuel Montsville (b. 1864, AL), Lemuel D. (b. 1867, AL), George Green (b. 1869, AL); spouse, Frances Elizabeth "Fannie" McClure (b. 1868, MS), married Oct. 23, 1890, Fayette County, Alabama; children, Claude (b. 1892, TX), Walter William (b. 1893, TX), Grady Samuel (b. 1896, OK), Floyd Edward (b. 1899, OK), John Lowell (b. 1901, TX), George (b. 1905, TX), Jesse (b. 1908, TX), Stephen F. (b. 1909, TX). *SR; A1b, e, f; A4a, b, d, g.*

ARCHER, LINTON PRENTICE. Born Mar. 20, 1885, Bell County, Texas. Ht. 5 ft. 11 in., brown eyes, black hair, ruddy complexion, married. REGULAR RANGER June 5, 1917–July 31, 1917 (private, Co. D). Honorably discharged. Peace officer. REGULAR RANGER Oct. 6, 1917–Feb. 25, 1918 (private, Co. D). Discharged. REMARKS: In Sept. 1918 was chief of police in Calvert, Robertson County, Texas; was a city peace officer in Calvert in 1920. In 1930 was an auto salesman in Bell County. Died Oct. 16, 1938, Bell County, Texas. FAMILY: Parents, James Milton Archer (b. 1855, TX) and Laura Anne Elizabeth Rucker (b. 1858, TX); siblings,

Annie Elizabeth (b. 1880, TX), William T. (b. 1883, TX), Ada Belle (b. 1888, TX), Jessie Jenkins (b. 1891, TX), James Milton or Whitlow (b. 1894, TX); spouse, Connie Zetta or Zoline Middlebrook (b. 1899, AL), married Aug. 4, 1916, Bell County; daughter, Louise L. or G. (b. 1918, TX). *SR; 471; A1b, d, e, f, g; A3a; A4a; B1; C.*

ARMSTRONG, SALVEDORE A. "SAL." Born Apr. 8, 1880, Frio County, Texas. Ht. 6 ft. 1 in., gray eyes, brown hair, red complexion, married. Rancher and Dimmit County deputy sheriff, Big Wells, Dimmit County, Texas. SPECIAL RANGER Apr. 30, 1918–Jan. 15, 1919. REMARKS: Had been foreman of a stock ranch in 1910. In 1930 was a stock farmer in Zavala County, Texas. Died Apr. 16, 1949, Uvalde County, Texas. LAW ENFORCEMENT RELATIVES: Ranger T. D. Armstrong, cousin. FAMILY: Parents, George W. Armstrong (b. 1857, TX) and Caroline Droddy (b. 1862, TX); spouse, Lilly Lee Cude (b. 1879, TX), married Aug. 10, 1898, Frio County; children, Earl Cude (b. 1899, TX), Edith Bessie (b. 1901, TX), George William (b. 1903, TX), Jewel Pink (b. 1908, TX), Marie Vesper (b. 1910, TX), Sal Alvin (b. 1913, TX), Lee (b. 1915, TX), Travis (b. 1918, TX), Lillian L. (b. 1925, TX). *SR; 471; Assistant AG to Gardner, April 25, 1918, AGC; A1b, d, e, f, g; A2b; A3a; A4b, g.*

ARMSTRONG, THOMAS DOYLE "TOM." Born Aug. 13, 1887, Frio, Frio County, Texas. Ht. 5 ft. 11 in., gray eyes, brown hair, medium complexion. Ranchman. REGULAR RANGER May 18, 1916–June 1, 1917 (private, Co. A). Resigned. REMARKS: In June 1917 lived in Alice, Jim Wells County, Texas. In 1920 was a well driller in Pearsall, Frio County. In 1930 was a road laborer in Frio County. In 1936 lived in Maverick County, Texas. A Thomas "Tom" Armstrong died Apr. 13, 1978, Comal County, Texas. LAW ENFORCEMENT RELATIVES: Ranger Sal Armstrong, cousin. FAMILY: Parents, Thomas Armstrong (b. 1850, TX) and Elizabeth Craven (b. 1851, TX); siblings, Samuel (b. 1880, TX), Buergo, twin brother to Thomas (b. 1887, TX), William (b. 1888, TX); spouse, Anna Ruth Compton (b. 1906, AL), married about 1929; children, Tom D., Jr. (b. 1930, TX), Mary Jeane (b. 1936, TX). *SR; 471; A1d, f, g; A2a, b, e; A3a; A4a, b.*

ARNOLD, CHARLES HENRY. Born Feb. 21, 1877, Fort Stockton, Pecos County, Texas. Ht. 5 ft. 7 in., blue eyes, brown hair, fair complexion, married. Real estate agent, San Antonio, Bexar County, Texas. REGULAR RANGER June 29, 1918–Feb. 1, 1919 (sergeant, unassigned, worked under Captain W. M. Hanson). Honorably discharged. REMARKS: Had been a Bexar County deputy sheriff under John P. Campbell. Letterhead in 1918: "C.H. Arnold & Co., Moore Building—South Texas lands." In 1920 was a prison system auditor in San Antonio. A Charles Henry Arnold died Nov. 29, 1927, Bexar County, Texas. FAMILY: Parents, Henry Arnold (b. 1847, KY) and Mary (b. 1852, TX); spouse, Ethel (b. 1879, TX), married about 1910; sons, Charles, Jr. (b. 1915, TX), Martin (b. 1916, TX). *SR; 471; Hanson to Harley, June 29, 1918, AGC; Arnold to Johnston, Jan 30, Feb 1, 1919, AGC; A1d, e, f; A3a; C.*

ARRINGTON, JOBE [JACOB?] MICHEL. Born Aug. 15, 1881, Lynchburg, Virginia. Ht. 5 ft. 6 in., gray eyes, dark hair, married. Special county officer, Wichita Falls, Wichita County, Texas. SPECIAL RANGER Oct. 19, 1918–Jan. 15, 1919. REMARKS: As special county officer 1918–1919, captured draft evaders. In 1930 was a watchman, living in Dallas, Dallas County, Texas. FAMILY: Spouse, Ida (b. 1890, TX), married about 1908; daughters, Ethel M. (b. 1909, TX), Effie (b. 1911, TX), Anna Belle (b. 1913, TX). *SR; 471; A1f, g; A3a.*

ARRINGTON, MOSES LEE. Born Apr. 24, 1884, Granbury, Hood County, Texas. Ht. 6 ft. ½ in., brown eyes, dark hair, fair complexion, married. Attorney, Granbury. LOYALTY RANGER July 8, 1918–Feb. 1919. REMARKS: Partner in firm of Arrington and Robertson, Lawyers, Granbury. In 1930 a Mose L. Arrington (b. 1884, TX) was a farmer in Palo Pinto County, Texas. Mose Lee Arrington died Oct. 1931, Palo Pinto County, Texas. FAMILY: Parents, John C. Arrington (b. 1860, TX) and Sarah Jane Grice (b. 1865, TX); siblings, George, Luther (b. 1886, TX), Hettie (b. 1891, TX); spouse #1, Willie or Millie (b. 1882, MS), married about 1910; spouse #2, Dina (b. 1900, TX), married about 1928. *SR; 471; Arrington to Harley, Feb 22, 1919, AGC; A1d, e, f, g; A2b; A3a; A4e.*

ASBURY, JOHN THOMAS. Born Nov. 10, 1873, Fort Worth, Tarrant County, Texas. Ht. 5 ft. 8 in., brown eyes, brown hair, fair complexion, married. Farmer, Baird, Callahan County, Texas. SPECIAL RANGER May 30, 1917–Dec.

1917 (attached to Co. C). REMARKS: Had been a dry goods clerk, grocery clerk, cowpuncher. Died Mar. 1, 1937, Callahan County, Texas. LAW ENFORCEMENT RELATIVES: Callahan County constable at Baird (1900) Willis C. Asbury, father. FAMILY: Parents, Willis C. Asbury (b. 1848, KY) and Cynthia C. (b. 1851, GA); sister, Ocoola (b. 1885, TX); spouse, Lucy Annie (b. 1876, TX), married about 1895; sons, James (b. 1896, TX), John (b. 1903, TX). *SR; A1b, d, e, f; A3a; C.*

ASHER, JOHN (or JOHNNIE) HARRISON. Born Aug. 4, 1889, Wartburg, Morgan County, Tennessee. Ht. 5 ft. 11 in., blue eyes, brown hair, dark complexion, married. Peace officer, Amarillo, Potter County, Texas. REGULAR RANGER Feb. 15, 1921–Apr. 22, 1921 (private, Co. B). Discharged "For the good of the service." REMARKS: Had been a farmer in Randall County, Texas; in 1930 was a farmer living in Dallas County, Texas. Died Apr. 23, 1973, Arlington, Tarrant County, Texas. FAMILY: Parents, James Washington Asher (b. 1866, TN) and Isadora J. Brown (b. 1870, TN); siblings, Laura (b. 1891, AL), Clifton McKinley (b. 1894, TX), Willie Mae (b. 1904, TX), Stonewall (b. 1908, TX); spouse, Bettie (b. 1896, TX), children, Johnny (b. 1913, TX), Violet Loraine (b. 1915, TX), Pawnee (b. 1916, TX), Evelyn (b. 1918, TX). *SR; 471; A1d, f, g; A2a, b; A3a; A4b, g.*

ASKEW, ROBERT G. Born Apr. 1881, Licking, Texas County, Missouri. Ht. 5 ft. 8 in., blue eyes, black hair, fair complexion. Soldier. REGULAR RANGER Sept. 1, 1911–Jan. 31, 1912 (private, Co. C). Discharged—reduction in force. REMARKS: Had served in the 16th Infantry Dec. 31, 1901–Dec. 30, 1904, and in the 17th Infantry July 22, 1909-Oct. 30, 1911. In 1910 was stationed at Fort McPherson, Blackhall, Fulton County, Georgia. *SR; 471; A1e.*

ASKEY, WALTER H. Born Aug. 1871, Gonzales County, Texas. Ht. 5 ft. 9 in., brown eyes, brown hair, dark complexion, married. Ranchman, Sisterdale, Kendall County, Texas. LOYALTY RANGER Aug. 16, 1918–Feb. 1919. REMARKS: In 1930 still living in Kendall County. Died Nov. 7, 1946, Bastrop County, Texas. LAW ENFORCEMENT RELATIVES: Ranger John Eckford Gilliland, cousin-by-marriage; Ranger Herff A. Carnes, cousin; Ranger Quirl B. Carnes, cousin; Wilson County, Texas sheriff (Dec. 31, 1917–Jan. 1, 1937) Alfred Burton Carnes, cousin. FAMILY: Parents, Elijah Clinton "Clint" Askey (b. 1845, TX) and Elizabeth Susan Carnes (b. 1850, LA); siblings, Katherine, William Clinton (b. 1872, TX), Cora (b. 1879); spouse, Katharine (b. 1872, AR), married about 1899. *SR; 1503:547; A1b, f, g; A2b; A4b, g.*

ATEN, CALVIN GRANT. Born Dec. 7, 1868, Abingdon, Illinois. Ht. 5 ft. 9 in., gray eyes, brownish gray hair, florid complexion, married. REGULAR RANGER Apr. 1, 1888–Sept. 1, 1890 (private, Frontier Battalion, Co. D). Ranchman, Adrian, Oldham County, Texas. LOYALTY RANGER June 1, 1918–Feb. 1919. REMARKS: Had lived in the Austin, Travis County, Texas area prior to 1888. Was employed on the XIT Ranch in the Texas Panhandle; sometime after 1910 established his own farm/ranch in Donley County, Texas. Died Apr. 1, 1939, Lelia Lake, Donley County, Texas; buried in Citizen's Cemetery, Clarendon. LAW ENFORCEMENT RELATIVES: Ranger and sheriff (Fort Bend County, Texas, Aug. 21, 1889–Nov. 4, 1890; Castro County, Texas, May 9, 1893–Jan.1895) Ira Aten, brother; Ranger Eddie Aten, brother. FAMILY: Parents, Elder Austin Cunningham Aten (b. 1832, OH) and Catherine "Kate" Eveline Dunlap (b. 1833, OH or VA); siblings, Angeline E. (b. 1854, IL), Thomas Q. "Tommie" (b. 1856, IL), Clara B. (b. 1858, IL), Frank L. (b. 1861, IL), Ira A. (b. 1863, IL), Edwin Dunlap "Eddie" (b. 1870, IL); spouse, Mattie Jo Kennedy (b. 1862, TX), married May 2, 1894 in Round Rock; children, Cassie (b. 1894, TX), Calvin Warren (b. 1896, TX), Darrell Lamar (b. 1899, TX), Rena May (b. 1901, TX), Quinn (b. 1903, TX), Lannie Lillian (b. 1905, TX), Austin Turner (b. 1912, TX), Moody Evelyn (b. 1917, TX). *SR; 471; 172:I, 276; 1503:94,188; A1a, b, e, g; A4a, b, g.*

ATTWELL, SAMUEL B. (Name spelled ATWELL in some census records.) Born Sept. 1873, Columbia, Maury County, Tennessee. Ht. 5 ft. 10 in., brown eyes, black hair, dark complexion. Railroad special agent, Harris County, Texas. SPECIAL RANGER Mar. 23, 1917–Oct. 1, 1918 (attached to Co. C). REMARKS: Had been a cotton inspector in Houston, Harris County. In 1920 was a steel and iron contractor in Fort Worth, Tarrant County, Texas. A Samuel B. Atwell (note spelling) died July 23, 1926, Tarrant County, Texas. FAMILY: Parents, Leonard H. Attwell (b. 1841, KY) and Celia G. (b. 1846, KY); siblings, Edith A. (b. 1868, KY), Florence O. (1870, TN), Ashley W. (1871, TN), Leonard

Harrold, Jr. (1875, TN), Mary S. (1877, TN), Celia Adrian (1879, TN), Bartie J. (b. 1884, TX). *SR; A1b, d, f; A2b; A5a.*

AULTMAN, HENRY OGAR. Born Mar. 18, 1886, Kissimmee, Osceola County, Florida. Ht. 6 ft., hazel eyes, light hair, light complexion, married. Ranchman, enlisted in El Paso County, Texas. REGULAR RANGER May 17, 1916–Aug. 15, 1916 (private, Co B). Resigned. REMARKS: In 1918 was in the "cow business" in El Paso County, Texas. In 1930 was a cowman, living in Beaumont, Jefferson County, Texas. Died May 3, 1966, Harris County, Texas. FAMILY: Spouse, Katherine, married before 1916, divorced by 1930. *SR; 471; A1g; A2a, b; A3a.*

AUSTIN, VALERY EDWARD. Born Mar. 27, 1863, Weimar, Colorado County, Texas. No physical description, married. Real estate agent, Galveston, Galveston County, Texas. LOYALTY RANGER June 14, 1918–Feb. 1919. REMARKS: "Austin & Co., Real Estate and Rental Agents." Died May 2, 1938, Galveston, Galveston County, Texas. FAMILY: Parents, Edward Tailer Austin (b. 1823, CT or NY) and Marie Estelle Hebert (b. 1831, LA); siblings, Mary Adele (b. 1858, TX), Henrietta (b. 1859, TX), Hebert (b. 1861, TX), Estelle Emily (b. 1865, TX), Henry "Harry" (b. 1868, TX), Edward Tailer "Eddie" (b. 1870, TX); spouse, Ida Lewis Smith (b. 1863, VA), married Oct. 20, 1885, Lexington, Virginia. *SR; A1b, d, e, f, g; A4a, b, c, g; B1; C.*

AVANT, ABNER MATHIS. Born Mar. 1862, Round Lake, Gonzales County, Texas. Ht. 6 ft. 3 in., gray eyes, gray hair, light complexion, married. Rancher, Marfa, Presidio County, Texas. SPECIAL RANGER Apr. 25, 1917–Dec. 1917 (attached to Co. C). Rancher, Marfa. SPECIAL RANGER Apr. 22, 1918–Mar.15, 1919. REMARKS: Had been sheriff of Atascosa County, Texas from Nov. 6, 1894–Nov. 8, 1904. In 1910 was a real estate dealer in San Antonio, Bexar County, Texas. Owner of A. M. Avant Livestock and Land Co., Marfa, 1917–1919. Chairman of Marfa draft board, 1918. In 1920 was a real estate dealer in Marfa. Died July 29, 1925, Bexar County, Texas. FAMILY: Parents, Abner Avant (b. 1832, TN) and Alethia Liman Jones Elder (b. 1840, GA); siblings, Mary E. (b. 1858, TX), Ella T. (b. 1860, TX), Robert F. (b. 1866, TX), Benjamin E. (b. 1868, TX), Ula B. (1874, TX); spouse, Ida C. Johnson (b. 1865, TX), married May 14, 1883, Gonzales County; children, Blanche (b. 1884, TX), Abner Byron (b. 1885, TX), Benjamin A. (b. 1887, TX). *SR; Avant to Harley, Dec 31, 1917, AGC; Avant to Hutchings, April 27, 1917, AGC; Hanson to Harley, Feb 8, 1918, AGC; 1503:17; HC, Mar 15,1918; A1a, b, d, e, f, g; A2b; A4a, b, g.*

AVRIETT, EDMUND L. "EDD." Born Dec. 1879, Milano, Milam County, Texas. Ht. 5 ft. 8 in., gray eyes, dark hair, dark complexion. Lumberman. REGULAR RANGER Oct. 5, 1909–Feb. 1, 1911 (private, Co C; promoted to sergeant Oct. 31, 1910). Honorably discharged. REMARKS: In 1910 was living in Austin, Travis County, Texas; in 1920 was an electrician working for the Texas Power and Light Company, living in Temple, Bell County, Texas. In 1930 was an electrician in Waco, McLennan County, Texas. An Edmund L. Avriett died Mar. 11, 1944, McLennan County, Texas. LAW ENFORCEMENT RELATIVES: Ranger Hall Avriett , brother; Angelina County deputy sheriff (1910) Ben A. Avriett, father. FAMILY: Parents, Benjamin A. Avriett (b. 1853, LA) and Elizabeth Phoebe (b. 1856, AR); siblings, Walter A. (b. 1876, TX), Millie Emma (b. 1878, TX), H. (Hall) Thomas (b. 1882, TX), John C. (b. 1884, TX); spouse, Willie Stella (b. 1892, TX), married about 1914; son, Edwin Benjamin (b. 1919, TX). *SR; A1b, d, e, f, g; C.*

AVRIETT, HALL THOMAS. Born June 22, 1882, Milam County, Texas. Ht. 5 ft. 11 in., gray eyes, dark hair, medium complexion. Deputy sheriff. REGULAR RANGER Apr. 12, 1909–Feb. 1, 1911 (private, Co. C). Honorably discharged. REMARKS: On Sept. 9, 1909, he and Ranger Goff White killed a man by mistake; in 1913 they were indicted for murder in Trinity County, Texas. As of Sept. 1918 was foreman, Owens Lumber Company, Fort Worth, Tarrant County, Texas. In 1930 was a lumber yard foreman living in San Angelo, Tom Green County, Texas. Died Dec. 18, 1947, Tom Green County, Texas. LAW ENFORCEMENT RELATIVES: Ranger Edmund L. Avriett, brother; Angelina County deputy sheriff (1910) Ben A. Avriett, father. FAMILY: Parents, Benjamin A. Avriett (b. 1853, LA) and Elizabeth Phoebe (b. 1856, AR); siblings, Walter A. (b. 1876, TX), Millie Emma (b. 1878, TX), Edmund L. "Eddie" (b. 1879, TX), John C. (b. 1884, TX); spouse, Wilbur Gertrude (b. 1893, AR), married about 1914; daughter, Joyce (b. 1929, TX). *SR; 471; Rogers to Hutchings, May 15, 1913, AGC; A1d, e, g; A3a; C.*

BAHR, AUGUST THEODORE JACKSON "JACK AUGUST." Born Nov. 29, 1889, Shawneetown, Gallatin County, Illinois. Ht. 5 ft. 7 in., blue eyes, light brown hair, ruddy complexion. Special agent, Fort Worth, Tarrant County, Texas. SPECIAL RANGER Sept. 30, 1919–Dec. 31, 1919. REMARKS: His commission was issued at request of Adjutant General Harley. Had been chief special agent, Commercial Acid Company, St. Louis, Missouri. Died in 1936, Illinois. FAMILY: Parents, Ernst Frederick Ferdinand Bahr (b. 1846, Germany) and Caroline C. Scheelinger (b. 1856, OH); siblings, Jesse Ernst (b. 1876, IL), Charles (b. 1878), Matilda (b. 1880), Augusta (b. 1883), Susa Millspaugh (b. 1884, IL), Jacob Scheelinger (b. 1886, IL), William Frederick (b. 1901, IL); spouse, Lillie Mildred Bingsten (b. 1897, KS). *SR; A1d, e; A3a; A4a, g.*

BAILEY, CHARLES H. Born Sept. 1876, Lexington, Fayette County, Kentucky. Ht. 6 ft., blue eyes, gray hair, light complexion, married. Special officer, Dallas, Dallas County, Texas. REGULAR RANGER Sept. 28, 1920–Dec. 17, 1920 (Headquarters Co., Emergency Co. No. 1). Resigned. REMARKS: Was described as a *carrancista* agent in the Lower Rio Grande Valley in 1914. In 1920 said he'd been a special officer for 15 years. In 1930 a Charles Bailey, born about 1876, KY, was living in Dallas County, working as an oil field "commissary man." *SR; 471; BDH, Sept 29, 1914; A1g.*

BAILEY, HARRY MELVIN. Born Mar. 5, 1884, Chillicothe, Illinois. Ht. 5 ft. 8 in., brown eyes, dark hair, fair complexion, married. Division accountant, various railroads, San Antonio, Bexar County, Texas. SPECIAL RANGER Feb. 13, 1918–Nov. 8, 1918. REMARKS: In 1910 was a freight office clerk in Peoria, Peoria County, Illinois. Had been a railroad special agent, Atchison, Topeka, & Santa Fe Railroad. In 1918 was a special agent for the I&GN Railroad. Had been deputy sheriff in San Miguel and Bernalillo Counties, New Mexico. Was an operative, Ben Williams Detective Agency, El Paso, El Paso County, Texas. His SPECIAL RANGER commission was revoked when he ceased working for the railroads. In 1920 was a federal accountant in Los Angeles, Los Angeles County, California. A Harry Bailey (b. Mar. 5, 1884) died May 1969, Oceanside, San Diego County, California. FAMILY: Parents, Frank M. Bailey (b. 1860, WI) and Lizzie A. (b. 1854, MO); brother, W. Randolph (b. 1889, IL); spouse, Alice Fern (b. 1884, WI); son, Harry M. (b. 1914, TX). *SR; A1d, e, f; A2b; A3a.*

BAILEY, HENRY PAGE. Born Apr. 24, 1895, Pleasanton, Atascosa County, Texas. Ht. 5 ft. 8 in., brown eyes, dark complexion. Rancher, Carrizo Springs, Dimmit County, Texas. SPECIAL RANGER Dec. 27, 1917–Apr. 1918 (Co. C Volunteers—station: Indio Ranch). Discharged. REMARKS: In 1910 was a ranch hand in Val Verde County. In 1930 was a rancher in Uvalde County, Texas. Died July 2, 1944, Harris County, Texas; buried in Sabinal Cemetery. FAMILY: Parents, Samuel Lee Bailey (b. 1842, TN) and Sarah Page (b. 1851, TX); siblings, Rosa Lee (b. 1880, TX), Susie Sementhia (b. 1882, TX), Samuel Wright (b. 1884, TX),

Maggie "Carrie" (b. 1886, TX), Annie Mae (b. 1888, TX), Albert Thomas (b. 1890, TX), Jim (b. 1890), Benjamin F. "Frank" (b. 1892); spouse Hazel M. Durban or Durham (b. 1907, TX), married about 1924; sons, Albert, Cecil Page (b. 1930, TX). *SR; A1e, g; A2e; A3a; A4b, g; C.*

BAILEY, MARVIN EUGENE. Born Dec. 31, 1878, Riddleville, Karnes County, Texas. Ht. 5 ft. 11 in., blue eyes, black hair. Hotel man, enlisted in Brewster County, Texas. REGULAR RANGER Sept. 7, 1905–Aug. 19, 1906 (private, Co. C). Resigned to be deputy clerk of Karnes County, Texas. Stenographer, Karnes City, Karnes County. REGULAR RANGER June 5, 1908–May 1911 (sergeant, Co. C; promoted to captain, Co. B, Mar. 1, 1910; demoted to sergeant, Co. B, Feb. 3, 1911). Resigned. REMARKS: Had been a "medical student" in 1900. Was city marshal of Navasota, Grimes County, 1917. Was a life insurance agent living in Navasota in 1920 and 1930. A Marvin E. Bailey died Aug. 8, 1953, Harris County, Texas. FAMILY: Parents, Dr. T. K. Bailey (b. 1828, AL) and Mary Catherine (b. 1849, AL); brother, Pleasant B. (b. 1872, TX); spouse, Ellen Ione (b. 1880, TX), married about 1911. *SR; A1b, d, f, g; A3a; C.*

BAKER, ALFRED RANDOLPH. Born Aug. 26, 1885, Uvalde, Uvalde County, Texas. Ht. 6 ft. 1 in., blue eyes, brown hair, dark complexion. Laborer. REGULAR RANGER Oct. 3, 1906–1909 (private, Co. A; transferred to Co. B, Nov. 27, 1908). Discharged. Peace officer. REGULAR RANGER July 24, 1910–Nov. 1910 (private, Co. B). Resigned /was fired. Peace officer, Harlingen, Cameron County, Texas. REGULAR RANGER Sept. 12, 1911–Oct. 23, 1912 (private, Co. B). Resigned. REMARKS: Deputy constable, Cameron County, 1910–1911. Deputy sheriff, Val Verde County, Texas, 1913. Applied to become a mounted Customs inspector at Eagle Pass, Apr. 1913. Worked as a ranch manager, Cuatro Cienegas, Coahuila, Mexico, ca. 1917. In 1930 was deputy sheriff of Hidalgo County, living in Edinburg, Hidalgo County, Texas. Died Oct. 4, 1950, San Antonio, Bexar County, Texas. LAW ENFORCEMENT RELATIVES: Ranger (and Hidalgo County sheriff, Nov. 3, 1914–Nov. 1, 1930) Anderson Yancy Baker, brother; Ranger Joseph Eugene Baker, brother, Ranger Frank Patterson Baker, brother; Ranger John Rufus Bates, cousin; Ranger Lawrence H. Bates, cousin; Ranger Winfred F. Bates, cousin; Texas quarantine guard (Brownsville, 1915–1917) Arthur A. Bates, cousin. FAMILY: Parents, Thomas Gillespie Baker (b. 1851, AL) and Melverdia Jane Bates (b. 1859, TX); siblings, Frances Ellen (b. 1874, TX), Anderson Yancy (b. 1876, TX), Thomas Howard (b. 1878, TX), Joseph Eugene (b. 1880, TX), Harry Carroll (b. 1882, TX), Dudley (b. 1884, TX), Florine Alice (b. 1889, TX), Walter (b. 1891, TX), Frank Patterson (b. 1893, TX), Marcella Cornelia (b. 1896, TX); spouse, Lillian Jones (b. 1891, TX), married Aug. 25, 1912. *SR; 471; AG to Bailey, Nov 16, 1910, AGC; BDH, Dec 24, 1910; Sanders to Hutchings, Oct 23, 1912, AGC; MR, Co. B, Apr 30, 1913, AGC; Baker to Hutchings, Apr 8, 12, 1913, AGC; 172:I, 242; 1503:256; A1d, g; A2b; A3a; A4b.*

BAKER, FRANK PATTERSON. Born Sept. 3, 1893, Uvalde, Uvalde County, Texas. Ht. 6 ft., blue eyes, brown hair, light complexion. Mechanic, enlisted in Cameron County, Texas. REGULAR RANGER Aug. 5, 1915–Nov. 1915 (private, Co. D). Dismissed/fired. Mechanic, enlisted in Cameron County, Texas. REGULAR RANGER May 10, 1916–Nov. 30, 1916 (private, Co. A). Resigned. Texas quarantine guard, Hidalgo, Hidalgo County, Texas. SPECIAL RANGER Aug. 1, 1917–Jan. 17, 1919 (attached to Co. C). REMARKS: Had been a scout prior to enlisting in Rangers. Was a Texas quarantine guard, Hidalgo, Apr. 1917–Jan. 1919. Died May 4, 1921, Hidalgo County, Texas. LAW ENFORCEMENT RELATIVES: Ranger (and Hidalgo County sheriff, Nov. 3, 1914–Nov. 1, 1930) Anderson Yancy Baker, brother; Ranger Joseph Eugene Baker, brother; Ranger Alfred Randolph Baker, brother; Ranger John Rufus Bates, cousin; Ranger Lawrence H. Bates, cousin; Ranger Winfred F. Bates, cousin; Texas quarantine guard (Brownsville, 1915–1917) Arthur A. Bates, cousin. FAMILY: Parents, Thomas Gillespie Baker (b. 1851, AL) and Melverdia Jane Bates (b. 1859, TX); siblings, Frances Ellen (b. 1874, TX), Anderson Yancy (b. 1876, TX), Thomas Howard (b. 1878, TX), Joseph Eugene (b. 1880, TX), Harry Carroll (b. 1882, TX), Dudley (b. 1884, TX), Alfred Randolph (b. 1885, TX), Florine Alice (b. 1889, TX), Walter (b. 1891, TX), Marcella Cornelia (b. 1896, TX). *SR; 471; Ransom to Hutchings, Nov 2, 1915, AGC; AG to Ransom, Nov 3, 1915, AGC; 1503:256; A1d, e, f; A3a; A4b; C.*

BAKER, JOSEPH EUGENE. Born Mar. 16, 1880, Uvalde, Uvalde County, Texas. Ht. 5 ft., 10 in., blue eyes, brown hair, light complexion. Deputy sheriff, Cameron County, Texas. REGULAR RANGER Sept. 11, 1915–Dec. 9, 1915 (private,

Co. D). Discharged for "drunk and conduct unbecoming." Peace Officer, Hidalgo County, Texas. REGULAR RANGER May 18, 1916–Feb. 10, 1917 (private, Co. D, Co. A). Discharged—reduction in force. Jailer, Hidalgo County. REGULAR RANGER Dec. 31, 1917–May 1, 1918 (private, Co. G, F; promoted to sergeant, Co. G, May 1, 1918). Discharged or resigned (unknown). REMARKS: Had been a teamster in Uvalde County. Was Hidalgo County jailer for his brother Anderson Yancy Baker, the sheriff. Died Dec. 31, 1923, Edinburg, Hidalgo County, Texas. LAW ENFORCEMENT RELATIVES: Ranger (and Hidalgo County sheriff Nov. 3, 1914–Nov. 1, 1930) Anderson Yancy Baker, brother; Ranger Alfred Randolph Baker, brother; Ranger Frank Patterson Baker, brother; Ranger John Rufus Bates, cousin; Ranger Lawrence H. Bates, cousin; Ranger Winfred F. Bates, cousin; Texas quarantine guard (Brownsville, 1915–1917) Arthur A. Bates, cousin. FAMILY: Parents, Thomas Gillespie Baker (b. 1851, AL) and Melverdia Jane Bates (b. 1859, TX); siblings, Frances Ellen (b. 1874, TX), Anderson Yancy (b. 1876, TX), Thomas Howard (b. 1878, TX), Harry Carroll (b. 1882, TX), Dudley (b. 1884, TX), Alfred Randolph (b. 1885, TX), Florine Alice (b. 1889, TX), Walter (b. 1891, TX), Frank Patterson (b. 1893, TX), Marcella Cornelia (b. 1896, TX) *SR; 471; Ransom to Hutchings, Dec 11, 1915, AGC; Johnston to Baker, Jan 14, 1919, AGC; 1503:256; A1d, f; A3a; A4b; C.*

BAKER, JULES JOSEPH. Born Jan. 23, 1878, Houston, Harris County, Texas. Ht. 6 ft., blue eyes, black hair, dark complexion, married. REGULAR RANGER—served 5 months in 1907 (private, Co. A). Brand inspector, Colorado City, Mitchell County, Texas. REGULAR RANGER Apr. 11, 1921–June 9, 1921 (private, Co. A). Resigned. Peace officer, Teague, Freestone County, Texas. RAILROAD RANGER Aug. 5, 1922—unknown. Discharged or resigned—unknown. REMARKS: In 1900 was a guard at a state prison farm, living in Fort Bend County, Texas. In 1910 was a house carpenter in Bakersfield, Kern County, California. World War I Draft Registration document states he is a carpenter and New Mexico mounted policeman living in Carlsbad, Eddy County, New Mexico. A Jules Baker died Sept. 8, 1931, Harris County, Texas. LAW ENFORCEMENT RELATIVES: State prison farm guard (1900) William H. Baker, brother. FAMILY: Parents, William H. Baker (b. 1850, TX) and Nannie E. (b. 1854, TX); siblings, William H. (b. 1874, TX), M. J. (b. 1875, TX), Nannie M. (b. 1879, TX); spouse Carrie Abna Henderson (b. 1883, TX), married Nov. 15, 1908, Mitchell County; daughter, Olene (b. 1909, CA). *SR; 471; HC, Oct 26, 28, 30, 1910, Apr 2, 1918; A1b, d, e; A3a; A4b; B1; C.*

BAKER, THOMAS ALLISON "TOM." Born Apr. 9, 1879, Medina City, Bandera County, Texas. Ht. 6 ft. ½ in., brown eyes, red hair, florid complexion, married. Stock farmer, Mason, Mason County, Texas. SPECIAL RANGER Dec. 21, 1917–Jan. 15, 1919. REMARKS: Chief deputy sheriff, Mason County, 1930. Died Dec. 25, 1937, Mason County, Texas. FAMILY: Parents, William Baker (b. 1846, TX) and Eliza (b. 1852, TX); siblings, Virginia (1877, TX), William (b. 1881, TX), Benjamin (b. 1884, TX), Charles (b. 1886, TX), Mary (b. 1889, TX), Nolan (b. 1892, TX), Nathan (b. 1894, TX); spouse, Nina (b. 1875, TX), married about 1902; daughter, Lucile (b. 1903, TX). *SR; A1b, d, f, g; A2b; A3a.*

BALL, ZACHARY (or ZACHARIAH) TAYLOR. Born Oct. 20, 1848, Carroll County, Georgia. Farmer, Gary, Panola County, Texas. LOYALTY RANGER July 13, 1918–Feb. 1919. FAMILY: Parents, William Franklin Ball (b. 1812, NC) and Margaret Martha Morris (b. 1819, NC); siblings, Margaret A. (b. 1838, GA), Sampson E. (b. 1841, GA), Sarah (b. 1843, GA), Benjamin (b. 1845, GA), Martha (b. 1852, TX), Mary (b. 1854, TX), Rosa Anna Jane (b. 1856, TX), Jefferson D. (b. 1861, TX); spouse, Rosa Malissa Essery (b. 1857, TN), married Feb. 21, 1879, Panola County; children, Ida Lee (b. 1880, TX), Bessie Bee (b. 1882, TX), Mattie J. (b. 1889, TX), William F. (b. 1891, TX). *SR; A1b, d, e; A4a, b, g.*

BALLARD, JOHN HOUSTON. Born May 29, 1890, Floresville, Wilson County, Texas. Ht. 5 ft. 11 in., brown eyes, brown hair, dark complexion. Ranchman, Falfurrias, Brooks County, Texas. SPECIAL RANGER Feb. 7, 1916–Dec. 22, 1917 (attached to Co. C). Discharged. REMARKS: In 1910 was a bookkeeper for a lumber yard in Wilson County, Texas. As of June 1917 was working as pay clerk in Falfurrias. In Dec. 1917 worked for Ed C. Lasater, Falfurrias; in Dec. 1918, still worked for Ed Lasater and owned a small ranch. Applied for another SPECIAL RANGER commission; AG was agreeable. In 1920 was a bookkeeper in Brooks County. Was Brooks County sheriff, Nov. 4, 1924–Jan. 1937. Died Nov. 2, 1962, Bexar County, Texas. FAMILY: Parents, Benjamin F. Ballard (b. 1844, IL) and Lizzie A. (b. 1860, AL); siblings, Mary (b. 1887, TX), Gertrude A. (b. 1897, TX), Edith Fern (b. 1901, TX); spouse, Maude Ludwig (b. 1894, VA), married about 1916; children, Virginia (b. 1917, TX), John H., Jr. (b. 1920, TX), Mary K. (b. 1922, TX), Patrick (b. 1925, TX)), Nancy (b. 1927, TX). *SR; Ballard to Harley, Dec 25, 1918, AGC; Johnston to Ballard, Jan 10, 1919, AGC; Ballard to Johnston, Jan 13, 1919, AGC; 1503:68; A1d, e, g; A2a, b, e; A3a; A4b.*

BALLEW, THOMAS BIRD. Born Aug. 19, 1873, Calhoun, Gordon County, Georgia. Ht. 6 ft., blue eyes, gray hair, fair complexion, married. Cattleman, Marfa, Presidio County, Texas. SPECIAL RANGER Dec. 11, 1917–Jan. 15, 1919. REMARKS: In 1910 was a real estate agent in Presidio County; in 1917, owned a ranch near Polvo, Presidio County. In 1930 was a building contractor, living in El Paso, El Paso County, Texas. A Thomas B. Ballew died Aug. 9, 1945, El Paso County, Texas. FAMILY: Spouse, Amanda Lee Arendell (b. 1876, TX), married Sept. 20, 1896, Erath County, Texas; children, Edna (b. 1899, TX), Lucile (b. 1901, TX), Elmoe T. (b. 1903, TX), Mattie M. (b. 1905, TX). *SR; Ballew to Harley, Oct 9, 1917, AGC; Ballew to AG Dept. Jan 17, 1919, AGC; A1e, g; A2e; A3a; C.*

BARBEE, WILLIS MONROE. Born Mar. 16, 1888, Hico, Hamilton County, Texas. Ht. 5 ft. 10 in., blue eyes, brown hair, light complexion. Peace officer. REGULAR RANGER Nov. 11, 1911–Mar. 25, 1912 (private, Co. C). Discharged, reduction in force. Brand inspector, Sweetwater, Nolan County, Texas. REGULAR RANGER July 14, 1917–Apr. 30, 1918 (private, Co. C; transferred to Co. D, Sept. 1, 1917; transferred to Co. M, Jan. 1, 1918; transferred to Co. B, Apr. 15, 1918). Resigned by Apr. 30, 1918. REMARKS: Second enlistment form states born near Fairy, Hamilton County. In 1900 a Willis Barbee, age 12, was an orphan living with a family in Fisher County, Texas, along with one sister, Dora. In 1910 Willis M. Barbee was a grocery store clerk in Sweetwater. In 1930, owned a service station in Tom Green County, Texas. Died Aug. 8, 1968, San Angelo, Tom Green County, Texas; buried in Ozona Cemetery, Crockett County, Texas. FAMILY: Parents, James Monroe Barbee (b. 1859) and Amanda K. Taylor (b. 1864, TX); had 5 siblings; spouse, Katherine Lenora "Kate" Beall (b. 1891, TX), married Aug. 3, 1912, Sweetwater; children, Willis Beall (b. 1914, TX), Kathryn (b. 1915, TX), Eloise (b. 1921, TX). *SR; 471; MR, Co. A, Jan–Mar, 1912, AGC; AG to Barbee, Dec 21, 1917, AGC; Assistant AG to Fox, Apr 30, 1918, AGC; A1d, e, g; A2a, b; A3a; A4a, b; B1.*

BARBER, JOHN EDWARD. Born Oct. 11, 1866, Rockport, Aransas County, Texas. Ht. 6 ft. 1 in., blue eyes, black hair, light complexion, married. Farmer, Tivoli, Refugio County, Texas. LOYALTY RANGER July 9, 1918–Feb. 1919. REMARKS: Had been a butcher in Rockport. Died Mar. 7, 1945, Refugio County, Texas. FAMILY: Parents, John Albert Barber (b. 1818, LA) and Elizabeth "Betsy" Kokernot (b. 1831, LA); siblings, Amos Hamilton (b. 1847, TX), Addison L. (b. 1849, TX), George Albert (b. 1851, TX), David William (b. 1854, TX), Amelia or Amanda (b. 1855, TX), Elizabeth Carolyn (b. 1858, TX), Bettie Virginia (b. 1860), Clara Francis (b. 1863, TX), Martha Jane (b. 1868); spouse, his cousin Augusta Eliza Barber (b. 1869, TX), married June 30, 1887; children, Edna E. (b. 1888, TX), Alda Ella (b. 1889, TX), Elmer David (b. 1892, TX), Archie Edward (b. 1894, TX), Fred Herbert (b. 1897, TX), John Clyde "Dick" (b. 1899, TX). *SR; Barber to Harley, Feb 22, 1919; A1aa, d, e, g; A4a, b, g; C.*

BARDER, SAMUEL AARON. Born Sept. 18, 1889, Jacobs Well, Hays County, Texas. Ht. 6 ft. 1 in., blue eyes, brown hair, fair complexion. Farmer, Hays County. REGULAR RANGER Apr. 3, 1916–Dec. 31, 1916 (private, Co. D). Resigned. Stockman, Henley, Hays County. RAILROAD RANGER Aug. 17, 1922–Sept. 26, 1922. Discharged. REMARKS: Is also said to have been born in Wimberly, Hays County. Served 2 years 8 months in Co. E, 2nd Texas Infantry; sharpshooter, 1915–1916. Died Nov. 27, 1963, Medina County, Texas. FAMILY: Parents, John Ernest Barder, Sr. (b. 1862, Germany) and Georgia Ann English (b. 1868, Texas); siblings Jesse James (b. 1891, TX), John Eablis (b. 1893, TX), Albert Jefferson (b. 1896, TX), Nellie (b. 1898, TX), Lillie (b. 1900, TX), Etta Emma (b. 1903, TX), Linda Ray (b. 1905, TX), Louella (b. 1908, TX), Alma Dora (b. 1911, TX). *SR; 471; A1d, e, f; A2a, b; A3a; A4a, b, g.*

BARGSLEY, JOHN LEWIS. Born Apr. 8, 1863, Hood County, Texas. Ht. 6 ft. 5 in., blue eyes, light brown hair, light complexion, married. REGULAR RANGER—three years under Captains Jones and Sieker. Carpenter, San Antonio, Bexar County, Texas. REGULAR RANGER Sept. 28, 1920–Feb. 15,

1921 (private, Headquarters Co.). Discharged. Cowboy, San Antonio. RAILROAD RANGER Aug. 19, 1922–Oct. 17, 1922 (Co. A). Resigned. REMARKS: In 1910 did "odd jobs" in Uvalde County, Texas; in 1930 was a farmer living in Frio County, Texas. Died May 29, 1937, Uvalde County, Texas. FAMILY: Parents, John Bargsley (b. 1829, MS or LA) and Sarah Lucretia Arrington (b. 1834, AR); siblings, Nancy Ann (b. 1857, TX), Thomas M. (b. 1859, TX), James C. (b. 1861, TX), Sarah J. (b. 1865, TX), Charles (b. 1867, TX), Mary Frances (b. 1869, TX), Amanda L. (b. 1872, TX), William M. (b. 1875, TX), Ada Lena (b. 1877); spouse, Georgia Annie Boales (b. 1867, TX), married about 1888; children, Albert Charlie (b. 1889, TX), Ora (b. 1891, TX), George L. (b. 1894, TX), Roy Edwin (b. 1897, TX), William Henry (b. 1898, TX), Joseph M. (b. 1903, TX), twins Alvin M. and Alice Myrtle (b. 1906, TX). *SR; 471; A1aa, a, e, f, g; A2b; A3a; A4a, g.*

BARKER, ANDREW CHARLES "ANDY." Born Jan. 9, 1891, Taylor, Williamson County, Texas. Ht. 5 ft. 11 in., gray eyes, brown hair, dark complexion. Farmer. REGULAR RANGER Apr. 1, 1915–Aug. 1915 (private, Co. B). Resigned. REGULAR RANGER Jan. 1916–Sept. 1916 (private, Co. B). Stockman, Fort Stockton, Pecos County, Texas. SPECIAL RANGER Oct. 21, 1916–Sept. 5, 1917 (attached to Co. B). Brand inspector, Panhandle and Southwestern Cattlemen's Association. REGULAR RANGER Sept. 6, 1917–June 8, 1918 (private, Co. B). Discharged—fired. REMARKS: Was among those discharged when Co. B was disbanded because of the Porvenir massacre. Was a mounted Customs inspector at Presidio, Presidio County, Texas in 1919. In 1920 was a clerk for an oil company, living in San Antonio, Bexar County, Texas. An Andrew Charles Barker died Feb. 6, 1954, Kerr County, Texas. LAW ENFORCEMENT RELATIVES: Ranger and Pecos County sheriff (Nov. 8, 1904–Jan.1, 1927) Dudley Snyder Barker, uncle. FAMILY: Parents, Robert Edgar Barker (b. 1856, TX) and Mary L. Lucas (b. 1861, TN); siblings, Lula A. (b. 1881, TX), George V. (b. 1883, TX), James E. (b. 1885, TX), Lizzia A. (b. 1887, TX), Robert L. (b. 1894, TX), Harvey M. (b. 1896, TX), Ned (b. 1898, TX); spouse, Luta (b. 1880, TX). *SR; 471; AA, May 31, 1917; General Orders No. 5, June 4, 1918, AGC; 1503:410; A1d, f; A2b; A3a; A4b.*

BARKER, GEORGE EPHRIAM. Born July 20, 1866, Davisville, Benton County, Alabama. Ht. 5 ft. 8 in., blue eyes, black hair, dark complexion, married. Railroad auditor, San Antonio, Bexar County, Texas. SPECIAL RANGER Feb. 12, 1918–Jan. 15, 1919. REMARKS: As a youth had lived in Comanche County, Texas. In 1920 was an auditor for the MKT (Katy) Railroad in Wichita County, Texas. Died Nov. 23, 1951, Marion County, Texas. FAMILY: Parents, Abiah Morgan Barker (b. 1843, AL) and Martha Elizabeth Bowling (b. 1847, AL); siblings Albun Eustace (b. 1867, AL), William Green (b. 1869, AL), Mary Lee "Mollie" (b. 1871, TX); spouse Cora Urilla Womble (b. 1873, TX), married Apr. 1, 1888; children, William Leander (b. 1889, TX), Loyd Morgan (b. 1890, TX), Ellen Ruth (b. 1892, TX), George Wayne (b. 1894, TX), Brice Curtis (b. 1895, TX), Carl Eugene (b. 1897, TX). *SR; A1b, d, f; A2b; A4a, b, g.*

BARKLEY, JAMES M. Born Feb. 1862, Tarrant County, Texas. No physical description, married. Stockman, Guthrie, King County, Texas. LOYALTY RANGER June 12, 1918–Jan. 15, 1919. REMARKS: In 1880 was a cowboy living in Wichita Falls, Wichita County, Texas; later was a stock inspector, living in Judkins, Woodward County, Oklahoma. In 1910 census his wife was listed as head-of-household—he was a stockman, she was manager of ranch headquarters. In 1920 census he was head-of-household—a stock dealer, living in Fort Worth, Tarrant County. A J. M. Barkley died Dec. 25, 1920, Wichita County, Texas. FAMILY: Parents, Dr. B. F. Barkley (b. 1823, KY) and M. E. (b. 1827, KY); siblings, Francina A. (b. 1850, KY), Leonidas M. (b. 1854, KY), Rowena G. (b. 1857, TX), Laura J. (b. 1860, TX), Lillian M. (b. 1864, TX); spouse, Maude B. (b. 1862, TX), married about 1908; stepdaughter, Margaret Minter (b. 1894, TX). *SR; A1a, b, d, e, f; C.*

BARKOW, GUSTAVE PAUL HERMAN "GUS." Born Oct. 19, 1891, Seguin, Guadalupe County, Texas. Ht. 5 ft. 11 in., gray eyes, brown hair, married. Railroad special agent, Waco, McLennan County, Texas. SPECIAL RANGER Aug. 10, 1917–Dec. 15, 1917; Dec. 1917–Jan. 15, 1919 (reenlisted Dec. 1917). Special agent, Santa Fe and Southern Pacific Railroads, Houston, Harris County. RAILROAD RANGER Aug. 21, 1922–Oct. 15, 1922. Discharged. REMARKS: As of May 1917 was a special agent for the Texas and Pacific Railway Company in Marshall, Harrison County, Texas. A Gus Barkow was listed as a city probation officer in the 1917 Houston City Directory. Was a railroad special agent in 1920, living in Victoria, Victoria County, Texas.

In 1930 was secretary for a chemical company, living in Wilmington, New Castle County, Delaware. Died March 1, 1972, Houston, Harris County, Texas. FAMILY: Parents, Dr. Gustaf Barkow (b. 1847, Germany) and Carolina (b. 1873, TX); spouse, Maude E. (b. 1895, TX), married about 1913; daughters, Gussie Eloise (b. 1917, TX), Mary J. (b. 1924, TX). *SR; 471; Barkow to Harley, Dec 20, 1917, AGC; A1d, f, g; A2a, b, e; A3a; A5a.*

BARLER, WILLIE LEE "LEE." Born Jan. 2, 1874, Llano, Llano County, Texas. Ht. 5 ft. 8 in., blue eyes, light hair, ruddy complexion, married. Ranchman, El Paso County, Texas. REGULAR RANGER Apr. 9, 1915–Mar. 19, 1919 (private, Co. C; promoted to captain, Co. E, Aug. 24, 1917). Honorably discharged—Co. E was disbanded. Peace officer, Del Rio, Val Verde County, Texas. REGULAR RANGER Nov. 1, 1921–Jan. 3, 1922 (private, Co. C). Resigned. REMARKS: Deputy sheriff, Llano County, four years. As of May 1917 had spent past 17 years on the border, including three years in Chihuahua and Coahuila, Mexico. In 1920 lived in Del Rio, Val Verde County, Texas; in 1930 was a Customs inspector, living in Terrell County, Texas. His photo was the cover of the Apr. 10, 1939, issue of *Life* magazine. Died Nov. 16, 1951, Del Rio, Val Verde County, Texas; buried in Llano. FAMILY: Parents, Miles Barler (b. 1832, OH) and Jane Buttery (b. 1838, England); siblings, Villita "Litty" (b. 1858, TX), John A. (b. 1961, TX), Betty Ann (b. 1866, TX), Cora (b. 1870, TX), Eugene Miles (b. 1876, TX), Jessie Jane (b. 1881, TX); spouse, Euna Bernice Jackson (b. 1889, TX), married Mar. 8, 1908, divorced before Sept. 1918; daughter Isla Gayle (b. 1909, TX). *SR; 471; Almond to Hutchings, Apr 12, 1915, AGC; Robinson to Ferguson, May 22, 1917, AGC; A1b, e, f, g; A2b; A3a; A4a, g.*

Captain W. L. Barler. *Photo courtesy Texas Ranger Hall of Fame and Museum.*

BARNES, EDWARD ANDREW. Born Oct. 13, 1873, Eureka, Greenwood County, Kansas. Ht. 5 ft. 10 in., brown eyes, iron gray hair, dark complexion, married. Special agent, Missouri, Kansas, Texas (MKT) Railroad, Dallas, Dallas County, Texas. SPECIAL RANGER Dec. 28, 1917–Jan. 15, 1919. Special agent, MKT Railroad, Waco, McLennan County, Texas. RAILROAD RANGER July 26, 1922–Dec. 2, 1922 (Co. B). Discharged. Special agent, MKT Railroad, Waco. SPECIAL RANGER July 6, 1925–July 6, 1927; Nov. 7, 1927–Nov. 7, 1928; Dec. 5, 1928–Dec. 5, 1929; Dec. 18, 1929–Dec. 18, 1930; Jan. 8, 1931–Jan. 7, 1932; Jan. 15, 1932–Jan. 18, 1933; Jan. 25, 1933–Jan. 22, 1935; June 1, 1935–Aug. 10, 1935. REMARKS: As a young man had lived in Arkansas and the Choctaw Nation. Prior to December 1917, had been a Texas peace officer and special agent for some 14 years. An Edward Andrew Barnes, Sr. died Jan. 15, 1959, Dallas County, Texas. FAMILY: Parents, A. B. Barnes (b. 1840, PA) and California "Callie" (b. 1857, TN); siblings, Charles H. (b. 1860, MO), Mary Z. (b. 1866, AR), Lulu (b. 1872, KS), Zelda (b. 1877, Choctaw Nation); spouse, Jessie (b. 1885, MO); son Edward, Jr. (b. 1907, TX). *SR; A1b, d, g; A3a.*

BARNES, JOHN FRANKLIN. Born June 25, 1888, Gatesville, Coryell County, Texas. Ht. 5 ft. 10 in., blue eyes, black hair, dark complexion, married. Lumberman, Lampasas, Lampasas County, Texas. SPECIAL RANGER July 26, 1917–Dec. 1917 (attached to Co. C). REMARKS: Attended Texas A&M College 1904–1907. Died July 22, 1949, McLennan County, Texas. FAMILY: Parents, Walter Franklin Barnes (b. 1862, TX) and Alice Willingham (b. 1869, TX); sister, Myrtle (b. 1891, TX); spouse, Winifred Bonner (b. 1893, TX); son, John Wooten. *SR; A1e, f; A2b; A3a, A4a, b, g.*

BARNETT, ALONZO B. "LONNIE." Born May 19, 1883, near Shannon, Lee County, Mississippi. Ht. 5 ft. 7 in., blue eyes, brown hair, dark complexion. Cowboy, Gainesville, Cooke County, Texas. REGULAR RANGER May 3, 1921–July 16, 1923 (private, Co. B). Discharged. REMARKS: Had worked as a farm hired hand in Foard County, Texas; in 1918 worked as a carpenter in Cooke County. FAMILY: Parents, Aaron T. Barnett (b. 1860, MS) and Sallie (b. 1854, AL); siblings, Fannie (b. 1883, MS), Felix Arnold (b. 1885, MS), Gertrude (b. 1888, MS), Bessie (b. 1890, TX), Gracie May (b. 1893, TX), Beatrice (b. 1895, TX). *SR; 471; A1d, e, g; A3a.*

BARNETT, DEWITT TALMAGE "BOOG" or "BUG." Born Aug. 23, 1888, Files Valley, Hill County, Texas. Ht. 5 ft. 5 in., brown eyes, brown hair, light complexion. Cowboy, enlisted at Marfa, Presidio County, Texas. REGULAR RANGER Aug. 21, 1918–Mar. 15, 1919 (private, Co. D; transferred to Co. B). Honorably discharged. Stockman, Marfa. REGULAR RANGER Aug. 24, 1919–Sept. 16, 1919 (private, Co. A). Resigned. REMARKS: Had worked on a stock ranch in Val Verde County, Texas. World War I Draft Registration document filed in Cochise County, Arizona where he was a chauffer. In 1920 was a rancher in Brewster County, Texas. Died Dec. 9, 1982, Alpine, Brewster County, Texas. LAW ENFORCEMENT RELATIVES: Ranger Joe Graham Barnett, brother. FAMILY: Parents, Francis Marion "Frank" Barnett (b. 1863, AL) and Chicora Caroline Graham (b. 1866, TX); siblings, Joe Graham (b. 1890, TX), Anna Lee (b. 1892, TX), Frankie (b. 1894, TX), Sidney (b. 1896, TX). *SR; 471; Special Orders No. 21, Mar 10, 1919, WC; 1518; A1e, f; A2a, b; A3a; A4a, b; B1.*

BARNETT, FRANKLIN "FRANK." Born July 1867, Pettis County, Missouri. Ht. 6 ft. 1 in., gray eyes. Special agent, Fort Worth and Denver City Railroad, Fort Worth, Tarrant County, Texas. SPECIAL RANGER Jan. 3, 1918–Jan. 15, 1919. REMARKS: Had been a railroad detective in Sedalia, Pettis County in 1900. In 1910 was detective for FW&DC Railroad in Fort Worth; as of 1918 had been chief special agent, FW&DC Railroad at Fort Worth for the past 14 years. In 1930 was a railroad conductor in Cleburne, Johnson County, Texas. LAW ENFORCEMENT RELATIVES: Sedalia Chief of Police Robert W. Barnett, father. FAMILY: Parents, Robert Wickliffe Barnett (b. 1836, KY) and Malinda Perkins (b. 1842, IN); siblings, Charles E. (b. 1860, IL), Cyrus (b. 1861), Everett B. (b. 1862, IL), Nettie F. (b. 1864, IL), Viola (b. 1869, MO), Anna (b. 1875, MO), Lillie (b. 1877, MO), James A. (b. 1882, MO). *SR; A1a, b, d, e, g; A4a, b, g.*

BARNETT, J. C. Born Aug. 1856, Thornton, Limestone County, Texas. Ht. 5 ft. 7 in., blue eyes, gray hair, fair complexion, married. Railroad night watchman, Mart, McLennan County, Texas. SPECIAL RANGER Feb. 12, 1918–Jan. 15, 1919. *SR.*

BARNETT, JOE GRAHAM "BUSH." Born Aug. 28, 1890, Files Valley, Hill County, Texas. Ht. 5 ft. 9 in., blue eyes, brown hair, married. Ranchman, enlisted at Ysleta, El Paso County, Texas. REGULAR RANGER May 16, 1916–Jan. 28, 1917 (private, Co. B). Discharged. Cowboy, enlisted at Ysleta. REGULAR RANGER Nov. 8, 1918–unknown (private, Co. L; note: no Warrant of Authority issued). Ranchman, San Angelo, Tom Green County, Texas. SPECIAL RANGER Dec. 20, 1929–Jan. 30, 1930. Discharged. REMARKS: On Dec. 8, 1913 killed Will Babb at Langtry, Texas; was acquitted. As of Apr. 1917, lived in Sterling City, Sterling County, Texas; according to his WWI Draft Registration, June 1917, lived in Alpine, Brewster County, Texas, suffered from chronic appendicitis. December 1917 was manager of a ranch 65 miles south of Marathon, Brewster County. Between 1918 and 1925 worked as a cowboy and as part-time lawman, e.g. private security for Big Lake Oil Company; deputy sheriff in Big Lake, Reagan County, Texas and Rankin, Upton County, Texas. On July 23, 1925, killed Kirtley Watson at Big Lake; was acquitted. On Nov. 8, 1927, was appointed a state license and weight inspector. In 1929 was city marshal of Presidio, Presidio County, Texas.

In Dec. 1929 was a private investigator at San Angelo. Was a rancher in Brewster County in 1930. On Dec. 6, 1931, was killed in Rankin by Sheriff Will Fowler, who was acquitted. LAW ENFORCEMENT RELATIVES: Ranger DeWitt Talmage Barnett, brother. FAMILY: Parents, Francis Marion "Frank" Barnett (b. 1863, AL) and Chicora Caroline Graham (b. 1866, TX); siblings, DeWitt Talmage (b. 1888, TX), Anna Lee (b. 1892, TX), Frankie (b. 1894, TX), Sidney (b. 1896, TX); spouse, Annie Laurie Couger (b. 1896, TX), married about 1915; children, Maude C. (b. 1916, TX), Talmage Graham (b. 1918, TX), Billie C. (b. 1923, TX), Jerry Files (b. 1924, TX), Mary Ann (b. 1929, TX). *SR; AA, Apr 26,1917; Barnett to Harley, Dec 15, 1917, AGC; 1518; A1e, f, g; A2b, e; A3a; A4b.*

BARNHILL, PINKNEY LAMBERT "PINK." Born Dec. 22, 1865, Austin County, Texas. Ht. 5 ft. 10 in., blue eyes, dark hair, dark complexion, married. REGULAR RANGER—five years under Captains Rogers and Brooks. Stockman (King Ranch employee), Kingsville, Kleberg County, Texas. SPECIAL RANGER Jan. 27, 1916–Jan. 15, 1919. REMARKS: In 1900–1910 was a farmer in Lee County, Texas. In 1920 was a "coach trucker" in the railroad shop in Kleberg County; in 1930 was a night watchman on the King estate, Kingsville. Died July 3, 1940, Kleberg County, Texas. FAMILY: Parents, William Freeman Barnhill (b. 1819, GA) and Nancy O'Donnell (b. 1823, TN); siblings, Elisa (b. 1843, TX), Caroline (b. 1845, TX), Francis E. (b. 1848, TX), Angelina (b. 1849, TX), William H. (b. 1850, TX), Nancy (b. 1852, TX), John (b. 1855, TX), Ellen (b. 1859, TX), Portia (b. 1867, TX); spouse, Luna A. (b. 1877, TX), married about 1894; children, William Sanders (b. 1898, TX), Lorena (b. 1902, TX), Herbert (b. 1904, TX), Portia (b. 1906, TX), Lackie (b. 1909, TX), Woodrow (b. 1918, TX). *SR; 471; A1a, d, e, f, g; A4a, b; B1, C.*

BARRETT, ROBERT JACKSON. Born Feb. 26, 1869, Randolph County, Alabama. Ht. 5 ft. 10 in., brown eyes, brown hair, fair complexion, married. Merchant, Anson, Jones County, Texas. SPECIAL RANGER Apr. 31, 1917–Dec. 1917 (attached to Co. C). REMARKS: Had worked as a cotton ginner in Bell County, Texas. As of 1910 was selling hardware in Anson; still living in Anson in 1930. Died July 21, 1955, Jones County, Texas. FAMILY: Parents, William E. Barrett (b. 1832, S.C.) and Mary J. Allen (b. 1839, GA); siblings, Thomas J. (b. 1856, GA), Isabella C. (b. 1858, GA), Sophronia (b. 1860, GA), Mary Molly (b. 1862, GA), Charles W. (b. 1865, AL), John Henry (b. 1869, AL), James Milton (b. 1872, AL), David Earnest (b. 1874); spouse, Anna A. (b. 1875, AL); children, Tula E. (b. 1894, TX), Reuben R. (b. 1898, TX), Henrieta (b. 1904, TX). *SR; A1a, d, e, g; A2b; A4b, g.*

BARRIENTES, ABEL G. Born Nov 5, 1879, Rio Grande City, Starr County, Texas. Ht. 5 ft. 5 in., brown eyes, dark hair, dark complexion, married. Farmer and contractor, Snyder, Scurry County, Texas. SPECIAL RANGER Mar. 21, 1918–Jan. 15, 1919. REMARKS: Had been a soldier (captain?) and a peace officer in Snyder and Lubbock, Lubbock County, Texas. Died July 28, 1932, Scurry County, Texas. FAMILY: Spouse, Maria (b. 1886, Mexico), married about 1906; children, Celia (b. 1908, TX), Abel Colquitt (b. 1910, TX), Leonides (b. 1917, TX), Lola (b. 1921, TX). *SR; Barrientes to AG, Oct 5, 1917, AGC; A1g; A2e; C.*

BARROW, ARCHIE B. Born Jan. 16, 1877, Macon County, Alabama. Ht. 6 ft., blue eyes, dark hair, medium complexion. Merchant, Hamlin, Jones County, Texas. SPECIAL RANGER June 2, 1917–Dec. 1917 (attached to Co. C). REMARKS: In 1910 was a furniture merchant in Rotan, Fisher County, Texas. As of Sept. 1918 was a merchant in Eastland, Eastland County, Texas. In 1930 was a furniture company manager in Abilene, Taylor County, Texas. An Archie Burrell Barrow died Nov. 15, 1961, Taylor County, Texas. FAMILY: Parents, Jerry Barrow (b. 1851, AL) and Mary (b. 1856, GA); siblings, Elnor (b. 1876, AL), Mary G. (b. 1879, AL), Tennie (b. 1880, AL), Jerry (b. 1881, AL), Maude (b. 1883, AL), David (b. 1885, AL), Jennie (b. 1887, AL), Annie (b. 1890, AL), Bessie (b. 1893, AL), Stella (b. 1895, TX), Grady (b. 1897, TX). *SR; A1b, d, e, g; A2b; A3a.*

BARTELL, SAMUEL ENGLEHARDT "SAM." Born Jan. 8, 1862, Milford, Davis (now Geary) County, Kansas. Ht. 5 ft. 11 in., gray eyes, gray hair, dark complexion. Peace officer, San Antonio, Bexar County, Texas. REGULAR RANGER May 24, 1916–Aug. 15, 1916 (private, Co. D). Resigned. REMARKS: Had been a U.S. marshal in Oklahoma City, Oklahoma County, Oklahoma. In 1910 was a deputy sheriff in Oklahoma City. In 1930 was a constable in Oklahoma City. Died Nov. 12, 1944, Oklahoma City, Oklahoma.

FAMILY: Parents, Englehardt I. Bartell (b. 1824, Germany) and Cynthia (b. 1832, IL) or Mary Alice Southwell (b. 1836, IL); siblings, Rowland G. (b. 1852, IA), William Nelson (b. 1853), Edward C. (b. 1855, TX), Francis Marion (b. 1857, MO), Mary Margaret (b. 1860, KS), Daniel J. (b. 1864, KS) Caroline (b. 1867, KS), Earnest Sylvanus (b. 1869, KS), Robert Holtby (b. 1874, KS); spouse #1, Alta (b. 1878, MO), married about 1894; children, Carl (b. 1895, OK), Bernice (b. 1896, OK), Fay (b. 1899, OK); spouse #2, Mary E. (b. 1876, KS), married about 1909; spouse #3, Ola M. (b. 1878, TX), married about 1923; stepchildren, twins Ocia C. and Pauline Elliott (b. 1910, TX), Max S. B. Elliott (b. 1912, TX). *SR; 471; AG to Bartell, May 26, 1916, AGC; A1aa, a, d, e, g; A4a, b, g.*

BARTLETT, THOMAS EDWARD. Born Jan. 1874, Augusta, Richmond County, Georgia. Ht. 5 ft. 9 in., gray eyes, gray hair, dark complexion, married. Real estate broker, Schulenburg, Fayette County, Texas. SPECIAL RANGER June 11, 1918–Jan. 15, 1919. REMARKS: Had been a real estate agent in Denver, Denver County, Colorado. In 1930 was again a real estate agent in Denver. FAMILY: Spouse # 1, unknown, married about 1900; spouse #2, Lillian G. Galbreath (b. 1893, CO), married about 1912; children, Maxine (b. 1912, CO), Thomas E., Jr. (b. 1917, CA). *SR; A1e, f, g; A4a.*

BARTON, PHILIP ERWIN. Born Oct. 24, 1879, near Kilgore, Rusk County, Texas. Ht. 6 ft., brown eyes, black hair, brunette complexion, married. Cotton buyer, Kilgore, Gregg County, Texas (note: Kilgore straddles the county line between Rusk and Gregg Counties). LOYALTY RANGER June 12, 1918–Feb. 1919. REMARKS: Continued to be a cotton broker in Gregg County. Died Sept. 25, 1965, Kilgore, Gregg County, Texas. FAMILY: Parents John Andrew Virgil Barton (b. 1853, TX) and Bryan Marsh Erwin (b. 1857, TX); siblings, Augustin Madison (b. 1876, TX), Dr. Virgil Henry (b. 1878, TX), Andrew (b. 1881, TX), Julian Wiggins (b. 1884, TX), Emily Belle (b. 1887, TX), Josie Bryan (b. 1890, TX), John Cherry "Jack" (b. 1892, TX), Pheriba (b. 1894, TX), Hugh Mitchell (b. 1896, TX); spouse, Mary Isabel "Mabel" Kay (b. 1878, TX), married Dec. 30, 1903; children, Virgil Luther (b. 1904, TX), Philip Lee (b. 1906, TX), Martha (b. 1909, TX), Bryan Augustin (b. 1918, TX). *SR; A1b, d, f; A2b; A3a; A4b, g.*

BASS, RILEY M. Born July 1873, Hackneyville, Coryell County, Texas. Ht. 5 ft. 10 in., blue eyes, light hair, light complexion, married. Special officer, Gatesville, Coryell County. SPECIAL RANGER May 23, 1917–Jan. 1918 (attached to Co. C). REMARKS: Had been a deputy sheriff. In 1910 was living in San Antonio, Bexar County, Texas, working as a teamster. In Jan. 1918, when the AG cancelled his Warrant of Authority, Bass was or had been a Wells Fargo Guard in San Antonio. Died Mar. 3, 1918, San Antonio, Bexar County, Texas. FAMILY: Parents, Elihu H. Bass (b. 1833, IN or IA) and Parthenia Ann Gentry Ballard (b. 1844, AL); siblings, Mary Allice (b. 1865, TX), Marthy E. (b. 1867, TX), Arthur Lee (b. 1870, TX), Cora B. (b. 1876, TX), Elihu M. (b. 1879, TX), Calvin (b. 1884, TX), Henry H. (b. 1887, TX); spouse, Dora or Nora (b. 1875, TX), married about 1893; children, Lou N. (b. 1894, TX), Lonzo Riley (b. 1896, TX), Charles Lee (b. 1899, TX), Linda Allice (b. 1899, TX), Elise (b. 1905, TX), Thomas (b. 1907, TX). *SR; Campbell to Harley, Jan 29, Mar 13, 1918, AGC; A1b, d, e; A2b; A3a; A4b.*

BATES, JAMES CARROLL. Born Mar. 12, 1882, Comanche, Comanche County, Texas. Ht. 6 ft., brown eyes, brown hair, fair complexion. REGULAR RANGER 1900 (sergeant, Co. F). City marshal, San Angelo, Tom Green County, Texas. REGULAR RANGER Aug. 22, 1917–Aug. 31, 1918 (captain, Co. F). Resigned—Co. F was disbanded. REMARKS: Had been a Tom Green County deputy sheriff; deputy city marshal, San Angelo, 1907–1909; city marshal, San Angelo, 1909–1917. In April 1918, bought a small ranch near Marathon for $25,000. In 1920 was a salesman in San Angelo. In 1927 was San Angelo police chief. On Jan. 11, 1929 was arrested for conspiring to violate Prohibition Act; on Jan. 13, 1929, resigned as police chief; was reportedly sentenced to two years in a federal penitentiary. As of Apr. 1930 was a laborer in the "Road Camp" at the Federal Industrial Institution, Talcott, Summers County, West Virginia. Died June 8, 1946, San Angelo, Tom Green County, Texas. LAW ENFORCEMENT RELATIVES: Federal Bureau of Investigation agent (1918) L. E. Bates, brother. FAMILY: Parents, Reuben Columbus Bates (b. 1847, GA) and Mary Margaret Lanham (b. 1855, TX); siblings, Beulah Ann (b. 1874, TX), Luther Edwin (b. 1876, TX), Flora Alice (b. 1880, TX), Terrell Kiefer (b. 1885, TX), Isaac Whitt (b. 1888, TX), Mary Elizabeth (b. 1890, TX), Fannie Mae

(b. 1895, TX), Harriet Lanham (b. 1899, TX); spouse, Mary Newby (b. 1882, TX), married Oct. 5, 1930, San Angelo. *SR; 471; Harley to Martin, Aug 23, 1918, AGC; HC, Mar 29, 1911; AA Feb 5, 1914; Dubois to Ferguson, May 24, 1917, AGC; Davis to Whom, May 21, 1917, AGC; Bates to Ferguson, Apr 20, 1917, AGC; Bates to Harley, Apr 6, 1918, RRM; 1518; A1e, f, g; A2b; A3a; A4a, b, g.*

BATES, JOHN RUFUS. Born Dec. 25, 1878, Uvalde, Uvalde County, Texas. Ht. 5 ft. 9 in., hazel eyes, dark hair, dark complexion. Stockman, enlisted at Marfa, Presidio County, Texas. REGULAR RANGER Oct. 3, 1917–June 1918 (private, Co. B; transferred to Co. D, June 8, 1918 because Co. B was disbanded.) Resigned. REMARKS: Had been a cattle breeder in Uvalde County in 1900; in 1930 he and his mother were raising cattle in Clint, El Paso County, Texas. Died Nov. 8, 1949, Clint, El Paso County, Texas. LAW ENFORCEMENT RELATIVES: Ranger Lawrence Hughlett Bates, cousin; Ranger Winfred Finis Bates, cousin; Ranger Anderson Yancy Baker, cousin; Ranger Joseph Eugene Baker, cousin; Ranger Alfred Randolph Baker, cousin; Ranger Frank Patterson Baker, cousin; Texas quarantine guard (Brownsville, 1915–1917) Arthur A. Bates, cousin. FAMILY: Parents, Finis Carroll Bates (b. 1851, AR) and Amy Tennessee Pulliam (b. 1855, TX); siblings, Felix Monroe (b. 1872, TX), Arminta Mettie (b. 1874, TX), Elijah Carroll (b. 1876, TX), Edgar Pool (b. 1882, TX). *SR; 471; A1b, d, g; A2b; A3a; A4a, b, g.*

BATES, LAWRENCE HUGHLETT. Born June 11, 1876, Uvalde, Uvalde County, Texas. Ht. 6 ft. 1 in., dark eyes, dark hair, white complexion. REGULAR RANGER 1899–1902 (?). Wholesale dealer, Brownsville, Cameron County, Texas. SPECIAL RANGER June 15, 1917–Dec. 1917 (attached to Co. C). REMARKS: City marshal, Brownsville, 1902–1904; Special agent, U.S. Treasury Department, San Antonio, Bexar County, Texas, 1904–June 1910; Deputy constable, Cameron County, Sept. 1910; insurance broker, Brownsville, 1911; State Representative, 77th District, Brownsville, 1914–1917. In 1914 was appointed as a Lieutenant Colonel in the Texas National Guard on Governor Ferguson's staff. In 1920 was a wood salesman in Fort Worth, Tarrant County, Texas. LAW ENFORCEMENT RELATIVES: Ranger Winfred Finis Bates, brother; Texas quarantine guard Arthur A. Bates, brother (Brownsville, 1915–1917); Ranger John Rufus Bates, cousin; Ranger Anderson Yancy Baker, cousin; Ranger Joseph Eugene Baker, cousin; Ranger Alfred Randolph Baker, cousin; Ranger Frank Patterson Baker, cousin. FAMILY: Parents, Balis Anderson Bates (b. 1846, AL) and Sarah Frances Prather (b. 1856, TX); siblings, Arthur Anderson (b. 1872, TX), William Balis (b. 1874, TX), Izora (b. 1878, TX), Sam Bennett, Winfred Finis (b. 1883, TX), George Akers, Columbus Earl (b. 1888, TX), Bertie Ione, Lenore (b. 1891, TX), Lucile (b. 1894, TX), Balis Addison (b. 1898, TX). *SR; 471; Bates file, 137; EPMT, June 17, 190, Dec 1, 1914; BDH, Nov 3, 1910, Aug 1, Nov 30, 1914, Jan 8, 16, 1915; SAE, Feb 2, 1913; A1b, d, e, f; A3a; A4a, b; A6a.*

BATES, WINFRED FINIS. Born Jan. 1, 1883, Uvalde, Uvalde County, Texas. Ht. 5 ft. 8 ½ in., blue eyes, brown hair, fair complexion. REGULAR RANGER 1902–1905 (sergeant, Co. A). Criminal officer, enlisted at Shelby County, Texas. SPECIAL RANGER Aug. 18, 1905–unknown (attached to Co. D). Oil operator, Houston, Harris County, Texas. REGULAR RANGER Mar. 29, 1915–June 15, 1915 (private, Co. C; transferred to Co. B, Apr. 1, 1915). Resigned. REMARKS: Arizona Rangers, 1907–unknown. In government service, Panama Canal Zone, while Canal was being constructed. Worked in Brazil on railroads; returned to Texas in 1912. Traveling salesman for Texas Oil Co., Brownsville, Cameron County, 1912; in 1912 was transportation superintendent for a Mexican subsidiary of Standard Oil; later, special officer for the Texas Company. Apparently joined Houston police department. In 1915 was paymaster, Standard Oil of Louisiana. In 1916, oil promoter with headquarters in San Antonio, Bexar County, Texas. In 1920 was an oil pipeline manager, living in Fort Worth, Tarrant County, Texas. In 1930 was a pipeline right-of-way agent in Tulsa, Tulsa County, Oklahoma. Died Oct. 27, 1969, San Antonio, Bexar County, Texas. LAW ENFORCEMENT RELATIVES: Ranger Lawrence Hughlett Bates, brother; Texas quarantine guard (Brownsville, 1915–1917) Arthur A. Bates, brother; Ranger John Rufus Bates, cousin; Ranger Anderson Yancy Baker, cousin; Ranger Joseph Eugene Baker, cousin; Ranger Alfred Randolph Baker, cousin; Ranger Frank Patterson Baker, cousin. FAMILY: Parents, Balis Anderson Bates (b. 1846, AL) and Sarah Frances Prather (b. 1856, TX); siblings, Arthur Anderson (b. 1872, TX), William Balis (b. 1874, TX), Lawrence Hughlett

(b. 1876, TX), Izora (b. 1878, TX), Sam Bennett, George Akers, Columbus Earl (b. 1888, TX), Bertie Ione, Lenore (b. 1891, TX), Lucile (b. 1894, TX), Balis Addison (b. 1898, TX); spouse, Arah E. (b. 1886, AR), married about 1918. *SR; Bates to Harley, Apr 11, 1918, AGC; BDH, Apr 9, 1912; General Orders No. 2, Apr 1, 1915, AGC; AG to Sanders, Apr 6, 1915, AGC; Bates to Fox, June 8, 1915, AGC; Bates to Fox, June 9, 1915, WC; Bates to Hutchings, July 18, 1916, AGC; 319: 324–325, 327–331; A1d, f, g; A2a, b; A4b.*

BATSELL, JAMES MADISON. Born Apr. 11, 1866, Sherman, Grayson County, Texas. Ht. 5 ft. 10 in., blue eyes, gray hair, light complexion, married. Texas quarantine guard, Brownsville, Cameron County, Texas. SPECIAL RANGER Feb. 5, 1918–Jan. 15, 1919. REMARKS: Customs inspector, Brownsville, 1911–1916; mounted Immigration inspector, Brownsville, 1916; policeman, Brownsville, 1917; Texas quarantine guard, Brownsville, 1917–1918. Died Mar. 3, 1920, Cameron County, Texas; buried in West Hill Cemetery, Grayson County, Texas. FAMILY: Parents, Charles William Batsell (b. 1839, KY) and Elizabeth Clement (b. 1845, TX); stepmother, Rosa Florence Thomas (b. 1855, KY); siblings, Tom Annie (b. 1868), Charles William (b. 1869, TX); spouse, Fannie Lucia Dodge (b. 1867, IL), married Jan. 5, 1888; children, Jim H. (b. 1891, TX), Harold W. (b. 1894, TX), Stella (b. 1902, TX). *SR; BDH, Jan 29, Feb 1, 1915, Mar 21, 24, Apr 6, May 8, 1916, Feb 27, 1917; Collins to Harley, Feb 1, 1918, AGC; A1b, d; A4a, b; C.*

BAYLOR, ALBERT SEARCY. Born Oct. 29, 1869, Lavaca County, Texas. No physical description, married. Stockman, Uvalde, Uvalde County, Texas. LOYALTY RANGER June 17, 1918–Feb. 1919. REMARKS: An Albert S. Baylor died May 17, 1929, Bexar County, Texas. FAMILY: Parents, John Robert Baylor (b. 1823, KY) and Emily Jane Hanna (b. 1825, LA); siblings, John William (b. 1847, TX), Walker Keith (b. 1848, TX), Henry Weidner (b. 1849, TX), Sophie Elizabeth (b. 1850, TX), Anna Louise (b. 1853, TX), Thomas Perry (b. 1856, TX), George Wythe (b. 1858, TX), Francis (b. 1861, TX), Emma (b. 1864), Sidney Johnson (b. 1865, TX); spouse, Anne Laurie Beaumont (b. 1874, TX), married Oct. 20, 1899; children, Albert Searcy (b. 1903, TX), William Beaumont (b. 1904, TX), Felice (b. 1908, TX), Louise "Lou"(b. 1909, TX), Edward Randall (b. 1914, TX). *SR; A1a, b, d, e; A2b, e; A4a, g; B1.*

BEAKLEY, JAMES C. Born May 1865, Maury County, Tennessee. Ht. 5 ft. 11 in., blue eyes, light hair, fair complexion, married. Merchant, Dunn, Scurry County, Texas. SPECIAL RANGER Aug. 9, 1917–Dec. 1917, Jan. 17, 1918–Jan. 15, 1919 (attached to Co. C). REMARKS: Had been a farmer in Scurry County. In 1930 was a real estate agent in Scurry County. A James C. Beakley died July 8, 1944, Mitchell County, Texas. FAMILY: Parents, John H. Beakley (b. 1834, TN) and Lizza (b. 1847, SC); brother, Samuel S. (b. 1869, TN); spouse, Rachel Sarah "Sallie" (b. 1862, AL); children, Jessie L. (b. 1896, TX), Margaret G. (b. 1889, TX), Horace or Harris D. (b. 1892, TX). *SR; A1b, d, e, f, g; A2b.*

BEALL, CHARLES PRYOR. Born Jan. 7, 1883, Oakville, Live Oak County, Texas. Ht. 6 ft., blue eyes, brown hair, dark complexion. Peace officer, enlisted at Valentine, Jeff Davis County, Texas. REGULAR RANGER Mar. 1, 1915–Nov. 30, 1915 (private, Co. B). Resigned. Deputy sheriff, El Paso County, and brand inspector, Cattle Raisers' Association of Texas, El Paso, El Paso County, Texas. REGULAR RANGER Apr. 12, 1916–Sept. 1916 (private, Co. B, served at least through Sept. 1916). Resigned. Stockman, Sierra Blanca, Hudspeth County, Texas. SPECIAL RANGER Mar. 9, 1917–Dec. 1917. REMARKS: In 1930 was a Customs inspector, living in El Paso County. LAW ENFORCEMENT RELATIVES: Ranger William Erastus Beall, brother. FAMILY: Parents, Sebastian Beall (b. 1833, GA) and Mary Cavitt (b. 1853, MS or TX); siblings, William E. (b. 1874, TX), Jesse E (b. 1878, TX); spouse Ruby (b. 1900, GA), married about 1927; son, William (b. 1929, TX). *SR; 471; EPMT, Feb 23, 1916; Orndorff to Ferguson, Feb 26, 1917, AGC; A1d, e, f, g; A3a.*

BEALL, THOMAS DAVIDSON. Born Sept. 26, 1878, Bryan, Brazos County, Texas. Tall, slender, light blue eyes, light brown hair. Ranchman. REGULAR RANGER Apr. 18, 1918–Aug. 31, 1918 (private, Co. N, Hudspeth Scouts). Discharged—Co. N was disbanded. REMARKS: In 1930 was a farmer, living in Hudspeth County, Texas. Died June 30, 1969, El Paso, El Paso County, Texas. FAMILY: Parents, Thomas Jeremiah Beall (b. 1836, GA) and Margaret Nancy Ragsdale (b. 1843, MS); sisters, Mary L. (b. 1867, TX), Susan Neal (b. 1871, TX), Nancy Harrison "Nannie" (b. 1873, TX), Florence Ragsdale (b. 1875, TX); spouse,

Helen Hill Jones (b. 1895), married about 1930; children, Thomas Jeremiah (b. 1934, TX), Margaret Ragsdale (b. 1939, TX). *SR; 471; A1b, g; A2a, b, e; A3a; A4b.*

BEALL, WILLIAM ERASTUS. Born Mar. 25, 1874, Oakville, Live Oak County, Texas. Ht. 5 ft. 5 in., gray eyes, black hair, dark complexion, married. REGULAR RANGER—served a few months under Captain Fox. Ranchman, enlisted in Presidio County, Texas. REGULAR RANGER Apr. 16, 1918–Aug. 31, 1918 (private, Co. N, Hudspeth Scouts). Discharged—Co. N was disbanded. REMARKS: Had been a rancher in Sierra Blanca, El Paso County (now Hudspeth County), Texas. In 1920 was working as a cowboy on a cattle ranch in Spencer, Weston County, Wyoming. Died Apr. 16, 1920, Newcastle, Weston County, Wyoming. LAW ENFORCEMENT RELATIVES: Ranger Charles Pryor Beall, brother. FAMILY: Parents, Sebastian Beall (b. 1833, GA) and Mary Cavitt (b. 1853, MS); siblings, Charles Pryor (b. 1883, TX), Jesse E. (b. 1878, TX); spouse Ruth Gober Garlick (b. 1892, TX), married Jan. 31, 1911, Texas; children, Evalyn Medina (b. 1912, TX), Earl (b. 1916, TX). *SR; 471; A1b, d, e, f; A3a; A4b.*

BEALL, WILLIAM OTTO. Born Sept. 20, 1887, Dora, Nolan County, Texas. Ht. 6 ft. 2 in., blue eyes, brown hair, light complexion, married. Banker, Hamlin, Jones County, Texas. SPECIAL RANGER June 4, 1917–Dec. 1917 (attached to Co. C). REMARKS: In 1930 was a bank cashier in Petrolia, Clay County, Texas. Died Oct. 1, 1943, Austin, Travis County, Texas. FAMILY: Parents, William Malcolm Beall (b. 1861, TX) and Harietta Hawkins; sister, May (b. 1896, TX); spouse, Velna Crawford (b. 1884, TX), married 1909, Hamlin; children, W. O., Jr. (b. 1913, TX), Rodney (b. 1916, TX), Henrietta (b. 1918, TX), Malcolm (b. 1920, TX). *SR; 471; A1d, e, g; A3a; A4c; C.*

BEAN, JOHN M. Born Apr. 2, 1880, Jasper, Jasper County, Texas. Ht. 5 ft. 11 ¼ in., blue eyes, brown hair, fair complexion. Cowboy and peace officer, enlisted in El Paso, El Paso County, Texas. REGULAR RANGER June 15, 1915–Oct. 21, 1915 (private, Co. B). Resigned. REMARKS: Constable at Rogers, Bell County, Texas, 1911. El Paso County deputy sheriff, 1913. In 1918 working as a mechanic in Hudspeth County, Texas; in 1930 was a cotton farmer, still living in Hudspeth County. LAW ENFORCEMENT RELATIVES: Ranger Joseph Cecil Bean, uncle; U.S. Customs inspector (as of Sept. 1918) James B. Bean, brother. FAMILY: Parents, William Breckenridge Bean (b. 1856, TX) and Martha Caroline H. Turner (b. 1857, TX); brothers, James Breckenridge (b. 1879, TX), William Robert (b. 1892, TX). *SR; 471; SAE, Sept 24, 1911; EPMT, July 4, 1913; A1b, g; A3a; A4b, g.*

BEAN, JOSEPH CECIL "JOE." Born Aug. 19, 1874, Magnolia Springs, Jasper County, Texas. Ht. 5 ft. 11 in., brown eyes, brown hair, dark complexion. Stockman. REGULAR RANGER Jan. 1, 1912–Jan. 31, 1912 (private, Co A). Discharged—reduction in force. REMARKS: Sheriff, Terrell County, Nov. 6, 1906–Nov. 8, 1910 (was defeated for reelection). Lumberyard owner, Sanderson, Terrell County, 1911. Lived in El Paso, El Paso County, Texas Dec. 1917, Sept. 1918, Feb. 1920; in 1920 was an oil well driller in El Paso County. In 1930 was a farmer in Bay City, Matagorda County, Texas. Died Apr. 25, 1947, Brewster County, Texas. LAW ENFORCEMENT RELATIVES: Ranger John M. Bean, nephew; U.S. Customs inspector (as of Sept. 1918) James B. Bean, nephew. FAMILY: Parents, James Bean (b. 1825, GA) and Maratha or Martha Sarah Jane Garrett (b. 1830, GA); siblings, John Egbert (b. 1851, LA), Robert Jacob (b. 1852, TX), James (b. 1854, TX), Sarah Susan Jane (b. 1855, TX), William Breckenridge (b. 1856, TX), Jesse Alexander (b. 1858, TX), Benjamin Franklin (b. 1859, TX), Rebecca Elizabeth (b. 1860, TX), Rose Ella (b. 1862, TX), Price Lafayette (b. 1864, TX), Winnie (b. 1866, TX), Minnie (b. 1867, TX), Ira Levi (b. 1869, TX), Ancil (b. 1872, TX); spouse, Mary/Mollie (b. 1893, TX), married by Sept. 1918, divorced by 1930. *SR; 471; AA, Nov 10, 1910, Feb 12, 1920; HC, Apr 26, 1911; MR, Co. A, Jan 1912; Bean to Hobby, Dec 1, 1917, AGC; 1503:488; A1b, d, e, f, g; A3a, A4a, b, g; C.*

BEARD, ALEXANDER GLENN. Born June 27, 1884, Austin, Travis County, Texas. Ht. 6 ft., gray eyes, brown hair, fair complexion, married. Peace officer, enlisted in Austin. REGULAR RANGER May 11, 1916–Mar. 15, 1919 (private, Co. B; transferred to Co. D when Co. B was disbanded, June 8, 1918). Honorably discharged. REMARKS: Town marshal, Marfa, Presidio County, Texas, 1919. Was a bodyguard for an oil company in Tampico, Mexico; in 1930 was an oil company field superintendent, living in San Antonio, Bexar County, Texas. Worked for the

Sinclair Refining Company in Fort Worth, Tarrant County, Texas from 1932 until his death. Died Feb. 20, 1941, Fort Worth, Tarrant County, Texas; buried in Austin Memorial Park, Austin, Travis County, Texas. FAMILY: Parents, James Willis Beard (b. 1855, TX) and Mary Jane Glenn (b. 1862, TX); siblings, James Edgar (b. 1882, TX), William DeWitt (b. 1886, TX), Nancy Maud (b. 1888, TX), Andrew Jay (b. 1890, TX), Thomas Alfred (b. 1893, TX), Bessie Lee (b. 1894, TX), Laura May (b. 1897, TX), George Carl (b. 1900, TX), twins Claud Weller and Clyde Rutledge (b. 1902, TX); spouse #1, Laura A. Brodie (b. 1887, TX), married Apr. 15, 1909; children, Frank McLaughlin (b. 1909, TX), Laura Isabelle (b. 1912, TX); spouse #2, Essie Irene Hunter (1896, TX), married Dec. 6, 1923, South Carolina; children, Betty Caroline (b. 1924, TX), Mary Patricia (b. 1930, TX). *SR; 471; General Orders No. 5, June 4, 1918, AGC; Beard to Towns, Mar 17, 1919, AGC; Special Orders No. 21, Mar 10, 1919, WC; 488: 44–45; A1d, e, f, g; A2b, e; A3a; A4a, b, g.*

BEARD, JAMES I. No birth information or personal description. REGULAR RANGER 1919—unknown (private, Co. A; transferred to Co. B when Co. A was disbanded, Mar. 10, 1919). Discharged or resigned, unknown. *Special Orders No. 21, Mar 10, 1919, WC.*

BEARD, RUBEN SIMONTON "RUBE." Born Aug. 8, 1891, Montgomery, Montgomery County, Texas. Ht. 5 ft. 10 in., blue eyes, red hair, fair complexion, married. Banker, farmer, cattleman, Littlefield, Lamb County, Texas. LOYALTY RANGER July 24, 1918–Jan. 1919. REMARKS: In 1930 was a salesman of mill supplies in El Paso, El Paso County, Texas. A "Renuben" Beard, born Aug. 8, 1891, died in Oct. 1973; his Social Security number was issued in Texas and his last known address was Cairo, Grady County, Georgia. FAMILY: Parents, Samuel Nathaniel Beard (b. 1857, SC) and Laura W. Simonton (b. 1869, TX); siblings, Louie Arnold (1889, TX), Samuel Nicholas (1890, TX), Laura Francis "Annie" (b. 1900, TX); spouse, Lucy Pope (b. 1897, TX), married by June 1917, divorced by 1930; daughter, Jean Pope (b. 1917, TX). *SR; A1d, e, f, g; A2a, e; A3a; A4b.*

BEASLEY, CECIL STINSON. Born May 22, 1886, Campbell, Hunt County, Texas. Ht. 6 ft., blue eyes, brown hair, medium complexion, married. First assistant game commissioner, Austin, Travis County, Texas. SPECIAL RANGER Apr. 1, 1917–Jan. 15, 1919 (attached to Co. C; reenlisted Dec. 12, 1917; was reinstated Dec. 28, 1917). Discharged. REMARKS: In late 1918 was a share farmer living in Campbell. In 1930 was captain, State Fishing Commission, living in Galveston, Galveston County, Texas; wife was living in Campbell. A Cecil S. Beasley died Oct. 22, 1946, Hunt County, Texas. FAMILY: Parents, John Franklin Beasley (b. 1847, TN) and Mary Mahalia "Callie" (b. 1850, TX); siblings, Sarah Cora (b. 1873, TX), Sam D. (b. 1876, TX), Maude (b. 1877, TX), Thomas Montrose (b. 1880, TX), Jessie F. (b. 1885, TX), John F., Jr. (b. 1888, TX), William Homer (b. 1889, TX), Roger Mills (b. 1892, TX); spouse, Floy (b. 1891, TX), married about 1908. *SR; A1d, e, g; A3a; A4b, g; C.*

BEASLEY, HENRY W. ALLEN. Born Feb. 1867, Rancho, Gonzales County, Texas. Ht. 5 ft. 11 in., blue eyes, dark hair, fair complexion, married. Guard, Texas Oil Co., Humble, Harris County, Texas. SPECIAL RANGER Mar. 23, 1918–Jan. 15, 1919. Guard, Houston, Harris County. REGULAR RANGER Sept. 30, 1920–Feb. 15, 1921 (private, Headquarters Co; Emergency Co. No. 1). Discharged. Special agent, T&P Railroad, Houston. RAILROAD RANGER Aug. 1, 1922–Mar. 22, 1923. Discharged. REMARKS: As of Mar. 23, 1918 had 20 years experience as a peace officer. In 1930 was a bottling company salesman, living in Houston. FAMILY: Parents, Dr. John F. Beasley (b. 1829, LA) and Mary J. (b. 1841, AL); siblings Leslie (b. 1865, TX), Pierre (b. 1870, TX), Lela (b. 1874, TX), Corine (b. 1876, TX); spouse, Mary J. "Mollie" (b. 1868, TX), married about 1889; children, Florence E. (b. 1890, TX), Viron F. (b. 1892, TX), Ruby M. (b. 1896, TX), Harvey B. (b. 1899, TX). *SR; A1a, b, d, e, f, g.*

BEASLEY, JAMES MADISON. Born Mar. 14, 1869, Milburn, McCulloch County, Texas. Ht. 5 ft. 7 in., dark eyes, dark complexion, brown hair. Merchant, Mercury, McCulloch County, Texas. LOYALTY RANGER June 11, 1918–Jan. 1919. REMARKS: Died May 21, 1926, McCulloch County, Texas; buried in Beasley Family Cemetery, Sam McCollum Ranch, McCulloch County. FAMILY: Parents, John Beasley (b. 1813, GA) and Mary Guest (b. 1830, TN); siblings, Sarah E. (b. 1851), Andrew Jackson (b. 1853, MO), John Randolph (b. 1855, MO), Christopher C. (b. 1857), Victoria Josephene

(b. 1861, TX), Amanda Jane (b. 1864, TX), Thomas Jefferson (b. 1867, TX), Benjamin Franklin (b. 1870, TX) plus seven half-siblings born to his father's first wife. *SR; A1a, e, f; A4b, g; C.*

BEATY, ROBERT EDWARD. Born Dec. 20, 1873, San Saba, San Saba County, Texas. Ht. 6 ft., blue eyes, brown hair, florid complexion, married. Rancher, Alpine, Brewster County, Texas. SPECIAL RANGER Dec. 26, 1917–Jan. 15, 1919. REMARKS: Owned a ranch in southern Brewster County. In 1930 was a drug store merchant in Reagan County, Texas. FAMILY: Spouse, Nannie (b. 1875, TX), married about 1910. *SR; AG to Beaty, Dec 17, 1917, AGC; A1b, f, g; A3a.*

BEAUMIER, OSCAR LAWRENCE. Born Jan. 1882, Brenham, Washington County, Texas. Ht. 5 ft. 11 in., black eyes, black hair, dark complexion, married. Machinist, enlisted in Austin, Travis County, Texas. REGULAR RANGER May 12, 1916–May 31, 1916 (private, Co. B). Resigned. REMARKS: Note length of service. Was a garage mechanic and an iron worker/machinist. Died Feb. 11, 1955, Brenham, Washington County, Texas. FAMILY: Father, Louis Beaumier (1847, Canada); siblings, Louis Mack (b. 1872, TX), Blanche (b. 1874, TX), Walter (b. 1876, TX); spouse, Mae (b. 1885, TX, married about 1908. *SR; 471; A1a, d, e, f, g; A4g; C.*

BECK, JOHN CALEB. Born Mar. 13, 1874, Kaufman County, Texas. Medium height, medium build, gray eyes, dark brown hair, married. Bank cashier, Frost, Navarro County, Texas. LOYALTY RANGER June 19, 1918–Jan. 1919. REMARKS: In 1930 was a bank vice-president in Navarro County. Died Feb. 12, 1932, Frost, Navarro County, Texas; buried in Frost Cemetery. FAMILY: Parents, William Jasper Beck (b. 1851, AL) and Cordelia Artemesia McPeters (b. 1850, TX); brothers, Erastus R. (b. 1877, TX), William J. (b. 1879, TX); spouse #1, Mary V. Tullos (b. 1876, TX), married about 1894; children, Alice (b. 1895, TX), Harris S. (b. 1899, TX); spouse #2, Clyde Daniel (b. 1885, TX), married Nov. 16, 1916; son, John K. (b. 1921, TX). *SR; A1b, d, e, f, g; A2b; A3a; A4b, g.*

BECKETT, STAFFORD E. Born Aug. 1888, Hebron, Thayer County, Nebraska. Ht. 6 ft. 1 in., brown eyes, black hair, medium dark complexion, married. Immigration Service, Ysleta, El Paso County, Texas. REGULAR RANGER Oct. 4, 1919–Feb. 2, 1920 (private, Co. B). Resigned. REMARKS: Immigration inspector, El Paso, El Paso County, May 1916. Resigned from Rangers along with his captain, Charles Stevens, in protest against the AG's actions. Apparently became a federal Prohibition agent in El Paso, Feb. 1920. Died Mar. 21, 1921, El Paso County, Texas. FAMILY: Spouse, Rose R. (b. 1890, CO), as a widow in 1930 was a schoolteacher in Denver, Colorado; children, Robert (b. 1913, NE), Dorothy (b. 1915, CO). *SR; 471; EPMT, May 19, 1916; Beckett to Cope, Feb 3, 1920, AGC; Beckett to Aldrich, May 7, 1920, AGC; Aldrich to Beckett, July 30, 1920, AGC; Beckett to Smith, Mar 13, 1920, AGC; A1f; g; C.*

BEDFORD, GEORGE EMORY "BIT." Born Aug. 7, 1867, Gadsden, Etowah County, Alabama. Ht. 6 ft. 4 in., blue eyes, light hair, fair complexion, married. Salesman, Stamford, Jones County, Texas. SPECIAL RANGER May 31, 1917–Dec. 1917 (attached to Co. C). REMARKS: Eastland County, Texas sheriff, Nov. 4, 1902–Nov. 3, 1908. In 1910 was a bookkeeper for a general store in Eastland, Eastland County. In 1920 was deputy sheriff in Eastland County; at the time of his death was chief of police in Cisco, Eastland County. Killed by the "Santa Claus" bank robbers, Dec. 23, 1927, Cisco, Eastland County, Texas; buried in Oakwood Cemetery, Cisco. FAMILY: Parents, Jonas Monroe Bedford (b. 1817, NC) and Ann Sappington Owens (b. 1836, GA); siblings, Jessie V. (b. 1864, AL), Lawson Albert (b. 1867, AL), Lucy (b. 1870, AL), H. F. (b. 1871, AL), Nevada (b. 1871, AL), Myrtle Estelle (b. 1875, AL), Joe Mulkey (b. 1877, AL), Ira Hawkins (b. AL), also several half siblings born to his father's previous wife; spouse, Lela Leona McCleskey (b. 1870, AL); children, Goodner (b. 1895, TX), Loma (b. 1898, TX), Georgia Lucille (b. 1905, TX), Ernest Marcelle (b. 1910, TX). *SR; 1503:165; A1a, e, f; A4b; C.*

BEEZLEY, CARRY W. Born Dec. 1854, La Grange, Fayette County, Texas. Ht. 5 ft. 10 ½ in., blue eyes, red hair, sandy complexion, married. Guard for Wells Fargo, San Antonio, Bexar County, Texas. SPECIAL RANGER Dec. 23, 1916–Jan. 1918 (attached to Co. C). Jan. 1918, AG ordered his WA cancelled. REMARKS: In 1900 was a railroad locomotive fireman, living in Bell County, Texas; in 1910 was railroad locomotive engineer, living in Brownwood, Brown County,

Texas; in 1930 lived in Austin, Travis County, Texas with a son and his family. Died July 11, 1936, Travis County, Texas. FAMILY: Spouse, Martha I. (b. 1861, TX); children, Charlie B. (b. 1882, TX), Clarence V. (b. 1884, TX), Clyde William (b. 1886, TX), Claudie C. (b. 1888, TX), Julie M. (b. 1889, TX), Homer Lee (b. 1891, TX), Alma B. (b. 1894, TX), Rubin M. (b. 1896, TX), Bunice D. (b. 1898, TX), Thomas (b. 1902, TX), Howard (b. 1904, TX), Myrtle (b. 1906, TX). *SR; Beezley to Harley, Dec 26, 1917, AGC; Campbell to Harley, Jan 29, 1918, AGC; A1d, e, g; A3a; A4a; C.*

BELCHER, WILLIAM WARREN. Born Sept. 9, 1892, Morgan, Bosque County, Texas. Ht. 6 ft., gray eyes, brown hair, light complexion, married. Peace officer, Wichita Falls, Wichita County, Texas. REGULAR RANGER Mar. 1, 1921–Aug. 31, 1921 (private, Emergency Co. No. 1; transferred to Co. B, Apr. 1, 1921). Discharged. Peace officer, Wichita Falls. SPECIAL RANGER Oct. 29, 1923–Mar. 5, 1925. Special agent, FW&DC Railroad, Wichita Falls. SPECIAL RANGER Oct. 1, 1931–Jan. 20, 1933. REMARKS: In 1918 was an engine foreman for the Santa Fe Railroad, living in Amarillo, Potter County, Texas. From Mar. 1, 1921 to Aug. 31, 1921 was classified as a REGULAR RANGER without pay. FAMILY: Parents, William Pritchett "Billie" Belcher (b. 1869, GA) and Ola (b. 1874, TX); siblings, Ina (b. 1898, TX), Virgil (b. 1900, TX), Lloyd (b. 1904, TX); spouse, Muriel I. (b. 1897, TX), married about 1919; son, William W., Jr. (b. 1920, TX). *SR; 471; A1d, e, g; A2e; A3a; A4g.*

BELL, CLARENCE LESLIE. Born Feb. 9, 1895, Valentine, Jeff Davis County, Texas. Ht. 5 ft. 7 in., gray eyes, light hair, fair complexion. Ranchman. REGULAR RANGER Apr. 16, 1918–June 1, 1918 (private, Co. N, Hudspeth Scouts). Resigned. REMARKS: In 1930 was a rancher living in Jeff Davis County. Died Feb. 24, 1976, Smith County, Texas (another source lists Beckville, Panola County, Texas as last known address). FAMILY: Parents, William E. Bell (b. 1861, AL or GA) and Sallie or Callie (b. 1867, MS); siblings, Fannie (b. 1884, TX), Nina (b. 1885, TX), Lizzie (b. 1888, TX), Ford (b. 1890, TX), Willie (b. 1893, TX), Howard (b. 1898, TX), John O. (b. 1901, TX), Nona O. (b. 1904, TX), Alec (b. 1906, TX); spouse, Lonice (b. 1897, TX); sons, Clarence H. (b. 1922, TX), Charles M. (b. 1924, TX), Thomas W. (b. 1926, TX). *SR; 471; A1d, g; A2a, b; A3a.*

BELL, MARSHALL LEE "LEE." Born Oct. 1868, Palo Pinto, Palo Pinto County, Texas. Ht. 5 ft. 9 in., brown hair, brown eyes, dark complexion, married. Brand inspector, Midland, Midland County, Texas. SPECIAL RANGER July 6, 1917–Jan. 15, 1919 (attached to Co. C; reenlisted/WA was reinstated Dec. 20, 1917). Discharged. REMARKS: His station was El Paso, El Paso County, Texas. In 1930 was a cattle inspector for the Cattle Raisers' Association in El Paso. One of his sons, George Allen Bell, was a National League baseball player in 1930. Lee died Dec. 27, 1954, El Paso County, Texas. FAMILY: Parents, Irbin Hall Bell (b. 1843, MO) and Eliza Quintella Cowden (b. 1849, AL); siblings, Irbin C. (b. 1871, TX), Ora E. (b. 1873, TX), Ruth M. (b. 1878, TX), Oscar (b. 1881, TX), Charles (b. 1887, TX); spouse, Eula Mae Rountree (b. 1872, IL), married about 1890; children, Selma Dawson (b. 1891, TX), Ruth (b. 1892, TX), Frank Lee (b. 1897, TX), George Allen (b. 1902, TX), Robert P. (b. 1904, TX), Eula Lee (b. 1907, TX). *SR; A1b, d, g; A2b; A4a, b, g.*

BELL, SILAS "SIE." Born Mar. 2, 1877, Carrizo Springs, Dimmit County, Texas. Ht. 5 ft. 10 in., blue eyes, brown hair, fair complexion. Cowboy, enlisted in El Paso County, Texas. REGULAR RANGER Sept. 24, 1917–unknown (private, Co. E; promoted to sergeant, Co. E, Oct. 1, 1918). REMARKS: Had been a well driller in Dimmit County. As of 1914 had been an Atascosa County, Texas, deputy sheriff in Pleasanton for many years. Lived in Pleasanton, June 1915; in Sept. 1918 was living in Eagle Pass, Maverick County, Texas. A Silas Bell died Mar. 1934, Maverick County, Texas. FAMILY: Parents, Jonathan Reuben Bell (b. 1851, MS) and Elizabeth "Lizzie" English (b. 1849, TX); siblings, Martha Alice (b. 1870, TX), Maggie O. (b. 1872, TX), Amanda (b. 1874, TX), Lafayette "Fayette" "Fate" (b. 1879, TX), Mary S. "Mollie" (b. 1882, TX), Samuel (b. 1885, TX), Levi (b. 1888, TX), Daniel. *SR; 471; Burmeister to Hutchings, Dec 21, 1914, AGC; Belcher to Harley, Oct 11, 1917, AGC; Barler to Harley, Oct 12, 1917, AGC; A1b, d; A2b; A3a; A4a, b, g.*

BELL, TOM WARREN. Born Dec. 10, 1885, Lee County, Texas. Ht. 6 ft., blue eyes, brown hair, light complexion, married. Stock farmer, Turkey, Hall County. SPECIAL RANGER July 24, 1918–Jan. 15, 1919. FAMILY: Parents, Thomas Hale Bell (b. 1841, TX) and Susan Jakinthic Caruthers (b. 1855, TX); siblings, Annie Laura (b. 1878,

TX), Frank Forest (b. 1881, TX), Elma Iola (b. 1894, TX); spouse, Zula B. Crump (b. 1893, TX), married about 1910; sons, Thomas W. (b. 1912, TX), Orvil Doc (b. 1915, TX). *SR; A1d, f, g; A2b; A3a; A4g.*

BELLAMY, OSCAR NEWTON. Born Nov. 1859, Carnesville, Franklin County, Georgia. Ht. 5 ft. 10 in., blue eyes, brown hair, red complexion, married. Railroad conductor, Corpus Christi, Nueces County, Texas. SPECIAL RANGER Dec. 12, 1916–Dec. 12, 1918 (reinstated Dec. 29, 1917). Discharged—commission had expired. Railroad conductor, Corpus Christi. SPECIAL RANGER Jan. 11, 1919–Dec. 31, 1919. REMARKS: Prior to becoming a Ranger had lived in Mexico for 15 years. Nueces County deputy sheriff, Corpus Christi; chief deputy sheriff, 1913–1916. Probably died before 1930. LAW ENFORCEMENT RELATIVES: Nueces County deputy sheriff and Ranger Raymond Bellamy, son. FAMILY: Parents, Archibald Newton Bellamy (b. 1830, GA) and Harriet Ann Spigner (b. 1840, AL); siblings, William (b. 1861, GA), Victoria L. (b. 1863, GA), Walter E. (b. 1872, GA), Robert L. (b. 1874, GA), Minnie D. (b. 1877, GA), Martha B. (b. 1879, GA); spouse, Rosa M. (b. 1867, TX), married about 1886; children, Vesta B. (b. 1888, TX), Raymond (b. 1890, TX), Gertrude F. (b. 1893, TX), Boyd P. (b. 1896, TX), Sidney (b. 1902, Mexico), Earl (b. 1905, Mexico), Richard C. (b. 1909, Mexico). *SR; BDH, Oct 21, 1913, Mar 19, 1914, May 19, 1916; Stayton to Ferguson, Nov 29, 1916, AGC; AG to Stayton, Dec 1, 1916, AGC; Bellamy to Hutchings, Dec 1, 12, 13, 1916, May 16, 1917, AGC; Wright to Ferguson, May 21, 1917, AGC; A1a, b, d, f, g; A4b.*

BELLAMY, RAYMOND. (Listed as BELLEMY in Ranger Service Records.) Born Mar. 18, 1890, Yoakum, DeWitt County, Texas. Ht. 5 ft. 8 in., blue eyes, light hair, light complexion. Peace officer, enlisted at Harlingen, Cameron County, Texas. REGULAR RANGER Oct. 22, 1915–Dec. 6, 1915 at least (private, Co. D). Discharged. REMARKS: Note length of service. Had lived in Mexico for many years before becoming a Ranger. Was a jailer, Corpus Christi, Nueces County, Texas, 1913; in Mar. 1916 was a Nueces County deputy sheriff. Killed Constable Pat Feely in a shooting scrape, Mar. 25, 1917. Died Jan. 21, 1966, Liberty County, Texas; was married at the time of his death. LAW ENFORCEMENT RELATIVES: Nueces County deputy sheriff and Ranger Oscar N. Bellamy, father. FAMILY: Parents, Oscar N. Bellamy (b. 1859, GA) and Rosa M. (b. 1867, TX); siblings Vesta B. (b. 1888, TX), Gertrude F. (b. 1893, TX), Boyd P. (b. 1896, TX), Sidney (b. 1902, Mexico), Earl (b. 1905, Mexico), Richard C. (b. 1909, Mexico); spouse, unknown. *SR; 471; 497:131, 132; BDH, Oct 21, 1913; EPMT, Mar 16, 1916; SAE, Mar 26, 1917; A1d, f; A2a, b; A3a.*

BENGE, THOMAS F. Born Oct. 1867, Red River County, Texas. Ht. 5 ft. 11 in., gray eyes, light hair, fair complexion, married. Rancher, Millersview, Concho County, Texas. SPECIAL RANGER Aug. 29, 1918–Feb. 1919. REMARKS: Concho County sheriff Nov. 4, 1902–Nov. 6, 1906. As of Mar. 1919 had 14,000 acres stocked with cattle and sheep near Millersview; letterhead—"T. F. Benge, Stock Farmer, Dealer in Cattle, Millersview." Died Sept. 17, 1921, Concho County, Texas; he was shot. FAMILY: Parents, Robert Titus Benge (1845, TX) and Sophia W. Young (1849, TX); siblings, Laura L. (b. 1870, TX), Sallie A. (b. 1872, TX), Charlie J. (b. 1874, TX), Smythia H. (b. 1877, TX), Archer H. (b. 1880, TX), William Young (b. 1883, TX), Ora B. (b. 1885, TX); spouse, Lura Daisy Boykin (b. 1874, TX), married Dec. 24, 1888, Concho County; children, Edna (b. 1892, TX), Lucille (b. 1896, TX), Robert Frank (b. 1899, TX), Willie (b. 1902, TX), Daisy Ann (b. 1904, TX), Thomas Fiern, Jr. (b. 1905, TX), Charles Jack (b. 1907, TX), Sophia (b. 1909, TX), Boykin (b. 1912, TX). *SR; 1503:128; A1d, e, f; A4b.*

BENNETT, JAMES EDWARD "ED." Born Sept. 18, 1889, Lexington, Lee County, Texas. Ht. 5 ft. 11 in., brown eyes, black hair, dark complexion, married. Locomotive fireman, enlisted in Bexar County, Texas. SPECIAL RANGER Aug. 7, 1916–Dec. 1917. REMARKS: Had been a farmer. Had also been a fireman for the Laredo, Webb County, Texas fire department. In 1930 was a locomotive engineer, living in Webb County. Died Nov. 3, 1967, San Antonio, Bexar County, Texas; buried in San Fernando #3, Roselawn Cemetery, San Antonio. LAW ENFORCEMENT RELATIVES: Ranger John William Bennett, brother. FAMILY: Parents, William Riley Bennett (b. 1864, TX) and Lucy Thomas Fisher (b. 1867, NC); siblings, John William (b. 1886, TX), Berta Ethel (b. 1888, TX), Annie Jo (b. 1892, TX), Albert Ernest (b. 1894, TX), Carrie Isabel (b. 1897, TX), Lillie May (b. 1899, TX), Claude Lillian (1902, TX), Blanche Irene (b. 1905, TX), Roy Thomas (b. 1908, TX); spouse, Jessie E.

(b. 1898, TX); children, Leonard (b. 1917, TX), Jessie M. (b. 1923, TX), Annie Joe (b. 1928, TX). *SR; A1d, e, f, g; A2b, e; A4b, g.*

BENNETT, JOHN WILLIAM. Born Nov. 14, 1886, Smithville, Bastrop County, Texas. Ht. 6 ft., black eyes, black hair, fair complexion, married. Locomotive fireman, enlisted in Webb County, Texas. SPECIAL RANGER Aug. 10, 1916–Dec. 1917 (attached to Co. C). REMARKS: Lived in Laredo, Webb County, for several years in early 1900s; moved to San Antonio, Bexar County, Texas by 1920; in 1930 was a locomotive engineer, living in San Antonio. Died Nov. 22, 1941, San Antonio, Bexar County, Texas; buried in San Fernando #3, Roselawn Cemetery, San Antonio. LAW ENFORCEMENT RELATIVES: Ranger James Edward Bennett, brother. FAMILY: Parents, William Riley Bennett (b. 1864, TX) and Lucy Thomas Fisher (b. 1867, NC); siblings, Berta Ethel (b. 1888, TX), James Edward (b. 1889, TX), Annie Jo (b. 1892, TX), Albert Ernest (b. 1894, TX), Carrie Isabel (b. 1897, TX), Lillie May (b. 1899, TX), Claude Lillian (1902, TX), Blanche Irene (b. 1905, TX), Roy Thomas (b. 1908, TX); spouse, Pearl Ward (b. 1888, TX), married June 17, 1907; children, Cora Lee (b. 1908, TX), Mildred Laura (b. 1911, TX), John William, Jr. (b. 1919, TX), Pearl Loraine (b. 1920, TX). *SR; A1d, f, g; A2b; A4b, g.*

BENNIS, JOSEPH GERALD. Born Sept. 18, 1894, Punxsutawney, Jefferson County, Pennsylvania. Ht. 5 ft. 11 in., hazel eyes, dark hair, light complexion. Special agent for Chino Copper Co.—worked for T. B. Cunningham, El Paso, El Paso County, Texas. SPECIAL RANGER June 24, 1919–Dec. 31, 1919. REMARKS: In 1930 was a lawyer in El Paso. Died May 23, 1950, El Paso, El Paso County, Texas. FAMILY: Parents, Michael W. Bennis (b. 1866, PA) and Ida L. Quinlisk (b. 1869, PA); siblings, Aloysius B. (b. 1892, PA), Margaret (b. 1899, PA); spouse, Valerie Loring (b. 1897, IN), married about 1923; daughter, Valerie Emma (b. 1927, TX). *SR; Cunningham to Aldrich, June 28, 1919, AGC; A1e, f, g; A3a; A4g; C.*

BENSON, ROY HENRY. Born Sept. 26, 1884, Galveston County, Texas. Ht. 6 ft. 1 in., blue eyes, brown hair, blonde complexion, married. Dairy farmer, Dickinson, Galveston County. LOYALTY RANGER July 5, 1918–Feb. 1919. REMARKS: In 1930 was a stockman in Galveston County. A Roy H. Benson died March 30, 1935 in Galveston County, Texas. FAMILY: Parents, Henry Benson (b. 1847, TX) and Olivia (b. 1859, TX); siblings, Ida (b. 1877, TX), Marcus C. (b. 1880, TX), Grover C. (b. 1886, TX); spouse, Kathleen B. (b. 1888); son Royal H. (b. 1926, TX). *SR; A1b, d, f, g; A3a; C.*

BENSON, THOMAS LUDLOW. Born Dec. 16, 1876, Dayton, Rhea County, Tennessee. Ht. 5 ft. 9 ½ in., blue eyes, light hair, light complexion, married. Farmer and real estate agent, Mercedes, Hidalgo County, Texas. LOYALTY RANGER Sept. 19, 1918–Feb. 1919. REMARKS: In 1930 was an insurance agent in Kenedy, Karnes County, Texas. A Thomas Ludlow "Burson" died Mar. 15, 1942, Karnes County, Texas. FAMILY: Parents, William Barkley Benson (b. 1844, TN) and Julia Ann Collins (b. 1847, TN); siblings, Nora (b. 1870, TN), Harriet "Hattie" (b. 1872, TN), Jennie (b. 1874), Otto (b. 1881), Katherine "Kate" (b. 1882), Edgar (b. 1884), Rose (b. 1888); spouse, Sallye R. (b. 1884, TX), married about 1901; daughter, Katherine (b. 1906, TX). *SR; A1b, f, g; A2b; A3a; A4a, b, g.*

BENSON, WILLIAM W. "WILLIE." Born June 1877, Hookerville, Burleson County, Texas. Ht. 5 ft. 10 in., dark eyes, dark hair, light complexion. Ranchman, Olney, Young County, Texas. LOYALTY RANGER July 24, 1918–Feb. 1919. REMARKS: Young County deputy sheriff for several years. A W. W. Benson died Mar. 18, 1941, Young County, Texas. FAMILY: Parents, Seaborn Martin Jasper Benson (b. 1852, AL) and Marinda Augusta "Inda" Wood (b. 1861, TX); siblings, Edwin P. (b. 1879, TX), George M. (b. 1880, TX), Jacob or Joseph H. (b. 1883, TX), Mary (b. 1885, TX), Charles (b. 1886, TX), Maude (b. 1888, TX), Horace (b. 1890, TX), Roy (b. 1895, TX), Bernice (b. 1897, TX), Seaborn M. (b. 1898, TX), Clyde (b. 1901, TX), William H. (b. 1907, TX). *SR; A1b, d, f; A4b, g; C.*

BENTLEY, WILLIAM V. Born Nov. 1857, Franklin County, Alabama. Ht. 5 ft. 11 in., gray eyes, dark hair, fair complexion. Salesman. REGULAR RANGER Apr. 8, 1918–Oct. 1, 1918 (private, Co. M). Discharged/fired. REMARKS: As a young man, was a saloon keeper in Hill County, Texas; in 1910 had a horse farm in Scurry County, Texas. Assaulted a waiter in a San Antonio, Bexar County, Texas café, Oct. 2, 1918. In 1930 was a banker in Dallas, Dallas

County, Texas. A W. V. Bentley died Feb. 15, 1937, Tarrant County, Texas. FAMILY: Parents, John G. Bentley (b. 1829, AL) and Catherine (b. 1836, AL); siblings, Americus F. (b. 1853, AL), Sam (b. 1855, AL), John Harvey (b. 1859, AL), James A. (b. 1864, AL), Lula D. (b. 1866, AL), Sidney (b. 1871, AL), Robert (b. 1873, AL), Freddie (b. 1876, TX), Arthur (b. 1879, TX); spouse, Sarah Belle (b. 1861, MO), married about 1881; daughters, Gladdis (b. 1885, TX), Willie (b. 1889, TX). *SR; 471; Hanson to AG, Oct 9, 1918, AGC; A1aa, b, d, e, g; C.*

BERRY, HEWELL VERGNE. Born Sept. 19, 1879, Sebree, Webster County, Kentucky. Ht. 5 ft. 7 in., gray eyes, light brown hair, light complexion, married. Railroad conductor, enlisted in Bexar County, Texas. SPECIAL RANGER July 22, 1916–Dec. 1917. REMARKS: In 1900 was a private in the U.S. military forces "in the field" in the Philippines. By 1910 was living in San Antonio working for the railroad as a brakeman. In 1930 was a railroad conductor in San Antonio. Died May 8, 1959, Bexar County, Texas. FAMILY: Mother, Nannie Berry (b. 1850, KY); sister, Mary (b. 1878, KY); spouse, Musie (b. 1880, TX), married about 1907; children, Ethel May (b. 1908, TX), Hewell, Jr. (b. 1914, TX), John D. (b. 1917, TX), Myrtle Virginia (b. 1925, TX). *SR; A1b, d, e, f, g; A2b, e; A3a.*

BERRY, JOHN TAYLOR. Born June 1868, Granville, Kentucky. Ht. 5 ft. 10 in., blue eyes, light hair, light complexion, married. Lumberman, Hamlin, Jones County, Texas. SPECIAL RANGER June 2, 1917–Dec. 1917 (attached to Co. C). REMARKS: May have resided in Anson, Taylor County, Texas instead of Hamlin. In 1900 had been manager of a lumber yard in Cisco, Eastland County, Texas. By 1930 was the proprietor of a lumber company in Cisco. A John Taylor Berry died Aug. 26, 1952, Martin County, Texas. FAMILY: Parents, Jonathan Taylor Berry (b. 1834, KY) and Mary Courteney Smith (b. 1840, KY); siblings, William T. (b. 1860, KY), Ellen F. (b. 1862, KY), George W. (b. 1866, KY), Courtney S. (b. 1870, KY), Bettie H. (b. 1874, KY), Alice C. (b. 1875, KY), Chas. S. (b. 1877, KY), Piggie (b. 1884, TX); spouse #1, Nellie (b. 1873, LA), married about 1895; spouse #2, Turner A. (b. 1882, LA). *SR; Dodson to Ferguson, May 18, 1917, AGC; Cunningham to Ferguson, May 18, 1917, AGC; A1a, b, d, g; A2b; A4a, b.*

BEVERLY, THOMAS HUGHSTON (or HOUSTON). Born July 6, 1886, McKinney, Collin County, Texas. Ht. 5 ft. 9 ½ in., gray eyes, brown hair, fair complexion. Lawyer, enlisted in Austin, Travis County, Texas. REGULAR RANGER Dec. 29, 1917–Mar. 31, 1918 (private, Co. M). Resigned for a better paying job as a special employee of the federal Bureau of Investigation, at Eagle Pass, Maverick County, Texas. REMARKS: Attended Texas A&M. FAMILY: Parents, Haywood T. "Harry" Beverly (b. 1857, TX) and Hulda E. (b. 1861, TX); siblings, Fitzhugh (b. 1884, TX), Isabella (b. 1891, TX). *SR; 471; Cunningham to Harley, Apr 1, 1918, AGC; U.S. Commissioner, No. 335, Del Rio, FRC-FW; A1d, e; A3a; A4b.*

BEVERLY, WILLIAM MIDDLETON "BOB." Born May 5, 1875, Ringgold, Catoosa County, Georgia. Ht. 5 ft. 11 ½ in., brown eyes, black hair, dark complexion, married. Brand inspector, Cattle Raisers' Association of Texas, Dalhart, Dallam County, Texas. SPECIAL RANGER Oct. 5, 1918–Jan. 15, 1919. REMARKS: Was classified as a REGULAR RANGER without pay. Had been a farm laborer in Johnson County, Texas. Was Midland County, Texas, sheriff Nov. 3, 1908–Nov. 5, 1912. In 1920 was a cattle rancher in Nara Vista, Quay County, New Mexico. In 1930 was a rancher in Lovington, Lea County, New Mexico. Served 10 years as a livestock inspector for the New Mexico Sanitary Board. Died Apr. 16, 1958, El Paso, El Paso County, Texas; funeral services in Lovington, buried in Lubbock, Lubbock County, Texas. FAMILY: Parents, John Purnell Beverly (b. 1831, NC) and Missouri Alice Israel (b. 1843, NC); siblings, Anna Elizabeth (b. 1873, GA), Beulah Benton (b. 1877, GA), Jessie Purnell (b. 1878, GA), Adaline Alice (b. 1879, GA); spouse #1, Nancy Ona Elizabeth "Leet" Rammadge (b. 1868, SC), married Nov. 6, 1895, Chickasaw Nation, Oklahoma Indian Territory; children, James Purnell (b. 1896, OK), Alicia H. (b. 1898); spouse #2, Leah Belle Walker (b. 1876), married Feb. 23, 1905, Midland; daughter, Nora Bob (b. 1906, TX); spouse #3, Amanda Bell "Manda" Cagle (b. 1883, TN); children Bennie Lee (b. 1916, OK), William Walter (b. 1924, NM). *SR; Moses & Rowe to Harley, Sept 13, 1918, AGC; Johnston to Moses & Rowe, Oct 14, 1918, AGC; EPT, Apr 17, 1958; 1503:373; A1b, d, f, g; A2b; A4a, b, g.*

BEVILL, WILLIAM HAROLD "WILL." Born Nov. 11, 1872, Hornsby's Bend, Travis County, Texas. Ht. 6 ft., blue eyes, light hair, light complexion. Farmer, enlisted at Austin, Travis County. REGULAR RANGER Dec. 15, 1917–Oct. 1, 1918 (private, Co. F). Resigned. REMARKS: Was a farm laborer and a "gin engineer." Died Oct. 10, 1918, Travis County, Texas. FAMILY: Parents, A. J. Bevill (b. 1835, TN) and Nancy Gilbert (b. 1845, SC); siblings, Mackinvale Elizabeth "Mackie" (b. 1867, TX), Jaretta (b. 1870, TX), Hyson M. (b. 1875, TX), George Y. (b. 1878, TX), Lude E. (b. 1882, TX). *SR; 471; Robinson to Harley, Oct 22, 1918, AGC; A1b, d, e; A3a; A4b; C.*

BICKLER, GEORGE WASHINGTON. Born Oct. 5, 1893, Austin, Travis County, Texas. Ht. 5 ft. 7 in., gray eyes, brown hair, fair complexion. Stenographer, Austin. SPECIAL RANGER Nov. 18, 1916–Jan. 4, 1917 (attached to Co. C). Resigned. REMARKS: In 1920 he and one brother were bakers in Gorman, Eastland County, Texas. In 1930 was deputy district clerk, Texas Supreme Court in Austin. Died July 18, 1983, Bell County, Texas. FAMILY: Parents, Johann Jacob Bickler (b. 1849, Germany) and Martha Lungkwitz (b. 1855, TX); siblings, Jennie Marie (b. 1875, TX), Camilla Therese (b. 1876, TX), Harry Pitt (b. 1879, TX), Max Hermann (b. 1881, TX), Katherine Magdaline (b. 1883, TX), Viola (b. 1886, TX), Jacob F. (b. 1888, TX), Ralph Adolph (b. 1891, TX); spouse #1, Mary Belle Gandy (b. 1895, TX), married June 10, 1924, Austin; daughter, Margaret Elizabeth (b. 1926, TX); spouse #2, Emma Leta Purcell (b. 1903), married May 12, 1956. *SR; A1d, f, g; A2a, b, e; A4a, b; B1.*

BIGGIO, WILLIAM JAMES. Born Feb. 26, 1877, Rockport, Aransas County, Texas. Ht. 6 ft. 1 in., gray eyes, black hair, dark complexion. Wells Fargo guard and clerk, San Antonio, Bexar County, Texas (enlisted in Webb County, Texas). SPECIAL RANGER July 25, 1917–Jan. 1918 (attached to Co. C). Warrant was cancelled, probably because he left Wells Fargo's employ. REMARKS: In late 1918 was working as manager for American Railway Express in Laredo, Webb County. In 1930 was working for the city of Corpus Christi, Nueces County, Texas; retired from the city water and gas department. Died Jan. 23, 1947, Corpus Christi, Nueces County, Texas; buried in Old Bayview Cemetery, Corpus Christi. FAMILY: Parents, Willis or William Biggio (b. 1843, Italy) and Rebecca Manahan (b. 1852, LA); siblings, Chester (b. 1879, TX), Rebecca (b. 1881, TX), John (b. 1884, TX), Albert (b. 1887, TX); spouse (?) #1, Petra Gonzalez (b. 1879, TX); daughter, Petra (b. 1901, TX); spouse #2, Hettie May Anderson (b. 1885, TX); daughters, Willie Lee (b. 1921, TX), Mary Rebecca (b 1924, TX). *SR; Campbell to Stockton, July 27, 1917, AGC; Campbell to Harley, Jan 29, 1918, AGC; A1d, e, f, g; A2b, e; A3a; A4b, g.*

BILBERRY, EVERT M. Born Nov. 15, 1883, Mason County, Texas. Ht. 6 ft. 1 in., black eyes, black hair, dark complexion, married. Cowboy. REGULAR RANGER June 1, 1918–Aug. 31, 1918 (private, Co. N, Hudspeth Scouts). Discharged—Co. N was disbanded. REMARKS: As a young man was a farmer in Stonewall County, Texas. Lived in Sierra Blanca, Hudspeth County, Texas 1918–1930. In 1920 was proprietor of a restaurant; in 1930 was a proprietor of a filling station. An E. M. Bilberry died Jan. 4, 1953, Reeves County, Texas. FAMILY: Parents, Livingston Sevier Bilberry (b. 1840, TN) and Martha E. "Mattie"(b. 1850, TN); siblings, William G. (b. 1871, TX), Mary C. (b. 1872, TX), John Henry (b. 1874, TX), Mabry E. (b. 1875, TX), Louisa or Louanna E. (b. 1879, TX); spouse #1, Hattie Garrett (b. 1887, TX), married 1907, Stonewall; daughter, Etta Valete (b. 1908, TX); spouse #2, Roxie J. (b. 1892, TX); stepchildren, Clayton M. Garrett (b. 1912, TX), Mary L. Garrett (b. 1922, TX), Madelene Garrett (b. 1924, TX). *SR; 471; A1b, d, e, f, g; A3a; A4b, g; C.*

BILLINGS, DANIEL DRAPER. Born July 3, 1877, Howard County, Arkansas. Medium height, medium build, brown eyes, dark hair, married. Cotton buyer, Kirkland, Childress County, Texas. LOYALTY RANGER June 1, 1918–Feb. 1919. REMARKS: Was connected with the Kirkland Mercantile Company, Feb. 1919; in 1930 was an automobile salesman in Abilene, Taylor County, Texas. FAMILY: Parents, George Henry Billings (b. 1849, AR) and Eliza Tennessee Draper (b. 1858, AR); siblings, Rosala (b. 1872, AR), Margaret Elizabeth (b. 1874, AR), Casey Rebecca (b. 1879, AR), Charles Watson (b. 1882, AR), Georgia E. (b. 1890, AR); spouse, Addie Foster (b. 1877, TX), married about 1902; daughters, Sara Belle (b. 1903, TX), Bessie May (b. 1905, TX). *SR; A1b, d, e, f, g; A3a; A4b, g.*

BILLINGS, WILLIAM C. Born Jan. 13, 1885, Smiley, Gonzales County, Texas. Ht. 5 ft. 10 in., blue eyes, brown hair, red complexion, married. Rancher, Bruni, Webb

County, Texas. SPECIAL RANGER May 7, 1918–Jan. 15, 1919. REMARKS: Was a rancher in Laredo, Webb County in 1930. Died 1939, Webb County, Texas. FAMILY: Parents, Algernon Sidney Billings (b. 1849, TN) and Lucinda Medora Wheat (b. 1854); stepmother, Mary Ella O'Neal (b. 1860, TX); siblings, George A. (b. 1875, TX), Robert Gibson (b. 1877, TX), Susanna (b. 1879, TX), Thomas B. (b. 1879), Algernon Sidney (b. 1884, TX), John (b. 1889, TX), Frank R. (b. 1891, TX), Alice Lillian (b. 1893, TX), Mary Etta (b. 1894, TX), Daniel (b. 1896, TX), Bryan J. (b. 1899, TX), Arthur (b. 1900, TX); spouse Lillie Duderstadt (b. 1886, TX); children, Lilian (b. 1908, TX), Floyd (b. 1912, TX). *SR; A1b, d, e, f, g; A3a; A4a, b.*

BILLINGSLEY, ALBERT WALTER. Born Oct. 8, 1888, Mathis, San Patricio County, Texas (one source lists Olmos Ranch, Bee County, Texas). Ht. 6 ft., brown eyes, black hair, dark complexion, married. Cowboy. REGULAR RANGER Nov. 3, 1915–Dec. 1915 (private, Co. D). Discharged. Guard, Big Lake Oil Co., Big Lake, Reagan County, Texas. SPECIAL RANGER Jan. 3, 1931–July 20, 1932. Resigned. REMARKS: In Sept. 1918 was working on a farm in Hidalgo County, Texas. Sheriff of Reagan County, Mar. 11, 1929–Jan. 1, 1931, and Nov. 8, 1932–Jan. 1, 1957. Died May 13, 1972, Falls County, Texas. FAMILY: Parents, Albert Walter Billingsley (b. 1862, TX) and Martha D. "Mattie" Johnson (b. 1863, KY); siblings, Edna Isabelle (b. 1884, TX), Celeste (b. 1886, TX), Alta (b. 1890, TX), Iona Marian (b. 1892, TX), William Thornton (b. 1894, TX), Martha Jane (b. 1896, TX); spouse #1, Kitty Oleta (b. 1900, TX), married about 1920; spouse #2, Ruth Claunch (b. 1895, TX), married about 1923. *SR; 471; 1503:430; A1d, g; A2a, b; A3a; A4a, b.*

BILLINGSLEY, JAMES POLLARD. Born Aug. 3, 1854, Alvarado, Johnson County, Texas. Ht. 5 ft. 10 ½ in., blue eyes, dark hair, light complexion, married. President, First State Bank, Hermleigh, Scurry County, Texas. SPECIAL RANGER Oct. 1, 1917–Jan. 15, 1919 (reenlisted, WA was renewed Dec. 8, 1918). REMARKS: Had been a farmer in Scurry County. Died July 30, 1919, Tarrant County, Texas; buried in Dunn Cemetery, Dunn, Scurry County. FAMILY: Parents, William C. Billingsley (b. 1824, AR) and Arena Kirkland (b. 1829, IL); siblings Wm. W. (b. 1846, TX), Vienna (b. 1849, TX); spouse, Willie (b. 1869, KY), married about 1890; children, Roger W. (b. 1891, TX), Jessie J. (b. 1893, TX), Alonzo Nathan (b. 1896, TX), James P., Jr. (b. 1901, TX), Hugh F. (b. 1905, TX), Bryan (b. 1907, TX). *SR; A1aa, a, d, e; A2b; A3a; A4b.*

BILLS, LEE C. Born Apr. 1876, Sylvan, Lamar County, Texas. Ht. 5 ft. 6 in., gray eyes, black hair, married. Deputy sheriff, enlisted at Harlingen, Cameron County, Texas. REGULAR RANGER Sept. 21, 1915–Dec. 1915 (private, Co. D). Discharged. City marshal, Rotan, Fisher County, Texas. SPECIAL RANGER Apr. 21, 1917–May 1, 1918 (attached to Co. C). City marshal, Rotan. REGULAR RANGER May 1, 1918–Mar. 10, 1919 (private, Co. C; 1919, Co. D; was suspended, Feb. 6, 1919; was reinstated). Honorably discharged. Special agent, MKT Railroad, De Leon, Comanche County, Texas. RAILROAD RANGER Oct. 10, 1922–Dec. 30, 1922. Discharged. REMARKS: Note length of 1915 service. As of Apr. 1917 had 8 years experience as a peace officer. Died June 20, 1960, Eastland County, Texas; buried in DeLeon Cemetery. FAMILY: Parents, John Aquila Bills (b. 1831, TN) and Mary Matilda "Molly" Wright (b. 1839, TN); siblings, John W. (b. 1859, TN), M. Sophroney (b. 1862, TX), Mattie E. (b. 1864, TX), Thomas Henry (b. 1867, TX), Edwin E. (b. 1869, TX), George Walter (b. 1870, TX), Robert A. (b. 1873, TX), Alice (b. 1875, TX), Olga (b. 1979, TX), Bessie (b. 1884, TX); spouse, Kate Florence Nance (b. 1880, TX), married about 1899; daughters, Pauline (b.1902, TX), Katherine (b. 1904, TX). *SR; 471; McKenzie to Woodul, May 3, 1918, AGC; Special Orders No. 21, Mar 10, 1919, WC; A1a, b, d, e, g; A2b; A4a, b, g.*

BINFORD, CLEM BARKSDALE. Born Mar. 1, 1880, Marysville, Cooke County, Texas. Ht. 5 ft. 10 in., blue eyes, brown hair, fair complexion, married. Farmer, Marysville. LOYALTY RANGER June 15, 1918–Feb. 1919. REMARKS: Still farming in Cooke County in 1930. Died July 21, 1956, Smith County, Texas. FAMILY: Parents, W. C. Binford (b. 1850, VA) and Malinda (b. 1858, TX); stepfather, Will E. Pybus (b. 1859, TN); siblings, Rupert (b. 1876, TX), Daisy (b. 1883, TX); stepsister, Jennie A. Pybus (b. 1882, TX); spouse, Lora (b. 1882, TX), married about Apr. 1910; children, Daisy (b. 1911, TX), Lora Dale (b. 1913, TX), Janice Elizabeth (b. 1915, TX), Thomas C. (b. 1917, TX), Jewell (b. 1919, TX), Sadie K. (b. 1921, TX). *SR; A1b, d, e, f, g; A2b; A3a.*

BINFORD, EUGENE BEASLEY "GENE." Born Sept. 22, 1872, Marshalltown, Marshall County, Iowa. Ht. 5 ft. 9 ¾ in., blue eyes, brown hair, fair complexion, married. Rancher, Wildorado, Oldham County, Texas. LOYALTY RANGER June 8, 1918–Feb. 1919. REMARKS: Had been a lawyer in general practice in Oldham County. Died Oct. 7, 1934, Potter County, Texas. FAMILY: Parents, Thaddeus Binford (b. 1840, OH) and Angelica "Angie" Beasley (b. 1844, OH); sisters, Margaret "Maggie" (b. 1866, IA), Mamie (b. 1869, IA), Jessie F. (b. 1876, IA); spouse, Kathryn W. Cabot (b. 1888, IL), married Aug. 10, 1910; daughters, Barbara Fern (b. 1918, TX), Nancy Jean (b. 1921, TX). *SR; A1b, d, e, g; A2b, e; A3a; A4a, b.*

BINGHAM, CHARLES THOMAS. Born Oct. 1870, Laurman [*sic*] County, Missouri. Ht. 5 ft. 10 in., gray eyes, brown hair, florid complexion, married. Mining engineer, Bridgeport, Wise County, Texas. LOYALTY RANGER June 6, 1918–Feb. 1919. REMARKS: In 1930 was marshal, Bridgeport. A Charles Thomas Bingham died Mar. 18, 1954, Wise County, Texas. FAMILY: Parents, William H. Bingham (b. 1842, MO) and Louisa F. "Lou" (b. 1846, MO); siblings, Edwin S. (b. 1872, TX), Elbert (b. 1874, MO), Walter M. (b. 1878, MO); spouse, Maggie (b. 1876, TX), married about 1890; children, Clarence (b. 1891, TX), Claude "Bud" (b. 1893, TX), Edna H. (b. 1898, TX), Mildred L. (b. 1911, TX). *SR; A1b, d, e, f, g; C.*

BIRD, JOSEPH WILSON. Born Feb. 1866, near Waco, McLennan County, Texas. Gray eyes, gray hair, dark complexion, married. Stock farmer, Westbrook, Mitchell County, Texas. LOYALTY RANGER June 3, 1918–Feb. 15, 1919. REMARKS: At some point was a deputy sheriff for 21 months. Was Mitchell County sheriff, July 11, 1907–Nov. 3, 1908. In 1910 had been a real estate agent in Mitchell County. In 1930 was a stock farmer in Mitchell County. Died Dec. 27, 1942, Mitchell County, Texas. FAMILY: Parents, Wilson Robeson Bird (b. 1812, SC) and Nancy B. Teal (b. 1835, NC); siblings, Alabama (b. 1856, TX), John M. (b. 1859, TX); spouse, Rossie Ann (b. 1874, TX), married Feb. 19, 1891, McLennan County; son, Ollie Teal (b. 1892, TX). *SR; 1503:378; A1aa, b, e, f, g; A2b; A4b.*

BISHOP, LUCKETT PEMBERTON "LEO." Born May 7, 1892, Bastrop, Bastrop County, Texas. Ht. 5 ft. 11 ½ in., brown hair, brown eyes, light complexion. Peace officer. REGULAR RANGER Feb. 19, 1914–Jan. 31, 1915 (private, Co. A). Discharged. REMARKS: As a teen lived in Houston, Harris County, Texas. Lived in Brownsville, Cameron County, Texas, Mar. 1915; by May 1917 was working as a brakeman for the GH&SA Railroad in San Antonio, Bexar County, Texas. Died Nov. 20, 1965, San Antonio, Bexar County, Texas. LAW ENFORCEMENT RELATIVES: Ranger Thomas Sumpter Bishop, brother; deputy U.S. marshal, Southern District of Texas (1914–1915) Thomas P. Bishop, father. FAMILY: Parents, Thomas Pemberton Bryce Bishop (b. 1856, TX) and Laura Letitia Green (b. 1861, TX); siblings, Susan Drucella (b. 1880), Edna Lutticia (b. 1882), Milton Joseph (b. 1883), Margaret Amanda (b. 1884), Thomas Sumpter (b. 1886, TX); spouse, Lola Mary Thompson (b. 1899, TX), married Apr. 25, 1917, Victoria, Texas; son, L. P., Jr. (b. 1920, TX). *SR; 471; BDH, Nov 26, 1914; AG to Commanding Officer, Co. A, Jan 13, 1915, AGC; Kingsville Record, Mar 12, 1915; A1e, f; A2a, b; A3a; A4a, b.*

BISHOP, THOMAS SUMPTER. Born July 20, 1886, Harold or Harrell, Wilbarger County, Texas. Ht. 5 ft. 9 ½ in. blue eyes, light hair, light complexion, married. Special agent, GH&SA Railroad, Austin, Travis County, Texas. SPECIAL RANGER July 12, 1917–Jan. 15, 1919 (attached to Co. C; WA was reinstated Dec. 22, 1917). REMARKS: In 1910 was an assistant transfer agent for SP railroad in Houston, Harris County, Texas. Died May 2, 1927, San Antonio, Bexar County, Texas. LAW ENFORCEMENT RELATIVES: Ranger Luckett P. Bishop, brother; deputy U.S. marshal, Southern District of Texas (1914–1915) Thomas P. Bishop, father. FAMILY: Parents, Thomas Pemberton Bryce Bishop (b. 1856, TX) and Laura Letitia Green (b. 1861, TX); siblings, Susan Drucella (b. 1880), Edna Lutticia (b. 1882), Milton Joseph (b. 1883), Margaret Amanda (b. 1884), Luckett Pemberton (b. 1892, TX); spouse, Evalyn Rebecca Sams (b. 1886, TX), married June 5, 1910, Houston; children Margaret Elizabeth (1911, TX), Evalyn Gordon (b. 1913, TX), Florence Letitia (b. 1915, TX), Thomas Sams (b. 1919, TX). *SR; A1e, f, g; A2b; A3a; A4a, b.*

BLACK, AUGUSTUS LEE (or LEE ROY). Born Oct. 1870, Marcus, Georgia. Ht. 5 ft. 10 in., gray eyes, brown hair, fair complexion, married. Manager, Palmetto Lumber Co., Oakhurst, San Jacinto County, Texas. LOYALTY RANGER

June 5, 1918–Feb. 1919. REMARKS: By 1920 was manager of a lumber mill in Jasper, Jasper County, Texas; in 1930 still living in Jasper. Died June 27, 1950, Jasper County, Texas. FAMILY: Parents, Thomas Black (b. 1842, GA) and Carrie (b. 1842, GA); siblings, Marshall (b. 1871, GA), Wesley Parks (b. 1872, GA), Lucy A. (b. 1876, GA), Walter E. (b. 1878, GA), Oscar T. (b. 1879, GA); spouse, Ermine Amos (b. 1876, TX), married about 1897; children, Una E. (b. 1898, TX), Bernice (b. 1903, TX), Gwinn Augusta (b. 1905, TX), Boyd (b. 1908, TX), Joe (b. 1910, TX), Fred (b. 1913, TX). *SR; A1b, d, e, f, g; A2b, e; A3a.*

BLACK, EDWARD MONTROSE "TROZY." Born Aug. 28, 1884, Ben Franklin, Delta County, Texas. Ht. 6 ft. 3 in., gray eyes, dark hair, fair complexion, married. Farmer, Ben Franklin. LOYALTY RANGER July 1, 1918–Feb. 18, 1919. REMARKS: Still farming in Delta County in 1930. Died June 5, 1964, Cooper, Delta County, Texas; buried in Oaklawn Cemetery, Cooper. FAMILY: Parents, James Buchanan Black (b. 1865, AR) and Lou Ella Richardson (b. 1866, AR); siblings, Delmar (b. 1886, TX), Maidee (b. 1889, TX), James B., Jr. (b. 1892, TX), Erwin (b. 1896, TX); spouse, Ethel Eliza Barrett (b. 1886, AR), married Dec. 28, 1911; children, Dallas Welcome (b. 1912), Katheryn Ethelda (b. 1919, TX), Virginia Jett (b. 1922, TX). *SR; A1d, e, f, g; A2b; A3a; A4a, b, g.*

BLACK, FRANK AUSTIN. Born Feb. 18, 1885, Boston, Suffolk County, Massachusetts. Ht. 5 ft. 11 ½ in., gray eyes, black hair, dark complexion, married. Foreman. REGULAR RANGER Dec. 28, 1917–Mar. 21, 1919 (private, Co. L). Honorably discharged—Co. L was disbanded. Ranger, Fabens, El Paso County, Texas. REGULAR RANGER Apr. 21, 1919–Feb. 10, 1921 (private, Co. B; transferred to Co. F, July 1, 1920). Discharged. REMARKS: Had served briefly as a policeman in Columbus, New Mexico. FAMILY: Spouse, Ruth. *SR; 471; Special Orders No. 21, Mar 10, 1919, WC; A3a.*

BLACKWELL, CHARLES JOURDAN. Born Oct. 19, 1865, St. Francis County, Arkansas (listed in Ranger Service Record as Weatherford, Parker County, Texas). Ht. 6 ft. 1 in., gray eyes, dark hair, dark complexion. Farmer, Weatherford, Parker County. REGULAR RANGER July 30, 1915–July 1, 1918 (private, Co. A). Resigned. Captain of Guards, Gulf Refining Company, Port Arthur, Jefferson County, Texas. SPECIAL RANGER July 1, 1918–Nov. 12, 1918. Placed on active duty. REGULAR RANGER Nov. 12, 1918–June 20, 1919 (private, Co. A; transferred to detached duty Jan. 10, 1919). Discharged and reenlisted under the new law. REGULAR RANGER June 20, 1919–Feb. 15, 1921 (transferred to Headquarters Co.; promoted to sergeant, Headquarters Co., Oct. 1, 1919; promoted to captain of Emergency Co. No. 1, Oct. 1, 1920). Discharged—Emergency Co. No. 1 was disbanded. Peace officer, Weatherford. RAILROAD RANGER Aug. 16, 1922–Jan. 1, 1923 (Co. B). Discharged. Peace officer, Weatherford. REGULAR RANGER Apr. 18, 1923–Feb. 21, 1925 (private, Co. A). Honorably discharged. Farmer, Del Rio, Val Verde County, Texas. SPECIAL RANGER Nov. 14, 1925–Jan. 1, 1926. Peace officer, Rankin, Upton County, Texas. SPECIAL RANGER Nov. 17, 1927–Mar. 7, 1928. Peace Officer, Del Rio. SPECIAL RANGER Jan. 29, 1931–Jan. 28, 1932; Feb. 2, 1932–Jan. 20, 1933. Special officer, Roswell Hotel, Del Rio. SPECIAL RANGER June 7, 1933–Jan. 22, 1935. Discharged. REMARKS: In 1926 was police chief in Amarillo, Potter County, Texas. Died Oct. 9, 1935, Del Rio, Val Verde County, Texas. LAW ENFORCEMENT RELATIVES: Ranger Samuel Clay Blackwell, son; Ranger Clell M. Blackwell, son. FAMILY: Parents, Robert Buchanan Blackwell (b. 1829, TN) and Mary Jane Baggett (b. 1838, TN); brothers, Arch (b. 1859, TN), Robert (b. 1863, TN); spouse Sarah Elizabeth Lee Pickard (b. 1872, TX), married June 8, 1889, Parker County; children, Stella Pauline (b. 1890, TX), Jessee Elizabeth (b. 1892, TX), Samuel Clay (b. 1895, TX), Clell Miller (b. 1898, TX), Cole Younger (b. 1902, TX), Bedford Forrest (b. 1905, TX), Lawrence Lee (b. 1909, TX). *SR; 471; Blackwell to Harley, Nov 21, 1918, AGC; Special Orders No. 1, Jan 9, 1919, WC; 142; A1b, d, e; A4b; C.*

BLACKWELL, CLELL MILLER. Born Dec. 10, 1898, Weatherford, Parker County, Texas. Ht. 5 ft. 9 in., dark eyes, black hair, dark complexion, married. Mechanic, Weatherford. REGULAR RANGER Jan. 31, 1920–Feb. 2, 1925 (private, Co. A). Discharged. REMARKS: Served in Army in World War I. In 1930 was a county employee, driving a tractor, Presidio County, Texas. Died Aug. 16, 1976, Bexar County, Texas. LAW ENFORCEMENT RELATIVES: Ranger and sometime county peace officer Charles J. Blackwell, father; Ranger Samuel Clay Blackwell, brother. FAMILY: Parents, Charles Jourdan Blackwell (b. 1865, AR) and Sarah

B

Texas Ranger Captain Charles J. Blackwell. *Photo courtesy Texas Ranger Hall of Fame and Museum.*

Elizabeth Pickard (b. 1872, TX); siblings, Stella Pauline (b. 1890, TX), Jessee Elizabeth (b. 1892, TX), Samuel Clay (b. 1895, TX), Cole Younger (b. 1902, TX), Bedford Forrest (b. 1905, TX), Lawrence Lee (b. 1909, TX); spouse, Sallie Bob Moore (b. 1903, TX), married about 1923; children, Blanche Lee (b. 1928, TX), Clell Miller, Jr. (b. 1932, TX), Doris Lenore (b. 1933, TX). *SR; 471; A1d, e, f, g; A2a, b, e; A3a; A4b.*

BLACKWELL, JOSEPH MILTON (also spelled MELTON). Born Dec. 21, 1869, Polk County, North Carolina. Ht. 6 ft. 2 in., gray eyes, gray hair, dark complexion, married. Deputy sheriff and farmer, Leonard, Fannin County, Texas. LOYALTY RANGER June 16, 1918–Feb. 1919. REMARKS: In 1930 was a cotton farmer in Fannin County. Died Apr. 6, 1948, Leonard, Fannin County, Texas. FAMILY: Parents, John M. Blackwell (b. 1845, NC) and Louessa J. (b. 1849, SC); siblings, Nancy E. (b. 1867, SC), Sarah R. H. (b. 1868, SC), William H. (b. 1875, SC), John J. (b. 1877, NC), Hattie M. (b. 1878, NC), George Washington (b. 1881, SC), Minnie (b. 1886, TX), Walter R. (b. 1887, TX), Clara (b. 1889, TX), Tony (b. 1893, TX); spouse, Wilma Augusta Key (b. 1875, SC), married July 5, 1891, Fannin County; children, Maud (b. 1894, TX), Ina (b. 1897, TX), twins Andrew and Ozie (b. 1903, TX), Oma (b. 1905, TX), Lola (b. 1907, TX), Clara (b. 1909, TX), Pauline "Pearly" (b. 1912, TX). *SR; A1a, b, e, d, f, g; A2b; A3a; A4b.*

BLACKWELL, SAMUEL CLAY "CLAY." Born Feb. 4, 1895, Weatherford, Parker County, Texas. Ht. 5 ft. 11 in., brown hair, brown eyes, light complexion. Peace officer, Laredo, Webb County, Texas. REGULAR RANGER Aug. 1, 1919 –Jan. 30, 1921 (private, Co. C). REMARKS: In 1918 had been a farm hand in Aledo, Parker County. LAW ENFORCEMENT RELATIVES: Ranger and sometime county peace officer Charles J. Blackwell, father; Ranger Clell M. Blackwell, brother. FAMILY: Parents, Charles Jourdan Blackwell (b. 1865, AR) and Sarah Elizabeth Pickard (b. 1872, TX); siblings, Stella Pauline (b. 1890, TX), Jessee Elizabeth (b. 1892, TX), Clell Miller (b. 1898, TX), Cole Younger (b. 1902, TX), Bedford Forrest (b. 1905, TX), Lawrence Lee (b. 1909, TX). *SR; 471; A1d, e; A3a; A4b.*

BLAINE, JOHN EDWARD. Born Oct. 2, 1888, Argentine, Kansas. Ht. 5 ft. 6 in., brown eyes, brown hair, light complexion, married. Commercial agent for Edenborn Line, Louisiana Railway & Navigation Company, Dallas, Dallas County, Texas. SPECIAL RANGER Dec. 12, 1917–Jan. 15, 1919. REMARKS: Had been a newspaper reporter in Temple, Bell County, Texas. In 1930 was the proprietor of a fire truck manufacturing company in Dallas. Died Dec. 6, 1973, El Paso, El Paso County, Texas. FAMILY: Parents, William B. Blaine (b. 1861, IL) and Clara Griswell (b. 1863, VT); brothers, Thomas P. (b. 1898, TX), Willie (b. 1903, TX); spouse, Anna Halbert Randolph (b. 1891, TX), married May 7, 1913; sons, John Edward (b. 1914, TX), William Randolph (b. 1918, TX). *SR; AG to Blaine, Dec 11, 1917, AGC; Blaine to Harley, Dec 12, 1917, AGC; A1d, e, f, g; A2a, b, e; A3a; A4b.*

BLAIR, JOHN. Born June 1883, Waco, McLennan County, Texas. Ht. 5 ft. 6 in., brown eyes, light hair, fair complexion. Peace officer. REGULAR RANGER June 6, 1918–July 23, 1918 (private, Co. D). Resigned at Marfa, Presidio County, Texas. REMARKS: Note length of service. *SR; 471.*

BLAIR, THOMAS W. (Listed as W. T. in Ranger Service Records.) Born Jan. 1869, Pelham, Grundy County, Tennessee. Ht. 5 ft. 6 in., gray eyes, light hair, light complexion, married. Manager, Red Front Livery—Automobile Service, Livery and Transfer, Palacios, Matagorda County, Texas. LOYALTY RANGER June 6, 1918 –Jan. 1919. REMARKS: Had been a house carpenter in Matagorda County. In 1930 was a building contractor in Alvarado, Johnson County, Texas. FAMILY: Parents, William Thomas Blair (b. 1833, TN) and Violet L. Baird (b. 1837, TN); siblings, Alice (b. 1856, TN), Martin (b. 1858, TN), William (b. 1861, TN), James (b. 1863, TN), Robert (b. 1865, TN), Joseph (b. 1866, TN); spouse, Amanda E. (b. 1868, TX), married about 1889. *SR; A1aa, a, e, f, g; A4b, g.*

BLOCKER, ABNER PICKENS. Born Jan. 30, 1856, on the family ranch near Austin, Travis County, Texas. Ht. 5 ft. 10 in., dark eyes, dark hair, dark complexion, married. Brand Inspector, Sansom, Uvalde County, Texas. SPECIAL RANGER Jan 22, 1919–Dec. 31, 1919. REMARKS: Beginning in 1877 and for the next 17 years was a trail driver, delivering longhorn cattle from Texas to buyers in various states as far north as the Canadian border; delivered the first herds of south Texas cattle to the newly-formed

XIT ranch in the Texas Panhandle. In 1887 farmed cotton. In 1890 worked on his brother's Chupadero Ranch near Eagle Pass, Maverick County, Texas. In the late 1890s was a rancher in La Salle County, Texas; in the early 1900s returned to the Chupadero Ranch. In July 1913 had been a brand inspector at Del Rio, Val Verde County, Texas for the Cattle Raisers' Association of Texas. Died Aug. 9, 1943, Bexar County, Texas. FAMILY: Parents, Abner Pickens Blocker (b. 1822, SC) and Cornelia Randolph Murphy (b. 1826, AL); siblings, William Butler (b. 1850, AL), Mary F. (b. 1850, AL), John Rufus (b. 1850, SC), Macon W. (b. 1852, SC), Samuel J. (b. 1857, TX), Abbey M. (b. 1858, TX), Anna (b. 1860, TX), Nancy (b. 1862, TX); spouse, Florence Baldwin (b. 1880, England), married in 1896, daughter, Fay (b. 1901, TX). *SR; Moses & Rowe to Harley, Jan 13, 1919, AGC; 172:I, 594; A1a, b, e, f; A4a, b; C.*

BLOXOM, JOHN R., JR. Born Feb. 1891, Dora, Nolan County, Texas. Ht. 6 ft., gray eyes, brown hair, dark complexion. Stock farmer and Nolan County deputy sheriff for three years. REGULAR RANGER Apr. 2, 1918–Jan. 10, 1919 (private, Co. C; was suspended June 27, 1918, because of allegations of abuse of authority; was reinstated Sept. 10, 1918). Discharged/fired. REMARKS: In Dec. 1918 he and J. B. Nalls killed a man in Ranger, Eastland County, Texas. They were fired from the Texas Rangers on Jan. 10, 1919, by order of Governor W. P. Hobby. In Feb. 1919 Bloxom was convicted of murder and sentenced to two years in the state penitentiary. *SR; 471; Yarbrough to Harley, Jan 4, 1919, AGC; Harley to McKenzie, June 27, 1918, AGC; Harley to Brelsford, June 27, 1918, WC; Brelsford to Harley, June 15, 29, 1918, WC; Moorman to Hobby, June 28, 1918, WC; Oxford to Harley, June 28, 1918, WC; Bloxom to Harley, July 1, 1918, WC; Suiter to Hobby, Dec 22, 1918, WC; Special Orders No. 1, Jan 9, 1919, AGC; LWT, Feb 23, 1919.*

BLUM, HENRY. Born Mar. 1871, Strasbourg, France. Ht. 5 ft. 8 in., blue eyes, dark brown hair, dark complexion. Detective (deputy sheriff), county attorney's office, El Paso, El Paso County, Texas. SPECIAL RANGER May 6, 1918–July 4, 1918. Commission was revoked. REMARKS: Note short length of Ranger service. Had been a peace officer for some time in El Paso. Was controversial because of his efforts to combat liquor violations. *SR; Folsom to Hudspeth, Aug 18, 1917, AGC; Hudspeth to Hutchings, Aug 23, 1917, AGC; Hudspeth to Harley, Oct 13, 1917, AGC; Dudley to Harley, Oct 27, Dec 11, 1917, July 5, 1918, AGC; Howe to Harley, Nov 28, 1917, AGC; Harley to Dudley, Dec 15, 19176, AGC; Harley to Davis, July 3, 1918, AGC; Davis to Harley, July 5, 1918, AGC.*

BOGGS, GEORGE EVERATT. Born Apr. 28, 1885, Kaufman, Kaufman County, Texas. Tall, medium build, blue eyes, black hair. Cotton buyer and real estate, Kaufman. LOYALTY RANGER July 1, 1918–Feb. 1919. REMARKS: In 1910 was a rural mailman in Kaufman. Died Feb. 16, 1966, Kaufman County, Texas. FAMILY: Parents, James A. Boggs (b. 1849, GA) and Helen C. (b. 1854, MS); siblings, James T. (b. 1877, TX), William Malcolm (b. 1880, TX), Frank H. (b. 1881, TX), Guy E. (b. 1887, TX), Jane E. (b. 1891, TX). *SR; A1d, e, f, g; A2a, b; A3a.*

BOHART, CHARLES. Born Jan. 1890, Newton County, Missouri. Ht. 5 ft. 7 in., brown eyes, brown hair, dark complexion. Liveryman, Kleberg County, Texas. SPECIAL RANGER Aug. 26, 1916–Dec. 1917. *SR; Scarborough to Hutchings, Aug 26, 1916, AGC.*

BOHLS, ARTHUR WILLIAM. Born Dec. 23, 1883, Travis County, Texas. Ht. 6 ft. 1 in., blue eyes, light hair, fair complexion. Salesman, Travis County. SPECIAL RANGER Feb. 2, 1918–Jan. 15, 1919. REMARKS: In 1930 was a wholesale grocery salesman living as a lodger in Bakersfield, California. Died July 8, 1953, Travis County, Texas. FAMILY: Parents, Louis Bohls (b. 1859, TX) and Mary Fuchs (b. 1865, TX); siblings, Walter (b. 1885, TX), Eldom F. (b. 1887, TX), Lillie (b. 1888, TX), Lenora (b. 1890, TX), Leona (b. 1893, TX), Frederick G. (b. 1896, TX), Mary (b. 1898, TX), William (b. 1900, TX), Gertrude (b. 1903, TX), Irene (b. 1907, TX); spouse, Constance Wieman, married about 1925. *SR; A1e, f, g; A3a; A4g; C.*

BONNER, JOHN SUMMERFIELD. Born Apr. 25, 1873, Lufkin, Angelina County, Texas. Ht. 5 ft. 8 ½ in., blue eyes, dark hair, fair complexion, married. President of Bonner Oil Co., Houston, Harris County, Texas. LOYALTY RANGER July 2, 1918–Feb. 1919. Humble Oil Co. executive, Houston. SPECIAL RANGER Jan. 9, 1932–Jan. 8, 1933; Mar. 18, 1933–Jan. 22, 1935. Discharged. REMARKS: Died June 30, 1939, Harris County, Texas. FAMILY: Parents, William

Henry Bonner (b. 1831, AR) and Malinda Blackburn (b. 1832, MS); siblings, Mary (b. 1864, TX), Thomas J. (b. 1865, TX), W. G. (b. 1867, TX), Benjamin F. (b. 1869, TX), Estell V. (b. 1876, TX); spouse, Mamie Edna Ewing (b. 1880, TX), married Oct. 7, 1900; sons, John S., Jr. (b. 1902, TX), Louis Franklin (b. 1909, TX). *SR; A1b, d, f, g; A2b; A3a; A4a, b, g; B2.*

BOONE, ALFRED. Born Mar. 6, 1867, Frank Pierce, Johnson County, Iowa. Ht. 5 ft. 9 ½ in., blue eyes, light hair, light complexion. Railroad station agent, Fabens, El Paso County, Texas. SPECIAL RANGER May 17, 1918–Jan. 15, 1919; Jan. 28, 1928–Jan. 27, 1929; Jan. 26, 1929–Jan. 26, 1930; Jan. 29, 1930–Jan. 1, 1931; Feb. 9, 1931–Jan. 18, 1933. Warrant of Authority cancelled. REMARKS: Had been a telegraph operator. Deputy sheriff, El Paso County, two years. FAMILY: Parents, Abner Boone (b. 1828, PA) and Almira A. Simonton (b. 1832, PA); siblings, William Alpheus (b. 1854, IA), Marcellia (b. 1857), Mary J. (b. 1857, IA), Alonzo (b. 1860, IA), Arressia (b. 1861, IA), Benoni (b. 1871, IA), Pearl (b. 1881, IA); spouse #1, unknown, married about 1888; spouse #2, Vivian Ranard (b. 1871, IN), married about 1907. *SR; A1b, d, e, f, g; A4a, b.*

BOOTHE, FRANK HENRY. Born June 19, 1877, DeWitt County, Texas. Tall, stout, blue eyes, light hair, married. Merchant, Lagarto, Live Oak County, Texas. LOYALTY RANGER June 15, 1918–Feb. 1919. REMARKS: Had been a farmer in DeWitt County. In 1910 was a grocery salesman in Yoakum, Lavaca County, Texas. In 1930 was a farmer in Bee County, Texas. Died Mar. 24, 1941, Bee County, Texas. FAMILY: Parents, Lee C. Boothe (b. 1853, AL) and Nannie (b. 1856, TX); siblings, Otis (b. 1874, TX), Minnie (b. 1876, TX), Joseph (b. 1878, TX); spouse, Lena Edna (b. 1880, TX), married about 1900. *SR; A1b, d, e, g; A3a; C.*

BOREN, JAMES MINUS. Born Mar. 1870, Carroll County, Arkansas. No physical description, married. Stock farmer, Post City, Garza County, Texas. LOYALTY RANGER June 7, 1918–Feb. 1919. REMARKS: In 1910 was Garza County judge. In 1930 still a stock rancher in Post. A J. M. Boren died Nov. 15, 1937, Garza County, Texas. FAMILY: Parents, George Boren (b. 1850, AR) and Sarah A. (b. 1848, TN); siblings, John (b. 1869, AR), Martha J. (b. 1872, AR), Barbary E. (b. 1874, AR); spouse, Della Bailey "Ella" (b. 1878, LA), married about 1900; children, James Walter (b. 1901, TX), Mildred (b. 1903, TX), Barbara E. (b. 1909, TX). *SR; 172:I, 648; A1b, e, f, g; A2b; A4g.*

BORROUM, JOHN STOVALL. Born Aug. 24, 1884, Minera, Webb County, Texas. Short, stout, brown eyes, dark hair. Employed by A. Deutz & Brother, Hardware, Laredo, Webb County. SPECIAL RANGER June 25, 1918–Jan. 15, 1919. FAMILY: Parents, Thomas Borroum (b. 1860, TX) and Sallie (b. 1863, OH); brother, Willie D. (b. 1889, TX); spouse, Beulah L. (b. 1888, TX), married about 1907; daughter, Margaret (b. 1907, TX). *SR; A1d, e; A3a.*

BOUNDS, JOHN EARL. Born Dec. 24, 1880, Perry County, Alabama. Ht. 6 ft., brown eyes, black hair, dark complexion, married. Auto merchant, Stamford, Jones County, Texas. SPECIAL RANGER May 31, 1917–Dec. 1917 (attached to Co. C). REMARKS: Had been a farmer in Jack County, Texas. J. E. Bounds died Dec. 12, 1918, Jones County, Texas. FAMILY: Parents, James Bounds (b. 1830, AL) and Mary (b. 1847, AL); siblings, M. E. (b. 1867, AL), William (b. 1870, AL), Artalie (b. 1872, AL), James E. (b. 1874, AL), Robert Wallace (b. 1877, AL); spouse, Lucinda Annie Elizabeth (b. 1883, MO); children, Artie Mildred (b. 1908, TX), Sybil E. (b. 1910, TX), James Herbert (b. 1913, TX), John E. (b. 1918, TX). *SR; Register to Ferguson, May 18, 1917, AGC; Cunningham to Ferguson, May 18, 1917, AGC; A1b, e, f, g; A2b; A3a.*

BOWEN, MILTON L. Born 1873, Bowen, Grainger County, Tennessee. Ht. 6 ft. 2 in., blue eyes, gray hair, fair complexion. Real estate agent, Littlefield, Lamb County, Texas. SPECIAL RANGER Jun. 17, 1916–Dec. 1917. REMARKS: Had been a salesman for the "Armstrong Company" in Washington, D.C. In 1930 was a real estate solicitor in San Antonio, Bexar County, Texas; the 1930 census has birth year as ca. 1876. FAMILY: Parents, John Perry Bowen (b. 1827, TN) and Jennie V. Noah (b. 1835, TN); siblings, Hughey (b. 1859, TN), Sidney E. (b. 1863, TN), William (b. 1866, TN), Mary (b. 1868, TN), Robert (b. 1876, TN). *SR; A1a, b, e, g; A4b.*

BOWMAN, JOHN TIBAUT "TIBAUT." Born Sept. 8, 1883, Belton, Bell County, Texas. Medium height, medium build, gray eyes, dark hair, married. No occupation given. Evidently enlisted as a REGULAR RANGER in Nov. 1917, because he received railroad passes. The AG assigned him to Co. C, with station at Austin, Travis County, Texas. State official. REGULAR RANGER Jan. 7, 1918–unknown (Headquarters Co.). Banker, Austin: SPECIAL RANGER May 11, 1933–unknown. REMARKS: In 1910 was a stenographer for the Texas Railroad Commission, living in Austin. As of Sept. 1918 was an investment banker in Austin. Died May 9, 1937, Travis County, Texas. FAMILY: Mother, Mollie (b. 1861, TX); siblings, Thornton (b. 1885, TX), Annabyrd (b. 1889, TX); spouse, Mary Gladys G. (b. 1896, TX), married about 1917; children, J. Tibaut (b. 1918, TX), W. G. (b. 1920, TX), Robert Hardy (b. 1923, TX). *SR; Spindle to Harley, Nov 6, 1917, AGC; AG to General Manager, Nov 13, 1917, AGC; 172:I, 677; A1e, f, g; A2e; A3a; C.*

BOXLEY, ALONZO DAVID "LON." Born Apr. 16, 1879, Como, Panola County, Mississippi. Ht. 6 ft., blue eyes, light hair, light complexion, married. Rancher and farmer, Barstow, Ward County, Texas. LOYALTY RANGER June 5, 1918–Feb. 1919. REMARKS: A Lon David Boxley died Dec. 24, 1942, Reeves County, Texas. FAMILY: Parents, R. M. Boxley (b. 1834, TN) and Susan (b. 1845, TN); siblings, J. Benj. (b. 1871, MS), Katy (b. 1868, MS), Mollie (b. 1866, MS); spouse, Sara N. (b. 1882, TX), married about 1899. *SR; A1b, e; A3a; C.*

BOYD, CECIL. Born Dec. 25, 1896, El Paso, El Paso County, Texas. Ht. 5 ft. 6 in., blue eyes, light brown hair, light complexion. Cowboy, enlisted in Hudspeth County, Texas. REGULAR RANGER Sept. 11, 1917–Dec. 15, 1917 (private, Co. B). Discharged. Cowboy, enlisted in Hudspeth County. REGULAR RANGER Apr. 20, 1918–July 11, 1918 (private, Co. N—Hudspeth Scouts). Discharged. REMARKS: His parents and grandparents had ranching interests in Mexico for many years. FAMILY: Parents, John James Boyd (b. 1860, TX) and Cora Adams (b. 1869, AR); siblings, James Gordon (b. 1893, TX), Mary Mattie (b. 1895, NM), Palmer John (b. 1899, TX), Bennett (b. 1901), Corine (b. 1904, Mexico). *SR; 471; Fox to Harley, Dec 13, 1917, AGC; A1e, f; A3a; A4e.*

BOYD, ROBERT ABRAHAM "ABE." Born Aug. 1894, Kingsland, Llano County, Texas. Ht. 5 ft. 9 in., gray eyes, light hair, light complexion, married. Stockman, Mission, Hidalgo County, Texas. REGULAR RANGER Mar. 19, 1921–Nov. 30, 1922 (private, Co. D). Resigned. Ranchman. REGULAR RANGER Sept. 1, 1923–Feb. 1, 1924 (private, Co. E). Resigned. REMARKS: While in Co. E was stationed in San Antonio, Bexar County, Texas. Still raising cattle in Mission in 1930. FAMILY: Parents, Robert Boyd (b. 1853, AL) and Harriett A. (b. 1870, TX); siblings, Blanche E. (b. 1890, TX), Alvon or Alma R. (b. 1892, TX), Ollie (b. 1897, TX), Norton (b. 1904, TX); spouse, Marion (b. 1897, TX), married about 1920. *SR; 471; A1d, e, g.*

BOYD, WILLIAM A. Born 1862, Waco, McLennan County, Texas. Ht. 5 ft. 10 in., blue eyes, gray hair, fair complexion, married. Peace officer, Waco. SPECIAL RANGER Nov. 22, 1915–Nov. 1, 1917 (attached to Co. C). Discharged. Peace officer, Waco. SPECIAL RANGER Nov. 18, 1917–Dec. 1917 (attached to Co. C). REMARKS: In 1920 was an officer for "Bankers Association" in Waco. In 1930 a W. A. Boyd, age 67, born in Texas, was managing a poultry and dairy farm in Tarrant County, Texas. FAMILY: Parents, William George Boyd (b. 1829, TN) and Minerva J. Misell (b. 1834, TN); siblings, William (b. 1852, TN), George M. (b. 1853, TN), Jennie (b. 1856, TN), Judson (b. 1858, TN), Elizabeth A. (b. 1860, TN), Joseph N. (b. 1865, TX), Marcus M. (b. 1867, TX), James Henry (b. 1870, TX), Mitchell (b. 1873, TX), Lucy A. (b. 1874, TX), Nora. M. (b. 1877, TX); spouse #1, unknown, died before 1920; spouse #2 (possibly), Mary J. (b. 1884, NJ), married about 1922. *SR; A1a, b, f, g; A4b.*

BOYKIN, MELVIN FRED. Born Sept. 20, 1883, Concho County, Texas. Ht. 5 ft. 10 ½ in., brown eyes, dark hair, fair complexion. Ranchman, Dryden, Terrell County, Texas. REGULAR RANGER May 7, 1918–Feb. 1, 1919 (private, Co. M). Honorably discharged. REMARKS: As a teenager lived in Pauls Valley, Chickasaw Nation, Indian Territory. By 1930 was a carpenter living in San Antonio, Bexar County, Texas. Was a member of the first board of directors of the Texas State Association of Ex-Rangers. Died May 5, 1968, Bexar County, Texas. FAMILY: Parents, Francis M. Boykin (b. 1846, TX) and Martha J. (b. 1860, AR); siblings, Lola B. (b. 1891, TX), Oscar C. (b. 1888, TX); spouse, Janie Alma Rush (b. 1888, TX), married July 3, 1924, in Texas, divorced by 1930. *SR; 471; Special Orders No. 3, Jan 20, 1919, AGC; Harley to Tobin, June 28, 1919, AGC; 470:94 A1d, g; A2a, b; A3a; A4b.*

BOYNTON, ALEXANDER. Born Apr. 1, 1877, Unionville, Putnam County, Missouri. Ht. 5 ft. 8 in., blue eyes, brown hair, fair complexion, married. Rancher, Crystal City, Zavala County, Texas. SPECIAL RANGER Sept. 23, 1915–unknown (was attached to Co. C). REMARKS: Was vice-president of the Winter Garden Irrigation Co., of which T. A. Coleman was president. Boynton's ranch was in Dimmit County, Texas. Had been an architect for a builder in San Antonio, Bexar County, Texas; in 1920 was a real estate agent in San Antonio. In 1930 was an oil producer in San Antonio. FAMILY: Father, unknown (b. ME); stepmother, Sophie (b. 1839, Canada); spouse, Anna R. (b. 1880, TX), married about 1904; son, Warren (b. 1906, TX). *SR; Boynton to Ferguson, Sept 14, 1915, AGC; AG to Boynton, Sept 21, 1915, AGC; A1e, f, g; A6a.*

BOYNTON, OSCAR P. Born June 1872, Pinehill, Rusk County, Texas. No personal description. Merchant, Long Branch, Panola County, Texas. LOYALTY RANGER June 10, 1918–Jan. 15, 1919. REMARKS: In 1900 was a prison guard at the Rusk Wate Penitentiary, Cherokee County, Texas. In 1910 was an oil field driller living in Caddo Parish, Louisiana. In 1930 was a merchant living in Henderson, Rusk County, Texas. FAMILY: Parents, Andrew Jackson Boynton (b. 1836, GA) and Martha E. Benford (b. 1848, AL); siblings, John Benford (b. 1869, TX), Leila (b. 1875, TX), Jessie (b. 1879, TX); spouse, Odie Ingram (b. 1882, MS), married about 1922. *SR; A1b, d, e, g; A4b, g.*

BRACEWELL, JAMES ASBURY. Born Oct. 1893, Hockley, Harris County, Texas. Ht 5 ft. 9 ½ in., blue eyes, sandy hair, ruddy complexion, married. Contractor, Fort Worth, Tarrant County, Texas. REGULAR RANGER Nov. 18, 1920–Jan. 18, 1921 (Emergency Co. No. 2). Resigned to become an oil company special agent in Breckenridge, Stephens County, Texas. Special agent, Fort Worth. SPECIAL RANGER Mar. 29, 1927–Mar. 29, 1928; Apr. 17, 1928–Apr. 17, 1929. Special agent, Marland Oil Co., Fort Worth. SPECIAL RANGER Apr. 19, 1929–Apr. 19, 1929. Special agent, Continental Oil Co., Fort Worth. SPECIAL RANGER May 1, 1930–Jan. 1, 1931; Feb. 5, 1931–Jan. 20, 1933. REMARKS: Died in 1951 in Tulsa, Oklahoma. FAMILY: Parents, Windor Crouch Bracewell (b. 1865, LA) and Love America Syphrett (b. 1870, AL); siblings, Mickle E. (b. 1891, TX), Nathan C. (b. 1899, TX), Micah A. (b. 1902, TX), Windor Anita (b. 1905, TX), Lois (b. 1908, TX), Eunice (b. 1910, TX), Luther Earl (b. 1913, TX); spouse, Nellie (b. 1895, TX), married about 1919. *SR; 471; Bracewell to Aldrich, Jan 12, 21, 1921, AGC; A1e, f, g; A4b, c; B2.*

BRADFORD, CLYDE A. Born Nov. 1884, Round Rock, Williamson County, Texas. Ht. 6 ft. 1 ¼ in., blue eyes, brown hair, medium complexion, married. Merchant, Austin, Travis County, Texas. SPECIAL RANGER Oct. 24, 1918–Jan. 15, 1919. REMARKS: In 1910 was city marshal of El Centro, Imperial County, California. In 1920 was a paint merchant in Austin. In 1930 was an insurance agent in Austin. A Clyde Andrew Bradford died Feb. 23, 1956, Travis County, Texas. FAMILY: Parents, Christopher Columbus Bradford (b. 1852, AL) and Lula V. Coffee (b. 1861, MO); siblings, Wallis C. (b. 1888, TX), Dewey Charles (b. 1897, TX), Thelma V. (b. 1900, TX); spouse, Myrtle M. (b. 1888, IL), married about 1910; children, Louise T. (b. 1911, CA), Charles W. (b. 1913, TX). *SR; A1e, f, g; A2b; A4g.*

BRADY, HUBERT PATRICK. Born Mar. 13, 1895, Floresville, Wilson County, Texas. Ht. 6 ft., blue eyes, red hair, red complexion. Stockman. REGULAR RANGER May 16, 1916–Dec. 1, 1916 (private, Co. A). Resigned/honorably discharged. Stockman, Carrizo Springs, Dimmit County, Texas. SPECIAL RANGER May 30, 1917–Dec. 1917 (attached to Co. C). Peace officer, Carrizo Springs. REGULAR RANGER Oct. 1, 1920–June 30, 1923 (private, Co. D). Resigned. REMARKS: Served in the Navy, 1917–1919. On July 1, 1923, became a mounted Immigration inspector. In 1930 was chief patrol inspector, Laredo, Webb County, Texas. Later became district supervisor of Border Patrol with headquarters in San Antonio, Bexar County, Texas. Retired from Border Patrol, 1954. Was chief deputy sheriff, Zavala County, Texas. In 1949 served as first president of the Texas Ex-Rangers Association and served on the organization's first board of directors. Died Sept. 6, 1957, Bexar County, Texas; buried in Ft. Sam Houston National Cemetery, San Antonio. LAW ENFORCEMENT RELATIVES: Ranger and Dimmit County sheriff (Nov. 1954–Jan. 1973) Tom Giles Brady, brother; Border Patrolman Paul H. Brady, brother. FAMILY: Parents, Thomas H. Brady (b. 1864, TX) and Kate (b. 1873, NY); siblings, Paul H. (b. 1893, TX), Ramon H. (b. 1897, TX), Mary A. (b. 1899, TX), Stella (b. 1901, TX), Tom G. (b. 1902,

TX), Reginald (b. 1904, TX), James (b. 1905, TX); spouse, Margaret (b. 1901, TX), married about 1923; children, W. P. (son, b. 1925, TX), Marilyn Patricia (b. 1926, TX). *SR; 471; Gardner to Hutchings, Apr 25, May 30, 1917, AGC; 1000:iii, 112–113; LWT, Aug 7, 1921; 469: 64; Wright to Barton, Sept 13, 1921, WC; 470: 35, 43, 102; 319: 412; A1d, e, f, g; A2b, e; A3a, b.*

BRAHAN, ROBERT W. Born 1869, Seguin, Guadalupe County, Texas. Ht. 6 ft., gray eyes, gray hair, fair complexion. Insurance agent, Houston, Harris County, Texas. SPECIAL RANGER July 2, 1918–Dec. 31, 1919. REMARKS: Was a traveling salesman, living in Huntsville, Walker County, Texas in 1900. A Robert Weakley Brahan died Dec. 26, 1924, Walker County, Texas. FAMILY: Parents, Haywood Brahan (b. 1841, AL) and Mattie Jeannie Jefferson (b. 1843, MS); sister, Annie (b. 1868, TX); spouse, Anna Robinson (b. 1872, ME), married about 1897; children, Charles Haywood (b. 1897, TX), Catherine (b. 1906, TX). *SR; A1a, b, d, f; A3a; A4a, g; C.*

BRANOM, CURTIS "CURT." Born Oct. 12, 1874, Cumby, Hopkins County, Texas. Ht. 5 ft. 7 in., gray eyes, brown hair, fair complexion. Stockman, Cumby. LOYALTY RANGER June 11, 1918–Feb. 1919. REMARKS: As of Sept. 1918 worked for the Cumby Gin Company; managed a cotton gin in Cumby in 1920 and 1930. Died Sept. 9, 1949, Hopkins County, Texas. FAMILY: Parents, Albert Branom (b. 1848, TX) and Sarah M. E. Ward (b. 1850, TX); sister, Louise (b. 1878, TX); spouse, Sallie Weaver (b. 1880, TX), married June 9, 1907; daughter, Thelma (b. 1909, TX). *SR; A1b, f, g; A2b; A3a; A4a, b.*

BRATTON, JOSEPH OSCAR "JOE." Born Oct. 15, 1886, Pflugerville, Travis County, Texas. Ht. 6 ft. 1 ½ in., blue eyes, red hair, fair complexion, married as of Jan. 1918. Peace officer. REGULAR RANGER May 11, 1916–July 15, 1916 (private, Co. B). Resigned. Peace officer. REGULAR RANGER Jan. 2, 1918–Sept. 1918 (private, Co. F). Resigned. Peace officer, Austin, Travis County. SPECIAL RANGER Feb. 28, 1933–Feb. 27, 1935. REMARKS: 1918 enlistment form says born near Round Rock, Travis County; 1933 enlistment form says born in Austin. Died July 12, 1944, Travis County, Texas. FAMILY: Parents, John Bratton (b. 1856, TX) and Mary Priscilla Wood (b. 1859, TX); siblings, May Belle (b. 1879, TX), Elvie Jane (b. 1881, TX), Archer Rex (b. 1882, TX), John Wayne (b. 1889, TX), Woodie Estelle (b. 1894, TX); spouse, Alma Mussett (b. 1894, TX), married about 1913; children, Willis Lynn (b. 1914, TX), Priscilla Estelle (b. 1918, TX). *SR; 471; A1d, e, f, g; A4a, g; C.*

BRAZIEL, JOHN NEWTON. Born Oct. 8, 1879, Cleburne, Johnson County, Texas. Ht. 6 ft., blue eyes, dark hair, tan complexion, married. Farmer, Point, Rains County, Texas. LOYALTY RANGER July 3, 1918–Feb. 27, 1919. REMARKS: Had been a constable and deputy sheriff. Died May 3, 1935, Rains County, Texas. FAMILY: Parents, Thomas Butler Braziel (b. 1847, GA) and Elizabeth Goosby (b. 1854, TN); siblings, Nancy T. (b. 1869, TN), William M. "Bill" (1871, TN), Alonzo Rapiness (b. 1873, TN), Nora A. (b. 1876, TX), Otis Alexander (b. 1881, TX), Horace (b. 1883), Thomas Butler (b. 1886, TX); spouse, Lula Brooks (b. 1887, GA); sons, Leo McCallom (b. 1911, TX), John Elby (b. 1913, TX). *SR; A1b, f; A3a; A4a, b, g; C.*

BREHMER, OSCAR C. Born Feb. 28, 1881, Comal County, Texas. Ht. 5 ft. 10 ½ in., gray eyes, brown hair, married. Farmer and ranchman, near New Braunfels, Comal County. LOYALTY RANGER June 15, 1918–Feb. 1919. REMARKS: Still farming in Comal County in 1930. Died Oct. 16, 1959, Comal County, Texas. FAMILY: Parents, Carl or Karl Friedrich Brehmer (b. 1832, Prussia) and Emme Hartung (b. 1855, TX); siblings, Louisa Alma (b. 1876, TX), Agnes Emma (b. 1878, TX), Frieda (b. 1885, TX); spouse, Ottilie "Tilla" Jonas (b. 1892, TX), married about 1913; children, Norman Oscar (b. 1919, TX), Lola May (b. 1921, TX), Melba L. (b. 1925, TX). *SR; A1b, d, e, f, g; A2b, e; A3a; A4a, b, g.*

BRIGHTMAN, OSWELL OLIVER. Born Apr. 20, 1868, near Saint Mary's, Refugio County, Texas. No physical description, married. Merchant and cotton buyer, Comanche, Comanche County, Texas. LOYALTY RANGER June 17, 1918–Feb. 1919. REMARKS: Had been president of a mining company in Comanche County. In 1930 was manager of a cotton and grain warehouse in Comanche. Died Mar. 5, 1959, Comanche, Comanche County, Texas. FAMILY: Parents, Lyman Brightman (b. 1828, IN) and Harriet Catherine Howard (b. 1838, GA); siblings, Nancy Violeta (b. 1857, TX), Lieuen Russell (b. 1859, TX), Thomas Claver (b. 1860, TX), Mary Elizabeth (b. 1862, TX), Lyman

Howard (b. 1866, TX), William Sidney (b. 1871, TX), Robert Edward (b. 1873, TX), Sarah "Sally" (b. 1875, TX), Cannie (b. 1879, TX); spouse, Alma Buford Wiley (b. 1867, MS), married Dec. 12, 1890, Coleman, Texas; children, Alma May (b. 1892, TX), Harriet Eunice (b. 1894, TX), Dwight Moody (b. 1897, TX), Oswell Oliver, Jr. (b. 1905, TX), Lella V. (b. 1907, TX), Grace Yancy (b. 1911, TX). *SR; A1a, b, d, e, f, g; A2b; A4a, b, g.*

BRIGMAN, MARTIN A. Born May 1859, Cherokee County, Texas. Ht. 5 ft. 9 in., blue eyes, white hair. Real estate agent, Hillsboro, Hill County, Texas. LOYALTY RANGER June 8, 1918–Feb. 1919. Realtor, Hillsboro. RAILROAD RANGER Sept. 9, 1922–Dec. 29, 1922 (Co. B). Discharged. REMARKS: Had been a farmer and in the livestock business. In 1918 he stipulated: "I am only to devote such time as I can spare from my regular employment, and service at my option to be limited to Hill County." Letterhead: "Jackson-Brigman Co., Real Estate and Loans." Was still a real estate agent in Hillsboro in 1930. A Mart A. Brigman died Feb. 5, 1932, Hill County, Texas. FAMILY: Parents, Rev. R. C. Brigman (b. 1823, SC) and Sarah A (b. 1825, GA); siblings, Permelia A. (b. 1847, AL), Rebecca A. (b. 1848, AL), Mary (b. 1849, AL), Joshua (b. 1851, TX), George H. (b. 1853, TX), Jane (b. 1855, TX), William (b. 1856, TX), Larina (b. 1859, TX). *SR; A1aa, a, f, g; A4g; C.*

BRISCOE, JONATHAN PAYNE. Born Aug. 19, 1881, Goliad County, Texas. Medium height, slender build, gray eyes, red hair, married. Stockman, Hebbronville, Jim Hogg County, Texas (enlisted in Frio County, Texas). SPECIAL RANGER May 3, 1918–Jan. 15, 1919. REMARKS: In 1910 was a stock farmer in Frio County; in Sept. 1918 was working for stockman and Special Ranger Henry Edds, Hebbronville. In 1930 still living in Jim Hogg County. Died Mar. 19, 1960, Webb County, Texas. FAMILY: Parents, Andrew Birdsall Briscoe (b. 1841, TX), and Annie Frances Payne (b. 1852, IN); siblings, Carrie Payne (b. 1872, TX), Mary (b. 1874, TX), Birdsall Paremas (b. 1876, TX); spouse #1, Blanch Hugo; children, Evelyn Blanch (b. 1905, TX), Hugo Payne (b. 1907, TX); spouse #2, Effie M. Holman, married about 1909. *SR; A1e, g; A2b; A3a; A4a, b.*

BRISCOE, LEIGH ADOLPHUS, SR. "DOLPH." Born Sept. 1, 1890, Fulshear, Fort Bend County, Texas. Ht. 5 ft. 11 in., blue eyes, blonde hair, blonde complexion, married. Stockman, Uvalde, Uvalde County, Texas. SPECIAL RANGER May 22, 1917–Dec. 1917 (attached to Co. C). REMARKS: In May 1917 was a deputy sheriff in Uvalde County. In 1930 was raising cattle in Uvalde County. Died July 15, 1954, Uvalde County, Texas; buried in Briscoe Cemetery, Fort Bend County. His son, Dolph, Jr., would become the 40th governor of the state of Texas. FAMILY: Parents, Judge Leigh "Lee" Adolphus Briscoe (b. 1867, TX) and Lucy Amanda Wade (b. 1864, MS or TX); siblings, William Pelham (b. 1888, TX), Lucy Louise (b. 1894, TX), Minnie Leigh (b. 1895, TX); spouse, Georgie Garvey Briscoe, his cousin (b. 1888, TX), married Oct. 1, 1913; son, Dolph, Jr. (b. 1923, TX). *SR; Bickett to Ferguson, May 16, 1917, AGC; Briscoe to Hutchings, May 21, 1917, AGC; Johnson to Hutchings, May 19, 1917, AGC; AG to Johnson, May 21, 1917, AGC; 172:I, 740; A1d, e, g; A2b, e; A4a, b, g.*

BRITE, CHARLES ETHRIDGE. Born Feb. 3, 1884, San Angelo, Tom Green County, Texas. Ht. 5 ft. 10 ½ in., brown eyes, brown hair, fair complexion. Bookkeeper, Crystal City, Zavala County, Texas. SPECIAL RANGER July 16, 1916–Jan. 1918 (attached to Co. C). Merchant, enlisted in Presidio County, Texas. SPECIAL RANGER Jan. 29, 1918–Jan. 15, 1919. REMARKS: In 1930 was a poultry farmer in Leon County, Texas. Died June 26, 1930, Leon County, Texas FAMILY: Parents, William Thomas Brite (b. 1856, TX) and Mary Hester Neill (b. 1861, TX); siblings, Samuel Silas (b. 1882), Willie (b. 1885, TX), Thomas Stuart (b. 1886), Asa Grande (b. 1888, TX), Mary Louisa (b. 1889), James Irwin (b. 1891, TX), Alsa S. (b. 1893), Jerome Duck (b. 1894, TX), Martha Helen (b. 1896, TX), John Wells (b. 1898), Benjamin Lowe (b. 1902, TX), Joe Murray (b. 1904, TX), Jay Bailey (b. 1907, TX); spouse, Mary D. (b. 1885, TX), married about 1920; daughter, Mary Margaret (b. 1921, TX). *SR; AG to Taylor, July 8, 1916, AGC; Taylor to AG, July 16, 1916, AGC; A1d, e, f, g; A2b, e; A3a; A4a, b, g; B1.*

BRITE, JOHN WILLIAM. Born Mar. 1873, Bexar County, Texas. Ht. 5 ft. 10 in., gray eyes, brown hair, dark complexion, married. Ranchman, Comstock, Val Verde County, Texas. SPECIAL RANGER Dec. 3, 1917–Jan. 1919 (Co. A Volunteers). REMARKS: In 1900 was living in Sutton County, Texas. By 1910 was a stockman in Val Verde County; still living in Val Verde County in 1930. A John

William Brite died Apr. 16, 1955, Val Verde County, Texas. FAMILY: Spouse, Mattie B. (b. 1874, TX), married about 1893; children, Thomas R. (b. 1895, TX), Annie Laura (b. 1897, TX), Richard Joseph (b. 1899, TX), Ellison (b. 1905, TX), Marion "Buster" (b. 1908, TX). *SR; A1d, e, f, g; C.*

BROOKS, BEN HILL, JR. Born June 17, 1893, Dallas, Dallas County, Texas. Ht. 5 ft. 10 in., gray eyes, light brown hair, light complexion, married. Labor superintendent, Mercedes, Hidalgo County, Texas. LOYALTY RANGER June 1, 1918–Feb. 1919. REMARKS: For past 6 years had been a county and city peace officer. In 1930 was a contractor, still living in Mercedes. A Benjamin Hill Brooks, Jr. died Feb. 9, 1950, Hidalgo County, Texas. FAMILY: Parents, Ben Brooks (b. 1863, LA) and Maryetta (b. 1865, IN); siblings, Barrett Jackson (b. 1895, TX), Wilfred (b. 1897, TX), Ronald (b. 1899, TX), Joseph Terrell (b. 1900, TX); spouse, Aracille (b. 1898, Mexico), married about 1913; children, Marietta (b. 1914, Mexico), Morris (b. 1917, Mexico), Billy (b. 1927, Mexico). *SR; A1d, f, g; A3a; C.*

BROOKS, CHARLES M. Born Jan. 4, 1890, Bastrop, Bastrop County, Texas. Ht. 5 ft. 8 in., brown eyes, brown hair, fair complexion, married as of 1922. Peace officer. REGULAR RANGER Apr. 1, 1915–Jul. 10, 1916 (private, Co. B). Resigned to join the El Paso, Texas, police force. Special Ranger, El Paso [*sic*]. RAILROAD RANGER Aug. 16, 1922–unknown (Co A). REMARKS: Prior to Apr. 1915 had been a deputy U.S. marshal and a deputy sheriff. In Apr. 1915 accidentally shot himself in the leg. In 1920 was deputy sheriff at Ysleta, El Paso County. A C. M. Brooks died Apr. 13, 1925, El Paso County, Texas. FAMILY: Parents, Robert Brooks (b. 1859, TX) and Sarah E. "Sallie" (b. 1867, TX); brother, Robb T. (b. 1893, TX); spouse, Bessie (b. 1895, TX); children, Charles M. (b. 1918, TX), Dora Elizabeth (b. 1919, TX). *SR; 471; EPMT, Apr 14, 1915, Jul 13, 1916, Apr 2, 1919; Petition to Harley, [May 1919], AGC; A1d, e, f; A2b, e; A3a.*

BROOKS, ERNEST T. Born Nov. 16, 1873, Pine Apple, Wilcox County, Alabama. Ht. 5 ft. 7 ½ in., gray eyes, auburn hair, dark complexion, married. Lawyer, Anson, Jones County, Texas. SPECIAL RANGER May 31, 1917–Dec. 1917 (attached to Co. C). REMARKS: In 1900 was a lawyer living in Bell County, Texas; in 1930 was practicing law in Abilene, Taylor County, Texas. Died Mar. 3, 1954, Abilene, Taylor County, Texas. FAMILY: Brother, Alonzo Alsie "Lon" (b. 1972, AL); spouse, Mamie Fergus (b. 1878, TX), married Oct. 30, 1899, Killeen, Bell County; children, Meryl McCall (b. 1901, TX), Aubrey Henderson (b. 1903, TX), Maurice V. (b. 1905, TX), Frances (b. 1911, TX). *SR; Dodson to Ferguson, May 18, 1917, AGC; Cunningham to Ferguson, May 18, 1917, AGC; A1d, e, f, g; A2b; A3a; A4b.*

BROOKS, JOSEPH B. "JOE." Born July 9, 1890, Laredo, Webb County, Texas. Ht. 5 ft. 8 in., brown eyes, light brown hair, medium complexion, married as of 1919. Stockman. REGULAR RANGER Feb. 20, 1915–Feb. 15, 1923 (private, Co. A; reenlisted Feb. 20, 1917; Jan. 10, 1919 was transferred to detached duty). Ranger, Austin, Travis County, Texas. REGULAR RANGER June 11, 1919 (private, Headquarters Co.; promoted to sergeant, June 17, 1919; commissioned as captain, Oct. 1, 1919; was transferred to command Emergency Co. No. 1, Feb. 15, 1921. His commission expired Feb. 15, 1923). Captain, wharf police, Galveston, Galveston County, Texas. SPECIAL RANGER Apr. 18, 1927–Apr. 16, 1928; Apr. 10, 1928–Apr. 10, 1929; Apr. 17, 1929–Apr. 15, 1930; Apr. 16, 1930–Jan. 1, 1931 (commission was extended to Jan. 20, 1933); July 22, 1933–Jan. 22, 1935; Discharged. REMARKS: In 1912 was a Laredo motorcycle policeman. In 1913 was a Webb County deputy constable. FAMILY: Spouse, Maude (b. 1890, KS), married about 1919; son, Joseph Bertrand, Jr. (b. 1923, TX). *SR; 471; LWT, Sept 1, 1912, Jan 19, May 6 11, 25, June 8, 1913, Oct 12, 1919; Special Orders No. 1, Jan 9, 1919, WC; Hanson to AG, July 17, 1919, WC; Hobby to Cope, Sept 21, 1920, WC; Brooks to Cope, Dec 17, 1920, WC; Cope to Brooks, Jan 15, 19, 1921, WC; A1g; A2e; A3a.*

BROOKS, SAM RAYMOND. Born July 8, 1894, Rodessa, Caddo Parish, Louisiana. Ht. 5 ft. 6 ½ in., dark brown eyes, dark hair, dark complexion. Newspaper reporter, Beaumont, Jefferson County, Texas. SPECIAL RANGER Aug. 1, 1919–Dec. 31, 1919. REMARKS: Was commissioned at request of Governor Hobby. In 1917 had worked for the Beaumont Chamber of Commerce. In 1920 was an assistant secretary in a government office in Austin, Travis County, Texas. In 1930 was a newspaper reporter in Austin. Died Sept. 19, 1968, Harris County, Texas. FAMILY: Spouse, Gladys Iona Whitfield (b. 1901, TX), married about 1922; children,

Bettie Jane (b. 1923, TX), Virginia Payne Holly (b. 1928, TX), Sam Raymond, Jr. (b. 1940, TX). *SR; A1f, g; A2a, b, e; A3a.*

BROPHY, JERRY EDMUND. Born Nov. 15, 1889, Bell County, Texas. Ht. 5 ft. 4 in., brown eyes, brown hair, fair complexion. Clerk, Austin, Travis County, Texas. SPECIAL RANGER May 10, 1918–Jan. 15, 1919. REMARKS: In 1920 was an accountant living in Houston, Harris County, Texas. In 1930 was a representative of the Texas Oil Company, living in Eugene, Lane County, Oregon. FAMILY: Parents, Edmund Isaac Brophy (b. 1855, TX) and Ida Flume (b. 1864, TX); siblings, Annie Litia (b. 1884, TX), Lenora Mae (b. 1887, TX), Eanes Barker (b. 1895, TX), John A. "Jack" (b. 1892, TX); spouse, Mildred (b. 1899, NC), married about 1928. *SR; A1d, f, g; A3a; A4a, b, g.*

BROWN, BAYLOR B. Born Aug. 23, 1889, Ranger, Eastland County, Texas. Ht. 5 ft. 6 in., blue eyes, light hair, fair complexion. Secretary to general manager of International and Great Northern Railroad, enlisted in Harris County, Texas. SPECIAL RANGER Feb. 28, 1917–Dec. 1917. REMARKS: In 1920 was a bank trust officer in Fort Worth, Tarrant County, Texas; in 1930 was listed as a lawyer in Fort Worth. Died June 1, 1975, in Fort Worth, Tarrant County, Texas. FAMILY: Spouse, Lillie V. (b. 1892, TX), married about 1919. *SR; Williamson to Hutchings, Feb 25, 1917, AGC; AG to Williamson, Feb 26, 1917, AGC; A1f, g; A2a, b; A3a.*

BROWN, GEORGE CALVIN. Born Dec. 19, 1877, Oakville, Live Oak County, Texas. Ht. 5 ft. 9 in., gray eyes, brown hair, fair complexion, married. Stockman (J. T. Tigner Ranch), Marfa, Presidio County, Texas. SPECIAL RANGER Mar. 2, 1918–ca. Oct. 5, 1918. Resigned to join Immigration Service. Rancher, Presidio, Presidio County. REGULAR RANGER Sept. 27, 1919–Jan. 31, 1920 (private, Co. A). Resigned. Ranchman, Presidio. REGULAR RANGER Feb. 28, 1920–Mar. 31, 1920 (private, Co. A). Resigned. Ranch hand, Presidio. REGULAR RANGER Oct. 30, 1920–Oct. 31, 1923 (private, Co. A). Resigned. REMARKS: In 1910 was a stock farmer in McMullen County, Texas. In 1930 was a public health inspector in Presidio. FAMILY: Parents, Robert H. Brown (b. 1848, TX) and Amanda E. (b. 1853, TX); siblings, Volney M. (b. 1877, TX), Maude V. (b. 1881, TX), Royal H. (b. 1883, TX), Vasmer (b. 1886, TX), Carlos (b. 1891, TX), Bryan (b. 1899, TX); spouse, Margaret "Maggie" (b. 1882, TX), married about 1903; children, Julius (b. 1905, TX), twins Joseph C. and Francis E. (b. 1908, TX), Grace (b. 1912, TX). *SR; 471; Johnston to Brown, Oct 7, 1918, AGC; Brown to Aldrich, Apr 2, 1920, AGC; 470: 43; A1b, d, e, f, g; A3a.*

BROWN, GEORGE EARL. Born Feb. 2, 1868, Robertson County, Texas. No physical description, married. Farmer and stockman, Franklin, Robertson County. LOYALTY RANGER June 5, 1918–Feb. 1919. REMARKS: In 1900 was tax assessor in Robertson County; in Feb. 1919 was vice president of the First National Bank of Franklin. In 1920 and 1930 was a farmer in Robertson County. Died Apr. 27, 1933, Robertson County, Texas. FAMILY: Parents, George Brown (b. 1844, TX) and Fannie Ford; spouse #1, Missouri A. (b. 1878; d. 1900); son, George Earl (b. 1899); spouse #2, Edna Mitchell (b. 1878, TX), married about 1902; children, Edna Earl (b. 1904, TX), Vernon (b. 1905, TX), James Mitchell (b. 1908, TX), Charles Alexander (b. 1915, TX), Martha Ann (b. 1917, TX), John Robert "Jack" (b. 1921, TX). *SR; A1d, e, f, g; A4a, b; C.*

BROWN, JAMES A. Born Nov. 1885, Kosse, Limestone County, Texas. Ht. 6 ft., brown eyes, black hair, dark complexion, married. Private detective, Texas and Pacific Railroad, Dallas, Dallas County, Texas. SPECIAL RANGER May 26, 1917–July 26, 1917. Was placed on active duty. REGULAR RANGER July 26, 1917–Sept. 21, 1917 (private, Co. C). Discharged—"not satisfactory." Peace officer, Dallas. RAILROAD RANGER Oct. 20, 1922–Nov. 4, 1922. Discharged—"no good." REMARKS: Had worked in Los Angeles, Los Angeles County, California for the Thiel Detective Agency, the Southern Pacific Railroad, the Ray C. Seely Co., and the City of Los Angeles. *SR; 471.*

BROWN, JAMES EUGENE. Born Jan. 1872, London, Michigan. Ht. 5 ft. 7 ¼ in., blue eyes, brown hair, fair complexion, married. Oil producer, San Antonio, Bexar County, Texas. SPECIAL RANGER May 14, 1918–Jan. 15, 1919. REMARKS: "Military schooling, private investigator, deputy sheriff." In 1910 lived in Reeves County, Texas. In 1930 was an oil company promoter in San Antonio. FAMILY: Parents, James Brown (b. 1840, Ireland) and Carrie (b. 1842, MI); siblings, Nettie B. (b. 1867, NY), George M. (b. 1873, OH); spouse #1, Minnie M. (b. 1878, GA), married about 1895; spouse #2, Beatrice (b. 1889,

GA), married by 1920; sons, James (b. 1918, TX), Frederick "Buddy" (b. 1919, TX); spouse #3, Hazel (b. 1885, OH), married about 1927. *SR; A1a, b, e, f, g.*

BROWN, ROBERT DUEROC "ROB." Born May 6, 1878, Goliad, Goliad County, Texas. Ht. 5 ft. 8 ½ in., brown eyes, black hair, dark complexion, married. Deputy sheriff, enlisted at Mission, Hidalgo County, Texas. REGULAR RANGER Jan. 1, 1920–July 31, 1920 (private, Co. D). Resigned. Peace officer, Brownsville, Cameron County, Texas. REGULAR RANGER June 22, 1925–Mar. 31, 1926 (sergeant, Co. D). Resigned. REMARKS: In 1910 was a farmer in Goliad County. Had been a Customs inspector for 3 ½ years and a deputy sheriff for 12 years. As of Sept. 1918 was a city policeman in Mission. Was fluent in Spanish. Died of a gunshot wound, Apr. 20, 1929, Cameron County, Texas; buried in Buena Vista Cemetery, Brownsville. FAMILY: Parents, Robert A. Brown (b. 1839, TN or TX) and Mary Samantha Parker (b. 1844, TX); spouse, Minnie Mirim Fuller (b. 1879, TX), married Sept. 15, 1897, Charco, Goliad County; children, Clifton Dueroc (b. 1898, TX), Katharyn Estelle "Kate" (b. 1904, TX). *SR; 471; A1d, e, f; A3a; A4a, g; C.*

BROWN, THOMAS TYRE "TOM." Born Oct. 1, 1872, Caldwell County, Texas. Short, medium build, blue eyes, brown hair, married. Farmer and stock raiser, Luling, Caldwell County. SPECIAL RANGER Feb. 7, 1917–Dec. 1917. REMARKS: Had been a Caldwell County deputy sheriff; Sheriff W.M. Ellison requested that he be commissioned. Died Jan. 10, 1938, Caldwell County, Texas; buried in Luling City Cemetery. FAMILY: Parents, Robert Adkins Brown (b. 1847, AR) and Eugenia Ellison (b. 1854, TX); siblings, Anna Lucy (b. 1875, TX), Cassandra (b. 1876, TX), Minnie Pearl (b. 1879, TX), Robert Eugene (b. 1881, TX), Augustus Ellison (b. 1883, TX), Florence Ella (b. 1886, TX), Carroll Harris (b. 1888, TX), Ethel (b. 1890, TX), Clarence Elmo (b. 1893, TX), Ernest Evan (b. 1897, TX); spouse, Maggie Teas (b. 1874, TX), married Apr. 27, 1892; children, Carrie M. (b. 1893, TX), Gus T. (b. 1894, TX), La Val D. (b. 1896, TX), Nora Blanche (b. 1898, TX), Tom (b. 1904, TX), Victor (b. 1908, TX), Robert A. (b. 1913, TX). *SR; Ellison to Hutchings, Feb 2, 1917, AGC; AG to Brown, Feb 8, 1917, AGC; A1b, d, e, f, g; A2b; A3a; A4b.*

BROWNFIELD, ALBERT RAY. Born July 26, 1885, Nolan County, Texas. Medium height, medium build, blue eyes, dark brown hair, married. Stockman, Brownfield, Terry County, Texas. LOYALTY RANGER June 21, 1918–Feb. 1919. REMARKS: Died July 29, 1963, Terry County, Texas. FAMILY: Parents, Marion Virgil Brownfield (b. 1854, IA) and Ann Elizabeth Hornbeck (b. 1855); siblings, Alfred Marion (b. 1876, TX), Almer Lee (b. 1878, TX), Alva Dee (b. 1887, TX), Alice Effie (b. 1892, TX), Allie Francis (b. 1915, TX); spouse, Allie Doll Pyeatt (b. 1888, TX), married about 1909; children, Marian, Albert Ray, Jr. (b. 1915, TX). *SR; A1e, f, g; A2b; A3a; A4b, g.*

BRUNI, LOUIS HENRY. Born Apr. 1886, Laredo, Webb County, Texas. Ht. 5 ft. 9 in., brown eyes, brown hair, fair complexion, married. Stockman, Bruni, Webb County. SPECIAL RANGER Aug. 24, 1918–Jan. 15, 1919. REMARKS: Owned the 7—Ranch; letterhead: "L.H. Bruni, Dealer in Cattle, Horses and Mules, Bruni, Texas." Died Feb. 12, 1947, Laredo, Webb County, Texas. FAMILY: Parents, Antonio Mateo Bruni (b. 1856, Italy) and Consolacion Henry (b. 1858, TX); siblings, Fred Henry (b. 1880, TX), Mateo Angel Henry (b. 1881, TX), Antonio Henry (b. 1883, TX), Maria Micaela Henry (b. 1885, TX), Leopoldo Henry (b. 1887, TX), Loris (b. 1889, TX), Herminia (b. 1891, TX), Adela Henry (b. 1893, TX), Herlinda Henry (b. 1899, TX); spouse, Annie Rieser (b. 1885, IL), married about 1907; daughter, Lamar (b. 1910, TX). *SR; A1d, f, g; A4a, b.*

BRUNNER, COLE K. Born Apr. 1891, Lock Haven, Pennsylvania. Ht. 5 ft. 8 in., blue eyes, brown hair, light complexion, widower. Ranchman, enlisted in Harlingen, Cameron County, Texas. REGULAR RANGER Aug. 30, 1915–Oct. 31, 1915 (private, Co. D). Resigned. REMARKS: In Nov. 1914, was at Sanderson, Terrell County, Texas. Was employed on the Blocker & Jennings Ranch. Upon resignation from Rangers returned to Sanderson. FAMILY: Spouse, Corine Maury, married Nov. 1914, Sanderson. *SR; 471; EPMT, Nov 25, 1914; Ransom to Hutchings, Nov 2, 3, 7, AGC.*

BRUNSON, GLENN (also spelled GLEN) SAMUEL. Born July 16, 1890, Midland, Midland County, Texas. Ht. 6 ft., brown eyes, light hair, light complexion. Cattle raiser, Midland. SPECIAL RANGER June 26, 1917–Dec. 8, 1917 (attached to Co. C). REMARKS: AG revoked his commission until after the draft board acted on his case. Died July 13, 1982, Tom Green County, Texas. FAMILY: Parents, William Hodge Brunson (b. 1853, GA) and Annie Lee Cook (b. 1864, AL); siblings, Alma (b. 1894, TX), Lois W. (b. 1904, TX), Annie Lee (b. 1906, TX); spouse, Nellie Elkin (b. 1894, TX), married Dec. 26, 1921; children, Glen Samuel, Jr. (b. 1922, TX), Nellie Elken (b. 1926, TX), Shirley (b. 1929, TX). *SR; Harley to Brunson, Dec 8, 1917, AGC; A1d, e, f, g; A2a, b, e; A3a; A4a, b, g; B1.*

BRUTON, WILLIAM THOMPSON. Born Oct. 15, 1871, Farmerville, Union County, Louisiana. Ht. 5 ft. 6 in., gray eyes, dark hair, light complexion, married. Planter and stockman, Lovelady, Houston County, Texas. LOYALTY RANGER June 4, 1918–Feb. 12, 1919. REMARKS: Letterhead—"W.T. Bruton Farm and Ranch, Registered Poll Angus Cattle, Registered Poland China Hogs, Lovelady, Tex." Still farming in Lovelady in 1930. Died May 11, 1940, Houston County, Texas; buried in Evergreen Cemetery, Lovelady. FAMILY: Parents, Dr. William David M. Bruton (b. 1825, NC) and Mary Ann Thompson (b. 1839, MS); siblings, Catherine E. (b. 1854, NC), James (b. 1857, NC), Nannie or Mary Irene (b. 1860, LA), Mollie E. (b. 1866, LA), John Calvin (b. 1876, LA); spouse #1, Lillian Harriss (b. 1870, AL), married about 1892; daughter, Irene R. (b. 1893, TX); spouse #2, Leila A. (b. 1873, TN), married about 1911; children, William Thomas, Jr. (b. 1913, TX), Lucile Florence (b. 1915, TX). *SR; A1a, b, d, f, g; A2e; A4g; C.*

BRYANT, OSCAR W. Born Oct. 20, 1877, Chilton, Falls County, Texas. Ht. 5 ft. 6 in., gray eyes, black hair, dark complexion. Stockman, Plainview, Hale County, Texas. SPECIAL RANGER Jan. 14, 1917–Jan. 1918 (Co. B Volunteers). Honorably discharged. REMARKS: Bryant's Captain of Co. B Volunteers, J. C. Rawlings, found Bryant's character questionable and returned his commission to the AG. In 1910 was a bookkeeper in a hardware store in Plainview. In 1920 was a carpenter in Amarillo, Potter County; still lived in Amarillo in 1930. FAMILY: Father (probably), Martin Luther Bryant (b. 1849, SC); spouse #1, Lena Ford (b. 1886, TX), married about 1907, by Sept. 1918 he was "unmarried" (a Lena Gertrude Bryant died in 1914, Hale County); spouse #2, Jane (b. 1877, MO), married sometime between 1920 and 1930. *SR; Rawlings to Harley, Jan 24, 1918, AGC; A1b, e, f, g; A2b; A3a; A4a, b, g.*

BUCHANAN, JOSEPH BENJAMIN. Born May 1, 1890, Iredell, Bosque County, Texas. Ht. 6 ft., gray eyes, brown hair, fair complexion, married. Stockman, Austin, Travis County, Texas. SPECIAL RANGER Dec. 7, 1917–unknown. Ranchman. REGULAR RANGER Mar. 1, 1921–Dec. 26, 1921 (private, Co. A). REMARKS: Was killed in action on Dec. 26, 1921, Presidio County, Texas. FAMILY: Spouse, Lucille H. (b. 1897, TX), married as of Sept. 1917. *SR; 471; A1f; A3a; C.*

BUCHANAN, MARION BEVERLY "BEV." Born Dec. 16, 1889, Farmers Branch (Dallas), Dallas County, Texas. Ht. 5 ft. 11 in., dark gray eyes, light hair, fair complexion. Stockman, Plainview, Hale County, Texas. SPECIAL RANGER Dec. 6, 1917–Feb. 1918 (Co. B Volunteers). Discharged—Co. B Volunteers was disbanded in Feb. 1918. REMARKS: Died Jan 27, 1969, Friona, Parmer County, Texas. LAW ENFORCEMENT RELATIVES: Ranger William Young Buchanan, father (was a Ranger in 1871 under Capt. June Peak). FAMILY: Parents, William Young "Daddy Bill" Buchanan (b. 1856, MO) and Nancy "Nannie" Gassaway Lillard (b. 1862, TN); siblings, Mary Myra (b. 1887, TX), Jerome Dudley (b. 1891, TX), Edith Evlyn (b. 1900, TX), Susan (b. 1900, TX); spouse, Opal Whiteside; son, Billie Gene (b. 1927, TX). *SR; Rawlings to Harley, Dec 6, 1917, AGC; A1d, e, f; A2b, e; A3a; A4b.*

BUCK, EUGENE. Born Feb. 26, 1863, Brownsville, Cameron County, Texas. Ht. 5 ft. 8 in., gray eyes, light brown hair, light complexion, married. Deputy sheriff, Carrizo Springs, Dimmit County, Texas. SPECIAL RANGER Dec. 27, 1917–unknown (captain, Co. C Volunteers—station: Indio Ranch). Retired, Carrizo Springs. SPECIAL RANGER Sept. 19, 1931–Jan. 20, 1933. REMARKS: Had been a grocery merchant. Dimmit County sheriff, Nov. 8, 1904–Nov. 5, 1912; Dimmit County deputy sheriff, 1913. In Sept. 1913 he and deputy sheriff Candelario Ortiz were captured by gunrunners, who killed Ortiz. Buck died Dec. 18, 1942, Carrizo Springs, Dimmit County, Texas, buried in Mount Hope Cemetery, Carrizo Springs. FAMILY: Parents, James Madison Buck (b. 1832, LA) and Martha Ann Rowland (b. 1839, AL); siblings, Charles James (b. 1861, TX), Sarah Ann (b. 1864, TX), John Lee (b. 1866, TX), Martha Jane (b. 1867, TX), Leroy (b. 1870, TX), Mary Elizabeth (b. 1871, TX), Louis Perry (b. 1875, TX), Beatrice Maud (b. 1878, TX), Lela Lillian (b. 1880, TX), Dora Mabel (b. 1884, TX);

spouse, Oma E. Campbell (b. 1868, TX), married Mar. 12, 1886 (Buck was a widower by 1930 census); foster son/step son, Harry (b. 1894, NM). *SR; LWT, Nov 24, 1912, Sept 14, 21, Oct 5, 12, 19, 26, Nov 2, 23, 30, 1913, May 17, 1914; BDH, June 3, Sept 26, Oct 7, 1914, Jan 15, July 12, 1915; Cunningham to Harley, Dec 31, 1917, WC; Buck to Harley, May 13, 1919, AGC; 1503:160; A1a, b, d, e, f, g; A2b; A4b; B1.*

BURDETT, ROBERT LEE. Born June 1881, Sprinkle, Travis County, Texas. Ht. 6 ft., blue eyes, light brown hair, fair complexion. Peace officer. REGULAR RANGER Oct. 6, 1911–June 1912 (private, Co. C). Discharged. Peace officer. REGULAR RANGER Feb. 1, 1915–June 7, 1915 (private, Co. B). Killed in action on June 7, 1915, Fabens, El Paso County, Texas. REMARKS: Lived in Austin, Travis County, until he enlisted in the Rangers. FAMILY: Parents, Samuel Burdett (b. 1856, TX) and Elizabeth A. "Lizzie" (b. 1856, MD); siblings, Jessie (b. 1879, TX), Mary (b. 1887, TX). *SR; 471; AG to Fox, June 10, 1915, WC; EPMT, June 8–10, 13, July 3, 24, 1915; A1b, d, e; A2b.*

BURFORD, WILLIAM EDWARD. Born Dec. 5, 1883, Osage, Colorado County, Texas. Ht. 5 ft. 8 in., gray eyes, dark hair, fair complexion, married. Farmer, Weimer, Colorado County. REGULAR RANGER July 31, 1918—Was enlisted by AG and assigned to Co. M. Notation on his Warrant of Authority: "Was sworn in went back to Weimar and declined to accept position." Notation on Service Record: "Was enlisted but never placed on active duty." Policeman, Yoakum, Lavaca County, Texas. RAILROAD RANGER Aug. 5, 1922–Feb. 10, 1923 (Co. C). Resigned. Peace officer, Yoakum. REGULAR RANGER Feb. 10, 1923–Apr. 30, 1925 (private, Co. D). Resigned. REMARKS: Had been a farmer in Fayette County, Texas and DeWitt County, Texas. As Railroad Ranger was assigned to Texas and Pacific Railroad at Marshall, Harrison County, Texas. Died July 8, 1926, Colorado County, Texas. FAMILY: Father, Davie E. Burford (b. 1862, TX); siblings, Verna B. (b. 1885, TX), Robert F. (b. 1888, TX); spouse, Nannie E. (b. 1883, TX), married about 1908; daughters, Kathryn W. (b. 1909, TX), Hazel F. (b. 1920, TX). *SR; 471; A1d, e, f, g; A3a; C.*

BURLESON, STEPHEN MACKEY "STEVE." Born Dec. 3, 1877, Buda, Hays County, Texas. Ht. 5 ft. 10 in., blue eyes, brown hair, ruddy complexion. Ranchman. REGULAR RANGER May 26, 1916–Nov. 30, 1916 (private, Co. D). Resigned. Ranchman, enlisted in Jim Hogg County, Texas. REGULAR RANGER Jan. 1, 1917–Jan. 28, 1917 (private, Co. A). Was fired. REMARKS: In 1910 was the editor of a local paper in Hays County; in 1920 was a peace officer in Cisco, Eastland County, Texas. Died Apr. 25, 1924, Stephens County, Texas; buried in Live Oak Cemetery, Manchaca, Hays County. LAW ENFORCEMENT RELATIVES: Ranger David Crockett Burleson, father (served under Captain James Hughes Callahan in 1855). FAMILY: Parents, David Crockett Burleson (b. 1837, TX) and Louisa "Lou" Weir (b. 1844, MS); siblings, C. A. (b. 1862, TX), Joseph (b. 1868, TX), Sarah Griffin "Sallie" (b. 1872, TX), Martha Jane "Jennie" (b. 1875, TX), Lou (b. 1880, TX), Lizzie S. (b. 1881, TX), Mary Lener (b. 1885, TX). *SR; 471; Craighead to Hutchings, Dec 25, 1916, AGC; A1b, d, e, f; A2b; A3a; A4a, b, g.*

BURNS, CYRUS EUGENE. Born Oct. 20, 1872, McCulloch County, Texas. Medium height, medium build, blue eyes, black hair, married. Farmer, Burkett, Coleman County, Texas. LOYALTY RANGER June 8, 1918–Feb. 1919. REMARKS: Died Feb. 8, 1965, Burkett, Coleman County, Texas. FAMILY: Parents, Thomas Burns (b. 1837, Ireland) and Mary E. (b. 1850, TX); siblings, Alice A. (b. 1868, TX), William T. (b. 1870, TX); spouse, Mary Jane Pruitt (b. 1874, TX), married in 1893; children, Ethel (b. 1894, TX), Edith Elizabeth (b. 1900, TX), Carl Eugene (b. 1909, TX), Gordon Allen (b. 1912, TX). *SR; A1a. b, f, g; A2a, b; A3a; A4a, b, g.*

BURNS, JOHN PERLES, JR. Born Aug. 10, 1888, Taylor, Williamson County, Texas. Ht. 5 ft. 10 in., blue eyes, light hair, fair complexion. Farmer, Taylor. LOYALTY RANGER June 8, 1918–Feb. 1919. REMARKS: Died Mar. 25, 1970, Taylor, Williamson County, Texas. FAMILY: Parents, John P. Burns (b. 1859, TX) and Melinda (b. 1856, TX); brother, Herbert Ervin (b. 1886, TX). *SR; A1d, g; A2a, b; A3a.*

BURNS, LEWIS THOMAS "TOM." Born Dec. 5, 1876, near Yoakum, DeWitt County, Texas. Ht. 5 ft. 10 in., brown eyes, black hair, dark complexion, married. Stock farmer, Yoakum. SPECIAL RANGER June 22, 1918–Jan. 15, 1919. REMARKS: In 1900 had been manager of a stock ranch in Victoria County, Texas. By 1910 was a farmer in DeWitt County; still a stock farmer in DeWitt County in 1930. Died Aug. 17, 1963, DeWitt County, Texas. FAMILY: Parents, Lewis Burns

(b. 1851, TX) and Annie Mary White (b. 1857, TX); siblings, James Columbus (b. 1878, TX), Mary Ann (b. 1880), Frank William (b. 1883, TX); spouse, Myra Angelina Boothe (b. 1877, TX), married June 15, 1898, DeWitt County; children, Annie Lee (b. 1900, TX), Lewis Thomas, Jr. (b. 1909, TX). *SR; A1b, d, e, g; A2a, b; A3a; A4a, b.*

BURRIS, CLAUDE CLINTON. Born Oct. 14, 1873, Clinton, East Feliciana Parish, Louisiana. Ht. 5 ft. 9 ¾ in., brown eyes, gray hair, dark complexion, married. Farmer, Fort Stockton, Pecos County, Texas. LOYALTY RANGER June 10, 1918–Feb. 18, 1919. REMARKS: Had been a farmer in Johnson County, Texas; in 1930 was a public school officer, living in McCamey, Upton County, Texas. Died May 20, 1934, Upton County, Texas. FAMILY: Parents (probably), J. J. Burris (b. 1848, LA) and Julia M. (b. 1850, LA); sisters, Bessie Lee (b. 1874, MS), E. Virginia (b. 1877, MS); spouse, Ella V. (b. 1879, TN or TX), married about 1902. *SR; A1b, d, e, f, g; A2b; A3a; A4b.*

BURROW, GEORGE O. Born Sept. 1853, Holly Springs, Marshall County, Mississippi. Ht. 6 ft. 1 in., blue eyes, blonde hair, light complexion, widower. Stockman, enlisted in Val Verde County, Texas. SPECIAL RANGER (attached to Co. C—station: Del Rio) Dec. 19, 1916–Dec. 1917. REMARKS: Had worked for Wells Fargo for 6 years. As a young man had lived in Red Oak, Ellis County, Texas and Kinney County, Texas; was living in Val Verde County by 1900. A George Oliver Burrow died Apr. 1, 1924, Val Verde County, Texas. FAMILY: Parents, William Burrow (b. 1825, TN) and Sarah (b. 1825, TN); siblings, Mary (b. 1850, MS), Richard (b. 1851, MS), Reuben (b. 1857, MS); spouse, Luann (b. 1852, MS or AL), married about 1878; children, Sallie E. (b. 1879, TX), Oliver G. (b. 1885, TX), Helen (b. 1889, TX); stepdaughter, Emma Long (b. 1871, TX). *SR; A1a, b, d, e; A2b.*

BURWELL, CHARLES BLAIR. Born June 6, 1897, Cotulla, La Salle County, Texas. Ht. 6 ft. 1 in., gray eyes, brown hair, light complexion. Ranchman. REGULAR RANGER Sept. 1, 1917–Jan. 1920 (private, Co. A; transferred to Co. I, Dec. 21, 1917). Stockman, Kingsville, Kleberg County, Texas. SPECIAL RANGER Dec. 28, 1925–Feb. 1, 1927. Discharged. Brand inspector, Texas and Southwestern Cattle Raisers' Association, Kingsville. SPECIAL RANGER May 7, 1927–May 7, 1928; May 30, 1928–May 30, 1929; June 13, 1929–June 13, 1930. Discharged. REMARKS: In the 1950s managed the Laureles division of the King Ranch. Died Aug. 4, 1964, Kleberg County, Texas. LAW ENFORCEMENT RELATIVES: Ranger William Marvin Burwell, brother; Ranger (1891–1903) and La Salle County sheriff (Nov. 8, 1898–Nov. 6, 1900) and Potter County, Texas sheriff (Nov. 8, 1910–Nov. 5, 1918) William M. Burwell, uncle; Ranger Captain J. H. Rogers, uncle. FAMILY: Parents, Charles B. Burwell (b. 1868, TX) and Ada S. (b. 1872, TX); siblings, Lucy T. (b. 1892, TX), Beatrice (b. 1895, TX), William Marvin (b. 1900, TX), Catherine (b. 1904, TX), Ralph (b. 1914, TX). *SR; 471; AG to Sanders, Dec 21, 1917, AGC; 319: 381; 1503:321, 418; A1b, d, e, f; A2b, A3a.*

BUSBY, CHARLES C. Born Apr. 1876, Weesatche, Goliad County, Texas. Ht. 6 ft., gray eyes, dark brown hair, fair complexion, married. Ranchman, La Pryor, Zavala County, Texas. SPECIAL RANGER May 12, 1917–Jan. 15, 1919 (attached to Co. C—station: La Pryor). REMARKS: Letterhead: "C.C. Busby, Manager '77' Ranch, Col. I.T. Pryor, Owner—La Pryor." A Charles Cornelius Busby died Jan. 23, 1957, Zavala County, Texas. FAMILY: Parents, Robert B. Busby (b. 1849, TX) and Margaret E. Gibson (b. 1854, TX); siblings, Sarah E. (b. 1874, TX), Bamma Lee (b. 1877, TX), Julia E. (b. 1884, TX), Lola E. (b. 1889, TX); spouse, Onida (b. 1875, TX), married about 1899; children, Robert (b. 1901, TX), Inez (b. 1904, TX), Jack (b. 1907, TX). *SR; Pryor to Ferguson, May 8, 1917, AGC; AG to Busby, May 16, 1917, AGC; A1b, d, f; A2b; A4a.*

BUSTER, ARTHUR LEE. Born Sept. 16, 1886, Temple, Bell County, Texas. Ht. 5 ft. 10 ½ in., brown eyes, black hair, dark complexion, married. Deputy tax collector, Anson, Jones County, Texas. SPECIAL RANGER May 31, 1917–Dec. 1917 (attached to Co. C—station: Anson). REMARKS: In 1920 was a bank teller in Anson. In 1930 was business manager for a sanitarium in Stamford, Jones County. Died Dec. 19, 1938, Jones County, Texas; buried in Mount Hope Cemetery, Anson. FAMILY: Parents, John Green Buster (b. 1866, AR) and Margaret Savinia Gaither (b. 1864, TX); siblings, Cordelia Hester (b. 1889, TX), Lillie Pearl (b. 1894, TX), John Omer (b. 1902, TX); spouse, Bess Putman (b. 1891, AL); children, Margarette (b. 1917, TX), Dorothy M. (b. 1920, TX). *SR; Dodson to Ferguson, May 18, 1917,*

AGC; Cunningham to Ferguson, May 18, 1917, AGC; A1d, f, g; A2b; A3a; A4a, b.

BUSTER, JOHN ERASTUS. Born Dec. 30, 1851, Albany, Clinton County, Kentucky. Ht. 5 ft. 11 in., blue eyes, dark hair, light complexion, married. Farmer, Lewisville, Denton County, Texas. LOYALTY RANGER May 5, 1918–Feb. 18, 1919. REMARKS: Had lived in Grayson County, Texas. By 1880 was living in Denton County; in 1900 census was listed as a "ginner" in Denton County. Died June 11, 1937, Lewisville, Denton County, Texas. FAMILY: Parents, John P. Buster (b. 1814, KY) and Martha Jane Lair (b. 1820, KY), siblings, Parish (b. 1835, KY), Martha E. (b. 1837, KY), Evaline (b. 1840, KY), Waller (b. 1843, KY), Frances Ann (b. 1845, KY), Oliver C. (b. 1846, KY), Sarah Ellen (b. 1849, KY); spouse #1, unknown (b. MO); son, Lair (b. 1890, TX); spouse #2, Emma Sanola Mayfield (b. 1873, GA), married Dec. 1894; children, Reagan (b. 1896, TX), Willola (b. 1898, TX), Emmett (b. 1899, TX), Joella F. (b. 1913, TX). *SR; A1aaa, aa, a, b, d, f, g; A4a, g; C.*

BUTLER, MARVIN NEWTON. Born July 15, 1894, Kenedy, Karnes County, Texas. Ht. 6 ft. 3 in., blue eyes, light hair, light complexion. Stockman. REGULAR RANGER Dec. 28, 1917–Dec. 1, 1918 (private, Co. K). Resigned. REMARKS: Was a Texas A&M College football star. As of 1928 lived in Karnes City, Karnes County. In 1930 was Karnes County tax collector. Died June 26, 1969, Bexar County, Texas. LAW ENFORCEMENT RELATIVES: Ranger Sykes C. Butler, uncle; Ranger William B. Butler, cousin. FAMILY: Parents, Theodore Green Butler (b. 1871, TX) and Martha Louise "Mattie" Seale (b. 1874, MS); siblings, Annie Lucile (b. 1897, TX), Norine Louise (b. 1901, TX), Theodore G. (b. 1907, TX), Marc (b. 1909, TX); spouse, Hattie M. Livingston (b. 1895, TX), married about 1919; children, William Livingston "Billie" (b. 1921, TX), Marvin Teddy (b. 1927, TX), Martha (b. 1929, TX). *SR; 471; 319: 125; A1d, e, f, g; A2a, b, e; A3a; A4a, b, g; B1.*

BUTLER, SIDNEY W. Born Mar. 1870, Helena, Karnes County, Texas. Ht. 6 ft. 2 in., brown eyes, dark hair, married. Cowman, enlisted in Zavala County, Texas. SPECIAL RANGER (attached to Co. C—station: Crystal City) July 11, 1916–Aug. 7, 1917. REMARKS: Was a ranchman in Zavala County in 1910. Died Aug. 7, 1917, Bexar County, Texas. LAW ENFORCEMENT RELATIVES: Ranger Sykes C. Butler, cousin; Ranger William Bryan Butler, distant cousin; Ranger Marvin N. Butler, distant cousin. FAMILY: Parents, James B. Butler (b. 1832, MS) and Elizabeth Wallace Burris (b. 1831, OH); siblings, John Woodward (b. 1856, TX), Seaborn G. (b. 1857, TX), Holland (b. 1859, TX), Leander G. (b. 1861, TX), Burnell (b. 1862, TX), James Stanton (b. 1863, TX), Albert Andrew (b. 1867, TX), Ophelia E. (b. 1876, TX); spouse, Ada Robertson (b. 1879, TX), married Mar. 23, 1895, Frio County, Texas; children, Albert (b. 1897, TX), Mary (b. 1900, TX), Dennis (b. 1901, TX), Mattie (b. 1905, TX). *SR; A1b, d, e; A4a, b, g.*

BUTLER, SYKES CHARLES. Born Dec. 1867, Kenedy, Karnes County, Texas. Ht. 6 ft., blue eyes, auburn hair, light complexion, married. Ranchman, Kenedy. SPECIAL RANGER Jan. 16, 1918–Jan. 15, 1919. REMARKS: Letterhead: "S.C. Butler, Dealer in and Breeder of High Grade and Registered Hereford Cattle—Kenedy." Died Apr. 8, 1946, Bexar County, Texas; buried in Butler Cemetery, Kenedy. LAW ENFORCEMENT RELATIVES: Ranger William B. Butler, son; Ranger Marvin N. Butler, nephew; Ranger Sidney W. Butler, cousin. FAMILY: Parents, William Green Butler (b. 1834, MS) and Adeline Riggs Burris (b. 1838, OH); siblings, Newton G. (b. 1858, TX), Helen Adeline (b. 1860, TX), Louisa M. (b. 1862, TX), Emmett W. (b. 1864, TX), Marion (b. 1866, TX), Cora Ann (b. 1870, TX), Theodore Green (b. 1872, TX), William Green (b. 1876, TX); spouse, Emma Jane Seale (b. 1869, MS), married Dec. 30, 1890; children, Addie Mae (b. 1891, TX), Myrtle E. (b. 1893, TX), William Bryan (b. 1896, TX), Emma Eva (b. 1898, TX), Bessie (b. 1901, TX), Nell (b. 1910, TX). *SR; A1b, d, e; A4a, b, g; C.*

BUTLER, THOMAS B. Born Aug. 1870, Columbia, Caldwell Parish, Louisiana. Ht. 5 ft. 11 ½ in., dark eyes, black hair, dark complexion, married. Special agent, St. Louis Southwestern Railroad, Palestine, Anderson County, Texas. SPECIAL RANGER Jan. 3, 1919–Dec. 31, 1919. Special agent, International & Great Northern Railroad, Palestine. RAILROAD RANGER Aug. 10, 1922–Aug. 10, 1924 (Co. A). Discharged—enlistment expired. Special agent, I&GN Railroad, Palestine. SPECIAL RANGER June 30, 1925–Jan. 29, 1928; Jan. 17, 1928–Jan. 17, 1929; Jan. 23, 1929–Jan. 11, 1931; Feb. 24, 1931–Jan. 20, 1933; Jan. 20, 1933–Jan.

19, 1935; May 29, 1935–Aug. 10, 1935. Discharged. LAW ENFORCEMENT RELATIVES: Ranger T. B. Butler, Jr., son. REMARKS: Had lived in Bowie County, Texas in 1910. FAMILY: Parents, Thomas Blewett Butler (b. 1834, AL) and Aurelia Medora Hundley (b. 1850, AR); siblings, Ruby (b. 1867, LA), Fannie (b. 1869, LA), Blanche (b. 1873, LA), Frederick (b. 1875, LA), Alma (b. 1877, LA), Lilly A. (b. 1878, LA), Clara (b. 1880, LA); spouse, Dora (b. 1872, AL), married about 1891; children, Lola (b. 1893, TX), Earnest (b. 1895, TX), a daughter (b. 1904, TX), Thomas (b. 1913, TX). *SR; 471; Johnston to Williamson, Jan 20, 1919, AGC; Williamson to Harley, Jan 24, 1919, AGC; A1b, e, g; A4b.*

BUTLER, WILLIAM BRYAN. Born Nov. 17, 1896, Kenedy, Karnes County, Texas. Ht. 5 ft. 10 in., blue eyes, light hair, light complexion. Stockman, Karnes County. REGULAR RANGER Dec. 22, 1917–Mar. 17, 1919 (private, Co. K). Resigned. REMARKS: Died Aug. 8, 1969, Karnes County, Texas; buried in Butler Cemetery, Kenedy. LAW ENFORCEMENT RELATIVES: Ranger Sykes C. Butler, father; Ranger Marvin N. Butler, cousin; Ranger Sidney W. Butler, distant cousin. FAMILY: Parents, Sykes C. Butler (b. 1867, TX) and Emma Jane Seale (b. 1869, MS); siblings, Addie Mae (b. 1891, TX), Myrtle E. (b. 1893, TX), Emma Eva (b. 1898, TX), Bessie (b. 1901, TX), Nell (b. 1910, TX); spouse, Alice Kathryne Rutledge (b. 1901, TX), married Jan. 10, 1924; daughter, Lasca (b. 1941, TX). *SR; 471; A1d, e, g; A2a, b, e; A3a; A4b, g.*

BUTTRILL, CLYDE. Born Sept. 16, 1879, Beeville, Bee County, Texas. Ht. 5 ft. 6 in., brown eyes, brown hair, dark complexion. Stockman, Marfa, Presidio County, Texas. SPECIAL RANGER Dec. 28, 1917–June 7, 1918 (station: Marfa). Resigned. REMARKS: Mar. 27, 1911, was appointed brand inspector, Alpine (Brewster County, Texas) district, for Panhandle Stockmen's Association. Oct. 1911, resigned this position. Oct. 1916, was a Brewster County deputy constable at Alpine. June 7, 1918, resigned from Rangers to enter U.S. Immigration Service at Presidio. Aug. 1919—had been furloughed from Immigration Service because of lack of appropriations. Applied for a Special Ranger commission. Operated a ranch and a large irrigated farm on the Rio Grande near Santa Helena, about 100 miles from Alpine, 1916–1920. As of 1917 had 10 years' experience as a peace officer. Died May 16, 1932, Alpine, Brewster County, Texas. FAMILY: Parents, William Alston Buttrill (b. 1832, MS) and Anne E. Wilson (b. 1844, TX); brother, Lucius F. (b. 1867, TX). *SR; AA, Mar 30, 1911, Oct 5, Nov 9, 1916, Nov 4, 1920; EPMT, Oct 8, 1911; Harrell to Ferguson, May 15, 1917, AGC; AG to Higgins, May 17, 1917, AGC; Turney to Hutchings, May 29, 1917, AGC; Buttrill to AG, Aug 23, 1919, AGC; Turney to Hobby, Oct 20, 1919, AGC; A1b, d, e, f; A3a; A4g; B2; C.*

BYNUM, RUFUS SINCLAIR "RUFE." Born June 23, 1879, Waxahachie, Ellis County, Texas. Ht. 5 ft. 10 ½ in., blue eyes, black hair, light complexion, married. Ranchman, San Antonio, Bexar County, Texas, enlisted in Presidio County, Texas. SPECIAL RANGER Sept. 12, 1917–Dec. 1917 (attached to Co. C—station: Marfa). Stockman, San Antonio, enlisted in Presidio County. SPECIAL RANGER Jan. 9, 1918–Jan. 15, 1919. REMARKS: Was a rancher in the Big Bend, Texas. In 1920 was a stock rancher in San Antonio. Died Dec. 21, 1960, San Antonio, Bexar County, Texas; buried in Mission Cemetery, San Antonio. FAMILY: Parents, Rufus Sinclair Bynum (b. 1850, NC) and Sarah Eugenie Bridgers (b. 1855, MS); brother, Frank Duane (b. 1877, TX); spouse, LaVera Gibson (b. 1878, TX), married Dec. 20, 1899, in Waxahachie; children, Elizabeth (b. 1901, TX), Emily (b. 1904, TX), twins, LaVera and Rufus Sinclair (b. 1915, TX). *SR; Bynum to Hudspeth, Sept 5, 1917, AGC; AG to Bynum, Sept 6, 1917, AGC; A1d, e, f; A2b; A3a; A4b; B2.*

BYRD, STEPHEN JOHNSON "STEVE." Born Oct. 18, 1886, Jackson, Cape Girardeau County, Missouri. Ht. 5 ft. 6 in., brown eyes, sandy hair, fair complexion, married. Ranchman, enlisted in Zavala County, Texas. SPECIAL RANGER May 17, 1917–Dec. 1917 (attached to Co. C—station: La Pryor). REMARKS: In 1920 was a stock farmer in Dimmit County, Texas. Died Feb. 10, 1972, Frio County, Texas. FAMILY: Parents, William Charles Byrd (b. 1845, MO) and Mary Jane "Mollie" Evans (b. 1849, MO); siblings, Ella (b. 1869, MO), Catherine Isabella (b. 1871, MO), Emma (b. 1873, MO), Dena Alberta (b. 1874, MO), Mattie (b. 1877, MO), Edward Ruddell (b. 1879, MO), Mollie May (b. 1881, MO), William Charles (b. 1883, MO), Ashsah Lorena (b. 1891, MO); spouse, Frances Elizabeth "Bess" Dimmitt (b. 1889, MO), married Oct. 19, 1910; children, Stephen Johnson (b. 1914, TX), Mary Evelyn (b. 1916, TX). *SR; A1e, f; A2a, b; A3a; A4a, b, g.*

CAIN, D. C. Born 1879, Franklin, Warren County, Ohio. Ht. 5 ft. 9 in., gray eyes, black hair, dark complexion, married. Stock farmer, Plainview, Hale County, Texas. SPECIAL RANGER Dec. 15, 1917–Feb. 1918 (Co. B Volunteers—station: Plainview). Discharged—Co. B Volunteers was disbanded. *SR; Rawlings to Harley, Dec 23, 1917, AGC.*

CAIN, JAMES JACOB. Born Jan. 8, 1876, Wilkes-Barre, Luzerne County, Pennsylvania. Ht. 5 ft. 6 in., brown eyes, dark hair, dark complexion, married. Railroad brakeman, San Antonio, Bexar County, Texas. SPECIAL RANGER July 22, 1916–Dec. 1917. REMARKS: As a young boy lived in Milam County, Texas. Had been a railroad switchman in Austin, Travis County, Texas. In 1930 was a railway conductor in San Antonio. Died Oct. 6, 1942, San Antonio, Bexar County, Texas. FAMILY: Parents, Henry Cain (b. 1835, Ireland) and Mary (b. 1846, Ireland); siblings, Patrick (b. 1865, MA), Margarett (b. 1868, PA), Brigett (b. 1870, PA), Mary (b. 1874, PA), Celia (b. 1878, PA), Katherine "Kate" (b. 1880, TX); spouse, Katherine Cecelia Wolf (b. 1878, TX), married June 27, 1900, Austin; children, Harry Edward (b. 1902, TX), James Robert (b. 1904, TX), John Charles (b. 1907, TX), Joseph A. (b. 1910, TX), Mary Katherine (b. 1916, TX), Francis Patrick (b. 1918, TX). *SR; A1b, d, e, g; A2b; A3a; A4b.*

CALLAN, LEO ALPHONSE. Born May 9, 1878, Coleman County, Texas. Medium height, medium build, blue eyes, dark brown hair, married. Stockman, Llano, Llano County, Texas. SPECIAL RANGER Mar. 1, 1918–Jan. 15, 1919. REMARKS: In 1900 was a printer/pressman living in Menard County, Texas. In 1918 was a cowman living in San Antonio, Bexar County, Texas. In 1920 was manager of a "convenience house" in San Antonio; still living in San Antonio in 1930. A Leo A. Callan died June 21, 1937, Bexar County, Texas. FAMILY: Parents, James Joseph Callan (b. 1833, D.C.) and Margaret M. Sheen (b. 1844, MO); siblings, Joseph T. (b. 1861, TX), James (b. 1864, TX), Iranaeus or Israel (b. 1867, TX), Mary V. (b. 1870, TX), Louis G. (b. 1871, TX), Austin B. (b. 1874, TX), John B. (b. 1875, TX), Claude (b. 1881, TX), Margaret (b. 1888, TX); spouse, Thursey Belle (b. 1881, TX), married about 1900; daughters, Mary Lee (b. 1901, TX), Gwendolyn (b. 1904, TX). *SR; A1b, d, e, f, g; A3a; A4b; C.*

CAMPBELL, FRANK R. Born Apr. 1879, Chicago, Cook County, Illinois. Ht. 6 ft. 1 in., blue eyes, brown hair, fair complexion, married. Chief special agent, St. Louis Southwestern Railroad (Cotton Belt), Tyler, Smith County, Texas. SPECIAL RANGER Jan. 11, 1918–Jan. 15, 1919. REMARKS: In 1900 was a railroad brakeman in Hunt County, Texas. In 1920 was a railroad yard master living in Commerce, Hunt County. In 1930 was a train master in Berwin, Cook County, Illinois. FAMILY: Mother (?), Anna C. Brown (b. 1857, IA); spouse, Leota Giles (b. 1881, TX), married about 1899. *SR; Campbell to Harley, Jan 1, 30, 1918, AGC; A1b, d, e, f, g.*

CANALES, ALBINO T. Born July 1879, La Calera Ranch, Jim Wells County, Texas. Ht. 5 ft. 10 in., brown eyes, black hair, dark complexion, married. Rancher, Premont, Jim Wells County. LOYALTY RANGER July 25, 1918–Feb. 1919. REMARKS: Managed three ranches in Jim Wells, Duval, and Jim Hogg counties for his father, Andres Canales. Brother of State Representative Jose T. Canales, who got him the Ranger commission and in 1919 conducted a controversial legislative investigation of the Texas Rangers. An Albino T. Canales died Sept. 2, 1951, Jim Wells County, Texas. FAMILY: Parents, Andres Canales (b. 1852, Mexico) and Thomasa (b. 1858, Mexico); siblings, Jose T. (b. 1877, TX), Andres C. (b. 1882, TX), Jesus Maria (b. 1886, TX), Maria G. (b. 1888, TX), Profedes (b. 1890, TX), Herlinda (b. 1893, TX), Thomasa (b. 1896, TX); spouse, Rafaela G. (b. 1886, TX), married about 1905; children, Virginia (b. 1911, TX), Gustavo (b. 1913, TX), Maria Gracia (b. 1919, TX). *SR; Canales to Woodul, July 22, 1918, AGC; Woodul to Canales, July 26, 1918, AGC; 319: 51, 456; A1b, d, f, g; A2e; C.*

CARDWELL, OLIVE DEETS. Born Mar. 22, 1888, Oak Forest, Gonzales County, Texas. Ht. 6 ft. 3 in., brown eyes, brown hair, dark complexion. Stockman. REGULAR RANGER Apr. 1, 1914–Jan. 15, 1917 (private, Co. A; transferred to Co. C as sergeant, Oct. 1, 1915). Resigned. Honorably discharged. Brand Inspector, Cattle Raisers' Association of Texas, Post City, Garza County, Texas. SPECIAL RANGER Jan. 20, 1917–May 26, 1919 (attached to Co. C; suspended Oct. 1917 because of sheriff's complaints; reinstated/warrant renewed, Dec. 22, 1917). Discharged—no longer a brand inspector. REMARKS: In January 1918, while a brand inspector and Special Ranger, was reclassified as a Regular Ranger without pay, to avoid the draft. In 1920 was a clothing merchant in Post; in 1930 was an insurance agent in Garza County. Died Mar. 7, 1957, Garza County, Texas. LAW ENFORCEMENT RELATIVES: Ranger Percy Aubrey Cardwell, distant cousin; Uvalde County, Texas sheriff (Nov. 3, 1908–Nov. 8, 1910) Oscar T. Cardwell, father. FAMILY: Parents, Oscar Talbot Cardwell (b. 1862, TX) and Frances "Frankie" Lowry (b. 1866, TX); siblings, Alvis Lowry (b. 1886, TX), Clytie (b. 1892, TX), Wilda Lois (b. 1895, TX); spouse, Annie Elizabeth Rogers (b. 1886, TX). *SR; 471; AG to Sanders, Sept 27, 1915, AGC; Corpus Christi Democrat, June 13, 1915; [AG] to Ferguson, Sept 8, 1915, WC; Robinson to Anderson, Oct 10, 1917, AGC; AG to Moses & Rowe, Oct 11, 1917, AGC; Spiller to Harley, Oct 13, 1917, AGC; Lockhart to Harley, Dec 6, 1917, AGC; Moses & Rowe to Harley, May 28, 1919, AGC; 1503:503; A1d, e, f, g; A2b; A3a; A4a, b, g.*

CARDWELL, PERCY AUBREY. Born Nov. 15, 1892, Gonzales, Gonzales County, Texas. Ht. 6 ft. 2 in., gray eyes, brown hair, fair complexion. Clerk. REGULAR RANGER June 18, 1917–Apr. 15, 1919 (private, Co. C; promoted to sergeant, Asst. Quartermaster, Ranger Force, Nov. 12, 1917; applied for a transfer to Co. G as sergeant, Aug. 22, 1918; transferred to Co. G as sergeant, Aug. 31, 1918). Resigned. REMARKS: Resigned on Mar. 24, 1919, effective Apr. 15, 1919, because he had been passed over for promotion to Quartermaster captain. In 1930 was a real estate broker in San Antonio, Bexar County, Texas. A Percy Cardwell died Nov. 25, 1957, Bexar County, Texas. LAW ENFORCEMENT RELATIVES: Ranger Olive Deets Cardwell, distant cousin; Uvalde County, Texas sheriff (Nov. 3, 1908–Nov. 8, 1910) Oscar T. Cardwell, distant relative. FAMILY: Parents, William A. Cardwell (b. 1863, TX) and Katherine Edna "Kate" Lincicum or Linecum (b. 1864, TX); siblings, Lottie Kate (b. 1887, TX), William E. (b. 1889, TX), Thomas Almond (b. 1897, TX); spouse, Emma K. (b. 1899, TX), married about 1924. *SR; 471; Cardwell to Harley, Aug 22, 1918, AGC; [Cardwell] to Rowe, Aug 31, 1918, AGC; Cardwell to Harley, Mar 24, 1919, AGC; Harley to Cardwell, Mar 27, 1919, AGC; 1503:503; A1d, e, g; A2b; A3a; A4a, b.*

CARGILE, LEE. Born Jan. 21, 1895, De Leon, Comanche County, Texas. Ht. 5 ft. 8 in., brown eyes, black hair, dark complexion. Farmer, Polar, Kent County, Texas. SPECIAL RANGER Aug. 20, 1917–Dec. 8, 1917 (attached to Co. C). Commission revoked by the AG; he was of draft age. REMARKS: Schoolteacher, Kent County, 1915–1917. As of June 1918 was a constable at Polar, Kent County. In 1920 was a telegraph operator in Kent County. In 1930 was a public school teacher in Lubbock County, Texas. As of Apr. 1940 lived in Amarillo, Potter County, Texas. Died Oct. 2, 1969, Lubbock County, Texas. FAMILY: Parents, William Jesse Cargile (b. 1858, TX) and Mary Jane Underwood (b. 1859, TX); siblings, John Franklin (b. 1889, TX), Albert C. (b. 1892, TX), William Jefferson "Jeff" (b. 1893, TX), Charlie Edward (b. 1898, TX), Emma M. (b. 1900, TX); spouse, Laura B. (b. 1900, TX), married about 1923. *SR; Petition to*

Ferguson, May 17, 1917, AGC; Cargile to Hutchings, June 4, Aug 7, 1917, June 14, 1918, AGC; AG to Cargile, June 7, Aug 17, 1917, June 11, 1918, July 1, 1919, AGC; Culberson to Hobby, Feb 28, 1919, AGC; Adamson to Harley, [Dec 1919], AGC; A1e, f, g; A2a, b; A3a; A4a, b, g.

CARLISLE, JAMES NEWTON. Born Feb. 1871, Chickasaw County, Mississippi. Ht. 5 ft. 8 in., blue eyes, light hair, fair complexion, married. Salesman, Austin, Travis County, Texas. SPECIAL RANGER Jan. 8, 1918–Jan. 15, 1919. REMARKS: By 1880 was living with his widowed mother in Austin, Travis County, Texas. In 1910 was a saloon bartender in Austin. By 1920 was a farmer in Travis County; still a farmer in Austin in 1930. Died Apr. 28, 1934, Travis County, Texas. FAMILY: Parents, James Newton Carlisle (b. 1837, SC) and Mary E. Dibbrell (b. 1846, MS); siblings, Catherine R. (b. 1869, MS), Glenn G. (b. 1873, MS), Mary (b. 1875, MS); spouse, Sadie (b. 1877, England), married about 1913; son, James N., Jr. (b. 1916, TX). *SR; A1a, b, d, e, f, g; A4a, b; C.*

CARLSON, FRANK A. Born June 1861, Austin, Travis County, Texas. Ht. 6 ft., black eyes, black hair, dark complexion, married. Master mechanic, I&GN Railroad, San Antonio, Bexar County, Texas. SPECIAL RANGER Jan. 12, 1918–Jan. 14, 1919. REMARKS: Had been a farmer in Gainesville, Cooke County, Texas. In 1910 was a railroad master mechanic in Wichita Falls, Wichita County, Texas. In 1930 was a grocery merchant in San Antonio. FAMILY: Parents, John Carlson (b. 1832, Sweden) and Hannah or Emma (b. 1840, Sweden); siblings, Greta (b. 1859, TX), Nancy (b. 1869, MO), Willie (b. 1871, MO), William (b. 1875, MO), Dora (b. 1877, MO); spouse, Anna M. Housh (b. 1867, W.VA), married about 1887; children, Willie M. (b. 1887, TX), John C. (b. 1893, TX), Frank R. (b. 1897, TX), Howard (b. 1903, MO). *SR; A1a, b, d, e, f, g.*

CARLTON, OSWALD SNIDER. Born Oct. 25, 1868, Brundidge, Alabama. Ht. 5 ft. 10 in., gray eyes, brown hair, fair complexion, married. Life insurance agent, Dallas, Dallas County, Texas. SPECIAL RANGER June 10, 1918–Jan. 15, 1919. Retired life insurance company president and landowner, Houston and Livingston, Polk County, Texas. SPECIAL RANGER Sept. 20, 1933–1935. REMARKS: In 1933 he stated: "20 years a private special or honorary Ranger." Died Feb. 19, 1934, Livingston, Polk County, Texas. FAMILY: Parents, Dr. Snider Miles Carlton (b. 1830, GA) and Nancy Clark Satterwhite (b. 1829, GA); siblings, Elijah H. (b. 1855, AL), Catherine Rebecca (b. 1858, AL), Lobal Alva (b. 1860, AL), Mary Ellena (b. 1862, AL), Sallie Ada (b. 1864, AL); spouse, Johnnie King Mendez (b. 1871, AL), married about 1891; sons, Alva L. (b. 1894, TX), Oswald S. (b. 1899, TX). *SR; A1b, d, e, f, g; A4a, b; C.*

CARNES, HERFF ALEXANDER. Born May 23, 1879, Fairview, Wilson County, Texas. Ht. 5 ft. 7 in., blue eyes, medium complexion, brown hair. Farmer. REGULAR RANGER Feb. 13, 1903–Aug. 8, 1911 (private, Co. D; promoted to sergeant, Co. D, Feb. 1907—On Feb. 1, 1911 Co. D was redesignated as Co. A). Resigned in August 1911 to become a mounted Customs inspector in El Paso district; remained in Customs service until his death on Dec. 3, 1932, El Paso, El Paso County as the result of gunshot wounds inflicted by smugglers on Dec. 1, 1932; buried in Restlawn Cemetery, El Paso. LAW ENFORCEMENT RELATIVES: Ranger Quirl Bailey Carnes, brother; Wilson County sheriff (Dec. 31, 1917–Jan. 1, 1937) Alfred Burton Carnes, brother; Ranger David Franklin Webb, grandfather; Ranger John Eckford Gilliland, brother-in-law; Ranger Grenade Donaldson "Don" Gilliland, nephew; Ranger Walter H. Askey, cousin; Ranger David Cornelius Webb, cousin; Ranger Grover Cleveland Webb, cousin; Ranger Lake Thomas Webb, cousin; deputy sheriff, deputy U.S. marshal Ralph Blackburn Gilliland, nephew; U.S. Border Patrolman Thomas Joseph Carnes, nephew; FBI agent Robert Webb "Bob" Carnes, nephew; Wilson County sheriff (Nov. 4, 1952–Jan. 1, 1961) David Donaldson "Don" Carnes, nephew; El Centro, California policeman, Tom J. Carnes, Jr., great-nephew. FAMILY: Parents, Joseph Milton Carnes (b. 1846, LA) and Mary Catherine Webb (b. 1854, TX); siblings, William D. (b. 1871, TX), Atlanta Lee (b. 1873, TX), Walter Webb (b. 1875), Alfred Burton (b. 1877, TX), Lola Lillian (b. 1882, TX), Quirl Bailey (b. 1884, TX), Vivian Ida (b. 1887, TX), Ada Blanche (b. 1889, TX), Tommie Cole (b. 1891, TX), Webb McNeil (b. 1897, TX); spouse, Letha Lenore Lux (b. 1893, TX), married Sept. 1, 1912, Dallas, Texas; children, Hughes Alfred (b. 1913, TX), Mary Elizabeth (b. 1913, TX), Dr. David Milton (b. 1927, TX). *SR; 471; 1000:iii, 4, 45–48, 117; 319: 340; 470: 76, 80–81; Hughes to Walker, Apr 13, Mar 9, 1911, AGC; AG* *to Rodgers, Feb 3, 1911, AGC; Hughes to Colquitt, Feb 14, 1911,CP; Carnes to Hutchings, Aug 7, 1911, WC; Assistant AG to Hughes, Aug 24, 1911, WC; EPMT, Aug 10, Oct 4, 1911, June 20, 26, 1912, Feb 12, 1913, Feb 17, Apr 26, 29, 1914, Oct 8, 9, 1915, Jan 29, Feb 1, 9, 1916; Morris to Harley, May 5, 1919, AGC; 1503:547; A1d, f; A2b; A3a; A4a, b, g; B2.*

CARNES, QUIRL BAILEY. Born June 1, 1884, Fairview, Wilson County, Texas. No personal description. REGULAR RANGER 1907–July 31, 1910 (private, Co. B; Co. A, 1909–1910). Killed in action July 31, 1910, San Benito, Cameron County, Texas; buried at Floresville, Wilson County. LAW ENFORCEMENT RELATIVES: Ranger Herff A. Carnes, brother; Wilson County sheriff (Dec. 31, 1917–Jan. 1, 1937) Alfred Burton Carnes, brother; Ranger David Franklin Webb, grandfather; Ranger John Eckford Gilliland, brother-in-law; Ranger Grenade Donaldson "Don" Gilliland, nephew; Ranger Walter H. Askey, cousin; Ranger David Cornelius Webb, cousin; Ranger Grover Cleveland Webb, cousin; Ranger Lake Thomas Webb, cousin; deputy sheriff, deputy U.S. marshal Ralph Blackburn Gilliland, nephew; U.S. Border Patrolman Thomas Joseph Carnes, nephew; FBI agent Robert Webb "Bob" Carnes, nephew; Wilson County sheriff (Nov. 4, 1952–Jan. 1, 1961) David Donaldson "Don" Carnes, nephew; El Centro, California policeman, Tom J. Carnes, Jr., great-nephew. FAMILY: Parents, Joseph Milton Carnes (b. 1846, LA) and Mary Catherine Webb (b. 1854, TX); siblings, William D. (b. 1871, TX), Atlanta Lee (b. 1873, TX), Walter Webb (b. 1875), Alfred Burton (b. 1877, TX), Herff A. (b. 1879, TX), Lola Lillian (b. 1882, TX), Vivian Ida (b. 1887), Ada Blanche (b. 1889, TX), Tommie Cole (b. 1891, TX), Webb McNeil (b. 1897, TX). *471; 1000: 4, 41–47; 464: 39–40; 470: 71, 74–78; 424: 207; Assistant AG to Johnson, Aug 4, 18, 1910, WC; BDH Aug 1–3, 1910; Funeral notice, Aug 2, 1910, WC; reports on the San Benito ambush, July 31–Aug 14, 1910, WC; 1503:547; A1d; A4a, b, g; B2.*

CAROTHERS, GILBERT SPROLE. Born Aug. 28, 1883, Austin, Travis County, Texas. Ht. 6 ft. 2 in., blue eyes, dark hair, red complexion. Ranch foreman, Rio Grande City, Starr County, Texas. SPECIAL RANGER June 11, 1918–Jan. 15, 1919. FAMILY: Parents, William S. Carothers (b. 1840, PA) and Sarah J. "Sallie" (b. 1844, TX); siblings, Katie (b. 1864, TX), Fannie (b. 1867, TX), Carrie (b. 1869, TX), Alice (b. 1871, TX), Frank (b. 1880, TX). *SR; A1b, d; A3a; A5a; A6a.*

CARPENTER, S. J. Born Sept. 1877, Cooper County, Missouri. Ht. 6 ft., blue eyes, brown hair, fair complexion. Contractor, Laredo, Webb County, Texas. REGULAR RANGER Dec. 9, 1919–Feb. 10, 1921 (private, Co. C). Discharged. *SR; 471.*

CARR, WILLIAM D. Born Sept. 1879, Georgetown, Williamson County, Texas. Ht. 5 ft. 8 in., dark eyes, dark hair, dark complexion, married. Stockman. REGULAR RANGER May 31, 1916–Apr. 18, 1917 (private, Co. B). Resigned. FAMILY: Parents (probably), Simeon B. Carr (b. 1857, TX) and Mariah E. (b. 1856, TX). *SR; 471; A1b.*

CARROLL, EDWARD A. "ED." Born Feb. 27, 1890, Athens, Henderson County, Texas. Ht. 5 ft. 7 ½ in., gray eyes, brown hair, fair complexion, married. Insurance agent, Athens. LOYALTY RANGER June 6, 1918–Feb. 1919. REMARKS: Had been a deputy sheriff for 5 years. As of June 1917 was a stockman, farmer, and insurance man in Palestine, Henderson County. FAMILY: Parents, William T. Carroll (b. 1857, TX) and Nannie (b. 1870, TX); siblings, Willie T. (b. 1894, TX), Grace (b. 1896, TX), John W. (b. 1898, TX), Marion (b. 1900, TX); spouse, Mary (probably Lammons) (b. 1895, TX). *SR; A1d, e, f, g; A3a.*

CARROLL, JAMES DOUGLAS. Born Mar. 13, 1874, Caldwell, Burleson County, Texas. Ht. 5 ft. 9 in., gray eyes, brown hair, light complexion, married. Furniture merchant, Corsicana, Navarro County, Texas. LOYALTY RANGER July 25, 1918–Feb. 1919. REMARKS: 1st Texas Volunteer Infantry, 1898, in Spanish-American War. In 1910 was manager of a furniture store in Austin, Travis County, Texas. In 1920 lived in Henderson County, Texas. In 1930 was an insurance agent in Corsicana. A J. D. Carroll died Jan. 27, 1943, Navarro County, Texas. FAMILY: Spouse, Eva F. (b. 1880, TX), married about 1903; children, Evalyn (b. 1903, TX), Benjamin Douglas (b. 1906, TX), Virginia (b. 1912, TX), Jean Mallard (b. 1918, TX). *SR; A1b, d, e, f, g; A2e; A3a; C.*

CARSON, CLYDE LESLIE. Born Nov. 11, 1880, Blanco, Blanco County, Texas. Ht. 5 ft. 9 in., brown eyes, dark hair, dark complexion. Farmer. REGULAR RANGER Aug. 21, 1918–Mar. 8, 1919 (private, Co. G). Discharged. REMARKS: In 1910 was a butcher living in Travis County, Texas. In 1930 was an oil company watchman in Winkler County, Texas. Died July 5, 1931, Winkler County, Texas. FAMILY: Parents, Joseph Thomas Carson (b. 1856, TX) and Sallie Emma Goza (b. 1860, TX); siblings, Elmer Thompson (b. 1879, TX), Emma Goza (b. 1883, TX), Myrtle Mattie (b. 1885, TX), Thomas Benjamin (b. 1888, TX), Edwin Bates (b. 1890, TX), Herbert Hansel (b. 1891, TX), Joseph Wilmer (b. 1893, TX), Claude Vernon (b. 1896, TX), Lela May (b. 1898, TX), Nettie Blanch (b. 1900, TX), Ray Wallace (b. 1903, TX). *SR; 471; A1d, e, g; A3a; A4g; C.*

CARSON, FREDRIC L. Born Feb. 1871, Kansas. Ht. 5 ft. 9 in., blue eyes, dark hair, dark complexion, married. Superintendent of motive power, SA&AP Railroad, San Antonio, Bexar County, Texas. SPECIAL RANGER May 26, 1917–Jan. 15, 1919 (reinstated—warrant renewed Dec. 27, 1917). Discharged. REMARKS: Ranger Service Record states born in Oakland, California, however all census documents state born in Kansas. In 1880 was living in Perry, Jefferson County, Kansas. In 1900 was "foreman boss" in Topeka, Shawnee County, Kansas. In 1930 census living in San Antonio, still listed as born in Kansas. A Fredric Leon Carson died Mar. 12, 1949, Bexar County, Texas. FAMILY: Parents, Leondas F. Carson (b. 1850, MO) and Nettie A. (b. 1850, PA); siblings, Elmo (b. 1875, KS), Kate (b. 1876, KS); spouse, Stella McNary (b. 1873, IN), married about 1895; children, Harlan John (b. 1896, KS), Ermyn Mc. (b. 1898, KS), Leon Donald (b. 1902, KS), Clement Corwin (b. 1911, TX), Mary Adel (b. 1913, TX). *SR; Chamberlain to Hutchings, May 31, 1917, AGC; AG to Chamberlain, June 1, 1917, AGCV; A1b, d, f, g; A2b.*

CARTA, CHARLES ARTHUR "CHARLEY." Born June 1, 1882, Brackettville, Kinney County, Texas. Ht. 5 ft. 7 in., brown eyes, brown hair, ruddy complexion. Cowboy, Del Rio, Val Verde County, Texas. REGULAR RANGER Oct. 18, 1917–July 31, 1921 (private, Co. E; transferred to Co. F, Dec. 8, 1919; transferred to Co. D, Feb. 15, 1921). Resigned. Ranchman, Del Rio. REGULAR RANGER Oct. 21, 1921–June 30, 1924 (private, Co. C; transferred to Co. A, April 1, 1923). Resigned. REMARKS: Sept. 1918 WWI Draft Registration form lists his occupation as "State Ranger," registered in Eagle Pass, Maverick County, Texas; claims two broken ribs. Died Feb. 23, 1956, Del Rio, Val Verde County, Texas. LAW ENFORCEMENT RELATIVES: Ranger John A. Carta, brother. FAMILY: Parents, Richard Edward Carta (b. 1858, TX) and Margaret Elizabeth Beckett (b. 1863, TX); siblings, James Richard (b. 1880, TX), Lucy Ann (b. 1883, TX), Andrew Pickney (b. 1886, TX), John Allen (b. 1888, TX), Susan E. (b. 1890, TX), Samuel Martin (b. 1893, TX), Wesley Franklin (b. 1895, TX), Miriam Hope (b. 1897, TX), Joseph Edward (b. 1899, TX). *SR; 471; A1d; A3a; A4a, b, g.*

CARTA, JOHN ALLEN. Born Aug. 5, 1888, Brackettville, Kinney County, Texas. Ht. 5 ft. 7 in., brown eyes, dark hair, ruddy complexion. Cowboy. REGULAR RANGER Oct. 11, 1917–May 1918 (private, Co. E). Discharged. REMARKS: Died Oct. 7, 1918, in France; was a private in the U.S. Army, buried in Brookwood American Cemetery, Brookwood, England. LAW ENFORCEMENT RELATIVES: Ranger Charles A. Carta, brother. FAMILY: Parents, Richard Edward Carta (b. 1858, TX) and Margaret Elizabeth Beckett (b. 1863, TX); siblings, James Richard (b. 1880, TX), Charles Arthur (b. 1882, TX), Lucy Ann (b. 1883, TX), Andrew Pickney (b. 1886, TX), Susan E. (b. 1890, TX), Samuel Martin (b. 1893, TX), Wesley Franklin (b. 1895, TX), Miriam Hope (b. 1897, TX), Joseph Edward (b. 1899, TX). *SR; 471; A1d; A3a; A4a, b, g.*

CARTER, ARTHUR. Born Aug. 1863, Fayetteville, Fayette County, Texas. Ht. 5 ft. 11 in., gray eyes, sandy hair, sallow complexion, married. Druggist, Cheapside, Gonzales County, Texas. LOYALTY RANGER June 8, 1918–Feb. 1919. FAMILY: Parents, Thomas Carter (b. 1823, England) and Mary (b. 1838, England); siblings, twins Eliza and Mary (b. 1858, TX), Joseph (b. 1860, TX), Anna (b. 1861, TX), Lancelot Abbotts (b. 1869, TX), Jane (b. 1873, TX); spouse, Maggie (b. 1867, England), married about 1888. *SR; A1a, b, e, g.*

CARTER, HENRY F. Born Aug. 1854, Springfield, Greene County, Missouri. Ht. 6 ft. 1 in., gray eyes, gray hair, light complexion. Ranchman, Langtry, Val Verde County, Texas. SPECIAL RANGER Dec. 6, 1917–unknown (private, Co. A Volunteers—station: Comstock). REMARKS: Capt. James B. Murrah commanded the Co. A Volunteers. *SR; A1f.*

CARTER, JAMES "JIM." Born Oct. 1868, Austin, Travis County, Texas. No personal description. Deputy sheriff, Sierra Blanca, Hudspeth County, Texas. REGULAR RANGER April 23, 1918–Aug. 31, 1918 (private, Co. N, Hudspeth Scouts). REMARKS: In 1910 was a bartender in Sierra Blanca; was deputy sheriff, El Paso County, 1915–1918. FAMILY: Stepmother, Christiana A. Carter (b. 1854, TX). *SR; 471; Moore to Ransom, Nov 14, 1917, AGC; Ransom to Harley, Nov 19, 1917, AGC; A1e, f.*

CARTER, LEONARD BARTON. Born Mar. 4, 1880, Dale, Caldwell County, Texas. Ht. 5 ft. 4 in., brown eyes, black hair, dark complexion, married. Stockman, Pearsall, Frio County, Texas. REGULAR RANGER Dec. 17, 1917–Oct. 20, 1921 (private, Co. I; transferred to Co. C, June 21, 1919). Discharged. REMARKS: Died Mar. 29, 1956, Val Verde County, Texas. FAMILY: Parents, Leftridge Scott Carter (b. 1852, KY) and Margaret Ellen "Maggie" Robbins (b. 1856, TX); siblings, Iris Fainey (b. 1884, TX), Leftridge Oscar (b. 1886, TX), Leona Gertrude (b. 1887, TX), Sarah Albertine (b. 1890, TX), Ethel Awilde (b. 1893, TX), Charles Culberson (b. 1896, TX); spouse, Dorrie or Donnie or Dora Hokit (b. 1889, TX); children, May Belle (b. 1914, TX), Leonard (b. 1915, TX). *SR; A1b, d, f; A2b; A3a; A4b.*

CARTER, RICHARD CLAYTON. Born May 14, 1889, Waynesboro, Burke County, Georgia. Ht. 5 ft. 7 in., blue eyes, brown hair, light complexion. Ranchman: REGULAR RANGER May 11, 1916–Nov. 17, 1916 (private, Co. B). Resigned. REMARKS: In 1910 was a cowboy in Chaves County, NM; by June 1917 was a bartender in Redford, Presidio County, Texas. FAMILY: Parents, Edward A. Carter (b. 1841, GA) and Augusta S. (b. 1847, GA); siblings, May S. (b. 1876, GA), Robert L. (b. 1878, GA), Lillian (b. 1880, GA), Georgia B. (b. 1883, GA), Cora Gertrude (b. 1890, GA); spouse, Lusia (b. 1899, TX), married about 1917; son, Arthur (b. 1918, TX). *SR; A1d, e, f; A3a.*

CARTER, THOMAS MILLER. Born May 1867, Palo Pinto County, Texas. Ht. 6 ft. 2 in., gray eyes, brown hair, fair complexion, married. Farmer, rancher, and merchant, Graford, Palo Pinto County. LOYALTY RANGER June 21, 1918–Feb. 18, 1919. REMARKS: A Thomas Miller Carter died Oct. 24, 1935, Palo Pinto County, Texas. FAMILY: Parents, Christopher Lawson Carter (b. 1818, VA) and Anne Smith Ross (b. 1825, MO); siblings, Ross (b. 1843), Pleasant (b. 1845), Shapley Prince (b. 1847, MO), Ella (b. 1851, MO), Lawrence Sulivan (1854, MO), Elizabeth (b. 1855, TX), Peter Ross (b. 1860, TX), Christopher L. (b. 1863, TX), Mary A. "Mamie" (b. 1865, TX), Catherine Ross (b. 1870, TX); spouse, Ola M. Kuykendall (b. 1870, TX), married about 1897; daughter, Nannie (b. 1900, TX). *SR; A1b, d, e, f; A4b, g; C.*

CARVER, PLEASANT STELL "PLES." Born May 13, 1891, Fairview, Wilson County, Texas. Ht. 5 ft. 11 in., gray eyes, brown hair, fair complexion, married. Stockman. REGULAR RANGER Apr. 10, 1918–Aug. 1918 (private, Co. M). Resigned. REMARKS: In 1910 worked in a barber shop in Floresville, Wilson County. Before June 1917 had been a seaman in the U.S. Navy for 1 year 4 months and had been dishonorably discharged. In June 1917 was a foreman on the Muir Ranch, Kinney County, Texas. In 1930 was proprietor of a barber shop in Eagle Pass, Maverick County, Texas. Died Nov. 16, 1953, Quemado, Maverick County, Texas. FAMILY: Parents, John W. Carver (b. 1855, AR) and Emily Marion Brown (b. 1862, TX), siblings, Evamay (b. 1877, TX), John T. (b. 1880, TX), Jennie (b. 1883, TX), William Tullus (b. 1888, TX), Effie Ann (b. 1889, TX), Mabel C. (b. 1895, TX), Herman (b. 1900, TX), Florence E. (b. 1905, TX); spouse, Winnie Mae Musgrave (b. 1899, TX), married Oct. 11, 1917, Uvalde, Texas; children, June (b. 1919, TX), James (b. 1921, TX), Margie (b. 1923, TX). *SR; 471; A1d, e, g; A2b, e; A3a; A4a, b, g.*

CASH, WALTER C. Born Feb. 1870, Goliad, Goliad County, Texas. Ht. 6 ft. 1 in., black eyes, black hair, dark complexion, married. Livestock dealer, Goliad, Goliad County. LOYALTY RANGER June 6, 1918–Feb. 1919. REMARKS: Still working as a livestock speculator in Goliad in 1930. A Walter Clarke Cash died Apr. 2, 1943, DeWitt County, Texas. FAMILY: Parents, John C. Cash (b. 1830, VA or TN) and Mary Spiers (b. 1847, MS); siblings, Virginia (b. 1854, MS), Ann (b. 1856, MS), William (b. 1857, MS), Martha (b. 1859, MS), Mary (b. 1864, TX), Cora Lee (b. 1869, TX), Ludorah (b. 1872, TX), Maggie (b. 1875, TX), Arthur Thomas (b. 1879, TX), Jim J. (b. 1884, TX), Rufus Clifton (b. 1886, TX); spouse, Lillie A. (b. 1876, TX), married about 1893; children, Birdie (b. 1895, TX), Dora (b. 1896, TX), Temple Walter (b. 1898, TX), Fay Lea (b. 1902, TX). *SR; A1a, b, d, f, g; A3a; A4g; C.*

CASON, ROBERT LEE. Born Dec. 29, 1864, Titus County, Texas. (Ranger Service Records list birthplace as Morris County, Texas; Morris County was established in 1875 and had been a part of Titus County before then.) No physical description, married. Farmer, Daingerfield, Morris County. LOYALTY RANGER June 1, 1918–Feb. 1919. REMARKS: Morris County sheriff, Nov. 8, 1904–Nov. 6, 1906. Died Aug. 26, 1932, Cason, Morris County, Texas. FAMILY: Parents, John Washington Cason (b. 1818, SC) and Thursa Jane Scott (b. 1826, SC); siblings, William M. (b. 1847, GA), Ada S. (b. 1849, GA), Sarah A. (b. 1851, GA), Doritha Ella (b. 1852, TX), Mary Jane (b. 1854, TX), James Jefferson (b. 1856, TX), Jane (b. 1858), Lula Maude (b. 1860, TX), John Morgan (b. 1861, TX); spouse, Beulah Bell Kimbell (b. 1869, TX), married Jan. 5, 1887, Pittsburg, Camp County, Texas; children, William Leon (b. 1889, TX), Griffin Eugene (b. 1891, TX), Eunice (b. 1897, TX), Aubrey Add (b. 1900, TX). *SR; 1503:384; A1b, d, e, g; A2b; A4a, b, g.*

CASSELS, ALBERT EDWARDS. Born Sept. 28, 1872, Indiana. Ht. 5 ft. 9 in., brown eyes, gray hair, fair complexion, married. Bank guard, Milmo National Bank, Laredo, Webb County, Texas. SPECIAL RANGER Sept. 2, 1918–Jan. 14, 1919. REMARKS: In 1910 was a saloon bartender in Brenham, Washington County, Texas. In Sept. 1918 on WWI Draft Registration document stated had one eye, broken leg. Died Sept. 11, 1924, Webb County, Texas. FAMILY: Parents, Green Cassels (b. 1822, TN) and Malesia (b. 1837, IL); siblings, John W. (b. 1870, MO), Thomas L. (b. 1875, IN), James H. (b. 1878, TX); spouse, Sadie (b. 1874, GA), married about 1907. *SR; A1b, d, e; A3a; C.*

CATHEY, MARCUS EARL. Born Feb. 22, 1886, Gatesville, Coryell County, Texas. Ht. 5 ft. 9 in., blue eyes, light brown hair, fair complexion. Bookkeeper. REGULAR RANGER Oct. 3, 1911–July 1912 (private, Co. A; transferred to Co. C as sergeant, Oct. 6, 1911). Resigned. REMARKS: In 1910 was a traveling salesman living in Lampasas, Lampasas County, Texas. In 1918 was circulation manager for the *Beaumont Journal*, Jefferson County, Texas. In 1920 was a real estate agent in Waco, McLennan County, Texas. Died Aug. 8, 1949, Harris County, Texas. FAMILY: Spouse, Annie Louise Sanders (b. 1888, TX), married about 1907; son, Earl G. (b. 1908, TX). *SR; A1e, f; A3a; C.*

CAUSEY, THOMAS NEWTON. Born Jan. 6, 1876, Wellborn, Brazos County, Texas. Ht. 5 ft. 11 in., blue eyes, brown hair, light complexion, married. Timberman and contractor, Woodville, Tyler County, Texas. LOYALTY RANGER June 13, 1918–Feb. 1919. REMARKS: Had been a lumberman in a lumber yard in Kirbyville, Jasper County, Texas. In 1930 lived in Houston, Harris County, Texas. Died Oct. 10, 1938, Harris County, Texas. FAMILY: Parents, Philip Newton Causey (b. 1841, GA) and Mary C. (b. 1850, SC); siblings, Luke T. (b. 1872, TX), Anna Eudora (b. 1874, TX); spouse, Lissie J. (b. 1878, MS), married about 1902; children, Ervyn B. (b. 1902, TX), Herman U. (b. 1903, TX), Ross T. (b. 1906, TX), Dott E. (b. 1908, TX), L. T. (b. 1910, TX). *SR; A1b, e, f, g; A3a; A4a, b, g; C.*

CAVENDER, PERRY. Born Jan. 29, 1876, Indian Gap, Comanche County, Texas. Ht. 6 ft., blue eyes, light hair, sandy complexion. Cowboy. REGULAR RANGER Dec. 24, 1917–Dec. 20, 1918 (private, Co. F). Discharged. REMARKS: In the 1930 U.S. Census was listed as a prisoner in the New Mexico State Penitentiary with the job of "gate keeper," Santa Fe, Santa Fe County, New Mexico. Died Mar. 31, 1966, Tom Green County, Texas (Social Security Death Index lists death date as June 15, 1966). FAMILY: Mother, Ellen (b. 1855, AR); brother, Gus (b. 1878, TX); spouse unknown, married about 1910; son, K. M. (b. TX). *SR; A1b, g; A2a, b; A3a.*

CAVITT, JOSEPHUS FRANKLIN "JOE." Born Nov. 17, 1867, Robertson County, Texas. No physical description, married. Farmer and oil miller, McGregor, McLennan County, Texas. LOYALTY RANGER June 17, 1918—Feb. 1919. REMARKS: Had been a hardware merchant in McGregor. In 1930 was a tenant farmer in McLennan County. Died June 11, 1952, Valley Mills, Bosque-McLennan County, Texas; buried in Cavitt Cemetery, Wheelock, Robertson County, Texas. FAMILY: Parents, Volney Cavitt (b. 1824, TN) and Clara Jane Sparks (b. 1837, TX); siblings, Annie Jane (b. 1856, TX), Sheridan A. (b. 1858, TX), James Volney (b. 1861, TX), Minerva E. (b. 1862, TX), Belvidere Brooks (b. 1864, TX), William Sparks (b. 1865, TX), Cora (b. 1869, TX), Andrew Sidney (b. 1871, TX), Ruth Ann (b. 1873, TX). Florence (b. 1875, TX), Samuel Earle (b. 1877, TX), Elizabeth (b. 1880, TX); spouse, Mary "Mollie" Caufield (b. 1868, TX), married May 16, 1896; son, Volney (b. 1897, TX). *SR; A1a, b, d, e, f, g; A2b; A4b, g.*

CHADICK, ISAAC STOKELY or STOKES. Born July 7, 1889, Taylorsville, Alabama. Ht. 5 ft. 10 in., blue eyes, light brown hair, light complexion. Deputy sheriff, Cameron County, Texas. REGULAR RANGER Aug. 2, 1915–Sept. 20, 1915 (private, Co. D.) Discharged. REMARKS: Deputy sheriff, Cameron County, 1912–1915. In 1920 was team foreman for the U.S. Quartermaster in Hidalgo County, Texas. Died July 3, 1927, Hidalgo County, Texas. LAW ENFORCEMENT RELATIVES: Ranger W. D. Chadick, brother. FAMILY: Parents, Charles W. Chadick (b. 1846, TN) and Charlotte C. (b. 1855, AL); siblings, William D. (b. 1886, AL), Christine S. (b. 1892, AL), Charles Paul (b. 1896, AL). *SR; 471; A1d, f; A2b; A3a.*

CHADICK, WILLIAM DAVIDSON. Born Aug. 8, 1886, Taylorsville, Alabama. Ht. 5 ft. 10 in., blue eyes, black hair. Farmer and cattle raiser, Mercedes, Hidalgo County, Texas. LOYALTY RANGER June 1, 1918—Feb. 1919. REMARKS: In 1930 U.S. Census was listed as "Commissioner for Government" in Mercedes. Died Sept. 10, 1938, Hidalgo County, Texas. LAW ENFORCEMENT RELATIVES: Ranger I. S. Chadick, brother. FAMILY: Parents, Charles W. Chadick (b. 1846, TN) and Charlotte C. (b. 1855, AL); siblings, Isaac S. (b. 1889, AL), Christine S. (b. 1892, AL), Charles Paul (b. 1896, AL). *SR; A1d, f, g; A3a; C.*

CHAMBERLAIN, GEORGE E. Born Sept. 1868, Monroe, Ouachita Parish, Louisiana. Ht. 5 ft. 7 in., gray eyes, gray hair, ruddy complexion, married. Land and tax agent, SA&AP Railroad, San Antonio, Bexar County, Texas. SPECIAL RANGER Mar. 13, 1917–Dec. 1917 (attached to Co. C). Land and tax agent, San Antonio. SPECIAL RANGER Mar. 1, 1918–Jan. 14, 1919. REMARKS: Had been a railway postal clerk in San Antonio. In 1920 was a railroad land commissioner in San Antonio. A George Eugene Chamberlain died Aug. 19, 1925, Bexar County, Texas. FAMILY: Parents, G. Chamberlain (b. 1832, MO) and Louisa H. (b. 1837, TN); spouse, Mamie Jefferies (b. 1874, TX), married about 1899; son, Jefferies (b. 1900, TX). *SR; Harley to Chamberlain, Mar 1, 1918, AGC; A1a, b, d, f; C.*

CHANDLER, JOHN SMITH "JOHNNY." Born Dec. 1, 1894, Coventry, Wilson County, Texas. Ht. 5 ft. 6 in., blue eyes, brown hair, light complexion, married. Brand inspector, Pecos, Reeves County, Texas. SPECIAL RANGER Dec. 27, 1917–Feb. 19, 1919. REMARKS: Had been a farmer near Pandora, Wilson County; in 1930 was a farmer living in Stockdale, Wilson County. Died Apr. 29, 1973, Austin, Travis County, Texas. FAMILY: Parents, James Edward Chandler (b. 1869, TX) and Alice "Ankie" Smith (b. 1878, TX); spouse, Margie Jane Jackson (b. 1897, TX), married about 1915; children, Winfred B. (b. 1916, TX), Johnny S. (b. 1918, TX), Arthur W. (b. 1920, TX), Darline (b. 1925, TX), James Edward (b. 1928, TX). *SR; Harley to Kiser, Feb 19, 1919, AGC; A1d, e, f, g; A2a, b, e; A3a.*

CHAPMAN, GEORGE WALLACE. Born July 27, 1894, Pleasanton, Atascosa County, Texas. Ht. 5 ft. 11 in., brown eyes, light hair, fair complexion, married. Peace officer, Cotulla, La Salle County, Texas. REGULAR RANGER Sept. 1, 1917–Oct. 11, 1917 (private, Co. A). Honorably discharged because was drafted. Deputy sheriff, Cotulla. REGULAR RANGER Mar. 20, 1920–Feb. 22, 1921 (private, Co. C). Resigned. Contractor, Cotulla. RAILROAD RANGER Aug. 11, 1922–Nov. 1, 1922 (Co. A). Resigned. REMARKS: In 1917 tried to beat the draft by enlisting in Rangers. The Cotulla draft board complained to the AG, who dismissed him from the Rangers. In 1918 got a discharge from the Army on a dependency claim; the local draft board was outraged. In 1930 was deputy sheriff and jailer in Cotulla. Died Oct. 29, 1952, LaSalle County, Texas. FAMILY: Parents, George W. Chapman (b. 1853, TX) and May (b. 1859, TX); sisters, Ethel (b. 1877, TX), Annie (b. 1879, TX), Ruby B. (b. 1881, TX), Flora L. (b. 1883, TX), Kate M. (b. 1890, TX), Rosie (b. 1891, TX), Stella Maud (b. 1893, TX); spouse, Wilmina Wightman (b. 1905, MI), married about 1921; children, Anita E. (b. 1922, TX), Wallace G. (b. 1926, TX), Ethel Gwendolyn (b. 1929, TX). *SR; 471; Sanders to Harley, Oct 11, 1917, AGC; AG to Sanders, Oct 15, 1917, AGC; Hamilton to Harley, July 24, 1918, AGC; 1515; A1d, e, g; A2e; A3a; C.*

CHASTAIN, RICHARD B. Born June 1862, McKinney, Collin County, Texas. Ht. 5 ft. 7 in., blue eyes, brown hair, light complexion. Carpenter, enlisted in Culberson County, Texas. REGULAR RANGER Apr. 16, 1918–June 1, 1918 (private, Co. N, Hudspeth Scouts). Resigned. Mechanic, Sierra Blanca, Hudspeth County, Texas. RAILROAD RANGER Aug. 21, 1922–Jan. 15, 1923. Discharged. REMARKS: Was a Regular Ranger for 2 years 8 months in the 1890s. In 1900 was a carpenter in Presidio County, Texas; in 1910 was in the construction business, El Paso, El Paso County, Texas. In 1930 was a county officer living in Sierra Blanca. LAW ENFORCEMENT RELATIVES: Presidio County sheriff (Nov. 24, 1906–Jan. 1918) and Ranger Milton B. Chastain, brother; Alpine, Brewster County, Texas town marshal Murphy Trot Chastain, brother; Ranger James B. Gillett (author of the classic *Six Years With the Texas Rangers 1875–1881*), brother-in-law. FAMILY: Parents, Joseph Inman Chastain (b. 1826, TN) and Martha Luraine Vowell (b. 1826, TN); siblings, Jonas William (b. 1844, TN), Sandy Preston (b. 1845, TN), Martha Frances (b. 1848, TN), Murphy Trot (b. 1850, TN), Thomas Scott (b. 1852, TN), Tabitha Genettie (b. 1854, TN), George Murray (b. 1858, TX), Joseph Albert (b. 1860, TX), Milton Board (b. 1864, TX), Mary Lou (b. 1867, TX); spouse, Annie H. (b. 1870, TX), married about 1894, divorced sometime before 1930; children, Rubie W. (b. 1898, TX), Theodore Gillett (b. 1900, TX), Bascom (b. 1902, TX). *SR; AA, June 29, 1911; Knight to Harley, Aug 12, 1918, AGC; 1503:424; A1a, b, d, e, g; A4g.*

CHAVEZ, SEBASTIAN T. Born Sept. 18, 1883, San Antonio, Bexar County, Texas. Ht. 5 ft. 2 in., brown eyes, black hair, dark complexion. Cowboy. REGULAR RANGER Dec. 18, 1917–unknown (private, Co. G; still in Rangers as of Oct. 1918). Discharged or resigned, unknown. REMARKS: Had been honorably discharged from the Army. As of Dec. 1917 worked at Remount Station No. 3, Fort Sam Houston, San Antonio. In Sept. 1918 was a Ranger stationed in El Paso, El Paso County, Texas. In 1920 was an oil field laborer living in San Antonio. Died Apr. 23, 1964, Harris County, Texas. FAMILY: Parents, Sebastian Chavez (b. 1835, NM) and Asuncion (b. 1849, Mexico); siblings, Marie (b. 1878, TX), Laura (b. 1881, TX), George (b. 1886, TX). *SR; 471; Stevens to Woodul, Aug 22, 1918, WC; A1d, f; A2a, b; A3a.*

CHERRYHOMES, THOMAS ROY "ROY." Born Apr. 11, 1886, Chico, Wise County, Texas. Ht. 6 ft., gray eyes, brown hair, light complexion, married. Stock farmer, Jacksboro, Jack County, Texas. LOYALTY RANGER July 19, 1918–Feb. 1919. REMARKS: Lived 18 miles northeast of Jacksboro; as of 1930, still a stock farmer in Jacksboro. Died Mar. 11, 1933, Wichita County, Texas. FAMILY: Parents, Thomas Henry Cherryhomes (b. 1861, TX) and Sarah A. "Sallie" (b. 1864, TN); sister, Alice Bertha (b. 1884, TX); spouse, Virginia Tipton (b. 1890, TX), married June 9, 1907; children, Mildred (b. 1908, TX), Helen (b. 1910, TX), Thomas Tipton (b. 1914, TX), Robert Roy (b. 1920, TX). *SR; A1d, e, f, g; A2b; A3a; A4a, b, g.*

CHESSHER, JAMES PRIOR. Born Oct. 17, 1859, Guadalupe County, Texas. Ht. 5 ft. 11 in., blue eyes, brown hair, ruddy complexion. Peace officer, Luling, Caldwell County, Texas. REGULAR RANGER Dec. 10, 1917–Sept. 9, 1918 (private, Co. I). Resigned for a better-paying job as a guard for the Gulf Refining Co. at Port Arthur, Jefferson County, Texas. REMARKS: Had been a farmer in Gonzales County, Texas, and Guadalupe County. Died Jan. 4, 1945, Guadalupe County, Texas. FAMILY: Parents, John Baptist Chesher (note spelling discrepancy) (b. 1823, TN) and Susan J. Elkins (b. 1830, TN); siblings, James Edmond (b. 1855, TX), Hester Ann (b. 1858, TX), Mary Jane (b. 1862, TX), John Baptist (b. 1863, TX), Susan Estelle (b. 1866, TX), Sarah Martha (b. 1869, TX), Laura D. (b. 1873, TX), Bettie Dehan (b. 1875, TX), Edmond D. (b. 1876, TX), Richard Emert (b. 1878, TX), Walter Anderson (b. 1880, TX), Daniel S. (b. 1882, TX), Almer Howell "Allie" (b. 1887, TX), Minnie Daisy (b. 1888, TX); spouse, Cornelia Williams (b. 1860, TX), married about 1877, divorced by 1910; children, George Young (b. 1882, TX), Lena (b. 1884, TX), Rosie (b. 1885, TX), Maud (b. 1888, TX), Cornelia (b. 1889, TX), Jimmie (b. 1892, TX), Coleman (b. 1895, TX), Nina (b. 1897, TX), Claude (b. 1898, TX). *SR; 471; Chessher to Harley, Oct 1, 1918, AGC; A1aa, a, d, e, f; A2b; A3a; A4b, c, d, g.*

CHESSHIR, SAMUEL PAT. Born Feb. 8, 1873, Bogata, Red River County, Texas. Ht. 5 ft. 7 in., gray eyes, brown hair, light complexion. Ranch foreman. REGULAR RANGER Mar. 26, 1918–Aug. 31, 1921 (private, Co. A; transferred to Co. K, Mar. 10, 1919 when Co. A was disbanded; transferred to Co. D, June 20, 1919, reenlisted under the new law). Discharged—reduction in force. REMARKS: In 1919 was evidently stationed at Norias Ranch, Willacy County, Texas. In 1930 was a cattle inspector for a ranch in Kenedy County, Texas; in 1955 lived at Norias. Died Nov. 23, 1962, King Ranch, Kingsville, Kleberg County, Texas. FAMILY: Parents, Nathaniel (Daniel) Chesshir (b. 1824, VA) and Sarah "Sallie" Raulston (b. 1826, TN); siblings, Elizabeth

Jane (b. 1845, TN), James Riley (b. 1846), Margarette Frances (b. 1848, TX), William Butler (b. 1851), Jasper Newton (b. 1853), Sarah Catherine (b. 1856), Cordelia (b. 1857), Nancy Adeline (b. 1860), John Daniel (b. 1862), Moses (b. 1866, TX), Caldonia (b. 1868, TX). *SR; 471; Special Orders No. 21, Mar 10, 1919, WC; 319: 155; A1a, d, f, g; A3a; A4a, b.*

CHILDERS, JOSEPH GRAY, JR. Born Feb. 3, 1889, Bell County, Texas. Ht. 5 ft. 11 in., brown eyes, brown hair, dark complexion. Stockman/cattle dealer, Cotulla, La Salle County, Texas. SPECIAL RANGER July 11, 1917–Jan. 15, 1919 (attached to Co. C; Jan. 3, 1918 was reinstated/WA was renewed). Discharged. REMARKS: In 1920 owned a cattle ranch in Cotulla. Died Mar. 24, 1932, La Salle County, Texas. LAW ENFORCEMENT RELATIVES: Ranger Preston A. Childers, brother. FAMILY: Parents, Joseph Gray Childers (b. 1863, TX) and Josephine Anna Simmons (b. 1868, AR); siblings, Eula G. (b. 1885, TX), Beatrice (b. 1887, TX), Preston (b. 1891, TX), Lucile (b. 1893, TX). *SR; Childers to Harley, Apr 30, 1918, AGC; A1d, e, f; A2b; A3a; A4g.*

CHILDERS, MILAS A. Born Jan. 18, 1891, San Diego, Duval County, Texas. Ht. 5 ft. 10 in., brown eyes, black hair, dark complexion. Ranchman, Asherton, Dimmit County, Texas. SPECIAL RANGER Dec. 27, 1917–Jan. 15, 1919 (Co. C Volunteers, stationed at Indio Ranch). REMARKS: In 1930 was living in Val Verde County, Texas. A Milas Albert Childers died Nov. 28, 1944, Val Verde County, Texas. FAMILY: Parents, B. Samuel Childers (b. 1854, VA) and Trena or Ruma (b. 1860, MS); siblings, Mary Norma (b. 1887, TX), Nora (b. 1889, TX), Jenette (b. 1893, TX), Elizabeth "Lizzie" (b. 1895, TX), Ruma or Trena Susie (b. 1897, TX), Samuel B., Jr. (b. 1899, TX); spouse, Carrie Belle Southall (b. 1898, TX), married about 1922; children, Lucilla (b. 1922, TX), Irene (b. 1924, TX), James R. (b. 1925, TX), Betty Jean (b. 1926, TX). *SR; A1d, e, g; A2e; A3a; C.*

CHILDERS, PRESTON ARMOUR. Born Jan. 2, 1891, Temple, Bell County, Texas. Ht. 5 ft. 8 in., brown eyes, dark hair, ruddy complexion. Farmer, Temple. SPECIAL RANGER July 14, 1917–Dec. 1917 (attached to Co. C). Ranchman, Cotulla, La Salle County, Texas. SPECIAL RANGER Apr. 29, 1918–Jan. 15, 1919. REMARKS: As of June 1917 was a farmer in Falls County, Texas. In 1930 was a dairy farm manager in Bell County. Died Nov. 20, 1977, Bell County, Texas. LAW ENFORCEMENT RELATIVES: Ranger Joseph G. Childers, Jr., brother. FAMILY: Parents, Joseph Gray Childers (b. 1863, TX) and Josephine Anna Simmons (b. 1868, AR); siblings, Eula G. (b. 1885, TX), Beatrice (b. 1887, TX), Joseph G., Jr. (b. 1889, TX), Lucile (b. 1893, TX); spouse, Lucile Scott (b. 1893, TX), married about 1919; children, Gwen (b. 1921, TX), Joseph Scott (b. 1930, TX), William Carroll (b. 1932, TX). *SR; A1d, g; A2a, b, e; A3a; A4g.*

CHILTON, HUGH ANDERS. Born Sept. 19, 1879, Marlin, Falls County, Texas. Ht. 5 ft. 8 in., brown eyes, brown hair, light complexion. Peace officer, Marlin. LOYALTY RANGER June 6, 1918–Feb. 18, 1919. REMARKS: As of 1918 had spent about 12 years as deputy sheriff, constable, and deputy city marshal; in 1920 was a fire department inspector in Marlin. In 1930 was an insurance agent in Marlin. Died Oct. 1, 1961, Marlin, Falls County, Texas; buried in Marlin Cemetery. FAMILY: Parents, Lysias Brown Chilton (b. 1849, AL) and Ida Pauline Anders (b. 1860, TX); siblings, Ida Pauline "Jackie" (b. 1879, TX), Annie Louise (b. 1881, TX), Lysias Brown, Jr. (b. 1883, TX), Horace Lee (b. 1887, TX), Albert Hunter (b. 1890, TX); spouse, Mabel Bertha Smith (b. 1897, GA), married June 8, 1925. *SR; A1b, e, f, g; A2b; A3a; A4b.*

CHILTON, PHILIP HALE. Born Jan. 13, 1854, Morristown, Hamblen County, Tennessee. No physical description, married. Doctor, Alpine, Brewster County, Texas. SPECIAL RANGER Feb. 4, 1918–Jan. 14, 1919. REMARKS: Was Texas quarantine officer at Terlingua, Brewster County. Had been a physician in Comanche, Comanche County, Texas. Died Jan. 19, 1929, Jim Wells County, Texas. FAMILY: Parents, William Richard Chilton (b. 1821, TN) and Elizabeth Keith Scruggs (b. 1825, TN); siblings, James William (b. 1848, TN), Charles Garnett (b. 1850, TN), Richard Scruggs (b. 1852, TN), George Alexander (b. 1856, TN), Joseph Ewing (b. 1858, TN), John Bell (b. 1860, TN), Frederick Douglas (b. 1861, TN), Samuel Porter (b. 1864, TN), Rufus Jarnagin (b. 1866, TN), Keith (b. 1869, TN); spouse, Sophronia Ellen Wright (b. 1864, TX), married July 2, 1894, Texas; children, Catherine D. (b. 1895, TX), Philip H. (b. 1898, TX). *SR; Collins to Harley, Feb 1, 1918, AGC; A1aa, a, d, e; A2b; A4a, b, g.*

CHOATE, DANIEL BOONE "BOONE." Born Nov. 21, 1870, DeWitt County, Texas. No physical description, married. Farmer, Kenedy, Karnes County, Texas. LOYALTY RANGER June 7, 1918–Feb. 1919. REMARKS: In 1930 was a U.S. Customs inspector, Robstown, Nueces County, Texas. Died Nov. 30, 1935, Nueces County, Texas. FAMILY: Parents, John Henry Choate (b. 1847, MS) and Juliet "Julia" Friar (b. 1850, TX); brother, F. Beauregard (b. 1861, TX); spouse, Nancy Parsons (b. 1877, TX), married Aug. 30, 1893, Karnes County; children, Julia (b. 1897, TX), Ima (b. 1898, TX), John Henry (b. 1895, TX). *SR; A1b, d, e, g; A4a, b, c, g; C.*

CLAIBORNE, W. H. Born July 1871, Union County, Tennessee. Ht. 5 ft. 10 in., blue eyes, iron gray hair, married. Peace officer. REGULAR RANGER Jan. 10, 1918–Nov. 1, 1918 (sergeant., Co. M; was reduced to private, Sept. 10, 1918). Resigned. REMARKS: Lived in Fort Bend County, Texas in 1916. In 1920 was a prison guard at the state prison in Huntsville, Walker County, Texas. In 1930 was a farm overseer in Wharton County, Texas. FAMILY: Spouse, Mary (b. 1878, TX), married about 1912; children, Martha Lee (b. 1916, TX), W. H. (b. 1921, TX). *SR; 471; A1f, g; A2e.*

CLARK, FRANK BYLER. Born Aug. 22, 1873, Banquette, Nueces County, Texas. Ht. 5 ft. 10 in., brown eyes, dark gray hair, dark complexion, married. Stockman, Realitos, Duval County, Texas. SPECIAL RANGER Apr. 30, 1918–Jan. 14, 1919. REMARKS: Died Jan. 16, 1956, Hebbronville, Jim Hogg County, Texas. FAMILY: Parents, D. Hines Clark (b. 1838, LA) and Adolphine C. Sack (b. 1841, TX); siblings, William (b. 1856, TX), Archy (b. 1859, TX), Phillip (b. 1861, TX), Ada (b. 1863, TX), H. Forest (b. 1865, TX), Clarence W. (b. 1867, TX), Alice C. (b. 1869, TX), Thomas H. (b. 1875, TX); spouse, Lillie Maude David (b. 1887, TX), married Oct. 17, 1905, San Diego, Duval County; children, Lidy Ethel (b. 1907, TX), Frank Byler (b. 1909, TX), Forest Hines (b. 1911, TX), Cotton Wright (b. 1914, TX), James David (b. 1916, TX), Ollie Maude (b. 1918, TX), Leta Matilda (b. 1920, TX), Lillie Geneva (b. 1922, TX), Ada Thomas (b. 1929, TX). *SR; A1a, d, e, f, g; A2b, e; A3a; A4a, b, g.*

CLARK, GEORGE W. Born May 1851, Clinton County, Indiana. No physical description, married. Carpenter, Friona, Parmer County, Texas. LOYALTY RANGER June 7, 1918–Feb. 1919. REMARKS: In 1920 was an insurance agent in Parmer County. FAMILY: Spouse, Sarah Jennie (b. 1871, OH), married about 1887. *SR; 471; A1e, f.*

CLARK, HARVEY ROBERT. Born May 22, 1891, Schulenburg, Fayette County, Texas. Ht. 5 ft. 9 in., blue eyes, light hair, fair complexion, married. Lawyer, La Grange, Fayette County. REGULAR RANGER Feb. 14, 1918–July 29, 1918 (assigned to AG's office). Resigned. REMARKS: In 1930 had a private law practice in Schulenburg. Died June 6, 1956, Colorado County, Texas. FAMILY: Parents, Dr. Isaac Edgar Clark (b. 1861, TX) and Ella Wolters (b. 1863, TX); sister, Cleo A. (b. 1889, TX); spouse, Ruby M. (b. 1899, TX), married about 1917; son, Isaac Edgar (b. 1919, TX). *SR; 471; Clark to AG, Apr 25, 1918, AGC; Clark to AG, Aug 30, 1918, AGC; A1e, g; A2b, e; A3a; A4b, g.*

CLARKE, RUFINO. (First name spelled RUFUIO on Ranger Service Records; last name spelled CLARK on some census records.) Born 1852, Cerralvo, Nuevo Leon, Mexico. Ht. 5 ft. 8 in., brown eyes, mixed gray hair, fair complexion, married. Ranchman, Rio Grande City, Starr County, Texas. LOYALTY RANGER July 13, 1918–Feb. 1919. REMARKS: Immigrated to the U.S. in 1870; became a naturalized U.S. citizen. Had lived and worked in Duval County, Texas. In 1920 was a stockraiser in Starr County. Died Sept. 22, 1921, Starr County, Texas. FAMILY: Spouse, Clotilda or Matilda Palacios Guerra (b. 1863, TX), married about 1881, Rio Grande City; children, Jacobo (b. 1882, TX), Emelia (b. 1884, TX), Sofia (b. 1886, TX), Clotilda (b. 1888, TX), Fidela (b. 1890, TX), Constancia (b. 1891, TX), Adelaida (b. 1895, TX). *SR; A1b, d, e, f; A2b; A4b.*

CLARKSON, WILLIAM. Born Jan. 21, 1858, Charleston, Charleston County, South Carolina. Ht. 5 ft. 5 in., blue eyes, iron gray hair, fair complexion, married. Foundry shop owner, Corsicana, Navarro County, Texas. SPECIAL RANGER July 9, 1918–Jan. 14, 1919. REMARKS: Letterhead: "Oil City Iron Works, William Clarkson, William Clarkson, Jr., Founders, Machinists, Structural Iron Workers, Corsicana." In 1930 lived in Oklahoma City, Oklahoma County, Oklahoma. Died Sept. 1, 1941, Albuquerque, Bernalillo County, New Mexico. FAMILY: Parents, William Clarkson (b. 1832, SC) and Margaret

Susan Simons (b. 1832, SC); siblings, Thomas Simons (b. 1854, SC), Thomas Boston (b. 1856, SC), John Dawson (b. 1859, SC), Sarah Caroline (b. 1861, SC), Robert Heriot (b. 1863, SC), Margaret Simons (b. 1869, SC), Ida Clarke (b. 1873), Annie Thomasina (b. 1875), Frances Marion (b. 1877); spouse #1, Jennie Gullick (b. 1866, TX), married Jan. 21, 1885; children, Wiley G. (b. 1886, TX), William (b. 1888, TX), Rosetta T. (b. 1890, TX), Margaret (b. 1892, TX), Annie Beal (b. 1897, TX); spouse #2, Ruby Cherry Callahan (b. 1901, TX), married about 1930. *SR; A1a, b, d, e, f, g; A3a; A4b, g.*

CLAYBROOK, JOHN H. Born Feb. 1871, Bosque County, Texas. Ht. 6 ft., blue eyes, dark hair, dark complexion, married. Farmer and stockraiser, Perry, Falls County, Texas. LOYALTY RANGER June 7, 1918–Feb. 1919. REMARKS: Had been a merchant in Bosque County. In 1910 was a farmer in Perry. In 1930 was a stock farmer in Waco, McLennan County, Texas. A John Henry Claybrook died May 14, 1956, McLennan County, Texas. FAMILY: Parents (probably), Christopher Richard Claybrook (b. 1831, KY) and Rhoda Ann Lane (b. 1841, GA); siblings, William (b. 1862, TX), Mattie (b. 1864, TX), James (b. 1868, TX), Joseph Edwin (b. 1869, TX); stepmother, Sarah Anne McKissick (b. 1842, TX); siblings, Minnie (b. 1876, TX), Mary Marie (b. 1877, TX), Guy W. (b. 1879, TX); spouse #1, Mary H. "Mollie" Oakes (b. 1871, TX), married about 1898; sons, John H., Jr. (b. 1898, TX), Rudd A. (b. 1904, TX); spouse #2, Elizabeth (b. 1892, TX); stepson, Daniel B. Webster (b. 1917, TX). *SR; A1aa, a, b, d, e, f, g; A2b; A3a; A4b, g.*

CLENDENIN, WILLIAM H. Born Sept. 29, 1869, Alamance County, North Carolina. Ht. 5 ft. 6 in., brown hair, fair complexion, married. Lawyer, Emory, Rains County, Texas. LOYALTY RANGER July 9, 1918–Feb. 1919. REMARKS: Died Nov. 13, 1919, Emory, Rains County, Texas; buried in Emory. FAMILY: Parents, George A. Clendenin (b. 1837, NC) and Mary A. Roberson (b. 1845, NC); siblings, Joseph S. (b. 1870, NC), Mary E. (b. 1872, NC), Sarah J. (b. 1876, NC), Dora I. (b. 1878, NC); spouse, Emma Settle (b. 1874, GA), married Nov. 13, 1898, Rains County; son, Willie Bailey (b. 1899, TX). *SR; A1b, d, e; A2b; A4b.*

CLEVELAND, LEROY. Born Feb. 5, 1898, Marfa, Presidio County, Texas. Ht. 5 ft. 9 ½ in., brown eyes, brown hair, light complexion. Ranchman. REGULAR RANGER Sept. 11, 1917–Dec. 15, 1917 (private, Co B). Discharged (because he was underage?). REMARKS: In 1930 may have been a filling station operator in Lubbock, Lubbock County, Texas. FAMILY: Parents, William H. Cleveland (b. 1859, TX) and Mary A "Mollie" Williams (b. 1864, TX); sister, Alexa (b. 1888, TX). *SR; Fox to Harley, Dec 12, 1917, AGC; A1d, g; A3a; A4b.*

CLINE, IRA W. Born Aug. 1, 1882, Pleasanton, Atascosa County, Texas. Ht. 5 ft. 11 in., brown eyes, brown hair, fair complexion. Deputy sheriff, Presidio County, Texas. REGULAR RANGER July 27, 1912–June 1915 (private, Co. A; transferred to Co. B, Feb. 1, 1915; promoted to sergeant, Co. B, Mar. 1915). Discharged. REMARKS: Was raised in Presidio County. Commissioned Presidio County sheriff, Jan. 26, 1918, succeeding the late M. B. Chastain. In July 1920 lost the primary election for sheriff to (Ranger) J. E. Vaughan. In 1930 was a hotel detective in El Paso, El Paso County, Texas. An Ira W. Cline died Jan. 6, 1965, El Paso County, Texas. FAMILY: Parents, James Cline (b. 1853, TX or MS) and Ella E. (b. 1860, TX); siblings, Joel (b. 1871, TX), Minnie (b. 1880, TX), Della (b. 1886, TX), Peter Buford (b. 1888, TX), Ester (b. 1892, TX), Elsie (b. 1894, TX), Thomas B. "Tom" (b. 1895, TX), Travis C. (b. 1895, TX), Bowie (b. 1900, TX); spouse, Frances (b. 1900, TX), married about 1920; sons, Ira (b. 1921, TX), Jacob (b. 1923, TX), Francisco "Frank" (b. 1925, TX). *SR; 471; Bates to Ferguson, June 9, 1915, WC; AA, Sept 27, 1917, July 29, 1920; 1503:424; A1f, g; A2b, d, f, g; A2b, e; A3a.*

CLOUD, JAMES COLLINS. Born Apr. 13, 1875, Kurten, Brazos County, Texas. Ht. 5 ft. 7 in., brown eyes, black hair, dark complexion, married. Farmer, Bryan, Brazos County. LOYALTY RANGER June 8, 1918–Feb. 1919. REMARKS: Died Dec. 17, 1966, Brazos County, Texas. FAMILY: Parents, William Wilson Cloud (b. 1837, GA or SC) and Sarah Jane Smith (b. 1846, GA or SC); siblings, Virginia, Mary Ruth (b. 1867, GA), Fannie E. (b. 1869, GA or TX), William Elisha (b. 1871, TX), Robert A. (b. 1873, TX), Caroline "Carrie" (b. 1878, TX), Ella Lee (b. 1880, TX); spouse, Paralee A. Jones (b. 1879, TX), married in 1899, Brazos County; sons, Jesse James (b. 1900, TX), Webster W. (b. 1904, TX), Clarence I. (b. 1908, TX), Raymond E. (b. 1910, TX). *SR; A1b, d, e, f, g; A2b; A3a; A4b.*

COBB, DENT N. Born Oct. 1884, Encinal, La Salle County, Texas. Ht. 5 ft. 11 in., gray eyes, light brown hair, light complexion, married. Rancher, Rio Grande City, Starr County, Texas. SPECIAL RANGER May 8, 1918–Jan. 15, 1919. REMARKS: Immigration inspector, Laredo, Webb County, Texas, 1914. Customs inspector, Brownsville, Cameron County, Texas, 1914. Deputy collector of Customs, Hidalgo, Hidalgo County, Texas, 1914–1915. Deputy collector of Customs, Rio Grande City, 1916–June 1917. Resigned. In Apr. 1918 owned a ranch near Rio Grande City. FAMILY: Parents, Winfield Scott Cobb (b. 1849, AL) and Sarah H. Eaken (b. 1859, TX); siblings, Josie May (b. 1887, TX), William Scott (b. 1889, TX), Timothy Buckley (b. 1896, TX); spouse, Sallie Estelle (b. 1889, TX), married about 1907. *SR; LWT, Jan 11, Feb 22, 1914, Oct 10, 1915, Mar 11, 1917; BDH, Sept 10, 1914, Feb 13, 1915, May 4, 1916, June 26, 1917; Marks to Hanson, Apr 15, 1918, AGC; A1d, e; A4a, b.*

COCHRAN, JOHN W. Born Oct. 1871, Pike County, Georgia. Ht. 5 ft. 11 in., brown eyes, brown hair, light complexion, married. Farmer, Lonie, Childress County, Texas. LOYALTY RANGER June 4, 1918–Jan. 1919. REMARKS: Childress County sheriff, Nov. 6, 1906–Nov. 8, 1910. Soldier, Volunteer, Spanish-American War, 1 year, 3 months. In 1930, still farming in Childress County. A John William Cochran died Mar. 25, 1942, Childress County, Texas. FAMILY: Parents, Martin C. Cochran (b. 1821, GA) and Mary (b. 1839, SC); siblings, Nancy (b. 1868, GA), William (b. 1869, GA), Richard (b. 1873, GA), Samuel (b. 1876, GA), Sarah (b. 1879, GA); spouse, Annie (b. 1878, TX), married about 1905; daughters, Annie M. (b. 1906, TX), Lilly F. (b. 1910, TX), Eleanor (b. 1913, TX). *SR; 1503:102; A1a, b, d, e, f, g; C.*

COFFEE, WALTER DOUGLAS. Born July 25, 1882, Kyle, Hays County, Texas. Ht. 5 ft. 11 in., blue eyes, ruddy complexion, brown hair. Ranchman, Big Spring, Howard County, Texas. LOYALTY RANGER June 5, 1918–Feb. 1919. REMARKS: In 1910 was partner in a grain shed in Big Spring. Reportedly died Oct. 29, 1947, Alameda, California; buried in Mount Olive Cemetery, Big Spring. FAMILY: Parents, Lilburn Warren Coffee (b. 1850, AR) and Margaret Goode (b. 1856, TX); siblings, Lula Edna (b. 1875, TX), "Little Buddy" (b. 1880, TX), Jerry (b. 1884, TX), Rubye (b. 1886, TX), Margaret Elizabeth "Maggie" (b. 1888, TX), Lilburn Warren (b. 1892, TX), Nellie (b. 1894, TX), Solis (b. 1896, TX), Lillian Lee (b. 1898, TX); spouse, Sarah Ruth Moore (b. 1901, TX), married Sept. 9, 1926, Big Spring; sons, Robert Lee (b. 1926, TX), Walter Douglas, Jr. (b. 1927, TX). *SR; 471; A1d, e, f; A2e; A3a; A4a, b, c.*

COFFEE, WOODSON "WOODS." Born Mar. 1, 1862, Gonzales County, Texas. No physical description, married. Banker, First State Bank, Miami, Roberts County, Texas. LOYALTY RANGER June 10, 1918–Feb. 18, 1919. REMARKS: As a young man was a sheep herder and cattle driver in Indian Territory (now Oklahoma) and the Texas Panhandle; owned a cattle ranch in Throckmorton County, Texas in the late 1880s. In 1906 became county judge, Roberts County. In 1910 was a bank president in Roberts County. Moved to Amarillo, Potter County, Texas in 1926; in 1930 was a wheat farmer living in Amarillo. Died June 12, 1953, Amarillo, Potter County, Texas. FAMILY: Parents, Mansel Coffee (b. 1840, AL) and Georgia A. Reynolds (b. 1845, MS); siblings, Logan Alonzo (b. 1865, TX), Cleve (b. 1868, TX), Henry (b. 1869, TX), Hatty (b. 1873, TX), James (b. 1876, TX), Glenn (b. 1879, TX); spouse #1, Ollie Dickens (or Pickens) Stribling (b. 1868, TX), married Aug. 14, 1890, Throckmorton County; children, Ruth (b. 1891, TX), Benjamin Stribling (b. 1892, TX), Grace (b. 1894, Indian Territory, now OK), Woodson, Jr. (b. 1895, TX), Roy C. (b. 1897, TX), Oran (b. 1898, TX), Ollie (b. 1901), Jack (b. 1904, TX); spouse #2, Velda Bangs, married in 1932. *SR; 471; A1aa, b, d, e, g; A2b; A4a, b.*

COFFIN, ALBERT LLEWELLEN. Born June 22, 1848, Farmington, Franklin County, Maine. Ht. 5 ft. 8 in., gray eyes, light hair, light complexion. Carpenter, San Antonio, Bexar County, Texas. SPECIAL RANGER Jan. 2, 1917–Jan. 29, 1918 (attached to Co. C). Discharged—WA was cancelled. His WA was cancelled when he left Wells Fargo's employ. REMARKS: Was a Union Civil War veteran (private, infantry, 1863–1865), living in Brackettville, Kinney County, Texas in 1890. In 1893, 1894, and 1900 was a driver for Wells Fargo and Company Express living in San Antonio; in 1920 was a carpenter for an express company in San Antonio. FAMILY: Parents, Coburn Bartholomew Coffin (b. 1831, ME) and Abigail Cole True (b. 1828, ME); siblings, John Nelson (b. 1850, ME), Julia True (b. 1857,

ME); spouse, Fanny (b. 1867, TX), married about 1892; son, Coburn (b. 1895, TX), stepchildren, Earl Riggs (b. 1883, TX), Ruby K. Riggs (b. 1886, TX). *SR; Campbell to Harley, Jan 29, 1918, AGC; A1aaa, aa, d, f; A4b, g; A5a.*

COGDELL, DAVID M. Born Mar. 1884, Marshall County, Mississippi. Ht. 5 ft. 11 in., brown eyes, dark complexion, black hair. Stock farmer, Abilene, Taylor County, Texas. LOYALTY RANGER June 8, 1918–Feb. 1919. REMARKS: Had lived in Palo Pinto County, Texas; in 1910 was a dry goods merchant in Haskell, Haskell County, Texas. In 1930 was a stock raiser living in Childress, Childress County, Texas. A David Munsey Cogdell died Nov. 15, 1964, Scurry County, Texas. FAMILY: Parents, David M. Cogdell (b. 1853, TN) and Susie J. (b. 1861, MS); siblings, Maggie L. (b. 1882, MS), Holland C. (b. 1888, MS), Reginald Gordon (b. 1891, TX), twins Ernest L. and Earl E. (b. 1894, TX), Willard A. (b. 1898, TX), Mary Sue (b. 1902, TX); spouse #1, Lillian (b. 1886, TX), married about 1910; spouse #2, Johnny N. (b. 1892, TX), married about 1919; children, Johnny Sue (b. 1920, TX), David M., Jr. (b. 1922, TX), Martha A. (b. 1926, TX). *SR; A1d, e, f, g; A2b, e; A3a.*

COKER, LEONIDAS B. "L. B.," "LEE," "LEON." Born Apr. 1866, Smithville, Monroe County, Mississippi. Ht. 6 ft. 2 ½ in., gray eyes, gray hair, dark complexion, married. Real estate agent and farmer, Georgetown, Williamson County, Texas. LOYALTY RANGER June 7, 1918–Feb. 1919. REMARKS: Deputy sheriff, briefly. Had been a farmer living in Galveston County, Texas; in 1910 was a dairy farmer in Williamson County. An L. B. Coker died Apr. 10, 1928, Williamson County, Texas. FAMILY: Parents, Benjamin Franklin Coker (b. 1833, AL) and Martha Jane Wright (b. 1835, TN); siblings, William Henry (b. 1861, MS), Lucian D. (b. 1863, MS), Loretta J. (b. 1869, MS), A. M. "Shark" (b. 1872, MS), R. Lem (b. 1874, MS), Albert J. (b. 1876, MS), Martha Bell "Mattie" (b. 1878, MS); spouse, Elizabeth M. (b. 1869, VA), married about 1888; children, Lena M. (b. 1891, TX), Velma A. (b. 1894, TX), Winnie M. (b. 1895, TX), Burness (b. 1898, TX), Lora B. (b. 1897, TX), Dean (b. 1902, TX), Mary (b. 1906, TX). *SR; A1a, b, d, e, f; A4b; C.*

COKER, ROBERT AUGUSTUS. Born Dec. 2, 1873, Amity, Clark County, Arkansas. Ht. 6 ft. 1 in., brown eyes, black hair, dark complexion, married. Farmer, Athens, Henderson County, Texas. LOYALTY RANGER June 6, 1918–Feb. 1919. REMARKS: Parker County deputy sheriff, 3 years. Game warden, 2 years. In 1930 was a farmer living in Wood County, Texas. A Robert A. Coker died Oct. 21, 1941, Wood County, Texas. FAMILY: Parents, James F. Coker (b. 1841, AL) and Susan F. Ashcroft (b. 1843, AL); siblings, Richard Monroe (b. 1859, AL), Wesley James (b. 1866, AL), Lillie L. (b. 1862, AL); spouse, Maria W. "Mae" Limbaugh (b. 1877, AL), married about 1896; children, Olivia (b. 1897, TX), C. Milton (b. 1900, TX), Charley Woodson (b. 1902, TX). *SR; A1b, d, f, g; A3a; A4a, b, g; C.*

COLE, ALLEN. Born Mar. 29, 1879, Kenosha, Kenosha County, Wisconsin. Ht. 5 ft. 10 ½ in., blue eyes, brown hair, light complexion, married. Ranchman, enlisted in Hudspeth County, Texas. REGULAR RANGER Sept. 6, 1917–June 8, 1918 (private, Co. B). Discharged/fired—was one of five men fired when Co. B was disbanded as a result of the Porvenir massacre. REMARKS: Had been a special deputy sheriff. In 1910 was a clerk, living in Kenosha. In Sept. 1918 was a ranch laborer in Hudspeth County while his wife and children lived in Chicago, Illinois. The word "Deceased" is written across the face of his WWI Draft Registration form; the form is dated Sept. 1918, but there is no death date noted. Another source states died Oct. 25, 1918. FAMILY: Grandmother, Mary Allen (b. 1819, NY); sister, Harriet (b. 1880, WI); spouse, Louise D. Baker (b. 1885, TN), married Nov. 1903; children, John Allen (b. 1904, WI), William Hale (b. 1906, WI), Elizabeth Louise (b. 1908, WI). *SR; 471; A1d, e; A3a; A4b.*

COLE, JOHN PEARCY. Born Mar. 1870, Waxahachie, Ellis County, Texas. No physical description, married. Stock farmer, Pride, Dawson County, Texas. LOYALTY RANGER June 17, 1918–Feb. 19, 1919. REMARKS: Had been a farmer in Hill County, Texas. In 1930 was manager of an oil company in Levelland, Hockley County, Texas. A John Persy Cole died Mar. 10, 1942, Lubbock County, Texas. FAMILY: Spouse, Lizzie Bell (b. 1872, TX), married about 1893; children, John P., Jr. (b. 1894, TX), Winnie E. (b. 1895, TX), James C. (b. 1896, TX), Augustus B. (b. 1899, TX), Clarance H. (b. 1902, TX), Pearcy G. (b. 1904, TX), Ben W. (b. 1906, TX), Lizzie B. (b. 1909, TX), Cecil B. (b. 1912, TX), Louis G. (b. 1917, TX), Emma Lara (b. 1921, TX). *SR; A1d, e, g.*

COLE, LUTHER LEE. Born Jan. 26, 1866, Habersham, Habersham County, Georgia. Ht. 5 ft. 11 in., brown eyes, black hair, dark complexion, married. Merchant and farmer, Alto, Cherokee County, Texas. LOYALTY RANGER July 3, 1918–Feb. 1919. REMARKS: As early as 1870 lived in Alto; as of 1918 had lived in Cherokee County for the last 49 years. Had been a peace officer for several years. In Jan. 1919 owned general stores in Alto and Red Lawn. Died Mar. 27, 1932, Harris County, Texas; buried in Mount Zion Cemetery, Cherokee County, Texas. FAMILY: Parents, Aaron Shannon Cole (b. 1836, SC) and Harriet Emily Addis (b. 1838, SC); stepmother, Martha Hannah Barnes (b. 1850, TX); siblings, Harrison (b. 1859, GA), Rox Anna (b. 1860, GA), Martha (b. 1861, GA), probably twins John Ellis and Mary Alice (b. 1869, GA), Garnet B. (b. 1871, TX), Lula U. (b. 1873, TX), Emily J. (b. 1875, TX), twins Jerusha E. and Joanna V. (b. 1876, TX), Emory Walter (b. 1878, TX), Elmer F. (b. 1879, TX), Clark Perry (b. 1882, TX), Mary Ethel (b. 1884, TX), Pearl (b. 1885, TX), Dora E. (b. 1888, TX), Jewel W. (b. 1891, TX); spouse #1, Martha A. Knoy (b. 1864, TX), married about 1887; children, Ethel Soleta (b. 1888, TX), Myrtle L. (b. 1890, TX), Ruby I. (b. 1892, TX), Mabel (b. 1893, TX), Margaret Odessa "Maggie" (b. 1896, TX), Howard Richard (b. 1898, TX), Velma (b. 1900, TX), Reba (b. 1901, TX), Hazel (b. 1903, TX); spouse #2, Marion I. (b. 1877, TX), married about 1907; children, Ann, Kitty Luther; spouse #3, Leah (b. 1886, TX), married before 1920; daughter, Velma (b. 1916, TX). *SR; A1b, d, e, f; A2b; A4b.*

COLE, STEUBEN RUE "RUE." Born Sept. 1888, Grandview, Johnson County, Texas. Ht. 5 ft. 11 in., blue eyes, dark brown hair, fair complexion. Ranchman, Sterling City, Sterling County, Texas. REGULAR RANGER June 11, 1915–Jan. 10, 1916 (private, Co. B; transferred to Co. A, Aug. 1915). Resigned. REMARKS: As of Jan. 1916, lived in Sterling City. In July 1920 applied for a job as a fireman on the Union Pacific Railroad at Denver. FAMILY: Parents, John Byrd Cole (b. 1863, AL) and Lula Adeline Morrow (b. 1865, TX); siblings, Leonile (b. 1885, TX), Frank Waiverly (b. 1886, TX), Irving (b. 1891, TX), John Jacob (b. 1893, TX), Marguerite (b. 1897, TX), Wendell Odell (b. 1907, TX). *SR; Hutchings to Fox, June 14, 15, 1915, AGC; Hutchings to Cole, June 12, 1915, AGC; Cole to Hutchings, Jan 14, 1916, AGC; Cole to AG, July 28, 1920, AGC; A1d, e, f; A3a; A4b, g.*

COLE, THOMAS J. Born July 1888, Buda, Hayes County, Texas. Ht. 6 ft. 3 in., blue eyes, brown hair, medium complexion, married. Peace officer, Austin, Travis County, Texas. REGULAR RANGER Sept. 30, 1920–Aug. 31, 1921 (private., Headquarters Co., Emergency Co. No. 1; transferred to Headquarters Co., Feb. 15, 1921). Resigned. Peace officer, Austin. RAILROAD RANGER July 29, 1922–Sept. 2, 1922 (Co. D). Discharged. REMARKS: Policeman, Austin, 1916. In 1920 and 1930 was a barber in Austin. A Thomas Jefferson Cole died Sept. 14, 1930, Travis County, Texas. FAMILY: Parents, John D. Cole (b. 1855, TX) and Mary C. (b. 1872, TX); siblings, John D. (b. 1891, TX), Oliver H. D. R. (b. 1894, TX); spouse, Anna (b. 1890, TX), married about 1911; daughters, Agnes (b. 1913, TX), Mary D. (b. 1920, TX). *SR; 471; SAE, June 21, 1916; A1d, e, f, g; C.*

COLEMAN, EDWARD E. Born Feb. 1872, Centerville, Leon County, Texas. Ht. 5 ft. 9 in., brown eyes, black hair, dark complexion, married. REGULAR RANGER 1893–1895 (Co. A). Ex-sheriff, Frio County, Texas (Nov. 3, 1914–Nov. 5, 1918), Pearsall. SPECIAL RANGER Nov. 2, 1918–Jan. 15, 1919. REMARKS: Between 1893–1918 had been a peace officer of one kind or another; was also a barber and farm owner. Constable, deputy sheriff, Frio County. In 1918 had not been a candidate for reelection as sheriff. LAW ENFORCEMENT RELATIVES: Ranger C. H. Coleman, brother. FAMILY: Parents, Robert Bruce Coleman (b. 1831, AL) and Mary Louisa Reed (b. 1841, AL); siblings, William Hunter (b. 1857, TX), McAlpin (b. 1858, TX), Wiley (b. 1860, TX), Robert Bruce (b. 1862, TX), Keturah "Kitty" (b. 1864, TX), Kibbie (b. 1867, TX), John (b. 1869, TX), Dan (b. 1871, TX), Oliver (b. 1874, TX), Charley (b. 1879, TX); spouse, Edna Haynes (b. 1877, TX), married Sept. 21, 1898, Frio County; sons, Roy H. (b. 1899, TX), Stanly (b. 1901, TX), Marace (b. 1903, TX), Dan (b. 1904, TX), John (b. 1905, TX), Ned (b. 1908, TX). *SR; 471; LWT, Aug 15, 1915; Coleman to Hutchings, May 10, 1916, AGC; Coleman to Hobby, June 1, 1918, AGC; Moses to Harley, Sept 24, 1918, AGC; Coleman to AG, June 4, 1918, AGC; 1503:199; A1b, d, e; A2c; A4b, g.*

COLEMAN, MARION MONROE "MONROE." Born Sept. 21, 1873, Falls County, Texas. Tall, slender, gray eyes, sandy hair, married. Groceryman, Comanche, Comanche

County, Texas. LOYALTY RANGER May 31, 1918–Feb. 1919. REMARKS: Still a grocery merchant in Comanche in 1930. Died May 14, 1954, Comanche County, Texas. LAW ENFORCEMENT RELATIVES: Marlin, Falls County city marshal (1900) Marion Marcus Coleman, father. FAMILY: Parents, Marion Marcus Coleman (b. 1845, MO) and Esther Adeline Conoly (b. 1847, TN); siblings, John B. (b. 1868, TX), Archie L. (b. 1872, TX), Chesley Conoly (b. 1876, TX), T. T. (b. 1878, TX); spouse, Annie Louise (b. 1874, TX), married about 1895; children, Chesley S. (b. 1896, TX), Millard Monroe (b. 1898, TX), Thelma (b. 1902, TX), Annie (b. 1904, TX), Mary Simms (b. 1906, TX), Tom A. (b. 1909, TX), Lollie (b. 1913, TX), Chrystine (b. 1918, TX). *SR; A1a, b, e, g; A2e; A3a.*

COLEMAN, THOMAS ATLEE "TOM." Born June 5, 1860, Goliad, Goliad County, Texas. Ht. 5 ft. 10 ½ in., married. Rancher, San Antonio, Bexar County, Texas. SPECIAL RANGER June 20, 1916–Dec. 1917 (attached to Co. C—station: Austin). Rancher, San Antonio. SPECIAL RANGER Feb. 7, 1918–Jan. 14, 1919. REMARKS: One of the biggest cattlemen in Texas. In 1915 appointed as a lieutenant colonel in the Texas National Guard on Governor Ferguson's staff. In Sept. 1917 was appointed collector of Customs of the new San Antonio district—the old Laredo and Eagle Pass districts. In 1920 census listed his occupation as "capitalist." Died Mar. 30, 1923, Bexar County, Texas. FAMILY: Parents, Thomas Matthew Coleman (b. 1833, TX) and Margaretta Susan Atlee (b. 1840, TN); sister, A. M. (b. 1862, TX); stepmother, Frances Humphreys (b. 1853, TN); spouse, Birdie Keeran (b. 1859, CA), married June 16, 1886, Victoria County, Texas; children, Marguerete (b. 1890, TX), Claude (b. 1892, TX), Mary (b. 1895, TX), Elizabeth (b. 1900, TX), Thomas A., Jr. (b. 1905, TX). *SR; 319: 79–80, 507; AG to Coleman, Nov 3, 1915, AGC; 172:II, 200; LWT, Oct 30, 1910, May 11, 1913, Sept 23, Oct 7, 1917, Mar 20, 1921; 520: 271–272, 373, 386; A1aa, a, b, d, e, f; A4b, c, g; B1; C.*

COLEMAN, THOMAS PATRICK "TOM." Born Jan. 8, 1874, Richmond, Fort Bend County, Texas. Ht. 5 ft. 8 ½ in., dark eyes, dark brown hair, dark complexion, married. Farmer, Rosenberg, Fort Bend County, Texas. LOYALTY RANGER June 15, 1918–Feb. 18, 1919. REMARKS: Died Nov. 23, 1958, Rosenberg, Fort Bend County, Texas. FAMILY: Parents, Thomas Patrick Coleman (b. 1836, Ireland) and Julia Parrott (b. 1849, MS); siblings, Maria "Mary" (b. 1862, TX), William (b. 1868, TX), James (b. 1876, TX), Abby (b. 1878, TX), Julia Ann (b. 1880, TX), Rosa (b. 1883, TX); spouse, Natalie Roberts (b. 1887, TX), married Aug. 20, 1904, Rosenberg; children, Sidney (b. 1908, TX), Tom, Jr. (b. 1912, TX). *SR; A1b, d, e, f; A2b; A3a; A4a; B2.*

COLLEY, ENOCH MILTON. Born Mar. 20, 1880, Austin, Travis County, Texas. Ht. 5 ft. 10 in., brown eyes, brown hair, fair complexion. Peace officer, Austin, Travis County. REGULAR RANGER Dec. 15, 1917–Mar. 15, 1918 (private, Co. M). Resigned. Peace officer, Austin. RAILROAD RANGER July 29, 1922–Nov. 2, 1922. Discharged. REMARKS: As of Dec. 1917 had 10 years' experience as a peace officer. In Dec. 1917 was an investigator for the Travis County district attorney and for the past year had been working for a constable. Died Mar. 21, 1944, Travis County, Texas. FAMILY: Parents, James Polk Colley (b. 1847, TN) and Eliza Ann Smedley (b. 1852, TX); siblings, Siras (b. 1873, TX), James Henry (b. 1878, TX), Early T. "Earl" (b. 1882, TX), William Theodore (b. 1885, TX), Annie M. (b. 1890, TX), Abe (b. 1892, TX), Walter R. (b. 1895, TX), Mary Maud (b. 1897, TX). *SR; Hornsby to Harley, Dec 13, 1917, AGC; Matthews to Harley, Dec 14, 1917, AGC; White to Harley, Dec 14, 1917, AGC; Colley to Harley, Dec 15, 1917, AGC; Cunningham to Harley, Mar 13, 1918, AGC; A1b, d, e, g; A3a; A4g; C.*

COLLEY, GEORGE WALTON (or WASHINGTON). Born Sept. 5, 1875, Blanco, Blanco County, Texas. Ht. 5 ft. 8 in., gray eyes, black hair, medium complexion. Farmer, enlisted in Travis County, Texas. REGULAR RANGER Nov. 1, 1911–Jan. 31, 1912 (private, Co. A). Discharged—reduction in force. REMARKS: In 1918 was an auto mechanic for the Pierce Oil Company, Fort Worth, Tarrant County, Texas; still lived in Tarrant County in 1930. Died Apr. 27, 1971, Tarrant County, Texas. FAMILY: Parents, Albert Wytche Colley (b. 1836, GA) and Martha Louisiana "Lou" Ferguson (b. 1850, AL); siblings, William Naman (b. 1872, TX), Teresa Saphronia (b. 1874, TX), Berry Bradford (b. 1878, TX), Cordelia F. (b. 1879, TX), Laura Matilda (b. 1881, TX), Albert Herbert (b. 1885, TX); spouse #1, Marguerite "Maggie" Reed (b. 1879, MS), married about 1899; adopted son, David Earl (b. 1909); spouse #2, Zulema "Emma"

Mellado (b. 1892, Mexico), married Sept. 7, 1912; children, Pearl (b. 1913, TX), George Louis (b. 1914, TX), Madeline Frances (b. 1919, TX). *SR; 471; A1b, d, e, f, g; A2a, b; A3a; A4b, g.*

COLLINS, DOLPHIN EUGENE STOUT. (Listed as E. I. in Ranger Service Records.) Born Sept. 13, 1872, Howell, Howell County, Missouri. Ht. 5 ft. 6 ½ in., brown eyes, brown hair, fair complexion, married. Merchant and stockman, Channing, Hartley County, Texas. LOYALTY RANGER June 11, 1918–Feb. 1919. REMARKS: In 1930 was a banker in Hartley County. Died July 30, 1950, Hartley County, Texas. FAMILY: Spouse, Zera Scruggs (b. 1873, TX), married about 1892; children, Jack C. (b. 1893, TX), Grace C. (b. 1896, TX), Mary L. "Jenkie" (b. 1898, TX), Eugene S., Jr. (b. 1901, TX), Ida "Biddie" Mae (b. 1903, TX), Toliaferro Ware (b. 1911, TX), Frank (b. 1913, TX). *SR; A1a, b, d, e, f, g; A4b; C.*

COLLINS, HENRY WARREN "HARRY" "RIP." Born Feb. 26, 1896, Weatherford, Parker County, Texas. Ht. 6 ft. 1 in., gray eyes, brown hair, medium complexion, married. Peace officer. REGULAR RANGER Apr. 2, 1918–June 29, 1918 (private, Co. M). Discharged. Baseball player, Austin, Travis County, Texas. SPECIAL RANGER Jan. 24, 1931–Apr. 30, 1932. Peace officer and ball player, Austin. REGULAR RANGER May 1, 1932–Jan. 18, 1933 (placed on detached duty by AG). Discharged. Deputy sheriff, Travis County. REGULAR RANGER Sept. 1, 1937–Dec. 31, 1940 (private, Headquarters Co.). Resigned to take office as Travis County sheriff. REMARKS: 1915–1917 was star football player for Texas A&M College. From 1919–1933 was a professional baseball pitcher. Travis County sheriff, Nov. 5, 1940–Jan. 1, 1949. From 1950–1959 was Bryan, Brazos County, Texas police chief; retired. Died May 27, 1968, Bryan, Brazos County, Texas. FAMILY: Parents, Henry W. Collins (b. 1872, TX) and Mary (b. 1874, KY); spouse #1, Letitia Ethel "Letty" Parmele (b. 1896, TX), married about 1917; children, James Parmele (b. 1921, TX), Charlotte Marie (b. 1922, TX), Henry Warren (b. 1928, TX); spouse #2, Ruth Duff, married sometime after 1946. *SR; 471; AG to Cunningham, Apr 3, May 7, 1918, AGC; Assistant AG to Collins, May 29, 1918, AGC; 172:II, 217; 319: 109; 522: 184–185; 1503:495; A1d, e, g; A2a, b, e; A3a; A4a, b.*

COLLYNS, CECIL BAYLY. Born Feb. 20, 1878, Johnson County, Texas. Ht. 5 ft. 11 in., gray eyes, dark hair, fair complexion. Peace officer, Fort Worth, Tarrant County, Texas. SPECIAL RANGER July 31, 1918–Jan. 15, 1919. REMARKS: As of Sept. 9, 1918 was a Texas National Guard lieutenant in the Adjutant General's office, Austin, Travis County, Texas. In 1930 was an insurance agent in Fort Worth. In Nov. 1937 traveled to El Paso, El Paso County, Texas to promote establishment of a race track in El Paso. Died Apr. 1, 1976, Fort Worth, Tarrant County, Texas. FAMILY: Parents, Charles William Bayly Collyns (b. 1872, England) and Pearl Collins (b. 1878, TX); spouse, Dorothy Garrard (b. 1906, TN), married Nov. 18, 1936. *SR; A1g; A2a, b; A4a, b, g; B2.*

COLQUITT, RAWLINS MURRELL. Born Apr. 22, 1887, Terrell, Kaufman County, Texas. Ht. 5 ft. 8 in., brown eyes, brown hair, medium complexion, married. Insurance agent, Houston, Harris County, Texas. SPECIAL RANGER Jan. 14, 1918–Jan. 15, 1919. Insurance agent, Dallas, Dallas County, Texas. SPECIAL RANGER June 1, 1932–unknown. REMARKS: Was Texas Governor Oscar B. Colquitt's son. In 1910 was secretary for the Texas Railroad Commission, living in Austin, Travis County, Texas. In 1917 was an officer in Bankers Health & Accident Assn., Inc., Dallas (listed in the Houston, Texas City Directory). In 1918 was an agent for the Pan American Life Insurance Company, Houston. Died May 19, 1941, Dallas, Dallas County, Texas. FAMILY: Parents, Oscar Branch Colquitt (b. 1861, GA) and Alice Fuller Murrell (b. 1866, LA); siblings, Sydney Burkholter (b. 1888, TX), Oscar Branch (b. 1890, TX), Mary Alice (b. 1894, TX), Walter Fuller (b. 1899, TX); spouse, Josephine Elizabeth Heard (b. 1895, AR), married Oct. 7, 1914, San Antonio, Bexar County, Texas (one source states married in Little Rock, Arkansas); children, Rawlins M., Jr. (b. 1916, TX), Oscar Branch III (b. 1918, TX). *SR; A1e, f; A2e; A3a, A4a, b, g; A5a; B1; C.*

COLQUITT, WALTER HOMER. Born May 20, 1886, Shreveport, Caddo Parish, Louisiana. Ht. 5 ft. 7 in., gray eyes, gray hair, dark complexion, married. Rancher, Marfa, Presidio County, Texas. SPECIAL RANGER Jan. 2, 1918–Jan. 14, 1919. Rancher, Marfa. SPECIAL RANGER Dec. 26, 1933–unknown. REMARKS: "Three years as a Special Ranger under Capt. Fox." Died Jan. 30, 1947, Culberson

County, Texas. LAW ENFORCEMENT RELATIVES: Ranger Will K. Colquitt, brother. FAMILY: Parents, Robert Kellam Colquitt (b. 1859, AL) and Alice May Johnson (b. 1861, LA); siblings, Roberta May "Robbie"(b. 1882, LA), Thomas Francis (b. 1884, LA), William Kellam (b. 1896, LA); spouse, Ola Eugenia Nicholls (b. 1885, TX), married June 30, 1909; children, Jack Nicholls (b. 1915, TX), Robert Eugene (b. 1919, TX), Ola Eugenia (b. 1924, TX). *SR; A1d, e, f, g; A2e; A3a; A4a; C.*

COLQUITT, WILLIAM KELLAM "WILL." Born Sept. 20, 1896, Shreveport, Caddo Parish, Louisiana. Ht. 5 ft. 9 in., blue eyes, brown hair, fair complexion. Rancher, Marfa, Presidio County, Texas. SPECIAL RANGER May 9, 1917–Dec. 1917 (attached to Co. C). REMARKS: In 1920 was a ranch owner living with his brother, Homer, in Presidio County. Died Apr. 21, 1927, El Paso County, Texas. LAW ENFORCEMENT RELATIVES: Ranger W. Homer Colquitt, brother; Ranger James Buchanan Gillett, father-in-law. FAMILY: Parents, Robert Kellam Colquitt (b. 1859, AL) and Alice May Johnson (b. 1861, LA); siblings, Roberta May "Robbie" (b. 1882, LA), Thomas Francis (b. 1884, LA), Walter Homer (b. 1886, LA); spouse, Leota Gillett (b. 1898, TX), married sometime after Jan. 1920; two children (one is probably Will Milton, b. 1923, TX). *SR; A1d, e, f; A2e; A4a, g; C.*

COLVERT, CARL LEE. Born Nov. 20, 1881, Birmingham, Jefferson County, Alabama (1910 census record lists birthplace as Iowa). Ht. 5 ft. 9 in., brown eyes, brown hair, dark complexion. Railroad brakeman, enlisted in Atascosa County, Texas. SPECIAL RANGER July 17, 1916–Dec. 1917. REMARKS: In 1918 was a brakeman for the San Antonio, Uvalde, & Gulf Railroad, Pleasanton, Atascosa County, Texas. FAMILY: Spouse, Theresa (b. 1889, AL), married about 1907; daughter, Theresa (b. 1908, AL). *SR; A1e; A3a.*

CONE, WILLIAM THOMAS. Born Aug. 29, 1873, Headville, Robertson County, Texas. Ht. 5 ft. 11 in., blue-gray eyes, dark hair, fair complexion, married. Special agent, T&P Railroad, Fort Worth, Tarrant County, Texas. SPECIAL RANGER Feb. 12, 1918–Jan. 15, 1919. Special agent, T&P Railroad, Ft. Worth. RAILROAD RANGER Sept. 1, 1922–Sept. 1, 1924. Discharged—WA expired. Special agent, T&P Railroad, Big Spring, Howard County, Texas. SPECIAL RANGER Aug. 6, 1925–Apr. 19, 1928 (reenlisted Apr. 19, 1927, Ft. Worth). Discharged. Special agent, T&P Railroad, Fort Worth. SPECIAL RANGER July 24, 1928–July 24, 1929; Aug. 5, 1929–July 29, 1930; July 29, 1930–Mar. 1, 1931. Discharged when left the T&P Railroad's employ. REMARKS: In 1910 was city marshal, Arlington, Tarrant County. Apr. 19, 1927, enlistment form has Kosse, Robertson County, as birthplace. A William T. Cone died Dec. 17, 1941, Tarrant County, Texas. FAMILY: Parents, John T. Cone (b. 1837, GA) and Mahala (b. 1835, MS); siblings, Charles B. (b. 1870, TX), Norman R. (b. 1872, TX), Mary A. (b. 1877, TX); spouse, Nancy Wilkins (b. 1880, TX), married about 1899; children, Nina (b. 1902, TX), Elizabeth (b. 1903, TX). *SR; AG to Coppage, Feb 9, 1918, AGC; A1b, d, e, f; A2b; A3a; C.*

CONLEY, JOHN THOMAS. Born Feb. 8, 1885, Luling, Caldwell County, Texas. Ht. 5 ft. 8 in., blue eyes, brown hair, fair complexion. Farmer. REGULAR RANGER Dec. 24, 1917–Apr. 1918 (private, Co. I). Resigned. REMARKS: In 1930 was deputy sheriff, Caldwell County. A John T. Conley died Feb. 5, 1949, Caldwell County, Texas. FAMILY: Parents, Nimrod T. Conley (b. 1851, TN) and Sarah A. Springs (b. 1851, IL); siblings, Andrew Jackson (b. 1872, TX), Charles (b. 1875, TX), William Levi (b. 1877, TX), Ernest K. (b. 1880, TX), Alice (b. 1882, TX), Hardy S. (b. 1886, TX), Sam (b. 1889, TX), Sidney F. Alex (b. 1891, TX). *SR; A1b, d, f, g; A3a; A4a, b; C.*

CONNALLY, THOMAS. Born Nov. 1868, Dublin, Ireland. Ht. 5 ft. 6 in., blue eyes, dark hair, florid complexion, widower. Constable, La Vernia, Wilson County, Texas. REGULAR RANGER Dec. 22, 1917–unknown (private, Co. K; was still in Co. K as of Sept. 10, 1918). Discharged or resigned—unknown. REMARKS: Still living in Wilson County in 1920. FAMILY: Children, Charles (b. 1892, TX), Annie (b. 1895, TX), Janie (b. 1898, TX), Leora (b. 1900, TX). *SR; 471; 1000: iii, 69–70; Wright to Harley, Sept 7, 1918, WC; A1e, f.*

CONNER, JOSEPH FRANK "FRANK." Born Jan. 12, 1862, near Lampasas, Lampasas County, Texas. Ht. 5 ft. 11 in., gray eyes, dark hair, dark complexion, married. Brand inspector, Midland, Midland County, Texas. LOYALTY RANGER June 24, 1918–Jan. 11, 1919. REMARKS: In 1910 did "odd jobs" in Dawson County, Texas. Dawson County sheriff, Nov. 8, 1910–Nov. 3, 1914. About Feb. 1919 resigned as brand inspector to become range boss for the C.C. Slaughter Cattle Co. on their ranch in Hockley and Cochran Counties, Texas. In 1920 was living in Slaton, Lubbock County, Texas. A J. F. Conner died July 16, 1925, Swisher County, Texas (another source states he died July 19, 1925, Slaton). FAMILY: Parents, John Fletcher Conner (b. 1827, AR) and Mary Tolbert Tartelott (b. 1828, TN); siblings, Clarissa Ann (b. 1848), Elizabeth A. (b. 1849), Sarah Serena (b. 1851, TX), Rachel Drucilla (b. 1852), Hiram Jasper (b. 1854, TX), Daniel Henry (b. 1856, TX), Silas Marion (b. 1858, TX), John Fletcher (b. 1859, TX), Polly Anita (b. 1863, TX), Mary Caroline (b. 1865, TX), Rebecca Theodoca (b. 1868, TX), Dollie T. (b. 1871, TX), Eliza Emma (b. 1874, TX); spouse, Mary Frances "Mollie" Poe (b. 1872, TX), married Apr. 12, 1888, Fort McKavitt, Menard County, Texas; children, Eula, James Franklin (b. 1890, TX), Pearl L. (b. 1893, TX), Hught Hausfer (b. 1895, TX), William "Will" F. (b. 1896, TX), Robert Slaughter (b. 1898, TX), Joseph Jack (b. 1900, TX), Dollie Belle (b. 1904, TX), Silas D. "Si" (b. 1906, TX), Mary Rita (b. 1908, TX), Thelma Annie (b. 1909, TX). *SR; Slaughter to Harley, Mar 13, 1919, AGC; Harley to Slaughter, Mar 17, 1919, AGC; 1503:149; A1a, b, e, f; A2b; A3a; A4g.*

CONNER, WILLIAM MAXWELL "MAX." Born July 29, 1877, Montgomery County, Texas. Short, slender, blue eyes, light hair. Bookkeeper and deputy sheriff, Eagle Lake, Colorado County, Texas. LOYALTY RANGER June 7, 1918–Feb. 18, 1919. REMARKS: In Feb. 1919 was manager of the Eagle Lake Lumber Co.; still manager of a retail lumber company in Eagle Lake in 1930. A Maxwell Conner died June 9, 1960, Colorado County, Texas. FAMILY: Parents, Henry Conner (b. 1839, MD) and Emily N. (b. 1845, TX); siblings, Mary "Mollie" (b. 1873, TX), Allen (b. 1880, TX), Henry (b. 1882, TX), Alice (b. 1885, TX). *SR; A1d, e, f; A2b; A3a.*

CONNOR, GEORGE WASHINGTON "BUCK." Born Nov. 22, 1880, San Saba, San Saba County, Texas. Ht. 5 ft. 4 ½ in., hazel eyes, gray hair, fair complexion. Stockman, enlisted in El Paso County, Texas. REGULAR RANGER May 1, 1916–May 31, 1916 (private, Co. D). Resigned—honorably discharged. REMARKS: Note length of service. In Sept. 1916 lived in Quincy, California; was a magazine writer. Had served under Gen. Hugh Scott in the Philippines. In Sept. 1918 was a motion picture assistant producer living in Los Angeles, California. FAMILY: Father, W. L. Connor, living in West Virginia in 1918. *SR; Connor to AG, Sept 11, 1916, AGC; AG to Connor, Sept 18, 1916, AGC; EPMT, May 8, June 4, 1916; A3a.*

CONRO, LEVI R. Born Nov. 1854, Clinton County, New York. Ht. 5 ft. 10 ¾ in., blue eyes, gray hair, fair complexion, married. City recorder and tax collector, Goldthwaite, Mills County, Texas. LOYALTY RANGER June 10, 1918–Feb. 19, 1919. REMARKS: Deputy sheriff in the early 1890s. In 1900 was a saloon keeper in Goldthwaite. Was city marshal, Goldthwaite, 1915. In 1930, was city recorder in Goldthwaite. An L. R. Conro died Mar. 15, 1933, Mills County, Texas. FAMILY: Parents, Russel Conro (b. 1820) and Polly (b. 1820, NY); siblings, Marion R. (b. 1846, NY), Amelia A. (b. 1849, NY), George S. (b. 1851, NY), Ella A. (b. 1859, NY); spouse, Sarah J. "Sallie" (b. 1860, TX), married about 1882; children, Leila A. (b. 1884, TX), Lee Roy (b. 1887, TX), Lucille O. (b. 1895, TX). *SR; A1aaa, aa, d, e, g; C.*

COOK, CHARLES. Born Jan. 11, 1874, Clinton, DeWitt County, Texas. Ht. 5 ft. 10 ½ in., blue eyes, dark hair, fair complexion, married. Automobile dealer, Cuero, DeWitt County. LOYALTY RANGER June 5, 1918–Feb. 1919. REMARKS: As of Sept. 1918 was proprietor of Cook and Day Motor Company, Cuero. In 1930 was an agent for the Texas Oil Company, living in Cuero. A Charles Cook died Jan. 1, 1942, DeWitt County, Texas. FAMILY: Parents, Fredreich Cook (b. 1830, Bavaria) and Henrietta (b. 1838, Prussia); siblings, Oliver (b. 1860, TX), Walter (b. 1862, TX), Felix (b. 1865, TX), Henrietta (b. 1868, TX), Jessie (b. 1871, TX), Dora (b. 1877, TX), Fredreich (b. 1880, TX); spouse, Melanie (b. 1879, TX), married about 1898; children, Raymond (b. 1903, TX), Dorothy (b. 1907, TX). *SR; A1b, d, e, f, g; A3a; C.*

COOK, JOHN CLIFFORD "CLIFF." Born July 3, 1893, Lockhart, Caldwell County, Texas. Ht. 5 ft. 11 in., dark eyes, black hair, dark complexion. Ranchman, enlisted in Travis County, Texas. REGULAR RANGER May 27, 1916–Aug. 31, 1916 (private, Co. D). Resigned. REMARKS: Applied for reenlistment in Rangers in May 1917. As of June 1917 worked for his father in Buda, Hays County, Texas. Lived in Dallas County, Texas in the 1920s; in 1930 was a farmer in Bosque County, Texas. A John Cliff Cook died June 19, 1937, McLennan County, Texas. FAMILY: Parents, Levi C. Cook (b. 1850, TX) and Mary J. (b. 1857, KY); siblings, Emma A. (b. 1883, TX), Henrietta L. (b. 1885, TX), Mattie M. (b. 1888, TX), Ellan A. (b. 1892, TX), Ruth (b. 1896, TX); spouse, Mabyn Rosetta Morrison (b. 1889, TX), married about 1922; children, Mabyn R. (b. 1922, TX), John C., Jr. (b. 1924, TX), Moffett C. (b. 1925, TX), Lince Connell (b. 1927, TX), Vara La Rue (b. 1928, TX). *SR; 471; Cook to Hutchings, May 24, 1917, AGC; A1d, e, g; A2b, e; A3a.*

COOK, LOUIS JACKSON. Born Nov. 10, 1867, Homer, Claiborne Parish, Louisiana. Ht. 5 ft. 7 in., gray eyes, dark hair, light complexion. Garageman, Baird, Callahan County, Texas. SPECIAL RANGER June 1, 1917–Dec. 1917 (attached to Co. C). REMARKS: In 1930 was a grocery merchant in Putnam, Callahan County. Died July 13, 1939, Falls County, Texas. FAMILY: Parents, John Thomas Cook (b. 1846, MS) and Susan Lou Jackson (b. 1848, LA); siblings, James Columbus (b. 1869, LA), William Raleigh (b. 1872, TX), Milton Henry (b. 1875), Ira Eugene (b. 1877, TX), John Taylor (b. 1882, TX), Mattie Susie (b. 1884, TX), Ezra (b. 1886, TX), Fred Hood (b. 1888, TX), John Hiram. *SR; A1a, b, d, f, g; A2b; A4a, b.*

COOPER, HUBERT NEWTON. (Listed as HERBERT NEWTON in Ranger Service Records.) Born Sept. 6, 1891, Galveston, Galveston County, Texas. Ht. 5 ft. 9 in., blue eyes, light hair, light complexion. Newspaperman, Abilene, Taylor County, Texas. SPECIAL RANGER June 11, 1917–Dec. 17, 1917. Honorably discharged. REMARKS: Had lived in Waco, McLennan County, Texas. In June 1917 was employed by the Abilene Printing Company. In 1920 was a reporter for a publishing company living in Ranger, Eastland County, Texas; in 1930 was a newspaper journalist living in Austin, Travis County, Texas. Died May 1, 1973, Bell County, Texas. FAMILY: Parents, Oscar Henry Cooper, a graduate of Yale College who taught in Texas colleges and was one-time president of Baylor University, Waco (b. 1852, TX) and Mary Bryan Stewart (b. 1867, LA); siblings, Oscar H., Jr. (b. 1887, TX), Jackson Stewart (b. 1889, TX), Mary S. (b. 1901). *SR; Register to Ferguson, May 18, 1917, AGC; Cunningham to Ferguson, May 18, 1917, AGC; Cooper to AG, Nov 14, 1917, AGC; A1d, e, f, g; A2a, b; A3a; A4a, b.*

COOPER, JOHN A. Born Aug. 1871, Mount Pleasant, Titus County, Texas. Ht. 6 ft., blue eyes, brown hair, red complexion, married. Salesman, Mount Pleasant. LOYALTY RANGER June 17, 1918–Feb. 1919. REMARKS: Constable, deputy sheriff, Titus County, 4 years. Titus County sheriff, Nov. 8, 1910–Nov. 7, 1916. In 1920 was a real estate agent in Mount Pleasant. A John A. Cooper died Oct. 11, 1926, Lamar County, Texas. FAMILY: Parents, William Cooper (b. 1826, NC) and Ann Kendrick Flippen (b. 1833, TN); siblings, Mary (b. 1853, TX), William A. (b. 1856, TX), Roda (b. 1857, TX); spouse #1, probably Annie Ray, married about 1890; daughter, Jessie (b. 1896, TX); spouse #2, Emma (b. 1880, TX), married about 1901; children, Lorna or Lorene (b. 1902, TX), Annie (b. 1905, TX), Edward or Edmond (b. 1908, TX), Lester (b. 1909, TX), stepson, Charlie Whitten (b. 1897, GA); spouse #3, Minnie Gray (b. 1889, AR); daughter, Aline (b. 1916, TX); spouse #4, Paige Randall (b. 1895, TX), married about 1922, she was widowed by 1930; daughters John Alice (b. 1922, TX), Mary (b. 1925, TX). *SR; Johnson to Harley, Aug 30, 1918, AGC; 1503:491; A1e, f.*

COOPER, JOHN MILOS. Born Jan. 20, 1879, Karnes County, Texas. Ht. 5 ft. 11 in., gray eyes, black hair, fair complexion, married. Ranchman. REGULAR RANGER Aug. 30, 1918–Nov. 1, 1918 (private, Co. F). Discharged. REMARKS: In Sept. 1918 was a Ranger in Mercedes, Hidalgo County, Texas. Had been a dairyman in Bexar County, Texas. In 1920 was proprietor of a restaurant in San Antonio, Bexar County. A John M. Cooper died Oct. 15, 1923, Bexar County, Texas. FAMILY: Parents, George W. Cooper (b. 1842, MS) and Elizabeth Ricks (b. 1848, MS); siblings, Louis (b. 1866, TX), Martha J. (b. 1867, TX), Robert D. (b. 1869, TX), Thomas E. (b. 1872, TX), Emily (b. 1874, TX), Katy Ruth (b. 1876, TX), James A. (b. 1878, TX), George (b. 1882, TX), Sylvester (b. 1884, TX), Abbie (b. 1887, TX), Benjamin (b. 1889, TX), Bessie (b. 1891, TX); spouse, Bertha "Birdie" (b. 1884, TX), married about 1901, she was widowed by 1930; daughters, Georgie E. (b. 1903, TX), Lola Mae (b. 1907, TX). *SR; A1b, d, e, f, g; A2b; A3a; A4b.*

CORDER, BENJAMIN THEODOR "THEODOR." Born Feb. 9, 1884, Junction, Kimble County, Texas. Ht. 6 ft. 3 in., blue eyes, brown hair, light complexion, married. Ranchman, enlisted in Presidio County, Texas. SPECIAL RANGER Dec. 14, 1917–Jan. 15, 1919. REMARKS: In 1910 was the "cattle foreman" for the Big Canyon Ranch in Terrell County, Texas. As of Sept. 1918 was a ranchman in Sanderson, Terrell County. In 1930 was a rancher, living in El Paso, El Paso County, Texas. LAW ENFORCEMENT RELATIVES: Kimble County sheriff (Nov. 4, 1890–Nov. 3, 1896) Noah H. Corder, father. FAMILY: Parents, Noah Hubbard Corder (b. 1855, TX) and Mary Caroline Schrier (b. 1855, TX); siblings, Josephine "Josey" (b. 1880, TX), J. Eugene (b. 1882, TX), Mary Elizabeth "Mollie" (b. 1887, TX), John Montgomery (b. 1888, TX), Herbert Thomas (b. 1891, TX), Richard Emmett (b. 1895, TX), Winnie; spouse, Emma (b. 1888, TX), married about 1911; children, Daisey L. (b. 1915, TX), Benjamin T., Jr. (b. 1917, TX). *SR; 1503:307; A1d, e, f, g; A3a; A4a, b, g.*

CORN, GEORGE HOUSTON. Born Dec. 3, 1872, Paris, Lamar County, Texas. Ht. 5 ft. 8 in., gray eyes, dark hair, light complexion, married. Drayman, Baird, Callahan County, Texas. SPECIAL RANGER May 30, 1917–Dec. 1917 (attached to Co. C). REMARKS: Callahan County sheriff, Nov. 5, 1918–Jan. 1, 1923. Was also a justice of the peace for some time. In 1930 was a county road worker in Callahan County. Died Dec. 10, 1961, Baird, Callahan County, Texas. FAMILY: Parents, Sam Houston Corn (b. 1845, TX) and Caroline A. Dewitt (b. 1848, OH); siblings, William Dewitt (b. 1867, TX), Martha A. (b. 1869, TX), Mary (b. 1874, TX), Charles (b. 1878, TX); spouse, Emma A. Bradley (b. 1882, AL), married Feb. 4, 1897, Lamar County, Texas; children, Annie May (b. 1898, TX), Irvin D. (b. 1905, TX), Opal C. (b. 1908, TX), Raymond Carl (b. 1911, TX), Jerry H. (b. 1914, TX), Lowell Cleo (b. 1916, TX), Benjamin F. (b. 1918, TX), Weldon Burnett (b. 1921, TX). *SR; Corn to Harley, Feb 22, 1919, AGC; 1503:84; A1b, d, f, g; A2b, e; A3a; A4a, b, g.*

CORNETT, RUFUS MARCELLUS. Born Jan. 27, 1879, Young County, Texas. Medium height, medium build, gray eyes, brown hair, married. Real estate agent, Groom, Carson County, Texas. LOYALTY RANGER July 8, 1918–Feb. 1919. REMARKS: In 1920 was a bookkeeper for an oil company in Amarillo, Potter County, Texas. A Rufus M. Cornett died Apr. 11, 1948, Matagorda County, Texas. FAMILY: Parents, William Lafayette Cornett (b. 1846, KY) and Mary M. Davis (b. 1850, MO); siblings, Maud (b. 1882, TX), William Augustas (b. 1883, TX), Ophelia (b. 1885, TX), Jefferson Alva (b. 1887, TX), Arnolia "Nola" (b. 1890, TX); spouse, Effie (b. 1887, TX), married about 1907. *SR; 471; A1b, d, e, f; A2b; A3a; A4g.*

COTTON, DAVID N. Born June 1870, Brooksville, Coosa County, Alabama. Ht. 5 ft. 10 in., blue eyes, black hair, dark complexion, married. Watchman, I&GN Railroad, Mart, McLennan County, Texas. SPECIAL RANGER Oct. 14, 1916–Jan. 1918 (was reinstated—WA renewed Dec. 27, 1917). REMARKS: As a young teen he and two brothers had been "servants" in a household in Coosa County. In 1910 was a house carpenter in McLennan County. Died Jan. 26, 1918, McLennan County, Texas. FAMILY: Parents, according to one source, Merrill Jasper Cotton (b. 1831, GA) and Cordelia Savannah Thompson (b. 1834, GA); siblings, Mary E. (b. 1852, AL), Lennard (b. 1856, AL), Cordelia (b. 1861, AL), Osa (b. 1870, AL), Author (b. 1872, AL), Merrill (b. 1873, AL); spouse, Mollie (b. 1871, TX), married about 1888; children, Lula A. (b. 1890, TX), J. P. Davis (b. 1893, TX), J. D. (b. 1901, TX), Vera (b. 1903, TX). *SR; 471; Jones to Hutchings, Oct 7, 1916, AGC; AG to Jones, Oct 9, 1916, AGC; A1aa, a, b, e; A4a, b.*

COTULLA, SIMON. Born Oct. 9, 1878, Atascosa County, Texas. Medium height, medium build, brown eyes, brown hair, married. Butcher, Cotulla, La Salle County, Texas. LOYALTY RANGER June 5, 1918–Feb. 19, 1919. REMARKS: Died Nov. 25, 1962, Cotulla, La Salle County, Texas; buried in Old Cotulla Cemetery. FAMILY: Parents, Joseph Cotulla or Kotulla (b. 1846, Poland) and Mary Rieder (b. 1854, TX); siblings, Carolina (b. 1873, TX), Edward (b. 1875, TX), Luisa (b. 1877, TX), Mary (b. 1881, TX), Joseph (b. 1884, TX), William (b. 1885, TX), Emma (b. 1888, TX), John Henry (b. 1890, TX); spouse #1, Mattie Alice Taylor, married Nov. 6, 1904; children, Earnest Roy (b. 1905, TX), William Paul (b. 1907, TX); spouse #2, Lillian Taylor (b. 1882, TX), married after 1926. *SR; Cardwell to Strawn, July 11, 1918, AGC; A1b, d, e, f, g; A2a, b; A3a; A4b; B1.*

COUSINS, FLOYD ALLAN. Born May 24, 1884, Burkeville, Newton County, Texas. Ht. 6 ft., brown eyes, black hair, dark complexion, married. Druggist, Bronson, Sabine County, Texas. LOYALTY RANGER July 9, 1918–Feb. 1919. REMARKS: As a teenager was a farm laborer on the family farm in San Augustine County, Texas. In 1920 was a drug salesman in Fort Worth, Tarrant County, Texas; in 1930, lived in Dallas, Dallas County, Texas. FAMILY: Parents, James Clark Cousins (b. 1855, TX) and Susan Serena "Renie" Woods (b. 1856, TX); siblings, Eva Mellie (b. 1881, TX), Beulah (b. 1883, TX), C. Dochia (b. 1885, TX), Ava (b. 1888, TX), Elvin (b. 1890, TX), Ollie S. (b. 1892, TX), Lillie; spouse, Lena Erskine (b. 1889, TX), married about 1915; sons, Floyd Erskine (b. 1917, TX), Don E. (b. 1919, TX). *SR; A1b, d, f, g; A3a; A4a, b.*

COVEY, JOHN EDGAR. Born Jan. 1866, Cass County, Texas. Ht. 5 ft. 9 in., blue eyes, light hair, fair complexion, married. Hardware merchant, Bryan, Brazos County, Texas. LOYALTY RANGER June 8, 1918–Feb. 1919. REMARKS: Was connected with the Cole Hardware Co. in Bryan. FAMILY: Parents, John W. Covey (b. 1839, GA or AL) and Mary A. "Mollie" Wilks (b. 1842, GA); sisters, Eula Jackson (b. 1864, TX), Minnie (b. 1866, MO); stepfather as of 1880 census, Mason D. Cole (b. 1831, AL); half-siblings, Houston William Cole (b. 1874, TX), Jeff Cole (b. 1876, TX), Merna Cole (b. 1878, TX), Hattie Cole (b. 1879, TX); spouse, Edna (maiden name probably Christian) (b. 1883, TX), married about 1903; children, John Oliver, Edgar Cole (b. 1904, TX), Albert Bryan (b. 1918, TX). *SR; A1aa, b, e, f, g; A4a, b.*

COWDEN, JAX M. "MOE." Born Aug. 21, 1883, Palo Pinto, Palo Pinto County, Texas. Ht. 6 ft. ¼ in., brown eyes, brown hair, dark complexion, married. Cowman, Midland, Midland County, Texas. LOYALTY RANGER June 14, 1918–Feb. 19, 1919. REMARKS: In 1918–1919 was manager, Guaranty Cattle Loan Company, Midland, of which W. H. Cowden was vice president. In 1930 was a cattle rancher in San Angelo, Tom Green County, Texas. Death date unknown (probably Mar. 6, 1959, Bexar County, Texas); buried in Tom Green County. FAMILY: Parents, William Henry Cowden (b. 1853, LA or TX) and Mary "Mamie" Salvage (b. 1861, GA); siblings, Hallie (b. 1881, TX), Ertha Lee (b. 1881), Bernice C. (b. 1885, TX), Raymond Francis (b. 1887, TX), Henry Brunson (b. 1888, TX), Ruth (b. 1891), Gilbert Hamby (b. 1891, TX), William Hart (b. 1893, TX), Benjamin Liddon (b. 1895, TX), Jerry Eugene (b. 1897, TX), George E. (b. 1899, TX), Mary Francis (b. 1901, TX); spouse, Josephine Leach (b. 1887, NC), married about 1908; children, Susan (b. 1909, TN), Jax M., Jr. (b. 1913, TX), Dorothy (b. 1915, TX), Hallie Jean (b. 1916, TX). *SR; AG to Cowden, July 29, 1918, AGC; A1d, f, g; A2b; A3a; A4a, b, g.*

COX, BENJAMIN LAFAYETTE "BEN." Born Jan. 28, 1877, Canton, Van Zandt County, Texas. Ht. 5 ft. 11 in., blue eyes, brown hair, fair complexion, married. Lawyer, Abilene, Taylor County, Texas. SPECIAL RANGER June 15, 1917–Dec. 1917 (attached to Co. C). REMARKS: Had been a schoolteacher in Canton. Was a general practice attorney in Abilene in 1930. FAMILY: Parents, Tilman L. Cox (b. 1834, AL) and Nancy A. (b. 1838, AL); siblings, Theo B. (b. 1856, TX), Sarah (b. 1858, TX), Martha (b. 1861, TX), Matilda J. (b. 1864, TX), Louisa (b. 1867, TX), Marion L. (b. 1870, TX), Mary A. (b. 1872, TX), Cathren (b. 1875, TX); spouse, Nellie Hord (b. 1889, TX), married about 1912; daughters, Elizabeth (b. 1916, TX), Nancy Nell (b. 1921, TX). *SR; Register to Ferguson, May 18, 1917, AGC; Cunningham to Ferguson, May 18, 1917, AGC; A1a, b, d, f, g.*

COX, DEE W. Born Aug. 16, 1887, Carlsbad, Eddy County, New Mexico. Ht. 5 ft. 9 ½ in., dark eyes, black hair, dark complexion, married. Cattleman, enlisted in Amarillo, Potter County, Texas. REGULAR RANGER Sept. 1, 1909–Sept. 15, 1911 (private, Co. B). Resigned. Peace officer, enlisted at Austin, Travis County, Texas. REGULAR RANGER Dec. 22, 1917–Feb. 15, 1921 (private, Co. M; transferred to Co. D or Co. B?, June 1, 1918; transferred to Co. A; reenlisted under the new law, June 20, 1919). Discharged. Peace officer, Fort Worth, Tarrant County, Texas. RAILROAD RANGER Feb. 7, 1923–Mar. 24, 1923. Discharged. REMARKS: 1909 enlistment form and WWI Draft Registration form both give birthplace as Cloudcroft, Otero County, New Mexico; 1917 enlistment form gives Carlsbad. Before enlisting in the Rangers had been a peace officer in Grimes County, Texas. In 1920 was a Ranger living in Presidio County, Texas. In 1930 was a special police officer for a railroad company living in Clovis, Curry County, New Mexico. Died Sept. 10, 1960, Gallup, McKinley County, New Mexico; buried in Sunset Gardens, Gallup. FAMILY: Parents, Jesse Cox (1850, LA) and Mary Rose "Rosie" Orr (b. 1870, TX); siblings, Maude (b. 1889, TX), Ola (b. 1891, TX), Iva (b. 1894, IN), Roy (b. 1896, TX); spouse, Charlene Chinniccie "Charley" George (b. 1889, TX), married June 17 or Aug. 19, 1911, Nolan County, Texas; son, Malcolm (b. 1912, TX). *SR; 471; Mills to AG, Jan 18, 1919, AGC; Cox to Hutchings, July 2, 4, 1911, AGC; AG to Cox, July 3, 1911, AGC; Assistant AG to Cox, Apr 1, 1918, AGC; Cox to Cunningham, May 15, 1918, AGC; Claiborne to Harley, June 1, 1918, AGC; A1d, f, g; A3a; A4g; B1.*

COX, UMPHREY BATES "BATES." Born Oct. 5, 1876, Hamilton County, Illinois. Tall, medium build, blue eyes, light hair, married. Adjusting agent, Thurber, Erath County, Texas. LOYALTY RANGER, June 15, 1918–Feb. 1919. REMARKS: Had been a farmer in Erath County. Erath County sheriff, Nov. 6, 1906–Nov. 8, 1910. In 1920 was a field man for T&P Coal Co. in Erath County; in 1930 was a coal and oil claim agent in Erath County. Died Dec. 4, 1950, Erath County, Texas. FAMILY: Parents, Vanburen Cox (b. 1838, TN) and Minerva (b. 1844, TN); siblings, Marita (b. 1871, TN), William (b. 1874, TN), Nancy A. (b. 1875, IL), Sarah B. (b. 1876, IL), James (b. 1878, IL); spouse, Julia A (b. 1876, TX), married about 1895; daughters, Juanita B. (b. 1895, TX), Elsie (b. 1901, TX). *SR; Peacock to Colquitt, Mar 23, 1914, AGC; 1503:176; A1b, d, e, f, g; A2b; A3a.*

COX, WILLIAM WALKER "WALKER." Born Aug. 4, 1882, Burleson County, Texas. Tall, stout, gray eyes, black hair, married. Farmer, Rosebud, Milam County, Texas. LOYALTY RANGER June 7, 1918–Feb. 1919. REMARKS: Died Oct. 16, 1954 of a self-inflicted gunshot wound, Milam County, Texas. FAMILY: Parents, David Oridary Cox (b. 1852, TX) and Susan Matilda "Mattie" Perry (b. 1862, TX); siblings, Iona C. (b. 1878, TX), Leona K. (b. 1879, TX), Charles M. (b. 1887, TX), Jessie H. (b. 1888, TX), Lillie L. (b. 1890, TX), Essie B. (b. 1892, TX), Robert P. (b. 1894, TX), Austin B. (b. 1895, TX), Mattie L. (b. 1897, TX), Lola (b. 1899, TX), Pauline (b. 1902, TX); spouse, Eva Wingo (b. 1888, TX), married about 1907; children, Janelle (b. 1909, TX), Allan (b. 1911, TX), Loraine (b. 1913, TX), Clifton (b. 1919, TX). *SR; A1d, e, f, g; A2b; A3a; A4b.*

CRAFT, WILLIAM BENTFORD. Born June 22, 1885, Farmer, Archer County, Texas. Ht. 5 ft. 11 in., gray eyes, black hair, dark complexion, married. Cattleman, Jacksboro, Jack County, Texas. LOYALTY RANGER July 22, 1918–Feb. 19, 1919. REMARKS: Died July 13, 1964, Jack County, Texas. FAMILY: Spouse #1, Eula May (b. 1885, TX), married about 1907; children, Clint V. (b. 1908, TX), Elsie May (b. 1909, TX), J. D. (b. 1912, TX), William B. (b. 1917, TX), Greta Louise (b. 1919, TX), Elizabeth P. (b. 1921, TX); spouse #2, Mabel (b. 1898, TX), married about 1927; stepson, Bert Nelms (b. 1918, TX). *SR; A1e, f, g; A2a, b; A3a.*

CRAGG, HOWARD TILLMAN. Born Jan. 20, 1892, Carrizo Springs, Dimmit County, Texas. Ht. 6 ft. 1 ½ in., brown eyes, black hair, dark complexion. Cowboy. REGULAR RANGER June 12, 1916–Jan. 15, 1919 (private, Co. A). Resigned. REMARKS: As of June 1917 was a Ranger in Raymondville, Cameron County, Texas. Was a cowman in Dimmit County in 1920. Died Mar. 26, 1942, Harlingen, Cameron County, Texas. LAW ENFORCEMENT RELATIVES: Ranger Peter F. Tumlinson, grandfather; Ranger Peter F. "Captain" Tumlinson, great-grandfather; Rangers Lott Tumlinson (Co. A, 1903–1904), Peter C. Tumlinson, Benjamin Thomas Tumlinson, Jr., distant cousins; Rangers John Jackson "Captain" Tumlinson, William Riley "Buck" Taylor, William Walter Taylor, Joseph A. Taylor, William Alonzo Taylor, Elmer Josiah Taylor, Thomas Creed Taylor, Captain William L. Wright, Charles Hays Wright, Emanuel Avant Wright, Milam H. Wright, distant relatives; Sheriff (Dimmit County, Nov. 2, 1880–Nov. 4, 1890), and La Salle County, Texas, (Nov. 8, 1892–Jan. 1893) Joseph Tumlinson, great-uncle. FAMILY: Parents, Richard Cragg (b. 1860, TX) and Mary Ann Tumlinson (b. 1865, TX); siblings, James Edward (b. 1882, TX), Sarah Ann (b. 1885, TX), Myrtle Martha (b. 1887, TX), William Peter (b. 1889, TX), Joseph Aaron (b. 1894, TX), Thomas Richard (b. 1896, TX), Leonard Eastwood (b. 1900, TX), Cordelia (b. 1902, TX), Charles Elmo (b. 1906, TX), Jesse Bertran (b. 1907, TX); spouse #1, Mozelle (Norrelle?) Smith (b. 1894), married about 1931; daughter, Ada Marjean (b. 1935, TX); spouse #2, Ruth Mix (b. 1896), married about 1939, New York, New York. *SR; 1503:160, 321; A1d, f; A2b, e; A3a; A4a, b.*

CRAIG, WALTER AWALT. Born Sept. 10, 1884, Burton, Washington County, Texas. Ht. 5 ft. 9 ¾ in., brown eyes, brown hair, fair complexion, married. Stockman, Hockley, Webb County, Texas. SPECIAL RANGER May 31, 1918–Jan. 14, 1919. REMARKS: Had lived in Williamson County, Texas and Hardin County, Texas. In 1920 was a stockman living in Laredo, Webb County, Texas. Letterhead: "W.A. Craig, General Dealer in Livestock, Laredo." A Walter A. Walt Craig died June 25, 1922, Harris County, Texas. FAMILY: Parents, Jasper G. Craig (b. 1855, TX) and Johanna (b. 1855, TX); sister, Willie (b. 1883, TX); spouse, Maria Sanchez (b. 1897, TX). *SR; A1d, f, g; A3a; A6a; C.*

CRAIGHEAD, CHARLES ARCHER "CHARLIE." Born Aug. 26, 1879, near Sutherland Springs, Wilson County, Texas. Ht. 5 ft. 9 in., blue eyes, black hair, dark complexion. Brand inspector, Panhandle Cattle Raisers' Association for 4 years. REGULAR RANGER June 1908–Mar. 20, 1911 (private, Co. D, which became Co. A on Feb. 1, 1911). Resigned. Cowboy for the Elsinore Cattle Co., Fort Stockton, Pecos County, Texas. SPECIAL RANGER Jan. 7, 1918–May 21, 1919. Resigned to become a constable at Marfa, Presidio County, Texas. REMARKS: From 1911–1913 was a Marfa policeman. June 1913 resigned to become a deputy U.S. marshal for the Western District of Texas. Jan. 1914 resigned to become a mounted Customs inspector in the Big Bend. By Nov. 1917 was a cowpuncher for the Elsinore Cattle Co. In 1919 was Marfa constable. Spent 18 years as brand inspector for Cattle Raisers' Association of Texas, mainly around Hebbronville, Jim Hogg County, Texas. Died Nov. 19, 1951, Kleberg County, Texas; buried in Hebbronville. LAW ENFORCEMENT RELATIVES: Ranger and Jim Hogg County sheriff (May 12, 1916–Aug. 18, 1921) J. P. N. "Pat" Craighead, brother; Wilson County sheriff (Nov. 6, 1894–Nov. 8, 1898) John S. Craighead, father. FAMILY: Parents, John Sutherland Craighead (b. 1847, TN) and Mary Isabella McAlister (b. 1846, MS); siblings, Sarah Agnes (b. 1871, TX), John Alexander (b. 1873, TX), James Patterson Nelson (b. 1875, TX), William C. (b. 1878, TX), Robert M. (b. 1883, TX), Mary Isabell (b. 1885, TX); spouse, Brent Nichols, married Nov. 1911, Marfa. *SR; 471; BDH, Oct 3, 20, 21, Nov 5, 1910; AG to Hughes, Oct 3, 1910, WC; Bailey to Newton, Oct 31, 1910, AGC; Hughes to Newton, Nov 4, 1910, WC; SAE, Mar 27, 1911; EPMT, Apr 19, Nov 21, 1911, Mar 16, 1912, Feb 3, 1913, Jan 22, 1914; AA, June 5, 1913, Nov 22, 1917; Barker to AG, Dec 10, 1917, AGC; AG to Barker, Dec 17, 1917, AGC; Metcalfe to Harley, June 16, 1919, AGC; 1000: 116, 121–122; 470: 79; 1503:288, 546; A1b, d, g; A2b; A3a; A4a, b.*

CRAIGHEAD, JAMES PATTERSON NELSON "PAT." Born Feb. 3, 1875, Sutherland Springs, Wilson County, Texas. Ht. 5 ft. 9 in., brown eyes, black hair, dark complexion. Deputy sheriff. REGULAR RANGER Mar. 1, 1910–May 12, 1916 (private, Co. A; transferred to Co. D, Oct. 1, 1910; returned to Co. A, Feb. 1911). Resigned. REMARKS: July 31, 1910 lost a leg in the San Benito ambush. Was Jim Hogg County, Texas, sheriff May 12, 1916–Aug. 18, 1921. Died Aug. 18, 1921, Hebbronville, Jim Hogg County, Texas (Texas Death Index records his place of death as Bexar County, Texas). LAW ENFORCEMENT RELATIVES: Ranger Charles A. Craighead, brother; Wilson County sheriff (Nov. 6, 1894–Nov. 8, 1898) John S. Craighead, father. FAMILY: Parents, John Sutherland Craighead (b. 1847, TN) and Mary Isabella McAlister (b. 1846, MS); siblings, Sarah Agnes (b. 1871, TX), John Alexander (b. 1873, TX), William C. (b. 1878, TX), Charles A. (b. 1879, TX), Robert M. (b. 1883, TX), Mary Isabell (b. 1885, TX); spouse (?), Mary Brooks, married Oct. 26, 1902. *SR; 471; 470: 76, 79; 1000: 48–49; 4214: 207; BDH, Sept 7, 1910; MR, Co. D, Oct–Dec 1910, AGC; Statement of Drs. Wooten and Steiner, Feb 22, 1911, AGC; SAE, Feb 21, 1913, May 15, 1916; Thompson to Hutchings, Feb 24, 1916, AGC; Craighead to Hutchings, Dec 25, 1916, AGC; 1503:288, 546; 470:79; A1b, d, e, f; A2b; A3a; A4a, b.*

CRAVEY, FLETCHER. Born May 23, 1874, Comal, Comal County, Texas. Ht. 5 ft. 11 in., brown eyes, gray hair, dark complexion, widower. Special Agent, I&GN Railroad, Laredo, Webb County, Texas. SPECIAL RANGER May 18, 1918–Jan. 15, 1919. Special Agent, I&GN Railroad, Laredo. RAILROAD RANGER Aug. 22, 1922–Aug. 22, 1924 (Co. A). Discharged. Special agent, I&GN Railroad, Laredo. SPECIAL RANGER June 30, 1925–Oct. 21, 1926. Discharged. REMARKS: Had been a farmer in Bandera County, Texas; was a ranchman. In 1930 was a farm foreman in Edwards County, Texas. Died Sept. 9, 1945, Caldwell County, Texas; buried in Pipe Creek Cemetery, Bandera County. LAW ENFORCEMENT RELATIVES: Ranger James Cravey, brother. FAMILY: Parents, Charles Henry Cravey (b. 1825, GA) and Mary Eleanor Holland (b. 1835, MS); siblings, Charles H. (b. 1850, TX), Mary Elizabeth (b. 1852, TX), Alexander (b. 1854, TX), John "Jack" (b. 1855, TX), Benjamin Franklin (b. 1857, TX), Henry (b. 1858, TX), Mont "Doc" (b. 1859, TX), Martha (b. 1863, TX), Melvina (b. 1868, TX), Florida (b. 1870, TX), James (b. 1872, TX), Nellie Elnora (b. 1877, TX); spouse, Eva Lena (or Avalina) Stevens (b. 1877, TX), married Nov. 20, 1894; children, Myrtle (b. 1895, TX), Viola Ray (b. 1897, TX), Maude Margaret (b. 1897, TX), Douglas Gus (b. 1900, TX), Louis Fletcher (b. 1902, TX), Katherine L. (b. 1904, TX), Mable (b. 1906, TX). *SR; A1b, d, g; A2b; A3a; A4a, b, g; B2.*

CRAVEY, JAMES. Born Mar. 8, 1872, Anhalt, Comal County, Texas. Ht. 5 ft. 8 in., blue eyes, brown hair, fair complexion, married. Watchman, I&GN Railroad, enlisted in Williamson County, Texas. SPECIAL RANGER May 17, 1918–June 10, 1918. REMARKS: Had been a farmer in Kerr County, Texas and Bandera County, Texas. Was killed June 10, 1918, Taylor, Williamson County, Texas; buried in Bandera Cemetery. LAW ENFORCEMENT RELATIVES: Ranger Fletcher Cravey, brother. FAMILY: Parents, Charles Henry Cravey (b. 1825, GA) and Mary Eleanor Holland (b. 1835, MS); siblings, Charles H. (b. 1850, TX), Mary Elizabeth (b. 1852, TX), Alexander (b. 1854, TX), John "Jack" (b. 1855, TX), Benjamin Franklin (b. 1857, TX), Henry (b. 1858, TX), Mont "Doc" (b. 1859, TX), Martha (b. 1863, TX), Melvina (b. 1868, TX), Florida (b. 1870, TX), Fletcher (b. 1874, TX), Nellie Elnora (b. 1877, TX); spouse, May Belle Stevens (b. 1881, TX), married Feb. 10, 1897; children, Richard G. (b. 1898, TX), Lester J. (b. 1901, TX), Raymond I. (b. 1904, TX), Gladys M. (b. 1906, TX), Lura Belle (b. 1913, TX). *SR; A1b, d, e, f; A2b; A4a, b, g; B2.*

CRAWFORD, CHARLES M. Born May 1891, Crandall, Kaufman County, Texas. Ht. 5 ft. 10 in., blue eyes, brown hair, fair complexion. Clerk, Austin, Travis County, Texas. SPECIAL RANGER Jan. 19, 1921–Sept. 5, 1924 (attached to Co. A). Discharged—WA expired. Texas Quartermaster General, Austin. SPECIAL RANGER Sept. 23, 1927–Sept. 23, 1928. Discharged. *SR; A1f.*

CRAWFORD, WALTER JOSHUA. Born Feb. 25, 1873, Mount Vernon, Franklin County, Texas. Med. height, med. build, gray eyes, light hair, married. Lawyer, enlisted in Jefferson County, Texas. SPECIAL RANGER Jan. 27, 1919–Dec. 31, 1919. REMARKS: Was a partner in the law firm of Smith & Crawford, Beaumont, Jefferson County. Was campaign manager for Governor William P. Hobby. Died Feb. 19, 1924, Jefferson County; buried in Magnolia Cemetery, Beaumont. FAMILY: Parents, Joshua Crawford (b. 1841, GA) and Louisiana E. (b. 1845, LA); siblings, Ida "Texas" (b. 1866, TX), Maggie (b. 1867, TX), Eddie (b. 1871, TX), Daisy (b. 1876, TX), Lillie (b. 1878, TX); spouse, Cora Estelle Shults (b. 1875, TX), married about 1902; children, Alexine (b. 1909, TX), Walter J., Jr. (b. 1914, TX). *SR; 172:II, 396; BDH, Jan 12, 1918; Johnston to Crawford, Jan 13, 27, 1919, AGC; A1a, b, d, e, f, g; A2b; A3a; A4b.*

CREAGER, WILLIAM MADISON. (Listed in Ranger Service Records as W. M. CRAGER.) Born Feb. 1, 1869, Collin County, Texas. Gray eyes, light hair, light complexion, married. Merchant, Lorenzo, Crosby County, Texas. LOYALTY RANGER June 3, 1918–Feb. 1919. REMARKS: In 1920 was secretary for a sheet-metal company in Dallas, Dallas County, Texas. Died Nov. 20, 1922, Wichita County, Texas; buried in Eastview Memorial Cemetery, Vernon, Wilbarger County, Texas. FAMILY: Parents, James Ashley Creager (b. 1841, TX) and Janetta Anne Cave (b. 1847, KY); siblings, Alice (b. 1868, TX), James H. (b. 1871, TX), Daniel Taylor (b. 1872, TX), Joseph Scott Baker (b. 1874, TX), A. R. (b. 1878, TX), George Ross (b. 1880, TX), Janetta Jane "Nettie" (b. 1882, TX), Mary Nina (b. 1886, TX), Logan Harry (b. 1887, TX), Epsie Lee (b. 1891, TX); spouse, Mattie K. Dooley (b. 1870, MO), married Mar. 28, 1891. *SR; A1b, d, e; A2b; A3a; A4b; B2.*

CRITTENDEN, FRANK COLLINS. Born Feb. 22, 1885, Polk County, Tennessee. Ht. 6 ft., blue eyes, light hair, fair complexion, married. Stockman, Liberty Hill, Williamson County, Texas. REGULAR RANGER June 4, 1918–Apr. 19, 1919 (private, Co. D). Resigned at Marfa, Presidio County, Texas because of illness in his family. REMARKS: Had been a Williamson County deputy sheriff. In July 1919 applied from Van Horn, Culberson County, for reinstatement in the Rangers. In 1920 was a stock buyer, living in Bertram, Burnet County, Texas. Was Burnet County sheriff Nov. 2, 1920–Jan. 1, 1923. In 1930 was deputy sheriff, living in Huntsville, Walker County, Texas. FAMILY: Mother, Mary (b. 1853, TN); spouse #1, Gertrude (b. 1883, AR), married about 1909; children, Mildred (b. 1914, TX), Frank (b. 1917, TX), Lillian (b. 1920, TX); spouse #2, Ethel (b. 1891, TX); stepdaughter, Thelma Jardin (b. 1912, TX). *SR; 471; Assistant AG to Crittenden, May 28, 1918, AGC; Crittenden to Harley, July 2, 1919, AGC; Aldrich to Crittenden, July 16, 1919, AGC; Crittenden to Aldrich, July 14, 1919, AGC; 1503:76; A1d, e, f; A3a.*

CRITTENDEN, WILLIAM ROBERT. Born Mar. 1, 1860, Notasulga, Macon County, Alabama. Ht. 6 ft. 1 in., blue eyes, brown hair, dark complexion, married. Farmer, Forney, Kaufman County, Texas. LOYALTY RANGER July 5, 1918–Feb. 1919. REMARKS: By 1880 lived in Smith County, Texas. In 1920 was living with a son and grandchildren in Forney; both men were widowers. Died Oct. 31, 1920, Smith County, Texas. FAMILY: Parents, William D. Crittenden (b. 1836, GA) and Mary J. E. "Bettie" (b. 1839, GA); siblings, Anna R. (b. 1862, AL), John R. (b. 1865, AL); spouse, Mary Susan Harvey (b. 1862, GA), married about 1881; children, John Harvey (b. 1882, TX), Gordon McCorkle (b. 1886, TX), Christopher Columbus (b. 1891, TX). *SR; A1aa, a, b, d, e, f; A3a; B2; C.*

CROCKETT, JAMES EDWARD. Born Sept. 30, 1885, Llano, Llano County, Texas. Ht. 6 ft. 1 in., light brown eyes, black hair, dark complexion, married. Farmer, Cross Plains, Callahan County, Texas. SPECIAL RANGER June 9, 1917–Dec. 1917 (attached to Co. C). REMARKS: Died Oct. 4, 1929, Abilene, Taylor County, Texas. FAMILY: Parents, James David Crockett (b. 1862, TX) and Mary Jane Sawyer (b. 1864, MS); siblings, Maud Emma (b. 1884, TX), Callie (b. 1887, TX), William Roy (b. 1889, TX), Ancil Francis (b. 1891, TX), Clarence Sawyer (b. 1893, TX), Alvie Taylor (b. 1896, TX), Oscar D. (b. 1899, TX), Ross David (b. 1904, TX); spouse, Annie Pearl McDaniel (b. 1889, TX), married Apr. 15, 1906, Cross Plains; children, Alta I. (b. 1907, TX), Darwin Troy (b. 1910, TX). *SR; A1d, e, f; A3a; A4g; B1; C.*

CROFT, EWELL LEE. Born Aug. 15, 1891, Edgar, DeWitt County, Texas. Ht. 5 ft. 10 ½ in., blue eyes, red hair, ruddy complexion. Railroad brakeman, enlisted in Atascosa County, Texas. SPECIAL RANGER July 17, 1916–Dec. 1917. REMARKS: In June 1917 was a brakeman for the Kansas City, Mexico & Orient Railroad, living in Hamlin, Jones-Fisher County, Texas; in 1920 lived in Pleasanton, Atascosa County. In 1930 worked in a smelter in Douglas, Cochise County, Arizona. FAMILY: Parents, Jessie Zachariah Croft (b. 1870, TX) and Rebecca Jane Custer (b. 1871, AL); siblings, Luther Reagan (b. 1890, TX), Lydia M. (b. 1894, TX), Effie J. (b. 1898, TX), Ray L. (b. 1905, TX), Rachel E. (b. 1908, TX), Jewell M. (b. 1913, TX); spouse, Georgia Jay (b. 1896, TX), married about 1918; children, Roger E. (b. 1919, TX), Rebecca Jay (b. 1920, TX), Doris (b. 1923, TX), Dorothy Lois (b. 1925, TX), Mary Louise (b. 1927, TX). *SR; A1d, e, f, g; A2e; A3a; A4b, g.*

CROSS, HORACE DEVANI. Born Mar. 31, 1900, Greenville, Hunt County, Texas. Ht. 5 ft. 8 in., brown eyes, brown hair, fair complexion. Merchant, enlisted in Hidalgo County, Texas. REGULAR RANGER Jan. 26, 1918–Apr. 1918 (private, Co. G, Co. K). Resigned—was under age. REMARKS: In Sept. 1918 was a farmer living in Wills Point, Van Zandt County, Texas. Died Oct. 26, 1974, Brewster County, Texas. FAMILY: Parents, Ewing S. Cross (b. 1860, TX) and Eula M. (b. 1875, TX); siblings, Joe M. (b. 1882, TX), Verna M. (b. 1884, TX), Claud (b. 1887, TX), Trixie (b. 1889, TX), Charley (b. 1891, TX), Dick Leo (b. 1895, TX), Frank (b. 1903, TX), Tommie (b. 1911, TX). *SR; A1d; A2a, b; A3a.*

CROSS, JOSEPH JEFFERSON. Born Oct. 12, 1883, Weatherford, Parker County, Texas. Ht. 6 ft., dark eyes, black hair, dark complexion, married. Grocery merchant, Megargel, Archer County. LOYALTY RANGER June 1, 1918–Feb. 14, 1919. REMARKS: Deputy sheriff for 10 years. In Feb. 1919 was proprietor of City Garage, Auto Supplies in Megargel; in 1930 was a farmer in Megargel. Died Aug. 15, 1963, Fort Worth, Tarrant County, Texas. FAMILY: Parents, Jacob H. Cross (b. 1860, TX) and Martha Lucretia "Lou" Johnson (b. 1863, TX); siblings, Dovie Ann (b. 1886, TX), Nettie Pearl (b. 1891, TX), Nancy Ludie (b. 1893, TX), Roy Richard (b. 1902, TX), Edith Evalyene (b. 1903, TX); spouse, Elizabeth Amanda Mayes (b. 1887, TX), married Jan. 1, 1905, Young County, Texas; children, Virgil Andrew (b. 1906, TX), Francis Cleburne or Clephane (b. 1908, TX), Jacob Brandell "Jake" (b. 1911, TX), Walter Woodrow (b. 1914, TX), Bessie Fay (b. 1916, TX), Lillian Lee (b. 1922, TX), Joe Lacy (b. 1925, TX). *SR; A1d, e, f, g; A2a, b; A4a, b, g; B1, 2.*

CROSSON, JOHN. Born May 25, 1896, Alpine, Brewster County, Texas. Ht. 5 ft. 11 in., blue eyes, brown hair, red complexion. Ranchman, Marfa, Presidio County, Texas. SPECIAL RANGER May 9, 1917–Dec. 1917 (attached to Co. C). Ranchman, Marfa. REGULAR RANGER Oct. 4, 1919–Apr. 30, 1921 (private, Co. F; transferred to Co. C, Feb. 15, 1921). Resigned. REMARKS: As a young boy had lived in El Paso, El Paso County, Texas. In 1920 was a Ranger stationed in Del Rio, Val Verde County, Texas. In 1930 was a pipe fitter for an oil company in Los Angeles County, California. Died Apr. 4, 1974, Presidio, Presidio County, Texas. LAW ENFORCEMENT RELATIVES: Ranger Thomas C. Crosson, uncle; Ranger William Davis, uncle; Ranger B. Hillsman Davis, cousin. FAMILY: Parents, John Edmond Crosson (a "cattle doctor" as of 1900) (b. 1867, TX) and

Tymie Musgrave (b. 1878, TX); stepfather, Oscar Ebinger (b. 1881, CA). *SR; 471; Fox to Davis, Dec 13, 1917, AGC; A1d, f, g; A2a, b; A3a; A4g.*

CROSSON, THOMAS CLEMENT. Born Mar. 9, 1873, San Antonio, Bexar County, Texas. Ht. 5 ft. 10 ½ in., blue eyes, gray hair, light complexion, married. Stockman, Marfa, Presidio County, Texas. SPECIAL RANGER Jan. 8, 1918–Jan. 15, 1919. REMARKS: In 1900 was a bookkeeper living in Alpine, Brewster County, Texas. By 1910 was a ranch owner in Brewster County. In 1920 owned a ranch in Marfa; still a ranchman in Marfa in 1930. Died June 14, 1930, Presidio County, Texas. LAW ENFORCEMENT RELATIVES: Ranger John Crosson, nephew; Ranger William Davis, brother-in-law; Ranger B. Hillsman Davis, nephew. FAMILY: Parents, George Crosson (b. 1825, Ireland) and Ann Elizabeth Healy (b. 1842, LA); siblings, Sarah Ellen (b. 1860, CA), Catherine Agnes (b. 1863, TX), John E. (b. 1867, TX), George F. (b. 1869, TX), Maymee A. (b. 1871), Lizzie A. (b. 1875, TX), Charles W. (b. 1879, TX); spouse, Christina Campbell (b. 1879, MI), married Dec. 7, 1898, Alpine. *SR; A1b, d, e, f, g; A3a; A4b, g; B1; C.*

CROW, EMMETT MAYHOUGH (First name spelled EMMITT in some sources.) Born July 1879, Leake County, Mississippi. Ht. 6 ft. 2 in., brown eyes, black hair, fair complexion, married. Peace officer, enlisted in Austin, Travis County, Texas. REGULAR RANGER Sept. 3, 1917–Sept. 13, 1917 (private, Co. D). Resigned. REMARKS: Note length of service: 10 days. In 1920 and 1930 was farming in Bell County. Died Nov. 27, 1959, Bell County, Texas. LAW ENFORCEMENT RELATIVES: Ranger and city policeman John F. Crow, brother. FAMILY: Parents, John N. Crow (b. 1858, MS) and Sofronia (b. 1850, AL); siblings, George (b. 1875, MS), Mitty (b. 1877, MS), Tom (b. 1886, MS), Lacy (b. 1889, TX), John (b. 1891, TX); spouse #1, Ethel Lee Thompson (b. 1885, TX), married about 1903; children, Lena (b. 1905, TX), Ora Lee (b. 1908, TX), Clara (b. 1909, TX), Watt (b. 1910, TX), Docia (b. 1913, TX), Emmett, Jr. (b. 1917, TX), Bertha Mae (b. 1924, TX), Wilse (b. 1924, TX), Ivy (b. 1926, TX), Hellen (b. 1927, TX); spouse #2, Helen Hargrove; daughter, June Lanette (b. 1940, TX). *SR; A1b, d, f, g; A2b, e; A4b.*

CROW, JOHN FURMAN. Born Aug. 1891, Oenaville, Bell County, Texas. Ht. 5 ft. 11 in., blue eyes, brown hair, light complexion, married. Police officer, Rogers, Bell County. REGULAR RANGER Apr. 16, 1920–Feb. 15, 1921 (private, Co. A). Discharged. Peace officer, Rogers. REGULAR RANGER Mar. 19, 1921–Nov. 31, 1923 (private, Co. C; transferred to Co. A, Oct. 1, 1923). Discharged. Special officer, Southern Pacific Railroad, Houston, Harris County, Texas. SPECIAL RANGER Dec. 17, 1923–Dec. 31, 1924. Discharged—left SP's employ. Game warden, Falfurrias, Brooks County, Texas. REGULAR RANGER Feb. 15, 1933–Oct. 31, 1933 (private, Co. D). Resigned. REMARKS: In 1920 was manager of a pool hall in Rogers; during 1923–1924, was a special officer (night patrolman) for the SP Railroad in Houston and El Paso, El Paso County, Texas. In 1930 was a game warden on a state game reserve in Brooks County, Texas. Died Mar. 25, 1959, Kleberg County, Texas. LAW ENFORCEMENT RELATIVES: Ranger Emmett M. Crow, brother. FAMILY: Parents, John N. Crow (b. 1858, MS) and Sofronia (b. 1850, AL); siblings, George (b. 1875, MS), Mitty (b. 1877, MS), Emmett M. (b. 1879, MS), Tom (b. 1886, MS), Lacy (b. 1889, TX); spouse #1, Ollie (b. 1891, TX), married about 1909; children, Ruby L. (b. 1913, TX), Delmar (b. 1915, TX), Ruthelle (b. 1917, TX); spouse #2, Elleen (b. 1907, TX), married about 1924. *SR; 471; 470:43; A1d, e, f, g; A2b; A3a.*

CRUMPLER, HENRY. Born Feb. 1890, Magnolia, Columbia County, Arkansas. Ht. 6 ft. 1 in., gray eyes, black hair, dark complexion. Salesman and guard, Laredo, Webb County, Texas. SPECIAL RANGER Jan. 17, 1917–Mar. 21, 1917 (attached to Co. C). Discharged. REMARKS: Note length of service. As of June 1917 lived in Laredo where he was a salesman for a motor car company based in San Antonio, Bexar County, Texas. In 1930 was a hotel proprietor, Laredo. A Henry Crumpler died June 9, 1958, Nueces County, Texas. FAMILY: Spouse, Maud (b. 1891, LA), married about 1923. *SR; A1e, f, g; A2b; A3a.*

CULLINAN, MICHAEL PATRICK. Born Jan. 1866, Sharon, Mercer County, Pennsylvania. Ht. 5 ft. 7 ½ in., blue eyes, gray hair, fair complexion, married. President, Border Gas Company, Laredo, Webb County, Texas. SPECIAL RANGER July 24, 1918–Jan. 14, 1919. REMARKS: By 1900 was working for a gas company, living in Corsicana, Navarro

County, Texas. In 1920 census was identified as "Dr. M. P. Cullinan," gas company manager, Laredo. Died Jan. 20, 1927, Webb County, Texas. FAMILY: Parents, John Cullinan (b. 1835, Ireland) and Mary F. (b. 1837, Ireland); siblings, Margaret A. (b. 1858, PA), Joseph S. (b. 1861, PA), Mary E. (b. 1868, PA), Anna (b. 1870, PA), Catherine (b. 1872, PA), Jennie (b. 1874, PA), John (b. 1878, PA); spouse, Minnie A. (b. 1865, NY), married about 1892; children, Joseph L. (b. 1892, PA), Francis (b. 1895, PA), Mort (b. 1903, TX). *SR; A1b, d, f, g; C.*

CULP, GEORGE CHAPLIN (or CHAPMAN). Born Aug. 3, 1882, Gainesville, Cooke County, Texas. Ht. 6 ft. 4 in., blue eyes, auburn hair, light complexion, married. Farmer, enlisted in Potter County, Texas. REGULAR RANGER Aug. 9, 1909–Oct. 14, 1910 (private, Co. B). Honorably discharged. Railroad special officer, Amarillo, Potter County. SPECIAL RANGER Sept. 18, 1929–Sept. 18, 1930. Discharged—warrant expired. REMARKS: Had been a farmer in Causey, Roosevelt County, New Mexico. In 1917 was a farmer in Payne County, Oklahoma. In 1930 was a railroad officer, living in Wichita Falls, Wichita County, Texas. George Chaplin Culp died July 13, 1950, Wichita County, Texas. FAMILY: Parents, Albert Shirley Culp (b. 1829, KY) and Sarah S. Walker (b. 1848, MO); siblings, Victoria Willie (b. 1874, TX), Josephine (b. 1876, TX), Elizabeth Olivia (b. 1878, TX), Allie T. (b. 1880, TX), John C. (b. 1885, TX), Clara A. (b. 1887, TX), Beulah Mae (b. 1891, TX); spouse, Flora Ethel Edwards (b. 1891, OK), married about 1915; children, Albert R. (b. 1917, TX), Willie Fay (b. 1918, OK), Ruth (b. 1919, TX), Beulah May (b. 1921, TX), John Leonard (b. 1923, TX). *SR; 471; A.W. Brown affidavit, Feb 11, 1910, WC; A1b, d, e, f, g; A2e; A3a; A4a, b, g; C.*

CULPEPPER, CORNELIUS VANDERBILT. Born Apr. 20, 1880, Lavaca, Lavaca County, Texas. Ht. 5 ft. 8 ½ in., blue eyes, dark hair, dark complexion. Mechanic, Comstock, Val Verde County, Texas. SPECIAL RANGER Dec. 3, 1917–Jan. 15, 1919 (Co. A Volunteers). REMARKS: Had been a railroad car repairman in Val Verde County: in 1920 was a garage mechanic. In 1930 was a lumberman in a lumber yard in Comstock. Died Aug. 5, 1972, San Antonio, Bexar County, Texas. FAMILY: Parents, Francis Ogle Thorpe (or Francis Orren) Culpepper (b. 1856, TX) and Eliza Jane Richardson (b. 1858, AL); siblings, Ura Viola (b. 1879, TX), John Orren (b. 1882, TX), Darius Ivan (b. 1885, TX), Cora Olive (b. 1887, TX), Lois Elizabeth (b. 1889, TX), Alva Allen (b. 1900, TX), Ella Lola (b. 1892, TX), Robert Ray (b. 1896, TX); spouse, Lois F. Anderson (b. 1897, TX), married Dec. 29, 1917, Seguin, Guadalupe County, Texas; son, Claude Brotherton (b. 1922, TX). *SR; A1d, e, f, g; A2a, b; A3a; A4a, b, g; B1.*

CUMMINGS, ARTHUR P. "SUG." Born July 1886, Haskell, Haskell County, Texas. Ht. 5 ft. 6 in., gray eyes, brown hair, married as of Jan. 1926. Stockman, enlisted in Val Verde County, Texas. REGULAR RANGER Feb. 1, 1915–June 13, 1915 (private, Co. B). Discharged/fired. Stockman, San Angelo, Tom Green County, Texas. REGULAR RANGER Jan. 29, 1924–May 14, 1927 (private, Co. E; transferred to Headquarters Co., Mar. 1, 1925; transferred to Co. B, Sept. 1, 1925). Discharged. REMARKS: In May 1915 was "under a cloud" because of his performance in the fight in which Rangers Eugene Hulen and Joe Sitter were killed. His 1926 enlistment form gives his height as 5 ft. 9 ½ in.; in 1915 enlistment form it was 5 ft. 6 in. Had been a stockraiser in Van Horn, El Paso County, Texas. In 1930 was a U.S. Customs inspector, living in Del Rio, Val Verde County. FAMILY: Parents, Seaton Cummings (b. 1858, TX), and Octavia (b. 1861, KY); siblings, Bonnie L. (b. 1880, TX), Roy Seaton (b. 1882, TX), Charles N. (b. 1884, TX), Fanny (b. 1888, TX), Gertrude (b. 1890, TX); spouse, Daisy (b. 1889, TX), married about 1924. *SR; 471; EPMT, May 31,1915; 422:77; 1: I, 1532–1535; MR, Co B, May, June, 1915, AGC; AG to Fox, June 2, 3, 4, 1915, AGC; McKay to Hutchings, June 2, 1915, WC; Hutchings to Fox, June 5, 1915, WC; Bates to Ferguson, June 9, 1915, WC; Jester to AG, June 8, 1915, WC; 319: 106, 113; A1d, e, g; A3a.*

CUNNINGHAM, AARON WASHINGTON. Born Oct. 1866, Cooke County, Texas. Ht. 5 ft. 11 in., blue eyes, black hair, medium complexion. Peace officer, Harlingen, Cameron County, Texas. REGULAR RANGER Feb. 15, 1921–Aug. 31, 1921 (captain, Co. C). Resigned. REMARKS: Note length of service. In 1910 was deputy sheriff, Montague County, Texas; was Montague County sheriff Nov. 5, 1912–Nov. 7, 1916. In 1930 was a city inspector, living in Cameron County. An Aaron W. Cunningham died Nov. 27, 1945, Wise County, Texas. (Some sources state he died Dec. 27, 1941, Lane County, Oregon.) FAMILY: Parents, Aaron or

Abner Webster Cunningham (b. 1839, MS) and Nancy Caroline or Nancy Molly E. Magee (b. 1842, MS); siblings, James T. (b. 1861, AR), Abner W. (b. 1863, TX), Solomon (b. 1868, AR), William (b. 1871, AR), Lahitha (b. 1873, AR), Clementine (b. 1875, AR), John (b. 1878, TX); spouse #1, Mary Elizabeth West (b. 1868, AL), married about 1885; children, Lizzie B. (b. 1886, TX), William Vander (b. 1891, TX), Elmer H. (b. 1894, TX), Wallace Dixon (b. 1895, TX); spouse #2, Mary (b. LA), married about 1903; spouse #3, Esther Annie Lanning (b. 1869, AR), married before 1930, Saint Jo, Montague County. *SR; 471; 1503:379; A1a, b, d, e, f, g; A3a; A4a, b, g; C.*

CUNNINGHAM, JAMES F. Born Aug. 1860, Renick, Randolph County, Missouri. Ht. 5 ft. 9 in., gray eyes, light hair, fair complexion, married. Lawyer, Abilene, Taylor County, Texas. SPECIAL RANGER Apr. 23, 1917–Dec. 1917 (attached to Co. C). REMARKS: In a Confidential letter, Governor Ferguson ordered Adjutant General Hutchings to commission Cunningham in the Rangers. As a boy, Cunningham lived in South Fork, Fulton County, Arkansas. Was a lawyer in Abilene by 1900. A James F. Cunningham died Dec. 14, 1933, Taylor County, Texas. FAMILY: Parents, J. F. Cunningham (b. 1834, TN) and Emily (b. 1834, VA); siblings, Maud M. (b. 1862, MO), Wm. Fleming (b. 1865, AR), Adela B. (b. 1870, AR); spouse, Leila M. Oliver (b. 1863, TN), married about 1884; children, May (b. 1886, TX), Natalie (b. 1888, TX), Maud (b. 1891, TX), Alice (b. 1894, TX), Oliver (b. 1899, TX), Viola (b. 1904, TX). *SR; Ferguson to Hutchings, Apr 23, 1917, AGC; A1a, b, d, e, f, g; C.*

CUNNINGHAM, JAMES FRANK. Born Feb. 3, 1879, Comanche, Comanche County, Texas. Ht. 5 ft. 6 in., dark gray eyes, black hair, dark complexion married. Trapper, Telegraph, Kimble County, Texas. SPECIAL RANGER Aug. 1, 1918–Nov. 10, 1918. Discharged/fired. His commission was revoked for alleged abuses. REMARKS: In 1910 was a manager for a cattle ranch in Concho County, Texas. In Sept. 1918 described a "crippled left hand" on his WWI Draft Registration form. In 1930 his two daughters were pupils living in the Methodist Orphanage in Waco, McLennan County, Texas. FAMILY: Spouse, Allie (b. 1881, TX), married about 1904; children, Sam F. (b. 1906, TX), Lillian F. (b. 1912, TX), Rachel (b. 1914, TX). *SR; AG to Cunningham, July 23, 1918, AGC; Johnston to Hanson, Oct 23, 1918, AGC; Cunningham to Harley, Aug 26, 1918, AGC; Hanson to Harley, Nov 13, 1918, AGC; Henry to Harley, Dec 6, 1918, AGC; Latta to Harley, Dec 29, 1918, AGC; Cunningham to AG, Dec 30, 1918, AGC; A1e, f, g; A3a.*

CUNNINGHAM, KINLOCK FAULKNER. Born Mar. 23, 1874, Comanche County, Texas. Ht. 6 ft. 1 in., gray eyes, black hair, married. Peace officer. REGULAR RANGER Dec. 10, 1917–Feb. 7, 1919 (captain., Co. M). Discharged/fired. REMARKS: Had been a state prison farm manager, 1915. Was fired from Rangers because during a Feb. 7, 1919 shooting scrape in Austin, Travis County, Texas he killed Ranger Bert C. Veale; was charged with murder. In 1920 was a real estate dealer living in Comanche, Comanche County. Died Oct. 31, 1937, Goree, Knox County, Texas. FAMILY: Parents, Richard Tankersley Cunningham (b. 1844, TX) and Letitia or Lutitia Wright (b. 1847, AR); siblings, James Mitchell (b. 1866, TX), John Franklin (b. 1867, TX), Elias Isades (b. 1869, TX), Elena Elizabeth (b. 1872), Elzora Leona (b. 1876, TX), Effie May (b. 1879, TX), Lewis Theophilus (b. 1880, TX), Richard Aaron (b. 1883, TX), Dolly Ora (b. 1885, TX), William Cleveland (b. 1888, TX); spouse, Lillie Eliza Grundy (b. 1885, TX), married June 17, 1911. *SR; 471; Manley to Hutchings, Jan 18, 1915, AGC; Cunningham to Harley, Jan 5, 1918, WC; LWT, Feb 9, 1919; A1d, f; A3a; A4b; C.*

CUNNINGHAM, P. A. (probably PINKNEY ANDERSON) "TIPP." Born Nov. 1846, Obion County, Tennessee. Ht. 5 ft. 5 in., gray eyes, gray hair, fair complexion, married. Stockman, Celeste, Hunt County, Texas. SPECIAL RANGER Jan. 29, 1918–Jan. 15, 1919. REMARKS: In the 1910 and 1920 census records, a P. A. "Tipp" Cunningham (b. 1847, TN) was a hotel manager/proprietor in Celeste. A P. A. Cunningham died July 7, 1926, Hunt County, Texas. FAMILY (probably): Parents, Anson A. R. Cunningham (b. 1806) and Sarah Hubert (b. 1811, TN); siblings, Marion (b. 1831, TN), Columbus (b. 1833, TN), Esther (b. 1835, TN), Eliphus (b. 1836, TN), Sarah Jane (b. 1838, TN), Mansfield (b. 1840, TN), Jackson (b. 1842, TN), Mary Caroline "Mollie" (b. 1847, TN), Susan Elizabeth (b. 1851, TN); spouse #1, Mary H. (b. 1854, TN); children, Cora J. (b. 1874, TN), Walter L. (b. 1879, TX); spouse #2, Sarah J. Shank (b. 1865, MS), married May 20, 1885; son, Wilbur Anson (b. 1888, TX). *SR; A1aaa, aa, b, e, f; A2c; A3a; A4a, b, g; C.*

CUNNINGHAM, THOMAS BRAHAN. Born June 22, 1881, Bexar County, Texas. Ht. 6 ft., brown eyes, brown hair, fair complexion, married. Special agent, El Paso & Southwestern Railroad, El Paso, El Paso County, Texas. SPECIAL RANGER Mar. 7, 1918–Jan. 14, 1919. Commission was renewed Jan. 30, 1919–Dec. 31, 1919. REMARKS: June 1918 was special agent in El Paso for the Chino Copper Company. Was a private detective with offices at 614 First National Bank Building, El Paso. In 1930 was assistant general manager for a copper company, El Paso. Died Mar. 29, 1931, El Paso County, Texas. FAMILY: Parents, Edward Hall Cunningham (b. 1833, AR) and Mary Narcissa Anne Brahan (b. 1842, MS); siblings, Edward B. (b. 1873, TX), Eva Locke (b. 1876, TX), Sue D. (b. 1879, TX), Narcissa (b. 1884, TX); spouse, Blanche Hall (b. 1886, KS), married about 1902. *SR; EPMT, Mar 14, 15, 1916; Hobby to Harley, Mar 7, 1918, AGC; Cunningham to Brahan, May 11, 1918, AGC; Cunningham to Harley, June 10, 1918, AGC; A1b, d, f, g; A3a; A4b; C.*

CUNNINGHAM, THOMAS MARTIN. Born Feb. 11, 1859, De Kalb County, Alabama. Ht. 6 ft., blue eyes, gray hair, fair complexion, married. President, Bank of Miami, Miami, Roberts County, Texas. LOYALTY RANGER June 13, 1918–Feb. 1919. Had been a "freighter" in Johnson County, Texas. Was a stockman and cattle rancher in Roberts County in 1900 and 1910. FAMILY: Parents, William Johnathan Cunningham (b. 1832, TN) and Talitha A. Baxter (b. 1835, AL); siblings, Florida R. (b. 1861, AL), John A. (b. 1866, AL), James L. (b. 1867, AL), Robert E. Lee (b. 1871, TX), Mary (b. 1873, TX), Joseph J. (b. 1876, TX), Lilly J. (b. 1879, TX); spouse, Froney (b. 1857, MO), married about 1882; stepdaughter, Josie King (b. 1876, Cherokee Nation). *SR; A1b, d, e, f; A2b; A4g.*

CUNNINGHAM, WILLIAM JOHN. Born Oct. 1870, Baxter County, Arkansas. Ht. 5 ft. 11 in., blue eyes, dark hair, fair complexion, married. Lawyer, Abilene, Taylor County, Texas. SPECIAL RANGER June 16, 1917–Dec. 1917 (attached to Co. C). REMARKS: As a boy lived in Kaufman County, Texas. Was a lawyer in Abilene by 1900. A W. J. Cunningham died Sept. 5, 1952, Taylor County. Texas. FAMILY: Parents, Abner Webster Cunningham (b. 1839, MS) and Nancy Caroline (b. 1841, MS); siblings, James T. (b. 1861, AR), Abner Webster (b. 1863, TX), Aaron W. (b. 1866, TX), Solomon M. (b. 1868, AR), Labethe (b. 1873, AR), Clementine (b. 1875, AR), John W. (b. 1878, TX), Robert L. (b. 1882, TX), Dee M. (b. 1885, TX); spouse #1, Birdie (b. 1873, TN), married about 1894; children, Myrtle May (b. 1900, TX), Florence (b. 1903, TX), Webster John (b. 1905, TX); spouse #2, Harriett (b. 1877, TN), married about 1909. *SR; Register to Ferguson, May 18, 1917, AGC; Cunningham to Ferguson, May 18, 1917, AGC; A1a, b, d, e, f, g; A2b; A4b.*

CUPPLES, CHARLES TUCKER. Born June 10, 1864, Hardin County, Tennessee. Ht. 5 ft. 10 in., blue eyes, light hair, light complexion. Deputy sheriff, Val Verde County, Texas, 1907–1916. REGULAR RANGER June 17, 1916–Nov. 1, 1916 (private, Co. C). Resigned. REMARKS: Had been deputy sheriff, Edwards County, Texas in 1900. In 1930 was a sheep and goat rancher in Del Rio, Val Verde County. Census records in 1880 and 1900 list place of birth as Illinois. Died Aug. 19, 1944, Val Verde County, Texas; buried in Restlawn Cemetery, Del Rio, Val Verde County. FAMILY: Parents, Calvin J. Cupples and Mary Wallace (b. 1836, TN); sister, Tennessee Bell (b. 1860, TN); spouse, Lucy Laura Sweeten (b. 1865, TX), married April 18, 1886, Uvalde, Texas; children, Mary D. (b. 1887, TX), Lola Elizabeth (b. 1889, TX). *SR; 471; AG to Almond, June 19, 29, 1916, AGC; A1b, d, e, g; A4a, b, g; C.*

CURNUTTE, ROBERT HENRY. (Listed as CARNUTTE in Ranger Service Records.) Born June 17, 1875, Elliott County, Kentucky. Ht. 5 ft. 7 in., gray eyes, graying black hair, dark complexion, married. Banker, Snyder, Scurry County, Texas. LOYALTY RANGER May 31, 1918–Feb. 1919. REMARKS: In 1900 was a schoolteacher in Limestone County, Texas. In 1910 was a bank cashier in Snyder; still living in Snyder in 1930. A R. H. "Curnnitt" died Dec. 23, 1934, Taylor County, Texas. FAMILY: Parents, William Washington Curnutte (b. 1851, KY) and Lucy Ann Vencill (b. 1852, VA); siblings, Lula Virginia (b. 1878, KY), Claudie Candace (b. 1884, TX), Gussie S. (b. 1887, TX), John Dyer (b. 1890, TX), James Vencill (b. 1893, TX); spouse, Mollie Banks Thomas (b. 1881, TX), married about 1901; children, Lois L. (b. 1903, TX), Lila B. (b. 1905, TX), Robert H., Jr. (b. 1909, TX), Mary Vencill (b. 1922, TX). *SR; A1b, d, e, f, g; A2b, e; A4b, g.*

CURTIS, JESSE ROBERT. Born July 20, 1874, Russellville, Pope County, Arkansas. Ht. 5 ft. 8 in., gray eyes, brown hair, light complexion, married. Farmer, Clyde, Callahan County, Texas. SPECIAL RANGER June 14, 1917–Dec. 1917 (attached to Co. C). REMARKS: In 1910 was a blacksmith living in Taylor County, Texas; was farming in Callahan County in 1920 and 1930. FAMILY: Spouse, Sarah E. (b. 1877, TX), married about 1896; children, Albert E. (b. 1897, TX), Reba Jewel (b. 1899, TX), Rubie Jessie (b. 1901, TX), Alvin (b. 1903, TX), Granville (b. 1905, TX), Leva (b. 1907, TX), Clarence (b. 1911, TX), Melvin (b. 1913), Pauline (b. 1916, TX). *SR; A1e, f, g; A3a.*

CUSTER, EDWARD DEKALB. Born Feb. 10, 1869, Marion County, Alabama. Ht. 5 ft. 10 ½ in., black eyes, black hair, light complexion, married. Brand inspector, Sheep and Goat Raisers' Association of Texas, enlisted in Val Verde County, Texas. SPECIAL RANGER Apr. 13, 1917–Dec. 1917 (attached to Co. C). REMARKS: In 1880 lived in Bandera County, Texas; by 1900 was a stock raiser in Edwards County, Texas. Was Edwards County sheriff Nov. 5, 1918–Jan. 1, 1927. Died Apr. 14, 1952, Uvalde County, Texas; buried in Barksdale, Edwards County. FAMILY: Parents, Robert Jackson "Bob" Custer (b. 1844, AL) and Mary Jane Hamilton (b. 1845, MS); siblings, John Francis Alexander (b. 1871, TX), William Claborn (b. 1875, TX), Marion F. (b. 1879, TX), Ebenezer (b. 1881, TX); spouse, Etta Jane Butler (b. 1874, TX), married about 1897; children, George C. (b. 1897, TX), Earl E. (b. 1899, TX), Gilbert L. (b. 1900, TX), Jasper L. (b. 1902, TX), Fred F. (b. 1904, TX), Edna M. (b. 1909, TX). *SR; 471; La Crosse to AG, Apr 13, 1917, AGC; 1503:169; Almond to Hutchings, Apr 13, 1917, AGC; A1a, b, d, e, f, g; A2b; A4a, b, g.*

DANNELLEY, JOHN LEONIDAS. Born Feb. 15, 1881, San Jacinto County, Texas. Ht. 5 ft. 9 ½ in., blue eyes, dark hair, fair complexion, married. Lawyer, Laredo, Webb County, Texas. SPECIAL RANGER May 8, 1918–Jan. 15, 1919. REMARKS: Identified as "Lonnie" in 1900 census. In 1930, lived in San Antonio, Bexar County, Texas. Died Apr. 22, 1966, Elgin, Bastrop County, Texas. LAW ENFORCEMENT RELATIVES: Ranger W. A. Dannelley, brother. FAMILY: Parents, Anthony Oratio Dannelley (b. 1848, TX) and Iona Theodosia "Doshie" Capers (b. 1861, LA); siblings, Nellie (b. 1878, TX), Flora (b. 1885, TX), Willie A. (b. 1887, TX), Alva Oratio (b. 1889, TX), Clara Margaret (b. 1891, TX), Ollie Elizabeth (b. 1893, TX), Preston (b. 1898, TX), Henry O. (b. 1901, TX); spouse, Ida (b. 1896, TX), married about 1917. *SR; A1b, d, e, g; A2a, b; A3a; A4b; B2.*

DANNELLEY, WILLIAM ANTHONY "WILLIE." Born Nov. 19, 1887, San Jacinto, Walker County, Texas. Ht. 5 ft. 9 in., gray eyes, dark hair, fair complexion, married. Merchant, Hebbronville, Jim Hogg County, Texas. SPECIAL RANGER Mar. 22, 1918–Jan. 15, 1919. REMARKS: In March 1918 was also the county and district clerk of Jim Hogg County; in 1930 was county judge, Jim Hogg County. Died Nov. 28, 1954, Hays County, Texas. LAW ENFORCEMENT RELATIVES: Ranger John L. Dannelley, brother. FAMILY: Parents, Anthony Oratio Dannelley (b. 1848, TX) and Iona Theodosia "Doshie" Capers (b. 1861, LA); siblings, Nellie (b. 1878, TX), John L. (b. 1881, TX), Flora (b. 1885, TX), Alva Oratio (b. 1889, TX), Clara Margaret (b. 1891, TX), Ollie Elizabeth (b. 1893, TX), Preston (b. 1898, TX), Henry O. (b. 1901, TX); spouse, Elnora Lanie E. Wyrick (b. 1890, TN), married Dec. 15, 1907, Waco, McLennan County, Texas; children, Jack (b. 1911, TX), Eloise (b. 1915, TX). *SR; Dannelley to Woodul, Mar 16, 1918, AGC; Assistant AG to Dannelley, Mar 19, 1918, AGC; A1d, g; A3a; A4b; C.*

DARBY, JAMES P. "JIM." Born Nov. 1875, Weimar, Colorado County, Texas. Ht. 5 ft. 11 ½ in., brown eyes, auburn hair, red complexion, married. Claims agent, SA&AP Railroad, Beeville, Bee County, Texas. SPECIAL RANGER May 24, 1917–Jan. 15, 1919 (attached to Co. C; was reinstated—WA was renewed, Dec. 22, 1917). Discharged. Claims agent, Beeville. SPECIAL RANGER Aug. 5, 1933–unknown. REMARKS: Deputy city marshal, Weimar, 1898–1899. Bee County deputy sheriff, 1901–1910. Special agent, SA&AP Railroad, 1920–1930. A James P. Darby died July 5, 1939, Harris County, Texas. FAMILY: Parents, James A Darby (b. 1832, KY) and America S. (1843, KY); siblings, Eustace T. (b. 1865, TX), Ambrose (b. 1868, TX), Clyde (b. 1872, TX), Earle W. (b. 1881, TX); spouse, Jessie M. (b. 1885, MO), married about 1907; children, James Wilson (b. 1909, TX), Dorothy Elaine (b. 1917, TX), Jessie Lorine (b. 1918, TX). *SR; Chamberlain to Hutchings, May 31, 1917, AGC; AG to Chamberlain, June 1, 1917, AGC; Earnest to Harley, Dec 21, 1917, AGC; AG to Earnest, Dec 22, 1917, AGC; A1b, d, e, f, g; A2e; C.*

D

DARLINGTON, CLAUDE. Born July 28, 1883, Taylor, Williamson County, Texas. Ht. 6 ft., blue eyes, dark hair, ruddy complexion. Farmer. REGULAR RANGER Dec. 11, 1917–Mar. 15, 1919 (private, Co. M; promoted to sergeant, unknown date). Honorably discharged—Co. M was disbanded. Ranchman, Taylor. REGULAR RANGER July 1, 1919–Aug. 15, 1919 (private, Co. C). Resigned. Ranchman. REGULAR RANGER Mar. 28, 1920–Apr. 30, 1924 (private, Headquarters Co.; transferred to Co. C, May 11, 1922; transferred to Co. A, Jan. 1, 1923; transferred to Co. E, Sept. 1, 1923). Resigned. Ranger [*sic*], San Antonio, Bexar County, Texas. REGULAR RANGER May 5, 1924–June 27, 1924 (private, Co. E). Discharged. REMARKS: On May 5, 1924 enlistment form: "Reg. Ranger without pay." In 1930 was a special policeman, Taylor. A Claude Darlington died July 22, 1962, Williamson County, Texas. FAMILY: Parents, Ben Darlington and Sallie Appleton Barker (b. 1864, TX); siblings, Susie (b. 1885, TX), Frank (b. 1888, TX). *SR; 471; Special Orders No. 21, Mar 10, 1919,WC; 470:43; A1d, e, f, g; A2b; A3a; A4a, b, g.*

DAVENPORT, JOSEPH EUGENE. Born May 12, 1885, Leesville, Louisiana. Ht. 6 ft. 3 in., blue eyes, brown hair, fair complexion. REGULAR RANGER Oct. 1911–Jan. 31, 1912 (private, Co. B). Discharged—reduction in force. REGULAR RANGER Feb. 1915–Oct. 1915 (private, Co. A; transferred to Co. D, Aug. 1915). Discharged or resigned—unknown. Express guard, enlisted in Cameron County, Texas. SPECIAL RANGER Jan. 13, 1917–July 19, 1917 (attached to Co. C). Resigned. REMARKS: In 1910 was a farm laborer on his father's farm in Karnes County, Texas. Dec. 1915 became a quarantine guard at Brownsville, Cameron County, Texas. Oct. 1917 became a mounted Immigration inspector at El Paso, El Paso County, Texas. In 1920 was a mounted Customs inspector in the El Paso area; in 1930 was still a U.S. Customs inspector in El Paso. FAMILY: Parents, James Nathan Davenport (b. 1853, MS) and Mary Ann Hamilton (b. 1862, LA); siblings, Charles (b. 1884, LA), James Thomas (b. 1887, LA), George Arthur (b. 1897, TX), Dick, Lola (b. 1904, TX); spouse, Mary Bell Dean (b. 1896, AR), married about 1920; sons, James Deane (b. 1920, TX), Joseph Eugene, Jr. (b. 1927, TX). *SR; 471; MR, Co. B, Oct 1911–Jan 1912; LWT, Feb 4, 1912; 508:66; Sanders to Hutchings, Feb 21, 1915, AGC; Co D Scout Reports, Aug–Sept, 1915, RRM; 319: 38; BDH, Dec 12, 14, 15, 20, 1915, Oct 4, 1917; 463: 91–92; U.S. Commissioner, El Paso, Nos. 288, 393, FRC-FW; A1d, e, f, g; A2e; A3a; A4b.*

DAVID, LOYD ALLEN. Born July 14, 1894, Lapara Ranch, Bee County, Texas. Ht. 5 ft. 11 ½ in., brown eyes, dark brown hair, fair complexion. Mechanic, enlisted at Alice, Jim Wells County, Texas. REGULAR RANGER Nov. 1, 1917–Jan. 15, 1919 (private, Co. A). Resigned. REMARKS: Had lived in Nueces County, Texas. In 1920 was a garage machinist in Jim Hogg County, Texas; in 1930 was a county road supervisor in Jim Hogg County. Died Aug. 21, 1974, Odem, San Patricio County, Texas. FAMILY: Parents, Walter Monroe David (b. 1863, TX) and Melissa Ella "Lissie" Weed (b. 1867, TX); siblings, Cylah Walter (b. 1887, TX), Ella Lee (b. 1889, TX), Velma Lura "Belle" (b. 1890, TX), Lewie Terrel (b. 1894, TX), Raymond Mack (b. 1897, TX), Ralph (b. 1900, TX), Martin Lyle (b. 1902, TX), Cloma Corine (b. 1906, TX); spouse, Cora Helen Duvall (b. 1901, Indian Territory/OK), married July 11, 1920, San Antonio, Bexar County, Texas; children, Lyda Belle (b. 1921, TX), Lloyd Allen (b. 1927, TX). *SR; 319: 19; A1d, e, f, g; A2a, b, e; A3a, A4a, b, g.*

DAVIDSON, THOMAS JACK. Born Jan. 18, 1882, Galveston, Galveston County, Texas. Ht. 5 ft. 4 in., blue eyes, brown hair. Real estate agent, Austin, Travis County, Texas. REGULAR RANGER Aug. 21, 1918–unknown (private, Co. not listed; June 20, 1919, reenlisted under the new law, Co. B). Discharged or resigned—unknown. REMARKS: In 1910 was a real estate agent in Galveston. A Thomas J. Davidson died Feb. 13, 1935, Denton County, Texas. FAMILY: Parents, Robert Vance Davidson (b. 1853, NC) and Laura Harrison Jack (b. 1858, TX); siblings, Nancy (or Anne) Knox (b. 1880, TX), William "Wilber" Sevier (b. 1886, TX), Robert Vance, Jr. (b. 1889, TX). *SR; 471; A1d, e; A3a; A4g; B2; C.*

DAVIES, LUTHER. Born July 1882, Blacksburg, Cherokee County, South Carolina. Ht. 5 ft. 10 ½ in., brown eyes, black hair, dark complexion, married. Stockman, Naples, Morris County, Texas. LOYALTY RANGER June 4, 1918–Feb. 1919. REMARKS: Had been a dry goods salesman in Morris County in 1910. A Luther Davies died May 4, 1953, Morris County, Texas. FAMILY: Parents, John L. Davies (b. 1831, NC) and Sarah (b. 1841, SC); sisters, Mary L. (b. 1877, SC), Edna J. (b. 1879, SC); spouse, Cora Lee

Singletary (b. 1883, TX), married about 1906; children, Mina Frances (b. 1907, TX), Sarah Catherine (b. 1909, TX), William Luther (b. 1919, TX). *SR; A1d, e, f; A2e; A4b; C.*

DAVIS, BENNETT HILLSMAN. Born Aug. 29, 1896, El Paso, El Paso County, Texas. Ht. 5 ft. 11 in., blue eyes, light hair, fair complexion. Ranchman, Marfa, Presidio County, Texas. SPECIAL RANGER May 9, 1917–Dec. 1917. REMARKS: Was ranch hand, living in Marfa in 1920. In 1930 was an oil agent for Texaco Co. in Marfa. Died June 25, 1982, Marfa, Presidio County, Texas. LAW ENFORCEMENT RELATIVES: Ranger William W. Davis, father; Ranger Thomas Crosson, uncle; Ranger John Crosson, cousin. FAMILY: Parents, William W. Davis (b. 1870, TX) and Elizabeth "Lizzie" Crosson (b. 1877, TX); brothers, George Crosson (b. 1898, TX), Thomas Clement (b. 1901, TX); spouse #1, Agnes D. Smith (b. 1898, TX), married about 1921; daughter, Eloise D. (b. 1921, TX); spouse #2, Mary Elizabeth Runkles (b. 1920, TX), married Aug. 7, 1950; daughter, Vickee Lee (b. 1951, TX). *SR; A1d, e, f, g; A2a, b, e; A4g.*

DAVIS, EDWARD FREDERICK. Born Aug. 22, 1873, Hertfordshire County, England. Ht. 5 ft. 10 ½ in., brown eyes, black hair, dark complexion, married. Farmer, Denton, Denton County, Texas. LOYALTY RANGER May 31, 1918–Feb. 1919. REMARKS: Came to Texas in 1879, became a naturalized U.S. citizen in 1882. Lived in Dallas County, Texas, in 1880; was farming in Denton County from 1900 through 1930. Died Oct. 30, 1941, Denton County, Texas. FAMILY: Siblings, Sarah (b. 1857, England), Alfred (b. 1861, England), Charles (b. 1867, England), Emily (b. 1869, England), Annie (b. 1872, England); spouse, Emma S. Marks (b. 1876, IA), married about 1896; sons, Kenneth (b. 1899, TX), John (b. 1902, TX), Wallace Earl (b. 1903, TX). *SR; A1b, d, e, f, g; A2b; A3a; A4b.*

DAVIS, EDWARD TYRA. Born Apr. 24, 1873, Canton, Cherokee County, Georgia. Ht. 5 ft. 9 ½ in., blue eyes, light hair, fair complexion, married. Stockman, brand inspector, Cattle Raisers' Association of Texas, Paducah, Cottle County, Texas. SPECIAL RANGER May 19, 1917–Jan. 15, 1919 (attached to Co. C; was reinstated/WA was renewed, Dec. 20, 1917); May 26, 1926–Feb. 1, 1927; Feb. 18, 1927–Feb. 18, 1928; Feb. 24, 1928–May 13, 1928. Died May 13, 1928, Cottle County, Texas. REMARKS: In 1918 was classified as a Regular Ranger without pay. In 1920 lived in Paducah. In 1926, said he had been a Special Ranger for 6 years. FAMILY: Parents, Tyra B. Davis (b. 1834, SC) and Sarah Elizabeth Mason (b. 1844, GA); siblings, Silas Elathan (b. 1860, GA), Thomas Jefferson (b. 1863, GA), William Arthur (b. 1866, GA), Amanda L. (b. 1869, GA), Minnie (b. 1871, GA); spouse, Mattie Lee Anderson (b. 1883, GA), married about 1900; children, Gussie (b. 1901, TX), Edna (b. 1902, TX), Gordon Tyra (b. 1904, TX), Lucile (b. 1911, TX). *SR; A1a, d, e, f; A3a; A4b; C.*

DAVIS, HOWARD E. Born Jan. 17, 1888, St. Louis, St. Louis County, Missouri. Ht. 5 ft. 10 in., blue eyes, black hair, dark complexion. Clerk, enlisted in Harris County, Texas. SPECIAL RANGER Mar. 10, 1917–Dec. 1917. REMARKS: Enlistment form states: "Chief Pass Bureau." As of June 1917 was a U.S. government stenographer, Federal Training Camp, Houston, Harris County. In 1920 was a clerk for the railroad, living in Portland, Multnomah County, Oregon. FAMILY: Parents, Rice W. Davis (b. 1860, MO) and Christina (b. 1865, MO); brother, John N. (b. 1890, MO); spouse, Marcia A. (b. 1889, TX). *SR; A1d, e, f; A3a.*

DAVIS, JAMES B. Born Feb. 1864, Leander, Williamson County, Texas. Ht. 6 ft., brown eyes, brown hair, dark complexion, married. Hotel man, Fort Davis, Jeff Davis County, Texas. SPECIAL RANGER July 24, 1916–Dec. 1917. REMARKS: Until 1900 lived in Williamson County. Was Jeff Davis County sheriff Nov. 8, 1904–Nov. 3, 1914; still living in Jeff Davis County in 1920. A James Brown Davis died June 25, 1929, Jeff Davis County, Texas. FAMILY: Parents, Robert B. Davis (b. 1841, MO) and Arminta (b. 1843, MO), siblings, Robert E. (b. 1865, TX), Mary D. (b. 1867, TX), George W. (b. 1869, TX), Thos. H. (b. 1871, TX), S. H. (b. 1875, TX), Emmett E. (b. 1882, TX); spouse, Laura Augusta (b. 1869, TX), married about 1884; children, Alvin H. (b. 1889, TX), Winnie E. (b. 1891, TX), Elsie I. (b. 1901, TX). *SR; Hudspeth to Ferguson, July 11, 1916, AGC; AG to Hudspeth, July 17, 1916, AGC; Davis to Hutchings, July 28, 1916, AGC; 1503:285; A1a, b, d, e, f; A2b; C.*

DAVIS, JOHN H., SR. Born Nov. 1857, Brandon, Hill County, Texas. Ht. 5 ft. 10 in., light brown eyes, dark hair, fair complexion, married. Farmer, Chalk, Cottle County,

Texas. LOYALTY RANGER June 10, 1918–Feb. 1919. REMARKS: Had lived in Hill County through 1900; was a Hill County deputy sheriff for 5 years. By 1910 was farming in Cottle County; in 1920 owned a cotton gin in Cottle County. A John Davis died Mar. 9, 1927, Cottle County, Texas. FAMILY: Parents, James R. Davis (b. 1829, TN) and Margaret (b. 1833, Scotland); siblings, Nancy B. "Nannie" (b. 1855, TX), Mary A. (b. 1863, TX), James William (b. 1865, TX); spouse #1, Mollie M. Harris (b. 1862, TX); sons, James Fred (b. 1882, TX), John H., Jr. (b. 1887, TX), Carl (b. 1889, TX), Ransom (b. 1891, TX); spouse #2, Duff (b. 1886, TX), married about 1904; children, Morgan D. (b. 1912, TX), Ruth M. (b. 1914, TX), Steven Emmitt (b. 1916, TX), M. Ellen (b. 1919, TX). *SR; A1aa, a, b, d, e, f, g; A3a; A4b; C.*

DAVIS, J. R. Born Feb. 1886, Dahlonega, Lumpkin County, Georgia. Ht. 5 ft. 11 in., dark eyes, dark hair, dark complexion. Special agent, Nacogdoches, Nacogdoches County, Texas. SPECIAL RANGER Dec. 26, 1917–Jan. 15, 1919. *SR.*

DAVIS, LEVI. Born Mar. 2, 1876, Rancho, Gonzales County, Texas. Tall, slender, blue eyes, black hair. REGULAR RANGER Dec. 15, 1908–Sept. 30, 1910 (private, Co. A). Discharged—Co. A was disbanded. Peace officer. REGULAR RANGER Oct. 3, 1910–Sept. 12, 1911 (private, Co. B; promoted to sergeant, May 1911). Resigned to accept a position in Houston, Harris County, Texas. REMARKS: In Apr. 1913 was a Starr County deputy sheriff. William Sterling described him as "one of the most dangerous gunfighters I ever knew." [*319:36*] WWI Draft Registration document, Oct. 1917, states "In insane asylum." Died Jan. 1, 1940. FAMILY: Parents, Levi Jefferson Davis (b. 1834, SC) and Nancy Eliza Smith (b. 1848, MS); siblings, James Robert (b. 1867, TX), Mary A. (b. 1870, TX), Hiram Pinkney (b. 1872, TX), Avie (b. 1874, TX), Mack (b. 1877, TX), Myrtle (b. 1881, TX), Nonnie (b. 1884, TX), Lois (b. 1887, TX), Rufus Figh (b. 1889, TX). *SR; 471; 464:39, MR, Co. B, Jan–Aug 1911, AGC; SAE, Sept 16, 1911; BDH, Apr 9, 10, 1913; A1b, d, e; A3a; A4b, g; B2.*

DAVIS, VIRGIL S. GOULD "GOULD." Born Jan. 22, 1890, Blowout, Blanco County, Texas. Ht. 6 ft. 1 ½ in., blue eyes, sandy hair, light complexion. Ranchman, Blowout. SPECIAL RANGER Aug. 23, 1917–Dec. 1917 (attached to Co. C). REMARKS: In 1910 was a hired hand on a ranch in Douglas, Cochise County, Arizona. WWI Draft Registration card lists a crippled foot. Was a stockman in Blanco County by June 1917; still a stock farmer in Blanco County in 1930. Died June 13, 1945; buried in Davis Cemetery, Llano County, Texas. FAMILY: Parents, William Othello Davis (b. 1859, TX) and Bettie Florence Rabb (b. 1863, TX); siblings, Alfred (b. 1881, TX), Z. M. P. "Pike" (b. 1883, TX), W. Othello, Jr. (b. 1886, TX), Hiram Abiff (b. 1892, TX); spouse, Willie Beatrice McDonald (b. 1896, TX), married Nov. 2, 1919; children, Willie Beatrice (b. 1926, TX), Gould, Jr. (b. 1930, TX). *SR; A1d, e, f, g; A2e; A3a; A4b.*

DAVIS, WILLIAM BRANICK. Born Dec. 21, 1885, Junction, Kimble County, Texas. Ht. 5 ft. 11 in., blue eyes, brown hair, ruddy complexion, widowed. Cowboy. REGULAR RANGER Oct. 1, 1917–Mar. 10, 1919 (private, Co. E; transferred to Co. M, Sept. 1918). Honorably discharged—Co. M was disbanded. REMARKS: Had been a sheep trader in Kimble County; in 1920 was a cattle ranch fence rider in Maverick County, Texas. A William Branick Davis died Mar. 24, 1954, Harris County, Texas. FAMILY: Mother, Agnes (b. 1852, TX); spouse, Leota (b. 1892, MO), married in 1910; son, Von B. (b. 1912, TX). *SR; 471; Special Orders No. 21, Mar 10, 1919, WC; Davis to Harley, June 22, 1919, AGC; A1d, e, f; A3a; C.*

DAVIS, WILLIAM D. Born Oct. 1864, Nashville, Davidson County, Tennessee. Ht. 5 ft. 10 ½ in., blue eyes, brown and gray hair, fair complexion, married. Railroad conductor, Houston, Harris County, Texas. SPECIAL RANGER June 5, 1918–Jan. 15, 1919. REMARKS: Deputy U.S. marshal for 2 years. In 1930 was an attorney in Houston. A William Dudley Davis died July 9, 1931, Harris County, Texas. FAMILY: Parents, William Davis (b. 1839, Ireland) and Kate E. (b. 1844, TN); siblings, Sarah (b. 1860, TN), twins John and Michael (b. 1862, AL), Edward (b. 1868, TN), James R. (b. 1873, TN); spouse, Mayme A. (b. 1873, IL), married about 1894; children, Marie Winters (b. 1895, TX), Andrew Russel (b. 1897, TX). *SR; A1a, b, e, f, g; C.*

DAVIS, WILLIAM W. Born Jan. 1870, Brazos County, Texas. Ht. 6 ft. 1 in., blue eyes, light hair, light complexion. Peace officer. REGULAR RANGER Dec. 8, 1917–Mar. 21, 1919 (captain, Co. L). Discharged—Co. L was disbanded. REGULAR RANGER July 1, 1919–Feb. 10, 1921 (captain,

Ranger Captain Will W. Davis. *Photo courtesy Art Robertson, Las Cruces, New Mexico.*

Co. F). Honorably discharged—Co. F was disbanded. REMARKS: Had been a quicksilver miner in Brewster County, Texas. Governor Hobby appointed him as a reserve Ranger captain on May 19, 1919. He had been a peace officer in El Paso when his uncle, Charles Davis, was mayor. In 1919, his cousin was mayor of El Paso. LAW ENFORCEMENT RELATIVES: Ranger Bennett Hillsman Davis, son; Ranger Thomas Crosson, ex-brother-in-law; Ranger John Crosson, nephew. FAMILY: Parents, Bennett Hillsman Davis (b. 1832, TN) and Ruth D. Wilson (b. 1842, LA); sisters, Edna E. (b. 1869, TX), Lucille (b. 1871, TX); spouse #1, Elizabeth Crosson (b. 1876, TX), married about 1896, divorced by 1906; children, Bennett Hillsman (b. 1897, TX), Clement (b. 1902, TX); spouse #2, Buena B. (b. 1890), married about 1906, she died before 1920; son, William W., Jr. (b. 1910, TX); adopted son, John W. (b. 1908, TX). *SR; 471; Hobby to Harley, May 19, 1919, AGC; Burges to Harley, May 3, 1919, AGC; Special Orders No. 21, Mar 10, 1919, WC; Holliday to Harley, Mar 5, 1919, AGC; A1a, b, d, e, f; A4b.*

DAWS, ALBERT C. "A. C.," "BUCK." Born Oct. 8, 1860, Hood County, Texas (one source states born in Eliasville, Young County, Texas). No physical description, married. Stock raiser, Throckmorton, Throckmorton County, Texas. LOYALTY RANGER June 14, 1918–Jan. 15, 1919. REMARKS: Still a stock rancher in Throckmorton County in 1930. Died Dec. 23, 1943, Baylor County, Texas. FAMILY: Parents, John Joseph Daws (b. 1834, VA) and Ellen (b. 1836, LA); siblings, Samuel (b. 1857, TX), Virginia L. (b. 1859, TX), Richard (b. 1864, LA), Wm. (b. 1866, LA), Hettie Alice (b. 1867, TX), Robert (b. 1872, TX), Lucy (b. 1876, TX); spouse, Essie or Isie Lacy (b. 1874, TX), married June 10, 1894, Eliasville; children, Durer (b. 1895, TX), May B. (b. 1899, TX), Frank (b. 1903, TX). *SR; A1aa, b, d, e, f, g; A4g; C.*

DAWSON, JAMES C. Born Sept. 1871, Lampasas, Lampasas County, Texas. Ht. 5 ft. 11 in., blue eyes, gray-brown hair, red complexion, married. Coal, wood, and oil dealer, Snyder, Scurry County, Texas. LOYALTY RANGER June 5, 1918–Feb. 19, 1919. REMARKS: Had been a teamster in Scurry County. A James C. Dawson died Mar. 26, 1954, Scurry County, Texas. FAMILY: Parents, Thomas P. Dawson (b. 1839, TN) and Helen Greenwood (b. 1846, TX); siblings, Robert Bruce (b. 1866, TX), Martha E. (b. 1869, TX), Romalus (b. 1874, TX), Harriet F. "Hattie" (b. 1877, TX), Faye (b. 1879, TX), William Maxwell (b. 1881, TX), Phillip Napoleon (b. 1885, TX); spouse, Lula B. Standifer (b. 1875, TX), married about 1898; daughter, Dura M. (b. 1898, TX). *SR; A1b, d, e, f; A4a, b, g; B1; C.*

DAY, ALONZO RUDOLPH. Born July 8, 1881, Eastland, Eastland County, Texas. Ht. 5 ft. 9 ½ in., gray eyes, brown hair, light complexion, married. District clerk, Baird, Callahan County, Texas. SPECIAL RANGER May 29, 1917–Dec. 1917 (attached to Co. C). REMARKS: Had been deputy district clerk in Eastland County. Was deputy sheriff (office deputy), Eastland County, 3 years. In 1910 was a furniture merchant in Callahan County; in 1920 was an oil lease speculator, living in Baird. In 1930 was an insurance salesman in Fort Worth, Tarrant County, Texas. Died Sept. 6, 1963, Tarrant County, Texas. LAW ENFORCEMENT RELATIVES: Ranger Frank E. Day, nephew; Justice of the Peace (1900, Eastland County) Samuel J. Day, brother. FAMILY: Parents, William Hart Day (b. 1835, TN) and Elizabeth Sweatt (b. 1843, TN); siblings, Samuel (b. 1868, TN), Sallie (b. 1871, TN), W. Hart (b. 1873, TN), C. H. (b. 1876, TX), Eugene Franklin (b. 1877, TX), Jesse Coe (b. 1884, TX); spouse, Etta Mae Coffman (b. 1884, TX), married 1904; children, Marguerite (b. 1907, TX), Norman (b. 1909, TX), Melvin (b. 1912, TX). *SR; A1b, e, f, g; A3a; A4b; B1.*

DAY, FRANK ELLIS. Born Feb. 4, 1889, Eastland, Eastland County, Texas. Ht. 5 ft. 9 in., gray eyes, brown hair, fair complexion, married. Banker, Eastland. LOYALTY RANGER June 5, 1918–Feb. 1919. Oil business, Eastland. SPECIAL RANGER Aug. 26, 1919–Dec. 31, 1919. REMARKS: In 1910 had been deputy district clerk in Eastland County. As of June 1917 was cashier, First State Bank, Eastland. Was still an oil producer in Eastland County in 1930. Died Apr. 8, 1963, Eastland County, Texas. LAW ENFORCEMENT RELATIVES: Ranger Alonzo R. Day, uncle; Justice of the Peace (1900, Eastland County) Samuel J. Day, father. FAMILY: Parents, Samuel James Day (b. 1868, TN) and Annie Elizabeth Keahey (b. 1871, TX); siblings, George Eugene, Mabel Elizabeth, Montie Iona (b. 1892, TX), Sallie E. (b. 1893, TX), Mary Hart (b. 1895, TX), Samuel James (b. 1901, TX), William Melton (b. 1905, TX); spouse, Rose E. Simmons (b. 1890, TX), married about 1909; daughters, Edna M. (b. 1910, TX), Elizabeth A. (b. 1913, TX), Dorothy (b. 1916, TX). *SR; A1d, e, f, g; A2b; A3a; A4a, b; B1.*

DAY, JOHN T. Born Oct. 1867, De Soto County, Mississippi. Ht. 5 ft. 10 in., blue eyes, light hair, blonde complexion, married. Merchant, Hamlin, Jones County, Texas. SPECIAL RANGER June 2, 1917–Dec. 1917 (attached to Co. C). REMARKS: Had been a hardware merchant in Rotan, Fisher County, Texas; still sold hardware in Hamlin in 1930. FAMILY: Parents, Job Bishop Day (b. 1831, PA) and Ann Sophira Tate (b. 1843, TN); siblings, Eugene R. (b. 1869, MS), James Bishop "Jim" (b. 1876, MS), F. S. (b. 1878, MS); spouse, Eula (b. 1872, AL), married about 1894; children, John Edward (b. 1894, TX), Elizabeth (b. 1901, TX), Blanche Louise (b. 1910, TX). *SR; A1a, b, e, f, g; A2e; A3a; A4a, b.*

DEAN, JOHN MORTIMER. Born Nov. 17, 1860, Anderson County, South Carolina. Ht. 5 ft. 6 ¼ in., blue eyes, dark hair, fair complexion, married. Farmer and stockman, Grand Saline, Van Zandt County, Texas. LOYALTY RANGER June 5, 1918–Feb. 1919. REMARKS: Belonged to the "Western Division, South Carolina 'Red Shirt' Cavalry, 1876–1878." In 1900 census, was living in Van Zandt County, listed as "Legislator." In 1910 was a bank president in Van Zandt County. In 1920 was a cattle rancher in Eagle, McCurtain County, Oklahoma. FAMILY: Parents, Robert Baylis Dean (b. 1837, SC) and Sarah Amanda Burress (b. 1840, SC); siblings, William Lewis (b. 1858, SC), Robert Baylis (b. 1861, SC), Leonora Palmira (b. 1865, SC), Major Augustus (b. 1868, SC), Amy Lillian (b. 1870, SC), Luther Edwin (b. 1873, SC), Annie Eulala (b. 1875, SC), Waddy A. (b. 1877, SC); spouse, Christiana "Coonie" Ellis (b. 1868, TX), married about 1887; children, Floyd Ellis (b. 1889, TX), Amie Louceille (b. 1891, TX), Earley Alton (b. 1894, TX), Boyce C. (b. 1896, TX), John Luster (b. 1900, TX), Major Mortimer (b. 1903, TX), Wayne Henry (b. 1906, TX), Alma E. (b. 1909, TX), John Mortimer, Jr. (b. 1912, TX). *SR; A1aa, a, b, d, e, f; A4b, g.*

DEES, MYRON ADOLPH. Born June 21, 1877, Bandera County, Texas. Tall, medium build, gray eyes, dark hair, married. Stockman, Llano, Llano County, Texas. LOYALTY RANGER Apr. 7, 1918–Feb. 1919. REMARKS: As a small child lived in Atascosa County, Texas. In 1910 was a farmer living in Bighill Township, Osage County, Oklahoma. WWI Draft Registration document (Sept. 1918) states "lost right eye." In 1930 was a rancher in Llano. A Myron A. Dees died Dec. 29, 1961, Travis County, Texas. FAMILY: Parents, Edgar Calhoun Dees (b. 1850, LA) and Clara Ann Strickland (b. 1855, TX); siblings, N. E. (b. 1874, TX), Alfred Oliver (b. 1879, TX), Iona (b. 1891, TX), Willoughby Jerome (b. 1893, TX), Sidney (b. 1899, TX); spouse, Emma Valore or Valvie White (b. 1878, TX), married Dec. 7, 1898, Llano County; children, M. O. (b. 1902, TX), Bertice (b. 1904, TX), Matt Moss (b. 1906, TX), Ethel T. (b. 1908, OK). *SR; A1b, d, e, f, g; A2b, c; A3a; A4a, g.*

DE LA GARZA, MIGUEL. Born May 1871, Randado Ranch, Jim Hogg County, Texas (Note: Jim Hogg County was not established until 1913; 1880 US Census records indicate Rendado [*sic*] Ranch in Zapata County, Texas.) Ht. 5 ft.

9 in., brown eyes, gray hair, dark complexion, married. Rancher, Randado. LOYALTY RANGER Aug. 2, 1918–Feb. 1919. REMARKS: Randado was located near Hebbronville, Jim Hogg County. In 1910, Miguel de la Garza was county treasurer, Zapata County. FAMILY: Parents, Bernardo de la Garza (b. 1837, Mexico) and Margarita Garcia (b. 1840, Mexico); siblings, Rosita (b. 1864, Mexico), Ignacio (b. 1865, TX), Maria (b. 1866, TX); spouse, Inez or Ines F. (b. 1872, Mexico), married about 1893; children, Guadalupe (b. 1895, TX), Ignacio (b. 1897, TX), Margarita (b. 1899, TX), Maria L. (b. 1903, TX), Miguel (b. 1905, TX), twins Rafael and Hortensia (b. 1908, TX). *SR; A1b, d, e; A4a.*

DE MULLOS, CARLOS. Born June 1872, Douglas, Arizona. Ht. 5 ft. 9 in., brown eyes, black hair, dark complexion. Wrangler, enlisted in Hidalgo County, Texas. REGULAR RANGER Aug. 5, 1918–Aug. 31, 1918 (private, Co. G). Resigned. REMARKS: Note length of service. Had been a government employee, 1902–1918. *SR; Stevens to Harley, Dec 14, 1917, Jan 4, 1918, AGC; Arnold to Cardwell, Sept 6, 1918, AGC; De Mullos to AG, Sept 12, 1918, AGC.*

DENALSANO, WALTO LEON. Born 1869, Monterrey, Nuevo Leon, Mexico. Ht. 5 ft. 9 in., gray eyes, black hair, dark complexion, married. Deputy game warden, Eagle Pass, Maverick County, Texas. SPECIAL RANGER Feb. 12, 1917–Dec. 1917; Feb. 11, 1918–Jan. 15, 1919. REMARKS: Immigrated to the United States in 1889, became a naturalized citizen. Had served 15 years in the regular Army as a musician; honorably discharged. Served in the 3rd Texas Infantry Regiment, 1898–1899. Had been a constable and deputy sheriff. Had been a Wells Fargo guard. In 1920 owned a tailor shop in Eagle Pass. Died Dec. 4, 1951, Bexar County, Texas. FAMILY: Spouse, Mary (or Marie) Gaines (b. 1887, TX), married Oct. 16, 1901, Eagle Pass; children, Walto L., Jr. (b. 1905, TX), Chiara (b. 1914, TX). *SR; BDH, Jan 23, 1915; Denalsano to AG, Jan 26, 1917, Aug 23, 1919, AGC; AG to Denalsano, Jan 30, 1917, AGC; Denalsano's Monthly Report, Nov, 1917, AGC; A1f; A2e; A3b; A4a; C.*

DENISON, FRANK WILLIS, JR. Born Sept. 1, 1890, Belton, Bell County, Texas. Ht. 5 ft. 9 ¾ in., gray eyes, brown hair, light complexion. Mining engineer and manager of a coal mine, McDade, Bastrop County, Texas. SPECIAL RANGER July 17, 1917–Dec. 1917 (attached to Co. D). REMARKS: Grew up in Bell County; spent adult life as a mine operator in Bastrop County. Died Aug. 25, 1971, Bastrop County, Texas. FAMILY: Parents, Frank Lambdin Denison (b. 1868, TX) and Caroline Isabelle "Callie" Sanders (b. 1871, TX); siblings, Susie Bess (b. 1892, TX), Marie Elizabeth (b. 1894, TX), James Swayne (b. 1896, TX), Gippie Evangeline (b. 1900, TX), Fla Downs (b. 1908, TX), Raleigh Edmond (b. 1909, TX), twins Jack Wright and William Powers "Mack" (b. 1914, TX); spouse, Myrtle E. Hood (b. 1894, TX), married about 1919; son, Frank Willis, Jr. (b. 1921, TX). *SR; A1d, e, f, g; A2a, b, e; A3a; A4b.*

DENSON, BENJAMIN F. Born Dec. 1850, Brandon, Rankin County, Mississippi. Ht. 6 ft. 1 in., blue eyes, light hair, light complexion. Brand inspector, Panhandle & Southwestern Cattle Raisers' Association, Amarillo, Potter County, Texas. SPECIAL RANGER Mar. 16, 1918–Jan. 15, 1919. REMARKS: In 1900 and 1910 was a cattle and brand inspector in Kansas City, Jackson County, Missouri. In 1920 was a livestock inspector in Fort Worth, Tarrant County, Texas. A B. F. Denson died Oct. 5, 1925, Williamson County, Texas. FAMILY: Parents, Shadrack Denson (b. 1809, TN) and Eliza Williams (b. 1814, MS); siblings, Elizabeth (b. 1839, MS), Martha (b. 1843, MS), Florence (b. 1845, MS), Shadrack (b. 1846, MS); spouse, Mattie (b. 1861, KY), married about 1878; children, Eula L. (b. 1878, TX), Samuel B. (b. 1880, TX). *SR; 471; Hudspeth to Hobby, Jan 25, 1918, AGC; A1aaa, a, d, e, f; A2b; A4b, g.*

DESPAIN, DUNCAN LEMONS "BUD." Born Dec. 14, 1879, Durell, Atascosa County, Texas. Ht. 5 ft. 10 ½ in., blue eyes, brown hair, red complexion. Ranchman, Laredo, Webb County, Texas. SPECIAL RANGER Mar. 16, 1917–July 23, 1917. Discharged. Ranchman, Laredo. REGULAR RANGER July 1, 1919–Sept. 20, 1919 (private, Co. C). Resigned. REMARKS: Had been a railroad brakeman in San Antonio, Bexar County, Texas. Sometime between July 23, 1917 and July 1, 1919 was a mounted Immigration inspector. In Nov. 1919 became a Webb County deputy sheriff. Died June 13, 1945, Webb County, Texas; buried in City Cemetery, Laredo. FAMILY: Parents, John Wesley DeSpain (b. 1835, TN) and Elizabeth Ann Arnold (b. 1842, TX); siblings, John Wesley (b. 1864, TX), Simpson Franklin (b. 1866, TX), Daniel Arnold (b. 1869, TX), Keziah (b. 1871, TX), Matilda

(b. 1873, TX), Marshall Bey (b. 1876, TX), Fannie. *SR; 471; LWT, Nov 9, 1919; A1e, f, g; A3a; A4a, b, g; C.*

DIAL, JACKSON "JACK." Born Mar. 1866, Grapevine, Tarrant County, Texas. Ht. 5 ft. 8 ½ in., brown hair, brown eyes, dark complexion, widower. Barber, Stamford, Jones County, Texas. SPECIAL RANGER May 31, 1917–Dec. 1917 (attached to Co. C). REMARKS: Was a barber in Jones County by 1900. A Jack Dial died Mar. 12, 1928, Dallas County, Texas. FAMILY: Parents, Dr. Garlington Coker Dial (b. 1832, SC or TN) and Mary J. (b. 1842, AL); siblings, Bell (b. 1859, TX), Isaac William (b. 1862, TX), Arthur (b. 1872, TX), Elbert (b. 1873, TX), Garlington (b. 1877, TX), Mary J. "Molly" (b. 1880, TX), Amy (b. 1885, TX); spouse #1, unknown, died before 1900; son, Lewis R. (b. 1896, OK); spouse #2, Anna L. (b. 1863, KY), married before 1920. *SR; Register to Ferguson, May 18, 1917, AGC; Cunningham to Ferguson, May 18, 1917, AGC; A1a, b, d, e, f; A4b; C.*

DIAL, JAMES LAWRENCE. Born June 15, 1876, Floresville, Wilson County, Texas. Ht. 5 ft. 8 in., blue eyes, dark hair, light complexion, married. Stockman, enlisted in Val Verde County, Texas. REGULAR RANGER Nov. 20, 1917–Mar. 10, 1919 (private, Co. E; transferred to Co. M, Feb. 1918). Discharged—Co. M was disbanded. Ranchman, San Antonio, Bexar County, Texas. REGULAR RANGER Dec. 4, 1919–Feb. 10, 1921 (private, Co. F; promoted to sergeant May 17, 1920). Discharged. Cattle Dealer, San Antonio. RAILROAD RANGER Aug. 23, 1922–Nov. 19, 1922 (Co. A). Discharged—reduction in force. REMARKS: Was said to have been born in Fairview, Wilson County. In Sept. 1919 was a mounted policeman in San Antonio. Died Nov. 18, 1955, Atascosa County, Texas; buried in Fairview. FAMILY: Parents, James Laurens Dial (b. 1839, LA) and Mary Minervia Runels (b. 1856, TX); sisters, Annie S. (b. 1874, TX), twins Mozilla and Estella (b. 1886, TX); spouse, Jennie Carver, married June 2, 1907, Floresville; children, Jack Alfred (b. 1909, TX), Eva May (b. 1912, TX). *SR; 471; Special Orders No. 21, Mar 10, 1919, WC; Dial to AG, Sept 10, 1919, AGC; 1000: iii, 126–127; A1b, d, e, f; A3a; A4b; B1; C.*

DILLARD, EDWIN POTTER. Born June 30, 1873, Uvalde, Uvalde County, Texas. Ht. 5 ft. 6 in., blue eyes, light brown hair, light complexion, widower. Stockman, Uvalde. REGULAR RANGER Aug. 18, 1915–Jan. 21, 1916 (private, Co. A). Resigned. REMARKS: Died Mar. 8, 1928, Uvalde, Uvalde County, Texas. FAMILY: Parents, Allen Butcher Dillard (b. 1825, TN) and Elizabeth Sellend Sophronia Patterson (b. 1830, AL); siblings, Tallithie Jane (b. 1847), Allen George (b. 1848, TX), Sophronia A. (b. 1850, TX), Nancy Elizabeth (b. 1852, TX), Susiana (b. 1854), Alpha James (b. 1857, TX), Sarah A. (b. 1859), Jefferson Davis (b. 1861), Mary Maud (b. 1865, TX), Joseph Henry (b. 1869, TX), Flora Elizabeth (b. 1871, TX), John Theophiles (b. 1877, TX); spouse, Roxianna Gilbert (b. 1876, TX), married Sept. 6, 1893, she died in 1907; children, Mamie Bethel (b. 1896, TX), Henry Merle (b. 1897, TX), Willie Ira (b. 1899, TX), Edwin Potter "Jack" (b. 1901, TX), Ruby Anna belle (b. 1904, TX). *SR; 471; A1b, d, e; A2b; A4a, b, g.*

DILWORTH, J. C. Born Oct. 1891, Gonzales, Gonzales County, Texas. Ht. 5 ft. 8 in., blue eyes, black hair, fair complexion, married. Ranchman. REGULAR RANGER Aug. 27, 1918–Feb. 1, 1919 (private, no company listed; transferred to Co. K, Jan. 1, 1919). Resigned. Farmer, Corpus Christi, Nueces County, Texas. RAILROAD RANGER Aug. 16, 1922–Sept. 15, 1922. Discharged. REMARKS: In 1930 a James C. Dilworth, born about 1893 in Texas, was a U.S. Customs officer living in San Antonio, Bexar County, Texas. He was a widower with two sons. *SR; 471; Aldrich to Edelstein, Sept 8, 1919, AGC; A1g.*

DINWIDDIE, SETH THOMAS. Born Oct. 7, 1859, Red River County, Texas. No personal description. Farmer, Clarksville, Red River County. LOYALTY RANGER June 28, 1918–Feb. 1919. REMARKS: Red River County sheriff Oct. 20, 1893–Nov. 8, 1898 and Nov. 4, 1902–Nov. 6, 1906 and Nov. 5, 1912–Nov. 15, 1912. Died Aug. 12, 1922. FAMILY: Parents, William Jasper Dinwiddie (b. 1812, KY) and Lucy Elizabeth Gilliam (b. 1819, VA or MO); siblings, Harriett Ann (b. 1840, TN), Charles Robert (b. 1842, TN), Sarah William (b. 1844, TN), Jedidiah (b. 1846, TN), James Bradley (b. 1848, TN), Mary Susan (b. 1850, TN), Ballard Alvin (b. 1853, on wagon train to Texas), William Jasper (b. 1856, TX), Martha Jane (b. 1857), Lucy Elizabeth (b. 1862, TX). *SR; 1503:434; A1aa, a, f; A4a, b, g.*

DISSLER, JOHN. Born May 9, 1883, Boerne, Kendall County, Texas. Ht. 6 ft. 1 in., brown eyes, brown hair, light complexion. Ranchman, Comstock, Val Verde County, Texas. SPECIAL RANGER Jan. 31, 1918–Jan. 15, 1919 (Co. A Volunteers). REMARKS: One source says born in Kendalia, Kendall County. Died Nov. 1, 1952, Val Verde County, Texas. FAMILY: Parents, Charles Dissler (b. 1846, Switzerland) and Sarah Elizabeth "Lizzie" Edge (b. 1853, GA); siblings, Henry William (b. 1880, TX), Charles Franklin (b. 1887, TX), Benjamin Harrison (b. 1889, TX); spouse, Nellie McFaddin (b. 1897, TX), married July 19, 1919, Rock Springs, Edwards County, Texas; son, John McFaddin (b. 1931, TX). *SR; A1b, e, f; A2b, e; A3c; A4b; B1.*

DONALDSON, JOHN L. Born Dec. 27, 1887, The Grove, Coryell County, Texas (one source cites birthplace as Drew County (?), Arkansas). Ht. 5 ft. 11 in., blue eyes, brown hair, light complexion, widower, as of July 1918. Stock farmer and peace officer, The Grove. SPECIAL RANGER July 15, 1918–Jan. 15, 1919. Inspector, Houston, Harris County, Texas. SPECIAL RANGER June 21, 1933–June 20, 1935. REMARKS: Peace officer, Coryell County, ca. 1910–1918. Enlisted in the Army, was honorably discharged Jan. 1919. In 1930 lived in Gatesville, Coryell County. A John Lee Donaldson died Jan 6, 1960, Coryell County, Texas. FAMILY: Parents, John Edward Donaldson (b. 1863, AR) and Ida Lee Veazy (b. 1869, AR); siblings, Nettie Abbie (b. 1890, AR), Flora (b. 1892, TX), Guy (b. 1894, TX), Rex (b. 1896, TX), William Fay (b. 1898, TX), Thomas Cecil "Ace" (b. 1900, TX), Marshall (b. 1903, TX), Abner (b. 1905, TX), Neta J. (b. 1908, TX); spouse #1, Clara A. (b. 1894, TX), married about 1910; spouse #2, Annie M. (b. 1889, TX), married about 1921; son, Earl B. (b. 1921, TX). *SR; Mayfield to Harley, July 15, 18, 1918, AGC; Priddo to Colquitt, July 17, 1918, AGC; Assistant AG to Donaldson, July 22, 1918, AGC; A1d, e, g; A2b; A3a; A4b.*

DOOLEY, JOHN H. Born 1871, Deport, Lamar County, Texas. Ht. 6 ft. 1 ½ in., hazel eyes, light hair, light complexion, married. Farmer, Clarksville, Red River County, Texas. LOYALTY RANGER June 8, 1918–Feb. 1919. Rancher, Clarksville. RAILROAD RANGER Sept. 9, 1922–Mar. 15, 1923. Discharged—"services & conduct splendid." REMARKS: In 1920 was managing a cotton gin in Clarksville. As of 1922, said he had been a peace officer for 20 years. As a Railroad Ranger was stationed at Texarkana, Bowie County, Texas, guarding the Kansas City Southern Railroad. In 1930 was working for the highway department, still living in Clarksville. John Hiram Dooley died May 28, 1951, Grayson County, Texas; buried in Garland Cemetery, Red River County. FAMILY: Parents, John Esom Dooley (b. 1843, AR) and Nancy M. Grant (b. 1840, TN); siblings, Sarah M. (b. 1872, TX), Mary E. (b. 1879, TX); spouse, JoElla G. Garland (b. 1879, TX), married about 1913; sons, Joseph H. (b. 1915, OK), Jack W. (b. 1917, TX). *SR; A1b, f, g; A2b; A4a, b, g.*

DOUGHERTY, MARCELLUS BURTON, JR. Born June 6, 1895, Arroyo Colorado, Hidalgo County, Texas. Ht. 5 ft. 9 in., blue eyes, light hair, light complexion. Texas quarantine guard. REGULAR RANGER May 18, 1916–Aug. 31, 1916 (private, Co. D). Resigned. Express guard, Brownsville, Cameron County, Texas. SPECIAL RANGER Dec. 18, 1916–Mar. 31, 1917 (attached to Co. C). Discharged. REMARKS: In Mar. 1917 was appointed by sheriff as caretaker of Cameron County courthouse, to succeed his late father. In Jan. 1918 was a Cameron County deputy sheriff at Brownsville. A Marcelous [*sic*] Dougherty died Oct. 29, 1918, Cameron County, Texas. LAW ENFORCEMENT RELATIVES: Ranger and Hidalgo County deputy sheriff (1900) Marcellus Dougherty, father. FAMILY: Parents, Marcellus Dougherty (b. 1860, TX) and Emma B. (b. 1873, TX); siblings, Anita (b. 1894, TX), Eduardo Burton or Barton "Eddie"(b. 1899, TX), Lily (b. 1902, TX), Emma (b. 1905, TX), Maggie (b. 1907, TX), Ida (b. 1910, TX). *SR; 471; BDH, Mar 5, 1917, Jan 2, 1918; A1d; A3a; C.*

DOWDY, JAMES F. "JESSE." Born July 1872, Florence, Lauderdale County, Alabama. Ht. 5 ft. 10 in., blue eyes, dark hair, light complexion, married. Hardware dealer, Fluvanna, Scurry County, Texas. SPECIAL RANGER Aug. 14, 1917–Dec. 1917 (attached to Co. C). REMARKS: Had lived in Scurry County since 1893. In 1920 was a druggist for Home Town Drug Store in Scurry County; still a drug salesman in Scurry County in 1930. A Jessie Franklin Dowdy died Jan. 4, 1953, Scurry County, Texas. FAMILY: Parents, James T. Dowdy (b. 1851, AL) and Mary J. (b. 1850, AL); siblings, John T. (1870, AL), Mary (b. 1874, AL), Sarah (b. 1877, AL), Martha (b. 1880, AL); spouse, Margaret (b. 1878, AL), married about 1896; children, James Clarence (b. 1896, TX), Cora (b. 1899, TX), Ruby (b. 1901, TX). *SR; Merrell to AG, July 9, 1917, AGC; A1b, e, f, g; C.*

DOWE, JAMES WATSON. Born Dec. 16, 1881, Wadesville or Wanesville (?), Edwards County, Texas. Ht. 5 ft. 11 in., brown eyes, dark hair, dark complexion, married. Deputy sheriff, Asherton, Dimmit County, Texas. SPECIAL RANGER Apr. 30, 1918–Sept. 1, 1918. Discharged because in August he'd joined the Immigration Service as an inspector at Eagle Pass, Maverick County, Texas. REMARKS: Dimmit County deputy sheriff, ca. 1912–1918. In 1930 was a border patrolman living in Webb County, Texas. Died Apr. 19, 1954, Laredo, Webb County, Texas. LAW ENFORCEMENT RELATIVES: Ranger Orin C. Dowe, cousin. FAMILY: Parents, Judge Samuel Thomas Dowe (b. 1853, MS) and Bonney Mary Leavitt (b. 1857, TX); siblings, Myrtle J. (b. 1884, TX), Mildred J, (b. 1885, TX), Fannie J. (b. 1887, TX), Samuel Thomas, Jr. (b. 1889, TX); stepmother, Lucie A. (b. 1855, LA); brother, Leslie Howard (b. 1895, TX); spouse, Bertie Dalton Brown (b. 1894, TX), married July 4, 1916; children, James Watson, Jr. (b. 1917, TX), Thomas Wheatfield (b. 1919, TX), Virginia (b. 1921, TX). *SR; Gardner to Harley, Aug 30, 1918, AGC; Assistant AG to Gardner, Apr 25, 1918, AGC; A1d, f, g; A2b, e; A3a; A4a.*

DOWE, ORIN CURTICE. Born June 11, 1883, Cuero, DeWitt County, Texas. Ht. 5 ft. 10 ½ in., blue eyes, black hair, light complexion, married. Rancher, Marfa, Presidio County, Texas. SPECIAL RANGER Dec. 15, 1917–Apr. 12, 1918. On Apr. 12, 1918 went on active duty. REGULAR RANGER Apr. 12, 1918–Aug. 1918 (private, Co. B; transferred to Co. D, June 8, 1918 when Co. B was disbanded). Resigned. REMARKS: Prior to 1917 enlistment had been a mounted Customs inspector for 11 years in the Big Bend, including 5 years as inspector in charge at Marfa. In 1919 was a Customs inspector and small rancher in the Big Bend. In 1930 was a rancher in Marfa. Died June 6, 1970, El Paso County, Texas. LAW ENFORCEMENT RELATIVES: Ranger James W. Dowe, cousin. FAMILY: Parents, William Percy Dowe (b. 1857, MS) and unknown (b. TX); siblings, Almon (b. 1885, TX), Rowland Howard (b. 1886, TX), Lorenzo (b. 1888, TX), Jeanette (b. 1889, TX); stepmother, Eliza (b. 1869, England); sisters, Ora or Ola (b. 1896, TX), Ada (b. 1898, TX); step-brothers, Walter Myers (b. 1889, TX), Robert Myers (b. 1890, TX); spouse #1, Delia Shoemake (b. 1886, TX), married about 1909; daughter, Eva (b. 1910, TX), stepson, Riley Gaurley (b. 1904, TX); spouse #2, Millie, married before Sept. 1918. *SR; 471; Woodul to Dowe, July 3, 1918, AGC; Dowe to Harley, July 6, 1918, AGC; General Orders No. 5, June 4, 1918, AGC; Walter Rushin's statement, June 14, 1915, WC; AA, May 13, 20, 1915; 1:I, 1556–1558; A1aa, d, e, g; A2a, b; A3a; A4b.*

DOWNING, SCOTT MURPHY. Born Nov. 2, 1870, Boonville, Dallas County, Iowa. Ht. 5 ft. 8 ½ in., blue eyes, light hair, light complexion, married. Stockman, Canyon, Randall County, Texas. LOYALTY RANGER June 15, 1918–Feb. 1919. REMARKS: Was a farmer in Oklahoma between 1895–1910. Died Apr. 2, 1935, Canyon, Randall County, Texas; buried in Canyon. FAMILY: Parents, John Herdman Downing (b. 1827, OH) and Nancy Mustard (b. 1825, OH); siblings, George Washington (b. 1849, OH), twins James H. and Mary Elizabeth (b. 1852, IA), Ruth Josephine (b. 1855, IA), Francis Alva (b. 1857, IA), Rachel Cora (b. 1860, IA), Parthena Loretta (b. 1865, IA); spouse, Bessie Elizabeth Hunt (b. 1877, IA), married Oct. 29, 1893, Davis County, Iowa; children, Okla Faye (b. 1895, OK), Ruth Francis (b. 1897, OK), John Levi (b. 1899, OK), Gladys (b. 1901, OK), Marie (b. 1905, OK), Marion S. (b. 1908, OK), Neal H. (b. 1911, TX), Esther E. (b. 1913, TX), Jack Devere (b. 1916, TX), Scott M. (b. 1919, TX). *SR; A1b, d, f, g; A4a, b, g; B2; C.*

DOWNS, JAMES B. Born Jan. 1865, Waco, McLennan County, Texas. Ht. 6 ft. 1 in., blue eyes, light hair, light complexion, married as of Dec. 1917. REGULAR RANGER, 1894 (Co. B). Stock farmer, real estate, Lockney, Floyd County, Texas. SPECIAL RANGER Dec. 11, 1917–Mar. 18, 1918 (Co. B Volunteer—station: Plainview). Discharged. REMARKS: Mar. 1918 letterhead: "J. B. Downs Land, Cattle & Loan Co., Lockney." FAMILY: Parents, William A. Downs (b. 1821, GA) and Elizabeth Thomas Kemp (b. 1821, GA); siblings, Hannah Lenora (b. 1852, AR), Benjamin Oliver (b. 1856, TX), twins Louisa Lucy Sue and Elizabeth (b. 1859, TX), twins William and Sarah L. (b. 1862, TX); spouse, Ora Peters (b. 1879, TX), married May 7, 1899, Smith County, Texas; children, Ryan (b. 1896, TX), Gen (b. 1907, TX). *SR; 471; Rawlings to Harley, Dec 12, 1917, AGC; Downs to Harley, Mar 18, 1918, AGC; A1a, b, d, f; A2c; A4a, b, g.*

DRAKE, MILLARD OTHO. Born Aug. 28, 1881, Tilden, McMullen County, Texas. Ht. 5 ft. 10 ½ in., brown eyes, brown hair, light complexion. Cowboy, enlisted in

Culberson County, Texas. REGULAR RANGER Apr. 16, 1918–Aug. 31, 1918 (private, Co. N—Hudspeth Scouts). Discharged. REMARKS: In the 1910 census, a Millard O. Drake, age 28, managed a pool hall in Irion County, Texas; married with two children. A Millard O. Drake died Feb. 1, 1928, Tom Green County, Texas. FAMILY: Parents, F. M. Drake (b. 1838, TX) and Margaret A. (b. 1841, TX); siblings, James H. (b. 1858, TX), N. E. (b. 1864, TX), Hugh (b. 1866, TX), S. B. (b. 1867, TX), Adelia (b. 1869, TX), William T. (b. 1872, TX), Mary E. (b. 1875, TX); spouse (?), Myra (b. 1887, TX), married about 1905; children (?), Frances (b. 1906, TX), Lea D. (b. 1909, TX). *SR; 471; A1b, e; A3a; C.*

DRAPER, ASA LEE. Born May 15, 1880, Mineral Wells, Palo Pinto County, Texas. Ht. 5 ft. 8 in., blue eyes, brown hair, fair complexion, married. Ranchman, Hebbronville, Jim Hogg County, Texas. SPECIAL RANGER Apr. 30, 1918–Jan. 15, 1919. REMARKS: Still a stock rancher in Jim Hogg County in 1930. Died July 23, 1953, Jim Hogg County, Texas. LAW ENFORCEMENT RELATIVES: Ranger John C. Draper, brother. FAMILY: Parents, John Jasper Draper (b. 1849, MS) and Charlotte C. "Lottie" (b. 1854, AR or MO); siblings, Eudotia "Docia" L. (b. 1872, TX), Arminta Ellen (b. 1874, TX), James William (b. 1875, TX), John Coats (b. 1877, TX), Mary A. (b. 1879, TX), Samuel J. F. (b. 1880, TX); spouse, Myrtle H. (b. 1889, TX), married about 1907; son, Alfred L. (b. 1909, TX). *SR; A1d, f, g; A3a; A4b; C.*

DRAPER, JOHN COATS. Born Apr. 9, 1877, Palo Pinto, Palo Pinto County, Texas. Ht. 5 ft. 7 in., blue eyes, light hair, red complexion, married. Brand inspector, Cattle Raisers' Association of Texas, Hebbronville, Jim Hogg County, Texas. SPECIAL RANGER Apr. 30, 1917–Dec. 1917 (attached to Co. C); Jan. 19, 1918–Jan. 15, 1919. In 1918 was classed as a Regular Ranger without pay. REMARKS: In 1910 was a stockman on a horse ranch in Carlsbad, Eddy County, New Mexico. Was Jim Hogg County deputy sheriff at least 5 years. Brand inspector, Cattle Raisers' Association of Texas, 1910–1917. Was stock rancher in Jim Hogg County in 1930. A J. C. Draper died May 2, 1930, San Patricio County, Texas. LAW ENFORCEMENT RELATIVES: Ranger Asa Draper, brother. FAMILY: Parents, John Jasper Draper (b. 1849, MS) and Charlotte C. "Lottie" (b. 1854, AR or MO); siblings, Eudotia "Docia" L. (b. 1872, TX), Arminta Ellen (b. 1874, TX), James William (b. 1875, TX), Mary A. (b. 1879, TX), Samuel J. F. (b. 1880, TX), Asa L. (b. 1880, TX); spouse, Tena Lucille Nymeyer (b. 1882, ID), married about 1904 in Hebbronville; children, Dorothy L. (b. 1908, NM), John E. (b. 1912, NM). *SR; Allen to Ferguson, Apr 26, 28, 1917, AGC; Hutchings to Draper, May 2, 1917, AGC; Craighead to Hutchings, Apr 14, 1917, AGC; Draper to Ferguson, Apr 24, 1917, AGC; Craighead to Ferguson, Apr 24, 1917, AGC; Draper to Harley, Dec 24, 1917, AGC; Craighead to Harley, Jan 9, 1918, AGC; Acting AG to Moses & Rowe, Jan 12, 1918, AGC; Moses & Rowe to Draper, Jan 16, 1918, AGC; A1b, d, e, g; A2b; A3a; A4a, b.*

DRAPER, JOHN FIELDS. Born July 1868, Manor, Travis County, Texas. Ht. 5 ft. 8 in., black eyes, black hair, dark complexion, married. Rancher, Del Rio, Val Verde County, Texas. SPECIAL RANGER May 16, 1916–Dec. 1917 (attached to Co. C). REMARKS: Had been an Edwards County deputy sheriff several times. In 1916 had a small ranch on the Edwards County line. In 1930 was a cattle inspector, living in Del Rio. Died Nov. 27, 1953, Val Verde County, Texas. FAMILY: Parents, John Milton Draper (b. 1808, TN) and Susan Fitzgerald Johnson (b. 1827, TN), siblings, Harriet Cummings (b. 1846), Sarah Phoebe (b. 1850, TN), James Polk (b. 1851, TN), Mary Elizabeth (b. 1852, TN), David Johnson (b. 1855, TN), Edward Bradley (b. 1857, TN), Joseph Robert (b. 1859, TN), Emma Grace (b. 1861, TN), Andrew Jackson (b. 1863), Virginia E. (b. 1864, TX), Samuel Milton "Tony" (b. 1865, TX); spouse, Carrie Balou (b. 1872, TX), married about 1897; sons, Johnnie F. (b. 1898, TX), Sam Murdock (b. 1900, TX), James Claude (b. 1902, TX), Jack (b. 1909, TX). *SR; Almond to Hutchings, May 18, 1917, AGC; A1a, b, e, f, g; A4g; C.*

DRISKILL, EVERETT D. Born Jan. 30, 1893, Baird, Callahan County, Texas. Ht. 5 ft. 7 ½ in., brown eyes, brown hair, light complexion, married. Banker, Baird. SPECIAL RANGER June 1, 1917–Dec. 1917 (attached to Co. C). REMARKS: Had been a dry goods clerk in Baird. In June 1917 was assistant cashier for the Home National Bank, Baird. Died Feb. 4, 1951, Los Angeles, California. LAW ENFORCEMENT RELATIVES: Ranger John A. Driskill, brother; Baird city marshal (1930) James C. Berringer, father-in-law. FAMILY: Parents, Samuel Lafayette Driskill (b. 1852, MO) and Elizabeth Berniece "Bettie" Day (b. 1864, TX); siblings, Ford Lafayette (b. 1885, TX), Homer Day

(b. 1887, TX), John Alexander (b. 1895, TX), Jeanette (b. 1897, TX); spouse, Corinne Berringer (b. 1891, TX). *SR; A1d, e, f, g; A2f; A3a; A4b.*

DRISKILL, JOHN ALEXANDER. Born June 16, 1895, Baird, Callahan County, Texas. Ht. 5 ft. 8 ½ in., blue eyes, light hair, fair complexion. Ranchman and telephone business, Baird. SPECIAL RANGER June 4, 1917–Dec. 1917 (attached to Co. C). REMARKS: In 1930 was a cattle farmer in Baird. Died Feb. 22, 1960, Tarrant County, Texas. LAW ENFORCEMENT RELATIVES: Ranger Everett D. Driskill, brother. FAMILY: Parents, Samuel Lafayette Driskill (b. 1852, MO) and Elizabeth Berniece "Bettie" Day (b. 1864, TX); siblings, Ford Lafayette (b. 1885, TX), Homer Day (b. 1887, TX), Everett D. (b. 1893, TX), Jeanette (b. 1898, TX); spouse, name unknown (b. 1903, TX), married about 1925. *SR; A1d, e, g; A2b; A3a; A4b; B1.*

DRODDY, SALVADOR A. Born Aug. 1861, Bee County, Texas. Ht. 5 ft. 10 in., blue eyes, light hair, light complexion, married. Butcher, Refugio, Refugio County, Texas. LOYALTY RANGER July 10, 1918–Feb. 1919. REMARKS: In 1880 was "running stock" in Bee County. In 1910 was a saloon owner in Refugio. Still lived in Refugio in 1930. Died Mar. 26, 1940, Refugio County, Texas. FAMILY: Parents, Calvin Droddy (b. 1825, IL) and Ellen Boales (b. 1838, TX); siblings, Elizabeth (b. 1856, TX), William Alexander (b. 1858, TX), Caroline (b. 1864, TX), Ellen Jenny (b. 1866, TX), Thomas Calvin (b. 1868, TX); stepmother, Beatrice Fain (b. 1825, MS); spouse, Sarah Elizabeth or Elizabeth C. Carlisle (b. 1866, TX), married May 1, 1882, Papalote, Bee County, Texas; sons, John Maurice (b. 1883, TX), William Worth (b. 1886, TX), Salvador John (b. 1890, TX). *SR; A1aa, a, b, d, e, f, g; A3a; A4b, g; C.*

DUBOSE, BEN BENNETT. Born Feb. 14, 1894, Mathis, San Patricio County, Texas. Ht. 5 ft. 8 in., gray eyes, brown hair, dark complexion. Stockman. REGULAR RANGER Aug. 16, 1915–Oct. 31, 1915 (private, Co. D). Dismissed. Peace officer. REGULAR RANGER May 12, 1916–Dec. 6, 1916 (private, Co. A). Resigned. REMARKS: Died Apr. 1971, Laredo, Webb County, Texas. LAW ENFORCEMENT RELATIVES: Ranger Edwin Morgan Dubose, father; Ranger Henry G. "Judge" Dubose, uncle; one-time justice of the peace Friendly H. Dubose, grandfather. FAMILY: Parents, Edwin Morgan Dubose (b. 1870, TX) and Ella B. Newberry (b. 1870, TX); siblings, Forrest (b. 1889), Edwin (b. 1896, TX), Gladys (b. 1903, TX). *SR; 471; Ransom to Hutchings, Nov 2, 1915, AGC; AG to Ransom, Nov 3, 1915, AGC; Polk to Hutchings, July 19, 1916, AGC; A1e; A2a; A3a; A4a, b, g; A6a.*

DUBOSE, EDWIN MORGAN. Born Feb. 24, 1870, Banquette (Rancho Seco), Nueces County, Texas. Ht. 5 ft. 10 ½ in., black eyes, black hair, dark complexion, married. REGULAR RANGER 1898–1900 (Co E). Resigned. REGULAR RANGER 1904 (Co. D). Discharged. Stockman, Alice, Jim Wells County, Texas. REGULAR RANGER Sept. 1, 1917–Mar. 10, 1918 (private, Co. A). Resigned. Stockman and peace officer, Alice. SPECIAL RANGER May 3, 1918–May 21, 1918. Fired—AG revoked his WA, perhaps on May 21, 1918. Peace officer, Mathis, San Patricio County, Texas. SPECIAL RANGER July 1, 1933–Jan. 22, 1935. Discharged. REMARKS: Deputy U.S. marshal, Southern District of Texas, 1889. U.S. Customs inspector, 1903; Customs inspector 1910–1912; resigned. Mounted Customs inspector, 1914–1917. In 1917 captured draft dodgers. In 1918 lived in Beeville, Bee County, Texas. In 1930 was a poultry farmer in San Patricio County. In 1959, lived in San Patricio County. LAW ENFORCEMENT RELATIVES: Ranger Henry G. "Judge" Dubose, brother; Ranger Ben B. Dubose, son; one-time justice of the peace Friendly H. Dubose, father. FAMILY: Parents, Friendly Hartwell Dubose (b. 1834, AL) and Martha C. "Mattie" Fusselman (b. 1841, OH); siblings, John W. (b. 1869, TX), Henry G. "Judge" (b. 1873, TX), Charles Byler "Charley" (b. 1877, TX), Thomas Turpin (b. 1880, TX); half-siblings, Ella Jane Byler (b. 1861, TX), Rufus Franklin Byler (b. 1864, TX), Rhoda Frances Byler (b. 1865, TX); spouse, Ella B. Newberry (b. 1870, TX), married July 28, 1888; children, Forrest (b. 1889), Ben (b. 1894, TX), Edwin (b. 1896, TX), Gladys (b. 1903, TX). *SR; 471; Co. B Scout Report, Oct, 1910, WC; LWT, Mar 12, Aug 13, Oct 8, 1911, July 7, 1912, Mar 1, May 10, Aug 23, 1914; SAE, Oct 9, 1911; BDH, Apr 27, May 9, Aug 17, 18, 20, 21, Sept 11, 22, Oct 3, 23, Nov 11, 13, Dec 8, 9, 1914, Jan 13, Feb 4, Mar 16, Apr 2, May 10, July 6, Aug 13, 1915, Aug 5, 1916; 319: 369–370, 410–411; Sanders to Harley, Mar 10, 1918, AGC; Woodul to Dubose, May 245, 1918, AGC; Dubose to Provost Marshal, Dec 12, 1918, AGCV; A1a, b, e, f, g; A4a, b, g; B2.*

DUDLEY, JOHN LEE. Born July 1874, Columbus, Colorado County, Texas. Ht. 5 ft. 5 in., dark blue eyes, dark brown hair, dark complexion, married. Brakeman, I&GN Railroad, enlisted in Bexar County, Texas. SPECIAL RANGER July 22, 1916–Dec. 1917. REMARKS: In 1920–1930 lived in Laredo, Webb County, Texas, worked for the railroad as a brakeman and a locomotive fireman. A John Lee Dudley died Feb. 2, 1940, Anderson County, Texas. FAMILY: Parents, Hm. A. Dudley (b. 1848, NC) and Mary L. (b. 1854, TX); siblings, John L. (b. 1873, TX), Ellmore or Elmo M. (b. 1876, TX), Nana E. (b. 1878, TX), Louanna (b. 1880, TX); spouse, Margaret V. "Maggie" Haines (b. 1880, TX), married about 1898; children, John L., Jr. (b. 1899, TX), Lucy B. (b. 1902, TX). *SR; A1b, d, e, f, g; C.*

DUNAGAN, THOMAS MARION, JR. Born Aug. 31, 1889, Dallas County, Texas. Ht. 5 ft. 11 in., blue eyes, light hair, fair complexion. Auto mechanic. REGULAR RANGER Mar. 28, 1918–Dec. 31, 1918 (private, Co. L). Resigned. REMARKS: Had been a gunner's mate 1st class in the Navy; in 1910 was stationed on the *USS Virginia*, Hampton Roads, Virginia. In June 1917 was an auto mechanic for Speedway Filling Station in El Paso, El Paso County, Texas. In 1930 was a commercial automobile accessories salesman in Dallas, Dallas County. A Thomas Dunagan died Apr. 28, 1963, Dallas County, Texas. FAMILY: Spouse, Dana (b. 1896, TX), married about 1924. *SR; 471; A1e, g; A2b; A3a.*

DUNAWAY, JAMES DALLAS. Born Feb. 12, 1874, Manchaca, Travis County, Texas. Ht. 5 ft. 9 ½ in., blue eyes, auburn hair, light complexion, married. City marshal, Llano, Llano County, 1903; resigned to join the Rangers. REGULAR RANGER July 10, 1903–Mar. 1, 1906 (private, Co. B). Resigned to run for Llano city marshal. Reenlisted. REGULAR RANGER Apr. 16, 1906–1907 (private, Co. A; promoted to sergeant, June 1906). Resigned. Peace officer. REGULAR RANGER Mar. 29, 1915–Oct. 31, 1915 (private, Co. C; transferred to Co. B, June 1, 1915). Discharged—fired for having assaulted a witness. REMARKS: Private detective. Deputy sheriff, Edwards County, 1914–1915; was fired. After being fired from the Rangers in 1915 he worked in Mexico, returning to the U.S. in 1918. Died Feb. 21, 1924, Llano County, Texas. FAMILY: Parents, William Dunaway (b. 1847, AR) and Mary Elizabeth King (b. 1857, GA); siblings, Arthur Hugh (b. 1877, TX), William Earnest (b. 1880, TX), Dollie Frederick (b. 1882, TX), Myrtle Mattie (b. 1883), Ruby Smith (b. 1888, TX), twins Buelah Mae and Eulah Ray (b. 1891, TX), Leland (b. 1893), Bessie (b. 1895); spouse #1, Anna L. Speegle (b. 1877, TX), married about 1894; children, Alva Ray (b. 1896, TX), James Dallas, Jr., Clive Speegle (b. 1898, TX), Fred (b. 1903); spouse #2, Hallie Dunlap (b. 1879, TX), married about 1905; son Dan (b. 1907, TX), Halline. *SR; 471; Petition, Feb 24, 1915, AGC; MR, Co. D, Feb 28, 1907, AGC; Clark to Ferguson, Mar 15, 1915, AGC; AG to Sanders, Mar 13, Apr 6, 1915, AGC; Sanders to Hutchings, Mar 15, 1915, AGC; AG to Almond, Apr 2, 1915, AGC; AG to Dunaway, Apr 2, 1915, AGC; MR, Co. B, June 1915, AGC; Fox to Hutchings, Nov 18, 1915, AGC; Martin to Ferguson, Oct 7, 1915, AGC; Ferguson to Hutchings, Oct 9, 1915, AGC; Martin to Hutchings, Oct 30, 1915, AGC; AG to Martin, Oct 28, 1915, AGC; Dunaway to Hobby, Feb 10, 1918, AGC; 319: 359, 360; 468; 271; A1b, d, e; A3a; A4b, g; C.*

DUNCAN, JAMES BAILEY. Born May 4, 1853, Marion County, Alabama. (Several census records and other sources state his birthplace was Mississippi.) Ht. 5 ft. 7 in., black eyes, black hair, florid complexion, married. Ex-peace officer, Kemp, Kaufman County, Texas. LOYALTY RANGER July 6, 1918–Feb. 1919. REMARKS: Was constable in Kaufman County in 1910. As of June 1918 had been a peace officer for the last 28 years. Died Jan. 4, 1925, Kemp, Kaufman County, Texas; buried in Kemp Cemetery. FAMILY: Spouse, Rhoda Melissa Franklin (b. 1857, TX), married June 7, 1877, Kaufman County; children, Leonidas (b. 1878, TX), Maude (b. 1883, TX), Roscoe Sellar (b. 1885, TX), Minnie I. (b. 1894, TX). *SR; Duncan to Hobby, June 1, 1918, AGC; EPMT, Aug 10, 1910; A1b, e, f; A2b; A4b; C.*

DUNCAN, VIRGIL M. Born Aug. 1887, Tyler, Smith County, Texas. Ht. 5 ft. 10 ½ in., blue eyes, light brown hair, fair complexion, married. Railroad brakeman, enlisted in Nueces County. SPECIAL RANGER July 17, 1916–Dec. 1917 (attached to Co. C). REMARKS: Had been a messenger for Wells Fargo in San Antonio. In 1920 was living in Pleasanton, Atascosa County, Texas. FAMILY: Spouse, Jennie W. (b. 1886, TX); children, Tommie A. (b. 1907, TX), Mary E. (b. 1917, TX). *SR; Duncan to Hutchings, Apr 6, 1917, AGC; A1f.*

DUNCAN, WILLIAM KENNETH. Born Nov. 27, 1897, Toyah, Reeves County, Texas. Ht. 5 ft. 9 in., dark brown hair, dark brown eyes, dark complexion. Cowboy. REGULAR RANGER Sept. 28, 1917–Apr. 1918 (private, Co. B). Resigned. REMARKS: Note age. Participated in the Porvenir massacre. Died May 24, 1975, Reeves County, Texas. LAW ENFORCEMENT RELATIVES: Ranger William T. Duncan, father. FAMILY: Parents, William Thomas Duncan (b. 1869, TX) and Annie Ledbetter Chalk (b. 1871, TX); siblings, Alice Zilah (b. 1891, TX), James Clyde (b. 1894, TX), Aubrey S. (b. 1902, TX); spouse (?), may have married Jewel Frost in June 1926; daughter (?), Mildred Dolores (b. 1930, TX). *SR; Fox to Woodul, Mar 30, 1918, AGC; Bud Weaver's affidavit, undated, WC; 470: 87, 88; A1d, e; A2a, b, e; A3a; A4b.*

DUNCAN, WILLIAM THOMAS. Born Mar. 1869, Kaufman, Kaufman County, Texas. Ht. 6 ft., black eyes, black hair, dark complexion, married. Rancher, Kent, Jeff Davis County, Texas. SPECIAL RANGER Jan. 2, 1918–Jan. 15, 1919. REMARKS: Deputy sheriff for 20 years. Had lived in Jeff Davis and Reeves counties since 1882. Was alone at his ranch most of the time—45 miles from the county seat. Died Nov. 19, 1922, Reeves County, Texas. LAW ENFORCEMENT RELATIVES: Ranger William K. Duncan, son. FAMILY: Parents, James Duncan (b. 1838, TX) and Elizabeth Jane Thomas (b. 1850, TX); siblings, Susan (b. 1867, TX), George Holmes (b. 1871, TX), James L. (b. 1873, TX), Joseph D. (b. 1874, TX), Martella "Tillie" (b. 1877, TX); spouse, Annie Ledbetter Chalk (b. 1871, TX), married July 29, 1889, Reeves County; children, Alice Zilah (b. 1891, TX), James Clyde (b. 1894, TX), William Kenneth (b. 1897, TX), Aubrey S. (b. 1902, TX). *SR; Duncan to Hobby, Nov 28, 1917, AGC; Duncan to Harley, Jan 5, 1918, AGC; A1a, b, d, e; A4b; C.*

DUNLAP, MARION LAFAYETTE. Born Sept. 6, 1877, Bandera County, Texas. Ht. 6 ft., gray eyes, light hair, light complexion, married. Stock farmer, Devine, Medina County, Texas. SPECIAL RANGER Jan. 12, 1918–June 1, 1918. Discharged. REMARKS: Died Oct. 11, 1918; buried in Moore Cemetery, Moore, Frio County, Texas. FAMILY: Parents, Robert J. Dunlap (b. 1837, IL) and Sarah Delilah Bond (b. 1845, AR); siblings, Eleanor (b. 1863, TX), John Henry (b. 1871, TX), Ida Elmira (b. 1873, TX), James Robert (b. 1875, TX), Archibald S. (b. 1880, TX), Wm. Cleveland (b. 1885, TX); spouse, Virgie Arzelia Nowlin (b. 1897, TX). *SR; A1b, d, f; A2b; A3a; A4b.*

DUNN, GEORGE BOLING. Born Sept. 23, 1866, Holly Springs, Marshall County, Mississippi. Ht. 5 ft. 6 ½ in., blue eyes, gray hair, light complexion, married. Stock farmer, Mobeetie, Wheeler County, Texas. LOYALTY RANGER June 7, 1918–Feb. 1919. REMARKS: Still living in Wheeler County in 1930. Died Jan. 25, 1952, Gray County, Texas. FAMILY: Father, William C. Dunn (b. 1837, OH); stepmother, Mary M. (b. 1858, MS); sister, Ella L. (b. 1880, TN); spouse, Mary Agnes (b. 1867, MO), married about 1887; sons, William B. (b. 1888, TX), Earl A. (b. 1890, TX), John L. (b. 1897, TX). *SR; A1a, b, d, e, g; A2b; A4g.*

DUNN, JAMES BLACKBURN. Born Mar. 2 (3?), 1863, Wheelock, Robertson County, Texas. Ht. 6 ft., blue eyes, light brown hair, fair complexion, married. Stock farmer and deputy sheriff, Buckley, Robertson County. LOYALTY RANGER June 3, 1918–Feb. 1919. REMARKS: Robertson County deputy sheriff, 1909–1918. Died Feb. 2, 1934, Wheelock, Robertson County, Texas; buried in Wheelock Cemetery. FAMILY: Parents, George Hayes Dunn (b. 1825, AL) and Nancy Jane Killough (b. 1846, TX); siblings, Mary Ann (b. 1861, TX), Isabella (b. 1865, TX), Josephine (b. 1866, TX), Willie (b. 1868, TX), Sallie E. (b. 1870, TX), George Ripley (b. 1871, TX), John C. (b. 1873, TX), Annette Woodward (b. 1875, TX), Samuel R. (b. 1877, TX), Nancy J. (b. 1879, TX), twins Ada Eugene and Ida (b. 1881, TX); spouse #1, Eula Jackson Covey (b. 1863, TX), married Dec. 7, 1881; children, Ralph Blackburn (b. 1882, TX), George Hayes (b. 1884, TX), James Mason "Jim" (b. 1887, TX), Edgar Covey (b. 1889, TX), Marshall Wilkes (b. 1892, TX), Ben Holt (b. 1895, TX), Sul Ross (b. 1898, TX), Katherine Almera (b. 1900, TX); spouse #2, Margaret Lola "Maggie" Kirby (b. 1889, TX), married Nov. 16, 1916; children, James Blackburn, II (b. 1918, TX), Aurelia (b. 1921, TX), Carl Cole (b. 1923, TX), Margaret Lynn (b. 1925, TX), Henry Caufield (b. 1926, TX). *SR; A1b, d, e, g; A2e; A4a, b, g; B1.*

DUNN, JOHN GLENN. Born Feb. 1, 1895, Del Rio, Val Verde County, Texas. Ht. 5 ft. 10 in., gray eyes, dark hair, dark complexion. Cowboy, enlisted in Val Verde County. REGULAR RANGER May 30, 1916–Oct. 14, 1916 (private, Co. C). Resigned to seek other employment. *SR; Almond to*

Hutchings, May 31, 1916, AGC; AG to Almond, June 2, 29, 1916, AGC; A3c.

DURAN, SANTOS DUARTE. Born Oct. 27, 1885, El Paso, El Paso County, Texas. Ht. 5 ft. 7 ½ in., brown eyes, brown hair, dark complexion, married. Ranchman. REGULAR RANGER Mar. 25, 1918–Nov. 1, 1918 (private, Co. L). Discharged. REMARKS: Had served 6 years in the Navy. In 1930 was an undertaker, living in El Paso, El Paso County. FAMILY: Spouse, Dolores "Lola" (b. 1885, TX), married about 1915; children, Ricardo (b. 1916, TX), Romeo (b. 1917, TX), Evangeline (b. 1921, TX). *SR; 471; Davis to Harley, Apr 4, 1918, AGC; A1f, g; A3a.*

DURHAM, GEORGE P., JR. Born Feb. 9, 1895, Sauz Ranch, Willacy County, Texas. Ht. 5 ft. 9 ½ in., brown eyes, black hair, dark complexion. Cowboy, Norias Ranch, Armstrong, Willacy County. SPECIAL RANGER June 6, 1917–Dec. 31, 1919 (attached to Co. C; was reinstated—WA was renewed, Dec. 22, 1917; a new WA was issued, Jan. 23, 1919). Discharged. Ranchman, Raymondville, Willacy County. SPECIAL RANGER Oct. 30, 1933–Jan. 22, 1935. Discharged. REMARKS: Willacy County deputy sheriff, 1923–1933. Died July 25, 1937, Willacy County, Texas. LAW ENFORCEMENT RELATIVES: Ranger George P. Durham, father. FAMILY: Parents, George Preston Durham (b. 1856, GA) and Caroline "Carry" Chamberlain (b. 1870, TX); siblings, Mary Louise (b. 1891, TX), Caroline "Carry" (b. 1893, TX), Bland Chamberlain (b. 1896, TX), Henrietta Waters (b. 1899, TX), Sarah (b. 1901, TX), Lavoyger L. (b. 1905, TX), Robert E. Lee (b. 1907, TX), Edward Chamberlain (b. 1908, TX), Hal John (b. 1911, TX). *SR; 471; 470:130; Kleberg to AG, May 10, 1917, AGC; 1511; A1d, f, g; A3a; A4b, g; C.*

DURST, STERLING ORLANDO. Born July 15, 1882, Madison County, Texas. Ht. 6 ft., brown eyes, brown hair, red complexion. Deputy game warden, Junction, Kimble County, Texas. REGULAR RANGER Sept. 1, 1918–Mar. 31, 1919 (private, Co. F; transferred to Co. K, Jan. 1, 1919). Resigned—honorably discharged. Peace officer, Junction. REGULAR RANGER Aug. 1, 1919–Feb. 15, 1920 (private, Co. E). Resigned. Peace officer, Junction. RAILROAD RANGER Aug. 4, 1922–Dec. 6, 1922. Resigned. REMARKS: 1919 enlistment gives his birthplace as Austin. As of April 1918 had been a peace officer off and on for the past 8 years. Kimble County sheriff Nov. 6, 1934–Jan. 1, 1939. Died Dec. 15, 1966, Kimble County, Texas. LAW ENFORCEMENT RELATIVES: Kimble County judge John S. Durst, father. FAMILY: Parents, John Sterling Durst (b. 1843, TX) and Lilla Ann Kittrell (b. 1854, TX); siblings, Austin M. (b. 1890, TX), Leon H. (b. 1893, TX), Kitrell Goree (b. 1894, TX). *SR; 471; Durst to Harley, ca. April 17, 1918, AGC; AG to Durst, Apr 23, 1918, AGC; Aldrich to Durst, Mar 22, 1919, AGC; Durst to Harley, June 17, 1919, AGC; 1503:307; A1d, e, f, g; A2a, b; A3a; A4a, b.*

DUSTIN, VYVIAN GLENROY. Born July 1, 1873, Maysville, Mason County, Kentucky. Ht. 6 ft. 2 in., gray eyes, brown hair, fair complexion, married. U.S. government clerk, Houston, Harris County, Texas. LOYALTY RANGER June 27, 1918–Feb. 1919. REMARKS: Had been a fireman for the East & West Texas Railway in Houston. Had been a Harris County deputy sheriff. In 1910 was chief clerk, U.S. Post Office, Houston; in 1917 was a Post Office foreman in Houston. In Feb. 1919 was a 1st lieutenant stationed at Fort Sam Houston, San Antonio, Bexar County, Texas. Died May 7, 1921, Bexar County, Texas. FAMILY: Parents, Zadoc Dustin (also spelled Duston) (b. 1827, NH) and Isabelle Drysdale (b. 1834, Scotland); siblings, Louis Albert (b. 1857, Cuba), Estelle (b. 1859, Cuba), Phebe T. (b. 1867, OH), Zadie H. (b. 1877, KY); spouse, Blanche E. (b. 1876, TX), married about 1898. *SR; A1b, d, e, f; A3a; A4b; A5a; C.*

DYCHES, PINKNEY F. Born July 24, 1884, Granger, Williamson County, Texas. Ht. 5 ft. 6 in., dark eyes, dark hair, dark complexion. Stockman, Marfa, Presidio County, Texas. REGULAR RANGER Dec. 15, 1919–Jan. 31, 1928 (private, Co. A). Resigned. Peace officer, Coleman, Coleman County, Texas. SPECIAL RANGER Nov. 24, 1928–Dec. 31, 1928. Discharged. REMARKS: Note length of service, 1928. Prior to 1919 had been a deputy constable, San Angelo, Tom Green County, Texas, for 2 years and city marshal, Frontenac, Kansas, for 2 years. Died Sept. 10, 1955, San Angelo, Tom Green County, Texas. FAMILY: Parents, William Dyches (b. 1858, TX) and Tabitha Allan "Tabbie" May (b. 1859, MS); siblings, Gertrude D. (b. 1880, TX), Josiah Allan (b. 1882, TX), Willie Mae (b. 1886, TX), Clyde William (b. 1888, TX); spouse, Susan Katherine Douglas Watson LeSueur, married July 21, 1930 in Lovington, Lea

County, New Mexico; was divorced and remarried. *SR; 471; 1:I, 1536–1537, 1558–1561; Hanson to Col. Smith, Assistant AG, Feb 9, 1920, WC; 470:43; A1d, e; A2b; A4a, b.*

DYCUS, CHARLES T. "CHARLIE." Born Dec. 31, 1871, Liberty Hill, Williamson County, Texas. Ht. 6 ft., gray eyes, gray hair, light complexion, married. Livestock commission agent, Farwell, Parmer County, Texas. LOYALTY RANGER June 6, 1918–Feb. 1919. REMARKS: In 1900 was a farmer in Chickasaw Nation, Indian Territory. In 1910 was a precinct constable in Parmer County. Was a Parmer County deputy sheriff. "Marshal for St. Louis Rocky Coal Mines" for 3 years. Died May 24, 1935, Parmer County, Texas. FAMILY: Parents, Toliver Lafayette Dycus (b. 1840, NC) and Sarah Catherine Smith (1847, TN); siblings, Tima Savannah (b. 1866, GA), Emma Caroline (b. 1868, TX), Altha B. (b. 1870, TX), Augustus (b. 1872, TX), Andrew Willis (b. 1879, TX), Albert Smith (b. 1881, TX), Delilah (b. 1882, TX); spouse #1, Ella Strand (b. 1880, AR), married about 1898; children, Ralph (b. 1899, TX), Millie (b. 1902, TX), Johnny (b. 1905, TX), Toliver (b. 1906, OK), Connell (b. 1908, TX), Augustus (b. 1910, TX); spouse #2, Fannie C. (b. 1885, GA), married about 1913; children, Charles Bernol (b. 1918, TX), Nova L. (b. 1921, TX), Tiny A. (b. 1924, TX), Julis Young (b. 1925, TX). *SR; A1b, d, e, f, g; A2b, e, A4a, b, g.*

EADS, JAMES TIPTON "TIP." Born May 10, 1874, Claiborne County, Tennessee. Ht. 5 ft. 10 in., blue eyes, brown hair, light complexion, married. Peace officer, McKinney, Collin County, Texas. REGULAR RANGER Mar. 9, 1921–Aug. 31, 1921 (private, Co. B). Discharged. REMARKS: Had been a farmer in Collin County. In 1930 was a bank collector in McKinney. FAMILY: Parents, Harvey Eads (b. 1853, VA) and Barbrey S. (b. 1854, TN); brother, Charley (b. 1876, TN); spouse, Julia McGill (b. 1876, TX), married about 1894; daughters, Myrtle E. (b. 1895, TX), Ollie F. (b. 1898, TX), Julia E. (b. 1914, TX). *SR; 471; A1b, d, e, f, g; A3a.*

EADS, RALPH. Born Feb. 6, 1891, Handley, Tarrant County, Texas. Ht. 6 ft. 1 in., brown eyes, brown hair, fair complexion. Ranchman, Encinal, La Salle County, Texas. SPECIAL RANGER July 20, 1916–Dec. 1917. FAMILY: Parents, Homer Eads (b. 1860, MS) and Missouri (b. 1867, GA); siblings, Homer J. (b. 1889, TX), Helen (b. 1894, TX), Miriam (b. 1896, TX), Josephine (b. 1896, TX). *SR; Coleman to Hutchings, July 17, 1916, AGC; AG to Coleman, July 18, 1916, AGC; Eads to AG, July 25, 1916, AGC; A1d; A3a.*

EARLY, WALTER U. "WAL." Born Aug. 1868, Parkersville, Lyon County, Kentucky. Ht. 5 ft. 5 in., gray eyes, gray hair, light complexion. Lawyer, Brownwood, Brown County, Texas. LOYALTY RANGER June 5, 1918–Feb. 1919. REMARKS: In 1910 was district attorney in Brown County. Died Dec. 18, 1939, Brown County, Texas. FAMILY: Parents, James M. Early (b. 1838, KY) and Frances E. "Fannie" Smith (b. 1848, KY); siblings, Alvie E. (b. 1862, KY), Lola L. (b. 1867, KY), Catherine D. "Kate" (b. 1869, KY), Maggie B. (b. 1875, KY), Clarence T. (b. 1877, KY), Firman R. (b. 1878, KY), Nellie (b. 1884, KY), Lela (b. 1886, KY). *SR; A1a, b, d, e, f; A4b; C.*

EARNEST, DAVID POOLE "POOL." Born Nov. 7, 1884, Mitchell County, Texas. Tall, slender, gray eyes, brown hair, married. Stockman, Sudan, Bailey County, Texas. LOYALTY RANGER June 11, 1918–Feb. 1919. REMARKS: Had been a stock farmer in Yoakum County, Texas. In 1930 was a rancher in Cochran County, Texas. Died Aug. 13, 1936. FAMILY: Parents, John David Earnest (b. 1857, AR) and Florence Itaska Chalk (b. 1864, TX); siblings, twins Wilks and Louis (b. 1886, TX), Mary Edith (b. 1887, TX), Joseph Porter (b. 1889, TX), William Ellis (b. 1891, TX), Richard Ware (b. 1892, TX), Leonel or Lemuel Thomas (b. 1894, TX), James Daniel (b. 1896, TX), Mary Florence (b. 1898, TX), Lilian B. (b. 1900, TX), Katie F. (b. 1902, TX); spouse, Mary or Mamie A. Jones (b. 1885, TX), married about 1905; children, Nell Ruth (b. 1907, TX), John D. (b. 1908, TX). *SR; A1d, e, f, g; A3a; A4b; B1.*

EASON, EDMUND PEARY "ED." Born Apr. 20, 1872, Brazos County, Texas. No physical description, married. Editor and publisher, Winters, Runnels County, Texas. LOYALTY RANGER June 17, 1918–Mar. 1919. REMARKS: Was an editor in Irion County, Texas in 1900; by 1910 was printer of the *Winters Enterprise* in Runnells County. In

1930 lived in Long Beach, Los Angeles County, California. Died May 28, 1949, Orange County, California. FAMILY: Parents, Thomas J. Eason (b. 1835, GA) and Jane Strotha (b. 1863, AL); siblings, Robert M. (b. 1860, AL), William G. (b. 1862, AL), Georgeana (b. 1865, AL), David M. (b. 1869, MS), Lucinda (b. 1875, TX); spouse, Bertha Gertrude Beaty (b. 1876, TX), married Jan. 26, 1896, Irion County; children, Ruth Carol (b. 1898, TX), Beaty H. (b. 1901, TX), Erma (b. 1907, TX), Ralph E. (b. 1916, TX). *SR; A1a, b, d, e, f, g; A2c, f; A4b.*

EAST, ARTHUR LEE. Born Aug. 28, 1882, Archer City, Archer County, Texas. Ht. 5 ft. 11 in., blue eyes, light hair, light complexion, married. Stockman, Kingsville, Kleberg County, Texas. SPECIAL RANGER Apr. 30, 1918–Jan. 15, 1919; Jan. 24, 1919–Dec. 31, 1919 (his commission was renewed). REMARKS: Had been a cattle dealer in Nueces County, Texas. As of July 1918 was a ranchman living in Sarita, Kenedy County, Texas. Died May 13, 1944, Bexar County, Texas; buried at La Parra Ranch, Kenedy County. LAW ENFORCEMENT RELATIVES: Ranger Roy E. East, brother; Ranger Tom T. East, brother. FAMILY: Parents, Edward Hudson East (b. 1846, IL) and Hattie Ragan (b. 1859, MO); siblings, Jno. (b. 1884, TX), Roy E. (b. 1886, TX), Norman (b. 1889, TX), Thomas (b. 1889, TX), Edward H., Jr. (b. 1899, TX), Allen B. (b. 1902, TX); spouse, Sarita J. "Sarah" Kenedy (b. 1889, TX) (granddaughter of Mifflin Kenedy, early partner of Capt. Richard King, founder of the King Ranch), married Dec. 8, 1910, Corpus Christi, Nueces County. *SR; 471; A1b, d, e, f; A3a; A4b; B2; C.*

EAST, ROY E. Born May 1886, Archer City, Archer County, Texas. Ht. 6 ft., blue eyes, brown hair, light complexion, married. Stockman, Norias Ranch, Armstrong, Kenedy County, Texas. SPECIAL RANGER Dec. 22, 1917–Jan. 15, 1919. REMARKS: Had been a cattle dealer in Nueces County, Texas. In 1920 was a ranchman in Kleberg County, Texas. A Roy Edward East died Mar. 1, 1941, Kleberg County, Texas. LAW ENFORCEMENT RELATIVES: Ranger Arthur Lee East, brother; Ranger Tom T. East, brother. FAMILY: Parents, Edward Hudson East (b. 1846, IL) and Hattie Ragan (b. 1859, MO); siblings, Jno. (b. 1884, TX), Roy E. (b. 1886, TX), Norman (b. 1889, TX), Thomas (b. 1889, TX), Edward H., Jr. (b. 1899, TX), Allen B. (b. 1902, TX); spouse, Ione (b. 1897, TX). *SR; A1b, d, e, f; C.*

EAST, THOMAS TIMMONS "TOM." Born Dec. 19, 1889, Archer City, Archer County, Texas. Ht. 6 ft. 1 in., blue eyes, red hair, light complexion, married. Ranchman, enlisted in Kleberg County, Texas. SPECIAL RANGER Apr. 18, 1918–Jan. 15, 1919; Jan. 24, 1919–Dec. 31, 1919 (commission was renewed). REMARKS: Partner in Russell and East Cattle Co. Son-in-law of R. J. Kleberg, Sr., an early King Ranch manager. In Mar. 1918, bandits raided his ranch near Hebbronville, Jim Hogg County, Texas. Died Nov. 29, 1943, Kleberg County, Texas. LAW ENFORCEMENT RELATIVES: Ranger Arthur Lee East, brother; Ranger Roy E. East, brother. FAMILY: Parents, Edward Hudson East (b. 1846, IL) and Hattie Ragan (b. 1859, MO); siblings, Arthur Lee (b. 1882, TX), Jno. (b. 1884, TX), Roy E. (b. 1886, TX), Norman (b. 1889, TX), Edward H., Jr. (b. 1899, TX), Allen B. (b. 1902, TX); spouse, Alice Gertrudis Kleberg (b. 1893, TX), married Jan. 30, 1915, in the new *casa grande* of Rancho Santa Gertrudis; children, Tom T., Jr. (b. 1917, TX), Robert Claude (b. 1919, TX), Alice Hattie C. (b. 1920, TX). *SR; 471; East to Woodul, Apr 18, 1918, AGC; Capt. Wright's report, Mar 7, 1918, WC; Hanson to Harley, Nov 15, 1918, WC; Hanson to East, Dec 10, 1918, WC; 319: 50, 471–472; 417: 588–589; 464: 73; A1b, d, e, f; A2e; A3a; A4b; C.*

EASTER, JOHN FRANKLIN. Born Feb. 13, 1877, Itasca, Hill County, Texas. Ht. 5 ft. 9 ½ in., gray eyes, dark hair, fair complexion. Farmer, Dimmitt, Castro County, Texas. LOYALTY RANGER July 5, 1918–Feb. 1919. REMARKS: Served in Co. A, 1st Texas Infantry in Spanish-American War. Died Oct. 24, 1947, Dimmitt, Castro County, Texas. FAMILY: Parents, William Franklin Easter (b. 1846, MS) and Prudence Pryor Major (b. 1855, KY); siblings, Baxter B. (b. 1872, TX), Sarah (b. 1874, TX), Lillie M. (b. 1879, TX), Jennie Lee (b. 1881, TX), Jasper E. (b. 1883, TX), Alexander R. (b. 1885, TX), Harriet (b. 1889, TX), Walter S. (b. 1892, TX); spouse, Catherine Gandy or Grandy (b. 1886, TX), married July 8, 1918, Amarillo, Potter County, Texas; children, Mary Katherine (b. 1919, TX), John Franklin (b. 1921, TX). *SR; A1b, d, e, f; A2b; A3a; A4a, b, g.*

EASTERLING, ALLEN CLAUDE. Born Dec. 6, 1881, Hallettsville, Lavaca County, Texas. Ht. 6 ft., blue eyes, brown hair, light complexion, married. Stockman, enlisted in Presidio County, Texas. SPECIAL RANGER Feb. 21, 1918–Jan. 15, 1919. REMARKS: In 1900 was a typesetter living in Hallettsville; was a newspaper editor in Floresville, Wilson County, Texas in 1910. In 1920 was a feed and grain merchant in Marfa, Presidio County, Texas. In 1930 was a rancher in Del Rio, Val Verde County, Texas. Died Apr. 20, 1932, Val Verde County, Texas. FAMILY: Parents, John Thomas Easterling (b. 1854, MS) and Winnie Luenna Neeley (b. 1859, MS); siblings, his twin brother, Floyd (b. 1881, TX), Earnest Victor (b. 1885, TX); spouse, Birdie Pearl (b. 1886, TX), married about 1907. *SR; Fox to Harley, Feb 21, 1918, AGC; A1d, e, f, g; A3a; A4a; A6a; C.*

ECKHARDT, OTTO LUDWIG. Born May 1861, DeWitt, DeWitt County, Texas. Ht. 6 ft. 1 ½ in., gray eyes, brown hair, dark complexion, married. Stockman and farmer, Goliad, Goliad County, Texas. SPECIAL RANGER July 2, 1918–Jan. 15, 1919; June 12, 1919–Dec. 31, 1919. REMARKS: Nephew of R. J. Kleberg, manager of the King Ranch. Had been a DeWitt County and Goliad County deputy sheriff, and in 1917 a Harris County, Texas stockman and deputy sheriff. In Jan. 1919 was leasing 15,000–20,000 acres of ranchland. Was commissioned by order of Gov. Hobby. In 1930 was a real estate agent living in Goliad, Goliad County. Died July 28, 1932, Goliad County, Texas. LAW ENFORCEMENT RELATIVES: Ranger Robert J. Eckhardt, brother; Ranger Tom T. East, cousin by marriage. FAMILY: Parents, Robert Christian Eckhardt (b. 1836, Prussia) and Caroline Louise Kleberg (b. 1840, TX); siblings, Johanna Clare "Jane" (b. 1859, TX), Lulu Rosa (b. 1863, TX), William Rudolph (b. 1865, TX), Helena Emily (b. 1868, TX), Robert J. (b. 1869, TX), Caroline (b. 1872, TX), Marcellus George (b. 1873, TX), Hedwig (b. 1876, TX), Oscar George (b. 1877, TX), Victor Caesar (b. 1881, TX), Joseph Carl (b. 1882, TX); spouse, Inez Wallace Blackwell (b. 1865, TX), married about 1883; children, John Robert (b. 1884, TX), Leanna Rose (b. 1887, TX), Robert C. (b. 1888, TX), Sarah Bell (b. 1890, TX), Zora Louise (b. 1895, TX), Inez D. (b. 1898, TX). *SR; Eckhardt to Ferguson, May 5, 1917, AGC; Eckhardt to Harley, June 2, 8, 1918, AGC; Binford to Harley, Feb 10, 1919, AGC; A1a, b, d, e, g; A4b, g; B1; C.*

ECKHARDT, ROBERT J. Born Nov. 1869, Yorktown, DeWitt County, Texas. Ht. 5 ft. 10 ½ in., gray eyes, blonde hair, fair complexion, married. Farmer and president, First State Bank and Trust Company, Taylor, Williamson County, Texas. SPECIAL RANGER June 29, 1918–Jan. 14, 1919. Chief Clerk, Texas Highway Department, Taylor. SPECIAL RANGER May 22, 1926–Feb. 1, 1927; Feb. 9, 1927–Apr. 19, 1927. Discharged—WA expired. REMARKS: Nephew of R. J. Kleberg, manager of the King Ranch. In 1926 was commissioned by order of the governor. Died Dec. 5, 1930, Williamson County, Texas. LAW ENFORCEMENT RELATIVES: Ranger Otto L. Eckhardt, brother; Ranger Tom T. East, cousin by marriage. FAMILY: Parents, Robert Christian Eckhardt (b. 1836, Prussia) and Caroline Louise Kleberg (b. 1840, TX); siblings, Johanna Clare "Jane" (b. 1859, TX), Otto L. (b. 1861, TX), Lulu Rosa (b. 1863, TX), William Rudolph (b. 1865, TX), Helena Emily (b. 1868, TX), Caroline (b. 1872, TX), Marcellus George (b. 1873, TX), Hedwig (b. 1876, TX), Oscar George (b. 1877, TX), Victor Caesar (b. 1881, TX), Joseph Carl (b. 1882, TX); spouse #1, Zuba Mumford (b. 1875, NY), married Dec. 28, 1892; daughter, Dorothy (b. 1894, TX); spouse #2, Ruby Henderson (b. 1888, TX), married about 1905; daughters, Elizabeth (b. 1906, TX), Henrietta (b. 1914, TX). *SR; Eckhardt to Harley, June 29, July 3, 1918, AGC; A1a, b, d, e, f; A4b.*

EDDS, JOHN JOSEPH. Born Nov. 21, 1891, Elmendorf, Bexar County, Texas. Ht. 5 ft. 7 in., dark eyes, black hair, dark complexion. Deputy sheriff, Wilson County, Texas. REGULAR RANGER Sept. 15, 1915–Mar. 31, 1916 (private, Co. D). Resigned. Customs Inspector. REGULAR RANGER Jan. 1, 1918–Dec. 10, 1921 (sergeant, Co. K; June 20, 1919 reenlisted under the new law, transferred to Co. D). Resigned. REMARKS: Wilson County deputy sheriff, 1913. Mounted Customs inspector, 1916–1917; lived in Floresville, Wilson County in May 1917. Held various law enforcement jobs in the 1920s. Ended his career as a guard at Kelly Air Force Base in San Antonio, Bexar County. Died Feb. 24, 1956, Bexar County, Texas; buried at Benavides, Duval County, Texas. LAW ENFORCEMENT RELATIVES: Ranger Henry Edds, cousin. FAMILY: Parents, Jesse Winfred Edds (b. 1844, AL) and Gertrude or Georgia C. (b. 1857, TX); siblings, Jessie (b. 1883, TX), Clara (b. 1892, TX), Georgia (b. 1894, TX). *SR; 471; SAE, Jan 20, 1913, June 18, 1916; BDH Apr 6, 14, 1916, Mar 19, May 4, 1917; LWT, June 18, 1916; 319: 45; 508:67; 1000: iii, 70; 469: 64; 1505; A1d; A2b; A3a; A4b, g.*

E

EDDS, WILLIAM HENRY. Born Nov. 1868, St. Mary's, Aransas County, Texas. Ht. 6 ft., blue eyes, light hair, blonde complexion, married. Ranchman, Hebbronville, Jim Hogg County, Texas. SPECIAL RANGER Feb. 2, 1918–Jan. 15, 1919 (attached to Co. K). REMARKS: Jan. 1919 letterhead: "Henry Edds, Cattle, Horses, Mules, Hebbronville." Died June 28, 1927, Wilson County, Texas. LAW ENFORCEMENT RELATIVES: Ranger John J. Edds, cousin. FAMILY: Parents, George G. Edds (b. 1841, AL) and Mary J. (b. 1837, AL or TN); step-brother, Frank Turner (b. 1866, TX); spouse, Retta (b. 1879, MS), married about 1902; son George Henry (b. 1903, TX). *SR; BDH, Nov 15, 1915; Craighead to Harley, Feb 2, 1918, AGC; Assistant AG to Edds, Feb 14, 1918, AGC; A1b, d, e, f, g; A2b; A4g.*

EDWARDS, LEONARD WALTON "LUPE." Born Aug. 1893, Lagarto, Live Oak County, Texas. Ht. 5 ft. 10 in., brown eyes, auburn hair, sandy complexion. Mechanic, enlisted in Hidalgo County, Texas. REGULAR RANGER May 8, 1915–Oct. 18, 1915 (private, Co. A; transferred to Co. D Aug. 1915). Resigned. REMARKS: Died Dec. 28, 1915, Mission, Hidalgo County, Texas. Was accidentally shot and died of his wound. LAW ENFORCEMENT RELATIVES: Hidalgo County deputy sheriff (1915–1920) George M. Edwards, brother. FAMILY: Parents, William C. Edwards (b. 1851, TX) and Susan Mills (b. 1854, MS); siblings, Timothy (b. 1873, TX), Lilly (b. 1876, TX), George M. (b. 1879, TX), Lois or Louise V. (b. 1881, TX), Wendy D. (b. 1886, TX), Kelly W. "Bitty" (b. 1889, TX). *SR; 471; Ransom to Hutchings, Oct 26, 1915, AGC; BDH, Dec 29, 1915; 319:49; A1b, d, e, f; A4b; B2.*

EDWARDS, SAMUEL VAUGHN "PETE." Born Apr. 1, 1859, Clairette, Erath County, Texas. Ht. 6 ft. ½ in., blue eyes, gray hair, fair complexion, married. REGULAR RANGER, 1882–1884 (private, Co. F). Rancher, Laredo, Webb County, Texas. LOYALTY RANGER June 14, 1918–Feb. 1919. Rancher, Laredo. SPECIAL RANGER Nov. 18, 1929–Nov. 18, 1930; Feb. 16, 1931–Oct. 5, 1931—deceased. REMARKS: La Salle County, Texas, sheriff Dec. 21, 1896–Nov. 8, 1898. Was a mounted Customs inspector, Laredo, 1899–1913; resigned as chief inspector. Had a ranch near Laredo as early as 1910. Married daughter of A. D. Adams, a Frio County, Texas, pioneer. In 1920 was one of the three directors of the Laredo National Bank. In 1922 was one of the wealthiest landowners in Webb County. In 1929 was commissioned at the request of Attorney General R. L. Bobbitt. Died Oct. 5, 1931, Webb County, Texas. LAW ENFORCEMENT RELATIVES: Customs inspector (1913–1914, Laredo) Lee Edwards, son. FAMILY: Parents, Samuel Vaughn Edwards (b. 1832, AR) and Elizabeth Salmon (b. 1833, IL); siblings, Joseph (b. 1854, TX), Thomas (b. 1857, TX), Mary Catherine (b. 1864, TX), Elizabeth (b. 1865, TX); spouse #1, unknown, married about 1883; son, Lee; spouse #2, Adelia Adams (b. 1887, TX), married about 1911 at Pearsall, Frio County, Texas; daughters, Ruth (b. 1916, TX), Rachael (b. 1918, TX). *SR; 471; Edwards to Hutchings, June 1, 1915, AGC; AG to Edwards, June 2, 1915, AGC; Edwards to Ferguson, June 18, 1917, AGC; 1000: 10; 319: 69, 414–415, 448, 451, 497; 1503:321; LWT Dec 4, 11, 1910, Jan 29, 1911, May 5, 1912, Jan 12, June 29, July 27, Oct 19, 1913, Nov 15, 1914, Nov 5, 1916, Apr 20, 1919, Jan 18, 1920; A1aa, a, b, e, f, g; B1; C.*

EDWARDS, WILLIAM W. Born 1870, Gadsden, Etowah County, Alabama. Ht. 5 ft. 7 in., brown eyes, gray hair, fair complexion, married. U.S. Secret Service agent, San Antonio, Bexar County, Texas. LOYALTY RANGER Aug. 1, 1918–Feb. 19, 1919. REMARKS: Had been a railroad conductor in Smithville, Bastrop County, Texas. In 1920 was a revenue officer in San Antonio. FAMILY: Parents, William Edwards (b. 1835, GA) and Scyntha (b. 1835, GA); siblings, Enoch (b. 1866, GA), Elijah (b. 1869, GA), Fannie (b. 1873, AL); spouse, Kittie L. Meredith (b. 1873, TN), married Sept. 6, 1893, Denton County, Texas; son, Thomas W. (b. 1894, TX). *SR; 471; A1b, e, f; A2c.*

EICKENROHT, RENO ANDREW. Born Jan. 10, 1891, Seguin, Guadalupe County, Texas. Ht. 5 ft. 10 ½ in., brown eyes, dark hair, fair complexion. Newspaperman. REGULAR RANGER Jan. 30, 1918–July 29, 1918 (private, Co. L). Discharged. REMARKS: In 1930 was editor of a newspaper in Seguin. FAMILY: Parents, Alfred Eickenroht (b. 1865, TX) and Elizabeth or Elise Breustedt (b. 1868, TX); brother, Marvin (b. 1898, TX); spouse, Edith Noel Dromgoole "Netta" Giffin (b. 1901, TX), married June 23, 1923, divorced in 1938. *SR; 471; Davis to Harley, Mar 14, Apr 14, 1918, AGC; A1d, f, g; A3a; A4b; A6a.*

EIDMAN, HUGH BRYAN. Born Jan. 20, 1883, Georgetown, Williamson County, Texas. Medium height, medium build, brown eyes, brown hair, married. Stockman, Bay City, Matagorda County, Texas. LOYALTY RANGER June 10, 1918–Oct. 23, 1918—deceased. REMARKS: Had been a retail merchant for men's clothing in Matagorda County. Died Oct. 23, 1918, Matagorda County, Texas. FAMILY: Parents, Seamon Oscar Eidman (b. 1832, Germany) and Virginia E. Gregory (b. 1853, TX); siblings, Charles Sidney "Sid" (b. 1871, TX), Kathryn Mary "Katie" (b. 1874, TX), Seamon Oscar (b. 1876, TX), Jennie (b. 1878, TX), Guy G. (b. 1880, TX), Kraft Hewitt (b. 1885, TX), Umbleton S. (b. 1887, TX); spouse, Beulah Nuckols (b. 1885, TX), married about 1908. *SR; A1d, e; A3a; A4g; C.*

ELLINGTON, FORREST MUNFIE. Born Jan. 10, 1883, Baird, Callahan County, Texas. Ht. 5 ft. 11 in., gray eyes, dark brown hair, fair complexion, married. Stock farmer, Harris, Terry County, Texas. LOYALTY RANGER June 18, 1918–Feb. 1919. REMARKS: In 1918 was a World War I Draft Board registrar in Terry County. In 1930 was city night watchman in Brownfield, Terry County. Died June 22, 1951, Terry County, Texas. FAMILY: Parents, George W. Ellington (b. 1850, KY) and Mary A. (b. 1859, TX); siblings, Marlin Wilson (b. 1887, TX), Millard Edgar (b. 1889, TX), Grace E. (b. 1893, TX), Floyd (b. 1895, Indian Territory, OK), Pearl (b. 1897, Indian Territory, OK); spouse, Caroline Edna (b. 1891, PA), married about 1912; children, Eileen (b. 1915, TX), Leonard (b. 1927, TX). *SR; A1d, f, g; A2b; A3a.*

ELLIOT, WILLIAM J. Born Dec. 1868, on the Indian Ocean. Ht. 5 ft. 10 in., blue eyes, brown hair, fair complexion, married. Ranchman, Spur, Dickens County, Texas. LOYALTY RANGER June 17, 1918–Feb. 1919. REMARKS: Immigrated to the United States in 1888, became a naturalized citizen. Had been a merchant in Dickens County. In 1930 was a stock farmer in Dickens County. A William James Elliott died July 3, 1942, Dickens County, Texas. FAMILY: Spouse, Elizabeth Duff (b. 1871, Turkey), married about 1899; children, Margaret A. (b. 1900, TX), Elizabeth "Bessie" (b. 1902, TX), Dorothy (b. 1903, TX), William (b. 1904, TX), Audrey (b. 1906, TX), twins Virginia and Isabell (b. 1908, TX). *SR; A1d, e, f, g; C.*

ELLIOTT, JOHN HENRY, JR. Born Feb. 1, 1888, Tyler, Smith County, Texas. Ht. 5 ft. 6 in., blue eyes, blonde hair, fair complexion, married. Yardmaster, T&P Railroad, Toyah, Reeves County, Texas. SPECIAL RANGER June 1, 1918–Sept. 1918. Resigned because he planned to move to Arizona. REMARKS: In 1920 was a switchman on a railroad, living in Bisbee, Cochise County, Arizona; in 1930 was an accountant for a copper mine in Ajo, Pima County, Arizona. FAMILY: Spouse, Alma (b. 1891, MO), married about 1908; children, John H. (b. 1912, LA), Florence R. (b. 1918, TX), Lula (b. 1921, AZ). *SR; Howard to Harley, Sept 10, 1918, AGC; A1f, g; A3a.*

ELLIS, ASA "ACE." Born Sept. 27, 1894, Menard, Menard County, Texas. Ht. 5 ft. 11 ½ in., blue eyes, light hair, fair complexion. Stockman, London, Mason County, Texas. SPECIAL RANGER July 24, 1917–Dec. 1917 (attached to Co. C). REMARKS: Ace Ellis died Nov. 7, 1958, Howard County, Texas. LAW ENFORCEMENT RELATIVES: Ranger Louis Ellis, brother. FAMILY: Parents, Irvin Wilson Ellis (b. 1856, TX) and Sonora Agnes Glasscock (b. 1867, TX); siblings, William (b. 1884, TX), Irve Wilson (b. 1886, TX), Louis Emmit (b. 1888, TX), Pinkney Abner (b. 1890, TX), Alta (b. 1893, TX), Alma (b. 1896, TX), Elton (b. 1898), Thelma (b. 1900, TX), Velma (b. 1902, TX), Eugenia Capitola (b. 1909, TX), Dulcie (b. 1911, TX). *SR; Ellis to Hutchings, July 19, 1917, AGC; AG to Ellis, July 20, 1917, AGC; A1d, e, f; A2b; A3a; A4b, g.*

ELLIS, BENJAMIN SMITH. Born June 19, 1861, La Fargeville, Jefferson Co., New York. No physical description, widower. Farmer and stockraiser, Ochiltree, Ochiltree County, Texas. LOYALTY RANGER June 11, 1918–Feb. 1919. REMARKS: As a child and young adult lived in Putnam County, Missouri. By 1910 was a stock farmer in Ochiltree County. In 1930 was a sporting goods salesman in Las Vegas, San Miguel County, New Mexico. Died June 18, 1953, Perryton, Ochiltree County, Texas. FAMILY: Parents, Benjamin Ellis (b. 1822, NY) and Mary Smith "Polly" Priest (b. 1827, NY); siblings, Herman Eastman (b. 1848, NY), Charlotte (b. 1852, NY), George Irvin (b. 1864, NY), William H. (b. 1871, MO); spouse #1, Lydia Jane Parrish (b. 1864, IL; d. 1915), married Nov. 15, 1890, Unionville, Putnam County; children, Carl (b. 1891, OK), Pearl (b. 1895, TX), Chancy (b. 1903), Helen (b. 1905, TX); spouse #2, Maria Louise Ground or Turner (b. 1876, TX), married in 1925. *SR; A1a, b, d, e, f, g; A2b; A4a, b, g; B1.*

E

ELLIS, JAMES M. "JIM." Born May 1878, Gonzales County, Texas. Ht. 6 ft. 1 ½ in., brown eyes, black hair, dark complexion, widower. Peace officer, Austin, Travis County, Texas. REGULAR RANGER June 5, 1919–June 20, 1920 (private, Co. D). Resigned. REMARKS: In early 1920 was stationed as a Ranger in Brewster County, Texas. Became a Stephens County, Texas, deputy sheriff; was charged with killing a man on Nov. 16, 1920, during a raid. FAMILY: Parents, Thomas Conley Ellis (b. 1835, MO) and Mary Ann Dilworth (b. 1841, TX); siblings, Frances R. "Fanny" (b. 1859, TX), Louisa E. "Lou" (b. 1860, TX), Eliza Ann "Lyde" (b. 1862, TX), Jesse Lee (b. 1865, TX), Mary E. "Mollie" (b. 1869, TX), Joseph Benton (b. 1870, TX), Robert P. (b. 1872, TX), Alsey M. (b. 1874, TX), Willie Jane (b. 1882, TX), Lavernia (b. 1887, TX); spouse, Julia D. Gattis (b. 1883, TN; d. 1912), married about 1904 in Leesville, Gonzales County; children, Raymond (b. 1906, TX), Theresa (b. 1908, TX). *SR; 471; AA, Oct 23, 1919, Jan 1, Mar 18, May 27, 1920; LWT, Jan 9, 1921; A1b, e, f; A4b, g; B2.*

ELLIS, LOUIS EMMIT. Born May 14, 1888, Menard, Menard County, Texas. Ht. 5 ft. 11 in., blue eyes, brown hair, light complexion, married. Ranchman, Kimble County, Texas. SPECIAL RANGER Aug. 6, 1917–Dec. 1917 (attached to Co. C). REMARKS: In 1910 was a stock farmer in Tom Green County, Texas. In 1920 was a stock farmer in Menard. Died Nov. 12, 1958, Mason, Mason County, Texas. LAW ENFORCEMENT RELATIVES: Ranger Ace Ellis, brother. FAMILY: Parents, Irvin Wilson Ellis (b. 1856, TX) and Sonora Agnes Glasscock (b. 1867, TX); siblings, William (b. 1884, TX), Irve Wilson (b. 1886, TX), Pinkney Abner (b. 1890, TX), Alta (b. 1893, TX), Ace (b. 1894, TX), Alma (b. 1896, TX), Elton (b. 1898), Thelma (b. 1900, TX), Velma (b. 1902, TX), Eugenia Capitola (b. 1909, TX), Dulcie (b. 1911, TX); spouse, Mary Jane Leslie (b. 1886, TX), married June 4, 1908, Mason; daughter, Joycelyn L. (b. 1911, TX). *SR; A1d, e, f; A2b; A3a; A4g; B1.*

ELLIS, WAYMAN DENZIL. Born Mar. 25, 1883, Beeville, Bee County, Texas. Ht. 5 ft. 5 ½ in., brown eyes, brown hair, fair complexion, married. Stockman, Midland County, Texas (also listed Armstrong, Kenedy County, Texas as residence). SPECIAL RANGER Jan. 22, 1918–Jan. 15, 1919. REMARKS: Had been a farmer in Goliad County, Texas. Died June 8, 1933, Bexar County, Texas. FAMILY: Parents, John V. Ellis (b. 1835, KY) and Drusillia A. (b. 1849, TX); siblings, Earl C. (b. 1876, TX), Ralph V. (b. 1878, TX), Ethel M. (b. 1879, TX), C. C. (b. 1888, TX), Marvin (b. 1892, TX); spouse, Lillie (b. 1888, TX), married about 1901; children, Alma (b. 1902, TX), John W. (b. 1906, TX). *SR; Assistant AG to Kleberg, Jan 29, 1918, AGC; A1b, d, e; A3a; C.*

ELLISON, DUNCAN CLYDE. Born Mar. 5, 1890, Laredo, Webb County, Texas. Ht. 5 ft. 11 ½ in., blue eyes, light hair, light complexion. Cowboy, enlisted in Presidio County, Texas. REGULAR RANGER Sept. 1, 1917–Mar. 1, 1918 (private, Co. B). Resigned. REMARKS: His early childhood was spent in the Oklahoma Indian Territory. In 1930 was the proprietor of an auto repair shop in Hudspeth County, Texas. Died Mar. 30, 1952, Sierra Blanca, Hudspeth County, Texas; buried in the Sierra Blanca Masonic Cemetery. FAMILY: Parents, Jacob Jonathon "Jake" Ellison (b. 1854, TX) and Caroline Belle Howard (b. 1859, TX); siblings, Willie (b. 1879), Robert Franklin (b. 1880, TX), Arthur Guy (b. 1883, TX), Howard (b. 1885), Thomas A. (b. 1886, TX); spouse, Thelma Icy Williams (b. 1899, TX), married Mar. 2, 1918; children, Duncan Clyde, Jr. (b. 1919, TX), Julia Mae (b. 1922, TX), Tom D. (b. 1925, TX), Betty Clide (b. 1927, TX). *SR; Fox to Hutchings, Aug 29, 1917, AGC; AG to Fox, Aug 31, 1917, AGC; Fox to Harley, Feb 22, 1918, AGC; A1d, g; A2b, e; A3a; A4b, g; B1, 2.*

ELMORE, GEORGE MONROE "TUSS." Born Nov. 19, 1870, Charleston, Delta County, Texas. Ht. 5 ft. 9 in., gray eyes, dark hair, fair complexion, married. Farmer, Charleston. LOYALTY RANGER June 11, 1918–Feb. 1919. REMARKS: Died Jan. 10, 1930; buried in Charleston Cemetery. FAMILY: Parents, Robert Van Buren Elmore (b. 1836, MO) and Mary Margaret Stewart (b. 1845, TX); siblings, Letha Molly (b. 1865, TX), Daniel Axen (b. 1867, TX), Stewart Bledsoe (b. 1871, TX), L. Columbus "Lum" (b. 1874, TX), Isaac William (b. 1876, TX), Elizabeth "Dolly" (b. 1878, TX), Birdie (b. 1880, TX), John Cleveland (b. 1884, TX); spouse, Sarah Bell (b. 1869, TX), married Jan. 16, 1890, Delta County; daughters, Mamie (b. 1891, TX), Allie (b. 1895, TX). *SR; A1b, d, e, f; A2c; A4b, g; B1.*

ELROD, JESSE LEE. Born Oct. 1889, Fannin County, Texas. Ht. 5 ft. 10 in., blue eyes, dark hair, light complexion, married. Stockman, Muleshoe, Bailey County, Texas.

LOYALTY RANGER June 17, 1918–Feb. 1919. REMARKS: Spent his early years in Durant, Choctaw Nation, Indian Territory (later Oklahoma). In 1930 was a rancher living in San Angelo, Tom Green County, Texas. Died Sept. 17, 1945, Tom Green County, Texas. FAMILY: Parents, William T. Elrod (b. 1862, TN) and Cordelia Holland (b. 1870, TX); siblings, Roy H. (b. 1892, Indian Territory), Carl C. (b. 1894, Indian Territory), Novilla (b. 1899, Indian Territory), Thomas (b. 1902, OK), Helen (b. 1904, OK), William H. (b. 1906, OK); spouse, Minnie H. (b. 1895, TX), married about 1916; sons, Hamlin K. (b. 1920, TX), Norman (b. 1922, TX). *SR; A1d, f, g; A4g; C.*

ENGELKING, CONRAD (CARL?) PHILLIP. Born June 2, 1887, Sealy, Austin County, Texas. Ht. 6 ft. 1 in., brown eyes, brown hair, fair complexion. Peace officer, enlisted in Austin, Travis County, Texas. REGULAR RANGER Dec. 11, 1917–Mar. 25, 1918 (private, Co. M). Resigned to work for the Bureau of War Risk Insurance in Washington, DC. REMARKS: Ranger Service Record lists his first name as Carl; World War I Draft Registration document dated June 1917 lists his first name as Conrad, an attorney, living in Austin, Travis County. In 1920 a C. P. Engelking (b. about 1890, TX) was an attorney living in Electra, Wichita County, Texas. Conrad Phillip Engelking died May 24, 1952, Wichita County, Texas. LAW ENFORCEMENT RELATIVES: Ranger Lucas J. Engelking, cousin. FAMILY (Persons listed here are related to Conrad Phillip Engelking): Parents, Sigismund "Sigmund" Engelking (b. 1843, TX) and Anna Irene Marie Johanna Zimmerman (b. 1851, Bohemia); siblings, Peter (b. 1872), Ferdinand Charley (b. 1872, TX), Sigismund, Jr. (b. 1875), Johanna (b. 1880, TX), Fritz W. (b. 1883, TX), Ernestine (b. 1884, TX), Julius Christian (b. 1885, TX), Martha (b. 1886, TX), Hermann (b. 1888, TX); spouse (of C. P. Engelking), Hilda (b. 1897, TX). *SR; Engelking to Hanson, Feb 10, 1918, RRM; Hanson to Engelking, Feb 11, 1918, RRM; [AG] to Engelking, Apr 23, 30, 1918, AGC; Cunningham to Harley, Apr 24, 1918, AGC; Assistant AG to McCall, May 13, 1918, AGC; A1d, f; A2b; A3a; A4b, g.*

ENGELKING, LUCAS JOSEPH. Born Apr. 21, 1885, Bellville, Austin County, Texas. Ht. 5 ft. 11 ½ in., blue eyes, brown hair, fair complexion. Peace officer, Brownsville, Cameron County, Texas. REGULAR RANGER Aug. 7, 1915–Sept. 1, 1915 (private, Co. D). Resigned. REMARKS: Note length of service. In 1910 was a saloon bartender in Brownsville. Was a 1st lieutenant, Texas National Guard, Brownsville. From Mar. 1914–June 1915 had been a policeman, Brownsville. In June 1917 was a sergeant, 2nd Texas Infantry, at Brownsville. In 1920 was a corporal in the Army, stationed at Fort Bliss, El Paso, El Paso County, Texas. In 1930 was a house carpenter, living in Houston, Harris County, Texas. Died Feb. 14, 1967, McLennan County, Texas. LAW ENFORCEMENT RELATIVES: Ranger Conrad (or Carl) Phillip Engelking, cousin. FAMILY: Parents, Charles Engelking (b. 1848, TX) and Louise Langehammer (b. 1855, TX); siblings, Gustav Adolph (b. 1874, TX), Valeska (b. 1876), Ida (b. 1877, TX), twins Charles and Ernst Gus (b. 1879, TX), Otto (b. 1890, TX), Frederick Frank or Franz (b. 1882), Amalie (b. 1887), Louise (b. 1888), Louis (b. 1890); spouse, R. Evelyn (b. 1895, TX), married about 1919; children, Dorris J. (b. 1920, TX), Donald Joseph (b. 1923, TX). *SR; 471; Ransom to Hutchings, Aug 28, 1915, AGC; BDH, Feb 28, Mar 3, Aug 4, Sept 9, Oct 31, Nov 4, 1914, Feb 1, Mar 6, Jun 24, 29, 1915, Jan 28, 1917; A1e, f, g; A2b, e, f; A2b, e; A4a, b.*

ERSKINE, FRED PAUL GARASCHE. Born June 11, 1885, Derby, Frio County, Texas. Ht. 5 ft. 6 in., blue eyes, light brown hair, light complexion. Stockman, enlisted in Willacy County, Texas. REGULAR RANGER, 1915–Sept. 1916 (private, Co. A). Resigned/honorably discharged—reduction in force. REMARKS: In 1910 was a telephone manager in Dimmit County, Texas. In May 1917 lived at Cometa, Zavala County, Texas; did ranch work. In 1930 was county road supervisor, Zavala County. Died June 10, 1958, Zavala County. Texas. FAMILY: Parents, Blucher Haynes Erskine (b. 1849, TX) and Adrian "Ada" Cotton (b. 1850, TX); brothers, Andrew Nelson (b. 1873, TX), John P. (b. 1875, TX), Blucher Haynes, Jr. (b. 1881, TX). *SR; 471; Erskine to Ferguson, May 24, 1917, AGC; A1d, e, f, g; A2b; A3a; A4a, b, g.*

ERWIN, CHARLES DERETZ. Born Mar. 19, 1883, Bryan, Brazos County, Texas. Ht. 5 ft. 8 in., blue eyes, dark hair, light complexion, married. Bookkeeper, Houston, Harris County, Texas. SPECIAL RANGER Aug. 10, 1918–Jan. 15, 1919. REMARKS: Had been a clerk for a grain company in Houston. In 1917 was bookkeeper and manager of the Houston Club. In 1920 was an insurance adjustor in

Houston; in 1930 was manager of a riding academy in Houston. Died Aug. 5, 1965, Harris County, Texas. FAMILY: Spouse, Harriet Delle (b. 1885, TX), married about 1907; daughter, Mary Charlotte (b. 1910, TX). *SR; A1e, f, g; A2a, b; A3a; A5a.*

EVANS, ANDREW J. "JACK." Born Mar. 1866, Shelby, Shelby County, Alabama. Ht. 5 ft. 10 ¼ in., blue eyes, brown hair, light complexion, married. Passenger conductor, I&GN Railroad, San Antonio, Bexar County, Texas. SPECIAL RANGER Aug. 11, 1916–Jan. 15, 1919 (attached to Co. C; was reinstated—WA renewed Dec. 26, 1917). Discharged. REMARKS: As a teenager and young adult had lived in Palestine, Anderson County, Texas. In 1930 was a passenger train conductor living in Alamo Heights, Bexar County, Texas. FAMILY: Parents (probably), William Evans (b. 1843, AL) and Amanda (b. 1846, AL); sister, Rhoda (b. 1864, AL); spouse, Willie A. (b. 1878, TX), married about 1897; children, Ruby (b. 1899, TX), Jack (b. 1903, TX). *SR; Evans to Harley, Dec 24, 1917, AGC; A1a, b, d, e, f, g.*

EVANS, ARTHUR P. Born Dec. 1871, Mount Vernon, Jefferson County, Illinois. Ht. 5 ft. 10 in., brown eyes, gray hair, dark complexion. Stockman, Comstock, Val Verde County, Texas. SPECIAL RANGER Dec. 27, 1917–Jan. 15, 1919 (Co. A Volunteers). REMARKS: Had been a stock herder in Tom Green County, Texas. In 1930 was a stock commissioner, living in Del Rio, Val Verde County. An Arthur Evans died Jan. 11, 1958, Val Verde County, Texas. FAMILY: Parents, George W. Evans (b. 1832, VA) and Martha B. (b. 1833, IL); sisters, Ida C. (b. 1862, IL), Alena N. (b. 1873, IL). *SR; A1b, d, g; A2b.*

EVANS, JAMES ROBERT "DOXIE." Born Mar. 15, 1873, Grand Prairie, Tarrant County, Texas. Ht. 5 ft. 10 in., brown eyes, dark hair, light complexion, married. Stock farmer, Meadow, Terry County, Texas. LOYALTY RANGER June 15, 1918–Feb. 1919. REMARKS: In 1900 was a stock farmer in Foard County, Texas. Also lived in Lynn County, Texas; in 1930 lived in Hockley County, Texas. A James Robert Evans died Mar. 8, 1947, Callahan County, Texas. FAMILY: Parents, G. W. Evans (b. 1840, MS) and Caroline A. Henington (b. 1843, MS); siblings, O. F. (b. 1863, MS), W. J. (b. 1865, MS), J. B. (b. 1867, MS), W. F. (b. 1870, TX), Anna E. (b. 1876, TX), Isaac (b. 1879, TX), Ruby (b. 1883, TX); spouse, Mary Elizabeth "Mollie" Emery (b. 1872, TX), married Aug. 13, 1893, Arlington, Dallas County, Texas; children, Pearl (b. 1895, TX), Elbert Allen (b. 1900, TX), Walter Bernice (b. 1902, TX), Robert Ian (b. 1904, TX), Roland J. (b. 1906, TX), Cecil L. (b. 1908, TX), Bernard Seymore (b. 1913, TX). *SR; A1a, b, d, e, f, g; A2b; A3a; A4b.*

EVANS, JOHN WESLEY. Born July 25, 1854, Fayetteville, Fayette County, Texas. Ht. 6 ft., blue eyes, gray hair, light complexion, married. City marshal, Eden, Concho County, Texas. SPECIAL RANGER Apr. 27, 1918–Jan. 15, 1919. REMARKS: As a child had lived in Colorado County, Texas; in 1900 was a farmer in Hays County, Texas. FAMILY: Parents, Dr. Isaiah Evans (b. 1815, PA) and Louisa Emma Roper (b. 1821, TN); siblings, Emily Jane (b. 1845, MO), Mary Ann (b. 1847, MO), Elizabeth Catherine (b. 1850, TX), Amanda Louisa (b. 1852, TX), Elijah Asbury (b. 1856, TX), Fannie Ellen (b. 1858, TX), Martha Virginia (b. 1860, TX), William Madison (b. 1863, TX); spouse, Camilla Jones (b. 1859, TX), married Nov. 2, 1876, Lavaca County, Texas; children, William I. (b. 1881, TX), Berta E. (b. 1886, TX), John W. (b. 1888, TX), Silas K. (b. 1890, TX), Camilla T. (b. 1892, TX), Lytton B. (b. 1897, TX). *SR; Evans to Harley, Jan 26, 1918, AGC; Harley to Kemp, Apr 2, 1918, AGC; A1aa, d, e, f; A2c; A4b, g; B2.*

EVANS, ROBERT HAMPTON "BOB." Born Apr. 2, 1874, Bagdad, Williamson County, Texas. Ht. 5 ft. 10 in., brown eyes, black hair, dark complexion. Stockman, Marfa, Presidio County, Texas. SPECIAL RANGER Jan. 3, 1918–Jan. 15, 1919. REMARKS: A Robert Hempton [*sic*] Evans died July 15, 1927, El Paso County, Texas. FAMILY: Parents (probably), Thomas Evans (b. 1835, TN or KY) and Lavinia Elizabeth Marley (b. 1839, TN); siblings, Angela "Angie" (b. 1864, TX), Martha "Mattie" (b. 1866, TX), Eudora (b. 1868, TX), John Graves (b. 1870, TX), William (b. 1872, TX), Virginia Lavinia (b. 1881, TX), May (b. 1885, TX); spouse, Eva M. (b. 1879, TX); stepchildren, Otho Joyce (b. 1904, CA), Helen Joyce (b. 1908, CA). *SR; Fox to Harley, Jan 3, 1917, AGC; A1b, f; A2b; A3a; A4b.*

EVANS, ROGER QUINCY. Born Apr. 3, 1892, Cameron, Milam County, Texas. Tall, stout, gray eyes, light brown hair. County agricultural agent, Baird, Callahan County, Texas. SPECIAL RANGER May 29, 1917–Dec. 1917 (attached to Co. C). REMARKS: Had been a schoolteacher. In 1917 was an agriculture agent with Texas Agricultural and Mechanical College. In 1920 was a real estate agent in Callahan County. A Roger Quincy Evans died Dec. 22, 1965, Callahan County, Texas. FAMILY: Parents, John Pinckney Evans (b. 1845, AL) and Inez Isadore Griffin (b. 1855, AL); siblings, Sarah C. (b. 1868, MS), Laurence Commodore (b. 1876, TX), Marcus L. (b. 1880, TX), Ida Elizabeth (b. 1885, TX), Ada Ines (b. 1887); spouse, Jean (1897, TX). *SR; A1b, f; A2b; A3a; A4b; B1.*

EVERETT, WILEY J., JR. Born Dec. 17, 1896, Llano, Llano County, Texas. Ht. 5 ft. 7 ½ in., gray eyes, brown hair, dark complexion. Stockman, Llano. SPECIAL RANGER May 21, 1917–Dec. 1917 (attached to Co. C). REMARKS: A Wiley K. Everett died Jan. 26, 1942, Llano County, Texas. LAW ENFORCEMENT RELATIVES: Llano County sheriff (Nov. 7, 1916–Nov. 2, 1920) W. J. Everett, father. FAMILY: Parents, Wiley J. Everett (b. 1853, TN) and Lutie Malinda (b. 1862, TX); siblings, Ola (b. 1882, TX), Mittie (b. 1883, TX), Zula (b. 1886, TX), Wiley May (b. 1891, TX), Virdie E. (b. 1898, TX), twins Iva and Ira (b. 1900, TX); spouse, Norma Eva Clawson (b. 1904, TX), married about 1922; children, Doris Louvayne (b. 1926, TX), Joyce (b. 1929, TX), W. J., Jr. (b. 1934, TX). *SR; Everett to Harley, Mar 1, 1918, AGC; 1503:344; A1d, e, f, g; A2e; A3a; C.*

EWING, MACK BRADLEY. Born Dec. 8, 1874, Cooper, Delta County, Texas. Ht. 5 ft. 6 in., brown eyes, brown hair, dark complexion. Farmer, Tell, Childress County, Texas. LOYALTY RANGER June 1, 1918–Feb. 1919. REMARKS: Spanish-American War veteran. In 1900 lived with relatives in Palestine, Anderson County, Texas. In 1910 was a dry goods salesman in Childress County. Died June 17, 1920, Tell, Childress County, Texas. FAMILY: Parents, Edley Ewing (b. 1845, TX) and Ellen Bradley (b. 1852, TX); siblings, Kathryn "Kate" (b. 1871, TX), Sarah Elizabeth "Lizzie" (b. 1872, TX), Albert Edley (b. 1877, TX), Maude (b. 1881, TX), Grace Clay (b. 1884, TX). *SR; A1d, e; A3a; A4b.*

FAGAN, JOHN FRANCIS. Born June 1, 1879, Waxahachie, Ellis County, Texas. Ht. 5 ft. 11 ½ in., blue eyes, dark hair, light complexion, married. Brakeman, I&GN Railroad, San Antonio, Bexar County, Texas. SPECIAL RANGER July 18, 1916–Dec. 1917 (attached to Co. C). Brakeman, I&GN Railroad, San Antonio. LOYALTY RANGER June 17, 1918–Feb. 1919. REMARKS: Was a private in the U.S. Army in the Spanish American War. Died Nov. 14, 1948, Cotulla, La Salle County, Texas; buried in Fort Sam Houston National Cemetery, San Antonio. FAMILY: Parents, Lawrence Christopher Fagan (b. 1851, NY) and Mary Ryan (b. 1844, NY); siblings, Phillip (b. 1867, CT), Lawrence (b. 1869, CT), Annie (b. 1871, CT), Nellie (b. 1873, CT), Pete (b. 1890); spouse, Josephine Marion McCaskill (b. 1884, TX), married Sept. 22, 1904, Allegheny City, Allegheny County, Pennsylvania; son, William Lawrence (b. 1906, PA). *SR; Fagan to Harley, Dec 24, 1917, AGC; A1b, e, f, g; A2b; A3a, b; A4a, b.*

FALLS, JEFFERSON DAVIS. Born May 5, 1861, Kings Mountain, Cleveland County, North Carolina. Ht. 5 ft. 9 in., gray eyes, brown hair, medium complexion, married. Sheriff, Throckmorton, Throckmorton County, Texas. LOYALTY RANGER June 8, 1918–Feb. 1919. REMARKS: Throckmorton County sheriff Nov. 8, 1910–Nov. 5, 1918. Died Nov. 2, 1950, Throckmorton County, Texas; buried in Throckmorton Cemetery. FAMILY: Parents, James Bivins Falls (b. 1825, NC or PA) and Mary Dunlap Dixon (b. 1833, NC); siblings, Lenora G. (b. 1855, NC), Mary Ann (b. 1857, NC), Edward Clayton (b. 1859, NC), Benjamin Dilworth (b. 1863, NC), George Calvin (b. 1865, NC), Mittie Ellen or Aletta (b. 1868, NC); spouse #1, Margaret Ann Adams (b. 1863, NC); daughter, Mary Wilson (b. 1879, NC); spouse #2, Hazel Anna Condron (b. 1869, TX), married about 1887; children, Harvey Thomas (b. 1887, TX), Cora M. (b. 1889, TX), Dona (b. 1890, TX), Mary E. (b. 1893, TX), Jeffie Ruth (b. 1895, TX), Ruby (b. 1897, TX), Talmage Franklin (b. 1898, TX), Luella S. (b. 1901, TX), Sallie B. (b. 1904, TX), Anna (b. 1906, TX), Frank R. (b. 1909, TX), Angelina (b. 1912, TX). *SR; Falls to Hobby, Sept 17, 1918, AGC; 1503:490; A1a, d, e, f; A2b; A3a; A4a, b, g; B1, 2.*

FARROW, JOHN HARRISON. Born Dec. 24, 1867, Chester County, Tennessee. Blue eyes, dark hair, dark complexion, married. Farmer, Itasca, Hill County, Texas. SPECIAL RANGER Jan. 12, 1918–Jan. 15, 1919. REMARKS: Spent his childhood in Tennessee and Mississippi. Was a farmer in Hill County by 1900. Died Oct. 5, 1939, Hill County, Texas. FAMILY: Parents, Samuel Wilks Farrow (b. 1831, SC) and Gilla Adeline Trice (b. 1842, TN); siblings, Avarilla B. (b. 1859, TN), William Lucean (b. 1861, TN), Samuel Lafayette (b. 1862, TN), Robert D. (b. 1866, TN), Eddy E. (b. 1870, TN), Carrie A. (b. 1872, MS), Wilks (b. 1873, TN); spouse, Ella V. Brown (b. 1876, TN), married Dec. 26, 1894, Henderson County, Tennessee; children, Earl D. (b. 1896, TX), Julia A. (b. 1900, TX), Donna (b. 1904, TX). *SR; 471; Leatherwood to AG, Jan 12, 1918, AGC; A1a, b, d, e, f; A2j; A4g; B1; C.*

FATHEREE, IRA NEAL. Born Sept. 26, 1883, Lone Oak, Hunt County, Texas. Ht. 5 ft. 11 in., hazel eyes, black hair, fair complexion. Special agent, T&P Railroad, Big Spring, Howard County, Texas. SPECIAL RANGER Dec. 21, 1917–Jan. 15, 1919. Special Agent, T&P Railroad, Big Spring. RAILROAD RANGER Dec. 30, 1922–Dec. 30, 1924. Discharged. Chief special agent, T&P Railroad, Dallas, Dallas County, Texas. SPECIAL RANGER Aug. 7, 1925–July 30, 1927; July 30, 1927–July 30, 1928; Aug. 2, 1928–Aug. 2, 1929; Aug. 5, 1929–Aug. 7, 1930; Aug. 7, 1930–Aug. 7, 1931; Aug. 24, 1931–Jan. 18, 1933; Feb. 10, 1933–unknown. REMARKS: Railroad special officer and agent from 1910 on. Died Aug. 10, 1955, Dallas County, Texas. FAMILY: Parents, Chauncy Lafayette "Bud" Fatheree (b. 1849, LA) and Almeda Josephine Harkey (b. 1852, GA); siblings, Earnest Arthur (b. 1874, TX), Charley (b. 1876, TX), Raymond Orville (b. 1878, TX), Percy Lafayette (b. 1880, TX), Wilna Mollie (b. 1886, TX), Edward Earle (b. 1888, TX); one source lists spouse, Marjorie Murphy; daughter, Dorothy. *SR; A1d, e, g; A2a; A3a; A4b.*

FAUBION, J. L. Born Nov. 1868, Waco, McLennan County, Texas. Ht. 5 ft. 8 in., blue eyes, dark hair, fair complexion. REGULAR RANGER 1892 (Co. D). Electrician, enlisted in Travis County, Texas. REGULAR RANGER Aug. 13, 1915–Mar. 31, 1916 (private, Co. A). Resigned. Peace officer. REGULAR RANGER Dec. 13, 1917–July 28, 1918 (private, Co. I; WA cancelled, new commission issued in Co. A, May 31, 1918). Resigned. REMARKS: Ranger enlistment form in 1917 has birthplace as Lamar County, Texas; 1918 enlistment has birthplace as Clarksville, Red River County, Texas. A John Luther Faubion, born Nov. 1869, lived in Lamar County in 1870; his father had been a bartender in Waco, McLennan County and at one time was a Ranger; this family lived in Red River County in 1871. John Luther Faubion died Oct. 24, 1947, McLennan County, Texas. FAMILY: John Luther Faubion's parents, John Milton Faubion (b. 1841, TN) and Julia Ann Harmon (b. 1847, TX); siblings, Leslie Harmon (b. 1871, TX), Lillian (b. 1875, TX), Maud M. (b. 1877, TX), Charles (b. 1894, TX). *SR; 471; Faubion to Ferguson, Aug 11, 1915, AGC; Sanders to Harley, Aug 1, 1918, AGC; A1a; A2b; A4a, b.*

FAUBION, JOSEPH EUGENE. Born Oct. 2, 1877, Hamilton, Hamilton County, Texas. Ht. 5 ft. 11 in., blue eyes, brown hair, dark complexion, married. Stockraiser. REGULAR RANGER Jan. 26, 1918–Aug. 1918 (private, Co. L). Discharged. REMARKS: Had been a farmer in Coryell County, Texas. In Sept. 1918 was working on a stock ranch in Hot Wells, Hudspeth County, Texas; wife was living in Hamilton County. In 1930 was a farmer in Hamilton County. Died Feb. 17, 1966, Harris County, Texas; buried in Ireland, Coryell County. FAMILY: Parents, Henry Thomas Faubion (b. 1848, TN) and Susan Medora "Dora" Harris (b. 1848, MO); siblings, Ava T. (b. 1871, MO), Jas. H. (b. 1872, MO), Cynthia A. (b. 1874, TX), Rufus Otto (b. 1876, TX), Jennie Pearl (b. 1881, TX); spouse, Alice Pearl Enochs (b. 1880, TX), married Nov. 6, 1896, Copperas Cove, Hamilton County; children, Lucy (b. 1897, TX), Thelma R. (b. 1899, TX), William Travis (b. 1901, TX), Annie P. (b. 1904, OK), Samuel H. (b. 1906, TX), Mary Katherine (b. 1907, TX), Walter E. (b. 1909, TX), Jennie Ruth (b. 1912, TX), Joe (b. 1915, TX), Clyde (b. 1917, TX), Alice Eugene (b. 1918, TX), J. E. (b. 1922, TX), James F. (b. 1927, TX). *SR; 471; Davis to Harley, Jan 26, 1918, AGC; AG to Davis, Jan 29, 1918, AGC; Harley to Davis, Aug 22, 1918, AGC; A1b, d, e, f, g; A2b; A3a; A4a, b, g; B1.*

FAUST, WALTER. Born July 26, 1878, New Braunfels, Comal County, Texas. Ht. 6 ft., gray eyes, blonde hair, fair complexion, married. Cashier, First National Bank, New Braunfels. LOYALTY RANGER Aug. 5, 1918–Feb. 19, 1919. REMARKS: By 1930 was bank president, New Braunfels. Died Sept. 1, 1933, Comal County, Texas; buried in Comal Cemetery, New Braunfels. FAMILY: Parents, Joseph Faust (b. 1845, Prussia) and Ida Forcke or Ida von Stein (b. 1858, TX); sister, Melita (b. 1893, TX); spouse #1, Lassie or Lottie W. Pfeuffer (b. 1882, TX), married Feb. 10, 1904, Comal County, divorced by 1920; son, Walter Pfeuffer, Jr. (b. 1905, TX); spouse #2, Vera (b. 1891, TX), married about 1922; son, Joseph (b. 1923, TX). *SR; A1b, d, e, f, g; A2e; A3a; A4b, g; B1; C.*

FEAGIN, JEFFERSON DAVIS. Born Aug. 1871, Clayton, Barbour County, Alabama. Ht. 5 ft. 8 in., hazel eyes, dark hair, fair complexion. Lumberman, Kirbyville, Jasper County, Texas. LOYALTY RANGER June 5, 1918–Feb. 1919. REMARKS: A Jefferson Davis Feagin died May 22, 1924, Dallas County, Texas. LAW ENFORCEMENT RELATIVES: Bullock County, Alabama sheriff (1880) Isaac B. Feagin, father. FAMILY: Parents, Isaac Ball Feagin (b. 1833, GA) and Sarah J. "Sallie" Hall (b. 1840, GA); siblings, Mary L. "Minnie" (b. 1865, AL), James (b. 1866, AL), Harriet Z. "Hattie" (b. 1869, AL), Joel D. (b. 1873, AL), Lucy H. (b. 1876, AL), Arthur Henry (b. 1878, AL), Isaac Ball (b. 1882). *SR; A1a, b, e; A3a; A4a, b; B1; C.*

FEILD, HARRY. Born June 15, 1886, Lake Victor, Burnet County, Texas. Ht. 6 ft. 1 in., blue eyes, dark hair, fair complexion, married. Farmer, Lake Victor. LOYALTY RANGER June 8, 1918–Feb. 1919. REMARKS: In Ranger Service Records, last name is spelled "Field." Died Aug 24, 1970, Burnet County, Texas. FAMILY: Parents, Albert A. "Andy" Feild (b. 1856, TX) and Harriet "Hattie" McGuire (b. 1862, CA); siblings, Albert Vernor (b. 1880, TX), Kate (b. 1882, TX), Ira Jack (b. 1891, TX); spouse, Cora M. (b. 1887, TX); children, Erwin G. (b. 1909, TX), Browery (b. 1912, TX), Evelyn (b. 1915, TX), Maurice (b. 1917, TX). *SR; A1d, e, f; A2a, b; A3a; A4b, g; B1.*

FELPS, HENRY "FLIP." Born Mar. 14, 1887, Johnson City, Blanco County, Texas. Ht. 5 ft. 11 ½ in., brown eyes, brown hair, dark complexion. Peace officer. REGULAR RANGER June 19, 1913–Aug. 1, 1915 (private, Co. B; reenlisted and transferred to Co. A, June 19, 1915). Resigned. REMARKS: One source gives birthplace as Miller Creek, Blanco County. In Apr. 1917 lived in San Benito, Cameron County, Texas; in 1920 worked in a cotton gin in Eden, Concho County, Texas. In 1930 was a truck farmer in Sierra County, New Mexico. Died Aug. 1936, Truth or Consequences, Sierra County, New Mexico. FAMILY: Parents, Riley Waggoner "Brice" Felps (b. 1832, TN) and Julia Ann Maddox (b. 1848, AL); siblings, twins Joseph and Selety C. (b. 1871, TX), Jacob (b. 1873, TX), Daniel (b. 1875, TX), John W. (b. 1877, TX), Riley W. (b. 1880, TX), James Robert (b. 1884, TX), twin sister, Isabella "Belle" (b. 1887, TX); spouse, Verona Erwin (b. 1890, TX), married about 1922; children, Ruth (b. 1922, NM), Lois (b. 1924, NM), Wade Henry (b. 1926, TX). *SR; 471; BDH, Apr 23, 1917; A1b, d, f, g; A3a; A4b, e; B1.*

FENLEY, IVY R. Born Sept. 1882, Uvalde, Uvalde County, Texas. Ht. 5 ft. 9 in., hazel eyes, brown hair, fair complexion. Peace officer and rancher, El Paso County, Texas. REGULAR RANGER June 8, 1915–June 30, 1916 (private, Co. B). Resigned. El Paso County Deputy sheriff, 1916–1930. SPECIAL RANGER May 25, 1917–Sept. 1, 1917 (attached to Co. C). Resigned. REMARKS: El Paso policeman, 1912–1915; in 1930 still deputy sheriff in El Paso. Died 1949, El Paso, El Paso County, Texas. LAW ENFORCEMENT RELATIVES: El Paso policeman (1918) Joel Tilden Fenley, brother. FAMILY: Parents, James Taylor Fenley (b. 1847, LA) and Matilda Jane Gibson (b. 1851, TX); siblings, Elizabeth (b. 1867, TX), William M. (b. 1869, TX), James Robert (b. 1871, TX), Annie L. (b. 1874, TX), Joel Tilden (b. 1876, TX), Florence L. (b. 1879, TX), Mae Bell (b. 1884, TX), Effie Maude (b. 1886, TX), Thomas Leslie (b. 1889, TX), Addie Earlene (b. 1892, TX), Otho Mone (b. 1896, TX); spouse, Emma Webster (b. 1890, PA), married about 1923; stepson, Sherman Webster (b. 1902, CO). *SR; 471; EPMT, June 10, July 25, 29, 1915, Feb 9, Nov 16, 17, 1916; Orndorff to Ferguson, Apr 5, 1917; Wroe to AG, Apr 13, 1917, AGC; AG to Orndorff, Apr 13, May 22, AGC; Bryant to Ferguson, May 18, 1917, AGC; A1d, g; A3a; A4a, b; B2.*

FERGUSON, WILLIAM ANDERSON. Born July 4, 1875, Jasper, Jasper County, Texas. Ht. 5 ft. 4 in., brown eyes, dark hair, dark complexion, married. Mechanic, Doucette, Tyler County, Texas. LOYALTY RANGER June 12, 1918–Feb. 1919. REMARKS: In 1920 was a stock raiser in Tyler County. In 1930 was a timber worker in Tyler County. Died Sept. 24, 1944, Tyler County, Texas; buried in Magnolia Cemetery, Woodville, Tyler County. FAMILY: Parents, Elijah Anderson Ferguson (b. 1847, TX) and Elizabeth Julia "Bettie" Eddy (b. 1851, TX); brother, Zeramia Kinsey (b. 1876, TX); spouse, Bunnie Jane Stewart (b. 1878, TX), married Jan. 29, 1899, Colmesneil, Tyler County; son, William Van Stewart "Billie" (b. 1906, TX). *SR; A1b, e, f, g; A2b; A3a; A4a, b; B1.*

FIELDS, CHARLES WILLIAM. Born June 10, 1884, Giddings, Lee County, Texas. Ht. 5 ft. 8 in., blue eyes, brown hair, fair complexion, married. Farmer and stockman, Dime Box and Giddings, Lee County. SPECIAL RANGER Dec. 7, 1918–Jan. 15, 1919. REMARKS: In 1910–1920 was manager of a cotton oil compress in Giddings. FAMILY: Parents, Dr. Jacob Alexander Fields (b. 1852, VA) and Mary Virginia "Mollie" Flack (b. 1858, TX); siblings, John D. (b. 1877, TX), Maud M. (b. 1879, TX); spouse, Florence R. (b. 1883, TX), married about 1904; children, Virginia I. (b. 1905, TX), Charles W., Jr. (b. 1909, TX). *SR; A1d, e, f; A3a; A4a, b, g.*

FINLEY, ALBERT ROSS. Born Aug. 7, 1888, Kaufman County, Texas. Ht. 5 ft. 6 in., blue eyes, light hair, fair complexion, married. Stockman, Uvalde, Uvalde County, Texas. LOYALTY RANGER May 31, 1918–Feb. 21, 1919. REMARKS: In June 1917 was deputy sheriff, Uvalde County. On WWI Draft Registration document, claimed "Rupture, cripple arm, cripple leg." Died Jan. 13, 1950, Uvalde, Uvalde County, Texas. FAMILY: Parents, Nicholas E. Finley (b. 1863, MS) and Sarah Caroline "Callie" Yates (b. 1872, TX); siblings, Nora O. (b. 1890, TX), Ara M. (b. 1892, TX), Lonnie Madison (b. 1895, TX), Ruth Elizabeth "Bettie" (b. 1897, TX); spouse, Wilda or Willie Lois Cardwell (b. 1895, TX), married Sept. 14, 1915, Uvalde; sons, Albert Ross, Jr. (b. 1916, TX), Nick Cardwell (b. 1917, TX). *SR; A1d, e, f; A2b, e; A3a; A4a, b; B1.*

FINLEY, ISAAC NEWTON. Born June 9, 1878, Livingston, Overton County, Tennessee. Ht. 5 ft. 9 in., gray eyes, brown hair, red complexion, married. Farmer, Abilene, Taylor County, Texas. SPECIAL RANGER June 7, 1917–Dec. 1917 (attached to Co. C). REMARKS: By 1900 was a farmer in Taylor County, Texas. In 1910 was doing odd jobs, living in Bronte, Coke County, Texas. As of Sept. 1918 was a farmer in Honey Grove, Fannin County, Texas; in 1920 was a farmer in Nolan County, Texas. WWI Draft Registration document stated was "blind in right eye." An Isaac Finley died Aug. 1, 1946, Potter County, Texas. FAMILY: Parents, George T. Finley (b. 1844, TN) and Delila Jane Qualls (b. 1852, TN); sisters, Martha A. (b. 1870, TN), Mary E. (b. 1873, TN); spouse, Lilly Pearl (b. 1881, AL), married about 1900; children, Roy E. (b. 1901, TX), George A. (b. 1903, TX), Lillie P. (b. 1906, TX), Floyd (b. 1911, TX), Myrtle (b. 1915, TX), Bill (b. 1917, TX). *SR; Register to Ferguson, May 18, 1917, AGC; Cunningham to Ferguson, May 18, 1917, AGC; A1b, d, e, f; A2b; A3a; A4g; B1, 2.*

FINNEY, JOHN RENFRO. Born Dec. 4, 1875, Sulphur Springs, Hopkins County, Texas. Ht. 5 ft. 10 in., black eyes, gray hair (bald), light complexion, married. Druggist, Wills Point, Van Zandt County, Texas. LOYALTY RANGER June 5, 1918–Feb. 1919. REMARKS: Died Apr. 2, 1936, Wills Point, Van Zandt County, Texas. LAW ENFORCEMENT RELATIVES: Peace officer (Hopkins County, 1880) F. E. Finney, father. FAMILY: Parents, Francis Elgin Finney (b. 1833, MD) and Laura T. Scott (b. 1834, AL); siblings, Catherine (b. 1855, AL), Jim (b. 1857, AL), Frank (b. 1862, TX), Ellen E. (b. 1864, TX), Mollie (b. 1868, TX), Lara (b. 1877, TX); spouse, Ammye Swank (b. 1876, TX), married Dec. 27, 1897; children, Clarance Jack (b. 1899, TX), Mary Guion (b. 1901, TX), Margaret (b. 1913, TX). *SR; A1b, d, e, f, g; A3a; B2; C.*

FISCHER, WILHELM "WILLIE." Born Oct. 10, 1868, Fischer's Store, Comal County, Texas. Ht. 6 ft. 1 in., blue eyes, brown hair, fair complexion, married. General merchandise merchant, Fischer's Store. LOYALTY RANGER June 13, 1918–Feb. 1919. REMARKS: Died Jan. 17, 1958, Guadalupe County, Texas; buried in Fischer Cemetery, Comal County. FAMILY: Parents, Hermann Fischer (b. 1828, Prussia) and Anna Lindeman (b. 1836, Prussia); siblings, Otto (b. 1856, TX), Emma (b. 1859, TX), Hermann (b. 1867, TX); spouse, Elfrieda Pantemuehl (b. 1870, TX), married Oct. 11, 1891; children, Alma (b. 1893, TX), Lola Florence (b. 1894, TX), Gilbert (b. 1896, TX), Paul (b. 1898, TX), Erika Elfrieda "Rikki" (b. 1899, TX), Hilmar F. (b. 1900, TX), Lothar (b. 1902, TX), Willie, Jr. "Bill" (b. 1904, TX), Elsa (b. 1905, TX), Lillian Eve (b. 1907, TX), Raymond (b. 1908, TX), Gertia (b. 1910, TX), Anne Marie (b. 1911, TX). *SR; A1a, b, d, e, f, g; A2b; A4a, b, g.*

FITZGERALD, COREA (CAREA?) AQUILLA. Born Mar. 1, 1869, Poplar Bluff, Butler County, Missouri. Ht. 5 ft. 6 in., gray eyes, brown hair, ruddy complexion, married. Ranchman, Big Spring, Howard County, Texas. LOYALTY RANGER June 5, 1918–Feb. 1919. REMARKS: Died Mar. 13, 1921, Big Spring, Howard County, Texas. FAMILY: Parents, Moses Christopher Fitzgerald (b. 1827, TN) and Louisa Marie Sparkman (b. 1827, TN); siblings, Thomas Frances (b. 1849, TN), William Humphus (b. 1851, TN), James Caldon (b. 1854, TN), John Leonard (b. 1856, TN), Rufus Aron (b. 1859, TN), Celia E. (b. 1862, MO), Theophilis Christopher (b. 1864, MO), Henry Luther (b. 1866, MO); spouse, Maggie M. Richardson (b. 1879, TX), married about 1895; children, Esther L. (b. 1897, TX), Handy L. (b. 1900, TX), Fred (b. 1902, TX), Ora (b. 1904, TX), Opal Selby (b. 1908, TX). *SR; A1a, d, e, f; A2b; A4a, b.*

FITZGERALD, RAYMOND. Born Dec. 18, 1881, Gonzales, Gonzales County, Texas. Ht. 5 ft. 8 ½ in., gray eyes, black hair, dark complexion, married. Stockman, Marfa, Presidio

County, Texas. SPECIAL RANGER Dec. 31, 1917–Jan. 15, 1919. REMARKS: In 1910 was a stockman in Nolan County, Texas. In 1930 was a rancher in Garza County, Texas. FAMILY: Parents, Robert Hubert Fitzgerald (b. 1852, TX) and Emma Frances Littlefield (b. 1852, TX); siblings, Cora (b. 1871, TX), Hubert (b. 1875, TX), Archie (b. 1876, TX), Nellie (b. 1878, TX), Jerald (b. 1884, TX), Ethel (b. 1886, TX); spouse #1, Janie Maye Beall (b. 1885, TX), married June 6, 1904, Sweetwater, Nolan County, divorced before 1926; daughter, Evelyn (b. 1905, TX); spouse #2, Diane (b. 1886, TX), married about 1926. *SR; A1b, d, e, f, g; A3a; A4b; B1.*

FITZGERALD, SAM MACK or MAX. Born Feb. 1880, Gonzales, Gonzales County, Texas. Ht. 5 ft. 7 in., brown eyes, brown hair, dark complexion. Rancher. REGULAR RANGER June 26, 1916–July 17, 1916 (private, Co. B). Resigned. REMARKS: Note length of service. A Samuel M. Fitzgerald died Oct. 15, 1949, Harris County, Texas. FAMILY: Parents, Milam M. Fitzgerald (b. 1844, TX) and Caroline Augusta Kokernot (b. 1848, TX); siblings, Blanche (b. 1873, TX), Johnnie or Maude (b. 1876, TX), Edna (b. 1877, TX), Mattie Josephine (b. 1882, TX), David Crockett (b. 1885, TX). *SR; A1b, d; A2b; A4b.*

FLEMING, WILLIAM ADOLPHUS "ADOLPH." Born Mar. 2, 1889, Cadiz, Bee County, Texas. Ht. 5 ft. 11 in., blue eyes, brown hair, ruddy complexion, married. Stockman. REGULAR RANGER Dec. 17, 1917–Feb. 10, 1918 (private, Co. G). Discharged. REMARKS: Note length of service. As of June 1917 was living in Clareville, Bee County. Spoke Spanish fluently. In 1920 was a shipyard carpenter, lived in Rockport, Aransas County, Texas. In 1930 worked for the U.S. Immigration Service, lived in Cotulla, LaSalle County, Texas. FAMILY: Parents, Benjamin Marshall Fleming (b. 1848, TX) and Margaret Ann "Maggie" Quinn (b. 1860, TX); siblings, Benjamin Harrison (b. 1886, TX), Margaret Ann (b. 1892, TX), Alice Celes (b. 1894, TX); spouse, Lena A. (b. 1888, TX), married about 1911. *SR; 471; Stevens to Harley, Dec 17, 1917, AGC; A1d, e, f, g; A3a; A4b.*

FLETCHER, EMMETT ALVERSON. Born Oct. 10, 1867, Beaumont, Jefferson County, Texas. Ht. 5 ft. 9 ½ in., blue eyes, dark hair, florid complexion, married. President, Romayor Gravel Company, Beaumont. LOYALTY RANGER Aug. 1, 1918–Feb. 1919. President, Romayor Gravel Company, Beaumont. SPECIAL RANGER Aug. 25, 1919–Dec. 31, 1919. REMARKS: Was commissioned at the request of Governor Hobby. In 1920 was a real estate agent in Beaumont; in 1930 was president of a gravel company in Beaumont. An Emmett A. Fletcher died Feb. 24, 1943, Jefferson County, Texas. LAW ENFORCEMENT RELATIVES: Ranger Harvey D. Fletcher, brother. FAMILY: Parents, William Andrew Fletcher (b. 1839, LA) and Julian Ann Long (b. 1846, GA); siblings, Harvey Davis (b. 1869, TX), Marion Keith (b. 1871, TX), Bertha Valentine "Vallie" (b. 1874, TX), Clyde William (b. 1876, TX); spouse #1, Mary Emma Caswell (b. 1867, TX), married Oct. 9, 1889, Jefferson County, divorced before 1910; spouse #2, Gladys (b. 1888, AL), married by 1920. *SR; Fletcher to Harley, Aug 2, 1918, AGC; A1a, b, e, f, g; A2c; A4a; C.*

FLETCHER, HARVEY DAVIS. Born Aug. 20, 1869, Beaumont, Jefferson County, Texas. Ht. 5 ft. 5 ½ in., brown eyes, dark hair, dark complexion, married. Newspaperman, Service Department of the *Beaumont Enterprise*, Beaumont. SPECIAL RANGER Aug. 14, 1919–Dec. 31, 1919. REMARKS: Was commissioned at the request of Governor Hobby. In 1900 was treasurer of a lumber company in Beaumont; in 1910 was a coal merchant in Beaumont. Died Jan. 3, 1920, Jefferson County, Texas. LAW ENFORCEMENT RELATIVES: Ranger Emmett A. Fletcher, brother. FAMILY: Parents, William Andrew Fletcher (b. 1839, LA) and Julian Ann Long (b. 1846, GA); siblings, Emmett Alverson (b. 1867, TX), Marion Keith (b. 1871, TX), Bertha Valentine "Vallie" (b. 1874, TX), Clyde William (b. 1876, TX); spouse, Florence Bertha Vaughan (b. 1872, TX), married Feb. 8, 1893, Beaumont; children, Vallie May (b. 1896), William Andrew (b. 1899, TX), Nicholas Vaughan "Nick" (b. 1906, TX). *SR; A1a, b, d, e, f; A2b, c; A4a.*

FLETCHER, LLOYD. Born Dec. 31, 1881, Cleburne, Johnson County, Texas. Ht. 5 ft. 11 ½ in., blue eyes, red hair, red complexion, married. U.S. government investigator, Plainview, Hale County, Texas. SPECIAL RANGER Dec. 10, 1917–Feb. 1918 (Co. B Volunteers). Discharged—Co. B Volunteers was disbanded. REMARKS: In Sept. 1918 was a special agent for the U.S. Department of Justice in Amarillo, Potter County, Texas. In 1930 was an attorney in Amarillo. FAMILY: Spouse, Florence (b. 1892,

OH), married about 1913; son, Lloyd, Jr. (b. 1915, TX). *SR; Rawlings to Harley, Dec 11, 1917, AGC; A1f, g; A2e; A3a.*

FLETCHER, ROBERT ROSS. Born Mar. 30, 1885, Greenville, Hunt County, Texas. Short, medium build, blue eyes, brown hair, married. Barber, Kingsville, Kleberg County, Texas. LOYALTY RANGER June 10, 1918–Feb. 1919. REMARKS: In 1910 was a farmer in Clinton, Hunt County. Died Oct. 28, 1941, Kleberg County, Texas. FAMILY: Parents, William Henry Fletcher (b. 1856, TN) and Frances Madora Ellis (b. 1853, TN); siblings, Ollie Sue (b. 1876, TN), Inez Elizabeth (b. 1878, TN), Carl Ellis (b. 1880, TN), William Cloy (b. 1881, TN), Annie Lee (b. 1883, TN), Eula Celestia (b. 1887, TX), Herbert Henry (b. 1889, TX), James Ray (b. 1891, TX), Jasper (b. 1895, TX); spouse #1, Lillian Coon (b. 1890, TX); sons, Raymond (b. 1909, TX), Robert (b. 1914, TX); spouse #2, Mary (b. 1892, AL), married before 1930; stepchildren, Johnnie Mae De Mauri (b. 1914, TX), John A. De Mauri (b. 1917, TX), Ara Ann De Mauri (b. 1922, TX). *SR; A1d, e, f, g; A3a; A4b, g; C.*

FLORES, FELIX. Born May 7, 1892, San Angelo, Tom Green County, Texas. Ht. 6 ft. 1 in., brown eyes, black hair, dark complexion, married. Automobile salesman, San Antonio, Bexar County, Texas. REGULAR RANGER June 18, 1918–Aug. 31, 1918 (no company, worked for Capt. W. M. Hanson; was enlisted on a temporary basis, WA to expire on Aug. 1, 1918 unless a position on the border was available). Discharged. Night guard, Lone Star Shipbuilding Co., Beaumont, Jefferson County, Texas. SPECIAL RANGER Oct. 5, 1918–Nov. 1, 1918. Discharged when ceased working for Lone Star Shipbuilding Co. REMARKS: In 1910 was a freight teamster in Tom Green County; in June 1917 was a farmer in Bexar County. In Mar. 1919 lived at Burkburnett, Wichita County, Texas. FAMILY: Parents, Juan "John" Flores (b. 1855, TX) and Virginia (b. 1863, Mexico); siblings, Juan M. (b. 1877, TX), Carolina (b. 1880, TX), Maggie (b. 1882, TX), Adolph (b. 1883, TX), Julia (b. 1885, TX), Albert (b. 1888, TX), Daniel (b. 1890, TX), Lissy (b. 1894, TX), Fred (b. 1896, TX); spouse, unknown; one child by 1917. *SR; 471; Woodul to Hanson, June 14, 1918, AGC; Crawford to Harley, Sept 26, 1918, AGC; Flores to Harley, Mar 21, 1919, AGC; A1d, e; A3a.*

FLOWERS, ELISHA B. Born Feb. 1863, Burkesville, Cumberland County, Kentucky. Ht. 5 ft. 10 in., hazel eyes, brown hair, dark complexion, married. Stockman, Uvalde, Uvalde County, Texas. SPECIAL RANGER Aug. 3, 1917–Jan. 15, 1919 (attached to Co. C; reinstated—WA renewed Jan. 7, 1918). Discharged. REMARKS: In Jan. 1919 was a livestock dealer and rancher at Uvalde. In 1930 was a rancher living in San Antonio, Bexar County, Texas. Died Mar. 13, 1942, Bexar County, Texas. FAMILY: Parents, Van B. Flowers (b. 1834, KY) and Emily (b. 1834, KY); siblings, Lockie C. (b. 1854, KY), Viola S. (b. 1857, KY), Jennie (b. 1859, KY), Laurah A. (b. 1865, KY), Van B. (b. 1868, KY), Hattie M. (b. 1872, KY), Charles (b. 1874, KY); spouse #1, Pearl M. (b. 1869, TX), married about 1889, she died before 1910; children, Leslie (1895, TX), Louise (b. 1903, TX); spouse #2, Mattie (b. 1877, TX), married about 1914. *SR; A1a, b, d, e, f, g; C.*

FLYNT, JAMES PETTY. Born Apr. 19, 1878, Kosse, Limestone County, Texas. Ht. 6 ft. 3 in., blue eyes, brown hair, fair complexion, married. Cotton buyer, Ballinger, Runnels County, Texas. REGULAR RANGER Apr. 13, 1918–Aug. 31, 1918 (captain, Co. D). Was a SPECIAL RANGER Aug. 31, 1918–Jan. 15, 1919. REMARKS: While a Regular Ranger captain was paid $50 a month. Runnels County sheriff Nov. 3, 1908–Nov. 3, 1914 and Nov. 2, 1920–Jan. 1, 1925. In 1920 was a grain dealer in Ballinger. In 1930 was a state game warden in Runnels County. Died Feb. 26, 1966, Runnels County, Texas. FAMILY: Parents, Sandy Frank Flynt (b. 1836, TN) and Emily "Emma" Brown (b. 1842, GA); siblings, Ellie (b. 1866, TX), Ervin Franklin (b. 1868, TX), Bobbie J. (b. 1871, TX), Thomas B. (b. 1873, TX), Bryant (b. 1877, TX), Mary A. (b. 1879, TX), Frank (b. 1882, TX); spouse, Carrie J. Patterson (b. 1876, AL), married about 1899; children, Carrie (b. 1900, TX), Marion (b. 1902, TX), Frank (b. 1904, TX), James Petty, Jr. "Jim" (b. 1907, TX), Joe Martin (b. 1910, TX), Herrell Patterson (b. 1913, TX), Janie Louise (b. 1921, TX). *SR; 471; To Whom . . . , Jan 26, 1918, AGC; Willingham to Hobby, Jan 28, 1918, AGC; Eason to Hobby, Jan 28, 1918, AGC; Flynt to Cardwell, [June 30, 1918], AGC; [AG] to Flynt, July 5, 1918, AGC; 1503:444; A1b, d, e, f, g; A2a, b, e; A3a; A4g.*

FOLTS, WILLIAM HARDEMAN. (Name at birth, William Hardeman; see family notes below.) Born Aug. 30, 1869,

Prairie Lea, Caldwell County, Texas. Ht. 5 ft. 10 ½ in., gray eyes, brown hair, fair complexion, married. Vice president, Austin National Bank, Austin, Travis County. LOYALTY RANGER July 18, 1918–Feb. 20, 1919. REMARKS: Died May 8, 1953, Travis County, Texas. FAMILY: Birth parents, William Polk "Gotch" Hardeman (b. 1816, TN) and Sarah Ann "Sallie" Hamilton (b. 1832, GA); siblings, Thomas Johnston (b. 1858, TX), John Hamilton "Jack" (b. 1860, TX), Will Ella (b. 1863, TX), Tully L. (b. 1866, TX); his mother died 3 months after he was born. By 1880 U.S. census he and his sisters were living with their uncle and aunt, Thomas W. Folts (b. 1827, NC) and Mary Etta Hamilton (b. 1845, GA); by the 1900 U.S. census, William had taken his adoptive parents' name. Spouse, Willie Keesee (b. 1873, TX), married 1892; children, Thomas Wesley (b. 1895, TX), Eleanor I. (b. 1898, TX). *SR; A1a, b, d, e, f; A2b; A3a; A4b; B1.*

FORD, ELGIN. Born June 30, 1889, Floresville, Wilson County, Texas. Ht. 6 ft. 1 in., brown eyes, brown hair, dark complexion, married. Ranchman. REGULAR RANGER May 12, 1916–Sept. 15, 1916 (Pvt., Co. A). Resigned. REMARKS: In June 1917 was a railroad guard in Floresville. In 1920 was a furniture salesman living in Bexar County, Texas. Died Aug. 2, 1939, San Patricio County, Texas. FAMILY: Parents, Patrick Henry Ford (b. 1862, TX) and Ida M. Harper (b. 1868, TX); siblings, Glenn Dora (b. 1891, TX), Ina (b. 1893, TX), Leona (b. 1895, TX), Clyde (b. 1897, TX), Della (b. 1898, TX), Edwin (b. 1901, TX), Clifford (b. 1904, TX), Newel (b. 1908, TX); spouse, Emma Robbins (b. 1889, TX); children, Wayne Elgin (b. 1912, TX), Thomas Earl (b. 1914, TX). *SR; 471; 1000: iii, 126–127; A1d, e, f; A3a; A4a, b, g; B1; C.*

FORREST, WILLIAM YOUNG. Born Oct. 8, 1877, Cherokee County, Texas. Tall, slender, blue eyes, black hair, married. Automobile dealer, Jacksonville, Cherokee County. LOYALTY RANGER June 3, 1918–Feb. 1919. REMARKS: Elected as city marshal, Jacksonville, Apr. 1911. Letterhead in 1919: "Parrish and Forrest, Ford Dealers, Jacksonville." Still a Ford dealer in Jacksonville in 1930. Died May 13, 1952, Cherokee County, Texas. FAMILY: Parents, William P. Forrest (b. 1856, TN) and Mary Belzoria "Mollie" Campbell (b. 1859, TX); siblings, James L. (b. 1879, TX), Ola M. (b. 1881, TX), Verna (b. 1883, TX), Wade J. (b. 1885, TX), Porter L. (b. 1888, TX); spouse, Della (b. 1883, TX), married about 1909; children, William Dean (b. 1909, TX), Roy Winfred (b. 1913, TX), Mary (b. 1914, TX), Henry Lee (b. 1924, TX). *SR; SAE, Apr 5, 1911; A1b, d, e, f, g; A2b; A3a; A4g.*

FORTUNE, LOUIS A. Born Jan. 29, 1887, Daix, France. Ht. 5 ft. 6 in., blue eyes, black hair, fair complexion, married. Locomotive fireman, enlisted in Bexar County, Texas. SPECIAL RANGER Aug. 5, 1916–Dec. 1917. REMARKS: Immigrated to the United States in 1896; became a naturalized citizen in 1913. In 1900 was a farm laborer in Gonzales County, Texas. In 1910 was a railroad fireman living in San Antonio, Bexar County. By May 1917 was a locomotive engineer for the I&GN Railroad living in San Antonio. In 1930 still an engineer living in San Antonio. A Louis Alemis Fortune died Dec. 1, 1954, Wilson County, Texas. FAMILY: Brothers, Dominick (b. 1863, France), John (b. 1871, France), Zenobio (b. 1877, France); spouse, Irene (b. 1897, TX), married about 1914; children, Louis Gerard (b. 1917, TX), Lucille (b. 1919, TX), John A. (b. 1921, TX), Hellen (b. 1922, TX). *SR; A1d, e, f, g; A2b, e; A3a.*

FOX, JAMES CHRISTOPHER. Born Feb. 4, 1876, San Saba, San Saba County, Texas. Ht. 5 ft. 9 in., blue eyes, brown hair, ruddy complexion. Carpenter, enlisted in Hidalgo County, Texas. REGULAR RANGER Mar. 23, 1918–unknown (private, Co. G as of Dec. 31, 1918). Discharged or resigned—unknown. REMARKS: Had been a deputy sheriff, Hidalgo County. FAMILY: Parents, Simon Fox (b. 1844, TN) and Laura Lavern Baker (b. 1857); siblings, Charles Anderson (b. 1874, TX), Frances Victoria (b. 1878, TX), Elizabeth Suzanne (b. 1879, TX). *SR; 471; Johnston to Baker, Jan 14, 1919, AGC; A1d; A3a; A4b.*

FOX, JAMES LESLIE. Born Aug. 21, 1891, Austin, Travis County, Texas. Ht. 6 ft. 1 ½ in., brown eyes, brown hair, light complexion. Peace officer. REGULAR RANGER Sept. 30, 1920–Nov. 4, 1920 (private, Headquarters Co., Emergency Co. No. 1). Resigned. REMARKS: Note length of service. In 1910 was a moving pictures operator in Austin. Motorcycle policeman, Austin, 1917. In 1920 was a truck driver, living in Austin. Died June 17, 1969, Travis County, Texas. LAW ENFORCEMENT RELATIVES: Ranger Captain James Monroe Fox, father; Travis County deputy sheriff (1911) T. O. Fox, uncle. FAMILY: Parents, James M. Fox (b. 1866, MO) and Addean (b. 1870, KY); sister, Lennie (b. 1889, TX); spouse, Eulalie (b. 1898, TX), married after 1910; daughters, Elizabeth (b. 1916, TX), Grace C. (b. 1919, TX). *SR; 471; Petition to Whom, May 19, 1917, AGC; A1d, e, f; A2a, b.*

FOX, JAMES MONROE. Born Nov. 1866, Houston, Texas County, Missouri. Ht. 5 ft. 11 in., brown eyes, brown hair, fair complexion, married. Constable, Austin, Travis County, Texas. REGULAR RANGER Oct. 5, 1911–May 31, 1918 (captain, Co. C; transferred as captain, Co. B on Feb. 1, 1915). Resigned because of Porvenir massacre scandal (Co. B was disbanded June 8, 1918). Peace officer. REGULAR RANGER June 6, 1925–Mar. 31, 1927 (captain, Co. A). Resigned. Watchman, Austin. SPECIAL RANGER Feb. 19, 1934–Jan. 22, 1935. Discharged. REMARKS: Deputy sheriff and jailer, Travis County. Constable, Travis County precinct 3—elected 1910, resigned Oct. 5, 1911, to become a Ranger captain. In 1920 was a traveling stock dealer living in Austin. His 1934 commission was requested by Gen. Henry Hutchings. Died Feb. 11, 1937, Travis County, Texas. LAW ENFORCEMENT RELATIVES: Ranger James Leslie Fox, son; Travis County deputy sheriff (1911) T. O. Fox, brother. FAMILY: Parents, James Campbell Fox (b. 1833, TN) and Martha Elizabeth Martin (b. 1840, TN); siblings, Nancy C. (b. 1858, MO), William B. (b. 1859, MO), Betty (b. 1864, MO), Susan E, (b. 1869, MO), Melissa M. (b. 1870, MO), Thomas O. (b. 1872, MO); spouse, Addean (b. 1870, KY), married about 1887; children, Lennie (b. 1889, TX), Leslie (b. 1891, TX). *SR; 471; AG to Fox, June 5, 1915, AGC; Fox to Harley, May 31, 1918, AGC; General Orders No. 5, June 4, 1918, AGC; F. H. Lancaster report, Oct 19, 1911, 1BI; AS, May 11, 1910, Mar 6, 17, 1911; SAE, Oct 6, 11, 1911; Corpus Christi Caller and Daily Herald, May 9, 1916; EPMT, Aug 9, 1915; 422: 87, 89; 425: 91; BDH, Nov 7, 1913, Apr 5, 1916; A1b, d, e, f, g; A4b; C.*

FRANCIS, JAMES A. Born Mar. 1878, New Orleans, Orleans Parish, Louisiana. Ht. 5 ft. 7 in., gray eyes, light brown hair, light complexion. Electrician. REGULAR RANGER Aug. 12, 1915–Sept. 12, 1915 (private, Co. A). Discharged. REMARKS: Note length of service. Had previously served about 15 years in the Texas National Guard. In 1910 was an electrician living in Austin, Travis County, Texas. In 1930 lived in Austin, worked as an electrician at the university. A James A. Francis died Aug. 8, 1945, Travis County, Texas. FAMILY: Parents, William Francis (b. 1810, LA) and Ernestine (b. 1836, LA); siblings, Elizabeth (b. 1855, LA), William (b. 1856, LA), Charles (b. 1858, LA), Catherine (b. 1861, LA), Harriett (b. 1862, LA), Thomas (b. 1866, LA), Stewart (b. 1868, LA), Robert (b. 1872, LA); spouse #1, Ruby (b. 1882, TX), married about 1907; spouse #2, Ruffie (b. 1895, TX), married about 1919; children, Mickey (b. 1920, TX), Charles (b. 1923, TX). *SR; 471; A1b, e, g; C.*

FRANKLIN, CLAUDE "PUDGE." Born Jan. 20, 1886, Tilden, McMullen County, Texas. Ht. 5 ft. 5 ½ in., blue eyes, dark hair, light complexion. Stockman. REGULAR RANGER Jan. 16, 1918–July 15, 1920 (private, Co. I; promoted to sergeant Oct. 1, 1918; reduced to private because of reduction in force—war over, Mar. 1, 1919; reenlisted under the new law as sergeant, Co. C, June 20, 1919). Resigned to go into business for himself. REMARKS: Atascosa County deputy sheriff for several years. In 1930 was an oil company salesman and bookkeeper, Cotulla, La Salle County, Texas. Died Nov. 28, 1960, Atascosa County, Texas. LAW ENFORCEMENT RELATIVES: Ranger Stephen L. Franklin, cousin. FAMILY: Parents, Ralph Silas "Rafe" Franklin (b. 1848, LA or TX) and Amanda Minerva Holland (b. 1856, MS); siblings, Murray (b. 1872, TX), Ralph S. (b. 1876, TX), Green Allen (b. 1878, TX), Felix West (b. 1880, TX), Rufus Chapman (b. 1882, TX), Amy (b. 1883, TX), Thomas (b. 1888, TX), John (b. 1891, TX), Margareth "Maggie" (b. 1892, TX), Samuel (b. 1895, TX), Julius (b. 1898, TX); spouse, Ida Mae Morgan (b. 1903, TX), married Mar. 31, 1926; children, Claude, Jr. (b. 1927, TX), Lottie Lee (b. 1929, TX). *SR; 471; Special Orders No. 21, Mar 10, 1919, WC; Franklin to Cope, Feb 2, 1920, AGC; LWT, July 25, 1920; A1d, e, f, g; A2a, b, e; A3a; A4b, g.*

FRANKLIN, JOURD BENNETT. Born Mar. 23, 1894, Tilden, McMullen County, Texas. Ht. 5 ft. 10 in., brown eyes, brown hair, dark complexion. Cowman. REGULAR RANGER June 10, 1918–June 19, 1919 (private, Co I). Resigned or was discharged. REMARKS: Was a stockman in McMullen County as early as 1918 and as late as 1930. Died Mar. 19, 1967, McMullen County, Texas. LAW ENFORCEMENT RELATIVES: Ranger Stephen L. Franklin, uncle. FAMILY: Parents, William P. Franklin (b. 1864, TX) and Kate "Katie"

O'Neil (b. 1873, TX); brother, Will C. (b. 1891, TX); spouse, Fay Martin, married after 1930; son, Jourd Bennett, Jr. (b. 1943, TX). *SR; 471; A1d, f, g; A2a, b, e; A3a; A4a.*

FRANKLIN, STEPHEN L. "STEVE." Born 1862, Tilden, McMullen County, Texas. Ht. 5 ft. 10 in., dark eyes, black hair, dark complexion, married. Ranch foreman, Monte Christo [*sic*], Hidalgo County, Texas. SPECIAL RANGER Jan. 23, 1918–Jan. 15, 1919; Jan. 30, 1919–Dec. 31, 1919 (commission was renewed). REMARKS: Was Tom T. East's foreman in Hidalgo and Starr Counties. In 1910 had been a farmer in Frio County, Texas; in 1910 and 1920 was a ranch manager in La Salle County; in 1930 was ranch foreman in Jim Hogg County, Texas while wife and family lived in San Antonio, Bexar County, Texas. A Steve Lee Franklin died Nov. 30, 1951, Bexar County, Texas. LAW ENFORCEMENT RELATIVES: Ranger Claude Franklin, cousin; Ranger Jourd B. Franklin, nephew. FAMILY: Parents, William Morris "Billy" Franklin (b. 1836, MS) and Eveline Drake Evans (b. 1839, TX); siblings, Lenora, Francis Middleton (b. 1858, TX), Alexander (b. 1860, TX), William P. (b. 1864, TX), Sarah (b. 1866, TX), Marah (b. 1869, TX); spouse, Janie or Jenny Kuykendall (b. 1870, TX), married about 1888; children, Cordelia (b. 1889, TX), Cleora (b. 1891, TX), EvaLea (b. 1893, TX), Eula J. (b. 1896, TX), Storcy (b. 1899, TX), Tom (b. 1901, TX), Esther (b. 1904, TX), W. Ames (b. 1908, TX), Vida (b. 1911, TX). *SR; 471; Acting AG to Mussey, Jan 16, 1918, AGC; Mussey to Woodul, Jan 18, 25, 1918, AGC; A1a, b, d, e, f, g; A2b; A4a, b.*

FRANKS, THOMAS CHAPMAN. Born Apr. 1, 1879, Pleasanton, Atascosa County, Texas. Ht. 5 ft. 10 ½ in., blue eyes, light hair, married. REGULAR RANGER 1902–1904 (Co. A). Stockman, Eagle Pass, Maverick County, Texas. REGULAR RANGER Apr. 16, 1918–May 31, 1918 (private, Co. M). Resigned to become a mounted Immigration inspector for better pay. REMARKS: Note length of service in 1918. In 1920 was Maverick County deputy sheriff. Living in Eagle Pass in 1930. A Tom C. Franks died Feb. 5, 1936, Maverick County, Texas. FAMILY: Parents, Lemuel Alse Franks (b. 1847, TX) and Caroline O. Chapman (b. 1854, TX); siblings, Edna E. (b. 1874, TX), Ida M. (b. 1876, TX), Lottie A. (b. 1881, TX), Nannie L. (b. 1883, TX), Nettie C. (b. 1885, TX), Fannie E. (b. 1888, TX), Ben A. (b. 1895, TX); spouse, Eva (b. 1885, TX), married about 1915. *SR; 471; Franks to Cunningham, May 28, 1918, AGC; 319: 324; A1b, d, f, g; A3a; A4a, b, g; B1, 2; C.*

FRAZIER, BEN. Born Aug. 15, 1882, Stratton, DeWitt County, Texas. Ht. 6 ft., gray eyes, black hair, dark complexion, married. Ranchman, Valentine, Jeff Davis County, Texas. SPECIAL RANGER Dec. 31, 1917–Jan. 15, 1919. REMARKS: In 1900 lived in Johnson City, Blanco County, Texas. In 1918 was living in Valentine, Jeff Davis County, Texas while ranching in Culberson County, Texas. In 1920 lived in Martin County, Texas. FAMILY: Parents, Ben Frazier (b. 1849, GA) and Nannie Ann Rice (b. 1866, TX); siblings, Nannie May "Mattie" (b. 1885, TX), Delia or Belva (b. 1887, TX), Tippie (b. 1889, TX), Dora Lee (b. 1892, TX), Patrick (b. 1895, TX), Florence Leticia (b. 1898, TX); spouse, Annie Maud (b. 1885, TX); son, Ben J. (b. 1918, TX). *SR; A1d, f; A3a; B1.*

FRAZIER, EARL BEN or BEN EARL. Born Jan. 27, 1886, Union, Wilson County, Texas. Ht. 5 ft. 9 in., black eyes, iron gray hair, dark complexion, married. Stock farmer, Cuero, DeWitt County, Texas. LOYALTY RANGER June 5, 1918–Feb. 1919. REMARKS: Had been a trader in Cuero. In 1920 was a real estate agent in Cuero. FAMILY: Spouse, Bulah Thomas (b. 1895, TX). *SR; A1f; A3a.*

FRYE, ROY JESSE. Born June 1, 1874, Fall Branch, Washington County, Tennessee. Ht. 6 ft., gray eyes, gray hair, medium complexion, married. Real estate broker, Plainview, Hale County, Texas. LOYALTY RANGER July 10, 1918–Feb. 1919. REMARKS: In 1910 was a pool hall keeper in Plainview; in 1930 was a house decorator in Plainview. Died Apr. 13, 1955, Hale County, Texas. FAMILY: Parents, Solomon Frye (b. 1850, VA) and Sarah M. (b. 1837, TN); siblings, George W. (b. 1872, TN), Mattie B. (b. 1879, TN); spouse, Mamie Cane (b. 1873, NC), married about 1898; children, Paul N. (b. 1899, TX), Mildred (b. 1903, TX), Fred (b. 1907, TX), Bishop (b. 1908, TX), Mattie B. (b. 1911, TX), Walter C. (b. 1913, TX), George (b. 1916, TX), Josephine Fay (b. 1918, TX). *SR; Frye to Harley, Jan 13, 1919, AGC; A1b, d, e, f, g; A2b, e; A3a.*

FULLER, MARSHALL ANDREW. Born Dec. 26, 1884, Dyer County, Tennessee. Ht. 5 ft. 10 ½ in., blue eyes, gray hair, dark complexion, married. Manufacturer of cottonseed products, Snyder, Scurry County, Texas. LOYALTY RANGER June 14, 1918–Feb. 1919. REMARKS: In Sept. 1918 was manager of Fuller Cotton Oil Company, Snyder. Was a director of the Snyder National Bank in Feb. 1919. In 1930 was a cattleman living in Fort Worth, Tarrant County, Texas. Died Aug. 5, 1960, Tarrant County, Texas. FAMILY: Parents, William A. Fuller (b. 1853, TN) and Elizabeth C. "Bettie" Justice (b. 1857, VA); siblings, Carrie (b. 1882, TN), Powell S. (b. 1883, TN); spouse, Lillian Mamie Maury (b. 1892, TX), married June 18, 1912, Snyder; sons, William (b. 1915, TX), Andrew (b. 1917, TX). *SR; A1d, e, f, g; A2b; A3a; A4b, g; B1.*

FULLER, NATHAN N. Born Feb. 19, 1889, San Marcos, Hays County, Texas. Ht. 5 ft. 9 in., gray eyes, brown hair. Laborer (mill man). REGULAR RANGER May 15, 1916–Feb. 11, 1920 (private, Co. B; transferred to Co. D, June 8, 1918 because Co. B was disbanded; transferred to Co. A, June 20, 1919—reenlisted under the new law). Resigned because of disagreement with his captain, Jerry Gray. Ranchman, Marfa, Presidio County, Texas. RAILROAD RANGER Aug. 22, 1922–Jan. 5, 1923 (Co. A). Discharged. REMARKS: Date of birth in 1900 federal census records listed as Feb. 1888; in World War I Draft Registration document listed as Feb. 19, 1891; in Social Security Death Index listed as Feb. 19, 1887. Was 5 ft. 9 in. when enlisted in 1916; was 5 ft. 11 in. when enlisted in June 1919. In 1930 lived in Fabens, El Paso County, Texas, worked for the county roads department. Died Feb. 14, 1973, Brewster County, Texas. FAMILY: Parents, Alarick P. "Allie" Fuller (b. 1857, VA) and Mary Lou Howard (b. 1861, TX); siblings, Ed (b. 1881, TX), Eva Della (b. 1882, TX), Sallie (b. 1885, TX), Berta (b. 1886, TX), Dora (b. 1891, TX), Jessie (b. 1892, TX); spouse, Aramita (b. 1904, TX), married about 1922; daughters, Dora (b. 1922, TX), Laura (b. 1927, TX). *SR; 471; General Orders No. 5, June 4, 1918, AGC; Fuller to Aldrich, Feb 11, 1920, AGC; A1d, g; A2a, b; A3a; A4b.*

FULLER, RALPH JOSEPH. Born Jan. 15, 1888, Bexar County, Texas. Ht. 5 ft. 9 in., blue eyes, brown hair, light complexion. Peace officer. REGULAR RANGER Nov. 20, 1918–Mar. 8, 1919 (private, Co. G). Discharged. REMARKS: In 1910 was a house carpenter in San Antonio, Bexar County; in June 1917 was a machinist helper working for the U.S. government at Fort Sam Houston, San Antonio. In 1920 was a warehouse foreman in San Antonio. World War I Draft Registration document stated, "One leg 1 in. shorter that the other." A Ralph Joseph Fuller died Dec. 6, 1941, Bexar County, Texas. FAMILY: Parents, Joseph Fuller (b. 1850, CT) and Mary Doran (b. 1856, Ireland); siblings, Edward J. (b. 1877, MO), Mansie (b. 1879, TX), Alice (b. 1882, TX), Willie (b. 1884, TX); spouse, Annie (b. 1891, TX), married about 1909, divorced by 1920. *SR; 471; Special Orders No. 20, Mar 8, 1919, AGC; Cardwell to Aldrich, Mar 11, 1919, AGC; A1d, e, f; A3a; B1; C.*

FULLERTON, JOHN WESLEY. Born Sept. 17, 1874, Wrightsboro, Gonzales County, Texas. Ht. 6 ft. 3 in., blue eyes, brown hair, light complexion, married. Farmer and rancher, Devine, Medina County, Texas. SPECIAL RANGER Jan. 9, 1918–Jan. 15, 1919. REMARKS: Had been a farmer in Frio County, Texas. In 1920 was a real estate salesman in Devine. In 1930 was a lumber yard salesman in San Antonio, Bexar County, Texas. Died Mar. 31, 1947, Bexar County, Texas. FAMILY: Parents, John Columbus Fullerton (b. 1847, TX) and Phila Armita Ward (b. 1852, MS); siblings, Horace (b. 1873, TX), Eula Lee (b. 1878, TX), Ida Virginia (b. 1879, TX), Philip Young (b. 1881, TX), Margaret "Maggie" (b. 1882, TX), Robert (b. 1882, TX), Sallie Ann (b. 1884, TX); spouse, Margaret Lavinia "Vina" Cude (b. 1860, TX), married about 1899; daughter, Ozella (b. 1900, TX). *SR; A1b, d, e, f, g; A2b; A3a; A4b; B2.*

FUQUA, HENRY EARL. Born Nov. 10, 1895, Amarillo, Potter County, Texas. Ht. 5 ft. 8 ½ in., blue eyes, light hair, light complexion, married. Banker, Amarillo. SPECIAL RANGER June 25, 1917–Dec. 1917 (attached to Co. C). REMARKS: Still a bank cashier in Amarillo in 1930. Died July 7, 1940, Cook Memorial Hospital, Fort Worth, Tarrant County, Texas; buried in Llano Cemetery, Amarillo. FAMILY: Parents, Wiley Holder Fuqua (b. 1862, MS) and Mary Ella Chestnut (b. 1866, TN); siblings, Ina (b. 1888, TX), Wayland H. (b. 1893, TX); spouse, Allee Benham (b. 1895, TX), married Feb. 4, 1915; children, Henry Earl, Jr. (b. 1916, TX), Wiley Holder (b. 1919, TX), Alice Elanor (b. 1923, TX), Constance (b. 1926, TX). *SR; 172:III, 34; A1d, e, f, g; A2e; A3a; A4b; B2; C.*

FURLONG, WILLIAM HARRISON. Born Aug. 10, 1874, Springfield, Hampden County, Massachusetts. Ht. 6 ft. 2 in., brown eyes, brown hair, fair complexion. Manager, Medina Lake Toll Road Company, San Antonio, Bexar County, Texas. LOYALTY RANGER May 31, 1918–Feb. 1919. REMARKS: In 1930 was secretary, Chamber of Commerce, San Antonio. A William H. Furlong, Jr., died Nov. 30, 1959, Aransas County, Texas. (a Florence Furlong also died in Aransas County.) FAMILY: Spouse #1, unknown, married about 1900, divorced before 1920; spouse #2, Florence (b. 1900, TX), married about 1920; children, Barbara (b. 1921, TX), William H., III (b. 1922, TX), James (b. 1924, TX). *SR; A1f, g; A2a, b, e; A3a.*

FUTCH, WILLIAM LEE. Born Feb. 9, 1866, Magnolia or McNeill, Columbia County, Arkansas. Ht. 5 ft. 7 in., brown eyes, black hair, married. Special officer, GC&SF Railroad, Coleman, Coleman County, Texas. SPECIAL RANGER Feb. 16, 1918–Jan. 15, 1919. Special officer, GC&SF Railroad, Coleman. RAILROAD RANGER July 18, 1923–July 18, 1925. Discharged. Special officer, GC&SF Railroad, Coleman. SPECIAL RANGER Aug. 8, 1925–Aug. 8, 1927; Dec. 6, 1927–Nov. 26, 1928; Nov. 26, 1928–Nov. 26, 1929; Dec. 19, 1929–Dec. 18, 1930; Jan. 8, 1931–Jan. 7, 1932; Jan. 25, 1932–Jan. 20, 1933; Mar. 31, 1933–Jan. 22, 1935; May 29, 1935–Aug. 10, 1935. Discharged. REMARKS: Coleman County sheriff Nov. 6, 1906–Nov. 3, 1914. Special officer, GC&SF Railroad, Sweetwater, Nolan County, Texas, 1917. Died Nov. 17, 1963, Coleman, Coleman County, Texas. FAMILY: Parents, David Futch (b. 1835, MS) or A. P. Futch (b. 1830, AL) and Mary Elizabeth Warnock (b. 1845, AR); siblings, Margaret S. (b. 1867, AR), Mary V. (b. 1868, AR), David P. (b. 1870, AR), Sary Jane (b. 1872, AR), Texas P. (b. 1875, AR), Robert Andrew (b. 1876, AR), Isaac M. (b. 1878, AR), Nancy Ann (b. 1880, AR), Fred A.; spouse, Hattie Mahala Jones (b. 1876, TX), married Sep. 18, 1898, New Castle, Texas; children, Neil David (b. 1900, TX), Jack Boone (b. 1901, TX), Allen Lee (b. 1905, TX), Garland Saerman (b. 1911, TX). *SR; 471; Futch to Hutchings, June 17, 1917, AGC; Futch to Woodul, Feb 11, 1918, AGC; AG to Futch, Feb 14, 1918, AGC; Futch to Harley, Feb 16, 1918, AGC; 1503:108; SAE, Nov 20, 1911; EPMT, Apr 26, 1914; A1d, g; A2a, b; A3a; A4a, b, g; B2.*

GAINES, CARROLL MONTGOMERY. Born Oct. 2, 1891, Matagorda, Matagorda County, Texas. Medium height, medium build, brown eyes, brown hair. Lawyer and farmer, Bay City, Matagorda County. LOYALTY RANGER June 10, 1918–Feb. 1919. REMARKS: In 1930 was an attorney in San Antonio, Bexar County, Texas. Died Nov. 13, 1965, Bexar County, Texas; buried in Cedarvale Cemetery, Bay City. LAW ENFORCEMENT RELATIVES: Ranger John P. Gaines, brother. FAMILY: Parents, John Wesley Gaines (b. 1864, MS) and Martha Lorena Montgomery (b. 1865, MS); siblings, Lorena (b. 1893, TX), John P. (b. 1894, TX), Richard Cohran (b. 1898, TX), Marian (b. 1902, TX), Lucile (b. 1906, TX); spouse, Marguerite Josephine Hamilton (b. 1892, TX), married Nov. 26, 1918, Matagorda; children, Carroll M., Jr. (b. 1919, TX), Marguerite (b. 1922, TX), Anna E. (b. 1924, TX). *SR; A1d, f, g; A2a, b, e; A3a; A4a, b, g; B1.*

GAINES, JOHN PIERCE. Born Sept. 13, 1894, Matagorda, Matagorda County, Texas. Ht. 5 ft. 11 in., brown eyes, brown hair, dark complexion. Texas Highway Department employee, Bay City, Matagorda County. SPECIAL RANGER July 18, 1919–Nov. 1, 1919. REMARKS: His WA, to expire on June 1, 1921, was cancelled on Nov. 1, 1919 because he left the employ of the Texas Highway Department. Was a 1st lieutenant in the U.S. Army during World War I. In 1920 was a bookkeeper in Matagorda; in 1930 was a real estate salesman in San Antonio, Bexar County, Texas. Died Dec. 6, 1957, Victoria County, Texas; buried in Fort Sam Houston National Cemetery, San Antonio. LAW ENFORCEMENT RELATIVES: Ranger Carroll M. Gaines, brother. FAMILY: Parents, John Wesley Gaines (b. 1864, MS) and Martha Lorena Montgomery (b. 1865, MS); siblings, Carroll M. (b. 1891, TX), Lorena (b. 1893, TX), Richard Cohron (b. 1898, TX), Marian (b. 1902, TX), Lucile (b. 1906, TX); spouse, Carmen, married in 1925, single again by 1930. *SR; A1d, f, g; A3a, b; A4a, b, g; B1.*

GALLAGHER, DAVID OWEN. Born Mar. 9, 1884, San Antonio, Bexar County, Texas. Ht. 5 ft. 11 ½ in., gray eyes, brown hair, light complexion. Ranchman, Rancho Los Venados, Bustamante, Zapata County, Texas. SPECIAL RANGER Aug. 16, 1918–Jan. 15, 1919. REMARKS: Was christened in St. Mary's Catholic Church, San Antonio, Oct. 17, 1886. In 1910 was a railroad brakeman living in San Antonio. Died Aug. 30, 1965, Webb County, Texas. FAMILY: Parents, James Nester Gallagher (b. 1848, NH) and Mary Calphurnia "Callie" Foreman (b. 1856, TX); siblings, Thomas (b. 1874, TX), Maggie (b. 1876, TX), James (b. 1878, TX), Jack (b. 1880, TX), Mattie (b. 1886, TX), Julius (b. 1888, TX), Stella (b. 1891, TX), Bessie (b. 1895, TX); spouse, Fannie (b. 1885, TX), married about 1902; daughter, Calphurnia (b. 1903, TX). *SR; A1d, e; A2a, b; A3c; A4b, h; A6a; B1.*

GALLOWAY, WASHINGTON SHOOK "SHOOK." Born Apr. 20, 1875, Jeddo, Bastrop County, Texas. Ht. 6 ft., blue eyes, red hair, florid complexion, married. Planter, Lockhart, Caldwell County, Texas. LOYALTY RANGER June 3,

1918–Feb. 1919. REMARKS: Had been a barber in Lockhart; in 1910 was a justice of the peace in Lockhart. As of Sept. 1918 was a farmer and cotton seed breeder in San Marcos, Hays County, Texas. A Washington S. Galloway died Dec. 14, 1956, Nueces County, Texas. LAW ENFORCEMENT RELATIVES: Constable (in Jeddo, Bastrop County, 1880) George W. Galloway, father. FAMILY: Parents, George Washington Galloway (b. 1845, KY) and Sarah Ann Elizabeth Camp (b. 1849, TX); sisters, Martha Elizabeth "Mattie" (b. 1867, TX), Aurelia Effie Viola (b. 1869, TX), Ella Ora (b. 1872, TX), Mary Ione Ettienne (b. 1879, TX), Beatrice Vivian (b. 1881, TX); spouse, Lula May Cockrell (b. 1875, TX), married Jan. 23, 1898, Caldwell County; children, Harry Shook (b. 1900, TX), Grace M. (b. 1905, TX). *SR; A1b, d, e, f; A2b; A3a; A4a, b, g; B1.*

GAMBLE, JAMES D. Born Nov. 27, 1868, Benton, Polk County, Tennessee. Ht. 5 ft. 9 in., blue eyes, red hair, fair complexion, married. Stock farmer, Canyon, Randall County, Texas. LOYALTY RANGER June 1, 1918–Feb. 1919. REMARKS: Had been sheriff, Polk County, Tennessee. In 1910 was employed by a boarding barn in Canyon. In Feb. 1919 was a director of the Canyon City Supply Co., a dry goods and grocery store. In 1920 was city mayor of Canyon. In 1930 was selling fire insurance in Canyon. Died July 31, 1936, Canyon, Randall County, Texas. FAMILY: Parents, William Montgomery Gamble (b. 1832, TN) and Margaret "Maggie" Denton (b. 1848, TN); siblings, Ida (b. 1870, TN), Ella (b. 1872, TN), Mary or Mayme (b. 1877, TN), Willie (b. 1879, TN), Oscar N. (b. 1882, TN), Charles W. (b. 1887, TN), Stella V. (b. 1889, TN), Henry C. (b. 1891, TN); spouse, Ada Redden (b. 1882, TX), married Oct. 15, 1907, Canyon; children, James Denton, Jr. (b. 1909, TX), Wilmoth (b. 1911, TX), Margaret (b. 1914, TX), Hal B. (b. 1919, TX), Rex Porter (b. 1924, TX). *SR; A1a, b, d, e, f, g; A2e; A4a.*

GARCIA, AMADOR E. Born Sept. 22, 1886, Webb County, Texas. Ht. 5 ft. 7 ½ in., brown eyes, black hair, fair complexion, married. Rancher, Los Ojuelos Ranch, Webb County. SPECIAL RANGER Mar. 5, 1918–Jan. 15, 1919. REMARKS: Born on his family's Los Ojuelos Ranch. Had been Webb County deputy sheriff. In 1922 was one of the wealthiest Webb County landowners—Los Ojuelos Ranch. Died Mar. 6, 1957, Webb County, Texas. FAMILY: Parents, Eusebio Garcia (b. 1859, Mexico) and Josefa Guerra (b. 1859, Mexico); sisters, Hermalinda (b. 1882, Mexico), Amalia (b. 1888, TX), Josephine (b. 1891, TX), Francisca (b. 1893, TX), Ofelia (b. 1901, TX); spouse, Mamie M. (b. 1888, TX), married about 1909; children, Anita Marie (b. 1913, TX), Esther Margarite (b. 1915, TX), Alberto (b. 1921, TX), Tirza (b. 1923, TX). *SR; 319:69, 76–80, 87–88, 509; A1d, e, f, g; A2a, b, e; A3a; A4g.*

GARDIEN, WILLIAM LANGFORD. Born Mar. 1862, Mobile, Mobile County, Alabama. Ht. 5 ft. 11 ½ in., blue eyes, black hair, dark complexion, married. Real estate and insurance broker, Gonzales, Gonzales County, Texas. LOYALTY RANGER June 4, 1918–Feb. 1919. REMARKS: In 1910 was a newspaperman in Houston, Harris County, Texas. A William Langford Gardien died May 27, 1921, Bexar County, Texas. FAMILY: Parents, Edmond N. Gardien (b. 1826, France) and Elizabeth C. (b. 1833, AL); siblings, Alice E. (b. 1858, France), Roger B. (b. 1860, France), A. (b. 1863, MS), J. T. (b. 1866, AL); spouse, Maude F. Kent (b. 1862, AR), married Feb. 2, 1887, Gonzales County; children, Edmond Kent (b. 1887, TX), William L, Jr. (b.1892, TX), Maude (b. 1892, TX), Loretta (b. 1894, TX), Carl S. (b. 1895, TX). *SR; A1aa, a, d, e, f; A4g; C.*

GARDNER, CHARLES E. Born Apr. 1870, Cincinnati, Hamilton County, Ohio. Ht. 5 ft. 7 in., brown eyes, brown hair, fair complexion, married. General manager, Texas Carriage and Top Company, Houston, Harris County, Texas. SPECIAL RANGER June 8, 1918–Jan. 15, 1919. REMARKS: Had been a carriage painter in South Bend, Indiana. In Jan. 1919 was president, Texas Carriage and Top Company. FAMILY: Spouse #1, Edith (b. 1877, Canada), married about 1898; spouse #2, A. R. (b. 1887, OH), married about 1904; spouse #3, Mayme A. (b. 1883, TX). *SR; A1d, e, f; A5a.*

GARDNER, WILLIAM THOMAS. Born Apr. 14, 1879, Big Foot, Frio County, Texas. Ht. 5 ft. 10 in., dark eyes, brown hair, dark complexion, married. Sheriff and tax collector (Nov. 5, 1912–Nov. 5, 1918), Carrizo Springs, Dimmit County, Texas. LOYALTY RANGER June 7, 1918–Feb. 1919. REMARKS: Dimmit County deputy sheriff for 2 years. May 1917 applied for a Ranger captaincy. In 1920 was a farmer in Dimmit County. In 1930 was a laborer in a pecan grove in Uvalde, Uvalde County, Texas. Died Aug. 20, 1945, Zavala County, Texas; buried in Mount Hope Cemetery, Dimmit

County. FAMILY: Parents, Joseph William Peter Gardner (b. 1851, LA) and Jennie Holmes (b. 1857, MO); stepmother, Lucy Lincoln Wingate (b. 1866, TX); siblings, Beulah Irene (b. 1884, TX), Margaret Graham "Maggie" (b. 1886, TX), John Edmund (b. 1889, TX), Nettie A. (b. 1891, TX), Ethel M. (b. 1892, TX), Alexander F. (b. 1894, TX), Martha Ann (b. 1896, TX); spouse, Olivia T. Howard (b. 1884, TX), married about 1903; children, Jennie H. (b. 1903, TX), Herbert Orin (b. 1905, TX), William Howard (b. 1907, TX), Vera O. (b. 1909, TX), Bruce Robert (b. 1911, TX), Welborne Truet (b. 1913, TX), Norma Agnes (b. 1915, TX), Woodrow Wilson (b. 1917, TX), Maurice E. (b. 1918, TX), Thomas Elmo "Tommie" (b. 1921, TX), Laura Ellen (b. 1923, TX), Mabelle Claire (b. 1925, TX). *SR; 471; 1503:160; LWT, Sept 14, 1913; Gardner to Ferguson, May 7, 1917, AGC; A1a, d, e, f, g; A2b, e; A4a, b, g; B2.*

GARLICK, HENRY STOWE. Born July 29, 1875, Cincinnati, Hamilton County, Ohio. Medium height, medium build, blue eyes, blonde hair, married. Physician and surgeon, Laredo, Webb County, Texas. SPECIAL RANGER July 1, 1918–Jan. 15, 1919. REMARKS: Was an ear, nose, and throat physician, lived in Cincinnati in 1910. Died Feb. 9, 1921, Webb County, Texas. FAMILY: Parents, Henry Smith Garlick (b. 1852, TX) and Ida Caroline Stowe (b. 1852, PA); siblings, Carrie (b. 1876, OH), William Hobart (b. 1884, OH), Robin Cairns (b. 1887, OH), Edgar Rutherford (b. 1890, OH), Matilda Ida (b. 1892, OH); spouse, Mary Alice Heekin (b. 1879, OH), married about 1906. *SR; A1d, e, f; A3a; A4a; C.*

GARLICK, WILLIAM FRED. Born 1897, Young County, Texas. Ht. 6 ft., blue eyes, light hair, fair complexion. Ranchman, enlisted in Presidio County, Texas. REGULAR RANGER Apr. 16, 1918–June 1, 1918 (private, Co. N, Hudspeth Scouts). Resigned. REMARKS: Later resided in Brite, Texas. In 1920 was living in Jeff Davis County, Texas. In 1930 worked for the state highway department in Sierra Blanca, Hudspeth County, Texas. FAMILY: Parents, William H. Garlick (b. 1868, TX) and Martha Jane (b. 1871, TX); siblings, Gober (b. 1893, TX), Kate (b. 1895, TX), Audrey (b. 1899, TX), Laurie (b. 1902, TX), Henry (b. 1914, TX); spouse, Julia Segura (b. 1900, TX), married about 1921; children, Lucia (b. 1922, TX), Fred W. (b. 1923, TX), Van (b. 1924, TX), Martha J. (b. 1927, TX), Israel (b. 1928, TX), Cecelia Emilla (b. 1930, TX), Otilia (b. 1931, TX), Marvin Wayne (b. 1934, TX), Lee Roy (b. 1936, TX), Evelyn Jeane (b. 1938, TX), James Russell (b. 1941, TX), Ida Mae (b. 1943, TX). *SR; 471; 1: I, 1651–1652; A1e, f, g; A2e.*

GARNER, HARPER EUGENE "EUGENE." Born Sept. 1, 1877, Kerrville, Kerr County, Texas. Ht. 5 ft. 10 in., blue eyes, sandy hair, red complexion, married. Ranchman, Hebbronville, Jim Hogg County, Texas. SPECIAL RANGER Apr. 27, 1918–Jan. 15, 1919. REMARKS: In 1930 was an oil field trucker in Jim Hogg County. LAW ENFORCEMENT RELATIVES: Ranger Lon Garner, brother. FAMILY: Parents, William W. Garner (b. 1848, MS) and Mariah Elmo Michaels (b. 1855, MO); siblings, James Lon (b. 1879, TX), William S. (b. 1881, TX), Newton U. (b. 1883, TX), Seleta Elmo (b. 1885, TX), Dolph H. (b. 1889, TX), Duff M. (b. 1889, TX); spouse, Ada (b. 1882, TX), married about 1904; children, Lucile E. (b. 1907, TX), Lonnie Eugene (b. 1909, TX), Roberta Mae (b. 1918, TX), Russell (b. 1922, TX). *SR; A1b, d, e, g; A2e; A3a; A4b.*

GARNER, JAMES LON "LON." Born June 7, 1879, San Patricio County, Texas. Ht. 5 ft. 9 ½ in., brown eyes, brown hair, fair complexion, married. Constable, El Paso, El Paso County, Texas. SPECIAL RANGER Dec. 21, 1918–Jan. 15, 1919. REMARKS: Policeman, El Paso, 1907–1915; rose to rank of captain. Constable, El Paso County, 1916–1917; deputy sheriff, El Paso County, 1919. In 1920 was a bank collector in Ranger, Eastland County, Texas. Deputy sheriff, Stephens County, Texas, 1930; lived in Breckenridge, Stephens County, Texas. A James Lon Garner died Nov. 8, 1958, Bell County, Texas. LAW ENFORCEMENT RELATIVES: Ranger H. Eugene Garner, brother. FAMILY: Parents, William W. Garner (b. 1848, MS) and Mariah Elmo Michaels (b. 1855, MO); siblings, H. Eugene (b. 1877, TX), William S. (b. 1881, TX), Newton U. (b. 1883, TX), Seleta Elmo (b. 1885, TX), Dolph H. (b. 1889, TX), Duff M. (b. 1889, TX); spouse, Lillie Myrtle (b. 1888, TX), married about 1906; children, Mabel (b. 1908, TX), Sybil (b. 1914, TX), Lon, Jr. (b. 1917, TX), Aubrey W. (b. 1924, TX). *SR; EPMT, Aug 13, 1913, July 9, 1914, Apr 25, Nov 20, 1915, Aug 3, 1916, Apr 12, 1919; Smith to AG, Aug 2, 1917, AGC; A1b, f, g; A2b; A3a; A4b.*

GARNER, JOHN RAYFORD. Born Apr. 9, 1871, Bibb County, Alabama. Ht. 6 ft. 2 in., blue eyes, dark gray hair, married. Peace officer, Longview, Gregg County, Texas. SPECIAL RANGER Jan. 6, 1917–Jan. 15, 1919 (attached to Co. C; was reinstated Jan. 4, 1918—WA was renewed). Discharged. REMARKS: Family living in Texas by 1880. Gregg County sheriff Nov. 2, 1920–Jan. 1, 1923. Died Apr. 7, 1931, Gregg County, Texas. FAMILY: Parents, William Jackson Garner (b. 1840, AL) and Rebecca Caroline Fulgham (b. 1842, AL); siblings, Sarah E. (b. 1861, AL), William J., III (b. 1864, AL), James Edward (b. 1865, AL), Della Laura (b. 1867, AL), Alpha Omega (b. 1872, TX), Rufus Parker (b. 1874, TX), Alabama (b. 1877, TX), Walter Riley B. (b. 1879, TX); spouse, Nancy Cyrena "Rena" Grimes (b. 1874, TX), married Oct. 14, 1891, Gregg County; children, Annie Rebecca (b. 1892, TX), John Walter (b. 1898, TX), Joby Rayford (b. 1904, TX). *SR; Hutchings to Meredith, Dec 30, 1916, AGC; AG to Garner, Jan 8, 1917, AGC; 1503:217; A1b, d, e, f, g; A2b, c; A4a, b.*

GARRETT, ALBERT HENRY. Born Oct. 24, 1884, Baird, Callahan County, Texas. Ht. 5 ft. 9 in., gray eyes, brown hair, light complexion, married. Merchant, Monahans, Ward County, Texas. LOYALTY RANGER June 7, 1918–Feb. 1919. REMARKS: In 1930 was a county road worker in Upton County, Texas. An Albert Henry Garrett died Apr. 29, 1936, Midland County, Texas. FAMILY: Parents, Hiram W. Garrett (b. 1850, IL) and Lucy A. (b. 1860, TX); siblings, Elizabeth "Lizzie" (b. 1881, CA), Sylvia (b. 1886, TX), Dora F. (b. 1889, TX), Liliany (b. 1891, TX), Milton (b. 1896, TX), Bessie Lee (b. 1900, TX); spouse, Annie Laurie Parker (b. 1886, TX), married about 1905; children, Haley N. (b. 1907, TX), Gordon D. (b. 1910, TX), Laura L. (b. 1912, TX), Annie May (b. 1914, TX), Albert H. (b. 1916, TX), Margaret E. (b. 1919, TX), Geraldine (b. 1923, TX), Paul D. (b. 1925, TX), George Lee (b. 1928, TX), Alberta Lee (b. 1934, TX). *SR; A1d, e, f, g; A2e; A3a; C.*

GARRETT, CHARLES C. Born July 25, 1873, Summerville, Chattooga County, Georgia. Medium height, medium build, married. Farmer, Brookshire, Waller County, Texas. LOYALTY RANGER June 4, 1918–Feb. 1919. REMARKS: His family lived in Texas by 1880. In 1900 was a jeweler living in Waller County; in 1910 was a furniture salesman in Waller County. By 1920 was the proprietor of a watch repair shop in Burnet, Burnet County, Texas. Died Nov. 21, 1935, Burnet County, Texas; buried in Pattison, Waller County. FAMILY: Parents, John Harris Garrett (b. 1825, SC) and Susan Jane Moore (b. 1834, GA or SC); siblings, Mary Jane (b. 1857, GA), J. Benjamin (b. 1860, GA), John Henry Morgan (b. 1863, GA), James Robert (b. 1868, GA), Albert Franklin (b. 1871, GA), Georgia E. (b. 1876, GA); spouse, Harriet Viola "Hattie" Jones (b. 1877, TX), married Jan. 5, 1897, Waller County; children, Nona (b. 1906, TX), Anna S. (b. 1908, TX), Lila L. (b. 1909, TX). *SR; A1a, b, d, e, f, g; A3a; A4b, g; B2; C.*

GARRETT, JOE AMYOT. Born Mar. 4, 1882, Arm, Mississippi. Ht. 5 ft. 11 in., brown eyes, dark hair, fair complexion, married. Packinghouse manager, Beaumont, Jefferson County, Texas. LOYALTY RANGER July 10, 1918–Feb. 1919. REMARKS: In 1910 was a store clerk in Village Mill, Hardin County, Texas. As of Sept. 1918 was manager of the Wilson Packing Company in Beaumont. Died Dec. 4, 1923, Jefferson County, Texas. FAMILY: Spouse, Marjorie N. (b. 1885, WI). *SR; A1e, f; A3a; C.*

GARRETT, YOUNG P. Born Feb. 1884, Coryell County, Texas. Ht. 6 ft. 1 in., gray eyes, black hair, married. Inspector, Waco, McClennan County, Texas. SPECIAL RANGER Dec. 29, 1917–Mar. 5, 1918 (attached to Co. M). Discharged/fired. (He had been commissioned on the understanding he would go to the border; he refused and was fired—Special Orders No. 2, 03/05/18.) REMARKS: Jan. 1918 letterhead: "Y. P. Garrett, Wholesale Real Estate, Waco." FAMILY: Parents, A. M. Garrett (b. 1857, TX) and Annie M. (b. 1864, LA); siblings, Teddy (b. 1886, TX), Annie B. (b. 1889, TX), Ambrose M. (b. 1898, TX), Elena J. (b. 1901, TX). *SR;471; Garrett to Harley, Jan 25, 1918, AGC; Assistant AG to Garrett, Feb 5, 1918, AGC; AG to Garrett, Mar 5, 1918, AGC; A1d, e.*

GARRISON, GODDARD KENT. Born July 12 or 13, 1883, Brooklyn, Kings County, New York. Ht. 5 ft. 8 ½ in., brown eyes, dark hair, fair complexion. Salesman of auto accessories, Waco, McLennan County, Texas. SPECIAL RANGER Sept. 14, 1917–Dec. 17, 1917; was reinstated (WA was renewed) Jan. 10, 1918–Jan. 15, 1919. REMARKS: In 1920 was an auto and carriage salesman, lived in Dallas, Dallas County, Texas. FAMILY: Parents, William Henry Garrison (b. 1852, MA) and Mary O. (b. 1860, NY); siblings, Florence O. (b. 1881, NY), Marion (b. 1887, NY), William

H., Jr. (b. 1886, TX). *SR; Garrison to Harley, Jan 8, 1918, AGC; Olson to Griffith, Sept 17, 1917, AGC; Olson to Hobby, Sept 17, 1917, AGC.; A1d, f; A3a; A6a.*

GATEWOOD, JULIAN L. Born Jan. 27, 1877, Tarrant County, Texas. Ht. 5 ft. 9 in., blue eyes, brown hair, light complexion. Brand inspector, Cattle Raisers' Association of Texas, Canadian, Hemphill County, Texas. SPECIAL RANGER June 27, 1917–Jan. 15, 1919 (was reinstated Dec. 20, 1917). Discharged. REMARKS: In 1918 was classed as a Regular Ranger without pay, to avoid the draft. In 1920 lived in Wheeler County, Texas; in 1930 was a cattleman living in Amarillo, Potter County, Texas. Died April 17, 1959, Wichita County, Texas. FAMILY: Parents, Atwell Bowcock Gatewood (b. 1829, VA) and Emily Oxier (b. 1842, IN); siblings, Ann Eliza (b. 1870, TX), Charles (b. 1871, TX), Rachel Elizabeth (b. 1872, TX), Eddie (b. 1877, TX), William (b. 1879, TX), Garvin Lewis (b. 1880, TX). *SR; Acting AG to GC&SF Railroad, Jan 9, 1918, AGC; A1b, d, f, g; A2b; A3a; A4a, b, g; B1.*

GENTRY, JAMES MILAM. Born Apr. 25, 1890, Goliad, Goliad County, Texas. Ht. 5 ft. 10 in., brown eyes, brown hair, light complexion, married. Deputy sheriff, Hidalgo County, Texas. REGULAR RANGER Jan. 10, 1918–Aug. 1, 1918 (private, Co. G). Discharged/fired. REMARKS: On July 31, 1918 he was discharged by Capt. Charles Stevens "for the good of the service." He moved to Goliad. In 1930 he was a government tick inspector living in Kenedy, Karnes County, Texas. Died Sept. 2, 1947, Charco, Goliad County, Texas; buried in Glendale Cemetery, Goliad. LAW ENFORCEMENT RELATIVES: Ranger Owen E. Gentry, cousin. FAMILY: Parents, Benjamin Franklin Gentry (b. 1861, GA) and Harriet Ella Bell (b. 1869, TX); siblings, Nannie Lillie (b. 1888, TX), Martha or Myrtle J. (b. 1893, TX), Eddie L. (b. 1895, TX), Cornelia (b. 1898, TX), twins Elbert W. and Delbert W. (b. 1900, TX), Ben J. (b. 1906, TX); spouse, Lucy Morton Sutherland (b. 1893, TX), married Apr. 16, 1916, Floresville, Wilson County, Texas; sons, Jim Milam (b. 1918, TX), Franklin (b. 1920, TX), Wilbur (b. 1921, TX). *SR; 471; Stevens to Woodul, Aug 2, 1918, AGC; Gentry to Harley, Aug 7, 1918, AGC; A1d, e, g; A2b; A3a; A4g; B2.*

GENTRY, OWEN EDWARD. Born July 30, 1893, Cuero, DeWitt County, Texas. Ht. 5 ft. 7in., light brown eyes, brown hair, light complexion, married. Game warden on the King Ranch, Kingsville, Kleberg County, Texas. SPECIAL RANGER July 2, 1917–Dec. 1917 (attached to Co. C). His commission was cancelled because he ceased working for the King Ranch. Ranchman, Hebbronville, Jim Hogg County. SPECIAL RANGER Aug. 12, 1932–Jan. 18, 1933. Discharged. REMARKS: Gentry said he was a Special Ranger under Captain Sanders from Oct. 1916–Dec. 1917. In 1920 was an oil company foreman in Ranger, Eastland County, Texas. In 1930 was a cattle raiser in Jim Hogg County, Texas. Died Nov. 1, 1969, Atascosa County, Texas; buried in Fairview Cemetery, Wilson County, Texas. LAW ENFORCEMENT RELATIVES: Ranger James M. Gentry, cousin. FAMILY: Parents, John B. Gentry (b. 1865, GA) and Josie E. (b. 1868, TX); siblings, Virgie (b. 1889, TX), Janie L. (b. 1893, TX), Mabel (b. 1896, TX), Ethel J. (b. 1899, TX), Preston (b. 1900, TX); spouse, Nettie King Hill (b. 1895, TX), married about 1922. *SR; Scarborough to Ferguson, June 4, 1917, AGC; Scarborough to Harley, Dec 5, 23, 1917, AGC; AG to Scarborough, Dec 7, 1917, AGC; Gentry to Harley, Dec 7, 1917, AGC; A1d, f, g; A2a, b; A3a; A4b, g; B1, 2.*

GERON, FRANK COLE. Born Mar. 14, 1876, Arthur City, Lamar County, Texas. Ht. 6 ft., brown eyes, black hair, dark complexion, married. Traveling salesman, Paris, Lamar County. LOYALTY RANGER July 10, 1918–Feb. 19, 1919. REMARKS: Had been a "stock policeman" in Paris. In 1930 was a patient in Texas State Hospital, Terrell, Kaufman County, Texas. Died Nov. 11, 1931, Kaufman County, Texas; buried in Evergreen Cemetery, Lamar County. FAMILY: Parents, Solomon Cary Geron (b. 1834, AL) and Mary Louisa Harrison (b. 1843, TX); siblings, Thomas Cary (b. 1867, TX), Mattie F. (b. 1872, TX), Clara D. (b. 1874, TX), Harrison Royston (b. 1882, TX), Mary Elizabeth "Bessie" (b. 1886, TX); spouse #1, Pearl Provine (b. 1878, TX), married July 6, 1898, Lamar County; son, Hampton P. (b. 1900, TX); spouse #2, Mildred Maude Wilkins (b. 1877, SC), married Nov. 4, 1911; step-son, Leeroy Kelton (b. 1906, TX). *SR; A1b, d, g; A3a; A4a, b, g; B2; C.*

GHOLSON, ALBERT FRANKLIN. Born Dec. 9, 1881, Evant, Coryell County, Texas. Ht. 6 ft. 2 in., blue eyes, brown hair, fair complexion, married. Stockman. REGULAR RANGER Sept. 1, 1917–Mar. 31, 1918 (private, Co. C; transferred to Co. L in late 1917; promoted to sergeant, Jan. 4, 1918).

Resigned to become a mounted Customs inspector in Apr. 1918. REMARKS: Had been a cattle herder in Garza County, Texas and a farmer in Lampasas County, Texas. Was a U.S. Customs inspector in 1918 in Presidio County, Texas; still a Customs inspector in Marfa, Presidio County in 1920. In 1930 was a Customs officer in Brewster County, Texas. Died Jan. 18, 1972, Hamilton County, Texas. LAW ENFORCEMENT RELATIVES: Ranger (1858 and 1860–1861) Benjamin F. Gholson, father; Ranger (1858) Samuel S. Gholson, uncle. FAMILY: Parents, Benjamin Franklin Gholson (b. 1841, TX) and Jane Adeline Langford (b. 1847, LA); siblings, Frances Electra "Fannie" (b. 1865, TX), Elydia Cordelia (b. 1867, TX), Emma Lee (b. 1870), Mantola Isola (b. 1872), Ada Lela (b. 1874, TX), Samuel Leroy "Roy" (b. 1875, TX), Almedia Eliza (b. 1879, TX), Katy Lena (b. 1880, TX); spouse, Orline Winn (b. 1884, TX), married about 1906, Lampasas, Lampasas County, Texas; children, Evelyn (b. 1907, TX), Edwin "Eddie" (b. 1911, TX), Francis (b. 1917, TX). *SR; 471; AG to Davis, Jan 29, 1918, AGC; Davis to Harley, Jan 4, Mar 31, 1918, AGC; 240:365–367; 333:33–34; A1d, f, g; A2a, b; A3a; A4a, b, g; B1.*

GIBSON, GEORGE, JR. Born Oct. 23, 1879, London, England. Ht. 5 ft. 10 ½ in., blue eyes, light hair, fair complexion, married, as of June 1918. Saddler, Kingsville, Kleberg County, Texas. SPECIAL RANGER Apr. 17, 1916–Dec. 1917 (attached to Co. C). King Ranch employee, Santa Gertrudis Ranch, Kingsville. SPECIAL RANGER June 27, 1918–Jan. 15, 1919; Jan. 30–Dec. 31, 1919 (commission was renewed). REMARKS: Immigrated with his family to the United States in 1886; became a naturalized citizen in 1908. World War I Draft Registration (Sept. 1918) states has "one leg." In 1930 was a commercial trader in leather goods, lived in Houston, Harris County, Texas. FAMILY: Parents, George Gibson (b. 1845, England) and Marie (b. 1846, England); siblings, Alexandria (b. 1881, England), Isabella (b. 1884, England), Maria Victoria (b. 1891, TX); spouse #1, Ann (b. 1893, TX), married about 1918; stepdaughter, Willie Love (b. 1912, TX); spouse #2, Blanch W. (b. 1892, TX); stepdaughter, Charlotte F. Swift (b. 1915, TX). *SR; 471; Scarborough to Hutchings, Apr 11, 1916, AGC; A1d, e, f, g; A3a.*

GIBSON, JAMES. Born Jan. 27, 1856, Frederick, Frederick County, Maryland. Ht. 5 ft. 11 in., black eyes, dark hair, dark complexion, married. SPECIAL RANGER under Capt. J. H. Rogers, dates unknown. Stockman, Alice, Jim Wells County, Texas. SPECIAL RANGER June 10, 1918–Jan. 15, 1919; Feb. 10, 1931–Jan. 20, 1933 (WA expired Feb. 9, 1932, was extended to Jan. 20, 1933). REMARKS: Brand inspector, Cattle Raisers' Association of Texas, Alice, 1911. Letterhead in 1918: "Gibson and King, Dealers in High Grade Cattle, James Gibson—Alice, E. R. King, Jr.—Corpus Christi." In 1930 was a cattle farmer in Jim Wells County. A James Gibson died Sept. 14, 1945, Jim Wells County, Texas. LAW ENFORCEMENT RELATIVES: Ranger Joshua Gregg Gibson, son. FAMILY: Parents, Joshua Gregg Gibson (b. 1823, VA) and Susan Hite Waters (b. 1828, MD); siblings, Frances Hite "Fannie" (b. 1848, MD), William Waters (b. 1850, MD), Agnes (b. 1853, MD), Francis Conway (b. 1859, MD), Ann Pottinger (b. 1860, WV), Robert (1868, MD), Hopkins (b. 1872, WV); spouse, Mollie Mary Hale (b. 1870, TX), married Sept. 4, 1888, Kerr County, Texas; children, Willie Agnes, James, Jr. (b. 1891, TX), Zanita Ann (b. 1894, TX), Joshua Gregg "Rufus" (b. 1899, TX), Sue Ann. *SR; 471; EPMT, Aug 19, 1911; A1aa, e, f, g; A2d; A3a; A4b, g; C.*

GIBSON, JAMES FRANKLIN. Born Nov. 15, 1889, Young County, Texas. Ht. 5 ft. 10 ½ in., blue eyes, light hair, light complexion, married. Stock farmer, Grow, King County, Texas. LOYALTY RANGER June 10, 1918–Feb. 1919. In 1930 was a cotton farmer in Cottle County, Texas. Died Nov. 16, 1948. FAMILY: Parents, John Franklin Gibson (b. 1859, TN) and Ada Lee Moore (b. 1863, TX); siblings, Jennie Lee (b. 1892, TX), John R. (b. 1895, TX), Haydn M. (b. 1898, TX), Archie L. (b. 1901, TX), Ada L. (b. 1905, TX); spouse, Vaughnie Mackey (b. 1893, TX), married about 1911; sons, Clyde F. (b. 1912, TX), Glen (b. 1916, TX). *SR; A1d, e, g; A3a; B2.*

GILL, SAMUEL LAMAR. Born Aug. 1883, Gambles Gully, Live Oak County, Texas. Ht. 5 ft. 11 ½ in., brown eyes, brown hair, brunette complexion, married. Livestock dealer, Raymondville, Willacy County, Texas. SPECIAL RANGER May 31, 1916–Dec. 1917 (attached to Co. C). Lawyer, Raymondville. SPECIAL RANGER Jan. 24, 1933–Jan. 22, 1935. (WA expired Jan. 23, 1934, was extended to Jan. 23, 1935). REMARKS: Peace officer, Cameron County, Texas and Hidalgo County, Texas for 7 years. Lived in Raymondville since 1904. Deputy sheriff, Raymondville, 1914–1916. Vice president and manager of Lacoma Mercantile Co., Raymondville, 1914. Partner in Harding-Lindahl Land Co., Raymondville, May 1916. Vice president, Raymondville State Bank, 1915–1917. In Nov. 1917 was commissioned as a 1st Lt., Infantry, National Army, at Camp Travis. In 1920 was a real estate salesman in Cameron County. In 1933 his Ranger commission was requested by Gen. Henry Hutchings. Died Oct. 19, 1966, Raymondville, Willacy County, Texas; buried in Raymondville. LAW ENFORCEMENT RELATIVES: Cameron County deputy sheriff (1915–1917) Leon Gill, brother. FAMILY: Parents, John Ben Milam "Buddy" Gill (b. 1849, MS) and Mary Thornton "Mamie" Gillett (b. 1858, TX); siblings, Leon (b. 1886, TX), Nellie or Maie M. (b. 1891, TX), Truman M. (b. 1899, TX); spouse, Sarah Kenedy (b. 1884, TX), married Feb. 7, 1907; adopted son, Kenedy Dryer (b. 1915, TX). *SR; Gill to Hulen, Apr 22, 1914, AGC; Gill to Hutchings, Mar 18, 1916, Apr 11, 1917, AGC; Gill to Vann, May 25, 1916, AGC; Gill to Harley, Dec 25, 1917, AGC; BDH, Oct 28, Nov 4, Dec 3, 1914, Aug 6, 1915, Sept 4, 1916, Nov 28, 1917; A1d, e, f, g; A2b; A4a, b, g.*

GILLIAM JAMES D. Born Mar. 1863, Ray Springs, Tennessee. Ht. 5 ft. 7 in., gray eyes, gray hair, light complexion, married. Railroad watchman, Childress, Childress County, Texas. SPECIAL RANGER Jan. 3, 1918–Jan. 15, 1919. REMARKS: Watchman, Fort Worth and Denver City Railroad, 1908–1917. In 1920 was a railroad special agent living in Childress. In 1930 was a house contractor in Childress. FAMILY: Spouse, Mary A. (b. 1872, TN), married about 1886; children, Jessie P. (b. 1886, TN), Elsie F. (b. 1890, TN), James D. (b. 1895, TX). *SR; AG to Barnett, Dec 27, 1917, AGC; A1d, e, f, g.*

GILLILAND, CARL. Born Oct. 14, 1879, Clay County, Tennessee. (According to one source, born Oct. 14, 1873.) Medium height, slender, blue eyes, married. Lawyer, Hereford, Deaf Smith County, Texas. LOYALTY RANGER June 14, 1918–Feb. 1919. REMARKS: Still living in Hereford in 1930. Carl Thomas Jefferson Gilliland died Sept. 18, 1948, Deaf Smith County, Texas; buried in Hereford. FAMILY: Parents, James K. Gilliland (b. 1840, TN) and Margaret Fancher Officer (b. 1847, TN); siblings, James Lee (b. 1871, TN), William Herbert (b. 1876, TN), Mary Emma (b. 1882, TN); spouse, Irene S. Estes (b. 1884, TX), married June 5, 1905, Hereford; children, Mary Margaret (b. 1908, TX), James Estes (b. 1911, TX). *SR; A1b, d, e, f, g; A2b, e; A3a; A4a, b, g; B2.*

GILLILAND, JOHN ECKFORD "ECK." Born Dec. 25, 1869, Wilson County, Texas. No physical description, married. Farmer, Floresville, Wilson County. LOYALTY RANGER June 15, 1918–Feb. 1919. REMARKS: Still farming in Floresville in 1930. Died Mar. 1, 1948, San Antonio, Bexar County, Texas; buried in Fairview, Wilson County. LAW ENFORCEMENT RELATIVES: Ranger Grenade Donaldson 'Don' Gilliland, son; Ranger Herff A. Carnes, brother-in-law, Ranger Quirl B. Carnes, brother-in-law; deputy sheriff, deputy U.S. marshal Ralph Blackburn Gilliland, son; Wilson County sheriff (1918–1938) Alfred Burton Carnes, brother-in-law; U.S. Border Patrolman Tom Carnes, nephew; FBI agent Bob Carnes, nephew; Wilson County sheriff (1953–1960) Don Carnes, nephew. FAMILY: Parents, Grenade Drake Gilliland (b. 1826, AL) and Maggie Donaldson (b. 1842, TN); siblings, James (b. 1856, TX), Sarah P. (b. 1865, TX), Drake (b. 1867, TX), Annie Irene (b. 1874, TX), Juliet Elizabeth "Bessie" (b. 1876, TX), Mary Haney "Mollie" (b. 1879, TX); spouse, Atlanta Lee "Attie" Carnes (b. 1873, TX), married Sept. 6, 1893, Wilson County; children, Willie Eckford (b. 1894, TX), Martin Taylor (b. 1896, TX), Grenade Donaldson "Don" (b. 1899, TX), Mary Lee (b. 1902, TX), Anna Burton "Berta" (b. 1906, TX), Ralph Blackburn (b. 1908, TX). *SR; A1b, e, f, g; A2b; A4a, b, g.*

GILLISPIE, J. P. Born March 1885, Fayette County, Kentucky. Ht. 5 ft. 10 in., blue eyes, light hair, fair complexion. Peace officer, Hempstead, Waller County, Texas. REGULAR RANGER Dec. 19, 1912–June 9, 1913 (private, Co. B). Resigned/fired; proved unsuitable as Ranger; AG ordered him discharged. REMARKS: As of March 1915, lived at Hempstead, was married. Was assistant to special agent for I&GN Railroad. Wanted to reenlist in the Rangers. *SR; Sanders to Hutchings, May 4, June 1, Aug 19, 1913, AGC; AG to Sanders, Jan 7, 1913, AGC; MR, Co. B, June 30, 1913, AGC; Gillispie to Hutchings, Mar 6, 1915, AGC.*

GILLON, JOHN ALEXANDER. Born July 10, 1881, Fredericksburg, Gillespie County, Texas. Ht. 6 ft. 2 in., gray eyes, light hair, light complexion. Brand inspector,

Sheep and Goat Raisers' Association, Sonora, Edwards County, Texas. SPECIAL RANGER Nov. 12, 1917–Dec. 1917 (attached to Co. C). Brand inspector, Sheep and Goat Raisers' Association, Rocksprings, Edwards County. SPECIAL RANGER Feb. 11, 1919–Dec. 31, 1919. Stockman, Rocksprings. REGULAR RANGER Sept. 9, 1921–Apr. 15, 1923 (sergeant, Co. C). Resigned. Ranchman. REGULAR RANGER Sept. 1, 1923–Feb. 21, 1925 (private, Co. E). Discharged. Ranchman, San Antonio, Bexar County, Texas. SPECIAL RANGER Dec. 17, 1925–Feb. 1, 1927. Discharged—WA expired. Peace officer, San Antonio. SPECIAL RANGER May 28, 1927–Sept. 27, 1928 (reenlisted—WA was renewed, Mar. 12, 1928 while he was a peace officer in Iraan, Pecos County, Texas). Discharged. Peace officer, Llano, Llano County, Texas. SPECIAL RANGER Dec. 1, 1931–Sept. 9, 1932. WA cancelled—expired on Nov. 30, 1932. Peace officer, Hondo, Medina County, Texas. SPECIAL RANGER Dec. 11, 1933–Jan. 14, 1935. (WA expired Dec. 10, 1934, extended to Dec. 10, 1935). Resigned. REMARKS: In 1910 was a cattle ranch manager in Kinney, Nueces County, Texas. Brand inspector, Sheep and Goat Raisers' Association, Oct. 1918, Apr. 1920. In 1927 his Special Ranger commission was requested by the Oklahoma Contracting Company. In 1930 was a U.S. peace officer living in San Antonio. Died Aug. 15, 1968, San Antonio, Bexar County, Texas. FAMILY: Parents, Alexander Gillon (b. 1840, Scotland) and Susan (b. 1850, MO); siblings, Margret (b. 1875, TX), Robert (b. 1879, TX); spouse #1, Ruby Kuykendall (b. 1884, TX), married Aug. 27, 1903, Llano County; children, Robert H. (b. 1905, TX), Susan Alethia (b. 1907, TX); spouse #2, Lynn O. (b. 1887, TX), married about 1922. *SR; 471; Gillon to Harley, Oct 16, 1917, AGC; Holland to Harley, Oct 24, 1917, AGC; Allison to Harley, Oct 16, 1917, AGC; AG to Clark, Nov 5, 1917, AGC; Gillon to Harley, Dec 31, 1917, Feb 14, 1918, AGC; Clark to Harley, Oct 12, 1918, AGC; Gillon to Cope, Jan 19, 1920, AGC; Stricklin to Aldrich, Apr 12, 1920, AGC; 470: 43; A1b, d, e, g; A2a, b, c; A3a.*

GIPSON, FELIX C. Born Mar. 1872, Hunt County, Texas. No physical description, married. Merchant, Dickens, Dickens County, Texas. LOYALTY RANGER July 2, 1918–Feb. 1919. REMARKS: Was a retail druggist in Dickens. A Felix C. Gipson died July 27, 1934, Lubbock County, Texas. FAMILY: Parents, James C. Gipson (b. 1841, TN) and Emily (b. 1843, TN); siblings, Louisa (b. 1866, TN), James N. (b. 1868, TN), Mary E. (b. 1870, TN), Jno. H. (b. 1874, TX), Kate (b. 1879, TX); spouse #1, Mollie E. Clay (b. 1878, TX), married about 1895; children, Lora C. (b. 1896, TX), Selma M. (b. 1899, TX), Mildred (b. 1902, TX), Foy C. (b. 1904, TX), Jack Donald (b. 1907, TX); spouse #2, Ada V. (b. 1881, TX), married about 1923. *SR; A1b, d, e, f, g; A4b; C.*

GIRDLEY, BEAUMONT CLIFFORD. Born Oct. 19, 1883, Garland, Dallas County, Texas. Ht. 5 ft. 9 in., blue eyes, dark brown hair, medium dark complexion, married. Stockman and cashier of the Midland National Bank, Midland, Midland County, Texas. LOYALTY RANGER June 5, 1918–Feb. 20, 1919. REMARKS: In 1930 was a real estate agent in Midland. Died Nov. 10, 1952, Midland County, Texas; buried in Resthaven Memorial Park, Midland, Texas. FAMILY: Parents, James Alexander Girdley (b. 1850, TN) and Louisa Ann Josephine "Lucy" Spillman (b. 1860, MO); sisters, Eugenia D. (b. 1881, TX), Willie (b. 1884, TX), Marian Josephine (b. 1886, TX), Lenis Alma (b. 1890, TX), Stella Leora (b. 1894, TX); spouse, Lucy Elizabeth Cowden (b. 1883, TX), married May 24, 1908; sons, James Frederick (b. 1909, TX), Beaumont Clifford, Jr. (b. 1920, TX). *SR; A1d, f, g; A2b; A3a; A4b; B2.*

GLASSCOCK, HENRY DOYLE. Born July 16, 1886, Lampasas, Lampasas County, Texas. Ht. 5 ft. 9 ½ in., blue eyes, brown hair, ruddy complexion, married as of 1931. Cowpuncher, enlisted in Val Verde County, Texas. REGULAR RANGER Sept. 22, 1917–Feb. 15, 1931 (private, Co. E; Co. F, Aug. 20, 1919; Co. C, Feb. 15, 1921). Discharged (end of administration). Peace officer, Alpine, Brewster County, Texas. REGULAR RANGER Sept. 1, 1931–Jan. 18, 1933 (private, Co. A). Discharged. REMARKS: Had been a ranch hand in Concho County, Texas. Died June 7, 1961, Brewster County, Texas. FAMILY: Parents, James S. Glasscock (b. 1837, IL) and Hulda (b. 1848, AR); brothers, James A. (b. 1879, TX), Thomas F. (b. 1882, TX), Marvin C. (b. 1891, TX); spouse, Pearl V. (b. 1908, LA), married about 1928. *SR; 471; Barler to Harley, Oct 12, 1917, AGC; 319: 200; 470: 43; 480: 25; A1d, e, f, g; A2b; A3c.*

GLASSCOCK, LEE H. (Listed as GLASCOCK, LEE in the Ranger Service Records.) Born Aug. 1867, Williamson County, Texas. Ht. 5 ft. 11 in., blue eyes, brown hair, light complexion, married. Ranchman, Marfa, Presidio County, Texas. SPECIAL RANGER May 11, 1917–Dec. 1917 (attached to Co. C); Jan. 9, 1918–Jan. 15, 1919. REMARKS: In 1918 enlistment, birthplace is listed as Austin, Travis County. In 1900 was a grocery clerk in Denver, Arapaho County, Colorado. In 1930 was an insurance salesman in Presidio County. A Lee Glasscock died Mar. 2, 1936, Presidio County, Texas. FAMILY: Parents, William L. Glasscock (b. 1834, AL) and Mattie Pierce Rawls (b. 1845, LA); brother, Walter (b. 1872, TX); spouse #1, Lena S. Burleson (b. 1868, TX), married Mar. 9, 1887; children, Hetta V. (b. 1888, TX), Lee H. (b. 1890, TX); spouse #2, Sophia (b. 1885, TX), married about 1911; daughter, Lee (b. 1922, TX). *SR; Hudspeth to Harley, Oct 16, 1917, AGC; Glasscock to Harley, Oct 27, 1917, AGC; A1b, d, g; A2b; A4b.*

GLICK, GEORGE ALVA. Born Sept. 12, 1893, Foster, Fort Bend County, Texas. Ht. 5 ft. 9 in., blue eyes, brown hair, light complexion, married as of Sept. 1929. Cowboy, enlisted in Harlingen, Cameron County, Texas. REGULAR RANGER Aug. 21, 1915–Dec. 1915 (private, Co. D). Discharged sometime earlier than Dec. 7, 1915. Special officer, T&NO Railroad (SP), Rosenberg, Fort. Bend County. SPECIAL RANGER Sept. 30, 1929–Sept. 30, 1930. Discharged. Special officer, T&NO Railroad, San Antonio, Bexar County, Texas. SPECIAL RANGER Oct. 9, 1930–Oct. 9, 1931; Oct. 2, 1931–Jan. 18, 1933; Jan. 23, 1933–Aug. 10, 1935. Discharged. REMARKS: Sept. 1929 enlistment gives height as 5 ft. 11 in. Died July 8, 1980, Richmond, Fort Bend County, Texas; buried in Morton Cemetery, Fort Bend County. FAMILY: Parents, George A. Glick (b. 1860, OH) and Henrietta Wheaton (b. 1874, TX); brother, Louis H. (b. 1891, TX); spouse, Clara Bernice Stuart (b. 1903, TX), married Jan. 22, 1922, Richmond. *SR; 471; Ransom to Hutchings, Dec 7, 1915, AGC; A1d, e, f, g; A2b; A3a; A4b, g; B2.*

GONZALES, WILLIAM JOHN "WILLIE." Born May 20, 1885 on the Newberry Ranch, Jim Hogg County, Texas. Ht. 5 ft. 11 in., blue eyes, black hair, dark complexion, married. Ranch foreman, Hebbronville, Jim Hogg County. SPECIAL RANGER May 6, 1918–Jan. 15, 1919. REMARKS: In 1930 owned a dairy farm in Laredo, Webb County, Texas. FAMILY: Spouse, Trinidad (b. 1886, TX), married about 1905; children, William, Jr. (b. 1907, TX), Nora (b. 1908, TX), Carlos (b. 1910, TX), Dora (b. 1914, TX), Hortensia (b. 1916, TX), James William (b. 1917, TX), Mary Louise (b. 1919, TX), George (b. 1923, TX), Roberto (b. 1924, TX). *SR; A1f, g; A2e; A3a.*

GONZALEZ, JUAN CANDELARIO. Born Dec. 27, 1873, Marín, Nuevo Leon, Mexico. Ht. 5 ft. 11 ½ in., brown eyes, dark hair, fair complexion, married. Deputy sheriff, Rio Grande City, Starr County, Texas. LOYALTY RANGER July 12, 1918–Feb. 19, 1919. Peace officer, Rio Grande City. REGULAR RANGER Aug. 11, 1919–Jan. 31, 1923 (private, Co. D). Resigned. Dealer, Rio Grande City. REGULAR RANGER May 5, 1923–Feb. 28, 1925 (private, Co. D). Discharged—reduction in force. Deputy sheriff, Starr County. REGULAR RANGER July 31, 1925–May 15, 1927 (private, Co. D). Discharged. REMARKS: Starr County deputy sheriff for 2 years; Starr County sheriff, Nov. 8, 1910–Nov. 3, 1914. Immigrated to the U.S. in 1879; became a naturalized U.S. citizen in 1910. In 1930 was city marshal, Rio Grande City. A Juan C. Gonzalez died Feb. 21, 1934, Starr County, Texas. FAMILY: Spouse, Emilia Clarke (b. 1887, Mexico), married about 1906; children, Emma (b. 1908, TX), Juan C., Jr. (b. 1912, TX), Elma Rose (b. 1922, TX). *SR; 471; Gonzalez to Colquitt, May 14, 1913, AGC; 1503:473; BDH, Dec 14, 1910, Jan 29, 1913; LWT, Dec 18, 1910; 470: 11, 47; 485: 244–245; 469: 64; A1f, g; A3a; C.*

GONZAULLAS, MANUEL TERRAZAS (sometimes spelled TRAZAZAS) "LONE WOLF." Obscure antecedents—No Service Record and "The personnel file indicates no history before entering the Texas Rangers." [*Jim Pribble, Personnel Officer, Department of Public Safety to Texas Ranger Senior Captain W. D. Wilson, Mar 30, 1982.*] Gonzaullas claimed he was born July 4, 1891, Cadiz, Spain. Export business, El Paso, El Paso County, Texas. REGULAR RANGER Oct. 1, 1920, Co. B; Sept 1, 1921 transferred to Co. C. In 1921 he became a federal Prohibition agent, reenlisting as a REGULAR RANGER on July 2, 1924. In Dec. 1925 he resigned to become a Prohibition agent again. Reenlisted as a REGULAR RANGER June 10, 1927–Jan. 18, 1933 (sergeant, Co. B, 1928–1931; promoted to captain). He and other Rangers were fired by the incoming governor, "Ma" Ferguson. Superintendent, Bureau of Intelligence, Department of Public Safety (DPS), Austin, Travis County, Texas. REGULAR RANGER Feb. 26, 1940–July 31, 1951

Texas Ranger Captain Manuel Terrazas "Lone Wolf" Gonzaullas. *Photo courtesy Texas Ranger Hall of Fame and Museum.*

(Captain, Co. B). Retired. REMARKS: His biographers relied on what he told them about his early life. Gonzaullas stated he was born of naturalized American parents who were visiting Spain at the time of his birth. Immigrated to the U.S. in 1893; became a naturalized American citizen. Was reared in El Paso. Allegedly served as a major in the Mexican Army at age 20. One source states that he performed special intelligence work for the U.S. government for 5 years and that in 1920 was a mining engineer living in El Paso. After leaving Ranger service in 1933, Gonzaullas became chief special agent for the Atlas Pipeline Company and the Spartan Refining Company. On Jan 1, 1935 he became chief investigator for the district attorney at Longview, Gregg County, Texas. When the Department of Public Safety was formed in 1935, he was named superintendent of the Bureau of Intelligence. Died Feb. 13, 1977, Dallas, Dallas County, Texas; his body was cremated. FAMILY: Parents, Manuel Gonzaullas (Spain) and Helen von Droff (Canada); spouse, Laura Isabel Scherer (b. 1898, NY), married in California. *471; Aldrich to Gonzaullas, July 16, Aug 6, Dec 30, 1920, AGC; Aldrich to Crawford, Oct 20, 1920, AGC; Aldrich to Brady, Nov 18, 27, 1920, AGC; Cope to Gonzaullas, Jan 4, 1920 [sic-1921], AGC; Gonzaullas to Cope, Jan 6, 1921, AGC; 319: 107, 200, 229; 463: 94; biographies: 168 and 172:III, 237; 842; 844; 1512; 1502; A1f; A2a, b; A4a.*

GOODLETT, JAMES BOOTH. Born Mar. 4, 1869, Thorpe Springs, Hood County, Texas. Ht. 5 ft. 9 in., blue eyes, dark hair, dark complexion, married. Loan agent, Quanah, Hardeman County, Texas. SPECIAL RANGER June 1, 1918–Oct. 24, 1918. Resigned because he had been appointed postmaster at Quanah. FAMILY: Parents, James Hervey Goodlett (b. 1839, SC) and Nancy Alabama Cook (b. 1851, TN); brother, Edgar Spartan (b. 1872, TX); spouse, Orlean Ballentine (b. 1872, TN), married about 1898; children, Joy (b. 1899, AL), Andrew Jack (b. 1907, TX). *SR; A1a, b, d, e, f, g; A4b, g.*

GOODLOE, GAIL BORDEN. Born Feb. 28, 1878, San Antonio, Bexar County, Texas. Ht. 5 ft. 10 ½ in., blue eyes, brown hair, fair complexion, married. Superintendent of transportation, SA&AP Railroad, San Antonio, Bexar County. SPECIAL RANGER May 27, 1917–Jan. 15, 1919 (attached to Co. C; was reinstated/WA renewed, Jan. 4, 1918). REMARKS: Still a railroad superintendent in San Antonio in 1930. Died Feb. 1, 1935, Bexar County, Texas. FAMILY: Parents, Calvin Goodloe (b. 1842, AL) and Matilda Tibbets "Mattie" Sneed (b. 1847, AR); siblings, Sebron Sneed (b. 1866, TX), Emma Sue (b. 1867, TX), Meranda (b. 1869, TX), Daisy Isabel (b. 1870, TX), John Calvin (b. 1872, TX); spouse, Elizabeth E. Smith (b. 1884, TX), married about 1904; children, Bessie Borden (b. 1905, TX), Gail Edward (b. 1908, TX). *SR; Chamberlain to Hutchings, May 31, 1917, AGC; AG to Chamberlain, June 1, 1917, AGC; A1b, d, e, f, g; A3a; A4b, g; C.*

GOODWIN, OSCAR W. "DOC." Born Aug. 1877, Murray, Calloway County, Kentucky. Ht. 5 ft. 9 in., brown eyes, light hair, fair complexion. Druggist, El Paso, El Paso County, Texas. REGULAR RANGER Apr. 6, 1914–Feb. 10, 1916 (private, Co. A; transferred to Co. B, Feb. 1, 1915). Died Feb. 10, 1916 of natural causes following an operation, El Paso, El Paso County, Texas. REMARKS: 1880 U.S. Census record indicates he was born about 1874. Had been an El Paso County deputy sheriff. In 1910 was a druggist at the smelter, El Paso. FAMILY: Parents, John J. Goodwin (b. 1839, TN) and Martha J. "Madie" (b. 1849, KY or TN); sister, Henryetta (b. 1868, KY). *SR; 471; AA, May 14, 1914; EPMT, July 16, Aug 31, Sept 22, 24, 25, 27, Oct 22, Nov 8, 11, 12, 14, 17, 18, 1914, Jan 2, 4, 12, 26, 30, 31, Feb 7, 16, 21, 22, Mar 16, Apr 14, July 25, 29, Aug 28, Sept 15, Oct 15, 1915, Feb 11–13, 1916; MR, Co. B, Feb 29, 1916, AGC; A1a, b, e; A2b.*

GOODWYN, FRANCIS EPPS, JR. Born Aug. 23, 1884, Lagarto, Live Oak County, Texas. Ht. 5 ft. 11 ½ in., gray eyes, black hair, fair complexion, married. Foreman, Norias Ranch (King Ranch employee), Armstrong, Willacy County, Texas. SPECIAL RANGER June 6, 1917–Dec. 31, 1919 (attached to Co. C; was reinstated/WA was renewed, Jan. 8, 1918 and Jan. 23, 1919). Discharged. REMARKS: Caesar Kleberg, a King Ranch manager, asked the AG to commission Goodwyn. In 1930 was a ranch foreman in Kenedy County, Texas; wife and family lived in Kingsville, Kleberg County, Texas. LAW ENFORCEMENT RELATIVES: Ranger James D. Goodwyn, brother; Ranger Richard L. Goodwyn, brother. FAMILY: Parents, Francis Epps Goodwyn (b. 1846, SC) and Nancy Frenesnick "Fannie" (b. 1851, LA); siblings, Rhydonia (b. 1872, TX), Thomas (b. 1878, TX), Mary Maud (b. 1879, TX), James D. (b. 1881, TX), Amanda or Bessie (b. 1889, TX), Richard L. (b. 1892, TX); spouse, Lennie (b. 1887, TX), married about 1910; children, Francis E. (b. 1912, TX), Robert C. (b. 1916, TX), Finley W. (b. 1919, TX), Lennie (b. 1922, TX). *SR; Kleberg to AG, May 10, 1917, AGC; Kleberg to Woodul, Dec 29, 1917, AGC; A1b, f, g; A3a.*

GOODWYN, JAMES DOBIE. Born Dec. 20, 1881, Ramireno, Zapata County, Texas. Ht. 5 ft. 6 ½ in., blue eyes, brown hair, fair complexion. Ranchman. SPECIAL RANGER Jan. 10, 1919–Dec. 31, 1919 (commission was renewed, Jan. 23, 1919). Discharged. REMARKS: In Sept. 1918 was living on the Norias Ranch, Willacy County, Texas. In 1930 was a tick inspector in Willacy County. Died Feb. 16, 1965, Kleberg County, Texas. LAW ENFORCEMENT RELATIVES: Ranger Francis E. Goodwyn, Jr., brother; Ranger Richard L. Goodwyn, brother. FAMILY: Parents, Francis Epps Goodwyn (b. 1846, SC) and Nancy Frenesnick "Fannie" (b. 1851, LA); siblings, Rhydonia (b. 1872, TX), Thomas (b. 1878, TX), Mary Maud (b. 1879, TX), Francis E., Jr. (b. 1884, TX), Amanda or Bessie (b. 1889, TX), Richard L. (b. 1892,

TX); spouse, Mary Curry (b. 1901, TX), married about 1920; children, Henry (b. 1923, TX), James (b. 1924, TX), Dom (b. 1928, TX), Fannie (b. 1929, TX), Fannie Frances (b. 1937, TX), Tomey Jackson (b. 1940, TX). *SR; A1b, e, g; A2b, e; A3a.*

GOODWYN, RICHARD LAWRENCE. Born Aug. 12, 1892, Live Oak County, Texas. Ht. 5 ft. 8 ½ in., blue-gray eyes, light hair, light complexion, married. Stockman, enlisted in Kleberg County, Texas. SPECIAL RANGER Dec. 6, 1917–unknown. REMARKS: World War I Draft Registration document states born in Ramireno, Zapata County, Texas. A Richard Lawrence Goodwyn died Feb. 27, 1962, Hidalgo County, Texas. LAW ENFORCEMENT RELATIVES: Ranger Francis E. Goodwyn, Jr., brother; Ranger James D. Goodwyn, brother. FAMILY: Parents, Francis Epps Goodwyn (b. 1846, SC) and Nancy Frenesnick "Fannie" (b. 1851, LA); siblings, Rhydonia (b. 1872, TX), Thomas (b. 1878, TX), Mary Maud (b. 1879, TX), James D. (b. 1881, TX); Francis E., Jr. (b. 1884, TX), Amanda or Bessie (b. 1889, TX); spouse #1, unknown; spouse #2, Rosa Morene Gilliam (b. 1928, OK), married June 11, 1944, Edinburg, Hidalgo County; son, Richard Leon (b. 1947, TX). *SR; Scarborough to Harley, Dec 5, 1917, AGC; AG to Scarborough, Dec 7, 1917, AGC; A1b, d, e; A2b, e; A3a; A4b.*

GOOLSBY, JOHN ARTHUR. Born Feb. 23, 1891, Jefferson, Marion County, Texas. Ht. 5 ft. 10 ½ in., blue eyes, dark hair, fair complexion, married. Constable, San Benito, Cameron County, Texas. REGULAR RANGER June 10, 1918–Oct. 31, 1918 (private, Co. G). Discharged. REMARKS: Peace officer in the Lower Rio Grande Valley, 1914–1917. Constable, precinct 4, Cameron County, 1917. In 1920 was a real estate salesman in San Benito. Cameron County sheriff Nov. 6, 1934–Jan. 1, 1941. In 1930 was a power company salesman in San Benito. Died June 25, 1970, San Benito, Cameron County, Texas. FAMILY: Parents, Joseph Leander Goolsby (b. 1861, TX) and Ora Lee Mims (b. 1869, TX); siblings, Mims A. (b. 1888), Lizzie L (b. 1893, TX), Barnie R. (b. 1898, TX), Robert Bernie (b. 1900, TX), Norma (b. 1903, TX), Joseph (b. 1906, OK); spouse, Cecille Williams (b. 1895, TX), married about 1912; children, Virginia (b. 1913, TX), John Arthur "Jack" (b. 1920, TX), Frances (b. 1923, TX), James Williams (b. 1931, TX). *SR; 471; Goolsby to AG, Aug 21, 1917, AGC; Stevens to Woodul, June 11, 1918, AGC; 1503:86; A1d, e, f, g; A2a, b, e; A4b, g.*

GOSSETT, JOHN WESLEY. Born Nov. 8, 1858, Somerset, Pulaski County, Kentucky. Ht. 5 ft. 10 in., blue eyes, black hair, light complexion, widower. Watchman, I&GN Railroad, Taylor, Williamson County, Texas. SPECIAL RANGER July 10, 1918–Sept. 12, 1918. REMARKS: Died Sept. 12, 1918, Williamson County, Texas. FAMILY: Parents, Joel T. Gossett (b. 1839, NC) and Salina Celina Duck (b. 1838, KY); siblings, James (b. 1859, KY), Thomas B. (b. 1862, KY), Mary M. (b. 1866, KY), Arizona Alice (b. 1867, KY), Charles (b. 1869, KY); spouse, Victoria Margaret Tarter (b. 1854, KY), married July 18, 1878, Kentucky; children, Robertus Wolford (b. 1879, KY), Marvin Howard (b. 1882, TX), Willard Homer (b. 1884, TX), Wilber P. (b. 1889, TX), Olin Thomas (b. 1895, TX). *SR; 471; Williamson to Harley, July 12, 1918, AGC; A1aa, a, d, e; A3a; A4b, g; C.*

GOUGER, ROLAND ANDY. Born Nov. 14, 1874, Floresville, Wilson County, Texas. Ht. 5 ft. 11 in., brown eyes, black hair, dark complexion, married. Ranchman, Asherton, La Salle County, Texas. SPECIAL RANGER July 15, 1918–Jan. 15, 1919. Stockman, Asherton. REGULAR RANGER Dec. 12, 1919–Feb. 10, 1921 (private, Co. C). Discharged. REMARKS: In 1900 was a druggist living in Atascosa County, Texas. Was deputy sheriff, Atascosa County. In Sept. 1918 was an agent for the Gulf Refining Company, lived in Cotulla, La Salle County. Was mayor, Cotulla, La Salle County. Had been a game warden. In 1930 was a produce dealer in Robstown, Nueces County, Texas. R. A. Gougher died Nov. 26, 1932, Nueces County, Texas. FAMILY: Parents, John Albritten Gougher (b. 1848, AR) and Martha Butler (b. 1850, TX); sister, Pocahontas J. (b. 1880, TX); spouse, Ruby B. (b. 1882, TX), married about 1901; children, Mollie (b. 1902, TX), Roland A., Jr. (b. 1907, TX), Louise (b. 1909, TX). *SR; 471; A1d, e, g; A3a; A4b; C.*

GRAHAM, HOSEA JOE or JOSEPH. Born Mar. 25, 1887, Magdalena, Socorro County, New Mexico. Medium height, medium build, light brown eyes, light brown hair. Cowboy. REGULAR RANGER Apr. 16, 1918–June 1, 1918 (private, Co. N—Hudspeth Scouts). Resigned. REMARKS: Enlistment form has Apr. 24, 1918 as date of enlistment; warrant of authority is dated Apr. 16, 1918. In June 1917 was a U.S. government scout living in Sierra Blanca, Hudspeth County, Texas. In 1930 was a farmer in El Paso County, Texas. FAMILY: Parents, John or Abraham Gerden

Graham (b. 1851, TX or SC) and Tibitha Cox (b. 1860, TX); siblings, Henry Cox (b. 1882, NM), Belle (b. 1885, NM), Abraham (b. 1886, NM), August Keene (b. 1893, NM), Tabitha B. (b. 1895, NM), Jessie Jane (b. 1898, NM); spouse, Mary E. Sheridan (b. 1869, LA), married about 1922. *SR; A1g; A3a; A4A, b, c, g; B1.*

GRAHAM, JOHN ALLEN. Born Feb. 25, 1892, Bandera County, Texas. Ht. 6 ft., blue eyes, light brown hair, light complexion, married. Farmer and stock raiser, enlisted in Hidalgo County, Texas. REGULAR RANGER Jan. 19, 1918–June 1918 (private, Co. G). Resigned. REMARKS: Had been a farmer in Tarpley, Bandera County. In 1920 and 1930 was a farmer in Medina County, Texas. Died June 21, 1957, Edwards County, Texas. FAMILY: Parents, Allen Graham (b. 1869, TX) and Della Olivia Kelley (b. 1872, TX); siblings, Claude Murray (b. 1890, TX), Archie Jackson (b. 1895, TX); spouse, Lena Olga Marquis (b. 1892, TX), married about 1915; children, Evelyn (b. 1917, TX), Elva (b. 1923, TX), Johnnie (b. 1926, TX), Allen Archie (b. 1928, TX), Robert Gene (b. 1932, TX). *SR; Stevens to Woodul, June 11, 1918, AGC; A1d, e, f, g; A2b, e; A3a; A4b, g.*

GRAHAM, JOSEPH MARTIN "JOE." Born June 11, 1872, Files Valley, Hill County, Texas. Ht. 5 ft. 8 in., gray eyes, brown hair, light complexion, married. Rancher, Del Rio, Val Verde County, Texas. SPECIAL RANGER Dec. 27, 1917–Jan. 15, 1919. REMARKS: Lived in Del Rio and ranched in Brewster County, Texas—owned the Rocilla Ranch near Marathon. Died July 4, 1963, Brewster County, Texas; buried in Marfa, Presidio County, Texas. FAMILY: Parents, Joseph E. Graham (b. 1832, KY) and Carolyn Ann Files (b. 1839, TX); siblings, Chicora Carolyn "Cora" (b. 1866, TX), Oscar Henry (b. 1869, TX), William Drew (b. 1872); spouse, Molly Elvira Stanley (b. 1872, TX), married Dec. 29, 1898; children, Frank Files (b. 1899, TX), Joe Stanley (b. 1902, TX), William David (b. 1905, TX), Carolyn Duchess "Carrie" (b. 1907, TX), Chickora B. (b. 1909, TX), Mae (b. 1912, TX), Jeff (b. 1915, TX), Lara (b. 1917, TX), Nina Alice (b. 1919, TX). *SR; A1a, e, f, g; A2b; A4b; B1.*

GRAHAM, WADE BARNES. Born Sept. 25, 1882, Palestine, Anderson County, Texas. Tall, slender, hazel eyes, black hair, married. Foreman for a boilermaking plant, Palestine. LOYALTY RANGER June 4, 1918–Feb. 1919. REMARKS: World War I Draft Registration document states "left eye out." In 1920 was a railroad workman; in 1930 was a railroad master mechanic, lived in Palestine. Died Sept. 23, 1956, Palestine, Anderson County, Texas. FAMILY: Parents, John Lydell Graham (b. 1857, AL or TX) and Mary Elizabeth Wade (b. 1862, LA); sisters, Laura May (b. 1885, TX), Marian C. "Totsy" (b. 1892, TX); stepfather, Joe E. Bietey (b. 1862, LA); spouse #1, Carrie May Moon (b. 1884), married about 1905, she died in Feb. 1907; son, Charles Lydell (b. 1905, TX); spouse #2, Margaret "Maggie" Campbell (b. 1887, LA), married Dec. 16, 1910, Louisiana; daughters, Mary Elizabeth (b. 1911, LA), Sarah Margaret (b. 1914, LA), twins Lois Cecelia and Lorretta Catherine (b. 1915, LA). *SR; A1b, d, e, f, g; A2b; A3a; A4a, b; B1.*

GRANTHAM, RODNEY GUY. Born July 20, 1873, Arkansas. Ht. 5 ft. 9 ½ in., blue eyes, sandy hair, red complexion. Brand inspector, Cattle Raisers' Association of Texas, Farwell, Parmer County, Texas. SPECIAL RANGER Sept. 21, 1918–June 16, 1919. Discharged. REMARKS: In 1880 lived in Bearhouse, Ashley County, Arkansas. In Oct. 1918 was classified as a REGULAR RANGER without pay, to avoid the draft. In 1920 was a general farmer in Kent County, Texas; in 1930 was a stock farmer in Big Lake, Reagan County, Texas. Died Feb. 27, 1948, Tom Green County, Texas. LAW ENFORCEMENT RELATIVES: Scurry County, Texas "county officer" (1900) Alonzo J. Grantham, brother. FAMILY: Parents, James Perstell Grantham (b. 1840, AL) and Lucretia Jane Sirmon (b. 1836, AL); siblings, Walter Joseph (b. 1861, AR), Alonzo James (b. 1864, AR), Luther DeWitt (b. 1867, AR), Francis Asbury (b. 1869), Florence Inez (b. 1871, AR), Lucy Obera (b. 1875, AR), Roscoe Cornelius (b. 1878), Hunter Simon (b. 1888); spouse #1, Addie Marie Duncan (b. 1881, TX), married Jan. 4, 1911, Post, Garza County, Texas; daughter, Cordelia (b. 1911, TX); spouse #2, Irene (b. 1880, TX), married about 1920; stepdaughters, Florence Elkins (b. 1902, TX), Kindred Elkins (b. 1904, TX), Frances Elkins (b. 1908, TX). *SR; Moses & Rowe to Harley, Sept 13, 1918, AGC; Johnston to Townes, Oct 28, 1918, AGC; A1a, b, d, e, f, g; A2b, e; A3a; A4b, g; B1.*

GRAVIS, CHARLES KEARNEY. Born Mar. 4, 1870, Corpus Christi, Nueces County, Texas. No physical description, married. Stockman, San Diego, Duval County,

Texas. LOYALTY RANGER Aug. 31, 1918–Feb. 19, 1919. REMARKS: Duval County sheriff Nov. 6, 1906–Feb. 1907, when he resigned. Rancher, Duval County, 1912. In 1912 was involved in a big political shootout with Mexicans, killed three. Letterhead in 1919: "Gravis Bros., Cattle Dealers, C. K. Gravis, W. C. Gravis, San Diego." Died Mar. 31, 1951, San Diego, Duval County, Texas. FAMILY: Parents, Francis Cooley Gravis (b. 1837, TX) and Elizabeth A. Doyle (b. 1841, GA); siblings, Henry (b. 1869), Irene Elizabeth (b. 1872, TX), James Collins (b. 1874, TX), Walter Corbet (b. 1877, TX); spouse, Jimmie Wright (b. 1878, TX), married Apr. 20, 1897, Beaumont, Jefferson County, Texas; children, Elizabeth Lelia (b. 1898, TX), Frank James (b. 1903, TX), Charles Kearney (b. 1904, TX). *SR; 1503:163; BDH, May 20, 1912; LWT, May 19, 26, June 16, 1912, Apr 19, 1914; A1a, b, d, e, f; A2b, c; A4a, g.*

GRAY, CHARLES NATHAN. Born Mar. 4, 1885, Mount Vernon, Lawrence County, Missouri. Ht. 5 ft. 8 in., blue eyes, brown hair, fair complexion, married. Railroad agent, Gulf Coast Lines, Kingsville, Kleberg County, Texas. SPECIAL RANGER May 21, 1918–Jan. 15, 1919. In Sept. 1918 was living in Dallas, Dallas County, Texas. Died Sept. 29, 1947, Dallas, Dallas County, Texas; buried in Restland Cemetery, Dallas. FAMILY: Parents, Seaman or Simpson David Gray (b. 1853, IL) and Eliza Jane Hickman (b. 1856, GA); siblings, Elmer E. (b. 1878, MO), Nellie (b. 1886, MO), Jewell (b. 1891, MO); spouse #1, Luella or Luelvia "Evelyn" Roberts (b. 1886, TX), married about 1910; sons, Nathan (b. 1912, TX), Gereling (b. 1916, TX); spouse #2, Ethel Venus Keith (b. 1896, IL), married Nov. 25, 1943. *SR; Acting AG to Gray, May 11, 1918, AGC; A1d, e, f; A2b; A3a; A4b.*

GRAY, GEORGE WASHINGTON. Born Feb. 1, 1866, Troy, Bell County, Texas. Ht. 5 ft. 10 in., blue eyes, gray hair, light complexion, married. Lumberman, Hamlin, Jones County, Texas. SPECIAL RANGER June 2, 1917–Dec. 1917 (attached to Co. C). REMARKS: In 1900 was a clerk in a lumber yard in Mitchell County, Texas. In 1920 was manager of a lumber yard in Hamlin. Died June 19, 1927, Nolan County, Texas. FAMILY: Parents, John Alexander Gray (b. 1827, TN) and Sarah Elizabeth "Izabel" Bryan (b. 1835, TX); siblings, James Rigdon (b. 1853, TX), Thomas A. (b. 1856, TX), Sophronia Pauline (b. 1858, TX), twins Emma C. and Emma P. (b. 1859, TX), Reuben J. (b. 1862, TX), Belle Z. (b. 1865, TX), John Carroll (b. 1869, TX), Seaborn (b. 1871, TX), Ida E. (b. 1873, TX), Dora (b. 1875, TX), Benjamin Frank (b. 1879, TX); spouse, Evelyn Turner (b. 1871, KY), married about 1887; children, Alvin Willard (b. 1889, TX), Claude Burton (b. 1893, TX), George W., Jr. (b. 1899, TX), Lillian (b. 1908, TX), Anna Beth (b. 1914, TX). *SR; Dodson to Ferguson, May 18, 1917, AGC; Cunningham to Ferguson, May 18, 1917, AGC; A1a, b, d, e, f; A2b; A3a; A4b, g.*

GRAY, JAMES WILLIAM. Born May 15, 1880, Denton, Denton County, Texas. Tall, medium build, blue eyes, black hair, married. Dry goods merchant, Pilot Point, Denton County. LOYALTY RANGER May 31, 1918–Feb. 1919. REMARKS: In 1920 and 1930 was a dry goods merchant in Denton, Denton County. Died Aug. 19, 1959, Denton, Denton County, Texas. FAMILY: Parents, Charles Berry Gray (b. 1854, TX) and Mary Celeste Bonds (b. 1862, AL); siblings, Susie (b. 1878, AL), C. B., Jr. (b. 1882, TX), Walter C. (b. 1884, TX), Eliza D. (b. 1886, TX), John R. (b. 1888, TX), twins Ruth and Ruby (b. 1895, TX); spouse, Bertie Rachel Silver (b. 1888, MO), married June 10, 1909, Pilot Point; children, Silver G. (b. 1914, TX), Pauline (b. 1915, TX), Dorothy Jim (b. 1916, TX), James William "Jack" (b. 1923, TX). *SR; A1d, e, f, g; A2b, e; A3a; A4a, b, g; B2.*

GRAY, JERRY D. Born Sept. 13, 1884, Marlin, Falls County, Texas. Ht. 5 ft. 10 ½ in., blue eyes, light brown hair, ruddy complexion, married. Deputy sheriff, Temple, Bell County, Texas. REGULAR RANGER May 28, 1917–Apr. 30, 1925 (captain, Co. D; transferred as captain to Co. B, May 19, 1919; transferred as captain to Co. A—reenlisted under the new law, June 20, 1919). Resigned. Farmer, Presidio, Presidio County, Texas. SPECIAL RANGER July 25, 1925–July 25, 1927. Discharged. Ranchman, Presidio. SPECIAL RANGER Sept. 12, 1927–Sept. 12, 1928; Mar. 4, 1930–June 1, 1930 (resigned—WA expired on Jan. 1, 1931); June 14, 1932– Jan. 18, 1933 (WA expired on June 13, 1933). Discharged. REMARKS: "Branded H on left side." Sometime between 1910 and 1917 was a policeman in Temple and a Bell County constable. After leaving the Rangers he farmed in Presidio County for 27 years. LAW ENFORCEMENT RELATIVES: Ranger Jerry Cope Gray, son (was issued a SPECIAL RANGER commission on June 14, 1932, at the age of 12!). FAMILY: Spouse, Myrtle L. (b. 1892, TX), married about 1916; son, Jerry Cope (b. 1920, TX).

Texas Ranger Captain Jerry Gray. *Photo courtesy Texas Ranger Hall of Fame and Museum.*

SR; 471; Smith to Ferguson, Apr 19, 1917, AGC; Gray to Ferguson, May 11, 1917, AGC; General Orders No. 5, June 4, 1918, AGC; Hobby to Harley, May 19, 1919, WC; 1: I, 1537; 204:II, 165; 422: 95; 470: 43; A1f, g; A2e; A3a.

GRAY, JOHN M. Born Oct. 1864, East Saginaw, Saginaw County, Michigan. Ht. 5 ft. 10 in., brown eyes, dark hair, dark complexion, married. Garage owner, Del Rio, Val Verde County, Texas. SPECIAL RANGER June 21, 1918–Jan. 15, 1919 (Co. A Volunteers). REMARKS: Had been a pioneer rancher in Val Verde County. In 1910 was a grain merchant in Val Verde County. Letterhead, 1919: "Sterling Garage, John M. Gray, Prop., Buick Automobiles and Accessories, General Repairing. Firestone Tires, Tubes and Accessories, Del Rio, Texas." In 1930 was a rancher living in Georgetown, Williamson County, Texas. A John M. Gray died Oct. 29, 1933, Williamson County, Texas. FAMILY: Parents, Charles M. Gray (b. 1835, England) and Mary A. (b. 1843, England); siblings, George (b. 1863, MI), Jessie (b. 1867, MI), Guy Masse (b. 1872, MI), Samuel W. H. (b. 1875, MI), Allen T. (b. 1878, MI), Alice (b. 1885, MI); spouse, Kate R. (b. 1870, TX), married about 1889; children, Walter Charles (b. 1890, TX), Margaret (b. 1898, TX), Alma R. (b. 1905, TX). *SR; 471; A1a, b, d, e, f, g; A2b; A4b, g.*

GRAY, WALTER H. Born Sept. 1876, Bail County [*sic*], Kentucky. No physical description, married. Undertaker, Seymour, Baylor County, Texas. LOYALTY RANGER June 12, 1918–Feb. 1919. REMARKS: In 1900 was a farmer in Collin County, Texas. By 1910 was an undertaker in Seymour. In 1920 was an undertaker and also a retail furniture salesman. In 1930 still living in Seymour. FAMILY: Spouse, Mattie C. (b. 1879, TX), married about 1898; children, Herbert E. (b. 1898, TX), Nelly N. (b. 1900, TX), Frances Hesbah (b. 1902, TX), Lucille (b. 1904, TX). *SR; A1d, e, f, g.*

GRAY, WILLIAM KIRKMAN. Born July 12, 1881, Louisiana. Ht. 5 ft.10 in., blue eyes, light hair, fair complexion. Oil business, Orange, Orange County, Texas. SPECIAL RANGER Feb. 28, 1918–Jan. 15, 1919. Capitalist, Lake Charles, Louisiana. SPECIAL RANGER Apr. 23, 1930–Jan. 1, 1931; Mar. 3, 1931–Mar. 2, 1932; Jan. 28, 1933–Jan. 27, 1935 (captain). REMARKS: Note 1930–1935 rank, and residence out of state. World War I Draft Registration document (Sept. 1918) states, "Registrant has lost one leg and one arm." FAMILY: Parents, John Geddings Gray (b. 1849, MS) and Mary F. Kirkman (b. 1858, KY); siblings, John G., Jr. (b. 1888, LA), Matilda G. (b. 1889, LA); spouse, Opal Hughes (b. 1897, LA), married Apr. 22, 1922; daughter, Matilda (b. 1924, LA). *SR; A1d, f, g; A3a; A4b.*

GREEN, JOHN WILKES BOOTH "BOOTH." Born Dec. 17, 1872, Spicewood, Burnet County, Texas. Medium height, slender, light blue eyes, dark brown hair, married. Clerk for a general merchandise company, Marble Falls, Burnet County. LOYALTY RANGER June 12, 1918–Feb. 1919. REMARKS: Still a grocery salesman in Marble Falls in 1930. FAMILY: Parents, Gustavus Edward Green (b. 1844, TX) and Millicent Rebecca Fowler (b. 1849, SC); siblings, Wiley Edward (b. 1869, TX), Guy G. (b. 1871, TX), Eula Zoe

(b. 1875, TX), Gustavus (b. 1879, TX), Lannie (b. 1883, TX), Lou (b. 1885, TX); spouse, Athena Lantista "Attie" Phelan (b. 1873, TX), married Nov. 26, 1901. *SR; A1b, d, e, f, g; A3a; A4b; B1.*

GREER, DAVID C. Born Nov. 1871, Honea Path, Anderson County, South Carolina. Ht. 5 ft. 8 in., brown eyes, black hair, dark complexion, married. Farmer, Crowell, Foard County, Texas. LOYALTY RANGER July 25, 1918–Mar. 1919. REMARKS: In 1910 was a real estate agent in Crowell; in 1930 was a cotton buyer in Crowell. FAMILY: Parents, David R. Greer (b. 1840, SC) and Hester A. (b. 1843, SC); siblings, M. J. (b. 1870, SC), E. E. (b. 1874, SC), E. G. (b. 1875, SC), Roena J. (b. 1877, SC), Julie Hester (b. 1880, SC), George P. (b. 1882, SC), John H. (b. 1885, SC), Louvenia S. (b. 1887, SC); spouse, Mary Modena (b. 1874, TX), married about 1905; son, Virgil (b. 1907, TX). *SR; A1b, d, e, f, g; A2b.*

GRIFFIN, KERVY WESLEY. Born Aug. 18, 1883, Ragland, St. Clair County, Alabama. Ht. 5 ft. 10 in., gray eyes, dark hair, brunette complexion, married. Farmer, Edgewood, Van Zandt County, Texas. LOYALTY RANGER Sept. 10, 1918–Feb. 1919. REMARKS: In 1920 was an auto dealer in Van Zandt County. In 1930 was an oil company leaser living in Terrell, Kaufman County, Texas. Died Aug. 28, 1975, Kaufman County, Texas. FAMILY: Parents, William Wesley Griffin (b. 1856, GA) and Sarah Emily Black (b. 1856, GA); siblings, Lucy E. (b. 1879, AL), David H. (b. 1881, AL), William O. (b. 1886, AL), Mattie J. (b. 1888, AL), Ennis E. (b. 1891, AL), Hettie Lee (b. 1893, AL); spouse, Tommie J. Owens (b. 1892, TX), married Sept. 29, 1907; son, Leon W. (b. 1912, TX). *SR; A1d, e, f, g; A2a, b; A4a, b.*

GRIFFIN, RAY. Born Jan. 19, 1888, Luling, Caldwell County, Texas. Ht. 6 ft., blue eyes, sandy hair, light complexion. Watchman, I&GN Railroad, Austin, Travis County, Texas. SPECIAL RANGER Sept. 2, 1916–Dec. 1917; May 17, 1918–Jan. 15, 1919. REMARKS: Had been an ordinary seaman in the U.S Navy for 2 years. *SR; Morris to Hutchings, Sept 2, 1917, AGC; A3a.*

GRIFFITTS, HOMER WILKINS. Born June 20, 1893, Austin, Travis County, Texas. Ht. 5 ft. 10 ½ in., brown eyes, brown hair, light complexion. Auditor, Austin, Travis County. SPECIAL RANGER Sept. 4, 1915–unknown (attached to Co. C). Auditor, Austin. REGULAR RANGER Dec. 21, 1917–unknown (unassigned; still in the Rangers as of Jan. 9, 1918). Discharged or resigned—unknown. REMARKS: In 1918 was classified as a REGULAR RANGER without pay. In 1918 was a clerk and in 1920 was a quartermaster in the Adjutant General's office, Austin. In 1930 was a real estate agent in Austin. Died July 6, 1958, Travis County, Texas. FAMILY: Parents, D. A. Griffitts (b. 1861, TN) and Lena S. (b. 1868, TX); sisters, Lula H. (b. 1887, TX), Hattie R. (b. 1889, TX), Norma (b. 1891, TX); spouse, Vivian (b. 1895, TX), married about 1917; daughters, Lena Elizabeth (b. 1919, TX), Sybil Enid (b. 1921, TX). *SR; 471; Acting AG to GC&SF Railroad, Jan 9, 1918, AGC; A1d, e, f, g; A2b, e; A3a.*

GRIMES, JAMES F. "FRANK." Born Oct. 13, 1891, Pendleton, Bell County, Texas. Ht. 6 ft. 2 ½ in., blue eyes, brown hair, light complexion, married. Journalist, Abilene, Taylor County, Texas. SPECIAL RANGER June 9, 1917–Sept. 13, 1917 (attached to Co. C). Honorably discharged. REMARKS: Corporal in the Texas National Guard for 6 years. In 1910 had been a weekly newspaper printer in Rodgers, Bell County. By 1918 was a journalist for the *Abilene Daily Reporter*. In 1930 was a newspaper editor, living in Abilene. A Frank Grimes died July 28, 1961, Abilene, Taylor County, Texas. FAMILY: Parents, Lewis Gault Grimes (b. 1846, TN) and Xantha Rosalie "Xanthie" Wooten (b. 1851, AL); siblings, Marcus E. (b. 1871, TN), Robert A. (b. 1877, TN), Willie H. (b. 1881, TN), Lee M. (b. 1883, TN), Lula B. (b. 1885, TX), Louis A. (b. 1887, TX), Marvin Leslie (b. 1889, TX), Bishop E. (b. 1894, TX); spouse, Mary E. (b. 1890, TX), married about 1917; children, Rudyard Kipling (b. 1917, TX), Mary Xantha (b. 1923), Francis (b. 1926, TX). *SR; Register to Ferguson, May 18, 1917, AGC; Cunningham to Ferguson, May 18, 1917, AGC; 172:III, 341–342; A1d, e, f, g; A2b, e; A3a; A4g.*

GRIMES, JAMES JESSE. Born Feb. 24, 1853, Bell County, Texas. Ht. 5 ft. 7 in., blue eyes, dark hair, fair complexion, married. Retired farmer, Bronte, Coke County, Texas. LOYALTY RANGER May 31, 1918–Feb. 1919. REMARKS: Deputy sheriff in Bell, Lampasas, and Coryell Counties for several years. In 1920 lived in Winters, Runnells County, Texas. FAMILY: Parents, James Alexander Grimes (b. 1824, TN) and Edna Angelina Beene (b. 1828, TN); siblings, twins

Mary E. "Lizzie" and Nancy J. "Nannie" (b. 1848, TX), J. Frank (b. 1850, TX), John Alexander (b. 1855, TX), Cora Permelia (b. 1858, TX), Robert Allen (b. 1862), Thomas L. (b. 1870); spouse, Lucy E. Bland (b. 1856, AR), married about 1872; children, Alice E. (b. 1874, TX), Annie Laura (b. 1876, TX), Frank A. (b. 1878, TX), Minnie B. (b. 1880, TX), Vida V. (b. 1885, TX), Jessie E. (b. 1887, TX), Bessie M. (b. 1888, TX), Robert Leslie (b. 1890, TX), Raymond Calvin (b. 1892, TX). *SR; A1aaa, aa, b, d, e, f; A4a, g; B1, 2.*

GRIMES, WILLIAM THOMAS "TOM." Born June 17, 1878, Bastrop, Bastrop County, Texas. Ht. 5 ft. 10 in., dark eyes, brown hair, dark complexion. Deputy sheriff, Bastrop County, 1912–1913. REGULAR RANGER Mar. 8, 1913–May 15, 1918 (private, Co. B; promoted to sergeant, Co. B, May 1, 1914; transferred to Co. A as sergeant, Mar. 8, 1915; reenlisted Mar. 10, 1917). Resigned to become a city detective in Port Arthur, Jefferson County, Texas, for better pay. REMARKS: On Dec. 31, 1917 applied for promotion to Ranger captain. In 1920 was a stockman on the Barfield Ranch, Live Oak County, Texas. A William Thomas Grimes died July 29, 1936, Jim Wells County, Texas. LAW ENFORCEMENT RELATIVES: Port Arthur chief of city detectives (1918) Roy Grimes, brother. FAMILY: Parents, William Henry Grimes (b. 1848, TX) and Mattie Bell Clark (b. 1854, MS); siblings, Robert Henry (b. 1875, TX), Ada Inez (b. 1877, TX), Roy (b. 1880, TX), Ethel Louise (b. 1882, TX), Willie Belle (b. 1890, TX); spouse, Nell (b. 1896, TX), married before Sept. 1918. *SR; 471; MR, Co. B, Mar–July 1914, AGC; Jenkins to Ferguson, Apr 17, 1917, AGC; Jones to Ferguson, Apr 17, 1917, AGC; Scarborough to Ferguson, Apr 15, 1917, AGC; Yturria to Ferguson, Apr 27, 1917, AGC; AG to Yturria, May 2, 1917, AGC; Wright to Ferguson, Apr 25, 1917, AGC; Hanson to Ferguson, Apr 19, 1917, AGC; Wood to Ferguson, May 21, 1917, AGC; Grimes to Hobby, Dec 31, 1917, AGC; Governor to Grimes, Jan 9, 1918, AGC; Grimes to Cope, Jan 12, 1918, AGC; Grimes to Cardwell, May 19, 1918, AGC; Grimes to Sanders, May 13, 1918, AGC; Garner to Hobby, Sept 28, 1918, AGC; A1b, d, e, f; A3a; A4a, b; C.*

GRISHAM, WILLIAM JACKSON. Born Dec. 9, 1872, Booneville, Prentiss County, Mississippi. Medium height, medium build, blue eyes, light brown hair, married. Oil and lease business, Wichita Falls, Wichita County, Texas. LOYALTY RANGER May 31, 1918–Feb. 1919. REMARKS: Had been a dry goods salesman in Decatur, Wise County, Texas and in Altus, Jackson County, Oklahoma. In September 1918 was a real estate agent in Wichita Falls. In 1930 was a crude oil producer, Wichita Falls. Died Feb. 19, 1952, Wichita Falls, Wichita County, Texas. FAMILY: Parents, Isaac C. Grisham (b. 1836, TN) and Elliott Jane "Sallie" Howard (b. 1837, SC); siblings, Alice (b. 1863, MS), Mittie V. E. (b. 1866, MS), Sarah E. (b. 1868, MS), Katie G. (b. 1870, MS), M. H. (b. 1876, MS), H. Thomas (b. 1877, MS), Oscar (b. 1879, MS), Minnie T. (b. 1881, MS); spouse #1, Lillie L. Woody (b. 1880, TX), married about 1898; children, Lillie D. (b. 1899, TX), Vaughn Isaac (b. 1901, TX); spouse #2, Callie Elizabeth Sweeton (b. 1883, TX), married about 1906; daughters, Helen E. (b. 1907, OK), Ruth S. (b. 1918, TX). *SR; A1b, d, e, f, g; A2b; A3a; A4a, b, g.*

GROSS, ABRAHAM J. "ABE." Born June 23, 1877, Washington County, Texas. Ht. 5 ft. 9 in., brown eyes, black hair, fair complexion. Lawyer, Waco, McLennan County, Texas. SPECIAL RANGER Nov. 29, 1917–Dec. 1917. REMARKS: As a small boy had lived in Lampasas, Lampasas County, Texas. Was a cashier in a dry goods store in Waco in 1900. In Jan. 1918 the AG wanted him to enlist as a Regular Ranger. An Abe Gross died July 19, 1944, McLennan County, Texas. FAMILY: Parents, Hymann L. Groos or Gross (b. 1846, Poland) and Rosa H. (b. 1856, NY); siblings, Benjamin G. (b. 1871, NY), Esther (b. 1874, TX), Violet L. (b. 1879, TX), Blanche (b. 1883, TX), Sarah (b. 1887, TX). *SR; Acting AG to Gross, Jan 9, 1918, AGC; A1b, d, e; A3a; C.*

GROVER, JAMES EDWARD. Born Nov. 1889, Victoria County, Texas. Ht. 5 ft. 10 in., gray eyes, black hair, dark complexion, married. Stockman, Austin, Travis County, Texas. REGULAR RANGER June 17, 1919–Oct. 16, 1919 (private, Co. D; transferred to Co. E on an unknown date). Discharged/fired by Capt. Anders for disobeying orders. REMARKS: Grover said he resigned because of his family's health; returned to San Antonio, Bexar County, Texas. In Aug. 1920 was a traveling salesman in East Texas, e.g. Greenville, Hunt County, Texas. FAMILY: Spouse, Evelyn Person (b. 1888, TX); children, Jessie Leslie (b. 1915, TX), Dorothy Evelyn (b. 1916, TX), James Edward (b. 1918, TX), Nell (b. 1920, TX). *SR; 471; Grover to Aldrich, Aug 25, 1920, AGC; A1f; A4a, b.*

GUILFORD, HENRY BOYD "BOYD." Born July 28, 1895, Oakville, Live Oak County, Texas. Ht. 5 ft. 9 ½ in., brown eyes, light brown hair, red complexion, married. Ranchman, Alta Vista, Jim Hogg County, Texas. SPECIAL RANGER Mar. 16, 1918–Jan. 15, 1919. Ranchman, Hebbronville, Jim Hogg County. SPECIAL RANGER Mar. 4, 1930–Jan. 1, 1931. Discharged/WA expired. REMARKS: As a young teen lived in Nueces County, Texas. As of June 1917 was a deputy sheriff in Jim Hogg County. Was enlisted in 1930 at the request of Attorney General Bobbitt. Died June 4, 1950, Jim Hogg County, Texas. FAMILY: Parents, unknown Guilford (b. GA) and Vashti Bathsheba "Bashie" Wright (b. 1874, TX); sister, Hellen A. (b. 1892, TX); stepfather, Reuben R. Holbein (b. 1876, TX); half-siblings, Ray (b. 1902, TX), twins Reuben and Robert (b. 1904, TX), Lorene (b. 1908, TX); spouse, Kallula Fly (b. 1894, TX), married Dec. 19, 1913, Oakville; children, Kallulu Fly (b. 1919, TX), Henry Boyd, Jr. (b. 1923, TX), Reuben Dalton (b. 1926, TX). *SR; A1d, e, g; A2b, e; A3a; A4b; B1.*

GUILLEMETTE, LOUIS. Born Sept. 6, 1888, Calvados, France. Ht. 5 ft. 5 in., brown eyes, light brown hair, ruddy complexion, married. Special agent, GH&SA Railroad (SP), San Antonio, Bexar County, Texas. SPECIAL RANGER July 29, 1918–Jan. 15, 1919. REMARKS: Immigrated to the United States 1905; became a naturalized citizen before 1917. In 1910 had been a private in the U.S. Army stationed at Fort Sheridan Military Reservation, Deerfield, Lake County, Illinois. Served two enlistments in the cavalry, was discharged June 1915. Deputy sheriff, Bexar County, 1916–1918. His Bexar County deputy sheriff's commission (1916–1918) was evidently in connection with his work as a railroad special agent. In 1920 was a special officer living in Galveston County, Texas. One source says he died in June 1928, Bexar County, Texas. FAMILY: Spouse, Sarah Martinez (b. 1898, TX), children, Louis, Jr. (b. 1915, TX), Alice Sarah (b. 1917, TX), Blanche (b. 1919, TX). *SR; AG to Guillemette, July 19, 26, 1918, AGC; Guillemete to Harley, July 29, 1918, AGC; A1e, f, g; A2e; A3a; A4a.*

GUNN, ELMER GARFIELD. Born July 14, 1889, Pine Bluff, Jefferson County, Arkansas. Ht. 6 ft. 1 in., gray eyes, red hair, light complexion, married. Lawyer, Yoakum, Lavaca County, Texas. LOYALTY RANGER May 31, 1918–Feb. 1919. REMARKS: In 1920 was a lawyer in Waco, McLennan County, Texas; in 1930 lived in Lubbock, Lubbock County, Texas. Died Nov. 27, 1962, Madisonville, Madison County, Texas. FAMILY: Parents, Albert Alexander Gunn (b. 1866, AR) and Epsy Louvania Bush (b. 1867, AR); siblings, James Clarence (b. 1887, AR), Minnie Ola (b. 1891, TX), Tommy Pearl (b. 1893, TX), Otho Randolph (b. 1896, TX); stepmother, Louisa H. "Lucy" Ray (b. 1875, GA); spouse, Hazel Willie Hill (b. 1890, TX), married Apr. 29, 1913, Bellville, Austin County, Texas; children, Stanley Elmer (b. 1914, TX), Beverly Mae (b. 1917, TX), Hazel Willie (b. 1919, TX), Louie Hamilton (b. 1921, TX). *SR; A1d, f, g; A2a, b; A3a; A4a, b, g.*

GUSTAFSON, OSCAR FRANKLIN. Born Aug. 8, 1869, Sweden. Ht. 5 ft. 10 in., blue eyes, light hair, light complexion, married. Brand inspector, Cattle Raisers' Association of Texas, Munday, Knox County, Texas. SPECIAL RANGER July 25, 1918–Jan. 15, 1919. REMARKS: Immigrated to the United States in 1883; became a naturalized citizen by 1910. Cowboy for years for the Swenson brothers on their ranches. In 1900 lived in Jones County, Texas; in 1910 lived in Throckmorton County, Texas. In 1920 was a cattle inspector living in Stamford, Jones County. Died Dec. 14, 1947, Jones County, Texas. FAMILY: Spouse, Lydia Jane Breland (b. 1881, TX), married July 14, 1895; children, Loris or Lewie Alfred (b. 1896, TX), Elmer O. (b. 1901, TX), Rayford B. (b. 1903, TX), Ira D. (b. 1911, TX), Mary V. (b. 1913, TX). *SR; Moses & Rowe to Harley, July 19, Sept 13, 1918, AGC; Harley to Moses & Rowe, July 22, 1918, AGC; A1d, e, f; A3a; B1.*

GUYNES, WILLIAM PATTERSON, JR. Born May 22, 1889, Kaufman County, Texas. Short, medium build, brown eyes, dark hair, married. Farmer. SPECIAL RANGER Dec. 12, 1917–Jan. 15, 1919. REMARKS: In June 1917 was a clerk in a dry goods store in Crandall, Kaufman County. In 1930 was a public weigher in a cotton yard in Kaufman County. Died May 31, 1961, Kaufman County, Texas; buried in Crandall City Cemetery. FAMILY: Parents, William Patterson Guynes (b. 1857, MS) and Martha O. "Mattie" Kelly (b. 1862, AL); siblings, Ruth A. (b. 1879, TX), Norvel Milington (b. 1881, TX), Henry (b. 1882), John Oscar (b. 1887, TX), Cara Bell (b. 1889), Harvey G. (b. 1891, TX), Peter Ellis (b. 1893, TX), Guy (b. 1895, TX), Ewell (b. 1901, TX); spouse, Ruth Norton (b. 1894, TN), married about 1916. *SR; A1d, e, f, g; A2b; A3a; A4b.*

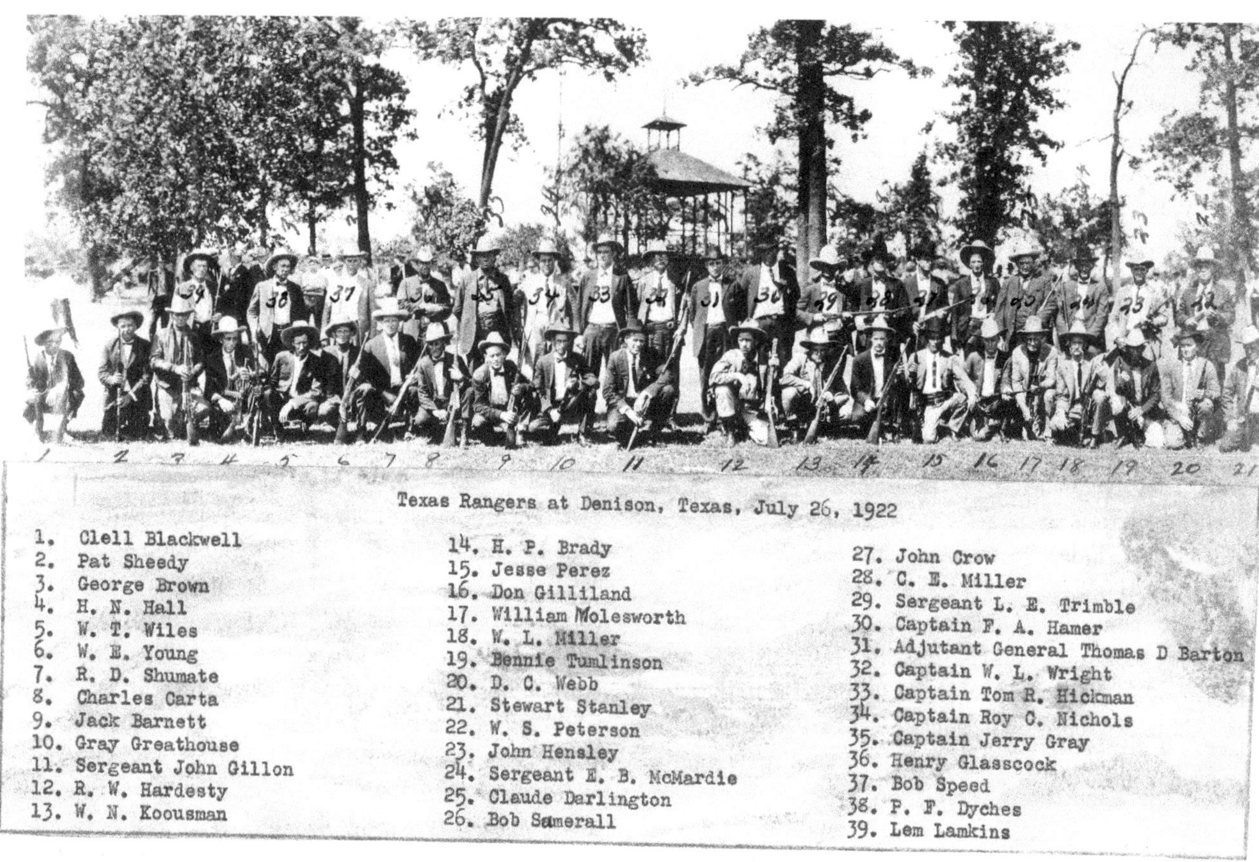

Photo courtesy Texas Ranger Hall of Fame and Museum.

Captain Tom Ross and his Company B. Seated left to right: Private James Lovett Seale, Private W. F. Sallis, Private Charles P. Middleton and Private Brown (no further identification). Standing left to right: Captain Ross and Private Roscoe Redus. *Photo courtesy Texas Ranger Hall of Fame and Museum.*

Captain Jerry Gray's Company A in the Big Bend in 1918. Captain Gray is second from left (with a holstered pistol on his saddle). Left to right, Ranger Arthur Miles, Captain Gray, Rangers Charles Hagler, Dewitt T. "Bug" Barnett, Jack Murdock, Sam Neill, A. G. Beard, Mark Langford, Frank Hillbolt, Dee Cox, Harold King, N. N. Fuller, Frank Crittenden, A. H. Woelber, and Bill Shurman. *Photo courtesy Texas Ranger Hall of Fame and Museum.*

Headquarters Company in Austin in 1919. Standing left to right: Rangers Frank Matthews, George Millard, C. J. Blackwell, J. R. Hunnicutt and Samuel Clay Blackwell. Second row left to right: Private John R. McMillan, Texas National Guard Colonel H. C. Smith, Senior Texas Ranger Captain William Martin Hanson and Sergeant Joe Brooks. In front sitting on the ground: Ranger S. O. Durst. *Photo courtesy Texas Ranger Hall of Fame and Museum.*

Captain John Sanders's Company A served as nightwatchmen for the giant King Ranch in the late summer and early fall of 1915 following the Norias Raid. Lined up at the Norias subheadquarters of the King Ranch left to right are Rangers George B. Hurst, C. J. Hanson, C. W. Price, Ben T. Tumlinson, Earl R. Wright, John A. Moran, John E. Hensley, Daniel Hinojosa, W. E. Holmes, Leonard Walker, Elmo D. Reid, W. Alonzo Taylor and Captain Sanders. *Photo courtesy Texas Ranger Hall of Fame and Museum.*

Company E Texas Rangers. *Photo courtesy Texas Ranger Hall of Fame and Museum.*

Texas Rangers East Texas 1923. *Photo courtesy Texas Ranger Hall of Fame and Museum.*

Company A, Texas Rangers was based in the lower Rio Grande Valley when this photograph was taken. Left to right: unidentified, unidentified, Ranger William J. McCauley, Captain Frank Johnson, Ranger Crosby Marsden, Ranger Oscar Rountree and Ranger Gus T. "Buster" Jones. *Photo courtesy Texas Ranger Hall of Fame and Museum.*

Company A lined up for the photographer. Kneeling left to right: Captain Joe Brooks, Sergeant Charles J. Blackwell, William E. Powers, S. O. Durst. Standing left to right: Frank Matthews, Jim Martin, Harrison Hamer and Tom Hickman. *Photo courtesy Texas Ranger Hall of Fame and Museum.*

Company B, Texas Rangers in Amarillo in 1909. Left to right: Ranger W. F. Sallis, Ranger C. P. Middleton, Ranger A. W. Brown; Ranger Captain Tom Ross, Sergeant Roscoe Redus and Ranger James L. Seale. *Photo courtesy Texas Ranger Hall of Fame and Museum.*

Company D was always willing to line up for pictures. Kneeling left to right: Sergeant Light Townsend, Captain W. L. Wright, Tom Brady and Webb County Deputy Sheriff W. B. Wright. Standing left to right are Rangers John E. Hensley, Dan Coleman, W. S. Peterson, unidentified, unidentified and John Sadler. *Photo courtesy Texas Ranger Hall of Fame and Museum.*

Five Texas Rangers pose on horseback on the giant King Ranch in front of the Norias subheadquarters, target of the Plan de San Diego raiders in August, 1915. Left to right are Rangers Howard C. Cragg, Ira J. Heard, Sam P. Chessher, Joe B. Brooks and Loyd A. David. *Photo courtesy Texas Ranger Hall of Fame and Museum.*

A Famous Ranger Photograph. This picture was taken in the Big Bend in the early 1920s and appeared in Walter Prescott Webb's classic history of the Rangers. One reason Webb chose this picture was the man who is second from the right. Ranger Arch Miller had only one arm. His other one had been amputated. However, as one observer put it, Miller was a whole lot better than some two armed Rangers. Left to right are Pete Crawford, a Texas game warden; Ray Miller (Arch Miller's brother); John Poole, Arch Miller, and Steve Bernett, justice of the peace. *Photo courtesy Texas Ranger Hall of Fame and Museum.*

Four members of Company A pose cradling their Model 1895 box magazine Winchester carbines. Left to right: Captain Joe Brooks, Sergeant Charles Blackwell, and Privates Tom Hickman and S. O. Durst. *Photo courtesy Texas Ranger Hall of Fame and Museum.*

Company D, Texas Rangers shown after seizing 3,000 quarts of tequila loaded on 37 horses in Duval County, Texas. The tequila had been brought across the Rio Grande from Mexico. Left to right: Customs Inspector Frank Smith, Ranger Herbert Brady, Ranger John J. Edds, Ranger D. C. Webb, Ranger Juan C. Gonzales, unidentified, unidentified, Ranger Captain William L. Wright. *Photo Courtesy Roy Wilkinson Aldrich Papers, Dolph Briscoe Center for American History, University of Texas at Austin.*

Four members of Company E, Texas Rangers at the Galveston Dock Strike of 1920. Left to right: Ranger Captain Roy Aldrich, Ranger Frank Black, Ranger Captain Charles Blackwell and Ranger W. W. "Bill" Molesworth. *Photo courtesy Roy Wilkinson Aldrich Papers, Dolph Briscoe Center for American History, University of Texas at Austin.*

Four members of Company E in 1918 pose on what appears to be the north bank of the Rio Grande. Left to right are Charlie Carta, Henry Glasscock, Dee Perkins and Captain W. L. Barler.
Photo courtesy Texas Ranger Hall of Fame and Museum

In 1921 a dock strike in Galveston paralyzed the port. Virtually the entire Ranger force was sent there to keep the peace. One of the companies was Captain Joe Brooks's contingent. Seated left to right are W. M. Molesworth, Sergeant Ed McCarthy, Jr., Captain Joe Brooks, J. M. Rooney, Benjamin T. Tumlinson, Jr. Standing left to right are J. W. Milam, D. W. Cox, T. T. Hawkins, John Bargsley, T. J. Cole, Claude Darlington and J. T. Martin. *Photo courtesy Texas Ranger Hall of Fame and Museum.*

Captain Will Wright's Company D at the Indian Crossing on the Rio Grande. Left to right: Captain Wright, Ranger Dan Coleman, Ranger Bill Dial, Ranger Tom Brady, Ranger John Sadler and Ranger Warren Smith. *Photo courtesy Captain M. T. Gonzaullas Collection, Texas Ranger Hall of Fame and Museum.*

HABY, JOHN WILLIAM "BILL." Born May 17, 1872, Castroville, Medina County, Texas. Ht. 5 ft. 7 in., brown eyes, dark hair, light complexion, married. Ranchman, Rio Frio, Real County, Texas. LOYALTY RANGER Aug. 29, 1918–Feb. 1919. REMARKS: In 1900 and 1910 was a cattle rancher living in Bandera County, Texas. In 1920 had a stock farm in Real County, Texas. Died Feb. 1, 1948, Leakey, Real County, Texas; buried in Leakey. FAMILY: Parents, Ambrose Haby (b. 1836, Germany) and Christina Beck (b. 1839, Germany); siblings, Ambrose (b. 1856, TX), Joseph (b. 1858, TX), Louis (b. 1859, TX), Mary (b. 1861, TX), Clothilda Christina (b. 1866, TX), Alois (b. 1868, TX), Amalia (b. 1869, TX), Mary Rosa (b. 1873, TX), Nicolas (b. 1875, TX), Mary Ida (b. 1876, TX), Alfred Alex (b. 1877, TX), Mary Pauline (b. 1879, TX); spouse, Monica Mamie Cooney McFadden (b. 1874, TX), married Jan. 21, 1896, Medina County; children, Bertha Louise "Bessie" (b. 1896, TX), Joseph Lee (b. 1898, TX), Maida (b. 1901, TX), Arnett A. (b. 1910, TX), Genevieve (b. 1916, TX). *SR; A1aa, a, b, d, e, f, g; A2b; A4a, b; B1.*

HAGLER, CHARLES HENRY. Born Mar. 17, 1895, Dallas County, Texas. Ht. 5 ft. 8 in., brown eyes, brown hair, fair complexion. Farmer. REGULAR RANGER June 5, 1918–Apr. 10, 1919 (private, Co. F). Resigned. REMARKS: In June, 1917 was a farmer living in Sherman, Grayson County, Texas. In 1920 was an oil field teamster in Grayson County. In 1930 was a barber shop proprietor in Sherman. Died Dec. 31, 1967, Dallas County, Texas; buried in Edgewood cemetery, Dallas, Dallas County. FAMILY: Parents, James Marion Hagler (b. 1856, MO) and Ella "Nellie" Payne (b. 1858, MO); siblings, Frederick L. (b. 1884, TX), Myrtle (b. 1886, TX), Bessie M. (b. 1889, TX), Marion "Mary" (b. 1892, TX), Estella Ora (b. 1893, TX), Nellie P. (b. 1897, TX); spouse, Myrtie (b. 1893, AL), married about 1923. *SR; 471; A1d, e, f, g; A2a, b; A3a; A4b, g; B1.*

HALE, CHARLES LEWIS. Born Feb. 4, 1883, Flatonia, Fayette County, Texas. Ht. 6 ft., blue eyes, brown hair. Peace officer, Karnes City, Karnes County, Texas. REGULAR RANGER Sept. 29, 1910–Feb. 1, 1911 (private, Co. B). Honorably discharged—reduction in force. REMARKS: In 1918 was a farmer in Bee County, Texas. In 1920 was a service car chauffer, living in Beeville, Bee County. In 1930 was an oil field truck driver in Bee County. A Charles Lewis Hale, Sr. shot and killed Ed Willoghby at the Pettus, Bee County, Texas racetrack. Charlie Lewis Hale died July 16, 1941, Nueces County, Texas. LAW ENFORCEMENT RELATIVES: Ranger Wiley Duff Hale, cousin. FAMILY: Parents, Adolphus D. Hale (b. 1841, AR) and Amanda Jane Fitzgerald (b. 1848, TX); siblings, William David (b. 1867, TX), Henry Rufus (b. 1869, TX), Adolphus Duff (b. 1870, TX), John Warren (b. 1871, TX), James Obedia (b. 1873, TX), Thomas Ira (b. 1876, TX), Mary Candace (b. 1878, TX), Nettie Lee (b. 1881, TX), Nancy Olivia (b. 1886, TX), Francis Alma "Fannie" (b. 1887, TX), Robert Bee (b. 1891, TX), Henry (b. 1896); spouse #1, Iola Caddel (b. 1908, TX), married about 1925; son, Charles L., Jr. (b. 1926, TX);

spouse #2, Ethel Pearl Ives (b. 1916), married Feb. 17, 1937, Bee County; son, James Morris (b. 1938, TX). *SR; 471; MR, Co. B, Jan–Feb 1911, AGC; A1b, d, f, g; A2b, e; A3a; A4a, b, g.*

HALE, GEORGE ALVAN. Born Dec. 8, 1890, Dodge City, Ford County, Kansas. Ht. 5 ft. 11 in., gray eyes, brown hair, light complexion, married. Special agent, AT&SF Railroad, Amarillo, Potter County, Texas. SPECIAL RANGER Dec. 31, 1917–Jan. 15, 1919. REMARKS: Grew up in Dodge City and Hutchinson, Reno County, Kansas. Had been a stenographer for a railroad in Hutchinson. Died Apr. 24, 1929, Potter County, Texas. LAW ENFORCEMENT RELATIVES: Dodge City, Kansas sheriff (1900) and Ranger Grant Hale, father. FAMILY: Parents, Grant Hale (b. 1864, IA) and Addie Spencer (b. 1871, KS); sister, Bernice (b. 1903, KS); spouse, Nell (b. 1896, TX). *SR; Hale to Harley, Dec 21, 1917, Jan 3, 1918, AGC; AG to Hale, Dec 26, 1917, AGC; Ad, e, f; A3a; C.*

HALE, J. GRANT. Born Dec. 1864, Nevada, Story County, Iowa. Ht. 5 ft. 6 in., brown eyes, gray hair, dark complexion, married. Superintendent, Special Service, AT&SF Railroad, Amarillo, Potter County, Texas. SPECIAL RANGER Dec. 31, 1917–Jan. 15, 1919. REMARKS: In 1900 was sheriff, Dodge City, Kansas. Died Mar. 31, 1934, Potter County, Texas. LAW ENFORCEMENT RELATIVES: Ranger George A. Hale, son. FAMILY: Parents, John Hale (b. 1833, KY) and Rachel J. (b. 1839, IN); siblings, William H. (b. 1860, IN), W. P. (b. 1861, IN), Charles E. (b. 1862, IA), Mary S. (b. 1867, IA), Susanna (b. 1870, IA), G. (b. 1878, IA); spouse, Addie Spencer (b. 1871, KS), married about 1890; children, George A. (b. 1890, KS), Bernice (b. 1903, KS). *SR; Hale to Harley, Dec 21, 1917, Jan 3, 1918, AGC; AG to Hale, Dec 26, 1917; A1a, b, d, e, f; C.*

HALE, WILEY DUFF "DUFF." Born Aug. 16, 1889, Ingram, Kerr County, Texas. Ht. 5 ft. 10 in., brown eyes, black hair, ruddy complexion, married. Peace officer, Menard, Menard County, Texas. REGULAR RANGER Jan. 3, 1918–Mar. 31, 1918 (private, Co. M). Resigned/fired. REMARKS: Note length of service. Capt. K.F. Cunningham took up Hale's warrant of authority because he had requested, and was denied, a transfer out of Co. M. As a boy lived in Bandera County, Texas. As of June 1917 was a pool hall owner in Menard. In 1920 was a stock farm foreman living in Menard County. Also owned a dairy business in Menard County. Died May 8, 1941, Menard County, Texas. LAW ENFORCEMENT RELATIVES: Ranger Charles L. Hale, cousin. FAMILY: Parents, Rufus Putnam Allen Hale (b. 1839, AR) and Clementine Virginia Crawford (b. 1858, TX); siblings, Martha Naomi (b. 1877, TX), Lila Leslie (b. 1879, TX), Fannie Edna (b. 1881, TX), Allen Bradley (b. 1883, TX), James Rufus (b. 1885, TX), Joseph or John Adolph (b. 1887, TX), Clementina Blanche (b. 1892, TX), Hester Felicia (b. 1896, TX); spouse #1, Bessie Gertrude Byrd (b. 1894, TX), married Jan. 1, 1915, Menard, Menard County; son, Robert (b. 1917, TX); spouse #2, Sallie Kirchner, married Sept. 17, 1939; stepsons, Sam Kirchner, Cecil Kirchner. *SR; AG to Cunningham, Jan 3, 1918, AGC; Hale to Harley, Jan 11, 1918, AGC; Cunningham to Harley, Apr 2, 1918, AGC; A1d, f, g; A3a; A4b, g; B2; C.*

HALE, WILL. Born July 30, 1876, Burnet County, Texas. Ht. 6 ft. 2 in., blue eyes, light hair, fair complexion, married. Ranchman, Talpa, Coleman County, Texas. LOYALTY RANGER June 26, 1918–Feb. 1919. REMARKS: In 1910 was a ranch foreman in Runnels County, Texas. Was a farmer in Talpa in 1930. A Will Hale died Apr. 23, 1931, Coleman County, Texas. FAMILY: Parents, Charles Hale (b. 1844, AL) and Mary (b. 1847, TN); siblings, E. Perry (b. 1867, TX), Idella (b. 1869, TX), Hansford (b. 1872, TX), Minnie (b. 1874, TX), Mary (b. 1879, TX); spouse, Hattie (b. 1876, TX), married about 1896; daughter, Eulabell (b. 1898, TX). *SR; A1a, b, e, f, g; A2b; A3a.*

HALE, WILLIAM F. Born Feb. 1871, Bexar County, Texas. No physical description, married. Roadmaster, I&GN Railroad, San Antonio, Bexar County. SPECIAL RANGER Jan. 17, 1918–Jan. 15, 1919. REMARKS: In 1900 was a railroad section foreman living in Medina County, Texas; still a railroad section foreman in 1930, living in Taylor, Williamson County, Texas. FAMILY: Parents, William C. Hale (b. 1825, TN) and Mary E. (b. 1842, AR); siblings, Rosa (b. 1866, TX), Susan (b. 1872, TX), Mary E. (b. 1874, TX), Thomas A. (b. 1878, TX); spouse #1, Lillie E. (b. 1875, TX), married about 1895; children, William C. (b. 1907, TX), Travis E. (b. 1909, TX), Charles (b. 1911, TX), Frances (b. 1913, TX); spouse #2, Ivy (b. 1878, TX), married by 1930. *SR; 471; A1b, d, e, g.*

HALEY, PATRICK DANIEL. Born Feb. 22, 1874, San Patricio, San Patricio County, Texas. Ht. 5 ft. 7 in., gray eyes, light hair, light complexion, married. Wells Fargo express guard, Brownsville, Cameron County, Texas. SPECIAL RANGER Dec. 18, 1916–Dec. 1917. REMARKS: May have been justice of the peace at Harlingen, Cameron County, in Feb 1910. Deputy sheriff, Cameron County, 1910–1915. Cattle buyer, Brownsville, Cameron County, 1915. Deputy constable, Cameron County, 1916. Deputy game warden, Cameron County, March–May 1917. Customs inspector, El Paso, El Paso County, Texas 1918. In 1920 was a cotton buyer for the New Orleans Company, Brownsville; in 1930 was a cotton broker in McAllen, Hidalgo County, Texas. FAMILY: Parents, John Haley (b. 1850, TX) and Kate (b. 1852, TX); siblings, Charles (b. 1873, TX), Minnie (b. 1876, TX), John L. (b. 1877, TX), Katy (b. 1880, TX); spouse, Bessie Hortence Layton (b. 1879, TX), married about 1899; children, Patrick Layton (b. 1901, TX), John L. (b. 1903, TX), Marian Kathleen (b. 1910, TX). *SR; BDH, Feb 5, Aug 9, Nov 26, 1910, Oct 1, Nov 11, Dec 7, 1912, Feb 1, Dec 23, 1913, Jan 21, Mar 28, 30, 31, Apr 4, 6, 7, May 25, Aug 11, Oct 28, Dec 3, 1914, Feb 23, July 12, Sept 1, Nov 1, 1915, Feb 10, 1916, Mar 29, May 5, Sept t, 7, 13, 1917; Campbell to Harley, Jan 29, 1918, AGC; A1b, d, e, f, g; A3a; A4g.*

HALL, ASA DOUGHERTY. Born May 31, 1893, Gainesville, Cooke County, Texas. Ht. 5 ft. 10 in., gray eyes, black hair, dark complexion. Cattleman, El Paso, El Paso County, Texas. SPECIAL RANGER June 29, 1917–Dec. 1917 (attached to Co. C). REMARKS: Operated a small ranch. State Senator Claude Hudspeth requested Hall's appointment as a Ranger to avoid the draft because Hall was the sole support of his widowed mother. In 1920 worked in a cigar store in El Paso. In 1930 was a bookkeeper for a title insurance company in Inglewood, Los Angeles County, California. Died Feb. 12, 1952, Los Angeles County, California. LAW ENFORCEMENT RELATIVES: El Paso police chief, El Paso County sheriff (Nov. 6, 1906–Nov. 8, 1910) Florence J. Hall, father. FAMILY: Parents, Florence James Hall (b. 1850, GA) and Agnes Elizabeth Norwood (b. 1853, LA); siblings, Willie James (b. 1875), Stella Louise (b. 1877), Frank Norwood (b. 1880, TX), Florence Belle (b. 1887, TX); spouse, Helen Aguirre (b. 1900, TX), married about 1918; daughter, Dixie Lee (b. 1919, TX). *SR; Hudspeth to Hutchings, June 22, 1917, AGC; 1503:173; A1d, e, f, g; A2a, f; A3a; A4g.*

HALL, HORACE CURLIN. Born Sept. 13, 1873, Union City, Tennessee. Medium height, medium build, brown eyes, dark hair, married. Physician, Texas quarantine officer, Laredo, Webb County, Texas. SPECIAL RANGER Feb. 21, 1918–Jan. 15, 1919. REMARKS: In 1930 was a medical doctor in Laredo, an eye, ear, nose, and throat specialist. Horace Curlin Hall died Feb. 2, 1931, Webb County, Texas. FAMILY: Parents, Kirk Hall (b. 1849, TN) and Eliza Curlin (b. 1855, TN); sisters, Omar (b. 1877, TN), Una (b. 1880, TN), Marrie Nell "Nellie" (b. 1887, TN), Elizabeth "Lizzie" (b. 1889, TX); spouse, Camilla (b. 1884, TX), married about 1901; children, Mary (b. 1902, TX), Horace C. (b. 1905, TX), Beverly S. (b. 1909, TX). *SR; Collins to Harley, Feb 1, 1918, AGC; A1b, d, f, g; A3a; A4b; C.*

HALL, HOWARD NATHAN "HAPPY." Born July 12, 1886, Hall Ranch, Helena, Karnes County, Texas. Ht. 6 ft., gray eyes, black hair, dark complexion, married. Stockman, Marfa, Presidio County, Texas. REGULAR RANGER Dec. 13, 1919–Nov. 22, 1920 (private, Co. A). Resigned from Rangers to enter federal service. Stockman and farmer. REGULAR RANGER Feb. 24, 1921–Aug. 5, 1923 (private, Co. A; transferred to Co. C, Jan. 1, 1923; transferred to Co. D, Apr. 1, 1923). Honorably discharged. REMARKS: Karnes County deputy sheriff, 2 years. Sergeant in Army intelligence, 21 months. Died June 3, 1971, Brownsville, Cameron County, Texas. FAMILY: Parents, Emory Horton Hall (b. 1852, GA) and Martha Jane "Mattie" Smith (b. 1857, TX); siblings, Alice Elizabeth (b. 1875, TX), Irene (b. 1877, TX), Emory Calvin (b. 1879, TX), Agnes Gertrude (b. 1881, TX), Nellie Lee (b. 1884, TX), Walter (b. 1889, TX), Seidel Seale "Ike" (b. 1893, TX), Edna H. "Patty" (b. 1895, TX); spouse #1, E. V. Fuller, married Mar. 10, 1911, lasted one month; spouse #2, Linnie Mae (b. 1899, TX), married after June 1917. *SR; 471; 470:43; A1d, e, f; A2a, b; A3a; A4a, b; B2.*

HALL, JERREY D. Born Mar. 1868, Weatherford, Parker County, Texas. Ht. 5 ft. 9 ½ in., black eyes, gray hair, dark complexion. Cowpuncher. REGULAR RANGER Apr. 12, 1918–July 1, 1918 (private, Co. F). Discharged/fired for drunkenness. REMARKS: Deputy U.S. marshal for 11 years. Brewster County deputy sheriff for 2 years. Soldier, 13 months' service during the Spanish-American War. *SR; 471.*

HALL, LARRY LIVINGSTON. Born Mar. 10, 1896, Cotulla, La Salle County, Texas. Ht. 5 ft. 11 in., gray eyes, brown hair, fair complexion, married. Stockman, Big Wells, Dimmit County, Texas. REGULAR RANGER Sept. 1, 1919–Dec. 31, 1921 (private, Co. C). Discharged. REMARKS: In 1930 was a U.S. Customs inspector living in Eagle Pass, Maverick County. A Larry L. Hall died Mar. 22, 1987, Maverick County, Texas. FAMILY: Parents, Thomas K. Hall (b. 1854, TX) and Catherine "Katy" (b. 1860, TX); siblings, Robert T. (b. 1884, TX), Mary S. (b. 1888, TX), Rebecca M. (b. 1889, TX), Julia K. (b. 1892, TX); spouse, Susie (b. 1904, TX), married about 1922. *SR; 471; LWT, Oct 3, 1920; A1d, e, g; A2b; A3a.*

HALL, OLLIE. Born June 1, 1872, Breckinridge County, Kentucky. No physical description, married. Farmer, Celina, Collin County, Texas. LOYALTY RANGER June 24, 1918–Feb. 1919. FAMILY: Parents, William Thomas "Tom" Hall (b. 1844, KY) and Lucy Catherine "Kate" Robertson (b. 1844, KY); siblings, Jessey J. (b. 1868, KY), Ollie's twin brother, Orrest (b. 1872, KY), Orpha (b. 1874, KY), Mary Ellen (b. 1876, KY), Samuel B. (b. 1878, KY), Henry Preston (b. 1880, KY); spouse, Novia A. Weeks (b. 1874, TX), married about 1894; children, Roy Elliot (b. 1898, TX), Bettie or Lurline (b. 1900, TX), Floyd W. (b. 1904, TX), Ollie Vernon (b. 1908, TX), A. C. (b. 1910, TX), Carl LeeRoy (b. 1915, TX), Mildred Lee (b. 1919, TX). *SR; A1b, d, e, f, g; A2f; A4b.*

HALL, WILLIAM H. Born Dec. 1858, Marshall, Calhoun County, Michigan. Ht. 5 ft. 11 in., blue eyes, light gray hair, light complexion, married. Wells Fargo express guard, San Antonio, Bexar County, Texas. SPECIAL RANGER Dec. 20, 1916–May 18, 1917 (attached to Co. C). Honorably discharged when he left Wells Fargo's employ. REMARKS: In 1900 was a railroad brakeman living in San Antonio. In 1910 was a San Antonio policeman. In 1920 was a warehouse watchman in San Antonio. A William Henry Hall died Jan. 29, 1944, Bexar County, Texas. FAMILY: Sister, Matie (b. 1873, MI); spouse, Sadie (b. 1869, MI). *SR; A1d, e, f; C.*

HALLMARK, WILLIAM PARKER. Born Oct. 20, 1873, Etowah County, Alabama. Short, stout, black eyes, married. Baker, Dublin, Erath County, Texas. LOYALTY RANGER July 1, 1918–Feb. 1919. REMARKS: Had been a restaurant proprietor in Dublin. In 1910 was the fire chief in Dublin. In 1930 was the Dublin postmaster. Died Nov. 10, 1967, Dublin, Erath County, Texas; buried in the New Dublin Cemetery. FAMILY: Parents, Jessie Ellis Hallmark (b. 1850, AL) and Milton "Mittie" Johanna McClusky (b. 1851, GA); siblings, Walter Freeman (b. 1871, AL), Susanna Rebecca L. (b. 1876, AL), Savannah Leona (b. 1878, AL), Jesse Bascom (b. 1880, AL), Lillie Bell (b. 1882, AL), James Howell (b. 1884, AL), Louisa Bell (b. 1888, AL), Joanna Pearl (b. 1891, AL); spouse, Charlise or Charlsie Leila Hagler (b. 1874, AL), married Nov. 15, 1891, Etowah County, Alabama; children, Johanna Beulah (b. 1893, TX), Leila Ruth (b. 1895, TX), William Pascal (b. 1898, TX). *SR; A1b, d, e, f, g; A2b, k; A3a; A4a, b, g.*

HAMER, DENNIS ESTILL. Born July 12, 1882, Pleasanton or Fairview, Atascosa County, Texas. Ht. 6 ft., blue eyes, light hair, blonde complexion. Stockman, Kingsville, Kleberg County, Texas. SPECIAL RANGER July 12, 1916–Dec. 1917 (attached to Co. C). Investigator. REGULAR RANGER Jan. 19, 1933–Jan. 24, 1935 (captain, Headquarters Co.). Discharged. REMARKS: Policeman, Houston, Harris County, Texas. Pay car guard, Grant Brothers Construction Company. In 1917–1918 was a city detective based in El Paso, El Paso County, Texas; had also been a city detective in Tucson, Pima County, Arizona. Was a mine owner in Mexico. Lived in Nogales, Santa Cruz County, Arizona for 27 years prior to his death. Died Jan. 5, 1967, Nogales, Santa Cruz County, Arizona; buried in Nogales City Cemetery. LAW ENFORCEMENT RELATIVES: Ranger Flavious L. Hamer, brother; Ranger Francis Augustus "Frank" Hamer, brother; Scurry County deputy game warden (1916–1917) and Ranger Harrison L. Hamer, brother; game warden and Ranger Francis A. Hamer, Jr., nephew. FAMILY: Parents, Franklin Augustus Hamer (b. 1853, IL) and Lou Emma Francis (b. 1860, TX); siblings, Francis Augustus "Frank" (b. 1884, TX), Sanford Clinton (b. 1886, TX), Harrison Lester (b. 1888, TX), Emma Patience "Pat" (b. 1894, TX), Alma Dell (b. 1898, TX), Flavious Letherage (b. 1900, TX), Mary Grace (b. 1891, TX); spouse, Grace, married Mar. 19, 1918. *SR; 471; McLemore to Johnston, Apr 7, 1918, AGC; Assistant AG to Orndorff, Apr 8, 1918, AGC; AG to Edwards, Apr 10, 1918, AGC; Governor to Johnston, Apr 20, 1918, AGC; Assistant AG to Hamer, Apr 10, 1918, AGC; AG to Scarborough, July 8, 1916, AGC;*

Taub to AG, Aug 22, 19167, AGC; AG to Taub, Aug 23, 1916, AGC; EPMT, Dec 26, 1917, Jan 8, Feb 3, 1918; A1d; A2a; A3a; A4a, b.

HAMER, FRANCIS AUGUSTUS "FRANK." Born Mar. 17, 1884, Fairview, Wilson County, Texas. Ht. 6 ft. 3 in., blue eyes, brown hair. REGULAR RANGER Apr. 21, 1906–Nov. 1908 (private, Co. C). Resigned (?). Peace officer, enlisted in Val Verde County, Texas. REGULAR RANGER Mar. 29, 1915–Nov. 8, 1915 (private, Co. C; from Aug. to Oct. attached to Co. B). Resigned. Brand inspector, Cattle Raisers' Association of Texas, San Angelo, Tom Green County, Texas. SPECIAL RANGER Nov. 8, 1915–Jan. 10, 1917 (attached to Co. C). WA revoked. Peace officer, Harlingen, Cameron County, Texas. REGULAR RANGER Oct. 1, 1918–June 19, 1919 (private, Co. F; promoted to sergeant ca. Oct. 12, 1918; placed on detached service, Apr. 1919). Resigned. Ranchman, Snyder, Scurry County, Texas. REGULAR RANGER Nov. 25, 1919–May 11, 1920 (private, Co. B; promoted to sergeant, Dec. 15, 1919). Honorably discharged. Peace officer, Austin, Travis County, Texas. REGULAR RANGER Sept. 1, 1921–June 30, 1925 (captain, Co. C; transferred as captain to Headquarters Co., Jan. 1, 1922). Resigned. SPECIAL RANGER July 1, 1925–Feb. 1, 1927. REGULAR RANGER Feb. 2, 1927–Feb. 1, 1933 (captain, Co. D; transferred as captain to Headquarters Co., May 1, 1927; reenlisted Feb 2, 1929, Feb. 2, 1931). Resigned. SPECIAL RANGER Feb. 1, 1946–Jan. 1, 1955. Commission expired. REMARKS: Cowboy and blacksmith in his youth. City marshal, Navasota, Grimes County, Texas, Dec. 1908–Apr. 1911. City detective (special officer for Mayor Rice), Houston, Harris County, Texas, 1911–1913. Special officer (worked against rustlers), Junction, Kimble County, Texas, 1913–1915. Brand inspector, Cattle Raisers' Association of Texas, Snyder, 1917. Federal Prohibition agent, El Paso, El Paso County, Texas and Austin, 1920; resigned Aug. 29, 1921. Special investigator for a Houston oil company. Special escape investigator for the Texas prison system; tracked down and ambushed Bonnie and Clyde, Feb. 10, 1934. Security guard firm partner (with Roy T. Rogers, ex-Houston police chief), Houston, Harris County, 1936–1949. Retired, sold out to his partner, Roy T. Rogers, 1949. Died July 10, 1955, Austin, Travis County, Texas. LAW ENFORCEMENT RELATIVES: Ranger Dennis E. Hamer, brother; Ranger Flavious L. Hamer, brother; Scurry County, Texas, deputy game warden (1916–1917) and Ranger Harrison L. Hamer, brother; game warden and Ranger Francis A. Hamer, Jr., son. FAMILY: Parents, Franklin Augustus Hamer (b. 1853, IL) and Lou Emma Francis (b. 1860, TX); siblings, Dennis Estill (b. 1882, TX), Sanford Clinton (b. 1886, TX), Harrison Lester (b. 1888, TX), Mary Grace (b. 1891, TX), Emma Patience (b. 1894, TX), Alma Dell (b. 1898, TX), Flavious Letheridge (b. 1900, TX); spouse #1, Molly, married Mar. 11, 1911, Dallas, Dallas County, Texas; spouse #2, Gladys Johnson Sims (b. 1891, TX), married May 12, 1917, New Orleans, Orleans Parish, Louisiana; sons, Francis Augustus, Jr. (b. 1919, CA), Billy Beckham (b. 1921, TX). *SR; 471; 901; Garrison to Redding, July 26, 1955, DPS; Curutta [?] to Harris [Sept 1918], AGC; AG to Hamer, Sept 7, 1918, AGC; Adamson to Harley, Sept 12, 1918, AGC; Harley to Hamer, Feb 3, 1919, AGC; Harley to Kleberg, June 28,*

A young Texas Ranger Francis Augustus "Frank" Hamer.
Photo courtesy Texas Ranger Hall of Fame and Museum.

Texas Ranger Flavius Hamer, a brother of Frank Hamer.
Photo courtesy Texas Ranger Hall of Fame and Museum.

Ranger Dennis Estill Hamer, another brother of Frank Hamer.
Photo courtesy Texas Ranger Hall of Fame and Museum.

1919, AGC; Hamer to Harley, July 8, 1919, AGC; Aldrich to Jackman, Mar 3, 1920, AGC; Aldrich to Rutledge, June 28, 1920, AGC; AS, July 12, 1910; AG to Sanders, Apr 6, 1915, AGC; AG to Hamer, Apr 2, 1915, AGC; AG to Almond, Apr 2, 1915, AGC; Hamer to AG, Apr 30, 1915, RRM; Spiller to Hutchings, Nov 1, 1915, AGC; AG to Spiller, Nov 2, 1915, AGC; Spiller to Hutchings, Nov 4, 1915, AGC; AG to Hamer, Nov 11, 1915, AGC; Hamer to AG, Nov 7, 1915, AGC; Spiller to Hutchings, May 5, 1916, AGC; Merrill to Ferguson, Dec 20, 1916, WC; [Hutchings] to Ferguson, Dec 21, 29, 1916, WC; Weems to Ferguson, Dec 12, 1916, WC; AG to Ferguson, Dec 21, 1916 [two letters], AGC; Wroe to AG, Dec 21, 28, 1916 [two letters], AGC; Weems to Ferguson, Dec 21, 1916, AGC; White to Hutchings, Dec 27, 1916, AGC; Hutchings to Ferguson, Dec 29, 1916, AGC; Hamer to Hutchings, Jan 10, 1917, AGC; AG to Hill, Jan 10, 1917, AGC; AG to Hamer, Jan 11, 1917, AGC; AG to Weems, Jan 3, 1917, AGC; Parrish to Hobby, Oct 3, 1917, RRM; Stevens to AG, Dec 7, 1919 WC; Aldrich to Stevens, Dec 10, 1919, WC; Stevens to AG, Dec 12, 1919, WC; Canales to Joint Investigation Committee, Feb 3, 1919, WC; 100:517–546; 172:III, 426–427; 840; 1517; EPMT, Aug 10, 1910, Sept 15, 1915; HC, Apr 2, 1918; LWT, Sept 4, 1921; 319: 106, 193, 197, 200, 202, 216, 381, 417–428; 1000: iii, 58, 118; 469: 63, 65; 470: 43, 72–73; 480: 26; 522: 370; biography—463; 901; 1519:128–155; A1d, g; A3a; A4b.

HAMER, HARRISON LESTER. Born Aug. 15, 1888, Fairview, Wilson County, Texas. Ht. 6 ft. 2 ½ in., blue eyes, light hair, light complexion, married. Ranchman, Snyder, Scurry County, Texas. REGULAR RANGER Oct. 23, 1918–Dec. 31, 1919 (private, Co. F; transferred to

Ranger Harrison Lester Hamer, yet another brother of Frank Hamer. *Photo courtesy Texas Ranger Hall of Fame and Museum.*

Co. K, Jan. 1, 1919; reenlisted under the new law and transferred to Co. D, June 20, 1919). Resigned, honorably discharged. Stockman, Fort Worth, Tarrant County, Texas. RAILROAD RANGER Oct. 2, 1922–Dec. 23, 1922. Resigned. Brand inspector, Sheep and Goat Raisers' Association, Del Rio. SPECIAL RANGER Apr. 9, 1927–Apr. 1, 1928; May 1, 1928–May 1, 1929; Aug. 22, 1929–Aug. 22, 1930. Discharged. Brand inspector, Sheep and Goat Raisers' Association, Big Lake, Reagan County, Texas. SPECIAL RANGER Sept. 25, 1930–Jan. 2, 1931. Discharged—WA expired; Jan. 3, 1931–Apr. 1, 1932. Placed on active duty. REGULAR RANGER Apr. 1, 1932–Jan. 18, 1933 (private, Co. D). Discharged. Peace officer, Del Rio. SPECIAL RANGER July 18, 1935–Aug. 10, 1935. Discharged. Security Division, Magnolia Petroleum Company, Beaumont, Jefferson County, Texas. SPECIAL RANGER Jan. 1, 1946–Jan. 1, 1947. REMARKS: Had been deputy game warden, Scurry County, 1916–1917. Deputy sheriff, bank guard, Ranger, Eastland County, Texas, Aug. 1918. Customs inspector, Del Rio, Val Verde County, Texas, 1925. Brand inspector, Sutton County Livestock Association. Auxiliary to the Military Police at Magnolia Petroleum Company, Beaumont, 1942–1945. Retired as head of the security division, Magnolia Petroleum Company, 1953. Lived with his son, C. P. Hamer, near Giddings, Lee County, Texas for the next 15 years, then lived in Del Rio, San Antonio, Bexar County, Texas, and Houston, Harris County, Texas. Was living in Houston in Feb. 1976. Died Aug. 24, 1977, Houston, Harris County, Texas; buried in Del Rio. LAW ENFORCEMENT RELATIVES: Ranger Dennis E. Hamer, brother; Ranger Flavious L. Hamer, brother; Ranger Francis Augustus "Frank" Hamer, brother; game warden and Ranger Francis A. Hamer, Jr., nephew. FAMILY: Parents, Franklin Augustus Hamer (b. 1853, IL) and Lou Emma Francis (b. 1860, TX); siblings, Dennis Estill (b. 1882, TX), Francis Augustus "Frank" (b. 1884, TX), Sanford Clinton (b. 1886, TX), Mary Grace (b. 1891, TX), Emma Patience (b. 1894, TX), Alma Dell (b. 1898, TX), Flavious Letheridge (b. 1900, TX); spouse, Frieda Inez "Freddie" Rainey (b. 1892, TX), married Aug. 10, 1907, Anson, Jones County, Texas; children, Beulah Sophia (b. 1908, TX), Clinton Paul (b. 1911, TX), Franklin Augustus (b. 1914, TX), Harrison Lester (b. 1915, TX), Frieda Wilna (b. 1918, TX), Daniel Vaughn (b. 1922, TX), Robert Lloyd (b. 1925, TX). *SR; 471; AA, Feb 17, 1976; Weems to Ferguson, Dec 21, 1916, AGC; Wroe to AG, Dec 28, 1916, WC; Hutchings to Ferguson, Dec 29, 1916, WC; AG to Weems, Jan 3, 1917, AGC; Hamer to Harley, July 5, 1918, AGC; Assistant AG to Buchanan, July 18, 1918, AGC; Governor to Hamer, Aug 31, 1918, AGC; Hamer to AG, Mar 23, 1919, AGC; Harley to Hamer, Mar 26, 1919, AGC; Brooks to Hamer, Nov 25, 1919, AGC; Aldrich to Hamer, Dec 4, 1919, AGC; Hamer to Aldrich, Dec 31, 1919, AGC; Cope to Hamer, Jan 6, 1920, AGC; 463:126; 470: 72–73; 319: 425; 1000: iii, 58–60; 1506; 1517; A1d, e, f, g; A2a, b; A3a; A4a, b.*

HAMILTON, AUSTIN TRAVIS. Born Feb. 12, 1882, Lampasas County, Texas. Ht. 6 ft., gray eyes, dark hair, dark complexion, married. Stock farmer, Lometa, Lampasas County. REGULAR RANGER Oct. 12, 1918–Oct. 17, 1919 (private, Co. F; transferred to Co. K, Jan. 1, 1919; reenlisted under the new law in Co. A, June 20, 1919). Resigned from Rangers because of conditions at home. REMARKS: Deputy sheriff, Lampasas County, several years. City marshal, Lometa, for one term. As of Sept. 1918 was a farmer, living in San Saba, Mills County, Texas. In 1930 was a peace officer in Goose Creek, Harris County. Died Feb. 21, 1944, Mills County, Texas. FAMILY: Parents, John Hamilton (b. 1844, TX) and Ella Jane (b. 1844, AL); siblings, Wayne (b. 1866, TX), Ellen R. (b. 1867, TX), Margaret (b. 1870, TX), Gertrude G. (b. 1873, TX), Florence (b. 1877, TX); spouse, Eula Mabel (b. 1882, TX), married about 1902; children, Jack (b. 1903, TX), Lillian (b. 1907, TX). *SR; 471; Kirby to Whom, Nov 3, 1914, AGC; White to Those, Nov 3, 1914, AGC; Davis to Whom, Nov 4, 1914, AGC; Jerry to Cardwell, Aug 8, 1918, AGC; Mace to Harley, Aug 21, 1918, AGC; Harley to Hamilton, Oct 14, 1918, Aug 15, 1919, AGC; Hamilton to Harley, Aug 15, 1919, AGC; A1b, d, e, f, g; A3a; C.*

HAMILTON, ERNEST FARLEY. Born Sept. 21, 1885, Audrain County, Missouri. Ht. 5 ft. 6 in., blue eyes, dark hair, ruddy complexion, married. Stockman. SPECIAL RANGER Jan. 5, 1918–Jan. 15, 1919 (attached to Co. E). REMARKS: As a youth had lived in San Angelo, Tom Green County, Texas. Had been a sheep man in Mule Creek, Kinney County, Texas. In 1918 was a rancher in Val Verde and King Counties, Texas; in 1920 lived in Del Rio, Val Verde County. Apparently was an inspector for the Sheep and Goat Raisers' Association. Died Feb. 20 1969, in Uvalde, Uvalde County, Texas. FAMILY: Parents, J. R. Hamilton (b. 1852, PA) and Flora (b. 1858, PA); siblings, Edith (b. 1877, TX), Russell (b. 1881, TX), Harry (b. 1882, MO), Martha (b. 1896, TX); spouse, Burissa (b. 1886, MS), married about 1906; sons, James B. (b. 1908, TX), Sherwood E. (b. 1910, TX). *SR; Barler to Woodul, Jan 9, 1918, AGC; A1d, e, f; A2a, b; A3a.*

HAMILTON, JAMES DAVID. Born Sept. 19, 1872, Nelson County, Kentucky. Tall, slender, brown eyes, dark brown hair, married. Farmer, Rockdale, Milam County, Texas. LOYALTY RANGER June 6, 1918–Feb. 1919. REMARKS: In 1920 was a butcher in a meat market in Rockdale. Died May 3, 1922, Milam County, Texas. FAMILY: Parents, David Hamilton (b. 1833, Ireland) and Mary Catherine (b. 1842, KY); siblings, Rebecca (b. 1866, KY), Edward (b. 1868, KY), John (b. 1870, KY); spouse, May Ella Henry (b. 1876, TX), married Dec. 20, 1894, Rockdale; children, Minnie May (b. 1896, TX), Laura (b. 1898, TX), Emma (b. 1904, TX), Ruth (b. 1910, TX), Hary W. (b. 1914, TX). *SR; A1a, b, d, e, f; A2b; A3a; A4b.*

HAMILTON, JIM HENRY "BUCK." Born Jan. 20, 1890, Maloney, Ellis County, Texas. Short, stout, blue eyes, brown hair, married. Bookkeeper, Kress, Swisher County, Texas. LOYALTY RANGER June 17, 1918–Feb. 1919. REMARKS: In June 1917 was a bookkeeper for Farmers' State Bank in Kress. In 1920 and 1930 was bookkeeper/manager of a grain elevator in Kress. Died June 7, 1951, Clovis, Curry County, New Mexico; buried in Kress. FAMILY: Parents, John Ake Hamilton (b. 1861, AL) and Sallie Ann Juliet Margerite Wood (b. 1870, TX); siblings, Minerva Hattie (b. 1888, TX), twins Bessie D. and Jessie Hogge (b. 1892, TX), twins Geneva Bam and Genoa Alice (b. 1894, TX), Mattie Bell (b. 1897, TX), Manly Pete (b. 1900, TX), Mary Bonnie (b. 1903, TX), John Wesley (b. 1908, TX), David Clinton (b. 1910, TX), William Horton (b. 1914, TX); spouse, Valera Alva "Vera" "Buddie" Beck (b. 1899, TX), married about 1916; children, Lenora M. "Lenna" (b. 1918, TX), Ruby Beatrice (b. 1920, TX), Ben Henry (b. 1920, TX), Alice Marie (b. 1923, TX), Tommy Jim (b. 1932, TX), Johnnie V. (b. 1934, NM). *SR; A1d, e, f, g; A2e; A3a; A4g; B1.*

HAMILTON, WILLIAM TIGG. Born July 4, 1878, Panola County, Mississippi. Ht. 6 ft. 3 in., gray eyes, brown hair, fair complexion, married. Deputy city marshal, De Leon, Comanche County, Texas. SPECIAL RANGER July 7, 1919–July 7, 1921. Discharged—WA was for 2 years. Special officer, Sinclair Oil Co. at De Leon. SPECIAL RANGER Aug. 29, 1927–Aug. 21, 1928. Discharged. City marshal, Cross Plains, Callahan County, Texas. SPECIAL RANGER Sept. 20, 1928–Sept. 20, 1929. Discharged. REMARKS: In 1930 was a city policeman in Cross Plains. FAMILY: Parents, James M. Hamilton (b. 1852, MS) and Lucy A. (b. 1848, MS); siblings, Daisey or Denny (b. 1885, MS), Henry (b. 1890, MS); spouse #1, Mary E. (b. 1877, MS), married about 1900; children, John M. (b. 1902, TX), Ethel L. (b. 1909, TX); spouse #2, Minnie O. (b. 1891, TX), son, Darwin R. (b. 1923, TX). *SR; A1b, d, e, f, g; A3a.*

HAMPTON, EDGAR GRAYSON. Born Dec.13, 1889, Vinton, Calcasieu Parish, Louisiana. Ht. 6 ft. ½ in., brown eyes, brown hair, ruddy complexion, married. Assistant bank cashier, Clyde, Callahan County, Texas. SPECIAL RANGER June 14, 1917–Dec. 1917 (attached to Co. C). REMARKS: By 1910 was assistant cashier, Clyde National Bank. Died May 29, 1966, Taylor County, Texas. FAMILY: Parents, John Preston Hampton (b. 1850, MS) and Alice M. (b. 1858, LA); siblings, Nena (b. 1876, LA), Nevill (b. 1880, LA), Ethel A. (b. 1885, LA), Iris (b. 1887, LA), Lillie B. (b. 1889, LA); spouse, Dixie (b. 1893, TX), married about 1912; daughter, Cecile (b. 1917, TX). *SR; AG to Hampton, Jun 18, 1917, AGC; A1d, e, f, g; A2a, b; A3a.*

HAMRICK, GEORGE THOMAS. Born Feb. 4, 1869, Shelby, Shelby County, Alabama. Ht. 5 ft. 9 in., gray eyes, black hair, olive complexion, married. Resident inspector for U.S. ships, employed by the U.S. Shipping Board, Emergency Fleet Corporation, Houston, Harris County, Texas. SPECIAL RANGER May 27, 1918–Jan. 15, 1919. REMARKS: In 1900 was a house carpenter in Birmingham, Jefferson County, Alabama. Was also a contractor/builder. Died Feb. 16, 1919, Harris County, Texas. FAMILY: Parents, William H. Hamrick (b. 1834, TN or GA) and Margaret Elizabeth Nabors (b. 1847, AL); siblings, John H. (b. 1866, AL), Sarah J. "Sallie" (b. 1868, AL), William V. (b. 1875), Jesse P. (b. 1879, AL), Kate Nellie (b. 1882, AL); spouse, Alice Lillian Foster (b. 1877, NC), married May 1893, Jefferson County, Alabama; children, Harry William (b. 1895, AL), Grace Ora (b. 1897, AL), Frances Elizabeth "Frankie" (b. 1900, AL), Oscar Curtis (b. 1902, AL), Myrtle Christine (b. 1904, AL), Lillian Alice (b. 1906, TX), Bertha Louise (b. 1907, TX), Marguerite Elizabeth (b. 1909, TX), Harriet Willie (b. 1910, TX), Elmer George (b. 1912, TX). *SR; Assistant AG to Hamrick, Apr 10, 1918, AGC; Crowell to Woodul, May 20, 1918, AGC; A1a, d, f; A4a, b, g; B1; C.*

HANEY, JOHN. Born Jan.1862, Beirut, Lebanon. Ht. 5 ft. 9 in., brown eyes, black hair, dark complexion, married. Merchant, Beaumont, Jefferson County, Texas. SPECIAL RANGER Oct. 19, 1918–Jan. 15, 1919. REMARKS: Immigrated to the United States in 1885, became a naturalized citizen. In 1900 was a dry goods merchant in Austin, Travis County, Texas. In 1920 was manager of a drug store in Beaumont; still lived in Beaumont in 1930. FAMILY: Spouse, Mary (b. 1867, Lebanon); children, Sheehan (b. 1881, Lebanon), Joe (b. 1885, Lebanon), Jacob (b. 1891, TX), Lillie (b. 1898, TX). *SR; A1d, e, f, g.*

HANKS, MARSHALL BERNARD. Born Sept. 1884, Dallas, Dallas County, Texas. Ht. 5 ft. 7 in., dark eyes, dark hair, dark complexion, married. Publisher, Abilene, Taylor County, Texas. SPECIAL RANGER June 9, 1917–Dec. 1917 (attached to Co. C). REMARKS: Died Dec. 12, 1948, Taylor County, Texas. FAMILY: Parents, Robert Taylor Hanks (b. 1850, AL) and Mattie B. (b. 1854, VA); siblings, Bessie Page (b. 1886, TX), Manly (b. 1889, TX); spouse, Eva Mae (b. 1884, TX), married about 1907; children, Eva Mae (b. 1910, TX), Patty (b. 1917, TX); adopted daughter, Evelyn Jackson (b. 1910, TX). *SR; Register to Ferguson, May 18, 1917, AGC; Cunningham to Ferguson, May 18, 1917, AC; A1d, e, f, g.*

HANSEN, ERNST C. Born Nov 1, 1884, Denmark. Ht. 6 ft. 1 in., gray eyes, black hair, light complexion, married. Real estate broker, Fredericksburg, Gillespie County, Texas. LOYALTY RANGER July 12, 1918–Feb. 21, 1919. REMARKS: As of 1918 had lived in Gillespie County for 30 years except for one year in Los Angeles, California. Immigrated to the United States in 1887, was a naturalized citizen. Died Sept. 3, 1965, Gillespie County, Texas. FAMILY: Parents, Jens Hansen (b. 1846, Denmark) and Agatha (b. 1856, Denmark); siblings, Amalie (b. 1879, Denmark), Marie (b. 1880, Denmark), Waldemar R. (b. 1882, Denmark), Arthur J. (b. 1886, Denmark); spouse, Rosa (b. 1891, TX), married about 1907. *SR; A1d, e, f, g; A2a, b; A3a.*

HANSON, CORNELIUS JAMES. Born May 16, 1888, Rancho, Gonzales County, Texas. Ht. 5 ft. 11 in., dark eyes, brown hair, dark complexion. Oil driller, enlisted in San Antonio, Bexar County, Texas. REGULAR RANGER May 15, 1916–Nov. 30, 1916 (private, Co. A; reenlisted Oct. 24, 1916). Resigned. Oil business. REGULAR RANGER Sept. 11, 1917–May 26, 1919 (private, Co. A; transferred to Co. F, unknown date; transferred to detached duty, Jan. 1, 1919). Resigned. REMARKS: Resigned from Texas Rangers in May 1919 to become assistant to the president of the Rainbow Oil and Refining Co., at a much higher salary. As of January 1920 was an oil well driller in Live Oak County, Texas. Died Feb. 29, 1920, San Antonio, Bexar County, Texas. LAW ENFORCEMENT RELATIVES: Ranger captain William M. Hanson, father. FAMILY: Parents, William M. Hanson (b. 1866, TX) and Maldonetta C. (b. 1866, TX);

brothers, Mortimer M. (b. 1886, TX), William (b. 1892, TX), Wrathell King (b. 1895, TX); spouse, Elizabeth A. (b. 1895, TX). *SR; 471; Stevens to Harley, Jan 4, 1918, AGC; Special Orders No. 1, Jan 9, 1919, WC; Hanson to Harley, May 26, 1919, AGC; Hanson to Aldrich, May 26, 1919, AGC; C.J.H. [Hanson] to Aldrich, June 8, 1919, AGC; Aldrich to Hanson, June 10, 1919, AGC; Millard to Aldrich, Mar 1, 1920, AGC; Aldrich to Millard, Mar 3, 1920, AGC; A1e, f; A2b; A3a.*

HANSON, WILLIAM MARTIN. Born Feb. 1866, Rancho, Gonzales County, Texas. Ht. 6 ft. ½ in., gray eyes, light hair, fair complexion, married. Chief special agent, San Antonio Uvalde & Gulf Railroad, San Antonio, Bexar County, Texas. SPECIAL RANGER Dec. 24, 1917–Jan. 30, 1918. Placed on active duty. REGULAR RANGER Jan. 31, 1918–Sept. 4, 1919 (captain, Inspector of Ranger Force; captain, Headquarters Co., May 19, 1919; reenlisted under the new law, June 20, 1919). Resigned, but kept his WA—on indefinite leave. REMARKS: Deputy sheriff, Gonzales County, 1884—many years. Deputy U.S. marshal, 1898–1902, Western District of Texas. U.S. marshal, 1902–1906—Southern District of Texas; was reappointed but resigned. Land and oil company manager, near Tampico, Mexico, 1896–1914. In Spring 1911 was a Mexican government secret agent in San Antonio, Bexar County, Texas. Owned the 3,000-acre Hacienda Guadalupe, Victoria, Tamaulipas, Mexico, 1906–1914. In Jan. 1914, was arrested as a Huerta spy and deported to the U.S. Special agent, SAU&G Railroad, San Antonio, 1915–1917. Deputy sheriff, San Antonio to aid railroad special agent work, 1915–1917. From Sept. 1, 1919–Mar. 1921 was special investigator for the Fall Subcommittee of the U.S. Senate. Returned to San Antonio; in 1922 was appointed inspector, U.S. Department of the Interior. In 1923 was appointed director of District 22 of the Immigration Service, supervising the Texas border. Resigned in 1926 amid controversy. Served as bailiff of the corporation [municipal] court in San Antonio. Died Feb. 19, 1931, San Antonio, Bexar County, Texas. LAW ENFORCEMENT RELATIVES: Ranger Cornelius J. Hanson, son; Ranger Everett Anglin, distant cousin (Anglin's mother was Hanson's cousin). FAMILY: Parents, Cornelius J. Hanson (b. 1831, England) and Susan L. (b. 1837, GA); spouse, Maldonetta C. (b. 1866, TX), married about 1885; children, Mortimer M. (b. 1886, TX), Cornelius J. (b. 1888, TX), William (b. 1892, TX), Wrathell King (b. 1895, TX). *SR; 471; Ellsworth to Secretary of State, Mar 3, 1911, 812.00/884 and May 11, 1911, 812.00/1779, RDS; Hanson to Ferguson, Apr 19, 1917, AGC; Carl to Harley, Dec 9, 1917, AGC; AG to Hanson, Dec 21, 26, 1917, AGC; Hanson to Woodul, Dec 24, 1917, AGC; Hanson to Harley, Feb 1, 1918, AGC; Hanson to Harley, Feb 8, 27, Mar 5, 1918, RRM; Hanson to Engelking, Feb 11, 1918, RRM; Vann to Hanson, Apr 3, 1918, AGC; Hanson to Johnson, May 29, 1918, WC; Harley to Anders, July 12, 1918, WC; Harvey and Hart to Harley, July 16, 1918, WC; Erby E. Swift report, July 25, 1918, WC; Hanson to Harley, Aug 31, Oct 15, 1918, WC; Special Orders N0.1, Jan 9, 1919, WC; Canales to Joint Investigation Committee, Feb 3, 1919, WC; Hobby to Harley, May 19, 1919, WC; 1: I, 1225–1229, 1502, II, 2894–2977, 3223–3249, 3255–3256; Hanson file, 137; EPMT, Nov 27, 1910; HC, Mar 10, Apr 29, 1918; AA, Dec 11, 1919; Corpus Christi Caller and Daily Herald, May 12, 14, 1916; LWT, Dec 18, 1910, Feb 19, Mar 26, May 28, June 4, 11, 1911, Feb 11, June 16, Sept 15, 1912, Jan 5, Aug 24, Sept 7, 1913, Jan 25, Feb 1, June 7, Oct 25, 1914, July 5, 1915, June 25, Oct 29, 1916, Sept 7, 1919, Mar 7, 1920, Jan 30, 1921; BDH, Jan 21–29, 1914, July 22, Nov 12, 1915, Aug 5, 1916; 319: 28, 467; 424: 222–223, 229; 504: 111, 164, 167, 172, 173,272–273, 316–317, 408, 411, 415–416, 422–423, 470; A1b, e, f, g; C.*

HARBISON, PELTON BRUCE. Born Sept. 25, 1885, Goliad, Goliad County, Texas. Ht. 5 ft. 10 in., brown eyes, dark hair, dark complexion. Stockman, Hebbronville, Jim Hogg County, Texas. REGULAR RANGER Dec. 9, 1919–Aug. 19, 1921 (private, Co. C; transferred to Co. D, Feb. 15, 1921). Resigned. REMARKS: In 1918 was a barber in Goliad. On Aug. 19, 1921 was appointed sheriff of Jim Hogg County, succeeding Pat Craighead. Harbin resigned on Jan. 21, 1929. Later ranched and farmed near Hebbronville. Died Aug. 6, 1956, Harbison Ranch, Jim Hogg County, Texas; buried in Greenhill Cemetery, Hebbronville. LAW ENFORCEMENT RELATIVES: Goliad County sheriff (Nov. 8, 1932–Jan. 1, 1949) Clyde M. Harbison, brother. FAMILY: Parents, Alexander Harbison (b. 1824, NY) and Mary Pelton (b. 1853, PA); siblings, Clyde McAlpine (b. 1882, IL), Earl Malcolm (b. 1883, IL), Mary Hazel (b. 1887, TX), Reginald (b. 1892, TX); spouse, Helen Marie Sewell (b. 1896, MO), married Dec. 24, 1921, Hebbronville; children, Hazel Maurine (b. 1923, TX), Georgia Isabel (b. 1926, TX), Reginald Newton (b. 1927, TX), Donnia Ione (b. 1929, TX),

Alice Louise (b. 1931, TX), Ida Alleene (b. 1934, TX), Carie Lee (b. 1936, TX). *SR; 471; 470: 133–136; 1503:208, 288; LWT, Oct 3, 1920; A1d, e, g; A2b, e; A3a; A4a, b; B2.*

HARDESTY, ROY WESLEY. Born Dec. 15, 1885, Red Oak, Ellis County, Texas. Ht. 6 ft. 1 in., gray eyes, brown hair, dark complexion, married. Oil rig contractor, Wichita Falls, Wichita County, Texas. REGULAR RANGER May 5, 1921–Mar. 31, 1923 (private, Co. B). Resigned/fired: "not satisfactory." REMARKS: A Roy W. Hardesty died Apr. 13, 1968, Dallas, Dallas County, Texas. FAMILY: Parents, Benjamin Franklin Hardesty (b. 1864, TX) and Lillie Belle Butcher (b. 1868, TX); brothers, Floyd F. (b. 1896, TX), Herman G. (b. 1889, TX), Walton D. (b. 1891, TX); spouse, Dora B. (b. 1892, TX). *SR; 471; 470: 43; A1d, f, g; A2b; A3a; B1.*

HARDIE, JOT GUNTER. Born June 30, 1895, Dallas, Dallas County, Texas. Ht. 5 ft. 10 in., dark eyes, black hair, dark complexion. Rancher, Del Rio, Val Verde County, Texas. SPECIAL RANGER July 3, 1917–Dec. 1917 (attached to Co. C). REMARKS: Managed a small ranch of his brother's four miles west of Del Rio. Had been a lawyer for the U.S. government at Camp Funston, San Antonio, Bexar County, Texas. In 1920 was a lawyer in general practice in San Antonio; in 1930 was a land and cattle lawyer in San Antonio. Jot Gunter Hardie died Oct. 22, 1944, Bexar County, Texas. FAMILY: Parents, John Hardie (b. 1867, MS) and Eula M. Gunter (b. 1870, TX); siblings, Esther (b. 1893, TX), John F. "Jack" (b. 1897, TX); spouse, Elizabeth K. (b. 1896, TX), married about 1918. *SR; Hardie to Ferguson, Jun 3, 1917, AGC; A1d, f, g; A3a; C.*

HARDIN, ALBERT HARRISON. Born Dec. 17, 1887, Shreveport, Louisiana. Ht. 6 ft. 1 ½ in., brown eyes, black hair, dark complexion, married. Night watchman, I&GN Railroad, Taylor, Williamson County, Texas. SPECIAL RANGER Aug. 22, 1916–Dec. 14, 1916 (attached to Co. C). His commission was cancelled when he ceased working for the I&GN Railroad. REMARKS: In Sept. 1918 was a mechanic for the Oriental Oil Company living in Dallas, Dallas County, Texas. WWI Draft Registration form lists birth year as 1883; also states "has a withered arm." In 1920 worked for an oil company in Little Rock, Pulaski County, Arkansas. In 1930 was retired, living in Dallas, Dallas County. Died July 21, 1930, Dallas County, Texas. FAMILY: Parents, John Hardin (b. 1836, AR) and Penelope Ann Dyer (b. 1853, AR); sister, Johncye (b. 1891, TX); stepfather, Joseph H. Calloway (b. 1854, AR); half-siblings, Ola S. Calloway (b. 1894, TX), John T. Calloway (b. 1897, TX); spouse, Ora Malinda Stewart (b. 1884, TX), married about 1912, Dallas County; children, DeEstle (b. 1913, TX), Violet Penelope (b. 1916, AR), Harrison Brady (b. 1920, AR). *SR; Jones to Hutchings, Dec 12, 1916, AGC; AG to Jones, Dec 14, 1916, AGC; A1d, e, f, g; A3a; A4a, b; C.*

HARDIN, ARCHIE BUD. Born Jan. 22, 1897, Derden, Hill County, Texas. Ht. 5 ft. 9 in., gray eyes, light hair, fair complexion. Farmer, Blum, Hill County. SPECIAL RANGER Jan. 16, 1918–Jan. 21, 1918. Placed on active duty. REGULAR RANGER Jan. 22, 1918–Mar. 1, 1918 (private, Co. G). Discharged/fired. Got drunk and attacked two schoolteachers. Capt. Stevens disarmed him and took his commission away; the matter was hushed up. REMARKS: Died Dec. 29, 1960, Whitney, Hill County, Texas; buried in Peoria Cemetery, Hill County. FAMILY: Parents, Richard Henry "Pete" Hardin (b. 1873, TX) and Rosetta Ince (b. 1876, TX); siblings, Nannie Beth or Blanche (b. 1896, TX), Joe Bailey (b. 1900, TX), Edna Mae (b. 1904, TX); spouse, Hazel Eunice Griffith (b. 1902, TX). *SR; Stevens to Harley, Feb 27, 1918, AGC; A1d, e, f; A2b; A4a, b, g.*

HARDIN, MICHAEL OLIVER "MIKE." Born July 14, 1889, Bell County, Texas. Ht. 6 ft. 3 in., blue eyes, light hair, light complexion. Deputy sheriff, enlisted in El Paso County, Texas. REGULAR RANGER Apr. 15, 1918–Aug. 1918 (private, Co. L). Discharged. REMARKS: Had been a peace officer for many years. Was a well digger in Knowles, Eddy County, New Mexico. In Sept. 1918 was a farmer in San Jon, Quay County, New Mexico. In 1930 was a barber in Ysleta, El Paso County. Died Jan. 29, 1964, El Paso County, Texas. FAMILY: Parents, Daniel Elijah Hardin (b. 1836, SC) and Lucinda Jane Poole (b. 1841, TX); siblings, Daniel Seymour (b. 1861, TX), Walter B. (b. 1867, TX), Tully Bostic (b. 1868, TX), Early J. (b. 1872, TX), Elmer (b. 1877, TX), Curtis Carl (b. 1885, TX); spouse #1, unknown, married about 1907; spouse #2, Della (b. 1905, NM), married in 1925; sons, Daniel J. (b. 1926, AZ), M. O. (b. 1928, AZ). *SR; 471; Davis to Harley, Apr 14, 1918, AGC; A1d, e, g; A2a, b; A3a; A4b, g.*

HARDING, WILLIAM ARTHUR. Born Dec. 17, 1877, Fort Deposit, Lowndes County, Alabama. Ht. 5 ft. 10 ½ in., gray eyes, light hair, fair complexion, married. Railroad special agent, enlisted in Galveston County, Texas. SPECIAL RANGER May 23, 1918–Jan. 15, 1919. Special agent, GH&SA Railroad (SP), El Paso, El Paso County, Texas. RAILROAD RANGER July 23, 1923–Sept. 12, 1923. Resigned. REMARKS: Watchman, T&P Railroad, Dallas, Dallas County, Texas. As of 1923, had been a railroad special agent for 15 years. FAMILY: Spouse, Marguerite "Maggie" (b. 1887, TX), married about 1903. *SR; AS, Nov 18, 1910; A1e; A3a.*

HARGIS, WILLIAM BONAPARTE. Born Nov. 5, 1872, Nacogdoches, Nacogdoches County, Texas. Ht. 5 ft. 9 in., gray eyes, black hair, dark complexion, married. Schoolteacher, Pineland, Sabine County, Texas. LOYALTY RANGER July 4, 1918–Feb. 1919. REMARKS: Died July 17, 1953, Travis County, Texas. FAMILY: Parents, Berry Fancher Hargis (b. 1853, LA) and Nancy Ellen Brittain (b. 1855, LA); siblings, Ivy Jefferson (b. 1875, TX), Emma Angeline (b. 1879, TX), Nannie Ellen (b. 1882, TX); stepmother, Elizabeth Frances Dillard (b. 1858, TX); siblings, Elvie L. (b. 1885, TX), Tracy B. (b. 1890, TX), Hattie McCullough (b. 1892, TX), Richard A. (b. 1896, TX); spouse #1, Jennie Rose (b. 1878, TX), married Nov. 21, 1891, Nacogdoches; children, Werner Rose (b. 1903, TX), Herbert E. (b. 1907, TX), Frederick B. (b. 1910, TX); spouse #2, Yuma Day (b. 1891, TX), married about 1928. *SR; A1b, d, e, f, g; A2b; A3a; A4b, g; B1.*

HARGUS, VAN DAILY. Born Jan. 15, 1893, Arapaho, Custer County, Oklahoma. Ht. 5 ft. 11 in., gray eyes, light hair, light complexion. Peace officer, enlisted in Brewster County, Texas. REGULAR RANGER Jan. 16, 1919–Feb. 3, 1920 (private, Co. G; reenlisted under the new law in Co. B, June 20, 1919). Resigned same day and for same reason as Capt. Charles Stevens—refused to carry out what he felt was an illegal order to enforce Texas oil claims vs. Oklahoma. REMARKS: Constable, precinct 2, Brewster County, Nov. 1916. In 1930 was a farmer near Fabens, El Paso County, Texas. Died Aug. 14, 1936, El Paso County, Texas. FAMILY: Parents, James Alford Hargus (b. 1850, MO) and Louisa Tate (b. 1855, TX); siblings, James (b. 1883, TX), Henry M. "Mack" (b. 1885, Indian Territory), Ida (b. 1888, Indian Territory), George Washington (b. 1890, Indian Territory), Thomas (b. 1895, OK), Jacob (b. 1897, OK), Clara Agnes (b. 1899, OK); spouse, Clara (b. 1901, TX), married about 1919; children, unknown child (1923, TX), Richard E. (b. 1926, TX). *SR; 471; Hargus to Cope, Feb 3, 29, 1920, AGC; Cope to Hargus, Mar 4, 1920, AGC; Hargus to Aldrich, Mar 13, 1920, AGC; AA, Nov 16, 1916, Nov 22, 1917, June 5, 1919; A1d, e, f, g; A2e; A3a; A4b, g; C.*

HARKEY, JEFFERSON DAVIS. Born Mar. 5, 1863, San Saba, San Saba County, Texas. Ht. 5 ft. 10 in., blue eyes, dark hair, light complexion, married. Stockman, Dickens County, Texas. REGULAR RANGER July 27, 1905–ca. 1909 (private, Co. A). Stockman, Dickens, Dickens County. LOYALTY RANGER June 12, 1918–Feb. 1919. REMARKS: Second enlistment cites Richland, San Saba County as his birthplace. Dickens County sheriff Mar. 14, 1891–Nov. 6, 1900. In 1920 was president of a bank in Dickens. Died of a stroke Apr. 17, 1927, Dickens, Dickens County, Texas; buried in Dickens Cemetery. FAMILY: Parents, Daniel Riley Harkey (b. 1829, NC) and Margaret Ellen Smith (b. 1832, VA or AR); siblings, Joseph or Josiah Mathias (b. 1851, AR), Nancy Jane (b. 1852, AR), Julia Ann Louisa (b. 1854, AR), John Adams, (b. 1855, TX), Sarah Caroline (b. 1857, TX), James Thomas (b. 1858, TX), Levi Jacob (b. 1860, TX), Martha Ellen (b. 1861, TX), Polly Anna (b. 1864, TX), Daniel Riley (b. 1866, TX), Moses Isaac or Israel (b. 1867, TX), Eli Last (b. 1869, TX); spouse, Sally Matilda Hopkins (or Hopson), married Oct. 18, 1886, San Saba County; children, Jefferson Bernice (b. 1887, TX), Earl Joe (b. 1890, TX), M. Ola (b. 1892, TX), Roy Kennen (b. 1895, TX), Bertie L. (b. 1897, TX), Bernice B. (b. 1900, TX), Leon Blum (b. 1903, TX), Linnie (b. 1906, TX), D. R. (b. 1909, TX). *SR; 471; 1503:159; A1aa, a, d, e, f; A2b; A3a; A4a, b, g; B1.*

HARPER, JAMES H. Born June 1871, Leon County, Texas. Ht. 5 ft. 8 ½ in., blue eyes, brown hair, light complexion, married. Farmer, Crowell, Foard County, Texas. LOYALTY RANGER July 1, 1918–Feb. 1919. REMARKS: A James Harper died Feb. 4, 1964, Foard County, Texas. FAMILY: Parents, James Harper (b. 1825, FL) and Susan (b. 1838, TX); siblings, William (b. 1857, TX), John (b. 1860, TX), Eliza (b. 1861, TX); spouse, Amanda Ellen (b. 1878, TX), married about 1894; children, Claud (b. 1896, TX), James David (b. 1898, OK), Frank E. (b. 1902, TX), Amanda E.

(b. 1904, TX), Joseph Boyce (b. 1908, TX), Richard S. (b. 1910, TX). *SR; A1a, b, d, e, f; A2b.*

HARRELL, EDWARD HOGAN. Born Jan. 1868, Selma, Dallas County, Alabama. Ht. 5 ft. 11 in., blue eyes, gray hair, blonde complexion. Lumber dealer, Houston, Harris County, Texas. SPECIAL RANGER July 8, 1918–Jan. 15, 1919. REMARKS: Had been a stenographer and traveling salesman for M.T. Jones Lumber Company, Houston. Was engaged in creosoting lumber. Letterhead: "Ed. H. Harrell Co., Lumber, Houston, Texas." In 1930 was a retail dry goods merchant in Houston. FAMILY: Parents, Dr. Oscar F. Harrell (b. 1838, AL) and Marie Antoinette Mobley (b. 1842, AL); siblings, Caroline (b. 1861, AL), Jessie (b. 1865, AL), Sallie (b. 1866, AL); spouse, Ruby (b. 1879, GA). *SR; A1aa, a, b, e, g; A4b; A5a.*

HARRELL, MILES W. Born May 1866, Burkeville, Newton County, Texas. Ht. 5 ft. 10 in., gray eyes, red hair, fair complexion, married. Attorney, Cleveland, Liberty County, Texas. LOYALTY RANGER July 15, 1918–Feb. 1919. REMARKS: Had been a lawyer in Livingston, Polk County, Texas. In 1910 was postmaster in Cleveland. Deputy sheriff for several years. In Sept. 1918 was commissioned as justice of the peace, precinct 6, Cleveland. FAMILY: Spouse #1, Lucy J. (b. 1870, TX), married about 1890; sons, Benjamin Herbert (b. 1891, TX), William Burton "Bertie" (b. 1893, TX), Elma Lea (b. 1899, TX); spouse #2, Dovie H. (b. 1872, TX). *SR; Harrell to Hanson, Sept 14, 1918, AGC; A1d, e, f, g; A3a.*

HARRINGTON, WILLIAM LEE "LEE." Born Feb. 20, 1888, Madisonville, Madison County, Texas. Ht. 5 ft. 8 in., blue eyes, black hair, dark complexion, married. Brand inspector, Panhandle and Southwestern Cattle Raisers' Association, Alpine, Brewster County, Texas, 1915–1916. SPECIAL RANGER Oct. 28, 1916–Dec. 1917 (attached to Co. B); Mar. 20, 1918–Jan. 15, 1919. REMARKS: Constable, Brewster County, May–Aug. 1918. Resigned. A Lee Harrington (b. 1888, TX) was a cattle rancher in Benson, Cochise County, Arizona in 1920. William Lee Harrington died Aug. 11, 1954, Presidio County, Texas. FAMILY: Parents, James Bridges Harrington (b. 1847, MS) and Rebecca Jane Rogers (b. 1850, TX); siblings, Joseph Stevens (b. 1869, TX), Janie E. (b. 1871, TX), James Thomas (b. 1873, TX), Carrie Mae (b. 1876, TX), Cornelia B. (b. 1879, TX), Herbert Hudson (b. 1882, TX), LeeRoy Lloyd (b. 1884, TX), Francis (b. 1886, TX); spouse, Sadie Lou Crawford (b. 1895, TX), married Aug. 30, 1917. *SR; Petition to Ferguson, Sept 8, 1916, AGC; Wroe to AG, Sept 25, 1916, AGC; Hudspeth to Hobby, Jan 22, 1918, AGC; AA, Nov 4, 1915, Nov 8, 1917, May 16, Aug 15, 1918; A1b, d, f; A2b; A3a; A4g.*

HARRIS, ALONZO "LON." Born Apr. 14, 1880, Clarke County, Mississippi. Ht. 6 ft. 1 ½ in., gray eyes, black hair, dark complexion, married. Cattle buyer, Indian Gap, Hamilton County, Texas. LOYALTY RANGER Oct. 7, 1918–Feb. 1919. REMARKS: In 1910 was a farmer in Hamilton County. In Sept. 1918 was a manager for the Indian Gap Telephone Company, Hamilton County. A Lon Harris died Nov. 17, 1943, Hamilton County, Texas. FAMILY: Parents, William J. Harris (b. 1828, MS) and Susan (b. 1842, GA); siblings, Thomas (b. 1867, MS), George (b. 1870, MS), Jane (b. 1871, MS), Obedin B. (b. 1872, MS), Daniel Rier (b. 1874, MS), Oliver (b. 1876, MS), Mary (b. 1876, MS), Bob (b. 1877, MS), Lizzie (b. 1878, MS); spouse, Nora (b. 1886, TX), married about 1900; children, Lela W. (b. 1901, TX), Earl Herman (b. 1905, TX), Cora L. (b. 1909, TX). *SR; A1b, d, e, f; A3a; A4b; C.*

HARRIS, HEADLEY BRUCE. Born Nov. 6, 1876, Caldwell County, Texas. Medium height, medium build, brown eyes, black hair, married. Farmer, Fentress, Caldwell County. LOYALTY RANGER May 31, 1918–Feb. 1919. REMARKS: Died Oct. 11, 1921, Caldwell County; buried in Fentress Cemetery, Fentress. FAMILY: Parents, Berry B. Harris (b. 1842, AL) and Martha O. "Mattie" Polk (b. 1849, TN or TX); siblings, Robert Polk (b. 1876, TX), Lena (b. 1878, TX), Oran Milo (b. 1879, TX); spouse, Lizzie (b. 1877, TX), married about 1899; children, Elvin F. (b. 1900, TX), Lena Mae (b. 1905, TX). *SR; 429:220; A1b, d, e, f; A2b; A3a; A4a, b.*

HARRIS, IRWIN CULVER. Born Mar. 21, 1893, Grayson County, Texas. Ht. 5 ft. 8 in., brown eyes, brown hair, fair complexion. Bank teller. REGULAR RANGER Dec. 14, 1917–Jan. 22, 1918 (private, Co. I). Resigned. REMARKS: Note length of service. As of June 1916 worked at the Commercial National Bank, Sherman, Grayson County. Died Mar. 26, 1929, Grayson County, Texas. FAMILY: Parents, William Thomas or Thomas Monroe "Tom" Harris

(b. 1861, TX) and Vallonia Eva "Vallie" Culver (b. 1872, GA or AL); brothers, Henry W. (b. 1895, TX), W. Thomas (b. 1900, TX); spouse, Mamie Lee Nelson (b. 1900, TX); son, Irwin Culver, Jr. (b. 1924, TX). *SR; 471; Ryan to AG, Dec 19, 1917, AGC; A1d, e, f; A2e; A3a; A4a, b, g; C.*

HARRIS, J. CARSON. Born Apr. 15, 1877, Perry, Ralls County, Missouri. Ht. 6 ft. 3 in., gray eyes, light hair, fair complexion, married. Abstractor, Snyder, Scurry County, Texas. SPECIAL RANGER Mar. 11, 1918–Jan. 15, 1919. Salesman for Humble Oil and Refining Company, Houston, Harris County, Texas. SPECIAL RANGER May 7, 1919–Dec. 31, 1919. REMARKS: In 1910 was an electric company superintendent in Beeville, Bee County, Texas; census record states he is widowed with 3 living children, but they are not listed with him. World War I Draft Registration document, Sept. 1917, lists first name as "Jonette" but may be "Jouette;" was U.S. government Selective Service clerk in Scurry County. A Jouette Carson Harris died Feb. 7, 1930, Bexar County, Texas. FAMILY: Parents, E. Richard Harris (b. 1849, England) and Tennessee Carson (b. 1845, KY); sister, Minnie C. (b. 1880, MO); spouse #1, unknown, but may have been Mary Wickens; daughter may have been Emily Henrietta (b. 1901, OK); another spouse may have been Pearl Mae Churchill (b. 1906, TX), married Apr. 3, 1926, Brown County, Texas. *SR; A1b, d, e, f; A2b; A3a; A4b.*

HARRIS, TOBE MARION. Born Oct. 8, 1882, Timpson, Shelby County, Texas. Ht. 5 ft. 8 in., blue eyes, sandy hair, light complexion, married. Lumberman, Shepherd, San Jacinto County, Texas. LOYALTY RANGER July 2, 1918–Feb. 1919. REMARKS: Deputy sheriff, Nacogdoches and San Jacinto Counties for 5 years. A "Tabe" Harris died Oct. 27, 1918, Nacogdoches County, Texas. FAMILY: Parents, Stephen L. Harris (b. 1846, TX) and Isabel (b. 1854, TX); siblings, Oscar D. (b. 1884, TX), Orphie J. (b. 1885, TX), Ida Lee (b. 1888, TX), Georgia V. (b. 1889, TX), James D. (b. 1890, TX); spouse, Lena May (b. 1884, TX); children, Thelma (b. 1904, TX), Clyde (b. 1906, TX), Maud (b. 1907, TX), Edwin (b. 1909, TX), T. M. (b. 1918, TX). *SR; A1d, f; A2b; A3a.*

HARRIS, WILLIAM GREEN "WILL." Born Jan. 1881, Orange, Orange County, Texas. Ht. 5 ft. 9 ½ in., brown eyes, dark hair, light complexion, married. Farmer, Warren, Tyler County, Texas. LOYALTY RANGER June 14, 1918–Feb. 1919. REMARKS: Deputy sheriff for several years. FAMILY: Spouse, Maggie. *SR; A3a.*

HARRIS, WILLIAM TERRY. Born Jan. 10, 1877, Tilden, McMullen County, Texas. Ht. 5 ft. 10 in., blue eyes, black hair, ruddy complexion. Stockman. U.S. government scout (Cavalry scout, commissioned at Army's request), McKinney Springs, Brewster County, Texas. SPECIAL RANGER Aug. 29, 1917–Jan. 15, 1919 (was reinstated—WA renewed, Jan. 17, 1918). Discharged. REMARKS: In 1930 was a grocery merchant in Corpus Christi, Nueces County, Texas. FAMILY: Parents, William T. Harris (b. 1837, MS) and Amanda M. (b. 1847, TX); siblings, Millie A. (b. 1879, TX), Robert E. (b. 1880, TX), Dot (b. 1883, TX), Flora V. (b. 1884, TX), Birdie (b. 1888, TX); spouse #1, unknown, married about 1902; spouse #2, Myrtle Nolte (b. 1893, TX), married about 1920; children, Louise (b. 1921, TX), William Terry, Jr. (b. 1922, TX). *SR; 471; AG to Commanding General, Aug 17, 1917, AGC; A1d, e; g; A2b, e; A3a.*

HARVEY, JESS WILLIAM. Born July 25, 1887, Frankford, Collin County, Texas. Ht. 6 ft., brown eyes, dark hair, dark complexion, married. Real estate agent, Paducah, Cottle County, Texas. LOYALTY RANGER June 8, 1918–Feb. 21, 1919. REMARKS: In June 1917 was a county commissioner in Cottle County. In 1920 was an oil company promoter living in De Leon, Comanche County, Texas. FAMILY: Parents, James A. Harvey (b. 1862, VA) and Loula A. (b. 1867, TX); siblings, Fredrick C. (b. 1885, TX), Jettie E. (b. 1889, TX), Earnest A. (b. 1894, TX), Lottie C. (b. 1896, TX), John L. (b. 1898, TX), Clifford A. (b. 1900, TX); spouse, Emma Victoria Cameron (b. 1889, TX), married Feb. 16, 1908; children, Clara Geneva (b. 1910, TX), Murray Lynn (b. 1911, TX), Erma Lou (b. 1914, TX). *SR; A1d, e, f; A3a; A4b.*

HARVEY, WILLIAM ALAN. Born Feb. 3, 1883, Springfield, Greene County, Missouri. Ht. 5 ft. 8 ½ in., blue eyes, brown hair, fair complexion, married. Railroad brakeman, enlisted in Atascosa County, Texas. SPECIAL RANGER July 17, 1916–Dec. 1917. REMARKS: In Sept. 1918 was a druggist and baker in Atascosa County. FAMILY: Spouse, Mamie N. *SR; A3a.*

HARVICK, JAMES ADDISON or ADAM "AD." Born Aug. 6, 1879, San Saba, San Saba County, Texas. Ht. 6 ft., brown eyes, black hair, dark complexion. Brand inspector, Cattle Raisers' Association of Texas, San Angelo, Tom Green County, Texas. SPECIAL RANGER Jan. 11, 1917–Jan. 15, 1919 (was reinstated—WA renewed Dec. 20, 1917). Discharged. Brand inspector, Sheep and Goat Raisers' Association, Ozona, Crockett County, Texas. SPECIAL RANGER Apr. 18, 1927–Apr. 18, 1928. Discharged. REMARKS: In Jan. 1918 was classed as a REGULAR RANGER without pay, to avoid the draft. Had been a brand inspector, Cattle Raisers' Association of Texas, 1913–1916. Died June 11, 1953, Ozona, Crockett County, Texas. FAMILY: Parents, Adam Stricklin Harvick (b. 1837, AR) and Mary Serene Beasley (b. 1843, TN); siblings, Nancy Louisa (b. 1862, TX), Julia Isabelle (b. 1864, TX), Marth Wincy (b. 1865, TX), Mollie (b. 1869, TX), Annie Tabitha (b. 1871, TX), Lillie (b. 1873, TX), Kate Murray (b. 1875, TX), Cassie H. (b. 1877, TX), Pocahontas (b. 1883, TX), Stricklin Martin (b. 1885, TX). *SR; Spiller to Ferguson, Dec 26, 1916, AC; Acting AG to GC& SF Railroad, Jan 9, 1918, AGC; EPMT, Feb 11, 17, 19, June 23, 1913; SAE, Feb 13, 1913; AA, Feb 13, 1913; A1b; A2b; A3a; A4b.*

HARVIE, CRAWFORD. Born July 1872, Liverpool, England. Ht. 6 ft. 2 in., blue eyes, dark brown hair, light complexion, married. President, Border National Bank, El Paso, El Paso County, Texas. LOYALTY RANGER July 4, 1918–Feb. 21, 1919. REMARKS: On Service Record of July 4, 1918, listed occupation as "Laundryman." One source gives birthplace as West Derby, Lancashire County, England. Immigrated to U.S. in 1873, became a naturalized citizen. Was proprietor of a steam laundry in El Paso as early as 1910. Still proprietor of a laundry in El Paso in 1930. A Crawford Harvie died Sept. 22, 1956, El Paso County, Texas. FAMILY: Spouse #1, Mary G. (b. 1876, MA), married about 1897; children, Crawford W. (b. 1899, MA), Edith E. (b. 1901, MA), Eleanor J. (b. 1906, MA), George H. (b. 1909, TX); spouse #2, Annie J. Mead (b. 1895, IL); children, William Meade (b. 1915, TX), Annie Jane (b. 1919, TX); spouse #3, Anna E. (b. 1879, KS), married about 1923; stepdaughter, Ruth M. Hall (b. 1911, KS). *SR; A1d, e, f, g; A2b, e, g.*

HARVIN, JAMES A. Born Sept. 1872, Brenham, Washington County, Texas. Ht. 5 ft. 7 ½ in., gray eyes, red gray hair, light complexion, married. Rancher, Eagle Pass, Maverick County, Texas. SPECIAL RANGER Dec. 27, 1917–Jan. 15, 1919 (Co. C Volunteers). REMARKS: In 1900 was U.S. Customs inspector, Eagle Pass; 1912, collector of Customs, Eagle Pass. FAMILY: Parents, Richard A. Harvin (b. 1847, SC) and Catherine T. (b. 1853, VA); siblings, Stephen Vaughn (b. 1876, TX), Katie E. (b. 1882, TX); spouse, unknown. *SR; EPMT, Sept 18, 1912; A1d.*

HARWELL, OSCAR HENRY. Born Feb. 27, 1885, Putnam, Callahan County, Texas. Ht. 6 ft. 3 in., black eyes, black hair, dark complexion Farmer and stockman, Baird, Callahan County. SPECIAL RANGER June 1, 1917–Dec. 1917 (attached to Co. C). REMARKS: In 1930 was a baker living in Abilene, Taylor County, Texas. Later was a hotel proprietor. Died June 13, 1954, Phoenix, Maricopa County, Arizona; buried in Greenwood Memorial Park, Arizona. FAMILY: Parents, Lunsford Dillard Harwell (b. 1858, TX) and Margaret Elizabeth Hutchison (b. 1865, TX); siblings, Jimmie C. (b. 1884, TX), Margaret E. "Maggie" (b. 1886, TX), Ervin L. (b. 1888, TX), Olive Myrtle "Ollie" (b. 1890, TX), Earl O. (b. 1892, TX), Lora Mae (b. 1895, TX), Dolly (b. 1899, TX), Alton H. (b. 1905, TX); spouse, Eva Etta Fleming (b. 1892, TX), married about 1918. *SR; A1d, e, g; A3a; A4b, g; B1.*

HAUGHTON, CHARLES MELVILLE. Born Mar. 28, 1871, Richmond, Wayne County, Indiana. Ht. 6 ft. 2 in., blue eyes, brown hair, fair complexion, married. Farmer, Barstow, Ward County, Texas. LOYALTY RANGER June 6, 1918–Feb. 28, 1919. REMARKS: Had been a deputy sheriff. In 1910 was a field agent for a rubber company in Fort Stockton, Pecos County, Texas. In 1930 was a cattle buyer in Ysleta, El Paso County, Texas. A Charles M. Haughton died Nov. 9, 1945, El Paso County, Texas. FAMILY: Parents, Dr. Richard Elwood Haughton (b. 1827, IN) and Elizabeth L. "Lizzie" Mather (b. 1847, OH); siblings, Louanna or Louisiana (b. 1859, IN), Everett or Edward E. (b. 1863, IN), William Percival (b. 1873, IN), Henry Raymond (b. 1877), Ruth Anna (b. 1883); spouse #1 (probably), Emma Lee Johnson, married Oct. 11, 1904, Midland, Midland County, Texas; spouse #2, Rose (b. 1883, OH), married about 1909; children, John P. (b. 1914, OH), William W. (b. 1915, OH), twins Rosemary and Susan Elizabeth "Bettie" (b. 1916, TX). *SR; A1b, d, e, f, g; A2e; A4a, b, g; C.*

HAWKINS, RICHARD CREWS "RED." Born Aug. 16, 1887, Kyle, Hays County, Texas. Ht. 6 ft., brown eyes, red hair, fair complexion, married. Cowboy. REGULAR RANGER Nov. 25, 1911–Mar. 1914 (private, Co. B; reenlisted Nov. 25, 1913). Discharged without honor/fired. Brand inspector, Del Rio, Val Verde County, Texas. SPECIAL RANGER Jan. 3, 1918–Jan. 15, 1919. Ranchman. SPECIAL RANGER May 13, 1934–Jan. 22, 1935. Discharged. Peace officer, Galveston, Galveston County, Texas. REGULAR RANGER Feb. 19, 1935–Aug. 31, 1939 (captain, Co. C). Discharged. REMARKS: Brand inspector, Cattle Raisers' Association of Texas, 1915. Brand inspector, Del Rio, 1916–1919. Died Feb. 10, 1957, Galveston County, Texas. LAW ENFORCEMENT RELATIVES: Ranger Tell T. Hawkins, father. FAMILY: Parents, Telyphus T. "Tell" Hawkins (b. 1859, TX) and Baylor Louisa Cruz (b. 1868, TX); siblings, Joseph M. (b. 1885, TX), Thomas M. (b. 1889, TX), Lizzie (b. 1891, TX), Maggie L. (b. 1893, TX), Nexia Francis. (b. 1895, TX), Cecil R. (b. 1899, TX), Telyphus (b. 1901, TX), Idella (b. 1905, TX); spouse, Thelma (b. 1896, GA); children, Fred (b. 1915, TX), Florence (b. 1918, TX). *SR; 471; Sanders to Hawkins, Nov 23, 1911, AGC; Hawkins to York, Aug 24, 1913, AGC; Sanders to Hutchings, Nov 28, 1913, AGC; Assistant Quartermaster to Sanders, Dec 8, 1913, AGC; Walter Rushin's statement, June 14, 1915, WC; AA, May 13, 1915, Aug 28, 1919; BDH, Nov 11, 1912; 319: 424–425; A1d, e, f; A2b; A3a; A4g, h; A6a.*

HAWKINS, TELYPHUS T. "TELL." Born Apr. 1859, Seguin, Guadalupe County, Texas. Ht. 6 ft., blue eyes, light gray hair, light complexion, married. Stockman, Jourdanton, Atascosa County, Texas. SPECIAL RANGER Nov. 19, 1917–Jan. 15, 1919 (attached to Co. C). Stockman. REGULAR RANGER Sept. 23, 1920–Feb. 15, 1921 (private, Headquarters Co. Emergency Co. No. 1). Discharged. REMARKS: Hays County deputy sheriff for 15 years before enlisting in Rangers. Died Jan. 2, 1930, Galveston, Galveston County, Texas. LAW ENFORCEMENT RELATIVES: Ranger Richard "Red" Hawkins, son. FAMILY: Parents, Joseph Hawkins (b. 1828, AL) and Nampa or Narcissa F. Bales (b. 1828, AL); siblings, Elizabeth F. (b. 1855, TX), Miles (b. 1857, TX), Aurames (b. 1858, TX), William J. (b. 1861, TX), Thomas U. (b. 1865, TX); spouse, Baylor Louisa Cruz (b. 1868, TX), married about 1885; children, Joseph M. (b. 1885, TX), Richard C. (b. 1887, TX), Thomas M. (b. 1889, TX), Lizzie (b. 1891, TX), Maggie L. (b. 1893, TX), Nexia Francis (b. 1895, TX), Cecil R. (b. 1899, TX), Telyphus (b. 1901, TX), Idella (b. 1905, TX). *SR; 471; Petition to AG, Nov 2, 1917, AGC; Hawkins to Aldrich, Oct 30, 1920, AGC; A1aa, b, d, e, f; A4g, h; C.*

HAY, GROVER C. Born July 10, 1884, Kyle, Hays County, Texas. Medium height, medium build, hazel eyes, red hair. Locomotive fireman, I&GN Railroad, San Antonio, Bexar County, Texas. LOYALTY RANGER June 12, 1918–Feb. 1919. REMARKS: Had been a farmer in Hays County. In 1930 lived in San Antonio. FAMILY: Parents, Jacob L. Hay (b. 1844, OH) and Lizzie K. (b. 1857, TX); siblings, Ira B. (b. 1881, TX), Alice T. (b. 1887, TX), Lizzie Rozette (b. 1889, TX), Emma Vince (b. 1889, TX), John Carlyle (b. 1893, TX), Lawrence K. (b. 1896, TX); spouse #1, Mamie R. Thiele (b. 1892, TX), married about 1907; children, Charles L. (b. 1909, TX), Maurine (b. 1910, TX), Grover C., Jr. (b. 1911, TX); spouse #2, Billie (b. 1907, AR), married about 1928. *SR; A1d, e, f, g; A3a.*

HAYDEN, AUDIE THOMAS. Born Oct. 3, 1894, Mount Pleasant, Titus County, Texas. Ht. 5 ft. 11 in., brown eyes, black hair, dark complexion, married. Deputy sheriff, Mount Pleasant. REGULAR RANGER Dec. 19, 1919–Jan. 9, 1920 (private, Co. C). Honorably discharged. REMARKS: Note length of service. Had been an agent for the Magnolia Petroleum Company. In 1930 was an agent for an oil refinery, lived in Fort Worth, Tarrant County, Texas. Died Nov. 3, 1930, Tarrant County, Texas; buried in Rosehill Cemetery, Fort Worth. FAMILY: Parents, James Alexander Hayden (b. 1857, MO) and Margaret Louise Watts (b. 1864, MO); siblings, Alga Bell (b. 1880, MO), William Alexander (b. 1882, MO), Jimmie Lula (b. 1885, MO), Pearl May (b. 1886, TX), Gertrude (b. 1888, TX), Walter Clyde (b. 1897, TX), twins Hattie and Mattie Eunice (b. 1901, TX); spouse, Wiltha Idora "Lucille" Mitchell (b. 1896, TX), married Jan. 13, 1913, Titus County; children, James T. (b. 1915, TX), Dymple (b. 1917, TX). *SR; 471; Hayden to Cope, Oct 14, 1919, AGC; A1d, f, g; A2b; A3a; A4b.*

HAYES, TRAVIS. Born Sept. 25, 1880, Skidmore, Bee County, Texas. Ht. 5 ft. 6 in., blue eyes, dark hair, brunette complexion. Farmer, Skidmore. LOYALTY RANGER May 31, 1918–Feb. 1919. REMARKS: Had been constable, precinct 6, Bee County. Died Dec. 18, 1952, Skidmore, Bee County,

Texas; buried in Evergreen Cemetery, Skidmore. LAW ENFORCEMENT RELATIVES: Bee County judge William R. Hayes (1880), father. FAMILY: Parents, William Robert Hayes (b. 1835, MO) and Drucilla Amanda Fuller (b. 1840, AL); siblings, Fannie (b. 1864, TX), Mary (b. 1867, TX), Horace (b. 1869, TX), Lucy (b. 1872, TX), Homer (b. 1874, TX), Annie (b. 1877, TX), Vivian (b. 1882, TX). *SR; A1b, d, f; A2b; A3a; A4b, g; B1.*

HAYNES, BARON HENRY. Born Jan. 1870, Lavaca County, Texas. No physical description, married. Farmer, Weesatche, Goliad County, Texas. LOYALTY RANGER June 10, 1918–Feb. 1919. REMARKS: In 1900 was a physician in Goliad County. Goliad County sheriff Nov. 2, 1920–Jan. 1931. Died Feb. 5, 1931, Goliad County, Texas. FAMILY: Parents, Christopher C. Haynes (b. 1843, AL) and Margretta (b. 1847, TX); siblings, Annie (b. 1868, TX), Minnie (b. 1870, TX), Sean (b. 1874, TX), Willard (b. 1876, TX), Blanche (b. 1880, TX); spouse, Emma A. (b. 1868, TX), married about 1900; children, Ralph C. (b. 1902, TX), Meta M. (b. 1904, TX), Murrel J. (b. 1905, TX), Cleo (b. 1907, TX). *SR; 1503:208; A1b, d, e, f, g; A4b.*

HAYNES, CHARLES LANDON. (Listed in Ranger Service Records as C. L. HAYSNER.) Born Dec. 4, 1871, Lockhart, Caldwell County, Texas. Ht. 6 ft., blue eyes, light brown hair, light complexion, married. Railroad locomotive engineer, Rockport, Aransas County. LOYALTY RANGER June 6, 1918–Feb. 1919. REMARKS: As a young boy lived in Kimble County, Texas. In 1900 was a railroad fireman in San Antonio, Bexar County, Texas. Died in 1935. FAMILY: Parents, Joseph Eugene Haynes (b. 1842, TN) and Matilda Elizabeth "Bettie" Crenshaw (b. 1852, TX); siblings, Helen Eugenia (b. 1869, TX), Alice Louretta "Lita" (b. 1874, TX), Eva Perrie (b. 1876, TX), Joseph Eugene (b. 1881, TX); spouse, Lillie McElhaney (b. 1879, TX), married about 1898. *SR; A1b, d, f; A4a, b.*

HAYNES, WILLIAM HENRY. Born July 4, 1873, Iron Mountain, St. Francois County, Missouri. Ht. 5 ft. 8 ½ in., brown eyes, black hair, dark complexion, married. Stock farmer, Plainview, Hale County, Texas. SPECIAL RANGER Dec. 15, 1917–Mar. 1918 (Co. B Volunteers). Discharged. REMARKS: "Haynes will look after Briscoe Co." Had been a special agent for the AT&SF Railroad in Plainview. FAMILY: Spouse, Beula. *SR; Rawlings to Harley, Dec 23, 1917, AGC; A3a.*

HEAD, MARCELLUS C. Born Dec. 12, 1876, Lebanon, Wilson County, Tennessee. Ht. 5 ft. 8 in., gray eyes, light hair, blonde complexion, married. Stock farmer, Hansford, Hansford County, Texas. LOYALTY RANGER July 30, 1918–Feb. 1919. REMARKS: In 1910 was a farm laborer in Oklahoma Territory. In 1920 was a grain buyer in Hansford County. In 1930 was a farmer in Granite, Greer County, Oklahoma. FAMILY: Parents, Dr. J. C. Head (b. 1842, TN) and Roxanah (b. 1841, TN); siblings, Floy (b. 1875, TN), Eugene D. (b. 1875, TN), John B. (b. 1880, TN), Theodocia (b. 1881, TN), Irene (b. 1883, TN), Wiseman (b. 1886, TN); spouse, Estella McLeod (b. 1887, TX), married about 1906. *SR; A1b, d, e, f, g; A3a.*

HEARD, JAMES IRA "IRA." Born Mar. 13, 1895, Refugio, Refugio County, Texas. Ht. 5 ft. 7 in., dark eyes, brown hair, medium complexion. Clerk. REGULAR RANGER Sept. 1, 1917–Mar. 10, 1919 (private, Co. A). REMARKS: In June 1917 was deputy for the state Fish and Oyster Commission in Refugio County. In 1920 was an agent for an oil company in Refugio County. Died Nov. 30, 1946, Refugio County, Texas. FAMILY: Parents, A. Wilson J. Heard (b. 1863, TX) and Mary Elizabeth Doughty (b. 1865, AL); siblings, Allen William Lafette (b. 1886, TX), Joseph Clement (b. 1887, TX), Martha Annie (b. 1890, TX), John Wilson (b. 1898, TX), Mary Claire (b. 1903, TX); spouse, Pearl "Georgie" Simmons (b. 1897, TX). *SR; 471; Hensley to Harley, Mar 11, 1919, AGC; A1d, f; A2b; A3a; A4a, b, g.*

HEARN, ROY LEE. Born Jan. 15, 1891, Runge, Karnes County, Texas. Ht. 5 ft. 10 in., brown eyes, dark brown hair, dark complexion. Farmer, Leming, Atascosa County, Texas. REGULAR RANGER Dec. 9, 1919–Aug. 10, 1921 (private, Co. D). Resigned. REMARKS: Was raised near Fairview, Wilson County, Texas. Was a mounted Customs inspector, Dec. 26, 1921–Aug. 1, 1948; in 1930 was a U.S. Customs inspector in Alice, Jim Wells County, Texas. Retired to San Antonio, Bexar County, Texas. Died May 7, 1970, Bexar County, Texas; buried in Pearsall, Frio County, Texas. FAMILY: Parents, Jesse Lee Hearn (b. 1866, TX) and Mary Frances "Mollie" Chambles (b. 1871, TX); siblings, Eulen Doyel (b. 1892, TX), John Elzy (b. 1893, TX), Grace L.

(b. 1898, TX), Hazel Bell (b. 1907, TX). *SR; 471; 470:71, 103–105; 508: 93; 1000: iii, 128–129; A1d, e, g; A2a, b; A3a; A4a, b.*

HEDGECOKE, EUGENE ELDER. Born Aug. 30, 1879, Pilot Point, Denton County, Texas. Ht. 5 ft. 8 in., green eyes, black hair, dark complexion, married. Clerk, Plemons, Hutchinson County, Texas. LOYALTY RANGER June 10, 1918–Oct. 7, 1918. Was granted an honorable discharge because he was moving to New Mexico. REMARKS: In 1910 was a U.S. commissioner, lived in Endee, Quay County, New Mexico. In 1920 was a garage machinist in Endee. Still lived in Quay County in 1930. Died Nov. 15, 1955, Borger, Hutchinson County, Texas. FAMILY: Parents, John Monroe Hedgecoke (b. 1849, NC) and Minnie Belle Pitts (b. 1862, MO); siblings, Samuel Sidney (b. 1881, TX), John Monroe, Jr. (b. 1884, TX), Alpha Lou (b. 1886, TX), Minnie (b. 1889), Knox Pitts (b. 1892, TX), Fred (b. 1894, TX), Charles (b. 1900, TX); spouse, Ivey Inez McCormick (b. 1885, TX), married May 31, 1903, Plemons; son, Howard Eugene (b. 1906, NM). *SR; Hedgecoke to Harley, Sept 27, 1918, AGC; A1d, e, f, g; A2b; A3a; A4a, b, g; B2.*

HELTON, HENRY D. B. Born May 1870, Holly Springs, Cherokee County, Georgia. Ht. 5 ft. 8 in., blue eyes, light hair, light complexion, married. Farmer, Channing, Hartley County, Texas. LOYALTY RANGER June 14, 1918–Feb. 1919. REMARKS: Had been a farmer in Montague County, Texas and Canyon, Randall County, Texas. In 1930 was a farmer in Moore County, Texas. Died Dec. 7, 1946, Moore County, Texas. FAMILY: Parents, James L. Helton (b. 1872, GA) and Sarah (b. 1845, GA or SC); siblings, Lavinia (b. 1866, GA), William I. (b. 1868, GA), Christina (b. 1877, GA), Benjamin (b. 1878, GA); spouse, Manty E. "Lizzie" (b. 1870, GA), married about 1894; children, Horace E. (b. 1900, TX), Opal (b. 1903, TX), Walton (b. 1906, TX), Lella (b. 1908, TX). *SR; A1a, b, d, e, f, g; A2b.*

HENNE, HERBERT GEORGE. Born July 9, 1882, New Braunfels, Comal County, Texas. Ht. 5 ft. 8 ¼ in., gray eyes, blonde hair, fair complexion, married. Lawyer and farmer, New Braunfels. SPECIAL RANGER June 10, 1918–Dec. 31, 1919 (commission was renewed Jan. 15, 1919). Discharged. REMARKS: Letterhead: "Henne & Fuchs, Herbert G. Henne and John R. Fuchs, Attorneys at Law, New Braunfels, Texas." Was educated at the University of Texas, Austin. Was a Methodist. Died May 15, 1932, San Antonio, Bexar County, Texas; buried in Henne Plot, New Braunfels. FAMILY: Parents, Louis S. Henne (b. 1841, Germany) and Emilie (b. 1852, TX); siblings, Louis A. (b. 1875, TX), Adolph (b. 1877, TX), Emma (b. 1880, TX); spouse, Inez Dorothy Gordon (b. 1887, MO), married Sept. 26, 1912, Chillicothe, Missouri; daughter, Mary Jean (b. 1923, MO). *SR; A1d, e, f, g; A3a; A4b, g; C.*

HENRICH, STEVEN AUGUST. (Birth name was Johanson Augusta Henryes III.) Born Oct. 16, 1873, Clinton, DeWitt County, Texas (Helena, Karnes County, Texas?). Ht. 6 ft. 1 in., brown eyes, dark brown hair, fair complexion. Peace officer. REGULAR RANGER Aug. 13, 1915–Sept. 8, 1915 (private, Co. A). Discharged/fired. Note length of service. REMARKS: Was fired as a result of Austin brawl involving Capt. E. H. Smith. Had been a policeman, Dallas, Dallas County, Texas. In 1910 was a butcher living in Dallas, Dallas County, Texas. Was recommended for the Rangers in 1915 by J. F. "Jake" Wolters. In Jan. 1916 was reportedly in the Karnes City jail on a felony charge, still claiming to be a Texas Ranger. In 1920 was a peace officer in Columbus, Luna County, New Mexico. In 1930 was a laundryman in Tucson, Pima County, Arizona. Died Mar. 18, 1953, Tucson, Pima County, Arizona; buried in Evergreen Cemetery, Tucson. FAMILY: Parents, Johanson "Johnson" Augusta Henryes (b. 1827, Holland or Germany) and Lavinia Margaret Austin (b. 1838, TN); siblings, Johanna Elizabeth "Josie" (b. 1867, TX), Roberta (b. 1870, TX), LaBinde (b. 1872, TX); spouse #1, unknown, married about 1891; son, Lafayette Belle "Fate" (b. 1896, TX); spouse #2, Katherine "Katy" Robinson (b. 1890, Germany), married about 1908; children, Steven, Jr. (b. 1910, TX), Felipe "Phillip" (b. 1911, TX), Roberta (b. 1914, TX); spouse #3, Elsie Louela Cordes-Tes Hildebrandt (b. 1893, TX), married Apr. 21, 1921, El Paso County, Texas, later divorced; children, Patricia Oranelle, Felicia "Louise," Gloria Merilyn (b. 1923, TX), twins (?) Victoria and Victor (b. 1925, NM), Tex Yuma (b. 1926, AZ), Clinton Dewitt (b. 1930, AZ). (Note: Spelling of family name listed variously as Henryes, Henrys, Henries, Heinrich.) *SR; 471; Wolters to McKay, Aug 12, 1915, AGC; [AG] to Ferguson, Sept 8, 1915, WC; Depositions, Sept 8, 9, 1915, WC; Brown to Ferguson, Jan 2, 1916, WC; AG to Brown, Jan 4, 1916, WC; EPMT, July 12, 1915; 1521; A1a, b, d, e, f, g; A2e; A4b.*

HENRICHSON, HORACE COMLEY "COMLEY." Born May 3, 1887, Bluntzer, Nueces County, Texas. Ht. 6 ft., brown eyes, black hair, dark complexion, married. Stockman and farmer, Valley Wells, Dimmit County, Texas. SPECIAL RANGER May 7, 1918–Jan. 15, 1919. REMARKS: Deputy sheriff, Valley Wells, Apr. 1918. Died Feb. 23, 1934, Hidalgo County, Texas; buried in Weslaco, Hidalgo County. FAMILY: Parents, George Washington Henrichson (b. 1832, LA) and Charlotte Elizabeth Ashton (b. 1850, KY); siblings, George William (b. 1868, TX), Robert Lee (b. 1870, TX), John Edward (b. 1872, TX), James Hunter (b. 1875, TX), twins Ashton Charleston and Charleston Ashton (b. 1879, TX), Mary Olivia (b. 1883, TX); spouse, Lenora Jurdena Poole (b. 1889, TX), married Mar. 20, 1907; children, Lenora Charlotte (b. 1908, TX), Ruby Mary (b. 1909, TX), Horace Timon (b. 1912, TX), Edward Grover (b. 1914, TX), Clara Olivia (b. 1917, TX), Roy Day (b. 1923, TX). *SR; Assistant AG to Gardner, Apr 25, 1918, AGC; A1f; A3a; A4b, g; C.*

HENRY, DEMPSEY F. Born Apr. 1863, Brushy Creek, Anderson County, Texas. Ht. 5 ft. 11 in., brown eyes, black hair, dark complexion, married. Farmer, Athens, Henderson County, Texas. LOYALTY RANGER June 5, 1918–Feb. 1919. REMARKS: Had been deputy sheriff, constable, tax assessor, 4 years. Retired, living in Athens in 1930. FAMILY: Parents, Isaac Henry (b. 1818, AL or AR) and Mary Jane (b. 1825, AL or AR); brothers, Isaac (b. 1855, TX), George (b. 1858, TX), John (b. 1860, TX); spouse #1, Frances Aveline "Frankie" Richardson, married about 1901, she died in 1909; spouse #2, Hattie Moss (b. 1890, TX), married about 1914; son, Jim F. (b. 1915, TX). *SR; A1a, b, e, f, g; A2e; A4b.*

HENRY, JOHN QUINCY. Born Mar. 4, 1873, Byrd Township, Brown County, Ohio. Ht. 5 ft. 10 in., blue eyes, brown hair, dark complexion, widower. Rancher and county judge, Comstock, Val Verde County, Texas. SPECIAL RANGER Dec. 8, 1917–Jan. 15, 1919. REMARKS: Owned a ranch near Sanderson, Terrell County, Texas. In 1910 had been a school teacher in Flatonia, Fayette County, Texas. In 1920 was a lawyer in Val Verde County; in 1930 was a lawyer in general practice in Mission, Hidalgo County, Texas. Died Mar. 9, 1961, Mission, Hidalgo County, Texas; buried in Oak Hill Cemetery, Flatonia, Fayette County, Texas. FAMILY: Parents, George Quincy Henry (b. 1846, OH) and Sarah Martha Pickerill (b. 1848, OH); siblings, James Wilson (b. 1870, OH), Cora Malinda (b. 1875, OH); spouse, Bessie Burnes (b. 1873, TX), married Aug. 11, 1898, Flatonia, Fayette County, Texas, died before 1910; children, Martha Beatrice (b. 1900, TX), John Quincy (b. 1904, TX). *SR; A1b, d, e, f, g; A2b; A3a; B2.*

HENRY, LEE WILLIAM. Born Sept. 12, 1883, Goliad, Goliad County, Texas. Ht. 6 ft. 1 in., blue eyes, gray hair, fair complexion, married. Ranchman, Pearsall, Frio County, Texas. REGULAR RANGER Aug. 6, 1918–unknown (private, Co. I; still in Oct. 28, 1918). Discharged or resigned—unknown. REMARKS: As of Sept. 10, 1918 was serving as a Ranger in Austin, Travis County, Texas. In 1930 was a farmer in Frio County. Died Oct. 6, 1959, Frio County, Texas. FAMILY: Spouse, Eula Beatrice Mudd (b. 1894, TX), married Oct. 23, 1916, San Antonio, Bexar County, Texas; children, Vivian L. (b. 1918, TX), Roy L. (b. 1921, TX), Marshall (b. 1924, TX). *SR; A1e, g; A3a.*

HENSLEY, JOHN EDWARD. Born Dec. 28, 1880, Rockdale, Milam County, Texas. Ht. 5 ft. 9 ½ in., brown eyes, brown hair, dark complexion, married. Peace officer. REGULAR RANGER May 27, 1918–Mar. 10, 1919 (private, Co. A). Honorably discharged—Co. A was disbanded. Texas Ranger, Norias, Willacy County, Texas. REGULAR RANGER June 20, 1919–Feb. 21, 1925 (private, Co. D, reenlisted under the new law). Discharged. REMARKS: Deputy sheriff, Coleman County, Texas, 1909. Subsequent career: Texas Liquor Control Board agent; Immigration inspector; Hidalgo County, Texas, deputy sheriff and jailer; Brownsville, Cameron County, Texas policeman. In 1930 was a border patrolman in Donna, Hidalgo County, Texas. WWI Draft Registration document states, "Right arm crooked—has been broken." Died Apr. 28, 1948, Donna, Hidalgo County, Texas. FAMILY: Parents, William Edward Hensley (b. 1849, TX) and Sarah Alpina Wilkinson (b. 1859, TX); siblings, Arthur Rufus (b. 1879, TX), Lula M. (b. 1883, TX), Gertrude P. (b. 1885, TX), Lenora Bird "Birdie" (b. 1888, TX), Lela Elizabeth (b. 1890, TX), Jessie Florence (b. 1892), Oran H. (b. 1900, TX); spouse #1, Johnnie Mabel (b. 1887, TX), married about 1904; sons, Elgene (b. 1905, TX), Graham (b. 1910, TX); spouse #2, Lina M. Wright (b. 1898, TX), married about 1922; daughters, Zelda Glo (b. 1925, TX), Annette (b. 1929, TX). *SR; 471; Special Orders No. 21, Mar 10, 1919, WC; 469: 60; 470: 11, 43; A1a, d, e, f, g; A2b, e; A3a; A4g.*

HEPPEL, FRANK BARRETT. Born Jan. 28, 1875, Little Rock, Pulaski County, Arkansas. Ht. 5 ft. 8 ½ in., blue eyes, brown hair, fair complexion, married. Special agent, GC&SF Railroad, Dallas, Dallas County, Texas. SPECIAL RANGER Jan. 4, 1919–Dec. 31, 1919. Special officer, GC&SF Railroad, Dallas. RAILROAD RANGER July 10, 1923–July 10, 1925. WA expired. SPECIAL RANGER Oct. 16, 1925–Oct. 16, 1927; Dec. 10, 1927–Nov. 26, 1928. Superintendent of Special Service, GC&SF Railroad, Galveston, Galveston County, Texas. SPECIAL RANGER Nov. 26, 1928–Jan. 26, 1929; Dec. 19, 1929–Apr. 3, 1930. Discharged. REMARKS: Had been a tinner, Dallas Tinware Manufacturing Company, while living in Dallas in 1900. His 1925 enlistment form states "Smith Detective Agency." In 1930 was living in El Paso, El Paso County, Texas. A Frank B. Heppel died Jan. 3, 1934, Dallas County, Texas. FAMILY: Parents, William Heppel (b. 1825, England) and Martha (b. 1833, IL); brother, Charles (b. 1870, AR); spouse, Mary Redifer (b. 1875, MD or PA), married about 1893; children, William Samuel (b. 1894, TX), Marshall Frank (b. 1896, TX), Ora Lee (b. 1900, TX), Seth E. (b. 1901, TX). *SR; A1b, d, e, f, g; A3a; A5a; C.*

HERBST, ARTHUR WALLINGTON. Born June 1, 1874, Angola, Steuben County, Indiana. Ht. 5 ft. 10 in., blue eyes, gray hair, medium complexion, married. Special agent, SA&AP Railroad, San Antonio, Bexar County, Texas. SPECIAL RANGER Apr. 30, 1917–Dec. 31, 1919 (attached to Co. C; WA was reinstated Dec. 22, 1917; commission was renewed Jan. 27, 1919). Discharged. REMARKS: In 1900 was a railroad detective and in 1910 was a prison guard, living in Jackson, Jackson County, Michigan. In 1930 was a city detective in San Antonio. Died Dec. 2, 1941, San Antonio, Bexar County, Texas. FAMILY: Parents, William Herbst (b. 1829, Prussia) and Mary (b. 1837, PA); brother, John N. (b. 1871, IN); spouse, Louella Webb (b. 1875, MI), married about 1900; daughter, Ruth E. (b. 1906, MI). *SR; Earnest to Harley, Dec 21, 1917, AGC; AG to Earnest, Dec 22, 1917, AGC; Herbst to Harley, Apr 20, 1918, AGC; A1b, d, e, f, g; A3a; C.*

HERR, A. WOODWARD. Born Aug. 31, 1888, Louisville, Jefferson County, Kentucky. Ht. 5 ft. 10 ½ in., gray eyes, black hair, fair complexion. Traveling passenger agent, MKT Railroad, Fort Worth, Tarrant County, Texas. SPECIAL RANGER Oct. 19, 1917–June 27, 1918 (attached to Co. D). Discharged. Division passenger agent, MKT Railroad, Houston, Harris County, Texas. RAILROAD RANGER Nov. 22, 1923–Nov. 22, 1925. Discharged. SPECIAL RANGER July 16, 1928–June 14, 1929; June 14, 1929–June 14, 1930; June 14, 1930–June 14, 1931. Discharged. Division passenger agent, MKT Railroad, Fort Worth. SPECIAL RANGER June 14, 1931–Jan. 18, 1933; Jan. 31, 1933–Jan. 22, 1935. Discharged. REMARKS: An A. W. Herr died Mar. 24, 1958, Tarrant County, Texas. FAMILY: Parents, Alfred Herr (b. 1861, KY) and Alice (b. 1863, KY); siblings, Ruth (b. 1883, KY), John (b. 1886, KY). *SR; A1d, f, g; A2b; A3a.*

HERRERA, JOSE. Born Apr. 13, 1886, Laredo, Webb County, Texas. Medium height, slender, brown eyes, brown hair. Texas quarantine guard, Laredo, Webb County. SPECIAL RANGER Feb. 5, 1918–Jan. 15, 1919. REMARKS: Webb County deputy sheriff, 1915–1916. FAMILY: Parents, Jesus Herrera (b. 1844, TX) and Guadalupe (b. 1854, Mexico); siblings, Isidro (b. 1875, Mexico), Jesus (b. 1876, Mexico), Asilio (b. 1878, Mexico), Refujio (b. 1881, TX). *SR; Collins to Harley, Feb 1, 1920, AGC; LWT, Nov 7, 1915, July 16, 1916, Sept 5, 1920; A1d; A3a.*

HERZING, JOHN FRANK. Born Sept. 29, 1889, Brackettville, Kinney County, Texas. Ht. 6 ft. 1 in., blue eyes, light hair, light complexion, married as of July 1919. Cowboy, Kinney County. REGULAR RANGER Sept. 20, 1917–Mar. 1919 (private, Co. E). Discharged when Co. E was disbanded. FAMILY: Parents, John Herzing, Jr. (b. 1867, DC) and Auguste Senne (b. 1871, Germany); siblings, Henry Emil (b. 1891, TX), Fritz Charley (b. 1894, TX), Charlotte Therese "Lottie" (b. 1897, TX), Esther Lee (b. 1901, TX), Louis Henry (b. 1909, TX), Annie (b. 1911, TX); spouse, Tennie (b. 1901, TX); children, J. L. (b. 1922, TX), Cora Pearl (b. 1923, TX). *SR; 471; Barler to Friffiths, Sept 20, 1917, AGC; Barler to Harley, Oct 12, 1917, AGC; Herzing to Harley, July 8, 1919, AGC; A1d, e, f, g; A2e; A3a; A4b.*

HESTER, THOMAS IGNATIUS. Born Mar. 31, 1889, Village Mills, Hardin County, Texas. Tall, medium build, gray eyes, light brown hair, married. Contractor and druggist, Donna, Hidalgo County, Texas. LOYALTY RANGER May 31, 1918–Feb. 1919. REMARKS: His father, A. F. Hester, was a bank president at Donna. T. I. Hester was involved in mistreatment of local Mexicans. In Oct. 1918, Hester stated that he was 39 years old; in May, 1918, his enlistment form listed his age as 29. A Thomas I. Hester died Oct. 20, 1955, Hidalgo County, Texas. FAMILY: Parents, Albert Franklin Hester (b. 1847, MS) and Mary Jane "Mollie" Richardson (b. 1859, TX); siblings, Mary Amanda (b. 1884, TX), Andrew Franklin (b. 1885, TX), Forrest Edmund (b. 1891, TX), Maggie Kathleen (b. 1898, TX); spouse, Ada L. Feagin or Fagan (b. 1883, IA), married about 1910; daughter, Florence L. (b. 1912, TX). *SR; Hester's statement, Oct 13, 1918, WC; Abney and Hester to Hanson, Nov 7, 1918, WC; A1d, f, g; A2b; A3a; A4a, b, g.*

HEUERMANN, EDWARD JOSEPH. Born May 1, 1887, San Antonio, Bexar County, Texas. Ht. 6 ft. 1 in., gray eyes, light hair, fair complexion, married. Farmer, Odem, San Patricio County, Texas. REGULAR RANGER Jan. 1, 1916–Dec. 1916 (private, Co. A). Resigned. Farmer, Odem. SPECIAL RANGER Mar. 23, 1931–Jan. 20, 1933. Discharged—WA expired. REMARKS: Texas quarantine guard, Jan.–Aug. 1917. Was also a San Patricio County deputy sheriff and constable. Attended Texas A&M College. In Aug. 1917 became a 1st lieutenant in the infantry, served overseas. In 1920 was an oil field worker in San Patricio County. In WWII was a military intelligence agent. Became a prosperous farmer in San Patricio County. Died Feb. 9, 1968, Odem, San Patricio County, Texas. FAMILY: Mother, Ottilie (b. 1862, TX); siblings, Augusta L. (b. 1885, TX), William G. (b. 1886, TX). *SR; Barnes to AG, Feb 23, 1918, AGC; Heuermann to Hanson, May 1, 1919, AGC; Lucy to AG, Jun 1, 1920, AGC; Aldrich to Lucy, Jun 3, 1920, AGC; 319: 15, 195; A1d, f; A2a, b; A3a.*

HEY, BEN GOOCH. Born Aug. 4, 1872, Mason, Mason County, Texas. Ht. 5 ft. 7 in., dark gray eyes, brown hair, light complexion, married. Real estate and livestock commission agent, Junction, Kimble County, Texas. SPECIAL RANGER Dec. 20, 1917–Jan. 15, 1919. REMARKS: One source lists his given names as Ben Louis August. In 1910 was county clerk in Mason County. Died Mar. 11, 1940, Mason County, Texas; buried in Gooch Cemetery, Mason. FAMILY: Parents, T. Wilson Hey (b. 1837, England) and Johanna "Hannah" Korn (b. 1849, TX); siblings, Caroline (b. 1874, TX), Alice K. (b. 1875, TX), Sophia Catherina "Kate" (b. 1877, TX), Wilson Smith (b. 1878, TX), Mina Hannah (b. 1880, TX), Sophia V. (b. 1882, TX), Mary Ellen (b. 1883, TX), James Louis (b. 1885, TX), twins Nettie B. and Maggie G. (b. 1887, TX), Lena (b. 1891, TX), Walter S. (b. 1893, TX), Rob Roy (b. 1899, TX); spouse, Maud Dixie Kountz (b. 1884, TX), married Aug. 5, 1903; children, Dixie F. (b. 1904, TX), Mable Benellen (b. 1905, TX), Ruth C. (b. 1908, TX), Johanna K. (b. 1919, TX), Ruth S. (b. 1921, TX). *SR; A1b, d, e, f, g; A4b; C.*

HIBBERT, FRANK H. Born Aug. 1867, Galveston, Galveston County, Texas. No physical description, married. Contractor, Galveston. LOYALTY RANGER. June 14, 1918–Feb. 1919. REMARKS: Had owned a boarding and livery stable in Galveston. In 1920 was a sand-hauling contractor in Galveston. Died May 7, 1922, Galveston County, Texas. FAMILY: Parents, John Hibbert (b. 1828, England) and Ann (b. 1828, Ireland); siblings, William H. (b. 1855, TX), John B. (b. 1856, TX), Anne (b. 1869, TX); spouse, Lotta Welschhans (b. 1874, LA), married about 1890; sons, John Frederick (b. 1893, TX), Walter (b. 1903, TX). *SR; A1a, b, d, e, f; A3a; A4g; C.*

HICKEY, RICHARD TOLIVER. Born May 14, 1894, Navarro County, Texas. Ht. 5 ft. 8 in., brown eyes, black hair, dark complexion, married. Pressman, Dallas, Dallas County, Texas. REGULAR RANGER Feb. 23, 1921–May 31, 1921 (private, Co. B). Resigned. REMARKS: Note length of service. In 1930 was a printer in a print shop in Chicago, Cook County, Illinois. Died Nov. 6, 1967, South Houston, Harris County, Texas. FAMILY: Parents, William Alexander Hickey (b. 1852, TN) and Charlotte Temple Edington (b. 1853, TN); siblings, Mary Elizabeth (b. 1875, TN), Tennessee Victoria (b. 1877, TN), James Edgar (b. 1879, TN), Laura Catherine (b. 1881, TN), William Leslie (b. 1883, TX), Flora Mae (b. 1887, TX), Jessie (b. 1890), Lynnie (b. 1891), Joann A. (b. 1897, TX); spouse, Allie or Ollie (b. 1896, OK or AL), married about 1911. *SR; 471; A1d, f, g; A2a, b; A3a; A4b, g.*

HICKMAN, THOMAS RUFUS. Born Feb. 21, 1886 on the Hickman Ranch, Gainesville, Cooke County, Texas. Ht. 6 ft., brown eyes, brown hair, married, as of June 1931. Stockman, Gainesville, Cooke County. REGULAR RANGER June 16, 1919–Jan. 18, 1933 (private, Co. B; transferred to Headquarters Co., Feb. 1, 1920; promoted to sergeant, Oct. 1, 1920; captain of Emergency Co. No. 2, Nov. 22,

1920; transferred to Co. B when Emergency Co. No. 2 was disbanded, Feb. 15, 1921; reenlisted May 10, 1922, as captain of Co. B; captain of Headquarters Co., June 16, 1925; transferred to Co. B, May 1, 1927; reenlisted June 16, 1927; reenlisted June 16, 1929; reenlisted June 16, 1931). Discharged. Peace officer, Gainesville. REGULAR RANGER Jan. 23, 1935–Nov. 12, 1935 (captain, Co. B; captain, Headquarters Co., Sept. 1, 1935). Resigned over dispute with Governor James Allred over incorporating the Texas Rangers into the Department of Public Safety. REMARKS: Appointed deputy constable in Gainesville, 1907 until 1911 when he was appointed deputy sheriff. After resigning from the Rangers, joined security department of the Gulf Oil Company. Was a member of the Public Safety Commission, 1957 until 1961 when he became chairman. Died Jan. 29, 1962, Gainesville, Cooke County, Texas. FAMILY: Parents, Walker B. Hickman (b. 1849, KY) and Mary A. "Mollie" (b. 1857, KY); siblings, William B. (b. 1885, TX), Nannie (b. 1888, TX); spouse, Tina Martha Knight; sons, Thomas Rufus, Jr. (b. 1937, TX), David Benton (b. 1942, TX). *SR; 471; Hickman to Hulen, Apr 6, 1917, AGC; Hickman to AG, Apr 12, 15, 1917, AGC; AG to Hickman, Apr 14, 1917, AGC; Jennings to Hutchings, May 2, 1917, AGC; Culp to Ferguson, May 5, 1917, AGC; Herblin to Hutchings, May 6, 1917, AGC; Hickman to Hutchings, May 21, 1917, AGC; Dayton to Hutchings, Aug 21, 1917, AGC; AG to Dayton, Aug 22, 1917, AGC; Aldrich to Brady, Nov 26, 1920, AGC; 522: 388–389; 470: 43; 463: 102–111, 143–150, 161–163, 280; 319: 106–107, 112, 200, 202, 229, 520–521; 497:127–129; 172:III, 586; A1d, e; A2b, e; A3a.*

HICKS, ALEXANDER LINCOLN. Born July 4, 1867, Watertown, Jefferson County, New York. Ht. 5 ft. 8 in., blue eyes, gray hair, fair complexion, married. U.S. government employee, San Antonio, Bexar County, Texas. LOYALTY RANGER May 31, 1918–Feb. 1919. REMARKS: Was a carpenter, working for the U.S. Army in San Antonio; in 1920 was a clerk for the Army in San Antonio. Died May 2, 1922, San Antonio, Bexar County, Texas. FAMILY: Spouse #1, Pauline Mathilda Schneider (b. 1866, TX), married about 1892; children, Alexander P. (b. 1892, TX), Mary (b. 1893, TX), Carlina "Carrie" (b. 1896, TX), Lillian (b. 1901, TX), Josephine (b. 1908, TX); spouse #2, Fannie (b. 1868, TX). *SR; A1d, e, f; A2b; A4b.*

HICKS, STONEWALL JACKSON. Born Mar. 1862, Sturgeon, Boone County, Missouri. No physical description, married. Farmer, Comanche County, Texas. LOYALTY RANGER May 31, 1918–Feb. 1919. REMARKS: In 1910 had been a merchant in a general store in Comanche. In 1920 and 1930 was a bank clerk and then a bank collector in Comanche. Died Nov. 1, 1934, Comanche County, Texas. FAMILY: Parents, Absalom Hicks (b. 1823, MO) and Elizabeth F. Marney (b. 1824, MO); siblings, Luther C. (b. 1845, MO), Young E. (b. 1849, MO), Marian F. (b. 1852, MO), Janett W. (b. 1853, MO), James W. (b. 1854, MO), Susan Flora (b. 1857, MO), W. Elizabeth (b. 1858, MO), Sterling Price (b. 1867, TX); spouse, Sarah J. (b. 1859, MS), married about 1896; children, Stella (b. 1890, TX), Bessie (b. 1896, TX), Perry M. (b. 1898, TX), Edelia D. (b. 1902, TX). *SR; A1a, b, e, f, g; A4b; C.*

HIGHFILL, KNOX LIVINGSTON. Born June 9, 1887, Summerfield, Guilford County, North Carolina. Ht. 5 ft. 8 in., blue eyes, brown hair, light complexion, married. Inspector, San Antonio, Bexar County, Texas. SPECIAL RANGER May 5, 1919–Dec. 31, 1919. REMARKS: Was a horticulturalist and nurseryman, lived in Bee County in 1910; in 1917 worked for the Waxahachie Nursery Company, Dallas County, Texas. By 1930 was a house painter in Guilford County. At time of death was a retired plumber in Greensboro, Guilford County. Died Sept. 26, 1959, Greensboro, Guilford County, North Carolina, following a stroke; buried in Forest Lawn Cemetery, Greensboro. FAMILY: Parents, William Simpson Highfill (b. 1861, NC) and Sarah Doskey Canada (b. 1869, NC); siblings, Lissie L. (b. 1889, NC), William R. (b. 1891, NC), Marjorie Pearl (b. 1897, NC), Geneva (b. 1905, NC); spouse, Rosa Case (b. 1886, NC), married about 1918; daughters, Hollyee (b. 1920, TX), Estella (b. 1924, NC), Maxine (b. 1926, NC), Edith (b. 1928, NC). *SR; 471; A1d, e, g; A21; A3a.*

HILBURN, ALONZO BATES "LON." Born July 7, 1888, Pleasanton, Atascosa County, Texas. Ht. 5 ft. 10 in., blue eyes, sandy hair, light complexion, married. Horseman/wrangler—had been foreman of U.S. government remount station at Fort Sam Houston. Enlisted in Bexar County, Texas. REGULAR RANGER Dec. 14, 1917–Sept.

10, 1918 (private, Co. G). Discharged. REGULAR RANGER unknown–Dec. 1918 (reinstated and assigned to Co. F). Resigned. LAW ENFORCEMENT RELATIVES: Ranger Ernest Hilburn, brother. REMARKS: Died Jan. 24, 1966, Atascosa County, Texas. FAMILY: Parents, William Anderson Hilburn (b. 1862, TN) and Lula Christina Route (b. 1865, TX); siblings, Ernest (b. 1891, TX), Henderson (b. 1894, TX), Ruth Eloise (b. 1900, TX), Ila; spouse, Lydia W. Eckhart (b. 1890, TX), married Feb. 6, 1906, Atascosa County. *SR; 471; A1d, e; A2b; A3a; A4b, d, f.*

HILBURN, ERNEST. Born July 17, 1891, Pleasanton, Atascosa County, Texas. Ht. 5 ft. 11 ¼ in., blue eyes, dark hair, ruddy complexion. Laborer, Crystal City, Zavala County, Texas. SPECIAL RANGER July 24, 1916–Dec. 1917 (attached to Co. C). REMARKS: In June 1917 lived in Phoenix, Arizona, but "worked for the government" in Leon Springs, Bexar County, Texas. Died Feb. 6, 1928, Atascosa County, Texas. LAW ENFORCEMENT RELATIVES: Ranger Alonzo B. Hilburn, brother. FAMILY: Parents, William Anderson Hilburn (b. 1862, TN) and Lula Christina Route (b. 1865, TX); siblings, Alonzo B. (b. 1888, TX), Henderson (b. 1894, TX), Ruth Eloise (b. 1900, TX), Ila. *SR; Hilburn to Hutchings, May 26, 1917, AGC; AG to Taylor, July 8, 1916, AGC; Taylor to AG, July 16, 1916, AGC; Hilburn to AG, July 25, 1918, AGC; AG to Hilburn, July 29, 1918, AGC; A1d, e; A2b; A3a; A4b, d, e; B2.*

HILL, ARTHUR WOODS. Born May 12, 1878, Belton, Bell County, Texas. Ht. 6 ft. 2 in., blue eyes, sandy hair, sandy complexion, married. Brand inspector, Barnhart, Irion County, Texas. REGULAR RANGER Dec. 22, 1917–Mar. 1918 (private, Co. F). Discharged. REMARKS: Note length of service. Had been a peace officer. In 1910 was a farmer in Concho County, Texas. In Sept. 1918 was a U.S. Customs inspector at Presidio, Presidio County, Texas. In 1920 was a U.S. government scout living in Marfa, Presidio County. World War I Draft Registration document stated "Rheumatism in left leg." FAMILY: Parents, John A. Hill (b. 1852, AL) and Mary E. (b. 1857, TX); siblings, Eva L. (b. 1874, TX), Roy L. (b. 1891, TX); spouse, Lela Walker (b. 1882, TX), married about 1907; son, Guy W. (b. 1908, TX). *SR; Bates to Hill, Dec 21, 1917, AGC; Bates to Johnston, Dec 21, 1917, AGC; A1b, d, e, f; A3a.*

HILL, CHARLES W. Born Mar. 1869, Bastrop County, Texas. Ht. 5 ft. 11 in., brown eyes, dark hair, dark complexion, married. Farmer, Kingsville, Kleberg County, Texas. SPECIAL RANGER Apr. 15, 1918–Jan. 15, 1919. REMARKS: Was Bastrop County deputy sheriff, 1910–1911. In 1930 was a farmer living in Austin, Travis County, Texas. A Charles Watson Hill died Jan. 18, 1938, Travis County, Texas. FAMILY: Parents, Robert T. Hill (b. 1842, TX) and Lucinda Caldwell (b. 1844, TX); siblings, Amanda (b. 1870, TX), Annie S. (b. 1873, TX), Mary (b. 1875), John C. (b. 1976, TX), Walter H. (b. 1880, TX); spouse, Tennie Burleson (b. 1872, TX), married May 20, 1891; children, Robert A. (b. 1893, TX), Richard A. (b. 1898, TX). *SR; Scarborough to Harley, Apr 15, 1918, AGC; EPMT, 9, 10 Aug 1910; AS, July 14, 1911; A1a, b, d, f, g; A2b; A4b, g.*

HILL, GEORGE ORVILLE. Born Sept. 18, 1896, Cotulla, La Salle County, Texas. Ht. 6 ft., brown eyes, dark hair, fair complexion. Ranchman. REGULAR RANGER Dec. 26, 1917–July 16, 1918 (private, Co. I). Resigned to take a better-paying job with the U.S. Public Health Service. LAW ENFORCEMENT RELATIVES: Ranger Jesse J. Hill, uncle. REMARKS: Was a stockman in Webb County, Texas in 1920. A George O. Hill died June 10, 1962, Webb County, Texas. FAMILY: Parents, John "Jack" E. Hill (b. 1876, TX) and Emma E. (b. 1879, TX); siblings, Amy Christine (b. 1899, TX), Clifton C. (b. 1904, TX); spouse, K. Alice (b. 1902, TX). *SR; 471; Harley to Hill, July 17, 1918, AGC; A1d, e, f; A2b; A3a.*

HILL, GORDON. Born May 4, 1887, Austin, Travis County, Texas. Ht. 6 ft., gray eyes, brown hair, fair complexion. Ranchman, Harlingen, Cameron County, Texas. SPECIAL RANGER Sept. 8, 1915–Dec. 1917 (attached to Co. C). REMARKS: Participated in the Norias fight, Aug. 8, 1915. Didn't qualify for reappointment as SPECIAL RANGER because he was of draft age. REMARKS: A Gordon Hill died Oct. 29, 1918, Cameron County, Texas. LAW ENFORCEMENT RELATIVES: Ranger Lon C. Hill, father; Ranger John A. Hill, brother; Ranger Sam H. Hill, uncle; Ranger William H. Hill, cousin. FAMILY: Parents, Leonidas Carrington "Lon" Hill (b. 1862, TX) and Eustacia Dabney (b. 1864, TX); siblings, Paul (b. 1883, TX), Ida (b. 1885, TX), Lon C. (b. 1889, TX), John A. (b. 1892, TX),

Annie R. (b. 1894, TX), William H. (b. 1896, TX), Eustacia (b. 1898, TX). *SR; Hill to Harley, Jan 2, 1918, AGC; Gay, "Amazing," WC; 319: 34–35; 425: 92; 463: 58–59; A1d; A3a; A4g; C.*

HILL, JESSE JAMES. Born Dec. 27, 1882, Cotulla, La Salle County, Texas. Ht. 5 ft. 6 in., blue eyes, dark hair, light complexion. Stockman. REGULAR RANGER Dec. 1917 (?)–Feb. 1, 1919 (private, Co. I). Honorably discharged. REMARKS: Date of enlistment is approximate; no date is given in Service Record. In 1918 was a Ranger in Laredo, Webb County, Texas. In 1930 was a transfer truck driver in Laredo. LAW ENFORCEMENT RELATIVES: Ranger George O. Hill, nephew. FAMILY: Parents, George W. Hill (b. 1845, MO) and Eliza Jane (b. 1847, TX); siblings, Alta F. (b. 1869, TX), William (b. 1870, TX), Anna (b. 1873, TX), John "Jack" (b. 1876, TX); spouse #1, Henrietta; spouse #2, Guadalupe (b. 1900, Mexico), married about 1923. *SR; 471; A1b, d, g; A3a.*

HILL, JOHN AUGUSTUS. Born May 29, 1892, Beeville, Bee County, Texas. Ht. 5 ft. 11 in., blue eyes, black hair, light complexion. Stockman and farmer, Armstrong, Willacy County, Texas (1918 address: c/o Kleberg, Norias, Armstrong, Texas). SPECIAL RANGER Jan. 7, 1918–Dec. 31, 1919 (commission was renewed Jan. 23, 1919). Discharged. Oil business, San Antonio, Bexar County, Texas. SPECIAL RANGER Feb. 22, 1933–Feb. 26, 1934 (WA was extended to Feb. 26, 1934). Discharged. REMARKS: In May 1917 was deputy sheriff of Cameron County, Texas. Died Sept. 5, 1978, Harris County, Texas. LAW ENFORCEMENT RELATIVES: Ranger Lon C. Hill, father; Ranger Gordon Hill, brother; Ranger Sam H. Hill, uncle; Ranger William H. Hill, cousin. FAMILY: Parents, Leonidas Carrington "Lon" Hill (b. 1862, TX) and Eustacia Dabney (b. 1864, TX); siblings, Paul (b. 1883, TX), Ida (b. 1885, TX), Gordon (b. 1887, TX); Lon C. (b. 1889, TX), Annie R. (b. 1894, TX), William H. (b. 1896, TX), Eustacia (b. 1898, TX); spouse, Lilliam A. (b. 1909, CA), married about 1928. *SR; A1d, e, f, g; A2a, b; A4g; A3a.*

HILL, LEONIDAS CARRINGTON "LON." Born July 31, 1862, Manor, Travis County, Texas. Ht. 6 ft., gray eyes, black hair, married. Rancher, Harlingen, Cameron County, Texas. SPECIAL RANGER Aug. 28, 1915–Dec. 1917 (attached to Co. C); Jan. 28, 1918–Dec. 31, 1919 (commission was renewed Jan. 23, 1919). Discharged. REMARKS: In 1900 was a lawyer in Beeville, Bee County, Texas. In 1910 was a land promoter living in Austin, Travis County, Texas. For a time was one of the biggest landowners in the Lower Rio Grande Valley. Died May 5, 1935, Harlingen, Cameron County, Texas. LAW ENFORCEMENT RELATIVES: Ranger Gordon Hill, son; Ranger John A. Hill, son; Ranger Sam H. Hill, brother; Ranger William H. Hill, nephew. FAMILY: Parents, William Hickman Hill (b. 1822, TN) and Minerva Frances Vernon (b. 1832, TN); siblings, Elizabeth Ewing (b. 1847, TN), Sarah Hibernia (b. 1849, TN), Mary Ann (b. 1851, TN), Rowena Vick (b. 1854, TX), William Hickman (b. 1857, TX), Sam Houston (b. 1859, TX), John Augustus (b. 1865, TX), Frances Hickman "Fanny" (b. 1867, TX); spouse, Eustacia Dabney (b. 1864, TX), married Dec. 13, 1882, Austin County, Texas; children, Paul (b. 1883, TX), Ida (b. 1885, TX), Gordon (b. 1887, TX); Lon C. (b. 1889, TX), John Augustus (b. 1892), Annie Rooney (b. 1894, TX), William Hickman (b. 1896, TX), Eustacia Dabney (b. 1898, TX), George Pendexter (b. 1902, TX). *SR; 172:III, 614–616; 1: I, 1253–1265; BDH, Aug 17, Oct 17, 24, 1910; SAE, Oct 18, 1911; 319: 51–52, 350–351; 464: 11, 12; 485: 42–44; 520: 813; A1aa, b, d, e, f; A2b; A4a, g; B1.*

HILL, SAM HOUSTON. Born July 10, 1859, Austin, Travis County, Texas. Ht. 5 ft 7 ½ in., black eyes, black hair, dark complexion, married. REGULAR RANGER 1881–unknown. Rancher, San Angelo, Tom Green County, Texas. SPECIAL RANGER Feb. 25, 1918–Dec. 31, 1919 (commission was renewed, Jan. 23, 1919). Discharged. REMARKS: Was a partner in "Hill Commission Co., Livestock and Real Estate, San Angelo;" 1918 letterhead: "Sam H. Hill & Son, Breeders of Aberdeen-Angus Cattle and High-Grade Angora Goats." Was commissioned by order of Governor Hobby. In 1930 lived in Schleicher County, Texas. A Sam Houston Hill died June 12, 1933, Schleicher County, Texas. LAW ENFORCEMENT RELATIVES: Ranger William Hickman Hill, son; Ranger Lon C. Hill, brother; Ranger Gordon Hill, nephew; Ranger John A. Hill, nephew. FAMILY: Parents, William Hickman Hill (b. 1822, TN) and Minerva Frances Vernon (b. 1832, TN); siblings, Elizabeth Ewing (b. 1847, TN), Sarah Hibernia (b. 1849, TN), Mary Ann (b. 1851, TN), Rowena Vick (b. 1854, TX), William Hickman (b. 1857, TX), Leonidas Carrington (b. 1862, TX); John Augustus (b.

1865, TX), Frances Hickman "Fanny" (b. 1867, TX); spouse #1, Adela R. Mansfield (b. 1860, VA), married May 1, 1877, Manor, Travis County; children, William Hickman (b. 1878, TX), Ella Mansfield (b. 1880, TX); spouse #2, Judith B. Mansfield (b. 1862, VA), married Dec. 6, 1902. *SR; AG to Hill, Feb 21, 1918, AGC; Hill to Harley, Feb 25, Mar 5, 1918, AGC; A1aa, b, d, f, g; A2b; A4a, g; B1.*

HILL, WILLIAM HICKMAN. Born Feb. 19, 1878, Travis County, Texas. Ht. 5 ft. 8 in., brown eyes, black hair, fair complexion, married. Rancher, Christoval, Tom Green County, Texas. SPECIAL RANGER Apr. 26, 1918–Jan. 15, 1919; Jan. 23, 1919–Dec. 31, 1919 (commission was renewed.). REMARKS: Commission was sponsored by state Senator Claude Hudspeth. 1918 letterhead: "Sam H. Hill & Son, Breeders of Aberdeen-Angus Cattle and High-Grade Angora Goats." In 1920 and 1930 was a cattle and sheep rancher in Schleicher County, Texas. LAW ENFORCEMENT RELATIVES: Ranger Sam Houston Hill, father; Ranger Lon C. Hill, uncle; Ranger Gordon Hill, cousin; Ranger John A. Hill, cousin. FAMILY: Parents, Sam Houston Hill (b. 1859, TX) and Adela R. Mansfield (b. 1860, VA); sister, Ella Mansfield (b. 1880, TX); spouse #1, Beatrice Boyce (b. 1877, TX), married Feb. 19, 1900; daughters, Kate Adele (b. 1900, TX), Ella Hickman (b. 1902); spouse #2, Myrtle Reilly (b. 1886, TX), married July 7, 1923; daughter, Bettie Judith (b. 1925, TX). *SR; Assistant AG to Hill, Apr 29, 1918, AGC; Hill to Woodul, May 12, 1918, AGC; A1b, d, f, g; A3a; A4a, g.*

HILLBOLDT, FRANK WALTON. Born Oct. 20, 1882, Sealy, Austin County, Texas. Ht. 5 ft. 8 in., blue eyes, light brown hair, light complexion. Peace officer. REGULAR RANGER June 6, 1918–May 11, 1920 (private, Co. D; transferred to Co. B, Oct. 1918; reenlisted under the new law in Co. A, June 20, 1919). Resigned to enter the Customs Service. REMARKS: Had been a cowboy and a deputy sheriff, Columbus, Colorado County, Texas for several years. In 1910 was a saloon barkeeper in Wharton County, Texas. In 1930 was a federal officer in Hudspeth County, Texas. A Frank W. Hillbolt (note spelling) died July 9, 1946, Hudspeth County, Texas. FAMILY: Parents, Charles Sam Hillboldt (b. 1859, TX) and Lunice (b. 1865, TX); siblings, Charles (b. 1885, TX), Dallas (b. 1888, TX), Jack (b. 1890, TX), May Bell (b. 1899, TX), Waco (b. 1897, TX); spouse, Betty I. Johns (b. 1903, TX), married about 1924; sons, Grover Lee (b. 1931, TX), Frank James (b. 1934, TX). *SR; 471; Davis to Harley, Mar 31, 1918, AGC; Clark to Harley, Apr 2, 1918, AGC; A1d, e, g; A2b, e; A3a.*

HILLIARD, CLAUDE ABE. Born Aug. 21, 1879, Columbus, Lowndes County, Mississippi. Ht. 5 ft. 6 in., light gray eyes, brown hair, dark complexion, married. Farmer, Lockhart, Caldwell County, Texas. REGULAR RANGER July 1, 1919–unknown, still a Ranger as of Jan. 26, 1920 (private, Co. C). REMARKS: Was a private in Co. G, 7th Infantry Regiment. Had been a bookkeeper. In Sept. 1918 was a restaurant proprietor in Lockhart. In 1930 was an automobile salesman in Lockhart. Died Jan. 4, 1957; buried in Lockhart City Cemetery. FAMILY: Parents, William A. Hilliard (b. 1843, MS) and Sallie F. (b. 1843, MS); brother, James (b. 1874, MS); spouse, Margaret Elsie "Maggie" (b. 1883, TX), married about 1907. *SR; 429:54; A1b, d, e, f, g; A3a; A4b, g.*

HILLYARD, DANIEL MILTON. Born Feb. 22, 1880, Rogers, Bell County, Texas. Ht. 5 ft. 11 in., gray eyes, dark hair, light complexion, married. Banker, Ballinger, Runnels County, Texas. SPECIAL RANGER Apr. 15, 1918–Jan. 15, 1919 (station—Winters, Runnels County). REMARKS: Had been a farmer in Bell County in 1900. In Sept. 1918 was a banker, First National Bank, Winters. Died Nov. 24, 1921, Runnels County, Texas. FAMILY: Spouse, Minnie Lenorah Shurtleff (b. 1879, AR), married about 1898; daughter, Permelia Isabella (b. 1899, TX). *SR;471; Acting AG to Hillyard, June 27, 1918, AGC; A1d; A3a; B1; C.*

HINES, MARCUS WALTON. Born Oct. 1869, Kosciusko, Attala County, Mississippi. Ht. 6 ft. 2 in., blue eyes, light hair, light complexion, married. Peace officer, Karnes City, Karnes County, Texas. REGULAR RANGER May 15, 1911–Apr. 1, 1914 (private, Co. B; promoted to sergeant, Dec. 1, 1911). Resigned to become a mounted Customs inspector at Brownsville, Cameron County, Texas; was a Customs inspector at least through 1923. REMARKS: Deputy sheriff and constable, Karnes City, Karnes County for nearly 25 years before enlisting in the Rangers. Weighed over 300 pounds. Was one of the defenders of Norias on Aug. 8, 1915. Died Oct. 31, 1929, Hidalgo County, Texas. In 1930 his widow was a government inspector living in Mercedes,

Hidalgo County. FAMILY: Parents, Miller Arnold Hines (b. 1844, GA) and Mary Elizabeth Davis (b. 1837, MS); siblings, Lura V. (b. 1868, MS), Nathaniel J. (b. 1873, MS); spouse, Rhoda Alice Pace (b. 1876, TX), married Dec. 22, 1897. *SR; 471; 1: I, 1309–1312; Gay, "Amazing," WC; FR, 1913: 877, 879–880; MR, Co. B, July 31, 1913, AGC; Stevens to Woodul, June 10, 1918, WC; HC, Aug 9, 1915; EPMT, Oct 5, 1911; SAE, Oct 3, Nov 18, 1911; NYT, June 10, 1919; BDH, Feb 2, Apr 14, May 12, Sept 12, Dec 28, 1914, Jan 18, Apr 2, May 10, July 13, Aug 9, Oct 18, Nov 20, Dec 1, 1915, Apr 14, 24, 1916, Oct 2, 1917, Jan 28, 1918; 319: 34–35; 463: 58–59; 485: 246, 265; A1a, b, e, g; A4b, g; C.*

HINES, ROBERT E. Born Nov. 7, 1888, Holly Springs, Marshall County, Mississippi. Ht. 6 ft., blue eyes, light hair, light complexion, married. Lumber merchant, El Paso, El Paso County, Texas. LOYALTY RANGER June 6, 1918–Feb. 1919. REMARKS: In May 1917 was manager of Hines Lumber and Coal Co., El Paso. Died Feb. 1983; last known address, Covina, Los Angeles County, California. FAMILY: Parents, John T. Hines (b. 1861, Germany) and Annie H. (b. 1865, MS); siblings, Edward (b. 1892, MS), Pauline (b. 1899, MS); spouse, Ethel E. Gibson (b. 1888, CO); children, Ethel Elizabeth (b. 1914, TX), Robert Emmett, Jr. (b. 1921, TX), Sheila H (b. 1924, AZ). *SR; A1d, f, g; A2a, e, f; A3a.*

HINOJOSA, DANIEL. Born Apr. 26, 1878, Bluntzer, Nueces County, Texas. Ht. 5 ft. 10 in., gray eyes, black hair. Deputy sheriff, Harlingen, Cameron County, Texas. REGULAR RANGER Sept. 6, 1910–Feb. 1, 1911 (private, Co. A; transferred to Co. B, Oct. 22, 1910). Discharged—reduction in force. Peace officer. REGULAR RANGER June 7, 1918–Feb. 3, 1919 (private, Co. A). Resigned/fired. REMARKS: Sept. 1910 enlistment form gives height as 5 ft. 10 in.; Oct. 1910 enlistment form as 5 ft. 8 in. Special policeman, San Benito, Cameron County, 1911. Deputy sheriff, San Benito, 1912–1913. Constable, Cameron County, 1914. Deputy sheriff, San Benito, 1915. Was charged with receiving a bribe while a peace officer in 1917; a Cameron County court dismissed the charge—insufficient evidence. Hinojosa was fired from the Rangers as a result of the 1919 investigation of the organization. In 1924 was an Immigration inspector. A Daniel Hinojosa died Aug. 11, 1932, Cameron County, Texas. *SR; 471; MR, Co. B, Jan–Feb 1911, AGC; Cameron County grand jury report [Nov 1912], WC; BDH, Aug 3, Nov 2, 1911, Dec 7, 1912, June 12, Sept 16, 1913, Aug 1, 11, 1914, July 29, Sept 2, 1915, June 10, 1916, Sept 5, 1917; 5: 297; 469: 60; 470: 47; 137; C.*

HITT, JOHN F. Born Jan. 1861, Hopkins County, Texas. Ht. 5 ft. 9 in., brown eyes, dark gray hair, dark complexion, married. Farmer, Winnsboro, Wood County, Texas. LOYALTY RANGER June 3, 1918–Feb. 1919. REMARKS: Had been a farmer in Panola County, Texas. In 1910 was a life insurance man in Franklin County, Texas. Was also a cotton buyer and real estate salesman. In 1920 was a grocery store merchant in Winnsboro. A John F. Hitt died Oct. 2, 1929, Wood County, Texas. FAMILY: Spouse, Virginia "Jennie" Copland (b. 1863, IL), married about 1880; children, Willie A. (b. 1885, TX), John Lawrence (b. 1887, TX), Maxie (b. 1895, TX), Annie L. (b. 1897, TX), Leonard (b. 1899, TX). *SR; A1b, e, f; C.*

HODGE, WILLIAM ETHEL. Born June 30, 1866, Elgin, Bastrop County, Texas. Ht. 6 ft., blue eyes, dark hair, fair complexion, married. Peace officer, Brownwood, Brown County, Texas. REGULAR RANGER Sept. 1, 1917–Feb. 15, 1918 (private, Co. C). Discharged/fired as a result of a meatless day flap. Was reinstated in March. REGULAR RANGER Mar. 1, 1918–July 1, 1918 (private, Co. C). Resigned. REMARKS: Had lived in Eastland County, Texas. In 1910 was a farmer in Brown County. In 1920 was a farmer in Corona, Lincoln County, New Mexico. Died June 10, 1928, Brownwood, Brown County, Texas; buried in Greenleaf Cemetery, Brownwood. FAMILY: Parents, Robert Archibald Hodge (b. 1842, TX) and Nancy Susan Smith (b. 1842, MS); siblings, John Robert (b. 1868, TX), George Newell (b. 1870, TX), Edwin Fields (b. 1872, TX), Minnie Letitia (b. 1874, TX), Donald Reed (b. 1876, TX), Mary Eulena (b. 1878, TX), twins Neely B. and Burney (b. 1881, TX), Addie Alice (b. 1885, TX); spouse, Frances "Fannie" Miller (b. 1869, TX), married Aug. 9, 1885, San Saba County, Texas; children, Frank Ellis (b. 1886, TX), Charles Clinton (b. 1887, TX), Burney Miller (b. 1890, TX), Nanny May (b. 1892, TX), William Bryan (b. 1897, TX), Sarah Willard (b. 1899, TX), Sidney Douglas (b. 1902, TX). *SR; 471; Assistant AG to Ransom, Feb 13, 1918, AGC; Ransom to Woodul, Feb 16, 1918, AGC; Sandlin to Harley, Feb 16, 1918, AGC; Hodge to Harley, Feb 17, 1918;*

Beasley to Ferguson, Aug 18, 1917, AGC; Keane to Stevens, Apr 8, 1918, WC; Maxon to Harley, May 15, 1919, AGC; Brownwood News, July 26, 1918; A1b, d, e, f; A4b; B1.

HODGE, WILLIAM TERRY. Born June 6, 1884, Sparta, White County, Tennessee. Ht. 6 ft. 1 in., brown eyes, black hair, dark complexion, married. No occupation listed, Laredo, Webb County, Texas. SPECIAL RANGER June 10, 1918–Jan. 15, 1919. REMARKS: In 1920 was a produce merchant in Harlingen, Cameron County, Texas. In Sept. 1918 was a grain dealer for the Taylor Grain Company, San Benito, Cameron County. Was a produce buyer in Cameron County in 1930. Died July 26, 1955, Cameron County, Texas. FAMILY: Spouse, Estella L. (b. 1888, TX), married about 1907; children, Eunice S. (b. 1908, TX), Mildred T. (b. 1914, TX). *SR; Acting AG to Ryan, June 13, 1918, AGC; A1f, g; A2b; A3a.*

HODGES, ARTHUR BALL. Born Dec. 31, 1887, Junction, Kimble County, Texas. Ht. 6 ft. 1 in., gray eyes, brown hair, dark complexion, married. Stockman, Junction, Kimble County. SPECIAL RANGER June 23, 1917–Dec. 1917 (attached to Co. C). REMARKS: Had been a Kimble County deputy sheriff. Lived in Kimble County in 1930. An Arthur Ball Hodges died Sept. 11, 1945, Bexar County, Texas. FAMILY: Parents, Thomas Menefee Hodges (b. 1849, TX) and Sarah Missouri Loyless (b. 1852, TX); siblings, Mary E. (b. 1872, TX), Agnes (b. 1874, TX), George Waldemore W. (b. 1877, TX), Henry L. (b. 1879, TX), Thomas M., Jr. (b. 1881, TX), triplets Lucy, Lula and Eula (b. 1886, TX); spouse, Vinie E. (b. 1885, TX), married about 1907; daughter, Mildred E. (b. 1909, TX). *SR; Latta to Ransom, June 16, 1917, AGC; AG to Latta, June 21, 1917, AGC; A1b, d, e, g; A3a; A4b, g; C.*

HOERSTER, HENRY. Born Nov. 1864, Koockville, Mason County, Texas. Ht. 5 ft. 9 in., brown eyes, dark hair, dark complexion, married. Stockman, Koockville. SPECIAL RANGER Feb. 16, 1918–Jan. 15, 1919. REMARKS: In 1930 was a farmer in Mason County. A Henry Hoerster died Feb. 19, 1938, Mason County, Texas. FAMILY: Parents, Heinrich "Henry" Hoerster (b. 1814, Prussia) and Elisabeth Gammenthaler (b. 1824, Switzerland); siblings, Frederick "Fritz" (b. 1841, Prussia), Daniel (b. 1843, Prussia), John Anton (b. 1845, Prussia), William (b. 1850, TX), Carolina (b. 1852, TX), Sophia (b. 1854, TX), Wilhelmina (b. 1855, TX), Rosina (b. 1862, TX), Lydia (b. 1867, TX), John August Emil (b. 1870, TX), Henry John (b. 1872, TX), William Edward "Eddy" (b. 1874, TX), Alfred William E. (b. 1877, TX); spouse, Emilie Conradine Leifeste (b. 1864, TX), married July 22, 1886, Mason County, Texas; children, Martha Mathilda "Meta" (b. 1887, TX), August Samuel (b. 1889, TX), Edna Mathilda (b. 1891, TX), Daniel Johann (b. 1893, TX), Caleb Alexander (b. 1895, TX), twins Mathilda and Martha (b. 1899, TX), Louise "Lula" (b. 1901, TX), Henry (b. 1905, TX), Dessie (b. 1909, TX). *SR; A1aa, a, b, d, e, f, g; A4b, g; B1; C.*

HOFFMAN, ROBERT HAYES, JR. Born May 5, 1878, Denton County, Texas. No physical description, married. Chemist, Austin, Travis County, Texas. SPECIAL RANGER July 10, 1918–Jan. 15, 1919. REMARKS: In 1920 was a "state chemist" in Austin. In 1930 was a drug store proprietor in Denton, Denton County. Died Aug. 21, 1938, Denton, Denton County, Texas. FAMILY: Parents, Robert Hayes Hoffman (b. 1846, TN) and Mary Patterson Clark (b. 1848, MS); siblings, Claude E. (b. 1870, TX), Carl F. (b. 1873, TX), Myrtle E. (b. 1874, TX), William C. (b. 1876, TX), Nellie or Hellen (b. 1881, TX), Luther (b. 1888, TX); spouse, Eva May B. or S. (b. 1889, TX), married about 1913. *SR; A1b, d, e, f, g; A2b; A4b.*

HOGG, THOMAS ELIJAH or ELISHA "TOM." Born Aug. 20, 1887, Austin, Travis County, Texas. Ht. 6 ft. 1 ¾ in., blonde hair, gray eyes, fair complexion, married. Stock farmer, La Pryor, Zavala County, Texas. SPECIAL RANGER May 19, 1917–Dec. 1917. REMARKS: His father, James S. Hogg, was governor of Texas from 1891–1895. Tom Hogg served 2 years in the Marine Corps. In 1918 claimed poor eyesight on World War I Draft Registration document. In 1920 lived in Tyler, Smith County, Texas. In 1930 was in the oil business in San Antonio, Bexar County, Texas. Died in 1949; buried in Oakwood Cemetery, Austin. LAW ENFORCEMENT RELATIVES: Claimed to be Adjutant General Henry Hutchings's nephew. FAMILY: Parents, James Stephen Hogg (b. 1851, TX) and Sarah Ann "Sallie" Stinson (b. 1854, GA); siblings, William Clifford (b. 1875, TX), Ima (b. 1882, TX), Michael (b. 1885, TX); spouse, Margaret or Marie Wells (b. 1892, TX). *SR; Hogg to Hutchings, May 14, 1917, AGC; AG to Hogg, May 17, 1917, AGC; A1d, f, g; A3a; A4a, b, c; A5a; B1.*

HOGGETT, LOUIS SQUIRE. Born Aug. 1859, DeWitt County, Texas. Ht. 5 ft. 10 in., blue eyes, brown hair, light complexion, married. Stockman, Junction, Kimble County, Texas. SPECIAL RANGER Dec. 21, 1917–Jan. 15, 1919. REMARKS: In 1900 was a farmer in Bandera County, Texas. Died July 24, 1926, Kimble County, Texas. FAMILY: Parents, Jacob Hoggett (b. 1825, MS) and Mary Elizabeth Cooper (b. 1837, MS); brother, William S. (b. 1854, TX); spouse, Terissa R. Griffin (b. 1870, TX), married Nov. 7, 1888, Karnes County, Texas; children, Mansfield (b. 1889, TX), Etta E. (b. 1891, TX), Marlin J. (b. 1893, TX), Newton Jackson (b. 1896, TX), Selma (b. 1897, TX), Buenavista Irene (b. 1899, TX), Pierce S. (b. 1902, TX), Roy K. (b. 1905, TX), Ruth Lee (b. 1909, TX). *SR; AG to Latta, Dec 17, 27, 1917, AGC; A1aa, d, e; A2b; A4g; B1.*

HOGREN, SAMUEL. Born Jan. 1888, Vesta, Redwood County, Minnesota. Ht. 5 ft. 9 ¼ in., brown eyes, light brown hair, ruddy complexion, married. Clerk, enlisted in Austin, Travis County, Texas. REGULAR RANGER Feb. 20, 1914–no longer serving as of Apr. 1, 1914 (private, Co. C). Resigned. REGULAR RANGER May 13, 1914–unknown (reenlisted as private, Co. C). Resigned or discharged—unknown. REMARKS: Had served 5 years 2 months in 6th Company, Coast Artillery. Army enlistments dated Nov. 27, 1908 and Dec. 22, 1911. *SR; 472; Ag to General Manager, Mar 7, 1914, AGC; Hutchings to General Manager, Apr 1, May 13, 1914, AGC; A3d.*

HOGUE, CHARLES C. "CHARLEY." Born Nov. 1867, Cold Spring, San Jacinto County, Texas. Ht. 6 ft. 2 ½ in., blue eyes, brown hair, light complexion, married. Farmer and merchant, Cold Springs. LOYALTY RANGER June 5, 1918–Feb. 1919. REMARKS: Had been chief deputy sheriff, San Jacinto County, for 5 years. In 1930 still farming in San Jacinto County. A Charles Crow Hogue died Feb. 15, 1954, Liberty County, Texas. FAMILY: Parents, William Scott Hogue (b. 1817, SC) and Sarah A. Billingsly (b. 1826, AL); siblings, Eliza (b. 1848, AR or AL), Thomas W. (b. 1850, AR or AL), Virginia (b. 1852, AR or AL), Minnie Cornelia (b. 1855, AR or AL or TX), William (b. 1860, TX), Walter Robert (b. 1862, TX), Julius C. (b. 1865, TX), Gertrude (b. 1870, TX); spouse, Tina (b. 1860, TX), married about 1894; children, Sarah V. (b. 1897, TX), Fannie (b. 1899, TX), Nellie (b. 1902, TX), Douglas (b. 1905, TX). *SR; A1aa, a, b, d, e, f, g; A4b.*

HOLBEIN, REUBEN ROBERT. Born July 10, 1875, Corpus Christi, Nueces County, Texas. Ht. 6 ft., gray eyes, gray hair, dark complexion, married. Ranchman, Alta Vista, Jim Hogg County, Texas. SPECIAL RANGER May 6, 1918–Jan. 15, 1919. REMARKS: 1919 letterhead: "Reuben Holbein, Dealer in Horses, Mules, and Cattle, Alta Vista." Was a cattleman in Jim Hogg County in 1930. Died Nov. 24, 1961, Jim Hogg County, Texas. FAMILY: Parents, Reuben Holbein (b. 1828, England) and Sarah Hobbs (1836, England); siblings, Walter Franklin (b. 1858, TX), Frances Rebecca (b. 1860, TX), Lillian Augusta (b. 1862, TX), Georgina (b. 1865, TX), Richard King (b. 1868, TX), John McClane (b. 1873, TX); spouse, Bashie V. Wright (b. 1874, TX), married about 1901; children, Ray (b. 1902, TX), twins Reuben and Robert (b. 1903, TX), Lorene (b. 1908, TX), Edith Maye (b. 1911, TX), George William (b. 1915, TX); stepchildren, Hellen Guilford (b. 1893, TX), Boyd Guilford (b. 1895, TX). *SR; A1a, b, d, e, f, g; A2b; A3a; A4a, b, g.*

HOLDEN, HENRY CLINTON "CLINT." Born Aug. 30, 1879, Llano, Llano County, Texas. Ht. 6 ft., gray eyes, light hair, fair complexion. Ranchman. REGULAR RANGER May 16, 1916–Mar. 30, 1918 (private, Co. B). Resigned. Ranchman (lived at Bright's Ranch), Valentine, Jeff Davis County, Texas. SPECIAL RANGER Mar. 19, 1928–Mar. 13, 1929; Jan. 31, 1934–Jan. 22, 1935. Discharged. REMARKS: In 1900 and 1910 was a clerk/druggist in a retail drug store in Llano. In Jan. 1918 participated in the Porvenir massacre. As of Sept. 1918 was working on the L. C. Brite ranch in Presidio County, Texas. In 1920 was a stock farmer in Presidio County; in 1930 was a ranch foreman living in Porvenir, Presidio County. Died Sept. 5, 1962, Presidio County, Texas. FAMILY: Parents, Richard Franklin Holden (b. 1832, GA) and Emilie Rompf (b. 1841, Germany); siblings, Christopher Columbus (b. 1862, TX), Alice (b. 1864, TX), Kittie Margaret (b. 1866, TX), Ellen (b. 1867, TX), Thomas Jefferson (b. 1871, TX), Lyle (b. 1874, TX), twin sister Hettie Carrie (b. 1879, TX), William Arthur (b. 1882, TX); spouse, Lacy Mae (b. 1890, AR), married about 1909. *SR; 471; Fox to Hutchings, Sept 10, 1916, AGC; Fox to Woodul Mar 30, 1918, AGC; 422: 87; A1b, d, e, f, g; A2b; A3a; A4a, b, g.*

HOLLAN, JOHN GREEN. Born June 1869, DeWitt County, Texas. Ht. 5 ft. 11 ½ in., blue eyes, light hair, fair complexion, married. Peace officer, enlisted in Austin, Travis County, Texas. REGULAR RANGER Apr. 1, 1918–Feb. 1, 1919 (private, Co. M). Resigned to work for American Express Company as a guard. REMARKS: In 1910 was a jailer for DeWitt County. In Aug. 1920, wanted to reenlist in Rangers. As of 1920 had 20 years' experience as a peace officer in DeWitt County. Died Jan. 28, 1935, DeWitt County, Texas. FAMILY: Parents, Henry Harrison Hollan (b. 1825, MS) and Eliza Jane Hall (b. 1837, MS); siblings, Napolian Bonepart (b. 1854, TX), James Wade (b. 1857, TX), Samuel Tilden (b. 1876, TX); spouse, Julia Grace Alexander (b. 1874, TX), married about 1891; children, James Wade (b. 1892, TX), twins Kitty and Henry (b. 1893, TX), John Coleman (b. 1894, TX), Julia Grace (b. 1898, TX), Albert B. (b. 1901, TX), Davidson (b. 1902, TX). *SR; 471; Bailey to Cope, Aug 30, 1920, AGC; A1b, e, f, g; A2b; A4b, g.*

HOLLAND, JOHN GRADY "GRADY." Born Aug. 10, 1889, Summerville, Georgia. Ht. 6 ft., blue eyes, light brown hair, fair complexion, married. Druggist, Canyon, Randall County, Texas. LOYALTY RANGER June 4, 1918–Feb. 1919. REMARKS: Had been a ranchman and farmer. In 1930 was a pharmacist in a drug store in Mineral Wells, Palo Pinto County, Texas. FAMILY: Parents, John Thomas Holland (b. 1849, GA) and Alice Tallulah Lyle (b. 1860, GA); siblings, Hugh Lyndon (b. 1881, GA), Nellie Clyde (b. 1883, GA), Martha Annice "Mattie" (b. 1886, GA), Moses Lyle (b. 1896, TX); spouse, Olive (b. 1890, TX), married about 1912; sons, John Grady, Jr. (b. 1914, TX), David Cole (b. 1918, TX). *SR; A1d, e, f, g; A3a; A4b, g.*

HOLLAND, WARREN RICHARDSON. Born Dec. 1, 1886, Mason, Mason County, Texas. Ht. 5 ft. 9 ¾ in., blue eyes, red hair, light complexion. Cowboy. REGULAR RANGER May 1, 1918–Feb. 28, 1919 (private, Co. L). Resigned. REMARKS: In June 1917 was a city fireman in El Paso, El Paso County, Texas; in 1920 still a fireman in El Paso. Died Oct. 3, 1926, El Paso County, Texas. FAMILY: Parents, Whitmill Holland (b. 1839, KY) and Sarah Rebecca "Sallie" Sheffield (b. 1857, FL); siblings, William Farrington (b. 1881, TX), Marion (b. 1883, TX), Helen (b. 1888, TX), George Alfred (b. 1894, TX), brother by adoption, Thomas (b. 1910, TX). *SR; 471; A1b, d, f; A2b; A3a; A4b; B1.*

HOLLAND, WILLIAM MURRAY "MURRAY." Born Sept. 25, 1896, Tilden, McMullen County, Texas. Ht. 5 ft. 7 in., blue eyes, light hair, light complexion. Stockman, Tilden. SPECIAL RANGER May 27, 1918–Jan. 15, 1919. REMARKS: His father was McMullen County sheriff (Nov. 5, 1912–Nov. 1915) when he was shot and killed by Pat Eidson, city marshal of Beeville, Bee County, Texas. Murray Holland was McMullen County sheriff, Nov. 2, 1926–Jan. 1, 1937. Died May 11, 1978, Bee County, Texas. LAW ENFORCEMENT RELATIVES: McMullen County sheriff (1912–1915) William T. Holland, father. FAMILY: Parents, William Tolbert Holland (b. 1874, TX) and Virginia Ida Byrne (b. 1873, TX); siblings, Lorinne Cecelia (b. 1898, TX), Robert Edward (b. 1900, TX), Charles Rufus (b. 1906, TX), Ida Louise (b. 1910, TX); spouse, Mabel Claire Lewis (b. 1898, TX), married Nov. 3, 1919, Catholic church, Gussetville, Live Oak County, Texas; sons, William Murray (b. 1920, TX), Robert Ruckman (b. 1925, TX). *SR; 1503:367; A1d, e, f, g; A2a, b; A3a; A4a, b, g.*

HOLLEBEKE, EDMOND BIRNARD. (Last name spelled HALLEBEKE in Ranger Service Records.) Born Sept. 22, 1879, Belgium. Ht. 6 ft., blue eyes, light hair, light complexion. Cowboy. REGULAR RANGER Aug. 20, 1918–Mar. 10, 1919 (private, Co. L). Honorably discharged—Co. L was disbanded. REMARKS: Immigrated to the United States in 1884. In 1900 his family lived in Midland County, Texas. As of Sept. 1918 he was stationed in Ysleta, El Paso County, Texas. In 1930 he was a rancher in Culberson County, Texas. Later owned ranches throughout New Mexico. Died May 13, 1961, Carlsbad, Eddy County, New Mexico. FAMILY: Parents, Pieter Jacob Van Hollebeke (b. 1853, Belgium) and Emma De Houch (b. 1856, Belgium); siblings, August C. (b. 1876, Belgium), Jewell Cesar (b. 1877, Belgium), Jerome John (b. 1882, Belgium), Alphonse Emeil (b. 1885, TX), Octave Willie (b. 1886, TX), Leopold (b. 1890, TX), Rosie Belle (b. 1894, TX), Charley W. (b. 1896, TX), Dewey L. (b. 1900, TX). *SR; 471; Special Orders No. 21, Mar 10, 1919, WC; A1d, e, g; A3a; A4b.*

HOLLIS, JOHN RANSOM. Born Sept. 24, 1874, Hickory, Newton County, Mississippi. Ht. 6 ft. 1 in., blue eyes, dark hair, fair complexion, married. Farmer, Honey Grove, Fannin County, Texas. SPECIAL RANGER June 4, 1917–Dec. 1917 (attached to Co. C); Dec. 29, 1917–Jan. 15, 1919 (was reinstated, WA renewed). REMARKS: In 1930 was a real estate broker in Abilene, Taylor County, Texas. Died Jan. 11, 1958, Howard County, Texas. FAMILY: Parents, Uriah Wilburn Hollis (b. 1832, AL) and Eliza Eads Cox (b. 1839, AL); siblings, Martha N. (b. 1870, MS), M. A. (b. 1872, MS), Sim (b. 1880, TX); spouse, Margaret Agnes (b. 1880, AR), married about 1899; children, Eugene Carl (b. 1900, TX), John Brent (b. 1901, TX), Iva Alice (b. 1904, TX), Frances "Frankie" (b. 1907, TX), J. C. (b. 1918, TX), Nick (b. 1919, TX). *SR; 471; Register to Ferguson, May 18, 1917, AGC; Cunningham to Ferguson, May 18, 1917, AGC; AG to Hollis, June 22, 1917, AGC; Hollis to Harley, Dec 27, 1917, AGC; A1a, b, d, e, f, g; A2b, c; A3a; A4a.*

HOLLIS, JOHN ROBERT. Born Nov. 1869, San Antonio, Bexar County, Texas. Ht. 5 ft. 8 ½ in., blue eyes, brown hair, light complexion, married. Cowboy, Marathon, Brewster County, Texas. REGULAR RANGER Aug. 22, 1919–Aug. 31, 1921 (private, Co. E; transferred to Co. A, Feb. 15, 1921). Discharged. Ranchman, Marathon. RAILROAD RANGER Aug. 16, 1922–Feb. 18, 1923 (Co. A). Discharged. Ranchman, Marathon. REGULAR RANGER Mar. 31,1923–May 15, 1927 (private, Co. A; reenlisted Mar. 31, 1925; transferred to Co. B, July 1, 1925). Discharged. REMARKS: 1922 Service Record notation: "First-class man." In 1930 was Marathon town marshal. A John Robert Hollis died July 9, 1945, Brewster County, Texas. FAMILY: Spouse, Hulda Fisher (b. 1880, Switzerland), married about 1903; children, George M. Walter (b. 1904, CO), John R., Jr. (b. 1905, CO), Fannie (b. 1907, CO), Roy (b. 1910, TX), Jesse H. (b. 1912, TX), Mabel (b. 1914, TX), Thomas L. (b. 1916, TX), Hazel Helen (b. 1918, TX), Werner (b. 1923, TX), Arnold Adolph (b. 1925, TX). *SR; 471; 488: 58; A1d, e, f, g; A2e; C.*

HOLLIS, LAWRENCE W., JR. Born Aug. 1888, Anson, Jones County, Texas. Ht. 5 ft. 5 ½ in., blue eyes, dark brown hair, fair complexion. Doctor, Marfa, Presidio County, Texas. SPECIAL RANGER Feb. 6, 1918–Jan. 15, 1919. REMARKS: Was Texas quarantine officer at Presidio. In 1930 was a physician in general practice in Abilene, Taylor County, Texas. FAMILY: Parents, Dr. Lawrence W. Jones (b. 1863, TX) and Eva (b. 1864, MS); siblings, Eva May (b. 1884, TX), Beatrice (b. 1891, TX), Scott W. (b. 1895, TX); spouse, Helen (b. 1897, CO). *SR; Collins to Harley, Feb 1, 1918, AGC; A1d, e, f, g.*

HOLLOMAN, FERRELL EXUM "EX." Born Apr. 18, 1892, Guadalupe County, Texas. Ht. 5 ft. 8 in., blue eyes, brown hair, fair complexion. Peace officer, Seguin, Guadalupe County. REGULAR RANGER Dec. 10, 1917–Dec. 1, 1918 (private, Co. K). Discharged. REMARKS: Various spelling of his last name: Holloman, Hollamon, Hollomon. In 1930 was a carpenter in Seguin. Died Oct. 8, 1968, Guadalupe County, Texas. LAW ENFORCEMENT RELATIVES: U.S. Marshal (1910) Tom H. Holloman, father. FAMILY: Parents, Thomas H. Holloman (b. 1861, TX) and Mina (b. 1868, TX); siblings, Franky (b. 1890, TX), Polly (b. 1894, TX), Thomas, Jr. (b. 1896, TX); spouse, Hilda E. (b. 1901, TX), married about 1926. *SR; 471; A1d, e, f, g; A2a, b; A3a.*

HOLMAN, EBEN MALCUE. Born May 3, 1874, Ozark County, Missouri. Ht. 6 ft. 1 in., blue eyes, light hair, light complexion, married. Brand inspector, Cattle Raisers' Association of Texas, Amarillo, Potter County, Texas. SPECIAL RANGER June 27, 1917–Jan. 15, 1919 (was reinstated/WA renewed, Dec. 20, 1917). REMARKS: In 1918 was classed as a REGULAR RANGER without pay. Died Apr. 11, 1948, Potter County, Texas. FAMILY: Parents, Will Holman (b. 1849, KY) and Catherine A. Hunt (b. 1860, IL); siblings, Charles R. (b. 1871, MO), Elizabeth Jane (b. 1877, MO), Maggie (b. 1880, TX), Willie (b. 1882); spouse, Jennie Pearl Blanton (b. 1882, TX); children, Katherine Ola (b. 1900), Earnest (b. 1904, TX), Troy. *SR; Moses & Rowe to Harley, Oct 9, 1917, AGC; AG to Moses & Rowe, Oct 20, 1917, AGC; Moses to AG, Oct 22, 1917, AGC; Acting AG to FW&DC Railroad, Jan 11, 1918, AGC; Acting AG to GC&SF Railroad, Jan 9, 1918, AGC; A1a, d; A2b; A3a; A4a, b.*

HOLMES, WALTER MEREDITH. Born Oct. 4, 1877, near Lockhart, Caldwell County, Texas. Ht. 5 ft. 10 in., gray eyes, brown hair, dark complexion, married. Farmer and merchant, Lockhart, Caldwell County. LOYALTY RANGER Oct. 10, 1918–Feb. 1919. REMARKS: Had been a deputy sheriff, Lockhart, for 6 years under Sheriff J. J. Sanders. Was manager of the William Blanks Supply Co., 1907–1918. Was a farmer in Lockhart in 1930. Died Mar. 2, 1938, Caldwell County, Texas; buried in Lockhart City Cemetery. LAW ENFORCEMENT RELATIVES: Ranger W. Eli Holmes, probably his brother (W. Eli Holmes lists Walter M. Holmes' father as "next of kin" on his World War I Draft

Registration). FAMILY: Parents, Eli Woods Holmes (b. 1851, TN) and Bellzoria Sara Taylor (b. 1848, KY); siblings, William H. (b. 1874, TX), Cora C. (b. 1875, TX), Sallie B. (b. 1876, TX), Cage W. (Eli?) (b. 1879, TX), Martin Luther (b. 1890, TX), Nora M. (b. 1904, TX), Estelle (b. 1912, TX); spouse, Elizabeth B. "Lizzie" (b. 1888, TX), married about 1906; sons, William Walter (b. 1907, TX), Joe B. (b. 1911, TX). *SR; 429:50; A1b, e, f, g; A2b; A3a, e; A4b.*

HOLMES, WOODS ELI "ELI." Born Sept. 22, 1879, Lockhart, Caldwell County, Texas. Ht. 5 ft. 10 in., blue eyes, brown hair, light complexion. Farmer. REGULAR RANGER May 20, 1918–Feb. 15, 1919 (private, Co. A). Resigned. Peace officer, Lockhart. RAILROAD RANGER Aug. 19, 1922–Sept. 15, 1922 (Co. A). Discharged/fired for drunkenness. REMARKS: In Sept. 1918 was a Ranger in Alice, Jim Wells County, Texas, under Captain J. J. Sanders. World War I Draft Registration document states "right shoulder has been broken." Died Dec. 9, 1928; buried in Lockhart City Cemetery. LAW ENFORCEMENT RELATIVES: See Ranger Walter Meredith Holmes. FAMILY: Parents (probably) Eli Woods Holmes (b. 1851, TN) and Bellzoria Sara Taylor (b. 1848, KY); siblings, William H. (b. 1874, TX), Cora C. (b. 1875, TX), Sallie B. (b. 1876, TX), Walter M. (b. 1877, TX), Martin Luther (b. 1890, TX), Nora M. (b. 1904, TX), Estelle (b. 1912, TX). *SR; 471; 469: 60; 429:50; A1b, d; A3a; A4b.*

HOLODAY, FRANK LYN. Born Mar. 20, 1893, Henrietta, Clay County, Texas. Ht. 6 ft. ½ in., gray eyes, brown hair, married. Lawyer, Henrietta. REGULAR RANGER Apr. 13, 1918–July 31, 1918 (captain); transferred to SPECIAL RANGER Aug. 1, 1918–Jan. 15, 1919 (captain; was made SPECIAL RANGER—without pay—because of the low Ranger appropriation.) REMARKS: Acted in capacity of Ranger captain as special agent for Adjutant General's department. Last name spelled in various ways: Holoday, Holaday, Halady; most often spelled Holaday. In 1930 was a lawyer in general practice in Henrietta. A Frank Lynn Holaday died June 7, 1947, Somervell County, Texas. FAMILY: Parents, Job S. Holoday (b. 1852, OH) and Allace P. (b. 1866, IN); siblings, Sybil H. (b. 1897, TX), James R. (b. 1901, TX), Lewis B. (b. 1902, TX), Thomas L. (b. 1905, TX); spouse, Augusta (b. 1896, TX), married about 1917; children, Allace A. (b. 1918, TX), Joetta (b. 1920, TX), Robert Lewis (b. 1921, TX). *SR; 471; Acting Quartermaster to Holoday, Aug 3, 1918, AGC; A1d, e, f, g; A2b, e; A3a.*

HONEA, ROBERT FRANCIS. Born Mar. 1870, McKenzie, Carroll County, Tennessee. Ht. 6 ft., gray eyes, brown hair, dark complexion, married. Railroad special agent, Stamford, Jones County, Texas. SPECIAL RANGER May 31, 1917–Dec. 17, 1917 (attached to Co. C). REMARKS: In 1900 was a railroad agent in Frio County, Texas. In 1920 was an oil operator in Brownwood, Brown County, Texas. Died Nov. 7, 1957, Wichita County, Texas. FAMILY: Parents, Dr. David F. Honea (b. 1835, TN) and Martha Jane "Mattie" Roach (b. 1838, TN); siblings, James Henry (b. 1857, TN), Hiram Hopkins (b. 1859, TN), Mary (b. 1862, TN), John (b. 1864, TN), Joseph E. (b. 1873, TN); spouse, Susie Pearl (b. 1872, LA), married about 1892; son, Robert C. (b. 1893, LA). *SR; 471; Register to Ferguson, May 18, 1917, AGC; Cunningham to Ferguson, May 18, 1917, AGC; Honea to Harley, Jan 14, 1918, AGC; A1a, b, d, e, f; A2b; A4b; B1.*

HONSE, FRANK. Born Sept. 19, 1886, Comfort, Kendall County, Texas. Short, blue eyes, light hair, medium build, married. Well contractor, Kingsville, Kleberg County, Texas. REGULAR RANGER June 8, 1918–Nov. 4, 1918. On June 8, 1918, enlisted without pay. In Nov. 1918 was ordered to report for duty to Captain Sanders (Co. A); refused, turned in his commission. REMARKS: In 1920 was city water works superintendent, Kingsville. FAMILY: Spouse, Mae (b. 1890, TX); children, Frank, Jr. (b. 1908, TX), Edward F. (b. 1911, TX), Ruby Mae (b. 1913, TX). *SR; A1f; A3a.*

HOOKS, DAVID A. Born Oct. 5, 1858, Haw Ridge, Coffee County, Alabama. Ht. 5 ft. 10 in., blue eyes, black hair, dark complexion, married. Night watchman, I&GN Railroad, Sellers (20 miles east of Houston), Harris County, Texas. SPECIAL RANGER Oct. 1, 1917–Jan. 15, 1919 (attached to Co. C). REMARKS: Had been a guard at a Texas state farm convict camp, Fort Bend County, Texas. In 1910 lived in Montgomery County, Texas. In 1920 was a U.S. government warehouse guard, living in Houston, Harris County, Texas. Died Jan. 28, 1926, Houston, Harris County, Texas; buried at Willis, Montgomery County. FAMILY: Parents, John Franklin Hooks (b. 1801, GA) and his second wife Caroline Dowling (b. 1825, SC); siblings, Robert James (b. 1846, AL), Mary Ann (b. 1848, AL), Sarah Kristen (b. 1850, AL),

Benjamin Daniel (b. 1853, AL), Ellen (b. 1855, AL); spouse, Mary Susie Martin (b. 1871, AL), married Nov. 3, 1889, Montgomery County, Texas; children, Lottie (b. 1891, TX), Hubert Jackson (b. 1893, TX), Lennie (b. 1897, AL), Ruby (b. 1899, TX), Charles D. (b. 1903, TX). *SR; Williamson to Hutchings, Sept 26, 1917, AGC; AG to Williamson, Sept 27, 1917; AGC; _______ to Hutchings, Oct 6, 1917, AGC; A1aa, d, e, f; A3a; A4b, g; C.*

HOPE, EMMETT. Born Oct. 22, 1877, Blanco County, Texas. Ht. 6 ft., blue eyes, brown hair, fair complexion, married. Deputy city marshal, Robstown, Nueces County, Texas. REGULAR RANGER Dec. 18, 1917–Aug. 1918 (private, Co. M). Resigned. REMARKS: One source lists his full name as Beverly Emmett Hope. In 1920 was a café proprietor in Robstown. In 1930 was a house carpenter, lived in San Antonio, Bexar County, Texas. Died July 13, 1947, San Antonio, Bexar County, Texas; buried in Roselawn Memorial Park, San Antonio. FAMILY: Parents, Rector C. Hope (b. 1852, TX) and Gertrude Dansby or Dansbee (b. 1854, TX); siblings, Annie (b. 1872, TX), Samuel Richard (b. 1875, TX), Bula (b. 1880); spouse, Malinda Lou "Lou" Baker (b. 1874, AR), married about 1902; son, Byron Baker (b. 1909, TX). *SR; 471; Cunningham to Harley, Dec 21, 1917, Feb 19, Apr 13, 1918, AGC; A1b, d, e, f, g; A2b; A3a; A4b, g.*

HOPE, LANNES. Born Aug. 20, 1879, Murfreesboro, Rutherford County, Tennessee. Ht. 5 ft. 11 in., blue eyes, dark hair, light complexion, married. Farmer, Roaring Springs, Motley County, Texas. LOYALTY RANGER July 4, 1918–Feb. 1919. REMARKS: Had been a deputy sheriff. In 1900 was a farmer in Navarro County, Texas. In 1910 was a rice farmer living in Beaumont, Jefferson County, Texas. In 1930 was a jailer at the jail in Amarillo, Potter County, Texas. First name spelled various ways: Launes, Lannas, Lanner, Lannie. An L. Hope died Feb. 4, 1933, Potter County, Texas. FAMILY: Parents, Dr. Francis Manning Hope, a dentist (b. 1836, TN) and Nancy Ann Mitchel Rains (b. 1838, TN); siblings, Sarah J. (b. 1867, TN), Ellan F. (b. 1869, TN), Eufratus A. (b. 1870, TN), Jimmy C. (b. 1872, TN), Snow C. (b. 1877, TN); spouse, Rosa "Rosie" Rodgers (b. 1877, TX), married about 1899; children, Archie Ellis (b. 1900, TX), Viola (b. 1903, TX), Allie Mae (b. 1905, TX), Thelma (b. 1908, TX), Lannas Lu (b. 1912, TX). *SR; A1b, d, e, f, g; A3a; A4g; C.*

HOPPING, RICHARD COKE "COKE." Born Aug. 20, 1875, Hood County, Texas. Ht. 6 ft., gray eyes, black hair, dark complexion, married. Brand inspector, Cattle Raisers' Association of Texas, Littlefield, Lamb County, Texas. SPECIAL RANGER June 9, 1919–Dec. 31, 1919. REMARKS: Parmer County sheriff Nov. 8, 1910–Nov. 5, 1918. In 1930 was a real estate agent in Lubbock, Lubbock County, Texas. Died Sept. 29, 1954, Lubbock, Lubbock County, Texas. FAMILY: Parents, Wray Hopping (b. 1833, GA) and Susan Ann Nutt Landers (b. 1843, MO); siblings, Jesse S. (b. 1871, TX), Flora (b. 1873, TX); spouse, Leila Jessie Jones (b. 1875, AR), married Jan. 15, 1893, Rock Church, Paluxy, Texas; children, Laverna (b. 1894, TX), Flora Bess (b. 1897, TX), Jacob Wray (b. 1900, TX), Earl Leroy (b. 1903, NM), Sidney Coke (b. 1906, NM), Roberta Lillian (b. 1908, TX), Annie Patterson (b. 1911, TX), Dorothy Southerland (b. 1913, TX), Doris Amanda (b. 1915, TX). *SR; 1503:408; Hopping to Harley, Dec 31, 1917, AGC; Moses & Rowe to Harley, June 3, 1919, AGC; Aldrich to Moses & Rowe, June 4, 1919, AGC; A1d, e, f, g; A2b; A3a; A4b, c; B1, 2.*

HORD, EDWARD "ED." Born May 1861, Lavaca, Lavaca County, Texas. Ht. 5 ft. 8 in., blue eyes, light hair, fair complexion, married. Ranchman, Comstock, Val Verde County, Texas. SPECIAL RANGER Dec. 3, 1917–Jan. 15, 1919. REMARKS: In 1910 did iron construction work in Humble, Harris County, Texas. In 1930 was a stock rancher in Del Rio, Val Verde County. Died June 6, 1943, Val Verde County, Texas. FAMILY: Parents, John E. Hord (b. 1833, TN) and Frances E. (b. 1840, MS); siblings, Anna (b. 1859, TX), Sally (b. 1861, TX), Fanny (b. 1866, TX), M. Nancy (b. 1868, TX), Willie (b. 1873, TX); spouse, Easter Abigail M. (b. 1867, TX), married about 1885; son, William Edward "Bill" (b. 1911, TX). *SR; A1a, b, e, g; A2b; A4b; C.*

HORNSBY, EMORY. Born Sept. 18, 1885, Travis County, Texas. Ht. 5 ft. 9 in., brown eyes, brown hair, fair complexion, widower. Farmer, New Braunfels, Comal County, Texas. SPECIAL RANGER Dec. 19, 1917–Jan. 25, 1918. Placed on active duty. REGULAR RANGER Jan. 25, 1918–Mar. 15, 1918 (private, Co. M). Resigned because of a disagreement. REMARKS: In Sept. 1918 was a checking clerk at the Fort Worth stockyards, Tarrant County, Texas. Died July 10, 1925, Austin, Travis County, Texas; buried at Hornsby Bend, Travis County. His brother, Rogers, was a Hall-of-Fame baseball player and major league team manager. LAW ENFORCEMENT RELATIVES: Ranger William Watts Hornsby, grandfather; Ranger William Wallace Hornsby, uncle; Ranger John William Hornsby, cousin. FAMILY: Parents, Aaron Edward Hornsby (b. 1857, TX) and Mary Dallas Rogers (b. 1864, TX); siblings, Everett (b. 1884, TX), William W. (b. 1887, TX), Margaret "Maggie" (b. 1889, TX), Rogers (b. 1896, TX); spouse, Jaretta Jones (b. 1885, TX), married Oct. 28, 1908, Travis County, Texas (d. 1916, TX); son, Edward Yancy (b. 1909, TX). *SR; 471; Engelking to Cunningham, Mar 16, 1918, AGC; A1d, e, f; A3a; A4a, b, g.*

HORNSBY, JOHN WILLIAM. Born Jan. 8, 1870, Hornsby Bend, Travis County, Texas. Ht. 6 ft. 1 in., brown eyes, gray hair, medium complexion, married. Lawyer, Austin, Travis County. SPECIAL RANGER Oct. 17, 1919–Dec. 31, 1919. REMARKS: In 1910 was a land commissioner, lived in Houston, Harris County, Texas. Died Mar. 5, 1947, Travis County, Texas. LAW ENFORCEMENT RELATIVES: Ranger William Watts Hornsby, grandfather; Ranger William Wallace Hornsby, uncle; Ranger Emory Hornsby, cousin. FAMILY: Parents, Malcolm Morrison Hornsby (b. 1841, TX) and Leonora McLauren (b. 1843, MS); siblings, Margaret Adelia (b. 1862, TX), James Malcolm (b. 1864, TX), Lydia Lucinda (b. 1866, TX), Mollie Leonora (b. 1868, TX), Joseph Edward (b. 1872, TX), Helen Marcella (b. 1874, TX), Amanda Goodnight (b. 1875, TX), Katherine Isabel (b. 1877, TX), Sarah M. (b. 1879, TX), Bertha (b. 1881, TX), Hugh Morrison (b. 1883, TX), Edith Ethel (b. 1885, TX); spouse, Florence C. Stanley (b. 1872, TN), married June 20, 1893, Austin; children, Hazel (b. 1895, TX), Stanley C. (b. 1906, TX). *SR; A1b, e, g; A4b.*

HORNSBY, WILLIAM WALLACE. Born Oct. 8, 1850, Austin, Travis County, Texas. Ht. 5 ft. 8 in., brown eyes, gray hair, dark complexion, married. Stockman. REGULAR RANGER June 10, 1918–Jan. 1, 1919 (private, Co. A). Discharged—reduction in force; was one of the newest men. REMARKS: Had been a ranch foreman. In 1880 was a farmer in Brown County, Texas. A William Wallace Hornsby died Jan. 26, 1934, Travis County, Texas. LAW ENFORCEMENT RELATIVES: Ranger William Watts Hornsby, father; Ranger Emory Hornsby, nephew; Ranger John W. Hornsby, nephew. FAMILY: Parents, William Watts Hornsby (b. 1817, MS) and Lucinda Burleson (b. 1820, AL); siblings, Margaret (b. 1840, TX), Rebecca Anne (b. 1844, TX), Malcolm Morrison (b. 1841, TX), Helen Marcella (b. 1846, TX), Sarah Adelia (b. 1848, TX), Daniel (b. 1854, TX), Aaron Edward (b. 1857, TX), Moses Smith (b. 1859, TX); spouse, Martha Lucinda "Mattie" Kirksey (b. 1851, TX), married Nov. 2, 1870, Caldwell, Texas; children, James Wallace (b. 1871, TX), Cora A. (b. 1872, TX), Deward Franklin (b. 1874, TX), William Dale (b. 1881, TX), Alta (b. 1890, TX). *SR; 471; Hornsby's Scout Report, June 20–Dec 31, 1918, AGC; A1aa, b; A4b; C.*

HORTON, FRED B. Born Dec. 18, 1881, San Antonio, Bexar County, Texas. Tall, stout, brown eyes, dark hair, married. Stockman, Tilden, McMullen County, Texas. LOYALTY RANGER June 18, 1918–Feb. 1919. REMARKS: Still a stock farmer in McMullen County in 1930. Died Apr. 12, 1958, McMullen County, Texas. FAMILY: Parents, Fredrich Horton (b. 1830, PA) and Barbara (b. 1846, PA); siblings, May (b. 1875, NV), Ross (b. 1878, NV), Eck M. (b. 1879, TX), Lew M. (b. 1881, TX); spouse, Jane Francis (b. 1893, TX), married about 1915; son, Richard Porter (b. 1923, TX). *SR; A1b, d, e, f, g; A2b; A3a.*

HOUCHINS, JOHN FLEMING. Born June 24, 1883, Hallettsville, Lavaca County, Texas. Ht. 6 ft. ½ in., dark eyes, dark brown hair, dark complexion, married. Stockman, Hallettsville. LOYALTY RANGER May 31, 1918–Feb. 1919. REMARKS: In 1920 was a grain and produce merchant in Hallettsville. Died Feb. 25, 1934, Harris County, Texas. FAMILY: Parents, John Fleming Houchins (b. 1857, TX) and Susan Adaline Oliver (b. 1861, TX); siblings, Horace Greeley (b. 1880, TX), Warren Arthur (b. 1885, TX), Maud (b. 1890, TX), Oscar Wilbur (b. 1892, TX), Pickney Goodson (b. 1897, TX); spouse, Adele Wangerman (b. 1882, TX), married Dec. 6, 1905; son, John Fleming, Jr. (b. 1909, TX). *SR; A1d, e, f; A3a; A4a, b, g; C.*

HOUSTON, EDWIN W. Born Apr. 9, 1890, San Antonio, Bexar County, Texas. Ht. 6 ft. 3 ½ in., brown eyes, black hair, dark complexion. Farmer and ranchman, Welfare, Kendall County, Texas. LOYALTY RANGER Aug. 15, 1918–Feb. 1919. REMARKS: Letterhead in 1919: "Houston Ranch, M. G. Houston [mother?], Edwin Houston, Welfare." Still ranching in Kendall County in 1930. Died Sept. 19, 1974,

Bexar County, Texas. FAMILY: Parents, Reagan Houston (b. 1860, TX) and Martha "Mattie" Green (b. 1862, TN); siblings, Bettie Green (b. 1885, TX), Grey J. (b. 1886, TX), Reagan, Jr. (b. 1888, TX), MacLean (b. 1892, TX), Grafton (b. 1895, TX), Bruce (b. 1897, TX), Bryan (b. 1899, Martha (b. 1905, TX); spouse, Martha Fulton Green (b. 1901, TX), married about 1920; children, Rena (b. 1930, TX), Edwin, Jr. (b. 1936, TX). *SR; A1d, e, f, g; A2a, b, e; A3a; A4b, g.*

HOUSTON, THOMAS ARCHEBEL "TOM." Born Apr. 27, 1874, Cherokee, San Saba County, Texas. Ht. 5 ft. 7 ½ in., blue eyes, brown hair, fair complexion, married. Stock raiser, Cherokee. LOYALTY RANGER June 7, 1918–Feb. 1919. REMARKS: In 1930 still a stock rancher in San Saba County. FAMILY: Parents, John Thomas Houston (b. 1846, TN) and Sarah Elizabeth Keeney (b. 1847, MO); siblings, Robert M. (b. 1869, TX), Calvin M. (b. 1872, TX), Michael (b. 1876, TX), Martha A. (b. 1878, TX), Nora A. (b. 1879, TX); spouse, Elizabeth "Lizzie" (b. 1882, TX), married about 1901; children, Thelma (b. 1909, TX), Glendon (b. 1914, TX), Ima Jean (b. 1916, TX). *SR; A1b, e, f, g; A3a; A4b.*

HOWARD, JOHN BUIE. Born Aug. 11, 1872, Upshur County, Texas. Ht. 5 ft. 11 in., brown eyes, brown hair, dark complexion, married. Lawyer, Pecos, Reeves County, Texas. LOYALTY RANGER June 3, 1918–Feb. 1919. Lawyer, El Paso, El Paso County, Texas. SPECIAL RANGER Sept. 18, 1933–Jan. 22, 1935. REMARKS: Had been a lawyer in Martin County, Texas. One source states died in 1944, El Paso County, Texas. FAMILY: Parents, Jackson Connor "Jack" Howard (b. 1848, TX) and Laura Angeline Buie (b. 1852, TX); siblings, Pearl Rivers (b. 1874, TX), Lucy Margie (b. 1877, TX), Jackson Connor (b. 1880), Luke Lidney (b. 1882, TX), Anne Dee (b. 1885, TX), Kathleen (b. 1887, TX), Laura (b. 1890, TX); spouse #1, Margaret T. "Maggie" Childs (b. 1884, TX), married Mar. 15, 1902, Gregg County, Texas; daughter, Margaretta (b. 1907, TX); spouse #2, Mamie Ray Brown (b. 1886, TX), married about 1913; son, John B. (b. 1918, TX). *SR; A1b, e, f, g; A4b, g.*

HOWELL, JAMES MONROE. Born Dec. 17, 1870, Memphis, Shelby County, Tennessee. Ht. 5 ft. 7 in., dark gray eyes, medium dark hair, light complexion, married. Brand inspector, Panhandle & Southwestern Cattle Raisers' Association, Dalhart, Dallam County, Texas. SPECIAL RANGER June 24, 1918–Jan. 15, 1919; Aug. 20, 1919–Dec. 31, 1919. REMARKS: Had been a cattleman; was Hartley County deputy sheriff for 5 years. In 1930 was a stock farmer in Amistad, Union County, New Mexico. Died 1943, Texas. FAMILY: Parents, Eli Blackman (or Blackwell) Howell (b. 1844, TN) and Sinthy Adlin King (b. 1849, TN); siblings, Callie Jane (b. 1874, TN), John Thomas (b. 1877, TX), Andy Isaac (b. 1881, TX); spouse, Betty Anne Barnett (b. 1873, AR), married about 1895; children, Nora Mable (b. 1897, TX), John Thomas (b. 1898, TX), Bertha Adeline (b. 1900, OK), Mary Ellen (b. 1906, NM), Oscar James (b. 1911, TX), Lissie (b. 1912, NM). *SR; Hudspeth to Harley, June 15, 1918, AGC; A1b, e, f, g; A4b, g.*

HUDDLESTON, CLYDE EUGENE. Born May 21, 1893, Little River, Bell County, Texas. Ht. 6 ft. 1 in., brown eyes, brown hair, fair complexion, married. Peace officer, Waco, McLennan County, Texas. REGULAR RANGER Dec. 1, 1917–Sept. 10, 1918 (private, Co. F; transferred to Headquarters Co., Jan. 1918). Resigned. Investigator, Dallas, Dallas County, Texas. SPECIAL RANGER July 1, 1927–July 1, 1928. Salesman, Dallas. SPECIAL RANGER July 9, 1928–July 9, 1929; Oct. 17, 1929–Oct. 17, 1930; Oct. 22, 1930–Jan. 1, 1931. REMARKS: In June 1917 was a policeman in Waco. On Dec. 1, 1917 his occupation was automobile salesman. In 1920 was manager of a truck manufacturing company in Austin, Travis County, Texas. His 1927 and 1928 Ranger commissions were issued at the request of Lt. Governor Barry Miller. In 1930 was an oil lease salesman in Dallas. Died Sept. 11, 1935, Dallas County, Texas. FAMILY: Parents, William Marion Huddleston (b. 1871, AR) and Eugenia Lafayette Vinson (b. 1875, TX); siblings, Hershel (b. 1895, TX), Carrie (b. 1899, TX), Bertha (b. 1904, TX); spouse, Opal (b. 1895, TX), married about 1913; children, J. Virginia (b. 1915, TX), James H. (b. 1918, TX). *SR; 471; _____ to Huddleston, Apr 15, 1918, AGC; Carrington to Harley, Nov 21, 1917, AGC; Harley to Huddleston, Nov 26, 1917, AGC; Woodul to Huddleston, Jan 10, 1918, AGC; Assistant AG to Stevens, Jan 25, 1918, WC; Huddleston to Woodul, Mar 9, 1918, RRM; Assistant AG to Huddleston, Mar 12, 1918, RRM; A1d, e, f, g; A3a; A4a, b, g; C.*

HUDGINS, WILLIAM OSCAR. Born Feb. 15, 1883, Velasco, Brazoria County, Texas. Tall, medium build, blue eyes, brown hair, married. Stockman, Velasco. SPECIAL RANGER June 6, 1918–Jan. 15, 1919. REMARKS: In 1910 was a retail grocery merchant in Brazoria County. In 1920 was a banker in Velasco. Died Sept. 6, 1921, Brazoria County, Texas; buried in Hudgins Cemetery, Oyster Creek, Brazoria County. FAMILY: Parents, Samuel Houston Hudgins (b. 1859, TX) and Emma Henrietta Pinckard (b. 1859, AR); siblings, Samuel Wesley (b. 1884, TX), Alonzo Follett (b. 1885, TX), Thomas Longer (b. 1887, TX), Jennie Lee (b. 1890, TX), Lucretia or Lutitia (b. 1894, TX), Boyd Dewey (b. 1898, TX); spouse, Mary Lee Seaborn (b. 1887, TX), married about 1907; children, Erna Lee (b. 1907, TX), William O., Jr. (b. 1909, TX). *SR; A1d, e, f; A2b; A3a; A4a, g.*

HUDSON, ROBERT MARMADUKE "DUKE." Born Aug. 18, 1880, Wooten Wells, Robertson County, Texas. Ht. 5 ft. 5 in., blue eyes, brown hair, light complexion. Peace officer, enlisted in Brewster County, Texas. REGULAR RANGER May 8, 1906–1908 (private, Co. C). Resigned. Mail service. REGULAR RANGER Apr. 1, 1910–July 15, 1910 (private, Co. C). Resigned to accept a better paying position. REMARKS: In 1910 was a Ranger stationed in Austin, Travis County, Texas. In Sept. 1918 was a ginner living in Courtney, Grimes County, Texas. In 1920 and 1930 was farming in Grimes County. An R. M. Hudson died Dec. 28, 1931, Grimes County, Texas. FAMILY: Spouse, Ila M. Shepard (b. 1894, TX), married about 1912; children, Robert (b. 1914, TX), E. L. (b. 1916, TX), Gibson (b. 1918, TX), John (b. 1920, TX), George (b. 1925, TX), Harold Anderson (b. 1930, TX). *SR; 471; McBride to Newton, May 25, 30, 1910, AGC; MR, Co. C, Apr–Jul 1910, AGC; AG to Rogers, Aug 3, 1910, AGC; AS, Apr 3, 1910; 463: 28–31; 1000: 118; A1e, f, g; A2e; A3a; C.*

HUDSON, WILLIAM WILSON "WILSE." Born July 25, 1876, Dublin, Erath County, Texas. Ht. 6 ft., brown eyes, black hair, dark complexion, married. Special officer—guard for Texas Oil Co.'s pipeline at Mingus and vicinity—Sweetwater, Nolan County, Texas. SPECIAL RANGER May 29, 1918–Oct. 1918 (attached to Co. C). Discharged. REMARKS: Had been a special officer for the AT&SF Railroad, 1916–1918. In 1920 was a city night watchman in Sweetwater; in 1930 was a Sweetwater city policeman. A William W. Hudson died May 26, 1955, Nolan County, Texas. FAMILY: Parents (probably), Franklin Eugene Hudson (b. 1851, MD) and Mary Matild Daffern (b. 1855, TX); siblings, Harvey Eugene (b. 1873, TX), Eliza Emmaline (b. 1875, TX), Minnie (b. 1878, TX), Ada May (b. 1880, TX), Charles Henry (b. 1883, AR), Joe Tilliford (b. 1885, TX); spouse, Jessie (b. 1882, TX), married about 1900. *SR; McKenzie to Harley, May 29, 1918, AGC; John to Harley, Oct 2, 1918, AGC; A1f, g; A2b; A3a; A4b.*

HUFF, SIMEON LEROY "LEE." Born Apr. 28, 1876, Boonville, Prentiss County, Mississippi. Ht. 5 ft. 10 in., blue-gray eyes, black hair, dark complexion, married. Policeman, Waco, McLennan County, Texas. SPECIAL RANGER Feb. 9, 1917–Dec. 1917. Peace officer, Waco. RAILROAD RANGER Sept. 18, 1922–Sept. 18, 1924 (Co. A). Discharged. REMARKS: Birthplace is also listed as Coryell County, Texas. Was commissioned in 1917 by order of Governor Ferguson. In Oct. 1920, was Wichita Falls, Wichita County, Texas police chief. In 1930 was city detective in Waco. Died Oct. 21, 1931, McLennan County, Texas. FAMILY: Parents, James B. Huff (b. 1844, MS) and Sallie H. (b. 1851, MS); siblings, Dollie E. (b. 1868, MS), Minnie Z. (b. 1871, MS), Franklin L. (b. 1878, TX); spouse, Daisy (b. 1889, TX), married about 1905, divorced by 1920. *SR; 471; HC, Apr 19, 1911; Aldrich to Crawford, Oct 20, 1920, AGC; A1b, d, e, f, g; A2b; A3a.*

HUFFAKER, DUKE HUNTER "HUNTER." Born Aug. 1867, Kansas City, Jackson County, Missouri. Ht. 5 ft. 9 ½ in., brown eyes, gray hair, medium complexion, married. Doctor and Texas quarantine officer, El Paso, El Paso County, Texas. SPECIAL RANGER Feb. 5, 1918–Jan. 15, 1919. REMARKS: His superior requested a SPECIAL RANGER commission for him. Had received his medical education at the University of Kansas and practiced medicine in Kansas City until he developed tuberculosis in the late 1890s. Moved to El Paso where his health improved. Still a physician in El Paso in 1930. Died Dec. 29, 1942, El Paso County, Texas. FAMILY: Parents, Christopher Columbus Huffaker (b. 1823, MO) and Elizabeth H. Hunter (b. 1837, MO); siblings, Julia Catherine (b. 1860, MO), Christopher Columbus, Jr. (b. 1863, MO), John Mastin (b. 1865, MO), Nancy Simpson (b. 1872, MO); spouse, Lois Catherine Greer (b. 1885, MS), married Nov. 20, 1909, El Paso. *SR; Collins to Harley, Feb 5, 1918, AGC; Huffaker to Harley, Feb 14, 1918, AGC; A1a, b, d, e, f, g; A4b, g; C.*

HUGHES, COVEY M. Born Feb. 1870, Shiner, Lavaca County, Texas. Ht. 5 ft. 9 in., gray eyes, dark hair, dark complexion, married. County auditor, Wharton, Wharton County, Texas. LOYALTY RANGER June 20, 1918–Feb. 1919. REMARKS: Wharton County sheriff, Feb. 15, 1894–Nov. 6, 1894. In 1910 was postmaster in Wharton. In Jan. 1919 ran the Wharton branch of "W.G. Hill & Co., Public Accountants." FAMILY: Parents, Thomas H. Hughes (b. 1839, MS) and Sarah (b. 1840, MS); siblings, Clementine (b. 1860, TX), Darlina (b. 1863, TX), Tennessee (b. 1868, TX); spouse, Fannie M. (b. 1879, TX), married about 1895. *SR; Hughes to Harley, Jan 18 [?], 1919, AGC; 1503:529; A1a, e, f.*

HUGHES, HOWARD ROBARD. Born Sept. 9, 1869, Lancaster, Schuyler County, Missouri. Ht. 5 ft. 11 ¾ in., brown eyes, brown hair, dark complexion, married. Engineer, Houston, Harris County, Texas. SPECIAL RANGER Apr. 22, 1919–Dec. 31, 1919. REMARKS: His commission was issued at the request of Hon. Walter J. Crawford of Beaumont. In 1910 was a fuel oil operator in Houston; in 1920 manufactured drilling supplies in Houston. His son, Howard R., Jr., was a noted aviation pioneer. Howard, Sr. died Jan. 14, 1924, Harris County, Texas. FAMILY: Parents, Felix Turner Hughes (b. 1838, IL) and Jean Amelia Summerlin (b. 1844, IA); siblings, Gerta (b. 1866, MO), Rupert (b. 1872, MO), Felix (b. 1874, MO), Reginald (b. 1877, MO), Jean (b. 1880, IA); spouse, Allene Stone Gano (b. 1883, KY), married May 24, 1904, Dallas, Dallas County, Texas; son, Howard R., Jr. (b. 1905, TX). *SR; Johnston to Hughes, Jan 13, 1919, AGC; 172:III, 770–771; A1b, e, f; A4b; C.*

HUGHES, JOHN REYNOLDS. Born Feb. 11, 1855, Cambridge, Henry County, Illinois. Ht. 5 ft. 11 in., brown eyes, brown hair, dark complexion. Stock farmer. REGULAR RANGER Aug. 10, 1887–Jan. 31, 1915 (private, Co. D; promoted to sergeant, Co. D, 1893; promoted to captain, Co. D, July 4, 1893 ; became captain, Co. A when Co. D was redesignated Co. A, Feb. 1, 1911). Resigned. REMARKS: Grew up in Illinois and Kansas. Had been a cowboy and Indian trader. In 1915 was an alfalfa farmer at Ysleta, El Paso County, Texas. In 1910 and 1915 was superintendent of Ysleta Sunday school. Later became chairman of the board and largest stockholder of Citizens Industrial Bank of Austin, Travis County, Texas. Was guest of honor at the Texas Centennial Exposition, at Dallas, 1936. Died (committed suicide) June 3, 1947, Austin, Travis County, Texas. LAW ENFORCEMENT RELATIVES: Ranger William Hughes, brother. FAMILY: Parents, Thomas Hughes (b. 1813, OH) and Jane Bond (b. 1827, OH); siblings, Mary G. (b. 1847, OH), Erick (b. 1849, OH), Emery (b. 1851, IL), William T. (b. 1856, IL), twins Thomas Forster and Ella J. (b. 1860, IL). *SR (Incomplete Service Record); 471; Hughes to AG, Jan 5, Feb 27, AGC; Hughes to Hutchings, Feb 5, 1911, AGC; Hughes's report to Hutchings, Sept 1909–Jan 1911, RRM; [AG] to Colquitt, Feb 3, 1914, WC; Petition to Ferguson, Jan 3, 1916, WC; Colquitt to President, Feb 26, 1911, FR, 1911: 410; 319: 115, 340–347, 383–390, 395; 172:III, 773; 1516; SAE. Dec 9, 1911; AA, Oct 6, 1910; BDH, Sept 7, 1910, Mar 9–11, June 11, 15, 17, 19, July 13, 1914, Jan 30 , 1915; EPMT, Oct 9, 1910, May 28, 1914,*

Texas Ranger Captain John R. Hughes, one of the four "great" Ranger Captains. *Photo courtesy Texas Ranger Hall of Fame and Museum.*

Jan 14, 25, 31, 1915; EPH, Dec 31, 1936; 406: 301–303; 484: 309–312,320–321, 377; 468: 371; 464: 38, 39; 470: 165–166; 236: 207–209; 522: 419; 841; biography—472; A1aa, a, d, e, g; A2b; A4b, g.

HULEN, EUGENE B. Born Mar. 1879, Gainesville, Cooke County, Texas. Ht. 5 ft. 9 in., blue-gray eyes, light brown hair, fair complexion. Contractor. REGULAR RANGER Mar. 29, 1915–May 24, 1915 (private, Co. C, was commissioned by order of the governor; transferred to Co. B, Apr. 1, 1915). Killed in action May 24, 1915, at Candelaria (near Pilares), Presidio County, Texas. LAW ENFORCEMENT RELATIVES: Ranger John Augustus Hulen, brother. (John A. Hulen was a RAILROAD and SPECIAL RANGER. He was Texas Adjutant General, 1903–1907, general freight and passenger agent for the Trinity and Brazos Valley Railroad, and was a general in the Texas National Guard.) FAMILY: Parents, Harvey Hulen (b. 1845, MO) and Frances Mary Catherine "Fannie" Morter (b. 1849, VA); siblings, John Augustus (b. 1872, MO), Victor Harvey (b. 1874, MO), Ray (b. 1878, TX), Frank (b. 1881, TX), Harry (b. 1886, TX), Virginia Cygners (b. 1889, TX), Fannie (b. 1892, TX). *SR; 471; General Orders No. 2, Apr 1, 1915, AGC; AG to Sanders, Apr 6, 1915, AGC; Hutchings to Hulen, May 26, June 2, 4, 1915, WC; Fox to AG, May 27, 1915, AGC; McKay to Hutchings, June 2, 1915, AGC; Fox to Hutchings, Dec 8, 1916, WC; Hulen to Hutchings, Feb 27, 1915, AGC; 1:I, 1532–1535; AA, May 27, 1915; EPMT, May 27, 31, June 1, 1915; BDH, May 26, June 1, 1915; 422: 75–77; 470: 85; 488: 35–36; A1b, d; A2b; A4b.*

HUMPHREY, ALLEN ALEXANDER. Born July 4, 1888, Point, Rains County, Texas. Ht. 6 ft., blue eyes, sandy hair, fair complexion, married. Farmer, Point. LOYALTY RANGER July 8, 1918–Feb. 1919. REMARKS: Died June 8, 1946, Hunt County, Texas; another source states died on the family farm, Point, Rains County, Texas. FAMILY: Parents, Joseph Wesley Humphrey (b. 1847, NC) and Mary Jane Bellah (b. 1852, TX); siblings, Nancy Catherine (b. 1883, TX), Martha Ann (b. 1884, TX), Joseph Robert (b. 1896, TX); spouse, Lydia Lutitia "Lutie" Coats (b. 1884, TX), married Aug. 30, 1908; children, Mary Elizabeth (b. 1912, TX), Robert Lee "Robbie" (b. 1914, TX), Finis Alexander (b. 1915, TX), Joseph Roy (b. 1919, TX), Anna Catherine (b. 1920, TX), William Wesley "Billie" (b. 1923, TX). *SR; A1d, e, f, g; A2b; A3a; A4b, g.*

HUMPHREYS, ERNEST NEWTON. Born Oct. 7, 1893, Medina City, Bandera County, Texas. Ht. 5 ft. 7 in., gray eyes, light hair, light complexion, married. Ranchman, Juno, Val Verde County, Texas. SPECIAL RANGER June 7, 1917–Dec. 1917 (attached to Co. C). REMARKS: In June 1917 was a ranch hand for C. B. Hudspeth in Crockett County, Texas. Family lived in Fresno County, California in the mid-1920s. Was a ranch foreman in Val Verde County, Texas in 1930. Died Feb. 9, 1931. LAW ENFORCEMENT RELATIVES: Ranger Fred Humphreys, brother. FAMILY: Parents, Charles Lee "Charlie" Humphreys (b. 1867, TX) and Mary Leticia Crockett (b. 1865, TX); siblings, Nettie (b. 1889, TX), Ollie (b. 1891, TX), Fred (b. 1895, TX), Ada Don "Addie" (b. 1897, TX), George Andrew (b. 1899, TX), Albert (b. 1902, TX), Clara (b. 1905); spouse, Essie E. Mayes (b. 1895, TX), married about 1913; children, Sidney (b. 1914, TX), Ray (b. 1916, TX), Julia F. (b. 1918, TX), Viola (b. 1920, TX), Bernice D. (b. 1923, CA), Ernest, Jr. (b. 1925, CA). *SR; A1d, e, g; A2h; A3a; A4g; B1.*

HUMPHREYS, JAMES FREDERICK "FRED." Born Sept. 7, 1895, Medina City, Bandera County, Texas. Ht. 6 ft., gray eyes, dark hair, sandy complexion. Stockman, Juno, Val Verde County, Texas. SPECIAL RANGER June 6, 1917–Dec. 1917 (attached to Co. C). REMARKS: In June 1917 was a ranch hand for C. B. Hudspeth in Crockett County, Texas. Died Oct. 13, 1994, Val Verde County, Texas. LAW ENFORCEMENT RELATIVES: Ranger Ernest Humphreys, brother. FAMILY: Parents, Charles Lee "Charlie" Humphreys (b. 1867, TX) and Mary Leticia Crockett (b. 1865, TX); siblings, Nettie Lee (b. 1889, TX), Ollie (b. 1891, TX), Ernest N. (b. 1893, TX), Ada Don "Addie" (b. 1897, TX), George Andrew (b. 1899, TX), Albert (b. 1902, TX), Clara (b. 1905); spouse, Celma Kathleen Skinner; daughters, Patricia Ruth (b. 1934, TX), Arnolia Alice (b. 1937, TX). *SR; A1d, e; A2a, b, e; A3a; A4g.*

HUNNICUTT, J. R. Born July 4, 1894, Marlin, Falls County, Texas. Ht. 5 ft. 7 in., blue eyes, light hair, light complexion, married. Clerk. REGULAR RANGER Nov. 20, 1917–Mar. 31, 1919 (private, Co. D). Honorably discharged. Peace officer, Austin, Travis County, Texas. REGULAR RANGER July 11, 1919–Aug. 28, 1920 (private, Co. E; promoted to sergeant, Oct. 1, 1919). Resigned. Traveling salesman, San Antonio, Bexar County, Texas. SPECIAL

RANGER Feb. 2, 1928–Feb. 2, 1929; Mar. 4, 1929–Mar. 4, 1930; Apr. 10, 1930–Jan. 1, 1931 (WA expired). REMARKS: In 1917 was a clerk for the State Surveyor, lived in Marlin. In Sept. 1920 worked for Aransas Dock & Channel Co. at Aransas Pass, Nueces County, Texas. Other occupations included Customs inspector, Internal Revenue agent (1937–), soldier during WW II (Major: administrative officer/medical branch). Died Mar. 3, 1973, McLennan County, Texas; buried in Blue Ridge Cemetery, Falls County. FAMILY: Parents, Robert Smith Hunnicutt (b. 1853, TX) and Louisa Rosella Varnado (b. 1861, MS); siblings, Lilla (b. 1878, TX), Joanna (b. 1881, TX), Robert Jasper (b. 1883, TX), Florence (b. 1885, TX), Charles W. (b. 1887, TX), Walter S. (b. 1889, TX), Lee Varnado (b. 1891, TX), Anna A. (b. 1898, TX), Edward (b. 1900, TX), Thomas (b. 1902, TX); spouse, Lillie Grigsby Atchison (b. 1898, OK) (in 1920 was a trained nurse in Oklahoma), married Sept. 4, 1926; children, J. R., Jr. (b. 1929, TX), Martha Jean (b. 1932, TX), Doris Ruth (b. 1933, TX). *SR; 471; Special Orders No. 21, Mar 10, 1919, WC; Hanson to AG, July 17, 1919, WC; Hunnicutt to Cope, Aug 23, 1920, AGC; Cope to Brooks, Aug 23, 1920, AGC; Cope to Hunnicutt, Aug 28, 1920, AGC; Hunnicutt to Aldrich, Sept 11, 13, 14, 1920, AGC; AA, May 6, 1920 supplement, May 27, 1920 supplement, Aug 19, 1920; A1d, e, f, g; A2a, b, e; A3a; A4g.*

HUNT, EDWARD L. Born Mar. 1868, Newnan, Coweta County, Georgia. Ht. 5 ft. 11 in., blue eyes, brown hair, light complexion, married. Watchman, I&GN Railroad, Mart, McLennan County, Texas. SPECIAL RANGER Oct. 14, 1916–Jan. 15, 1919 (was reinstated Dec. 27, 1917). Special agent, I&GN Railroad, Mart. RAILROAD RANGER Aug. 20, 1922–Aug. 20, 1924 (Co. A). Discharged—enlistment expired. Special agent, I&GN Railroad, Mart. SPECIAL RANGER June 26, 1925–Jan. 26, 1927; Jan. 26, 1927–Jan. 26, 1928 (reenlisted; employed by Missouri Pacific Lines, Mart); Jan. 21, 1928–Jan. 14, 1929; Jan. 14, 1929–Jan. 11, 1930; Jan. 11, 1930–Jan. 7, 1931; Jan. 7, 1931–Jan. 7, 1932; Jan. 7, 1932–Jan. 18, 1933; Jan. 20, 1933–Jan. 19, 1935; May 29, 1935–Aug. 10, 1935. Discharged. REMARKS: Had been a house carpenter in 1900 in Limestone County, Texas and in 1910 in McLennan County. FAMILY: Parents, David A. Hunt (b. 1835, GA), and Eliza Jane Walker (b. 1836, GA); siblings, twins John Adams and Thomas Jefferson (b. 1859, GA), David Alexander (b. 1860, GA), Georgia A. (b. 1863, GA), Alice A. (b. 1866, GA); spouse, Gertie Howard (b. 1878, KY), married about 1900; sons, Howard H. (b. 1907, TX), Clarence E. (b. 1913, TX). *SR; Jones to Hutchings, Oct 7, 1916, AGC; AG to Jones, Oct 9, 1916, AGC; A1a, b, d, e, f, g; A4g.*

HUNT, JOHN WASHINGTON "WASH." Born Sept. 13, 1885, Liberty Hill, Williamson County, Texas. Ht. 5 ft. 11 in., brown eyes, brown hair, ruddy complexion, married, as of Mar. 1931. Farmer and peace officer, Gregory, San Patricio County, Texas. LOYALTY RANGER May 30, 1918–Feb. 1919. Farmer and ranchman, Gregory. SPECIAL RANGER Mar. 30, 1931–Jan. 20, 1933 (WA was extended to Jan. 20, 1933). REMARKS: As of Mar. 1931 had been a peace officer (deputy sheriff and constable) in San Patricio County for 20 years. Died Sept. 28, 1956, San Patricio County, Texas. FAMILY: Parents, Andrew Jackson Hunt (b. 1852, TN) and Sarepta Jane Williams (b. 1855, TX); siblings, Fredonia E. (b. 1876, TX), William H. (b. 1878, TX), Mary Jane (b. 1881, TX), James (b. 1888, TX), Lucy (b. 1890, TX), Claud (b. 1893, TX), Ira (b. 1895, TX); spouse #1, unknown; spouse #2, Mary Fay Green (b. 1888, IL), married about 1909; children, Jennie S. (b. 1908, TX), Mary A. (b. 1911, TX), Lola F. (b. 1914, TX), Myra Lou (b. 1920, TX), John W., Jr. (b. 1923, TX), Laura Eleanor (b. 1924, TX). *SR; 471; A1b, d, e, f, g; A2b, e; A3a; A4a, b, g.*

HUNT, ROBERT ERNEST. Born May 1, 1882, San Angelo, Tom Green County, Texas. Ht. 5 ft. 10 in., blue eyes, light hair, light complexion. Ranch hand, enlisted in El Paso County, Texas. REGULAR RANGER June 8, 1915–Apr. 11, 1916 (private, Co. B). Resigned. REGULAR RANGER Aug. 20, 1918–Oct. 15, 1918 (private, Co. L). Died Oct. 15, 1918, El Paso County, Texas, of Spanish influenza. FAMILY: Mother, Mrs. L. A. Hunt. *SR; 471; EPMT, June 10, Sept 15, 1915; EPH, Oct 16, 1918; A3a; C.*

HUNT, THOMAS JOEL (or JAMES). Born Nov. 11, 1871, San Augustine, San Augustine County, Texas. Ht. 6 ft. 2 in., blue eyes, dark hair, dark complexion, married. Assistant superintendent, I&GN Railroad, Mart, McLennan County, Texas. SPECIAL RANGER Feb. 2, 1918–Jan. 15, 1919. Roadmaster, T&BV Railroad, Teague, Freestone County, Texas. RAILROAD RANGER Nov. 24, 1922–Nov. 24, 1924. Discharged—WA expired. REMARKS: Had been a cowboy.

In the early 1900s lived in New Mexico. In 1930 was still a steam railroad roadmaster in Teague. Died Dec. 15, 1958, Stephenville, Erath County, Texas; buried in Greenwood Cemetery, Teague. FAMILY: Parents, Thomas Carlos Hunt (b. 1844, TX) and Martha Jane Rawls (b. 1849, MS); siblings, Rawls, Rosey (b. 1873, TX), John R. (b. 1875, TX), Edward (b. 1878, TX); spouse, Leila Eliza Cox (b. 1874, TX), married May 28, 1893, Ranger, Eastland County, Texas; sons, Robert Lee (b. 1897, TX), Thomas John (b. 1904, NM), John W. (b. 1905, NM), Joel T. (b. 1906, NM), James Edward (b. 1917, TX). *SR; AG to Williamson, Jan 28, 1918, AGC; A1b, f, g; A2b; A4b, g.*

HUNTER, CHRISTOPHER TAYLOR "KIT." Born Jan. 6, 1856, Guadalupe County, Texas. Ht. 5 ft. 10 in., blue eyes, black hair, ruddy complexion, married. Stockman, Cuero, DeWitt County, Texas. REGULAR RANGER Nov. 3, 1917–Mar. 10, 1919 (private, Co. D; transferred to Co. H, Jan. 1, 1918; transferred to Co. M, July 1, 1918). Honorably discharged when Co. M was disbanded. REMARKS: Had been assistant sergeant-at-arms for the Texas legislature in Austin, a private game warden for 3 years, a cattle buyer, and a peace officer at Cuero for many years. As of 1917 had been a peace officer for more than 40 years. Died Nov. 7, 1922, Cuero, DeWitt County, Texas. FAMILY: Parents, Robert Hunter (b. 1813, NC) and Cyrene Sutton (b. 1826, TN); brother, Samuel A. (b. 1854, TX); spouse, Marietta Georgia "Mary" Blair (b. 1862, TX), married Jan. 25, 1882, Clinton, DeWitt County; children, Lennie Lee (b. 1882, TX), Richard Alexander (b. 1884, TX), Gilfred May (b. 1887, TX), Catherine Ivey "Katie" (b. 1889, TX), Ruby Bell (b. 1891, TX), Claudie Ella (b. 1894, TX), William Bryan (b. 1896, TX), Joe Bailey (b. 1899, TX), Alice Elizabeth "Allie" (b. 1902, TX), Edwin Russell (b. 1905, TX). *SR; 471; Special Orders No. 21, Mar 10, 1919, WC; Davidson to Hobby, Sept 24, 1917, AGC; Hunter to Harley, Sept 29, 1917, AGC; Bailey to Harley, Sept 29, Oct 30, 1917, AGC; Hartman to Harley, Oct 12, 1917, AGC; Hudspeth to Harley, Oct 18, 1917, AGC; Hunter to Woodul, July 25, 1918, AGC; A1aaa, aa, a, d, e, f; A2b; A4b, g; B1, 2.*

HUNTER, GEORGE DAVID. Born Mar. 1866, Anderson County, Texas. No physical description, married. Texas quarantine officer, Galveston, Galveston County, Texas. SPECIAL RANGER Jan. 9, 1919–Dec. 31, 1919. REMARKS: In 1910 was a liquor dealer in a saloon in Teague, Freestone County, Texas. A George David Hunter died Nov. 5, 1923, Bexar County, Texas. FAMILY: Parents, John D. Hunter (b. 1843, GA) and M. E. (b. 1848, TN); brother, J. L. (b. 1867, TX); spouse, Pauline L. Jowers (b. 1872, TX), married Nov. 6, 1889, Anderson County; children, David (b. 1892, TX), Rena W. (b. 1894, TX), John Lanier (b. 1896, TX), Sofronia "Sophie" (b. 1899, TX). *SR; 471; A1a, b, e, f; A2c/d; C.*

HUNTER, JAMES LYNN "LYNN." Born Oct. 20, 1868, Fluvanna County, Virginia. Ht. 6 ft., dark eyes, black hair, dark complexion, widower. Ginner, Austin, Travis County, Texas. REGULAR RANGER Dec. 19, 1917–unknown (unassigned—Regular Ranger without pay; still in as of June 1918). REMARKS: Was connected with the Loyalty Ranger program. In 1920 was an oil promoter living in Austin. In 1930 was U.S. postmaster in Austin. Died Nov. 21, 1940, Travis County, Texas. FAMILY: Parents, William Michael Hunter (b. 1839, VA) and Mildred A. "Nannie" (b. 1842, VA); siblings, Lizzie M. (b. 1870, VA), George A. (b. 1874, VA); spouse #1, Alice Seeligson (b. 1869, TX), married May 22, 1893; spouse #2, Velma Scott (b. 1882, TX), married after 1920 and before 1930; step-son, Louis S. Wilkerson (b. TX). *SR; 471; Day to Harley, June 10, 1918, AGC; A1b, d, e, f, g; A2b; A4b.*

HUNTON, GEORGE PITTMAN. Born Jan. 26, 1883, Hillsboro, Hill County, Texas. Ht. 5 ft. 8 in., gray eyes, light hair, dark complexion, married. Deputy sheriff, Temple, Bell County, Texas. SPECIAL RANGER Aug. 16, 1917–Nov. 30, 1917 (attached to Co. D). Placed on active duty. Peace officer, Temple. REGULAR RANGER Nov. 30, 1917–Mar. 1, 1918 (private, Co. D). Resigned. REMARKS: In 1910 had been a newspaper printer in Tom Green County, Texas. Died Jan. 23, 1928, Bell County, Texas; buried in Temple, Bell County. LAW ENFORCEMENT RELATIVES: Sterling County, Texas constable (Precinct 1) O. H. Graham, brother-in-law. FAMILY: Parents, George W. Hunton (b. 1859, GA) and Lula Belle Pittman (b. 1861, GA); sisters, Emma (b. 1885, TX), Bessie (b. 1888, TX), Gracy (b. 1893, TX), Lulu F. (b. 1895, TX), Eva (b. 1898, TX), Meredith (b. 1900, TX); spouse, Malva L. (b. 1885, TX), married about 1905; daughters, Vaughn Mirva (b. 1910, TX), Malva C. (b. 1911, TX). *SR; 471; Smith to Gray, July 16, 1917, AGC; Graham to Harley, Jan 17, 1918, AGC; A1d, e, f; A3a; A4a, b, g; C.*

HUNTSUCKER, WILLIAM HARVEY. Born Sept. 26, 1878, Oxford, Lafayette County, Mississippi. Ht. 5 ft. 8 in., blue eyes, black hair, light complexion, married. Veterinarian, Rotan, Fisher County, Texas. LOYALTY RANGER June 5, 1918–Feb. 1919. REMARKS: As a young man had been a farmer in Lafayette County. Was police chief, Rotan, 1919. Still practicing veterinary medicine in Rotan in 1930. Died Mar. 28, 1949, Jones County, Texas; buried in Stamford, Jones County. FAMILY: Parents, William J. Huntsucker (b. 1854, MS) and Matilda J. Hill (b. 1856, MS); siblings, Richard (b. 1880, MS), Claudie M. (b. 1882, MS), Mandie L. (b. 1887, MS), Earl Moody (b. 1890, MS), Beulah R. (b. 1893, MS); spouse, Hattie R. Gregory (b. 1876, MS or AR), married about 1898 in Mississippi; children, Eustace Franklin (b. 1897, MS), William Estes (b. 1898, MS), Ira Carlton (b. 1903, TX). *SR; A1d, e, f, g; A2b; A3a; A4a, b.*

HURST, CLEVELAND CLARENCE "CLEVE." Born Mar. 7, 1886, Odem, San Patricio County, Texas. Ht. 6 ft. 1 in., blue eyes, dark hair, ruddy complexion. Ranchman. REGULAR RANGER Nov. 8, 1915–unknown (private, Co. D). Resigned (?). Ranchman. REGULAR RANGER Aug. 8, 1916–Jan. 6, 1917 (private, Co. D; transferred to Co. A, unknown date). Resigned. Peace officer. REGULAR RANGER Sept. 12, 1917–Mar. 31, 1918 (private, Co. C). Resigned to become a mounted Customs inspector. REMARKS: Nov. 1915, accidentally shot himself in the thigh. In Sept. 1918 was a Customs inspector in McKinney Springs, Brewster County, Texas. In 1920 was a Customs inspector living in Presidio County, Texas. In 1930 was a Customs officer in Hebbronville, Jim Hogg County, Texas. Died Mar. 28, 1963, Odem, San Patricio County, Texas; buried in Bethel Cemetery, Odem. LAW ENFORCEMENT RELATIVES: Ranger George B. Hurst, brother. FAMILY: Parents, David Hurst, Jr. (b. 1848, TN) and Elizabeth Smith (b. 1847, TN); siblings, Amanda Rose (b. 1871, TN), David Burton (b. 1872, TN), Sarah E. (b. 1873, TN), Charles (b. 1878, TX), Robert Lee (b. 1880, TX), Newton Sparks (b. 1882, TX), Edward C. (b. 1884, TX), George B. (b. 1888, TX); spouse, Zella Byrd (b. 1891, TX), married about 1925. *SR; Hurst to Harley, Apr 3, 1918, AGC; Ransom to Hutchings, Nov 27, Dec 11, 1915, AGC; 319: 15, 45; 508: 67; A1d, f, g; A2b; A3a; A4a, b, c, g; B1.*

HURST, GEORGE B. Born Sept. 30, 1888, Hope, Lavaca County, Texas. Ht. 6 ft. 1 in., gray eyes, brown hair, dark complexion. Farmer. REGULAR RANGER July 31, 1915–Mar. 18, 1919 (private, Co. A; reenlisted and promoted to sergeant, July 31, 1917; reduced to private and transferred to Co. B when Co. A was disbanded, Mar. 10, 1919). Resigned to accept a position as a Brooks County, Texas deputy sheriff. REMARKS: In Mar. 1920 applied to join the Customs Service at Alice, Jim Wells County, Texas. Was Brooks County sheriff, Nov. 7, 1922–Jan. 1, 1925. In 1930 was a government revenue officer living in Ozona, Crockett County, Texas. Died June 18, 1934, El Paso, El Paso County, Texas; buried in Bethel Cemetery, Odem, San Patricio County, Texas. LAW ENFORCEMENT RELATIVES: Ranger Cleveland C. Hurst, brother. FAMILY: Parents, David Hurst, Jr. (b. 1848, TN) and Elizabeth Smith (b. 1847, TN); siblings, Amanda Rose (b. 1871, TN), David Burton (b. 1872, TN), Sarah E. (b. 1873, TN), Charles (b. 1878, TX), Robert Lee (b. 1880, TX), Newton Sparks (b. 1882, TX), Edward C. (b. 1884, TX), Cleveland C. (b. 1886, TX). *SR; 471; Special Orders No. 21, Mar 10, 1919, WC; Hurst to Harley, Mar 18, 1919, AGC; Scarborough et al to AG, Sept 6, 1919, AGC; Tumlinson to Aldrich, Mar 10, 1920, AGC; 1503:68; 319: 15; 469: 60; A1d, g; A3a; A4a, b, c, g; C.*

HUSKEY, LEWIS CLARK. Born Dec. 5, 1860, Titus County, Texas. No physical description, married. Stockman, Albany, Shackelford County, Texas. LOYALTY RANGER June 13, 1918–Feb. 1919. REMARKS: In 1930 lived in Palo Pinto County, Texas. Died July 27, 1936, Palo Pinto County, Texas; buried in Albany Cemetery, Shackelford County. FAMILY: Parents, Silas Huskey (b. 1808, TN) and Elizabeth (b. 1830, MO); siblings, Priscilla (b. 1844, MO), Malissa (b. 1848, TX), Eliza (b. 1850, TX), Josephine (b. 1852, TX), Luella (b. 1854, TX), John P. (b. 1857, TX); spouse, Sarah M. "Sallie" Perkins (b. 1865, TX), married Sept. 23, 1883, Hopkins County, Texas; children, Charles F. (b. 1884, TX), Blanche (b. 1888, TX), Louis Hilliard "Hillie" (b. 1892, TX), Earnestine (b. 1896, TX), Nealey John (b. 1903, TX), Margaret Elizabeth (b. 1904, TX). *SR; A1aa, a, b, d, e, f, g; A4b, g; B1; C.*

HUTCHISON, JOHN W. Born 1871, Bryan, Brazos County, Texas. Ht. 5 ft. 6 in., gray eyes, light hair, fair complexion. Lawyer, enlisted in Travis County, Texas. SPECIAL RANGER

Mar. 26, 1918–Jan. 15, 1919. REMARKS: In 1920 was a lawyer in general practice in Houston, Harris County, Texas. A J. W. Hutchison died Oct. 22, 1924, Harris County, Texas. *SR; A1f; C.*

HUTCHISON, SIDNEY SILL. Born Mar. 3, 1871, Gillett, Karnes County, Texas. Ht. 6 ft., blue eyes, brown hair, light complexion; widowed. REGULAR RANGER (dates unknown—1 year under Capt. Rogers). Ranchhand. REGULAR RANGER Dec. 22, 1917–Dec. 15, 1920 (private, Co. K; reenlisted under the new law in Co. D, June 20, 1919). Discharged. REMARKS: As of Jan. 1920 was a Ranger in Starr County, Texas. Died Feb. 14, 1952, Karnes County, Texas. FAMILY: Parents, William Oscar Hutchison (b. 1848, KY) and Mary Jane Dromgoole (b. 1851, MS); siblings, Jane Kyle (b. 1873, TX), William Owen (b. 1876, TX), Charles Ernest (b. 1888, TX), Bertha Mae (b. 1891, TX); spouse, Ada Pearl Woolsey (b. 1881, TX), married about 1901; daughter, Lola May (b. 1903, TX). *SR; 471; A1b, e, f; A4b.*

HYATT, SIDNEY WILLIAM. Born May 3, 1886, Cypress Mill, Blanco County, Texas. Ht. 6 ft. 1 in., blue eyes, brown hair, dark complexion. Stockman and deputy sheriff, Johnson City, Blanco County. LOYALTY RANGER June 26, 1918–Feb. 1919. REMARKS: Was deputy sheriff of Blanco County from 1911–1918. In 1930 was farming in Blanco County. Died July 12, 1942, Blanco County, Texas; buried in Hyatt Family Cemetery, Blanco County. FAMILY: Parents, Edward John Hyatt (b. 1856, England) and Clara "Carrie" Burdett (b. 1860, England); siblings, Edward Burdett "Eddie" (b. 1882, TX), Clara Anne (b. 1884, TX), John Gordon (b. 1888, TX), Harvey Harry (b. 1890, TX), Regina D. (b. 1893), Gertrude Margaret (b. 1894, TX), Edith Kathleen "Kate" (b. 1896, TX), James Cecil Stanly (b. 1899, TX). *SR; A1d, e, f, g; A2b; A3a; A4b.*

HYDE, JAMES AUDLEY "AUDLEY." Born Jan. 29, 1889, Taylor, Williamson County, Texas. Ht. 6 ft. 1 in., gray eyes, light hair. Hotel clerk, Taylor. REGULAR RANGER Sept. 3, 1920–Nov. 29, 1920 (private, Headquarters Co.). Resigned/fired. City policeman, Taylor. REGULAR RANGER Dec. 6, 1920–Dec. 21, 1920 (Emergency Co. No. 1). Resigned/fired. REMARKS: Both his resignations had a notation on the Service Record: "Crook, won't do." In 1910 had been a baggage master for the railroad, living in Taylor. In 1930 was a railroad engineer, still living in Taylor. FAMILY: Parents, Joseph F. Hyde (b. 1855, NC) and Maud (b. 1866, IL); siblings, Nellie (b. 1887, TX), Homer Joseph (b. 1891, TX), Robert Burke (b. 1893, TX), Illene (b. 1897, TX). *SR; 471; A1d, e, f, g; A3a.*

HYDE, THOMAS CARLYLE "CARLIE." Born May 26, 1889, Kerr County, Texas. Ht. 6 ft. 2 in., blue eyes, brown hair, light complexion, married. Cowboy. REGULAR RANGER Mar. 25, 1918–May 1, 1918 (private, Co. L). Died May 1, 1918 at Ysleta, El Paso County, Texas of amoebic dysentery. REMARKS: Was in draft age, married with two children, classified No. 4. FAMILY: Parents, Benjamin J. Hyde (b. 1848, LA) and Martha Viola J. Wallace (b. 1854, TX); siblings, Johnie Benjamin (b. 1874, TX), Emma (b. 1876, TX), Lon Ethel (b. 1878, TX), Martha Anna (b. 1880, TX), Willie E. (b. 1883, TX), Minter Marion (b. 1885, TX), Lee Washington (b. 1892, TX), Lena May (b. 1896, TX); spouse (probably), Sudie Allen; one child (b.1912, TX), other child unknown. *SR; 471; Woodul to Davis, Apr 30, 1918, AGC; Davis to Cardwell, May 9, 13, 1918, AGC; Davis to Woodul, May 10, 1918, AGC; A1d; A2e; A3a; A4b; C.*

IGLEHART, DAVID TOM, JR. Born Sept. 1871, Bryan, Brazos County, Texas. Ht. 5 ft. 10 in., brown eyes, black hair, dark complexion, married. Ranchman, Austin, Travis County, Texas. SPECIAL RANGER Jan. 7, 1918–Jan. 15, 1919 (Headquarters Co.). REMARKS: In Jan. 1918 he was classed as a REGULAR RANGER. In 1920 was a cotton compressor living in Austin. A D. T. Iglehart died June 1, 1927, Travis County, Texas. FAMILY: Parents, David T. Iglehart (b. 1836, MD) and Mary H. Johnson (b. 1846, NC); sisters, Mary (b. 1866, TX), Julia (b. 1867, TX); spouse, Mattie B. Dunnington (b. 1876, TX). *SR; Acting AG to GC & SF Railroad, Jan 9, 1918, AGC; Acting AG to FW&DC Railroad, Jan 11, 1918, AGC; A1b, d, f; A5a; C.*

IKARD, SULLIVAN ROSS "SULLY." Born Sept. 20, 1883, Weatherford, Parker County, Texas. Ht. 5 ft. 8 in., gray eyes, brown hair, light complexion. Cowboy. REGULAR RANGER Aug. 11, 1918–Mar. 10, 1919 (private, Co. L). Honorably discharged—Co. L was disbanded. REMARKS: In 1910 was a stock ranch herder in Reeves County, Texas. In 1930 was manager of a cattle ranch in Wheeless, Cimarron County, Oklahoma. Died July 21, 1952, Reeves County, Texas. FAMILY: Parents, Lafayette Edward Ikard (b. 1838, AL) and Melinda Dulce Wright (b. 1842, GA); siblings, Isabella E. (b. 1872, TX), Robert Emmett (b. 1875, TX), Milton U. (b. 1878, TX), Willey May (b. 1880, TX), Floyd (b. 1881, TX), Mildred L. (b. 1886, TX), Upton Milton; spouse, Verne (b. 1897, TX), married about 1920; daughter, Bettie J. (b. 1922, NM). *SR; 471; Special Orders No. 21, Mar 10, 1919, WC; A1b, d, e, g; A2b; A3a; A4b.*

INGHAM, ANDY YOUNG. Born Feb. 1, 1881, Dallas County, Texas. Ht. 5 ft. 10 in., blue eyes, brown hair, fair complexion, married. Stock farmer, Texhoma, Sherman County, Texas. LOYALTY RANGER June 6, 1918–Feb. 1919. REMARKS: In 1920 was an oil well drilling contractor in Granite, Greer County, Oklahoma. In 1930 was a building contractor in Texhoma. Died Mar. 16, 1963 in Oklahoma; buried in Texhoma Cemetery, Sherman County, Texas. FAMILY: Parents, Orris James Ingham (b. 1835, NY) and Elizabeth Strader (b. 1849); siblings, Alice E. (b. 1872, TX), Harry J. (b. 1877, TX); spouse, Rela Vaughn (b. 1881, TX), married July 8, 1903, Stratford, Sherman County; children, Orris Hearn (b. 1904, TX), Evelyn Elizabeth (b. 1907, TX), Andy Young (b. 1911, TX), Annie Norene (b. 1915, TX), Margie Mayfield (b. 1917, TX), Virginia Duse (b. 1928, TX). *SR; A1d, e, f, g; A2a, e; A3a; A4b, g; B2.*

IRVIN, THOMAS ALVA "AL." Born Aug. 14, 1873, Hughes Springs, Cass County, Texas. Ht. 6 ft. 4 in., brown eyes, dark hair, dark complexion, married. Rancher and farmer, Abilene, Taylor County, Texas. SPECIAL RANGER May 31, 1917–Dec. 1917 (attached to Co. C). REMARKS: Had been Callahan County sheriff and tax collector, Nov. 6, 1900–Nov. 8, 1910. Died Nov. 26, 1949, Baird, Callahan County, Texas; buried in Cross Plains Cemetery, Cross Plains, Callahan County. FAMILY: Parents, William Russell Irvin (b. 1851, GA) and Ann Eliza Briggs (b. 1854, MS); siblings, Ora L. (b. 1877, TX), William Burris (b. 1879, TX), Lena (b. 1883, TX), Maggie (b. 1885, TX), Leonard (b. 1890, TX),

Bennie B. (b. 1891, TX), Eunice (b. 1893, TX), Beulah L. (b. 1895, TX); spouse #1, Laura Eva Aycock (b. 1874, TX), married Oct. 17, 1894, she died in 1897; spouse #2, Mamie Claire Aycock (b. 1879, TX), married Nov. 1, 1898, Callahan County; children, William Buell (b. 1899, TX), Irma Dean (b. 1901, TX), Freeda Lurlene (b. 1904, TX), Russell Briggs (b. 1906, TX); spouse #3, Mary Ollie Durbin (b. 1892); spouse #4, Effie M. Esman; son, Thomas Alred (b. 1935, TX). *SR; 1503:84; A1b, d, e, f; A2b, e; A3a; A4b, g; B1, 2.*

ISAACS, JOHN CHILDRESS. Born Jan. 31, 1866, Bosque County, Texas. Ht. 5 ft. 10 in., brown eyes, black hair, dark complexion, married. Cattleman, Canadian, Hemphill County, Texas. LOYALTY RANGER June 4, 1918–Feb. 1919. REMARKS: One source lists his birthplace as Snyder, Scurry County, Texas; another source lists birthplace as Comanche, Comanche County, Texas. In 1930 was a stock rancher in Canadian. Died Oct. 22, 1937, Canadian, Hemphill County, Texas. FAMILY: Parents, Josiah Childress Isaacs (b. 1824, TN) and Mary Jane Jacks (b. 1822, TN); siblings, Elizabeth (b. 1852, TX), William Conn (b. 1853, TX), Harriet Ellen (b. 1856, TX), George W. (b. 1857, TX), Eliza Jane (b. 1859, TX), Jefferson Davis (b. 1862, TX), Samuel Allen (b. 1864, TX); spouse, Viola B. (b. 1878, PA), married about 1890; children, William Calvin (b. 1904, TX), Anna Teresa (b. 1906, TX), John C., Jr. (b. 1901, TX), Quentin (b. 1919, TX). *SR; A1b, e, f, g; A2b; A4a, b, g; B1.*

IVEY, CURTIS LEON. Born Feb. 28, 1871, San Marcos, Hays County, Texas. Ht. 5 ft. 11 in., gray eyes, brown hair, medium complexion, married. Veterinarian, San Marcos. LOYALTY RANGER June 17, 1918–Feb. 1919. REMARKS: Died Dec. 31, 1953, McLennan County, Texas. FAMILY: Parents, Elijah P. Ivey (b. 1835, AL) and Mary Ann Saunders (b. 1842, AL); siblings, Mary Emma (b. 1859, LA), Milton Drew (b. 1861, LA), Sarah Cassie (b. 1863, LA), Susan Addis (b. 1866, LA), Claude Sanders (b. 1869, LA), Elmer Elijah (b. 1874, TX), Huling Clinton (b. 1876, TX), James Ford (b. 1878, TX), Paul Pressler (b. 1883, TX); spouse, Eulah E. Rodgers (b. 1869, MS), married Oct. 7, 1891, San Marcos; children, Leon C. (b. 1893, TX), Mary (b. 1896, TX), Frank E. (b. 1899, TX). *SR; A1b, d, e, f, g; A2b; A4b; B1.*

IVY, WILLIAM JOSHUA "JOSH." Born May 16, 1876, Huntington, Angelina County, Texas. Ht. 5 ft. 8 ½ in., blue eyes, brown hair, fair complexion, married. Stock farmer, Huntington. LOYALTY RANGER June 29, 1918–Feb. 1919. REMARKS: In 1920 was a timber contractor in Angelina County. In 1930 was an ice man in Angelina County. Died Oct. 23, 1949, Angelina County, Texas; buried in Jonesville Cemetery, Angelina County. FAMILY: Parents, Jamerson Wiggins Ivy (b. 1847, GA) and Martha J. "Jannie" Collins (b. 1855, TX); siblings, George Cyrus (b. 1872, TX), James Bobby (b. 1874, TX), Mary E. "Mollie" (b. 1878, TX), Delilia (b. 1882, TX), Susan "Sudie" (b. 1883, TX), Martha A. (b. 1884, TX), Nora E. (b. 1887, TX), Eveline (b. 1889, TX), Matilda (b. 1892, TX), John A. (b. 1894, TX); spouse, Alfa Omega "Minnie" Russell (b. 1880, TX), married about 1903; son, Bolivar (b. 1904, TX). *SR; A1a, b, d, e, f, g; A2b; A3a; A4b, g; B1.*

IZAGUIRRE, EDUARDO. Born Sept. 15, 1886, Camargo, Tamaulipas, Mexico. Ht. 5 ft. 9 in., brown eyes, black hair, dark complexion, married. Ranchman (owned the Agua Nueva Ranch), Jim Hogg County, Texas. SPECIAL RANGER May 1, 1918–Jan. 15, 1919; Aug. 6, 1919–Dec. 31, 1919. REMARKS: As of May 1918 had taken out his first naturalization papers. Jan. 1919 letterhead: "Eduardo Izaguirre, Agua Nueva Ranch, Raiser and Dealer in Cattle and Horses, Agua Nueva, Tex., Jim Hogg Co." *SR; A3c.*

JACKMAN, THOMAS J. Born Sept. 1869, San Marcos, Hays County, Texas. Ht. 5 ft. 11 in., brown eyes, blonde hair, blonde complexion. Peace officer, San Marcos. REGULAR RANGER June 28, 1919–Sept. 20, 1923 (private, Co. B; transferred to Co. A, July 1, 1920; reenlisted June 28, 1923). Resigned. REMARKS: Had been a cattle herder in the Creek Nation, Indian Territory. In 1930 was a police patrolman in Galveston, Galveston County, Texas. A Thomas J. Jackman died Aug. 3, 1943, Brazoria County, Texas. LAW ENFORCEMENT RELATIVES: Hays County sheriff (Nov. 8, 1892–Nov. 5, 1912) William T. Jackman, brother. FAMILY: Parents, Sidney Drake Jackman (b. 1826, KY) and Martha Rachel Slaven (b. 1834, MO); siblings, William T. (b. 1852, MO), Cora Francis (b. 1853, MO), Mary Belle (b. 1856, MO), Henry Clay (b. 1857, MO), Nathaniel D. (b. 1859, MO), Sidney J. (b. 1863, MO), Nora W. (b. 1867, TX); stepmother, Cass (b. 1838, MS); siblings, Edward B. (b. 1877, TX), Nellie N. (b. 1878, TX), Mark (b. 1881, TX). *SR; Jackman to Harley, May 25, 1919, AGC; Stevens to Harley, Aug 24, 1919, WC; 1503:250; 471; 470: 43; A1a, b, d, f, g; A2b; A4a, b, g.*

JACKSON, CECIL. Born Nov. 1885, Silver, Coke County, Texas. Ht. 6 ft., black eyes, black hair, dark complexion. Ranchman. REGULAR RANGER Sept. 4, 1917–unknown (private, Co. B). *SR; 471.*

JACKSON, FORD G. Born Nov. 6, 1895, Alpine, Brewster County, Texas. Tall, stout, blue eyes, dark brown hair. Texas quarantine guard (at Terlingua), Alpine. SPECIAL RANGER Feb. 4, 1918–Jan. 15, 1919. REMARKS: Had been a cowman. In 1930 was a ranch manager in Brewster County. A Ford Jackson died May 19, 1932, Bexar County, Texas. FAMILY: Parents, Joseph Daniel Jackson (b. 1861, TX) and Dorcas Ford (b. 1866, TX); sister, Una S. (b. 1890, TX); spouse, Emma Eugenie "Jene" Brannon (b. 1903, NY), married about 1924; daughter, Carolyn Jeanne (b. 1926, TX). *SR; Collins to Harley, Feb 1, 1918, AGC; A1d, e, g; A2b, e; A3a; A4a, b.*

JACKSON, OTHAR C. Born Dec. 1868, Coryell County, Texas. No physical description, married. Doctor, Voca, McCulloch County, Texas. LOYALTY RANGER July 24, 1918–Feb. 1919. REMARKS: Still in medical general practice in McCulloch County in 1930. An "Other Cols Jackson" died Nov. 30, 1933, McCulloch County, Texas. FAMILY: Parents, Joel W. Jackson (b. 1833, MS) and Susan A. (b. 1844, TX); siblings, Lula Jeanette (b. 1861, TX), Thula Thomas (b. 1863, TX), Luther (b. 1866, TX), Marion A. (b. 1871, TX), Anna (b. 1874, TX), Estea Ammy (b. 1879, TX); spouse, Ernis (b. 1883, KY). *SR; A1a, b, d, e, f, g; A2b; A4a, b, g.*

JAMES, CHARLEY BIRD. Born Feb. 23, 1873, Wright City, Warren County, Missouri. Ht. 5 ft. 9 in., gray eyes, dark hair, dark complexion, married. Railroad chief special agent, Teague, Freestone County, Texas. SPECIAL RANGER Dec. 29, 1917–Jan. 15, 1919. REMARKS: Had been a Dallas County deputy sheriff for 12 years. A Charley B. James died Nov. 22, 1940, Dallas County, Texas. FAMILY: Parents,

Thomas James (b. 1842, VA) and Catherine "Katie" (b. 1846, VA); siblings, Mary "Mollie" (b. 1869, VA), Thomas (b. 1875, MO), George (b. 1879, MO), Berdie (b. 1882, TX), Dunny (b. 1885, TX); spouse, Kate E. (b. 1886, TX); stepchildren, Mary K. Wright (b. 1906, TX), George Wright (b. 1907, TX). *SR; A1a, b, d, e, f; A2b; A3a.*

JAMES, DAVID LINDSEY. Born June 17, 1871, Fort Griffin, Shackelford County, Texas. Ht. 5 ft. 10 in., brown eyes, black hair, dark complexion. Stockman (had a ranch near Hot Wells), Marfa, Presidio County, Texas. SPECIAL RANGER Dec. 18, 1917–Jan. 15, 1919. REMARKS: As a young boy had lived in Brackettville, Kinney County, Texas. Jeff Davis County, Texas sheriff, Nov. 6, 1900–Nov. 8, 1904. Died Jan. 6, 1930, Bexar County, Texas; buried in Marfa. FAMILY: Parents, George W. James (b. 1825, MO Territory) and Lorena Lindsey (b. 1830, AR; d. 1875 in an Indian raid, Coleman County, Texas); siblings, George (b. 1850, AR), Margaret (b. 1855, AR), Sarah Catherine (b. 1860, TX), George Samuel (b. 1862, TX), Mary Ann (b. 1864, TX), William Jasper (b. 1867, TX), Cornelius (b. 1869, TX). *SR; Fox to Harley, Dec 18, 1917, AGC; 1503:285; A1b, d, e; A2b; A4a, b.*

JAMES, SIDNEY ALFRED. Born Nov. 26, 1877, Troy, Lincoln County, Missouri. Ht. 6 ft., blue eyes, light hair, light complexion, married. Merchant, Austin, Travis County, Texas. SPECIAL RANGER Aug. 31, 1916–Dec. 1917 (attached to Co. C). REMARKS: Was a deputy game warden in 1915. By Sept. 1918 was a merchant, farmer and stock raiser in Encinal, La Salle County, Texas. Still a retail merchant in Encinal in 1930. A Sidney A. James died Dec. 20, 1934, Webb County, Texas. FAMILY: Parents, Quincy James (b. 1856, MO) and Anne (b. 1854, MO); siblings, Jesse (b. 1879, MO), Kate (b. 1881, MO), John (b. 1885, MO), Henry (b. 1887, MO), Franklin (b. 1889, MO), Robert (b. 1891, MO), Joseph (b. 1894, MO); spouse, Katherine B. "Katie" (b. 1886, TX), married about 1908; son, Sidney A. (b. 1913, TX). *SR; BDH, Jan 23, 1915; A1b, d, e, f, g; A2b; A3a.*

JAMESON, LOUIS CALVIN. Born June 24, 1878, Whitewright, Grayson County, Texas. Ht. 6 ft., blue eyes, dark hair, fair complexion, married. Ranchman, Talpa, Coleman County, Texas. LOYALTY RANGER June 5, 1918–Feb. 1919. REMARKS: Had been a farmer in Runnels County, Texas. In 1920 was managing a ranch in Valera, Coleman County. Died Mar. 10, 1926, Runnels County, Texas. FAMILY: Parents, Thomas Allen Jameson (b. 1849, MS) and Laura Julina Clayton (b. 1858, MS); siblings, Eugina (b. 1878, TX), George Allen (b. 1879, TX), Samuel Jerome (b. 1881, TX), Finis Franklin (b. 1882, TX), twins Thomas Benjamin and William Henry (b. 1886, TX), Charles Jerome (b. 1889, TX), Amanda (b. 1892, TX), Dorintha Delana (b. 1894, TX), Emmitt Andrew (b. 1897, TX); spouse, Malinda Sophia Herring (b. 1881, TX), married about 1899; children, Elba B. (b. 1901, TX), Henry A. (b. 1905, TX), Ethel (b. 1907, TX), Louis C., Jr. (b. 1910, TX). *SR; A1e, f, g; A2b; A3a; A4a, b.*

JARRETT, THADDEUS JOHNSON "THAD." Born Oct. 6, 1881, Bosque, Bosque County, Texas. Ht. 5 ft. 11 in., brown eyes, brown hair, dark complexion, married. Ranchman, Comstock, Val Verde County, Texas. SPECIAL RANGER Dec. 3, 1917–Jan. 15, 1919 (Co. A Volunteers). REMARKS: In 1910 was an oil mill superintendent in Valley Mills, Bosque County. In 1930 was a livestock rancher in Val Verde County. Died Dec. 15, 1939, Bexar County, Texas; buried in Cedar Hill Cemetery, Del Rio, Val Verde County, Texas. FAMILY: Parents, Dr. E. V. Jarrett (b. 1854, GA) and Nancy Ellan Barnett (b. 1859, TX); sisters, Josie (b. 1883, TX), Mattie (b. 1886, TX); spouse, Irene Peters (b. 1886, TX), married Oct. 23, 1906, Valley Mills; son, Edward Virginius (b. 1908, TX). *SR; A1b, d, e, g; A2b; A3a; A4g; B1.*

JEFFERIES, ALAN TAYLOR. Born Sept. 13, 1889, Arkansas City, Cowley County, Kansas. Ht. 5 ft. 10 in., brown eyes, brown hair, fair complexion, married. Brand inspector, Cattle Raisers' Association of Texas and stock raiser, Clarendon, Donley County, Texas. SPECIAL RANGER June 26, 1917–Jan. 15, 1919 (attached to Co. C; was reinstated—WA renewed Dec. 20, 1917); June 12, 1919–Dec. 31, 1919. Brand inspector, Texas and Southwestern Cattle Raisers' Association, Clarendon. SPECIAL RANGER Apr. 22, 1927–Apr. 1, 1928; May 15, 1928–May 15, 1929; May 23, 1929–May 15, 1930; reenlisted May 15, 1930–Jan. 18, 1933 (reenlisted May 12, 1931/WA until Jan. 20, 1933); Feb. 1, 1933–Aug. 10, 1935 (WA extended to Jan. 31, 1935; reenlisted June 7, 1935). REMARKS: In Jan. 1918 was classed as a REGULAR RANGER without pay. Died Oct. 22,

1974, Donley County, Texas. FAMILY: Parents, James D. Jefferies (b. 1851, KY) and Elizabeth "Bettie" S. Warner (b. 1865, KY); sister, Hazel M. (b. 1891, KS); spouse, Kathleen (b. 1894, TX), married about 1919. *SR; Acting AG to FW&DC Railroad, Jan 11, 1918, AGC; Acting AG to GC&SF Railroad, Jan 9, 1918, AGC; Moses & Rowe to Harley, June 7, 1919, AGC; A1e, f, g; A2a, b; A3a; A4b, g.*

JEFFRIES, J. D. Born May 1890, Dallas, Dallas County, Texas. Ht. 5 ft. 9 in., gray eyes, light hair, fair complexion. Cowboy, enlisted in La Salle County, Texas. SPECIAL RANGER Nov. 6, 1916–Dec. 1917 (attached to Co. C). *SR.*

JENKINS, JOSEPH J. "JOE." Born July 8, 1867, Bastrop County, Texas. Ht. 6 ft. 1 ½ in., gray eyes, gray hair, dark complexion. Deputy sheriff. REGULAR RANGER Oct. 6, 1911–June 10, 1913 (private, Co. B). Resigned. REMARKS: Was wounded in Nov. 1912 shooting affray in Brownsville, Brown County, Texas. Had been a saw mill worker. In 1930 was a peace officer, a night watchman, in Bastrop. Died July 2, 1947. LAW ENFORCEMENT RELATIVES: Ranger John Holland Jenkins, father. FAMILY: Parents, John Holland Jenkins (b. 1823, AL) and Mary Jane Foster (b. 1826, MO); siblings, William Edward (b. 1847, TX), John Holland, Jr. (b. 1850, TX), James Northcross (b. 1853, TX), Sarah Ann (b. 1856, TX), Cicero Rufus (b. 1858, TX), Robert Lane (b. 1861, TX). *SR; 471; Sanders to Hutchings, Nov 10, 1912, WC; Sanders to Hutchings, June 16, 1913, AGC; 172:III, 930–931; BDH, Nov 11, 1912; A1b, d, e, g; A2b; A4b, g; B1.*

JENKINS, WILLIAM WARD. Born Jan. 19, 1887, Georgetown, Williamson County, Texas. Tall, medium build, light brown eyes, brown hair. Cowboy, enlisted in Hudspeth County, Texas. REGULAR RANGER Apr. 20, 1918–June 1, 1918 (private, Co. N—Hudspeth Scouts). Discharged. REMARKS: Was a farmer in Mitchell County, Texas in 1930. Died June 5, 1954, Mitchell County, Texas. FAMILY: Spouse, Ida Fay Goodwin (b. 1895, TX), married about 1920; daughter, Frances Fay (b. 1926, TX). *SR; 471; A1g; A2b, e; A3a.*

JENNINGS, CLYDE EDWARD. Born Dec. 9, 1888, Lindsay, Oklahoma. Ht. 6 ft., brown eyes, black hair, fair complexion, married. Policeman, Austin, Travis County, Texas. REGULAR RANGER Dec. 14, 1917–Mar. 31, 1918 (private, Co. I). Discharged/resigned? Peace officer, Austin. RAILROAD RANGER July 29, 1922–July 1, 1923. Discharged. REMARKS: Had been a streetcar conductor in Austin. Was a policeman in Austin from 1913–1917. In March 1918 wanted to resign from the Rangers and change jobs with W. M. Molesworth, an Austin policeman. In 1920 was a jailer in Austin. Was a real estate dealer in Corpus Christi, Nueces County, Texas in 1930. Died Nov. 23, 1971, Corpus Christi, Nueces County, Texas. FAMILY: Parents, Andy P. Jennings (b. 1859, TX) and Dora (b. 1868, Indian Territory); brother, Arthur (b. 1886, OK); spouse, Zelda B. (b. 1889, TX), married about 1919. *SR; 471; Molesworth to Harley, Mar 14, 1918, AGC; A1d, e, f, g; A2a, b; A3a.*

JESTER, SUE MACKIE "MACK." Born June 18, 1886, Manor, Travis County, Texas. Ht. 5 ft. 7 in., brown eyes, brown hair, fair complexion, married, as of 1918. Peace officer. REGULAR RANGER Oct. 6, 1911–Feb. 28, 1912 (private, Co. C). Discharged—reduction in force. Peace officer. REGULAR RANGER Feb. 1, 1915–Nov. 12, 1915 (private, Co. B). Resigned. Peace officer, San Antonio, Bexar County, Texas. REGULAR RANGER June 1, 1924–Feb. 21, 1925 (private, Co. E). Discharged. REMARKS: In 1910 was to be tried in Bastrop County, Texas for rape. Had been constable at Manor, deputy sheriff at Manor, 1911. Was Cameron County, Texas deputy sheriff, 1912; Manor city marshal, 1913–1914; city marshal, Calvert, Robertson County, Texas, 1917; Deputy U.S. marshal for the Western District of Texas 1918–1920, resigning on Feb. 29, 1920. A Mackey Jester, Jr. died July 29, 1928, Winkler County, Texas. FAMILY: Mother, Emma L. (b. 1862, NC); brothers, William Stephen (b. 1883, TX), Joe Gay (b. 1884, TX); spouse, Ruby (b. 1891, TX). *SR; 471; Jester to Hutchings, Apr 25, 1914, AGC; Jester to AG, Jan 8, 1915, AGC; AG to Fox, Oct 26, 1915, AGC; AG to Rutledge, Dec 15, 1915, AGC; U.S. Commissioner, El Paso, Nos. 236, 967, 1013, FRC-FW; 320:387; 321:350; 322:517; AS, Jan 1, 17, 20, 1910, Mar 27, May 30, 31, June 13, Aug 28, 1911; BDH, Feb 1, 22, Mar 13, Apr 2, 3, 24, May 4, 18, 1912, June 9, 1915; EPMT, Aug 8, 1915, July 27, 1919; A1d, e, f; A2b; A3a.*

JOHNSON, ADAM RANKIN, JR. Born Aug. 25, 1872, Burnet, Burnet County, Texas. Ht. 5 ft. 11 ¼ in., blue eyes, brown hair, medium complexion, married. Merchant, Burnet. SPECIAL RANGER May 31, 1918–Jan. 15, 1919.

Field consultant for the American Municipal Association, Austin, Travis County, Texas. SPECIAL RANGER Nov. 22, 1933–unknown. REMARKS: Served in the Spanish-American War and World War I. In 1920 was on the "Board of Control" in Austin. In 1930 was Austin city manager. According to the Texas Death Index, 1903–2000, he died Feb. 12, 1951, Travis County, Texas. His widow states he died Feb. 13, 1951, Austin, Travis County, Texas; buried in Oakwood Cemetery, Austin. FAMILY: Parents, Adam R. Johnson (b. 1834, KY) and Maria Josephine Eastland (b. 1845, TN); siblings, Elizabeth "Bettie" (b. 1866, TX), Robert E. (b. 1868, TX), Juliet (b. 1870, TX), Fannie (b. 1875, TX), William C. (b. 1879, TX), Ethel (b. 1882, TX), Mary R. (b. 1884, TX); spouse, Ruby Izora Brooks (b. 1874, TX), married Jan. 22, 1898, Burnet County, Texas; children, William Gary (b. 1899, TX), Lenna Kate (b. 1902, TX), Bettie (b. 1904, TX), Martha Jo (b. 1908, TX), Walter B. (b. 1911). *SR; A1b, d, e, f, g; A2b; A4a, b; B1, 2.*

JOHNSON, ALONZO MARTIN "LON." Born Oct. 3, 1883, Kyle, Hays County, Texas. Ht. 5 ft. 11 in., gray eyes, light hair, light complexion, married. Restaurant proprietor, San Antonio, Bexar County, Texas. SPECIAL RANGER May 11, 1918–Jan. 15, 1919. REMARKS: Proprietor of the Santa Monica Café at the I&GN Railroad depot. Captain W. M. Hanson endorsed his application for a commission. Still a café proprietor in San Antonio in 1930. Lon Martin Johnson died Aug. 26, 1932, Bexar County, Texas. FAMILY: Parents, Edward T. Johnson (b. 1856, TX) and Annie Laurie Yeoman (b. 1864, TX); siblings, Benjamin H. (b. 1885, TX), Thomas F. (b. 1888, TX), William E. (b. 1890, TX), Lucy I. (b. 1893, TX), Rack G. (b. 1895, TX), Sally E. (b. 1897, TX); spouse, Minnie Gertrude (b. 1888, MS), married before 1918, divorced by 1930; sons, Edward (b. 1911, TX), Albert (b. 1913, TX). *SR; Johnson to Hanson, Apr 9, 1918; Assistant AG to Hanson, Apr 25, 1918, AGC; A1d, f, g; A2b; A3a; A4g.*

JOHNSON, EDWARD ERNEST. Born Mar. 2, 1878, Frio Town, Frio County, Texas. Ht. 6 ft. 1 in., gray eyes, light hair, light complexion, married. Special agent, I&GN Railroad, Mart, McLennan County, Texas. SPECIAL RANGER Mar. 24, 1917–Jan. 15, 1919 (attached to Co. C; was reinstated/WA renewed, Dec. 27, 1917). REMARKS: Had been a railroad employee from 1895–1917. In 1930 was still a railroad agent in Mart. An Ernest Edward Johnson died Oct. 5, 1952, McLennan County, Texas. FAMILY: Parents, Newton Johnson (b. 1834, SC) and Cornelia J. Strait (b. 1842, AL); siblings, Celestia J. (b. 1867, AL), Mary E. (b. 1869, AL), Marcus A. (b. 1872, LA), Augusta A. (b. 1876, AL); spouse, Isabel McDonald (b. 1875, WY), married about 1904; children, twins Edward E., Jr. and Isabell (b. 1906, TX), Donald Newton (b. 1908, TX), Margaretta (b. 1909, TX), John Rutledge (b. 1915, TX). *SR; A1b, e, f, g; A2b; A3a; A4b.*

JOHNSON, FRANCIS NOEL "FRANK." No Service Record. Born Feb. 8, 1869, Hartsford, Tennessee. No physical description, married. REGULAR RANGER Jan. 28, 1907–Sept. 30, 1910 (captain, Co. A). Discharged when Co. A was disbanded. REMARKS: Mitchell County, Texas sheriff, Nov. 4, 1902–resigned July, 1907. Was a special policeman at Brownsville, Cameron County, Texas in Oct. 1910. In May, 1914 a Frank Johnson was a farm manager near Mission. In 1920, was a windmill dealer in Weatherford, Parker County, Texas. A Frank Johnson died Dec. 12, 1923, Parker County, Texas; one source states he died Jan. 1924, Weatherford, Parker County, Texas. FAMILY: Parents, Napoleon B. Johnson (b. 1844, GA) and Sarah Jane "Buddy" Williams (b. 1848, IL); siblings, Walter Anderson (b. 1871, TX), Samuel Matthew (b. 1874, TX), Charles Thomas (b. 1874, TX), Napoleon Bertram (b. 1878, TX), Willie M. (b. 1880, TX), Lotta Pearl (b. 1880, TX), Estella Ann (b. 1882, TX), John Earl (b. 1886, TX); spouse, Mattie E. Durett (b. 1867, IL), married Mar. 1894; children, Dorothy "Dot" (b. 1901, TX), Roy Edward (b. 1905, TX). *471; Canales to Campbell, Oct 25, 1910, AGC; Hughes to Newton, Nov 1, 1910, WC; 1503:378; BDH, Oct 1, 28, Nov 1, 1910, May 25, 1914; LWT, Feb 29, 1920; 464: 39, 40; 479: 72–73; A1b, e, f; A2b; A4a, b.*

JOHNSON, JOHN HENRY. Born Oct. 15, 1876, Corinth, Alcorn County, Mississippi. Ht. 5 ft. 11 in., blue eyes, black hair, dark complexion, married. Doctor, Sherwood, Irion County, Texas. LOYALTY RANGER June 5, 1918–Feb. 1919. REMARKS: Had been a physician in Upland, Upton County, Texas. In 1930 was a private practice physician in Fort Worth, Tarrant County, Texas. FAMILY: Parents, W. H. Johnson (b. 1850, MS) and Nancy E. Saunders (b. 1852, MS); siblings, Charles (b. 1870, MS), Sarah E. (b. 1872, MS), Rufus M. (b. 1873, MS), Mary E. (b. 1875, TN), Loney (b. 1878, MS); spouse, Maud L. (b. 1885, TX), married about 1909; children, Dorothy L. (b. 1910, OK), Margaret or

Marjorie E. (b. 1912, TX), Jack, Jr. (b. 1913, TX), Allie J. (b. 1916, TX). *SR; A1b, e, f, g; A3a.*

JOHNSON, JOHN WILLIAM "WILL." Born Mar. 31, 1889, Wesatche, Goliad County, Texas. Medium height, stout, blue eyes, light hair, married. Farmer, Charco, Goliad County. LOYALTY RANGER Sept. 28, 1918–Oct. 28, 1918 (his WA was cancelled). REMARKS: In 1920 was a retail meat merchant in Charco. In 1930 was the proprietor of a zoo in Laredo, Webb County, Texas. Died May 15 (or 22), 1967, Laredo, Webb County, Texas. FAMILY: Parents, James T. Johnson (b. 1852, TX or TN) and Martha (b. 1854, TX); siblings, Annie (b. 1874, TX), Laura A. (b. 1881, TX), Thomas H. (b. 1883, TX), Samuel A. (b. 1884, TX), Robert L. (b. 1887, TX), Mattie C. (b. 1891, TX), Delia (b. 1893, TX), Ellie O. (b. 1894, TX); spouse #1, Lillie Opal (b. 1889, TX), married about 1908, she died in 1918; sons, Walter (b. 1909, TX), Thomas (b. 1911, TX); spouse #2, Maria de la Garza (b. 1891, TX); children, Doris (b. 1923, TX), Ralph (b. 1924, TX), Raymond (b. 1926, TX), Alice (b. 1927, TX), James (b. 1932, TX). *SR; A1d, e, f, g; A2a, b, e; A3a.*

JOHNSON, LOUIS EDGAR "EDGAR." Born Jan. 30, 1876, Stephenville, Erath County, Texas. Ht. 6 ft. 1 in., blue eyes, brown hair, light complexion, married. Ector County, Texas sheriff and tax collector (Mar. 18, 1918–Jan. 1, 1923), Odessa. LOYALTY RANGER June 8, 1918–Feb. 1919. REMARKS: Had been an Ector County deputy sheriff for 3 ½ years. In 1930 was a trucker, lived in Ector County. FAMILY: Parents, J. B. Johnson (b. 1844, AL) and Rebecca (b. 1850, TX); brothers, E. L. (b. 1871, TX), F. W. (b. 1873, TX); spouse, Lida May (b. 1877, TX), married about 1898; son, Van E. (b. 1901, TX). *SR; Johnson to AG, Nov 19, 1918, AGC; 1503:167; A1b, e, f, g; A3a.*

JOHNSON, ROBERT HUDSON. Born Aug. 30, 1880, Fannin County, Texas. Ht. 5 ft. 10 ½ in., brown eyes, black hair, fair complexion, married. Peace officer. REGULAR RANGER Dec. 15, 1917–May 1, 1918 (private, Co. I). Discharged. REMARKS: Fisher County, Texas sheriff, Nov. 3, 1908–Nov. 8, 1910. In Oct. 1917 lived at Roby, Fisher County, applied for a Ranger captaincy. In Sept. 1918 was a canal rider for irrigation district #1 in Harlingen, Cameron County, Texas. In 1920 was a teamster doing general hauling in Harlingen. In 1930 was chief of police in Harlingen. Died Oct. 25, 1946, Harlingen, Cameron County, Texas. LAW ENFORCEMENT RELATIVES: Peace officer Horace Johnson, son; killed by bandits in an ambush. FAMILY: Parents, Robert White Johnson (b. 1843, AL) and Nancy Caroline Bryant (b. 1839, GA); siblings, at least 3 brothers and 1 sister, all born in Texas; spouse, Sarah Elizabeth "Bettie" Murray (b. 1880, TN), married about 1899; children, Horace (b. 1899, TX), Lois (b. 1901, TX), Annie Lee (b. 1904, TX), Ruth (b. 1906, TX), Luther (b. 1908, TX), Roberta Dee (b. 1909, TX), twins Mae and Fae (b. 1912, TX), Willis (b. 1915, TX), Rozelle (b. 1917, TX), Robert (b. 1921, TX), Ross (b. 1924, TX). *SR; 471; Capt. C.H. Strong, memo, Feb 16, 1918, RRM; Thomas et al to Whom, Oct 9, 1917, AGC; Buchanan to Harley, Oct 9, 1917, AGC; Weakley to Whom, Oct 8, 1917, AGC; 1503:184; A1b, d, f, g; A3a; A4b, g.*

JOHNSON, ROBERT L. Born Jan. 1868, Houston County, Texas. Ht. 5 ft. 11 ½ in., dark eyes, dark hair. Lawyer, Snyder, Scurry County, Texas. SPECIAL RANGER Sept. 28, 1918–Jan. 15, 1919. *SR.*

JOHNSON, THOMAS JESSE "TOM." Born May 24, 1880, Buda, Hays County, Texas. Ht. 5 ft. 9 in., brown eyes, black hair, ruddy complexion, married. Ranchman, Johnson City, Blanco County, Texas. SPECIAL RANGER Nov. 8, 1917–Jan. 15, 1919 (attached to Co. C). REMARKS: U.S. President Lyndon Baines Johnson was one of his nephews. According to the Texas Death Index, 1903–2000, Tom Jessie Johnson died Jan. 26, 1953, Blanco County, Texas. Other sources list date of death as Jan. 2, 1952, or Jan. 27, 1955, Johnson City; buried in Johnson City Masonic Cemetery. FAMILY: Parents, Samuel Ealey Johnson, Sr. (b. 1838, AL or GA) and Eliza Jane Bunton (b. 1849, KY); siblings, Mary Elizabeth (b. 1868, TX), Frank Barnett (b. 1870, TX), Ava Lee (b. 1872, TX), Lucy (b. 1875, TX), Samuel Ealey, father of Lyndon B. (b. 1877, TX), George Desha (b. 1883, TX), Kate (b. 1885, TX), Jessie Hermione (b. 1887, TX); spouse, Kittie Clyde Chapman (b. 1885, TX), married Oct. 4, 1904; children, Ava Elma (b. 1906, TX), Margaret Mable (b. 1907, TX), James Ealey (b. 1909, TX). *SR; A1f, g; A2b; A3a; A4a, b, g; B2.*

JOHNSON, WILLIAM A. Born May 1867, Fort Worth, Tarrant County, Texas. Ht. 5 ft. 11 in., blue eyes, dark brown hair, red complexion, married. Division special agent, I&GN Railroad, Laredo, Webb County, Texas. SPECIAL RANGER Jan. 11, 1918–Jan. 15, 1919. REMARKS: Had lived in San Antonio, Bexar County, Texas. Had been a deputy sheriff for 6 years; was district and county clerk in Edwards County for 10 years; was special agent for the I&GN Railroad, ca 1916–1918. FAMILY: Spouse, Mattie (b. 1876, TX), married about 1892; children, Zena M. (b. 1892, TX), Bessie M. (b. 1894, TX), Maude L. "Maddy" (b. 1896, TX), William A., Jr. (b. 1899, TX). *SR; Jones to Hutchings, Aug 14, 1916, AGC; Hanson to Johnson, May 29, 1918, WC; A1d, e.*

JOHNSON, WILLIAM JOSHUA. Born Feb. 9, 1883, Cookville, Titus County, Texas. Ht. 5 ft. 11 in., brown eyes, black hair, fair complexion, married. Physician, Cookville. LOYALTY RANGER June 17, 1918–Feb. 1919. REMARKS: In 1920 was the superintendent at the East Texas Hospital for the Insane, Rusk, Cherokee County, Texas. In 1930 was medical superintendent for the Southwestern Insane Asylum, San Antonio, Bexar County, Texas. Died Mar. 6, 1951, Bexar County, Texas. FAMILY: Parents, Claude Johnson (b. 1849, TX) and Antoinette (b. 1859, AL); siblings, Maggie J. (b. 1885, TX), Henrietta A. (b. 1889, TX), Clarence B. (b. 1892, TX); spouse, Alice (b. 1893, TX); children, Mary (b. 1917, TX), William (b. 1920, TX), Robert (b. 1923, TX). *SR; A1d, f, g; A2b; A3a.*

JOHNSON, WILLMAN (or WELMAN) EDGEFIELD. Born May 4, 1880, Atlanta, Fulton County, Georgia. Ht. 6 ft. 2 in., brown eyes, dark hair, florid complexion, married. Inspector of special service for Texas, SP Railroad, Houston, Harris County, Texas. SPECIAL RANGER May 10, 1917–Jan. 15, 1919 (attached to Co. C); was reinstated—WA renewed, Dec. 22, 1917. REMARKS: Had been inspector of special service for Texas, SP Railroad, 1911–1917. FAMILY: Spouse, Kittie Grant. *SR; White to Hutchings, May 7, 1917, AGC; Hutchings to White, May 10, 1917, AGC; A3a.*

JOHNSTON, HARRY MELVILLE. Born July 25, 1884, Austin, Travis County, Texas. Ht. 5 ft. 7 in., brown eyes, brown hair, fair complexion, married. Newspaper reporter, Austin. REGULAR RANGER Nov. 5, 1917–Feb. 13, 1919 (captain, quartermaster, Headquarters Co.; was suspended Feb. 7, 1919). Discharged/fired. REMARKS: On Feb. 7, 1919, participated in a drunken escapade leading up to a shooting scrape in which Captain K. F. Cunningham killed Ranger Bert C. Veale in Austin. REMARKS: In 1910 was a reporter for a daily newspaper in Houston, Harris County, Texas. In Jan. 1920 worked for the Texas Department of Insurance and Banking in Austin. Died May 25, 1927, Harris County, Texas. FAMILY: Parents, Rienzi Melville Johnston (b. 1849, GA) and Mary E. Parsons (b. 1852, GA); sisters, Hallie Rienzi (b. 1882, TX), Libbie Mary (b. 1886, TX); spouse #1, Beatrice Peeler (TX), married about 1907; spouse #2, Winifred May Graham (b. 1888, TX), married May 18, 1917; children, Harry, Jr. (b. 1918, TX), Mary Elizabeth (b. 1919, TX). *SR; 471; Special Orders No. 13, Feb 13, 1919, AGC; Aldrich to Caldwell, Jan 29, 1920, AGC; 172:III, 972–973; 172:III, 972–973; LWT, Feb 9, 1919; A1d, e, f; A2b, e; A3a; A4g.*

JOHNSTON, WILLIAM SCOTT "SCOTT." Born June 9, 1878, Texas. Medium height, medium build, blue eyes, black hair, married. Farmer, McLean, Gray County, Texas. LOYALTY RANGER June 15, 1918–Feb. 1919. FAMILY: Spouse, Willie N. (b. 1881, TX); married about 1899; children, Norman Scott (b. 1903, TX), Vernon L. (b. 1906, TX), William Elton (b. 1908, TX), Margaret (b. 1912, TX), Shirley A. (b. 1921, TX). *SR; A1e, f, g; A2e; A3a.*

JONES, ALLEN CARTER, III "DICK." Born Feb. 1884, Beeville, Bee County, Texas. Ht. 6 ft. ½ in., blue eyes, brown hair, light complexion, married. Ranchman, Alta Vista, Jim Hogg County, Texas. SPECIAL RANGER May 6, 1918–Jan. 15, 1919. REMARKS: As a youth attended West Texas Military Academy in San Antonio, Bexar County, Texas. In 1930 was a stock farmer in Beeville. An Allen Carter Jones died Nov. 10, 1957, Bexar County, Texas. FAMILY: Parents, William Whitby Jones (b. 1858, TX) and Louella Marsden (b. 1861, WI); siblings, Lorene (b. 1881, TX), Kathleen (b. 1885, TX), Catherine (b. 1887, TX), Alice (b. 1894, TX); spouse, Annie Gertrude Russell (b. 1894, TX), married about 1914; children, Luella (b. 1916, TX), Alice R. (b. 1920, TX), William W. (b. 1922, TX), Jeanne Gertrude (b. 1926, TX). *SR; A1d, f, g; A2b, e; A4g.*

JONES, FRED VAN. Born May 25, 1891, Nolan County, Texas. Ht. 5 ft. 4 in., brown eyes, brown hair, dark complexion. Stockman, enlisted in Travis County, Texas. SPECIAL RANGER Feb. 26, 1918–Jan. 15, 1919. REMARKS: In June 1917 was a cattle inspector for the Livestock

Sanitary Company of Texas, living in Blackwell, Nolan County. In 1920 and 1930 was a cattle ranchman living in Colorado City, Mitchell County, Texas. Died June 18, 1976, El Paso County, Texas. FAMILY: Parents, William C. Jones (b. 1857, TX) and Savanah L. (b. 1857, TX); siblings, Clide C. (b. 1883, TX), Otto Franklin (b. 1888, TX), Allie D. (b. 1893, TX); spouse, Lyle (b. 1904, TX), married about 1920; children, Fred V., Jr. (b. 1922, TX), Janie (b. 1929, TX). *SR; A1d, f, g; A2a, b, e; A3a.*

JONES, GEORGE LEE. Born July 26, 1897, Marfa, Presidio County, Texas. Ht. 5 ft. 10 in., brown eyes, dark hair, dark complexion. Rancher, Marfa. SPECIAL RANGER May 2, 1917–Dec. 1917 (attached to Co. C). REMARKS: His father allegedly used political influence to get Ranger commissions for George Lee and his brother. As of Aug. 1918 was a stock man in Jeff Davis County, Texas. Died July 15, 1977, El Paso County, Texas. LAW ENFORCEMENT RELATIVES: Ranger William Frank Jones, brother. FAMILY: Parents, William T. or J. Jones (b. 1861, AL) and Alice P (b. 1866, TX); siblings, Jessie M. (b. 1893, TX), William F. (b. 1896, TX), Allice R. (b. 1902, TX). *SR; Ferguson to Hutchings, [Apr 30, 1917], AGC; Jones to Hutchings, May 3, 1917, AGC; A1d, e, f; A2a, b; A3a.*

Ranger Gus T. "Buster" Jones. From *Trails and Trials of a Texas Ranger* by William Warren Sterling. Copyright 1959 by William Warren Sterling. Assigned 1968 to the University of Oklahoma Press. *Reprinted by permission of the publisher.*

JONES, GUSTAVE TINER "BUSTER" "GUS." Incomplete Service Record. Born July 17, 1883, San Angelo, Tom Green County, Texas. Ht. 5 ft. 6 in., blue eyes, brown hair, fair complexion, married. REGULAR RANGER Mar. 1908–July 1, 1910 (private, Co. A). Resigned to become a mounted Customs inspector. Bureau of Investigation agent (special government employee), El Paso, El Paso County, Texas. SPECIAL RANGER Mar. 31, 1917–Dec. 1917 (attached to Co. C); May 15, 1918–Jan. 15, 1919. REMARKS: Was deputy city marshal (night marshal) in San Angelo in 1903; Tom Green County deputy sheriff, 1904; Customs inspector at Brownsville, Cameron County, Texas 1910–1912; Immigration inspector, San Diego, California, 1912–1916; Bureau of Investigation and F.B.I. agent, 1916–1944; Bureau of Investigation special agent in charge of El Paso District, 1917; Bureau of Investigation division superintendent for West Louisiana, Texas, New Mexico, and Arizona, 1921; Bureau of Investigation special agent in charge, San Antonio, Bexar County, Texas 1922; F.B.I. agent, sent to Mexico City as civil attaché, 1939; F.B.I. agent assigned to foreign service as attaché, Mexico City, 1940; F.B.I. agent serving as liaison officer with British Intelligence, West Indies, 1943; retired as F.B.I. agent in 1944, in San Antonio; served as a security consultant for large industrial plants and U.S. and Mexican ranchers. Died Sept. 28, 1963, San Antonio, Bexar County, Texas. LAW ENFORCEMENT RELATIVES: Lieutenant, Co. A, Frontier Battalion W. W. Jones, father. FAMILY: Parents, William W. Jones (b. 1843, TX) and Viola M. Smith (b. 1858, AL); sister, Pearl Celeste (b. 1879, TX); spouse, Mary A. (b. 1887, TX). *SR; 471; Johnson to Newton, May 30, June 29, 1910, WC; AG to Johnson, June 2, 1910, WC; AG to Jones, Mar 28, 1917, AGC; Jones to Hutchings, July 13, 1917, AGC; Acting AG to*

Jones, June 5, 1918, AGC; U.S. Commissioner, El Paso, No. 892, FRC-FW; 319: 437–447; 464: 39, 40, 44; 504: 274–275, 408, 414; 1021:335; Jones file, 137; BDH, May 30, July 2, Oct 13, Nov 1, Dec 22, 1910, Feb 2, Aug 9, 1911, Jan 11, 1913, May 15, Aug 12, 1914, Jan 17, June 28, 1918; A1d, f, g; A2a; A3a; A4b.

JONES, HOLLIS WORTH "WORTH." Born July 25, 1898, Pine Hill, Rusk County, Texas. Ht. 5 ft. 10 ½ in., gray eyes, brown hair, light complexion. Texas quarantine guard, Brownsville, Cameron County, Texas. SPECIAL RANGER Feb. 5, 1918–Jan. 15, 1919. REMARKS: In 1920 was a drug store clerk in Brownsville. In 1930 was a newspaper reporter in El Paso, El Paso County, Texas. Died Nov. 24, 1986, El Paso County, Texas. FAMILY: Parents, Williams R. Jones (b. 1873, TX) and Eula (b. 1877, TN or LA); siblings, Levy (b. 1904, TX), Elizabeth (b. 1908, TX); spouse, Catherine Georges (b. 1904, MO), married about 1927; son, William Robert (b. 1930, TX). *SR; Collins to Harley, Feb 1, 1918, AGC; A1d, f, g; A2a, b, e; A3a.*

JONES, JAMES H. Born May 2, 1892, Bidias, Grimes County, Texas. Ht. 6 ft., dark eyes, dark hair, dark complexion. Well driller, enlisted in Hidalgo County, Texas. REGULAR RANGER June 24, 1916–Aug. 31, 1916 (private, Co. D). REMARKS: Note length of service. In June 1917 was a well driller living in El Paso County, Texas. On his WWI Draft Registration document stated had been a private in the Texas National Guard for two years. Also stated that he had tuberculosis. FAMILY: Parents, James Jones (b. 1868, MS) and Mallie (b. 1865, TX); brothers, Joseph (b. 1893, TX), John (b. 1895, TX), Jeff (b. 1897, TX). *SR; 471; Almond to Hutchings, July 9, 1916, AGC; A1d; A3a.*

JONES, JOHN R. Born April 17, 1859, Monroe County, Missouri. Ht. 6 ft. 2 in., blue eyes, gray hair, fair complexion, married. REGULAR RANGER "during part of 1885 & 1886 under Capt. McMurray." Superintendent, I&GN Railroad, San Antonio, Bexar County, Texas. SPECIAL RANGER Feb. 13, 1918–Jan. 15, 1919. RAILROAD RANGER Aug. 25, 1922–Feb. 19, 1923 (Co. A). Resigned. REMARKS: Had worked for the railroad since 1886. In 1930 managed his own farm in Salt River Township, Ralls County, Missouri. FAMILY: Parents, William A. Jones (b. 1831, VA) and Amanda (b. 1833, MO); siblings, Henry Edgar (b. 1854, MO), Lucy J. (b. 1856, MO), Sallie (b. 1865, MO), Annie B. (b. 1870, MO); spouse #1, unknown, married about 1880; spouse #2, Laura (b. 1871, IL), married about 1893; adopted son, Laurie (b. 1908, TX). *SR; Jones to Hutchings, July 29, 1916, AGC; A1aa, a, b, e, g.*

JONES, NAT B. "KIOWA." Born June 1871, Athens, Henderson County, Texas. Ht. 6 ft., brown eyes, brown hair, brown complexion. REGULAR RANGER 3 years 9 months including 1902. Brand inspector, Sheep and Goat Raisers' Association and stockman, Sonora, Sutton County, Texas. SPECIAL RANGER May 4, 1915–Sept. 22, 1917 (attached to Co. C; reenlisted/reappointed Jan. 24, 1917). Transferred to active duty. REGULAR RANGER Sept. 23, 1917–July 1, 1918 (private, Co. E). Resigned. SPECIAL RANGER July 29, 1918–Jan. 15, 1919. Brand inspector, Sheep and Goat Raisers' Association, enlisted in Val Verde County, Texas. SPECIAL RANGER Feb. 11, 1919–Dec. 31, 1919. Stockman,

Ranger Nat B. "Kiowa" Jones. *Photo courtesy Texas Ranger Hall of Fame and Museum.*

Kerrville, Kerr County, Texas. SPECIAL RANGER May 20, 1926–Feb. 1, 1927. Discharged/WA expired. REMARKS: May 1926 enlistment has birthplace as Goshen, Henderson County. Was appointed in 1915 at the request of Senator Claude Hudspeth to combat sheep thefts in Sutton County. In Apr. 1920 was an inspector for the Sheep and Goat Raisers' Association, at Juno, Val Verde County. A Nat B. Jones died Mar. 12, 1928, Kerr County, Texas. *SR; 471; Hudspeth to Ferguson, Apr 24, 1915, AGC; Ferguson to Hutchings, Apr 28, 1915, AGC; AG to Hudspeth, Apr 28, 1915, AGC; AG to La Crosse, Jan 9, Apr 13, 1917, AGC; AG to Barler, Nov 10, 1917, AGC; Stricklin to Aldrich, Apr 12, 1920, AGC; C.*

JONES, THOMAS STEVENS "TONY." Born Sept. 1, 1885, Old Jones Ranch, Bates, Kimble County, Texas. Ht. 6 ft. 2 in., blue eyes, brown hair, light complexion, married. Rancher, Junction, Kimble County. SPECIAL RANGER July 26, 1917–Jan. 15, 1919 (attached to Co. C; was reinstated/WA renewed, Dec. 27, 1917). Discharged. REMARKS: Graduated from Howard Payne University, Texas. Was a farmer and rancher in Kimble County all his life. Died Dec. 22, 1942, Bexar County, Texas; buried in Junction Cemetery. FAMILY: Parents, John Lafayette Jones (b. 1858, TX) and Lucy Elizabeth Stevens (b. 1863, TX); siblings, Maud M. (b. 1880, TX), Lillie Neal (b. 1882, TX), Clem Arvil (b. 1883, TX), Lola (b. 1892, TX); spouse, Viola Mae Bruce (b. 1887, TX), married Dec. 9, 1906, Old Hodges Hotel, Junction; children, Doris Faye (b. 1909, TX), John Lemuel (b. 1912, TX), Tommie Marietta (b. 1916, TX), Jack Spratt (b. 1920, TX). *SR; Latta to Ransom, July 26, 1917, AGC; Reid to Hutchings, July 26, 1917, AGC; Latta to Hutchings, July 26, 1917, AGC; AG to Latta, July 30, Dec 27, 1917, AGC; A1d, e, f, g; A2b; A3a; A4b; B2.*

JONES, WALTER FRANCIS. Born Dec. 17, 1889, Del Rio, Val Verde County, Texas. Ht. 6 ft. 1 in., blue eyes, brown hair, light complexion. Ranchman, Del Rio. SPECIAL RANGER May 19, 1917–Dec. 1917 (attached to Co. C). REMARKS: District Judge Joseph Jones at Del Rio asked Governor Ferguson to appoint Jones because there was friction between local peace officers and the military. The latter had confidence in Jones. In June of 1917 Jones was city attorney for Del Rio as well as a stockman. Was a lawyer in Del Rio in 1930. A Walter Francis Jones died Dec. 19, 1941, Bexar County, Texas. FAMILY: Parents, Joseph Jones (b. 1857, TX) and Mary F. (b. 1862, KS); siblings, Josephine (b. 1892, TX), John P. (b. 1894, TX); spouse, Bertha (b. 1893, TX), married about 1922. *SR; Jones to Ferguson, May 7, 1917, AGC; AG to Jones, May 18, 1917, AGC; A1d, e, f, g; A3a; C.*

JONES, WILL CURRIE. Born Apr. 14, 1874, Christoval, Tom Green County, Texas. Ht. 5 ft. 11 in., blue eyes, light hair, light complexion, married. Stockman, San Angelo, Tom Green County. REGULAR RANGER Dec. 21, 1917–Aug. 31, 1918 (private, Co. F). Resigned. REMARKS: Captain Bates (Co. F) gave him a letter of recommendation as a good peace officer. FAMILY: Spouse, Linabelle M. "Belle" (b. 1876, TX), married about 1899; children, Maggie B. (b. 1900, TX), Eugene W. (b. 1905, TX). *SR; Bates to Harley, Nov 9, 1917, AGC; Bates to Whom, Aug 31, 1918, AGC; AA, Apr 11, Nov 21, 1918; A1d, e, f; A3a.*

JONES, WILLIAM FRANK. Born Dec. 23, 1896, Fort Davis, Jeff Davis County, Texas. Ht. 5 ft. 10 in., gray eyes, dark hair, light complexion. Ranchman, Marfa, Presidio County, Texas. SPECIAL RANGER May 2, 1917–Dec. 1917 (attached to Co. C). REMARKS: His father allegedly used political influence to get William Frank and his brother commissions. LAW ENFORCEMENT RELATIVES: Ranger George L. Jones, brother. FAMILY: Parents, William T. or J. Jones (b. 1861, AL) and Alice P. (b. 1866, TX); siblings, Jessie M. (b. 1893, TX), George L. (b. 1897, TX), Allice R. (b. 1902, TX); spouse, Sargie O. (b. 1904, TX), married about 1923; daughter, Georgie Lee (b. 1924, TX). *SR; Ferguson to Hutchings [Apr 30, 1917], AGC; Jones to Hutchings, May 3, 1917, AGC; A1d, e, f, g; A3a; B2.*

JONES, WILLIAM JOSEPH. Born Oct. 8, 1892, Cedar Creek, Taney County, Missouri. Ht. 5 ft. 10 ½ in., brown eyes, dark hair, dark complexion, married. Mail carrier, Plemons, Hutchinson County, Texas. LOYALTY RANGER July 30, 1918–Feb. 1919. In 1930 was a garage mechanic in Stinnett, Hutchinson County. Died Oct. 19, 1976, Lamar County, Texas. FAMILY: Parents, James H. Jones (b. 1867, MO) and Alice M. (b. 1865, IL); siblings, Robert L. (b. 1898, MO), Georgia M. (b. 1907, MO); spouse, Rose L. (b. 1896, TX), married about 1915; children, Georgia Fern (b. 1917, TX), Sam Neven (b. 1918, TX), Robert James (b. 1928, TX). *SR; A1d, e, f, g; A2a, b; A3a.*

J

JORDAN, AARON CHOATE. Born July 25, 1875, Neosho, Newton County, Missouri. Ht. 5 ft. 8 in., gray eyes, dark hair, dark complexion, married. Stockman, Palo Pinto, Palo Pinto County, Texas. LOYALTY RANGER June 7, 1918–Feb. 1919. Stockman, Palo Pinto. SPECIAL RANGER Feb. 15, 1933–Jan. 8, 1935. Discharged. REMARKS: Had been a farmer in Palo Pinto County at least as early as 1900. Palo Pinto County sheriff, Nov. 8, 1910–Nov. 3, 1914; County commissioner, Palo Pinto County for 12 years. As of Feb. 1933 had been a Palo Pinto County deputy sheriff for 7 years. An Aaron C. Jordan died Oct. 1, 1948, Palo Pinto County, Texas. FAMILY: Parents, Jarman Lee Jordan (b. 1835, VA) and Nancy Emily Choate (b. 1836, TN); siblings, John Marion (b. 1859, TN), Martha Elizabeth (b. 1860, TN), Mary L. (b. 1867, TN), William E. (b. 1870, MO), Ella Lee (b. 1872, MO), Frances "Fanny" (b. 1874, MO), Clara Myrtle (b. 1877), Myrtha (b. 1879, MO); spouse, Jennie or Jane (b. 1876, TX), married about 1895; son, Thomas G. (b. 1898, TX). *SR; Connell to Hanson, Oct 2, 1919, AGC; 1503:402; A1b, e, g; A2b; A3a; A4b.*

JORDAN, THOMAS EDWIN. Born Oct. 9, 1878, Victoria County, Texas. Medium height, stout, brown eyes, light hair, married. Farmer, Victoria, Victoria County. LOYALTY RANGER June 10, 1918–Feb. 1919. REMARKS: In 1930 still a farmer in Victoria County. A Thomas Edwin Jordan died Sept. 2, 1947, Victoria County, Texas. FAMILY: Parents, George E. Jordan (b. 1852, VA) and Ella V. (b. 1852, TX); brother, Hugh North (b. 1875, TX); spouse, Susie Bell (b. 1889, TX), married about 1905; children, William Thomas (b. 1906, TX), Edith (b. 1908, TX), Clementine (b. 1912, TX), Jimmie E. (b. 1914, TX), Douglas (b. 1921, TX), Susie May (b. 1923, TX). *SR; A1b, d, e, g; A2b, e; A3a.*

JORDAN, WILEY D. Born Mar. 22, 1892, Fort Parker, Limestone County, Texas. Ht. 6 ft. 5 in., brown eyes, brown hair, light complexion. Cowboy. REGULAR RANGER Apr. 16, 1918–Aug. 31, 1918 (private, Co. N—Hudspeth Scouts). Discharged. REMARKS: In 1920 was a stock farm laborer in Presidio County, Texas. A Wiley D. Jordan died July 23, 1923, Presidio County, Texas. FAMILY: Parents, Andrew T. Jordan (b. 1848, VA) and Mattie (b. 1860, IL); siblings, Bryant W. (b. 1882, TX), Albert F. (b. 1888, TX); stepmother, Nancy C. (b. 1882, TX); half-brother, Calvin C. (b. 1900, TX). *SR; 471; A1b, d, f; A2b; A3a; A4b.*

JOSEPH, ROBERT LEE "LEE." Born Nov. 22, 1865, Chambers County, Texas. No physical description, married. President of Guaranty State Bank, San Antonio, Bexar County, Texas. LOYALTY RANGER June 21, 1918–Feb. 1919. REMARKS: Had been a bank president in Cuero, DeWitt County, Texas. Was a loan broker in Austin, Travis County, Texas in 1930. Died Jan. 1, 1936, Dallas County, Texas. FAMILY: Parents, Thomas Miller Joseph (b. 1823, CT) and Mary Minor Trueheart (b. 1824, VA); siblings, Fannie Overton (b. 1852, TX), Lucian Minor (b. 1853, TX), Margaret Beall (b. 1855, TX), Thomas Rogers (b. 1859, TX), Edgar Alexander (b. 1860, TX), Charles Henry Trueheart (b. 1863, TX), Henry Maury (b. 1870, TX); spouse, Lillian W. Thornton (b. 1865, TX), married Dec. 15, 1886; sons, Edgar E. (b. 1887, TX), Donald Lee (b. 1895, TX). *SR; A1a, b, d, e, f, g; A2b; A4b.*

JULIAN, JAMES LESTER "LESTER." Born Aug. 24, 1882, Berry, Fayette County, Alabama. Ht. 5 ft. 11 in., brown eyes, brown hair, dark complexion, married. Railroad conductor, Houston, Harris County, Texas. SPECIAL RANGER June 4, 1918–Jan. 15, 1919. REMARKS: Had lived in Orange County, Texas. In Sept. 1918 was a conductor for the Gulf Coast Line Railway in Houston. Still in Houston in 1920. FAMILY: Spouse, Lena Keith (b. 1886, GA), married July 22, 1907, Murray County, Georgia; children, Emily K. (b. 1911, TX), James, Jr. (b. 1914, TX). *SR; A1e. f; A3a; A4b; A5a.*

KEAHEY, THOMAS EDWIN. Born Feb. 2, 1885, Rockwall County, Texas. Ht. 5 ft. 8 ½ in., dark eyes, dark hair, dark complexion, married. Real estate agent, Rockwall, LOYALTY RANGER June 1, 1918–Feb. 1919. REMARKS: In 1920 was a real estate agent in Waco, McLennan County, Texas. Died Mar. 14, 1959, McLennan County, Texas. FAMILY: Parents, Joseph Henry Keahey (b. 1856, MS) and Ocenia Varena Teuton (b. 1862, TX); siblings, James Alvie (b. 1887, TX), Hallie Eugenia (b. 1890, TX), Gene Helbert (b. 1892, TX), John Robert (b. 1894, TX), Margaret Eva (b. 1897, TX), Ralph Waldo (b. 1900, TX), Ruth (b. 1908, TX), Paul Revere (b. 1908, TX); spouse, Grace Louise McCurry (b. 1890, TX), married Dec. 26, 1909; children, Thomas Hugh (b. 1911, TX), Mary Louise (b. 1913, TX), Bettie Allene "Lady Bettie" (b. 1916, TX). *SR; A1d, e, f; A2b; A3a; A4b, g; B1.*

KECK, FRANK RANDALL. Born Mar. 4, 1892, Cotulla, La Salle County, Texas. Ht. 6 ft. 1 in., brown eyes, brown hair, brunette complexion, married. Service car driver, Cotulla. LOYALTY RANGER June 29, 1918–Feb. 1919. REMARKS: Had worked as a clerk in his father's lumber and hardware business. In 1920 and 1930 was in the lumber business in Cotulla. Died Mar. 24, 1956, La Salle County, Texas. FAMILY: Parents, Thomas Randal Keck (b. 1862, IL) and Eva R. Freeman (b. 1873, TX); brother, Ray M. (b. 1894, TX); spouse, Fannie Mai (b. 1895, TX), married about 1913; children, Ruth Lareen (b. 1915, TX), Ray R. (b. 1924, TX). *SR; Cardwell to Strawn, July 11, 1918, AGC; A1d, e, f, g; A2b; A3a; A4b.*

KEENE, HENRY C. Born Oct. 30, 1892, Lexington, Holmes County, Mississippi. Ht. 5 ft. 8 in., brown eyes, black hair, dark complexion. Peace officer, enlisted in Cameron County, Texas. REGULAR RANGER Sept. 4, 1917–Feb. 15, 1921 (private, Co. A; transferred to Co. I, Dec. 21, 1917; transferred to Co. C; reenlisted under the new law, June 20, 1919; promoted to sergeant, July 15, 1920). Resigned. REMARKS: Had been city marshal and deputy sheriff, Lyford, Cameron County from 1915–1917. (Lyford is now in Willacy County following a reorganization in 1921.) In 1930 was a U.S. Health Service inspector in Laredo, Webb County, Texas. Died Jan. 14, 1987, Webb County, Texas. FAMILY: Parents, Henry Hunter Keene (b. 1871, MS) and Lillie Viola Parrish (b. 1871, MS); siblings, Mary A. (b. 1895, MS), Robert Angus (b. 1896, MS), Edwin H. (b. 1899, MS), Frank R. (b. 1905, MS), Lily E. (b. 1907, MS); spouse, Anela or Avela "Maria" Alanis or Alaniz (b. 1898, TX), married about 1920; children, Albert Oscar (b. 1926, TX), Irma Belia (b. 1938, TX). *SR; 471; Sanders to Hutchings, Sept 19, 1917, AGC; Sanders to Harley, Dec 11, 1917, AGC; AG to Sanders, Dec 21, 1917, AGC; Ryan to Keene, Jan 10, 1921, AGC; BDH, Aug 14, Dec 2, 1915, Feb 26, Mar 2, 3, Apr 5, 1916; LWT, Aug 22, Oct 10, 1920; A1d, e, f, g; A2a, b, e; A3a; A4b.*

KEERAN, CLAUDE ANDREW. Born Apr. 10, 1862, Stockton, San Joaquin County, California. Ht. 5 ft. 9 ½ in., gray eyes, brown hair, married. Stockman, enlisted in Victoria County, Texas. SPECIAL RANGER July 12, 1916–Dec. 1917 (attached to Co. C). Stockman, Inez, Victoria

County. SPECIAL RANGER April 26, 1918–Jan. 15, 1919. REMARKS: Had been a deputy U.S. marshal. In 1920 was a ranchman in San Antonio, Bexar County, Texas. Died Mar. 30, 1930, San Antonio, Bexar County, Texas; buried in Alamo Masonic Cemetery, San Antonio. FAMILY: Parents, John Newbanks Keeran (b. 1829, VA) and Mary Jane Tyner (b. 1841, AR); sister, Birdie (b. 1859, CA); spouse, Gertrude (b. 1885 or 1890, KY), married about 1901; children, Armel (b. 1902, TX), John N. (b. 1906, TX), Emily Reese (b. 1907, TX). *SR; A1d, e, f; A4b, g; B1; C.*

KELLIS, JOHN RUSK. Born Nov. 1, 1877, Peden, Mississippi. Ht. 6 ft. 2 in., gray eyes, dark hair, light complexion, married. Automobile dealer, Canton, Van Zandt County, Texas. LOYALTY RANGER June 14, 1918–Feb. 1919. REMARKS: In 1910 was deputy sheriff in Van Zandt County; Van Zandt County sheriff Nov. 8, 1910–Nov. 7, 1916. In 1930 was mayor of Canton. Died July 6, 1949, Van Zandt County, Texas; buried in Colfax Cemetery. FAMILY: Parents, James Henry Kellis (b. 1851, MS) and Mary Irwin Rusk (b. 1855, TX); brothers, Oliver J. (b. 1875, TX), Lewis K. (b. 1880, MS); spouse, L. Oren Mayne (b. 1883, TX), married about 1899; children, William Alton (b. 1900, TX), Lillie (b. 1905, TX). *SR; 1503:507; A1b, d, e, f, g; A2b; A3a; A4a, b, g.*

KELLY, EUGENE LEONARD "LENN." Born Jan. 12, 1882, Hallettsville, Lavaca County, Texas. Ht. 5 ft. 9 in., blue eyes, light hair, light complexion, married. Ranchman, Odessa, Ector County, Texas. SPECIAL RANGER Dec. 19, 1917–June 1918. Fired—WA was revoked in June 1918. Was reinstated, because his commission expired on Jan. 15, 1919. REMARKS: AG revoked his commission because a complaint had been lodged against him at San Angelo. Had a ranch near the El Paso County line. In 1920 was a retail drug merchant in Odessa. In 1930 was an oil field worker living in Odessa. An Eugene Lenn Kelly died Nov. 18, 1955, Ector County, Texas. FAMILY: Parents, Eugene Kelly (b. 1849, TX or MS) and Ida (b. 1865, TX); stepmother, Scottie L. (b. 1872, TX); half-brother, Garland K. (b. 1900, TX); spouse #1, Daisy Dell (b. 1878, AR), married about 1903; children, Lewis M. (b. 1903, TX), Eugene A. (b. 1903, TX), Richard G. (b. 1905, TX), Len (b. 1908, TX), Scottie Bird (b. 1909, TX), Vaughn (b. 1916, TX); spouse #2, Lyda R. (b. 1883, TX), married about 1923. *SR; Fox to Woodul, Dec 17, 1917, AGC; Kelly to Hanson, June 20, 1918, AGC; [Hanson] to Kelly, June 22, 1918, AGC; A1b, d, e, f, g; A2b; A3a.*

KELLY, OSCAR BLAND. Born Apr. 19, 1871, Coryell County, Texas. No physical description, married. Stock farmer, Post City, Garza County, Texas. LOYALTY RANGER June 7, 1918–Feb. 1919. REMARKS: First Garza County sheriff, June 15, 1907–Nov. 3, 1914. In 1930 was a sheep rancher living in Post. Died Feb. 29, 1964, Ontario, San Bernardino County, California; buried in Post, Garza County, Texas. FAMILY: Parents, Allen Preston Kelly (b. 1844, LA) and Sarah Elizabeth Bland (b. AR); spouse, Lulu Susan Elkins (b. 1880, TX), married Aug. 13, 1899; children, Max Allen (b. 1900, TX), Elwood B. "Bud" (b. 1902, TX), Knox (b. 1906, TX), Mary M. (b. 1914, TX), William Wilks (b. 1917, TX). *SR; 1503:203; A1e, f, g; A2f; A4b; B1.*

KELSO, EBER BENONA. Born Oct. 1892, Bartlett, Bell County, Texas. Ht. 5 ft. 11 in., blue eyes, black hair, light complexion. Accountant for the Texas Highway Department, Austin, Travis County, Texas. SPECIAL RANGER July 18, 1919–Dec. 31, 1919. REMARKS: Commission issued at request of Rollin J. Windrow and Governor Hobby. In 1930 was a garage proprietor living in Beaumont, Jefferson County, Texas. Died May 21, 1956, Harris County, Texas. FAMILY: Parents, Henry Reid Kelso (b. 1854, SC) and Leona Annetta Eastland (b. 1861, TX); siblings, Ala (b. 1883, TX), Grover (b. 1886, TX), Isla (b. 1887, TX), Allen H. (b. 1890, TX), Earl D. (b. 1894, TX), James Aubie (b. 1896, TX), Vivian (b. 1900, TX), Maurine (b. 1903, TX); spouse, Emma (probably Stafford) (b. 1900, TX), married about 1923. *SR; A1d, e, g; A2a, b, g.*

KEMPNER, ROBERT LEE. Born Jan. 21, 1883, Galveston County, Texas. Medium height, medium build, dark eyes. Cashier, Texas Bank and Trust Company, Galveston, Galveston County. LOYALTY RANGER June 12, 1918–Feb. 1919. REMARKS: Died Apr. 30, 1966, Galveston, Galveston County, Texas. FAMILY: Parents, Harris Kempner (b. 1837, Poland) and Eliza "Lyda" Seinsheimer (b. 1852, OH); siblings, Isaac H. (b. 1873, OH), Daniel Walter (b. 1877, TX), Hattie (b. 1880, TX), Stanley Eugene (b. 1885, TX), Frances "Fannie" (b. 1888, TX), Sarah (b. 1890, TX), Gladys (b. 1893, TX). *SR; Kempner to Harley, Jan 11, 1919, AGC; A1b, d, f, g; A2a, b; A3a; A4g.*

KENDRICK, ANTHONY ERASTUS "RASTUS." Born June 20, 1874, Hillsboro, Hill County, Texas. Ht. 6 ft. 1 in., brown eyes, black hair, light complexion, married. Stock farmer, Clyde, Callahan County, Texas. SPECIAL RANGER June 14, 1917–Dec. 1917 (attached to Co. C). REMARKS: Had lived in Callahan County at least since 1900. Died Feb. 2, 1928, Callahan County, Texas. FAMILY: Parents, Harvey R. Kendrick (b. 1855, MS) and Sarah Malinda Permilia McVicker (b. 1859, GA); siblings, Alma (b. 1878, TX), Elba (b. 1881, TX), Alice (b. 1883, TX), Nellie (b. 1885, TX), Roy (b. 1887, TX), Ethel (b. 1889, TX); spouse, Zelda A. Aycock (b. 1875, TX), married Dec. 24, 1902; children, Byron (b. 1903, TX), Ruby Leona (b. 1906, TX), Mel Harvey (b. 1908, TX), Lola Lee (b. 1910, TX), Oren Erastus (b. 1914, TX), Leon Elmore (b. 1920, TX). *SR; A1b, d, e, f, g; A2b; A3a; A4b; B1, 2.*

KENNEDY, ARTHUR V. Born Oct. 1859, New York, New York County, New York. Ht. 5 ft. 11 ½ in., gray eyes, brown-gray hair, light complexion, married. Railroad conductor, enlisted in Bexar County, Texas. SPECIAL RANGER Aug. 12, 1916–Dec. 1917. REMARKS: Had been a freight conductor for the I&GN Railway in San Antonio as early as 1891. FAMILY: Spouse #1, Elizabeth (b. 1876, England), married about 1898; spouse #2, Anna M. (b. 1881, TX), married about 1903; son, Arthur V. (b. 1913, TX). *SR; A1d, e, f; A5a.*

KENNEDY, STEPHEN RUFUS. Born Sept. 1, 1860, Ouachita County, Arkansas. No physical description, married. Stock farmer, Alanreed, Gray County, Texas. LOYALTY RANGER June 11, 1918–Feb. 1919. REMARKS: Had been a farmer in Hunt County, Texas. In 1930 was a retired stock farmer in McLean, Gray County. Died Feb. 11, 1949, Vacaville, Solano County, California; buried in Alanreed, Gray County, Texas. FAMILY: Parents, Stephen Kennedy (b. 1834, MO) and Nancy Sanford Cooper (b. 1833, AR); siblings, William T. (b. 1855, AR), James E. (b. 1857, AR), Mary M. (b. 1859, AR), Ermalinda Caroline (b. 1862, AR), William F. (b. 1864, AR), Robert Lee (b. 1866, AR), Matthew (b. 1870, TX), Elizabeth (b. 1872, TX), Lawrence B. (b. 1873, TX); spouse, Mary Amanda Green (b. 1866, GA), married May 8, 1884, Caddo Mills, Hunt County; children, Mary Eleanor (b. 1885, TX), William Milton (b. 1887, TX), James Lester (b. 1889, TX), Minnie Lou (b. 1892, TX), Stephen Hall (b. 1895, TX), Rufus Cary (b. 1905, TX). *SR; A1d, e, f, g; A2c, f; A4b; B1.*

KERCHEVILLE, McCROCKLIN "MACK." Born June 1882, Big Foot, Frio County, Texas. Ht. 6 ft. 1 ½ in., gray eyes, black hair, dark complexion, married. Lawyer, Devine, Medina County, Texas. SPECIAL RANGER Jan. 15, 1918–unknown. Deceased. REMARKS: In 1910 was a cotton buyer in Big Foot. FAMILY: Parents, Richard W. "Dick" Kercheville (b. 1853, TX) and Mary Elizabeth "Betty" Johnson (b. 1863, TX); siblings, Nellie I. (b. 1879, TX), Clarence (b. 1884, TX), Odell (b. 1887, TX), Berry W. (b. 1889, TX), Mary (b. 1892, TX); stepmother, Rose Laura Long (b. 1878, TX); half-brother, Frank; spouse, Mary Elizabeth "Lizzie" Laxon (b. 1881, TX), married about 1904; children, Melba Elizabeth (b. 1905, TX), Coronal Minerva (b. 1907, TX), Nellie Katherine (b. 1910, TX), Richard Hollie (b. 1912, TX). *SR; A1b, d, e, f; A4b, g.*

KERR, JOHN DEVILBISS. Born Aug. 12, 1873, San Antonio, Bexar County, Texas. Ht. 6 ft., brown eyes, dark red hair, light complexion, married. U.S. Army scout in the Big Bend, enlisted in Presidio County, Texas. SPECIAL RANGER Jan. 21, 1918–Jan. 15, 1919 (attached to Co. B). REMARKS: Had lived in New Mexico in the early 1900s. In 1910 was a theater manager in Plainview, Hale County, Texas. In 1920 lived in Marfa, Presidio County. FAMILY: Parents, Isaac Newton Kerr (b. 1836, TN) and Mary Hixie Harris (b. 1840, GA); siblings, Nellie (b. 1860, TX), Thomas Allen (b. 1862, TX), Mollie (b. 1864, TX), William Amos (b. 1867, TX), Ida Lee (b. 1870, TX); spouse, Mary E. Lackland (b. 1877, TX), married Nov. 15, 1893, Atascosa County, Texas; children, Albert O. (b. 1895, TX), Arthur D. (b. 1897, TX), Eva (b. 1904, NM), Clyde (b. 1908, NM). *SR; Fox to Woodul, Jan 21, 1918, AGC; 488: 44–45; A1b, e, f; A2b; A4b, g; B1.*

KERR, JOSEPH PERRY "PERRY." Born July 13, 1896, Lufkin, Angelina County, Texas. Ht. 6 ft., blue eyes, dark hair, fair complexion. Bookkeeper, Lufkin. REGULAR RANGER Aug. 1, 1919–Aug. 28, 1919 (private, Co. E). Resigned. REMARKS: Note length of service. In 1920 was a clerk in the railway office, Lufkin. In 1930 was a bottling company salesman in Lufkin. Died June 11, 1975, Harris County, Texas. FAMILY: Parents, Sam Heflin Kerr (b. 1870, TX) and Carrie Belle Hottle (b. 1870, LA); siblings, Harry McCool (b. 1892, TX), Sam H. (b. 1894, TX), Hannah Belle (b. 1897, TX), Dixon Gladney (b. 1899, TX), Gertrude

Kelley (b. 1901, TX), Rachel Jane (b. 1903, TX); spouse, Beulah Clark Chambers (b. 1902, TX), married about 1921; daughter, Lyska Marie (b. 1924, TX). *SR; 471; Aldrich to Kerr, Aug 1, 1919, AGC; Kerr to Aldrich, Aug 4, 1919, AGC; Aldrich to Singleton, Aug 15, 1919, AGC; A1d, e, f, g; A2a, b; A4b.*

KEY, JOHN GIBSON "GIP." Born Apr. 1858, Mount Lebanon, Bienville Parish, Louisiana. Ht. 5 ft. 7 ½ in., blue eyes, light hair, light complexion, married. Peace officer, Big Sandy, Upshur County, Texas. LOYALTY RANGER July 5, 1918–Feb. 1919. REMARKS: In Feb. 1919 was an agent for Aetna Insurance Co., at Big Sandy. In 1900 was a retail grocer and in 1910 was a hotel keeper, both in Upshur County. FAMILY: Parents, Martin William Key (b. 1828, SC) and Margaret (b. 1828, AL or SC); brother, William M. (b. 1857, LA); spouse, Mamie (probably Dozier) (b. 1874, TX), probably married Jan. 8, 1891, Gregg County, Texas; children, Bessie (b. 1893, TX), Gippie (b. 1898, TX), Henry (b. 1900, TX), Corine (b. 1902, TX), Clarence (b. 1907, TX), Carl (b. 1911, TX). *SR; A1a, b, d, e, f; A2c.*

KIEFER, EDGAR HUGH. Born Apr. 1872, Brenham, Washington County, Texas. Ht. 5 ft. 9 ½ in., brown eyes, dark hair, medium complexion, married. Publisher, Anson, Jones County, Texas. SPECIAL RANGER May 31, 1917–Dec. 1917 (attached to Co. C). REMARKS: Had been editor of the newspaper in Abilene, Taylor County, Texas. In 1930 again in the newspaper business in Abilene. Died Jan. 17, 1942, Taylor County, Texas; buried in Elmwood Cemetery, Abilene. FAMILY: Parents, J. Frank Kiefer (b. 1833, Germany) and Amanda M. Allen (b. 1835, LA); siblings, Rufus (b. 1862, TX), Frank (b. 1866, TX), Halbert (b. 1870, TX), Minnie (b. 1873, TX); spouse, Maggie May Patterson (b. 1873, TX), married Dec. 11, 1894, Rotan, Fisher County, Texas; children, Halbert (b. 1898, TX), Hazel J. (b. 1900, TX), Lallah L. (b. 1903, TX), Frank J. (b. 1907, TX), Margaret R. (b. 1915, TX). *SR; A1b, e, f, g; A4b; B1; C.*

KILBORN, OSCAR ELGIN. Born Feb. 8, 1886, Kendall County, Texas. Ht. 5 ft. 9 in., blue eyes, brown hair, fair complexion, married. Railroad policeman for the SP Railroad, San Antonio, Bexar County, Texas. SPECIAL RANGER June 6, 1918–Jan. 15, 1919. REMARKS: Had been a farmer in Atascosa County, Texas. In 1930 was a farmer in San Antonio. Died July 24, 1956, Bexar County, Texas. FAMILY: Parents, William Burton Kilborn (b. 1843, LA) and Martha Jane Wallace (b. 1858, MS); siblings, Ora Mae (b. 1879, TX), Luther Buckner (b. 1881, TX), Walter Elija (b. 1889, TX), Ray Quincy (b. 1891, TX), Arthur Ernest (b. 1894, TX), Caroline Alma "Carrie" (b. 1896, TX); spouse, Virginia E. Brown (b. 1886, TX), married Nov. 13, 1905, San Antonio; son, Raymond Luther (b. 1912, TX). *SR; A1d, e, g; A3a; A4g; B1.*

KILGORE, FREDERICK HOBER "FRED." Born Oct. 26, 1876, Austin County, Texas. Tall, stout, blue eyes, blonde hair, married. Farmer, Hempstead, Waller County, Texas. LOYALTY RANGER June 8, 1918–Feb. 1919. REMARKS: Was a farmer in Waller County from 1900 to his death. Died Apr. 4, 1927, Waller County, Texas. FAMILY: Parents, James C. Kilgore (b. 1832, AL) and Sarah A. (b. 1844, GA); siblings, Thomas E. (b. 1861, FL), Joseph A. (b. 1864, FL), Bettie B. (b. 1867, FL), Jennie M. (b. 1871, FL or TX), James (b. 1874, TX); spouse, Lucy (b. 1882, TX), married about 1902; children, Godfrey Dick (b. 1903, TX), Sallie May (b. 1908, TX), Ora Lee (b. 1911, TX). *SR; A1b, d, e, f, g; A2b; A3a.*

KING, HAROLD ATWOOD. Born Oct. 3, 1873, Jacksonville, Morgan County, Illinois. Ht. 5 ft. 11 ½ in., gray eyes, gray hair, fair complexion. Business manager for Fort Davis Auto Company, Fort Davis, Jeff Davis County, Texas. SPECIAL RANGER July 10, 1916–June 9, 1918 (was reinstated—WA renewed, Dec. 20, 1917). Resigned to go on active duty. Peace officer, Fort Davis. REGULAR RANGER June 10, 1918–Sept. 31 [*sic*], 1921 (private, Co. D; transferred to Co. B, unknown date; reenlisted under the new law as sergeant of Co. A, June 20, 1919). Discharged, reduction in force. REMARKS: Had lived in Big Bend since 1897. Was deputy sheriff of Jeff Davis County for 12 years and constable in Jeff Davis County for 3 years. In 1930 was a bank guard for a federal reserve bank in El Paso, El Paso County, Texas. Died Oct. 23, 1948, Jeff Davis County, Texas. FAMILY: Parents, John W. King (b. 1835, MA) and Eva "Lillian" Atwood (b. 1850, IL). *SR; 471; Petition to Fox, June 27, 19176, AGC; King to Ferguson, June 29, 1916, AGC; King to AG, July 15, 17, 1916, AGC; Hudspeth to Ferguson, July 11, 1916, AGC; AG to King, July 8, 1916, AGC; AG to Hudspeth, July 17, 1916, AGC; Eagle to Johnston, Dec 15, 1917, AGC; Harley* *to Eagle, Dec 16, 1917, AGC; 1: I, 1535–1537; AA, May 23, 1918; LWT, Oct 10, 1920; A1b, d, e, f, g; A2b, A3a.*

KING, JACOB LUTHER. Born Dec. 9, 1876, Lavaca County, Texas. Ht. 5 ft. 8 ¾ in., blue eyes, brown hair, fair complexion, married. Peace officer, Houston, Harris County, Texas (permanent address: San Antonio, Bexar County, Texas). SPECIAL RANGER July 28, 1919–Dec. 31, 1919. Special agent, Terminals, I&GN Railroad, San Antonio. RAILROAD RANGER Aug. 22, 1922–Aug. 22, 1924 (Co. A). Discharged. SPECIAL RANGER Oct. 5, 1925–Dec. 4, 1926. Discharged. REMARKS: Was city policeman/detective, San Antonio, in 1910, 1916. Commission in 1919 was issued at request of Gen. Jacob Wolters. In 1920 was a tractor salesman in San Antonio. In 1930 was a deputy sheriff in San Antonio. Died April 16, 1949, Bexar County, Texas. FAMILY: Parents, Sidney Pughley King (b. 1856, GA) and Nancy J. "Nannie" Young (b. 1855, GA); siblings, Lenora B. (b. 1880, TX), Grace (b. 1888, TX), Robert S. (b. 1892, TX); spouse, Hannah H. (b. 1879, Germany), married about 1899; daughters, Agnes D. (b. 1902, TX), Velma M. (b. 1908, TX). *SR; SAE, June 23, 1916; A1b, e, f, g; A2b; A3a; A4b.*

KING, RALPH McELREE or McELNE. Born Aug. 23, 1889, Alvarado, Johnson County, Texas. Ht. 5 ft. 10 in., blue eyes, auburn hair, light complexion, married. Stock farmer, Shafter Lake, Andrews County, Texas. LOYALTY RANGER June 13, 1918–Feb. 1919. REMARKS: In 1930 was a railroad station agent living in Cameron County, Texas. Died Nov. 23, 1968, Cameron County, Texas. FAMILY: Parents, Andrew King (b. 1856, GA) and Ida (b. 1860, TN); brothers, Lawrence R. (b. 1885, TX), Will A. (b. 1888, TX); spouse, Ruth H. Stacks (b. 1897, LA), married about 1915; children, Ida Ruth (b. 1916, TX), Oliver Ralph (b. 1918, TX), John M. (b. 1919, TX), Bert (b. 1925, TX), Myrtle Blanch (b. 1927, TX). *SR; A1d, e, f, g; A2a, b, e; A3a.*

KING, RICHARD, III. Born Dec. 17, 1884 on the Agua Dulce Ranch, Nueces County, Texas. Ht. 5 ft. 11 ½ in., brown eyes, brown hair, dark complexion, married. Rancher, Corpus Christi, Nueces County. LOYALTY RANGER June 5, 1918–Feb. 1919. REMARKS: His grandfather, Richard King, was the founder of the famous King Ranch, located in South Texas. Educated at the University of Missouri, studied agriculture. Was one of the trustees for the estate of his grandmother, Henrietta King. Was vice-president of the Corpus Christi National Bank. Died Mar. 4, 1974, Nueces County, Texas. LAW ENFORCEMENT RELATIVES: Ranger Richard Mifflin Kleberg, cousin; Ranger Robert Justus Kleberg, Jr., cousin; Ranger Tom T. East, cousin by marriage. FAMILY: Parents, Richard King, Jr. (b.1860, TX) and Elizabeth Pearl Ashbrook (b. 1865, MO); sisters, Minerva, Mary; spouse, Pierpont Heaney (b. 1890, TX), married about 1907; sons, Richard L. (b. 1909, TX), Alfred (b. 1917, TX). *SR; A1b, e, g; A2a, b; A3a; A4b.*

KING, WILLIAM HENRY. Born Mar. 1, 1859, Wilson County, Texas. No physical description, married. Lumber company manager, Stockdale, Wilson County. LOYALTY RANGER May 31, 1918–Feb. 1919. REMARKS: By 1930 had retired from the lumber company in Stockdale. Died Apr. 25, 1944, Stockdale, Wilson County, Texas. FAMILY: Parents, John Rhodes King (b. 1816, TN) and Eliza Wheeler (b. 1825, TN); siblings, Rachel Emma (b. 1853, TX), Martha Ann (b. 1855, TX), John Edwin (b. 1858, TX), Ruth Isabel (b. 1864, TX), Jesse Thwing (b. 1869, TX); spouse, Onie Page Wheeler (b. 1862, TX), married Oct. 25, 1882; children, John Rhodes (b. 1883, TX), Ethel (b. 1886, TX), Bernice (b. 1887, TX), James Milner (b. 1888, TX), Opal (b. 1891, TX), Isabel "Elizabeth" (b. 1899, TX). *SR; A1b, d, e, f, g; A2b; B2.*

KIRK, WILLIAM. Born July 31, 1893, Pine Bluff, Jefferson County, Arkansas. Ht. 5 ft. 8 ½ in., brown eyes, brown hair, dark complexion. Chauffeur, Austin, Travis County, Texas. REGULAR RANGER July 14, 1917–unknown but prior to Nov. 13, 1917 (private, Co. D). REMARKS: Was classed as a Regular Ranger without pay. Was chauffeur for Governor Ferguson, who ordered his appointment. As of Nov. 13, 1917 Kirk was no longer in the service of the state. *SR; 471; Ferguson to Hutchings, July 14, 1917, AGC; AG to General Manager, Nov 13, 1917, AGC; A3a.*

KIRKLAND, SAM ALMONTE "MONTIE." Born Dec. 29, 1891, Fisher County, Texas. Ht. 5 ft. 7 in., brown eyes, dark hair, ruddy complexion. Cowboy. REGULAR RANGER Sept. 22, 1917–Mar. 1, 1919 (private, Co. E). Discharged. REMARKS: In 1930 was manager of a grocery store in

Rocksprings, Edwards County, Texas. Died June 17, 1965, Edwards County, Texas. FAMILY: Parents, Samuel Kirkland (b. 1867, KY) and Della (b. 1874, TX); siblings, Joseph (b. 1892, TX), Fannie (b. 1896, TX); spouse, Ruth (b. 1902, TX), married about 1929. *SR; 471; Barler to Harley, Oct 12, 1917, AGC; A1d, e, f, g; A2b; A3a.*

KLAERNER, EDWARD HENRY. Born Nov. 30, 1886, Gillespie County, Texas. Ht. 5 ft. 11 ½ in., gray eyes, dark brown hair, light complexion. Real estate agent, Fredericksburg, Gillespie County. SPECIAL RANGER Dec. 20, 1916–Dec. 1917 (attached to Co. C). REMARKS: Was commissioned on Governor Ferguson's order. Died Oct. 15, 1918, El Paso County, Texas. FAMILY: Parents, John Klaerner (b. 1862, TX) and Amalia Basse (b. 1865, TX); siblings, Kilmer (b. 1888, TX), Felix (b. 1890, TX), Meta (b. 1892, TX), Walter (b. 1894, TX), Cora (b. 1895, TX), Edgar (b. 1897, TX). *SR; Ochs to Ferguson, Nov 23, 1916, AGC; Martin to Ferguson, Nov 25, Dec 14, 1916, AGC; Wroe to Hutchings, Dec 15, 1916, AGC; AG to Martin, Dec 16, 1916, AGC; A1d, e; A2b; A3a; A4b.*

KLAUS, THEODORE CHARLES "TED." Born Aug. 16. 1888, Cibolo, Guadalupe County, Texas. Ht. 5 ft. 10 in., gray eyes, light hair, light complexion, married. Peace officer. REGULAR RANGER Nov. 26, 1917–Jan. 23, 1919 (private, Co. D). Resigned to take a better position. REMARKS: Had been a bartender in his father's saloon in Taylor, Williamson County, Texas. In 1920 was a deputy for the Texas Game, Fish, and Oyster Commission, living in Austin, Travis County, Texas. In 1930 was an Austin city detective. FAMILY: Father, William F. Klaus (b. 1863, TX); sister, Anita (b. 1892, TX); spouse, Ada Boles (b. 1892, TX), married about 1909; daughter, Lucille (b. 1912, TX). *SR; 471; Matthews to Harley, Oct 27, 1917, AGC; A1e, f, g; A3a.*

KLEBERG, CAESAR. Born Sept. 20, 1873, Cuero, DeWitt County, Texas. Ht. 5 ft. 9 in., blue eyes, dark gray hair, ruddy complexion. Stockman (in 1911 was made manager of Norias Division of King Ranch). SPECIAL RANGER Nov. 30, 1917–Dec. 31, 1919 (attached to Co. C; commission was renewed Jan. 23, 1919). REMARKS: His commission was filed with Regular Rangers. In 1900 lived in Washington, DC; was secretary for his father who was a member of the U.S. House of Representatives, 1897–1903. Was nephew of Robert Justus Kleberg, Sr., general manager of the famous King Ranch in South Texas. Died Apr. 14, 1946, Rancho Santa Gertrudis, Kleberg County, Texas. LAW ENFORCEMENT RELATIVES: Ranger Richard Mifflin Kleberg, cousin; Ranger Robert Justus Kleberg, Jr., cousin; Ranger Otto Ludwig Eckhardt, cousin; Ranger Robert J. Eckhardt, cousin; Ranger Tom T. East, cousin by marriage. FAMILY: Parents, Rudolph Kleberg (b. 1847, TX) and Mathilde Elise Eckhardt (b. 1855, TX); siblings, Louise Indiana "Lulu" (b. 1877, TX), Augustus (b. 1879, TX), Alfred L. (b. 1881, TX), Matilda B. (b. 1884, TX). *SR; 471; Kleberg to Hutchings, July 20, 1915, AGC; Kleberg to AG, May 10, 1917, AGC; 172:III, 1135; 1:I, 1282–1286; 319: 474; 424: 147; A1b, d, f; A2b; A3a; A4b.*

KLEBERG, RICHARD MIFFLIN "DICK." Born Nov. 18, 1887, Corpus Christi, Nueces County, Texas. Ht. 5 ft. 10 ¾ in., gray eyes, black hair, swarthy complexion, married. Ranchman, Kingsville, Kleberg County, Texas. SPECIAL RANGER Apr. 4, 1918–Dec. 31, 1919 (commission was renewed Jan. 23, 1919). Cattleman, Corpus Christi. SPECIAL RANGER Apr. 10, 1931–unknown. REMARKS: His Ranger commissions were filed with Regular Rangers. His grandfather, Richard King, was the founder of the famous King Ranch in South Texas; his father was the King Ranch general manager. Richard M. was a Phi Beta Kappa graduate of the University of Texas; received a law degree in 1911. During WWI was an Army intelligence operative on the border and in Mexico. Served as U.S. congressman 1931–1944. Died May 8, 1955, Hot Springs, Arkansas; buried in Chamberlain Burial Park, Kingsville. LAW ENFORCEMENT RELATIVES: Ranger Robert Justus Kleberg, Jr., brother; Ranger Caesar Kleberg, cousin; Ranger Richard King, cousin; Ranger Otto Ludwig Eckhardt, cousin; Ranger Robert J. Eckhardt, cousin; Ranger Tom T. East, brother-in-law. FAMILY: Parents, Robert Justus "RJ" Kleberg (b. 1853, TX) and Alice Gertrudis King (b. 1862, TX); siblings, Henrietta Rosa (b. 1889, TX), Alice Gertrudis (b. 1893, TX), Robert Justus, Jr. (b. 1896, TX), Sarah Spohn (b. 1898, TX); spouse, Mamie E. Searcy (b. 1889, TX), married June 12, 1911, Brenham, Washington County, Texas; children, Mary Etta (b. 1913, TX), Richard M., Jr. (b. 1916, TX), Katherine (b. 1918, TX), Alice Gertrudis King (b. 1928, TX). *SR; 471; 172:III, 1136; 319: 472; 417: 592; A1d, e, f; A2e; A4b, c.*

KLEBERG, ROBERT JUSTUS, JR. Born Mar. 29, 1896, Corpus Christi, Nueces County, Texas. Ht. 5 ft. 10 in., blue eyes, brown hair, light complexion. Ranchman, Santa Gertrudis Ranch, Kingsville, Kleberg County, Texas. SPECIAL RANGER Aug. 19, 1918–Jan. 15, 1919; Jan. 23, 1919–Dec. 31, 1919 (commission was renewed Jan. 23, 1919). REMARKS: His commission was filed with Regular Rangers. His grandfather, Richard King, was the founder of the famous King Ranch in South Texas; his father was the King Ranch general manager. Robert, Jr. was very active in King Ranch management. Died Oct. 13, 1974, Houston, Harris County, Texas; buried at the King Ranch in South Texas. LAW ENFORCEMENT RELATIVES: Ranger Richard Mifflin Kleberg, brother; Ranger Caesar Kleberg, cousin; Ranger Richard King, cousin; Ranger Otto Ludwig Eckhardt, cousin; Ranger Robert J. Eckhardt, cousin; Ranger Tom T. East, brother-in-law. FAMILY: Parents, Robert Justus "RJ" Kleberg (b. 1853, TX) and Alice Gertrudis King (b. 1862, TX); siblings, Richard Mifflin (b. 1887, TX), Henrietta Rosa (b. 1889, TX), Alice Gertrudis (b. 1893, TX), Sarah Spohn (b. 1898, TX); spouse, Helen Mary Campbell (b. 1902, KS), married Mar. 2, 1926, Corpus Christi, Nueces County, Texas; daughter, Helen King "Helenita" (b. 1927, TX). *SR; 471; 172:III, 1136–1137; A1d, e, f; A2b, e; A3a; A4b, c.*

KLEMANN, NEWTON ROSWELL. Born Feb. 23, 1897, Eagle Pass, Maverick County, Texas. Ht. 5 ft. 9 in., dark eyes, brown hair, dark complexion. Manager, Farrar Lumber Company, Santa Maria, Cameron County, Texas. REGULAR RANGER Apr. 20, 1918–July 1, 1918 (private, Co. G). Resigned from Rangers to enlist in Army. REMARKS: Was recommended by Judge James B. Wells of Brownsville, Cameron County. Died Feb. 17, 1929, Willacy County, Texas. FAMILY: Parents, Herman Emil Klemann (b. 1858, KY) and Ramona Ransom (b. 1871, TX); siblings, Eleanor (b. 1890, TX), Herman Ransom (b. 1893, TX), Harvey C. (b. 1899, TX); spouse, Mattie May Sprouse, married about 1925; one child. *SR; 471; Klemann to Stevens, June 30, 1918, AGC; BDH, Apr 29, 1918; A1e, g; A2b; A3a; A4a.*

KLINGER, WALTER JOSIAH. Born Nov. 15, 1882, Shamokin, Northumberland County, Pennsylvania. Ht. 5 ft. 5 in., brown eyes, brown hair, light complexion, married. Bookkeeper, Plainview, Hale County, Texas. SPECIAL RANGER July 22, 1918–Jan. 15, 1919. REMARKS: In 1910 was the chief clerk at the Santa Fe railroad depot in Plainview. In 1930 was a real estate accountant in Plainview. Died Jan. 28, 1957, Hale County, Texas. FAMILY: Parents, Daniel D. Klinger (b. 1853, PA) and Hannah E. Young (b. 1853, PA); brothers, Joseph (b. 1876, PA), William A. (b. 1888, PA), Fredrick Harwood (b. 1890, PA), Harry D. (b. 1892, PA); spouse, Elizabeth West (b. 1884, Canada), married about 1917. *SR; A1d, e, f, g; A2b; A3a; A4b.*

KNIGHT, DENTON GIBBON "DAN." Born June 1857, San Antonio, Bexar County, Texas. Ht. 5 ft. 10 in., blue eyes, light hair, fair complexion, married. Ranchman, Presidio County, Texas. REGULAR RANGER Sept. 28, 1912–Feb. 15, 1914 (private, Co. A). Discharged. Ranchman. REGULAR RANGER Apr. 16, 1918–Aug. 31, 1918 (captain, Co. N, Hudspeth Scouts). Discharged; Co. N was disbanded because of the meager appropriation for the Rangers. REMARKS: Presidio County sheriff Nov. 8, 1892–Nov. 1906; in 1915 was a Customs inspector in the Big Bend. Died Mar. 16, 1929, Presidio County, Texas. FAMILY: Parents, George Knight (b. 1816, NY) and Frances (b. 1824, NY); siblings, Theodore T. (b. 1840, NY), Samuel A. (b. 1842, NY), Allen O. (b. 1844, NY), James E. (b. 1847, NY), Norela (b. 1849, NY), Harriet (b. 1854, TX), Mary (b. 1858, TX), William (b. 1862, TX), George, Jr. (b. 1864, TX), Joseph L. (b. 1867, TX); spouse, Mary B. "Mollie" Pool (b. 1876, TX), married about 1896; children, John G. (b. 1896, TX), Denton G. (b. 1899, TX), Henry Clay (b. 1902, TX), George P. (b. 1905, TX), Martin (b. 1906, TX), Theodore (b. 1908, TX), Dixie Lee (b. 1916, TX), Mary Lou (b. 1917, TX). *SR; 471; Jeter to Hutchings, Aug 3, 1914, AGC; Evans circular letter, June 4, 1915, AGC; AG to Knight, Aug 26, 1918, AGC; Special Orders No. 33, Aug 26, 1918, AGC; Knight to Harley, Aug 30, 1918, AGC; 1503:424; EPMT, Dec 7, 1913, July 11, Aug 8, 1915; A1aa, a, b, d, e, f; A4b.*

KOON, JAMES ARTEMUS "ARTIE." Born Mar. 10, 1885, Tupelo, Lee County, Mississippi. Ht. 5 ft. 10 ½ in., gray eyes, light hair, fair complexion, married. Garage manager, Spur, Dickens County, Texas. SPECIAL RANGER Aug. 17, 1918–Jan. 15, 1919. REMARKS: Died Oct. 9, 1968, Dallas County, Texas. LAW ENFORCEMENT RELATIVES: Ranger William H. Koon, brother. FAMILY: Parents, Joseph M. Koon (b. 1856, MS) and Beatrice E. (b. 1853, AL or MS); siblings,

Earlton (b. 1883, MS), Elton (b. 1883, MS), Walter (b. 1888, TX), William (b. 1890, TX); spouse, Jewel Winkler, married June 25, 1913; son, James Newton (b. 1931, TX). *SR; A1d; A2b, e; A3a; B1.*

KOON, WILLIAM HENRY. Born Feb. 10, 1890, Rogers, Bell County, Texas. Ht. 5 ft. 11 in., blue eyes, light hair, fair complexion. Ranchman. REGULAR RANGER Sept. 17, 1917–Apr. 16, 1918 (private, Co. C). Resigned to join Army. LAW ENFORCEMENT RELATIVES: Ranger James A. Koon, brother. REMARKS: Had been a garage owner in Burnet County, Texas. In 1930 was a farmer in Burnet County. Died Jan. 2, 1974, Travis County, Texas. FAMILY: Parents, Joseph M. Koon (b. 1856, MS) and Beatrice E. (b. 1853, AL or MS); siblings, Earlton (b. 1883, MS), Elton (b. 1883, MS), James A. (b. 1885, MS), Walter (b. 1888, TX); spouse, Annie (b. 1902, TX), married about 1926. *SR; 471; McKenzie to Harley, Apr 2, 1918, WC; Harley to Koon, Apr 2, 1918, WC; AG to McKenzie, Apr 30, 1918, AGC; A1d, g; A2a, b; A3a.*

KOONSMAN, MARTIN NICKLOS. Born Mar. 5, 1899, Duffau, Erath County, Texas. Ht. 5 ft. 7 in., gray eyes, light brown hair, light complexion. Stockman, Dickens, Dickens County, Texas. REGULAR RANGER Oct. 21, 1920–Apr. 1, 1925 (private, Co. B; reenlisted Oct. 21, 1922; promoted to sergeant, Jan. 1, 1923). Resigned to become a brand inspector, Texas and Southwestern Cattle Raisers' Association, for better pay. License inspector, Texas Highway Department, Dickens. SPECIAL RANGER Mar. 9, 1927–Mar. 9, 1928. License inspector, Texas Highway Department, Abilene, Taylor County, Texas. SPECIAL RANGER Apr. 12, 1928–Apr. 8, 1930 (reenlisted Apr. 8, 1929?). Discharged. REMARKS: Was a brand inspector for the Texas and Southwestern Cattle Raisers' Association in 1925. Was a state highway patrolman living in Abilene in 1930. Died Apr. 28, 1974, Jones County, Texas. FAMILY: Parents, James Patrick Koonsman (b. 1870, VA) and Nancy Harriet "Nannie" Hollis (b. 1871, TX); siblings, Nola E. (b. 1891, TX), Addie (b. 1893, TX), Emma L. (b. 1895, TX), John L. (b. 1902, TX), Samuel J. (b. 1905, TX), James (b. 1908, TX); spouse #1, Eunice Inez Higdon (b. 1908, TX), married June 18, 1929; children, Elizabeth "Betty" Jean (b. 1930, TX), Carroll Durwood (b. 1933, TX), Kenneth David (b. 1942, TX); spouse #2, Marie Dickson, married Dec. 5, 1957. *SR; 471; 470: 43; A1d, e, g; A2a, b; A3a; A4a, b.*

KORNEGAY, CLIFFORD. Born June 1872, Latrobe, Scott County, Mississippi. Ht. 5 ft. 9 in., blue eyes, dark hair, fair complexion, married. Farmer, enlisted in Travis County, Texas. SPECIAL RANGER Apr. 13, 1918–Jan. 15, 1919. REMARKS: Had been a deputy sheriff for 6 years. In 1900 was a cotton ginner in Tarrant County, Texas. In 1930 was a farmer and ginner in Runnels County. Died July 8, 1944, Real County, Texas. FAMILY: Parents, Alexander W. Kornegay (b. 1831, NC) and Mary J. (b. 1836, NC); siblings, Joel (b. 1862, MS), Mollie (b. 1865, MS), Dump (b. 1869, MS), Maggie (b. 1876, MS); spouse, Ola (b. 1877, GA), married about 1899; children, Loyle (b. 1901, TX), Clifford, Jr. (b. 1905, TX). *SR; A1b, d, f, g; A2b; A4b; B2.*

KOTHMANN, ELGIN OTTO. Born Dec. 15, 1887, Loyal Valley, Mason County, Texas. Ht. 6 ft. ¼ in., hazel eyes, brown hair, light complexion, married. Stockman, Mason, Mason County. SPECIAL RANGER Jan. 29, 1918–Jan. 15, 1919. REMARKS: 1919 letterhead: "Elgin O. Kothmann, Premier Ranch, Quality Herefords, Mason, Texas." In 1930 was still a stock farmer in Mason County. Died Feb. 3, 1938, McLennan County, Texas; buried at Premier Ranch Cemetery, Mason County, Texas. FAMILY: Parents, Heinrich Friedrich "Fritz" Kothmann (b. 1835, Germany) and Mary Miller Eversburg (b. 1847, TX); spouse, Anna Jordan (b. 1888, TX), married May 17, 1910; children, Henry Fritz (b. 1911, TX), Christian M. (b. 1913, TX), Karl W. (b. 1915, TX), Victor L. (b. 1917, TX), twins David and Dorothy (b. 1923, TX). *SR; AG to Sheriff, Dec 5, 1917, AGC; A1d, e, g; A2b; A3a; A4a, b, g; B1.*

KRING, JOSEPH HENRY. Born July 2, 1891, Beeville, Bee County, Texas. Ht. 6 ft., gray eyes, brown hair, married. Railroad locomotive fireman, Brownsville, Cameron County, Texas. SPECIAL RANGER July 15, 1918–Jan. 15, 1919. REMARKS: Had been a deputy sheriff for 1 ½ years. Died Sept. 5, 1969, Kingsville, Kleberg County, Texas. FAMILY: Parents, Henry Joseph Kring (b. 1869, TX) and Viola Smith (b. 1872, TX); siblings, Sidney James (b. 1896, TX), Lucille (b. 1897, TX), Earnest Lee (b. 1901, TX); spouse, Olive Mae Bennett (b. 1892, TX), married June 18, 1913; daughter, Lucille (b. 1915, TX). *SR; A1d, f; A2b; A3a; A4a, b.*

KROHN, ISAAC H. Born June 1889, Austin, Travis County, Texas. Ht. 6 ft., brown eyes, black hair. Farmer. REGULAR RANGER Oct. 10, 1911–Jan. 31, 1912 (private, Co. A). Discharged—reduction in force. REMARKS: Had been a clerk in a drug store in Austin. In 1920 was a cotton buyer, lived in Austin. FAMILY: Parents, Elias Krohn (b. 1851, Germany) and Rosa Melasky (b. 1859, TX); siblings, Jennett (b. 1887, TX), Lillian (b. 1891, TX), Edward (b. 1892, TX), Ray (b. 1895, TX), Goldye (b. 1897, TX). *SR; 471; A1d, e, f.*

KUYKENDALL, WILLIAM H. Born June 1860, Evergreen, Burleson County, Texas. Ht. 5 ft. 7 in., dark eyes, brown hair, medium complexion, married. Stockman, Llano County, Texas. SPECIAL RANGER Mar. 19, 1917–Jan. 15, 1919 (was reinstated—WA was renewed, Feb. 14, 1918). REMARKS: Was commissioned on Gov. Ferguson's orders. Llano County sheriff Nov. 3, 1908–Nov. 7, 1916. In 1920 was a stock dealer in San Antonio, Bexar County, Texas. In 1930 was a state game warden, lived in San Antonio. Died Feb. 22, 1939, Bexar County, Texas. FAMILY: Spouse #1, Althea E. Deats, married May 23, 1883; children, Ruby (b. 1884, TX), Etta (b. 1886, TX); spouse #2, Melinda Ricketson (b. 1866, GA), married Apr. 5, 1890, Llano County; children, Louis (b. 1891, TX), Emmett (b. 1893, TX), Willie (b. 1894, TX), Lennie (b. 1897, TX), Lorene (b. 1899, TX); spouse #3, Ella Long (b. 1877, TX). *SR; Wroe to Hutchings, Mar 16, 1917, AGC; AG to Martin, Mar 16, 1917, AGC; 1503:344; A1d, e, f, g; A2b, c; B1.*

LAAS, AUGUST EDWARD. Born Feb. 22, 1883, Colorado County, Texas. Tall, medium build, light brown eyes, brown hair, married. Farm manager, Floresville, Wilson County, Texas. LOYALTY RANGER June 22, 1918–Feb. 1919. REMARKS: Feb. 1919 letterhead: "Aug. E. Laas, Mule Dealer, Floresville." In 1930 was a grocery merchant in Floresville. Died Jan. 3, 1952, Wilson County, Texas. FAMILY: Parents, Christopher J. Laas (b. 1842, Germany) and Caroline Brune (b. 1849, TX); siblings, Annastine C. (b. 1869, TX), Charles F. (b. 1870, TX), Henry A. (b. 1872, TX), Hermanie Debra (b. 1876, TX), Christopher George (b. 1878, TX), Louis H. (b. 1888, TX); spouse, Nora Marie (b. 1887, TX), married about 1905. *SR; A1d, e, f, g; A2b; A3a; A4b.*

LACY, JOE LIPSCOMB. Born June 6, 1887, Crockett, Houston County, Texas. Ht. 5 ft. 11 ¾ in., gray eyes, brown hair, light complexion. Peace officer, Crockett. REGULAR RANGER Nov. 18, 1910–Feb. 1, 1911 (private, Co. C). Honorably discharged. REMARKS: Was deputy sheriff, Houston County. In 1920 was an undertaker in Crockett. Died Jan. 11, 1929, Dallas County, Texas; buried in Glenwood Cemetery, Crockett. LAW ENFORCEMENT RELATIVES: Crockett city marshal (1900) and Houston County sheriff (Nov. 6, 1906–Nov. 8, 1910) John C. Lacy, father. FAMILY: Parents, John Calhoun Lacy (b. 1850, AL) and Jennie (or Jane) Wortham (b. 1854, TX); siblings, Richard Henry (b. 1871, TX), Bulah (b. 1875, TX), Melchijah Wortham "Pick" (b. 1879, TX), Hortense (b. 1881, TX), John (b. 1883, TX), Mary M. (b. 1890, TX), Trixie (b. 1892, TX); spouse, Lalah or Leila Ponder (b. 1889, TX); children, Hortense (b. 1913, TX), twins Jennie and Johnnie (b. 1917, TX). *SR; AG to Lacy, Nov 16, 1910, AGC; 1503:267; AS, Nov, 1910; A1d, e, f; A2b, e; A3a; A4b; B1.*

LACY, THOMAS H. Born Mar. 1863, Retreat, Grimes County, Texas. Ht. 5 ft. 7 in., blue eyes, brown-gray hair, fair complexion, married. Watchman for the I&GN Railroad, Houston, Harris County, Texas. SPECIAL RANGER Mar. 26, 1917–Jan. 15, 1919 (was reinstated/WA renewed, Dec. 27, 1917). REMARKS: Grimes County sheriff Nov. 3, 1908–Sept. 5, 1912; deputy sheriff of Grimes County for 7 years. In 1920 was a railroad detective in Houston. Died Nov. 12, 1927, Harris County, Texas. FAMILY: Parents, Thomas H. Lacy (b. 1819, AL) and Eliza Jane (b. 1829, SC); siblings, Clara (b. 1849, AL), Elisha (b. 1849, AL), Pinkney (b. 1851, AL), Mary (b. 1851, AL), Caroline (b. 1857, TX), Celeste (b. 1859, TX), Emma (b. 1867, TX); spouse, Dora L. (b. 1876, TX), married about 1893; children, Mattie D. (b. 1896, TX), William Robbins (b. 1894, TX), Thomas F. (b. 1898, TX), Janie (b. 1899, TX), Philip (b. 1902, TX), Emma L. (b. 1904, TX), Olin (b. 1907, TX), Reeder Lyle (b. 1908, TX), Johnnie Mae (b. 1911, TX), Douglas (b. 1914, TX), George Neal (b. 1916, TX). *SR; EPMT, Aug 10, 1910; SR of T.N. Reneau; 1503:218; A1a, b, d, e, f, g; A2b; A4a.*

LAMB, RUFUS H. Born Nov. 1872, Union, Alabama. No physical description, married. Merchant, Asherton, Dimmit County, Texas. LOYALTY RANGER May 31, 1918–Feb.

1919. REMARKS: 1919 letterhead: "R. H. Lamb, Staple and Fancy Groceries, Shelf Hardware and Furniture, Asherton, Tex." In 1930 was the owner of a grocery store in Asherton. FAMILY: Parents, J. M. Lamb (b. 1826, SC) and Elizabeth (b. 1832, AL); siblings, Charles E. (b. 1858, AL), John B. (b. 1860, AL), Robert B. (b. 1862, AL), James R. (b. 1864, AL), Mary S. (b. 1866, AL), Hettie O. (b. 1869, AL), Alace (b. 1874, MS); spouse, Ada Anerson (b. 1879, KY); children, Mable (b. 1902, TX), Rufus, Jr. (b. 1903, TX), Morris E. (b. 1914, TX), James Malcolm (b. 1917, TX), George Murul (b. 1918, TX). *SR; A1a, b, d, f, g; B2.*

LAMKIN, JAMES LEMUEL "LEM." Born Jan. 29, 1877, Grapevine, Tarrant County, Texas. Ht. 5 ft. 8 in., blue eyes, light brown hair, light complexion, married. Peace officer, Garner, Parker County, Texas. REGULAR RANGER Apr. 1, 1921–July 31, 1925 (private, Co. B; transferred to Co. C, Apr. 1, 1923; transferred to Co. B, July 1, 1925). Resigned. REMARKS: Had been a locomotive fireman. In Sept. 1918 was a farmer in Garner. In 1930 was a state game warden living in Parker County. Died June 19, 1951, Parker County, Texas; buried in Bethesda Cemetery near Garner. FAMILY: Parents, John Hill Lamkin (b. 1853, TX) and Louisa Sophronia "Lou" Evans (b. 1858, MO); sisters, Mattie Thornhill (b. 1879, TX), Hattie Jane (b. 1884, TX); spouse, Mattie Lee Boyd (b. 1877, TX), married Oct. 10, 1895; children, Mattie Viola (b. 1896, TX), Louis David (b. 1902, TX), William Ralph (b. 1904, TX), Maggie Lee (b. 1912, TX), Woodrow Wilson (b. 1914, TX), Gertrude Lorene (b. 1919, TX). *SR; 471; 430:43; A1b, e, f, g; A2b; A3a; A4a, b; B1.*

LANE, JAMES CALVIN. Born Dec. 22, 1881, Center Point, Kerr County, Texas. Ht. 6 ft., blue eyes, brown hair, fair complexion, married. Barber, Floresville, Wilson County, Texas. LOYALTY RANGER June 13, 1918–Feb. 1919. REMARKS: A James Calvin Lane died July 3, 1954, Wilson County, Texas. FAMILY: Parents, Tarlton Lane (b. 1847, TN) and Margaret Caroline McElroy (b. 1858, TN); siblings, Samuel (b. 1883, TX), Frank (b. 1885, TX), Asa (b. 1887, TX), Myrtie (b. 1890, TX), Alice (b. 1893, TX), Olla (b. 1896, TX); spouse, Lillie Curington (b. 1890, TX). *SR; A1d, e, f; A2b; A3a; A4b.*

LANE, JOSEPH Y. "JOE." Born Oct. 1869, Greenville, Greene County, Tennessee. Ht. 6 ft., blue eyes, light hair, fair complexion, married. Farmer and county commissioner, Goodlett, Hardeman County, Texas. LOYALTY RANGER June 1, 1918–Feb. 1919. REMARKS: In 1920 was a cotton and grain farmer in Hardeman County. Still farming in Hardeman County in 1930. A Joseph Young Lane died June 9, 1944, Hardeman County, Texas. FAMILY: Parents, John Lane (b. 1835, NC) and Nancy C. (b. 1837, TN); siblings, Hugh T. (b. 1865, TN), Charles (b. 1871, TN), George F. (b. 1873, TN), Nancy Lee (b. 1875, TN), John E. (b. 1876, TN); spouse #1, unknown (b. TX), married about 1890; children, Bettie (b. 1895, TX), Ruby (b. 1897, TX), Jasper D. (b. 1899, TX), Mattie (b. 1903, TX); spouse #2, Lena (b. 1881, KY), married about 1908; children, Raymond (b. 1911, TX), Madine (b. 1914, TX), Loraine (b. 1916, TX). *SR; A1b, e, f, g; A2b.*

LANGFORD, EARL. Born Dec. 23, 1892, Pleasanton, Atascosa County, Texas. Ht. 5 ft. 6 ½ in., brown eyes, dark hair, dark complexion, married. Special policeman for the SP Railroad. REGULAR RANGER May 13, 1916–Aug. 20, 1916 (private, Co. B). Resigned. REMARKS: Note length of service. Langford stated that prior to enlisting in the Texas Rangers he'd been a special agent for the GH&SA Railroad and had been a deputy sheriff for two years. In June 1917 worked for the Texas Purchasing Company, El Paso, El Paso County, Texas. Claimed a "physical disability" at that time. As of Apr. 1919 was a chauffer for rancher R. Prior Lucas; applied for reenlistment in the Rangers. An Earl Langford died May 28, 1971, El Paso County, Texas. *SR; 471; Fox to Hutchings, May 16, 1916, WC; Lucas to Harley, Apr 2, 1919, AGC; Langford to Harley, Apr 9, 1919, AGC; A2b; A3a.*

LANGFORD, IVY BERRY. Born Feb. 27, 1886, Bandera, Bandera County, Texas. Ht. 5 ft. 6 in., brown eyes, brown hair, fair complexion, married. Traveling salesman, Brenham, Washington County, Texas. SPECIAL RANGER May 14, 1918–Jan. 15, 1919. REMARKS: Had been a dry goods salesman in San Antonio, Bexar County, Texas. In 1930 was a plumber, again living in Bexar County. Died Feb. 17, 1945, Bexar County, Texas; buried in San Antonio. FAMILY: Parents, Isaac Berry Langford (b. 1850, TX) and Elizabeth Jane Bird (b. 1856, TX); siblings, Samuel Milton (b. 1873, TX), William L. (b. 1874, TX), Benjamin Franklin (b. 1876, TX), Clarence (b. 1878, TX), Allie (b. 1880,

TX), Sarah May (b. 1882, TX), Leah (b. 1882, TX), Jennie Ethel (b. 1890, TX), Villa (b. 1894, TX); spouse, Hermione Bedwell (b. 1893, KS), married Dec. 12, 1912; son, Ivy B., Jr. (b. 1917, TX). *SR; A1d, e, g; A2b; A3a; A4a, b; B1, 2.*

LANGFORD, MARCUS L. "MARK." Born Apr. 1870, Williamson County, Texas. Ht. 6 ft. 1 ¾ in., blue eyes, light hair, fair complexion, married. Contractor. REGULAR RANGER June 1, 1918–Mar. 3, 1919 (private, Co. D). Resigned. Contractor, Georgetown, Williamson County. REGULAR RANGER June 13, 1919–Nov. 4, 1920 (private, Co. A; transferred to Co. F, Oct. 15, 1920). Resigned. REMARKS: Had been a carpenter in Burnet County, Texas. In 1930 was a building contractor in Brownwood, Brown County, Texas. A Marcus La Fayette Langford died May 19, 1939, Brown County, Texas. FAMILY: Parents, William A. Langford (b. 1842, NC) and Christina C. (b. 1836, Sweden); siblings, Joe F. (b. 1872, TX), Tennessee (b. 1874, TX), Georgie A. (b. 1876, TX), Maude (b. 1879, TX); spouse #1, Maude C. (b. 1873, MS), married about 1890; children, Earnest (b, 1891, TX), Alda M. (b. 1893, TX), Ivan (b. 1895, TX), Clyde (b. 1897, TX), Oran (b. 1898, TX), Elton (b. 1901, TX), Harper (b. 1905, TX), Rosa C. (b. 1908, TX), M. L., Jr. (b. 1911, TX); spouse #2, Merle M. (b. 1889, TX). *SR; 471; Langford to Aldrich, Sept 5, 6, 1920, AGC; Aldrich to Langford, Sept 15, 1920, AGC; 488:44–45; A1a, b, d, e, f, g; A2b.*

LANIER, GUION TAN DELUCRE "GUY." Born July 1856, Van Zandt County, Texas. No physical description, married. Farmer, Marquez, Leon County, Texas. LOYALTY RANGER July 4, 1918–Feb. 1919. REMARKS: Died Feb. 25, 1925, Leon County, Texas. FAMILY: Parents, Guion Henry Lanier (b. 1823, LA) and Sarah Ann Howith (b. 1834, TN); siblings, Martha Jane (b. 1850, TX), William Thomas (b. 1852, TX), Franklin Edward (b. 1854, TX), Jefferson Davis (b. 1857, TX), Nancy (b. 1860, TX), Samuel Rufus (b. 1866, TX); spouse, Mary Emma Winstead (b. 1860, TX), married about 1878; children, Edward C. (b. 1879, TX), Frederick (b. 1882, TX), Eula (b. 1884, TX), Beulah (b. 1886, TX), Zela M. (b. 1890, TX), Augustus Myers (b. 1893, TX), Ela (b. 1895, TX), Marvin M. (b. 1900, TX), Guy Gilbert (b. 1901, TX). *SR; A1aa, a, d, e, f; A2a, b; A4b; B1, 2.*

LARGENT, JOHN S. Born Feb. 1860, McConnelsville, Morgan County, Ohio. Ht. 5 ft. 11 in., blue eyes, brown hair, fair complexion, married. Farmer, Gageby, Hemphill County, Texas. LOYALTY RANGER June 10, 1918–Feb. 1919. REMARKS: Had been a farmer in Guide Rock, Webster County, Nebraska, 1880–1900. By 1910 lived in Hemphill County. FAMILY: Parents, Lewis Largent (b. 1831, OH) and Hannah Plucker or Hannah J. Hafer (b. 1835, OH); brother, Rufus M. (1856, OH); stepfather, Benjamin Crow (b. 1836, OH); half-siblings, Denman Floyd Crow (b. 1863, OH), George Crow (b. 1865, OH), Elizabeth Bell "Lizzie" Crow (b. 1867, OH); spouse, Vicie J. (b. 1864, IL), married about 1884 in Nebraska; children, Carlos C. (b. 1885, NE), Alta M. (b. 1888, NE), Cassandra L. "Cassie" (b. 1890, NE), Della O. (b. 1894, NE), John S. (b. 1908, NE). *SR; A1a, b, d, e, f; A4b; B1.*

LARGENT, THOMAS J., III "TOM." Born Dec. 1863, Sabine Parish, Louisiana. Ht. 5 ft. 10 in., gray eyes, black hair, sallow complexion, married. Engineer, enlisted in Kleberg County, Texas. SPECIAL RANGER July 19, 1916–Dec. 1917. REMARKS: In Ranger Service Records his birth year is listed as 1867. Had been an "engineer foreman" in Gonzales County, Texas and a machinist in Hidalgo County, Texas. In Mar. 1918 was deputy sheriff, Harlingen, Cameron County, Texas, In 1920 was a railroad pipe-fitter living in Kingsville, Kleberg County. In 1930 was post office overseer in Kingsville. A Thomas J. Largent died Sept. 14, 1942, Kleberg County, Texas. FAMILY: Parents, Thomas J. Largent, Jr. (b. 1825, AL) and Sarah Anna McLennon (b. 1839, MS); siblings, Martha J. (b. 1865, LA), Catherine H. (b. 1867, LA), John (b. 1871, LA), Charlotte (b. 1873, LA), Annie (b. 1875, LA), Charles (b. 1877, LA); spouse, Frances Anna Glasgow (b. 1866, TX), married June 26, 1884 in Guadalupe County, Texas; children, Kitty (b. 1885, TX), Lillie (b. 1886, TX), Mabel (b. 1888, TX), John (b. 1890, TX), Holly (b. 1893, TX), Wallace (b. 1896, TX), Thomas Jackson (b. 1898, TX), Anna May (b. 1900, TX), Emma Elizabeth (b. 1904, TX), Carl (b. 1906, TX). *SR; 471; AG to Scarborough, July 8, 1916, AGC: Largent to Hutchings, Sept 3, 1916, AGC; AG to Largent, Sept 5, 1916, AGC; Stevens to Woodul, Mar 27, 1918, WC; A1a, b, d, e, f, g; A2b; A4b.*

LARKIN, BAKER. Born Feb. 1864, Saint Tammany Parish, Louisiana. Ht. 5 ft. 9 in., hazel eyes, light complexion, dark hair, married. Watchman for the I&GN Railroad, Palestine, Anderson County, Texas. SPECIAL RANGER Mar. 24,

1917–Jan. 15, 1919 (attached to Co. C; was reinstated—WA renewed, Dec. 27, 1917). *SR.*

LARREMORE, EDWARD A. "ED." Born Feb. 21, 1876, Caldwell County, Texas. Ht. 5 ft. 9 in., brown eyes, red hair, fair complexion, married. Stockman, Cleburne, Johnson County, Texas. SPECIAL RANGER May 14, 1919–Dec. 31, 1919. REMARKS: Died May 27, 1941, Johnson County, Texas. LAW ENFORCEMENT RELATIVES: Caldwell County Sheriff (1880) Archibald Larremore, father. FAMILY: Parents, Archibald Y. Larremore (b. 1843, AR) and Nancy J. Montgomery (b. 1842, TX); siblings, Mary P. (b. 1866, TX), Wm. N. (b. 1869, TX), Sue (b. 1871, TX), Albert B. (b. 1879, TX); spouse, Lula (b. 1877, TX), married about 1898; adopted son , Eugene F. (b. 1915, TX). *SR; A1b, d, e, f, g; A3a; A4b; C.*

LATHAM, GROVER CLEVELAND "CLEVE." Born Jan. 29, 1885, Live Oak County, Texas. Ht. 6 ft. 1 in., gray eyes, brown hair, fair complexion, married. Ranch foreman, Raymondville, Willacy County, Texas. SPECIAL RANGER June 6, 1917–Dec. 31, 1919 (attached to Co. C; was reinstated—WA renewed, Dec. 22, 1917; commission renewed, Jan. 23, 1919). REMARKS: Worked for the King Ranch; was foreman at Norias Ranch, Armstrong, Kenedy County, Texas. Caesar Kleberg requested that he be commissioned. FAMILY: Parents, Louis Charles Latham (b. 1843, LA) and Agnes Russell (b. 1858, MS or AL); siblings, Charley Simon (b. 1879, TX), Houston C. (b. 1880, TX), Allen S. (b. 1882, TX), Lela I. (b. 1887, TX), Lula Pearl (b. 1889, TX), Louis E. (b. 1891, TX), Walter L. (b. 1898, TX); spouse, Eva (b. 1886, TX); daughter, Evaline (b. 1912, TX). *SR; Kleberg to AG, May 10, 1917, AGC; A1d, e, f; A3a; A4b; B1.*

LATHAM, JOHN BARKLEY. Born Jan. 19, 1886, Lineville, Clay County, Alabama. Ht. 6 ft. 1 in., blue eyes, brown hair, medium complexion, married. Western Union manager, Abilene, Taylor County, Texas. SPECIAL RANGER Aug. 8, 1917–Dec. 1917 (attached to Co. C). REMARKS: Had been a "clock inspector, telegraph" in Dallas, Dallas County. In 1930 was a cotton broker in Abilene. Died Feb. 20, 1949, Tarrant County, Texas. FAMILY: Spouse, Minnie G. (b. 1886, TX), married about 1910; daughters, Catherine Constance (b. 1919, TX), Betty F. (b. 1922, TX). *SR; Dodsen to Ferguson, July 19, 1917, AGC; AG to Latham, Aug 6, 1917, AGC; A1e, f, g; A2b, e; A3a.*

LAUGHLIN, JAMES THOMAS "TOM." Born Jan. 1865, San Marcos, Hays County, Texas. Ht. 5 ft. 11 ½ in., gray eyes, dark hair, dark complexion, married. Stockman. REGULAR RANGER Feb. 9, 1907–unknown (private, Co. C; reenlisted as sergeant, Co. C, Feb. 9, 1909). Peace officer. REGULAR RANGER Nov. 16, 1921–June 15, 1922 (private, Co. C). Resigned. Ex-Ranger, Del Rio, Val Verde County, Texas. REGULAR RANGER Aug. 1, 1922–Nov. 3, 1923 (private, Co. C; transferred to Co. A, Apr. 1, 1923). Resigned. Ex-city marshal, Del Rio. REGULAR RANGER May 15, 1927–Dec. 15, 1931 (private, Co. A; reenlisted as sergeant, Co. C, May 15, 1929; reenlisted, Feb. 9, 1931). Honorably discharged. REMARKS: As of Nov. 1921, had been chief of police, Austin, four years; deputy U.S. marshal, eight years. A James T. Laughlin died Apr. 24, 1943, Val Verde County, Texas. FAMILY: Parents, Thomas Jackson Laughlin (b. 1825, PA) and Rachel M. Halford (b. 1837, MO); siblings, Diana M. (b. 1862, TX), Elizabeth (b. 1867, TX), John N. (b. 1870, TX), William H. (b. 1871, TX), Charles M. (b. 1872, TX), Jessie (b. 1875, TX), Earnest (b. 1878, TX); spouse, Anna Laura McGeehee (b. 1875, TX), married Oct. 16, 1896, San Marcos; children, Rachel Lee (b. 1899, TX), Alfred J. (b. 1909, TX), Jack Thomas (b. 1915, TX), Frances (b. 1911, TX). *SR; Barton to Laughlin, Feb 10, 1921, AGC; Laughlin to Barton, Feb 12, 1921, AGC; U.S. Commissioner, Del Rio, No. 537, FRC-FW; AS, Jan 29, Feb 16, 1910, Apr 28, 1911; 470:43; A1b, d, e, f, g; A2b; A4b; B1.*

LAWRENCE, ERNEST. Born Nov. 4, 1878, Waller County, Texas. Tall, medium build, light gray eyes, light brown hair, married. Stockman, Hempstead, Waller County. LOYALTY RANGER June 10, 1918–Feb. 1919. REMARKS: Waller County sheriff May 11, 1927–Jan. 1934. An E. Lawrence died Jan. 29, 1934, Waller County, Texas; buried in Fields Store Cemetery, Waller County. FAMILY: Parents, George Williamson Lawrence (b. 1923, MO) and Sarah Wall "Sallie" Howell (b. 1832, AL); siblings, Alfred Martin (b. 1852, TX), George Williamson (b. 1855, TX), Ida Marie (b. 1857, TX), Susan Pauline (b. 1858, TX), Sarah Elizabeth (b. 1860, TX), Loo Madeline (b. 1862, TX), Grace (b. 1865, TX), Lee (b. 1868, TX), Hattie Jefferson (b. 1870, TX), Lola (b. 1872, TX), Ludwell (b. 1874, TX); spouse, Rene (b. 1882, TX), married about 1904; daughter, Lois (b. 1907, TX). *SR; 1503:520; A1d, f, g; A2b; A3a; A4b.*

LAY, WILLIAM HARRISON. Born Feb. 12, 1887, Louisville, Jefferson County, Kentucky. Ht. 5 ft. 9 in., blue eyes, brown hair, ruddy complexion, married. Peace officer, enlisted in Wichita County, Texas. REGULAR RANGER Oct. 17, 1920–Dec. 31, 1920 (private, Emergency Company). Honorably discharged—reduction in force. Peace officer, Wichita Falls, Wichita County. REGULAR RANGER June 1, 1936–May 31, 1938 (private, Co. E). Discharged. REMARKS: Had been a truck driver for a lumber company in Wichita Falls. In June 1917 was a lineman for a light and power company in Wichita County. In 1920 was a detective living in Wichita County. A William H. Lay died May 30, 1957, Wichita County, Texas. FAMILY: Spouse, Blanche Allen (b. 1894, TX); son, Wesley (b. 1917, TX). *SR; 471; Aldrich to Lay, Dec 20, 1920, AGC; Aldrich to Gonzaullas, Dec 30, 1920, AGC; Cope to Gonzaullas, Dec 30, 1920, AGC; Cope to Lay, Jan 5, 1921, AGC; Lay to Cope, Jan 7, 1921, AGC; A1e, f; A2b; A3a.*

LAYMANCE, THOMAS ISAAC "TOM." Born Apr. 1894, Athens, Henderson County, Texas. Ht. 5 ft. 11 in., brown eyes, brown hair, dark complexion, married. Farmer, Fort Worth, Tarrant County, Texas. REGULAR RANGER Apr. 6, 1921–Feb. 28, 1923 (private, Co. B). Resigned. REMARKS: In 1930 was a city policeman in Pasadena, Harris County, Texas. Died July 18, 1971, Harris County, Texas. FAMILY: Parents, Isaac Franklin Laymance (b. 1859, TX) and Harriet Andren "Hattie" Redding (b. 1869, TX); siblings, Andrew Jackson (b. 1887, TX), Zelma Clear (b. 1889, TX), Arly Joe (b. 1890, TX), John Joseph (b. 1896, TX), James Franklin (b. 1901, TX), Hattie A. (b. 1903, TX), Elbert (b. 1907, TX), Alma (b. 1907, TX), Farmer (b. 1909, TX); spouse, Pearl (b. 1901, TX), married about 1918; son, Thomas Douglass (b. 1919, TX). *SR; 471; 470:43; A1d, e, g; A4b; B1; C.*

LAYNE, GEORGE EDGAR. Born Dec. 1871, Boone County, Arkansas. Ht. 5 ft. 9 in., brown eyes, brown hair, medium complexion, married. Special agent, I&GN Railroad, San Antonio, Bexar County, Texas. SPECIAL RANGER May 16, 1918–Jan. 15, 1919. Special agent, I&GN Railroad, San Antonio. RAILROAD RANGER Aug. 19, 1922–Aug. 19, 1924 (Co. A). Discharged. Special agent, Missouri Pacific Railroad, San Antonio. SPECIAL RANGER Jan. 28, 1927–Jan. 28, 1928; Jan. 28, 1928–Jan. 14, 1929; Jan. 14, 1929–Jan. 11, 1930; Jan. 11, 1930–Jan. 7, 1931; Jan. 7, 1931–Jan. 7, 1932; Jan. 18, 1932–Jan. 18, 1933; Jan. 20, 1933–Jan. 19, 1935; May 29, 1935–Aug. 10, 1935. Discharged. REMARKS: Had been a railroad employee since 1882. A George Edgar Layne died Feb. 2, 1947, Anderson County, Texas. FAMILY: Parents, Leonard Layne (b. 1833, TN) and Sarah M. Sewell (b. 1833, TN); siblings, Cora P. (b. 1860, TN), Leonard M. (b. 1862, AR), Wm. E. (b. 1866, AR), Jacob R. (b. 1868, AR), Jonathan K. (b. 1870, AR), a sister F. R. (b. 1874, AR); spouse, Mary E. (b. 1872, TX), married about 1891; children, Wyatt (b. 1893, TX), Wayland (b. 1894, TX), Willis (b. 1898, TX), William (b. 1900, TX), Juanita (b. 1905, TX). *SR; A1a, b, d, e, f; A2b; B1.*

LAYNE, HUGH. Born July 14, 1882, Graham, Young County, Texas. Ht. 6 ft. 1 in., brown eyes, light brown hair, fair complexion, married. Stockman, Munday, Knox County, Texas. LOYALTY RANGER June 1, 1918–Feb. 1919. REMARKS: Had been a Knox County deputy sheriff. In 1910 had been manager of a lumber yard in Knox County. FAMILY: Parents, Thomas Asbury Layne (b. 1845, IN) and Susan Frances Howard (b. 1851, KY); siblings, Pleasant W. (b. 1871, TX), Elbridge O. (b. 1874, TX), Olga Lee (b. 1876, TX), Maggie (b. 1876, TX), Shannon (b. 1885, TX), Leona S. (b. 1889, TX); spouse, Addie Hathaway (b. 1885, LA), married about 1908. *SR; A1d, e; A3a; A4a, b.*

LAZENBY, WALTER HOWARD. Born Jan. 26, 1896, Waco, McLennan County, Texas. Ht. 5 ft. 8 in., blue eyes, light brown hair, fair complexion. Deputy sheriff, Waco. SPECIAL RANGER Jan. 26, 1918–June 1918. Resigned. REMARKS: In June 1917 was an automobile salesman for Brown Auto Company in Waco. In 1920 was a clerk in a meat market in Waco; in 1930 owned his own meat market in Waco. Died May 7, 1960, McLennan County, Texas. FAMILY: Parents, Walter N. Lazenby (b. 1870, TX) and Pearl C. (b. 1872, TX); siblings, Lucy (b. 1894, TX), Otto (b. 1902, TX), Alonia (b. 1904, TX), Mildred (b. 1908, TX); spouse, Bess E. (b. 1892, TX), married about 1921. *SR; A1d, e, f, g; A2b; A3a.*

LEAHY, DANIEL PHILLIP. Born Mar. 4, 1891, San Patricio, San Patricio County, Texas. Ht. 5 ft. 11 in., gray eyes, brown hair, medium complexion, married. Stockman. REGULAR

RANGER May 10, 1916–Aug. 28, 1916 (private, Co. A). Resigned. Ranchman, Eagle Pass, Maverick County, Texas. SPECIAL RANGER Apr. 3, 1933–unknown. REMARKS: Note length of service. In June 1917 was chief deputy sheriff in Maverick County. Died Oct. 22, 1955, Maverick County, Texas. FAMILY: Parents, Phillip Leahy (b. 1849, Ireland) and Cecelia (b. 1855, TX); siblings, Laura (b. 1883, TX), Harry (b. 1885, TX), William (b. 1886, TX), Maggie (b. 1890, TX), Dolly (b. 1894, TX), Edgar (b. 1903, TX). *SR; A1d, e, f; A2b; A3a.*

LEAVERTON, THOMAS HERBERT. Born Nov. 10, 1876, Houston County, Texas. Medium height, stout build, gray eyes, brown hair, married. Owner of T. H. Leaverton Lumber Company, Grapeland, Houston County. LOYALTY RANGER June 4, 1918–Feb. 24, 1919. REMARKS: Died May 2, 1929, Grapeland, Houston County, Texas. FAMILY: Parents, Henry Clay Leaverton (b. 1849, TX) and Julia D. Pritchard (b. 1854, SC); siblings, Eugene (b. 1871, TX), Lavinia (b. 1873, TX), Lillie Corrine (b. 1875, TX), Joe (b. 1879, TX), David Nunn (b. 1880, TX), Frank William (b. 1883, TX), Claude Clay (b. 1885, TX), Harold Adair (b. 1890, TX), Eudora (b. 1892, TX); spouse #1, Ruth Ann Taylor (b. 1877, TX), married Dec. 22, 1897, Houston County; son, William Frank (b. 1898, TX); spouse #2, Ada Mary Brimberry (b. 1873, AR), married Oct. 30, 1901, Houston County; daughter, Adabel (b. 1902, TX); spouse #3, Ella Brimberry (b. 1878, AR), married Jan. 1, 1905, Houston County. *SR; A1b, d, e, f, g; A3a; A4b, c; B1, 2.*

LE BLANC, ARTHUR JAMES. Born Aug. 17, 1875, Abbeville, Vermillion Parish, Louisiana. Ht. 5 ft. 8 in., brownish eyes, black hair, dark complexion, widower. Real estate agent, Port Arthur, Jefferson County, Texas. LOYALTY RANGER June 6, 1918–Feb. 1919. REMARKS: In May 1919 was a Port Arthur city commissioner. Still a real estate agent in Port Arthur in 1930. FAMILY: Parents, Richard Le Blanc (b. 1828, LA) and Evelina Emelia "Melina" Moore (b. 1835, LA); siblings, Richard (b. 1854, LA), twins Louis Alphonse and Marie Alphonsa (b. 1855, LA), Alice M. (b. 1857, LA), Evelina (b. 1861, LA), Oscar (b. 1864, LA), Noemi (b. 1866, LA), Pauline (b. 1869, LA), Camilla (b. 1871, LA), John (b. 1873, LA), Robert (b. 1878, LA); spouse #1, Cora Guidry (b. 1877, LA), married May 27, 1896, Lafayette, Lafayette Parish, Louisiana; children, Earl (b. 1897, LA), Ruby (b. 1898, LA), Henry (b. 1905, LA), Ida (b. 1907, LA); spouse #2, Leta M. (b. 1888, TX); step-son, John T. Blackwell (b. 1909, TX). *SR; A1b, d, f, g; A3a; A4b.*

LEDBETTER, FRANK WHITFIELD. Born Oct. 29, 1873, Hallettsville, Lavaca County, Texas. Ht. 5 ft. 8 ½ in., gray eyes, light gray hair, light complexion, married. Dentist, Yoakum, Lavaca County. LOYALTY RANGER July 19, 1918–Feb. 24, 1919. REMARKS: Prior to becoming a Ranger, had been a special deputy city marshal and a special deputy sheriff. In 1918 was chief of Yoakum division of the American Protective League. In 1919 was chairman of the Yoakum City Commission. Died Feb. 13, 1926, DeWitt County, Texas. FAMILY: Parents, Absalom A. Ledbetter (b. 1844, AL) and Julia Guitella Denson (b. 1853, MS); siblings, Charles M. (b. 1872, TX), Absalom A. (b. 1875, TX), Cassie (b. 1884, TX), Roger (b. 1889, TX), Fannie (b. 1891, TX); spouse #1, Alice Antoinette Moreland (b. 1879, TX), married July 7, 1897; children, Rosina (b. 1898, TX), Teresa (b. 1901, TX), Charles (b. 1903, TX); spouse #2, Frances A. "Fannie" (b. 1880, MS), married about 1905; daughters, Elizabeth (b. 1907, TX), Cassie Joe (b. 1910, TX). *SR; A1b, d, e, f, g; A2b; A3a; A4b; B1, 2.*

LEDBETTER, JAMES JOSEPH. Born May 18, 1860, Dallas County, Texas. Ht. 5 ft. 10 in., brown eyes, brown hair, light complexion. Special officer, Galveston Dry Dock and Construction Company, Galveston, Galveston County, Texas. SPECIAL RANGER Sept. 4, 1918–Jan. 15, 1919. Chief guard, Southern Dry Dock and Shipbuilding Company, Houston, Harris County, Texas. SPECIAL RANGER Apr. 19, 1919–Jan. 30, 1921. WA was cancelled. REMARKS: Had been a city policeman in Dallas, Dallas County in 1900 and 1910. In 1930 was a guard at the Federal Reserve Bank in Dallas. Died Nov. 28, 1939, Bexar County, Texas. FAMILY: Parents, Oliver Vincent Ledbetter (b. 1827, TN) and Margaret Fox (b. 1828, AL); siblings, Nathaniel B. (b. 1852, TX), Westly C. (b. 1854, TX), Minerva (b. 1856, TX), William Oliver (b. 1858, TX), Melvina M. (b. 1860, TX), Arthur L. (b. 1864, TX), Thomas J. (b. 1865, TX), Carroll E. (b. 1868, TX); spouse, Laura Keel (b. 1862, TX), married Nov. 3, 1883; son, Robert C. (b. 1885, TX). *SR; 471; A1a, d, e, g; A2b; A4b; B1, 2.*

LEE, FLINT. Born Dec. 30, 1885, Ames, Coryell County, Texas. Ht. 5 ft. 9 in., blue eyes, light hair, light complexion, married. Farmer, Levita, Coryell County. LOYALTY RANGER

June 12, 1918–Feb. 1919. REMARKS: In 1930 was a farmer and cattle trader in Coryell County. Died Feb. 16, 1963, Coryell County, Texas. FAMILY: Parents, Henry or Harvey Lee (b. 1859, TX) and Sarah Adeline "Addie" Roberts (b. 1858, TN); siblings, Robert Edward "Bob" (b. 1878, TX), Thomas "Tom or Bud" (b. 1880, TX), Cora (b. 1882, TX); spouse, Rose Victoria Wilhelm Liljeblad (b. 1889, TX), married about 1908; children, Loere (b. 1910, TX), Largus Moore (b. 1911, TX), Rosamond Amelia (b. 1915, TX), E. Milton (b. 1919, TX), David W. (b. 1920, TX), Sarah Nell (b. 1925, TX). *SR; A1b, d, f, g; A2a, b; A3a; A4a, b.*

LEEMAN, WILLIAM B. Born July 1866, Greenville, Hunt County, Texas. Ht. 5 ft. 10 ½ in., blue eyes, brown hair, light complexion, married. Garage business, Honey Grove, Fannin County, Texas. LOYALTY RANGER June 6, 1918–Feb. 1919. REMARKS: In 1910 was a cotton buyer in Fannin County. Was Fannin County sheriff Nov. 8, 1910–Nov. 3, 1914; had been Honey Grove city marshal for 6 years. In 1930 was a city policeman in Bonham, Fannin County. Died Oct. 8, 1946, Fannin County, Texas. FAMILY: Parents, Sam'l M. Leeman (b. 1815, KY) and Mary J. (b. 1830, KY); siblings, Mary (b. 1856, TX), Thomas W. (b. 1858, TX), Bettie J. (b. 1860, TX), Alice D. (b. 1862, TX), Charles A. (b. 1864, TX), Mitchell M. (b. 1869, TX); spouse, Annie L. (b. 1874, KY), married about 1896; children, Adelaide (b. 1901, TX), W. B., Jr. (b. 1903, TX), Wendell L. (b. 1907, TX). *SR; 1503:180; A1a, b, e, f, g; A2b.*

LEFEVERS, JOHN MARSHALL. Born Nov. 5, 1876, Maxey, Lamar County, Texas. Ht. 5 ft. 11 ¾ in., blue eyes, light hair, fair complexion, married. Real estate broker, Waco, McLennan County, Texas. LOYALTY RANGER June 4, 1918–Feb. 1919. REMARKS: Had been a farmer in Prairie Hill, Limestone County, Texas. In 1910 was manager of a livery stable in Mount Calm, Hill County, Texas. A John Lefevers died Aug. 19, 1969, McLennan County, Texas. FAMILY: Parents, James Lefevers (b. 1843, AL) and Amanda (b. 1834, AL); siblings, Amanda R. (b. 1865, AR), Sarah E. (b. 1867, AR), Henry A. (b. 1869, TX), Isaac J. (b. 1871, TX), Susan S. (b. 1873, TX), Caleb J. (b. 1875, TX); spouse, Mary Frances (b. 1876, TX), married about 1895; children, Harmon (b. 1896, TX), Rosa (b. 1900, TX), Ina A. (b. 1902, TX), Maureen A. (b. 1905, TX), J. H. (b. 1908, TX). *SR; A1b, d, e, f; A2b; A3a.*

LEHR, FRED PAUL. Born Apr. 27, 1886, Wichita, Sedgwick County, Kansas. Ht. 5 ft. 10 ½ in., gray eyes, dark hair, light complexion, married. Stockman, San Antonio, Bexar County, Texas. LOYALTY RANGER June 20, 1918–Feb. 1919. REMARKS: A Fred Paul Lehr died Feb. 14, 1943, Bee County, Texas. FAMILY: Spouse, Hulda or Hilda. *SR; A2b; A3a.*

LEIGH, JOHN SIDNEY. Born Feb. 29, 1876, Huntsville, Walker County, Texas. Ht. 5 ft. 10 ½ in., dark blue eyes, gray hair, light complexion, married. Night watchman, I&GN Railroad, Valley Junction, Robertson County, Texas. SPECIAL RANGER June 4, 1917–Jan. 15, 1919 (was reinstated—WA renewed, Dec. 27, 1917). Special officer, I&GN Railroad, Palestine, Anderson County, Texas. RAILROAD RANGER Aug. 14, 1922–Aug. 14, 1924 (Co. A). Discharged. Special agent, Terminals, I&GN Railroad, Palestine. SPECIAL RANGER Jan. 13, 1926–Oct. 16, 1926. Discharged. REMARKS: In 1930 was a real estate agent in Huntsville. Died Mar. 4, 1944, Walker County, Texas. FAMILY: Parents, John S. Leigh (b. 1853, AL) and Mary R. (b. 1879, TX); brothers, Robert H. (b. 1874, TX), Horatio F. (b. 1879, TX); spouse, Mary Nixon (b. 1878, TX), married about 1910. *SR; Williamson to Hutchings, May 31, June 5, 1917, AGC; AG to Williamson, June 1, 1917, AGC; A1b, f, g; A2b; A3a.*

LENZ, EMIL R. Born Sept. 1882, El Paso, El Paso County, Texas. Ht. 5 ft. 10 in., gray eyes, brown hair, medium complexion, married. Deputy sheriff. REGULAR RANGER Mar. 1, 1915–unknown (private, Co. B; still in, June 1915). Discharged. REMARKS: Was an Arizona Ranger for 1 year, 1908–1909; gave New York as birthplace when enlisted in Arizona Rangers. An Emil R. Lenz (b. 1882, NY) is listed in the 1910 census as a railroad officer living in Benson, Cochise County, Arizona with his wife and daughter; an Emil R. Lenz (b. 1882, NY) is listed in the 1920 census as a bank guard living in Los Angeles, Los Angeles County, California with his wife and three children. *SR; 471; A1e, f.*

LESLIE, ANDREW YELL. Born Mar. 18, 1864, Searcy County, Arkansas. No physical description, married. Stock farmer, Alvord, Wise County, Texas. LOYALTY RANGER June 17, 1918–Feb. 1919. REMARKS: Still a rancher in Alvord in 1930. FAMILY: Parents, Andrew Jackson Leslie (sometimes spelled Lesslie) (b. 1834, TN) and Malinda A.

Parks (b. 1842, AR); siblings, Luiza Octavane (b. 1856, AR), Samuel Gipson (b. 1858, AR), John Stephenson (b. 1861, AR), Blanch Tennessee (b. 1866, AR), Mary Elizabeth (b. 1868, TN), Robert E. (b. 1871, AR), Albert Jackson (b. 1874, AR), Wiley Harris (b. 1876, AR), Ruth Anise (b. 1879, AR), Grover Cleveland (b. 1884, AR); spouse, Elizabeth "Liza" "Lizzie" Bryan (b. 1865, TX), married about 1888; daughter, Lela M. (b. 1895, TX). *SR; A1b, e, g; A4a, b; B1.*

LESUEUR, WILLIAM LEE. Born Aug. 22, 1889, Coleman County, Texas. Ht. 5 ft. 11 ft., gray eyes, dark hair, dark complexion. Fireman, enlisted in Wichita County, Texas. REGULAR RANGER Oct. 18, 1920–Apr. 30, 1921 (private, Emergency Co. No. 2, Feb. 11, 1921). Resigned. REMARKS: Had been a house carpenter in Valera, Coleman County. In June 1917 was an oil field worker in Sour Lake, Hardin County, Texas. A William Lee Lesueur died Dec. 22, 1944, Galveston County, Texas. FAMILY: Parents, James W. Lesueur (b. 1855, AR) and Lee Ella (b. 1870, AR); siblings, Earnest (b. 1891, TX), Madison "Matt" (b. 1893, TX), James Preston (b. 1895, TX), Mary A. (b. 1897, TX), Jimmie (b. 1901, TX). *SR; 471; A1d, e; A2b; A3a.*

LEVERING, PAUL CHATTERTON. Born Mar. 31, 1874, Petersburg, Menard County, Illinois. Ht. 5 ft. 11 in., gray eyes, brown hair, fair complexion, married. Farmer, Big Wells, Dimmit County, Texas. LOYALTY RANGER June 18, 1918–Feb. 1919. Still farming in Dimmit County in 1930. A Paul C. Levering died July 29, 1953, Bexar County, Texas. FAMILY: Parents, Henry C. Levering (b. 1849, IL) and Julia Chatterton (b. 1855, IL); brothers, Roy C. (b. 1879, IL), Harry C. (b. 1886, IL); spouse, Margaret C. (b. 1882, IL), married about 1905. *SR; A1b, d, f, g; A2b; A3a; A4b.*

LEWIS, EDWIN P. Born June 1875, Denison, Grayson County, Texas. Ht. 5 ft. 11 in., brown eyes, dark hair, dark complexion, married. Passenger conductor, I&GN Railroad, enlisted in La Salle County, Texas. SPECIAL RANGER Aug. 8, 1916–Dec. 1917. REMARKS: Had been an employee of the I&GN Railroad from 1891–1916. In 1910 lived in Webb County, Texas. In 1920 and 1930 was a train conductor living in San Antonio, Bexar County, Texas. FAMILY: Spouse, Daisy (b. 1881, TX), married about 1903; children, Sydney (b. 1904, TX), Wilber (b. 1906, TX), Helen (b. 1909, TX), Edna (b. 1912, TX), Jack (b. 1917, TX). *SR; A1e, f, g.*

LEWIS, JAMES B. Born June 1869, Newport, Cocke County, Tennessee. Ht. 5 ft. 11 in., gray eyes, black hair, dark complexion, married. Lawyer, Hemphill, Sabine County, Texas. LOYALTY RANGER July 3, 1918–Feb. 1919. REMARKS: Had lived in Texas since 1880. Letterhead, 1919: "Minton & Lewis, Attorneys at Law, J. W. Minton, J. B. Lewis, Hemphill, Tex." FAMILY: Spouse, Hessie Whitehead (b. 1883, TX), married about 1908; children, Owen W. (b. 1909, TX), James B., Jr. (b. 1914, TX), Hellen M. (b. 1915, TX), Edna M. (b. 1918, TX). *SR; A1e, f, g.*

LEWIS, JOHN EDWARD. Born May 17, 1885, Marceline, Linn County, Missouri. Ht. 5 ft. 11 in., brown eyes, brown hair, light complexion, married. Machinist, Canadian, Hemphill County, Texas. LOYALTY RANGER July 10, 1918–Feb. 24, 1919. REMARKS: Was a machinist for the P&SF Railroad in Canadian. In 1930 was roundhouse foreman in Dalhart, Dallam County, Texas. Died Apr. 8, 1951. FAMILY: Parents, Charles Gilbert Lewis (b. 1857, MO) and Mary F. Glover; spouse, Mabel (b. 1894, TX), married about 1911. *SR; A1g; A3a; A4b; B1.*

LIEB, VICTOR EMANUEL. Born Mar. 17, 1883, Brenham, Washington County, Texas. Ht. 5 ft. 8 ½ in., gray eyes, brown hair, medium complexion, married. Civil engineer, McAllen, Hidalgo County, Texas. SPECIAL RANGER Aug. 4, 1919–Dec. 31, 1919. REMARKS: In Sept. 1918 was a civil engineer for the U.S. Reclamation Service living in El Paso, El Paso County, Texas. In 1930 was a petroleum geologist living in Houston, Harris County, Texas. Died Nov. 6, 1959, Harris County, Texas. FAMILY: Parents, Christian Charles Lieb (b. 1859, TX) and Mathilde Willibaldine Lehmann (b. 1862); sister, Irma Gwendolyn (b. 1891, TX); spouse, Sarah Katherine Varney (b. 1881, NY), married Oct. 25, 1911; children, Carl V. (b. 1914, TX), Betty E. (b. 1915, TX), Lewis Varney (b. 1918, TX). *SR; A1b, g; A2b, e; A3a; A4b; B1.*

LINCECUM, ADDISON L. Born May 1876, Long Point, Washington County, Texas. Ht. 5 ft. 9 in., brown eyes, brown hair, dark complexion, married. Physician, chief of the Texas Quarantine Service, Austin, Travis County, Texas. SPECIAL RANGER Aug. 1, 1917–June 17, 1918 (attached to Co. C). Discharged. REMARKS: Had been chief of the Texas Quarantine Service from 1914–1917. In 1920 and 1930 was a physician in general practice in El Campo, Wharton

County, Texas. An Addison L. Lincecum died Dec. 6, 1965, Lavaca County, Texas. FAMILY: Parents, Dr. Lucullas Garland Lincecum (b. 1828, MS) and Frances "Fannie" Rainwater (b. 1832, MS); siblings, John Louis (b. 1854, MS), Leander William (b. 1854, TX), Gideon (b. 1860, TX), twins James S. and John (b. 1859, TX), Ida (b. 1861, TX), Paschal B. (b. 1877, TX), Trinia (b. 1879), Teresa; spouse, Letha Elizabeth Gandy (b. 1877, TX), married about 1897; children, Barney G. (b. 1901, TX), Ruth (b. 1904, TX), Addison T. "Bill" (b. 1914, TX). *SR; 471; A1a, b, f, g; A2b; A4b, c; B1, 2.*

LINDSEY, DAVID. Born 1886, Jacksboro, Jack County, Texas. Ht. 5 ft. 10 in., brownish-gray eyes, brown hair, dark complexion. Stock farmer, Jacksboro. LOYALTY RANGER July 23, 1918–Feb. 1919. REMARKS: "Acted as a substitute for short training trip with Co. C, Colorado Rough Riders." Still a stock farmer in Jack County in 1930. FAMILY: Parents, John C. Lindsey (b. 1840, TX) and Martha R. (b. 1846, KY); brother, Ray G. (b. 1883, TX); spouse, Mary E. Walters (b. 1895, TX), married about 1906; children, Dave, Jr. (b. 1922, TX), Mary L. (b. 1924, TX), John Henry Ray (b. 1926, TX). *SR; A1e, f, g; A2e.*

LINN, MARK ORA. (Listed as LINN, O. M. in Ranger Service Records.) Born Jan. or June 18, 1875, Corsicana, Navarro County, Texas. Ht. 5 ft. 11 in., blue eyes, brown hair, light complexion. Rancher, Dalhart, Dallam County, Texas. LOYALTY RANGER July 5, 1918–Feb. 1919. REMARKS: Had been a stockman in El Paso, El Paso County, Texas. In 1920 was a livestock salesman living in Phoenix, Maricopa County, Arizona. In 1930 was again a ranchman in El Paso. FAMILY: Parents, G. A. Linn (b. 1835, KY) and Amanda F. (b. 1840, AL or TX); siblings, William M. (b. 1862, TX), George P. (b. 1866, TX), Rosie B. (b. 1869, TX), Lillie G. (b. 1871, TX), Linda C. (b. 1873, TX), Dasie A. (b. 1877, TX), a brother (b. 1880, TX); spouse #1, Kate (b. 1879, TX), married about 1908; spouse #2, Imogene (b. 1892, TX), married about 1918. *SR; Linn to Harley, July 30, 1918, AGC; Woodul to Linn, Aug 1, 1918, AGC; A1b, e, f, g; A3a.*

LIPSCOMB, WALKER BARBEE. Born Mar. 13, 1890, Luling, Caldwell County, Texas. Tall, medium build, blue eyes, light hair. Banker, Guaranty State Bank, San Antonio, Bexar County, Texas. LOYALTY RANGER June 24, 1918–Feb. 1919. REMARKS: In 1920 was a bank clerk in Los Angeles, Los Angeles County, California. Died May 8, 1929; buried in Luling City Cemetery. FAMILY: Parents, Willoughby W. Lipscomb (b. 1850, TN or MS) and Jessie O. (b. 1867, TX); siblings, Edward P. (b. 1888, TX), Ruth (b. 1892, TX), Louis (b. 1899, TX). *SR; 429:13; A1d, e, f; A3a.*

LIPSCOMB, WILLIAM CHILDS (or CHILES). Born Aug. 12, 1860, Washington County, Texas. No physical description, married. Farmer, Brenham, Washington County. LOYALTY RANGER June 8, 1918–Feb. 1919. REMARKS: Died May 18, 1950, Brenham, Washington County, Texas; buried in Prairie Lea Cemetery. FAMILY: Parents, Abner Eddins Lipscomb (b. 1823, AL) and Mary Ann Shivers (b. 1828, AL); siblings, twins Nancy Briley and Sinai Eddins (b. 1847, AL), Jesse Shivers (b. 1849, AL), Henrietta H. (b. 1852, MS), Carrie M. (b. 1857, TX), Abner S. (b. 1863, TX); spouse, Minnie W. Weaver (b. 1869, MO), married Dec. 27, 1892; children, Susie Childs or Chiles (b. 1893, TX), Abner Eddins (b. 1897, TX). *SR; A1a, d, e, f, g; A2b; A4b.*

LITTLE, JAMES. Born Feb. 28, 1874, Washington County, Texas. Medium height, medium build, brown eyes, black hair, married. Stockman and farmer, Burton, Washington County. LOYALTY RANGER June 11, 1918–Feb. 1919. REMARKS: Member of the American Protective League. Letterhead in 1919: "Boone and Little, Butcher Shop and Restaurant, Dealers in All Kinds of Live Stock and Hides, Burton, Tex." In 1920 and 1930 he and his wife operated a boarding house/hotel in Washington County. FAMILY: Spouse, Mamie (b. 1884, TX), married about 1903; children, M. C. (b. 1905, TX), Grace A. (b. 1916, TX), Jimmie N. (b. 1921. TX). *SR; A1f, g; A3a.*

LITTLE, JOHN J. Born Aug. 1860, Kendall County, Texas. Ht. 5 ft. 10 ½ in., blue eyes, gray hair, light complexion, married. Stockman, Pearsall, Frio County, Texas. SPECIAL RANGER Sept. 24, 1918–Jan. 15, 1919. REMARKS: Frio County sheriff Nov. 8, 1904–Nov. 6, 1906. FAMILY: Parents, Brice Little (b. 1834, Scotland) and Mary Kerbny (b. 1839, Ireland); siblings, David B. (b. 1862, TX), Mary (b. 1864, TX), Samuel L. (b. 1868, TX), Sarah (b. 1870, TX), George S. (b. 1874, TX), Edmond (b. 1879, TX); spouse, Sally Blockaller (b. 1867, TX), married Dec. 31, 1895, Frio

County; son, Bryce (b. 1897, TX). *SR; LWT, Mar 31, 1912; Thomas to Hutchings, June 11, 1917, AGC; 1503:199; A1b, d, e, f; B1.*

LIVINGSTON, HENRY LEE. Born Jan. 11, 1888, Runge, Karnes County, Texas. Ht. 5 ft. 11 in., blue eyes, brown hair, fair complexion, married. Yard watchman, SA&AP Railroad, San Antonio, Bexar County, Texas. SPECIAL RANGER May 16, 1918–June 14, 1918. Discharged. REMARKS: Note length of service; was discharged because he had resigned as railroad watchman. Had been constable, Kenedy, Karnes County in June 1917. In 1920 was a ranch overseer in Karnes County. Owned a night watching service in Houston, Harris County, Texas prior to 1960 when he retired to Victoria, Victoria County, Texas. Died Sept. 25, 1963, Victoria County, Texas; buried in Kenedy Cemetery, Karnes County. FAMILY: Parents, George B. Livingston (b. 1848, AL) and Eugenia Clarinda Cox (b. 1857, AL); siblings, Mabel M. (b. 1883, TX), Edna E. (b. 1891, TX), Otto R. (b. 1895, TX), Emma L. (b. 1897, TX); spouse, Vida Estelle Berry (b. 1889, TX), married about 1910; children, George H. (b. 1911, TX), GenaEle or Jennell (b. 1918, TX), James L. (b. 1919, TX). *SR; Herbst to Harley, June 14, 1918, AGC; A1d, e, f; A2a, b, e; A3a; A4a.*

LOCHWITZKY, ALEXANDER M. Born Aug. 1871, Petrograd, Russia. Ht. 5 ft. 3 in., brown eyes, brown hair, dark complexion, married. Special investigator, Texas attorney general's department, Austin, Travis County, Texas. SPECIAL RANGER Aug. 1, 1919–Dec. 31, 1919. Special investigator, Texas attorney general's department, Austin. REGULAR RANGER Feb. 16, 1921–unknown (private, Emergency Co. No. 1). REMARKS: In 1919 was commissioned by order of Governor Hobby. In 1919 was a major in the Texas National Guard. Immigrated to the United States in 1903, was naturalized in 1908. In 1910 lived in Richmond, Henrico County, Virginia. In 1930 was an officer in the U.S. Army living in Dayton, Montgomery County, Ohio. FAMILY: Spouse #1, unknown; spouse #2, Antoinette (b. 1896, Bohemia). *SR; 471; Lochwitzky to Cureton, Aug 15, 1919, AGC; Lochwitzky to Cope, Aug 19, 1919, AGC; A1e, f, g.*

LOCK, A. P. Born Oct. 1868, Kyle, Hays County, Texas. Ht. 6 ft., blue eyes, light brown hair, light complexion, married. Rancher. REGULAR RANGER Mar. 18, 1918–Oct. 1, 1918 (private, Co. G). Resigned. REMARKS: Had been a peace officer in DeWitt County for 4 years. Enlisted by Capt. Charles F. Stevens who wrote, "Recommended by Marcos Neives, U.S. Customs Inspector. In my judgement [*sic*] a good man." *SR; 471; Harrison to AG, Jan 29, 1919, WC.*

LOCKE, HENRY WILLIAM. Born Oct. 1875, Chicago, Cook County, Illinois. Ht. 6 ft. 3 in., brown eyes, brown hair, married. Special agent for the GH&SA Railway, El Paso, El Paso County, Texas. SPECIAL RANGER Oct. 8, 1917–July 1918 (attached to Co. C). Discharged. Special officer for the MKT Railroad, Dallas, Dallas County, Texas. SPECIAL RANGER May 28, 1930–May 28, 1931. REMARKS: Claimed to have been attached to Co. B, Frontier Battalion during Mabry's and Scurry's tenures as adjutant general; claimed to have served with Captains McDonald and Rogers. Was a private detective in Ft. Worth, Tarrant County, Texas in 1913; was a railroad investigator for the Special Service Department in Dallas. As of Sept. 1918 was a civilian employee of the Army Quartermaster Department, El Paso. In 1930 lived in Dennison, Grayson County, Texas. Died June 16, 1931, Grayson County, Texas. LAW ENFORCEMENT RELATIVES: Fort Worth city policeman (1910) Thomas Copp, stepfather. FAMILY: Mother, Bertha (b. 1852, Germany); stepfather, Thomas Copp (b. 1851, England); brother, Willie (b. 1869, IL); spouse, Sammie or Tommie. *SR; 471; A1b, e, g; A2b; A3a.*

LOCKWOOD, THOMAS STEPHEN. Born Aug. 5, 1889, San Antonio, Bexar County, Texas. Ht. 5 ft. 8 in., gray eyes, brown hair. Clerk, Austin, Travis County, Texas. SPECIAL RANGER Apr. 28, 1917–Dec. 1917 (attached to Co. C). REMARKS: As of June 1917 was a "state official, Adjutant General Department" in Austin. *SR; A3a.*

LOEWENSTEIN, JAMES L. "JIM." (Listed in Ranger Service Records as LOWENSTEIN.) Born May 13, 1884, Ysleta, El Paso County, Texas. Ht. 5 ft. 9 in., brown eyes, brown hair, dark complexion, married. Farmer, Ysleta. REGULAR RANGER Dec. 25, 1917–Feb. 1, 1918 (private, Co. L). Discharged/resigned to take a better paying job with the U.S. government. Rancher, Ysleta. SPECIAL RANGER Mar. 23, 1918–July 5, 1919 (attached to Co. L). WA was revoked. REMARKS: Note length of Regular Ranger service. In 1920 was a railroad machinist in El Paso County. In 1930 was an El Paso county jailer. Died Dec. 18, 1932, El Paso County, Texas. FAMILY: Parents, Moritz Loewenstein/Lowenstein (b. 1836, Germany) and Juanita Diaz Buchanan (b. 1857, TX); siblings, Moritz J. (b. 1874, TX), Isaac (b. 1875, TX), Albert (b. 1877, TX), Julius (b. 1879, TX), Juana (b. 1882, TX), George (b. 1886, TX), Joseph (b. William (b. 1889, TX), Gustav A. (b. 1894, TX), Julia (b. 1898, TX); spouse, Delfina Duran (b. 1892, TX), married about 1914; children, Bertha A. (b. 1914, TX), Emma (b. 1918, TX), Florence V. (b. 1921, TX), Alma G. (b. 1927, TX), James, Jr. (b. 1932, TX). *SR; 471; Acting AG to GC&SF Railroad, Jan 9, 1918, AGC; Acting AG to Davis, Jan 9, 1918, AGC; Davis to Harley, Jan 26, 1918, AGC; A1d, f, g; A2b, e; A3a; A4a, b.*

LONG, FRANCIS MARION. Born Dec. 4, 1849, New Albany, Floyd County, Indiana. No physical description, married. County surveyor, Goldthwaite, Mills County, Texas. LOYALTY RANGER June 7, 1918–Feb. 1919. REMARKS: Note age. By 1870 was a cattle driver living in Denton County, Texas. In 1880 was a trader in Coryell County, Texas. Died Dec. 12, 1925, Mills County, Texas; buried in Goldthwaite Cemetery. FAMILY: Parents, Peter Benjamin Long (b. 1824, IN) and Sarah "Sally" Arnold (b. 1825, IN); siblings, Vista A. (b. 1844, IN), Nancy A. (b. 1845, IN), Elizabeth (b. 1847, IN), Mildred Jane (b. 1851, IA), Augustus (b. 1854, IA), Sarah B. (b. 1856, IA); stepmother, Pernecia (b. 1840, OH); siblings, Pernecia (b. 1860, MO), James E. (b. 1863, AR), Serena Carlson (b. 1866, TX), George (b. 1867, TX), Daniel (b. 1870, TX), Rebecca Ellen (b. 1874, AR); spouse #1, Rachal S. Carter (b. 1861, TX), married about 1879; son, George W. (b. 1879, TX); spouse #2, Nancy Magdaline "Maggie" Gazaway (b. 1863, TX), married Dec. 23, 1883, Denton County, Texas; children, Sarah Maud (b. 1884, TX), James Coke (b. 1887, TX), Bessie (b. 1889, TX), Albert Augustus (b. 1893, TX). *SR; A1aa, a, b, f; A2b; A4a, b; B2.*

LONG, FRED W. Born Oct. 1871, Iuka, Tishomingo County, Mississippi. Ht. 6 ft., blue eyes, dark hair, married. Peace officer, Hillsboro, Hill County, Texas. SPECIAL RANGER Jan. 7, 1919–Dec. 31, 1919. REMARKS: In 1911 was city marshal of Itasca, Hill County, and on the executive committee of the City Marshals and Chiefs of Police Union of Texas. Hill County sheriff Nov. 3, 1914–Nov. 5, 1918. As of 1919 had been a peace officer for 25 years. In Jan. 1920 was appointed as assistant special agent in the Texas attorney general's office, Austin, Travis County, to enforce Prohibition. In 1930 was proprietor of a filling station in Hillsboro. A Fred Whitson Long, Sr. died July 23, 1961, Hill County, Texas. FAMILY: Parents, Richard Barton Long (b. 1828, AL) and Letitia Ann Jourdan (b. 1842, TN); brothers, Horace Champion (b. 1873, MS), Adolphus Barton (b. 1875, MS); spouse, Etta Clark (b. 1873, TX), married June 10, 1896, Gregg County, Texas; children, Richard Clark (b. 1899, TX), Fred William (b. 1905, TX), Minnie Beall (b. 1908, TX). *SR; 1503:258; HC, Mar 29, 1911; AA, Jan 29, 1920; A1b, d, f, g; A2b; A4b, g.*

LONG, GEORGE J. Born Feb. 1887, Springfield, Greene County, Missouri. Ht. 5 ft. 6 in., blue eyes, light hair, ruddy complexion, married. Railroad brakeman, enlisted in Atascosa County, Texas. SPECIAL RANGER July 17, 1916–Dec. 1917. REMARKS: Still a railroad brakeman living in Pleasanton, Atascosa County in 1930. A George James Long died May 28, 1960, Atascosa County, Texas. FAMILY: Spouse, Della Diane (b. 1897, TX), married about 1915; children, George James, Jr. (b. 1919, TX), Mary (b. 1924, TX), Joe Bailey (b. 1931, TX). *SR; A1f, g; A2b, e.*

LONG, JAMES FRANKLIN. Born May 31, 1874, Weatherford, Parker County, Texas. Ht. 5 ft. 7 in., blue eyes, brown hair, light complexion, married. Farm manager, Thalia, Foard County, Texas. LOYALTY RANGER July 9, 1918–Feb. 1919. REMARKS: In 1920 and 1930 was a farmer living in Crowell, Foard County. Died Nov. 27, 1951, Foard County, Texas. FAMILY: Parents, James Franklin Long (b. 1829, NC) and Angeline Jane Bell (b. 1830, NC); siblings, William Cicero (b. 1850, GA), twins Martha Ann and Mary Ann (b. 1854, TX), Wiley Harrison (b. 1856, TX), Andrew Baxter (b. 1858, TX), George Washington (b. 1860, TX), Joseph Emory (b. 1865, TX), Thomas Jefferson (b. 1868, TX), Eppie Amanda (b. 1875, TX); spouse, Mary Josephine "Josie" (b. 1886, TX), married about 1906; children, Bernice I. (b. 1907, TX), Robert J. (b. 1909, TX), James E. (b. 1921, TX). *SR; A1aa, e, f, g; A2b; A3a; A4b; B1.*

LONG, JOHN HENRY. Born Oct. 10, 1873, Leesville, Gonzales County, Texas. Ht. 6 ft., brown eyes, red hair, red complexion, married. Detective, San Antonio, Bexar

County, Texas. REGULAR RANGER July 12, 1918–Feb. 21, 1919 (not assigned to a company; on detached service, Jan. 9, 1919). Discharged/resigned. REMARKS: As of 1918 had been a peace officer for 16 years, 9 of them a detective; had been a Ranger for 4 years. In 1918 was enlisted by W. M. Hanson; was stationed in San Antonio and worked undercover. In Mar. 1919 was chief of police at Ranger, Eastland County, Texas. In 1930 was proprietor of a filling station in San Antonio. Died Nov. 11, 1957, San Antonio, Bexar County, Texas; buried in San Jose Cemetery, San Antonio. FAMILY: Parents, William Long (b. 1852, LA) and Teresa (b. 1856, TX); brothers, Clement (b. 1877, TX), Benjamin F. (b. 1880, TX), James F. (b. 1883, TX); spouse, Virginia Abigail Holmes (b. 1876, AR), married Nov. 23, 1893, Atascosa County, Texas; children, Helen (b. 1895, TX), William H. (b. 1896, TX), George F. (b. 1899, TX), Burgess (b. 1902, TX), Bryant (b. 1906, TX), Evelyn (b. 1909, TX). *SR; 471; Hanson to Arnold and Chapa, July 8, 1918, AGC; Special Orders No. 1, Jan 9, 1919, WC; Long to Hobby, Feb 21, Mar 12, 1919, AGC; Aldrich to Long, Mar 4, 1919, AGC; Long to Aldrich, Mar 19, 1919, AGC; A1b, d, f, g; A2b, c; A3a; B1.*

LONGORIA, JOHN LUTHER. Born Mar. 13, 1887, Van Alstyne, Grayson County, Texas. Ht. 5 ft., 11 in., gray eyes, dark complexion, black hair. Carpenter, Mercedes, Hidalgo County, Texas. REGULAR RANGER Apr. 26, 1918–May 1918 (private, Co. G). Resigned. REMARKS: Note length of service. Prior to enlisting in the Rangers, had been deputy city marshal in Mercedes for 3 years, including 1915–1917. Had also been a railroad fireman in Aransas Pass, San Patricio County, Texas. In Apr. 1917 was a partner in Longoria & Meredith, General Contractors and Builders, Mercedes. *SR; 471; Longoria to Ferguson, Apr 27, 1917, AGC; AG to Longoria, May 1, 1917, AGC; A1e; A3a.*

LONSFORD, JAMES BENJAMIN "BEN." Born Oct. 27, 1885, Van Alstyne, Grayson County, Texas. Medium height, medium build, brown eyes, brown hair, married. Real estate agent, Corsicana, Navarro County, Texas. LOYALTY RANGER June 29, 1918–Feb. 1919. REMARKS: Letterhead in 1919: "J. L. Lonsford & Son, Real Estate, J. L. Lonsford, J. B. Lonsford, Corsicana." In Jan. 1919 planned to move to Wichita Falls, Wichita County, Texas. In 1920 was an oil refinery "stillman" living in Iowa Park, Wichita County. Died Mar. 28, 1953, Dallas County, Texas. FAMILY: Parents, Jackson Lee Lafayette Lonsford (b. 1861, TN) and unknown George; sister, Kate E. (b. 1892, TX); spouse, Katie Carrol (b. 1891, TX), married about 1910; son, Benjamin Rex (b. 1911, TX). *SR; A1d, f; A2b; A3a; B1.*

LORENZ, ROYAL WADE "WADE." Born Feb. 10, 1896, Stockdale, Wilson County, Texas. Ht. 5 ft. 9 in., blue eyes, light hair, florid complexion. Deputy sheriff. REGULAR RANGER Dec. 21, 1917–Mar. 3, 1919 (private, Co. K). Resigned. REMARKS: Had been a stockman and stock trader. Died Feb. 12, 1930, Wilson County, Texas; buried in Stockdale. FAMILY: Parents, William Adam Lorenz (b. 1865, TX) and Leonora Smith (b. 1869, TX); siblings, Wilhelmina B. "Winchie" (b. 1889, TX), Ludia A. (b. 1891, TX), Henry John (b. 1892, TX), Elizabeth "Birdie" (b. 1899, TX), Winston W. (b. 1916, TX); spouse, Bernice (b. 1898, TX), married after 1920; son, Royal Wade (b. 1925, TX). *SR; 471; 1000:iii, 128–129; A1d, e, f, g; A2b, e; A3a; B1.*

LOTT, WILL T. Born Oct. 1880, Goliad, Goliad County, Texas. Ht. 5 ft. 11 in., brown eyes, brown hair, dark complexion. Ranchman, enlisted in Sinton, San Patricio County, Texas. REGULAR RANGER Mar. 29, 1915–Apr. 30, 1915 (private, Co. A). Resigned; had a bad arm, unfit for duty. REMARKS: Note length of service; had trouble with his arm and spent most of his time in a sanatorium in San Antonio, Bexar County, Texas; returned to his home in Goliad. Died Mar. 29, 1956, Goliad County, Texas. FAMILY: Parents, Will W. Lott (b. 1854, TX) and Pinkie A. (b. 1860, TX); siblings, Augier D. (b. 1885, TX), Walter (b. 1887, TX), Lottie L. (b. 1894, TX), Stuart P. (b. 1898, TX). *SR; 471; Sanders to Hutchings, Apr 10, 11, 17, 19, 27, 1915, AGC; AG to Sanders, Apr 12, 1915, AGC; A1e; A2b.*

LOVE, RICHARD COATES "DICK." Born Jan. 19, 1878, Abilene, Taylor County, Texas. Ht. 5 ft. 8 in., brown eyes, black hair, dark complexion, married. Cattleman, enlisted in Hudspeth County, Texas. REGULAR RANGER June 1, 1918–Aug. 31, 1918 (private, Co. N, Hudspeth Scouts). Discharged. REMARKS: Was a prominent rancher near Sierra Blanca, Hudspeth County. Died Apr. 6, 1936, Indian Hot Springs, Hudspeth County, Texas. LAW ENFORCEMENT RELATIVES: First sheriff of Borden County, Texas (Mar. 17, 1891–Nov. 3, 1896) Tom D. Love, brother; Hudspeth County sheriff (Nov. 6, 1984 -1989) Richard Ivy "Dick" Love, grandson. FAMILY: Parents, Leonard Robert Love (b. 1839, MS) and Francis Jane "Fanny" Powell (b. 1849, MS); siblings, Thomas Decator (b. 1862, TX), Wert Eugene (b. 1866, TX), twins Mary Elizabeth "Lizzie" and George Wesley (b. 1869, TX), Robert Wade (b. 1871, TX), John Rowdy (b. 1880, TX), Jimmie (b. 1881), Charlie; spouse #1, Emma Sheridan (b. 1879), married about 1898; son (b. 1898, TX); spouse #2, Harriet "Hattie" Christian (b. 1896, NM), married about 1919. *SR; 471; Thomason to Hanson, June 15, 1919, AGC; 1503:47, 271; A1b, f, g; A2b; A3a; A4a, b, g.*

LOVE, THOMAS H. Born Oct. 1870, Pointe Coupee Parish, Louisiana. Ht. 5 ft. 8 in., gray eyes, dark hair, red complexion, married. Assistant superintendent, I&GN Railroad, San Antonio, Bexar County, Texas. SPECIAL RANGER Feb. 13, 1918–Jan. 15, 1919. Assistant superintendent, I&GN Railroad, San Antonio. RAILROAD RANGER Aug. 31, 1922–Feb. 19, 1923 (Co. A). Resigned. REMARKS: Had been a railroad roadmaster. A Thomas Henry Love died May 8, 1948, Bexar County, Texas. FAMILY: Parents, William A. Love (b. 1849, LA) and Susanne Bailey (b. 1845, LA); spouse, Medora "Dora" Winters (b. 1874, TX), married Oct. 31, 1894, Frio County, Texas; son, Franklin N. (b. 1895, TX). *SR; Jones to Hutchings, Aug 31, Sept 7, 1916, AGC; AG to Jones, Sept 5, 1916, AGC; Hutchings to Jones, Sept 8, 1916, AGC; A1a, b, d, f; A2b, c.*

LOW, SAMUEL DONELSON WARREN "SAM." Born Jan. 1874, Washington County, Texas. No physical description, married. Farmer, enlisted in Travis County, Texas. SPECIAL RANGER Sept. 17, 1918–Jan. 15, 1919. REMARKS: Had been a lumber dealer in Brenham, Washington County. In 1920 was prison system commissioner living in Huntsville, Walker County, Texas. In 1930 was a farmer living in Brenham. Died May 6, 1939, Washington County, Texas. FAMILY: Parents, Theodore Augustus Low (b. 1849, TN) and Cecelia L. (b. 1852, TX); siblings, Theo (b. 1876, TX), Coral (b. 1877, TX); spouse, Ruth M. "Maggie" (b. 1874, TX), married about 1894; son, Samuel D. W., Jr. (b. 1896, TX). *SR; A1b, d, f, g; A2b; A3a; A4b; B2.*

LOWE, WILLIAM ADOLPHUS, JR. "DOLF." Born Feb. 13, 1886, McMullen County, Texas. Tall, slender, gray eyes, brown hair, married. Stockman, Tilden, McMullen County. LOYALTY RANGER June 8, 1918–Feb. 1919. REMARKS: Had been a stockman in San Antonio, Bexar County, Texas. Died May 24, 1923, Bexar County, Texas. FAMILY: Parents, William A. Lowe (b. 1857, TX) and Mae Ellen Beall (b. 1858, TX); siblings, Ethel (b. 1879, TX), James Guy (b. 1881, TX), Arthur Jean (b. 1884, TX), Roy Beall (b. 1888, TX), Mattie May (b. 1890, TX), Mabel Moss (b. 1893, TX); spouse, Georgia Reed Martin (b. 1887, TX), married about 1907; children, Mabel Moss (b. 1908, TX), Arthur Jean (b. 1910, TX). *SR; A1d, e, f; A2b; A3a; A4a, b.*

LUBBOCK, JAMES LEE "JIM." Born Oct. 20, 1872, San Antonio, Bexar County, Texas. Ht. 5 ft. 5 ½ in., blue eyes, dark brown hair, fair complexion, married. Farmer, Bexar County. REGULAR RANGER May 13, 1916–Nov. 1, 1916 (private, Co. B, detached service—San Antonio). Discharged—reduction in force. REMARKS: In Sept. 1918 was farming in Skidmore, Bee County, Texas. In 1930 was a free-lance trader living in San Antonio. A Jim Lee Lubbock died Mar. 18, 1954, Kerr County, Texas. FAMILY: Parents, Frank Richard Lubbock (b. 1847, TX) and Mary Elizabeth Grayson (b. 1845, TX); siblings, Earl, Frank Grayson (b. 1868, TX), William Robertson (b. 1870, TX), Bessie (b. 1878, TX); spouse #1, Mabel Ross (b. 1877, TX or MD), married about 1893; children, Edith (b. 1899, TX), Grayson (b. 1900, TX), Dorothe (b. 1902, TX), Leola (b. 1905, TX), Marjorie (b. 1910, TX); spouse #2, Henrietta (b. 1897, TX), married about 1919; children, James, Jr. (b. 1922, TX), John (b. 1923, TX), Joe (b. 1927, TX), Jay (b. 1928, TX), Estella (b. 1930, TX). *SR; 471; Wilson to AG Department, July 4, 1916, AGC; AG to Wilson, July 6, 1916, AGC; AG to Lubbock, Sept 30, Oct 19, 1916, AGC; A1b, d, f, g; A2b; A3a; A4a.*

LYNCH, ISAAC LAWRENCE "IKE." Born May 1857, Mills Springs, Wayne County, Kentucky. Ht. 6 ft., blue eyes, light hair, light complexion, married. Dairyman, Anahuac, Chambers County, Texas. LOYALTY RANGER July 17, 1918–Feb. 1919. REMARKS: Had been a farmer and a rural-route mail carrier in Bell County, Texas. In 1930 lived in Houston, Harris County, Texas. Died Feb. 4, 1940, Harris County, Texas. LAW ENFORCEMENT RELATIVES: Ranger William West Lynch, nephew. FAMILY: Parents, Isaac P. Lynch (b. 1821, KY) and Elizabeth J. (b. 1826, TN); siblings,

James A. (b. 1851, KY), Mary L. "Mollie" (b. 1853, KY), John A. (b. 1854, KY), Charles (b. 1860, KY), David (b. 1862, KY); spouse, Martha T. "Pinkie" (b. 1869, TX), married about 1885; children, David (b. 1885, TX), Oscar (b. 1887, TX), Elizabeth (b. 1889, TX), Ruth (b. 1896, TX), Ike Lawrence, Jr. (b. 1899, TX), Sam (b. 1902, TX), Sadie (b. 1904, TX). *SR; A1aa, a, b, d, e, f, g; A2b.*

LYNCH, WILLIAM WEST. Born Feb. 1890, Pendleton, Bell County, Texas. Ht. 5 ft. 7 ½ in., brown eyes, brown hair, light complexion, married. Banker, Pendleton. SPECIAL RANGER Aug. 7, 1917–Dec. 1917 (attached to Co. C). REMARKS: Was appointed on Governor Ferguson's order. In 1920 was vice president of a bank in Temple, Bell County. LAW ENFORCEMENT RELATIVES: Ranger Ike L. Lynch, uncle. FAMILY: Parents, James Allen Lynch (b. 1851, KY) and Idellah Newton Thompson (b. 1862, LA); siblings, Mary Lee (b. 1881, TX), James Henry (b. 1883, TX), Charles Parker (b. 1885, TX), Elizabeth (b. 1890, TX); spouse, Clara May (b. 1894, TX). *SR; Ferguson to Hutchings, Aug 7, 1917, AGC; A1d, f; B1, 2.*

McALISTER, PAUL. Born May 31, 1884, Wichita Falls, Wichita County, Texas. Ht. 6 ft., brown eyes, light complexion, brown hair. Farmer, enlisted in Hidalgo County, Texas. REGULAR RANGER Nov. 22, 1911–Feb. 1, 1912 (private, Co. C). Honorably discharged—reduction in force. Deputy sheriff, San Diego, Duval County, Texas. SPECIAL RANGER Oct. 5, 1915–Jan. 14, 1916 (attached to Co. C). WA revoked by order of governor. REMARKS: In 1912 was Cameron County deputy sheriff. On Aug. 9, 1912, killed Brownsville city marshal José Crixell; was tried in 1913 and acquitted. In 1915, Archie Parr asked that McAlister's commission as a Special Ranger be revoked; it was. Was a Corpus Christi, Nueces County, Texas policeman; resigned in 1925 to become a Game, Fish, and Oyster commissioner. On July 5, 1925, was one of four men killed in a shooting affray outside a Corpus Christi brothel. LAW ENFORCEMNT RELATIVES: Corpus Christi policeman (1925) Burl McAlister, brother. FAMILY: Parents, Jerome McAlister (b. 1846, MO or KY) and Emma Hanks Henderson (b. 1861, TX); siblings, Mary (b. 1889, TX), Burl (b. 1890, TX), Nellie (b. 1896, TX); spouse, Olive Lynn "Ollie" Watson (b. 1884, TX), married Nov. 4, 1903, Corpus Christi; children, Robert King (b. 1904, TX), Francis (b. 1906, TX), Oliver (b. 1908, TX). *SR; 471; Fox to Hutchings, Aug 10, 1912, AGC; Sanders to Hutchings, Mar 28, Oct 23, 1913, AGC; AG to Sanders, Oct 25, 1913, AGC; Hutchings to Fox, Nov 4, 1913, AGC; Fox to Hutchings, Nov 4, 1913, AGC; Kleberg to Hutchings, Sept 25, Nov 30, 1915, AGC; AG to Ferguson, Sept 30, 1915, AGC; AG to Kleberg, Nov 22, Dec 4, 1915, AGC; Hutchings to McAlister, Jan 14, 1916, AGC; Parr to Hutchings, Jan 12, 1916, AGC; Hutchings to Ferguson, Jan 14, AGC; SAE, Jan 23, 1913; BDH, Dec 26, 1911, Jan 3, 31, Apr 12, June 6, Aug 10–16, 20–30, Sept 2, 4, Nov 22, Dec 16, 19, 21, 1912, Feb 26, Apr 2, 4, 8, 9, 16, Sept 24, Oct 6, 30, Nov 1–8, 10, 11, 15, 18, 1913, Aug 26, 1915; 485:48; 428; A1e, f; A2b; A3a; A4a, b; B2.*

McALPINE, ALEXANDER DUNCAN "ALEX." Born Feb. 3, 1875, Grimes County, Texas. Medium height, medium build, blue eyes, dark hair, married. Physician, Navasota, Grimes County. LOYALTY RANGER June 5, 1918–Feb. 1919. REMARKS: Still practicing medicine in Navasota in 1930. Died Jan. 13, 1953, Grimes County, Texas. FAMILY: Parents, Dr. John Anderson McAlpine (b. 1843, NC) and Willie Cabeen Cameron (b. 1857, LA); siblings, Gladys, Walter, Euphemia Maude (b. 1877, TX), Lela Beatrice (b. 1880, TX), John Gwyn (b. 1881, TX), Marcus Randolph (b. 1884, TX), Willie Sterrett (b. 1886, TX), Robert Burns (b. 1889, TX), Nellie Ethridge (b. 1891, TX), Bessie Vivian (b. 1895, TX); spouse, Ruby Lee Wilson (b. 1888, TX), married June 11, 1911, Honey Grove, Fannin County, Texas; daughters, Ruby Alixe (b. 1914, TX), Mary (b. 1916, TX). *SR; A1b, d, e, g; A2b; A3a; A4a, b.*

McBEE, CHARLES W. Born Feb. 25, 1897, Rock Springs, Edwards County, Texas. Ht. 6 ft. 1 in., blue eyes, ruddy complexion, light hair. Cowboy. REGULAR RANGER May 1, 1918–unknown (private, Co. E). REMARKS: In 1930 was a U.S. Border Patrolman in Val Verde County, Texas. A Charles McBee died Jan. 16, 1973, Val Verde County, Texas. FAMILY: Parents, Frank Marion McBee (b. 1849, TN) and America (1853, TX); siblings, Louisa (b. 1869, TX), William (b. 1875, TX), Olie J. (b. 1877, TX), Samuel M. (b. 1881, TX), Laura T. (b. 1884, TX), David J. (b. 1887, TX); spouse, Laura "Lily" Brite (b. 1898, TX), married about 1919; children, Brancie Marie (b. 1920, TX), Will J. (b. 1923, TX), Elsie (b. 1926, TX), Jack Mey (b. 1933, TX). *SR; 471; A1d, e, f, g; A2b, e; A3a.*

McBRIDE, PETER. Born Aug. 3, 1863, Corpus Christi, Nueces, County, Texas. Ht. 5 ft. 9 in., blue eyes, dark gray hair, red complexion, married. Stockman, Realitos, Duval County, Texas. SPECIAL RANGER Apr. 30, 1918–Jan. 15, 1919. REMARKS: Died Nov. 22, 1957, Realitos, Duval County, Texas; buried in Corpus Christi. FAMILY: Parents, James McBride (b. 1827, Ireland) and Mary Dunn (b. 1836, Ireland); siblings, Margaret (b. 1855, TX), Catherine (b. 1859, TX), Mary (b. 1866, TX), James (b. 1869, TX), Dennis (b. 1871, TX), Julia (b. 1875, TX); spouse, Minnie Alice Priour (b. 1870, TX), married Aug. 18, 1890, Corpus Christi; children, Gerald Francis (b. 1891, TX), James M. (b. 1893, TX), Anna Belle (b. 1895, TX), Julian Peter (b. 1898, TX), Marie Mary (b. 1901, TX), Katherine Agnes (b. 1903, TX), Clarence Joseph (b. 1906, TX), Florence Ruby (b. 1908, TX), Bennett (b. 1910, TX), Dennis Priour (b. 1911, TX), Minnie Alice (b. 1914, TX). *SR; A1a, d, f, g; A2b; A4a, b.*

McCALLUM, EMMETT BRUCE. Born May 10, 1883, Mitchell County, Texas. Tall, medium build, brown eyes, brown hair, married. Stock farmer. REGULAR RANGER Jan. 9, 1918–Jan. 1918 (private, Co. G). Discharged. REMARKS: Note length of service. In Sept. 1918 was working for Inspiration C. C. Company, Globe, Gila County, Arizona. In 1920 was again farming in Mitchell County. Died Apr. 9, 1952, San Patricio County, Texas. FAMILY: Parents, William C. McCallum (b. 1847, TN) and Laura (b. 1846, AL); spouse, Willie Myrtle (b. 1890, TX), married about 1907; children, Madolyn L. (b. 1908, TX), Emmett B. (b. 1909, TX), Elga (b. 1916, TX). *SR; 471; A1e, f; A2b; A3a.*

McCAMPBELL, JAMES HOWELL "HOWELL." Born Aug. 8, 1895, Jim Wells County, Texas. Ht. 6 ft. 1 in., gray eyes, light brown hair, fair complexion, married. Ranchman, Hebbronville, Jim Hogg County, Texas. REGULAR RANGER Jan. 7, 1918–May 15, 1918 (private, Co. B). Resigned. SPECIAL RANGER July 27, 1918–Jan. 15, 1919. REMARKS: In Jan. 1918, participated in the Porvenir massacre. 1919 letterhead: "R. H. McCampbell, J. H. McCampbell, Live Stock, Hebbronville." In 1930 was a rancher and cattleman in Brownsville, Cameron County, Texas. Died Oct. 13, 1955, Nueces County, Texas. FAMILY: Parents, Ralph H. McCampbell (b. 1870, TX) and Martha Ella Dinn (b. 1871, TX); spouse, Louella Mae Lynn (b. 1893, IA), married Feb. 2, 1916, Alpine, Brewster County, Texas; sons, Ralph (b. 1917, TX), Richard "Dick" (b. 1921, TX). *SR; 471; LWT, Aug 6, 1911; A1d, f, g; A2b, e; A3a; A4a; B1.*

McCARTHY, EDWARD, JR. "ED." Born Dec. 7, 1881, most probably in Galveston, Galveston County, Texas. Ht. 5 ft. 10 in., dark gray eyes, fair complexion, married. Lawyer and court reporter, Houston, Harris County, Texas. REGULAR RANGER Sept. 28, 1920–Sept. 28, 1922 (private, Headquarters Co.; promoted to sergeant, Oct. 1, 1920; transferred to Emergency Co. No. 1, Jan. 15, 1921). Discharged. REMARKS: Appointed by order of Governor Hobby, re: Galveston strike. "Mr. McCarthy under agreement with Governor Hobby, was to be enlisted as a sergeant during pendency of Galveston situation. This enlistment as a private per telegram of AG pending adjustment of his status." Died June 16, 1925, Harris County, Texas. FAMILY: Parents, Edward McCarthy (b. 1858, TX) and Pauline Helen Brown (b. 1861, TX); spouse, Elizabeth Ellen (b. 1885, TX), married about 1905; children, Edward (b. 1909, TX), Dorrance (b. 1913, TX). *SR; A1b, e, f, g; A2b; A3a; B1.*

McCAULEY, WILLIAM J. "WILLIE," "BILLY." Born Feb. 9, 1873, Longview, Harrison County, Texas. Ht. 5 ft. 7 in., gray eyes, brown hair. REGULAR RANGER 1899, 1902–1907 (private, Co. B; reenlisted as sergeant, Co. B, Aug. 2, 1905; transferred as sergeant to Co. A, 1907–1910). Died of natural causes on Sept. 23, 1910, Marlin, Falls County, Texas. REMARKS: Buried in Wichita Falls, Wichita County, Texas. State would not pay medical expenses. LAW ENFORCEMENT RELATIVES: Ranger captain William J. McDonald, uncle. FAMILY: Parents, John H. McCauley (b. 1842, NC) and Mary T. McDonald (b. 1851, MS); siblings,

Eula May (b. 1875, TX), John Henry (b. 1877, TX), Mary (b. 1879, TX), Dott (b. 1882, TX), Don M. (b. 1888, TX). *SR; 471; MR, Co. A, Sept 1910, AGC; Johnson to Phelps, Aug 14, 1910, WC; McDonald to AG, Sept 24, 1910, AGC; AG to McDonald, Nov 22, 1910, AGC; BDH, Sept 26, 2920; AS, Sept 25, 26, 27, 1910; HC, Sept 25, 1910; 319:336, 350, 353 ff; 464:39, 40; 468:143, 200, 322, 364; 479:72–73; A1b, d; A4a, b.*

McCLAMROCH, ROBERT SIDNEY. Born Aug. 29, 1890, Jackson, Hinds County, Mississippi. Ht. 5 ft. 10 in., blue eyes, black hair, dark complexion, married. Manager, West Lumber Company (a sawmill and lumber manufacturing plant), Westville, Trinity County, Texas. LOYALTY RANGER June 13, 1918–Feb. 26, 1919. Discharged. REMARKS: He stipulated that he'd be a Loyalty Ranger "provided my duties as such do not require me to leave my place of residence & business and apply only to enforcement of 'The Hobby Loyalty Act.'" In 1920 was an accountant for a lumber company in Orange, Orange County, Texas. In 1930 was vice president of a bank in Beaumont, Jefferson County, Texas. Died Nov. 21, 1951, Jefferson County, Texas. FAMILY: Parents, Albert McClamroch (b. 1862, MS) and Jennie (b. 1859, MS); siblings, Lolla B. (b. 1893, MS), Harris (b. 1896, MS); spouse, Nettie Dickens (b. 1896, TX), married about 1914; daughter, Jeanette (b. 1921, TX). *SR; A1d, e, f, g; A2b; A3a.*

McCLANAHAN, MARION RAY. Born Mar. 10, 1892, Greer County, Oklahoma. Ht. 6 ft., gray eyes, medium complexion, light hair. Schoolteacher and farmer, Carrizo Springs, Dimmit County, Texas. SPECIAL RANGER May 27, 1917–Dec. 1917 (attached to Co. C). REMARKS: Died Jan. 5, 1945, Bexar County, Texas. FAMILY: Parents, James or John P. McClanahan (b. 1856, MO) and Lula "Lou" (b. 1860, TX); siblings, John Wesley (b. 1879, TX), Willie (b. 1881, TX), Jesse Harvey (b. 1882, TX), Charles Vernon (b. 1887, TX), Myrtle (b. 1894, Indian Territory), twins Arthur Byron and Oscar Barney (b. 1897, Indian Territory), Dorsey (b. 1905, OK). *SR; A1d, e; A2b; A3a.*

McCLELLAN, JAMES DIXIE "JIMMIE." Born Oct. 20, 1885, Snyder, Scurry County, Texas. Ht. 5 ft. 7 in., blue eyes, light hair, light complexion. Ranchman, enlisted in El Paso County, Texas. REGULAR RANGER Mar. 12, 1918–Feb. 21, 1919 (private, Co. L). Resigned to enter U.S. Immigration Service at Ysleta, El Paso County. REMARKS: Was an "old cowpuncher." Had been a policeman and deputy constable. WWI Draft Registration document, Sept. 1918, states "bad right eye." On June 14, 1919 applied for reenlistment in the Rangers. In 1920 was a foreman in the Union Stockyards in El Paso, El Paso County. A James D. McClellan died June 15, 1952, El Paso County, Texas. FAMILY: Mother, Beulah (b. 1867, TX); siblings, Georgia (b. 1886, TX), Arthur (b. 1893, TX), Quinn (b. 1894, TX). *SR; 471; Davis to Harley, Mar 14, 1918, AGC; McClellan to Harley, Feb 1, June 4, 1919, AGC; Harley to McClellan, Feb 4, 1919, AGC; A1e, f; A2b; A3a.*

McCLOY, J. BERTRAND. Born Nov. 9, 1879, Richmond, Fort Bend County, Texas. Ht. 5 ft. 9 in., brown eyes, brown hair, dark complexion, married. Stockman, Beaumont, Jefferson County, Texas. SPECIAL RANGER Jan. 7, 1918–Jan. 15, 1919. REMARKS: As of Sept. 1918 was a stockraiser in Beaumont, employed by the Texas Cattle Raisers' Association. In 1920 was a cattle and mule buyer in Beaumont. Died Sept. 14, 1961, Harris County, Texas. FAMILY: Parents, Dr. Jno. McCloy (b. 1830, MS) and Ann W. (b. 1849, TX); sisters, Bessie (b. 1868, TX), Burlah (b. 1877, TX); spouse, Mary "Madie" (b. 1879, TX), married about 1904; daughters, Bessie (b. 1905, TX), Ruth (b. 1909, TX). *SR; A1b, f, g; A2b; A3a.*

McCLURE, ELMER BERTIE. Born Aug. 18, 1885, Austin, Travis County, Texas. Ht. 6 ft. 1 in., blue eyes, brown hair, medium complexion, married. Labor foreman, Marfa, Presidio County, Texas. REGULAR RANGER Aug. 21, 1919–Nov. 30, 1920 (private, Co. A). Resigned to become a Prohibition enforcement agent. Peace officer, Austin. REGULAR RANGER Mar. 27, 1923–Aug. 3, 1923 (private, Headquarters Co.). Resigned. Ranchman, Wichita Falls, Wichita County, Texas. RAILROAD RANGER Aug. 23, 1923–Feb. 26, 1925. Discharged. Special agent, Phillips Petroleum Company, Breckenridge, Stephens County, Texas. SPECIAL RANGER Nov. 1932–Nov. 1934 (reenlisted Sept. 18, 1933). REMARKS: In 1933, as a special agent for Phillips Petroleum Co., was based in Amarillo, Potter County, Texas. Elmer Birdie McClure died May 8, 1944, Stephens County, Texas. FAMILY: Parents, William LaFayette McClure (b. 1862, TX) and Julia Margaret Buttery (b. 1866, TX);

siblings, Burney L. (b. 1887, TX), Ethel (b. 1889, TX), Willie S. (b. 1893, TX), Mabel (b. 1897, TX), Walter, Pearl. *SR; 471; A1d, f; A2b; A3a.*

McCOMBS, DAVID IVEY. Born Dec. 1863, Hill County, Texas. Ht. 5 ft. 7 in., brown eyes, dark hair, ruddy complexion, married. Farmer, Sweetwater, Nolan County, Texas. REGULAR RANGER May 20, 1918–July 1, 1918 (private, Co. C). Resigned to run for sheriff of Kent County, Texas. REMARKS: Note length of service. Kent County sheriff Nov. 6, 1906–Nov. 3, 1914; lived in Clairemont. Applied for a Ranger captaincy. Died Sept. 4, 1928, Kent County, Texas. FAMILY: Mother, Eda A. (b. 1845, MO); siblings, William B. (b. 1861, TX), Mary E. (b. 1865, TX); spouse, Fannie P. (b. 1869, TX), married about 1890; children, Roscoe P. (b. 1892, TX), Edith L. (b. 1894, TX), Louis W. (b. 1895, TX), Willie C. (b. 1896, TX), Vera G. (b. 1898, TX), Hallie A. (b. 1901, TX), David I. (b. 1903, TX), Fannie B. (b. 1905, TX), Mack A. (b. 1906, TX), Bertie M. (b. 1908, TX). *SR; Higgins to Hobby, Oct 9, 1917, AGC; Smith to Hobby, Oct 9, 1917, AGC; Buchanan to Hobby, Oct 10, 1917, AGC; Petition to Hobby, Oct 10, 1917, AGC; McCombs to Woodul [June, 1918], AGC; McKenzie to Harley, June 29, 1918, AGC; 1503:303; EPMT, Aug 10, 1910; A1a, d, e, f; A2b.*

McCORMICK, JAMES W. Born Feb. 1885, Fort Smith, Sebastian County, Arkansas. Ht. 5 ft. 10 in., blue eyes, black hair, dark complexion, married. Barber. REGULAR RANGER Mar. 27, 1920–Apr. 23, 1920 (private, Headquarters Co.). Discharged. Peace officer, enlisted in Wichita County, Texas. REGULAR RANGER Oct. 18, 1920–Dec. 31, 1920 (no company listed). Honorably discharged—reduction in force. Peace officer, Wichita Falls, Wichita County. REGULAR RANGER Feb. 15, 1921–Apr. 18, 1922 (sergeant, Co. B). Resigned to become Wichita Falls police chief. Peace officer, Wichita Falls. REGULAR RANGER Apr. 13, 1923–Oct. 7, 1924 (sergeant, Co. C). Resigned. SPECIAL RANGER Oct. 7, 1924–Mar. 6, 1925 (Regular Ranger without pay). Discharged. Deputy sheriff, Wichita Falls. REGULAR RANGER Aug. 3, 1926–May 15, 1927 (Headquarters Co.). Discharged. Peace officer. REGULAR RANGER Jan. 16, 1935–May 31, 1938 (captain, Headquarters Co.; transferred to Co. E, June 25, 1936). Discharged. *SR; 471; Aldrich to Gonzaullas, Dec 30, 1920, AGC; Cope to Gonzaullas, Dec 30, 1920, AGC; Cope to Davenport, Jan 5, 1921, AGC; Cope to McCormick, Jan 5, 1921, AGC; Munroe to Aldrich, Sept 9, 1921, WC.*

McCOY, S. M. Born July 1885, Cotulla, La Salle County, Texas. Ht. 5 ft. 11 in., blue eyes, light hair, light complexion, married. Stockman, San Antonio, Bexar County, Texas. REGULAR RANGER Dec. 14, 1917–Jan. 15, 1918 (private, Co. G). Discharged. Peace officer, San Antonio. RAILROAD RANGER Aug. 12, 1922–Sept. 7, 1922 (Co. A). Resigned. REMARKS: Note length of service. Was born and raised in Cotulla. Enlisted by Capt. Charles F. Stevens who wrote, "S. M. McCoy is a good horseman, is well acquainted with the frontier and speaks Spanish." As of Dec. 1916 had worked at the Army Quartermaster remount depot at Fort Sam Houston as a foreman. For the last 7 years had lived in San Antonio. *SR; 471; Barnett to Whom, Dec 10, 1917, AGC; McCoy to AG, Dec 13, 1917, AGC; Stevens to Harley, Dec 14, 1917, AGC; Frederick to Whom, Dec 20, 1916, AGC.*

McCRACKEN, WILLIAM ROSS. Born Nov. 28, 1881, Bee County, Texas. Ht. 6 ft., blue eyes, brown hair, light complexion, married. Farmer and stock raiser (worked on a ranch of a Mr. Flato), enlisted in Kleberg County, Texas. SPECIAL RANGER Dec. 6, 1917–Jan. 15, 1919. REMARKS: Had been a railroader in Nueces County, Texas. FAMILY: Spouse, Vella M. (b. 1891, TX), married about 1908. *SR; Scarborough to Ferguson, June 4, 1917, AGC; Scarborough to Harley, Nov 30, Dec 5, 1917, AGC; AG to Scarborough, Dec 7, 1917, AGC; A1e; A3a.*

McCULLOCH, WILLIAM HAMILTON. Born Feb. 14, 1885, Detroit, Wayne County, Michigan. Tall, medium build, brown eyes, dark hair. 1st lieutenant and aide, active duty, Adjutant General's office, Austin, Travis County, Texas. SPECIAL RANGER Dec. 17, 1919–Dec. 31, 1919. No WA; enlistment form was not notarized; thus, Dec. 31, 1919 is merely the presumed ending date. *SR; A3a.*

McCULLUM, E. B. No service record. No information of birth. No personal description. REGULAR RANGER Jan. 1918–Jan. 31, 1918 (private, Co. G). Discharged/fired. REMARKS: Note length of service. Capt. Stevens fired him for unreliability: lying, etc. McCullum moved to Colorado. *471; Stevens to Woodul, May 3, 1918, AGC.*

McCURDY, FRANK B. Born Sept. 8, 1876, Galveston, Galveston County, Texas. Ht. 5 ft. 10 ½ in., blue eyes, black and gray hair, light complexion, married. Printer, Houston, Harris County, Texas. SPECIAL RANGER Oct. 22, 1918–Jan. 15, 1919; Mar. 16, 1934–unknown. REMARKS: By 1918 owned his own printing company in Houston. A Frank B. McCurdy died Jan. 4, 1938, Harris county, Texas. FAMILY: Parents, George Thomas McCurdy (b. 1845, GA) and Anna (b. 1853, MS); sisters, Lila E. (b. 1879, TX), Rue (b. 1883, TX), Georgia Ann (b. 1885, TX); spouse, Margaret "Maggie" (b. 1879, TX), married about 1897. *SR; A1b, d, e, f, g; A2b; A3a; A4a, b.*

McCUTCHEON, WILLIAM WILLIS. Born Apr. 9, 1873, Sweet Home, Lavaca County, Texas. Ht. 5 ft. 11 in., gray-blue eyes, light hair, light complexion. Rancher and merchant, Limpia, Jeff Davis County, Texas. SPECIAL RANGER June 23, 1917–Dec. 1917 (attached to Co. C); May 13, 1918–Jan. 15, 1919. REMARKS: Letterhead: "B. B. McCutcheon, W. W. McCutcheon, Cattle, Limpia, Texas." He also owned a general store. Was endorsed by Capt. J. M. Fox. Died Jan. 9, 1941, Jeff Davis County, Texas. FAMILY: Parents, Willis William McCutcheon (b. 1836, TX) and Mary "Mollie" Bennett (b. 1843, TX); siblings, Mary Elizabeth "Lizzie" (b. 1868, TX), Bennett B. (b. 1871, TX), Jesse P. (b. 1875, TX), Sallie (b. 1878, TX); spouse, Valda L. Hackney (b. 1888, TX), married about 1910. *SR; Hudspeth to Hutchings, June 14, 1917, AGC; AG to Hudspeth, June 19, 1917, AGC; AG to Stewart, Sept 27, 1917, AGC; AG to McCutcheon, Dec 18, 1917, AGC; A1b, d, e; A2b; A3a; A4a; g.*

McDONALD, GEORGE N. Born July 1889, Franklin, Robertson County, Texas. Ht. 5 ft. 8 ½ in., gray eyes, black hair, dark complexion. Farmer, Luling, Caldwell County, Texas. SPECIAL RANGER June 4, 1918–Nov. 21, 1918. Discharged. REMARKS: Was deputy constable, Luling, in 1916. In 1920 was a stock trader in Luling. FAMILY: Spouse, Aline (b. 1890, TX); son George W. (b. 1914, TX). *SR; 471; SAE, May 5, 1916; A1f.*

McDONALD, JOHN THOMAS (1). Born Oct. 1883, Henrietta, Clay County, Texas. Ht. 5 ft. 9 ½ in., brown eyes, black hair, dark complexion, married. Stockman, Plainview, Hale County, Texas. SPECIAL RANGER Dec. 22, 1917–Feb. 1918 (Co. B. Volunteers). Discharged. REMARKS: Was said to be "well fixed" financially. *SR; Rawlings to Harley, Dec 23, 1917, AGC.*

McDONALD, JOHN THOMAS (2). Born Oct. 26, 1883, Fort Worth, Tarrant County, Texas. Ht. 5 ft. 9 ½ in., gray eyes, black hair, dark complexion, married. Brand inspector, Panhandle and Southwestern Stockmen's Association, Tulia, Swisher County, Texas. SPECIAL RANGER June 24, 1918–Jan. 15, 1919. REMARKS: Was appointed at Senator Claude Hudspeth's request. Was farming in Bovina, Parmer County, Texas while living in Tulia. *SR; Hudspeth to Harley, June 15, 1918, AGC; A3a.*

McDONALD, WILLIAM D. Born July 1867 on the Gila River, Arizona. Ht. 5 ft. 10 ¾ in., blue eyes, brown hair, fair complexion, married. Cowboy, Laredo, Webb County, Texas. SPECIAL RANGER June 18, 1918–Oct. 16, 1918. Discharged/fired. REMARKS: Gave his address as c/o I&GN Railroad, Laredo; got commission under false pretenses: did not work for I&GN Railroad. Adjutant General revoked his commission by Oct. 16, 1918. *SR; Williamson to Johnston, Oct 12, AGC.*

McDOWELL, BERT JAMES. Born Sept. 1880, Pittsburg, Camp County, Texas. Ht. 5 ft. 10 in., blue eyes, brown hair, light complexion, married. Insurance agent, Del Rio, Val Verde County, Texas. SPECIAL RANGER May 4, 1917–Dec. 1917 (attached to Co. C). REMARKS: Was a mounted Customs inspector from 1900–1911; was U.S. marshal, Western District of Texas, 1912–1913; on Feb. 24, 1913, resigned as U.S. marshal to rejoin Customs. Was a Val Verde County deputy sheriff in 1919. In 1930 was U.S postmaster in Del Rio. Died Mar. 8, 1943, Val Verde County, Texas. FAMILY: Spouse, Ada Lou or Lou Ada Upshaw (b. 1891, TX), married about 1909; daughter, Geraldine "Jewel" (b. 1910, TX). *SR; EPMT, July 15, 1911, Dec 20, 1912, Feb 25, 26, 1913; BDH, Feb 12, 1910; SAE, Dec 13, 1911, Feb 26, 1913; AA, Feb 27, 1913, Sept 18, 1919; A1e, f, g; A2b; A4b; B1.*

McDOWELL, HORACE HARRISON. Born Mar. 26, 1884, Bradford, Pennsylvania. Medium height, slender, blue eyes, light hair, married. Stockman, Victoria, Victoria County, Texas. LOYALTY RANGER June 7, 1918–Feb. 1919. REMARKS: In 1910 had been a stockman in Refugio County,

Texas. FAMILY: Parents, Jessie C. McDowell (b. 1848, PA) and Caroline (b. 1854, PA); spouse, Katherine Waldine (b. 1889, TX), married about 1908; children, Jesse "Jack" (b. 1909, TX), Catherine (b. 1911, TX). *SR; A1d, e, f, g; A3a.*

McELROY, JOHN L. Born Jan. 1866, Philadelphia, Philadelphia County, Pennsylvania. Ht. 5 ft. 8 ½ in., blue eyes, gray hair, light complexion. Railroad auditor, San Antonio, Bexar County, Texas. LOYALTY RANGER June 26, 1918–Feb. 24, 1919. REMARKS: Still a railroad auditor in San Antonio in 1930. FAMILY: Parents, E. J. McElroy (b. 1840, PA) and Annie (b. 1844, PA); siblings, Annie R. (b. 1869, VA), Arthur Jas. (b. 1871, VA), Mary C. (b. 1874, VA), Joseph (b. 1878, VA), Kate (b. 1879, VA), Willie (b. 1882, VA); spouse, Kate M. (b. 1881, TX), married about 1921. *SR; A1b, d, e, f, g.*

McELROY, WILL A. Born Aug. 29, 1882, Bluff Springs, Travis County, Texas. Ht. 5 ft. 10 in., blue eyes, brown hair, light complexion, married. Commercial secretary, Gilmer, Upshur County, Texas. SPECIAL RANGER Jan. 8, 1918–Jan. 15, 1919. Retired, Houston, Harris County, Texas. SPECIAL RANGER Dec. 14, 1934–Jan. 22, 1935. Discharged. REMARKS: Had been a grocery man in Hays County, Texas. In 1920 was a motor company department head in Houston. In 1930 was president of a life insurance company in Houston. A Will Allen McElroy died July 13, 1942, Harris County, Texas. FAMILY: Spouse, Cotta Killian (b. 1884, GA), married about 1904; sons, Killian (b. 1906, TX), Nolte (b. 1909, TX), Ethelbert (b. 1913, TX). *SR; A1e, f, g; A2b; A3a.*

McFARLAND, THOMAS CARLISLE "CARL." Born Mar. 1869, Bonham, Fannin County, Texas. No physical description, married. Salesman, Fort Worth, Tarrant County, Texas. SPECIAL RANGER Mar. 21, 1918–Jan. 15, 1919. REMARKS: Had lived in Lavaca County, Texas, and Victoria, Victoria County, Texas. LAW ENFORCEMENT RELATIVES: Ranger Van Earl McFarland, brother. FAMILY: Parents, Dr. Thomas Jefferson McFarland (b. 1837, AL) and Caroline Pauline Jayne (b. 1842, TX); siblings, Marion Minter (b. 1865, MS), Pauline (b. 1867, TX), Van Earl (b. 1873, TX), Julliette (b. 1876, TX), A. Jessie (b. 1878, TX), Caroline Belle (b. 1880, TX); spouse, Appollonia "Lonie" Collier (b. 1870, TX), married June 5, 1895, Victoria; children, Grace (b. 1896, TX), Clyde (b. 1902, TX). *SR.*

McFARLAND, VAN EARL. Born Feb. 25, 1873, Fannin County, Texas. Ht. 6 ft., blue eyes, light hair, fair complexion, married. Physician (Texas quarantine officer), Eagle Pass, Maverick County, Texas. SPECIAL RANGER Feb. 7, 1918–Jan. 15, 1919. REMARKS: His superior requested that he be commissioned. Continued to practice medicine in Maverick County through 1930. Died June 27, 1942, Maverick County, Texas. LAW ENFORCEMENT RELATIVES: Ranger T. C. McFarland, brother. FAMILY: Parents, Dr. Thomas Jefferson McFarland (b. 1837, AL) and Caroline Pauline Jayne (b. 1842, TX); siblings, Marion Minter (b. 1865, MS), Pauline (b. 1867, TX), Thomas Carlisle (b. 1869, TX), Julliette (b. 1876, TX), A. Jessie (b. 1878, TX), Caroline Belle (b. 1880, TX); spouse, Olive Emma Townsend (b. 1881, TX), married Dec. 12, 1900, Eagle Pass; children, Van Haile (b. 1902, TX), Jessie (b. 1904, TX), Olive (b. 1907, TX), Sharp (b. 1910, TX), Pauline (b. 1914, TX). *SR; Collins to Harley, Feb 1, 1918, AGC; A1b, d, e, f, g; A2b; A3a; A4b; B1.*

McFARLANE, SAMUEL J. Born July 1889, Peshtigo, Marinette County, Wisconsin. Ht. 5 ft. 6 in., dark brown hair. Clerk. REGULAR RANGER Dec. 1, 1913–Feb. 10, 1914 (private, Co. C). Discharged without honor/fired—he deserted. REMARKS: Had been a soldier in the cavalry and infantry for 6 years; in 1910 was a member of the 22nd U.S. Infantry, stationed in Alaska. In 1920 was a traveling salesman for a harness company living in Big Rock, Pulaski County, Arkansas. FAMILY: Parents, James Laughlin McFarlane (b. 1848, Canada) and Rebecca Van Doren (b. 1853, WI); sisters, Matie (b. 1880, WI), Rebecca (b. 1882, WI); spouse, Elinor (b. 1898, AR). *SR; 471; A1d, e, f; A4b.*

McFARLIN, JAMES LAUGHLIN "JIM." Born Apr. 28, 1860, Waxahachie, Ellis County, Texas. Ht. 6 ft. 1 in., gray eyes, iron gray hair, dark complexion, married. Stock farmer, Channing, Moore County. LOYALTY RANGER June 13, 1918–Feb. 24, 1919. REMARKS: Had been a deputy sheriff in Hardeman County for several years and was interim sheriff, Hardeman County, for three months. Had also lived in Parker County, Texas. Was still a stock farmer in Moore County in 1920. FAMILY: Parents, Benjamin Porter McFarlin (b. 1825, TN) and Erixene Carolina McKnight (b. 1828, TN); siblings, Elizabeth (b. 1848, TN), Mosana Extrene (b. 1850, TN), Sarah (b. 1853, TX), Edward Page

(b. 1855, TX), Roxanna Augusta (b. 1857, TX), Benjamin Porter (b. 1862, TX), Robert B. (b. 1866, TX); spouse, Allie E. (b. 1860, TX), married about 1882; children, Claud (b. 1883, TX), Iona (b. 1885, TX), Ben (b. 1887, TX), Jimmie (b. 1888, TX), Roland B. (b. 1902, TX). *SR; 471; A1aa, b, d, e, f; A4b.*

McGAFFEY, ALFRED BIRD. Born Sept. 1, 1878, Caldwell County, Texas. Ht. 5 ft. 8 in., gray eyes, light hair, fair complexion, married. Peace officer. REGULAR RANGER Dec. 19, 1917–unknown (private, Co. F). Never reported for duty. REMARKS: Had been a cotton classifier in Caldwell County. Around Nov. 1917 was a secret agent for a Mexican faction. Is listed in the 1917 Houston, Texas City Directory as "Alfred B. McGaffey, trade: secret service." He asked his friend Adjutant General Harley for a secret service position. Harley informed him the AG Department didn't engage in secret service work, offered him a job as a Ranger private. In Sept. 1918 was a manager for Lillenthal Bros. in Houston, Harris County, Texas. In 1920 was a house carpenter in Luling, Caldwell County. An Alfred B. McGaffey died Nov. 1, 1950, Collin County, Texas. FAMILY: Parents, Charles Neal McGaffey (b. 1852, TX) and Annie Bell Beaufort (b. 1856, MD); siblings, Melville Otis (b. 1877, TX), Annie Bell, Lilla Beaufort, Charles Neal, May McCollister; spouse, Sallie K. (b. 1881, TX), married about 1898; children, Annie V. (b. 1902, TX), Chas. R. (b. 1904, TX), Alfred B. (b. 1906, TX), twins Elizabeth and Abigail (b. 1916, TX). *SR; 471; McGaffey to Harley, Dec 8, 1917, AGC; AG to McGaffey, Dec 15, 1917, AGC; A1b, e, f; A2b; A3a; A4b; A5a; B1.*

McGEE, J. L. Born 1871, Urbana, Champaign County, Ohio. Ht. 5 ft. 9 ½ in., blue eyes, light gray hair, ruddy complexion, married. Clerk, Austin, Travis County, Texas. SPECIAL RANGER Mar. 22, 1916–May 25, 1916 (attached to Co. C). Discharged. REMARKS: Note length of service. *SR.*

McGEE, JAMES ALPHUS "JINKS." Born Aug. 22, 1874, West Station, McLennan County, Texas. Ht. 5 ft. 10 in., brown eyes, dark hair, dark complexion, married. Stockman, Abilene, Taylor County, Texas. SPECIAL RANGER June 14, 1917–Dec. 1917 (attached to Co. C). REMARKS: Letterhead: "Jinks McGee & Co., Mules and Horses, Abilene." Died Jan. 8, 1952, Abilene, Taylor County, Texas; buried in Masonic Cemetery, Abilene. FAMILY: Parents, Alphus McGee and M. A. (b. 1858, TX); stepfather, F. T. Wood (b. 1856, AR); sister, E. M. Wood (b. 1879, TX); spouse, Bettie Warren Graves (b. 1879, TX), married about 1897; sons, J. B., Graves Alphus (b. 1902, TX). *SR; Register to Ferguson, May 18, 1917, AGC; Cunningham to Ferguson, May 18, 1917, AGC; Wagstaff to Hutchings, June 15, 1917, AGC; McGee to Harley, Dec 25, 1917, AGC; A1b, d, e, f; A3a; A4b.*

McGEE, PHILIP PEARESON "PHIL." Born Nov. 1877, Richmond, Fort Bend County, Texas. Ht. 5 ft. 11 ½ in., gray eyes, dark hair, dark complexion. Brand inspector, Cattle Raisers' Association of Texas, Houston, Harris County, Texas. SPECIAL RANGER July 23, 1917–June 4, 1918 (attached to Co. C; reinstated/WA renewed, Dec. 20, 1917). Died June 4, 1918, Harris County, Texas. REMARKS: In 1918 was classed as a Regular Ranger without pay, to avoid the draft. FAMILY: Parents, Thomas McGee (b. 1850, GA or AL) and Mary (b. 1856, MO); sister, Lizzy (b. 1875, TX). *SR; Acting AG to GC&SF Railroad, Jan 9, 1918, AGC; Moses to Harley, Sept 4, 1918, AGC; A1b, d; A2b.*

McGILL, OAKLEY. Born Dec. 3, 1887, Corsicana, Navarro County, Texas. Ht. 6 ft. ½ in., brown eyes, black hair, dark complexion, married. Stockman, Plainview, Hale County, Texas. SPECIAL RANGER Dec. 8, 1917–Feb. 14, 1918 (Co. B Volunteers). Discharged—Co. B Volunteers disbanded. REMARKS: As of 1917, had lived in Lamb County, Texas for 17 years. Died June 19, 1929, Hale County, Texas. FAMILY: Parents, Thomas McGill (b. 1857, TN) and Inez (b. 1866, AR); siblings, Elmer (b. 1885, TX), Jewell (b. 1889, TX), Tommie (b. 1892, TX), Manly (b. 1894, TX); spouse, Azzie (b. 1890, TX); children, Glenna (b. 1913, TX), Azzie Lee (b. 1914, TX). *SR; 471; Rawlings to Harley, Dec 8, 1917, AGC; A1d, f; A2b; A3a.*

McGLOIN, GEORGE D. Born Mar. 1872, San Patricio, San Patricio County, Texas. Ht. 5 ft. 8 in., blue eyes, gray hair, light complexion, married. Stockman (in San Patricio County) and banker (Guaranty State Bank), San Antonio, Bexar County, Texas. SPECIAL RANGER Oct. 5, 1918–Jan. 15, 1919. REMARKS: Prior to Ranger service had been county clerk in San Patricio County. Died Aug. 31, 1924,

San Patricio County, Texas. FAMILY: Parents, Patrick Gilbert McGloin (b. 1844, Ireland) and Mary Ann Malloy (b. 1849, LA); siblings, Gilbert (b. 1871, TX), James (b. 1873, TX), Frank D. (b. 1878, TX), Mary Isabell "Mabel" (b. 1879, TX), Phillip H. (b. 1881, TX), Roger Bernard (b. 1882, TX), Wm. J. (b. 1884, TX); spouse, Annie Pearl Williamson (b. 1886, TX). *SR; Webb to Harley, Sept 23, 1918, AGC; A1b, d, e; A2b; A4a.*

McGREGOR, JOHN DOUGAL or DOUGLAS. Born Jan. 14, 1859, Brenham, Washington County, Texas. Ht. 5 ft. 10 ½ in., blue eyes, light hair, fair complexion, married. Physician and rancher, Van Horn, Culberson County, Texas. SPECIAL RANGER Jan. 18, 1917–Jan. 15, 1919 (reinstated/WA renewed, Dec. 28, 1917). REMARKS: Letterhead: "J. D. McGregor & Sons, Breeders of High Grade and Thoroughbred Hereford Cattle, Lobo, Culberson County." Was one of the biggest ranchers in the area; owned all the land from Lobo to Hot Wells and Van Horn. In 1930 was a cattle trader in El Paso, El Paso County, Texas. Died Aug. 26, 1941, El Paso County, Texas. FAMILY: Parents, Christopher Gilbert McGregor (b. 1827, NC) and William Anna Wilkinson (b. 1831, NC); brothers, William Harvey (b. 1853, AL), James C. (b. 1855, NC), Gilbert C. (b. 1861, TX); stepfather, Thomas E. Woods (b. 1827, AL); siblings, Thomas Edward Woods (b. 1866, TX), Alice Josephine Woods (b. 1868, TX), twins Mary Lorain and Mary Lee Woods (b. 1875, TX); spouse, Harriet "Hattie" Smyley (b. 1860, AL), married 1883, Pleasant Hill, Alabama; children, Flint (b. 1884, TX), John Douglas (b. 1886, TX), Agnes (b. 1889, TX), Malcolm (b. 1899, TX). *SR; McGregor to Ferguson, Sept 23, 1916, AGC; Fox to Hutchings, Jan 11, 1917, AGC; AG to Daugherty, Jan 12, 1917, AGC; McGregor to Hutchings, Jan 18, 1917, AGC; Daugherty to Fox [Jan 1917], AGC; A1aa, a, b, d, e, g; A2b; A4a.*

McINTOSH, PIKE K. Born Jan. 1, 1888, Rosebud, Falls County, Texas. Ht. 5 ft. 11 in., blue eyes, light hair, light complexion. Farmer, Rosebud. LOYALTY RANGER June 7, 1918–Feb. 24, 1919. REMARKS: In 1930 was a farmer in Schleicher County, Texas. Died Apr. 5, 1968, Eldorado, Schleicher County, Texas. FAMILY: Parents, John D. McIntosh (b. 1855, AL) and Mary Lou McGowan (b. 1852, AR); siblings, Norman (b. 1884, TX), Edward (b. 1890, TX), Joseph Dixon (b. 1892, TX); spouse, Pauline C. Crim (b. 1891, TX), married in Falls County. *SR; A1d, e, f, g; A2a, b; A3a; A4b.*

McKENZIE, SAMUEL "SAM." Born Feb. 24, 1875, Oakville, Live Oak County, Texas. Ht. 5 ft. 8 in., blue eyes, brown hair. REGULAR RANGER Mar. 1903–1909 (private, Co. D; transferred to Co. B, Aug. 2, 1905). Resigned (?). Peace officer. REGULAR RANGER Aug. 3, 1911–Jan. 1, 1912 (private, Co. B; promoted to sergeant, Sept. 1911; reduced to private by Capt. Sanders for insubordination, Dec. 12, 1911). Resigned. Peace officer. REGULAR RANGER May 15, 1917–Mar. 31, 1919 (private, Co. C; promoted to sergeant of Co. C, Oct. 1917). Discharged. Peace officer, Alice, Jim Wells County, Texas. REGULAR RANGER Nov. 29, 1919–Feb. 15, 1921 (private, Co. E; promoted to sergeant of Co. E, 1920). Discharged. REMARKS: In a 1919 letter, McKenzie stated that he'd enlisted in the Rangers in 1900. In 1910 was deputy sheriff of Presidio County, Texas; from 1912–1913 was deputy sheriff of Webb County, Texas; in 1913–1916 was a mounted Customs inspector. In Apr. 1921 was deputy sheriff of Brewster County, Texas; was city detective in Laredo, Webb County, Texas for many years. In 1919 his reenlistment was uncertain because he had pleaded guilty to violation of criminal statute while a Ranger—had played poker, which legally constituted gambling. Died July 13, 1941, Laredo, Webb County, Texas. FAMILY: Was the adopted son of John McKenzie (b. 1830, Scotland) and Mary (b. 1848, VA). *SR; Bailey to Beckham, Aug 26, 1910, AGC; Hutchings to Sanders, Jan 1, 1912, WC; Assistant AG to Sanders, Jan 11, 1912, WC; Assistant AG to McKenzie, Jan 11, 1912, WC; McKenzie to Hutchings, Mar 20, 1917, AGC; McKenzie to Harley, Apr 2, 1918, WC; Given to Hobby, Mar 31, 1919, AGC; McKenzie to Hobby, July 11, 1919, AGC; Harley to Taylor, July 30, 1919, AGC; Secretary to Bonham, Aug 11, 1919, AGC; Governor to Bonham, Aug 12, 15, 1919, AGC; Harley to Hobby, Aug 12, 1919, AGC; McKenzie to Cope, Nov 7, 1919, AGC; BDH, Aug 19, 1911, Jan 3, 4, 1912, May 13, Sept 24, Nov 28, Dec 12, 1914, Jan 6, 13, Feb 1, Aug 20, Sept 2, Oct 11, 12, 30, Nov 5, 27, 1915, Feb 9, Mar 13, Apr 8, July 12, 1916; LWT, Nov 12, Dec 3, 1911; Jan 14, 21, Aug 18, 1912, Jan 5, Apr 20, Aug 3, Sept 21, Oct 26, Nov 2, 1913, Oct 17, 1915, Apr 3, 1921; SAE, Sept 16, Oct 25, Nov 2, Dec 1, 2, 1911; AA, Feb 12, Oct 7, 14, 1920; 319:48, 195, 350, 353–362; 464:39, 41–43; 468:322, 365; 508:66; A1a, b, d; A2b; A3a.*

McKINLEY, PRESTON MITCHELL. Born Jan. 23, 1884, Sevier County, Arkansas. Ht. 5 ft. 10 in., blue eyes, brown hair, medium complexion, married. Saddler, Miles, Runnels County, Texas. LOYALTY RANGER June 21, 1918–Feb. 24, 1919. REMARKS: Had been a saddle maker since he was 16 years old. In Sept. 1918 was a harness maker for Schoellkopf Saddlery Company in Dallas, Dallas County, Texas. In 1920 was manager of a leather shop in Vernon, Wilbarger County, Texas. In 1930 was a hardware salesman in Vernon. A Preston M. McKinley died Dec. 28, 1962, Tom Green County, Texas. FAMILY: Parents, William Washington McKinley (b. 1848, AR) and Mary E. (b. 1861, GA); siblings, Henry (b. 1872, AR), Evalina (b. 1878, AR), Cora (b. 1880, AR), Horace J. (b. 1886, AR), William K. (b. 1889, AR), James N. (b. 1892, TX), George A. (b. 1895, TX), Granville E. (b. 1899, TX); spouse, Lillie M. (b. 1887, MS), married about 1904; daughters, Bertha Fay (b. 1906, TX), Ethel M. (b. 1909, TX). *SR; A1b, d, e, f, g; A2b; A3a; A4a.*

McKINNEY, ALLEN L. Born Nov. 1898, Bee County, Texas. Ht. 6 ft., gray eyes, brown hair, fair complexion. Mechanic, Alta Vista, Jim Hogg County, Texas. SPECIAL RANGER Aug. 13, 1918–Jan. 15, 1919. REMARKS: Note age. In 1930 was a traveling dry goods salesman living in Beeville, Bee County. FAMILY: Parents, John G. (b. 1870, AL) and Mary A. (b. 1870, TN); siblings, Lee (b. 1894, TX), Albert (b. 1896, TX), Harry (b. 1901, TX), Johney Lorine (b. 1904, TX); spouse, Cherry K. (b. 1902, OK), married about 1926. *SR; A1e, f, g.*

McKINNEY, CARL SIDNEY. Born July 17, 1881, Bloomington, Monroe County, Indiana. Ht. 5 ft. 10 ½ in., gray eyes, dark hair, fair complexion, married. Customs broker and forwarding agent, Laredo, Webb County, Texas. SPECIAL RANGER July 1, 1918–Jan. 15, 1919; Sept. 2, 1932–unknown. REMARKS: 1919 letterhead: "C. S. McKinney, Customs Broker and Forwarding Agent, Laredo." Had been a furniture salesman and a railroad clerk. A Carl S. McKinney died Sept. 2, 1933, Webb County, Texas. LAW ENFORCEMENT RELATIVES: Monroe County, Indiana sheriff (1870) Lawson McKinney, father. FAMILY: Parents, Lawson E. McKinney (b. 1838, IN) and Eliza L. Carman or Corman (b. 1842, IN); siblings, Grant Elmore (b. 1863, IN), Morton Craig (b. 1865, IN), Ethel Grace (b. 1866, IN), Coburn M. (b. 1869, IN), Mackie (b. 1873, IN), Roy Andrew (b. 1877, IN); spouse, Gertrude Winter (b. 1881, NM), married about 1907; daughter, Anne (b. 1908, TX). *SR; A1a, b, d, e, f; A2b; A3a; B2.*

McKNIGHT, ALBERT DENSON "AB." Born July 29, 1877, Bartlett, Williamson County, Texas. Ht. 5 ft. 9 in., brown eyes, dark hair, dark complexion, married. Deputy sheriff, Sonora, Sutton County, Texas. REGULAR RANGER Oct. 22, 1917–May 1918 (private, Co. E). Discharged. REMARKS: Was planning to run for Sutton County sheriff; thus had to resign from Rangers. Capt. Barler wanted to get rid of him anyway. Had been a peace officer in Oklahoma and deputy sheriff in Sutton County. In May 1917 was constable, precinct 1, in Sutton County. Was a brand inspector for the Sheep and Goat Raisers' Association in 1918. Was a house carpenter by trade. Died Oct. 27, 1927, Tom Green County, Texas; buried in McKnight Cemetery, Hollis, Harmon County, Oklahoma. FAMILY: Parents, Edward Harmon McKnight (b. 1840, MS) and Catherine Emily Mumford (b. 1848, TX); siblings, Sallie Rogers (b. 1866, TX), Bettie Ann (b. 1868, TX), Thomas (b. 1871, TX), James Samuel (b. 1874, TX), Albert's twin sister Allie, twins Edward Harmon and Edwin H. (b. 1881, TX), Mary W. (b. 1884, TX), Kathlyn (b. 1888, TX); spouse #1, Rosella Troxell (b. 1877, TX), married Apr. 6, 1897; son, Presley (b. 1904, OK); spouse #2, Maudie Harris, married Sept. 22, 1927. *SR; [McKnight] to Hutchings, May 22, 1917, AGC; Hanson to Woodul, Apr 22, 1918, AGC; Moore to Harley, Dec 19, 1918, AGC; McKnight to Hobby, Mar 24, 1919, AGC; A1b, d, f; A2b; A3a; A4a, b.*

McLAUGHLIN, ALBERT DOUGLAS. Born Apr. 20, 1860, Hopkins County, Texas. Ht. 5 ft. 10 ½ in., blue eyes, brown hair, fair complexion, married. Banker, Hamlin, Jones County, Texas. SPECIAL RANGER June 2, 1917–Dec. 1917 (attached to Co. C). REMARKS: In 1900 was a deputy sheriff living in Sulphur Springs, Hopkins County. In 1910 was a bank president in Hamlin. In 1920 was a real estate agent in Hamlin. Died Oct. 13, 1932, Jones County, Texas. FAMILY: Parents, Thomas McLaughlin (b. 1835, IN) and Mary Ann Hargrave (b. 1835, IN); siblings, William E. (b. 1856, TX), Sterling Price (b. 1862, TX), Lucy May (b. 1865, TX), Margaret R. (b. 1867, TX), Francis Ellen (b. 1870, TX), Dora (b. 1871, TX), Laura Lee (b. 1874, TX), Martha Aline (b. 1878, TX); spouse, Fannie Sparks (b. 1870, TX), married June 9, 1897, Hopkins County. *SR; Dodson to*

Ferguson, May 18, 1917, AGC; Cunningham to Ferguson, May 18, 1918, AGC; A1aa, a, d, e, f; A2b; A4a, b.

McMAHON, MARSHALL HILL. Born July 27, 1879, Madisonville, Madison County, Texas. Ht. 5 ft. 10 in., brown eyes, brown hair, dark complexion, married. Stockman, Cotulla, La Salle County, Texas. SPECIAL RANGER May 11, 1918–Jan. 15, 1919. REMARKS: Had been a deputy sheriff of La Salle County in 1916; owned several ranches; letterhead: "M. H. McMahon, Dealer in All Kinds of Cattle, Cotulla, Texas." Died Sept. 4, 1936, La Salle County, Texas. FAMILY: Parents, Marshall McMahon (b. 1847, TX) and Annie E. (b. 1853, IL); siblings, Ira (b. 1873, TX), Walter (b. 1877, TX), Olley C. (b. 1881, TX), Sallie A. (b. 1885, TX), Briton or Burton Lock (b. 1894, TX); spouse, Bettie L. (b. 1886, TX), married about 1905; children, Walter (b. 1906, TX), Gladys (b. 1909, TX). *SR; LWT, June 25, 1916; A1b, d, e, f, g; A2b; A3a.*

McMILLAN, JAMES ALEXANDER. Born June 18, 1863, Randolph County, Georgia. No physical description, married. Farmer, Lindale, Smith County, Texas. LOYALTY RANGER June 8, 1918–Feb. 1919. REMARKS: Died Oct. 1, 1947, Tyler, Smith County, Texas; buried in Sand Flat Cemetery, Sand Flat Community, Smith County. FAMILY: Parents, John Leonard McMillan (b. 1815, NC) and Julia Ann McDonald (b. 1840, NC); siblings, Mary Elizabeth "Mollie" (b. 1866, AL), Jessie Clifton (b. 1867, AL), John G. (b. 1874, AL), Hammett Pinson (b. 1880, AL); spouse, Dora Josephine Sears (b. 1873, TX), married Dec. 29, 1892, Smith County; children, Carl Isaac (b. 1895, TX), Eunice L. (b. 1896, TX), Leonard Benton (b. 1897, TX), Lois B. (b. 1901, TX). *SR; A1e; A2b; A3a; A4b.*

McMILLAN, JOHN ROBERT. Born May 25, 1879, Hallettsville, Lavaca County, Texas. Ht. 6 ft. 2 in., blue eyes, brown hair, fair complexion, married. Civil engineer, Hico, Hamilton County, Texas. REGULAR RANGER Sept. 19, 1918–July 1919 (private, Co. D; reenlisted under the new law in Headquarters Co., June 20, 1919). Resigned. Civil engineer, Hico. SPECIAL RANGER Aug. 11, 1919–Dec. 31, 1919. REMARKS: Had been Hico city marshal in 1910. Resigned from Rangers in July 1919 to become police chief, Hico. In 1920 was again Hico city marshal. In 1930 was city secretary, Hico. Died May 15, 1939, Hamilton County, Texas. FAMILY: Parents, William James McMillan (b. AL) and Martha (b. 1854, LA); siblings, William (b. 1882, TX), Lilly (b. 1890, TX), Lola (b. 1893, TX); spouse #1, unknown; spouse #2, Lida Busch (b. 1898, TX), married about 1912; daughters, Marguerite L. (b. 1914, TX), Roberta (b. 1923, TX), Pansy (b. 1927, TX). *SR; 471; Harley to McMillan, Aug 11, 1919, AGC; McMillan to Aldrich, Sept 4, 1919, AGC; Aldrich to McMillan, Sept 8, Dec 17, 1919, AGC; Aldrich to Dunlap, Oct 20, 1919, AGC; A1b, d, e, f, g; A2b; A3a; B1.*

McMILLAN, SAMUEL JAMES "SAM." Born Nov. 13, 1872, Quitman, Wood County, Texas. Ht. 5 ft. 8 ½ in., brown eyes, brown hair, dark complexion, married. Collector, Decatur, Wise County, Texas. LOYALTY RANGER June 10, 1918–Feb. 1919. REMARKS: Evidently worked for a wholesale and retail hardware, cotton, and grain company in Decatur. World War I Draft Registration document, Sept. 1918, stated was a collector for the Lelland Company in Decatur. In 1920 was a barber in Decatur. A J. S. McMillan died Dec. 11, 1937, Wise County, Texas. FAMILY: Parents, Rufus C. McMillan (b. 1842, TX) and Ophelia Lafayett McCurry (b. 1846, GA); siblings, Dora (b. 1867, TX), Sarah (b. 1870, TX), William (b. 1877, TX); spouse, Mary Jane (b. 1880, TX), married about 1896; children, Rufus (b. 1898, TX), Margaret (b. 1905, TX), Mary F. (b. 1912, TX). *SR; A1a, b, e, f; A2b; A3a; A4a, b; B2.*

McMORDIE, EDGAR B. Born Apr. 1872, Round Rock, Williamson County, Texas. Ht. 6 ft., brown eyes, gray hair, light complexion, married. Salesman, Gatesville, Coryell County, Texas. REGULAR RANGER Feb. 15, 1921–Aug. 31, 1922 (private, Headquarters Co.). Resigned. Peace officer, Waco, McLennan County, Texas. RAILROAD RANGER Sept. 1, 1922–Sept. 1, 1924 (Co. B). Discharged. Peace officer, Gatesville, Coryell County. REGULAR RANGER Nov. 25, 1927–Nov. 30, 1928 (private, Headquarters Co.). Resigned. SPECIAL RANGER Dec. 1, 1928–Dec. 1, 1929. REMARKS: In 1910 was a teacher at the Gatesville State Reformatory. Coryell County sheriff Feb. 28, 1910–Nov. 3, 1914. Applied for a Ranger captaincy in May 1917. Was police chief in Mexia, Limestone County, Texas in 1930–1931. Died Jan. 19, 1941, Coryell County, Texas; buried in the Gatesville City Cemetery. FAMILY: Parents, Frank McMordie (b. 1832, TN) and Mary Louisa McGuire (b. 1839, TN); siblings, Arthur (b. 1870, TX), Susie (b. 1881, TX); spouse, Mattie O.

True (b. 1889, TX), married about 1914. *SR; 471; Baggett to Hutchings, Nov 27, 1914, AGC; McMordie to Ferguson, May 5, 1917, AGC; 1503:132; A1d, e, f, g; A2b; B1.*

McMURREY, WILLIAM "WILLIE," "WILL." Born Dec. 17, 1889, Sweet Home, Lavaca County, Texas. Ht. 5 ft. 10 in., blue eyes, red hair, fair complexion, married. A King Ranch foreman—Norias Ranch, Armstrong, Willacy County, Texas. SPECIAL RANGER Jan. 10, 1918–Jan. 15, 1919. Ranchman, Hebbronville, Jim Hogg County, Texas. SPECIAL RANGER Nov. 22, 1929–Nov. 22, 1930; Sept. 14, 1931–unknown. REMARKS: In 1929 was commissioned at the request of Attorney General Bobbitt. Died May 31, 1980, Jim Wells County, Texas. FAMILY: Mother, Lula (b. 1866, TX); siblings, Vingy (b. 1882, TX), Lizzy (b. 1884, TX), Lula J. (b. 1885, TX), Frank J. (b. 1888, TX); stepfather, Louis D. Gravell (b. 1862, TX); siblings, Allie Gravell (b. 1895, TX), Georgia Gravell (b. 1899, TX); spouse, Anna (b. 1893, TX), married about 1914; daughter, Mildred (b. 1915, TX). *SR; 471; A1d, g; A2q, b; A3a.*

McMURTRY, ROBERT LEE. Born Jan. 25, 1884, Stony, Denton County, Texas. Ht. 5 ft. 7 ½ in., brown eyes, black hair, dark complexion, married. Cattleman and brand inspector for the Cattle Raisers' Association of Texas, Tulia, Swisher County, Texas. SPECIAL RANGER June 27, 1917–Jan. 15, 1919 (attached to Co. C; reinstated—WA renewed, Dec. 20, 1917). REMARKS: Briscoe County, Texas sheriff Nov. 3, 1908–Nov. 5, 1912. In 1918 was classed as a Regular Ranger without pay to avoid the draft. Was an uncle of Pulitzer Prize-winning author Larry Jeff McMurtry. Died Oct. 2, 1971, Potter County, Texas. FAMILY: Parents, William Jefferson McMurtry (b. 1858, MO) and Louisa Frances Williams (b. 1859, MO); siblings, Charles Thomas (b. 1878, MO), James Langston (b. 1880, TX), Edward Dawson (b. 1882, TX), Lawrence Carroll (b. 1885, TX), Albert Leroy (b. 1887, TX), Laura Grace (b. 1889, TX), John Scott (b. 1891, TX), Joseph Homer (b. 1893, TX), Irene Mae (b. 1895, TX), William Jefferson (b. 1900, TX), Margaret Alice (b. 1905, TX); spouse #1, Nora Talley (b. 1887, TN), married Dec. 19, 1906, Clarendon, Donley County, Texas; children, Francis Lenoir (b. 1910, TX), Lee Helvey (b. 1913, TX); spouse #2, Mary Polk (b. 1900, TX), married Mar. 21, 1926; daughters, Roberta (b. 1931, TX), Carol Young (b. 1934, TX), Rose Mary (b. 1936, TX). *SR; Acting AG to GC&SF Railroad, Jan 9, 1918, AGC; 1503:67; A1d, e, f; A2a, b; A3a; A4b.*

McNAMARA, MICHAEL MATHIS "MIKE." Born June 30, 1891, Waco, McLennan County, Texas. Ht. 5 ft. 8 in., gray eyes, black hair, brunette complexion. Farmer, Waco. SPECIAL RANGER Aug. 28, 1918–Dec. 31, 1919 (WA was renewed, Jan. 25, 1919). Insurance agent, Dallas, Dallas County, Texas. SPECIAL RANGER Apr. 11, 1933–Apr. 10, 1935 (WA was extended to Apr. 10, 1935). FAMILY: Parents, John McNamara (b. 1844, Ireland) and Ruth Childress (b. 1856, TX); siblings, John Bolivar (b. 1877, TX), Guy James (b. 1878, TX), Eugene Addis (b. 1879, TX), Emmett Parnell (b. 1888, TX), Ruth Mary (b. 1893, TX), Joseph Weldon (b. 1895, TX). *SR; A1d, e, f; A3a; A4b; B1.*

McQUEEN, JOHN C. Born 1892, Pineville, Arkansas. Ht. 6 ft., blue eyes, light hair, light complexion. Ranchman, Laredo, Webb County, Texas. REGULAR RANGER Mar. 30, 1920–June 1, 1920 (private, Co. C). Resigned. REMARKS: Note length of service. *SR; 471; Aldrich to McQueen, May 4, 1920, AGC.*

MADDOX, GUY OWEN. Born May 17, 1890, Beaver Dam, Ohio County, Kentucky. Ht. 5 ft. 10 ½ in., blue eyes, auburn hair, light complexion. Special officer. REGULAR RANGER Dec. 16, 1910–Feb. 1, 1911 (private, Co. C; transferred to Co. B, Jan. 15, 1911). Discharged—reduction in force. REMARKS: Note length of service. Had been a policeman in Austin, Travis County, Texas in 1910. In June 1917 was a merchant, "Maddox & Bro.," in Edna, Jackson County, Texas. Died Aug. 13, 1960, Harris County, Texas. FAMILY: Mother, Carrie (b. 1845, KY); siblings, Nora M. (b. 1885, KY), Vern P. (b. 1887, KY); spouse, Elsie (b. 1893, TX); daughters, Clarice (b. 1913, TX), Vivian (b. 1915, TX). *SR; MR, Co. C, Jan 1911, AGC; MR, Co. B, Feb 1911, AGC; AS, July 4, 1910; A1d, e, f; A2b; A3a.*

MAGEE, EDGAR S. Born Feb. 11, 1875, Cuero, DeWitt County, Texas. Ht. 6 ft. 4 in., brown eyes, dark hair, dark complexion. Stock hand. REGULAR RANGER Sept. 7, 1905–Mar. 1906 (private, Co. C). Resigned or was discharged—unknown. Ranchman, REGULAR RANGER June 2, 1916–Feb. 10, 1917 (private, Co. D). Discharged—reduction in force. Peace officer. REGULAR RANGER Mar.

1, 1917–May 1, 1918 (private, Co. A). Resigned. REGULAR RANGER May 3, 1918–Sept. 20, 1918 (private, Co. I). Discharged. REMARKS: Was an Arizona Ranger in 1907; in 1918 was foreman of the Sterling Ranch, Hidalgo County, Texas. An Edgar S. Magee died Apr. 18, 1950, Bexar County, Texas. *SR; 471; 319:419; A2b; A3a.*

MAGEE, LORENZA BERKLIN. Born July 28, 1887, Rancho, Gonzales County, Texas. Ht. 5 ft. 11 in., gray eyes, brown hair, dark complexion. Stock hand, Nixon, Gonzales County. REGULAR RANGER May 17, 1916–unknown (private, Co. D). Resigned. REMARKS: Prior to Ranger service had been city marshal of Nixon and deputy sheriff of Gonzales County; in 1917 lived in Nixon; wanted to reenlist. In 1920 was a lumber salesman in Nixon. A Lorenza Magee died Aug. 23, 1965, Taylor County, Texas. FAMILY: Parents, Cornelius Norflet Magee (b. 1848, MS) and Julia Ann McCulloch (b. 1853, MS); siblings, Felix Toliver (b. 1876, MS), Eulalia Estella (b. 1878, TX), Effie D. (b. 1879, TX), Cornelius Oscar (b. 1882, TX), Althea L. (b. 1890, TX); spouse, Bessie Ferguson, married sometime after 1920. *SR; 471; Tom to Ransom, May 16, 1916, AGC; Magee to Hutchings, May 21, 1917, AGC; A1b, d, e, f; A2b; A3a; A4b.*

MAGRUDER, WILLIAM BELHAVEN HAMILTON "HAMILTON." Born Feb. 16, 1894, San Antonio, Bexar County, Texas. Ht. 5 ft. 11 in., blue eyes, light hair, light complexion. Stockman, enlisted in Val Verde County, Texas. SPECIAL RANGER July 3, 1917–Dec. 1917 (attached to Co. C). In 1920 was an oil broker in Comanche County, Texas. In 1930 was a petroleum engineer living in San Antonio. Died July 28, 1970, San Antonio, Bexar County, Texas. FAMILY: Father, Alexander Stephen Magruder (b. 1864, LA); spouse (?), Lydia (b. 1894, TX), married about 1924. *SR; A1f, g; A2a, b; A4a.*

MAHONY, GARY M. Born July 24, 1880, Eureka, Navarro County, Texas. Ht. 5 ft. 7 ½ in., blue eyes, brown hair, light complexion, married. Merchant, Ratcliff, Houston County, Texas. LOYALTY RANGER June 6, 1918–Feb. 1919. REMARKS: Letterhead: "G. M. Mahoney's Department Store, Ratcliff, Texas." Died June 28, 1968, Houston County, Texas. FAMILY: Parents, Henry D. Mahoney (b. 1843, SC) and Carrie E. (b. 1844, SC); siblings, Seth C. (b. 1866, SC), Sallie T. (b. 1868, SC), Carrie L. (b. 1870, SC), Kate (b. 1872, SC), Volon (b. 1876, TX), Refer T. (b. 1878, TX), Irene (b. 1883, TX), Toycie (b. 1884, TX); spouse, Jessie B. (b. 1880, TX); children, Alina (b. 1907, TX), Gary Max (b. 1913, TX), Carry Nell (b. 1919, TX). *SR; A1b, d, f; A2a, b, e.*

MALLARD, AMERICUS RANKIN. Born Mar. 27, 1886, Maury County, Tennessee. Ht. 5 ft. 11 ½ in., gray eyes, brown hair, dark complexion, married. Barbershop owner, Coolidge, Limestone County, Texas. LOYALTY RANGER July 20, 1918–Feb. 1919. REMARKS: In 1920 and 1930 was a cotton buyer in Coolidge. FAMILY: Parents, William Marcus Lafayette Mallard (b. 1844, TN) and Harriet Josephine (b. 1848, TN); siblings, T. P. (b. 1873, TN), Hod (b. 1878, TN), Hattie (b. 1879, TN), W. L., Jr. (b. 1881, TN), Hyter (b. 1889, TX); spouse, Willia (b. 1888, TX), married about 1909; son, Will Harden (b. 1915, TX). *SR; A1d, e, f, g; A3a; A4b.*

MALONE, CHARLES ANDREWS. Born Mar. 19, 1880, Mount Vernon, Franklin County, Texas. Ht. 5 ft. 8 in., gray eyes, brown hair, fair complexion, married. Rancher, Plainview, Hale County, Texas. SPECIAL RANGER Dec. 7, 1917–Mar. 1918 (Co. B Volunteers). Discharged. REMARKS: Owned a 50,000-acre ranch in Cochran County, Texas. Had been a cotton ginner in Taylor County, Texas. In 1910 owned an electric light and ice plant in Plainview. Died Dec. 23, 1960, Hale County, Texas. FAMILY: Parents, Robert Cuthbert Malone (b. 1849, GA) and Elizabeth Frances "Betty" Andrews (b. 1851, SC); siblings, Evelyne Elizabeth (b. 1872, TX), Ada C. (b. 1877, TX), John C. (b. 1882, TX), Robert M. (b. 1885, TX), Lucy (b. 1888, TX), Tom H. (b. 1891, TX), Brantley U. (b. 1893, TX); spouse, Kate H. (b. 1887, IA), married about 1910; children, Katherine E. (b. 1911, TX), Robert C. (b. 1912, TX). *SR; Rawlings to Harley, Dec 7, 1917, AGC; A1b, d, e, g; A2b; A3a; A4b.*

MALONE, JAMES NATHANIEL "NAT." Born Aug. 10, 1894, Kenedy, Karnes County, Texas. Ht. 5 ft. 8 in., brown eyes, brown hair, dark complexion, married. Cowboy, enlisted in Val Verde County, Texas. REGULAR RANGER May 10, 1916–Oct. 31, 1916 (private, Co. A). Discharged. Cowpuncher, Del Rio, Val Verde County. SPECIAL RANGER May 31, 1917–Oct. 22, 1917 (attached to Co. C). Went on active duty. REGULAR RANGER Oct. 23, 1917–Mar. 10, 1919 (private, Co. E; transferred to Co. M, unknown date).

Honorably discharged—Co. M was disbanded. Ranch hand, Del Rio. REGULAR RANGER Mar. 1, 1921–May 20, 1921 (private, Co. C). Resigned. REMARKS: In 1917 as a Special Ranger evidently worked on the Bedell Moore estate, which had property on the Rio Grande. Died July 9, 1924, San Antonio, Bexar County, Texas. LAW ENFORCEMENT RELATIVES: Constable (in Val Verde County in 1900) James M. Ussery, uncle. FAMILY: Parents, Nathaniel Beryl Malone (b. 1871, TX) and Pearl Ussery (b. 1879, TX); sister, Jessie Pearl (b. 1896, TX); spouse, Ruby Estelle Langley (b. 1901, TX), married Apr. 29, 1919; children, one son, one daughter. *SR; 471; Almond to Hutchings, May 31, 1917, AGC; Special Orders No. 21, Mar 10, 1919, WC; A1d, f; A2b; A4a, b; B1.*

MALONE, JOHN. Born June 21, 1896, Beeville, Bee County, Texas. Ht. 6 ft. 1 in., blue eyes, brown hair, light complexion. Ranchman, Marfa, Presidio County, Texas. SPECIAL RANGER May 15, 1917–Dec. 1917 (attached to Co. C). REMARKS: Cowboy, raised on the border. One resource states he was "Founder and president, Best Western and Master Hosts Hotels." Died Apr. 25, 1963, Albuquerque, Bernalillo County, New Mexico. FAMILY: Parents, Ira S. Malone (b. 1853, TX) and Paloma Elizabeth Walton (b. 1861, TX); siblings, Beulah (b. 1887, TX), F. J. (b. 1891, TX), Lela (b. 1893, TX), May (b. 1899, TX). *SR; Davis to Harley, Jan 26, 1918, AGC; A1e, f, g; A2a; A4b.*

MANN, JAMES SCOTT. Born Feb. 26, 1879, Colmesneil, Tyler County, Texas. Ht. 5 ft. 9 in., hazel eyes, red hair, light complexion, married. Physician, Browndel, Jasper County, Texas. LOYALTY RANGER June 1, 1918–Feb. 1919. REMARKS: In 1910 was a contract physician in Liberty County, Texas. In Sept. 1918 was the physician for the Shirley Lumber Company in Jasper County. Was a medical doctor in West Columbia, Brazoria County, Texas in 1930. Died Aug. 24, 1949, Tyler County, Texas; buried Magnolia Cemetery, Woodville, Tyler County. FAMILY: Parents, Samuel Edward Mann (b. 1847, TX) and Minerva Ann Enloe (b. 1856, TX); siblings, William Edward (b. 1871, TX), Thomas Cullee (b. 1873, TX), David Aden (b. 1876, TX), Samuel Lindsey (b. 1880, TX), George M. (b. 1883, TX), twins Ester Francis and Earnest Franklin (b. 1885, TX), John Bunyan (b. 1892, TX); spouse, Lou Ettie Triplett (b. 1881, TX), married Feb. 4, 1903, Woodville; children, Annie L. (b. 1904, TX), Edna Helen (b. 1911, TX), James Scott, Jr. (b. 1916, TX). *SR; A1d, e, g; A2b; A3a; A4a, b; B1.*

MANRY, ARTHUR LEE. Born Nov. 20, 1873, Trinity, Trinity County, Texas. Ht. 5 ft. 8 in., brown eyes, dark hair, dark complexion, married. Railroad conductor, Brownsville, Cameron County, Texas. SPECIAL RANGER Apr. 12, 1918–Jan. 15, 1919. Railroad conductor, Kingsville, Kleberg County, Texas. SPECIAL RANGER Aug. 14, 1919–Dec. 31, 1919. REMARKS: Died Dec. 2, 1932, Kleberg County, Texas. FAMILY: Parents, Jno. L. Manry (b. 1845, MS) and Ella E. (b. 1852, VA); siblings, Wm. F. (b. 1872, TX), Ella (b. 1876, TX), Pearl (b. 1879, TX); spouse, Louisa (b. 1885, TX), married about 1909; daughters, Lois Bernice (b. 1911, TX), Minnie Lee (b. 1916, TX). *SR; A1b, d, f, g; A2b; A3a.*

MARKS, FRED EMANUEL. Born Feb. 4, 1873, Rio Grande City, Starr County, Texas. Ht. 5 ft. 8 in., brown eyes, brown hair, fair complexion, married. Druggist, Rio Grande City. LOYALTY RANGER July 11, 1918–Oct. 20, 1918. Went on active duty. REGULAR RANGER Oct. 21, 1918–Dec. 8, 1919 (no company, on detached service in San Antonio, Bexar County, Texas; reenlisted under the new law, private, Headquarters Co., June 20, 1919). Resigned. REMARKS: Had been deputy sheriff for 5 years and deputy U.S. marshal for 3 years. In 1916 was an informant at Rio Grande City for the federal Bureau of Investigation. In 1918 worked for Ranger Capt. William M. Hanson in San Antonio. His resignation was not accepted until Mar. 13, 1920. Died Oct. 12, 1920, San Antonio, Bexar County, Texas; buried in Rio Grande City. FAMILY: Parents, Ernest Marks (b. 1835, France) and Josephila Peña (b. 1857, Mexico); sisters, Sarah C. (b. 1875, TX), Eve (b. 1877, TX), Ernestine (b. 1879, TX); sister-by-adoption, Lorenza Torres (b. 1867, TX); spouse, Santos N. (b. 1879, TX), married about 1900; daughters, Santos Minerva (b. 1901, TX), Carmen (b. 1903, TX), Norah (b. 1908, TX), Edna (b. 1917, TX). *SR; 471; Marks to Hanson, Nov 7, 1918, WC; Marks to Harley, May 6, 1919, WC; Hanson to AG, July 17, 1919, WC; Marks to Cope, Dec 8, 1919, AGC; Cope to Marks, Mar 13, 1920, AGC; Chapa to Cope, Oct 12, 1920, AGC; A1b, e, f; A3a.*

MARSHALL, JOHN. Born 1888, Austin, Travis County, Texas. Ht. 5 ft. 11 ½ in., gray eyes, light hair, dark complexion. Stockman. REGULAR RANGER May 19, 1920–July 31,

1920 (private, Co. F). Resigned. REMARKS: Note length of service. *SR; 471.*

MARSHALL, WILLIAM F. Born June 1870, Indianapolis, Marion County, Indiana. Ht. 5 ft. 6 in., blue eyes, dark hair, married. Postmaster, Mineral, Bee County, Texas. LOYALTY RANGER May 31, 1918–Feb. 1919. REMARKS: Prior to Ranger service, had been deputy sheriff. 1918 letterhead: "W. F. Marshall, Groceries and Confections, Mineral, Tex." Still a grocery store proprietor in Bee County in 1930. A William F. Marshall died Jan. 23, 1953, Bee County, Texas. FAMILY: Spouse, Mellie M. (b. 1872, TX), married about 1895; children, Edith E. (b. 1895, TX), John E. (b. 1898, TX), Ida M. (b. 1901, TX), Marion N. (b. 1906, TX), Nellie (b. 1909, TX). *SR; Marshall to Harley, July 2, 1918, AGC; A1d, e, f, g; A2b.*

MARTIN, ANDREW HARRIS. Born Sept. 20, 1852, Saline County, Arkansas. Ht. 5 ft. 11 in., gray eyes, gray hair, dark complexion, married. Ranchman, Comstock, Val Verde County, Texas. SPECIAL RANGER Dec. 3, 1917–Jan. 15, 1919 (Co. A Volunteers). REMARKS: Had been a stock raiser in Kimble County, Texas, before settling in Val Verde County by 1900. Died Nov. 8, 1928, Comstock, Val Verde County, Texas; buried in Comstock Cemetery. FAMILY: Parents, James Henry (or Hutchinson) Martin (b. 1826, MO) and Mary Lee Rowland (b. 1834, AL); siblings, Martha Jane (b. 1855, AR), Francis Emily (b. 1860, MO), James Alexander (b. 1863, TX), twins John and Sallie (b. 1866, TX), Mary Isabella (b. 1869, TX), William Allen (b. 1870, TX), Robert Henry (b. 1873, TX), Susan (b. 1875, TX); spouse, Anna M. Sandherr (b. 1858, AR), married about 1877; children, Charlie (b. 1878, TX), Maud (b. 1879, TX), Dee (b. 1881, TX), Colonel Griffith (b. 1884, TX), Natt (b. 1886, TX), Buck Barber (b. 1889, TX), Georgia (b. 1891, TX), Andrew H., Jr. (b. 1896, TX), Roland (b. 1899, TX), William Hugh (b. 1902, TX). *SR; A1a, b, d, e, f; A2b; A4a, b; B1, 2.*

MARTIN, CHARLES L. Born Feb. 1876, Johnson County, Texas. Ht. 5 ft. 8 in., hazel eyes, brown hair, light complexion. Farmer, Westover, Baylor County, Texas. LOYALTY RANGER June 21, 1918–Feb. 1919. In 1910 was a livestock dealer in Hill County, Texas. In 1930 still farming in Baylor County. FAMILY: Parents, Charles Love Martin (b. 1840, GA) and Phoebe Elizabeth Easter (b. 1844, MS); siblings, R. S. (b. 1867, AL), John B. (b. 1869, AL), Bettie (b. 1874, TX), Doc K. (b. 1878, TX), Arthur (b. 1879, TX), Hugh (b. 1881, TX), Joseph (b. 1883, TX), Nora G. (b. 1888, TX), Emma (b. 1889, TX), Theodocia (b. 1891, TX); spouse, Anna B. (b. 1895, MO), married about 1919; son, Charles, Jr. (b. 1921, TX). *SR; A1b, d, e, f, g; A4a, b.*

MARTIN, ELDRED CLEMON "DRED." Born Jan. 25, 1876, Rusk, Cherokee County, Texas. Medium height, medium build, married. Peace officer, Rusk. LOYALTY RANGER June 3, 1918–Feb. 1919. Had been a prison guard at the state penitentiary at Rusk. In 1920 was a service car driver in Rusk and in 1930 was a bus driver in Rusk. Died Oct. 28, 1932, Cherokee County, Texas. FAMILY: Parents, Mathew W. Martin (b. 1835, SC) and Arcilla S. Martin (b. 1842, SC); siblings, William A. (b. 1859, TX), Martha Jane (b. 1862, TX), Florence D. (b. 1866, TX), Mary C. "Betty" (b. 1868, TX), Matt (b. 1872, TX), Alley (b. 1874, TX), Miller (b. 1879, TX), Emma (b. 1882, TX); spouse, Sarah Belle Sublett (b. 1885, TX), married June 21, 1901, Cherokee County. *SR; A1b, d, e, f, g; A3a; A4a.*

MARTIN, FRANK. Born Oct. 1867, San Antonio, Bexar County, Texas. Ht. 5 ft. 9 in., gray eyes, gray hair, fair complexion, married. Deputy sheriff and King Ranch foreman, Raymondville, Willacy County, Texas. SPECIAL RANGER June 6, 1917–Nov. 25, 1917 (attached to Co. C). Killed Nov. 25, 1917, while trying to make an arrest at Raymondville. REMARKS: On Aug. 8, 1915 was a defender of the Norias Ranch and was seriously wounded. Caesar Kleberg requested that he be commissioned. FAMILY: Spouse, Natalia Mendez (b. 1867, Mexico), married May 9, 1897, Cameron County, Texas; son, Frank (b. 1899, TX). *SR; Kleberg to AG, May 10, 1917, AGC; 1:I, 1277; Gay, "Amazing," WC; BDH, July 9, 1915, Nov 26, Dec 1, 1917; 319:30–32; 425:91–92; A1d; B1.*

MARTIN, GROVER CLEVELAND. Born Aug. 1, 1884, Oglesby, Coryell County, Texas. Ht. 5 ft. 9 in., blue eyes, light hair, light complexion, married. Farmer, Copperas Cove, Coryell County. LOYALTY RANGER June 17, 1918–Feb. 1919. REMARKS: In 1910 was a farmer in Damsite, Hardeman County, Texas. In 1930 was farming in Coryell County. Died Nov. 17, 1945, Falls County, Texas; buried in

Gatesville, Coryell County. FAMILY: Parents, Francis Marion Martin (b. 1842, MS) and Sarah Sebrina Magee (b. 1852, MS); siblings, Peter Clarence (b. 1869, MS), Kate D. (b. 1871, MS), Leandra or Lena (b. 1878, TX), Morton B. (b. 1880, TX), Silas R. (b. 1882, TX), twins Alma A. and Bertha G. (b. 1887, TX), Homer Paul (b. 1890, TX), Vera (b. 1891, TX), Francis M. (b. 1895, TX), Bonner A. (b. 1898, TX); spouse, Eppie Mae Perryman (b. 1883, TX), married Jan. 9, 1910, Tarrant County, Texas; children, Sarah L. (b. 1912, TX), Grover C., Jr. (b. 1920, TX), Lella R. (b. 1922, TX). *SR; A1d, e, g; A2b; A3a; A4a, b; B1, 2.*

MARTIN, JAMES FISHER. Born May 6, 1874, Karnes County, Texas. Ht. 5 ft. 8 in., blue eyes, black hair, dark complexion, married. Brand inspector, Cattle Raisers' Association of Texas, Pleasanton, Atascosa County. SPECIAL RANGER Nov. 21, 1918–Jan. 15, 1919. REMARKS: Had been a brand inspector for the Cattle Raisers' Association for many years. Moses & Rowe law firm requested that he be commissioned. A James Fisher Martin died Apr. 24, 1949, Karnes County, Texas. FAMILY: Spouse, Callie F. (b. 1882, TX), married about 1900; children, Willie S. (b. 1901, TX), Alice K. (b. 1904, TX), Edna (b. 1913, TX), Lilla (b. 1918, TX), Mattie (b. 1921, TX), J. F. (b. 1923, TX). *SR; Moses & Rowe to Harley, Nov 4, 1918, AGC; Johnston to Moses & Rowe, Nov 18, 1918, AGC; A1f, g; A2b; A3a.*

MARTIN, JAMES TAYLOR. Born Mar. 28, 1875, Sulphur Springs, Hopkins County, Texas. Ht. 5 ft. 10 ½ in., blue eyes, brown hair, light complexion, married. Peace officer, Gilmer, Upshur County, Texas. REGULAR RANGER Aug. 12, 1919–Apr. 30, 1921 (private, Headquarters Co.). Discharged. REMARKS: Also gave birthplace as Gilmer. Was city marshal, Gilmer, in 1910. Died Feb. 12, 1959, Upshur County, Texas. FAMILY: Parents, Gilbert Preston "Gib" Martin (b. 1848, TX) and Sarah "Dink" Lee (b. 1852, TX); siblings, William Lee (b. 1871, TX), Ella Eleanor (b. 1872, TX), George Rogers (b. 1878, TX), Mary Esther (b. 1880, TX), Gilbert Preston (b. 1882, TX), Suda Winifred (b. 1884, TX), Anna Lanora (b. 1885, TX), Sarah Gilbert (b. 1887, TX); spouse, Lenna Dell Tittle (b. 1881, GA), married July 12, 1898, Hopkins County; children, Willie Pearl (b. 1900, TX), James or Jack Albert (b. 1901, TX), Exa V. (b. 1904, TX). *SR; 471; Hanson to Martin, Aug 5, 8, 1919, AGC; Martin to Cope, Mar 9, Aug 26, 1920, AGC; Cope to Martin, Mar 10, Aug 26, 1920, AGC; Aldrich to Millard, Mar 10, 1920, AGC; A1b, d, e, f; A2b; A3a; A4a, b.*

MARTIN, JOHN CHARLES "JACK." Born Aug. 23, 1881, Roanoke, Randolph County, Alabama. Tall, slender, black eyes, black hair, married. Hardware business, Clarkesville, Red River County, Texas. SPECIAL RANGER Jan. 23, 1919–Dec. 31, 1919. REMARKS: Red River County sheriff Nov. 3, 1914–Nov. 5, 1918. Died Apr. 29, 1939, Sacramento, Sacramento County, California. FAMILY: Father, Charles A. Martin (b. 1854, GA); sisters, Fanny, Alice; spouse, Delilah Roberts (b. 1884, TX), married May 2, 1902; children, John Morris (b. 1903, TX), Tommie or Fannie Mae (b. 1905, TX), Travis Leon (b. 1908, TX), Marvin Lee (b. 1912, TX), Melvin Ford (b. 1914, TX), John, Jr. (b. 1917, TX), Liberty Loan (b. 1918, TX), Joe Bailey (b. 1919, TX), Charles Henry (b. 1922, TX), Slaton Eugene (b. 1925, TX), Janice Jean (b. 1926, TX). *SR; 1503:434; A1d, e, f; A2e; A3a; A4b.*

MARTIN, JOHN GEORGE. Born July 3, 1880, Burleson County, Texas. Ht. 6 ft. 1 in., brown eyes, brown hair, medium complexion, married. Watchman, I&GN Railroad, San Antonio, Bexar County, Texas. SPECIAL RANGER Oct. 7, 1918–Jan. 15, 1919. REMARKS: In 1910 and again in 1930 was a machine shop stationary engineer in San Antonio. In 1920 was an express company guard in San Antonio. A John George Martin died Feb. 7, 1955, Bexar County, Texas. FAMILY: Spouse #1, unknown; spouse #2, Alice A. (b. 1884, TX), married about 1900; son, Bernard (b. 1901, TX); spouse #3, Daisy (probably Hatton) (b. 1884, IA), married about 1928. *SR; A1e, f, g; A2b; A3a.*

MARTIN, JOSEPH ARCH "ARCH." Born Jan. 13, 1895, Brazoria, Brazoria County, Texas. Ht. 5 ft. 9 in., brown eyes, brown hair, ruddy complexion, married. Farmer, Sweeny, Brazoria County. LOYALTY RANGER June 5, 1918–Feb. 24, 1919. REMARKS: Had been a peace officer. In 1920 was a horse trader living in Sour Lake, Hardin County, Texas. FAMILY: Parents, McWillie Martin (b. 1868, TX) and Elloise M. (b. 1871, TX); siblings, Furnace E. "Furnie" (b. 1892, TX), Catherine Eulalie (b. 1901, TX), Gertude Nadine (b. 1904, TX), Harris M. "Harry" (b. 1907, TX), Hellen (b. 1911, TX); spouse, Gladys (b. 1900, TX); son, J. A., Jr. (b. 1918, TX). *SR; A1d, e, f; A3a.*

MARTIN, ROBERT BRUCE. Born Apr. 25, 1875, Vance, Tuscaloosa County, Alabama. Ht. 5 ft. 11 in., brown eyes, brown hair, dark complexion, married. Railroad trainmaster, Houston, Harris County, Texas. SPECIAL RANGER Jan. 3, 1919–Dec. 31, 1919. Trainmaster, T&BV Railroad, Teague, Freestone County, Texas. RAILROAD RANGER Nov. 25, 1922–Mar. 17, 1923. Discharged. REMARKS: Was commissioned in 1919 at the request of Fuller Williamson. In 1920 was a railroad superintendent at Palestine, Anderson County, Texas. In 1930 was a train examiner living in Alexandria, Rapides Parish, Louisiana. Died Dec. 1952, Shreveport, Caddo Parish, Louisiana. FAMILY: Parents, William Bruce Martin (b. 1840, TN) and Wilmoth Catherine Crunk (b. 1841, TN); siblings, Henry (b. 1864, TN), James P. (b. 1866, TN), Augusta B. (b. 1868, TN), Brent (b. 1873, AL), Charles (b. 1878, AL), Franklin (b. 1879, AL); spouse #1, Edna W. Schooler (b. 1877, MS), married Sept. 1898, Birmingham, Jefferson County, Alabama; sons, Robert Roy (b. 1901, AL), George (b. 1905, AL); spouse #2, Lucille (b. 1878, AL), married about 1905; children, Louise (b. 1907, TX), Bruce (b. 1913, TX). *SR; Johnston to Williamson, Jan 20, 1919, AGC; Williamson to Harley, Jan 24, 1919, AGC; A1b, d, f, g; A3a; A4b.*

MARTIN, THOMAS J. Born Sept. 1869, Uvalde, Uvalde County, Texas. Ht. 5 ft. 8 in., dark eyes, dark hair, dark complexion, married. Stockman and farmer, Spofford, Kinney County, Texas. SPECIAL RANGER Mar. 25, 1918–Jan. 15, 1919. REMARKS: In 1930 still a stockman and farmer in Kinney County. FAMILY: Parents, Francis M. Martin (b. 1834, OH or KY) and Dicy Ann (b. 1838, AL); brother, Henry G. (b. 1867, TX); spouse, Mildred M. (b. 1873, MO or NY), married about 1909; daughter, Harriett (b. 1909, TX). *SR; A1a, b, e, f, g.*

MARTIN, W. H. Born Sept. 1884, Beeville, Bee County, Texas. Ht. 6 ft. 1 in., gray eyes, red hair, ruddy complexion. Cowpuncher. REGULAR RANGER Oct. 20, 1917–Feb. 12, 1918 (private, Co. E; transferred to Co. M, unknown). Discharged/fired. REMARKS: Was fired for disobeying orders and for conduct unbecoming; the Army at Eagle Pass, Maverick County, Texas had complained about him. Prior to his Ranger service, had been deputy sheriff of McCulloch County, Texas. *SR; 471; Cunningham to Harley, Feb 13, Mar 13, 1918, AGC.*

MARTIN, WILLIAM EDWARD. Born Aug. 19, 1889, Leesville, Gonzales County, Texas. Ht. 6 ft. 1 in., blue eyes, dark hair, dark complexion. Farmer. REGULAR RANGER June 2, 1916–Jan. 6, 1917 (private, Co. D; transferred to Co. A, unknown). Resigned/honorably discharged—reduction in force. REMARKS: In Aug. 1917 was living in Gonzales County and trying to reenlist in the Rangers. In 1930 was a poultry farmer in Gonzales County. Died July 9, 1951, Gonzales County, Texas. FAMILY: Parents, William Orville Martin (b. 1858, TX) and Lydia A. (b. 1870, TX); siblings, Elmo C. (b. 1891, TX), Maggie C. (b. 1894, TX), Ima G. (b. 1897, TX), Lydia A. (b. 1899, TX); spouse, Myrtle Marie Hood (b. 1898, TX), married Mar. 3, 1920. *SR; 471; Martin to Hutchings, Aug 6, 1917, AGC; A1d, e, f, g; A2b; A3a; A4b.*

MARTINEZ, MERCURIO. Born Oct. 27, 1876, San Ignacio, Zapata County, Texas. Ht. 5 ft. 8 ½ in., brown eyes, black hair, fair complexion, married. Texas quarantine guard, San Ignacio. SPECIAL RANGER Feb. 5, 1918–Jan. 15, 1919. REMARKS: In 1900 and 1910 was a schoolteacher in Zapata County. Had been treasurer of Zapata County. His superior requested in 1918 that he be commissioned. Died Oct. 15, 1966, Webb County, Texas. FAMILY: Parents, Proceso Martinez (b. 1841, Mexico) and Jesus (b. 1849, Mexico); siblings, Adolfo (b. 1870, TX), Serafin (b. 1872, TX), Eudosio (b. 1874, TX), Delfina (b. 1878, TX), Proceso U. (b. 1884, TX); spouse #1, unknown; spouse #2, Guadalupe (b. 1864, Mexico), married about 1910. *SR; Collins to Harley, Feb 1, 1918, AGC; A1b, d, e, f; A2a, b; A3a.*

MASON, JAMES N. P. Born Mar. 1871, Leander, Williamson County, Texas. Ht. 5 ft. 8 in., blue eyes, brown hair, fair complexion, married. Bank cashier, enlisted in McCulloch County, Texas. SPECIAL RANGER May 23, 1916–Dec. 1917 (attached to Co. C). REMARKS: In May 1920 was cashier of First State Bank, Melvin, McCulloch County. Had been a dry goods merchant in Irion County, Texas and a furniture merchant in Lampasas County, Texas. A James N. Mason died June 28, 1927, Lampasas County, Texas. FAMILY: Parents, Charles C. Mason (b. 1847, NC) and Sarah Jane Wells (b. 1852, TX); siblings, Frances C. (b. 1873, TX), Sarah J. (b. 1876, TX), Charles C. (b. 1878, TX), Elizabeth F. (b. 1880, TX), Alpheus L. (b. 1882, TX), Maggie D. (b. 1885, TX), Ernest D. (b. 1888, TX); spouse, Beulah Y. (b. 1871, TX), married about 1894; children, Oriz N. (b. 1896, TX),

George L. (b. 1898, TX), Mattie Corinne (b. 1901, TX). *SR; Mason to AG, May 17, 1920, AGC; A1b, d, e, f, g; A2b; A4b.*

MASTERSON, NEILL TURNER. Born June 1, 1884, Brazoria, Brazoria County, Texas. Ht. 5 ft. 6 in., gray eyes, light hair, light complexion, married. Cattleman, enlisted in Harris County, Texas. SPECIAL RANGER Feb. 11, 1918–Jan. 15, 1919. REMARKS: Was also a lawyer, practiced in Houston, Harris County. Died Feb. 28, 1947, Brazoria County, Texas. FAMILY: Parents, Judge Harris H. Masterson (b. 1856, TX) and Sallie Stewart Turner (b. 1861, NC); siblings, Harris H., Jr. (b. 1881, TX), Raina (b. 1883, TX), Travis (b. 1885, TX), Birchall (b. 1896, TX); spouse, Elizabeth Mary "Libbie" Johnston (b. 1887, TX), married about 1906; children, Neill T., Jr. (b. 1908, TX), Elizabeth (b. 1909, TX), Harris, III (b. 1915, TX). *SR; A1d, e, f, g; A2b; A3a; A4a, b.*

MATHEWS, CHRISTOPHER COLUMBUS. Born Nov. 22, 1973, Palestine, Anderson County, Texas. Ht. 5 ft. 6 in., brown eyes, brown hair, dark complexion, married. Peace officer, Lufkin, Angelina County, Texas (for past 8 years). SPECIAL RANGER Feb. 5, 1916–Dec. 1917 (attached to Co. C). Farmer, Lufkin. RAILROAD RANGER Aug. 29, 1922–Nov. 16, 1922. Discharged. Railroad employee, Lufkin. SPECIAL RANGER Mar. 27, 1926–Feb. 1, 1927. Discharged—WA expired. REMARKS: On 1916 enlistment form gave birthplace as Tennessee Colony, Anderson County. In 1910 was county constable, Angelina County. In Sept. 1918 was marshal, city of Lufkin. As of 1926 had been a deputy sheriff and city marshal of Lufkin. In 1930 was a loan company officer in Lufkin. Died Apr. 4, 1940, Angelina County, Texas. FAMILY: Parents, J. W. Mathews (b. 1835, AL or GA) and Lula (b. 1858, TX); brothers, Edward (b. 1875, TX), Marcus (b. 1879, TX); spouse #1, unknown, married about 1897; children, Norma (b. 1898, TX), Etta M. (b. 1901, TX); spouse #2, Marianne "Minnie" (b. 1881, TX), married about 1907; children, Melvin (b. 1912, TX), Clyde (b. 1915, TX), Jack P. (b. 1919, TX). *SR; HC, Apr 20, 1911; A1b, e, f, g; A2b; A3a.*

MATTHEWS, FRANK W. Born June 1872, Liberty Hill, Williamson County, Texas. Ht. 6 ft., blue eyes, brown hair, light complexion, married. Peace officer, San Antonio, Bexar County, Texas. REGULAR RANGER July 1, 1919–Mar. 8, 1920 (private, Co. C; transferred to Headquarters Company, Aug. 8, 1919; transferred to Co. E, Oct. 29, 1919). Resigned to become a guard for Lone Star Oil and Refining Co. at Wichita Falls, Wichita County, Texas. Peace officer, San Antonio. REGULAR RANGER Mar. 27, 1920–Apr. 22, 1920 (private, Headquarters Company). Discharged. Investigator, San Antonio. RAILROAD RANGER Aug. 18, 1922–Oct. 31, 1922. Discharged. REMARKS: Had been a policeman in Austin, Travis County; was a policeman in Beaumont, Jefferson County; was a security guard for Greene Consolidated Copper Company in Sonora, Mexico for 1 or 2 years, where he commanded an armored auto used to move gold ore from Cananea through Yaqui country to the railroad; was a city detective in San Antonio in 1910; was a special officer for the T&P Railroad in Texarkana, Bowie County, Texas in 1918. In Apr. 1920 was "Captain of Receiver Guards, Red River," at Wichita Falls during the Texas-Oklahoma boundary dispute. LAW ENFORCEMENT RELATIVE: Travis County sheriff (Nov. 4, 1902–Nov. 2, 1920) George S. Matthews, cousin. FAMILY: Parents, John T. Matthews (b. 1824, TN) and Lenora N. (b. 1838, SC); siblings, Abner E. (b. 1859, TX), Samuel H. (b. 1861, TX), Sydney I. (b. 1863, TX), Wesley I. (b. 1866, TX), Sarah J. (b. 1875, TX); spouse #1, Mattie K. (b. 1872, TX), married about 1893, divorced by 1910; children, Addie L. (b. 1894, TX), Floyd E. (b. 1898, TX), Maggie (b. 1900, TX); spouse #2, Ethyl (b. 1891, MS), married by 1920. *SR; Matthews to Harley, Jan 9, 1918, AGC; Matthews to Aldrich, Mar 31, Apr 26, 1920, AGC; Davenport to Cope, Jan 3, 1921, AGC; HC, Sept 9, 1910; AS, Jan 20, Sept 9, 10, 1910; 1503:494–495; A1b, d, e, f.*

MAXEY, FRANK LUSTER. Born July 30, 1885, Joplin, Jasper County, Missouri. Ht. 5 ft. 4 in., brown eyes, dark hair, dark complexion. Merchant, Anson, Jones County, Texas. SPECIAL RANGER May 31, 1917–Dec. 1917 (attached to Co. C). REMARKS: In 1930 was a hardware merchant in Dallas, Dallas County, Texas. Died July 27, 1965, Dallas County, Texas. FAMILY: Parents, James Jackson Maxey (b. 1857, MO) and Henrietta Martin (b. 1868, MO); siblings, Henry Clark (b. 1887, MO), Sadie Jewell (b. 1889, MO), Myrtle Mae (b. 1891, MO), Mabel Alberta (b. 1896, MO), Herman Martin (b. 1897, MO), Galen Spencer (b. 1900, TX), Leta L. (b. 1903, TX), Creola B. (b. 1905, TX); spouse, unknown Chaffin, married Aug. 9, 1942; one child.

SR; Dodson to Ferguson, May 18, 1917, AGC; Cunningham to Ferguson, May 18, 1917, AGC; A1e, f, g; A3a; A4a, b.

MAXWELL, JOHN W. Born Apr. 12, 1874, Collin County, Texas. Ht. 6 ft. 4 ½ in., blue eyes, brown hair, red complexion, widower. Real estate agent, Gainesville, Cooke County, Texas. SPECIAL RANGER Nov. 19, 1918–Jan. 15, 1919. REMARKS: A John Wesley Maxwell died Mar. 18, 1919, Travis County, Texas. FAMILY: Parents, Zachary T. Maxwell (b. 1850, MO) and Rebecca Missouri Mitchell (b. 1850, MO); siblings, Mose, Maggie L. (b. 1869, MO), Corwin (b. 1871, MO), Martha L. (b. 1872, MO), Dora L. (b. 1881, TX), Zachra T. (b. 1885, TX), Dewit T. (b. 1889, TX); spouse, Maude (b. 1877, TX), married about 1897; children, Eunice (b. 1899, TX), Earl (b. 1901, TX), Johnnie M. (b. 1903, TX), Ethie M. (b. 1908, TX). *SR; A1b, e; A2b; A3a; A4a, b.*

MAY, JOSEPH D. "JOSIE." Born Sept. 20, 1872, State Springs, Calhoun County, Mississippi. Ht. 5 ft. 11 in., gray eyes, brown hair, married. Retired grocery merchant, Omaha, Morris County, Texas. LOYALTY RANGER July 15, 1918–Feb. 1919. REMARKS: Letterhead: "J. D. May, Dealer in Staple and Fancy Family Groceries, Omaha, Tex." A Josie D. May died May 12, 1953, Morris County, Texas. FAMILY: Parents, Dr. Jonathan H. May (b. 1835, AL) and Nancy P. "Nannie" (b. 1843, SC); brothers, John T. (b. 1867, MS), Jonathan E. (b. 1870, MS), Willie B. (b. 1872, MS), Jimmie (b. 1879, MS); spouse #1, unknown; spouse #2, Sadie Bell (b. 1886, TX), married about 1906; children, Nannie L. (b. 1907, TX), Thomas (b. 1914, TX). *SR; A1a, b, d, e, f, g; A2b; A3a.*

MAY, WILLIAM P. Born June 1872, Taylor, Williamson County, Texas. Ht. 5 ½ ft. 11 in., gray eyes, dark hair, fair complexion, married. Stockman, Laredo, Webb County, Texas. SPECIAL RANGER Feb. 21, 1918–Jan. 15, 1919. REMARKS: A William P. May died Nov. 25, 1920, Webb County, Texas. FAMILY: Parents, William May (b. 1838, MS) and Jennie or Janie Langham (b. 1846, TX); brother, Henry (b. 1869, TX); spouse, Alma (b. 1876, TX), married about 1899. *SR; A1a, b, d, e, g; A2b.*

MAYBERRY, WALTER EARNEST. Born May 5, 1887, Gatesville, Coryell County, Texas. Ht. 6 ft. 3 ½ in., gray eyes, light brown hair, light complexion, married. Cattleman, Austin, Travis County, Texas. SPECIAL RANGER Dec. 30, 1916–Dec. 20, 1917 (attached to Co. C). Went on active duty. REGULAR RANGER Dec. 21, 1917–Feb. 13, 1919 (unassigned, served without pay in the AG's office; promoted to sergeant, Headquarters Co., June 28, 1918; suspended, Feb. 7, 1919). Discharged/fired, Feb. 13, 1919. Peace officer. REGULAR RANGER—reinstated as sergeant, Nov. 25, 1919. Custodian, Camp Mabry, Austin; June 1, 1922–June 1, 1924 (Pvt., Co. B). Discharged—WA expired. REMARKS: On Feb. 7, 1919, witnessed Capt. Cunningham's killing of Ranger Bert Veale; was suspended. Mayberry's last appearance on state payroll: Quartermaster's Branch, AG's department, Camp Mabry storekeeper at $125/month. In 1930 worked in the U.S. Customs office in Laredo, Webb County, Texas. Died June 11, 1956, Austin, Travis County, Texas. FAMILY: Parents, Thomas Alfred Mayberry (b. 1864, TX) and Willie Ann Winfield (b. 1861, AR); siblings, James Thomas (b. 1882, TX), John Allen (b. 1884, TX), Sallie Ann (b. 1889, TX), Robert Lee (b. 1892, TX), Willie Alvera (b. 1894, TX); spouse, Lucile Randerson (b. 1892, TX), married Sept. 1, 1915, Austin; sons, Robert Thomas (b. 1920, TX), James Edward (b. 1921, TX). *SR; 471; Special Orders No. 13, Feb 13, 1919, AGC; LWT, Feb 9, 1919; 463:114; A1d, g; A2b; A3a; A4a, b.*

MAYES, WILL. Born 1866, Coleman County, Texas. Ht. 5 ft. 11 in., blue eyes, black hair, dark complexion, married. Brand inspector, Cattle Raisers' Association of Texas, Richmond, Fort Bend County, Texas. SPECIAL RANGER Nov. 26, 1918–Jan. 15, 1919. REMARKS: Had been brand inspector for the Cattle Raisers' Association of Texas for many years; that organization requested that he be commissioned. *SR; Moses to Rowe, Nov 21, 1918, AGC.*

MAYFIELD, JOHN. Born Sept. 1868, Austin, Travis County, Texas. Ht. 6 ft. 2 in., gray eyes, gray hair, dark complexion. Farmer, enlisted in Collin County, Texas. REGULAR RANGER Aug. 14, 1911–Oct. 15, 1911 (private, Co. A). Honorably discharged. REMARKS: Note length of service. *SR; MR, Co. A, Oct 31, 1911, AGC.*

MAYFIELD, THOMAS SHANNON "TOM." Born June 16, 1880, Leesville, Gonzales County, Texas. Ht. 6 ft. 2 in., brown eyes, brown hair, dark complexion, married. Contractor, Pharr, Hidalgo County, Texas. LOYALTY RANGER June 6, 1918–Feb. 1919. REMARKS: In 1901, became an Hidalgo County deputy sheriff at San Juan Plantation; served until 1916. In 1908 was also assistant manager of Closner (San Juan) Plantation; in 1910 was superintendent of a sugar plantation. Was a rancher, contractor and developer in Hidalgo County in 1919. Was an oil company employee in Tampico, Mexico from 1921–1941; returned to Lower Valley from Mexico in 1941. Was Hidalgo County constable from 1942–1952. Died Nov. 24, 1966, San Juan, Hidalgo County, Texas; buried in Hillcrest Memorial Park, Edinburg, Hidalgo County. FAMILY: Parents, John T. Mayfield (b. 1849, MO) and Margaret Celestia Anderson (b. 1857, TX); siblings, Jerushia Mariah (b. 1881, TX), Fannie Mattie (b. 1887, TX), Maggie John (b. 1889, TX), Asa P. (b. 1893, TX); spouse, Woody Denley Edwards (b. 1888, TX), married about 1908; daughters, Lillian (b. 1909, TX), Vivienne Lucille (b. 1918, TX). *SR; 471; Sanders to Mayfield, Jan 27, 1915, AGC; Fall Committee, I, 1287–1296, 1321–1323; BDH, May 9, 1910, June 19, 1912, Dec 1, 1914, Feb 7, May 9, 1916; NYT, June 10, 1919; 319:25, 27, 35–38, 51; 424:218; 485:37; A1d, e, f; A2b; A3a; A4a; B1.*

MAYFIELD, WALTER. Born Sept. 18, 1878, Brownsville, Cameron County, Texas. Ht. 5 ft. 9 in., blue eyes, red hair, red complexion, married. Ranchman, enlisted in Jeff Davis County, Texas. REGULAR RANGER June 1, 1918–Aug. 31, 1918 (private, Co. N—Hudspeth Scouts). Discharged—Co. N was disbanded. REMARKS: One source states he was born in Brown County, Texas; family was living in Brown County in 1880. Had been a cattle raiser in El Paso County, Texas. In 1920 was a house carpenter in Valentine, Jeff Davis County. In 1930 was a laborer on a stock ranch in Jeff Davis County. Died Oct. 9, 1960, in Big Spring, Howard County, Texas. FAMILY: Parents, Henry Southerland Mayfield (b. 1844, TX) and Zillah Ann Boyd (b. 1842, MO); siblings, Luther (b. 1873, TX), Lola Belle (b. 1875, TX), Eula (b. 1876, TX); spouse, Rachel Telford (b. 1882, AR), married July 15, 1903; children, Leon (b. 1904, NM), George H. (b. 1906, NM), Alonzo Odem (b. 1909, TX), Joe T. (b. 1911, NM), Eula (b. 1913, NM), Walter, Jr. (b. 1915, NM), James A. (b. 1917, NM), Ralph (b. 1920, TX). *SR; 471; A1b, d, e, f, g; A2b; A3a; A4b; B1, 2.*

MEADOWS, WILLIAM DUDLEY. Born Jan. 1869, Irving College, Tennessee. Ht. 5 ft. 8 in., blue eyes, gray hair, fair complexion, married. County commissioner, Austin, Travis County, Texas. SPECIAL RANGER Apr. 13, 1918–Jan. 15, 1919. REMARKS: Had been a farmer in Milam County and Runnels County, Texas. In 1920 was a county commissioner in Runnels County. In 1930 was a cotton seed salesman in Runnels County. FAMILY: Parents, W. M. Meadows (b. 1822, TN) and Sarah (b. 1832, TN); siblings, Ida (b. 1858, TN), Parriet (b. 1862, TN), Thula B. (b. 1865, TN), Minnie (b. 1867, TN), Aubrey (b. 1871, TN), Marion (b. 1874, TN); spouse, Lillie (b. 1872, TN), married about 1890; children, William Cloyce (b. 1891, TN), Thomas Allen (b. 1892, TN), Thelma (b. 1897, TX). *SR; A1b, d, e, f, g.*

MEEKS, THOMAS HOUSTON. Born July 16, 1882, Clarke County, Mississippi. Ht. 5 ft. 11 in., gray eyes, auburn hair, fair complexion, married. Assistant superintendent, SP Railroad, Houston, Harris County, Texas. SPECIAL RANGER Aug. 16, 1918–Jan. 15, 1919. REMARKS: In 1910 was a railroad dispatcher in Muskogee, Muskogee County, Oklahoma. In 1930 was assistant to the vice president of a railroad company, living in Houston. Died June 6, 1966, Galveston County, Texas. FAMILY: Spouse, Violet L. (b. 1885, TX), married about 1905; son, Thomas G. (b. 1917, LA). *SR; A1e, f, g; A2a, b; A3a.*

MEGEE, ROBERT ERNEST. Born Nov. 18, 1886, Hutto, Williamson County, Texas. Ht. 5 ft. 11 in., gray eyes, light brown hair, fair complexion, married. Automobile dealer, Austin, Travis County, Texas (enlisted in Galveston County, Texas). SPECIAL RANGER July 20, 1917–Dec. 1917 (attached to Co. C). REMARKS: In 1920 and 1930 was a wholesale oil distributor living in San Antonio, Bexar County, Texas. FAMILY: Parents, John T. Megee (b. 1844, TN) and Annie R. (b. 1858, TX); sisters, Alice N. (b. 1882, TX), Johnnie (b. 1884, TX), Lena (b. 1885, TX), Anna (b. 1890, TX), Willie (b. 1893, TX), Mattie Louise (b. 1895, TX); spouse, Francis H. (b. 1895, TX), married about 1915; son, Robert E., Jr. (b. 1923, TX). *SR; A1d, e, f, g; A3a.*

MELLARD, FRANK COURTNEY "COURTNEY." Born Feb. 27, 1878, Gonzales, Gonzales County, Texas. Ht. 5 ft. 11 in., gray eyes, brown hair, light complexion, married. Ranchman, enlisted in Presidio County, Texas. SPECIAL RANGER Dec. 8, 1917–Jan. 15, 1919. REMARKS: In Jan. 1919, owned Marfa agency for Oberland and Willys-Knight automobiles. Died Feb. 17, 1970, Brewster County, Texas. FAMILY: Parents, Robert T. "Bob" Mellard (b. 1849, MS) and Sallie Lytle Wilson (b. 1854, TX); siblings, Willie May (b. 1880, TX), Lytle (b. 1882, TX), J. W. (b. 1895, TX); spouse, Helen A. Buchanan (b. 1878, VA), married Aug. 1, 1900, Scurry County, Texas; sons, Malcolm (b. 1902, TX), Rudolph (b. 1904, TX), Kenneth (b. 1909, TX). *SR; A1e, f; A2a, b, c; A3a; A4a; B2.*

MELTON, GEORGE W. Born June 1869, Ellington, Reynolds County, Missouri. Ht. 5 ft. 10 in., blue eyes, dark hair, fair complexion, married. County commissioner, Edna, Jackson County, Texas. LOYALTY RANGER July 27, 1918–Feb. 1919. REMARKS: In Feb. 1919 was manager of a family-owned garage at Edna. In 1930 was manager of a tin shop in Edna. FAMILY: Spouse, Barbara A. (b. 1871, MO), married about 1895; children, Harry M. (b. 1895, MO), Hazel (b. 1897, MO), Herbert L. (b. 1899, MO), Homer C. (b. 1902, MO), Helen (b. 1905, MO), William Howard (b. 1909, MO), Herma J. (b. 1913, TX). *SR; A1b, d, e, f, g.*

MELTON, WILLIAM SHERROD. Born Nov. 1858, Bienville Parish, Louisiana. Ht. 6 ft. 1 in., gray eyes, iron gray hair, dark complexion, married. Farmer, Cottonwood, Callahan County, Texas. SPECIAL RANGER May 29, 1917–Dec. 1917 (attached to Co. C). FAMILY: Spouse, Fannie J. (b. 1858, TX), married about 1877; children, Ada L. (b. 1878, TX), Lula D. (b. 1879, TX), W. Eugene (b. 1882, TX), Nonnie (b. 1886, TX). *SR; A1b, d, e, f, g.*

MERCER, JAMES BEAUMOND. Born May 6, 1881, Travis County, Texas. Ht. 6 ft. 3 ½ in., gray eyes, dark brown hair, light complexion. Farmer, enlisted in Travis County. REGULAR RANGER Nov. 20, 1911–Sept. 1912 (private, Co. C; promoted to sergeant, 1912). Resigned/honorably discharged. REMARKS: When he resigned in 1912 he returned to his home in Burnet, Burnet County, Texas. In June 1917 lived in Kerrville, Kerr County, Texas; applied to reenlist in Rangers. As of Sept. 1918 was a stock foreman on the ranch of Mrs. M. E. Mercer in Kerrville. FAMILY: Spouse, Viola. *SR; 471; Mercer to Hutchings, June 28, 1917, AGC; SAE, Dec 25, 1911; BDH, Dec 26, 1911, Feb 1, 6, Apr 12, May 20, 25, 28, July 13, Aug 29, Sept 9, 1912; A3a.*

MERREM, EDGAR JACOB. Born Dec. 10, 1866, La Grange, Fayette County, Texas. Ht. 6 ft. 1 in., dark eyes, dark hair, fair complexion, married. Merchant (general merchandise), Shiner, Lavaca County, Texas. LOYALTY RANGER May 30, 1918–Feb. 24, 1919. REMARKS: Died Apr. 21, 1943, Shiner, Lavaca County, Texas. FAMILY: Parents, Edgar Abraham Merrem (b. 1827, Germany) and Natalie Clara Walz (b. 1835, Prussia); siblings, Ludwig (b. 1855), Clara Elizabeth (b. 1856, TX), Leona (b. 1858), August (b. 1859), Ernst (b. 1860, TX), Emma (b. 1864, TX), Kuno Henry (b. 1869, TX), William Sidney (b. 1872, TX); spouse, Willie Ann Llena Crane (b. 1865, TX), married about 1893; children, Mary Elizabeth, La Delle, Edgar Leon (b. 1894, TX), Leslie Crane (b. 1895, TX), William Elmo (b. 1899, TX), Mabel Lee (b. 1901, TX). *SR; 471; Merrem to Harley, Feb 2, 1919, AGC; A1a, b, e, f; A4a, b.*

MERRICK, JOSEPH A. Born May 1872, Benton County, Arkansas. Ht. 5 ft. 9 in., gray eyes, brown hair, light complexion, married. Stock farmer, Lakeview, Hall County, Texas. SPECIAL RANGER July 24, 1918–Jan. 15, 1919. FAMILY: Parents, Britton A. Merrick (b. 1847, MO) and Mary L. (b. 1848, TN); siblings, Marth "Mattie" (b. 1869, AR), Saunders (b. 1874, AR), Emma (b. 1876, MO), Clarence E. (b. 1880, MO), John C. (b. 1896, TX); spouse, Dovie (b. 1878, TX), married about 1900; daughters, Kedron M. (b. 1901, TX), Jodie B. (b. 1908, TX). *SR; A1a, b, d, e.*

MERRILL, WILLIAM T. Born Feb. 1879, Somerville, Burleson County, Texas. No physical description, married. Stockman, Stephenville, Erath County, Texas. LOYALTY RANGER June 27, 1918–Feb. 1919. REMARKS: In 1920 and 1930 was an oil field trader in Stephenville. FAMILY: Parents, Lemuel Pruitt Merrill (b. 1848, GA) and Sarah Antonia Hiner (b. 1860, TX); siblings, Joseph (b. 1876, TX), Charles H. (b. 1881, TX), Minnie L. (b. 1884, TX), M. J. (b. 1885, TX), H. L. (b. 1886, TX), L. P. "Luck" (b. 1888, TX), Lottie (b. 1891, TX), Mary A. (b. 1894, TX), John Hiner (b. 1896, TX), Novi P. (b. 1898, TX); spouse, Myrtle M. (b. 1881, TX), married about 1903; children, Fred R. (b. 1904, TX), Roy L. (b. 1906, TX), Charles M. (b. 1910, TX), Lola (b. 1913, TX), William J. "Billy" (b. 1918, TX). *SR; A1b, d, e, f, g; A4b.*

METZ, REINHARDT HENRY, JR. Born Aug. 31, 1884, Gillett, Karnes County, Texas. Ht. 5 ft. 11 in., brown eyes, dark hair, dark complexion, married. Drugstore owner, Gillett. SPECIAL RANGER Jan. 25, 1918–Jan. 15, 1919. REMARKS: Had been a deputy sheriff. Died Feb. 15, 1930, Wilson County, Texas; buried in Gillett Cemetery. FAMILY: Parents, Reinhardt Henry Metz (b. 1855, TX) and Pauline Jacob (b. 1861, TX); siblings, Mary Louise (b. 1882, TX), Pauline Emily (b. 1886, TX), Herman Peter (b. 1888, TX), Josephine (b. 1897, TX), Rowena (b. 1900, TX); spouse, Louise Johanna Schaefer "Loula" (b. 1883, TX); children, Milam Sutton (b. 1910, TX), Pauline Louise (b. 1915, TX). *SR; A1d, f, g; A2b; A3a; A4b.*

MIDDLETON, CHARLES PAXTON. Born Oct. 22, 1874, Bastrop, Bastrop County, Texas. Ht. 5 ft. 6 in., brown eyes, dark brown hair, dark complexion, married. Salesman, enlisted in Tarrant County, Texas. REGULAR RANGER Mar. 2, 1909–Apr. 15, 1909 (private, Co. B). Resigned. REGULAR RANGER May 30, 1909–unknown (private, Co. B). Resigned or was discharged—unknown. Watchman, I&GN Railroad, Houston, Harris County, Texas. SPECIAL RANGER Jan. 29, 1917–Oct. 1918 (was reinstated—WA renewed, Dec. 27, 1917). Discharged. REMARKS: A Charles P. Middleton died Nov. 17, 1925, Harris County, Texas. FAMILY: Spouse, Sallie E. (b. 1882, TX), married about 1907. *SR; 471; see also SR for Ranger Allen P. Roberts; Middleton to Williamson, Nov 20, 1916, AGC; Williamson to Whittington, Nov 22, 1916, AGC; Williamson to Hutchings, Jan 26, 1917, AGC; AG to Williamson, Jan 27, 1917, AGC; A1e, f; A2b; A3a.*

MILAM, JAMES W. Born Apr. 1863, Birmingham, Jefferson County, Alabama. Ht. 5 ft. 10 in., brown eyes, dark gray hair, dark complexion, married. Deputy sheriff, Houston, Harris County, Texas. REGULAR RANGER Sept. 30, 1920–Feb. 15, 1921 (private, Headquarters Co., Emergency Co. No. 1). Discharged. REMARKS: Was a deputy sheriff in 1915. Had lived in Harris County as early as 1910. Was a peace officer in Houston in 1930. FAMILY: Spouse #1, unknown, married about 1885; children, James W., Jr. (b. 1888, TX), Effie (b. 1893, TX), Edna (b. 1895, TX); spouse #2, Annie (b. 1871, TX), married about 1900; spouse #3, Earnestine Hoffman (b. 1877, TX), married about 1915. *SR; 471; HC, July 4, 1915; A1b, e, f, g; A3a.*

MILES, BASSETT R. Born Oct. 16, 1872, Richmond, Fort Bend County, Texas. Ht. 6 ft., brown eyes, black hair, dark complexion, married. Contractor, Luling, Caldwell County, Texas (enlisted in Bexar County, Texas). SPECIAL RANGER Aug. 6, 1918–Jan. 15, 1919. REMARKS: Had been a hardware merchant and the Luling city postmaster. In 1920 was an oil field clerk in Luling. Died Aug. 15, 1949; buried in Luling City Cemetery. FAMILY: Parents, R. A. Miles (b. 1842, KY) and L. J. (b. 1852, KY); sister, Mary A. (b. 1878, TX); spouse, Blanche L. Andrews (b. 1874, TX), married about 1896; daughters, Willynn (b. 1897, TX), Glenn (b. 1899, TX). *SR; A1b, d, e, f; A3a.*

MILES, WILLIAM ARTHUR. Born May 27, 1883, Chilton, Falls County, Texas. Ht. 5 ft. 11 in., brown eyes, dark brown hair, dark complexion. Peace officer. REGULAR RANGER Sept. 1917–Mar. 1, 1918 (private, Co. C). Resigned. Peace officer. REGULAR RANGER June 6, 1918–Mar. 10, 1919 (private, Co. D). Honorably discharged—reduction in force. REMARKS: In Aug. 1919 applied for reenlistment; was a plain clothes officer in the Wichita Falls, Wichita County, Texas police department. In 1910 had been a Falls County deputy sheriff. In Oct. 1919, was a special agent, MKT Railroad at Wichita Falls. In 1920 was a federal officer living in Wichita Falls. FAMILY: Parents, William A. Miles (b. 1849, MS) and Anna E. (b. 1859, AR); siblings, Lou Ella (b. 1878, TX), Eliza G. (b. 1880, TX), Rupert (b. 1885, TX), Campbell P. (b. 1888, TX), George C. (b. 1892, TX), May (b. 1896, TX); spouse, Susie Ethel (b. 1885, TX), married about 1901. *SR; 471; Gray to Miles, June 4, 1918, AGC; Special Orders No. 21, Mar 10, 1919, WC; Monday to Harley, Mar 11, 1919, AGC; Harley to Monday, Mar 15, 1919, AGC; Miles to Aldrich, Mar 21, 1919, AGC; Miles to Harley, Aug 31, 1919, AGC; Brooks to Breniman, Oct 6, 1919, AGC; A1b, d, e, f; A3a; A4b.*

MILES, WILLIAM T. Born Nov. 1871, Clarksville, Habersham County, Georgia. Ht. 6 ft., brown hair, brown eyes, dark complexion. Road foreman. REGULAR RANGER Dec. 15, 1917–Feb. 21, 1925 (private, Co F; reenlisted under the new law in Co. B, June 20, 1919; transferred to Co. A, Feb. 1, 1920; reenlisted June 20, 1921; reenlisted June 20, 1923; promoted to sergeant, Sept. 1, 1923; transferred to Co. E, Sept. 19, 1923). Honorably discharged—reduction in force. Sergeant of wharf police, Galveston, Galveston County, Texas. SPECIAL RANGER Feb. 11, 1932–unknown (Feb. 11, 1933?). REMARKS: A William Thomas Miles died

Jan. 19, 1947, Galveston County, Texas. FAMILY: Parents, Thomas Mitchell Miles (b. 1839, GA) and Nancie Magness (b. 1843, GA); siblings, Mary Estelle (b. 1869, GA), John P. (b. 1874, GA), Sarah Elizabeth (b. 1877, GA), Francis C. (b. 1878, GA); spouse, Elizabeth R. Quarles (b. 1872), married about 1898; daughter, Willie Victoria (b. 1900, TX). *SR; 471; 470: 43; A1b, f, g; A2b; A4a, b.*

MILHOAN, MILES. Born May 24, 1889, Sebastian County, Arkansas. Tall, slender, blue eyes, brown hair, married. Farmer, White Deer, Carson County, Texas. LOYALTY RANGER July 15, 1918–Feb. 1919. REMARKS: Had been a peace officer: Carson County deputy sheriff as of June 1917. In 1930 was a wheat farmer in Oldham County, Texas. Died Jan. 19, 1967, Oldham County, Texas. FAMILY: Parents, John D. Milhoan (b. 1864, OH) and Martha C. "Marthy" (b. 1869, TN or MS); siblings, Newton (b. 1892, AR), Maude (b. 1893, AR), John L. (b. 1897, AR), Lizzie (b. 1899, AR), Everett L. (b. 1903, OK), Joe (b. 1909, TX); spouse, Ruth Meadows (b. 1888, AR), married about 1913; children, Zoe (b. 1915, TX), Dan M. (b. 1917, TX), Denton or Peyton I. (b. 1919, TX), Charles H. (b. 1920, TX), Homer L. (b. 1922, CO), Louella (b. 1924, CO), Chester (b. 1925, CO), Hazel (b. 1928, TX), Mary Ann (b. 1930, TX). *SR; A1d, g; A2a, b, e; A3a.*

MILLARD, GEORGE MICHAEL. Born July 1868, Basingstoke, Hampshire County, England. Ht. 5 ft. 11 ½ in., brown eyes, gray hair, dark complexion, married. Peace officer, San Antonio, Bexar County, Texas. REGULAR RANGER June 20, 1919–Jan. 1, 1920 (private, Headquarters Co.). Resigned because he couldn't live on a Ranger's salary. REMARKS: Was a naturalized U.S. citizen. Had been a liveryman in Kissimmee, Osceola County, Florida. In 1930 was a Railway Express guard in San Antonio. A G. M. Millard was a Bexar County deputy sheriff in 1915–1916 and a deputy U.S. marshal at Eagle Pass in May, 1920. A George Millard died Oct. 10, 1940, Bexar County, Texas. FAMILY: Parents, James Elwin Millard and Dora Frances; spouse, Mary L. (b. 1877, FL), married about 1897; children, Violet (b. 1898, FL), Lawrence (b. 1902, TX). *SR; 471; Millard to Cope, Dec 18, 1919, Feb 27, 1920, AGC; Cope to Millard, Mar 1, 1920, AGC; LWT, Oct 24, 1915; SAE, Jan 22, 1916; U.S. Commissioner, Del Rio, No. 556, FRC-FW; A1d, e, f, g; A2b; B1.*

MILLER, ANDREW NEAL. Born Jan. 11, 1855, Groesbeck, Limestone County, Texas. Ht. 5 ft. 10 in., gray eyes, gray hair, light complexion, married. Cattleman, Oakwood, Leon County, Texas. LOYALTY RANGER June 11, 1918–Feb. 25, 1919. REMARKS: Letterhead: "A. N. Miller, Dealer in Livestock, Oakwood." Had been a bookkeeper for a dry goods store in Oakwood. In 1930 was city marshal, Oakwood. Died July 10, 1931, Limestone County, Texas. FAMILY: Parents, Meredith Neal Miller (b. 1829, TX) and Lucy Eller Oliver (b. 1836, TN); siblings, Mary Ella (b. 1860, TX), Aline (b. 1863, TX), Lucrecia (b. 1866, TX), William O. (b. 1869, TX), Rosena (b. 1871, TX), Ora (b. 1875, TX), Sam Houston (b. 1882, TX); spouse #1, unknown, married about 1875; spouse #2, Norah E. Ward (b. 1868, TX); spouse #3, Mattie Greer Lane (b. 1874, MS), married about 1904; daughter, Lillian Aline (b. 1906, TX). *SR; A1aa, a, e, f, g; A2b; A4a.*

MILLER, CHARLES EDWARD "CHARLIE." Born June 9, 1895, Miguel, Frio County, Texas. Ht. 5 ft. 11 in., gray eyes, brown hair, light complexion, married. Trainman, San Antonio, Bexar County, Texas. REGULAR RANGER Dec. 10, 1919–Sept. 8, 1921 (private, Co F; transferred to Co. C, Feb. 15, 1921). Discharged. Peace officer. REGULAR RANGER Oct. 1, 1921–Sept. 30, 1922 (private, Co. C; transferred to Headquarters Co., May 11, 1922). Resigned. Peace officer, San Antonio. REGULAR RANGER Aug. 6, 1923–Oct. 31, 1923 (private, Headquarters Co; transferred to Co. E, Sept. 12, 1923). Discharged. Special officer, SP Railroad, Houston, Harris County, Texas. RAILROAD RANGER Dec. 17, 1923–Dec. 23, 1924. Discharged. Peace officer. REGULAR RANGER Dec. 23, 1924–Feb. 21, 1925 (private, Co. E). Discharged. Special officer, SP Railroad, San Antonio. SPECIAL RANGER May 9, 1928–May 9, 1929. Brand inspector, Sheep and Goat Raisers' Association of Texas, San Antonio. SPECIAL RANGER June 3, 1929–June 3, 1930; June 14, 1930–Jan. 20, 1931 (WA expired); June 14, 1931–unknown (June 14, 1933?). Peace officer, Mountain Home, Kerr County, Texas. SPECIAL RANGER June 16, 1933–Oct. 18, 1933. Discharged; Nov. 3, 1933–Jan. 22, 1935 (WA was extended to Nov. 2, 1935). Inspector, Sheep and Goat Raisers' Association of Texas, Kerrville, Kerr County. SPECIAL RANGER June 21, 1935–Aug. 10, 1935. Discharged. REMARKS: June 1935 commission was requested by Schreiner Brothers. Died Dec. 8, 1971,

San Angelo, Tom Green County, Texas; buried in State Cemetery, Austin, Travis County, Texas. FAMILY: Spouse #1, Marie (b. 1893, TX); stepchildren, Myrtle Minicia (b. 1910, TX), Louis Minicia (b. 1912, TX); spouse #2, Eva A. Meyers (b. 1901, TX), married about 1928; sons, Robert Albert (b. 1934, TX), Frost Woodhull (b. 1937, TX), Charles Schreiner (b. 1942, TX). *SR; 901; A1f, g; A2b, e; A3a; B2.*

MILLER, CHARLES RICHARD. Born Aug. 22, 1875, Hays County, Texas. Ht. 6 ft. 1 in., blue eyes, dark hair, fair complexion, married. Brand inspector, Cattle Raisers' Association of Texas, Dilley, Frio County, Texas. SPECIAL RANGER Mar. 29, 1918–Jan. 15, 1919. REMARKS: Cattle Raisers' Association requested a Special Ranger commission for him. REMARKS: Had been a farmer and cattle buyer. In 1930 was a livestock inspector in Dilley. Died Mar. 18, 1933, Bexar County, Texas. FAMILY: Parents, John William Miller (b. 1848, England) and Mary Frances Meeks (b. 1846, MO or TX); sister, Nellie; step-siblings, Lucie Lessum (b. 1866, TX), Robert Lessum (b. 1868, TX); spouse, Julia Clary (b. 1878, TX), married about 1894; children, Otis Clary (b. 1901, TX), Irene (b. 1906, TX). *SR; Acting AG to Moses & Rowe, Apr 2, 1918, AGC; Moses & Rowe to Harley, Sept 13, 1918, AGC; A1b, e, f, g; A2b; A4b.*

MILLER, CLAY ESPY "ESPY." Born Oct. 23, 1895, San Saba, San Saba County, Texas. Ht. 5 ft. 11 in., brown eyes, dark hair, dark complexion. Stockman, Fort Davis, Jeff Davis County, Texas. SPECIAL RANGER June 4, 1917–Dec. 1917 (attached to Co. C). In June 1917 was ranch manager for his uncle, J. W. Espy, in Fort Davis. Claimed a "physical disability" on his World War I Draft Registration. Died Mar. 12, 1960, El Paso County, Texas. FAMILY: Parents, Walter Spurgeon Miller (b. 1871, TX) and Lena Elizabeth Espy (b. 1875, TX); siblings, Rosalie (b. 1892, TX), John Keesey (b. 1902, TX), Audry (b. 1915, TX). *SR; Hudspeth to Ferguson, May 17, 1917, AGC; AG to Hudspeth, May 31, 1917, AGC; AG to Miller, May 31, 1917, AGC; Tobin to Shelton, Dec 10, 1917, AGC; A1d, e, f; A2b; A3a; B1, 2.*

MILLER, HUGH. Born Jan. 6, 1862, San Marcos, Hays County, Texas. Ht. 5 ft. 9 in., gray eyes, black hair, dark complexion, married. Sheriff, San Saba, San Saba County, Texas. SPECIAL RANGER Oct. 5, 1916–Jan. 15, 1919 (WA was reinstated Dec. 20, 1917) (attached to Co. C). Stockman and peace officer, Waco, McLennan County, Texas. RAILROAD RANGER Aug. 1, 1922–Aug. 1, 1924 (Co B). Discharged. REMARKS: San Saba County sheriff Nov. 6, 1906–Nov. 7, 1916. Was also a cowman; had also worked for the Cattle Raisers' Association of Texas. In Jan 1918 was classified as a Regular Ranger, for draft purposes. In 1930 was a sheep rancher in San Saba County. Died Feb. 28, 1944, San Saba County, Texas. FAMILY: Parents, Hugh Miller (b. 1832, MO) and Sarah Ann Mayes (b. 1837, MO); siblings, Stephen Richard (b. 1855, TX), Martha (b. 1857, TX), Mary Agnes (b. 1859, TX), Alexander (b. 1866, TX), Frances (b. 1869, TX), Daniel (b. 1871, TX), Elijah Hollin (b. 1874, TX); spouse, Emma S. Huffstutler (b. 1866, TX), married Oct. 10, 1883, Lampasas County, Texas; children, Pearl (b. 1884, TX), Zenobia (b. 1886, TX), Lula Agie (b. 1888, TX), Richard (b. 1891, TX), Annie E. (b. 1892, TX), Alice C. (b. 1894, TX). *SR; Miller to Ferguson, June 5, 1915, AGC; Flack to Ferguson, June 5, 1916, AGC; AG to Miller, June 7, 1915, AGC; AG to Flack, June 7, 1915, AGC; Wroe to Hutchings, Oct 2, 1916, AGC; AG to Miller, Oct 3, 9, 1916, AGC; Neal to Harley, Dec 18, 1917, AGC; Acting AG to GC&SF Railroad, Jan 9, 1918, AGC; 1503:454; EPMT, Aug 10, 1910; A1a, b, d, e, f, g; A2b; A4b; B1.*

MILLER, JOHN ARCH "ARCHIE." Born Mar. 29, 1894, Llano, Llano County, Texas. Ht. 6 ft. 2 in., blue eyes, light brown hair, light complexion, married; single as of Dec. 1931. Ranchman, REGULAR RANGER Nov. 25, 1918–Feb. 17, 1920 (private, Co G; reenlisted in Co. B under the new law, June 20, 1919). Resigned. Ranchman, Marathon, Brewster County, Texas. RAILROAD RANGER Aug. 16, 1922–Jan. 5, 1923 (Co A). Discharged. Ranchman, Marathon. REGULAR RANGER Mar. 31, 1923–Jan. 18, 1933 (private, Co. A; reenlisted Mar. 31, 1925; transferred to Co. B, July 1, 1925; reenlisted Mar. 31, 1927; transferred to Co. C, May 15, 1927; reenlisted Mar. 31, 1931; promoted to sergeant, Co. C, Dec. 15, 1931). Discharged. Inspector, Del Rio Wool Mohair Co., Marathon. SPECIAL RANGER Nov. 21, 1933–Nov. 20, 1934. Resigned. Peace officer, La Pryor, Zavala County, Texas. SPECIAL RANGER June 26, 1935–Oct. 1, 1935. Discharged. REMARKS: Resigned on Feb. 17, 1920, for the same reason as his captain, Charles Stevens—refused to carry out what he considered an illegal order to enforce Texas oil claims on the Oklahoma border. In Nov. 1918 an Archie Miller was constable of precinct 3, Brewster

County. FAMILY: Parents, Thomas J. Miller (b. 1857, TX) and Mary L. (b. 1862, TX); siblings, Raymond (b. 1879, TX), Katie E. (b. 1881, TX), Matthew R. (b. 1883, TX), Francis T. (b. 1886, TX), Claud (b. 1888, TX), Frederick (b. 1896, TX); spouse, Irma (b. 1896, TX), married about 1913. *SR; 471; Miller to Aldrich, Nov 17, 1919, AGC; Aldrich to Miller, Dec 12, 1919, AGC; Miller to Cope, Feb 17, 1920, AGC; Aldrich to Miller, Mar 3, 9, 1920, AGC; AA, Nov 2, Dec 19, 1918, Feb 20, June 5, 1919; 488: 58, 59; 319: 200; 843; A1d, e, f, g; A3a.*

MILLER, ROBERT MARION "BOB." Born July 3, 1878, Georgetown, Williamson County, Texas. Ht. 6 ft. 2 in., blue eyes, brown hair, light complexion, married. Deputy sheriff, Paint Rock, Concho County, Texas. REGULAR RANGER Sept. 1, 1917–Apr. 8, 1918 (private, Co. C; Dec. 1917 transferred to Co. M). Resigned Apr. 1, 1918. Honorably discharged. Peace officer, Paint Rock. SPECIAL RANGER Mar. 3, 1927–Mar. 3, 1928. Weight inspector, Texas Highway Department, Paint Rock. SPECIAL RANGER Mar. 5, 1928–Mar. 5, 1929. Peace officer, Paint Rock. SPECIAL RANGER Mar. 7, 1929–Mar. 7, 1930. Deputy sheriff, Littlefield, Lamb County, Texas. SPECIAL RANGER Jan. 24, 1933–Aug. 25, 1934. Discharged (WA was revoked). REMARKS: Concho County constable and deputy sheriff, 1903–1917; Concho County sheriff Nov. 2, 1920–Jan. 1, 1927. In Dec. 1921 was tried for murder. Died Sept. 1, 1951, McCulloch County, Texas; buried in Union Band Cemetery, San Saba County, Texas. FAMILY: Parents, Marion Luther "Lute" Miller (b. 1856, TX) and Katherine Dixie "Katie" Ellison (b. 1863, TX); siblings, John N. (b. 1880, TX), Thomas R. (b. 1884, TX), James Fred (b. 1886, TX), Vernon E. (b. 1889, TX), George W. (b. 1891, TX), Alta M. (b. 1894, TX), Michael M. (b. 1896, TX), Luther C. (b. 1898), Myrtle; spouse, Alma Myrtle Barton (b. 1879, TX), married June 20, 1897, San Saba County; children, Bernice Ethel (b. 1898, TX), Myrtle Leon (b. 1900, TX), Mattie Marion (b. 1904, TX), Estell "Stella Bob" (b. 1907, TX), Opal Lee "Dude" (b. 1910, TX), Charles Robert (b. 1915, TX). *SR; 471; Miller to Ferguson, Aug 10, 1917, AGC; Dubois to Ferguson, Aug 10, 1917, AGC; Hill to Ferguson, Aug 16, 1917, AGC; Howze to Ferguson, Aug 16, 1917, AGC; Kemp to Ferguson, Aug 16, 1917, AGC; Ransom to Harley, Oct 19, 1917, AGC; AG to Cunningham, Dec 19, 1917, AGC; Moses to Harley, Dec 19, 1917, AGC; Assistant AG to Mrs. Harrison, Mar 7, 1918, RRM; Cunningham to Harley, Mar 3, 1918, RRM; Engleking to Cunningham, Mar 16, 1918, AGC; 1503:128; A1b, e, f, g; A2b; A3a; A4b; B2.*

MILLER, WILLIAM L. "BILL." Born about 1863, Gonzales, Gonzales County, Texas. Ht. 6 ft., blue eyes, sandy hair, ruddy complexion, widower. Express guard, enlisted in Webb County, Texas. SPECIAL RANGER Mar. 30, 1918–unknown. Ranchman, Laredo, Webb County. REGULAR RANGER Oct. 14, 1918–Dec. 3, 1923 (private, Co I; reenlisted under the new law in Co. C, June 20, 1919; transferred to Co. D, Feb. 15, 1921; reenlisted, Co. D, June 20, 1921). Discharged. REMARKS: In 1910 was a stock inspector at Laredo. FAMILY: Parents, John W. Miller (b. 1828, SC) and Nancy P. (b. 1833, GA or MS); siblings, Jesusa (b. 1851, TX), Annetta (b. 1853, TX), twins Mary and Martha (b. 1855, TX), Nancy (b. 1858, TX), Thomas B. (b. 1865, TX), Samuel (b. 1868, TX), John M. (b. 1870, TX), twins Lewis E. and Lou E. (b. 1873, TX); spouse, unknown; children, Mollie (b. 1892, TX), Bulia (b. 1894, TX), Wm., Jr. (b. 1898, TX). *SR; 471; LWT, Sept 25, 1921; 469: 64; A1aa, a, b, e, f.*

MILLICAN, LEANDER RANDON. Born Aug. 27, 1853, Millican, Brazos County, Texas. Ht. 5 ft. 10 in., gray eyes, gray hair, dark complexion, married. Minister, Allamore, Hudspeth County, Texas. SPECIAL RANGER July 8, 1919–Dec. 31, 1919. REMARKS: Was enlisted by Adjutant General Harley. Had been deputy sheriff of Lampasas County in 1874. Became a Baptist minister in 1875. Was a missionary for the Texas and Southern Baptists all the rest of his life, organizing and building churches in various western counties in Texas. Died Apr. 18, 1938, El Paso County, Texas; buried at Paisano Baptist Encampment. LAW ENFORCEMENT RELATIVES: Washington County, Texas, Constable (1839), Navasota County, Republic of Texas, Sheriff (1841), and Brazos County Sheriff (1843) Elliott M. Millican, father. FAMILY: Parents, Dr. Elliott McNeil Millican (b. 1806, SC) and Marcella Elizabeth Boyce (b. 1822, KY); siblings, Elliott M. (b. 1841, TX), William H. (b. 1844, TX), Jasper (b. 1846, TX), Susan Elizabeth (b. 1848, TX), Marcella (b. 1854, TX), Marcellus Randall (b. 1856, TX), Willie Wilbur Ashby (b. 1858, TX); spouse, Georgia Katherine Saunders (b. 1855, TX), married Feb. 13, 1878 in Blanco County, Texas; children, Elliott Randon (b. 1879,

TX), Lola (b. 1881, TX), Adoniram Judson "A. J." (b. 1885, TX). *SR; 172:IV, 746; A1aa, b, d, f; A2b; A4a, b; B1.*

MILSAP, JOHN V. "BUCK." Born 1871, near Paris, Lamar County, Texas. Ht. 5 ft. 6 in., blue eyes, dark hair, fair complexion, married. Farmer and ginner, Hamlin, Jones County, Texas. SPECIAL RANGER June 4, 1917–Dec. 1917 (attached to Co. C). Farming and ginning, Hamlin. LOYALTY RANGER June 3, 1918–Feb. 1919. REMARKS: As of 1918, had been a deputy sheriff. In 1930 was a cow trader in Hamlin. Died June 14, 1933, Jones County, Texas. FAMILY: Parents, John H. Milsap (b. 1847, MS) and Rhoda G. (b. 1853, MS); siblings, Mary M. (b. 1872, TX), S. A. (b. 1874, TX), N. H. (b. 1876, TX), Thomas P. (b. 1878, TX), Jessie G. (b. 1883, TX); spouse, Annie Bell Nixon (b. 1871, TX), married June 17, 1891, Jones County; children, Aubrey Hibbs (b. 1892, TX), Arthur B. (b. 1894, TX), Sallie M. (b. 1899, TX). *SR; Dodson to Ferguson, May 18, 1917, AGC; Cunningham to Ferguson, May 18, 917, AGC; A1b, e, f, g; A2b, c.*

MIMS, ROYLE KELLY "ROY." Born Aug. 13, 1877, Marion, Perry County, Alabama. Medium height, stout build, blue eyes, brown hair, married. Banker, Laredo, Webb County, Texas. SPECIAL RANGER June 15, 1918–Jan. 15, 1919. REMARKS: President, First State Bank & Trust Co., Laredo. Died June 5, 1958, Webb County, Texas. FAMILY: Parents, William H. Mims (b. 1841, MS or GA) and Annie (b. 1858, AL); brother, Wm. Henry (b. 1880, TN); spouse, Reba B. (b. 1881, TX), married about 1903; children, Royle B. (b. 1907, TX), William H. (b. 1909, TX), Rebecca A. (b. 1915, TX), Lula M. (b. 1918, TX). *SR; A1b, d, e, f; A2b; A3a.*

MOBLEY, EDWARD M. Born Aug. 1868, Murfreesboro, Pike County, Arkansas. Ht. 5 ft. 7 ½ in., blue eyes, light brown hair, medium complexion, married. Chief special agent, Kansas City, Mexico & Orient Railroad, San Angelo, Tom Green County, Texas. SPECIAL RANGER Dec. 31, 1917–Jan. 15, 1919. REMARKS: Had lived in Texas since 1869. As of Feb. 1919, had 17 years' experience as a peace officer in San Angelo and vicinity—several years deputy sheriff; deputy U.S. marshal, Western District of Texas, 1893–1895; Howard County, Texas sheriff Nov. 8, 1906–Nov. 8, 1910; special agent, KM&O Railroad, 1911–1919. In 1930 was tax commissioner for a railroad company in San Angelo. Died July 7, 1935, Tom Green County, Texas. FAMILY: Parents, Jonathan Mobley (b. 1846, AR) and Lucy Ann Brock (b. 1847, AR); siblings, Beverly L. (b. 1873, TX), Lucy E. (b. 1876, TX), R. F. (b. 1877, TX), A. J. (b. 1879, TX), Ellen C. (b. 1882, TX), Melbourne A. (b. 1884, TX), Arthur W. (b. 1886, TX); spouse, Portia Ellis Christian (b. 1877, TX), married 1896, Lee County, Texas; sons, Guy Reuelle (b. 1900, TX), Willard (b. 1904, TX). *SR; Mobley to Rogers, Sept 27, 1910, AGC; AG to Mobley, Dec 29, 1917, AGC; 1503:269; A1a, b, e, f, g; A2b; A4a, b; B1.*

MOLESWORTH, WILLIAM M. Born Apr. 1867, County Clare, Ireland. Ht. 5 ft. 8 in., blue eyes, light hair, light complexion, married. Peace officer. REGULAR RANGER Mar. 29, 1918–May 15, 1927 (private, Co. I. Honorably discharged Feb. 1, 1919; order was rescinded, restored to duty Feb. 1919; reenlisted under the new law June 20, 1919, as a private, Co. C; reenlisted June 20, 1921 as a private, Headquarters Co.; reenlisted June 20, 1923; reenlisted June 20, 1925). Discharged. Peace officer, Austin, Travis County, Texas. SPECIAL RANGER (station—CD Ranch, Fort McKavett, Menard County, Texas) Oct. 19, 1927–July 13, 1928. Resigned. REMARKS: Immigrated to the United States in 1886; became a naturalized citizen. Enlistment form June 20, 1925, lists birthplace as County Cork, Ireland; all U.S. census records list birthplace as England. Had been a stockraiser in Uvalde County, Texas. In Mar. 1918 was a policeman in Austin. In 1930 was manager of a golf club in Austin. Died Aug. 11, 1956, Travis County, Texas. FAMILY: Parents, John Molesworth (b. 1819, England) and Mary Newall (b. 1826, England); siblings, Edward Newall H. (b. 1848, England), Frederick N. (b. 1850), Mary Frances (b. 1852), Sarah Emma (b. 1854), Harriet Eleanor (b. 1857, England), John (b. 1858, England), Margaret E. (b. 1860, England), Lawrence Teesdale (b. 1864, England), Marion P. (b. 1869, England); spouse, Emily Jane C. (b. 1867, Ireland), married about 1894; children, Kathleen (b. 1895, TX), Hilda M. (b. 1898, TX), Edward W. (b. 1902, TX), Frances E. (b. 1905, TX). *SR; 471; Molesworth to Harley, Mar 14, 1918, AGC; A1d, e, f, g, i; A2b, g; A4a, b.*

MONKHOUSE, GEORGE A. Born Oct. 1871, Lockhart, Caldwell County, Texas. Ht. 5 ft. 9 in., black eyes, black hair, dark complexion, married. Stockman, Floresville, Wilson County, Texas. LOYALTY RANGER June 13, 1918–Feb. 1919.

REMARKS: ". . . spent about 10 yrs. as deputy sheriff." In 1930 was a Ford Motor Co. salesman in Marfa, Presidio County, Texas. FAMILY: Parents, John Monkhouse (b. 1845, England) and Alice (b. 1854, KY or TX); siblings, Wm. S. (b. 1870, TX), Hettie L. (b. 1875, TX), Edmond J. (b. 1878, TX), Kate E. (b. 1880, TX); spouse, Bessie Lou (b. 1876, TX), married about 1894; children, Vera (b. 1895, TX), Velma (b. 1898, TX), Alberta (b. 1901, TX), Clark R. (b. 1904, TX), Hettie Lou (b. 1908, TX). *SR; A1b, d, e, f, g.*

MONROE, JODA or JODIE D. Born Sept. 10, 1867, Hall, Georgia. Ht. 6 ft. 1 in., blue eyes, light and slightly gray hair, fair complexion, married. Merchant, Snyder, Scurry County, Texas. LOYALTY RANGER June 1, 1918–Feb. 1919. REMARKS: In 1920 owned a grocery business in Snyder. In 1930 was a rancher in Scurry County. Died July 22, 1955, Scurry County, Texas. FAMILY: Parents, John Wesley Monroe (b. 1845, SC) and Martha Jane Martin (b. 1846, GA); siblings, Dolphus Marion (b. 1872, TX), Mina (b. 1872, TX), Charles M. (b. 1873, TX), Bertha M. (b. 1875, TX), John William (b. 1877, TX), Thomas David (b. 1878, TX), Mary Ann (b. 1880, TX), Lula Jane (b. 1883, TX), Robert B. (b. 1885, TX); spouse, Vashti McCauley (b. 1871, TX), married about 1890; children, Zada (b. 1895, TX), Dwight W. (b. 1899, TX), Thomas (b. 1905, TX). *SR; A1a, b, e, f, g; A2b; A4a, b.*

MONTGOMERY, JOHN DANIEL. Born Nov. 14, 1875, Green County, Kentucky. Ht. 5 ft. 11 in., blue eyes, brown hair, fair complexion, married. Special watchman, Waco, McLennan County, Texas. SPECIAL RANGER Aug. 1, 1918–Jan. 15, 1919. REMARKS: In Sept. 1918 was a special watchman for the Saint Louis and San Francisco Railroad Company in Waco. In 1920 was a Waco city fireman. A John D. Montgomery died June 19, 1935, McLennan County, Texas. FAMILY: Parents, William D. Montgomery (b. 1845, KY) and Synthia E. McGlasson (b. 1857, KY); siblings, Ada W. (b. 1871, KY), Henry T. (b. 1879, KY); spouse, Allie Elizabeth (b. 1873, MS), married about 1897; daughter, Cecil M. (b. 1901, TX). *SR; A1b, e, f; A2b; A3a; A4b.*

MONTGOMERY, JOHN WILLIAM. Born June 9, 1884, Bell County, Texas. Ht. 5 ft. 10 in., brown eyes, black hair, dark complexion. Brand inspector, Cattle Raisers' Association of Texas, Abilene, Taylor County, Texas. SPECIAL RANGER June 2, 1916–Jan. 15, 1919 (attached to Co. C; WA was reinstated Dec. 20, 1917). Special officer, Frisco Lines, Fort Worth, Tarrant County, Texas. RAILROAD RANGER Sept. 2, 1922–Sept. 2, 1924. Discharged. REMARKS: As of June 1916, "deputy sheriff and field inspector." In Jan. 1918 was reclassified as a REGULAR RANGER without pay, to avoid the draft. In 1930 census records is listed as a "State Ranger," living in Fort Worth. World War I Draft Registration document describes: "one arm missing right above the elbow." FAMILY: Mother, L. A. (b. 1862, VA); brother, Ira (b. 1877, TX); spouse, Nellie (b. 1893, IL), married about 1917; children, Joseph (b. 1918, TX), Virginia (b. 1920, TX). *SR; Acting AG to CG&SF Railroad, Jan 9, 1918, AGC; Acting AG to FW&DC Railroad, Jan 11, 1918, AGC; A1d, f, g; A3a.*

MONTGOMERY, MARVIN DILLARD. Born Mar. 15, 1881, Florence, Williamson County, Texas. Ht. 5 ft. 9 in., blue eyes, brown hair, fair complexion, married. Stock farmer, Happy Union, Hale County, Texas. SPECIAL RANGER Nov. 27, 1917–Feb. 1918 (Co. B Volunteers). Discharged. REMARKS: "Has resided on the plains for 27 yrs, is cool headed and will look after Randall Co. He's a stock farmer & a man of excellent reputation." Had been in the garage business in Tulia, Swisher County, Texas. In 1930 was a wholesale drug salesman in Amarillo, Potter County, Texas. Died July 21, 1945, Potter County, Texas. FAMILY: Parents, Charles Iverson Montgomery (b. 1849, AL) and M. Lovie Shofner (b. 1860, TN); siblings, Alden W. (b. 1878, TX), Sadie (b. 1887, TX), Alma (b. 1896, TX), Frank Shofner (b. 1896, TX); spouse, Mary (b. 1891, IL), married about 1912. *SR; A1b, d, e, f, g; A2b; A3a; A4b.*

MOON, REASON BURRELL. Born July 1888, Blevins, Falls County, Texas. Ht. 5 ft. 10 ½ in., brown eyes, brown hair, fair complexion, married. Salesman, Anson, Jones County, Texas. SPECIAL RANGER May 31, 1917–Dec. 1917. REMARKS: In 1920 was an automobile salesman in Wichita County, Texas. In 1930 was an auto supplies salesman in Plainview, Hale County, Texas. Died Jan. 28, 1962, Dallas County, Texas; buried in Hillcrest Cemetery, Temple, Bell County, Texas. FAMILY: Parents, William Todd Moon (b. 1851, LA) and Louisa Jane Seale (b. 1853, AL); siblings, Mary Mondelthia "Monnie" (b. 1876, TX), Aura "Arrie" (b. 1878, TX), Ella (b. 1883, TX); stepmother, Elizabeth

Minerva Farmer (b. 1850, KY); step-siblings, Blake Farmer (b. 1889, TX), Sadie Farmer (b. 1891, TX); spouse, Lena Belle Strawn (b. 1892, TX), married May 28, 1912; children, Louise A. (b. 1914, TX), Maxine E. (b. 1916, TX), Kenneth Allen (b. 1918, TX), Jack F. (b. 1920, TX), William S. (b. 1922, TX), Bobby Jean (b. 1928, TX). *SR; A1b, d, f, g; A2b, e; A4a, b.*

MOOR, EARL THEODRICK. Born Jan. 9, 1885, Orangeville, Fannin County, Texas. Ht. 5 ft. 8 ¾ in., blue eyes, light hair, light complexion, married. Clerk, Austin, Travis County, Texas. SPECIAL RANGER July 18, 1917–Dec. 1917. REMARKS: In 1920 and 1930 was an oil company salesman, living in Fort Worth, Tarrant County, Texas. Died Mar. 28, 1941. FAMILY: Parents, Austin Henry Moor (b. 1842, AL) and Eliza Jane Inzer (b. 1844, AL); siblings, Florrah Montague (b. 1872, MS), Mary Alice (b. 1875, MS), James Balch (b. 1875, MS), Pearl Hesseltine (b. 1881, MS); spouse, Dean Welborn (b. 1889, TX), married about 1910; children, Elizabeth Jane (b. 1911, TX), Francis Austin (b. 1915, TX). *SR; A1f, g; A3a; A4a, b.*

MOORE, CHARLES ROBERT. Born June 1874, Indianola, Calhoun County, Texas. Ht. 5 ft. 6 in., gray eyes, dark hair, fair complexion. REGULAR RANGER Sept. 1909–Apr. 1913 (private, Co. D; as of Feb. 1911 was private, Co A—formerly Co. D; promoted to sergeant, July 15, 1912). Resigned. REMARKS: In 1900 was an Infantry soldier. Before enlisting in the Rangers had been a railroad conductor in Mexico and had been an El Paso County deputy sheriff. May well have prevented a presidential assassination at the Oct. 16, 1909, meeting in El Paso of Presidents William Howard Taft and Profirio Díaz. Was appointed a deputy U.S. marshal for the Western District of Texas, at El Paso, Apr. 5, 1913. Was serving as such when he died on Apr. 7, 1914 in El Paso from complications after an operation. LAW ENFORCEMENT RELATIVES: Ranger F. R. Moore, brother. FAMILY: Parents, William Moore (b. 1840, ME) and Frances (b. 1845, Germany); siblings, Wm. A. (b. 1864, TX), Geo. O. (b. 1867, TX), Frank R. (b. 1868, TX), Kate L. (b. 1871, TX), Henry D. (b. 1878, TX). *SR; 471; Hughes to Hutchings, report Sept 1909–June 1911, RRM; Moore to AG, May 21, 1912, WC; Dougherty to Hughes, June 1, 2, 1912, WC; Moore to Hughes, June 2, 1912, WC; Colquitt to Hutchings, June 10, 1912, WC; Hughes to AG, Apr 8, 1912, AGC; Moore and Webster to Hutchings, Feb 27, 914, AGC; AG to the Moores, Apr 1, 1914, AGC; EPMT Apr 16,1911, Oct 9, 1912, Apr 6, 7, June 17, Dec 20, 1913, Jan 18, Apr 8, 9, 1914; EPH, Jan 25, 1912; SAE, Apr 16, Nov 5, 1911; 403: 448–449 ff; A1b, d, e.*

MOORE, FRANCIS R. "FRANK." Born July 1868, Indianola, Calhoun County, Texas. Ht. 5 ft. 10 in., dark eyes, dark hair, dark complexion, married. Passenger conductor, Victoria, Victoria County, Texas. SPECIAL RANGER June 13, 1918–Jan. 15, 1919. LAW ENFORCEMENT RELATIVES: Ranger Charles Robert Moore, brother. FAMILY: Parents, William Moore (b. 1840, ME) and Frances (b. 1845, Germany); siblings, Wm. A. (b. 1864, TX), Geo. O. (b. 1867, TX), Kate L. (b. 1871, TX), Charles R. (b. 1874, TX), Henry D. (b. 1878, TX); spouse, Lasta A. Doubek (b. 1878, AR), married about 1901; daughters, Lasta Harrington (b. 1902, TX), Kathleen M. (b. 1904, TX). *SR; A1a, b, d, e, f, g; A2b.*

MOORE, JACK. Born 1886, San Saba, San Saba County, Texas. Ht. 5 ft. 9 in., black eyes, black hair, dark complexion. Peace officer. REGULAR RANGER May 12, 1916–Nov. 31, 1916 (private, Co B). Resigned. *SR; 471.*

MOORE, JEFFERSON BEAUREGARD "JEFF." Born Dec. 15, 1861, Lake County, California. Ht. 6 ft., brown eyes, gray hair, dark complexion, married. Ranchman, Del Rio, Val Verde County, Texas. SPECIAL RANGER Dec. 8, 1917–Jan. 15, 1919 (Co. A Volunteers—station: Comstock). REMARKS: Had a livery stable in Crockett County, Texas. Crockett County sheriff Nov. 6, 1900–Nov. 6, 1906. In 1910 was a bank cashier in San Angelo, Tom Green County, Texas. In Feb. 1919 was president, Sheep and Goat Raisers' Association of Texas; lived in Del Rio. Died Jan. 19, 1937, Val Verde County, Texas; buried in Masonic Cemetery, Del Rio. FAMILY: Spouse, Earnest Theodosia Heaner (b. 1861, SC), married May 31, 1882, Seguin, Guadalupe County, Texas; children, Katie Eugenia (b. 1883, TX), Winella Ellafore (b. 1885, TX), E. Imogene (b. 1887, TX), Ernest (b. 1889, TX), Jefferson William (b. 1892, TX), Ruby (b. 1895, TX), Thomas Dewey (b. 1898, TX). *SR; Cunningham to Harley, Aug 26, 1918, AGC; 1503:136; A1d, e, f, g; A4b.*

MOORE, JOHN W. Born Sept. 1871, Kaufman County, Texas. No physical description, married. Banker, Estelline,

Hall County, Texas. LOYALTY RANGER July 10, 1918–Feb. 1919. REMARKS: Had been a hardware salesman in Hall County. Hall County sheriff Nov. 8, 1904–July 1907. In 1910 was president of a bank in Estelline. FAMILY: Spouse, Congress E. (b. 1886, TX), married about 1901; son, Samuel H. (b. 1903, TX). *SR; 1503:228; A1d, e, f.*

MOORE, JOHN WARE. Born Oct. 22, 1873, Center Point, Kerr County, Texas. Ht. 6 ft. 3 in., blue eyes, brown hair, florid complexion, married. REGULAR RANGER—served 4 years under Capt. Rogers. Brand inspector, Cattle Raisers' Association of Texas, Alpine, Brewster County, Texas. SPECIAL RANGER Jan. 9, 1918–Jan. 15, 1919. REMARKS: As of Jan. 1918, had been a brand inspector for the Cattle Raisers' Association for 12 years. According to World War I Draft Registration document, had a "stiff leg." A John Ware Moore died May 1, 1920, Kerr County, Texas. LAW ENFORCEMENT RELATIVES: Ranger James "Jim" Moore, brother; Mounted Customs Inspector (1911–1915), Hudspeth County sheriff (Aug. 25, 1917–Jan. 1, 1929), El Paso County peace officer (1930), and Ranger W. Harrison "Harry" Moore, brother. FAMILY: Parents, Andrew Simpson Moore (b. 1838, TN) and Mary Emaline Goss (b. 1850, TX); siblings, Kate (b. 1870, TX), James (b. 1875, TX), Daisy L. (b. 1879, TX), Harrison (b. 1886, TX), Jennie Ann (b. 1888, TX); spouse, Cayloma Minnie (b. 1885, TX). *SR; Sanders to Hutchings, Mar 20, 1912, CP; Moore to Harley, Jan 7, 1918, AGC; 1503:270; EPMT, July 6, 1913; AA, Oct 19, Nov 9, 1916, July 26, 1917, Jan 23, 1919; A1b, d, f; A2b; A3a; A4b.*

MOORE, RUFUS ADOLPHUS. Born Oct. 8, 1882, Tilden, McMullen County, Texas. Ht. 5 ft. 11 in., gray eyes, light hair, light complexion. Ranchman, Del Rio, Val Verde County, Texas. SPECIAL RANGER Dec. 21, 1916–Dec. 1917 (attached to Co. C). REMARKS: Val Verde county sheriff Almond requested his immediate appointment. Moore would be paid by the G. Bedell Moore Estate, which owned nearly all the Rio Grande frontage between Del Rio and Eagle Pass. Moore would be a replacement for Ranger Delbert Timberlake, who had resigned. A Rufus A. Moore died Dec. 21, 1941, Val Verde County, Texas. FAMILY: Parents, Rufus A. Moore (b. 1853, TN) and Cora M. Lowe (b. 1863, TX); sister, Fay (b. 1889, TX); spouse, Katherine. *SR; Almond to Hutchings, Dec 21, 1916, AGC; A1d; A2b; A3a; A4a, b.*

MOORE, W. HARRISON "HARRY." Born May 16, 1886, Center Point, Kerr County, Texas. Ht. 5 ft. 11 ½ in., gray eyes, black hair, dark complexion, married, as of May 1910. REGULAR RANGER 1904 (private, Co. D). Ranch hand, enlisted in Terrell County, Texas. REGULAR RANGER May 1, 1909–Feb. 28, 1910 (private, Co. D). Discharged. Ranch hand, enlisted in El Paso County, Texas. REGULAR RANGER May 3, 1910–July 5, 1911 (private, Co. D, which on Feb. 1, 1911 became Co. A). Discharged. REMARKS: Resigned in 1911 to become a mounted Customs inspector in the El Paso district, 1911–1915. Hudspeth County sheriff Aug. 25, 1917–Jan. 1, 1929. In 1930 was a county peace officer living in El Paso, El Paso County. LAW ENFORCEMENT RELATIVES: Ranger John Ware Moore, brother; Ranger James "Jim" Moore, brother. FAMILY: Parents, Andrew Simpson Moore (b. 1838, TN) and Mary Emaline Goss (b. 1850, TX); siblings, Kate (b. 1870, TX), John W. (b. 1873, TX), James (b. 1875, TX), Daisy L. (b. 1879, TX), Jennie Ann (b. 1888, TX); spouse #1 (?), married before 1910; spouse #2 (?), Alice R. (b. 1896, TX), married about 1915; sons, Lenox Ware (b. 1917, TX), Harry, Jr. (b. 1920, TX). *SR; 471; MR, Co D, May–Dec, 1910, AGC; Hughes to AG, Jan 5, 1911, RRM; Hughes to Hutchings, July 7, 1911, AGC; Hughes to Walker, July 23, 1911, AGC; MR, Co A, July, 1911, RRM; Petition to Hutchings, Aug 16, 1915, AGC; Moore to Ransom, Nov 14, 1917, AGC; Ransom to Harley, Nov 19, 1917, AGC; Vaughan to Captain, June 30, 1919, AGC; Moore to Cope, Dec 4, 1919, AGC; 1503:270; EPMT, June 20, 26, 1912, Feb 12, 1913; 1000: 116; A1d, f, g; A2e; A3a; A4b; B2.*

MOORING, CHARLES EVERETT "CHARLIE." Born Mar. 14, 1879, Shiro, Grimes County, Texas. Ht. 6 ft., blue eyes, brown hair, fair complexion, married. Farmer, Shiro. LOYALTY RANGER June 4, 1918–Feb. 1919. REMARKS: On World War I Draft Registration document, Sept. 1918, stated he was a "jitney driver, farmer, state detective," living in Shiro. In 1930 was a taxi driver in Kerville, Kerr County, Texas. FAMILY: Parents, Patrick Mooring (b. 1837, NC) and Rebecca (b. 1849, SC); siblings, Mary (b. 1869, TX), Lew S. (b. 1871, TX), Sallie (b. 1878, TX), Mabel (b. 1881, TX); spouse, Cora Lee (b. 1886, AR), married about 1912. *SR; A1d, e, f, g; A3a.*

MOORMAN, CULL C. Born Jan. 11, 1891, Comanche County, Texas. Ht. 5 ft. 10 in., brown eyes, brown hair, dark complexion, married. Oil and investments, Dallas, Dallas

County, Texas. SPECIAL RANGER July 7, 1919–Dec. 31, 1919. REMARKS: Commissioned at request of Governor Hobby. World War I Draft Registration document states has "ulcerated stomach." Had been a banker at the F&M State Bank, Ranger, Eastland County, Texas. In 1920 was a bank president in Dallas. In 1930 was an oil production operator living in Ranger. Died Apr. 28, 1964, Potter County, Texas. FAMILY: Parents, James M. Moorman (b. 1850, AL) and Mary (b. 1850, AL); siblings, Eva (b. 1879, TX), Hansen (b. 1882, TX), Otis (b. 1885, TX), Daniel (b. 1887, TX); spouse, Lila Love (b. 1891, TX), married about 1912; daughter, Mildred (b. 1920, TX). *SR; A1d, f, g; A2a, b; A3a.*

MORAN, JOHN AUGUST. Born Jan. 22, 1886, Mason, Mason County, Texas. Ht. 5 ft. 10 in., blue eyes, black hair, ruddy complexion. Peace officer. REGULAR RANGER Nov. 1, 1917–Dec. 12, 1918 (private, Co. A). Died Dec. 12, 1918, Mason, Mason County, Texas of influenza. REMARKS: Had been a pool hall proprietor in 1910 in Mason. FAMILY: Father, Martin Moran (b. 1846, MA); siblings, Elizabeth "Lizzie" (b. 1883, TX), Katherine "Katie" (b. 1888, TX), Martin Van Buren (b. 1892, TX), Annetta (b. 1893, TX), Clara (b. 1897, TX). *SR; Banks to Hutchings, June 1, 1917, AGC; Sanders to Willis, Oct 12, 1917, AGC; Sanders to Harley, Dec 13, 1918, AGC; Johnston to Moran, Dec 13, 1918, AGC; 469: 60; A1b, d, e; A2b; A3a.*

MORGAN, THOMAS I. "TOM." Born Feb. 1868, Camp Colorado, Coleman County, Texas. Ht. 6 ft. 2 in., blue eyes, light hair, light complexion, married. Peace officer, San Angelo, Tom Green County, Texas. REGULAR RANGER Dec. 21, 1917–Aug. 31, 1918 (private, Co. F; promoted to sergeant, June 1, 1918.) Discharged. REMARKS: Had lived in Brownwood, Brown County, Texas. In 1910 was a farmer in Tom Green County. In 1920 was a jailer in Alpine, Brewster County, Texas. In 1930 was a policeman in San Angelo. FAMILY: Parents, Richard C. Morgan (b. 1826, GA) and Melvina F. St. Clair (b. 1837, AR); siblings, Jefferson Davis (b. 1862, TX), John J. (b. 1863, TX), Martin W. (b. 1865, TX), Hulday (b. 1875, TX), George W. (b. 1877, TX), Hellen (b. 1880, TX); spouse, Georgia (b. 1870, TX), married about 1893; children, Cecil (b. 1893, TX), Ira (b. 1894, TX), Otis (b. 1897, TX), Sterling (b. 1899, TX), Loveta (b. 1910, TX). *SR; Bates to Harley, Nov 9, 1917, AGC; AA, Apr 11, 1918; A1a, b, d, e, f, g; B1.*

MORLEY, JOHN LIVINGSTONE. Born Jan. 2, 1892, Detroit, Wayne County, Michigan. Ht. 6 ft. 1 in., gray eyes, dark brown hair, dark complexion. Bookkeeper. REGULAR RANGER Feb. 16, 1914–sometime prior to May 13, 1914 (private, Co. C). REMARKS: Had been a salesman in Austin, Travis County, Texas. In 1920 was an accountant for a movie theater in Dallas, Dallas County, Texas. Died Feb. 23, 1962, Jim Wells County, Texas. FAMILY: Parents, Wesley John Morley (b. 1856, Canada) and Grace Downey Livingstone (b. 1866, Canada or MI); sister, Florence Dorothy (b. 1895, MI); spouse, Mary Katherine McCallum (b. 1898, TX); children, Jane Darling (b. 1926, TX), John McCallum (b. 1927, TX). *SR; 471; AG to General Manager, May 13, 1914, AGCA1d, e, f; A2b, e; A4a, b.*

MORRIS, ALEXANDER ROSCOE "ROSCOE." Born Sept. 13, 1885, Dale, Caldwell County, Texas. Ht. 5 ft. 9 in., blue eyes, light hair, light complexion. Cowboy, Sonora, Sutton County, Texas. REGULAR RANGER Mar. 22, 1921–Apr. 30, 1921 (private, Co. C). Discharged/fired. REMARKS: Note length of service. Was fired because of allegations that he was a bootlegger. In 1910 had been a guard at a state prison farm, Fort Bend County, Texas. In June, 1920, was an inspector for the Sheep and Goat Raisers' Association. Died Dec. 30, 1958, Travis County, Texas; buried in Jeffrey Cemetery, Caldwell County. FAMILY: Parents, Alexander Morris, Jr. (b. 1853, TX) and Winnie Ellen West (b. 1860, TX); siblings, L. Edward (b. 1879, TX), Margaret Frances "Maggie" (b. 1881, TX), Ida Bell (b. 1884, TX), George W. (b. 1888, TX), Docie O. (b. 1890, TX), Thomas J. (b. 1892, TX), Martin Alton (b. 1894, TX), Lester Lee (b. 1896, TX), Virgil Otis (b. 1900, TX). *SR; 471; Morris to Barton, Sept 20, 1921, AGC; A1d, e; A2b; A3a; A4b.*

MORRIS, RICHARD LEE. Born Nov. 18, 1889, Sweetwater, Nolan County, Texas. Ht. 5 ft. 11 in., brown eyes, black hair, fair complexion, married, as of Dec. 1917. Warehouseman. REGULAR RANGER Oct. 5, 1911–June 30, 1912 (private, Co. A; transferred to Co. C, Oct. 6, 1911). Discharged. Electrician. REGULAR RANGER Dec. 14, 1917–Apr. 1918 (private, Co. I). Discharged. REMARKS: In 1920 was a trucking company foreman in San Antonio, Bexar County, Texas. In 1930 was an electrical engineer for an ice plant in Houston, Harris County, Texas. LAW ENFORCEMENT RELATIVES: Constable (precinct 3, Travis County, Texas,

Oct. 1911) and Police Chief (Austin, Travis County, 1915–1918) Will J. Morris, father. FAMILY: Parents, William J. Morris (b. 1861, TX) and Carrie Grace Neville (b. 1866, TX); siblings, Mary Louise (b. 1886, TX), Carrie Maude (b. 1888, TX), McLendon (b. 1899, TX), Nevill Mallory (b. 1906, TX); spouse, Frances Monroe Sawyer (b. 1892, TX), married July 23, 1912, Austin; daughter, Sarah Lee (b. 1920, TX). *SR; 471; MR, Co. C, June, 1912; SAE, Oct 11, 1911; A1d, e, f, g; A3a; A4b.*

MORRISON, ANDREW HARRIS. Born June 24, 1889, Franklin County, Iowa. Ht. 6 ft., blue eyes, brown hair, light complexion, married. Stock farmer, Plainview, Hale County, Texas. SPECIAL RANGER Dec. 14, 1917–Mar. 1918 (Co. B Volunteers). Discharged. REMARKS: Is listed as a REGULAR RANGER. In 1930 was a cook in a café in Plainview. Died Oct. 9, 1974, Brown County, Texas. FAMILY: Parents, Horace H. Morrison (b. 1846, OH) and Rosa (b. 1853, IA); brother, Otto E. (b. 1891, IA); spouse, unknown, married before June 1917; daughter, Audry E. (b. 1916, MO). *SR; 471; Rawlings to Harley, Dec 23, 1917, AGC; A1e, g; A2a, b; A3a.*

MORRISSET, JOHN MADISON. Born Apr. 17, 1863, Waverly, Humphreys County, Tennessee. Ht. 5 ft. 11 in., blue eyes, brown-gray hair, fair complexion, married. Stock farmer, Abilene, Taylor County, Texas. SPECIAL RANGER June 4, 1917–Dec. 1917. REMARKS: Had been a farmer in Callahan County, Texas. Died Jan. 19, 1955, Shackelford County, Texas. FAMILY: Parents, John Madison Morrissett (b. 1832, TN) and Cynthia Ann Matthews (b. 1827); spouse, Annie Louetta Hancock (b. 1866, NC), married Jan. 26, 1888, Clyde, Callahan County; children, Emma Cleora (b. 1889, TX), Isabelle (b. 1891, TX), Russell Hart (b. 1894, TX), Kendrick Kuykendall (b. 1896, TX), R. W. (b. 1900, TX), J. B. (b. 1902, TX). *SR; Hutchings to Nordyke, June 18, 1917, AGC; A1d; A2b; A4b.*

MORSE, HENRY DE WITT, JR. Born June 15, 1893, Houston, Harris County, Texas. Ht. 5 ft. 8 ½ in., blue eyes, light brown hair, blond complexion. Peace officer, enlisted in Houston. REGULAR RANGER May 15, 1916–July 31, 1916 (private, Co. D). Resigned/fired. Investigator, Houston. SPECIAL RANGER Apr. 21, 1933–Apr. 26, 1934. Discharged—arrested on a criminal charge. REMARKS: Note length of service in 1916. Was evidently fired over unauthorized possession of an Army .38 revolver. Had been a sergeant in Co. A, 3rd Texas Infantry regiment. Died Sept. 2, 1952, Harris County, Texas. FAMILY: Parents, Henry D. Morse, Sr. (b. 1872, TX) and Willie E. (b. 1874, TX); brothers, Robert E. (b. 1896, TX), Lawrence A. (b. 1898, TX); spouse, Ella Mae (b. 1888, OH), married between June 1917 and Jan. 1920. *SR; 471; AG to Test, Sept 2, 1916, AGC; Test to Hutchings, Sept 4, 1916, AGC; A1d, e, f; A2b; A3a.*

MORTON, STANLEY. Born Aug. 11, 1877, Lawrenceburg, Anderson County, Kentucky. Ht. 5 ft. 11 in., gray eyes, gray hair, fair complexion. Ex-Immigration officer, Brownsville, Cameron County, Texas. REGULAR RANGER Dec. 15, 1919–May 15, 1921 (private, Co. D). Resigned. REMARKS: Had held a variety of positions in Brownsville: traffic policeman, 1915; fire marshal, street supervisor, special police officer, building inspector, city sanitary inspector, 1916; fire marshal, 1917; Immigration inspector before enlisting in the Rangers. In 1930 was a "US government patrol inspector" in San Antonio, Bexar County, Texas. In 1910 census record is listed as William S. Morton. A Stanley Morton died Oct. 8, 1965, Bexar County, Texas. FAMILY: Parents, William Morton (b. 1841, KY) and Sallie M. (b. 1845, KY); siblings, Claude S. (b. 1868, KY), Samuel B. (b. 1870, KY), Hibert (b. 1872, KY), Annie M. (b. 1873, KY), Susie (b. 1880, KY). *SR; 471; Aldrich to Morton, Jan 28, 1921, AGC; BDH, Aug 30, 1915, Feb 3, 9, May 2, June 7, July 18, Aug 3, 1916, Mar 10, 1917; 485: 187ff; A1b, d, e, g; A2b; A3a.*

MOSELEY, LEE B. Born Aug. 1881, Fairview, Wilson County, Texas. No physical description, single. Merchant, Floresville, Wilson County (enlisted in Karnes County, Texas). REGULAR RANGER Aug. 30, 1911–Oct. 31, 1911 (private, Co. B). Resigned. REMARKS: Note length of service. Had been a Wilson County deputy sheriff, at Floresville. FAMILY: Mother, Eliza Ann (b. 1830, MO or LA); sister, Agness (b. 1884, TX). *SR; Sanders to Hutchings, Aug 31, 1911, AGC; SAE, Oct 12, 13, Nov 15, 17, 27, 1911; A1d, e.*

MOSELEY, WILLIAM THOMAS "TOM." Born 1885, Tarpley, Bandera County, Texas. Ht. 6 ft. 1 in., gray eyes, brown hair, fair complexion. Brand inspector, Cattle Raisers'

Association of Texas, Kingsville, Kleberg County, Texas. SPECIAL RANGER July 23, 1915–Jan. 15, 1919 (attached to Co. C; WA was reinstated Dec. 20, 1917, Jan. 7, 1918). REMARKS: Was enlisted in 1915 by direction of the governor. In May 1916, a Tom Moseley was described as a Kleberg County deputy sheriff; in July 1916 a W.T. Moseley was described as a Customs inspector at Kingsville. Jan. 1918 enlistment form gives birthplace as Frio County, Texas. In Oct. 1920 was still a brand inspector and was transferred to Alpine, Brewster County, Texas. Kleberg County sheriff Nov. 7, 1922—resigned Aug. 1935. A W. Thomas Moseley died Feb. 2, 1940, Kleberg County, Texas. FAMILY: Spouse, Beulah Violet Stark (b. 1897, TX), married about 1920; sons, William T., Jr. (b. 1924, TX), Richard Stark (b. 1926, TX). *SR; 471; Kleberg to Hutchings, July 20, 1915, AGC; Spiller to Hutchings, May 5, 1916, AGC; Capt. Will Wright's report, Mar 7, 1918, WC; 1503:313; BDH, Aug 15, 21, Oct 8, 1914, Sept 24, 1915, May 13, July 14, Sept 16, 1916; AA, Oct 7, 1920; A1g; A2b, e.*

MOSS, EDGAR JOHNSON. Born Aug. 3, 1883, Llano County, Texas. Tall, stout, blue eyes, light hair, married. Stockman, Llano, Llano County. LOYALTY RANGER June 4, 1918–Feb. 1919. FAMILY: Parents, James Ragsdale Moss (b. 1843, TX) and Delia Johnson (b. 1857, MS); siblings, Zella (b. 1872, TX), Matthew M. (b. 1880, TX), Leola (b. 1881, TX), Lillian (b. 1882, TX), Inez (b. 1885, TX), James R. (b. 1886, TX), William B. (b. 1889, TX), Andrew J. (b. 1890, TX), Mary (b. 1892, TX), Attilla L. (b. 1894, TX), Richard Olney (b. 1896, TX); spouse, Ethel (b. 1892, TX); children, Edgar, Jr. (b. 1918, TX), Mary Lee (b. 1919, TX); Dorothy (b. 1922, TX). *SR; A1d, e, f, g; A3a; A4b.*

MOTLEY, ROBERT A. Born Apr. 1871, Motley, Rusk County, Texas. Ht. 5 ft. 9 in., blue eyes, dark hair, fair complexion, married. Druggist, banker, and farmer, Overton, Rusk County. LOYALTY RANGER June 7, 1918–Feb. 24, 1919. REMARKS: In Mar. 1919 was president, First Guaranty State Bank, Overton. Was still a bank president in Overton in 1930. A Robert Anderson Motley died June 16, 1935, Rusk County, Texas. FAMILY: Parents, Dr. J. W. Motley (b. 1837, AL) and Ann E. (b. 1845, AL); siblings, Dr. John G. (b. 1862, TX), Maud (b. 1867, TX), James W. (b. 1872, TX), Luke (b. 1874, TX), Soleta A. (b. 1876, TX), Gooch (b. 1878, TX); spouse, Ora A. (b. 1881, TX), married about 1901; daughters, Leah Hartman (b. 1902, TX), Nell L. (b. 1906, TX), Ruth A. (b. 1913, TX). *SR; A1b, d, e, f, g; A2b.*

MOYNAHAN, THOMAS PATRICK. Born Jan. 23, 1883, Taylor, Williamson County, Texas. Ht. 5 ft. 8 in., gray eyes, dark hair, fair complexion, married. Railroad conductor, enlisted in Bexar County, Texas. SPECIAL RANGER July 29, 1916–Dec. 1917. REMARKS: Had been a railroad brakeman. As of Sept. 1918 worked for the T&GN Railroad Company in San Antonio, Bexar County. In 1930 was a railroad watchman in San Antonio. Died Jan. 26, 1945, Bexar County, Texas. FAMILY: Mother, Mary (b. 1835, Ireland); sisters, Katie (b. 1873, KY), Bessie (b. 1877, KY); spouse, Elizabeth "Lizzie" Fagan (b. 1886, TX), married about 1908; children, Thomas, Jr. (b. 1909, TX), Edward M. (b. 1915, TX), Clayde Elizabeth (b. 1917, TX), Agnes Rose (b/ 1921, TX). *SR; A1d, e, f, g; A2b, e; A3a.*

MUIL, CHARLES GORDON. Born Jan. 30, 1977, Scotland. Ht. 6 ft., gray eyes, auburn hair, fair complexion, married. Lumber and hardware, San Diego, Duval County, Texas. LOYALTY RANGER Aug. 28, 1918–Feb. 24, 1919. REMARKS: "citizen of U.S. and Texas." Letterhead: "A. L. Muil & Son, Lumber, Hardware, Pipe, Casing, Fittings and Supplies, Mrs. A. L. Muil, Chas. Muil, San Diego, Tex." Immigrated to the United States in 1878; naturalized citizen in 1888. A Charles Muil died Oct. 15, 1965, Bexar County, Texas. FAMILY: Parents, Adam Muil (b. 1833, Scotland) and Lizzie P. (b. 1834, Scotland); siblings, Biscay L. (b. 1878, At Sea), Robert S. (b. 1880, TX), Alice F. (b. 1883, TX); spouse, Lillian Hoffman (b. 1886, TX). *SR; A1d, e, f; A2b; A3a.*

MUNDINE, JOHN HARMAN "BABE." Born Nov. 7, 1887, Lexington, Lee County, Texas. Ht. 5 ft. 8 in., brown eyes, brown hair, dark complexion, married. Farmer and stockman, Lexington. LOYALTY RANGER Sept 23, 1918–Feb. 1919. REMARKS: Was deputy sheriff; city marshal of Lexington. In 1930 was a stock raiser in Uvalde, Uvalde County, Texas. A John Harmon Mundine died Aug. 16, 1938, Bexar County, Texas. FAMILY: Parents, John Harmon or Patrick Mundine (b. 1861, TX) and Alice C. Holman (b. 1865, TX); siblings, Corinne (b. 1899, TX), Quintus (b. 1902, TX); spouse, Lochie (b. 1890, TN), married about 1911; daughters, Charlie Belle (b. 1912, TX), Alice Grace (b. 1916, TX), Lochie Virginia (b. 1918, TX), Johnnie Jeanne (b. 1924, TX). *SR; A1d, e, g; A2b; A3a; A4b.*

MUNN, JOHN SPENCER. Born Dec. 31, 1876, La Grange, Fayette County, Texas. Ht. 5 ft. 8 in., blue eyes, black hair, dark complexion, married. Stockman, Junction, Kimble County, Texas. SPECIAL RANGER June 18, 1917–Dec. 1917 (attached to Co. C). Stockman, Junction. RAILROAD RANGER Aug. 5, 1922–Aug. 12, 1922. Discharged. Stockman, Junction. REGULAR RANGER Aug. 18, 1922–Nov. 30, 1922 (private, Headquarters Co.). Discharged. REMARKS: Resigned in Dec. 1917 because he'd been appointed postmaster in Junction. In 1930 was city secretary in Junction. Died Nov. 4, 1955, Kimble County, Texas. FAMILY: Parents, Daniel F. Munn (b. 1843, TX) and Martha A. "Mattie" Spencer (b. 1847, MS); siblings, Walter T. (b. 1866, TX), M. Ida (b. 1869, TX), Daniel Talbert (b. 1871, TX), Henry J. (b. 1872, TX), Minnie (b. 1874, TX), R. Guy (b. 1878, TX), Kate (b. 1881, TX), Willie May (b. 1885, TX), Margaret (b. 1886, TX); spouse, Birdie Mary Turner (b. 1882, TX), married Aug. 8, 1904, Junction; children, twins Gay E. and Ray (b. 1909, TX), John Max (b. 1923, TX). *SR; Latta to Ransom, Dec 6, 1917, AGC; A1b, d, g; A2b; A3a; A4a, b.*

MURCHISON, CLAUD. Born Sept. 24, 1876, Austin, Travis County, Texas. Ht. 5 ft. 8 in., blue eyes, brown hair, fair complexion, married. Special agent (private detective), Austin and San Antonio, Bexar County, Texas. SPECIAL RANGER Aug. 30, 1916–Aug. 31, 1918 (attached to Co. C; commission renewed Dec. 1917). Commission expired—wasn't renewed in 1918 because certain charges had been raised against Murchison. REMARKS: Murchison stated in Aug. 1916 that he'd been a deputy sheriff in Wilson, Bexar, Dallas, and Harris counties, and had served as special investigator for 15 years "and at present retained on regular payroll of S.W.T. & T. Co. and Texas Company." Operated a private detective and security service. In 1920 was a special agent in Fort Worth, Tarrant County, Texas. Died July 8, 1932, Bexar County, Texas; buried in Oakwood Cemetery, Austin. FAMILY: Parents, Duncan James Murchison (b. 1842, TN) and Virginia Holman (b. 1847, TX); siblings, Frank (b. 1872, TX), Ivan (b. 1878, TX), Stella (b. 1881), Duncan J. (b. 1884); spouse #1, Louise Calder (b. 1877, TX), married June 25, 1896, Harris County; children, Eula (b. 1898, TX), John Weston (b. 1905, TX), Felda (b. 1912, TX); spouse #2, Ethel (b. 1897, TX), married as of Sept. 1918. *SR; Tallichet to Ferguson, Aug 15, 1916, AGC; Wolters to Ferguson, Aug 15, 1916, AGC; Wolters to Hutchings, Aug 15, 1916, AGC; John to Ferguson, Aug 15, 1916, AGC; Moore to Ferguson, Aug 15, 1916, AGC; Holman to Ferguson, Aug 15, 1916, AGC; AG to Wolters, Aug 19, 1916, AGC; Murchison to AG, Aug 30, 1916, AGC; AG to Murchison, Aug 31, 1916, AGC; Murchison to Hutchings, Sept 5, 1916, AGC; Murchison to Hobby, Oct 29, 1917, AGC; Governor to Murchison, Nov 3, 1917, AGC; AG to Murchison, Nov 5,1917, AGC; Murchison to Woodul, Nov 10, 1917, AGC; Woodul to Cardwell, Dec 26, 1917, AGC; Cardwell to Tobin, Aug 23, 1918, AGC; Murchison to Harley, Aug 31, 1918, AGC; A1d, e, f; A2b; A3a; A4b; B1.*

MURDOCK, WILLIAM "JACK." Born Sept. 2, 1887, San Antonio, Bexar County, Texas. Ht. 5 ft. 11 in., black eyes, black hair, dark complexion, married. Cowboy, San Antonio. REGULAR RANGER May 14, 1918–Mar. 10, 1919 (private, Co. B). Honorably discharged—reduction in force. REMARKS: Enlisted by Ranger Captain William M. Hanson, who wrote: "Lived in Mexico several years, speaks Spanish fluently, good shot, and splendid rider, broke horses for the Government for 14 months past. Does not drink, bears a good reputation, and is very energetic." In 1930 was a stockyard laborer in San Antonio. A Jack Murdock died Sept. 20, 1980, Bexar County, Texas. FAMILY: Parents, Louis Murdock (b. 1863, SC) and Mary Elizabeth (b. 1866, LA); brothers, Louis (b. 1888, TX), Edward (b. 1889, TX), Frederic (b. 1892, TX), Thomas (b. 1895, TX); spouse #1, Naomi (b. 1876, TX), married about 1909; children, William Louis (b. 1909, TX), Leona (b. 1911, TX), Raymond (b. 1914, TX); step-son, Clarence Calhoun (b. 1906, TX); spouse #2, Hazel Posey (b. 1905, TX), married about 1926; children, Rennie (b. 1927, TX), Judie Faye (b. 1932, TX); spouse #3, Maria Antonia Endrizzi; children, Jack W. (b. 1936, TX), Rose Marie (b. 1939, TX), Eddie (b. 1942, TX), John (b. 1943, TX), Helen Francis (b. 1944, TX), Edith Naomi (b. 1945, TX), Thomas Ralph (b. 1948, TX). *SR; 471; Special Orders No. 21, Mar 10, 1919, WC; A1d, e, f, g; A2b, e; A3a.*

MURPHY, JAY G. Born July 1882, Kingsville, Tennessee. Ht. 5 ft. 8 in., gray eyes, light brown hair, ruddy complexion. Lineman. REGULAR RANGER Dec. 11, 1917–Apr. 1918 (private, Co. G). Resigned. REMARKS: "7 yr 5 mo in Army excellent discharge from Army; stock experiences of 6 yr in N.M. and Texas." Was recommended by James B. Wells and Sheriff Vann of Cameron County, Texas. *SR; 471; Wells* *to Whom, Dec 11, 1917, AGC; Stevens to Harley, Dec 13, 1917, AGC; AG to Stevens, Dec 14, 1917, AGC.*

MURRAH, DANIEL "DAN." Born Aug. 1870, Bartlett, Bell County, Texas. Ht. 5 ft. 11 in., blue eyes, gray hair, dark complexion. Ranchman, Comstock, Val Verde County, Texas. SPECIAL RANGER Dec. 27, 1917–Jan. 15, 1919 (Co. A Volunteers). REMARKS: Had been a farmer in Big Valley, Mills County, Texas. Died July 22, 1930, Val Verde County, Texas. LAW ENFORCEMENT RELATIVES: Ranger Captain James B. Murrah, brother; Ranger Jake R. Murrah, brother; Ranger James E. Murrah, nephew. FAMILY: Parents, James Madison Murrah (b. 1834, TN, MS, or AL) and Malinda Abigail Powers (b. 1833, TN, MS, or AL); siblings, James B. (b. 1856, TX), Jake R. (b. 1860, TX), Esther (b. 1868, TX). *SR; A1d, e; A2b; B1.*

MURRAH, JACOB RICHARD "JAKE." Born Aug. 1860, Middletown, Goliad County, Texas. Ht. 6 ft., blue eyes, dark hair, dark complexion, married. Ranchman, Comstock, Val Verde County, Texas. SPECIAL RANGER Dec. 3, 1917–Jan. 15, 1919 (Co. A Volunteers). REMARKS: Had been a cattle dealer in Mills County, Texas. In 1930 was a rancher in Val Verde County. Died Feb. 13, 1934, Val Verde County, Texas. LAW ENFORCEMENT RELATIVES: Ranger Captain James B. Murrah, brother; Ranger Dan Murrah, brother; Ranger James E. Murrah, son. FAMILY: Parents, James Madison Murrah (b. 1834, TN, MS, or AL) and Malinda Abigail Powers (b. 1833, TN, MS, or AL); siblings, James B. (b. 1856, TX), Esther (b. 1868, TX), Dan (b. 1870, TX); spouse, Fannie Horde (b. 1865, TX), married about 1882; children, James E. (b. 1884, TX), Rufus H. (b. 1885, TX), Myrtle (b. 1889,TX), William J. (b. 1893, TX), Daniel (b. 1896, TX), Tol Landon (b. 1898, TX), Eno R. (b. 1900, TX), Malinda A. (b. 1905, TX). *SR; A1d, e, g; A2b; A4a; B1.*

MURRAH, JAMES BUCKLEY. Born Aug. 1856, Goliad County, Texas. Ht. 5 ft. 11 in., gray eyes, gray hair, fair complexion, married. Ranchman, Comstock, Val Verde County, Texas. SPECIAL RANGER Dec. 1, 1917–Jan. 15, 1919 (captain, Co. A Volunteers). REMARKS: His ranch fronted on the Rio Grande just below the mouth of the Devil's River. Had been a stock man in San Angelo, Tom Green County, Texas. In 1920 was a rancher in San Antonio, Bexar County, Texas. Died Mar. 17, 1924, Bexar County, Texas. LAW ENFORCEMENT RELATIVES: Ranger Jake R. Murrah, brother; Ranger Dan Murrah, brother, Ranger James E. Murrah, nephew. FAMILY: Parents, James Madison Murrah (b. 1834, TN, MS, or AL) and Malinda Abigail Powers (b. 1833, TN, MS, or AL); siblings, Jake R. (b. 1860, TX), Esther (b. 1868, TX), Dan (b. 1870, TX); spouse, Paulina Mills (b. 1869, CA), married Jan. 7, 1891; daughters, Pauline Hazel (b. 1894, TX), Elizabeth Belding "Bess" (b. 1900, TX). *SR; Murrah to Harley, Aug 13, 1918, AGC; A1aa, e, f; A2b; A4b; B1, 2.*

MURRAH, JAMES EDWARD. Born May 11, 1884, Brown County, Texas. Ht. 5 ft. 11 in., blue eyes, light hair, fair complexion, married. Ranchman, Comstock, Val Verde County, Texas. SPECIAL RANGER Dec. 3, 1917–Jan. 15, 1919 (Co. A Volunteers). REMARKS: In 1930 was still a rancher in Val Verde County. LAW ENFORCEMENT RELATIVES: Ranger Jake R. Murrah, father; Ranger Captain James B. Murrah, uncle; Ranger Dan Murrah, uncle. FAMILY: Parents, Jake R. Murrah (b. 1860, TX) and Fannie Horde (b. 1865, TX); siblings, Rufus H. (b. 1885, TX), Myrtle (b. 1889,TX), William J. (b. 1893, TX), Daniel (b. 1896, TX), Tol Landon (b. 1898, TX), Eno R. (b. 1900, TX), Malinda A. (b. 1905, TX); spouse, Ethel (b. 1894, TX), married about 1917; son, J. R. (b. 1927, TX). *SR; A1d, e, g; A3a; A4a.*

MURRAY, J. R. Born 1895, Burnet County, Texas. Ht. 5 ft. 10 in., gray eyes, black hair, fair complexion. Salesman, San Antonio, Bexar County, Texas. SPECIAL RANGER May 27, 1918–July 1918. Resigned because of illness. REMARKS: Left for New York to receive treatment for cardiac problems. *SR; Hanson to Harley, July 18, 1918, AGC.*

MURRELL, FESTUS EUGENE. Born Sept. 9, 1878, Mount Vernon, Franklin County, Texas. Ht. 5 ft. 11 in., blue eyes, light brown hair, light complexion, married. Salesman, Henrietta, Clay County, Texas. LOYALTY RANGER July 4, 1918–Feb. 1919. REMARKS: World War I Draft Registration document states "one finger on right hand missing." In Sept. 1918 worked for the Texas Company in Henrietta. In 1930 was an oil company representative in Amarillo, Potter County, Texas. Died Apr. 7, 1951, Tarrant County, Texas. FAMILY: Parents, William Murrell (b. 1834, AL) and Laura Musgrove (b. 1859, AL); brother, John (b. 1868, TX); spouse

#1, Mittie V. Eubanks (b. 1880, TX), married Nov. 23, 1899, Bowie County, Texas; son, Clarence (b. 1902, TX); spouse #2, Margaret Eloise (b. 1889, TX), married about 1917; children, Virginia Delight (b. 1918, TX), Jackson Campbell (b. 1920, TX). *SR; A1b, d, e, f, g; A2b, c, e; A3a.*

MUSSEY, HART, JR. Born Apr. 21, 1879, San Antonio, Bexar County, Texas. Ht. 5 ft. 10 ½ in., blue eyes, dark hair, light complexion, married. Ranch employee, Kingsville, Kleberg County, Texas. SPECIAL RANGER Apr. 30, 1918–Jan. 15, 1919; Jan. 24, 1919–Dec. 31, 1919 (commission was renewed Jan. 24, 1919). REMARKS: Was Tom East's foreman at Monte Christo, Hidalgo County, Texas. Caesar Kleberg requested that he be commissioned. Had been a vegetable broker in Starr County, Texas. In 1930 was an oil leaser living in Corpus Christi, Nueces County, Texas. Died Sept. 18, 1972, Kleberg County, Texas. FAMILY: Parents, Hart Mussey, Sr. (b. 1843, KY) and Sophronia Presnall (b. 1847, TX); sisters, Laura Presnell (b. 1875, TX), Mabel (b. 1877, TX); spouse, Marie Anais "Mayme" Rachal (b. 1879, TX), married about 1904; daughters, Rachal (b. 1904, TX), Mary Louise (b. 1906, TX), Lucy Margaret (b. 1909, TX). *SR; Acting AG to Kleberg, Jan 16, 1918, AGC; A1b, e, f, g; A2a, b; A4a, b.*

MYERS, EDWIN CLARK. Born Oct. 1, 1879, Goliad County, Texas. Ht. 5 ft. 6 ½ in., gray eyes, brown hair, blond complexion, married. Ranchman, Limpia, Jeff Davis County, Texas. SPECIAL RANGER Oct. 10, 1917–Jan. 15, 1919 (attached to Co. C). REMARKS: Served 5 months as a quarantine guard at Limpia. In Jan. 1919 lived in Schulenburg, Fayette County, Texas. In 1930 was a painter in Schulenburg. Died May 21, 1941, Schulenburg, Fayette County, Texas; buried in the St. Rose of Lima Catholic Cemetery. LAW ENFORCEMENT RELATIVES: Ranger Tom G. Myers, cousin. FAMILY: Parents, William Edwin Myers (b. 1846, MS) and Minnie Willie Clark (b. 1857, TX); siblings, twins Bayard McLary and Byron (b. 1884, TX), Clarence Bing (b. 1888, TX), Marguerite Ima (b. 1894, TX); spouse, Adele Mary Richter (b. 1885, TX), married Nov. 12, 1912; children, William Clark (b. 1914, TX), Harvey Sommerfield (b. 1916, TX), Ima Felton (b. 1917, TX), Mary Adele (b. 1921, TX), Helen Grace (b. 1923, TX), Julia Irene (b. 1925, TX), Fredrick Bayard (b. 1928, TX). *SR; AG to Myers, Oct 5, 1917, AGC; A1b, f, g; A2b; A3a; A4a, b; B1, 2.*

MYERS, GRAHAM WILSON. Born Oct. 1885, Hampton, Hamilton County, Texas. Ht. 5 ft. 9 ½ in., blue eyes, light hair, light complexion, married. Farmer, Clyde, Callahan County, Texas. SPECIAL RANGER June 7, 1917–Dec. 1917 (attached to Co. C). REMARKS: Died in 1918. FAMILY: Parents, John W. Myers (b. 1845, MS) and Ada A (b. 1856, MS); siblings, Georgie (b. 1876, TX), Mary (b. 1880, TX), Asmith (b. 1882, TX), Zelika (b. 1887, TX), Kirby (b. 1889, TX), Annie (b. 1892, TX), Separa (b. 1885, TX); spouse, Elgie Maud Scott (b. 1893, TX); daughter, Lady Syble (b. 1917, TX). *SR; Hutchings to Nordyke, June 18, 1917, AGC; A1b, d, f, g; A4b; B1.*

MYERS, THOMAS GREEN "TOM." Born May 23, 1882, Beeville, Bee County, Texas. Ht. 5 ft. 11 in., blue eyes, dark brown hair, fair complexion. Peace officer, enlisted in Presidio County, Texas. REGULAR RANGER May 15, 1916–unknown (private, Co. B). Resigned. REMARKS: Resigned sometime prior to June 8, 1918, when Co. B was disbanded. As of Sept. 1918 was a "vulcanizer" living in Marfa, Presidio County. In 1920 was a government construction crew foreman in Marfa. Died Apr. 22, 1933. LAW ENFORCEMENT RELATIVES: Ranger Edwin C. Myers, cousin. FAMILY: Parents, Green Benjamin Myers (b. 1841, MS) and Mary Rebecca "Mollie" McKinney (b. 1845, MS); siblings, Ora Lee (b. 1867, TX), James William (b. 1869, TX), Nancy Rejane (b. 1870, TX), Moses McKinney "Mack" (b. 1873, TX), Harriet Elizabeth (b. 1876, TX), Mary Elizabeth (b. 1878, TX), Birdie Pearl (b. 1885, TX); spouse #1, Augusta R. "Gussie" Black (b. 1888, TX), married Apr. 1918; spouse #2, Anita Young (b. 1895, TX), married 1931. *SR; MR, Co. B, July 31, 1917, AGC; 1000: iii, 129; A1d, f; A3a; A4a, b; B1, 2.*

MYNATT, JEFF D. Born Aug. 1857, Anderson County, Texas. Ht. 5 ft. 10 in., gray eyes, dark gray hair, fair complexion. Peace officer. REGULAR RANGER Dec. 29, 1917–May 1, 1918 (private, Co. F). Resigned. Peace officer, Tyler, Smith County, Texas. SPECIAL RANGER Sept. 12, 1918–Jan. 15, 1919. REMARKS: Was commissioned in Sept. 1918 at request of the Chief Special Agent, I&GN Railroad, Houston, Harris County, Texas. As of Dec. 1917, Mynatt stated that he'd been first deputy sheriff, Wichita County, 1883–1886, deputy U.S. marshal, Northern District of Texas and Eastern District of Texas for several years, sheriff of Woodward County, OK, for 2 years, special agent, I&GN

Railroad, 2 years. FAMILY: Parents, R. M. Mynatt (b. 1815, TN) and Elizabeth (b. 1816, TN); siblings, Perk (b. 1842, AL), E. F. (b. 1847, AL), O. (b. 1850, AL), Campbell (b. 1854, AL), twin brother J. C. (b. 1857, TX); spouse, Ella Clounch (b. 1860, TX), married about 1879; sons, Rufus Foster (b. 1879, TX), Don W. H. (b. 1885, TX). *SR; Mynatt to AG, Dec 27, 197, AGC; Williamson to Harley, Sept 3, 1918, AGC; A1aa, a, b, d; A2f.*

MYRES, SAMUEL DALE. Born Nov. 22, 1871, Cleburne, Johnson County, Texas. Ht. 5 ft. 8 in., brown eyes, brown hair, fair complexion. Saddlery manufacturer, Sweetwater, Nolan County, Texas. LOYALTY RANGER, June 6, 1918–Feb. 1919. REMARKS: Ex-mayor of Sweetwater; several times deputy sheriff. In 1930 was a leather merchant in El Paso, El Paso County, Texas. Died July 2, 1953, El Paso County, Texas; buried in Evergreen Cemetery, El Paso. FAMILY: Parents, David Rittenhouse Myres (b. 1839, PA) and Mary Jane Dale (b. 1849, KY); siblings, Morris Carlos (b. 1875, TX), Fannie Rice (b. 1878, TX), Annie Earl, William Ewing (b. 1883, TX), Charles Clifton (b. 1888, TX); spouse #1, Drusa Ann Rogers (b. 1871, TN), married Oct. 14, 1894; children, Samuel D, Jr. (b. 1899, TX), Willie L. (b. 1903, TX), Melrose (b. 1906, TX); spouse #2, Evangeline Forkner (b. 1901, MO). *SR; 172:IV, 918; A1b, d, e, f, g; A2b; A4b; B1.*

MYZELL, E. R. Born 1876, Dresden, Weakley County, Tennessee. Ht. 5 ft. 10 ½ in., brown eyes, black hair, dark complexion. Peace officer, Texarkana, Bowie County, Texas. SPECIAL RANGER Jan. 21, 1918–May 1918. Resigned. REMARKS: Was a watchman for the SLSW Railroad at Texarkana. Had apparently been one for 5 years. His superior requested that he be commissioned. In 1900 an Emmett Myzell (born Dec. 1875, TN) was a saw-mill laborer in Little River, Little River County, Arkansas. *SR; Campbell to Harley, Jan 30, 1918, AGC; A1d.*

NABERS, SIDNEY ALONZO. Born June 18, 1884, Pleasant Ridge, Union County, Mississippi. Medium height, medium build, brown eyes, brown hair. Ranchman. REGULAR RANGER Apr. 18, 1918–Aug. 31, 1918 (private, Co. N—Hudspeth Scouts). Discharged—Company N was disbanded. REMARKS: In Sept. 1918 was a ranchman in Sierra Blanca, Hudspeth County, Texas. In 1930 was a switchman in the railroad yards in El Paso County, Texas. FAMILY: Mother and stepfather, Iglarena (b. 1865, AL) and Andrew Byrd (b. 1872, AL); siblings, Cora (b. 1889, MS), Alice (b. 1890, MS); spouse, May (b. 1879, OH), married about 1929. *SR; 471; A1d, g; A3a.*

NALLS, JAMES BERRY "BERRY." Born 1868, Columbia County, Arkansas. Ht. 5 ft. 10 in., dark eyes, dark hair, dark complexion. Peace officer. REGULAR RANGER Sept. 1, 1917–Jan. 10, 1919 (private, Co. C). Discharged/fired. REMARKS: He and Ranger John Bloxom, Jr. were fired and convicted of murder. Nalls was sentenced to 3 years in prison. Before enlisting in the Rangers, Nalls had been a constable and deputy sheriff in San Saba, San Saba County, Texas for 10 years. In 1910 was a jail "keeper" in San Saba. In 1920 was San Saba deputy sheriff. FAMILY: Parents, Bartlett Nalls (b. 1837, AR) and Mary Ann Elizabeth Rowsey (b. 1841, AR); siblings, John H. (b. 1860, AR), Mary (b. 1863, AR), Robert B. (b. 1866, AR), Thomas Oscar (b. 1869, AR), Stella (b. 1872, AR), Sallie (b. 1874, TX), Dicey (b. 1876, TX); spouse, Lou (b. 1873, TX), married about 1890; children, Noel Alvis (b. 1893, TX), Lena (b. 1896, TX), George (b. 1904, TX). *SR; 471; Beasley to Ferguson, Aug 18, 1917, AGC; Moore to Ferguson, Aug 9, 197, AGC; Special Orders No. 1, Jan 9, 1919, AGC; LWT, Feb 2, 1919; A1a, b, e, f, g; A3a; A4b.*

NEIL, CHARLES EDGAR. Born Nov. 1, 1880, Henderson, Rusk County, Texas. Ht. 6 ft., gray eyes, dark hair. Farmer, Floydada, Floyd County, Texas. LOYALTY RANGER June 15, 1918–Feb. 1919. REMARKS: Had been a hardware merchant in Hill County, Texas. Died Dec. 6, 1953, Potter County, Texas. FAMILY: Parents, James P. Neil (b. 1843, TN) and Catherine L. (b. 1846, SC); brother, Robert W. (b. 1878, TX); spouse, Ottie (b. 1883, TX), married about 1902; children, Eveline (b. 1904, TX), Charles E., Jr. (b. 1919, TX). *SR; A1d, e, f, g; A2b; A3a.*

NEILL, SAMUEL H. "SAM." Born Sept. 1856, Lockhart, Caldwell County, Texas. Ht. 5 ft. 10 in., blue eyes, black hair, light complexion, married. Peace officer. REGULAR RANGER Mar. 1, 1918–Apr. 15, 1920 (private, Co. B; transferred to Co. D when Co. B was disbanded on June 8, 1918; reenlisted in Co. A under the new law, June 20, 1919). Discharged—because of his age. REMARKS: Moved to the border in 1873. Served as a mounted Customs inspector for almost four years. On Dec. 25, 1917 was one of the defenders of the Brite Ranch during a raid by Mexicans. REMARKS: Had been a mail carrier in Carrizo Springs, Dimmit County, Texas, and a carpenter in El Paso, El Paso County, Texas. Died Sept. 27, 1923, Presidio County, Texas.

LAW ENFORCEMENT RELATIVES: Ranger T. T. "Van" Neill, son. FAMILY: Parents, George C. Neill (b. 1821, TN) and Nancy (b. 1826, TX); siblings, Josephina (b. 1850, TX), Agnes (b. 1852, TX), George (b. 1854, TX); stepmother, Elizabeth (b. 1841, IA); siblings, Barclay (b. 1862, TX), Menta D. (b. 1867, TX), Dicy (b. 1868, TX); step-sister, Mattie Cole (b. 1858, TX); spouse #1, Mary E. (b. 1863, TX); son, Trevaniel T. (b. 1878, TX); spouse #2, Sarah Jane (b. 1864, TX), married about 1896; daughter, Lovey (b. 1899, TX). *SR; 471; Fox to Harley, Feb 2, 918, AGC; Finley et al. to Harley, Feb 22, 1918, AGC; Fox to Woodul, Mar 2, 1918, AGC; General Orders No. 5, June 4, 1918, AGC; 1: I, 1540–1552; EPMT, Aug 8, 1915, Jan 4, 1916; 422: 85–87; 470: 85–88; A1aa, a, b, d, e, f; A2b.*

NEILL, TREVANIEL TUL "VAN." Born Oct. 7, 1878, Carrizo Springs, Dimmit County, Texas. Ht. 5 ft. 11 in., gray eyes, black hair, dark complexion, married. Foreman, Brite Ranch, Presidio County, Texas. SPECIAL RANGER Aug. 12, 1918–Jan. 15, 1919. REMARKS: Was one of the defenders of the Brite Ranch during raid by Mexicans on Dec. 25, 1917. REMARKS: Had been a silver mine laborer in Shafter, Presidio County. In 1930 had a cattle ranch in El Paso, El Paso County, Texas. Died July 13, 1950, El Paso County, Texas. LAW ENFORCEMENT RELATIVES: Ranger Sam H. Neill, father. FAMILY: Parents, Samuel H. Neill (b. 1856, TX) and Mary E. (b. 1863, TX); stepmother, Sarah Jane (b. 1864, TX); sister, Lovey (b. 1899, TX); spouse, Delia A. "Addie" Smith (b. 1883, TX), married about 1905; children, Travaniel T., Jr. (b. 1907, TX), Mary Elizabeth (b. 1908, TX), Alma A. (b. 1912, TX). *SR; 470: 87; A1b, d, e, f, g; A2b; A3a.*

NELSON, FLOYD SILAS. Born Mar. 31, 1889, Collin County, Texas. Ht. 6 ft., gray eyes, light hair, fair complexion. Department manager, Dallas, Dallas County, Texas. SPECIAL RANGER Aug. 30, 1918–Jan. 15, 1919. REMARKS: Jan. 1919 was Exalted Ruler of Austin Lodge 201, Benevolent and Protective Order of Elks. Had been a salesman in a dry goods store in McKinney, Collin County. In 1930 was vice president of an investment company in Dallas, lived in University Park, Dallas County. FAMILY: Parents, J. S. Nelson (b. 1865, TX) and Tikie (b. 1861, TX); sister, May (b. 1893, TX); spouse, Ruth Finch (b. 1895, TX), married about 1927; daughter, May Ruth (b. 1928, TX). *SR; A1e; A2e; A3a.*

NESBITT, JAMES WILLIAM "WILLIE." Born Feb. 6, 1876, Collin County, Texas. Medium height, medium build, gray eyes, light hair, married. Farmer, Scotland, Archer County, Texas. LOYALTY RANGER Jun. 1, 1918–Feb. 1919. REMARKS: In 1930 was a farmer in Lubbock County, Texas. Died May 11, 1940, Tom Green County, Texas. FAMILY: Parents, George William Nesbitt (b. 1846, LA) and Agnes Louise "Lizzie" (b. 1857, IN or OH); brothers, John T. (b. 1873, TX), George S. (b. 1879, TX), Frank P. (b. 1887, TX); spouse, Lillie Belle Flannigan (b. 1879, TX), married Jan. 7, 1897, Saint Paul's Church; children, Eva (b. 1898, TX), Bernard (b. 1900, TX), Julian (b. 1902, TX), Cleder (b. 1904, TX), Paul Morton (b. 1907, TX), Olive (b. 1909, TX), Vincent N. (b. 1913, TX), Dorothy (b. 1915, TX), Floyd P. (b. 1918, TX), Gladys E. (b. 1922, TX), J. Glen (b. 1924, TX). *SR; A1b, e, g; A2b; A3a; A4a; B1.*

NEUMANN, PAUL. Born Dec. 19, 1884, Haw Creek, Fayette County, Texas. Ht. 6 ft. 1 in., blue-gray eyes, dark hair, fair complexion, married. Merchant, Woodsboro, Refugio County, Texas. LOYALTY RANGER July 13, 1918–Feb. 1919. REMARKS: Died Jan. 8, 1944, Refugio County, Texas. FAMILY: Parents, Otto Neumann (b. 1853, Germany) and Wilhelmina Caroline Werbach (b. 1850, At Sea); brothers, Herman Emil (b. 1876), Marvin Alfred (b. 1880); spouse, Hilda (b. 1897, TX), married about 1915; daughters, Gladys A. (b. 1916, TX), Lucile (b. 1918, TX), Geraldine (b. 1920, TX). *SR; A1d, e, f, g; A2b; A3a; A4b.*

NEVILL, FRANK. Born June 15, 1880, Austin, Travis County, Texas. Medium height, medium build, blue eyes, light hair, married. Stockman, Angleton, Brazoria County, Texas. LOYALTY RANGER June 4, 1918–Feb. 1919. LAW ENFORCEMENT RELATIVES: Ranger (1874–1882) and Presidio County, Texas sheriff (Nov. 7, 1882–Nov. 6, 1888) Charles Lilburn Nevill, half-brother. REMARKS: In 1930 was deputy sheriff in Humble, Harris County, Texas. Died July 6, 1975, Harris County, Texas. FAMILY: Parents, Zachariah Lewis Nevill (b. 1833, VA) and Sarah Temperance Townsend (b. 1841, TX); siblings, James Kendall (b. 1865, AK or TX), Carrie Grace (b. 1866, TX), Edwin Watts (b. 1869, TX), Zachariah Lee (b. 1872, TX), John B. (b. 1874, TX), Harvey P. (b. 1876, TX); spouse, Viola Bruner (b. 1886, TX), married Dec. 17, 1901, Angleton; children, Ivan Bruner (b. 1903, TX), John Lewis (b. 1905, TX),

Carrie Delores (b. 1907, TX), Frank Paul (b. 1910, TX). *SR; 1503:424; 1509:381–383; A1e, f, g; A2a, b; A3a; A4b; B1.*

NEWBERRY, GEORGE WASHINGTON (1). Born May 8, 1888, Eureka Springs, Carroll County, Arkansas. Ht. 5 ft. 11 ½ in., light brown eyes, dark hair, dark complexion. Cowboy, Del Rio, Val Verde County, Texas. SPECIAL RANGER May 30, 1916–Oct. 10, 1916 (attached to Co. C but was recruited by and commanded by Sheriff John W. Almond of Val Verde County). Resigned. REMARKS: Had been deputy city marshal and constable, Texas City, Galveston County, Texas. After leaving the Rangers was a non-commissioned officer in the U.S. Cavalry during World War I; saw active combat in Europe. Died Dec. 3, 1959, California; buried in Fort Rosecrans National Cemetery, California. FAMILY: Parents, William Jasper Newberry (b. 1844, AR) and Esther M. Pittman (b. 1845, KY); siblings, Rosey D. (b. 1882, AR), Sterling P. (b. 1885, AR); may have been married to Amy Hartfield (b. England); may have had two daughters. *SR; Almond to Hutchings, May 31, 1916, AGC; AG to Almond, June 2, 29, 196, AGC; A1d; A3b, c; A4a, b.*

NEWBERRY, GEORGE WASHINGTON (2). Born Apr. 4, 1881, Lagarto, Live Oak County, Texas. Ht. 5 ft. 7 in., dark eyes, dark complexion, married. Merchant, Barnhart, Irion County, Texas. LOYALTY RANGER June 8, 1918–Feb. 24, 1919. REMARKS: Had been a hardware merchant in Nueces County, Texas. As of Sept. 1918 was a merchant for the L. B. Cox Company in Barnhart. In 1930 was a grain merchant in San Angelo, Tom Green County, Texas. A George W. Newberry died Dec. 13, 1930, Tom Green County, Texas. LAW ENFORCEMENT RELATIVES: Ranger James H. Newberry, cousin. FAMILY: Parents, George W. Newberry (b. 1852, AL) and Mollie (b. 1857, VA); siblings, Cyrus (b. 1877, TX), Ila (b. 1880, TX); spouse, Meriam (b. 1888, TX), married about 1905; sons, Clyde (b. 1907, TX), Harrell (b. 1912, TX), Winston (b. 1915, TX). *SR; A1b, e, f, g; A2b; A3a; A4a.*

NEWBERRY, JAMES HENRY. Born Jan. 28, 1868, Live Oak County, Texas. Ht. 5 ft. 9 in., gray eyes, black hair, dark complexion, married. Claims agent, SA&AP Railroad, San Antonio, Bexar County, Texas. SPECIAL RANGER June 1, 1917–Jan. 15, 1919 (attached to Co. C; WA was reinstated Dec. 22, 1917). REMARKS: In Jan. 1919 was vice president and general manager, Fredericksburg & Northern Railroad Co., Fredericksburg, Gillespie County, Texas; in 1920 held same position, lived in San Antonio. Had also lived in Yoakum, Lavaca County, Texas. Died Nov. 20, 1959, Bexar County, Texas. LAW ENFORCEMENT RELATIVES: Ranger George W. Newberry (2), cousin. FAMILY: Parents, Henry Bascomb Newberry (b. 1838, GA) and Sarah Frances Boatright (b. 1840, GA); siblings, Susan Elizabeth (b. 1857, AL), Joseph J. (b. 1861, TX), Saluda Mayo (b. 1864, TX), Ella Beulah (b. 1870, TX), Mary Arvillia (b. 1873, TX), Robert Walter (b. 1875, TX), Albert Sidney (b. 1880, TX); spouse, Elizabeth "Lizzie" (b. 1870, TX), married about 1889; sons, Harvey B. (b. 1890, TX), S. Henry (b. 1895, TX), Presnall (b. 1905, TX). *SR; Chamberlain to Hutchings, May 31, June 2, 1917, AGC; Earnest to Harley, Dec 21, 1917, AGC; AG to Earnest, Dec 22, 1917, AGC; A1aa, b, e, f, g; A2b; A4a; B1.*

NEWMAN, JOHN McGEE "MAX" OR "MACK." Born Mar. 27, 1886, Ennis, Ellis County, Texas. Ht. 6 ft., brown eyes, dark hair, red complexion. Laborer and city marshal, Menard, Menard County, Texas. REGULAR RANGER Sept. 26, 1917–June 8, 1918 (private, Co. B). Discharged/fired. REMARKS: Was one of five Co. B Rangers fired for participating in the Porvenir massacre. In May 1917 was city marshal of Menard. Served in Army in World War I. In July 1919 lived in Douglas, Cochise County, Arizona. Was a smelter employee for the Phelps Dodge Corporation in Douglas. In 1930 was a city police officer in Menard. Died Dec. 23, 1948, Menard County, Texas. FAMILY: Parents, Seberon M. Newman (b. 1849, AL) and Malinda (b. 1848, AL); spouse, unknown, married about 1908, divorced by 1920; daughter, Iris (b. 1911, TX). *SR; 471; General Orders No. 5, June 4, 1918, AGC; Newman to Ferguson, May 17, 1917, AGC; Newman to Harley, July 11, 1919, AGC; Aldrich to Newman, Aug 6, 1919, AGC; A1f, g; A2b; A3a.*

NEWMAN, THOMAS BLACKLEY "TOM." Born Apr. 21, 1890, El Paso, El Paso County, Texas. Ht. 5 ft. 10 ½ in., blue eyes, light hair, light complexion, married. Builder, El Paso. SPECIAL RANGER July 16, 1917–Dec. 1917 (attached to Co. C). REMARKS: Owned Newman Investment Co., El Paso. Died Sept. 1, 1965, El Paso County, Texas. FAMILY: Spouse, Hannah Hill (b. 1894, WV), married about 1915; sons, Tom B., Jr. (b. 1918, TX), Charles H. (b. 1927, TX), William Campbell (b. 1929, TX). *SR; AG to Newman, July 13, 1917, AGC; A1f, g;A2a, b; A3a.*

NEWSOM, JAMES GARRETT. Born Jan. 17, 1880, Eagle Lake, Colorado County, Texas. Ht 5 ft. 10 in., blue eyes, light hair, light complexion. [Locomotive ?] Fireman, enlisted in Colorado County. REGULAR RANGER May 10, 1916–Sept. 15, 1916 (private, Co. A). Resigned. REMARKS: Was evidently fired for drinking. In Sept. 1918 was a night watchman for the Gunter Hotel in San Antonio, Bexar County, Texas. Was a hotel timekeeper in San Antonio in 1930. FAMILY: Parents, Eaton Pugh Newsom (b. 1841, TN) and Anna Smithson (b. 1855, TX); siblings, Musa (b. 1874, TX), Mary (b. 1875, TX), Earnest (b. 1878, TX), Bessie (b. 1882, TX), Donavant (b. 1884, TX), Thomas (b. 1887, TX), John (b. 1892, TX); spouse #1, Mary Thatcher (b. 1889, TX), married about 1907; spouse #2, Mattie E. Lewis (b. 1894, TX), married about 1917; son, John B. (b. 1918, TX). *SR; Williamson to Hutchings, Sept 21, 1916; Williamson to State Comptroller, Sept 21, 1916, AGC; A1b, d, e, g; A3a; A4a.*

NEWTON, THOMAS MEYERS. Born May 29, 1858, Medina County, Texas. No physical description, married. Ranchman, Alpine, Brewster County, Texas. SPECIAL RANGER Feb. 7, 1918–Jan. 15, 1919. REMARKS: Was a Texas quarantine guard at Terlingua, Brewster County. His superior requested that he be commissioned. In 1920 was manager of a quicksilver mine in Alpine. Died Feb. 4, 1924, San Antonio, Bexar County, Texas. FAMILY: Parents, William Carroll Newton (b. 1822, AL) and Amanda Melvina Fitzalan Earnest (b. 1824, AL); siblings, Elisa (b. 1843, MS), Elizabeth (b. 1845, MS), Julia (b. 1847, MS), twins Joice and William (b. 1849, MS), Clara (b. 1852, MS), Mary (b. 1854, MS), James (b. 1855, TX), John (b. 1859, TX); spouse, Ida M. Casey (b. 1864, TN), married Nov. 1, 1893, San Antonio; children, Bessie (b. 1894, TX), Louis Oge (b. 1896, TX), Mabel (b. 1898, TX). *SR; Collins to Harley, Feb 1, 1918, AGC; A1aa, d, e, f; A2b; A4a, b.*

NEWTON, WILLIAM ROWLAND. Born Sept. 1, 1873, Harrison, Boone County, Arkansas. Ht. 5 ft. 10 in., dark eyes, black hair, brunette complexion, married. Physician and surgeon, Cameron, Milam County, Texas. SPECIAL RANGER Feb. 20, 1918–Jan. 15, 1919. REMARKS: Jan. 1919 letterhead: "Cameron Hospital, Dr. W. R. Newton, Dr. E. Richard, Cameron, Texas." In 1930 still a surgeon in the hospital in Cameron. Died May 21, 1938, Milam County, Texas. FAMILY: Parents, George Washington Newton (b. 1835, AR) and Nancy Ann Eliza Brown (b. 1846, AR); siblings, Jefferson David (b. 1867, AR), Dixie E. (b. 1868, AR), John H. (b. 1870, AR), Mary E. J. (b. 1875, AR), George W. (b. 1878, AR), Martha E. (b. 1879, AR), Laura Hester (b. 1880, AR), Ann Jennie (b. 1881, AR), Minnie E. (b. 1883, AR); spouse #1, Martha Ella Whiteside, married about 1896; spouse #2, Matilda Julia Mondrik (b. 1886, TX), married May 17, 1906, Milam County; children, William Joseph (b. 1909, TX), George W. (b. 1914, TX), Mary (b. 1915, TX), Frank M. (b. 1917, TX), Nannie C. (b. 1918, TX), Josephine (b. 1920, TX). *SR; A1b, e, f, g; A2b; A3a; A4a, b; B1, 2.*

NICHOLS, DWIGHT MOODY. Born Mar. 9, 1885, Karnes County, Texas. Medium height, medium build, light blue eyes, brown hair, married. Stockman and farmer, Kenedy, Karnes County. LOYALTY RANGER June 7, 1918–Feb. 1919. REMARKS: Died Sept. 4, 1966, Karnes County, Texas; buried in Kenedy City Cemetery. FAMILY: Parents, Andrew Monroe Nichols (b. 1859, TX) and Helen Adeline Butler (b. 1860, TX); siblings, Bruce James (b. 1877, TX), Sykes P. (b. 1890, TX), Ethel A. (b. 1893, TX); spouse, Pauline K. Conrad (b. 1893, TX), married Feb. 20, 1912, DeWitt County, Texas; children, Gladys (b. 1914, TX), D. M., Jr. (b. 1916, TX). *SR; A1d, e, f; A2a, b; A3a; A4a; B1, 2.*

NICHOLS, EVERETT EARL. Born Jan. 6, 1889, Kerr County, Texas. Ht. 5 ft. 11 in., brown eyes, dark brown hair, dark complexion. Farmer. REGULAR RANGER Oct. 20, 1911–Jan. 31, 1912 (private, Co. A). Discharged—reduction in force. REMARKS: In 1930 was a farmer in Kerr County. Died Mar. 18, 1944, Kerr County, Texas; buried in Nichols Cemetery, Kerr County. FAMILY: Parents, John Frederick Nichols (b. 1866, TN) and Ruth Ingram (b. 1871, CA); siblings, Emmet Harvey (b. 1890, TX), Wesley Frederick (b. 1892, TX), John Rufus (b. 1895, TX), Nettie Alice (b. 1897, TX), William Allen (b. 1899, TX), Mary Blanche (b. 1900, TX), Melissa R. (b. 1905, TX), Lucy E. (b. 1909, TX); spouse #1, Margaret Lowrance, married Dec. 15, 1915, Kerr County; spouse #2, Eula Bertha Holliman (b. 1896, TX), married about 1918; children, Elizabeth (b. 1919, TX), Turner W. (b. 1920, TX), Alice Nell (b. 1923, TX), Evelyn (b. 1926, TX), Viola (b. 1927, TX), Everett, Jr. (b. 1929, TX), Bertha May (b. 1931, TX), Rebekah Ann (b. 1936, TX), Emma Chloe (b. 1938, TX), Beverlay A. (b. 1941, TX). *SR; 471; MR, Co. A, Jan, 1912, AGC; A1d, e, g; A2b; A3a; A4a, b; B1, 2.*

NICHOLS, MILFORD WILSON. Born Mar. 6, 1876, Hye, Blanco County, Texas. Ht. 5 ft. 9 in., blue eyes, light brown hair, light complexion, married. Stock farmer, Loyal Valley, Mason County, Texas. LOYALTY RANGER July 17, 1918–Feb. 1919. REMARKS: "a farmer all his life." Died Feb. 3, 1963, Kerr County, Texas. FAMILY: Mother, Caroline (b. 1852, TX); siblings, Pleasanton N. (b. 1874, TX), George H. (b. 1878, TX), Maria A. (b. 1882, TX), Maude E. (b. 1888, TX), Eulah M. (b. 1893, TX); spouse, Rosa J. (b. 1888, TX); children, Eva E. (b. 1918, TX), Milford W., Jr. (b. 1919, TX). *SR; A1d, e, f; A2b; A3a.*

NICHOLS, ROY CARLISLE. Born Feb. 29, 1876, Richmond, Fort Bend County, Texas. Ht. 5 ft. 9 ½ in., brown eyes, dark brown hair, dark complexion, married. Peace officer, Rio Hondo, Cameron County, Texas. REGULAR RANGER Feb. 15, 1921–Mar. 31, 1927 (captain, Headquarters Co.; transferred to Co. C, Jan. 1, 1922; reenlisted Feb. 15, 1923; reenlisted Feb. 15, 1925). Resigned. Peace officer, Marshall, Harrison County, Texas. SPECIAL RANGER Jan. 22, 1930–Jan. 1, 1931. Discharged. REMARKS: As of Dec. 1919, had been a peace officer continuously for the last 15 years. In Sept. 1918 had been a state prison guard in Brazoria County, Texas. In 1930 was deputy sheriff in Marshall. Died Sept. 25, 1947, Fort Bend County, Texas. FAMILY: Spouse, Nellie (b. 1893, TX), married about 1911; children, Roy (b. 1914, TX), Emma Aldridge (b. 1924, TX). *SR; 471; Nichols to Cope, Dec 5, 1919, AGC; 470: 43; A1g; A2b, e; A3a.*

NICHOLSON, JAMES M. "JIM." Born Feb. 1860, Cotton, Arkansas. Ht. 5 ft. 6 ½ in., blue eyes, dark brown hair, light complexion, married. Night watchman, I&GN Railroad, Spring, Harris County, Texas. SPECIAL RANGER Dec. 10, 1917–Jan. 15, 1919 [?]. REMARKS: His superior requested that he be commissioned. Had been a penitentiary guard in Little Rock, Pulaski County, Arkansas, and a boarding house operator in Ada, Pontotoc County, Oklahoma. In 1920 was a special agent for the railroad in Palestine, Anderson County, Texas. FAMILY: Spouse #1, Doe (b. 1858, MS), married about 1880; children, Frederick (b. 1886, AR), James (b. 1891, AR), Pearl (b. 1894, AR); spouse #2, Rachel A. (b. 1858, FL), married about 1910. *SR; Williamson to Harley, Dec 6, 1917, AGC; AG to Williamson, Dec 7, 1917, AGC; A1d, e, f.*

NOTON, WILLIAM DALE. Born May 28, 1875, Travis County, Texas. Ht. 5 ft. 4 ½ in., brown eyes, brown hair, fair complexion, married. Farmer, enlisted in Travis County. SPECIAL RANGER Jan. 28, 1918–Jan. 15, 1919. REMARKS: In 1930 was a stockman in Travis County, living in Austin. Died Mar. 28, 1935, Travis County, Texas. FAMILY: Parents, Thomas Smith Noton (b. 1841, England) and Marion Mitchell (Canada); siblings, La Rue (b. 1873, TX)), Mary Jane; spouse, Lillian Burleson "Lily" Deats (b. 1885, TX), married Nov. 16, 1904, Austin; children, William Dale (b. 1904, TX), Marion Pauline (b. 1908, TX), Robert Pierson (b. 1910, TX), La Rue "Ruth" (b. 1916, TX), James Thomas (b. 1919, TX). *SR; A1b, d, e, f, g; A2b; A3a; A4a, b.*

NUNNERY, JAMES C. Born 1871, Travis County, Texas. Ht. 5 ft. 9 in., dark brown eyes, black hair, dark complexion. Farmer. REGULAR RANGER Oct. 13, 1911–Jan. 31, 1912 (private, Co. A and Co. C). Discharged—reduction in force. *SR; 471; Nunnery to Hutchings, Mar 2, 1913, AGC; BDH, Jan 31, 1912.*

NUTT, JOHN WILLIAM "WILL." Born Sept. 1867, Bee County, Texas. No physical description, married. Stockman, Beeville, Bee County. LOYALTY RANGER Jan. 1, 1918–Feb. 24, 1919. REMARKS: Letterhead: "J.W. Nutt, Dealer in High Class Steers, High Class Horses and Mules, Beeville." Was a stockraiser in Bee County in 1930. A John W. Nutt died Sept. 14, 1932, Bee County, Texas. FAMILY: Parents, John A. Nutt (b. 1835, MS or NC) and Nancy S. (b. 1851, MO); siblings, Pascal (b. 1869, TX), E. Lu (b. 1870, TX), Henry A. (b. 1872, TX), Jennettie (b. 1876, TX), Oscar R. (b. 1878, TX); spouse, Mary (b. 1870, TX), married about 1886; children, Evie (b. 1887, TX), Leona (b. 1889, TX), Boyd (b. 1891, TX), Allee T. (b. 1893, TX), Carl (b. 1895, TX). *SR; A1a, b, d, e, f, g; A2b.*

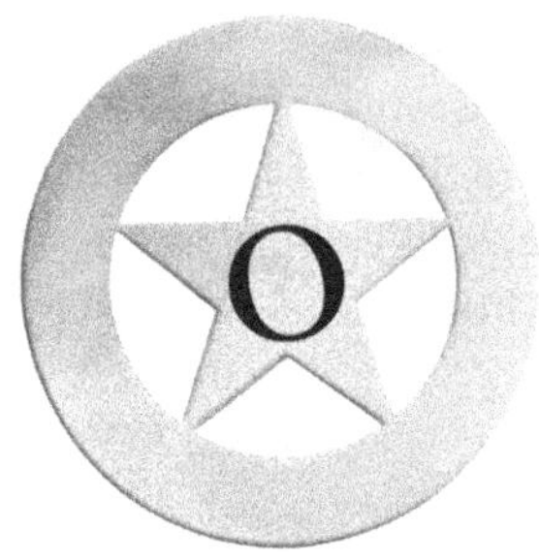

OBERSTE, ALBERT WILLIAM. Born Nov. 12, 1886, Hartman, Johnson County, Arkansas. Ht. 5 ft. 6 in., blue eyes, brown hair, fair complexion, married. Stock farmer, Plainview, Hale County, Texas. SPECIAL RANGER Dec. 20, 1917–Feb. 1918 (private, Co. B Volunteers). Discharged—Co. B Volunteers was disbanded. REMARKS: In June 1917 was a mechanic at the E. N. Egge Auto Company in Plainview. In 1920 was an auto dealer in Amarillo, Potter County, Texas. In 1930 was an appliance salesman in Amarillo. Died Sept. 10, 1953, Oklahoma; buried in Fairlawn Cemetery, Oklahoma City, Oklahoma County, Oklahoma. FAMILY: Parents, Hugo Oberste (b. 1855, Germany) and Maria Theresa Sprenger (b. 1854, Germany); siblings, Rosa (b. 1882, AR), Leo (b. 1889, AR), Louie (b. 1891, AR), Emil (b. 1893, AR), Emma (b. 1896, AR); spouse, Clyde Varnell (b. 1893, AR), married about 1913. *SR; Rawlings to Harley, Dec 23, 1917, AGC; A1b, e, f, g; A3a; A4b.*

O'BRIEN, THOMAS EDMUND. Born Jan. 12, 1886, Rusk, Chambers County, Texas. No personal description. Farmer, Lacoste, Medina County, Texas. LOYALTY RANGER Sept. 2, 1918–Feb. 1919. REMARKS: A Thomas O'Brien died July 10, 1966, Medina County, Texas. FAMILY: Parents, Frank Philip O'Brien (b. 1850, VA) and Emma (b. 1860, TX); siblings, Alice (b. 1888, TX), Charles P. (b. 1899, TX). *SR; A1e, f; A2a, b.*

ODEM, DAVID CHARLES "DAVE." Born Feb. 14, 1857, Campbelltown, Live Oak County, Texas. Ht. 6 ft., gray eyes, gray hair, fair complexion, married. Farmer and stockman, Sinton, San Patricio County, Texas. LOYALTY RANGER May 31, 1918–Feb. 24, 1919. REMARKS: San Patricio County sheriff Nov. 4, 1884–Nov. 2, 1886 and Nov. 8, 1892–Nov. 3, 1914. President, Sinton State Bank, 1919. Was a member of the Sinton Townsite Company which developed Sinton and assisted in the development of the town of Odem, San Patricio County. Died Nov. 10, 1925, Santa Rosa Hospital, San Antonio, Bexar County, Texas; buried on the Odem Ranch, San Patricio County. FAMILY: Parents, David Charles Odem (b. 1812, MS or 1820, LA) and Elizabeth Timmon (b. 1825, Ireland); siblings, Cecelia (b. 1849, NY), Michael (b. 1854, TX), John Edward (b. 1859, TX); spouse, Adaline Gertrude Gallagher (b. 1862, TX), married Oct. 2, 1878, Live Oak County; children, Elizabeth Mary (b. 1879, TX), Hubert E. "Bert" (b. 1882, TX), Margaret U. (b. 1884, TX), David C. "Dave" (b. 1886, TX), Carolina "Carrie" (b. 1888, TX), James F. "Jim" (b. 1890, TX), William T. "Willie" (b. 1892, TX), Bryan S. (b. 1896, TX). *SR; 471; 1503:452; LWT, Mar 14, 1915; 319: 15; A1aa, a, d, e, f; A2b; A4a, b.*

ODEN, LOUIS DEAN. Born Nov. 7, 1865, Frio County, Texas. Ht. 5 ft. 10 in., blue eyes, light hair, light complexion, married. Deputy sheriff. REGULAR RANGER Dec. 22, 1917–Feb. 1, 1918 (private, Co. L). Resigned for a better job as an El Paso mounted policeman. REMARKS: In 1910 was a farmer in Calexico, Imperial County, California. Returned to Texas; on Oct. 18, 1912, was appointed an El Paso County deputy sheriff, assigned to Smeltertown. In 1920 and 1930 was a city policeman in El Paso. Died Apr.

6, 1948, El Paso County, Texas. FAMILY: Parents, Aaron Louis Dean Oden (b. 1843, TX) and Peggy Caroline Hayes (b. 1845, TX); brother, Sam Houston (b. 1862, TX); spouse, Sannie Carr (b. 1884, TX), married about 1901, divorced before 1920; children, Louisa Ozella (b. 1903, TX), Louis Dean (b. 1906, TX). *SR; 471; Davis to Harley, Jan 26, Feb 4, 1918, AGC; EPMT, Oct 19, 1912; EPH, June 24, 1913; A1aa, a, b, e, f, g; A2b; A4a, b; B2.*

ODOM, DORSEY PANE "DORSE." Born Apr. 25, 1890, Cross Plains, Callahan County, Texas. Ht. 5 ft. 10 in., blue eyes, brown hair, fair complexion, married. Farmer, Baird, Callahan County. SPECIAL RANGER June 2, 1917–Dec. 1917. REMARKS: Died May 26, 1946, Callahan County, Texas. FAMILY: Parents, Robert P. Odom (b. 1856, TX) and Katie A. (b. 1862, TN); siblings, Edward S. (b. 1883, TX), Ivon (b. 1885, TX), Gussie M. (b. 1892, TX), Robert Price (b. 1895, TX), Ralph H. (b. 1898, TX), Ora (b. 1900, TX); spouse, Lala (b. 1896, TX), married about 1910; sons, Blan (b. 1912, TX), Billie D. (b. 1925, TX), Tom Lyne (b. 1928, TX). *SR; A1d, e, f, g; A2b; A3a.*

ODOM, JACOB M. Born Dec. 8, 1872, Gillette, Karnes County, Texas. Ht. 5 ft. 9 in., gray eyes, dark hair, dark complexion, married. Forest patrolman, Groveton, Trinity County, Texas. LOYALTY RANGER June 12, 1918–Feb. 1919. REMARKS: Had been a farmer and ice man in Karnes County and Gonzales County, Texas. In 1920 and 1930 was a stock farmer in Trinity County. Died Apr. 30, 1943, Trinity County, Texas. FAMILY: Parents, Justice Odom (b. 1836, LA) and Louisa A. (b. 1853, TX); sisters, Lou S. (b. 1874, TX), Eveolin M. (b. 1876, TX), Shirley (b. 1879, TX); spouse, Callie C. (b. 1884, TX), married about 1899; children, Erna (b. 1903, TX), James "Jim" (b. 1905, TX), Roy (b. 1910, TX). *SR; A1b, d, e, f, g; A2b; A3a.*

OGDEN, RALPH ROGERS. Born July 13, 1874, Ogden Ranch, Hill County, Texas. Ht. 6 ft., gray eyes, dark hair, light complexion, married. Farmer and trader, Austin, Travis County, Texas. SPECIAL RANGER Aug. 26, 1918–Jan. 15, 1919; Aug. 23, 1927–Aug. 23, 1928. Oil and ranching, Austin. SPECIAL RANGER, Apr. 26, 1933–unknown. REMARKS: In 1920 was an "agriculturalist" in Austin. In 1930 was an oil lease salesman in Austin. Died Apr. 19, 1944, Oklahoma. FAMILY: Parents, Charles Vance "Charley" Ogden (b. 1850, AR) and Mary Elizabeth Rogers (b. 1846, TN); siblings, Allen Maude (b. 1876, TX), Ezekiel Clay (b. 1877, TX), Della Morse (b. 1879, TX), Mary Vance (b. 1881, TX); spouse, Ethel Johnson (b. 1885, TX), married about 1905. *SR; A1b, e, f, g; A3a; A4a.*

OGG, LESTER E. Born Sept. 1881, Bellville, Austin County, Texas. Ht. 5 ft. 7 ¾ in., blue-gray eyes, brownish-gray hair, fair complexion, divorced. Accountant and contractor, enlisted in Dallas County, Texas. REGULAR RANGER Aug. 26, 1915–Sept. 8, 1915 (private, Co. D). Discharged. REMARKS: Note length of service. Ogg said he resigned from Rangers because the glare of the sun in South Texas was affecting his eyes. On his enlistment form Ogg stated that he had lived on West Texas ranches, was for several years paymaster for a mining company in Mexico, and was familiar with sections of the border. In Apr. 1916 he was arrested in El Paso for forgery, and the Burns Detective Agency, Houston, was investigating him for passing worthless checks. FAMILY: Parents, Edward Charles Ogg (b. 1854, TX) and Sarah Ella Bethany (b. 1859, TX); siblings, Edna E. (b. 1878, TX), Walter (b. 1879, TX), Harry Bethany (b. 1883, TX), Herbert Manley (b. 1889, TX), Reese Blake (b. 1892, TX), Virginia H. (b. 1893, TX). *SR; 471; Ogg to Hutchings, Sept 11, 1915, AGC; Burns Agency to Hutchings, June 2, 1916, AGC; AG to Burns, June 7, 1916, AGC; EPMT, Apr 22, 1916; A1d, e; A4a.*

O'KEEFE, DAVID MARVIN "MARVIN." Born Nov. 27, 1887, Waxahachie, Ellis County, Texas. Tall, stout, gray eyes, black hair. Stock farmer, Panhandle, Carson County, Texas. LOYALTY RANGER July 8, 1918–Oct. 20, 1918. Died Oct. 20, 1918, Carson County, Texas. FAMILY: Parents, James E. O'Keefe (b. 1849, AL) and Mary U. (b. 1860, IL); siblings, Rufus (b. 1877, TX), Sidney J. (b. 1879, TX), Thomas A. (b. 1884, TX), John R. (b. 1890, TX), Dussie A. (b. 1895, TX), Onie (b. 1897, TX). *SR; A1d, e; A2b; A3a.*

OLIPHANT, GEORGE CLEVELAND "CLEVE." Born Dec. 9, 1884, Kenedy, Karnes County, Texas. Ht. 5 ft. 10 ½ in., light blue eyes, light brown hair, light complexion. Ranch hand. REGULAR RANGER Dec. 24, 1917–Jan. 13, 1919 (private, Co. K). Discharged. REMARKS: Had been a deputy sheriff. In 1930 was a construction worker (carpenter) in Corpus Christi, Nueces County, Texas. LAW ENFORCEMENT

RELATIVES: Ranger J. Boone Oliphant, brother. FAMILY: Mother, Ella S. (b. 1859, TX); siblings, Zora (b. 1881, TX), Nora (b. 1883, TX), Boone (b. 1888, TX), Leila (b. 1890, TX); spouse, Nettie (b. 1892, TX), married about 1905; stepchildren, Conrad Butner (b. 1912, TX), Gertrude Butner (b. 1917, TX). *SR; 471; A1d, e, f, g; A3a.*

OLIPHANT, JAMES BOONE "BOONE." Born Apr. 16, 1888, Karnes City, Karnes County, Texas. Ht. 6 ft., brown eyes, dark hair, dark complexion. Ranchman. REGULAR RANGER Nov. 13, 1915–Oct. 15, 1917 (private, Co. B). Resigned. REGULAR RANGER Dec. 16, 1917–June 8, 1918. Discharged/fired. REMARKS: In Dec. 1917 Capt. Fox received permission to reenlist Oliphant, of whom he thought highly. Oliphant had worked on the TO Ranch in Mexico in 1914. He was fired from the Rangers on June 8, 1918 for having participated in the Porvenir massacre—Co. B was disbanded. In 1930 was a ranch worker in Uvalde, Uvalde County, Texas. Died Jan. 29, 1969, Uvalde County, Texas. LAW ENFORCEMENT RELATIVES: Ranger G. Cleveland Oliphant, brother. FAMILY: Mother, Ella S. (b. 1859, TX); siblings, Zora (b. 1881, TX), Nora (b. 1883, TX), Cleveland (b. 1884, TX), Leila (b. 1890, TX); spouse, Ruth Barker English (b. 1897, TX), married about 1916; children, James B., Jr. (b. 1917, TX), Frank (b. 1920, TX), Grover L. (b. 1922, TX), Eugene (b. 1924, TX), Tom (b. 1926, TX), Willie (b. 1928, TX), Ella Louise (b. 1934, TX). *SR; 471; Fox to Harley, Dec 13, 1917, AGC; Harley to Fox, Dec 13, 1917, AGC; EPMT, Dec 2, 1915; 422: 87; 470: 87, 88; A1d, e, f, g; A2a, b, e; A3a.*

OLIVER, JOHN JEFFERSON. Born Feb. 10, 1883, Seguin, Guadalupe County, Texas. Ht. 5 ft. 10 in., hazel eyes, light hair, fair complexion. Stockman, Marathon, Brewster County, Texas. SPECIAL RANGER Dec. 31, 1917–Jan. 15, 1919 (?) (attached to Co. F). REMARKS: Capt. Carroll Bates, Co. F, requested that he be commissioned. FAMILY: Parents, John Goodwin Oliver (b. 1851, TX) and Fannie I. (b. 1858, TX); siblings, Phines R. (b. 1877, TX), Lola (b. 1879, TX), Wallace W. (b. 1880, TX), Florence H. (b. 1884, TX), Edwin E. (b. 1886, TX), John Moore (b. 1888, TX), Hugh G. (b. 1890, TX), Colin McC. (b. 1892, TX), Thomas H. (b. 1895, TX), Elsberry Lane (b. 1897, TX), Paula (b. 1900, TX). *SR; A1d; A3a.*

OLSON, GILBERT NATHAN. Born Jan. 2, 1884, Pearsall, Frio County, Texas. Ht. 5 ft. 10 ½ in., blue eyes, brown hair, fair complexion. Merchant, Hebbronville, Jim Hogg County, Texas. SPECIAL RANGER Apr. 29, 1918–Jan. 15, 1919. REMARKS : Had been a house carpenter in Duval County, Texas. Died Aug. 16, 1950, Bell County, Texas. FAMILY: Parents, Gilbert H. Olson (b. 1838, Norway) and Emma (b. 1851, Norway); siblings, Hantz (b. 1872, TX), Peter A. (b. 1876, TX), Sarah C. (b. 1878, TX). *SR; A1b, e; A2b; A3a.*

ORBERG, JOE. (Ranger Service Records spelling: OREBERG, JOE.) Born May 15, 1875, Stockholm, Sweden. Ht. 5 ft. 11 ½ in., blue eyes, brown hair, light complexion, married. Peace officer, Austin, Travis County, Texas. REGULAR RANGER Feb. 15, 1921–Feb. 21, 1925 (private, Co. B; reenlisted in Headquarters Co., Feb. 15, 1923). Discharged. Equipment inspector, State Highway Department, Austin. SPECIAL RANGER Mar. 23, 1927–Mar. 31, 1927. Discharged. REMARKS: Note length of SPECIAL RANGER service. As of Sept. 1918 was a naturalized U.S. citizen living in Manor, Travis County; occupation, "soldier." Died Dec. 29, 1932, Travis County, Texas. *SR; 471; 470: 43; A2b; A3a.*

ORENBAUN, THOMAS ALEXANDER "ALEX." Born Sept. 29, 1861, Oakwood, Leon County, Texas. Ht. 6 ft. 2 ½ in., blue eyes, brown hair, fair complexion. Carpenter, Hillsboro, Hill County, Texas. LOYALTY RANGER June 8, 1918–Feb. 1919. REMARKS: "I am only to devote such time as I can spare from my regular employment and service at my option to be limited to Hill County." Still a carpenter in Hill County in 1930. Died Apr. 27, 1934. FAMILY: Parents, Thomas Richard Orenbaun (b. 1827, VA) and Saphronia Coker (b. 1836, AL); siblings, James Buchanan (b. 1856, TX), Isabella Mary (b. 1859, TX), Andrew (b. 1864, TX), Franklin (b. 1867, TX), Lewis (b. 1869, TX), George (b. 1871, TX), Saphronia (b. 1874, TX), Virginia (b. 1876, TX). *SR; A1d, f, g; A4c.*

ORMAND, GARLAND. Born May 2, 1881, Brandon, Rankin County, Mississippi. Ht. 6 ft. 2 in., dark eyes, dark hair, dark complexion, married. Retail League director, Llano, Llano County, Texas. SPECIAL RANGER Jan. 31, 1918–July 30, 1918. Saloon proprietor, Llano. SPECIAL RANGER July 30, 1918–Jan. 15, 1919 (attached to Co. C). Café owner and proprietor, Bartlett, Williamson County, Texas. SPECIAL RANGER Mar. 24, 1934–Jan. 22, 1935. Discharged. REMARKS: A Garland Ormand died Sept. 8, 1956, Travis County, Texas. FAMILY: Parents, Columbus Edward Ormand (b. 1850, MS) and Charlena Meggs Boggs (b. 1854, MS or AR); siblings, V. M. (b. 1870, MS), Sallie A. (b. 1873, MS), Mary Eugenia (b. 1874, MS), Emma (b. 1876, MS), Maud (b. 1885, MS), Verbry M. (b. 1885, AR), Cora L. (b. 1888, AR), Marvin (b. 1893, TX), Homer (b. 1896, TX); spouse, Addie Evalina Bardin (b. 1890, TX), married June 14, 1908, Llano; children, Carl Edwin (b. 1911, TX), Earline (b. 1916, TX), Garland, Jr. (b. 1921, TX). *SR; AG to Ormand, July 27, 1917, AGC; Petition, July 1917, AGC; A1b, d, f, g; A2b; A3a; A4b.*

ORTH, LEONARD ALLEN. Born May 23, 1875, Denver, Arapahoe, Colorado. Ht. 5 ft. 11 ¾ in., blue eyes, brown hair, light complexion, married. Ice company manager, Yoakum, DeWitt County, Texas. LOYALTY RANGER May 31, 1918–Feb. 1919. REMARKS: As a boy lived in Hiawatha, Brown County, Kansas. In 1920 was a machinist at a phosphate plant in Mount Pleasant, Maury County, Tennessee. In 1930 was supervising engineer in an ice plant in Dallas, Dallas County, Texas. Died June 16, 1958, Dallas County, Texas. FAMILY: Parents, C. H. Orth (b. 1840, OH) and Mary E. (b. 1843, MA); siblings, Tommie (b. 1866, PA), Willie (b. 1868, PA), Stokely (b. 1877, KS), Mary (b. 1879, KS); spouse, Alma Riedel (b. 1878, TX), married Jan. 1, 1902; children, Harry R. (b. 1908, TX), Rosa Louise E. (b. 1909, TX). *SR; A1b, e, f, g; A2b; A3a; A4b.*

OSGOOD, JESSE GRAY. Born July 1, 1889, Carrizo Springs, Dimmit County, Texas. Ht. 5 ft. 6 ½ in., blue eyes, brown hair, ruddy complexion. Ranchman, Del Rio, Val Verde County, Texas. REGULAR RANGER Dec. 6, 1919–Sept. 30, 1921 (private, Co. F). Discharged. REMARKS: As a boy had lived in Santa Cruz County, Arizona Territory. FAMILY: Parents, James B. Osgood (b. 1864, TX) and Annie J. (b. 1866, TX); siblings, James Leslie (b. 1887, TX), Willis A. (b. 1891, TX), Gussie B. (b. 1896, TX), Curtis (b. 1898, TX), Leeta (b. 1903, TX), Andy (b. 1906, TX), Carl (b. 1909, TX); stepmother, Nora (b. 1889, TX); sister, Eva (b. 1919, TX). *SR; 471; A1d, e, f; A3a.*

OTTING, ALVAH A. Born Dec. 1, 1889, Falls City, Richardson County, Nebraska. Ht. 5 ft. 10 in., brown eyes, dark hair, fair complexion, married. Merchant, Austin, Travis County, Texas. SPECIAL RANGER Sept. 17, 1918–Jan. 1, 1919. Special representative, Business Men's Assurance Co., Austin. SPECIAL RANGER Apr. 18, 1934–unknown. REMARKS: Lived in Austin as early as 1900. In 1910 was a grocery salesman in Austin. In 1920 had his own grocery store in Los Angeles, Los Angeles County, California. Returned to Austin by 1930, was an insurance salesman. Died Mar. 10, 1948, Travis County, Texas. FAMILY: Parents, Fred Otting (b. 1849, Germany) and Minnie (b. 1854, MO); siblings, Gus F. (b. 1880, MO), Harry (b. 1885, MO), Daisy (b. 1887, MO); spouse, Lutie M. (b. 1894, TX), married about 1913. *SR; A1d, e, f, g; A2b; A3a.*

OWEN, IRA D. Born June 20, 1880, Magnolia, Columbia County, Arkansas. Ht. 6 ft. 3 in., blue eyes, light hair, fair complexion. REGULAR RANGER Oct. 23, 1911–Jan. 31, 1912 (private, Co. C). Discharged—reduction in force. REMARKS: In 1910 was a farm manager in Hidalgo County, Texas. In 1920 was a U.S. government Immigration inspector in Calexico, Imperial County, California. In 1930 was an Immigration inspector in Nogales, Santa Cruz County, Arizona. FAMILY: Spouse, Dorothy K. Nichols (b. 1895, CA), married about 1914; children, Harold K. (b. 1914, CA), Donald C. (b. 1917, CA), Lilian B. (b. 1919, CA), Keith N. (b. 1922, AZ). *SR; 471; BDH, Jan 31, 1912; A1e, f, g; A2h; A3a.*

OWENS, BERIE. Born Aug. 25, 1892, Dallas County, Texas. Tall, slender, brown eyes, light brown hair, married. Lumberman, Comstock, Val Verde County, Texas. SPECIAL RANGER Apr. 27, 1918–Jan. 15, 1919. REMARKS: Service Record states: "This young man was put in [Selective Service] class 5 on account crippled hand." World War I Draft Registration document states: "Has lost all fingers on right hand." Had been assistant manager of Eagle Pass Lumber Company in Brownsville, Cameron County, Texas. In 1930 was a hardware store manager in George West, Live Oak County, Texas. Died Nov. 3, 1972, Live Oak County, Texas. FAMILY: Parents, Rufus D. Owens (b. 1860, AL) and Lura A. (b. 1871, TX); siblings, Clide (b. 1890, TX), Marian E. (b. 1895, TX), Maud (b. 1898, TX); spouse, Iva Lee Rhode (b. 1896, TX), married about 1917; daughter, Mary Alyce (b. 1927, TX). *SR; 471; A1d, g; A2b, e; A3a.*

OWENS, HORACE WEBSTER. Born Oct. 31, 1885, Smith County, Texas. Tall, stout, blue eyes, light hair, married. Paint contractor, Teague, Freestone County, Texas. LOYALTY RANGER, July 1, 1918–Jan. 15, 1919. REMARKS: Died Apr. 22, 1945, Freestone County, Texas. FAMILY: Parents, George Lott Owens (b. 1843, AR) and Laura Virginia Robbins (b. 1847, AL); siblings, Frances Elizabeth (b. 1866, TX), John Edwin (b. 1868, TX), Thomas M. (b. 1870, TX), G. L. (b. 1873, TX), Myrta Mae (b. 1876, TX), Fred L. (b. 1878, TX), William Lee (b. 1881, TX), Augustus Garland (b. 1883, TX), Clara V. (b. 1889, TX), Samuel Roy (b. 1892, TX); spouse, Willie May Howell (b. 1891, TX); children, Horace Weldon (b. 1910, TX), Opal J. (b. 1912, TX), Webster Wroe (b. 1914, TX). *SR; 471; A1f; A2b; A3a; A4b.*

OWENS, TROY RANDOLPH. Born Apr. 18, 1894, Lampasas, Lampasas County, Texas. Ht. 5 ft. 10 ½ in., blue eyes, brown hair, ruddy complexion. Cowpuncher. REGULAR RANGER Oct. 1, 1917–Mar. 10, 1919 (private, Co. E). Discharged—Co. E was disbanded. Rancher, Rocksprings, Edwards County, Texas. REGULAR RANGER Aug. 27, 1919–Aug. 31, 1921 (private, Co. F; transferred to Co. A, Oct. 15, 1920). Discharged—reduction in force. Rancher, Rocksprings. REGULAR RANGER Oct .1, 1921–Mar. 10, 1922 (private, Co. C). Discharged. REMARKS: In June 1917 was a ranch man living in Paint Rock, Concho County, Texas. In 1930 was a farmer in Edwards County. Died Oct. 9, 1979, Edwards County, Texas. FAMILY: Parents, Kyle Owens (b. 1872, TX) and Queen V. (b. 1877, TX); siblings, Lida N. (b. 1896, TX), Alton W. (b. 1899, TX); spouse, Ray E. Harris (b. 1903, TX), married about 1925; son, Troy Ray (b. 1929, TX). *SR; 471; Barler to Harley, Oct 12, 1917, AGC; Owens to Harley, June 23, 1919, AGC; Aldrich to Owens, Aug 15, 1919, AGC; A1d, f, g; A2a, b, e; A3a.*

OYERVIDES, MIGUEL. Born Sept. 29, 1874, Lockhart, Caldwell County, Texas. Ht. 6 ft., brown eyes, black hair, fair complexion, married. Clerk. REGULAR RANGER Oct. 16, 1911–Jan. 20, 1912 (private, Co. C). Discharged—reduction in force. REMARKS: Had been a saloon bartender in Austin, Travis County, Texas. In Sept. 1918 was an Austin city policeman. In 1920 was a dry goods store clerk in Austin. Still living in Austin in 1930. In many census records, name is Anglicized to "Michael" Oyervides. A Michael G. Oyervides died Nov. 6, 1941, Travis County, Texas. FAMILY: Parents, Teodor "Theodore" Oyervides (b. 1839, Mexico) and Tivorcia (b. 1849, Mexico); siblings, Casus (b. 1873, TX), Frank (b. 1879, TX), Lorena (b. 1882, TX), Jose "Joseph" (b. 1885, TX), Jenaro (b. 1887, TX); spouse #1, Aurelia Gonzales (b. 1879, TX), married Feb. 4, 1893, Travis County; sons, Teodor (b. 1897, TX), Miguel, Jr. (b. 1900, TX), Adolph (b. 1901, TX); spouse #2, Frances (b. 1891, TX), married about 1910; children, Angelina (b. 1914, TX), Marguerita (b. 1916, TX), Frances (b. 1918, TX), Edward (b. 1921, TX). *SR; 471; BDH, Jan 31, 1912; A1d, e, f, g; A2b; A3a; B1.*

Ranger Captain Henry Lee Ransom was easily the most controversial Ranger of this period. He had more notches on his guns than almost any Ranger. Although he appears in this photograph to be a rather benign businessman, he was anything but. Front row seated left to right: Captain Ransom; M. G. "Blaze" Delling, former Ranger and U.S. Immigration Inspector; and R. M. "Duke" Hudson, former Ranger and sheriff, Anderson County. Second row seated: Ranger Jim Dunaway and A. Y. Baker, former Ranger and sheriff, Hidalgo County. Third row standing: unidentified, Ranger Jules Baker, unidentified, Ranger Levi Davis and Ranger Lee Anders. *Photo courtesy Texas Ranger Hall of Fame and Museum.*

There always seemed to be a Texas Ranger named Wright in a group of Rangers. In this photo left to right are Ranger H. P. "Red" Brady, Ranger J. C. "Doc" White, unidentified, Ranger Herff A. Carnes and Ranger Milam Wright. *Photo courtesy Captain M. T. Gonzaullas collection, Texas Ranger Hall of Fame and Museum.*

Rangers at Del Rio. Ranger Captain Frank Hamer (second from left) and portions of two Ranger companies. To Hamer's left is Ranger Lon Willis. The two men to Hamer's right are unidentified. On the second row behind Hamer are Ranger Captain W. L. Barler, unidentified and Ranger Charles Miller. Third row left to right are Ranger Henry Glasscock, Ranger John Carta, Ranger Charles Carta, and Ranger Oscar Latta. *Photo courtesy Roy Wilkinson Aldrich Papers, Dolph Briscoe Center for American History, University of Texas at Austin.*

Rangers P. F. Dyches (left) and Ranger Clay Blackwell astride mules in Dimmit County in 1920. *Photo courtesy Roy Wilkinson Aldrich Papers, Dolph Briscoe Center for American History, University of Texas at Austin.*

Senior Texas Ranger Captain William Martin Hanson (second from right on the back row in a white linen suit with a bow tie) poses with the members of a posse he commanded. Sitting in front is a group of WWI draft dodgers who had earlier killed one Ranger and wounded another. Hanson took command and arrested them without further casualties. None of the other members of the posse are identified nor are the draft dodgers. *Photo courtesy of the Texas Ranger Hall of Fame and Museum.*

Texas Ranger Captain Monroe Fox and Company C in 1911. Fox is standing in front of his company who are on their horses. Left to right are Ranger R. L. Morris; Ranger R. L. Burdett, Ranger Sue M. "Mack" Jester, Ranger Jim Mercer, Ranger R. G. Askew and Ranger M. C. Cathey. *Photo courtesy Texas Ranger Hall of Fame and Museum.*

Texas Ranger Herff Carnes (left) poses with Ranger Pat Craighead whose lower leg was amputated because of a wound suffered in an ambush near Brownsville. *Photo courtesy Texas Ranger Hall of Fame and Museum.*

Texas Rangers (left to right) Charlie Price, John Caraway, Charlie Blackwell and Will Erskine. *Photo courtesy Dolph Briscoe Center for American History, University of Texas at Austin.*

Texas Rangers and U.S. Customs River Guards at Rio Grande City, May, 1915. Standing on the steps left to right: River Guards Charles Hayes Wright, Edwin M. Dubose and Joe Taylor; Ranger "Lupe" Edwards; Deputy Sheriff Bennie [H. G. ?] Dubos. Front row standing and sitting left to right: Ranger Roy Aldrich, Deputy U.S. Marshall Rader and Ranger Captain J. E. Davenport. *Photo courtesy Roy Aldrich Collection, Dolph Briscoe Center for American History, University of Texas at Austin.*

Texas Rangers Marvin Butler (left) and John Edds (right) in a 1918 photograph. *Photo courtesy Dolph Briscoe Center for American History, University of Texas at Austin.*

The Rangers at Longview in 1919. Sitting left to right: Senior Ranger Captain William Martin Hanson; Texas National Guard Brigadier General Jacob F. Wolters; Ranger Captain Roy Aldrich. Standing left to right: Ranger Captain Joe Brooks, Ranger Fred Graves, Ranger D. E. Singleton and Ranger J. R. Hunnicutt. *Photo courtesy Roy Wilkinson Aldrich Papers, Dolph Briscoe Center for American History, University of Texas at Austin.*

Unique photograph of Rangers and ex-Rangers in Austin, Texas, at the 1920 trial of H. L. "Hod" Roberson who was tried for killing Foote Boykin in Sierra Blanca four years earlier. Front row left to right: unknown, Harry Moore, and Charlie Bell. Second row left to right: Charles Craighead, Oscar Latta, unknown, Frank Hamer, Jeff Vaughn, unknown, Ira Cline, Red Hawkins, unknown. Third row left to right: unknown, H. L. Roberson, Captain W. L. Barler, former Captain John Hughes, Captain Monroe Fox, Captain Roy Aldrich, unknown, Pat Craighead, unknown. *Photo courtesy Dolph Briscoe Center for American History, University of Texas at Austin.*

William W. Sterling shown here (third from left) posing for the camera with four Knox County lawmen (not identified) loved to have his picture taken. He was a special Ranger, then a regular Ranger, a Ranger captain and finally adjutant general. *Photo courtesy Texas Ranger Hall of Fame and Museum.*

By the early 1920s most of the Rangers of the previous decade had retired, been fired, were cattle inspectors, were employed by various federal law enforcement agencies or were dead. Illustrative of this fact is this comparatively rare photograph for the period of the entire forty-one-man Ranger force. In the front row (sixth from left and following) are Captain Frank Hamer, Governor Pat Neff, Adjutant General T. D. Barton, Captains William L. Wright, Roy W. Aldrich and Jerry Gray. Although there is a sprinkling of Rangers who had served in the earlier decade in the back rows, most were new Rangers. To our knowledge the identifications below the photograph are correct. *Photo courtesy Texas Ranger Hall of Fame and Museum.*

Chomping on their cigars, four Rangers pose for the camera near Presidio in 1921. Left to right are C. L. Blackwell, Howard Hall, Lee Trimble and John Crow. *Photo courtesy Texas Ranger Hall of Fame and Museum.*

Captain John Sanders's Company A at Alice, Texas in 1916. Left to right: unidentified, Ranger Charlie Wright, Ranger Elgin Ford, Ranger Cleve Hearst, unidentified and unidentified. *Photo courtesy Roy Wilkinson Aldrich Collection, Dolph Briscoe Center for American History, University of Texas at Austin.*

Captain William L. Wright's Company D near Laredo in 1917. Left to right are Ranger Bryan Butler, Ranger Rex Holland, Ranger Harold Adams, Ranger Cleve Oliphant, Ranger Dionicio Acosta, Ranger Sanders Peterson, Ranger Marvin Butler, Ranger John Sutton, Ranger Wright Wells, Ranger Tom Connally, Ranger Monroe Wells and Captain Wright. *Photo courtesy Roy Wilkinson Aldrich Papers, Dolph Briscoe Center for American History, University of Texas at Austin.*

Captain Will Davis's Company L, Texas Rangers lined up for a photograph in September, 1918, on the north bank of the Rio Grande at Ysleta, Texas, downriver from El Paso. Left to right are Sergeant J. G. Perkins, A. J. Robertson, Edd Hallebeke, J. D. McClellan, S. R. Ikard, Frank Black, R. E. Hunt, W. R. Holland, Santos Duran, B. L. Pennington, T. E. Perkins and Captain Davis. *Photo courtesy Art Robertson, Jr., Las Cruces, New Mexico.*

R.E. Hunt.
W.R. Holland
Santos Duran.
B.F. Pennington.
T.E. Perkins.
Captain

Left to right: Ranger Jim Dunaway, Captain Tom Ross, and Ranger Milam Wright. From *Trails and Trials of a Texas Ranger* by William Warren Sterling. Copyright 1959 by William Warren Sterling. Assigned 1968 to the University of Oklahoma Press. *Reprinted by permission of the publisher.*

Captain William L. Wright's Company D was probably the best Ranger company on the border when commanded by Captain Wright. In this photo left to right are Captain Wright, Ranger John Edds, Sergeant Wright Wells and Ranger Tom Connally. *Photo courtesy Texas Ranger Hall of Fame and Museum.*

PACE, CHARLES D. "CHARLIE." Born Apr. 3, 1871, Kenedy, Karnes County, Texas. Ht. 5 ft. 8 in., blue eyes, brown hair, dark complexion. Farmer, Kenedy. REGULAR RANGER Sept. 15, 1911–Apr. 9, 1912 (private, Co. B). WA was cancelled. Farmer, Kenedy. REGULAR RANGER Dec. 17, 1912–Apr. 18, 1913 (private, Co. B). WA was cancelled. REMARKS: Discharged for medical reasons. Was a farmer in Karnes County in 1920. In 1930 was Kenedy justice of the peace. Died Mar. 31, 1949, Karnes County, Texas. FAMILY: Parents, John Daniel Pace (b. 1839, AR) and Katherine E. "Kate" Campbell (b. 1844, OH); siblings, Nancy Isabella (b. 1872, TX), Rhoda Alice (b. 1875, TX), Daniel A. (b. 1883, TX). *SR; 471; Sanders to Hutchings, Mar 3, 1913, AGC; AG to Sanders, Mar 5, 1913, AGC; LWT, Jan 21,1912; 508: 66; A1b, d, e, g; A2b; A4a; B2.*

PALMER, JOHN C. Born 1873, Dewey County, Oklahoma. Ht. 5 ft. 7 in., brown eyes, dark gray hair, ruddy complexion. Moulder, enlisted in Austin, Travis County, Texas. REGULAR RANGER Jan. 3, 1918–Apr. 1918 (private, Co. F). Discharged/fired. REMARKS: Went AWOL, sold his weapons, bounced checks. *SR; 471; AG to General Manager, Jan 4, 1918, AGC; Caruthers to Harley, Apr 4, 1918, AGC; Bates to Harley, Apr 4, 1918, AGC; Bates to Harley, Apr 6, 1918, RRM; Assistant AG to Tevis, Apr 30, 198, AGC.*

PARCHMAN, JAMES LEMUEL. Born Nov. 1856, Seguin, Guadalupe County, Texas. Ht. 5 ft. 11 in., blue eyes, gray hair, light complexion, married. Stockman. REGULAR RANGER May 1, 1918–Aug. 31, 1918 (private, Co. F). Resigned. REMARKS: Had been a Bee County, Texas deputy sheriff about 30 years ago; a Menard County, Texas deputy sheriff and constable about 20 years ago. Had also lived in Irion County, Texas. In 1910 and 1920 was a stockman and ranch foreman in San Angelo, Tom Green County, Texas. Still living in San Angelo in 1930. A J. L. Parchman died Feb. 10, 1940, Tom Green County, Texas. FAMILY: Parents, Whitfield M. Parchman (b. 1831, TN) and Mary E. (b. 1837, MS); siblings, John W. (b. 1856, TX), Permelia Louisa (b. 1859, TX), Ivy (b. 1862, TX), Thomas (b. 1864, TX), Emma (b. 1868, TX), Edward (b. 1871, TX), King (b. 1874, TX), Clifton B. (b. 1879, TX); spouse #1, unknown, married about 1877; son, Whitfield (b. 1877, TX); spouse #2, Julia A. (b. 1869, AR), married about 1887. *SR; 471; Bates to Whom, Aug 31, 1918, AGC; Parchman to Harley, Sept 26, 1918, AGC; Johnston to Parchman, Oct 2, 1918, AGC; A1aa, a, b, d, e, f, g; A2b.*

PARKER, BENJAMIN J. "BEN." Born Jan. 1, 1868, Elkhart, Anderson County, Texas. Ht. 5 ft. 8 in., blue eyes, dark hair, fair complexion, married. Farmer, Elkhart. LOYALTY RANGER June 6, 1918–Feb. 1919. REMARKS: Had served 6 years as deputy sheriff. Still farming in Anderson County in 1930. A Ben J. Parker died Jan. 17, 1956, Anderson County, Texas. FAMILY: Parents, John Parker (b. 1839, TX) and Lucinda Ellen Rosson (b. 1848, TN); siblings, Sephronia (b. 1870, TX), Irena (b. 1874, TX), Lucinda (b. 1875, TX), Ann Nancy (b. 1878, TX), Marth (b. 1879, TX); spouse,

Docia Kennedy (b. 1873, TX), married about 1891; children, Lucinda (b. 1893, TX), Estelle (b. 1894, TX), Ross (b. 1895, TX), Charm (b. 1898, TX), Joe Bailey (b. 1903, TX), Lorena (b. 1906, TX), John H. "Jack" (b. 1908, TX), Flora (b. 1912, TX). *SR; A1b, d, e, f, g; A2b; A4a, b.*

PARKER, CLARENCE EDGAR. Born Feb. 18, 1891, McComb, Pike County, Mississippi. Ht. 5 ft. 10 in., brown eyes, brown hair, fair complexion, married. Railroad brakeman, enlisted in Atascosa County, Texas. SPECIAL RANGER July 17, 1916–unknown. REMARKS: In June 1917 was a railroad brakeman in Carrizo Springs, Dimmit County, Texas. In 1920 was a railroad conductor in Atascosa County. A Clarence Edgar Parker died Apr. 5, 1925, Limestone County, Texas. FAMILY: Spouse, Margaret E. (b. 1897, TX); daughters, Mildred (b. 1918, TX), Louise (b. 1919, TX). *SR; A1f; A2b, e; A3a.*

PARKER, FRANK. Born 1869, Karnes County, Texas. Ht. 5 ft. 11 ½ in., blue eyes, brown hair, light complexion, married. Stockman, enlisted in Callahan County, Texas. SPECIAL RANGER June 2, 1917–Dec. 1917 (attached to Co. C). REMARKS: In 1910 had been a cattle inspector in Fort Worth, Tarrant County, Texas. In Jan. 1911 was a brand inspector for the Cattle Raisers' Association of Texas. In 1920 was manager of his own ranch in Callahan County. FAMILY: Mother, Millie F. (b. 1850, MS); siblings, Zula M. (b. 1871, TX), Tasmell L. (b. 1873, TX), Ida J. (b. 1874, TX), Oliver (b. 1876, TX), George W. (b. 1878, TX); spouse, Totsie M. (b. 1877, TX), married about 1901; children, Wallis R. (b. 1902, TX), Nellie V. (b. 1905, TX), Doris (b. 1916, TX). *SR; AS, Jan 26, 1911; A1b, d, e, f.*

PARKER, GEORGE OSCAR "OSCAR." Born Nov. 14, 1881, Minter, Lamar County, Texas. Ht. 5 ft. 11 ½ in., brown eyes, black hair, brunette complexion, married. Banker, Abilene, Taylor County, Texas. SPECIAL RANGER June 8, 1917–Dec. 1917. REMARKS: Had been a clerk in the post office in Abilene. In 1920 was president of the First State Bank in Abilene. Died May 7, 1922, Taylor County, Texas. FAMILY: Spouse, Bonnie Mae (b. 1894, TX); children, Addie Lou (b. 1907, TX), Josephine (b. 1913, TX), George O., Jr. (b. 1915, TX), John M. (b. 1918, TX). *SR; Register to Ferguson, May 18, 1917, AGC; Cunningham to Ferguson, May 18, 1917, AGC; A1d, f, g; A2b; A3a.*

PARKER, HOWELL R. Born Feb. 12, 1856, Wetumpka, Elmore County, Alabama. No physical description, married. Machinist, Kirvin, Freestone County, Texas. LOYALTY RANGER July 7, 1918–Feb. 1919. REMARKS: Had also lived in Mexia, Freestone County. In 1920 was a cotton gin machinist in Kirvin. FAMILY: Parents, Joseph Baker Parker (b. 1812, GA) and Annie Townsend (b. 1820, AL); siblings, Nancy Elizabeth (b. 1841), William A. (b. 1843), John Elisha (b. 1844), Sarah Permelia (b. 1846, AL), Leonora Annie (b. 1849, AL), Eulalia Evalyn (b. 1851, AL), Phillip Henry (b. 1852, AL), Joseph Baker (b. 1854, AL), Ellen Cornelia (b. 1856), Samuel Townsend (b. 1858, AL), Thomas (b. 1858, AL), Tilla Varnado (b. 1861), Mattie Eva (b. 1863, AL); spouse, Mollie or Mattie C. (b. 1862, MS), married about 1895; son, Baker (b. 1898, TX); stepdaughters, Mollie or Mattie Bess Loader (b. 1888, TX), Charlia B. Loader (b. 1892, TX). *SR; A1a, e, f; A4b.*

PARKER, HUNTER C. Born Feb. 1873, Shelby County, Texas. No physical description, married. Ginner and farmer, Tenaha, Shelby County. LOYALTY RANGER July 2, 1918–Feb. 1919. REMARKS: Had been a mill worker and dry goods merchant in Shelby County. In 1930 was a flour and grain merchant in Tenaha. Died Jan. 8, 1959, Shelby County, Texas. FAMILY: Brother, R. T. (b. 1871, TX); spouse, Nora (b. 1882, TX), married about 1902; children, Winnie L. (b. 1903, TX), James H. (b. 1905, TX), Heber (b. 1914, TX), Ben P. (b. 1924, TX). *SR; A1d, e, f, g; A2b.*

PARKER, JOSHUA FLOY. Born Aug. 22, 1885, Snyder, Scurry County, Texas. Ht. 5 ft. 9 in., black eyes, brown hair, light complexion. Ranchman. REGULAR RANGER Sept. 11, 1917–Dec. 15, 1917 (private, Co. B). REMARKS: In June 1917 was a stockman in Presidio County, Texas. In 1930 was a U.S. Border Patrolman in Bowie, Cochise County, Arizona. FAMILY: Parents, William Calhoun Parker (b. 1860, TX) and Henry Ann Montgomery (b. 1864, TX); siblings, Dexter (b. 1887, TX), Roy (b. 1889, TX), Leila (b. 1892, TX), Ruby (b. 1894, TX), Frank (b. 1899, TX); spouse, Lynne (b. 1886, TX), married about 1923. *SR; Fox to Harley, Dec 13, 1917, AGC; A1d, g; A3a; A4b.*

PARKER, WILLIAM A. Born Oct. 1870, Parkersville, Lyon County, Kentucky. Ht. 6 ft., brown eyes, brown hair, dark complexion, married. Exporter, Waco, McLennan

County, Texas. SPECIAL RANGER July 24, 1918–Jan. 15, 1919. REMARKS: Was the Waco representative for Oliver Typewriter Co. In 1930 was an office supplies salesman in Waco. A William Archer Parker died Dec. 11, 1958, McLennan County, Texas. FAMILY: Parents, James E. Parker (b. 1844, KY) and Mary Jane Jackson (b. 1850, KY); siblings, Thomas N. (b. 1866, KY), Mollie P. (b. 1873, KY), Pernecy (b. 1875, KY), James E. (b. 1877, KY), Sarah E. (b. 1879, KY); spouse, Bertie B. (b. 1872, MO), married about 1898; children, William H. (b. 1899, Mexico), Bertie R. (b. 1904, TX). *SR; A1b, g; A2b; A4b.*

PARKS, EDGAR SAMUEL. Born Dec. 3, 1877, Madisonville, Monroe County, Tennessee. Ht. 6 ft. 2 in., brown eyes, black hair, dark complexion, married. Pump engineer, Clifton, Bosque County, Texas. LOYALTY RANGER June 7, 1918–Feb. 1919. REMARKS: In 1930 still a pump engineer for the railroad in Bosque County. An Edgar Samuel Parks died Dec. 29, 1956, Bell County, Texas. FAMILY: Spouse, Mollie R. Wood (b. 1878, TX), married about 1895; daughters, Katie L. (b. 1899, TX), Eddie M. (b. 1905, TX). *SR; A1d, e, f, g; A2b; A3a.*

PARKS, THOMAS CALEB. Born July 11, 1879, Blufton, Llano County, Texas. Ht. 5 ft. 10 ½ in., blue eyes, brown hair, fair complexion, married. Barber, Knox City, Knox County, Texas. LOYALTY RANGER June 4, 1918–Feb. 1919. FAMILY: Parents, Alexander Parks (b. 1860, AR) and Senie (b. 1860, TX); siblings, Sam I. (b. 1878, TX), Annie L. (b. 1885, TX), William J. (b. 1887, TX), Goldie (b. 1889, TX), Gray (b. 1891, TX), Paula (b. 1893, TX), Walter (b. 1895, TX), Roy (b. 1898, TX), Clayton (b. 1900, TX); spouse, Annie Ellen (b. 1885, TX), married about 1901; children, Cecil (b. 1902, TX), Willie Mamil (b. 1906, TX), Oswald (b. 1908, TX). *SR; A1b, d, e; A3a.*

PARMER, CLINTON LANE "CLINT." Born Mar. 1, 1865, Greenville, Alabama. Ht. 6 ft. 2 in., gray eyes, brown hair, fair complexion, divorced. Broker and planter, Waco, McLennan County, Texas. SPECIAL RANGER July 22, 1918–Jan. 15, 1919. REMARKS: Had been a deputy sheriff. Died Apr. 6, 1922, Bexar County, Texas. FAMILY: Parents, Dr. Clinton Dale Parmer (b. 1831, AL) and Eleanor Ann Oliver (b. 1837, AL); siblings, Walter O. (b. 1854, AL), Samuel E. (b. 1860, AL), Mary Frances (b. 1863, AL), Annie Dale (b. 1872, AL); spouse, Lizzie Alma Gentry (b. 1872, TN), married about 1895, Nashville, Tennessee, divorced by July 1918; children, Ruby (b. 1896, TX), Lottie (b. 1898, TX), Lorna (b. 1900, TX), Walter O. (b. 1902, TX), Clint L., Jr. (b. 1904, TX), Ellen (b. 1906, TX). *SR; 471; A1b, d, e, f; A2b; A4a, b.*

PARR, ARCHIBALD JACKSON "JACK." Born Jan. 15, 1886, near Greenville, Hunt County, Texas. Ht. 6 ft. 1 in., gray eyes, black hair, fair complexion, married. Barber, Anson, Jones County, Texas. SPECIAL RANGER May 31, 1917–Dec. 1917 (attached to Co. C). Barber, Anson. LOYALTY RANGER June 1, 1918–Feb. 1919. REMARKS: One source lists birthplace as Canton, Van Zandt County, Texas. Had been a farmer. In 1920 was a salesman for a motor car company in Anson. In 1930 was an auto salesman in Fort Worth, Tarrant County, Texas. Died Jan. 17, 1968, Tarrant County, Texas. FAMILY: Parents, Pinkney Elbert Parr (b. 1859, AR) and Mary Angelina Morris (b. 1867, MS); siblings, Ida Mae (b. 1881, TX), Zula Elizabeth (b. 1883, TX), James Berryman (b. 1889, TX), Edna Clementine (b. 1891, TX), Porter Elbert (b. 1893, TX), Donald Evander (b. 1897, TX), Clarence Braxton (b. 1899, TX), Charles Cecil (b. 1904, TX); spouse, Elma Stanford (b. 1890, TX), married Dec. 25, 1910, Anson; sons, Elbert Stanford (b.1912, TX), Archie J. (b. 1915, TX), Marvin Jack (b. 1919, TX). *SR; Dodson to Ferguson, May 18, 1917, AGC; Cunningham to Ferguson, May 18, 917, AGC; A1e, f, g; A2b; A3a; A4a, b.*

PARRISH, BYRON BRUCE. Born May 14, 1876, Mason, Mason County, Texas. Ht. 5 ft. 11 in., blue eyes, black hair, dark complexion, married. Criminal official (peace officer). REGULAR RANGER June 4, 1917–Feb. 17, 1918 (private, Co. D). Discharged. REMARKS: Peace officer in New Mexico, 1906–1908; in Oklahoma, 1910–1914. In 1915 applied to enlist in Rangers; Governor Ferguson recommended him for captain, but there were no vacancies. Ferguson ordered that he be enlisted. A position as private was held for Parrish but he declined because his mother was ill. In 1917–1918 Parrish left a trail of unpaid bills. In Sept. 1918 was a farmer in Eastland County, Texas. In 1919–1920 he was police chief of Ranger, Eastland County. In June 1920 he applied to enlist in the Rangers. In 1930 he was a radio salesman in Sabinal, Uvalde County,

Texas. Died June 17, 1931, Upton County, Texas. FAMILY: Parents, Darrington Alonzo Parrish (b. 1853, AL or LA) and Margaret Ann Fry (b. 1860, TX); siblings, Lucy, Bertha Barbara (b. 1878, TX), Buckner Burnes (b. 1880, TX), Darrington Alonzo (b. 1884), Earl Peter (b. 1888), Dude Asbury (b. 1890), Emma Gertrude (b. 1892), Bonnie Blue (b. 1895), Blannie Belle (b. 1899, TX); spouse #1, Annie G. Hope (b. 1872, TX), married June 4, 1905, Hill County, Texas; children, Byron J. (b. 1907, NM), Cleo Vernice (b. 1911, TX), Alta (b. 1912, CO); spouse #2, Della C. Buckelew (b. 1904, OK); daughters, Mary Imogene (b. 1929, TX), Ruby Mae (b. 1931, TX). *SR; 471; Parrish to Ferguson, Feb 22, 1915, AGC; Ferguson to Hutchings, Feb 26, 1915, AGC; Ferguson to Parrish, Feb 26, 1915, AGC; AG to Ferguson, Feb 26, 1915, AGC; Hutchings to Ferguson, Feb 27, 1915, AGC; AG to Sanders, Apr 6, 9, 12,1915, AGC; Sanders to Hutchings, Apr 4, 7, 11, 1915, AGC; AG to Parrish, Apr 12, 1915, AGC; Parrish to Hutchings, Apr 12, 1915, AGC; Parrish to AG, Apr 21, 1915, AGC; Parrish to Hobby, Oct 3, 1917, RRM; Barclay to Hobby, Oct 29, 1917, AGC; Capt. Co. D to Kemp, Oct 30, 1917, AGC; Governor to Barclay, Nov 2, 1917, AGC; Scoggins to AG, Nov 6, 1917, AGC; AG to Gray, Nov 10, 1917, AGC; Canfill to Hobby, Jan 25, 1918, AGC; Assistant AG to Chandler & Schultz, Apr 17, 1918, AGC; AG to Canfill, Mar 6, 1918, AGC; Parrish to Cope, Dec 26, 1919, Dec 26, 1920, AGC; A1b, f, g; A2b, e; A3a; A4a, b.*

PARSONS, ROBERT BRUCE. Born May 19, 1867, Woodville, Tyler County, Texas. Ht. 6 ft. 4 in., gray-blue eyes, black hair, dark complexion, married. Salesman, Sherman, Grayson County, Texas. LOYALTY RANGER June 8, 1918–Feb. 1919. REMARKS: As of Mar. 1919, Parsons stated that he had had more than 15 years' experience as a peace officer and could qualify as a Ranger captain. As of 1910 was a policeman in El Paso, El Paso County, Texas; in May 1911 resigned from the El Paso police force to become a deputy U.S. marshal at Beaumont, Jefferson County, Texas. In May 1915 was again an El Paso policeman. In July 1915 was appointed a deputy U.S. marshal in El Paso. In 1920 was a traveling salesman, living in San Antonio, Bexar County, Texas. Died in 1926 in Denton County, Texas. FAMILY: Parents, Edmund Jason Parsons (1821, TN) and Mary Ann Fulgham (b. 1830, MS); siblings, Virginia Ann (b. 1846, TX), William Jason (b. 1848, TX), Edmond James Wheat (b. 1849, TX), Samuel Zenus (b. 1855, TX), Enoch Craig (b. 1857, TX), Jason Micajah (b. 1861, TX); stepmother, Sarah Durdin (b. 1842, TX); siblings, General Lee (b. 1871, TX), C. Alexander (b. 1873, TX), Ernest O. (b. 1874, TX), M. Violet (b. 1876, TX), Evey (b. 1878, TX), Maggie (b. 1879, TX), Lula (b. 1880, TX), David Dudley (b. 1885, TX), Naomi (b. 1885, TX); spouse #1, Antonia Means (b. 1867, TX), married about 1890; daughter, Dardel (b. 1893, TX); spouse #2, Byra (b. 1872, WA). *SR; EPMT, May 30, July 24, 1911, May 23, July 14, 1915; A1b, e, f; A4a, b.*

PATTERSON, CABOT FRANK "FRANK." Born Sept. 27, 1879, Junction, Kimble County, Texas. Ht. 5 ft. 11 in., blue eyes, black hair, dark complexion. Deputy sheriff. REGULAR RANGER Sept. 19, 1917–Oct. 1, 1918 (private, Co. B). When Co. B was disbanded on June 8, 1918, he was one of seven men transferred to Co. D. Deserted—"Jumped his Company—off payroll." Game warden, Junction. SPECIAL RANGER Aug. 5, 1922–Dec. 1, 1922. Discharged (refused to turn in his WA). REMARKS: 1922 enlistment form states—"previous service: 1917–1920, Co. B." In 1920 was an oil well machinist in Kimble County. Kimble County sheriff Nov. 6, 1928–Jan. 1, 1933. A Cabot Patterson died Aug. 29, 1969, Frio County, Texas. FAMILY: Parents, Nicholas Cummings Patterson (b. 1855, TN) and Elizabeth Lumira Kounts (b. 1857, VA); siblings, Floyd Columbus (b. 1881, TX), Earl Cleveland (b. 1884, TX), Harry (b. 1888, TX), Olney (b. 1891, TX), Dixie Cummings (b. 1899, TX), Elizabeth (b. 1902, TX); spouse, Alice McKemie (b. 1892, AR), married Feb. 29, 1924. *SR; 471; General Orders No. 5, June 4, 1918, AGC; 1503:307; A1b, d, f, g; A2b; A3a; A4b.*

PATTERSON, GEORGE B. Born July 1877, Scotland. Ht. 5 ft. 9 in., gray eyes, brown hair, blond complexion, married. Ranch foreman, Catarina, Dimmit County, Texas. SPECIAL RANGER May 13, 1918–Jan. 15, 1919. REMARKS: Immigrated to the U.S. in 1883; became a naturalized citizen. Was a Dimmit County deputy sheriff, at Catarina. Sheriff requested a Special Ranger commission for Patterson. In 1920 was a truck farmer in Dimmit County. In 1930 was a farmer in San Patricio County, Texas. FAMILY: Spouse, Laura M. (b. 1898, NY), married about 1912; sons, Leonard G. (b. 1915, TX), George B., Jr. (b. 1917, TX), Howard D. (b. 1919, TX), Jack (b. 1921, TX). *SR; Assistant AG to Gardner, Apr 25, 198, AGC; A1f, g.*

PATTON, ORLANDO R. Born Apr. 16, 1881, Fulton, Itawamba County, Mississippi. Ht. 6 ft., blue eyes, black hair, fair complexion, married. Physician, Midway, Madison County, Texas. LOYALTY RANGER July 10, 1918–Feb. 1919. REMARKS: Was listed as a physician in the 1900 U.S. census when he was 19 years old. In 1920 and 1930 was a medical doctor in League City, Galveston County, Texas. Died Nov. 21, 1943, Galveston County, Texas. FAMILY: Parents, John W. Patton (b. 1843, MS) and Susan C. Martin (b. 1853, AL); siblings, Charles M. (b. 1873, MS), Alex (b. 1875, MS), Dr. Luther (b. 1879, MS), Lavonia (b. 1883, MS), Edgar (b. 1886, MS); spouse, Emma W. (b. 1892, TX), married about 1912; children, Carolyn (b. 1918, TX), John Charles (b. 1923, TX). *SR; A1d, e, f, g; A2b, e; A4a.*

PATTON, RICE MAXEY "MAX." Born Aug. 28, 1869, near Paris, Lamar County, Texas. Ht. 5 ft. 10 in., gray eyes, brown hair, light complexion, married. General claim agent, Texas Midland Railroad, Terrell, Kaufman County, Texas. SPECIAL RANGER Dec. 31, 1917–Jan. 15, 1919. REMARKS: Hunt County, Texas sheriff Nov. 3, 1896–Nov. 6, 1900. In 1910 and 1920 was a railroad claim agent in Greenville, Hunt County. An R. M. Patton died Feb. 20, 1943, Kaufman County, Texas. FAMILY: Parents, Robert J. Patton (b. 1832, AL) and Catherine Gail "Kittie" Burris (b. 1842, TX); siblings, William J. (b. 1861, TX), Robert B. (b. 1863, TX), Hattie A. (b. 1864, TX), Sarah C. "Sallie" (b. 1866, TX), Ellis B. (b. 1868, TX), Teoflies Hardiman (b. 1871, TX), Lulu Bell (b. 1874, TX); spouse, Berta Scales (b. 1875, AR), married Jan. 2, 1901, Paris, Texas; children, Max (b. 1904, TX), Ella Neta (b. 1906, TX). *SR; AG to Patton, Dec 26, 1917, AGC; 1503:273; A1b, d, e, f; A2b; A4a, b.*

PATTON, W. B. Born July 1890, Tulia, Swisher County, Texas. Ht. 5 ft. 10 ½ in., blue eyes, light hair, fair complexion. Stockman, enlisted at Laredo, Webb County, Texas. REGULAR RANGER Mar. 1, 1914–unknown; was still in as of July 24, 1914 (private, Co. B). *SR; 471; Sanders to Hutchings, July 24, 1914, WC.*

PATTON, WILLIAM BROOKS "BROOKS." Born Oct. 18, 1892, Allen, Lyon County, Kansas. Ht. 5 ft. 11 in., blue eyes, light hair, light complexion, married. Banker, Fowlerton, La Salle County, Texas. SPECIAL RANGER July 3, 1918–Jan. 15, 1919. FAMILY: Parents, William H. Patton (b. 1860, TX) and Mary A. (b. 1869, OH or PA); siblings, Flava L. W. (b. 1887, KS), Harry M. (b. 1889, KS); spouse, unknown; one child, unknown. *SR; Ad, e; A3a.*

PATTON, WILLIAM F. Born Aug. 1856, Gentryville, Douglas County, Missouri. Ht. 5 ft. 9 in., blue eyes, iron gray hair, fair complexion, married. Stock raiser, Miami, Roberts County, Texas. LOYALTY RANGER June 6, 1918–Feb. 1919. REMARKS: In 1920 was an oil dealer in Miami. In 1930 lived in Miami, retired. FAMILY: Parents, James Harvey Patton (b. 1820, TN) and Julian A. Rutherford (b. 1828, TN); siblings, James Horace (b. 1861, TX), Charlie (b. 1863, TX), John (b. 1864, TX), Thomas (b. 1867, TX); spouse, Minnie R. (b. 1865, TX), married about 1882; children, Lela or Leigh Ann (b. 1886, TX), B. Harvey (b. 1888, TX), J. Randle (b. 1892, TX). *SR; A1aa, a, d, f, g; B1.*

PAYTON, CROSS DANIEL. Born Jan. 5, 1882, Fayette, Howard County, Missouri. Ht. 5 ft. 9 in., gray eyes, brown hair, light complexion, married. Merchant, Abilene, Taylor County, Texas. SPECIAL RANGER June 6, 1917–unknown (attached to Co. C). REMARKS: Was a hardware merchant in Abilene. Died Feb. 10, 1952, Taylor County, Texas. FAMILY: Parents, Reuben Yelverton Payton (b. 1846, KY) and Mary Alice Shipley (b. 1854, MO); siblings, Lindsey Carson (b. 1872, MO), Albert Sidney (b. 1875, MO), Dora (b. 1880, MO), Lena (b. 1884, MO); spouse, Carrie Cowden (b. 1889, NM or TX), married July 11, 1909, Abilene; daughter, Paralee (b. 1911, TX). *SR; A1d, e, f, g; A2b; A3a; A4a, b.*

PEARCE, ALFRED COLE "FRED." Born Jan. 5, 1879, Walnut Springs, Bosque County, Texas. Ht. 5 ft. 10 in., blue-gray eyes, brown hair, red complexion, married. Attorney, Plainview, Hale County, Texas. SPECIAL RANGER Dec. 19, 1917–Feb. 1918 (Co. B Volunteers). Attorney, Plainview. SPECIAL RANGER Mar. 27, 1918–Jan. 15, 1919. REMARKS: 1919 letterhead: "Penry (L. C.), Pearce (Fred C.), and Bird (J. L.), Lawyers, Cisco, Texas." In 1930 was a lawyer in Lubbock, Lubbock County, Texas. Died Feb. 5, 1945, Los Angeles County, California. FAMILY: Parents, Alfred Cole Pearce (b. 1823, IL) and Margaret Louise Lattimore (b. 1846, AL); sisters, Fannie Mae (b.1873, TX), Maud Adner (b. 1876, TX); spouse, Sadie Montgomery (b. 1887, TX), married June 6, 1912, Canyon City, Texas; children, Louisa (b. 1914, TX), Fred C., Jr. (b. 1918, TX),

Monty (b. 1920, TX). *SR; Rawlings to Harley, Dec 11, 1917, AGC; A1f, g; A2f; A3a; A4a, b.*

PEARCE, GEORGE WASHINGTON. Born Mar. 31, 1876, Pleasanton, Atascosa County, Texas. Ht. 5 ft. 9 in., blue eyes, brown hair, dark complexion, married. Ranch foreman, Blanks Ranch, Lockhart, Caldwell County, Texas. LOYALTY RANGER June 15, 1918–Feb. 1919. REMARKS: Was a deputy sheriff for 6 years. In 1930 was a farmer in Dimmit County, Texas. A George Washington Pearce died Nov. 22, 1949, Blanco County, Texas. FAMILY: Parents, Jeremiah S. Pearce (b. 1839, AR) and Charity Melvinia McMains (b. 1846, MO), siblings, Cynthia C. (b. 1868, TX), Samuel Andrew (b. 1871, TX), Jesse Stuart (b. 1881, TX), Martha Agnes (b. 1884, TX), Ailsie Artie (b. 1889, TX); spouse, Donna Bell (b. 1883, NM), married about 1902; children, Lottie (b. 1903, TX), Bertha M. (b. 1907, TX), George (b. 1918, TX), Florence (b. 1919, TX). *SR; A1d, e, f, g; A2b; A3a; A4b.*

PEEBLES, JOHN JACKSON "JACKSON." Born Oct. 2, 1894, Johnson City, Carter County, Tennessee. Ht. 5 ft. 11 ½ in., blue eyes, light brown hair, light complexion. Deputy district clerk, Baird, Callahan County, Texas. SPECIAL RANGER June 1, 1917–unknown (attached to Co. C). REMARKS: Spent part of his youth in Ohio where his father was a minister. In 1930 had returned to Ohio where he was foreman for a brick company in Franklin Township, Columbiana County. A John J. Peebles died Dec. 6, 1961, Franklin County, Ohio. FAMILY: Parents, Henry M. Peebles (b. 1859, TN) and Alice (b. 1860, TN); siblings, Cliet E. (b. 1881, TN), Washington N. (b. 1884, TN), Charley N. (b. 1886, TN), Callie T. (b. 1890, TN), Ruth (b. 1898, TN), Georgia (b. 1904, OH); spouse, Velma D. (b. 1903, OH); daughters, Barbara R. (b. 1924, OH), twins Alice L. and Blanche L. (b. 1925, OH), Mary L. (b. 1927, OH), John J. (b. 1928, OH). *SR; A1d, e, g; Ai; A3a.*

PEEK, HENRY FRANKLIN. Born Dec. 1867, Cookeville, Putnam County, Tennessee. Ht. 6 ft. 1 in., blue eyes, dark hair, fair complexion, married. Farmer, Fate, Rockwall County, Texas. LOYALTY RANGER May 31, 1918–Feb. 1919. REMARKS: Died Jan. 13, 1954, Tarrant County, Texas. FAMILY: Parents, Robert Peek (b. 1800, VA) and Celina Harp (b. 1825, TN); siblings, Thomas (b. 1844, TN), Perlina (b. 1849, TN), Martha (b. 1851, TN), Francis (b. 1856, TN), Lucy (b. 1858, TN), twins Josephas and Josephine (b. 1860, TN), Samuel (b. 1865, TN); spouse, Paralee I. (b. 1872, MS), married about 1888; children, Henry N. (b. 1888, TX), Mitchell C. (b. 1890, TX), Robert J. (b. 1892, TX), Clyde F. (b. 1894, TX), Fred N. (b. 1908, TX), Edna M. (b. 1910, TX). *SR; A1aa, b, d, e, f; A2b; A4b; B1.*

PEEVEY, LEONIDAS LUCIEN "LON" or "LEON." Born Aug. 14, 1848, Barry County, Missouri. Ht. 5 ft. 10 ½ in., gray eyes, brown hair, light complexion, widower. Farmer, Abilene, Taylor County, Texas. SPECIAL RANGER June 30, 1917–unknown (Dec. 1917?) (attached to Co. C). REMARKS: Had been a jailer, a deputy sheriff, and a deputy U.S. marshal. Died May 12, 1927, Abilene, Jones County, Texas; buried in the Abilene Municipal Cemetery. LAW ENFORCEMENT RELATIVES: Ranger Tom Peevey, son. FAMILY: Parents, Judge Isaac Peevey (b. 1804, GA) and Waty Babbs (b. 1804, NC); siblings, Amanda A. (b. 1828, TN), Elizabeth (b. 1828, AL), Crawford (b. 1830, TN), Joseph G. (b. 1831, TN), Elvira (b. 1834, TN), Missouri (b. 1836, TN), Leroy (b. 1838, AL), Savanna (b. 1839, AL), Tennessee S. (b. 1840, AL), Emeline (b. 1841, AL), Nancy (b. 1843, TN), Martha (b. 1846, AL), Consininer (b. 1850, MO), Bartholomew G. (b. 1851, MO); spouse, Martha Jane Wilson (b. 1848, TX), married about 1870, Lamar County, Texas; children, Thomas Isaac (b. 1871, TX), Joseph White (b. 1873, TX), Emma Waite (b. 1875, TX), Mary Tennie (b. 1875, TX), Robert Oren (b. 1877, TX), Benjamin Littleton (b. 1879, TX), Elisha or Leonidas Lucien (b. 1880, TX), Nancy Pearl (b. 1882, TX), Zella Mabel (b. 1889, TX); stepdaughter, Georgia Alice Morrison (b. 1869, TX). *SR; A1aa, a, b, d, f; A2b; A4a, b; B1, 2.*

PEEVEY, THOMAS ISAAC "TOM." Born July 9, 1871, Paris, Lamar County, Texas. Ht. 5 ft. 8 in., brown eyes, brown hair, dark complexion, married. Farmer, Hawley, Taylor County, Texas. SPECIAL RANGER June 30, 1917–unknown (Dec. 1917?). REMARKS: In 1920 was a farm laborer in Chandler, Maricopa County, Arizona. In 1930 was a retail grocery merchant in Alhambra, Maricopa County. Died Apr. 8, 1961. LAW ENFORCEMENT RELATIVES: Ranger L. L. Peevey, father. FAMILY: Parents, Leonindas Lucien Peevey (b. 1848, MO) and Martha Jane Wilson (b. 1848, TX); siblings, Joseph White (b. 1873, TX), Emma Waite (b. 1875, TX), Mary

Tennie (b. 1875, TX), Robert Oren (b. 1877, TX), Benjamin Littleton (b. 1879, TX), Elisha or Leonidas Lucien (b. 1880, TX), Nancy Pearl (b. 1882, TX), Zella Mabel (b. 1889, TX); step-sister, Georgia Alice Morrison (b. 1869, TX); spouse, Malissia M. (b. 1878, TN), married about 1898. *SR; A1b, e, f, g; A4b; B1.*

PENICK, ROBERT EDWARD. Born July 4, 1891, Anson, Jones County, Texas. Ht. 5 ft. 10 ½ in., blue eyes, medium hair, medium complexion, married. Merchant, Stamford, Jones County. SPECIAL RANGER May 31, 1917–unknown (Dec. 1917?). REMARKS: In 1920 and 1930 was a hardware merchant in Wichita Falls, Wichita County, Texas. An R. E. Penick died Sept. 10, 1934, Wichita County, Texas. FAMILY: Parents, Robert Lee Penick (b. 1862, MO or KY) and Dottie L. Potts (b. 1861, LA); sister, Lelair E. (b. 1887, TX); spouse, Irmodene (1891, TX), married about 1917; children, Blanche M. (b. 1918, TX), Tom R. (b. 1919, TX), Mary Irmodene (b. 1922, TX). *SR; Register to Ferguson, May 18, 1917, AGC; Cunningham to Ferguson, May 18, 1917, AGC; A1d, e, f, g; A2b, e; A3a; A4b; B2.*

PENLAND, ROBERT LUTHER. Born June 2, 1874, Haysville, Clay County, North Carolina. Ht. 5 ft. 7 ½ in., blue eyes, gray hair, light complexion, married, as of Aug. 1934. Real estate dealer, Waco, McLennan County, Texas. LOYALTY RANGER June 4, 1918–Feb. 1919. Guard, Waco. SPECIAL RANGER Aug. 17, 1934–unknown. REMARKS: Had been a grocery salesman in Grayson County, Texas. In 1920 was an auto salesman in Waco. In 1930 was a real estate agent in Waco. Died Apr. 7, 1957, McLennan County, Texas. FAMILY: Parents, John A. Penland (b. 1851, NC) and Sarah Caroline "Sallie" Truitt (b. 1859, NC); brothers, James Marr (b. 1876, NC), Charles Monroe (b. 1878, NC), Arthur Nichols (b. 1881, NC), Will Hamilton (b. 1883, NC), Earl Paul (b. 1886, NC), George Harvey (b. 1888, NC); spouse #1, Julia M. (b. 1880, TX), married about 1899; children, Buford (b. 1903, TX), Maurice (b. 1909, TX), Pauline M. (b. 1911, TX); spouse #2, Grace J. (b. 1878, TX), married about 1916. *SR; A1d, f, g; A2b; A3a.*

PENN, JUSTO SABOR. Born Oct. 4, 1875, Austin, Travis County, Texas. Ht. 6 ft., brown eyes, light hair, fair complexion, married. Publisher, *Laredo Weekly Times*, Laredo, Webb County, Texas. LOYALTY RANGER June 4, 1918–Feb. 1919. REMARKS: Had been a reporter for the Laredo newspaper; by 1910 was a newspaper editor in Laredo. In 1930 was a county judge, Webb County. Died July 2, 1939, Bexar County, Texas. FAMILY: Parents, James Saunders Penn (b. 1846, MS) and Virginia Josephine Miller (b. 1851, VA); siblings, Amar (b. 1873, TX), Viva (b. 1874, TX), Viola (b. 1878, TX), Albert Mc. (b. 1885, TX); spouse, Elisa or Alicia Herrera (b. 1880, TX), married Aug. 14, 1901; children, Virginia (b. 1902, TX), Esther (b. 1903, TX), Alice (b. 1905, TX), Justo S., Jr. (b. 1908, TX), James H. (b. 1917, TX). *SR; 172:IV, 78; A1b, d, e, f, g; A2b; A3a; B1.*

PENNINGTON, BENJAMIN L. Born May 1861, Holland, Bell County, Texas. Ht. 5 ft. 10 in., brown eyes, light hair, light complexion, married. Ranchman. REGULAR RANGER Oct. 4, 1917–Oct. 12, 1918 (private, Co. B; transferred to Co. L, Mar. 1918). Died Oct. 12, 1918 of Spanish influenza. REMARKS: City marshal of Holland, 12 years; constable at Holland, 8 years. In Aug. 1915, while constable at Holland, was shot and wounded by the mayor. Had a drinking problem. LAW ENFORCEMENT RELATIVES: Ranger Joseph D. Jackson, uncle. FAMILY: Parents, John Pennington (b. 1830, MO) and Caroline Jackson (b. 1836, KY); sisters, Louann C. (b. 1856, TX), Elizabeth Sarah (b. 1858, TX); stepfather, R. B. Fewell (b. 1845, MS); sister, Roseanna Fewell (b. 1870, TX); spouse, Fannie E. (b. 1865, AR), married about 1882; children, Levi (b. 1883, TX), Clarence (b. 1886, TX), Raphael S. (b. 1888, TX), Virgil (b. 1891, TX), Zoleta "Zollie" (b. 1896, TX), Benjamin L. (b. 1900, TX). *SR; 471; EPMT, Oct 13, 1918; EPH, Oct 14, 1918; BDH, Aug 4, 1915; LWT, Aug 8, 1915; Jackson to Hutchings, Mar 27, 1917, AGC; AG to Jackson, Mar 29, 1917, AGC; Assistant AG to Fox, Jan 28, 1918, AGC; Davis to Harley, Mar 18, 23, 1918, AGC; Assistant AG to Davis, Mar 26, 1918, AGC; A1aa, a, b, d, e; A4a, b.*

PEREZ, JESSE, SR. Born Feb. 1869, San Antonio, Bexar County, Texas. Ht. 5 ft. 9 in., brown eyes, dark hair, dark complexion, married. REGULAR RANGER 1890–1892, 1906–1908—"2 yrs. under Capt. Lee Hall; 3 yrs under Capt. Hughes, 4 mo. under Capt. McDonald; 1 yr under Capt. Ross." Peace officer. REGULAR RANGER Mar. 16, 1918–July 31, 1920 (private, Co. G; resigned from Co. G Nov. 10, 1918; enlisted in Co. K, Nov. 18, 1918; reenlisted under the new law, Jan. 20, 1919). Resigned. Peace officer, Roma, Starr

County, Texas. REGULAR RANGER Mar. 19, 1921–Jan. 31, 1923 (private, Co. D). Resigned. REMARKS: Had been a Rough Rider in Spanish-American War. Chief deputy for 3 years under Sheriff John Closner of Hidalgo County, Texas. Deputy sheriff for 3 years under Sheriff A.Y. Baker of Hidalgo County. Deputy sheriff for 2 years under Sheriff John Tobin of Bexar County. In June, 1917, was liquidating his business enterprise in Mission, Hidalgo County. In 1930 was an Immigration inspector in Starr County. FAMILY: Spouse, unknown, married about 1895; son, Jesse Perez, Jr. (b. 1896, TX). *SR; 471; Perez to Ferguson, June 26, 1917, AGC; Perez to Stevens, June 11, 1918, WC; Wright to Barton, Sept 13, 1921, WC; BDH, June 7, 1912, May 9, June 26, Aug 14, 1914; 470: 35, 47; 485: 244–245; "Memoirs of Jesse Perez;" A1g.*

PERKINS, CHARLES F. Born Apr. 1879, Sweetwater, Nolan County, Texas. Ht. 5 ft. 11 in., blue eyes, brown hair, light complexion, married. Laborer. REGULAR RANGER Sept. 20, 1917–unknown—still in on Sept. 10, 1918 (private, Co. E.). REMARKS: Had been a deputy sheriff in Val Verde County, Texas and adjoining counties. In 1910 was an assistant section foreman for the railroad in Terrell County, Texas. FAMILY: Parents, Simion Perkins (b. 1842, IN) and Mary E. (b. 1854, KY); brother, George A. (b. 1872, KS); spouse, Eulah or Eulalie (b. 1883, TX), married about 1900; children, James L. (b. 1901, TX), Maudie L. (b. 1906, TX). *SR; Barler to Griffiths, Sept 20, 1917, AGC; Barler to Harley, Oct 12, 1917, AGC; MR, Co. E, Dec 31, 1917, AGC; A1b, e; A2b.*

PERKINS, JAMES CLARK. Born Aug. 1, 1890, Cameron, Milam County, Texas. Ht. 5 ft. 11 in., gray eyes, brown hair, fair complexion. Peace officer. REGULAR RANGER Aug. 25, 1917–Mar. 10, 1919 (private, Co. C; transferred to Co. L, Jan. 1918; promoted to sergeant, Mar. 1918). Honorably discharged—Co. L was disbanded. Ranger, Fabens, El Paso County, Texas. REGULAR RANGER June 20, 1919–July 3, 1919 (private, Co. A; reenlisted under the new law; was ordered to report to Captain Stevens July 1, 1919). Resigned because he refused to serve under Stevens. Returned to Cameron. Stockman. REGULAR RANGER Jan. 5, 1920–May 17, 1920 (sergeant, Co. F). Discharged/fired—perhaps for failure to pay debt to landlady. LAW ENFORCEMENT RELATIVES: Ranger T. E. Paul "Elzey" Perkins, brother (killed in action). FAMILY: Parents, Jessie Perkins (b. 1855, AL) and Nannie (b. 1862, TX); siblings, Elzey (b. 1884, TX), Leania M. (b. 1886, TX), Lillian (b. 1889, TX), Halliebyrd (b. 1895, TX); spouse, Opal Belle McCall (b. 1893, TX), married Nov. 25, 1925. *SR; 471; Acting AG to Davis, Jan 9, 1918, AGC; Assistant AG to Davis, Feb 14,1918, AGC; Davis to Harley, Mar 31, 1918, AGC; Special Orders No. 21, Mar 10, 1919, WC; Harley to Perkins, July 1, 3, 1919, AGC; Perkins to Harley, July 2, 1919, AGC; Hanson to Harley, July 1, 1919, AGC; Aldrich to Perkins, July 7, 16, 1919, AGC; Perkins to Aldrich, July 9, 21, 1919, AGC; Aldrich to Perkins, Mar 1, 1920, AGC; Davis to Cope, Apr 10, 1920, WC; Perkins to Cope, May 17, 22, 1920, AGC; Aldrich to Mrs. Schryer, May 29, 1920, AGC; A1d, e; A2a, b; A3a; A4b.*

PERKINS, JAMES PAUL "PAUL." Born July 11, 1874, Beeville, Bee County, Texas. Ht. 6 ft. 2 in., gray eyes, brown hair, dark complexion, married. Constable, enlisted in Bee County. REGULAR RANGER Dec. 21, 1917–Oct. 1, 1918 (private, Co. K). Resigned. REMARKS: Had been a deputy sheriff. In 1910 was a carpenter in Beeville. In 1920 was a boiler maker in San Antonio, Bexar County, Texas. In 1930 was a house carpenter in Aransas Pass, San Patricio County, Texas. Died Jan. 16, 1951, Bee County. Texas; buried in Prairie View Cemetery, Aransas Pass. FAMILY: Parents, James Calvin "Cap" Perkins (b. 1854, LA) and Sariah Elizabeth "Betsy" Garsee (b. 1855, TX); brother, Green Edward or Edgar (b. 1876, TX); spouse, Lula Dan Nichols (b. 1891, TX), married about 1907; children, Katherine F. (b. 1908, TX), James D. (b. 1910, TX), Ila D. (b. 1914, TX), Houston D. (b. 1920, TX), Elizabeth S. (b. 1923, TX), Barney R. (b. 1925, TX). *SR; 471; A1e, f, g; A2b; A3a; A4b.*

PERKINS, LONZO ANDREW "LON." Born Apr. 1869, Hays County, Texas. No physical description, married. Farmer, Rotan, Fisher County, Texas. LOYALTY RANGER June 10, 1918–Feb. 1919. REMARKS: In 1930 was living in Portland, San Patricio County, Texas. Died July 27, 1941, San Patricio County, Texas. FAMILY: Parents, George K. Perkins (b. 1825, MS) and Mariah P. (1840, TX); siblings, Laura P. (b. 1856, TX), Emma (b. 1858, TX), Anna (b. 1861, TX), Ida (b. 1863, TX), Mattie (b. 1865, TX), Alice (b. 1867, TX), Allison (b. 1871, TX), Rubie (b. 1874, TX), Oaklin (b. 1876, TX), Georgia (b. 1879, TX); spouse, May F. (b. 1868, TX), married about 1895; children, Roy L. (b. 1897, TX), Essie V. (b. 1900, TX), Liny A. (b. 1907, TX). *SR; A1a, b, e, g; A2b.*

PERKINS, T. E. Paul "ELZEY." Born Mar. 12, 1884, Milam County, Texas. Ht. 6 ft. ½ in., gray eyes, brown hair, medium complexion. Cowboy. REGULAR RANGER Sept. 1, 1918–Nov. 7, 1918 (private, Co. L). Killed in action, Nov. 7, 1918 near Fabens, El Paso County, Texas. LAW ENFORCEMENT RELATIVES: Ranger James Clark Perkins, brother. FAMILY: Parents, Jessie Perkins (b. 1855, AL) and Nannie (b. 1862, TX); siblings, Leania M. (b. 1886, TX), Lillian (b. 1889, TX), James Clark (b. 1890, TX), Halliebyrd (b. 1895, TX). *SR; 471; Davis to Harley, Nov 8, 1918, AGC; Davis to Low, Nov 12, 918, WC; 1: I, 1570; EPMT, Nov 9, 10, 14, 19, 1918; A1d; A2b; A3a.*

PERROW, HENRY CARRINGTON. Born Feb. 18, 1877, Nelson County, Virginia. Ht. 6 ft. 1 in., blue eyes, brown hair, light complexion, married. Switchman, I&GN Railroad, San Antonio, Bexar County, Texas. REGULAR RANGER Dec. 18, 1917–Mar. 1918 (private, Co. G). Resigned. REMARKS: For the past 5 yrs. had been a switchman for the I&GN Railroad at San Antonio. Had an honorable discharge from the Army. Worked on a ranch in Arizona for 18 months. In Sept. 1918 was a policeman in San Antonio. In 1930 was a police detective in San Antonio. Died Dec. 13, 1933, Bexar County, Texas. FAMILY: Parents, Ebel R. (b. 1839, VA) and Henrietta J. (b. 1850, VA); sister, May G. (b. 1879, VA); spouse, Mayme Emily (b. 1878, NE), married about 1900; daughter, Blanche L. (b. 1903, KS). *SR; 471; Stevens to Harley, Dec 18, 1917, AGC; Jones to Stevens, Dec 18, 1917, AGC; A1b, d, g; A2b; A3a.*

PETERSON, WILLIAM SANDERS. Born Aug. 6, 1864, Wrightsboro, Gonzales County, Texas. Ht. 5 ft. 10 ½ in., blue eyes, brown hair, light complexion, married, as of Dec. 1917; single, as of June 1919. Stockman, Kerrville, Kerr County, Texas. REGULAR RANGER Dec. 21, 1917–Feb. 21, 1925 (private, Co. K; reenlisted in Co. D under the new law, June 20, 1919; reenlisted June 20, 1921). Honorably discharged. REMARKS: In 1910 was doing odd jobs in Globe, Gila County, Arizona. As of Apr. 1916 had been a peace officer for 7 years, including 5 yrs. 3 months in the Arizona Rangers and an unspecified time as a Kerr County deputy sheriff. State senator Claude Hudspeth was his patron. Died June 18, 1929, Kerr County, Texas. LAW ENFORCEMENT RELATIVES: Ranger James Bailey Wright, cousin; Ranger Earl Ray Wright, cousin. FAMILY: Parents, William Caswell Peterson (b. 1835, NC) and Lucy Ann Wright (b. 1836, AL); siblings, Elizabeth Wright (b. 1860, MS), Leroy Clay (b. 1862, TX), John M. (b. 1866, TX), Sidney C. (b. 1868, TX), Walter Gray (b. 1869, TX), George Wright (b. 1870, TX), Henry Caswell (b. 1874, TX), Thomas (b. 1876, TX), Cornelia Ann (b. 1879, TX); spouse #1, Virginia Chester Williamson (b. 1866, TX), married Oct. 12, 1886, Kerr County; daughters, Mary Ethel (b. 1887, TX), Annie E. (b. 1889, TX); spouse #2, Stella Belle Bennett (b. 1871, TX), married about 1907. *SR; 471; Peterson to Hutchings, Apr 16, 1916, AGC; Hudspeth to Harley, Oct 26, 1917, AGC; 470: 35, 43; A1a, b, e; A2b, c; A4a, b; B1.*

PEVETO, ALVA BURTON. Born June 1, 1871, Cameron, Cameron Parish, Louisiana. Ht. 5 ft. 11 in., blue eyes, black hair, dark complexion, married. Transfer business, Orange, Orange County, Texas. LOYALTY RANGER July 3, 1918–Feb. 26, 1919. REMARKS: June 1919, the federal Bureau of Investigation was proceeding against him for bootlegging. Died Oct. 29, 1930, Orange County, Texas. FAMILY: Parents, John Peveto (b. 1821, LA) and Elizabeth Gillen (b. 1841, LA); siblings, Juril Hardamon (b. 1859, LA), William O. (b. 1861, LA), Missouri Isabella (b. 1863, LA), Martha Isadora (b. 1865, LA), Jessee H. (b. 1867, LA), twins Lucinda Belzora "Bella" and S. B. (b. 1869, LA), Preston (b. 1877, LA); stepmother, Mary or Pauline Hayes (b. 1837, TX). *SR; A1a, b, d, f; A2b, c; A4a, b, g.*

PEYTON, WILLIAM SNYDER. Born Dec. 25, 1884, Charlottesville, Albemarle County, Virginia. Ht. 5 ft. 6 in., blue eyes, light hair, fair complexion. Lawyer, San Antonio, Bexar County, Texas. LOYALTY RANGER May 31, 1918–Feb. 24, 1919. REMARKS: Was listed as a SPECIAL RANGER. 1919 letterhead: "W.S. Peyton, Attorney at Law, Gunter Building, San Antonio." Died Oct. 26, 1924, Bexar County, Texas. FAMILY: Parents, Francis Bradley Peyton (b. 1848, VA) and Marion Helen Beale (b. 1852, VA); siblings, Genevieve Gordon (b. 1879, VA), Marion Helen (b. 1880, VA), Francis Bradley, Jr. (b. 1882, VA), William Herbert (b. 1883, VA), Charles Livingston (b. 1888, VA), Phillip Barbour (b. 1891, VA); spouse, Lucy Peyton Maury (b. 1884), divorced by 1920. *SR; A1d, f; A2b; A3a; A4a, b.*

PHELPS, ROBERT CARROL, JR. Born Jan. 1881, Uvalde, Uvalde County, Texas. Ht. 5 ft. 11 in., blue eyes, brown hair, fair complexion, married. Government scout, enlisted in Presidio County, Texas. SPECIAL RANGER Mar. 19, 1917–Dec. 1917. REMARKS: Was commissioned at the request of the Army. *SR.*

PHELPS, WILLIAM EURA. Born Sept. 17, 1886, Uvalde, Uvalde County, Texas. Ht. 5 ft. 5 in., blue eyes, light hair, fair complexion, married. Deputy sheriff, Alpine, Brewster County, Texas. REGULAR RANGER July 1, 1919–Nov. 3, 1919 (private, Co. E). Resigned. Honorably discharged. REMARKS: Was constable at Alpine 1914–1916. In Feb. 1916, resigned to take charge of the smelter at the Study Butte mine. In 1917, lived in Terlingua. In Nov. 1918, became a deputy sheriff and jailer of Brewster County. In 1920 was a railroad special officer in Gallup, McKinley County, New Mexico. Died Jan. 22, 1949, Gallup, McKinley County, New Mexico; buried in Hillcrest Cemetery, Gallup. FAMILY: Parents, Robert Calloway Phelps (b. 1861, TX) and Marie Frances Parsons (b. 1867, TX); siblings, Robert Calloway, Jr. (b. 1883, TX), Jesse (b. 1891, TX), Mary Cordelia (b. 1892, TX); spouse, Rose Lee Druden (b. 1894, TX), married Feb. 16, 1910, Alpine; children, Eura Wilber (b. 1913, TX), Hugh Francis (b. 1914, TX), Rosemary (b. 1917, TX), William Lee (b. 1918, TX), Hollis Everett (b. 1920, NM). *SR; 471; AA, Feb 26, 1914, Mar 18, Apr 1, 15, July 29, 1915, Feb 24, 1916, Feb 15, June 14, Sept 27, 1917, Nov 21, 1918, June 26, July 10, Oct 2, 23, 1919; A1e, f; A3a; A4a, b; B1.*

PHILLIPS, CHARLES MORGAN. Born Sept. 19, 1877, Claiborne, Mississippi. Ht. 5 ft. 9 ½ in., hazel eyes, gray hair, light complexion. Labor agent for U.S. government, San Antonio, Bexar County, Texas. SPECIAL RANGER Jan. 3, 1919–either Jan. 15 or Dec. 31, 1919. Farmer, Bell County, Texas. RAILROAD RANGER Aug. 7, 1922–Dec. 30, 1922 (Co. B). Discharged. REMARKS: In Apr. 1917 wrote from Smithville, Bastrop County, Texas applying for a commission as a Ranger captain. Said he had considerable experience as a peace officer. FAMILY: Parents, Dr. (dentist) Curtis S. Phillips (b. 1850, IL) and Susan McCurdy (b. 1853, MS); siblings, Athea (b. 1875, MS), Horace (b. 1880, MS). *SR; Phillips to Ferguson, Apr 12, 1917, AGC; A1b, d; A3a; B2.*

PICKLE, MALCOLM LUCIUS. Born July 18, 1879, Palestine, Anderson County, Texas. Ht. 5 ft. 10 7/8 in., brown eyes, black hair, dark complexion, married. Special officer, Fort Worth, Tarrant County, Texas. SPECIAL RANGER Jan. 23, 1918–Jan. 15, 1919. REMARKS: Was a watchman, Saint Louis Southwestern Railroad. His superior requested that he be commissioned. Pickle stated that he had served the SLSW for 7 years. In 1920 lived in Tyler, Smith County, Texas. In 1930 was a railroad shop yard man in Athens, Henderson County, Texas. Died Nov. 20, 1953, El Paso County, Texas; buried in Oakwood Cemetery, Tyler. FAMILY: Parents, Ira William Pickle (b. 1848, AL) and M. Carrie or Cora Wynn (b. 1856, SC); siblings, Irene, Eugene Asberry, Daisey P. (b. 1877, SC), Edwina (b. 1888, TX); spouse, Lou Ella Tomlinson (b. 1877, TX), married about 1902, Smith County; children, Lillian Lorraine or Hattie (b. 1903, TX), Elsie Pauline (b. 1904, TX), Lamar Leonard "Jack" (b. 1905, TX), Harold Elwood (b. 1906, TX), Mary Evylyn (b. 1909, TX), Roy Darnell (b. 1912, TX), Dorothy Marie (b. 1916, TX). *SR; Campbell to Harley, Jan 1, 30, 1918, AGC; A1b, e, f, g; A2b; A4a, b; B1.*

PLACE, JOSEPH THOMAS "JOE." Born Oct. 25, 1887, Phoenix, Maricopa County, Arizona. Ht. 5 ft. 10 in., dark eyes, black hair, dark complexion, married. Farmer, El Paso, El Paso County, Texas. SPECIAL RANGER Apr. 22, 1918–Jan. 1, 1919. REMARKS: Was an El Paso County deputy sheriff. On Nov. 7, 1918, he and Ranger T. E. Paul "Elzey" Perkins were ambushed; Perkins was killed. In 1930 was a farmer in Solomonsville, Graham County, Arizona where he and his parents had lived when he was a boy. Died Aug. 17, 1970, Cottonwood, Arizona. FAMILY: Parents, William Atherton Place (b. 1853, IA) and Permelia Adeline "Addie" Riggins (b. 1852, IL); step brother, Wilson Orr (b. 1883, IL); spouse, Lena Virginia Gamble (b. 1889, NM), married about 1907; children, William (b. 1908, Mexico), George G. (b. 1910, Mexico), Joseph Davis (b. 1916, AZ), Mary Ella (b. 1923, AZ). *SR; Davis to Harley, Nov 8, 1918, Apr 21, 1919, AGC; A1d, f, g; A3a; A4g.*

POOL, JAMES FRANKLIN P. Born Oct. 10, 1871, Johnson County, Missouri. Ht. 5 ft. 10 in., brown eyes, gray hair, dark complexion, married. Merchant, Hamlin, Jones County, Texas. SPECIAL RANGER June 2, 1917–Dec. 1917. REMARKS: One source spells last name "P'Pool." In 1930 was a cotton broker living in Highland Park, Dallas County, Texas. Died July 2, 1942, Dallas County, Texas. FAMILY: Parents, William F. P. Pool (b. 1842, KY) and Sarah Ellen Jackson (b. 1848, IL); siblings, George G. P., Ella P., Charlie H. P. (b. 1865, KY), Nina J. P. (b. 1867, KY), Robert Allen P. (b. 1874, MO), Birdie Lillian P. (b. 1876, KY), Sarah Susan P. (b. 1879, MO); spouse, Lucy M. Davis (b. 1878, TX), married Dec. 4, 1898; daughters, Ruda Virginia P. (b. 1901, TX), Mary Ellen P. (b. 1904, TX). *SR; A1b, d, e, f, g; A4a.*

PORTER, CAREY CHOATE. Born Sept. 10, 1885, Caldwell, Burleson County, Texas. Ht. 6 ft., blue eyes, brown hair, fair complexion, married. Manager, Sugar Land Railway Company, Sugar Land, Fort Bend County, Texas. SPECIAL RANGER Jan. 21, 1918–late 1918. Died Oct. 18, 1918, Harris County, Texas. FAMILY: Parents, Curran R. Porter (b. 1854, TX) and Alice (b. 1857, TX); siblings, Ralph (b. 1880, TX), Oscar (b. 1882, TX), Ruth (b. 1891, TX), Thelma (b. 1897, TX); stepmother, Lizzie (b. 1864, KY); spouse, Helen. *SR; Porter to Woodul, Jan 26, 1918, AGC; A1b, d, e; A2b; A3a.*

PORTER, HAROLD ALONZO. Born Nov. 25, 1889, Hays County, Texas. Tall, slender, brown eyes, black hair, married. Farmer and stockman, Nursery, Victoria County, Texas. LOYALTY RANGER June 8, 1918–Feb. 1919. REMARKS: In 1930 still a farmer in Victoria County. Died Mar. 8, 1970, San Patricio County, Texas. FAMILY: Parents, William Alonzo Porter (b. 1860, KY) and stepmother Ida (b. 1874, AL); siblings, Lula May (b. 1895, TX), August (b. 1897, TX), Charley N. (b. 1898, TX), Falba (b. 1901, TX); spouse, Gertrude Annie Coffin (b. 1889, TX), married Jan. 2, 1913; daughters, Annie Ione (b. 1915, TX), Almarie (b. 1917, TX), Lottie Jean (b. 1924, TX), Haroldine (b. 1929, TX). *SR; A1e, f, g; A2a, b, e; A3a; A4b.*

POUNCEY, JESSE MERRILL. Born Nov. 14, 1879, Gonzales County, Texas. Ht. 5 ft. 10 ½ in., gray eyes, dark hair, dark complexion, married. Stockman and trader, Alpine, Brewster County, Texas. SPECIAL RANGER Jan. 31, 1918–Jan. 15, 1919. REMARKS: Deputy sheriff for 12 years. Owned a ranch near the Rio Grande 65 miles from Alpine. In 1930 was a real estate salesman in Alpine. Died Oct. 16, 1934, Bexar County, Texas; buried in the IOOF Cemetery. FAMILY: Parents, Anthony Wayne Pouncey, Jr. (b. 1854, TX) and Artelia Q. Ward (b. 1856, TX); spouse, Sarah Irma Magee (b. 1882, TX), married May 18, 1903, Gonzales County; children, Merrill Olivia (b. 1905, TX), Anthony Truman (b. 1907, TX), Temple Cone (b. 1914, TX). *SR; Pouncey to AG, June 10, 1919, AGC; A1b, d, f, g; A2b; A3a; A4a, b; B1.*

POWELL, FRANK. Born May 8, 1877, Hamilton, Ontario, Canada. Ht. 5 ft. 10 ½ in., blue eyes, brown hair, fair complexion, married. Motion picture director, San Antonio, Bexar County, Texas. LOYALTY RANGER June 21, 1918–Feb. 1919. REMARKS: Became a naturalized U.S. citizen at Cleveland. In 1910 was a guest in the Hotel King Edward, Manhattan, New York County, New York; was a stage actor. FAMILY: Mother, Mrs. Elizabeth Barber (her name as of Sept. 1918); spouse, unknown, married about 1907. *SR; A1e; A3a.*

POWELL, FRANK ROBERTS "BOB." Born Oct. 5, 1879, Albany, Shackelford County, Texas. Tall, slender, blue eyes, red hair, married. Abstracter, Dumas, Moore County, Texas. LOYALTY RANGER June 11, 1918–Feb. 24, 1919. REMARKS: One source lists birthplace as McLennan County, Texas; another lists Waxahachie, Ellis County, Texas as birthplace. In 1930 still proprietor of an abstract office in Dumas. Died Sept. 25, 1932, Potter County, Texas. FAMILY: Parents, John Henry Powell (b. 1850, AR) and Annie Elizabeth Roberts (b. 1861, TX); siblings, Annie B., Milton Howard, Hixie E. (b. 1879), Lillian Erie (b. 1882), Thomas Cole (b. 1884), John Clifton (b. 1886), Ruby Irene (b. 1891), Mary Fern (b. 1897); spouse, Loula Bell Parker (b. 1879, TX), married Oct. 4, 1903, Burnet County, Texas; sons, John Riley (b. 1904, TX), Bob (b. 1906, TX), Walter P. (b. 1908, TX). *SR; A1e, f, g; A2b; A3a; A4a, b; B1.*

POWERS, GEORGE P. "PAT." Born Aug. 1849, Tipperary, Ireland. Ht. 5 ft. 8 in., brown eyes, gray hair, dark complexion, married. Quarantine guard, El Paso, El Paso County, Texas. SPECIAL RANGER Feb. 23, 1918–Jan. 15, 1919. REMARKS: His superior requested that he be commissioned. In 1910 was a sanitation inspector for the city of El Paso. In Jan. 1919 resided at Glory Point Farm, El Paso, Route L, Box 576. In 1920 was manager of an alfalfa farm in El Paso County. Died Jan. 3, 1928, El Paso County, Texas. FAMILY: Spouse, Sarah A. (b. 1863, PA). *SR; Collins to Harley, Feb 1, 1918, AGC; AG to Powers, Feb 2, 1918, AGC; A1e, f, g; A2b.*

POWERS, WILLIAM EDWARD. Born Mar. 17, 1881, Nacogdoches, Nacogdoches County, Texas. Ht. 6 ft. 2 in., gray eyes, brown hair, light complexion, married. Peace officer, Gilmer, Upshur County, Texas. REGULAR RANGER Aug. 12, 1919–Jan. 31, 1920 (private, Headquarters Co.). Resigned because of wife's illness; she died. Peace officer, Wichita Falls, Wichita County, Texas. REGULAR RANGER Mar. 27, 1920–Apr. 23, 1920 (private, Headquarters Co.). Discharged. Peace officer, Wichita Falls. REGULAR RANGER Oct. 2, 1920–Dec. 31, 1920 (private, Emergency Co. No. 2). Honorably discharged. Peace officer, Wichita Falls. REGULAR RANGER Mar. 1, 1921–Apr. 30, 1921 (private, Emergency Co. No. 1). Honorably discharged. REMARKS: In Sept. 1918 was constable, precinct #1 in Gilmer. A William Edward Powers died Mar. 7, 1959, Nueces County, Texas. FAMILY: Spouse, Eunice L. (b. 1883, TX), married about 1901; daughter, Alta (b. 1908, TX). *SR; 471; Powers to Cope, Oct 1, 1920, AGC; Cope to Davenport, Jan 5, 1921, AGC; Cope to Powers, Jan 5, 1921, AGC; Powers to Barton, Feb 3, 1921, AGC; Davenport to Barton, Feb 4, 1921, AGC; A1e, f; A2b; A3a.*

PRATHER, JOHN HAMILTON. Born Nov. 1864, near Fort Worth, Tarrant County, Texas. Ht. 5 ft. 11 in., blue eyes, gray hair, red complexion, married. REGULAR RANGER—he served 16 or 17 months in Co. E, Frontier Battalion. Cowboy, Asherton, Dimmit County, Texas. SPECIAL RANGER Dec. 27, 1917–Apr. 1918 (private, Co. C Volunteers). Discharged. REMARKS: His station in 1917–1918: Indio Ranch. Had been a farmer in Midland County, Texas. In 1920 was a house carpenter in Nueces County, Texas. Died Dec. 30, 1932, Petronila, Nueces County, Texas; buried in Rose Hill Cemetery, Corpus Christi, Nueces County, Texas. FAMILY: Parents, John David Prather (b. 1841, MO) and Sarah Jane Bennett (b. 1834, KY); sister, Mary Ellen (b. 1860, TX); stepmother, Mollie Jo Scott (b. 1848, TX); sisters, Ada, Marinda; spouse, Frances Ellen Baker (b. 1874, TX), married Mar. 15, 1891, Zavala County, Texas; children, Ned William (b. 1893, TX), Mary Alva (b. 1894, TX), Edward Merle (b. 1896, TX), John Howard (b. 1899, TX), Thomas Bluford (b. 1900, TX), Ora Lee (b. 1902, TX), Martin Clyde (b. 1904, TX), Henry Harold (b. 1906, TX0, Sarah Louise (b. 1909, TX), John Davis (b. 1911, TX), Anderson Bates (b. 1913, TX). *SR; A1a, e, f, g; A2b; A4a, b.*

PREMONT, CHARLES. Born July 1867, Russia. Ht. 5 ft. 9 in., brown eyes, black hair, dark complexion. REGULAR RANGER about 2 years ca. 1892. Stockman, Alice, Jim Wells County, Texas. SPECIAL RANGER Feb. 14, 1917–unknown (Dec. 1917?). REMARKS: Immigrated to the United States ca. 1882; became a naturalized citizen in 1914. Had been a farmer and stockman in Nueces County, Texas. Died Nov. 7, 1941, Jim Wells County, Texas. *SR; 471; 319: 375; 470: 154; A1d, e, f; A2b.*

PRICE, CHARLES W. Born Mar. 21, 1888, Travis County, Texas. Ht. 6 ft. 2 in., brown eyes, brown hair, fair complexion. Farmer. REGULAR RANGER Oct. 6, 1911–Jan. 31, 1912 (private, Co. C). Discharged—reduction in force. Peace officer. REGULAR RANGER Apr. 27, 1915–June 11, 1918 (private, Co. A; reenlisted Apr. 27, 1917). Resigned. Peace officer, Alice, Jim Wells County, Texas. SPECIAL RANGER June 11, 1918–Jan. 15, 1919. Peace officer. REGULAR RANGER July 29, 1919–Dec. 1919. Resigned. Tax collector, Alice. SPECIAL RANGER Feb. 18, 1931–Jan. 20, 1934 (WA was extended). REMARKS: Was elected Travis County constable, precinct 6, Del Valle, in 1910; resigned in 1911 to join Capt. Fox's new Ranger company. In May 1913 became a Cameron County, Texas deputy sheriff—the county jailer. He resigned in May 1914 to become a Cameron County deputy constable. He resigned in Apr. 1915 to reenlist in the Rangers. In June 1918 he resigned to run for sheriff of Jim Wells County; Nov. 5, 1918, was elected by 99 votes and served as sheriff until Jan. 1, 1931. Was sheriff again Nov. 8, 1932 until his death on July 29, 1944. *SR; 471; Sanders to Hutchings, Apr 27, 1915, AGC; AG to Sanders, May 3, 1915, Apr 27, 1918, AGC; Wells to Sanders, Dec 5, 1915, AGC; Acting AG to Hanson, June 10, 1918, AGC; AG to Colt's, July 30, 1918, AGC; Hanson to Cardwell, July 30, 1918, AGC; Price to Harley, May 12, 1919, AGC; Tumlinson to Aldrich, Dec 15, 1919, AGC; 1503:290; AS, June 8, 1911; SAE, Oct 11, 1911; BDH, May 7, June 5, Sept 17, 19, 20, Dec 9, 1913, Jan 3, Mar 23, 31, May 6, July 18, 20, 21, Aug 13, 1914, Jan 21, Sept 14, 1915, Mar 9, Oct 26, 1917; LWT, Nov 14, 1920, Jan 9, 1921; La Prensa, Apr 11, June 1, 1916; 319: 32–33; 469: 60; 485: 229, 230; A1f; A2b; A3a.*

PRICE, GEORGE HARLEY. Born June 24, 1873, Cleveland, Cuyahoga County, Ohio. Ht. 5 ft. 11 in., blue eyes, light hair, light complexion, married. Railroad conductor, Kingsville, Kleberg County, Texas. SPECIAL RANGER July 9, 1918–Jan. 15, 1919. REMARKS: In Sept. 1918 was a railroad conductor for the Gulf Coast Lines, living in Kingsville. Still a railroad conductor living in Kingsville in 1930. FAMILY: Spouse, Louisa (b. 1885, Sweden), married about 1907; children, Alma (b. 1909, Mexico), Tom (b. 1911, TX), Waldine (b. 1913, TX), Betty (b. 1916, TX), Clara Belle (b. 1919, TX). *SR; Price to Harley, Aug 31, 1918, AGC; A1f, g; A3a.*

PRICE, WILLIAM SAMUEL. Born Jan. 8, 1861, Palestine, Anderson County, Texas. Ht. 5 ft. 10 in., blue eyes, dark gray hair, fair complexion, married. Banker and farmer, Kerens, Navarro County. LOYALTY RANGER June 27, 1918–Feb. 1919. REMARKS: Died Dec. 1, 1956, Navarro County, Texas; buried in Kerens Cemetery. FAMILY: Parents, Weyman Adair Price (b. 1836, AL) and Sarah Ann Gray (b. 1839, IL); siblings, Melvina (b. 1863, TX), John S. (b. 1869, TX), Louis (b. 1876, TX); spouse #1, Florence L. Coulson (b. 1865, TX), married Feb. 17, 1884; daughter, Hallie (b. 1888, TX); spouse #2, Nancy Tallulah "Lula" Hemphill (b. 1870, GA), married about 1895; sons, Harry D. (b. 1897, TX), Robert Eben (b. 1897, TX), Will Sidney (b. 1905, TX). *SR; A1b, d, e, f, g; A2b; A4b.*

PRIDGEN, OSCAR FITZGERALD. Born June 13, 1853, Marshall, Harrison County, Texas. Ht. 5 ft. 8 ½ in., gray eyes, gray hair, dark complexion, married. REGULAR RANGER—said that he'd served in the Rangers Apr.–June 1, 1875, under Capt. McNelly (Washington County Volunteer Militia) and 3 months in 1882 under Capt. Smith. Express guard, San Antonio, Bexar County, Texas. SPECIAL RANGER June 3, 1919–Dec. 31, 1919. REMARKS: Ranger Service Record indicates birth year as 1858; most other records cite an earlier date. Attended Texas Military Institute, Austin, Travis County, Texas in 1870. Worked for the Post Office Department; was assistant postmaster and postmaster in DeWitt County, Texas in 1900 and 1910. In 1930 was a county special agent in San Antonio. Died July 12, 1945, Bexar County, Texas. FAMILY: Parents, Texas state senator (1870–1872) Bolivar Jackson Pridgen (b. 1829, NC) and Martha Ann Williams (b. 1832, TN); siblings, William Edgar (b. 1857, TX), George McDuffy (b. 1859, TX), David Crockett (b. 1861, TX), Sidney (b. 1862, TX), Fanny (b. 1864, TX), Betty (b. 1866, TX); spouse, Mary A. "Mollie" Lowe (b. 1857, TX), married Nov. 22, 1876, DeWitt County, Texas; daughters, Martha Alice (b. 1877, TX), Maud (b. 1878, TX). *SR; 471; 525, V: 38A1aa, a, b, d, e, g; A2b; A4a, b, g.*

PRINCE, FREDERICK ELPHONZO "FRED." Born Oct. 10, 1858, Roxbury, Washington County, Vermont. No physical description, married. Basket and crate manufacturer, Pittsburg, Camp County, Texas. LOYALTY RANGER June 7, 1918–Feb. 1919. REMARKS: Was a woodworker in Massachusetts in 1900. Living in Camp County by 1910. In 1920 and 1930 was owner of a box factory in Pittsburg. Died Oct. 15, 1943, Pittsburg, Camp County, Texas. FAMILY: Parents, John Prince (b. 1825, VT) and Betsey Arminda Clark (b. 1832, VT); siblings, Ada Harriet (b. 1852, VT), George John (b. 1855, VT), Fred's twin Frank Alonzo, Loretta Mary (b. 1860, VT), Mary Bertha (b. 1862, VT), Jessie Aurora (b. 1867, VT); spouse, May Arnold (b. 1861, MI), married Nov. 19, 1884, Mount Pleasant, Michigan; children, Marian Arnold (b. 1890, MI), Walter Arnold (b. 1893, MI). *SR; A1aa, a, b, d, e, f, g; A2b; A4b; B2.*

PUCKETT, JOHN BYRON. Born July 29, 1876, Helena, Karnes County, Texas. Ht. 5 ft. 11 in., brown eyes, black hair, dark complexion, married. REGULAR RANGER 1902–1903 (private, Co. A). Stockman, enlisted in Cameron County, Texas. SPECIAL RANGER Mar. 5, 1918–Jan. 15, 1919. REMARKS: In 1900 was a railroad engine coaler in Karnes County. In 1910 was Hidalgo County, Texas deputy sheriff living in Mercedes. In Sept. 1918 was a rancher and stockman in Hidalgo County. Died Apr. 28, 1919, Raymondville, Cameron County, Texas. FAMILY: Parents, Thomas Harvey Puckett (b. 1825, IN) and Elmira Archer (b. 1838, MO); siblings, William P. (b. 1858, TX), Martha Elizabeth (b. 1859, TX), Hiram H. (b. 1860, TX), Jemima (b. 1864, TX), Mary Emma (b. 1865, TX), Thomas Dennis (b. 1867, TX), Arona (b. 1869, TX), Milton David (b. 1871, TX), Harmon (b. 1874, TX), Ella May (b. 1881, TX); spouse, Agnes Elizabeth Douglas (b. 1877, Mexico), married Sept. 19, 1902, Brownsville, Cameron County; children, Margaret Myrtle (b. 1903, TX), John Byron (b. 1904, TX), Douglas Harvey (b. 1906, TX), Charles Eldridge (b. 1908, TX), Robert Elsworth (b. 1909, TX), Mary Agnes (b. 1912, TX). *SR; 471; 319: 324; A1b, d, e, f; A2b; A3a; A4b; B1.*

PUCKITT, LITTLE WOOD "WOODY." Born July 2, 1890, Winnfield, Winn Parish, Louisiana. Ht. 6 ft. 6 in., brown eyes, black hair, dark complexion, married. Ranchman, enlisted in Kimble County, Texas. SPECIAL RANGER Aug. 6, 1917–Dec. 1917. REMARKS: In June 1917 was a rancher in Menard County, Texas. In 1920 was an oil field teamster in Menard County. In 1930 was a stock farmer in Kimble County. An L. W. Wood Puckett [*sic*], Sr. died July 18, 1957, Menard County, Texas. FAMILY: Parents, George W. Puckett [*sic*] (b. 1850, LA) and Arminda (b. 1853, AL); siblings, Wily (b. 1874, LA), Lou (b. 1874, LA), Arva U. (b. 1875, LA), Arla M. (b. 1879, LA), Sibby (b. 1883, LA), Jessy (b. 1890, LA), Dexter (b. 1892, LA); spouse, Alma M. (b. 1897, TX), married about 1916; children, Irva J. (b. 1917, TX), Little W., Jr. (b. 1921, TX). *SR; A1b, d, f, g; A2b; A3a.*

PULLIN, LOUIS ELDRIDGE. Born Dec. 5, 1877, Karnes County, Texas. Ht. 5 ft. 10 in., gray eyes, black hair, dark complexion, married. Farmer and peace officer, Runge, Karnes County. SPECIAL RANGER July 18, 1918–Jan. 15, 1919. REMARKS: In 1910 and 1920 was a farmer in Karnes County. In 1930 was deputy sheriff in McAllen, Hidalgo County, Texas. Died Aug. 27, 1945, Hidalgo County, Texas. LAW ENFORCEMENT RELATIVES: Ranger Thomas N. Pullin, uncle. FAMILY: Parents, John Andrew Jackson Pullin (b. 1857, TX) and Udora Josephine Haywood (b. 1856, TX); siblings, William Taylor (b. 1880, TX), Alice Mary (b. 1882, TX), Daniel Lafayette (b. 1886, TX), Andy Whitney (b. 1889, TX), twins Cora Elizabeth and Dora Caroline (b. 1892, TX), Bertha Josephine (b. 1894, TX), Lulu Irene (b. 1898, TX), Otis Beverly (b. 1901, TX); spouse #1, Minnie Nichols (b. 1881, TX), married Nov. 22, 1900; spouse #2, Lydia L. Appling (b. 1888, TX), married Nov. 16, 1902; children, Rhodia L. (b. 1903, TX), Preston (b. 1906, TX), Linnie (b. 1908, TX), Louise (b. 1916, TX), Lottie (b. 1919, TX), Milton Taylor (b. 1923, TX). *SR; A1b, e, f, g; A2b, e; A3a; A4a, b; B2.*

PULLIN, THOMAS NOLAN "TOM." Born Aug. 15, 1863, Lavaca County, Texas. Ht. 6 ft., blue eyes, white hair, light complexion, married. Farmer, Kenedy, Karnes County, Texas. REGULAR RANGER Dec. 22, 1917–May 1918 (private, Co. K). Resigned. REMARKS: Had resided in Karnes County for 35 years, had been a peace officer for 20 years. One source cites birthplace as Karnes County. Died Oct. 22, 1926, San Patricio County, Texas. LAW ENFORCEMENT RELATIVES: Ranger Louis E. Pullin, nephew. FAMILY: Parents, Hiram Rand Pullin (b. 1828, MS) and Candacy Ware Butler (b. 1838, MS); siblings, James H. (b. 1853, MS), Elizabeth (b. 1854, MS), John Andrew Jackson (b. 1857, TX), Sarah Jane (b. 1859, TX), Daniel (b. 1860, TX), Jesse Harmon (b. 1862, MS), William A. (b. 1865, TX), Henry Howard (b. 1868, TX), Maranda (b. 1871, TX), Green Berry (b. 1872, TX), Alfred Lee (b. 1873, TX), Easterlina (b. 1877, TX); spouse, Minerva Caroline Morgan (b. 1868, TX), married Aug. 23, 1883, Kenedy; children, John H. (b. 1884, TX), George W. (b. 1886, TX), Angie C. (b. 1887, TX), Bessie (b. 1890, TX), Willie (b. 1893, TX), Leonard (b. 1898, TX), Tom E. (b. 1903, TX), Vivian (b. 1905, TX), Lillie May (b. 1907, TX), Lenora (b. 1912, TX). *SR; 471; Lynch to Ferguson, Apr 11, 1917, AGC; Smiley to Hutchings, May 2, 1917, AGC; Murray to Ferguson, Aug 1, 1917, AGC; A1b, d, e, f, g; A2b; A4b; B1, 2.*

PURVIS, FRANK HARRIS. Born Aug. 18, 1893, Fort Worth, Tarrant County, Texas. Ht. 5 ft. 6 in., blue eyes, brown hair, ruddy complexion. Auto business, Fort Worth. SPECIAL RANGER July 13, 1917–July 18, 1917 (attached to Co. C), was reclassified as a REGULAR RANGER July 19, 1917–unknown (no company listed). REMARKS: Governor Ferguson ordered his appointment. World War I Draft Registration document states he is an auto salesman working for the U.S. government. FAMILY: Parents, Duff Purvis (b. 1861, TX) and Annie Francis (b. 1868, MO). *SR; 471; Ferguson to Hutchings, July 13, 1917, AGC; Hutchings to Purvis, July 14, 1917, AGC; A1d, e; A3a.*

PUTMAN, AMZY DARIUS. Born Sept. 19, 1896, Llano, Llano County, Texas. Ht. 6 ft., brown eyes, dark hair, dark complexion, married. Ranchman, Laredo, Webb County, Texas. REGULAR RANGER Dec. 19, 1919–Oct. 31, 1921 (private, Co. C). Discharged. REMARKS: In June 1918 was living and working on the Clark Farm in North Laredo. In 1930 was a labor foreman at an oil refinery in Baytown, Harris County, Texas. Died Apr. 8, 1931. FAMILY: Parents, Simeon Mercer Putman (b. 1854, TX) and Adeline Victoria Stone (b. 1861, TX); siblings, A. Velma (b. 1881, TX), Effie (b. 1882, TX), May (b. 1884, TX), Lea A. (b. 1886, TX), Merle E. (b. 1892, TX), Ona O. (b. 1894, TX), Beulah B. (b. 1901, TX), John D. (b. 1903, TX); spouse, Rebecca

(b. 1893, Mexico), married about 1918; children, Ruby (b. 1921, TX), Arthur (b. 1923, TX). *SR; 471; A1b, d, e, g; A3a; A4a, b, g.*

PUTNAM, CARL. Born April 25, 1895, Travis County, Texas. Ht. 5 ft. 8 in., blue eyes, light hair, fair complexion. Farmer, Austin, Travis County. SPECIAL RANGER Dec. 14, 1917–Aug. 1918. Discharged. REMARKS: In June 1917 was farm and ranch manager for Chester Thrasher, Travis County. In 1930 was a sewerage inspector in Austin. A Carl Putnam died June 19, 1932, Travis County, Texas. FAMILY: Adoptive parents, George D. Heisner (b. 1853, TX) and Martha L. (b. 1854, TX); brother, Roger Putnam (b. 1894, TX); adoptive sister, Bertha Heisner (b. 1882, TX); spouse, Ada (b. 1895, TX), married about 1919; son, Carl, Jr. (b. 1921, TX). *SR; A1d, e, f, g; A2b; A3a.*

PYLE, CHARLES R. Born Apr. 1865, Helena, Karnes County, Texas. Ht. 6 ft., blue eyes, brown hair, florid complexion, married. Night watchman, SA&AP Railroad, Yoakum, Lavaca County, Texas. SPECIAL RANGER May 1, 1918–Jan. 15, 1919. REMARKS: His superior requested a Special Ranger commission for Pyle. Varying dates of birth given on census records and Ranger Service Record: 1864, 1865, 1866, 1868. Had been a farmer and a furniture store owner in Yoakum. In 1930 was manager of a pressing shop in Yoakum. FAMILY: Parents, John F. Pyle (b. 1833, TN) and Sarah A. (b. 1838, AR); brother, Aloyze B. (b. 1872, TX); spouse, Dora E. Ross (b. 1865, TX), married Apr. 12, 1896, Karnes County; daughter, Dorothy (b. 1910, TX). *SR; Herbst to Harley, Apr 20, 1918, AGC; Ranger A. W. Herbst's Service Record; A1b, d, e, f, g; B1.*

PYLE, THEOPHILIS McCROCKLIN, JR. Born Dec. 9, 1871, Blanco, Blanco County, Texas. Ht. 5 ft. 9 in., gray eyes, black hair, dark complexion, married. Stockman, Clarendon, Donley County, Texas. SPECIAL RANGER June 24, 1918–Jan. 15, 1919. REMARKS: Was a brand inspector for the Panhandle & Southwestern Stockmen's Association. State senator Claude Hudspeth requested his commissioning. Had been a livestock dealer in Hall County, Texas. In 1930 was a city policeman in Clarendon. Died Dec. 31, 1937, Donley County, Texas. FAMILY: Spouse, Ada Lee Watson (b. 1871, TX), married Dec. 15, 1895, Longbranch, Guadalupe County, Texas; children, Claude W. (b. 1896, TX), Opal M. (b. 1901, TX). *SR; Hudspeth to Harley, June 15, 1918, AGC; A1d, e, f, g; A2b; A4b; B1.*

QUINN, JOHN OLAND "OLIE." Born Jan. 29, 1873, Tunnel Hill, Catoosa County, Georgia. Ht. 6 ft., gray eyes, black hair, medium complexion, married. Railroad yardmaster, Laredo, Webb County, Texas. SPECIAL RANGER Mar. 11, 1918–Jan. 15, 1919. REMARKS: Had been a railroad yardmaster for the last 15 years. Had been a railroad brakeman in Dodd, Fannin County, Texas and a railroad conductor in Baird, Callahan County, Texas. Died Oct. 21, 1925, Webb County, Texas. FAMILY: Parents, William R. Quinn (b. 1849, GA) and Virginia C. Harris (b. 1852, GA); brothers, William B. (b. 1876, GA), Jessee M. (b. 1879, GA); spouse, Lena May Rogers (b. 1878, AR), married about 1899; children, Jennie Louise (b. 1899, TX), Clyde (b. 1902, TX), Paul (b. 1904, TX), Ross (b. 1907, TX). *SR; A1b, d, e, f; A2b; A3a; A4b.*

RABB, FRANK. Born Mar. 6, 1866, near Corpus Christi, Nueces County, Texas. Ht. 5 ft. 10 in., gray eyes, gray hair, light complexion, married. Ranchman, Brownsville, Cameron County, Texas. SPECIAL RANGER July 25, 1918–Jan. 15, 1919. REMARKS: Was collector of Customs at Brownsville, 1913–1917. Feuded with prominent politicians such as Congressman John Nance Garner. Made an extended trip to Mexico, accompanying Venustiano Carranza when the latter made his triumphal entry into Mexico City in August 1914. Allegedly used his official position to prevent supplies from reaching Pancho Villa's troops when they were besieging the Carranza garrison in Matamoros in April, 1915. Was a large landowner in the Lower Rio Grande Valley. In 1920 U.S. census records, identified as a "capitalist" in Brownsville. In 1930 was a real estate operator in Brownsville. A Frank Rabb died Sept. 29, 1932, Hidalgo County, Texas. FAMILY: Parents, John William Rabb (b. 1825, TX) and Martha A. "Mattie" Reagan (b. 1826, TN); siblings, Elizabeth J. (b. 1849, TX), Margaret A. (b. 1851, TX), Green Alexander (b. 1854, TX), Thomas Lee (b. 1856, TX), Mary Louise (b. 1858, TX); spouse, Lillian Mary Starck (b. 1870, TX), married Mar. 9, 1887, Brownsville. *SR; Stevens to Woodul, Mar 23, 1918, WC; BDH, July 15, Nov 23, Dec 6, 1912, Jan 24, Mar 18, May 14, 15, June 30, July 30, 31, Aug 29, Sept 3, 8, 10, 11, 27, Oct 3, 24, 1913, Jan 5 Mar 11, Apr 9, July 116, 17, 19, 22, 24, 28, 29, 31, Aug 3, 9, 11, 17, 31, Sept 5, 7, 8, 11, Oct 5, 14, 19, 20, 26, 29, Nov 3, 7, 20, 23, 28, Dec 1, 12, 14, 18, 20, 23, 24, 26, 1914, Jan 1, 4, 9, 27–30, Feb 20, 27, Mar 1, 13, 16, July 24, Dec 16, 1915, June 10, 13, 26, 1916, Sept 29, 1917; EPMT, July 16, 23, 1914, Apr 2, 3, 4, 6, 1915; 8:659; 485:56; A1a, b, e, f, g; A2b; A4a, b.*

RAMSEY, HAL HARRISON. Born Apr. 14, 1867, Johnson Station, Tarrant County, Texas. Ht. 5 ft. 8 in., brown eyes, gray-black hair, dark complexion, married. Dentist, Baird, Callahan County, Texas. SPECIAL RANGER May 29, 1917–Dec. 1917 (attached to Co. C). REMARKS: In 1920 had his own dental office in Abilene, Taylor County, Texas; retired in Abilene by 1930. Died Dec. 4, 1959, Taylor County, Texas. LAW ENFORCEMENT RELATIVES: Ranger M.T. Ramsey, son. FAMILY: Parents, Seth Strange Ramsey (b. 1825, GA) and Martha Missouri Miller (b. 1828, GA); siblings, James Bailey (b. 1852, GA), John Pruitt (b. 1854, GA), Merrick Ford (b. 1855, TX), Harriet Elizabeth (b. 1857, TX), Jane L. (b. 1859, TX), Julien D. (b. 1861, TX), Seth Strange (b. 1863, TX), Adenia M. (b. 1869, TX), Mattie C. (b. 1870, TX); spouse, Kate Richardson (b. 1874, TX), married about 1892; children, Wayne Vetree (b. 1895, TX), Minton T. (b. 1896, TX), Hal H. (b. 1898, TX), David Seth (b. 1900, TX), Nena Kate (b. 1902, TX), Cala B. (b. 1904, TX), Norma (b. 1907, TX), Comette (b. 1911, TX). *SR; A1a, d, e, f, g; A2b, e; A4b.*

RAMSEY, MINTON TRAVIS. Born Aug. 1, 1896, Baird, Callahan County, Texas. Ht. 5 ft. 9 ¾ in., brown eyes, brown hair, dark complexion. Dental student, Baird. SPECIAL RANGER June 23, 1917–Dec. 1917. Honorably discharged. REMARKS: In Dec. 1917 asked to be released as a Texas Ranger in order to enlist in the enlisted reserve corps of the Medical Department. He was a senior dental student at the University of Tennessee, Memphis. By 1930 he was a practicing dentist in Abilene, Taylor County, Texas. Died Apr. 4, 1983, Taylor County, Texas. LAW ENFORCEMENT RELATIVES: Ranger Hal H. Ramsey, father. FAMILY: Parents, Hal H. Ramsey (b. 1867, TX) and Kate Richardson (b. 1874, TX); siblings, Wayne Vetree (b. 1895, TX), Hal H. (b. 1898, TX), David Seth (b. 1900, TX), Nena Kate (b. 1902, TX), Cala B. (b. 1904, TX), Norma (b. 1907, TX), Comette (b. 1911, TX); spouse, Avondell (b. 1899, TX), married about 1921; son, Minton T., Jr. (b. 1928, TX). *SR; Ramsey to AG, Dec 11, 1917, AGC; A1d, e, f, g; A2b; A3a; A4b.*

RANSOM, ELMORE WALTER "ELMO." Born Mar. 1, 1883, Fort Bend County, Texas. Tall, slender, blue eyes, brown hair, married. Tax collector, Richmond, Fort Bend County. LOYALTY RANGER June 18, 1918–Feb. 1919. REMARKS: In 1910 was deputy sheriff, Fort Bend County. Was still a tax collector in Fort Bend County in 1930. Died Feb. 24, 1936, Harris County, Texas. FAMILY: Parents, Robert Jerrod Ransom (b. 1835, MS) and Mary E. Bertrand (b. 1850, TX); siblings, Real Freeman (b. 1870, TX), N. Pearl (b. 1874, TX), Robie (b 1875), Mamie (b. 1877), Earle Cleveland (b. 1880, TX); spouse, Evelyn Dyer (b. 1889, TX), married about 1905; children, Thomas D. (b. 1907, TX), Mary Alice (b. 1912, TX), Evelyn (b. 1914, TX), Elmore W., Jr. (b. 1918, TX). *SR; A1e, f, g; A2b; A3a; A4a, b; B2.*

RANSOM, HENRY LEE. Born Dec. 29, 1870, Brenham, Washington County, Texas. Ht. 5 ft. 8 in., gray eyes, gray hair, fair complexion, married. Deputy sheriff, Mitchell County, Texas. REGULAR RANGER Feb. 14, 1905–Dec. 10, 1905 and May 1, 1908–Jan. 15, 1909 (private, Co. A). Resigned both times for better-paying positions. Peace officer. REGULAR RANGER July 20, 1915–Apr. 1, 1918 (captain, Co. D; transferred to Co. C, Feb. 1, 1917; reenlisted as captain, Co. C, July 19, 1917). Was killed accidentally on Apr. 1, 1918 in Sweetwater, Nolan County, Texas. REMARKS: Served in Philippines in Troop B, 1st Texas Cavalry. Was a peace officer beginning in 1902. Manager, H.S. Ranch, Mitchell County, 1905. City marshal, Colorado City, Mitchell County, 1907. Deputy sheriff, Hempstead, Waller County, Texas, 1909. Special police officer, Houston, Harris County, Texas, 1910–1911. Houston police chief, 1912; was fired. Managed state prison farm (1913–1915?). Ransom was arguably the most controversial of all the Ranger captains. In 1910 he killed prominent defense attorney James B. Brockman in Houston, and was acquitted. As a Houston special officer and police chief he employed harsh measures to impose law and order, beat up reporters, and shot a policeman in the neck. In 1915, he was given the assignment of crushing Hispanic rebellion under the notorious Plan de San Diego in South Texas. His tactics were ruthless. Ransom was buried in Hempstead. FAMILY: Parents, Egbert Bell Ransom (b. 1828, GA) and Eliza Jane Creed (b. 1842, IN); siblings, Victoria Adelaide (b. 1862, TX), Cora (b. 1867, TX), William Alford (b. 1870, TX); spouse #1, Martha Ella Cole (b. 1876, TX), married Jan. 6, 1892 near Sealy, Austin County, Texas, divorced about 1898; children, Beatrice (b. 1893, TX), Mary Ella; spouse #2, Anna Hope Cooke (b. 1887, TX); children, Ruby Lee (b. 1908, TX), Jonathan Lane (b. 1914, TX). *SR; 471; Bishop to Colquitt, Mar 1, 1913, AGC; Ransom to Hutchings, Sept 16, Dec 11, 1915, AGC; AG to Ransom, Dec 17, 1915, AGC; Ransom to Harley, Oct 19, 1917, AGC; Koon to Harley, Apr 1, 1918, WC; McKenzie to Harley, Apr 2, 1918, WC; Harley to McKenzie [Apr 2, 1918 ?], WC; Yarborough to Sheriff, Apr 3, 1918, WC; Harley to Koon, Apr 2, 1918, AGC; McKenzie to AG, Apr 2, 1918, AGC; HC, Oct 26–28, 30, 1910, Mar 6, Apr 15–23, 1911, July 20, 1915, Apr 2, 1918; SAE, Apr 20, 1911; BDH, Apr 22, 1913, July 22, Aug 7, 1915; AS, Oct 27, 30, Nov 6, 1910, Jan 17, Apr 18, 21, 23, 1911; EPMT, Oct 26, 1910, Apr 23, 1911, July 25, 1915; LWT, Jun 16, July 14, 1912, July 25, 1915; 319: 34,39, 43, 45, 47, 48; 417: 586–587; 425: 91; 479: 15–16, 72–73; 508: 67; biography: 1504; 154:365–366; A1a, b; A2b, e; A4a, b; B1.*

RANSON, GEORGE ERNEST. Born Aug. 31, 1885, Seymour, Baylor County, Texas. Ht. 5 ft. 10 in., gray eyes, brown hair, fair complexion, married. Farmer, Hawley, Jones County, Texas. SPECIAL RANGER June 26, 1917–Dec. 1917 (attached to Co. C). REMARKS: In 1930 was still farming in Jones County. Died Sept. 17, 1956, Brown County, Texas. FAMILY: Parents, Eugene Ranson (b. 1847, MO) and Mary M. (b. 1845, MO); sisters, Jennie E. (b. 1877, MO), Stella (b. 1881, TX), Maud (b. 1883, TX), Pearl (b. 1889, TX); spouse, Emma (b. 1883, TX), married about 1907; daughter, Kathrine (b. 1916, TX). *SR; Brooks et al. to Ferguson, June 4, 1917, AGC; AG to Brooks, June 21, 1917, AGC; A1d, g; A2b; A3a.*

RASCO, SAMUEL LODOVICK. Born Apr. 10, 1876, Madison County, Texas. Ht. 5 ft. 7 in., blue eyes, dark hair, dark complexion, married. Farmer and stockman, Madisonville, Madison County. LOYALTY RANGER July 16, 1918–Feb. 1919. REMARKS: In 1930 had a stock farm in North Zulch, Madison County. Died July 3, 1964, Brazos County, Texas. FAMILY: Parents, Joseph or Joel Terrell Rasco (b. 1846, GA) and Jemima Ann Mize (b. 1843, IL); siblings, Isaac (b. 1869, TX), Ollie (b. 1870, TX), Minnie (b. 1872, TX), William Thomas (b. 1874, TX), Emma (b. 1878, TX), Annie (b. 1880, TX); spouse #1, Alice Lydia Reed (b. 1877, TX), married Nov. 1, 1894; children, George W. (b. 1895, TX), Annie Pearl (b. 1896, TX), Joseph or Joel T. (b. 1899, TX), Mabel (b. 1903, TX); spouse #2, Mary Tranny or Frannie (b. 1885, TX), married about 1905. *SR; A1b, d, e, f, g; A2b; A3a, A4b, g.*

RATHER, CHARLES TAYLOR "CHARLEY." Born Jan. 11, 1882, Midway, Madison County, Texas. Ht. 6 ft., blue eyes, black hair, light complexion, married. Stock farmer, Belmont, Gonzales County, Texas. LOYALTY RANGER June 5, 1918–Feb. 1919. REMARKS: Died June 2, 1973, Gonzales County, Texas; buried in Belmont. FAMILY: Parents, George Anthony Rather (b. 1851, TN) and Willie Julia Law (b. 1858, AL); siblings, Albert Branch (b. 1884, TX), Eunice Isabella (b. 1886, TX), Mary Christian (b. 1889, TX), Aline Gabriella (b. 1892, TX); spouse, Inez Hollis Hodges (b. 1885, TX), married Feb. 7, 1909; children, Olivia (b. 1911, TX), Charlotte (b. 1915, TX), Willie I. (b. 1823, TX), Charles T. (b. 1925, TX). *SR; A1d, e, f, g; A2a, b; A3a; A4a, b; B1, 2.*

RAWLINGS, J. C. Born Oct. 1886, Brandenburg, Meade County, Kentucky. Ht. 5 ft. 8 in., blue eyes, light hair, fair complexion. Stock farmer, Plainview, Hale County, Texas. SPECIAL RANGER Nov. 22, 1917–Feb. 14, 1918 (captain, Co. B Volunteers). Discharged—Co. B Volunteers (9 men strong) was disbanded. REMARKS: Represented Walter Darlington farm loans firm of Kansas City, Missouri. *SR; Pearce to Harley, Oct 18, 1917, AGC; Rawlings to Harley, Dec 6, 1917, Jan 24, 1918, AGC.*

RAWLS, THOMAS H. "TOM." Born Mar. 1868, Bainbridge, Decatur County, Georgia. Ht. 5 ft. 8 in., blue eyes, brown hair, light complexion, married. Ranchman, Marfa, Presidio County, Texas. SPECIAL RANGER Feb. 16, 1917–Jan. 15, 1919 (reenlisted, May 3, 1918). REMARKS: In 1930 still a cattle rancher in Marfa. A T. N. or T. H Rawls died July 29, 1955, Presidio County, Texas. FAMILY: Parents, John Calhoun Rawls (b. 1830, GA) and Louisa Harris McDermio (b. 1831, GA); siblings, Sarah C. (b. 1862, GA), Joseph A. (b. 1864, GA), William O. (b. 1866, GA), Martha I. "Mattie" (b. 1869, GA), John T. (b. 1874, GA); spouse, Mary (b. 1875, TX), married about 1897; daughters, Myrtle (b. 1900, TX), Willie (b. 1902, TX). *SR; Wroe to Hutchings, Feb 12, 1917, AGC; Fox to Hutchings [Feb 1917], AGC; A1a, b, f, g; A2b; A4b.*

RAY, ASTOR LEWIS. Born Aug. 16, 1881, Reklaw, Cherokee County, Texas. Ht. 6 ft. 2 in., gray eyes, light brown hair, red complexion, married. Farmer, Riviera, Kleberg County, Texas. LOYALTY RANGER June 7, 1918–Feb. 1919. REMARKS: Had been a farmer in Nueces County, Texas. Was a stock farmer in Kleberg County in 1930. Died July 31, 1953, Kleberg County, Texas. FAMILY: Parents, Samuel F. Ray (b. 1848, AL) and Mackie L. (b. 1850, AL); siblings, Joseph H. (b. 1873, MS), George G. (b. 1875, MS), Magolene (b. 1878, TX), Johnie (b. 1884, TX), William (b. 1890, TX); spouse, Iva B. (b. 1884, TX), married about 1902; children, Samuel R. (b. 1903, TX), Maude T. (b. 1907, TX), Wilson A. "Jack" (b. 1913, TX). *SR; A1b, d, e, f, g; A2b; A3a.*

RAY, JOHN C. Born Aug. 1872, Sherburnville, Kankakee County, Illinois. Ht. 5 ft. 11 in., blue-gray eyes, black hair, dark complexion, married. Lumber salesman, Waco, McLennan County, Texas. SPECIAL RANGER Dec. 3, 1917–Dec. 21, 1919 (WA was renewed Jan. 25, 1919). REMARKS: Deputy sheriff, McLennan County; deputy game commissioner, State of Texas. Was still a traveling lumber salesman in Waco in 1930. A John Clarence Ray died Apr. 20, 1947, McLennan County, Texas. FAMILY: Spouse #1, Mary (b. 1882, TX), married about 1904; spouse #2, Wilma (b. 1876, TX). *SR; AG to Ray, Dec 1, 1917, AGC; Ray to Harley, Dec 3, 7, 1917, Feb 24, 1919 AGC; A1e, f, g; A2b.*

RAY, JOHN JONES, JR. Born Sept. 11, 1898, Greer County, Oklahoma. Ht. 5 ft. 11 in., brown hair, light complexion. Cowman, Diboll, Angelina County. Texas. LOYALTY RANGER Aug. 26, 1918–Feb. 25, 1919. FAMILY: Parents, John J. Ray (b. 1865, GA) and Mary L. (b. 1877, TX); brother, Gilbert T. (b. 1897, OK). *SR; A2e; A3a.*

REA, JESSE DAVID. Born July 26, 1878, Saltillo, Lee County, Mississippi. Ht. 5 ft. 10 ½ in., blue eyes, dark hair, dark complexion, married. Fire insurance agent, Rosebud, Falls County, Texas. SPECIAL RANGER July 20, 1918–Jan. 15, 1919. REMARKS: Letterhead: "Phoenix Assurance Company, Ltd. of London, Jesse D. Rea, Agent, Rosebud, Texas." Had been a farmer in Ellis County, Texas. Died May 5, 1943, Falls County, Texas. FAMILY: Parents, Thomas S. Rea (b. 1837, MS) and Mary Adeline Ridings (b. 1841, MS); siblings, William Thomas (b. 1858, MS), James (b. 1860, MS), Maggie (b. 1862, MS), Mary Susan (b. 1867, MS), Charles Randolph (b. 1868, MS), Emmett Theophilus (b. 1870, MS), Ella (b. 1873, MS), Viola Victoria (b. 1875, MS), Hattie Belle (b. 1880, MS), Bertha Sedalia (b. 1887, TX); spouse, Lillie McClure Henderson (b. 1877, TX), married about 1898; children, Edith Aileen (b. 1899, TX), Homer Earl (b. 1901, TX), Ruth (b. 1908, TX), Mary Naomi (b. 1911, TX). *SR; A1b, d, e, g; A2b; A3a; A4a, b.*

REAGAN, JOHN MARTIN, JR. Born Feb. 8, 1881, Kaufman County, Texas. Ht. 6 ft. ½ in., dark brown eyes, black hair, dark complexion, married. Provision salesman, Beaumont, Jefferson County, Texas. LOYALTY RANGER June 1, 1918–Feb. 1919. REMARKS: As a young man had done insurance work in Oak Cliff, Dallas County, Texas. As of Sept. 1918 was a traveling salesman for Houston Packing Company, living in Beaumont. In 1920 was a wholesale meat dealer in Beaumont. FAMILY: Parents, John Martin Reagan (b. 1852, MS) and Sallie McGaffey Jackson (b. 1858, TX); siblings, Thomas R. (b. 1878, TX), Robert L. (b. 1883, TX), Gypsie (b. 1886, TX), Sallie (b. 1889, TX), George K. (b. 1892, TX), Steven Rivers (b. 1896, TX); spouse, Maggie F. (b. 1885, TX), married about 1905; children, James O. (b. 1907, TX), John M. (b. 1908, TX), Virginia E. (b. 1912, TX), Peggy J. (b. 1915, TX), Mary A. (b. 1920, TX). *SR; A1d, e, f; A3a; B1.*

REDUS, ROSCOE. Born July 13, 1876, Devine, Medina County, Texas. Ht. 5 ft. 11 in., dark eyes, black hair, dark complexion. Stock farmer. REGULAR RANGER July 25, 1908–Jan. 12, 1910 (private, Co. B; ca. Oct. 1909 was promoted to sergeant). Discharged/fired—got drunk, rode horse through and shot up a saloon at Ysleta, El Paso County, Texas. REMARKS: His captain, Tom M. Ross, was also fired as a result of this escapade. Jan. 1911, was evidently an agent of the Justice Department in San Antonio, Bexar County, Texas. Dec. 1911, was a grand jury bailiff in San Antonio. By Sept. 1918 was a stock farmer in Bandera County, Texas, living in Medina Lake, Medina County. Died June 23, 1954, Bexar County, Texas. FAMILY: Parents, William Redus (b. 1839, AL) and Calpurnia Lignon Greenwood (b. 1849, MS); brothers, William Calhoun (b. 1871, TX), Aaron (b. 1874, TX), Greenwood (b. 1878, TX); spouse #1, Ruby Terrell (b. 1880, TX), married Apr. 24, 1901; daughter, Carmen (b. 1903, TX); spouse #2, Matilda Spettle (b. 1878, TX). *SR; 471; Ross to Newton, Jan 12, 1910, AGC; Ross to Newton, Jan 31, 1910, WC; A.W. Brown affidavit, Feb 11, 1910, WC; Assistant AG to Thorne, Apr 22,1910, AGC; Redus to AG, Apr 5, 1917, AGC; 496: 77; EPMT, Nov 19,1909, Jan 19, 1910; SAE, Sept 3, Dec 12,1911; A1b, d, e, f; A2b; A3a; A4a, b; B1, 2.*

REED, ALEXANDER HAMILTON "ALEX." Born Apr. 2, 1883, Goliad, Goliad County, Texas. Ht. 6 ft., brown eyes, black hair, fair complexion. Ranchman, Hebbronville, Jim Hogg County, Texas. SPECIAL RANGER Apr. 22, 1918–Jan. 15, 1919; Aug. 16, 1919–Dec. 31, 1919. REMARKS: In 1930 was a hotel manager in Beeville, Bee County, Texas. Died Apr. 15, 1952, Bee County, Texas. FAMILY: Parents, James P. Reed (b. 1849, TX) and Ida N. (b. 1851, TX); siblings, Thomas M. (b. 1875, TX), James E. (b. 1878, TX), Willie (b. 1881, TX), Alma (b. 1885, TX), George (b. 1891, TX); spouse, Anne Schvab (b. 1902, TX), married about 1920; son, Hamilton Schvab (b. 1930, TX). *SR; 319: 39; A1d, e, g; A2b, e; A3a.*

REED, ELMO DELROY. Born Jan. 17, 1897, Goliad, Goliad County, Texas. Ht. 6 ft. 2 in., brown eyes, brown hair, dark complexion. Ranchman. REGULAR RANGER Dec. 16, 1917–Apr. 1918 (private, Co. G; promoted to sergeant, Jan. 4, 1918). Resigned. Stockman. REGULAR RANGER May 7, 1918–Jan. 1, 1919 (private, Co. A). Discharged. Stockman, Goliad. SPECIAL RANGER Jan. 13, 1919–probably Dec. 31, 1919. REMARKS: On 1917 enlistment form: "Good horseman, speaks Spanish, and highly recommended." In 1920 was a student in pharmacy school; in 1930 was a prescription clerk in a drug store in Beeville, Bee County, Texas. Died June 8, 1971, Williamson County, Texas. FAMILY: Parents, Thomas M. (b. 1858, TX) and Almeda E. (b. 1874, TN); brothers, Demry M. (b. 1899, TX), Sylvester (b. 1900, TX), Thomas (b. 1905, TX); spouse #1, Mabel A.

Passmore (b. 1903, TX), married about 1922; sons, Elmo D., Jr. (b. 1923, TX), Bob Passmore (b. 1926, TX); spouse #2, Addie Belle Crawford; daughter, Jane (b. 1939, TX). *SR; 471; Stevens to Harley, Dec 17, 1917, Jan 4, 1918, AGC; Redway report [Nov 1918], WC; 469: 60; A1d, e, f, g; A2a, b, e; A3a; A4b.*

REED, WILLIAM GUY. Born Feb. 11, 1876, Batavia, Kane County, Illinois. Ht. 5 ft. 8 in., blue eyes, dark hair, dark complexion, married. Locomotive engineer, North Pleasanton, Atascosa County, Texas. SPECIAL RANGER Sept. 14, 1917–Dec. 1917. Locomotive engineer, Crystal City, Zavala County, Texas. LOYALTY RANGER July 24, 1918–Feb. 1919. REMARKS: As of May 1917 had been a locomotive engineer for the San Antonio, Uvalde & Gulf Railroad for several years. The railroad's general manager asked that Reed be commissioned. Reed stated that he'd been a deputy sheriff in Louisiana and a private, Co. H, 1st Louisiana Volunteers in the Spanish-American War. A William G. Reed died Dec. 27, 1928, Bexar County, Texas. FAMILY: Parents (probably), William Reed (b. 1839, NY) and Louise (b. 1853, IL); sister (probably), Cora (b. 1876, IL); spouse, Lena B. (b. 1882, KS); children, Harriet L. (b. 1907, LA), Nelson T. (b. 1910, LA), John H. (b. 1914, TX), twins Charles K. and Marjorie (b. 1918, TX). *SR; Ponder to Ferguson, May 7, 1917, AGC; Ponder to Hutchings, Sept 10, 1917, AGC; A1b, f, g; A2b; A3a.*

REESE, JOHN WALTER. Born June 3, 1879, Oakland, Colorado County, Texas. Ht. 5 ft. 8 ½ in., brown eyes, dark hair, dark complexion, married, as of Mar. 1916. Peace officer. REGULAR RANGER Jan. 23, 1910–July 18, 1910 (private, Co B; promoted to sergeant, Mar. 1910). Discharged/fired. Peace officer, enlisted in El Paso County, Texas. SPECIAL RANGER Mar. 12, 1916–Dec. 17, 1917. His commission was cancelled. Jan. 17, 1918 was recommissioned—until Jan. 15, 1919. His WA was cancelled. REMARKS: In 1900 was deputy sheriff in Fort Bend County, Texas. Was a peace officer in Columbus, Luna County, New Mexico, Aug. 1910. Was an El Paso County deputy sheriff, 1914–1917. Was a special agent for the GH&SA Railroad in El Paso, 1916. Was an El Paso police inspector in Sept. 1918 and Aug. 1919. Died Dec. 11, 1919, El Paso County, Texas. FAMILY: Parents, Samuel Houston Reese (b. 1860, TX) and Keron Blanche Minerva "Ketie" Townsend (b. 1856, TX); siblings, Nuddie Ella (b. 1877, TX), Spencer Herbert (b. 1880, TX), Keron Virginia "Sadie" (b. 1882, TX), Lillian Estelle (b. 1883, TX); spouse, Ethel Josephine Cox. *SR; Ross to Newton, Jan 31, 1910, AGC; AG to Ross, Feb 7, Mar 4, 1910, AGC; Thorne to Newton, Apr 9, 14, 1910, AGC; AG to Bailey, June 18, 1910, AGC; Bailey to Newton, July 20, 1910, AGC; Reese to Newton, July 27, 1910, AGC; Hudspeth to Hutchings, Mar 6, 1916, AGC; AG to Hudspeth, Mar 8, 1916, AGC; Reese to Hutchings, Mar 13, 1916, AGC; Assistant AG to Fryer, Apr 5, 1918, AGC; Reese to Harley, Aug 16, 1919, AGC; EPMT, Mar 14, Aug 10, 1910, Jan 16, 1914, Feb 6, 1918, Jan 30, Mar 3, May 13, Nov 8, 9, 12, 14, Dec 12, 13, 24, 1919; A1b, d; A2b; A3a; A4b; B1.*

REEVES, FRANK. Born Nov. 10, 1884, Albany, Clinton County, Kentucky. Ht. 6 ft. ½ in., blue eyes, brown hair, dark complexion, married. Stenographer, Stamford, Jones County, Texas. SPECIAL RANGER May 31, 1917–Dec. 1917. REMARKS: Had been a farmer in Young County, Texas. In 1930 was a newspaper reporter in Fort Worth, Tarrant County, Texas. Died Feb. 4, 1975, Tarrant County, Texas. FAMILY: Father, Edward G. Reeves (b. 1862, KY); siblings, Hattie F. (b. 1889, TX), Edward G. (b. 1892, TX); stepmother, Dovie (b. 1883, TX); sister, Dovie (b. 1899, TX); spouse, Nancy Jane (b. 1889, TX), married about 1909; son, Frank C. (b. 1910, TX). *SR; Register to Ferguson, May 18, 1917, AGC; Cunningham to Ferguson, May 18, 1917, AGC; A1d, e, g; A2a, b; A3a; A4b; B1.*

REEVES, MILLS QUARLES. Born Feb. 2, 1887, Anderson County, Texas. Ht. 5 ft. 9 in., brown eyes, black hair, fair complexion, married. County judge, Palestine, Anderson County. SPECIAL RANGER Aug. 10, 1918–Jan. 15, 1919. REMARKS: In 1910 was a lawyer in Anderson County. On World War I Draft Registration document, dated June 1917, stated "2nd Sergeant, Infantry, Texas Volunteer Guard." FAMILY: Mother, Willie (b. 1861, MS); sister, Mary (b. 1884, TX); spouse, unknown. *SR; A1d, e; A2b; A3a.*

RENEAU, JACOB WILLIAM DENTON "JAKE." Born July 4, 1870, Dandridge, Jefferson County, Tennessee. Ht. 5 ft. 9 in., brown eyes, dark hair, dark complexion, married. Farmer, Imperial, Pecos County, Texas. LOYALTY RANGER June 11, 1918–Feb. 1919. REMARKS: Had been a farmer in Grant County, Oklahoma Territory and a real estate agent in Linn County, Kansas. In 1930 was a real estate agent in Fort Worth, Tarrant County, Texas. Died Mar. 30, 1946, Oklahoma City, Oklahoma; buried in Oklahoma City. FAMILY: Parents, Samuel Russell Reneau (b. 1846, TN) and Barbara Ann Burchfield (b. 1853, TN); siblings, Mary Martha Jane (b. 1869, TN), Louvenia L. (b. 1872, TN), Julia Caroline (b. 1874, TN), George Thomas Seaton (b. 1876, TN), John Eagleton (b. 1878, TN), Sarah L. Priscilla (b. 1880, TN), Rachel L. Elizabeth (b. 1882, TN), Margaret Gallion (b. 1883, TN), James Columbus (b. 1885, TN), Amanda Frances (b. 1887, TN), Nellie Coleman (b. 1889, TN), Jesse Robert (b. 1891, TN); spouse, Delia Haley (b. 1881, MO or IL), married Sept. 20, 1899; children, Madella D. (b. 1901, OK), Fyrn U. (b. 1903, OK), Glore J. (b. 1905, OK), LaVaughn (b. 1907, OK), Jacob D., Jr. (b. 1909, KS), James Doyle (b. 1910, KS). *SR; A1b, d, e, f, g; A4b.*

RENEAU, THOMAS N. Born Feb. 19, 1868, San Felipe, Austin County, Texas. Ht. 5 ft. 11 in., blue eyes, dark hair, dark complexion. Peace officer. REGULAR RANGER Apr. 27, 1914–June 30, 1916 (private, Co. A; transferred to Co. D as sergeant; reenlisted Feb. 1, 1915). Resigned because of illness. Criminal officer, Houston, Harris County, Texas. SPECIAL RANGER Mar. 23, 1918–Jan. 15, 1919; Aug. 15, 1919–Dec. 31, 1919. Special officer, Gulf Coast Lines (GC&SF Railroad), Houston. RAILROAD RANGER Aug. 10, 1922–Aug. 10, 1924 (Co. D). Discharged. Peace officer, Houston. SPECIAL RANGER Oct. 18, 1934–Dec. 24, 1934. Resigned. REMARKS: Houston city detective, 1910–1913. Chief special agent, Houston Belt & Terminal Railway Co., Jan. 1919. As of Oct. 1934 had been a city detective, deputy U.S. marshal, Texas Ranger, chief special agent, Gulf Coast Lines, investigator for the Harris County district attorney. Died Aug. 16, 1937, Houston, Harris County, Texas; buried in Hollywood Cemetery, Houston. FAMILY: Parents, Thomas S. Reneau (b. 1830, TN) and Annie R. Munger (b. 1845, TX); siblings, Martha (b. 1866, TX), Annie R. (b. 1869, TX), Ella F. (b. 1870, TX), Lou Stella (b. 1874, TX), William Walther (b. 1877, TX), Maggie Lee (b. 1879, TX); spouse, Lillie Annie Brandt (b. 1874, TX), married Dec. 22, 1890; children, Lillian Aneta (b. 1892, TX), Nelson (b. 1896, TX). *SR; 471; AG to General Manager, May 13, 1914, AGC; Johnson to Hutchings, Aug 27, 1915, AGC; AG to Johnson, Aug 31, 1915, AGC; Ransom to Hutchings, Aug 26, 29, 1915, AGC; AG to Ransom, Aug 27, 1915, AGC; Reneau to Hutchings, May 10 1917, AGC; Reneau to Ferguson, May 10, 1917, AGC; AG to Reneau, May 15, 26, 1917, AGC; Petition to Hutchings [May 1917], AGC; Reneau to Hobby, Dec 8, 1917, AGC; Hammond to Hobby, Dec 8, 1917, AGC; Jones to Harley, Feb 24, 1919, AGC; Tevis to Hobby, Mar 7, 1919, AGC; Reneau to Hobby, Mar 17, 1919, AGC; HC, Apr 21, 1911; BDH, July 24, 1913, Aug 19, 1914, Aug 17, 1915; A1b; A2b; A4b.*

RHEW, AUSTIN. Born Mar. 5, 1875, Nuecestown, Nueces County, Texas. Ht. 5 ft. 5 in., blue eyes, light hair, light complexion, married. Farmer, Kingsville, Kleberg County, Texas. SPECIAL RANGER June 20, 1918–Jan. 15, 1919. REMARKS: In Sept. 1918 worked for Mrs. Henrietta M. King of the King Ranch, Kleberg County. In 1920 was a ranch foreman in Santa Monica, Los Angeles County, California. Died Aug. 13, 1937, Kleberg County, Texas. FAMILY: Spouse, Tacy (b. 1889, TX); sons, Herff (b. 1909, TX), Meldon J. (b. 1910, TX). *SR; A1d, f; A2b; A3a.*

RHODES, ERSKINE. Born Mar. 6, 1881, Frio County, Texas. Ht. 5 ft. 11 in., gray eyes, brown hair, dark complexion, married. Rancher, enlisted in Dimmit County, Texas. SPECIAL RANGER July 14, 1916–Dec. 1917; Apr. 30, 1918–Jan. 15, 1919. REMARKS: In Apr. 1918 was a Dimmit County deputy sheriff, at Cometa; the sheriff requested that he be commissioned. In Sept. 1918 was farming in Carrizo Springs, Dimmit County. Still a stock farmer in Dimmit County in 1930. Died Sept. 19, 1957, Hidalgo County, Texas. FAMILY: Mother, Sallie (b. 1855, TX); brother, Frank E. (b. 1883, TX); spouse, Helen Herick (b. 1885, IL or MO), married about 1909; daughters, Helen H. (b. 1914, TX), Genevieve "Jennie" D. (b. 1917, TX). *SR; Assistant AG to Gardner, Apr 25, 1918, AGC; A1d, e, f, g; A2b; A3a.*

RICH, NEWTON GILBERT. Born Feb. 22, 1881, Woodville, Jackson County, Alabama. Ht. 5 ft. 8 ½ in., blue eyes, light hair, light complexion, married. Roadmaster, I&GN Railroad, Navasota, Grimes County, Texas. SPECIAL RANGER Dec. 10, 1917–Jan. 15, 1919. REMARKS: The railroad's chief special agent requested that he be commissioned. FAMILY: Spouse, Mary (b. 1884, TX). *SR; Williamson to Harley, Nov 24, 1917, AGC; AG to Williamson, Nov 26, 1917, AGC; A1f; A3a.*

RICHARDS, STRATFORD HARRISON "STRAT." Born Jan. 30, 1882, Valley Mills, Bosque County, Texas. Ht. 6 ft. 1 in., blue eyes, black hair, medium complexion, married. Special agent, GH&SA Railroad, Ennis, Ellis County, Texas. SPECIAL RANGER Apr. 16, 1917–Jan. 15, 1919 (WA was reinstated Dec. 22, 1917). REMARKS: Was in the Special Service Department of the Southern Pacific Railroad. His superior requested that he be commissioned. In 1920 was a railroad special agent in Houston, Harris County, Texas. In 1930 was a farmer in Houston County, Texas. Died Jan. 4, 1960, Houston County, Texas. FAMILY: Parents, Charles Hampton Richards (b. 1832, AL) and Emily Wren (b. 1852, AR); brothers, John M. (b. 1876, TX), Patrick J. (b. 1887, NE), William P. (b. 1889, TX), Charles L. (b. 1892, TX); spouse, Lena (b. 1893, TX), married about 1908; son, Cull (b. 1910, TX). *SR; Buckner to Ferguson, Apr 10, 1917, AC; AG to Buckner, Apr 1, 1917, AGC; Wroe to AG, Apr 13, 1917, AGC; A1d, f, g; A2b; A3a; A4b.*

RICHARDS, WILLIAM HENRY. Born Jan. 23, 1866, Clayton, Barbour County, Alabama. Ht. 5 ft. 11 in., brown eyes, dark hair, brunette complexion, married. Farmer, San Augustine, San Augustine County, Texas. LOYALTY RANGER July 8, 1918–Feb. 1919. REMARKS: Died Apr. 28, 1948, San Augustine County, Texas; buried in Antioch Cemetery, San Augustine County. FAMILY: Parents, Robert J. Richards (b. 1835, AL) and Nancy L. Cox (b. 1837, AL); siblings, Nancy Louisa (b. 1861, AL), Robert Jimpsey (b. 1863, AL), Rachel Ann (b. 1867, AL), Julia E. (b. 1869, AL), Mary J. (b. 1871, AL), Rosa Mae (b. 1873, AL), James A. (b. 1875, AL); spouse, Minnie Veola Pickett (b. 1865, AL), married Nov. 27, 1887, Barbour County, Alabama; children, Maud (b. 1888, AL), Weltie Viola (b. 1890, AL), Brookie (b. 1891, AL), Rosa (b. 1894, AL), Robert "Bobby" (b. 1896, AL), Alma (b. 1898, AL), Benjamin (b. 1900, AL), William (b. 1902, TX), Sallie (b. 1905, TX), Earl (b. 1908, TX), Mary Lou (b. 1910, TX). *SR; A1b, d, e, f; A4a, b; B2.*

RIDEN, JESSE J. Born Sept. 1868, Hartville, Wright County, Missouri. Ht. 6 ft., gray eyes, dark hair, medium complexion, married. Constable, Loraine, Mitchell County, Texas. LOYALTY RANGER June 1, 1918–Feb. 1919. REMARKS: As a young man was a teacher in Hill County, Texas. Had been a peace officer for a number of years. In 1910 was constable, precinct 8, Jones County, Texas. Had been constable, precinct 5, Loraine, for several years. In 1920 was manager of a cotton gin in Loraine. FAMILY: Mother, Margaret M. (b. 1839, MO); sister, Abbie (b. 1882, TX); spouse, Bertie (b. 1892, LA), married about 1909; daughter, Margaret B. (b. 1909, TX). *SR; Secretary to Riden, Oct 3, 1917, AGC; A1d, e, f.*

RILEY, JAMES ROBERT. Born Apr. 7, 1880, Grayson County, Texas. Ht. 5 ft. 10 in., dark eyes, brown hair, dark complexion, married. Stockman, Dimmitt, Castro County, Texas. LOYALTY RANGER July 8, 1918–Feb. 1919. REMARKS: Died Mar. 19, 1961, Castro County, Texas. FAMILY: Parents, James Perry Riley (b. 1854, IL) and Elizabeth Jane Burleson (b. 1858, TX); siblings, S. C. (b. 1878, TX), George (b. 1881, TX), Lewis (b. 1885, TX), Earnest (b. 1887, TX), Lizzie (b. 1889, TX), Vivien (b. 1895, TX), Julia (b. 1898, TX); spouse, Annie (b. 1881, TX), married about 1902; children, Raymond J. (b. 1905, TX), Dorothy L. (b. 1908, TX), Frank or Furche (b. 1911, TX), Eva L. (b. 1914, TX), Elsie G. (b. 1916, TX), Vernice Marie (b. 1920, TX). *SR; A1b, d, e, f, g; A2b, e; A3a; A4b.*

RIPLEY, ROY STEPHEN. Born Feb. 22, 1887, San Antonio, Bexar County, Texas. Ht. 5 ft. 6 in., blue eyes, dark brown hair, white complexion. Salesman. REGULAR RANGER Oct. 11, 1911–Jan. 31, 1912 (private, Co. A). Discharged—reduction in force. REMARKS: In June 1917 was deputy district clerk, 45th Judicial District court, San Antonio. Had served in the Texas National Guard, was 1st lieutenant and company commander. Died Oct. 15, 1922, Bexar County, Texas. FAMILY: Parents, Pleas L. Ripley (b. 1850, LA) and Fanny M. (b. 1853, NC); sister, Janie L. (b. 1877, TX). *SR; EPMT, Oct 23, 1911; MR, Co. A, Jan 1912, AGC; Sluder to Ferguson, June 9, 1917, AGC; A1d, e, f; A2b; A3a.*

RISER, WILLIAM DAVID. Born Aug. 24, 1884, Jackson, Hinds County, Mississippi. Ht. 5 ft. 6 ½ in., blue eyes, dark hair, dark complexion, married. Editor-publisher, Big Lake, Reagan County, Texas. LOYALTY RANGER Aug. 26, 1918–Feb. 1919. REMARKS: In Feb. 1919 was apparently the Big Lake agent for Great Southern Life Insurance Co. Had been a printer in Upton County, Texas. In 1930 was a real estate agent in McCamey, Upton County. Died Feb. 14, 1962, Los Angeles, Los Angeles County, California; buried in Inglewood, Los Angeles County. FAMILY: Parents, David

Preacher Riser (b. 1852, MS) and May Shirley Pennebaker (b. 1865, LA); siblings, George Thomas (b. 1883, MS), Sallie A. "Ammie" (b. 1888, MS), Tully Griffin (b. 1890, MS), Roxie Mae (b. 1892, TX), Augustus Gamble (b. 1897, TX), Mattie Callie E. (b. 1900, TX); spouse, Carrie Ellen Wilson (b. 1890, TX), married May 17, 1908, Stiles, Reagan County; children, Iva Ellen (b. 1909, TX), Minnie May (b. 1912, TX), William D., Jr. (b. 1914, TX), Thomas Wilson (b. 1919, TX), Myrtle Frances (b. 1930, TX). *SR; A1e, f, g; A2f; A3a; A4b; B1, 2.*

ROBBINS, JOSEPH M. Born Nov. 7, 1868, Williamson County, Texas. Ht. 5 ft. 8 in., blue eyes, brown hair, light complexion, married. Deputy sheriff, Beaumont, Jefferson County, Texas. SPECIAL RANGER Oct. 3, 1918–Jan. 15, 1919. REMARKS: Was chief of night guards at Lone Star Shipbuilding Co., Beaumont. The company asked that he be commissioned. As of Jan. 21, 1919, was no longer employed by Lone Star. Had been a blacksmith in Frio County, Texas and an oil well driller in Atascosa County, Texas. In Mar. 1919 was farming near Laredo, Webb County, Texas. In 1930 still a stock farmer in Laredo. Died June 6, 1944, Webb County, Texas. FAMILY: Parents, Henry Chapel Robbins (b. 1817, AR) and Nancy Rebecca Kiser (b. 1832, AR); siblings, Mary Jane (b. 1855, TX), Anna Frances (b. 1858, TX), Luticia (b. 1860, TX), George (b. 1863, TX), Nancy Emma (b. 1866, TX), Joseph's twin sister Josephine (1868, TX), William Harrison (b. 1871, TX), Sallie Sarah (b. 1874, TX), Tlitha (b. 1876, TX); spouse, Lucy E. Little (b. 1871, TX), married Sept. 16, 1891, Pearsall, Frio County. *SR; 471; Crawford to Harley, Sept 26, 1918, AGC; A1b, d, e, f, g; A2b; A4a, b; B1, 2.*

ROBERSON, BENJAMIN FRANKLIN. Born Sept. 1868, Guadalupe County, Texas. Ht. 5 ft. 10 in., blue eyes, light hair, light complexion, married. Mechanic, San Juan, Hidalgo County, Texas. SPECIAL RANGER July 29, 1918–Jan. 15, 1919. REMARKS: In 1910 was a mechanical engineer in Nueces County, Texas. In Aug. 1916 a B. F. Roberson was a Kleberg County deputy sheriff. In 1920 was superintendent of water works in San Juan. Died Dec. 14, 1924, Hidalgo County, Texas. LAW ENFORCEMENT RELATIVES: Ranger Horace "Hod" Roberson, brother. FAMILY: Parents, Robert Wren Roberson (b. 1842, MO) and Mary (b. 1856, TX); brothers, Sidney (b. 1871, TX), Horace (b. 1875, TX), another (b. 1880, TX); spouse, Katie B. (b. 1871, TX), married about 1892; children, Raymond L. (b. 1894, TX), Irma P. (b. 1896, TX). *SR; BDH, Aug 12, 1916; A1b, e, f; A2b.*

ROBERSON, DAVID SETH "SETH." Born July 11, 1855, Polk County, Tennessee. Ht. 6 ft. 2 in., blue eyes, dark gray hair, light complexion. Night watchman, Devine, Medina County, Texas. SPECIAL RANGER Jan. 9, 1918–Jan. 15, 1919. REMARKS: Said he'd been a Texas Ranger, a "private ranger" (read: hired gun) for ranchers, and a justice of the peace. In 1920 was justice of the peace in Medina County. Died Feb. 19, 1924, Bexar County, Texas. FAMILY: Parents, Hiram Roberson (b. 1811, NC) and Nancy Crawford (b. 1818, NC); siblings, William Aaron (1838), Felix Webster (b. 1840, GA), George M. (b. 1841, GA), Hiram L. (b. 1842), John Madison (b. 1844, GA), Sarah Jane (b. 1846, GA), Louisa C. (b. 1847), Moses J. (b. 1849, GA), Mary A. (b. 1850, TN), Nancy A. (b. 1851, TN), James R. (b. 1853, TN), Harriet B. (b. 1856, TN), Martha Amanda (b. 1858, TN); spouse, Eva Crawford (b. 1875, TX), married Aug. 21, 1895, Frio County, Texas; children, Ina (b. 1896, TX), Eunice (b. 1898, TX), Alvah (b. 1899, TX), Edith (b. 1901, TX), Beulah (b. 1902, TX), Don (b. 1904, TX), Sabra (b. 1908, TX), Gordon H. (b. 1913, TX), Clester (b. 1916, TX). *SR; 471; Roberson to AG, Dec 6, 1917, AGC; A1a, b, d, e, f; A2b, c; A4a, b; B1.*

ROBERSON, HORACE LAWRENCE "HOD." Born Nov. 30, 1875, Staples Store, Guadalupe County, Texas. Ht. 6 ft. 1 in., brown eyes, light brown hair, light complexion. Stockman. REGULAR RANGER Oct. 11, 1911–July 1913 (private, Co. A; promoted to sergeant). Resigned. REGULAR RANGER Apr. 1, 1914–Sept. 4, 1914 (sergeant, Co. A). Resigned. Ranger [*sic*], Dickens, Dickens County, Texas. SPECIAL RANGER May 8, 1916–Jan. 15, 1919 (attached to Co. C; WA was reinstated Dec. 20, 1917). REMARKS: On 1911 enlistment form gave birthplace as San Antonio, Bexar County, Texas. In 1910–1911 was a Pullman conductor in San Antonio. Resigned from Rangers in 1914 to become foreman of huge TO Ranch in Chihuahua, Mexico. Killed several men, was defendant in sensational murder trial in El Paso, Texas. As of 1916, while appealing guilty verdict, worked as a brand inspector for the Cattle Raisers' Association of Texas, who requested he be commissioned as a SPECIAL RANGER. In 1918 was classified as a REGULAR RANGER without pay, to avoid the draft. He and fellow brand inspector (and ex-Ranger) Dave Allison were murdered in Seminole, Gaines County, on Apr. 1, 1923. LAW ENFORCEMENT RELATIVES: Ranger B. F. Roberson, brother. FAMILY: Parents, Robert Wren Roberson (b. 1842, MO) and Mary (b. 1856, TX); brothers, Benjamin F. (b. 1868, TX), Sidney (b. 1871, TX), another (b. 1880, TX). *SR; 471; Hughes to AG, Dec 4, 1911, WC; Wages to York, Mar 24, 1913, AGC; Hughes to AG, Apr 1, 1913, AGC; Tobin and Coy to Ferguson, Mar 13, 1916, AGC; Roberson to Ferguson, Mar 17, 1916, AGC; AG to Roberson, Mar 23, 1916, AGC; Crane to Hutchings, Apr 1, 1916, AGC; AG to Crane, Apr 22, 1916, AGC; Crane to AG, Apr 19, 1916, AGC; Ham to AG [ca. May 1, 1916], AGC; Ham to Ferguson [ca. May 15, 1916], AGC; Davis to Ham, May 18, 1916, AGC; AG to Ham, May 18, 1916, AGC; Spiller to Hutchings, May 5, 1916, AGC; Assistant AG to Collier, Dec 26, 1917, AGC; Acting AG to GC&SF Railroad, Jan 9, 1918, AGC; Acting AG to FW&DC Railroad, Jan 11, 1918, AGC; EPH, Jan 25, 1912; EPMT, Oct 23, Dec 3, 19, 1911, Jan 17, 19, 30, 22, 26, May 5, Nov 28, 30, Dec 1–5, 7, 14, 19, 1915, Apr 23, May 11, June 2, 7, 17, 20, 1916, June 1, 3, Oct 16, Nov 5, 11, 12, 14, 17, 18, 19, Dec 7, 1919; AA, July 2, 1914, Jan 21, 28, Dec 9, 1915, Oct 25, 1917; BDH, Jan 16, 1915; LWT, Aug 6, 1911; 319: 379–380; 463: 68;1501:246–248; 1020; A1b, e; A3a.*

ROBERTS, HUGH C. Born Dec. 19, 1883, Rusk, Cherokee County, Texas. Ht. 6 ft., blue eyes, brown hair, fair complexion, married. Stockraiser, Throckmorton, Throckmorton County, Texas. LOYALTY RANGER June 12, 1918–Feb. 1919. REMARKS: Lived in Abilene, Taylor County, Texas as a young man. In 1930 operated an "automobile laundry" in Abilene. FAMILY: Parents, Chas. Roberts (b. 1853, TN) and May D. (b. 1857, KY); sisters, Blanche (b. 1881, AL), June (b. 1886, TX); spouse, May (b. 1886, TX), married about 1904; children, J. W. (b. 1905, TX), ElRay (b. 1908, TX). *SR; A1d, e, f, g; A3a.*

ROBERTS, JOHN HENRY. Born Mar. 11, 1877, Byrdtown, Blanco County, Texas. Ht. 5 ft. 7 in., blue eyes, brown hair, light complexion, married. Teamster, Richland Springs, San Saba County, Texas. LOYALTY RANGER June 5, 1918–Feb. 1919. FAMILY: Spouse, Ollie Elizabeth Locklear (b. 1881, TX), married Feb. 26, 1900, Llano, Llano County, Texas; daughters, Beatrice Elizabeth (b. 1901, TX), Ollie Maude (b. 1903, NM), Jessie Gray (b. 1906, NM), Blanche Elizabeth (b. 1914, TX), Johneal Whitney (b. 1918, TX). *SR; A1d, f; A3a; A4b; B2.*

ROBERTS, JOSEPH B. Born about 1863, Tompkins County, Georgia. Ht. 5 ft. 7 in., blue eyes, brown hair, light complexion, married. Stockman, Ysleta, El Paso County, Texas. SPECIAL RANGER May 3, 1918–Jan. 15, 1919 (attached to Co. L). REMARKS: There is no Tompkins County in Georgia. In 1910 had been a drug store proprietor in Carlsbad, Eddy County, New Mexico. Letterhead in 1918: "Roberts-Kerr Cattle Co., Inc—Ranch 70 miles N. E. of El Paso—El Paso, J.B. Roberts, President and Gen. Mgr., A. F. Kerr, Secretary and Treas." In 1930 was time-keeper for the city of El Paso. A Joseph Barte Roberts died Nov. 26, 1934, El Paso County, Texas. FAMILY: Spouse #1, unknown, married about 1879; spouse #2, unknown; children, Josephine (b. 1890, TX), Bessie (b. 1898, TX), Joseph B., Jr. (b. 1901, TX); spouse #3, Theresa M. (b. 1874, TX), married about 1901. *SR; Roberts to Thomason, June 11, 1919, AGC; Thomason to Harley, June 13, 1919, AGC; A1e, f, g; A2b.*

ROBERTS, LIGHT DAVID. Born Aug. 13, 1882, Eagle Lake, Colorado County, Texas. Ht. 5 ft. 11 in., brown eyes, dark hair, fair complexion, married. Rice mill manager, Eagle Lake. LOYALTY RANGER June 12, 1918–Feb. 24, 1919. REMARKS: Was a Matagorda County deputy sheriff for 2 years. Was treasurer of International Rice Mills Co., Eagle Lake. In 1930 was still a rice broker in Eagle Lake. Died Sept. 22, 1956, Colorado County, Texas. FAMILY: Parents, Thomas Jefferson Roberts (b. 1840, LA) and Nancy Johnson (b. 1837, TX); siblings, James Eugene, Elizabeth, Mary Irene (b. 1866, TX), Thomas Jefferson (b. 1873, TX); spouse, Lorena (b. 1889, TX), married about 1908; children, Florence May (b. 1909, TX), Thomas C. (b. 1912, TX). *SR; A1d, f, g; A2b; A3a; A4a, b.*

ROBERTS, RAYMOND TRACY. Born Oct. 1, 1890, Raton, Colfax County, New Mexico. Medium height, slender, brown eyes, dark hair, married. Cowman, enlisted in Hudspeth County, Texas. REGULAR RANGER Apr. 27, 1918–Aug. 31, 1918 (private, Co. N—Hudspeth Scouts). Discharged—Co. N was disbanded. REMARKS: Had been a hired hand in

Coke County, Texas. In 1920 was a farm laborer in Coke County. In 1930 was manager of a ranch in El Paso, El Paso County, Texas. FAMILY: Parents, Rev. James H. Roberts (b. 1852, WV) and Ruth D. (b. 1854, OH); siblings, Lucy M. (b. 1881, OH), J. Horace (b. 1882, OH), Bessie M. (b. 1884, OH), James S. (b. 1887, OH), Julia D. (b. 1889, OH), Carl M. (b. 1892, NM), Walter B. (b. 1894, TX); spouse, Millie Mc. (b. 1888, TX), married about 1915; daughter, Emily Ruth (b. 1920, TX). *SR; 471; A1d, e, f, g; A3a.*

ROBERTS, ROSS L. Born Nov. 1886, Del Rio, Val Verde County, Texas. Ht. 5 ft. 9 in., gray eyes, light hair, blond complexion. Deputy sheriff. REGULAR RANGER Mar. 25, 1910–May 28, 1911 (private, Co. B; promoted to sergeant, Oct. 1910; reduced to private, Feb. 3, 1911). Honorably discharged. LAW ENFORCEMENT RELATIVES: Ranger Sidney Roberts, cousin. REMARKS: In 1930 was a rancher in Terrell County, Texas. A Ross Lucious Roberts died Feb. 28, 1963, Val Verde County, Texas. FAMILY: Parents, Joseph Roberts (b. 1851, TX) and Vernon (b. 1855, TX); siblings, Mary V. (b. 1880, TX), Howard J. (b. 1883, TX), Lucy (b. 1889, TX), James C. (b. 1892, TX); spouse, Carrie (b. 1887, TX), married about 1915. *SR; 471; Scout Report, Co. B, Oct 1910, WC; Hughes to Hutchings, Feb 5, 1911, AGC; MR, Co. B, Jan–Apr 1911, AGC; BDH, Oct 28, 1910, Jan 20, 1911; A1d, e, f, g; A2b.*

ROBERTS, SIDNEY. Born Sept. 1893, Del Rio, Val Verde County, Texas. Ht. 5 ft. 10 in., blue eyes, brown hair, ruddy complexion. Clerk. REGULAR RANGER Feb. 1, 1918–Oct. 1, 1918 (private, Co. E). Resigned. LAW ENFORCEMENT RELATIVES: Ranger Ross L. Roberts, cousin. FAMILY: Parents, Henry Pleasant Roberts (b. 1855, TX) and Rosalie Cotton (b. 1859, TX); siblings, Harrold J. (b. 1882, TX), Rosalie (b. 1883, TX), David P. (b. 1886, TX), Charles Cotton (b. 1889, TX), Ida S. (b. 1895, TX), Gladys (b. 1898, TX), Marian (b. 1905, TX). *SR; 471; A1d, e; A4b.*

ROBERTS, WILLIAM ARTHUR. Born July 12, 1873, Belton, Bell County, Texas. Ht. 5 ft. 9 ½ in., blue eyes, brown hair, fair complexion. Peace officer, enlisted in Terrell County, Texas. REGULAR RANGER Jan. 30, 1915–Nov. 7, 1916 (private, Co. B; promoted to sergeant ca. Sept. 1915). Resigned. REMARKS: Had been a deputy sheriff and special officer. In July 1918 was a deputy sheriff at Hurley, Grant County, New Mexico, at a mining camp. In Dec. 1919 lived in Sierra Blanca, Hudspeth County, Texas. FAMILY: Parents, Rev. Cornelius B. Roberts (b. 1837, MS) and Martha Ann Renick (b. 1841, MO); siblings, Benton A. (b. 1862, TX), Edgar E. (b. 1865, TX), Barton (b. 1867, TX), Walter (b. 1869, TX), Nancy "Flora" (b. 1875, TX). *SR; 471; Hutchings to Hulen, June 2, 1915, WC; Armstrong to AG, July 18, 1918, AGC; Assistant AG to Armstrong, July 22, 1918, AGC; Roberts to Hobby, Dec 4, 1919, AGC; BDH, Aug 9, 1915; EPMT, Sept 15, 1915; A1a, b; A3a; A4b.*

ROBERTS, WILLIAM FRANKLIN, JR. Born Aug. 16, 1888, Waldrip, McCulloch County, Texas. Ht. 5 ft. 8 in., blue eyes, brown hair, dark complexion, married. Postmaster and stockman, Lohn, McCulloch County. LOYALTY RANGER June 6, 1918–Feb. 1919. REMARKS: Was a postmaster in McCulloch County as early as 1910. In 1930 was a bank cashier in McCulloch County. FAMILY: Parents, William Franklin Roberts (b. 1842, MS) and Osa or Osie (b. 1863, MS); siblings, Lillian (b. 1886, TX), Gibbon (b. 1898, TX); spouse, Linnie L. (b. 1890, TX), married about 1913; son, W. James (b. 1922, TX). *SR; A1d, e, f, g; A3a.*

ROBERTSON, ARTHUR JAY "ART." (The first part of his Ranger Service Record is erroneously listed under A. J. ROBINSON.) Born May 12, 1882, Biadsville, Lincoln County, Arkansas. Ht. 5 ft. 8 ½ in., brown eyes, brown hair, dark complexion. Farmer and rancher, enlisted in El Paso County, Texas. REGULAR RANGER Dec. 28, 1917–Mar. 10, 1919 (private, Co. L). Honorably discharged—Co. L was disbanded. Government employee. REGULAR RANGER Feb. 18, 1921–Mar. 5, 1921 (private, Co. A). Resigned. REMARKS: 1921 Ranger enlistment form has height as 5 ft. 11 in., gray eyes, black hair, married. In 1919–1920 worked as a ditch rider for the U.S. Reclamation Service at Canutillo and Ysleta, El Paso County. Was an El Paso city detective. In 1930 was a Bureau of Reclamation ditch rider and a Dona Ana County, New Mexico, deputy sheriff living in La Mesa, Dona Ana County. Later served as Las Cruces, Dona Ana County, chief of police. At time of death was a justice of the peace in Las Cruces. Died Apr. 3, 1951, El Paso, El Paso County, Texas; buried in the Masonic Cemetery, Las Cruces. FAMILY: Siblings, Dan C., two sisters; spouse #1, unknown, married about 1907; spouse #2, Bessie R. (b. 1883, MO), married about 1912; spouse

#3, Natalia; son, Arthur, Jr. *SR; 471; Special Orders No. 21, Mar 10, 1919, WC; Petition to Harley [May 1919], AGC; Robertson to Cope, Apr 6, 1920, AGC; 114; A1f; A2b; A3a.*

ROBERTSON, HULING PARKER, JR. Born Jan. 12, 1887, Salado, Bell County, Texas. Ht. 6 ft. 1 in., brown eyes, brown hair, light complexion, married. Attorney, Belton, Bell County. SPECIAL RANGER July 23, 1917–Dec. 1917 (attached to Co. D). REMARKS: In 1930 was practicing law in Highland Park, Dallas County, Texas. Died Apr. 30, 1934, Kerr County, Texas; buried in Robertson Cemetery, Salado. FAMILY: Parents, Huling Parker Robertson (b. 1857, TX) and Mary Gatlin Cooke (b. 1861, VA); sister, Marie Christine (b. 1898, TX); spouse, Wilhelmina Pegram (b. 1887, TX). *SR; Ferguson to Hutchings, July 21, 1917, AGC; A1d, e, g; A2b; A3a; A4a, b.*

ROBERTSON, WADE HAMPTON. Born Jan. 9, 1877, Seward, Seward County, Nebraska. Ht. 5 ft. 8 in., blue eyes, black hair, fair complexion, married. Collector for Rodgers-Wade Furniture Co., Paris, Lamar County, Texas. LOYALTY RANGER June 29, 1918–Feb. 1919. REMARKS: Discusses arrests he made of deserters and draft dodgers. Died Feb. 7, 1962, Lamar County, Texas. FAMILY: Parents, James Henry Robertson (b. 1847, KY) and Lucy Edward Wingfield (b. 1849, MO); brothers, Edward (b. 1872, MO), Carl H. (b. 1875, NE); spouse, Carrie B. Currin (b. 1881, VA), married Aug. 19, 1905, Vernon, Wilbarger County, Texas; son, Elbert Stephens (b. 1909, TX). *SR; A1b, d, e, f, g; A2b; A3a; B1.*

ROBERTSON, WILLIAM JAMES TRAIN. Born Apr. 28, 1897, McGregor, McLennan County, Texas. Ht. 5 ft. 10 in., gray eyes, dark hair, ruddy complexion. Ranchman, Marathon, Brewster County, Texas. REGULAR RANGER July 1, 1919–Aug. 31, 1921 private, Co. B; transferred to Co. A, May 11, 1920). Discharged—reduction in force. Cattleman, Marathon. RAILROAD RANGER Aug. 16, 1922–Jan. 5, 1923 (Co. A). Discharged. REMARKS: A William Robertson, born Apr. 28, 1897, died June 26, 1978. FAMILY: Mother, Nannie (b. 1862, LA); siblings, Hallie (b. 1882, TX), Walter C. (b. 1884, TX), Mabel (b. 1887, TX), Edward J. (b. 1889, TX), Grace (b. 1890, TX), Mary (b. 1893, TX). *SR; 471; A1d; A2a, b; A3a.*

ROBINSON, A. J.—erroneous Ranger Service Record listing for ARTHUR J. ROBERTSON.

ROBINSON, D. W. Born Feb. 1886, Houston, Harris County, Texas. Ht. 5 ft. 9 in., blue eyes, dark hair, light complexion. Peace officer, Harris County. REGULAR RANGER May 29, 1916–July 23, 1916 (private, Co. D). REMARKS: Note length of service. Had been a Harris County peace officer for 10 years. A David W. Robinson was listed in the 1917 Houston, Texas City Directory; was a detective. *SR; 471; A5a.*

ROBINSON, FRANCIS M. Born Aug. 1872, Cameron, Milam County, Texas. Ht. 5 ft. 11 in., blue-gray eyes, dark hair, dark complexion, married. Deputy sheriff and night watchman. SPECIAL RANGER Sept. 12, 1916–unknown. Special officer, GH&SA Railroad, El Paso, El Paso County, Texas. SPECIAL RANGER Dec. 2, 1918–Jan. 15, 1919. REMARKS: Was a deputy sheriff at Valentine, Jeff Davis County, Texas, 1915, 1916. A Francis M. Robinson died Nov. 4, 1960, El Paso County, Texas. FAMILY: Parents, James W. Robinson (b. 1849, MS) and Matilda (b. 1844, AL); siblings, Della (b. 1878, TX), Hubert (b. 1881, TX), Docia (b. 1883, TX). *SR; Wroe to Hutchings, Sept 5, 1916, AGC; Johnston to Webster, Jan 20, 1919, AGC; EPMT, Aug 3, 4, 14, Oct 21, 1915, May 27, 1916; A1b, d; A2b.*

ROBINSON, GEORGE WASHINGTON. Born Apr. 24, 1889, Panna Maria, Karnes County, Texas. Ht. 6 ft. 1 in., gray eyes, brown hair, fair complexion, married. Peace officer, San Antonio, Bexar County, Texas. REGULAR RANGER Jan. 19, 1920–Sept. 9, 1920 (private, Co. F). Resigned. Peace officer, San Antonio. REGULAR RANGER Feb. 15, 1921–Aug. 31, 1921 (sergeant, Co. C). Discharged—reduction in force. REMARKS: As of 1920 had been a peace officer for 10 years. In Sept. 1920, resigned because his wife was ill and he'd gotten a better job with American Express at $140 a month at the I&GN depot in San Antonio. In 1930 was a finisher in a glass factory in San Antonio. Died May 30, 1975, Bee County, Texas. FAMILY: Parents, W. N. Robinson (b. 1852, VA) and Ella Lucrecia (b. 1860, TX); siblings, James Lee (b. 1884, TX), Ella May (b. 1887, TX), Bessie Estella (b. 1891, TX), Lilly Dewey (b. 1898, TX); spouse #1, Mattie L. (b. 1890, TX), married about 1910; spouse #2, Ethel Virginia Chestnutt (b. 1910, TX), married about 1929; daughters, Ada Lucretia (b. 1929, TX), Ida Bess (b. 1941, TX). *SR; 471; Cope to McCaskill, Jan 17, 1920, AGC; Robinson to Aldrich, Sept 9, 1920, AGC; Robinson to Cope,*

Sept 9, 1920, AGC; Aldrich to Robinson, Sept 14, 1920, AGC; A1d, e, f, g; A2a, b, e; A3a.

ROBINSON, HARRY H. Born Oct. 1872, Uvalde, Uvalde County, Texas. Ht. 5 ft. 10 in., blue eyes, brown hair, light complexion. Laborer. REGULAR RANGER Dec. 20, 1917–Feb. 1, 1919 (private, Co. M). Honorably discharged. REMARKS: Peace officer and laborer. In 1920 was city marshal in Eagle Pass, Maverick County, Texas. Maverick County sheriff July 8, 1929–Jan. 1, 1937. FAMILY: Parents, John Francis "Frank" Robinson (b. 1837, TX) and Mary P. Griner (b. 1846, TX or TN); siblings, John F., Jr. (b. 1869, TX), Robert Lee (b. 1875, TX), Edward (b. 1879, TX), Nannie (b. 1882, TX), Frankie (b. 1892, TX). *SR; 471; Cunningham to Harley, Dec 2, 1917, AGC; Special Orders No. 3, Jan 20, 1919, AGC; 1503:363; A1d, f; A3a; A4b.*

ROBINSON, THADDEUS PULASKI "TIP." Born July 7, 1878, Houston, Harris County, Texas. Ht. 5 ft. 11 in., brown eyes, brown hair, dark complexion. Mattress maker, Austin, Travis County, Texas. REGULAR RANGER Sept. 30, 1920–Mar. 31, 1921 (private, Emergency Co. No. 1; transferred to Co. B, Feb. 15, 1921). Resigned. Peace officer, Austin. SPECIAL RANGER Mar. 14, 1934–Jan. 22, 1935. Discharged. REMARKS: In 1910 was a fire wagon driver in Austin. World War I Draft Registration document indicates he was a laborer for Porter Brothers at the Army Supply Warehouse, Portsmouth, Norfolk County, Virginia, but his home was in Austin. As of 1917 was described as a lifelong resident of Travis County. Had been an Austin policeman for a number of years. Was recommended by Sheriff Matthews of Travis County. In Jan. 1921 was serving at Wichita Falls, Wichita County, Texas. His 1934 commission was requested by Sheriff Allen of Travis County. Died Oct. 8, 1935, Travis County, Texas. FAMILY: Parents, Thaddeus Pulaski Robinson (b. 1843, AL) and Mary Allen Renney (b. 1848, TX); siblings, Enoch William (b. 1867, TX), Mary Dean (b. 1869, AL), Lucy B. (b. 1871, TX), Eustis Hamilton (b. 1873, TX), Alfonso Jerome (b. 1875, TX), Athan P. (b. 1882, TX), Merril Pratt (b. 1886, TX). *SR; 471; Robinson to Harley, Dec 7, 1917, AGC; Robinson to Barton, Jan 30, 1921, AGC; A1d, e, f; A2b; A3a; A4a, b; B1.*

ROBUCK, ROBERT GREEN. Born Feb. 7, 1868, Runge, Karnes County, Texas. Ht. 5 ft. 9 ½ in., brown eyes, gray hair, florid complexion, married. Stockman, Karnes City, Karnes County. LOYALTY RANGER June 4, 1918–Feb. 1919. REMARKS: Had been a peace officer. In 1920 was Karnes County clerk. Died Nov. 27, 1941, Bell County, Texas. FAMILY: Parents, Rufus Green Robuck (b. 1832, AL) and Annie Elizabeth Pyle (b. 1838, TN); siblings, Elizabeth Jane (b. 1861, TX), Sarah Elvira (b. 1870, TX), Maude Ella (b. 1872, TX), Charles Henry (b. 1875, TX), Minnie Mae (b. 1878, TX), twins Arthula and Iola (b. 1881, TX); spouse, Julia Leigh Graves (b. 1875, TX), married Dec. 14, 1898; daughters, Elizabeth Julia (b. 1900, TX), Elvira Lee "Eva" (b. 1904, TX). *SR; A1a, b, d, e, f; A2a; A4b; B1.*

ROGERS, CLARENCE AARON. Born June 8, 1890, Waco, McLennan County, Texas. Ht. 6 ft. 1 in., blue eyes, light brown hair, blond complexion, married. Automobile dealer, Bowie, Montague County, Texas. LOYALTY RANGER June 5, 1918–Feb. 1919. REMARKS: In 1920 was an oil operator in Wichita Falls, Wichita County, Texas. In 1930 was president of Royalty Oil Company, Wichita Falls. Died June 11, 1970, Wichita County, Texas. FAMILY: Parents, Rev. Mathew Wesley Rogers (b. 1857, NC) and Texas Byrne Rhea (b. 1863, TX); siblings, Mathew P. (b. 1883, TX), Annie Mary (b. 1886, TX), Roswell W. (b. 1888, TX), Otis Rhea (b. 1902, TX), Robert Allie (b. 1904, TX); spouse, Merle Elizabeth Cook (b. 1892, TX), married June 10, 1913, Lorena, McLennan County; children, Clarence A., Jr. (b. 1919, TX), Gwendolen (b. 1925, TX), Herbert Cook (b. 1929, TX). *SR; A1f, g; A2a, b, e; A3a; A4a, b; B1.*

ROGERS, CLARK LAFAYETTE. Born Oct. 22, 1872, Logan County, Arkansas. Ht. 6 ft., brown eyes, red hair, fair complexion, married. Merchant, Stamford, Jones County, Texas. SPECIAL RANGER May 31, 1917–Dec. 1917 (attached to Co. C). REMARKS: Was a hardware merchant in Stamford in 1920. Died Jan. 10, 1955, Howard County, Texas. FAMILY: Parents, Robert Turner Rogers (b. 1834, NC) and Mary Daniel Reed (b. 1851, MS); siblings, Mary Emily (b. 1868, AR), John Thomas (b. 1870, AR), Emma Helen (b. 1875, AR), Annie Lee (b. 1877, AR), Margaret Lula (b. 1879, AR), Robert Marvin (b. 1881, AR), William Richard (b. 1884, AR), twins Edward Lucien and Jesse Cleveland (b. 1890, AR), Olive May (b. 1893, TX); spouse, Lailia R. Hunter (b. 1879, TN or MS), married about 1905; son, Conrad L. (b. 1907, TX). *SR; Register to Ferguson, May 18, 1917,*

AGC; Cunningham to Ferguson, May 18, 1917, AGC; A1b, e, f; A2b; A3a; A4b.

ROGERS, DUNCAN WESLEY. Born April 17, 1883, Hebron, Lawrence County, Mississippi. Ht. 5 ft. 9 ½ in., gray eyes, dark hair, light complexion. Special agent, Southern Pacific Railroad, enlisted in Jefferson County, Texas. SPECIAL RANGER Jan. 3, 1919–Dec. 31, 1919. Special agent, T&BV Railroad, Houston, Harris County, Texas. RAILROAD RANGER Oct. 7, 1922–Nov. 15, 1922 (Headquarters Co.). Discharged. REMARKS: As of Jan. 1919, had been a special deputy sheriff at Alexandria, Louisiana for 5 years; had worked for the Southern Pacific for the last 5 years. In 1930 was a city police officer in Houston. Died Sept. 12, 1935, Harris County, Texas. FAMILY: Brother, James Preston Rogers (b. 1885, MS); spouse, May (b. 1893, TX), married about 1924. *SR; Johnston to Webster, Jan 20, 1919, AGC; A1g; A2b; A3a.*

ROGERS, JOHN HARRIS. Born Oct. 19, 1863, Guadalupe County, Texas. Ht. 5 ft. 10 in., blue eyes, iron gray hair (as of 1929), light complexion, married. REGULAR RANGER Sept. 5, 1882–Jan. 31, 1913 (private, Co. E, Frontier Battalion; transferred to Co. F; promoted to sergeant, Oct. 19, 1892; appointed captain, Co. E, Jan. 1, 1893; captain, Co. E, Texas State Ranger Force, 1901–1911). Resigned. Peace officer, Austin, Travis County, Texas. REGULAR RANGER May 15, 1927–Nov. 1, 1930, (captain, Co. C; reenlisted May 15, 1929). Died Nov. 11, 1930 at Scott and White Hospital, Temple, Bell County, Texas. REMARKS: Served a total of 31 years in Rangers. In 1892 helped crush Catarino Garza revolution. In 1901 captured Gregorio Cortez. In Jan. 1911 resigned because he was a Prohibitionist. On Feb. 1, 1911, was appointed deputy U.S. marshal for the Western District of Texas, at El Paso, El Paso County, Texas. In 1913 was appointed U.S. marshal for the Western District of Texas; served for 8 years. Was a staunch Presbyterian. LAW ENFORCEMENT RELATIVES: Ranger Charles "Kid" Rogers, brother; Ranger (1891–1903) and La Salle County sheriff (Nov. 8, 1898–Nov. 6, 1900) and Potter County, Texas sheriff (Nov. 8, 1910–Nov. 5, 1918) William M. Burwell, brother-in-law; Ranger Charles B. Burwell, nephew; Ranger William Marvin Burwell, nephew. FAMILY: Brother, Charles Rogers; spouse, Harriet "Hattie" Burwell (b. 1874, TX), married about 1892; children, Lucille (b. 1893, TX), Pleasant B. (b. 1895, TX), Lapsley H. (b. 1898, TX). *SR; 471; Rogers to Hutchings, Feb 1, 1911, AGC; [Hutchings] to Rogers, Feb 3, 1911, AGC; 172:V, 664; SAE, Oct 25, 1911, Mar 23, 1913; AA, Jan 26, 1911, Feb 1, Dec 26, 1912, Mar 27, 1913; BDH, Nov 10, 1910, May 19, 1913, Apr 17, 1917; AS, Jan 13, 16, 1911; LWT, July 27, 1913; EPH, May 19, 1913; EPMT, Aug 17, Nov 16, 1910, Jan 20, Feb 5, Mar 24, Apr 28, June 22, 1911, Mar 29, Apr 17–19, July 21, Oct 17, 1912, Mar 25, 26, Apr1, 1913, Apr 6, 1914, July 8, 24, 1915; 319: 306, 309–11, 363–364, 366–382, 449–450, 496, 507–511; 421: 250, 252, 255, 256; 51: 145–149; 470: 164–165; 463: 22, 24, 25, 27–31, 66; 468: 260, 406, 407; 469: 57–58; biography: 1507; 1503:321, 418; A1b, d, e, f, g; A2b.*

ROGERS, OTTIS WOODWARD. Born Nov. 13, 1873, Anderson, Anderson County, South Carolina. Ht. 6 ft. 1 ½ in., blue eyes, black hair, dark complexion. Convict guard. REGULAR RANGER Sept. 25, 1910–June 13, 1911 (private, Co. C). Honorably discharged. REMARKS: In 1900 was a prison guard at Rusk-Wate Penitentiary, Cherokee County, Texas. In 1910 was a convict camp guard in Walker County, Texas. Died Feb. 10, 1938, Anderson County, Texas; buried in Olive Branch Cemetery, Anderson County. FAMILY: Parents, John Columbus "Hosia" Rogers (b. 1836, SC) and Savilla Welborn (b. 1835, SC); siblings, Joseph M. (b. 1853, SC), Thomas M. (b. 1855, SC), Mary A, (b. 1859, SC), Ozie G. (b. 1863, SC), William Ira (b. 1867, SC), Leah America (b. 1869, SC), Matilda Buena Vista (b. 1877, TX), Columbus Gustas (b. 1879, TX). *SR; 471; AG to Vanvleck, Jan 26, 1911, AGC; MR, Co. C, Jan 1911, AGC; A1aa, a, b, d, e; A3a; A4a, b; B2.*

ROLLINS, CALVIN EDGAR. Born Nov. 6, 1881, Spring Place, Murray County, Georgia. Ht. 5 ft. 10 in., blue eyes, brown hair, light complexion, married. Gaines County, Texas sheriff Mar. 24, 1914–Nov. 5, 1918, Seminole. LOYALTY RANGER June 18, 1918–Feb. 1919. REMARKS: In 1920 was manager of a clothing store in Gaines County. In 1930 was an automobile salesman in Gaines County. A Calvin Rollins died July 30, 1965, Gaines County, Texas. FAMILY: Parents, Robert Sebastian Rollins (b. 1842, GA) and Emily Denton (b. 1854, TN); siblings, Flora B. (b. 1877, GA), Maude Lee (b. 1879, GA), Oscar Buell (b. 1886, GA), Sarah Edith "Sadie" (b. 1889, TN), Homer (b. 1891, TX); spouse #1, unknown (b. TX), married about 1903; children, Mabel F. (b. 1905, TX), Doris A. (b. 1908, TX), Fred A. (b. 1910, TX), Alta A.

(b. 1913, TX); spouse #2, Pauline L. (b. 1893, TX), married about 1915. *SR; 1503:200; A1d, f, g; A2b; A3a; A4a, b.*

ROOKER, LORENZA BUNYAN. Born Aug. 9, 1875, Prairie County, Arkansas. Medium height, medium build, brown eyes, brown hair, married. Farmer, East Bernard, Wharton County, Texas. LOYALTY RANGER June 7, 1918–Feb. 1919. REMARKS: Was a constable at East Bernard in Mar. 1911. In 1920 was a farmer in Montgomery County, Texas. In 1930 was farming in Wharton County. Died Dec. 17, 1941, Wharton County, Texas. FAMILY: Parents, James Marion Rooker (b. 1833, SC) and Mary A. Hill (b. 1842, MS); siblings, Emma E. (b. 1859, MS), Joseph (b. 1861, MS), Ella N. (b. 1863, MS), James T. (b. 1865, MS), John W. (b. 1868, MS), Randolph A. (b. 1872, AR), Cora N. (b. 1873, AR), Leroy L. (b. 1877, AR), twins Mary O. and Martha O. (b. 1879, AR), Samuel (b. 1882, AR), Ava (b. 1884, AR), Elmer D. (b. 1886, AR); spouse, Francis (b. 1876, KY), married about 1905; children, Gladis (b. 1907, TX), Bessie May (b. 1908, TX), Marion (b. 1910, TX), Fancy or Annie B. (b. 1912, TX), Cora L. (b. 1914, TX). *SR; HC, Mar 17, 1911; A1b, f, g; A2b; A3a; A4a.*

ROONEY, JOHN MONROE "MONROE." Born July 31, 1895, Alpine, Brewster County, Texas. Ht. 5 ft. 11 in., blue eyes, light hair, fair complexion. Ranchman, Alpine. REGULAR RANGER Dec. 8, 1919–Feb. 10, 1921 (private, Co. E). Discharged. Ranchman, Alpine. RAILROAD RANGER July 26, 1922–July 29, 1924 (Co. D). Discharged. Special agent, Santa Fe (GC&SF) Railroad, Temple, Bell County, Texas. SPECIAL RANGER Aug. 3, 1925–Aug. 3, 1927; Dec. 6, 1927–Nov. 28, 1928; Nov. 28, 1928–Nov. 28, 1929; Dec. 19, 1929–Dec. 19, 1930. Chief special agent, GC&SF Railroad, Galveston, Galveston County, Texas. SPECIAL RANGER Jan. 10, 1931–Jan. 9, 1932; Jan. 26, 1932–Jan. 20, 1933; Apr. 1, 1933–Jan. 22, 1935; May 29, 1935–Aug. 10, 1935. Discharged. REMARKS: In 1930 was a railroad detective in Temple. FAMILY: Parents, Francis Joseph Rooney (b. 1867, Ireland) and Martha Seleta Chambers (b. 1877, NM); siblings, Katherine Seleta "Kittie" (b. 1898, TX), Francis Patrick (b. 1899, TX), Walter Roy (b. 1902, TX), Margret Anna (b. 1909, TX); spouse, Marguerite Rosa Granau (b. 1901, TX), married about 1925; son, John Monroe, Jr. (b. 1932, TX). *SR; 471; A1d, e, g; A2e; A3a; A4a, b.*

ROSS, CLAY EDWARD. Born Sept. 5, 1885, Kingston, Hunt County, Texas. Ht. 5 ft. 11 in., gray eyes, light hair, light complexion, married. Brand inspector, Dundee, Archer County, Texas. LOYALTY RANGER June 20, 1918–Feb. 1919. REMARKS: As of Sept. 1918 was a cattle inspector for the Texas Livestock Sanitary Commission, lived in Dundee. Had been a merchant and store keeper in 1910 in Randall County, Texas and in 1920 in Archer County. In 1930 was a stock farmer in Archer County. Died Feb. 22, 1957, Archer County, Texas. FAMILY: Parents, David Sanderson Ross (b. 1853, AL) and Mary Ann Skinner (b. 1855, AL); siblings, Columbus Eli (b. 1874), Mary Audelia (b. 1876, TX), Ila Ann (b. 1878), William Sanderson (b. 1880, TX), Joel Webb (b. 1883, TX), Bera J. (b. 1895); spouse, Clarissa Ellen Ralls (b. 1893, IL), married Nov. 14, 1909, Canyon, Randall County; children, Weldon E. (b. 1912, TX), Joseph C. (b. 1919, TX), Vera Pearl (b. 1921, TX), David S. (b. 1925, TX), Mary Ellen (b. 1929, TX), Pat A. (b. 1933, TX). *SR; A1d, e, f, g; A2b, e; A3a; A4a, b.*

ROSS, GUY GRIFFITH. Born Aug. 1888, Blanco, Blanco County, Texas. Ht. 6 ft. 1 ¼ in., gray eyes, black hair, dark complexion, married. Grain dealer, Blanco. LOYALTY RANGER June 7, 1918–Feb. 1919. REMARKS: In 1920 was a general store merchant in Blanco. In 1930 was a traveling hardware salesman in Blanco. Died Dec. 4, 1960, Bexar County, Texas; buried in Blanco Cemetery. FAMILY: Parents, Porter M. Ross (b. 1855, MO) and Mattie E. (b. 1855, TX); siblings, William A. (b. 1876, TX), Augustus A. (b. 1878, TX), Emmett Porter (b. 1879, TX), Vorie G. (b. 1884, TX), Melvin (b. 1886, TX), Arthur Storey (b. 1891, TX), Clarence B. (b. 1894, TX), Una L. (b. 1897, TX); spouse, May L. (b. 1891, TX), married about Feb. 1910; son, Charles E. (b. 1918, TX). *SR; A1d, e, f, g; A2b; A3a; A4b.*

ROSS, THOMAS M. "TOM." Born Aug. 1871, San Antonio, Bexar County, Texas. Ht. 6 ft., dark eyes, black hair, dark complexion. Peace officer, enlisted in Trinity County, Texas. REGULAR RANGER July 29, 1905–Feb. 28, 1910 (sergeant, Co. D; commissioned captain, Co. B, Feb. 1, 1907). Resigned/fired. Peace officer, Henderson Ranch, Van Court, Tom Green County, Texas. SPECIAL RANGER May 8, 1929–May 8, 1930. Discharged. Peace officer, San Antonio. SPECIAL RANGER June 6, 1930–Jan. 1, 1931; Feb. 19, 1931–Feb. 18, 1932. REMARKS: Feb. 1907 enlistment form states, "3 yr 10 mo with Capt. J. H. Rogers; 4 yrs 9 mo with Capt. Hughes." Was a corporal in Rogers's company; was a sergeant in Hughes's company. Was fired from Rangers in Feb. 1910 because his sergeant, Roscoe Redus, went on a rampage. Was the great-grandson of Col. Jose Antonio Navarro, one of the signers of the Texas Declaration of Independence, 1836. Operated the Ross Real Estate Company, San Antonio, 1910. Was Cameron County, Texas deputy sheriff, 1910–1911. Was special employee, federal Bureau of Investigation, fall of 1916; promoted to special agent but fired, Jan. 1917. Interpreter, federal district court, San Antonio, 1930–1945. In 1930 was a special investigator living in Atascosa County, Texas. Died Jan. 1, 1946, at his home in Rossville, Atascosa County, Texas. LAW ENFORCEMENT RELATIVES: Ranger J. Alexander Ross, brother. FAMILY: Parents, John C. Ross (b. 1841, Scotland) and Mary or Marie A. (b. 1845, TX); siblings, Jose A. (b. 1876, TX), Evander (b. 1878, TX), Hanna (b. 1880, TX), Alexander (b. 1885, TX). *SR; 471; AG to Ross, Jan 29, Feb 12, 23, 1910, WC; Ross to Newton, Jan 31, Feb 14, 19, 1910, WC; AG to Robertson, May 31, 1910, AGC; Assistant AG to Clark, Aug 25, 1910, AGC; Scout Report, Co. B, Oct 1910, WC; Canales to Campbell, Oct 25, 1910, AGC; Ross to Harley, Feb 9, 1919, AGC; EPMT, Nov 19, 1909, Feb 27, 1910; SAE, Dec 13, June 17, 1916; LWT, Nov 14, 1915, May 28, June 18, July 2, 16, Nov 5, 1916, Mar 4, Apr 22, 1917; BDH, Oct 3, Nov 3, Dec 1, 1910, Feb 25, July 13, 15, 17, 25, Aug 14, Nov 2, 1911, June 19, 25, 27, 1912, Sept 8, 13, 1915, June 12, July 12, 1916; La Prensa, June 13, 14, 1916; 464: 39–41; 319: 359; A1b, d, f, g.*

ROSSER, JAMES LEE "LEE." Born July 31, 1876, Floresville, Wilson County, Texas. Ht. 5 ft. 11 in., blue eyes, brown hair, florid complexion. Cowpuncher, enlisted in Wilson County. SPECIAL RANGER May 18, 1918–Sept. 20, 1918. Resigned. Went on active duty. Ranchman, Harlingen, Cameron County, Texas. REGULAR RANGER Sept. 21, 1918–Dec. 31, 1918 (private, Co. F). Discharged. REMARKS: On World War I Draft Registration document, states is a stockman working for rancher (and Special Ranger) Henry Edds in Hebbronville, Jim Hogg County, Texas. FAMILY: Parents, Ben F. Rosser (b. 1842, MO) and Texana A. (b. 1854, TN); siblings, Sarah (b. 1872, TX), JohnAnn (b. 1874, TX), Benjamin A. (b. 1878, TX), Kate (b. 1882, TX), Frank (b. 1887, TX). *SR; 471; Johnston to Baker, Jan 14, 1919, AGC; A1b, d; A3a.*

ROUNTREE, EDWIN BRUCE. Born July 18, 1885, Midland, Midland County, Texas. Ht. 5 ft. 6 in., gray eyes, black hair, dark complexion, married. Brand inspector, Cattle Raisers' Association of Texas, Midland. SPECIAL RANGER Sept. 16, 1918–Jan. 15, 1919. REMARKS: In 1930 was an automobile salesman in Midland. Died Jan. 25, 1960. FAMILY: Parents, Allen Barnett Rountree (b. 1846, IL) and Margaret Ann Reeves (b. 1846, IL); siblings, Ula Mae (b. 1871, IL), James Paul (b. 1872), Helen (b. 1887, TX); spouse, Roberta Ellen Scruggs (b. 1895, TX), married about 1913; sons, Edwin B., Jr. (b. 1918, TX), Robert D. (b. 1929, TX). *SR; Moses & Rowe to Harley, Sept 4, 23, 1918, AGC; AG to Moses & Rowe, Sept 10, 1918; Johnston to Moses & Rowe, Sept 24, 1918, AGC; A1f, g; A3a; A4a, b; B1.*

ROUNTREE, LEONIDAS JOHNSON "LEON," "LEE J." Born July 15, 1868, Dripping Springs, Hays County, Texas. Ht. 5 ft. 10 ½ in., gray eyes, gray hair, fair complexion, married. Editor, *Georgetown Commercial*, Georgetown, Williamson County, Texas. SPECIAL RANGER Mar. 13, 1918–Jan. 15, 1919. REMARKS: In 1920 was editor of a newspaper in Sulphur Springs, Hopkins County, Texas. By 1923 was editor of the *Bryan Daily Eagle*, Bryan, Brazos County, Texas. Served as Brazos County Representative to the Texas House of Representatives. Died on the floor of the House of Representatives, May 2, 1923, Austin, Travis County, Texas; buried at Bryan. LAW ENFORCEMENT RELATIVES: Ranger Oscar J. Rountree, cousin; Ranger Mason L. Rountree, cousin. FAMILY: Parents, Thomas P. "Tom" Rountree (b. 1840, AR) and Mary Kate Johnson (b. 1849, TX); siblings, Emma Lucille (b. 1871, TX), Emmet Granville (b. 1873, TX), Oscar Beverly (b. 1874, TX); stepfather, Granville McPherson (b. 1829, TN); siblings, Granville G. McPherson (b. 1882, TX), Melville McPherson (b. 1884, TX), Wallace B. (b. 1887, TX); spouse, Francis "Frannie" Mitchell (b. 1879, TX), married Apr. 2, 1909, Williamson County. *SR; AS, Feb 20, 1911; A1b, d, e, f; A2b; A4b.*

ROUNTREE, MASON LEE. Born Nov. 4, 1887, Blanco County, Texas. Ht. 5 ft. 4 in., gray eyes, dark brown hair, dark complexion. Cowboy, Sonora, Sutton County, Texas. REGULAR RANGER Oct. 23, 1915–ca. Apr. 30, 1916 (private, Co. D). Resigned—honorably discharged. REMARKS: Lived in Plainview, Hale County, Texas in

Apr. 1917. In June 1917 was working for J. H. Jordan and Company, Contractors, Hale County. In 1920 and 1930 lived in Maricopa County, Arizona. Died July 6, 1968, Hale County, Texas. LAW ENFORCEMENT RELATIVES: Ranger Oscar J. Rountree, brother; Ranger Lee J. Rountree, cousin. FAMILY: Parents, James Oscar Rountree (b. 1852, TX) and Mariah Louise "Lutie" Routh (b. 1860, AR); siblings, Oscar James (b. 1877, TX), Mona Ruth (b. 1879, TX), Montie (b. 1881, TX), Thomas Payne (b. 1883, TX), Austin (b. 1885, TX), Nellie (b. 1887, TX), Cora (b. 1888, TX); spouse, Maude N. (b. 1896, IA), married about 1919; adopted daughters, Bettie (b. 1915, AZ), Patricia J. (b. 1916, AZ). *SR; 471; AG to Rountree, Nov 2, 1915, Apr 7, 12, 1917; Ransom to Hutchings, Nov 7, 1915, AGC; Rountree to Hutchings, Feb 5, 1916, AGC; Rountree to Ferguson, Apr 1, 8, 1917, AGC; 319: 45; 508: 67; A1d, e, f, g; A2b; A3a; B1.*

ROUNTREE, OSCAR JAMES. No Service Record. Born Sept. 1, 1877, lived in Sonora, Sutton County, Texas until he was 25 years old. Was approximately 5 ft. 7 in. tall. REGULAR RANGER 1907–Feb. 1910 (private, Co. A). REMARKS: Cameron County, Texas deputy sheriff, Aug. 1910. Was hired as a bodyguard by Ed Roos of San Antonio, Bexar County, Texas who had a land dispute with millionaire D. B. Chapin. On Aug. 19, 1910, Chapin shot and killed Rountree in Breen's saloon in San Antonio. LAW ENFORCEMENT RELATIVES: Ranger Mason L. Rountree, brother; Ranger Lee J. Rountree, cousin. FAMILY: Parents, James Oscar Rountree (b. 1852, TX) and Mariah Louise "Lutie" Routh (b. 1860, AR); siblings, Mona Ruth (b. 1879, TX), Montie (b. 1881, TX), Thomas Payne (b. 1883, TX), Austin (b. 1885, TX), Mason L. (b. 1887, TX), Nellie (b. 1887, TX), Cora (b. 1888, TX). *471; MR, Co. A, Jan–Feb 1910, AGC; Assistant AG to Seale, Aug 24, 1910, AGC; SAE, Apr 15, Oct 25, Dec 8–16, 1911; BDH, Aug 19, 23, 24, 1910; AA, Dec 21, 1911; EPMT, Aug 22, 1910; AS, Aug 19, 21, 24, Sept 9, 1910, Feb 12–16, May 8, 22, 1911; 464: 39, 40; 1000: 118; A1b, d, e; A2b; A4b; B1.*

ROUTT, HENRY RUSSELL "RUSSELL." Born Feb. 10, 1879, Madison County, Alabama. Medium height, medium build, gray eyes, light hair, married. Ranchman, Live Oak Ranch, Laguna, Uvalde County, Texas. LOYALTY RANGER Sept. 1, 1918–Feb. 1919. REMARKS: By 1918 had lived in Texas 33 years, grew up in Medina County, Texas. In 1910 was a stock trader in San Antonio, Bexar County, Texas. In 1920 was a dry goods salesman in Uvalde, Uvalde County. In 1930 was a farmer in Bosque County, Texas. Died Nov. 1, 1962, Meridian, Bosque County, Texas; buried in McGregor Cemetery, McGregor, McLennan County, Texas. FAMILY: Parents, William Robert Routt (b. 1850, AL) and Lucy Ann Powell (b. 1854, AL); siblings, Lillie Lee (b. 1874, AL), Sudie Lafayette (b. 1877, AL), Lucy Peyton (b. 1884, AL), William Robert (b. 1887, TX), Georgia Mae (b. 1891, TX); spouse #1, Ada Styles (b. 1886, TX), married about 1906; daughter, Elizabeth (b. 1906, TX); spouse #2, Callie Roach (b. 1890, KY), married Dec. 31, 1922, McGregor. *SR; A1b, d, e, f, g; A2b; A3a; A4a, b; B2.*

ROWE, WALTER IVORY. Born Nov. 1889, Pleasant Hill, Travis County, Texas. Ht. 5 ft. 11 in., gray eyes, brown hair, dark complexion. Peace officer. REGULAR RANGER Sept. 1, 1917–Feb. 3, 1921 (private, Co. C; transferred to Co. D, Dec. 1, 1917; reenlisted in Co. E under the new law, June 20, 1919). Resigned. Peace officer, Fort Worth, Tarrant County, Texas. RAILROAD RANGER Oct. 17, 1922–Feb. 15, 1923 (Co. B). Resigned. Peace officer (special agent, MKT Railroad), Denison, Grayson County, Texas. RAILROAD RANGER Aug. 14, 1923–Aug. 14, 1925. Discharged. Peace officer, Denison. SPECIAL RANGER Apr. 6, 1926–Jan. 26, 1927; Jan. 26, 1927–Jan. 26, 1928; Feb. 28, 1928–Feb. 28, 1929; Mar. 4, 1929–Mar. 4, 1930; Mar. 7, 1930–Mar. 7, 1931; Mar. 8, 1931–Jan. 18, 1933; Jan. 27, 1933–Jan. 22, 1935; May 30, 1935–Oct. 10, 1935. Discharged. REMARKS: Was badly wounded by draft dodgers at Broaddus, San Augustine County, Texas on July 12, 1918. Applied for position of Ranger Quartermaster captain, Dec. 1918. Was the brother of S. C. Rowe, of the Fort Worth law firm of Moses & Rowe, attorneys for the Cattle Raisers' Association of Texas. Resigned from Rangers on Feb. 3, 1921, because he'd gotten a better job as special agent with the Frisco Railroad. A Walter I. Rowe died July 1, 1940, Grayson County, Texas. FAMILY: Mother, Mirria (b. 1851, England); brother, Sigmund Charles (b. 1881, England). *SR; 471; Acting AG to FW&DC Railroad, Jan 11, 1918, AGC; Anders to Harley, July 12, 1918, WC; L.B. Harvey's statements, July 13, 17, 1918, WC; Rowe to Woodul, July 24, 1918, WC; [Woodul] to Rowe, July 26, 1918, WC; Erby E. Swift report, July 25, 1918, WC; Rowe to Harley, Aug 29, 1918, AGC; [Cardwell] to Rowe, Aug 31, 1918, AGC; Moses & Rowe to*

Harley, Sept 13, 1918, AGC; Hanson to Judge Advocate, Oct 3, 1918, WC; Rowe to Hobby, Dec 7, 1918, AGC; Hanson to AG, July 17, 1919, WC; Rowe to Barton, Feb 3, 1921, AGC; 319: 195–196, 395; A1f, g; A2b; A3a.

ROWLAND, JOHN ROBERT. Born Oct. 20, 1861, Weston, Collin County, Texas. Ht. 6 ft., blue eyes, brown hair, light complexion, widower. Ranchman. REGULAR RANGER Dec. 2, 1911–Jan. 31, 1912 (private, Co. B). Discharged—reduction in force. REMARKS: Had been a hostler in Val Verde County, Texas. In 1910 was a stock farmer in Kinney County, Texas. Died Aug. 10, 1935, Del Rio, Val Verde County, Texas; buried in Brackettville, Kinney County. FAMILY: Parents, John W. Rowland (b. 1837, MO) and Amanda Ellen Wilson (b. 1844, MO); siblings, Thomas H. (b. 1860, TX), Mary E. (b. 1863, TX), Joseph (b. 1866, TX), Oliver (b. 1869, TX), Mack (b. 1874, TX), Archibald (1875, TX); spouse, Frances E. "Frannie" Hutchison (b. 1868, TX), married Mar. 6, 1884, Frio County, Texas; children, Lillian N. (b. 1884, TX), Roberta (b. 1886, TX), John Dennis (b. 1887, TX), Robert Victor (b. 1888, TX), Missouri (b. 1889, TX), Frank (b. 1902, TX). *SR; 471; A1d, e; A2b; A4b.*

RUBY, THOMAS E. Born Nov. 1871, Hays County Texas. Ht. 5 ft. 10 in., gray eyes, black hair, dark complexion, married. Road contractor, Buda, Hays County. SPECIAL RANGER Sept. 16, 1918–Jan. 15, 1919. REMARKS: Had been a farmer and "keeper" of a boarding house in Hays County. Died Sept. 24, 1921, Blanco County, Texas. FAMILY: Parents, Thomas Ruby (b. 1835, MO) and Sarah (b. 1835, MO); brother, John (b. 1858, TX); spouse, Emma Armstrong (b. 1875, TX), married Apr. 21, 1892, Travis County, Texas; children, Irene "Rene" A. (b. 1893, TX), Maurice E. (b. 1896, TX), Gladys (b. 1899, TX), Cecil (b. 1902, TX). *SR; A1b, d, e, f; A2b; B1.*

RUETER, HENRY ERNEST WILLIAM "WILL." Born Apr. 14, 1888, Jersey County, Illinois. Ht. 6 ft. 2 in., blue-gray eyes, brown hair, dark complexion. Stockman, Plainview, Hale County, Texas. SPECIAL RANGER Dec. 12, 1917–Mar. 1918 (Co. B Volunteers). Discharged. REMARKS: Was a rancher in "comfortable circumstances." In 1930 was a farmer in Cochran County, Texas. Died Mar. 18, 1940, Lamb County, Texas. *SR; Rawlings to Harley, Dec 12, 1917, AGC; A1f, g; A2b; A3a.*

RUMSEY, CHARLES STUART "CHARLIE." Born Aug. 28, 1891, Laredo, Webb County, Texas. Ht. 5 ft. 11 ½ in., brown eyes, brown hair, medium complexion. Packer, Laredo. REGULAR RANGER Sept. 1, 1913–Nov. 27, 1913 (private, Co. A). Resigned. REMARKS: Note length of service. As of June 1917 was a quarantine officer for the state of Texas, Station Laredo. In 1920 was working in the state labor agency office in Laredo. In 1930 was an automobile mechanic in San Antonio, Bexar County, Texas. Died Mar. 5, 1943, Bexar County, Texas. LAW ENFORCEMENT RELATIVES: Ranger Robert S. Rumsey, Jr., brother. FAMILY: Parents, Robert Henry Stuart Rumsey (b. 1851, England) and Mary Galvin (b. 1860, Ireland); siblings, Marie Stuart (b. 1876, IL), Robert Stuart (b. 1880, TX), twins John Stuart and James Stuart (b. 1883, Mexico), Ethel Stuart (b. 1886, TX), Viva Stuart (b. 1888, TX), Eva Stuart (b. 1890, TX); spouse, Celia (b. 1894, Mexico), married about 1917; sons, Charles S., Jr. (b. 1918, TX), Roberto (b. 1919, TX); adopted son, Edward (b. 1917, TX). *SR; 471; Hughes to AG, Sept 14, Oct 10, Dec 6, 1913; Acting AG to Hughes, Sept 2, 1913, AGC; Hughes to Acting AG, Aug 21, 1913, AGC; AG to General Manager, May 13, 1914, AGC; A1d, f, g; A2b; A3a; A4b.*

RUNYON, LAFAYETTE GRACEY. Born June 24, 1873, Weatherford, Parker County, Texas. Brown eyes, black hair, dark complexion. Carpenter, enlisted in Potter County, Texas. REGULAR RANGER Dec. 13, 1909–May 15, 1910 (private, Co. D). Resigned. REMARKS: In 1910 was a farmer in Dora, Roosevelt County, New Mexico. By Sept. 1918 was the local manager for the Singer Sewing Machine Company in Amarillo, Potter County. Was still managing the Singer office in 1930. Died Aug. 22, 1948, Gray County, Texas. FAMILY: Parents, Silas Samson Runyon (b. 1834, KY) and Mary Jane Wampler (b. 1835, IN); siblings, Willis (b. 1865, TX), Ben (b. 1868, TX), David (b. 1870, TX), Joseph (b. 1872, TX), Jed (b. 1876, TX), Augusta (b. 1878, TX); spouse, Mary L. (b. 1889, TX), married about 1920. *SR: 471; MR, Co. D, May, 1910, AGC; A1d, e, f, g; A2b; A3a; A4b.*

RUSHIN, WALTER. Born Nov. 1868, San Saba, San Saba County, Texas. Ht. 5 ft. 10 in., blue eyes, light brown hair, fair complexion. Ranchman, Marathon, Brewster County, Texas. REGULAR RANGER June 8, 1915–Jan. 15, 1916 (private, Co. B). Resigned. REMARKS: May 1915 was a Brewster County deputy sheriff. Had been a peace officer in Brewster County for a number of years. *SR; 471; AG to Rushin, Jan 2, 1912, AGC; Rushin to Ferguson, May 27, 1915, AGC; AG to Rushin, June 2, 1915, AGC; Fox to AG, June 14, 1915, WC; Rushin's statement, Jan 14, 1915, WC; Rushin to Hutchings, Mar 10, May 9, 1916, AGC; AG to Rushin, May 19, 1916, AGC; AA, May 13, 1915.*

RUSHING, FRANKLIN CHRISTOPHER "FRANK." Born Nov. 7, 1886, Lufkin, Angelina County, Texas. Ht. 5 ft. 7 in., brown eyes, brown hair, brunette complexion, married. Stockman, Rayville [*sic*], Trinity County, Texas. LOYALTY RANGER Sept. 2, 1918–Feb. 1919. REMARKS: AG's office stated there was no such place as Rayville in Trinity County. However, in Sept. 1918 on his World War I Draft Registration document, Rushing stated he was a cattle man in Rayville, Trinity County. That document also stated "one-eyed." In 1930 was a logging team foreman in Polk County, Texas. Died Jan. 5, 1978, Anderson County, Texas. FAMILY: Parents, Charles E. "Charlie" Rushing (b. 1855, MS) and Ader L. (b. 1867, AL); siblings, John C. (b. 1889, TX), Jessie J. (b. 1891, TX), William D. (b. 1893, TX), Charlie E. (b. 1895, TX), Jimmie (b. 1897, TX); spouse, Josie (b. 1884, TX), married about 1913; daughter, Frankie (b. 1925, TX). *SR; A1d, f, g; A2a, b; A3a; B2.*

RUSSELL, CHARLES ALEX. Born Aug. 28, 1888, Kosse, Limestone County, Texas. Ht. 5 ft. 9 in., brown eyes, brown hair, dark complexion. Farmer, Turkey, Hall County, Texas. SPECIAL RANGER Dec. 12, 1917–Feb. 1918 (Co. B Volunteers). REMARKS: Had been employed by Plainview Laundry, Plainview, Hale County, Texas. In 1930 was an insurance salesman in Turkey. Died May 23, 1962, Big Spring, Howard County, Texas. FAMILY: Mother, Katherine F. (b. 1867, TX); siblings, Willie I. (b. 1890, TX), Jesse A. (b. 1892, TX), James S. (b. 1894, TX), Roy L. (b. 1896, TX), Zona R. (b. 1898, TX); spouse #1, unknown, married about 1921; son, Charles B. (b. 1925, TX); spouse #2, Norma Katherine Wilcoxson (b. 1910, TX), married Dec. 23, 1928, Turkey. *SR; 471; Rawlings to Harley, Dec 11, 1917, AGC; A1e, f, g; A2b; A3a; A4b.*

RUSSELL, GROVER S. "SCOTT." Born Dec. 1887, Stephenville, Erath County, Texas. Ht. 5 ft. 10 in., brown eyes, black hair, dark complexion. Farmer, enlisted in Erath County. REGULAR RANGER Oct. 1, 1912–June 23, 1913 (private, Co. A). Killed June 23, 1913, in line of duty at Smeltertown, near El Paso, El Paso County, Texas. LAW ENFORCEMENT RELATIVES: Ranger Sam M. Russell, brother; pioneer peace officer Sam N. Russell, father. FAMILY: Sam N. Russell (b. 1856, AR) and Carrie May (b. 1868, GA); siblings, Lula M. (b. 1885, TX), Sam M. (1889, TX), Grady Hillman (b. 1892, TX), Claud Price (b. 1894, TX), William Bryan (b. 1895, TX), Winnie Howard (b. 1898, TX), Gayle (b. 1903, TX). *SR; 471; Hughes to AG, June 23, 1913, AGC; Hughes to Hutchings, June 24, 1913, WC; AG to Hughes, June 24, 1913, AGC; EPH, June 23–30, 1913; EPMT, Apr 23, June 24, 1913, Jan 26, 1915; BDH, June 24, 1913; LWT, June 29, 1913; A1d; A2b.*

RUSSELL, MAXWELL DENTON "MAX." Born Dec. 31, 1876, Menard, Menard County, Texas. Ht. 6 ft., gray eyes, light hair, light complexion, married. Stockman, Ballinger, Runnels County, Texas. SPECIAL RANGER Apr. 17, 1918–Jan. 15, 1919. REMARKS: Had been a peace officer for 12 years. In 1900 and 1910 was a tax assessor in Menard County. In 1930 was a rancher and stock farmer, listed in the U.S. Census records in both Menard County and Runnels County. A Max Russell died Nov. 20, 1957, McCulloch County, Texas. FAMILY: Parents, Joseph Oliver Russell (b. 1828, GA) and Sarah Jane Robertson (b. 1838, GA); siblings, Harriet (b. 1856), Richard Robertson (b. 1858, GA), James (b. 1861), Florence (b. 1864, GA), Levi Lynch (b. 1867, GA), William Walter (b. 1869, GA), Emma (b. 1871), Edward (b. 1873, TX), Jennie (b. 1878, TX), Thomas Peter (b. 1880, TX), Robert Longmire (b. 1882, TX); spouse, Alice Wilkinson (b. 1882, TX), married about 1907; daughters, Maxine (b. 1908, TX), Nell (b. 1912, TX). *SR; A1b, d, e, f, g; A2b; A3a; A4a, b.*

RUSSELL, R. L. Born July 1841, Frankfort, Franklin County, Kentucky. Ht. 5 ft. 8 ½ in., blue eyes, dark hair, dark complexion. Newspaper editor and correspondent, Lufkin, Angelina County, Texas. REGULAR RANGER Jan. 22, 1919–Mar. 31, 1919 (no Co. listed). Honorably discharged. REMARKS: Note age and length of service. *SR; 471.*

RUSSELL, SAMUEL MORRIS "SAM." Born Aug. 9, 1889, Stephenville, Erath County, Texas. Ht. 5 ft. 9 in., brown eyes, black hair, ruddy complexion. Farmer, enlisted in Erath County. REGULAR RANGER May 11, 1914–Sept.

30, 1914 (private, Co. A). Discharged. REMARKS: Note length of service. As of June 1917 was a teacher and farmer in Erath County. In 1920 was county attorney in Erath County. Died Oct. 19, 1971, Erath County, Texas. LAW ENFORCEMENT RELATIVES: Ranger Scott Russell, brother; pioneer peace officer Sam N. Russell, father. FAMILY: Parents, Sam N. Russell (b. 1856, AR) and Carrie May (b. 1868, GA); siblings, Lula M. (b. 1885, TX), Grover S. (b. 1887, TX), Grady Hillman (b. 1892, TX), Claud Price (b. 1894, TX), William Bryan (b. 1895, TX), Winnie Howard (b. 1898, TX), Gayle (b. 1903, TX). *SR; 471; EPMT, May 25, July 30, 1914; A1d, e, f; A2a, b; A3a.*

RUSSELL, WILLIAM E. Born Sept. 1871, Ojinaga, Chihuahua, Mexico. Ht. 5 ft. 10 in., blue eyes, brown hair, light complexion, married. Stockman, enlisted in Presidio County, Texas. SPECIAL RANGER May 1, 1918–Jan. 15, 1919. REMARKS: Immigrated to the United States in 1877; became a naturalized citizen. As of 1930 still a stock farmer in Presidio County. LAW ENFORCEMENT RELATIVES: Presidio County sheriff (Nov. 6, 1888–Nov. 8, 1892) William Russell, father. FAMILY: Parents, William Russell (b. 1839, KY) and Tomasa Rodriguez (b. 1845, Mexico); siblings, Lucia "Lucy" (b. 1866, Mexico), Anita (b. 1868, Mexico), Frank (b. 1876, Mexico); spouse, Lucia Hernandez (b. 1877, Mexico), married March 22, 1893, Presidio County; children, Anita (b. 1894, TX), Roberto (b. 1896, TX), Esther (b. 1898, TX), Tomasa (b. 1902, TX), Laura (b. 1904, TX), Guillermo "Willie" (b. 1906, TX), Jose "Joe" (b. 1912, TX), Elfega "Elva" (b. 1913, TX). *SR; 1503:424; A1b, d, e, f, g; A4b.*

RUTHERFORD, LIVINGSTON LEWELLAN "LIVEY." Born Dec. 23, 1875, Bastrop County, Texas. Tall, slender, blue eyes, light hair, married. Merchant, Ralls, Crosby County, Texas. LOYALTY RANGER June 3, 1918–Feb. 1919. REMARKS: Had been a farmer in Young County, Texas. In 1930 was manager of a wholesale oil station in Ralls. Died Mar. 23, 1934, Mitchell County, Texas. FAMILY: Parents, Calvin Rutledge Rutherford (b. 1840, TN) and Nancy Caroline Brown (b. 1843, NC); siblings, Augustus M. (b. 1864, AR), Mary M. (b. 1866, AR), James H. (b. 1868, AR), William Asa (b. 1870, AR), Joseph B. (b. 1871, AR), Thomas Clint (b. 1873, TX), Minnie Jan (b. 1878, TX), unnamed twins (b. 1880, TX), Calvin (b. 1881, TX), Robert B. (b. 1882, TX), Alice M. (b. 1884, TX), Rufus W. (b. 1886, TX); spouse, Willie or Willa (b. 1877, TX), married about 1898; son, Virgil H. (b. 1898, TX). *SR; A1b, d, g; A2b; A3a; A4a.*

RUTLEDGE, JAMES EMMETT. Born Apr. 23, 1874, Helena, Karnes County, Texas. Ht. 5 ft. 11 in., blue eyes, brown hair, light complexion, married. Railroad conductor, enlisted in Bexar County, Texas. SPECIAL RANGER Aug. 5, 1916–unknown. REMARKS: Had been a brakeman. In 1930 was still a railroad conductor in San Antonio, Bexar County. Died Feb. 24, 1959, San Antonio, Bexar County, Texas; buried in Southside Mission Burial Park, San Antonio. FAMILY: Parents, Emmett Elixir Rutledge (b. 1847, AL) and Martha Emily "Mattie" Malone (b. 1851, MS); siblings, Edward Dorman (b. 1870, TX), Abram Burwell "Burly" (b. 1872, TX), Frank Borroum (b. 1876, TX); spouse, Alice Alma Kelley (b. 1884, TX), married Aug. 27, 1902, San Antonio; children, Thelma A. (b. 1905, TX), Nell L. (b. 1909, TX), James E. (b. 1914, TX). *SR; A1b, f, g; A2b; A3a; A4a, b; B1, 2.*

RYAN, JOSEPH WILLIAM. Born Nov. 10, 1882, Brenham, Washington County, Texas. Medium height, stout, brown eyes, brown hair, married. Cattleman, Littlefield, Lamb County, Texas. LOYALTY RANGER June 28, 1918–Feb. 15, 1919. REMARKS: As of Sept. 1918 was a sheep raiser in Lamb County, living in Plainview, Hale County, Texas. In 1920 was an oil well rig operator in Fort Worth, Tarrant County, Texas. In 1930 was a general insurance manager in Amarillo, Potter County, Texas. FAMILY: Spouse, Lucy May O'Keefe (b. 1893, TX), married about 1912; son, Rufus E. (b. 1917, TX). *SR; A1e, f, g; A3a.*

RYAN, WILLIAM MATTHEW. Born July 9, 1880, Gonzales, Gonzales County, Texas. Ht. 5 ft. 10 in., brown eyes, gray hair. Peace officer. REGULAR RANGER Nov. 28, 1917–Feb. 10, 1921 (captain, Co. I; reenlisted under the new law as captain, Co. C, June 20, 1919). Discharged. Oil man, Laredo, Webb County, Texas. REGULAR RANGER June 16, 1925–Feb. 2, 1927 (captain, Co. D). Discharged. REMARKS: Was prominent in Laredo Council of Knights of Columbus. Was active in oil development and later served as a Webb County deputy sheriff. Died June 24, 1944, Laredo, Webb County, Texas. FAMILY: Parents, Patrick Ryan (b. 1849, Ireland) and Mary (b. 1850, Ireland); siblings, Margaret (b. 1869, PA), Robert (b. 1871, PA), Mary (b. 1873, PA),

Ranger Captain William M. Ryan. *Photo courtesy Texas Ranger Hall of Fame and Museum.*

Hannah (b. 1875, PA), Matthew (b. 1877, PA), Richard (b. 1881, TX), Nellie (b. 1884, TX), Alice (b. 1886, TX), Tom (b. 1889, TX). *SR; 471; McCallum to Ryan, Dec 1, 1917, AGC; Hobby at Harley, May 19, 1919, WC; LWT, Dec 9, 1917, Feb 22, 29, 1920, Feb 6, June 26, Nov 6, 1921; A1b, d, f; A2b; A3a.*

SACKVILLE, HOWARD ALLEN. Born Aug. 26, 1882, Petersboro, Ontario, Canada. Ht. 5 ft. 10 in., brown eyes, dark hair, dark complexion, married. Merchant, Dilley, Frio County, Texas. LOYALTY RANGER July 8, 1918–Feb. 1919. REMARKS: Parents listed in 1880 U.S. Census record in Frio County; 1900 U.S. Census record states Howard Sackville was born in Canada, immigrated to U.S. in 1887 and became a naturalized U.S. citizen. Had been a stock farmer in 1910. In 1930 was proprietor of a grocery store in Dilley. Died Nov. 27, 1946, Frio County, Texas. FAMILY: Parents, William Sackville (b. 1844, Canada) and Mary Isabella Sanderson (b. 1853, Canada); siblings, James S. (b. 1879, Canada), Margaret J. (b. 1892, TX); spouse, Minnie Harris (b. 1884, TX), married about 1910; daughters, Mary Ann (b. 1919, TX), Frances Elizabeth (b. 1921, TX). *SR; A1b, d, e, f, g; A2b; A3a; A4a, b.*

SADLER, GEORGE W. Born Mar. 12, 1882, Pearsall, Frio County, Texas. Ht. 6 ft. 1 ½ in., brown eyes, brown hair, light complexion, married. Stockman. REGULAR RANGER Dec. 18, 1917–Jan. 10, 1919 (private, Co. G). Resigned. Ranchman, Van Horn, Culberson County, Texas. SPECIAL RANGER May 17, 1935–Aug. 10, 1935. REMARKS: As a young man had lived in Llano County, Texas. As of Sept. 1918 was stationed in Sanderson, Terrell County, Texas; wife lived in Bigfoot, Frio County. Resigned in 1919 because he was married and couldn't live on his Ranger salary of $50 a month. Spoke Spanish fluently, was familiar with the border region. In 1930 was a ranch manager in Culberson County. A George Warrington Sadler died Jan. 16, 1955, Culberson County, Texas. LAW ENFORCEMENT RELATIVES: Ranger Lenn T. Sadler, brother; Ranger John W. Sadler, brother; Ranger William Sadler, brother; Ranger Tom H. Sadler, brother; Ranger Willis A. Sadler, distant cousin. FAMILY: Parents, James Kaine Sadler (b. 1848, TN) and Mary E. Berry (b. 1853, TX); siblings, Minnie Ollie (b. 1872, TX), Cora Lee (b. 1875, TX), Rebecca C. (b. 1877, TX), Tennessee (b. 1879, TX), Lenard Tillman (b. 1884, TX), John W. (b. 1886, TX), William D. (b. 1889, TX), Thomas (b. 1891, TX), Eva (b. 1893, TX); spouse, Maude Rogers (b. 1887, TX), married June 20, 1906, Frio County; daughter, Audrey. *SR; 471; Hanson to AG, Jan 29, 1919, WC; Aldrich to McQueen, Mar 13, 1919, AGC; A1b, d, g; A2b; A3a; A4a, b; B2.*

SADLER, JOHN W. Born Sept. 30, 1886, Pearsall, Frio County, Texas. Ht. 5 ft. 9 in., brown eyes, brown hair, dark complexion, married. Ranchman. REGULAR RANGER May 8, 1918–Oct. 15, 1918 (private, Co. G). Resigned. Ranchman, Hebbronville, Jim Hogg County, Texas. REGULAR RANGER Jan. 23, 1924–Jan. 18, 1933 (private, Co. D; reenlisted Jan. 23, 1926; reenlisted Jan. 23, 1929; reenlisted Jan. 23, 1931). Discharged. Peace officer (special officer for Atlas Pipeline Co., Longview), Falfurrias, Brooks County, Texas. SPECIAL RANGER July 27, 1933–Jan. 22, 1935. Discharged. REMARKS: A John W. Sadler died Nov. 30, 1942, Fannin County, Texas. LAW ENFORCEMENT RELATIVES: Ranger George W. Sadler, brother; Ranger Lenn T. Sadler, brother; Ranger William Sadler, brother; Ranger Tom H. Sadler, brother; Ranger Willis A. Sadler, distant cousin. FAMILY: Parents, James Kaine Sadler (b. 1848, TN) and Mary E. Berry (b. 1853, TX); siblings, Minnie Ollie (b. 1872, TX), Cora Lee (b. 1875, TX), Rebecca C. (b. 1877, TX), Tennessee (b. 1879, TX), George W. (b. 1882, TX), Lenard Tillman (b. 1884, TX), William D. (b. 1889, TX), Thomas (b. 1891, TX), Eva (b. 1893, TX); spouse, Letha Avis Long (b. 1892, TX), married about 1914 (Letha Avis Long was a sister of Lula Ellen Long, Ranger Lenard T. Sadler's wife). *SR; 471; 319 200; A1b, d, g; A2b; A3a; A4a, b.*

SADLER, LENARD TILLMAN "LENN." Born July 23, 1884, Pearsall, Frio County, Texas. Ht. 6 ft., brown eyes, brown hair, light complexion, married. Ranchman. REGULAR RANGER May 27, 1918–Sept. 15, 1918 (private, Co. G). Was killed by Ranger A. P. Lock on Sept. 15, 1918, Val Verde County, Texas. LAW ENFORCEMENT RELATIVES: Ranger George W. Sadler, brother; Ranger John W. Sadler, brother; Ranger William Sadler, brother; Ranger Tom H. Sadler, brother; Ranger Willis A. Sadler, distant cousin. FAMILY: Parents, James Kaine Sadler (b. 1848, TN) and Mary E. Berry (b. 1853, TX); siblings, Minnie Ollie (b. 1872, TX), Cora Lee (b. 1875, TX), Rebecca C. (b. 1877, TX), Tennessee (b. 1879, TX), George W. (b. 1882, TX), John W. (b. 1886, TX); William D. (b. 1889, TX), Thomas (b. 1891, TX), Eva (b. 1893, TX); spouse, Lula Ellen Long (b. 1890, TX), married July 15, 1908, Jourdanton, Atascosa County, Texas (Lula Ellen Long was a sister of Letha Avis Long, Ranger John W. Sadler's wife). *SR; 471; A1b, d; A2b; A3a; A4a, b; B1.*

SADLER, THOMAS H. "TOM." Born June 1891, Frio County, Texas. Ht. 5 ft., 10 in., blue eyes, brown hair, dark complexion, married. Ranchman. REGULAR RANGER Dec. 18, 1917–unknown (private, Co. G). REMARKS: Spoke Spanish, was a good horseman, was familiar with border region, came highly recommended. For the previous 19 months worked for the U.S. government at a remount station. In 1920 bought and sold livestock in San Antonio, Bexar County, Texas. In 1930 was a ranch hand in Culberson County, Texas, living with his brother, George. LAW ENFORCEMENT RELATIVES: Ranger George W. Sadler, brother; Ranger Lenn T. Sadler, brother; Ranger John W. Sadler, brother; Ranger William Sadler, brother; Ranger Willis A. Sadler, distant cousin. FAMILY: Parents, James Kaine Sadler (b. 1848, TN) and Mary E. Berry (b. 1853, TX); siblings, Minnie Ollie (b. 1872, TX), Cora Lee (b. 1875, TX), Rebecca C. (b. 1877, TX), Tennessee (b. 1879, TX), George W. (b. 1882, TX), Lenn T. (b. 1884, TX), John W. (b. 1886, TX); William D. (b. 1889, TX), Eva (b. 1893, TX); spouse, Lillie (b. 1895, TX); daughter, Hazel Lee (b. 1919, TX). *SR; 471; A1b, d, e, f, g; A2e; A4a, b.*

SADLER, WILLIAM D. Born Jan. 20, 1889, Bigfoot, Frio County, Texas. Ht. 5 ft. 9 ½ in., brown eyes, black hair, dark complexion, married. Ranchman. REGULAR RANGER Aug. 29, 1918–Nov. 10, 1918 (private, Co. G). Resigned. REMARKS: World War I Draft Registration document, June 1917, lists Atascosa County, Texas as birthplace. At that time was working for the "government" at Leon Springs, Bexar County, Texas. Worked on a ranch near the Rio Grande for J. A. Hill of Harlingen, Cameron County, Texas. Applied for a SPECIAL RANGER commission, gave J. A. and Lon Hill as references; was refused. In 1920 was a ranch manager in Hidalgo County, Texas. Died May 14, 1968, Bexar County, Texas; buried in Brummett Community Cemetery, Bigfoot. LAW ENFORCEMENT RELATIVES: Ranger George W. Sadler, brother; Ranger Lenn T. Sadler, brother, Ranger John W. Sadler, brother; Ranger Tom H. Sadler, brother; Ranger Willis A. Sadler, distant cousin. FAMILY: Parents, James Kaine Sadler (b. 1848, TN) and Mary E. Berry (b. 1853, TX); siblings, Minnie Ollie (b. 1872, TX), Cora Lee (b. 1875, TX), Rebecca C. (b. 1877, TX), Tennessee (b. 1879, TX), George W. (b. 1882, TX), Lenn T. (b. 1884, TX), John W. (b. 1886, TX), Thomas (b. 1891, TX), Eva (b. 1893, TX); spouse, Susie Arlee Jones (b. 1895, TX); sons, Eglane (b. 1916, TX), Roy Lee (b. 1919, TX). *SR; 471; Sadler to AG, June 15, 1918, AGC; Woodul to Sadler, June 18, 1918, AGC; A1b, d, e, f; A2a, b, e; A4a, b.*

SALLIS, WILLIAM FRED "WILL." Born July 4, 1881, Waller, Waller County, Texas. Ht. 5 ft. 8 in., gray eyes, dark hair, dark complexion. Salesman. REGULAR RANGER Apr. 20, 1909–1910 (private, Co. B). REMARKS: As a youth lived in Brenham, Washington County, Texas. In 1910 was a bartender in a saloon in Dallas, Dallas County, Texas. In 1920 was an oil operator in Wichita Falls, Wichita County, Texas. In 1930 was manager of a lunch stand in Dallas. Died July 27, 1953, Dallas County, Texas. FAMILY: Parents, James Milton Sallis (b. 1845, AL) and Sarah Elizabeth Johnson (b. 1855, TX); siblings, Jesse Seals (b. 1877, TX), Mary Alice

(b. 1879, TX), Byrd "Birdie" (b. 1887, TX); spouse, Helen B. Chappell (b. 1903, OK), married about 1920; sons, William Fred, Jr. (b. 1923, TX), James Milton (b. 1926, TX), Edwin Lee (b. 1932, TX). *SR; 471; A1d, e, f, g; A2b, e; A4a, b; B1.*

SALMON, ROMULUS SYLVANEUS "ROMIS." Born July 29, 1869, Stephenville, Erath County, Texas. Ht. 5 ft. 10 in., gray eyes, dark hair, ruddy complexion, married. Deputy sheriff, Kinney County. REGULAR RANGER Nov. 13, 1918–Jan. 1, 1919 (private, Co. E). Resigned. REMARKS: Had been a cow herder in Kinney County. In 1910 was a bartender in Kinney County. As of Nov. 1918 had been a Kinney County deputy sheriff for 18 years. In June 1919 lived in Spofford, Kinney County and applied for reenlistment in the Rangers. In 1920 was a restaurant proprietor in Spofford. Kinney County sheriff Nov. 2, 1920–Jan. 1, 1931, lived in Brackettville. Died Jan. 16, 1942, Val Verde County, Texas. LAW ENFORCEMENT RELATIVES: Texas State Policeman (1873) John Salmon, father. FAMILY: Parents, John Salmon (b. 1827, KY) and Mary Ann Jolly (b. 1830, IN); siblings, George Washington (b. 1853, TX), Eliza Jane (b. 1856, TX), John Baylor (b. 1859, TX), Elizabeth (b. 1860, TX), James F. (b. 1863, TX), Henry Edward (b. 1871, TX), Cassie Virginia (b. 1874, TX); spouse, Alice Spear (b. 1872, TX), married Dec. 21, 1888, Kinney County; children, Aaron (b. 1891, TX), Archie (b. 1892, TX), Bonny or Bennie (b. 1896, TX), Hazel (b. 1892, TX), Adolph (b. 1900, TX). *SR; 471; Clamp to Harley, June 28, 1919, AGC; 1503:312; 553:2; A1a, b, d, e, f, g; A2b; A4a, b.*

SAMMONS, CHARLES ELZY. Born May 10, 1876, Florence, Williamson County, Texas. Ht. 5 ft. 10 in., black eyes, black hair, dark complexion, married. Automobile dealer, Stamford, Jones County, Texas. SPECIAL RANGER May 31, 1917–Dec. 1917 (attached to Co. C). REMARKS: In 1920 was manager of a motor company in Abilene, Taylor County, Texas. In 1930 was a real estate agent in Abilene. Died Nov. 24, 1957, Taylor County, Texas. FAMILY: Parents, Andrew Jackson Sammons (b. 1846, TN) and Mary Elizabeth Henderson (b. 1852, AR); siblings, James William (b. 1870, TX), Josephine A. (b. 1873, TX), Rosa (b. 1878, TX), S. E. (b. 1881, TX), M. Emma (b. 1883, TX), Andy Jack (b. 1885, TX), Irene A. (b. 1888, TX), David Perry (b. 1890, TX), Benjamin Harrison (b. 1892, TX), Paul Rinon (b. 1895, TX); spouse #1, unknown (b. KY), married about 1900; children, Mack (b. 1903, TX), La Verne (b. 1905, TX); spouse #2, Dana E. Harkrider (b. 1883, TX); son, Chas. D. (b. 1924, TX). *SR; Register to Ferguson, May 18, 1917, AGC; Cunningham to Ferguson, May 18, 1917, AGC; AG to Sammons, June 13, 1917, AGC; A1b, f, g; A2b; A3a; A4a, b.*

SAMMONS, TIMOTHY EUGENE. Born Feb. 7, 1884, Floresville, Wilson County, Texas. Ht. 6 ft. 1 in., gray eyes, light hair, light complexion, married. City marshal, Shamrock, Wheeler County, Texas. SPECIAL RANGER July 1, 1919–Dec. 31, 1919. REMARKS: A Timothy Sammons died Mar. 15, 1956, Harris County, Texas. FAMILY: Parents, Wiley Benjamin Sammons (b. 1856, AR) and Dorcas Ophelia Owens (b. 1857, MS); siblings, Fred (b. 1881, TX), Loney N. (b. 1883, TX), Wiley B. (b. 1885, TX), Elizabeth May (b. 1889, TX), Arrena L. (b. 1891, TX), Ema (b. 1894, TX), Jessie F. (b. 1895, TX), Daisey W. (b. 1898, TX), Rosa L. (b. 1900, TX); spouse, Nellie Gray. *SR; A1d; A2b; A3a; A4a, b.*

SANCHEZ, DARIO. Born Dec. 19, 1854, Laredo, Webb County, Texas. Ht. 5 ft. 5 ½ in., married. Stockman, Laredo. LOYALTY RANGER June 14, 1918–Mar. 6, 1919. REMARKS: Owned a ranch near Encinal, Webb County. Webb County sheriff Nov. 2, 1886–Nov. 8, 1892; mayor of Laredo. In Dec. 1910 was vice president of the Laredo National Bank. In Jan. 1920 was reelected as one of the three directors of that bank. Died June 7, 1924, Webb County, Texas. FAMILY: Parents, Nicolas Sanchez (b. ca. 1820, TX) and Manuela (b. 1826, TX); siblings, Sanovia (b. 1843, TX), Roberto (b. 1846, TX), Lina (b. 1854, TX), Eustacia M. (b. 1858, TX), Jose (b. 1862, TX); spouse, Ofelia Benavides de la Garza (b. 1862, TX), married Nov. 26, 1885, Laredo; children, Elvira (b. 1888, TX), Nicolas (b. 1890, TX), Ofelia (b. 1892, TX), Dario, Jr. (b. 1893, TX), Ernestina (b. 1895, TX), Roberto (b. 1897, TX), Felipa (b. 1899, TX), Jose (b. 1901, TX), Marcelino (b. 1903, TX), Irene (b. 1908, TX). *SR; 1503:526; 172:V, 826; LWT, Dec 4, 1910, Jan 15, 1911, Nov 22, 1914, Sept 19, 1915, June 4, 1916, Jan 18, 1920; A1aaa, aa, a, b, d, e, f; A2b; A4b; B1, 2.*

SANDEL, HENRY LUTHER. Born July 24, 1887, Loma, Walker County, Texas. Ht. 6 ft. 1 in., blue eyes, brown hair, dark complexion, married. Merchant, Loma. LOYALTY RANGER June 6, 1918–Feb. 1919. REMARKS: In 1930 was a merchant in Navasota, Grimes County, Texas. Died Aug. 14, 1980, Richmond, Fort Bend County, Texas; buried in

Sheffield Cemetery, Pecos County, Texas. FAMILY: Parents, Thomas Henry Sandel (b. 1860, TX) and Mary Jane "Mollie" Sims (b. 1866, TX); siblings, Clara Lee (b. 1885, TX), Edgar Ray (b. 1889, TX), Samuel Nathan (b. 1891, TX), Harvey Bernice (b. 1893, TX), Lela Ethel (b. 1896, TX), Thomas Guinn (b. 1897, TX), Mary Lillian (b. 1899, TX), Wilmer Ernest (b. 1901, TX), Mattie Ella (b. 1904, TX); spouse, Bendina Brown Mitchell (b. 1889, TX), married Sept. 12, 1912, Crabbs Prairie, Walker County; children, Bennie J. (b. 1916, TX), Geraldine (b. 1917, TX), Lillian Iantha (b. 1920, TX), Mitchell Luther (b. 1924, TX). *SR; A1d, e, f, g; A2a, b, e; A3a; A4a, b; B1, 2.*

SANDERS, ALBERT FIELD "ALLIE." Born Oct. 2, 1889, La Vernia, Wilson County, Texas. Ht. 5 ft. 9 ½ in., black eyes, black hair, dark complexion. Peace officer, enlisted in Jim Wells County, Texas. REGULAR RANGER Dec. 10, 1917–Jan. 1, 1919 (private, Co. G; transferred to Co. I, July 1, 1918; transferred back to Co. G). Discharged. REMARKS: Said he had considerable experience as a peace officer. As of May 1917 was a state game warden in Alice, Jim Wells County. Had enlisted in the Field Artillery but failed his physical exam; had his exemption papers. In 1920 was living in Lockhart, Caldwell County, Texas. In 1930 was a county road worker in Lockhart. Died Jan. 17, 1951, Caldwell County, Texas. LAW ENFORCEMENT RELATIVES: Ranger Captain John J. Sanders, father; Ranger Jesse C. Sanders, brother. FAMILY: Parents, John J. Sanders (b. 1854, TX) and Maria C. (b. 1859, TX); siblings, Jesse (b. 1882, TX), John P. (b. 1883, TX), Elizabeth K. (b. 1887, TX), Gladys (b. 1897, TX), Walter H. (b. 1899, TX). *SR; 471; Sanders to Colquitt, Apr 24, 1914, AGC; Sanders to Stevens, Dec 7, 1917, AGC; Stevens to Harley, Dec 18, 1917, AGC; AG to Stevens, Dec 19, 21, 1917, AGC; Sanders to Woodul, Dec 20, 1917, AGC; AG to Sanders, Dec 21, 27, 1917, AGC; Reynolds to Townes, Jan 18, 1918, AGC; Acting AG to Caldwell County [Draft] Board, Jan 22, 1918, AGC; Harley to Bates, July 10, 1918; Sanders to Harley, Dec 31, 1918, AGC; Sanders to Cope, Dec 5, 1919, AGC; A1d, e, f, g; A2b; A3a.*

SANDERS, JESSE C. Born June 30, 1882, Lockhart, Caldwell County, Texas. Ht. 5 ft. 10 in., gray eyes, brown hair, dark complexion. REGULAR RANGER 1901–1903 (private, Co. A, Co. F). Peace officer. REGULAR RANGER June 3, 1915–Sept. 12, 1915 (private, Co. A, Co. B). Discharged. LAW ENFORCEMENT RELATIVES: Ranger Capt. John J. Sanders, father; Ranger Albert F. Sanders, brother. REMARKS: In July 1915 was transferred from Co. A (Captain Sanders) to Co. B (Captain Fox) on governor's order. In Jan. 1918 applied for reenlistment in Rangers. As of Sept. 1918 was a prison guard, state prison farm at Weldon, Houston County, Texas. In 1910 a J. C. Sanders was a town peace officer in Crystal City, Zavala County, Texas. In 1930 a J. C. Sanders was a county peace officer in Jefferson County, Texas. A Jessie Calvin Sanders died Apr. 19, 1935, Jefferson County, Texas. LAW ENFORCEMENT RELATIVES: Ranger Captain John J. Sanders, father; Ranger Albert F. Sanders, brother. FAMILY: Parents, John J. Sanders (b. 1854, TX) and Maria C. (b. 1859, TX); siblings, John P. (b. 1883, TX), Elizabeth K. (b. 1887, TX), Albert F. (b. 1889, TX), Gladys (b. 1897, TX), Walter H. (b. 1899, TX). *SR; 471; Sanders to Hutchings, May 4, June 10, 14, July 15, 1915, AGC; Ferguson to Hutchings, June 10, 1915, AGC; AG to Fox and Sanders, July 13, 1915, AGC; Fox to Hutchings, July 15, 1915, AGC; Sanders to Harley, Jan 2, 1918, AGC; BDH, Aug 9, 1915; 319: 320; 248: 14–16; A1d, e, f, g; A2b; A3a.*

SANDERS, JOHN JESSE. Born Apr. 16, 1854, Cold Spring, Polk County, Texas. Ht. 6 ft. 2 in., black eyes, black hair, dark complexion, married. Ex-sheriff, Lockhart, Caldwell County, Texas. REGULAR RANGER Feb. 1, 1911–Mar. 4, 1919 (captain, Co. B; reenlisted Feb. 1, 1913; reenlisted Feb. 1, 1915 as captain, Co. A; reenlisted, Feb. 1, 1917; suspended, Feb. 6, 1919). Relieved—fired. Special watchman, I&GN Railroad, Lockhart. RAILROAD RANGER Aug. 22, 1922–until his death, Feb. 6, 1924 (Co. A). REMARKS: Elected Lockhart city marshal, Jan. 1890; served until elected Caldwell County sheriff Nov. 8, 1898–Nov. 3, 1908. Became a cotton seed buyer. In 1914 played a prominent role in the Clemente Vergara case. Died Feb. 6, 1924, at the I&GN Hospital in Palestine, Anderson County, Texas; buried in the family plot at Lockhart. LAW ENFORCEMENT RELATIVES: Ranger Jesse C. Sanders, son; Ranger Albert F. Sanders, son. FAMILY: Parents, John W. Sanders and Harriet Blackwell; spouse, Mariah C. Hale (b. 1859, TX), married Sept. 2, 1880; children, Jesse C. (b. 1882, TX), John P. (b. 1883, TX), Elizabeth K. (b. 1887, TX), Albert F. (b. 1889, TX), Gladys (b. 1897, TX), Walter H. (b. 1899, TX). *SR; 471; Sanders to Newton, Feb 24,*

Captain John J. Sanders. *Photo courtesy Texas State Library.*

1910, AGC; F.H. Lancaster report, Oct 1911, 1BI; Lowry to Hutchings, July 12, 1914, AGC; Sanders to Hutchings, July 8, 15, 18, 21, 24, 30, 1914, WC; Hutchings to Sanders, July 22, 1914, WC; Grimes to Hutchings, Aug 3, 1914, WC; AG to Sanders, Mar 4, June 2, 1915, AGC; Sanders to Hutchings, Nov 14, Dec 19, 195, AGC; AG to Sanders, Oct 10, 1917, AGC; Sanders to Harley, Nov 4, 1917, AGC; McClintock to Harley, Feb 4, 1919, AGC; Harley to Davenport, Mar 15, 1919, AGC; 1503:79; AA, Apr 16, 1914; AS, Feb 26, Nov 11, 1910, Jan 28, 1911; EPMT, Jan 28, 1911; BDH, Feb 24, 1911, Nov 11–23, Dec 7, 1912, July 30, 1913, Feb 2, 1914; LWT, Apr 27, Aug 3, 1913, Apr 26, May 3, July 5, 19, Aug 30, 1914; 424: 208; 425: 78–79; 461: 391–392; 469: 60–62; 1520; A1d, e, f; A2b.

SANDIFER, WILLIAM WASHINGTON "WILL." Born Oct. 6, 1875, Franklin, Robertson County, Texas. Ht. 5 ft. 11 in., blue eyes, dark hair, brunette complexion, married. Farmer and stockman, Franklin. LOYALTY RANGER June 5, 1918–Feb. 1919. REMARKS: In 1930 was a farmer in New

Baden, Robertson County. Died May 3, 1952, Robertson County, Texas. FAMILY: Parents, James Jefferson Sandifer (b. 1851, MS) and Sarah Prudence "Sally" Patrick (b. 1856, TX); siblings, Alverta (b. 1874, TX), John (b. 1878, TX); spouse, Mollie J. McCormick (b. 1870, TX), married Dec. 20, 1896, Robertson County. *SR; A1b, d, e, f, g; A2b; A3a; B1.*

SANDLIN, CANADA VANGHAN. (Listed as CHARLES in Ranger Service Records.) Born Sept. 17, 1879, Bremen, Cullman County, Alabama. Ht. 5 ft. 11 in., blue eyes, brown hair, medium complexion, married. Water service foreman, St. Louis Brownsville & Mexico Railroad, Kingsville, Kleberg County, Texas. SPECIAL RANGER July 22, 1916–Dec. 1917; Mar. 16, 1918–Jan. 15, 1919. REMARKS: Had been a hired hand on a farm in Kaufman County, Texas in 1900. In 1910 was a laundry teamster in Houston, Harris County, Texas. In 1930 worked in a compress in Houston. Died July 27, 1960, Houston, Harris County, Texas; buried in Hollywood Cemetery, Houston. FAMILY: Parents, John M. Sandlin (b. 1855, AL) and Serepta Zeporah "Zip" Garrison (b. 1857, AL); siblings, Bell M., Rufus (b. 1877, AL), William A. (b. 1885, AL), Mary A. (b. 1890, AL); spouse, Katherine Lee "Katie" Ingraham (b. 1886, TX), married about 1904; sons, Wiley Garrett or Garrett Nathaniel (b. 1913, TX), Fallhey (b. 1916, TX), William Heard (b. 1919, TX). *SR; Sandlin to Hutchings, Sept 17, 1916, AGC; A1b, d, e, f, g; A2b, e; A3a; A4a, b.*

SANDS, WILLIAM B. Born Jan. 3, 1875, Mason, Mason County, Texas. Ht. 6 ft. 1 in., gray-blue eyes, dark hair, dark complexion. Cowpuncher. REGULAR RANGER Dec. 1, 1915–Sept. [?], 1916 (private, Co. B). Discharged/fired. REMARKS: Was fired for killing Army sergeant Owen Bierne on Sept. 21, 1917, in El Paso, El Paso County, Texas. His trial ended in a hung jury. As of Sept. 1918 was living in El Paso, working on the Hall Ranch in New Mexico. In 1920 was manager of a cattle ranch in La Union, Dona Ana County, New Mexico. A William Benjamen Sands died Apr. 17, 1946, Mason County, Texas. FAMILY: Parents, W. B. Sands (b. 1845, PA) and Mary Ellen (b. 1857, KS or MO); siblings, Clara (b. 1883, TX), Walter (b. 1886, TX), Ruth (b. 1890, TX); spouse, Teresa (b. 1883, Mexico). *SR; 471; McGregor to Ferguson, Sept 23, 196, RRM; EPMT, Dec 6, 1915, Oct 16, Nov 8, 25, 1919; EPH, Sept 26, 1916; BDH, May 23, 30, 1917; A1b, d, f; A2b; A3a.*

SANER, JAMES MONROE "MONROE." Born Dec. 7, 1855, Boerne, Kendall County, Texas. Ht. 5 ft. 7 in., gray eyes, brown hair, married. Farmer and stockman, Boerne. LOYALTY RANGER July 16, 1918–Mar. 6, 1919. REMARKS: As of 1918 had served as sheriff and deputy the last 30 years including Kendall County sheriff Nov. 3, 1908–Nov. 7, 1916. Died Aug. 26, 1923, Kendall County, Texas; buried in Boerne Cemetery. FAMILY: Parents, Patterson Douhitt Saner (b. 1822, NC) and Elizabeth Maness (b. 1832, TN); siblings, Phoebe Francisco (b. 1851, TX), Mary Josephine (b. 1853, TX), Rosilla Paloma (b. 1857, TX), John Jacob (b. 1860, TX), Thomas Patterson (b. 1861, TX); spouse, Lela Lenora Doughtrey (b. 1863, TX), married Oct. 22, 1879, Victoria, Victoria County, Texas; children, Felix Raymond (b. 1880, TX), Frank Alexander (b. 1882, TX), Thomas Benjamin (b. 1885, TX), James Monroe (b. 1887, TX), Margaret Rosa (b. 1889, TX), Mary Ellen (b. 1893, TX), Nora Alcester (b. 1896, TX), Josephine (b. 1898, TX), John William (b. 1902, TX), twins Elizabeth Madora and George Robert (b. 1906, TX). *SR; 1503:300; A1aa, a, d, e; A2b; A4a, b; B1.*

SAULSBERY, LEE. Born July 25, 1877, Guadalupe County, Texas. Ht. 6 ft. 2 in., brown eyes, black hair, ruddy complexion. Peace officer. REGULAR RANGER Nov. 30, 1917–May 1, 1920 (private, Co. D). REMARKS: Grew up in Bell County, Texas. As of Sept. 1918 was stationed in Austin, Travis County, Texas. In 1920 was serving in Brewster County, Texas. FAMILY: Parents, Morgan Saulsbery (b. 1852, KY) and Arminta Thompson (b. 1863, WV); siblings, Katie (b. 1879, TX), Mabel (b. 1881, TX), Morgan (b. 1885, TX), Monica (b. 1894, TX), Velma (b. 1899, TX); spouse, Ethel (b. 1892, TX); step-sons, Elwin Fogil (b. 1912, TX), Philip Fogil (b. 1914, TX). *SR; 471; Hanson to Judge Advocate, Oct 3, 1918, WC; Saulsbery to Cope, May 1, 1920, AGC; A1d, e, f; A3a.*

SAUNDERS, JAMES C. Born Aug. 1868, Banquette, Nueces County, Texas. Ht. 5 ft. 6 in., blue eyes, sandy hair, red complexion, married. Ranchman, Hebbronville, Jim Hogg County, Texas. SPECIAL RANGER Apr. 29, 1918–Jan. 15, 1919. REMARKS: Still a stock raiser in Hebbronville in 1930. A James Columbus Saunders died June 7, 1946, Jim Hogg County, Texas. LAW ENFORCEMENT RELATIVES: Ranger W. W. Saunders, brother. FAMILY: Parents, George Saunders (b. 1824, KY) and Sarah Watters Wright (b. 1844,

MS); siblings, Josephine Cook (b. 1863, TX), William W. (b. 1877, TX), twins Susie and Sarah (b. 1881, TX), Mary Ann "Annie" (b. 1883, TX); spouse, Rafaela Perez (b. 1887, TX), married about 1915; son, George Stephen (b. 1917, TX). *SR; A1b, d, f, g; A2b, e; A4a, b.*

SAUNDERS, WILLIAM WRIGHT "WILL." Born Sept. 23, 1877, Banquette, Nueces County, Texas. Ht. 5 ft. 6 in., blue eyes, brown hair, light complexion, married. Ranchman, Hebbronville, Jim Hogg County, Texas. SPECIAL RANGER Apr. 29, 1918–Jan. 15, 1919. REMARKS: In 1920 was a stockman, lived near his brother, James. LAW ENFORCEMENT RELATIVES: Ranger J. C. Saunders, brother. FAMILY: Parents, George Saunders (b. 1824, KY) and Sarah Watters Wright (b. 1844, MS); siblings, Josephine Cook (b. 1863, TX), James C. (b. 1868, TX), twins Susie and Sarah (b. 1881, TX), Mary Ann "Annie" (b. 1883, TX); spouse, Elizabeth Gonzales (b. 1898, TX); son, Benjamin B. (b. 1919, TX). *SR; A1b, d, f; A3a; A4a, b.*

SAVAGE, ROBERT RUSSELL "RUSSELL." Born June 23, 1881, Corpus Christi, Nueces County, Texas. Ht. 5 ft. 7 in., gray eyes, blond hair, light complexion, married. Lawyer, Corpus Christi. LOYALTY RANGER May 31, 1918–Feb. 1919. REMARKS: As of Sept. 1918 was city attorney for Corpus Christi. A Robert R. Savage died June 7, 1944, Nueces County, Texas. FAMILY: Parents, Robert Russell Savage (b. 1851, MS) and Mary Margaret or Martha Scott (b. 1853, TX); siblings, Charlotte Scott "Lottie" (b. 1875, TX), Beverly Rayburn (b. 1877, TX), James Scott (b. 1884, TX), Mary Laura (b. 1885, TX), John Edward (b. 1888, TX), Linton Sidbury (b. 1891, TX); spouse, Alice R. Borden (b. 1884, TX). *SR; A1d, e, f; A2b; A3a; A4a.*

SCANNELL, MILES JOSEPH. Born Dec. 18, 1895, Shafter, Presidio County, Texas. Ht. 6 ft., gray eyes, light brown hair, dark complexion. Ranchman. REGULAR RANGER Apr. 16, 1918–June 1, 1918 (private, Co N—Hudspeth Scouts). Discharged. REMARKS: As early as 1910 lived in Jeff Davis County, Texas. In June 1917 was a stock raiser in Valentine, Jeff Davis County. In 1919 he was a government scout for the 8th Cavalry in the Big Bend. He later became a Border Patrolman, rising to the rank of senior inspector. On Sept. 9, 1929, he was killed by a Mexican outlaw near Polvo (Redford), Presidio County, Texas. FAMILY: Parents, John Joseph "Jack" Scannell (b. 1860, Ireland) and Julia Fay Hopkins (b. 1870, TX); siblings, John Patrick, Ellen R. (b. 1893, TX), Mary A. (b. 1898, TX), Chandler H. (b. 1905, TX), Margaret F. (b. 1908, TX); spouse, Dorothy Cotter (b. 1904, TX), married about 1927; son, Jack C. (b. 1927, TX). *SR; 204:II, 334; 471; 1: 1651–1653; 330: 51; 422: 83; 470: 123; 488: 38, 44; 1:1652; 36:97; A1e, f, g; A2b; A3a; A4b.*

SCARBOROUGH, ELIAS B. "ELI." Born Aug. 26, 1877, Paige, Bastrop County, Texas. Ht. 6 ft., brown eyes, auburn hair, married. Farmer, Kingsville, Kleberg County, Texas. SPECIAL RANGER July 11, 1916–Nov. 5, 1918 (attached to Co. C; his commission was reinstated Dec. 27, 1917). Warrant of authority was cancelled because he moved out of the country. REMARKS: He was one of the scouts in the Kleberg County home guard unit organized by Sheriff J. S. Scarborough. Letterhead in Sept. 1916: "E. B. Scarborough, Real Estate, Loans and Insurance, Riviera, Kleberg County." Had been a farmer in Jackson County, Texas and Wheeler County, Texas. In 1920 was a farmer in McCulloch County, Texas. Died Feb. 21, 1964, Bowie County, Texas. LAW ENFORCEMENT RELATIVES: Ranger, Lee County sheriff (Nov. 4, 1890–Nov. 3, 1896 and Nov. 4, 1902–Nov. 8, 1910) and Kleberg County sheriff (Aug. 10, 1914–Jan 1, 1923) James S. Scarborough, Sr., uncle; Ranger, Kingsville chief of police (1930) and Kleberg County sheriff (Aug. 5, 1935–Jan. 1, 1973) James S. Scarborough, Jr., cousin; Lee County sheriff (Nov. 8, 1910–Nov. 5, 1918) William D. Scarborough, uncle; Kleberg County sheriff (Nov. 7, 1972–Jan. 1, 1989) James S. Scarborough III, distant cousin. FAMILY: Parents, Thomas Hicks Scarborough (b. 1846, LA) and Mary Elizabeth Erwin (b. 1860, TN); siblings, John T. (b. 1874, TX), Mary A. (b. 1880, TX); spouse #1, Ella (b. 1875, TX), married about 1889; sons, Barton (b. 1901, TX), Elias Neville (b. 1904, TX); spouse #2, Neta (b. 1885, TX); son, Robert E. Lee (b. 1919, TX). *SR; AG to Scarborough, July 8, 1916, AGC; Scarborough to Hutchings, July 11, Sept 10, 1916, AGC; Scarborough to Ferguson, June 4, 1917, AGC; Scarborough to Harley, Dec 23, 1917, AGC; AG to Scarborough, Dec 27, 1917, AGC; 1503:313, 330; A1b, d, e, f; A2a, b, e; A3a; B1.*

SCARBOROUGH, JAMES SPURGEON, SR. Born Dec. 1859, Louisiana. Ht. 6 ft., gray eyes, black (bald) hair, medium complexion, married. Kleberg County sheriff,

Kingsville, Texas. SPECIAL RANGER Apr. 27, 1918–Jan. 15, 1919. Real estate agent, Lexington, Lee County, Texas. SPECIAL RANGER Aug. 10, 1931–Jan. 20, 1933. Real estate agent and detective, Kingsville. SPECIAL RANGER June 10, 1933–Jan. 22, 1935. Discharged. REMARKS: Ranger Service Record lists birthplace as Colorado County, Texas. All census records indicate birthplace as Louisiana; in 1860 U.S. census, Scarborough lived with his family in Mansfield, DeSoto Parish, Louisiana. Lee County, Texas sheriff Nov. 4, 1890–Nov. 3, 1896, and Nov. 4, 1902–Nov. 8, 1910. Kleberg County sheriff Aug. 10, 1914–Jan. 1, 1923; in 1920 was also Kleberg County tax collector. A James Scarborough died Aug. 26, 1936, Kleberg County, Texas. LAW ENFORCEMENT RELATIVES: Ranger, Kingsville chief of police (1930) and Kleberg County sheriff (Aug. 5, 1935–Jan. 1, 1973) James S. Scarborough, Jr., son; Ranger E. B. Scarborough, nephew; Lee County sheriff (Nov. 8, 1910–Nov. 5, 1918) William D. Scarborough, brother; Kleberg County sheriff (Nov. 7, 1972–Jan. 1, 1989) James S. Scarborough III, grandson. FAMILY: Parents, Rev. Lawrence Hamilton Scarborough (b. 1808, GA) and Jane Chambers Hicks (b. 1817, TN); siblings, Nancy E. (b. 1844, LA), Thomas Hicks (b. 1846, LA), Martha J. (b. 1848, LA), Lawrence H. (b. 1849, LA), Mary A. E. (b. 1851, LA), Amanda A. (b. 1853, LA), Sarah P. (b. 1856, LA), William D. (b. 1860, LA), McDonald (b. 1864, TX); spouse, Portia (b. 1867, TX), married about 1894; sons, James S., Jr. (b. 1895, TX), William L. (b. 1906, TX). *SR; BDH, Sept 1, 1914; Scarborough to Hanson, Mar 1, 1919, AGC; Scarborough to Harley, Mar 7, 1919, AGC; Aldrich to Scarborough, Mar 7, 1919, AGC; 1503:313, 330; A1aa, a, e, f; A2b; A4a, b.*

SCARBOROUGH, JAMES SPURGEON, JR. Born Nov. 2, 1895, Giddings, Lee County, Texas. Ht. 6 ft. ½ in., blue eyes, light hair, light complexion. Bookkeeper, Kingsville, Kleberg County, Texas. SPECIAL RANGER May 30, 1917–Dec. 1917. REMARKS: Had been connected with R. J. Kleberg and Co., Bankers, for 4 years. In 1930 was Kingsville police chief. Kleberg County sheriff Aug. 5, 1935–Jan. 1, 1973. Died Dec. 5, 1978, Kleberg County, Texas. LAW ENFORCEMENT RELATIVES: Ranger, Lee County sheriff (Nov. 4, 1890–Nov. 3, 1896 and Nov. 4, 1902–Nov. 8, 1910) and Kleberg County sheriff (Aug. 10, 1914–Jan. 1, 1923) James S. Scarborough, Sr., father; Ranger Elias B. Scarborough, cousin; Kleberg County sheriff (Nov. 7, 1972–Jan. 1, 1989) James S. Scarborough III, son; Lee County sheriff (Nov. 8, 1910–Nov. 5, 1918) William D. Scarborough, uncle. FAMILY: Parents, James S. Scarborough, Sr. (b. 1859, LA) and Portia (b. 1867, TX); brother, William L. (b. 1906, TX); spouse, Isabel W. (b. 1899, TX), married about 1918; sons, James S., III (b. 1921, TX), Daniel Stripling (b. 1923, TX). *SR; 1503:313, 330; A1d, e, f, g; A2a, b, e; A3a.*

SCARBOROUGH, WILLIAM F. Born Jan. 1868, Caldwell, Burleson County, Texas. Ht. 6 ft. 2 ½ in., gray eyes, iron gray hair, light complexion, married. Cowman, Midland, Midland County, Texas. SPECIAL RANGER June 8, 1918–Jan. 15, 1919. REMARKS: "many years as deputy sheriff." Letterhead: "W. F. Scarborough, Breeder and Dealer in Hereford Cattle, Midland, Texas—Ranches in Winkler, Loving and Andrews Counties—Brand O—on left hip." A William Francis Scarborough died June 20, 1939, Winkler County, Texas. FAMILY: Parents, George W. Scarborough (b. 1842, LA or MS) and Elizabeth Rutland (b. 1846, LA or KY); spouse, Kara E. Wiman or Wyman (b. 1867, KY), married Mar. 28, 1886, Jones County, Texas; children, Hollister "Hollis" (b. 1887, TX), Leta E. (b. 1893, TX), Lucile (b. 1897, TX), Evelyn (b. 1906, TX). *SR; A1e, f; A2b, c; A4a, b.*

SCHEULTZ, ROBERT ALVIN "ALVIN." Born Dec. 15, 1883, Houston, Harris County, Texas. Ht. 5 ft. 9 ½ in., gray eyes, brown hair, dark complexion. Government officer ("Camp Logan and Ellington Field, enforcing War Department rules and all laws"), Houston. SPECIAL RANGER Oct. 13, 1917–Sept. 23, 1918. Resigned. REMARKS: "2 ½ yrs. Pinkerton Agency; 9 yrs. railroad service; 3 yrs. cotton compress." Died Aug. 9, 1953, Harris County, Texas. FAMILY: Parents, Adolph J. Scheultz (b. 1854, TX) and Mamie L. (b. 1861, TX); siblings, Elsie (b. 1882, TX), Loyd E. (b. 1888, TX). *SR; Scheultz to Tillotson, Sept 28, 197, AGC; AG to Scheultz, Oct 9, 1917, AGC; Scheultz to AG, 23 Oct 1917, AGC; Johnston to Scheultz, Sept 24, 1918, AGC; A1d, e, f; A2b; A3a.*

SCHNAUBERT, CHARLES OTTO. Born Jan. 1864, Indianola, Calhoun County, Texas. Ht. 5 ft. 10 in., blue eyes, gray hair, dark complexion, married. Ranchman, Comstock,

Val Verde County, Texas. SPECIAL RANGER Dec. 3, 1917–unknown (Co. A Volunteers). REMARKS: Had worked on farms in DeWitt County, Texas and McCulloch County, Texas. Died Feb. 4, 1948, Val Verde County, Texas. FAMILY: Parents, Otto Schnaubert (b. 1834, Germany) and Maria Elizabeth Noll (b. 1844, Germany); siblings, Lina (b. 1861, TX), Arthur (b. 1870, TX); spouse, Nellie (b. 1871, TX), married about 1889; children, Tommie E. (b. 1890, TX), Charles Robert (b. 1892, TX), Lillie (b. 1895, TX), Nellie (b. 1896, TX), Bettie (b. 1898, TX). *SR; A1a, b, d, e, f, g; A2b; A3a; A4a.*

SCHNELLE, WALTER GEORGE. Born May 13, 1884, Golden City, Barton County, Missouri. Ht. 6 ft., blue eyes, light hair, fair complexion, married. Irrigation engineer, with headquarters at Travelers' Hotel, San Antonio, Bexar County, Texas. SPECIAL RANGER Aug. 23, 1918–Jan. 15, 1919. REMARKS: "Stationed at points on the Rio Grande from Brownsville to Del Rio." As a youth had lived in Dallas, Dallas County, Texas. In 1920 was the district agent for a tractor company in San Antonio. FAMILY: Parents, H. G. Schnelle (b. 1850, Germany) and Anna (b. 1851, Germany); siblings, Tillie (b. 1877, IL), Anna (b. 1883, MO), Willie (b. 1887, MO), Lida (b. 1888, MO); spouse Ann Moore "Nannie" (b. 1886, TX). *SR; A1d, f; A3a.*

SCHUESSLER, JOHN HERMAN. Born Sept. 25, 1878, Castell, Mason County, Texas. Ht. 5 ft. 10 in., blue eyes, blond hair, light complexion, married. Stock farmer, Castell. LOYALTY RANGER July 20, 1918–Feb. 1919. REMARKS: World War I Draft Registration document states name is "John Charles Schuessler;" all other sources identify Schuessler as "J. H.," "John H.," or "John Herman." Died July 22, 1935, Mason County, Texas. FAMILY: Parents, Herman Schuessler (b. 1850, TX) and Wilhelmina "Mina" Leifeste (b. 1849, Germany); brothers, August Herman Alfred (b. 1875, TX), Emil Friedrich Carl (b. 1877, TX), Alvin Daniel (b. 1880, TX), Daniel August (b. 1883, TX), Adolph Max (b. 1888, TX); spouse, Ida Jordan (b. 1885, TX), married about 1904; children, Virginia Marie (b. 1906, TX), Francis May "Frannie" (b. 1913, TX), Johnida (b. 1916, TX), John H. (b. 1925, TX). *SR; A1b, d, e, f, g; A2b; A3a; A4b.*

SCHURMAN, STEPHEN FOSTER. Born Dec. 26, 1874, Pike County, Pennsylvania. Ht. 5 ft. 8 in., brown eyes, light gray hair, ruddy complexion. Farmer, Terrell, Kaufman County, Texas. REGULAR RANGER Dec. 14, 1917–Jan. 31, 1919 (private, Co. F, Co. L, Co. B). Honorably discharged. REMARKS: As of Sept. 1919 was a Ranger in Marathon, Brewster County, Texas. In 1920 was a farm laborer in Starrville, Smith County, Texas. An S. F. Sherman [*sic*] died Nov. 7, 1922, Anderson County, Texas. FAMILY: Parents (probably), Isaac William Schurman (b. 1838, Canada) and Isabella Miller (b. 1837, Scotland); brother (probably), Norman (b. 1863, Canada). *SR; 471; Schurman to AG, June 8, 1919, AGC; A1e, f; A2b; A3a; A4b.*

SCHWINN, FREDERICK S. Born June 20, 1889, Fort Scott, Robinson County, Kansas. Ht. 5 ft. 11 ½ in., blue eyes, brown hair, light complexion, married. Assistant superintendent, I&GN Railroad, Palestine, Anderson County, Texas. SPECIAL RANGER Mar. 22, 1918–Jan. 15, 1919. REMARKS: His business address in Jan. 1919 was Room 721, Mason Building, Houston, Harris County, Texas. In 1930 was a civil engineer in Houston. Died Dec. 2, 1968, Harris County, Texas. FAMILY: Mother, Lilly S. (b. 1866, MO); sister, May L. (b. 1894, IL); spouse, Patricia Barnes (b. 1882, NV), married about 1913; children, Frederick S., Jr. (b. 1915, LA), Elizabeth C. (b. 1918, TX), David (b. 1921, TX). *SR; A1d, f, g; A2a, b; A3a.*

SCOTT, FELIX CHARLES. Born Aug. 14, 1883, Llano, Llano County, Texas. Ht. 5 ft. 9 in., dark eyes, dark hair, dark complexion. Ranchman. REGULAR RANGER Jan. 3, 1918–Feb. 1, 1919 (private, Co. I). Honorably discharged. REMARKS: As early as 1910 lived in Laredo, Webb County, Texas. In 1930 was still a ranchman in Laredo. Died Nov. 3, 1934, Webb County, Texas. FAMILY: Parents, William M. (b. 1858, TX) and Belle E. (b. 1861, TX); siblings, Newt (b. 1884, TX), Mark P. (b. 1886, TX), Smith (b. 1888, TX), Annie Belle (b. 1891, TX), Lula (b. 1893, TX), Inez (b. 1897, TX), Bessie (b. 1899, TX), Kate (b. 1903, TX). *SR; 471; A1d, e, f, g; A2b; A3a.*

SCOTT, FRED. Born Mar. 1890, Cameron, Choctaw Nation (now Le Flore County), Oklahoma. Ht. 5 ft. 9 in., gray eyes, brown hair, fair complexion. Ranchman, enlisted at Alice, Jim Wells County, Texas. REGULAR RANGER May 10, 1916–unknown (private, Co. A). Resigned. *SR; 471.*

SCOTT, GEORGE W. Born Sept. 1871, Comfort, Kerr County, Texas. Ht. 6 ft. 1 ¾ in., gray eyes, black hair, dark complexion, widower. Brand inspector, Cattle Raisers' Association of Texas, Eagle Pass, Maverick County, Texas. SPECIAL RANGER Nov. 21, 1917–Jan. 15, 1919 (attached to Co. C). FAMILY: Parents, Warren Bemmas Scott (b. 1841, IA) and Eliza Rebecca Russell (b. 1844, TX); siblings, Armine R. (b. 1868, TX), Emma Lodima (b. 1870, TX), Julia Ann (b. 1874, TX), George Walter B. (b. 1876, TX), Lucia L. (b. 1878, TX), John V. (b. 1879, TX), Cynthia L. (b. 1883, TX); spouse (probably), Lou (b. 1869, TX), married about 1895. *SR; Moses to Harley, Nov 13, 1917, AGC; AG to Moses, Nov 17, 30, 1917, AGC; AG to Moses & Rowe, Jan 3, 1918, AGC; AG to Scott, Apr 4, 1918, AGC; A1a, b, d, e; A4a, g.*

SCOTT, HORACE VALENTINE. Born June 14, 1866, Canton, Van Zandt County, Texas. Ht. 5 ft. 8 in., blue eyes, light hair, light complexion, married. Stock farmer, Dumont, King County, Texas. LOYALTY RANGER July 5, 1918–Feb. 1919. REMARKS: Letterhead: "H. V. Scott, Raiser of Fine Cattle, Sheep, Hogs, Dumont, Tex." Had been a farmer in Bell County, Texas. In 1920 was a stock farmer in Cottle County, Texas. Died Jan. 3, 1924. FAMILY: Parents, Thomas Freeman Scott (b. 1830 or 1834, GA) and Hester Elmira McSween (b. 1838, GA); siblings, Mary Magdelina (b. 1861, TX), Francis Calaway (b. 1863, TX), Georgia Ann (b. 1867, TX), George Washington (b. 1869, TX), John Thomas (b. 1871, TX), Henrieta Josephine (b. 1874, TX), Asa Truman (b. 1876, TX), Nancy Elmira (b. 1878, TX); spouse, Martha B. Teel or Teal (b. 1870, TX), married about 1889; children, Ophelia V. (b. 1891, TX), John T. (b. 1893, TX), Solomon E. (b. 1894, TX), Horace, Jr. (b. 1896, TX), Jerry (b. 1901, TX). *SR; A1a, b, d, e, f; A4a, b.*

SCOTT, SAMUEL JORDAN, JR. Born Jan. 9, 1885, Freestone County, Texas. Medium height, medium build, brown eyes, black hair, married. Druggist, Donie, Freestone County. LOYALTY RANGER July 1, 1918–Feb. 1919. REMARKS: In 1920 was a farmer in Freestone County. In 1930 was proprietor of an oil station in Teague, Freestone County. A Samuel Jordan Scott died Mar. 18, 1956, Navarro County, Texas. FAMILY: Parents, Samuel J. Scott, Sr. (b. 1849, TX) and Mary E. "Mollie" (b. 1859, TX); brother, Oscar (b. 1889, TX); spouse, Mary Ethel (b. 1886, TX), married about 1907; children, Foy L. (b. 1909, TX), Reina or Roma (b. 1911, TX), Jack (b. 1913, TX), Evelyn (b. 1915, TX), Violet (b. 1917, TX), Max (b. 1921, TX). *SR; A1e, f, g; A2b; A3a; A4a, g.*

SCOTT, WILLIAM GEORGE BENJAMIN "GEORGE." Born Apr. 14, 1876, Mellow Valley, Clay County, Alabama. Ht. 5 ft. 10 ½ in., gray eyes, brown hair, fair complexion, married. Merchant, Baird, Callahan County, Texas. SPECIAL RANGER May 31, 1917–Dec. 1917 (attached to Co. C). REMARKS: Had been Callahan County clerk in 1910. In 1920 was a grocery merchant in Baird. FAMILY: Parents, Freeman T. Scott (b. 1853, GA) and Ella E. (b. 1859, AL); sister, Lizzie J. (b. 1878, TX); spouse, Adelia (b. 1878, TX), married about 1898; children, Maggie (b. 1900, TX), Anna M. (b. 1905, TX), G. B. "Jackie" (b. 1910, TX). *SR; A1b, d, e, f; A3a.*

SCOTT, WILLIAM M. Born June 1891, Waelder, Gonzales County, Texas. Ht. 6 ft., brown eyes, black hair, dark complexion, married. Clerk. REGULAR RANGER Dec. 13, 1917–Jan. 1, 1918 (private, Co. G). Resigned/fired. REMARKS: "Has had considerable experience with horses, a good rider, and speaks Spanish fluently." Was fired for drinking. He later became a lieutenant in the 10th Cavalry, participated in the battle of Nogales in 1918. LAW ENFORCEMENT RELATIVES: Ranger captain (commander of Co. F, Frontier Battalion, 1885–1888) William Scott, father. FAMILY: Father, William Scott. *SR; 471; Stevens to Harley, Dec 13, 1917, AGC; AG to Stevens, Dec 14, 1917, AGC; Scott to Harley, Dec 1, 1917, AGC; Rogers to Harley, Dec 12, 1917, AGC; Rogers to Hutchings, May 22, 1917, AGC; Bates to Hutchings, June 28, 1917, AGC; Chapa to Hutchings, June 28, 1917, AGC; Stevens to Harley, Jan 4, 1918, AGC; 416: 348.*

SCRUGGS, JAMES COLUMBUS. Born Dec. 23, 1875, Shelby County, Alabama. Ht. 5 ft. 10 in., blue eyes, light and a little gray hair, blond complexion, married. Stock farmer, Guymon [*sic*], Hansford County, Texas. LOYALTY RANGER July 27, 1918–Feb. 1919. REMARKS: His station is listed as Guymon, Texas County, Oklahoma. Had been a farmer in Stephens County, Oklahoma. In 1930 was a farmer in San Miguel County, New Mexico. Died Dec. 18, 1954, Las Vegas, San Miguel County, New Mexico; buried in Tiptonville Cemetery, Watrous, Mora County,

New Mexico. FAMILY: Parents, William Deason Scruggs (b. 1840, SC) and Salina Drucilla Varden Bailey (b. 1845, AL); sister, Elvira "Sadie" (b. 1878, AL); spouse, Sarah Thomas "Tommie" Burch (b. 1886, OK), married Dec. 1902, Chickasha, Oklahoma; children, Ernest Horace (b. 1903, OK), Ila Dale "Mickie" (b. 1905, OK), James Alva "Billy" (b. 1907, OK), Nora Thomas "Norecia" (b. 1909, OK), Artie Howard (b. 1911, OK), Francis Jewel "Fannie" (b. 1914, TX), Theo Fadie Christine (b. 1916, TX), Mary Louise "Mearcie" (b. 1918, TX), Jimmie June (b. 1921, NM), Alma Jean (b. 1925, NM), Truman Roscoe (b. 1927, NM). *SR; A1e, f, g; A3a; A4b.*

SCULLIN, HARRY. Born Oct. 1866, Leavenworth, Leavenworth County, Kansas. Ht. 5 ft. 8 in., brown eyes, black hair, ruddy complexion, married. Manufacturer. SPECIAL RANGER Sept. 14, 1916–Jan. 1, 1917 (attached to Co. B). Resigned. Manufacturer. SPECIAL RANGER Feb. 10, 1918–Jan. 15, 1919. REMARKS: Was president, Scullin Steel Co., St. Louis, Missouri. Was a Ranger groupie, often traveling to West Texas to ride with the Rangers. As a youth lived in New York City, New York. U.S. Census records for 1910, 1920, and 1930 each identify his home as St. Louis. FAMILY: Parents, John Scullin (b. 1836, NY) and Hannah Perry (b. 1841, Canada); siblings, May Eunice (b. 1862, Canada), Fred (b. 1872, MO), twins(?) Robert and Lanore Madeline (b. 1876, MO), Charles L.; spouse, Julia Woodward (b. 1869, IL), married about 1889; daughters, Mary (b. 1890, MO), Eugenia (b. 1892, MO). *SR; 471; Scullin to Hutchings, Aug 19, 1916, AGC; AG to Scullin, Aug 2, 21, 1916, AGC; Fox to Harley, Feb 10, 1918, AGC; A1a, b, d, e, f, g; A4a.*

SEAGO, WILEY NOAH. Born Aug. 1872, Tishamingo County, Mississippi. Ht. 5 ft. 8 in., blue eyes, black hair, dark complexion, married. Ranchman—worked for the King Ranch near Kingsville, Kleberg County, Texas. SPECIAL RANGER Oct. 31, 1916–Dec. 1917. REMARKS: In 1900 was foreman of Dillard Fant's Candelaria Ranch. In 1916 Caesar Kleberg recommended him for a Ranger commission. Died from a fall from a horse in 1924, New Mexico; buried in Highland Cemetery, Iowa Park, Wichita County, Texas. FAMILY: Parents, Joseph Eli Seago (b. 1847, MS) and Frances Angeline Bonds (b. 1847, MS); siblings, Etta (b. 1874), Joseph F. (b. 1878), John Doss (b. 1880, MS), twins (?) Chellie and Maggie (b. 1881, TX), George Alexander (b. 1882, TX), Simmons Leo (b. 1887, TX), Sinna D. (b. 1892, TX); spouse, Lelia Eva Foster (b. 1884); children, Mary Caroline, Angeline Mildred, Noah Foster (b. 1914, TX), Stephen Meeker (b. 1918, TX). *SR; Scarborough to Hutchings, Oct 26, 1916, AGC; AG to Scarborough, Oct 27, 1916; 319: 464; A41, b; B1, 2.*

SEALE, JAMES LOVETT. Born Sept. 7, 1887, Helena, Karnes County, Texas. Ht. 5 ft. 10 in., blue eyes, light hair, fair complexion. Deputy county clerk, Karnes County, Texas. REGULAR RANGER June 2, 1909–Mar. 1, 1910 (private, Co. B). Resigned/honorably discharged. Farmer. REGULAR RANGER Mar. 26, 1918–Jan. 1, 1919 (private, Co. M). Resigned. Peace officer, Karnes City, Karnes County. REGULAR RANGER Oct. 9, 1919–May 12, 1920 (private, Co. F). Resigned. Officer, GH&SA Railroad, El Paso, El Paso County, Texas. RAILROAD RANGER Dec. 31, 1923–Jan. 31, 1924. Discharged. Watchman, Del Rio, Val Verde County, Texas. SPECIAL RANGER Nov. 13, 1933–Jan. 22, 1935. Discharged. REMARKS: His family were pioneers in Karnes and Wilson Counties. He'd served two terms as a Karnes County deputy sheriff prior to 1909. In 1915, Eli C. Seale, his uncle, was tax collector and William J. Seale, his father, was district clerk of Karnes County. In May–July 1920, he was a Val Verde County deputy sheriff at Del Rio. Died July 14, 1961, Val Verde County, Texas. LAW ENFORCEMENT RELATIVES: Karnes County sheriff (1910) Eli C. Seale, uncle. FAMILY: Parents, William J. Seale (b. 1853, MS) and Addie J. (b. 1855, AR); brothers, E. B. (b. 1882, TX), William Calvin (b. 1890, TX). *SR; 471; EPMT, Nov 19, 1909; Wynn to Newton, Mar 2, 1910, AGC; Seale to Newton, Mar 5, 8, Oct 4, 1910, AGC; Assistant AG to Seale, Mar 7, Aug 24, 1910, AGC; AG to Peter, Mar 15, 1910, AGC; AG to Seale, Oct 5, 1910, AGC; Morris to Whom, June 19, 1915, AGC; Chambers to Hutchings, June 19, 1915, AGC; Smiley to Hutchings, June 19, 1915, AGC; Bailey to Hutchings, May 4, 1917, AGC; Seale to Hutchings, May 1, 1917, AGC; Cunningham to Harley, Apr 2, 1918, AGC; Seale to Cope, July 12, 1920, AGC; A1d, e; A2b; A3a.*

SEITZLER, THOMAS LAUGHLIN. Born Sept. 1873, Durant, Holmes County, Mississippi. No physical description, married. Garage owner, Terrell, Kaufman County, Texas. LOYALTY RANGER July 5, 1918–Mar. 6, 1919. REMARKS: Had lived in Fort Worth, Tarrant County,

Texas. In 1920 was a machinist in Ranger, Eastland County, Texas. In 1930 was an oil well supply machinist in Dallas, Dallas County, Texas. Died June 19, 1960, Dallas County, Texas. FAMILY: Brother, Benjamin George (b. 1874); spouse, Lillian May Lumley (b. 1878, TX), married about 1896; children, Ernest L. (b. 1910, TX), Pauline (b. 1912, TX), Mildred (b. 1913, TX), Tommie (b. 1915, TX). *SR; A1d, e, f, g; A2b.*

SHAFER, W. Born Aug. 1865, Luray, Page County, Virginia. Ht. 5 ft. 10 in., gray eyes, blond hair, blond complexion. Ranchman. SPECIAL RANGER Feb. 27, 1917–Dec. 1917. *SR.*

SHANK, SILAS. Born Sept. 16, 1873, Belton, Bell County, Texas. Ht. 6 ft. 1 in., blue eyes, brown hair, ruddy complexion, married. Brand inspector, Panhandle and Southwestern Stockmen's Association, El Paso, El Paso County, Texas. SPECIAL RANGER Mar. 12, 1918–Jan. 15, 1919. REMARKS: State Senator Claude Hudspeth, 25th District, signed his enlistment form. Died Sept. 22, 1938, El Paso County, Texas; buried in McCulloch County, Texas. FAMILY: Parents, William M. Shank (b. 1833, Germany) and Ellender Azubah Cottle (b. 1837, TX); siblings, Candace (b. 1857, TX), Charles L. (b. 1859, TX), Wm. J. (b. 1864, TX), twins James and Bettie (b. 1867, TX), Mary (b. 1869, TX), Silas's twin Paul (b. 1873, TX); spouse #1, Mamie Gober, married Feb. 1891; children, William Henry (b. 1892, TX), Ada (b. 1894, TX), Jessie (b. 1897, TX); spouse #2, Ysaura "Ora" (b. 1885, Mexico). *SR; 471; Hudspeth to Hobby, Jan 25, 1918, AGC; A1b, f; A2b; A3a; A4a, b; B2.*

SHANKLIN, JOHN FRAZIOR. Born Aug. 3, 1885, Prairie Lea, Caldwell County, Texas. Ht. 5 ft. 6 in., blue eyes, black hair, fair complexion. Salesman, San Antonio, Bexar County, Texas. REGULAR RANGER Aug. 6, 1918–Dec. 15, 1918 (private, Co. I). Resigned. REMARKS: As of Sept. 1918 was a sales clerk at Frank Brothers, Alamo Plaza, San Antonio. A John F. Shanklin died Feb. 19, 1950, Bexar County, Texas; buried in the Old Prairie Lea Cemetery. FAMILY: Parents, James R. Shanklin (b. 1850, VA) and Nannie (b. 1862, TX); siblings, Birdie (b. 1881, TX), Ray (b. 1886, TX), Willow (b. 1891, TX), Lois (b. 1892, TX), Nannie Lorene (b. 1894, TX), Nina (b. 1898, TX), Joe P. (b. 1900, TX). *SR; 471; 429:159; A1d, e; A2b; A3a.*

SHARP, ALONZO THOMAS. Born Aug. 1868, Colquitt, Miller County, Georgia. No physical description, married. Farmer, Beckville, Panola County, Texas. LOYALTY RANGER June 8, 1918–Feb. 1919. REMARKS: Lived in Panola County as early as 1880. Died in 1926. FAMILY: Parents, Sherrod Luther Sharp (b. 1839, SC) and Martha Evelyn "Mattie" Blanton (b. 1848, AL); siblings, John W. (b. 1867, AL), Luther (b. 1870, GA), Sallie (b. 1872, GA); spouse, Fannie Belle Metcalf (b. 1867, TX), married about 1898; children, Lawrence R. (b. 1889, TX), Lonnie B. (b. 1894, TX), Reuben S. (b. 1896, TX), Grace (b. 1900, TX), Mattie T. (b. 1903, TX), Bessie (b. 1907, TX), Quincy (b. 1909, TX). *SR; A1a, b, d, e, f; A4a.*

SHARP, JAMES ALPHUS. Born Mar. 20, 1879, New Hope, Drew County, Arkansas. Ht. 5 ft. 10 in., blue eyes, brown hair, light complexion, married. Farmer and stock raiser, Turkey, Hall County, Texas. LOYALTY RANGER July 2, 1918–Feb. 1919. REMARKS: Was a deputy sheriff. One source lists his birthplace as Howard County, Arkansas. In 1930 was a farmer in Briscoe County, Texas. Died in 1953, Oklahoma. FAMILY: Parents, Robert J. Sharp (b. 1847, AR) and Mary Elizabeth Rivers (b. 1851, AL); siblings, Elisa E. (b. 1870, AR), Martha J. (b. 1874, AR), Sarah E. (b. 1875, AR), John E. (b. 1881, AR), William Nelson (b. 1883, AR), Ross Henry (b. 1885, AR), Richard L. (b. 1888, AR), Luther (b. 1891, AR); spouse #1, Anna Pennington (b. 1881), married July 4, 1897, Howard County, Arkansas; spouse #2, Donie or Denna D. Brewer (b. 1881, AR), married Jan. 12, 1899, Howard County, Arkansas; children, Mary D. (b. 1907, AR), Henry C. (b. 1909, AR), Wesley A. (b. 1914, TX), Boy (b. 1917, TX). *SR; A1b, e, g; A3a; A4b.*

SHARP, WILLIAM RILEY. Born May 1859, Bosque County, Texas. Ht. 6 ft., gray eyes, gray hair, florid complexion, married. Stockman, Del Rio, Val Verde County, Texas. SPECIAL RANGER Jan. 17, 1917–unknown (attached to Co. C). Resigned as of Feb. 16, 1917. REMARKS: Note length of service. Was commissioned at request of Sheriff John W. Almond of Val Verde County, who had been asked to do so by the G. Bedell Moore Estate and the Val Verde Irrigation Co., which owned about 45 miles of Rio Grande riverfront between Del Rio and Eagle Pass. Had lived in Wilson County as a youth; had been a farmer in Burnet County, Texas. Died Feb. 7, 1938, Val Verde County, Texas. FAMILY:

Parents, Solomon Sharp (b. 1823, AR) and Evy Ann Starnes (b. 1827, VA); siblings, Penelope or Emaline (b. 1849, AR), Marion or Marvin D. (b. 1853, AR), Mary J. (b. 1855, AR), Amy Francis (b. 1856, AR), Levi (b. 1858, TX), George (b. 1860, TX), Jefferson (b. 1862, TX), Rebecca (b. 1863, TX), Harry or Harvey (b. 1864, TX), Nancy (b. 1866, TX), Sarah (b. 1869, TX); spouse, Nancy J. (b. 1860, TX), married about 1877; children, Levi (b. 1879, TX), Mertte (b. 1890, Mexico), Kate (b. 1892, Mexico). *SR; Almond to Hutchings, Jan 17, Feb 16, 1917, AGC; AG to Almond, Jan 19 1917, AGC; A1aa, a, b, e, f; A2b; A4b.*

SHARVER, ALONZO MARION. Born Apr. 27, 1881, Travis County, Texas. Medium height, medium build, blue eyes, black hair, married. Farmer and stockman, Newton, Newton County, Texas. LOYALTY RANGER June 24, 1918–Feb. 1919. REMARKS: Newton County sheriff Nov. 8, 1910–Nov. 3, 1914. In 1930 was a road building contractor in Newton. A. M. Sharver Sr. died May 7, 1951, Denton County, Texas. FAMILY: Parents, Henry Sharver (b. 1850, Germany) and Roxadel (b. 1856, TX or MS); siblings, Terry (b. 1875, TX), Henry (b. 1876, TX), Kate (b. 1878, TX), another brother (b. 1880, TX), Virgil G. (b. 1887, TX); spouse, Ellen Bertha "Ollie" Baker (b. 1892, TX), married Sept. 1916; son, A. M., Jr. (b. 1918, TX). *SR; 1503:391; A1b, e, g; A2b; A3a; B2.*

SHAW, JOE ROBERT. Born Jan. 11, 1888, Yoakum, Lavaca County, Texas. Ht. 5 ft. 9 in., blue eyes, brown hair, dark complexion, married. Ranchman. REGULAR RANGER July 5, 1918–Aug. 21, 1918 (private, Co. G). Killed in line of duty, Aug. 1, 1918, at Brownsville, Cameron County, Texas. REMARKS: On enlistment form: "This man is a good man." As of June 1917 was a ranchman in Harlingen, Cameron County. FAMILY: As of June 1917 had a wife and two children. *SR; 471; Stevens to Woodul, Aug 22, 1918, AGC; Harrison to Stevens, Aug 24, 1918, AGC; Shaw to AG, Oct 7, 1918, AGC; BDH, Aug 22, 24, 28, 1918; A3a.*

SHEEDY, PATRICK. Born Aug. 18, 1873, Brackettville, Kinney County, Texas. Ht. 5 ft. 5 in., brown eyes, brown hair, fair complexion, married. Cowpuncher, enlisted in Val Verde County, Texas. SPECIAL RANGER Feb. 16, 1917–Sept. 20, 1917 (attached to Co. C). Placed on active duty. REGULAR RANGER Sept. 20, 1917–Mar. 1, 1918 (private, Co. E). Resigned. Ranchman. REGULAR RANGER Apr. 1, 1922–Aug. 31, 1923 (private, Co. C; transferred to Co. A, Apr. 1, 1923). Fired for drunkenness. REMARKS: Had been a cattle drover. Was deputy sheriff and constable. As of Sept. 1918 was a river rider for the Val Verde Irrigation Company in Maverick County, Texas, lived in Del Rio, Val Verde County. In 1920 was a railroad foreman in Uvalde County, Texas. In 1930 was a watchman at a mine in Uvalde County. Died Mar. 23, 1932, Uvalde County, Texas. FAMILY: Parents, James Sheedy (b. 1825, Ireland) and Sarah (b. 1842, TX); siblings, Ellen (b. 1860, TX), Eliza (b. 1862, TX), James (b. 1864, TX), John (b. 1866, TX), Sarah (b. 1869, TX), Jessie (b. 1872, TX); spouse, Prudy (b. 1875, TX), married about 1892; children, Joseph (b. 1893, TX), Alpha A. (b. 1897, TX), Ora (b. 1902, TX), Patrick O. (b. 1905, TX), Almira P. (b. 1908, TX), Cora C. (b. 1912, TX). *SR; 471; Almond to Hutchings, Feb 16, 1917, AGC; Barler to Griffiths, Sept 20, 1917, AGC; Baler to Harley, Oct 12, 1917, AGC; 470: 43; A1a, d, e, f, g; A2b; A3a; B1.*

SHELTON, R. S. Born Mar. 1884, Albany, Shackelford County, Texas. Ht. 5 ft. 10 in., blue eyes, black hair, dark complexion. Engineer, Crystal City, Zavala County, Texas. SPECIAL RANGER July 17, 1916–unknown. REMARKS: Had been deputy sheriff. *SR; AG to Taylor, July 8, 1916, AGC.*

SHELY, GEORGE RUTLEDGE. Born Aug. 1, 1892, Uvalde County, Texas. Ht. 5 ft. 8 in., blue eyes, light hair, light complexion, married. Stockman, Marathon, Brewster County, Texas. REGULAR RANGER Aug. 25, 1919–Jan. 11, 1921 (private, Co. E.). Resigned. REMARKS: In 1930 was a farmer in Brewster County. Died about 1950 in Artesia, Eddy County, New Mexico. FAMILY: Parents, John Shely (b. 1867, TX) and Mary Ann Elizabeth McCall (b. 1871, TX); siblings, Ira (b. 1893, TX), Irene (b. 1899, TX); by 1900 lived with relatives: uncle, Charles Totty or Toddie (b. 1858, TX) and Theodocia M. (b. 1861, TX); spouse #1, unknown, married about 1913; had at least one child; spouse #2, Edna Virginia "Virgie" Mobley (b. 1891, TX), married about 1918. *SR; 471; AA, Nov 27, Dec 4, 1919, Aug 19, 1920; A1d, e, g; A3a; A4a, b; B2.*

SHELY, WILLIAM ALMOND. Born Dec. 20, 1894, Corpus Christi, Nueces County, Texas. Ht. 6 ft. 1 in., gray eyes, brown hair, medium complexion. Ranchman. REGULAR RANGER Dec 12, 1915–unknown (private, Co. D). Resigned to accept a commission in U.S. Army. REMARKS: In 1930 was a captain in the U.S. Army living in Stillwater, Payne County, Oklahoma. Rose to rank of colonel, received Legion of Merit. Died Nov. 18, 1946. LAW ENFORCEMENT RELATIVES: Ranger William Ysidro Shely, father; Ranger Warren Washington Shely, uncle; Ranger Josephus Shely, uncle; Ranger Lorenzo Dow Shely, uncle. FAMILY: Parents, William Ysidro Shely (b. 1868, MO) and Josephine Almond (b. 1867, TX); sisters, Dorothy M. (b. 1899, TX), Elizabeth (b. 1906, TX); spouse, Franklyn H. (b. 1893, TX), married about 1918; daughter, Josephine A. (b. 1920, WA). *SR; 471; Ransom to Hutchings, Dec 13, 1915, AGC; 319: 45, 357–358, 448; 508: 67; A1d, e, f, g; A3a; A4g.*

SHEPARD, THOMAS LANE. Born June 24, 1889, Gunsight, Stephens County, Texas. Ht. 6 ft., gray eyes, dark hair, medium complexion, married. Public school teacher, Merkel, Taylor County, Texas. SPECIAL RANGER Aug. 7, 1917–Dec. 1917 (attached to Co. C). Schoolteacher, Austin, Travis County, Texas. SPECIAL RANGER June 5, 1919–Dec. 31, 1919. REMARKS: June 1919, Governor Hobby ordered that Shepard be commissioned. In 1920 was a druggist in Austin. In 1930 was a pharmacist in Lubbock, Lubbock County, Texas. Died Jan. 2, 1937, Lubbock County, Texas. FAMILY: Parents, John Woodrow Shepard (b. 1853, AR) and Sarah Isabella Baggett (b. 1855, NC); brothers, Fleet D. (b. 1890, TX), Floyd Euvelle (b. 1893, TX); spouse #1, Hughie Jessica Gatliff (b. 1891, TX), married about 1909; children, John Lane (b. 1912, TX), Jessica Jean (b. 1919, TX); spouse #2, Minnie Lee Barrett (b. 1886, TN), married Sept. 2, 1925. *SR; Dodson to Ferguson, July 19, 1917, AGC; A1d, f, g; A2b; A3a; A4a, b; B2.*

SHEPHERD, C. M. Born Aug. 1871, Mobile, Mobile County, Alabama. Ht. 6 ft. 1 in., blue eyes, brown hair, fair complexion, married. Transportation inspector, Houston, Harris County, Texas. SPECIAL RANGER Feb. 16, 1918–Jan. 15, 1919. REMARKS: clerk. *SR.*

SHEPPARD, SIMEON C. Born Dec. 1852, Marion, Georgia. Ht. 6 ft. 2 in., blue eyes, gray hair, light complexion, married. Police detective, enlisted in McLennan County, Texas. SPECIAL RANGER Feb. 9, 1917–Jan. 15, 1919 (?). REMARKS: "by order of Governor." Had lived in McLennan County at least since 1870. Had been a farmer in McLennan County. In 1910 was a Waco, McLennan County, city detective. In 1920 was a private detective in Waco. Died Jan. 22, 1932, McLennan County, Texas. FAMILY: Siblings, Mary (b. 1847, GA), Samuel (b. 1851, GA), Harriet (b. 1853, GA), Joseph (b. 1857, GA); spouse, Myra Kirkland (b. 1856, MS), married about 1875; children, Alma G. (b. 1876, TX), Albert B. (b. 1879, TX), Simeon (b. 1880, TX), Robert (b. 1881, TX), Eugenia (b. 1885, TX), Ruby (b. 1886, TX), Joseph Ross (b. 1887, TX), John (b. 1890, TX), Hugh (b. 1893, TX), Kathreen (b. 1898, TX). *SR; A1a, b, d, e, f, g; A2b.*

SHIPLEY, AUBREY. Born Dec. 23, 1891, Greenville, Hunt County, Texas. Ht. 6 ft., gray eyes, light hair, fair complexion. Fireman. REGULAR RANGER Oct. 13, 1911–Jan. 31, 1912 (private, Co. A). Discharged—reduction in force. REMARKS: As of June 1917 was a "fire builder" for the M.K.T. Railroad in Greenville. Died Sept. 3, 1978, Tyler County, Texas. FAMILY: Parents, John F. Shipley (b. 1852, VA) and Mary V. (b. 1855, VA); siblings, William Vance (b. 1878, TX), Bertha (b. 1880, TX), Revie (b. 1882, TX), Myrtle (b. 1884, TX), Bird (b. 1888, TX), Lillian (b. 1894, TX). *SR; 471; A1d, e, f; A2a, b; A3a.*

SHOEMAKER, JAMES LINDSAY. Born Apr. 23, 1866, Quitman, Wood County, Texas. Ht. 5 ft. 9 in., blue eyes, brown hair, light complexion, married. Farmer, Alba, Wood County. LOYALTY RANGER June 13, 1918–Feb. 1919. REMARKS: "12–15 yrs experience as a peace officer." Had been proprietor of a livery stable in Wood County. Died Jan. 1, 1935, Dallas County, Texas; buried in Quitman City Cemetery. FAMILY: Parents, Oliver Wesley Shoemaker (b. 1831, GA) and Rachel Baker (b. 1839, TN); siblings, Mary M. (b. 1855, AL), Amanda J. (b. 1856, AL), John Wesley (b. 1858, TX), Thomas H. (b. 1860, TX), Catherine C. (b. 1863, TX), Elizabeth A. (b. 1869, TX); spouse, Mamie Goodwin (b. 1872, TX), married July 13, 1892, Wood County. *SR; A1b, d, e; A2b; A4a, b; B2.*

SHULTS, CHARLES ECHOLS "CHARLIE." Born Feb. 5, 1875, Llano, Llano County, Texas. Ht. 5 ft. 9 in., brown eyes, black hair, dark complexion, married. Stockman, Llano. SPECIAL RANGER May 10, 1917–Jan. 15, 1919 (WA was reinstated Jan 9, 1918). REMARKS: In 1930 was a cattle stockman in El Paso, El Paso County, Texas. Died Dec. 22, 1957, Alameda County, California. FAMILY Parents, Monroe

Houston Shults (b. 1846, AR) and Catherine T. Jennings (b. 1851, TX); siblings, Anna Belle (b. 1872, TX), James Garner (b. 1877, TX), Richard Henderson (b. 1879, TX), Minnie E. (b. 1882, NM), Etta Mae (b. 1885, TX), Mary C. (b. 1887, TX); spouse, Minnie Lindsey (b. 1877, TX), married Oct. 20, 1897, Llano; sons, Charles Othello (b. 1899, TX), Herman O. (b. 1901, TX), H. L. (b, 1904, TX), Marvin Eckhols (b. 1907, TX). *SR; AG to Caldwell, Jan 3, 1918, AGC; A1b, d, e, f, g; A2c, f; A3a; A4b.*

SHUMATE, RUDOLPH DANIEL. Born Apr. 24, 1877, Jacksboro, Jack County, Texas. Ht. 6 ft., gray eyes, light hair, light complexion, married. Peace officer, Brownwood, Brown County, Texas. SPECIAL RANGER Mar. 29, 1918–Jan. 15, 1919. Peace officer, Brownwood. REGULAR RANGER Feb. 4, 1919–Sept. 1, 1920 (Headquarters Co.; transferred to Co. G, June 20, 1919; reenlisted in Co. B under the new law, June 20, 1919; transferred to Co. A, July 1, 1920). Resigned. Peace officer, Brownwood. REGULAR RANGER Jan. 6, 1922–Feb. 21, 1925 (private, Co. C; transferred to Co. E, Nov. 1, 1924). Discharged. REMARKS: During the 7 years prior to becoming a Ranger, had been a Brown County constable, first deputy sheriff of Brown County, and Brown County jailer. Was dismissed. In 1920 resigned from the Rangers to become a federal Prohibition agent. Applied for reenlistment in Rangers, saying he'd made a mistake in resigning. As of Jan. 1, 1921, he'd resigned as a Prohibition agent. On Jan. 6, 1922, he reenlisted in the Rangers. In 1930 was a life insurance agent in Stanton, Martin County, Texas. Died July 13, 1945, McLennan County, Texas. FAMILY: Parents, Isaac Thomas Shumate (b. 1852, TN) and Elizabeth Caroline "Carrie" Parker (b. 1856, MO); siblings, John W. (b. 1879, TX), Isaac Elton (b. 1880, MO), Adolph (b. 1883, TX), Bessie E. (b. 1885, TX), Maud (b. 1886, TX), Paul O. (b. 1888, TX), Katie (b. 1890, TX), Gertrude (b. 1892, TX), Carrie W. (b. 1893, TX), Parker (b. 1897, TX), Gladys (b. 1899, TX); spouse #1, Corealice C. "Corrie" Couch (b. 1877, AL), married Feb. 25, 1895, McLennan County; children, Ernest E. (b. 1909, TX), Ruth (b. 1911, TX); another spouse (b. TX); daughter, Dreavon (b. 1921, TX); spouse #2 or 3, Vera G. (b. 1897, TX), married about 1926. *SR; 471; Pugh to Aldrich, May 27, 1919, AGC; Early to Cope, Dec 24, 1919, AGC; Shumate to Cope, Aug 24, 28, 31, 1920, AGC; AG to Shumate, Aug 27, 1920, AGC; Cope to Turner, Aug 27, 1920, AGC; Shumate to Aldrich, Sept 20, 1920, AGC; Shumate to Barton, Jan 1, 1921, AGC; 470: 43; A1b, d, f, g; A2b, e; A3a; A4g; B1.*

SIELSKI, HENRY MACDONALD. Born Apr. 18, 1888, Laredo, Webb County, Texas. Ht. 5 ft. 10 ¾ in., brown eyes, brown hair, fair complexion. Quarantine guard, Laredo. SPECIAL RANGER Feb. 20, 1918–Jan. 15, 1919. REMARKS: In 1920 was a broker in Eagle Pass, Maverick County, Texas. Died Dec. 27, 1968, Bexar County, Texas. FAMILY: Parents, Joseph Casimir Sielski (b. 1843, Poland) and Margaret Letitia McDonald (b. 1850, TX); siblings, Joseph Clinton (b. 1872, TX), Violet (b. 1873, TX), John Stewart (b. 1875, TX), Victor McGavrok (b. 1880, TX), Emilia (b. 1884, TX), Gerald (b. 1891, TX); spouse, Gene L. Fallon (b. 1897, TX), married about 1920; children, Betty Gene (b. 1921, TX), Marion MacDonald (b. 1926, TX), Henry MacDonald, Jr. (b. 1929, TX). *SR; Collins to Harley, Feb 1, 1918, AGC; A1d, f; A2a, b, e; A3a; A4g; B1.*

SIMPSON, ALBERT E. Born Aug. 1866, Town Creek, Lawrence County, Alabama. Ht. 6 ft., blue eyes, gray hair, light complexion, married. Farmer, San Antonio, Bexar County, Texas. SPECIAL RANGER Jun. 29, 1918–Jan. 15, 1919. REMARKS: In Apr. 1918 was a night yard watchman for the SA&AP Railroad at San Antonio. His superior requested a Special Ranger commission for Simpson. In 1930 was a real estate salesman in San Antonio. LAW ENFORCEMENT RELATIVES: Lawrence County, Alabama sheriff (1870) I. S. Simpson, father. FAMILY: Parents, I. S. Simpson (b. 1832, AL) and Ann Catherine (b. 1833, TN); sisters, Cora (b. 1855, AL), Emma (b. 1858, AL); spouse, Annie C. (b. 1872, TN), married about 1890; children, Marie (b. 1891, AL), Hall (b. 1894, AL), Julia (b. 1897, AL), Marjorie "Sadie" (b. 1900, AL), Eugene (b. 1903, AL), Annie Laurie (b. 1906, AL), Leslie W. (b. 1910, AL). *SR; Herbst to Harley, Apr 20, June 14, 1918, AGC; Acting AG to Herbst, June 18, 1918, AGC; A1a, b, d, e, f, g.*

SIMPSON, ALFRED ROBERT. Born Sept. 22, 1895, Velasco, Brazoria County, Texas. Ht. 6 ft. 1 in., blue eyes, brown hair, light complexion, married. Ranchman, Austin, Travis County, Texas. REGULAR RANGER Mar. 10, 1921–Aug. 31, 1921 (private, Co. C). Discharged. REMARKS: World War I Draft Registration document lists name as Robert A. Simpson; states "Cripple foot." In 1920 was a business college student in Travis County. FAMILY: Parents, Robert Simpson (b. 1863, TX) and Cecelia (b. 1868, AR); siblings, Edward (b. 1889, TX), Charles (b. 1890, TX), Ina (b. 1892, TX), Elcey (b 1893, TX), Addie (b. 1895, TX), Leonard (b. 1897, TX), Halley (b. 1898, TX), Gertrude (b. 1901, TX); as early as 1910 lived with uncle and aunt, Langston T. Miller (b. 1847, MO) and Nancy E. (b. 1855, AL). *SR; 471; A1d, e, f; A3a.*

SIMPSON, WILLIAM ALEXANDER. Born Aug. 22, 1883, Lordsburg, New Mexico. Ht. 6 ft. 1 in., brown eyes, brown hair, dark complexion, married. Peace officer, Ysleta, El Paso County, Texas. SPECIAL RANGER Mar. 23, 1918–Jan. 15, 1919 (attached to Co. L). Chief special agent, El Paso. SPECIAL RANGER Jan. 30, 1933–Jan. 22, 1935. Discharged. REMARKS: El Paso city policeman, 1911–1919; policeman, 1911, mounted policeman, 1913–1916, police sergeant, June 1916, captain of detectives, city of El Paso, 1919. In 1930 was a peace officer at the copper smelter in El Paso. A William A. Simpson died June 25, 1957, El Paso County, Texas. FAMILY: Mother, Sarah (b. 1856, CA); sister, Gertrude (b. 1886, TX); spouse, Anna Belle (probably Smith) (b. 1879, OH), married about 1913; adopted son, Gerald T. (b. 1903, OH). *SR; A1d, e, f, g; A2b; A3a.*

SINGLETON, DARWIN ELDRIDGE. Born Oct. 26, 1894, Lufkin, Angelina County, Texas. Ht. 6 ft. 1 in., blue eyes, brown hair, dark complexion, married. Soldier, Lufkin. REGULAR RANGER July 3, 1919–unknown (private, Co. D). Salesman and officer, Lufkin. REGULAR RANGER Nov. 2, 1923–Dec. 1, 1924 (no company listed). Resigned. REMARKS: Died Aug. 29, 1970, Alameda County, California. FAMILY: Parents, James Maxwell Singleton (b. 1865, TX) and Carrie E. Haygood (b. 1875, TX); siblings, Neill (b. 1898, TX), James Maxwell (b. 1904, TX), Darlene (b. 1905, TX), Jefferson Lafayette (b. 1907, TX), Eustes Byron (b. 1909, TX), William Madison (b. 1911, TX); spouse, Edna Crumpler (b. 1899, TX); sons, Darwin Eldridge, Jr. (b. 1927, TX), William Penn (b. 1930, TX). *SR; 471; Singleton to Harley, July 1, 1919, AGC; Hanson to AG, July 17, 1919, WC; A1d, e, f; A2a, e, f; A4a, b, g.*

SITTRE, JOHN BAPTIST. Born Feb. 18, 1890, Castroville, Medina County, Texas. Ht. 5 ft. 10 ½ in., brown eyes, red hair, light complexion. Ranchman, enlisted in Bexar County, Texas. REGULAR RANGER Dec. 18, 1917–Feb. 28, 1919 (private, Co. G). Discharged. REMARKS: In June 1917 was a stock farmer working for his uncle, Louis Burell, in Medina County. Died Aug. 8, 1939, Medina County, Texas; buried in Catholic Cemetery, Castroville. FAMILY: Parents, John Baptist Edward Sittre (b. 1867, TX) and Maria Rosa Burell (b. 1865, TX); brother, Joseph Hilary (b. 1891, TX); stepmother (as of 1897), Mary Josephine Haby (b. 1867, TX); siblings, Otto Riley (b. 1898, TX), Lillie Hilda (b. 1899, TX), Robert Oscar (b. 1902, TX), Edna Virginia (b. 1904, TX), Elisa "Elsie" (b. 1908, TX), Marissa (b. 1909, TX); spouse #1, Helen Marie Holloman, married about 1925; daughters, Rose Marie (b. 1926, TX), Grace Elisebeth (b. 1929, TX); spouse #2, Cora Holloman (b. 1896, TX); daughter, Johnnie Mae (b. 1931, TX). *SR; 471; Cardwell to Aldrich, Mar 11, 1919, AGC; A1d, g; A2b, e; A3a; A4b, g.*

SKINNER, JOHN FINNEY. Born May 13, 1873, Leesville, Gonzales County, Texas. Ht. 6 ft. 1 in., blue eyes, light hair, fair complexion, married. Stock raiser, Harlingen, Cameron County, Texas. SPECIAL RANGER Dec. 28, 1916–unknown. REMARKS: Recommended by Cameron County Sheriff W. T. Vann. Appointed on Governor Ferguson's order. Died July 8, 1946, Gonzales County, Texas. FAMILY: Parents, James Featherstone Skinner (b. 1826, SC) and Mary Jane Belfield Bryan (b. 1839, TN); siblings, Otho Ann (b. 1857, TX), Martha Frances (b. 1859, TX), Sarah Josephean (b. 1861, TX), Mary Catherine (b. 1866, TX), James C. (b. 1868, TX), Joseph H. (b. 1870, TX), Thomas Richman (b. 1875, TX), Amanda (b. 1878, TX), Julia (b. 1880, TX), Alexander Bright (b. 1883, TX); spouse, Mary Virginia "Jennie" Key (b. 1871, TX), married Nov. 14, 1894, Gonzales County; children, Walter R. (b. 1896, TX), Maude (b. 1898, TX), Derwood Upton (b. 1909, TX). *SR; Vann to Ferguson, Dec 15, 1916, AGC; Wroe to AG, Dec 21, 1916, AGC; A1b, d, e, f; A2b; A3a; A4a, b; B1, 2.*

SKINNER, WALTER SCOTT. Born Sept. 28, 1895, Daingerfield, Morris County, Texas. Ht. 5 ft. 11 in., blue eyes, brown hair, dark complexion, married. Ranchman, El Paso, El Paso County, Texas. SPECIAL RANGER July 19, 1917–Dec. 1917 (?) (attached to Co. C). REMARKS: In June 1917 was a cattle raiser on his father's ranch in Marathon, Brewster County, Texas. In 1920 was a rancher in El Paso, El Paso County. Died Dec. 29, 1982, Kerr County, Texas.

FAMILY: Parents, Sidney Prentice Skinner (b. 1863, AR) and Willia Getzendaner (b. 1869, TX); spouse, Adell (b. 1898, TX); son, Walter S. (b. 1919, TX). *SR; AG to Skinner, July 13, 1917, AGC; A1f; A2a, b; A3a; A4b.*

SKIPPER, WILLIAM PIERCE. Born Jan. 23, 1889, Ellis County, Texas. Ht. 5 ft. 11 in., brown eyes, black hair, dark complexion, married. Oil mill foreman, Kingsville, Kleberg County, Texas. SPECIAL RANGER July 18, 1916–Sept. 10, 1916 (attached to Co. C). Warrant of authority was revoked by order of Governor Ferguson. REMARKS: Note length of service. In 1920 was a traction engineer in Nueces County, Texas. Died Oct. 10, 1963, Kleberg County, Texas; buried in Chamberlain Cemetery, Kingsville. FAMILY: Parents, Henry Jefferson Skipper (b. 1854, GA) and Cynthia Evelyn Cornelious (b. 1860, TX); siblings, Arthur A. (b. 1879, TX), Henry Elmo (b. 1885, TX), Beulah Elizabeth (b. 1887, TX), Florence Leola (b. 1892, Indian Territory), Ethel May (b. 1894, TX), Desimoiselle (b. 1897, TX), Tina Estella (b. 1899, TX); spouse, Penecia or Louise (b. 1889, TX or 1899); daughters, Susie E. (b. 1913, TX), Lola A. (b. 1914, TX). *SR; Skipper to Hutchings, Aug 2, 1916, AGC; Hutchings to Scarborough, Sept 10, 1916, AGC; A1d, f; A2a, b; A3a; A4a, b, g; B1, 2.*

SLACK, HENRY CLAY. Born Dec. 1866, Webster Parish, Louisiana. Ht. 5 ft. 8 in., brown eyes, iron gray hair, dark complexion, married. Brand inspector, Panhandle and Southwestern Cattle Raisers' Association, Pecos, Reeves County, Texas. SPECIAL RANGER Mar. 15, 1918–Jan. 15, 1919. REMARKS: State Senator Claude Hudspeth asked Governor Hobby to commission Slack. Had been a provision dealer in Reeves County. In 1930 was a cattle trader in Pecos. A Henry Clay Slack died Feb. 29, 1944, Tarrant County, Texas. FAMILY: Parents, Richard Slack (b. 1830, MS) and Harriet Elizabeth Tyler (b. 1837, AL); siblings, William Marion (b. 1852, LA), Joseph F. (b. 1855, LA), Georgia Ann (b. 1857, LA), James (b. 1863, LA), Fancy (b. 1865, LA), Frank, Ophelia Ann (b. 1872, LA), Mary Ann (b. 1873, LA), Della (b. 1875, LA), Maidy Ann (b. 1877, LA); spouse, Malinda C. "Linnie" Maxey (b. 1870, TX), married Sept. 23, 1889, Pecos; children, Henry Clay, Jr. (b. 1890, TX), Evelyn E. (b. 1904, TX). *SR; Hudspeth to Hobby, Jan 25, 1918, AGC; A1aa, a, b, d, g; A2b; A3a; A4b.*

SLEDGE, LINDEN WILTON. Born Nov. 20, 1878, Littleton, Halifax County, North Carolina. Ht. 6 ft. ½ in., blue eyes, black hair, dark complexion, married. Agent for I&GN Railroad, Houston, Harris County, Texas. SPECIAL RANGER Mar. 23, 1917–Jan. 15, 1919 (WA was reinstated Dec. 27, 1917). REMARKS: Had been manager of a store in Hays County, Texas. In 1910 was a railroad agent in LaSalle County, Texas. In 1920 was a bank cashier in Rockdale, Milam County, Texas. In 1930 was an insurance agent in Rockdale. Died Oct. 8, 1932, Milam County. FAMILY: Parents, Clarence Linden Sledge (b. 1846, NC) and Martha Williamson "Pinkie" Mingea (b. 1849, VA); siblings, Lillian L. (b. 1873, NC), Lena J. (b. 1877, NC), Pinkie M. (b. 1880, NC), Mary A. (b. 1882, NC), Caledonia H. (b. 1884, TX), Clarence W. (b. 1887, TX); spouse, Margaret Emma Lockett (b. 1884, TX), married about 1908. *SR; A1b, d, e, f, g; A2b; A3a; A4g.*

SLOUGH, JOHN WESLEY. Born Jan. 16, 1862, Carthage, Leake County, Mississippi. Ht. 5 ft. 10 in., brown eyes, gray hair, dark complexion, married. Farmer, Cross Plains, Callahan County, Texas. SPECIAL RANGER June 6, 1917–Jan. 15, 1919 (attached to Co. C; WA was reinstated Jan. 9, 1918). REMARKS: Was deputy sheriff, then constable. Had been a farmer in Brown County, Texas. Died Dec. 12, 1925, Taylor County, Texas; buried in Pleasant Valley Cemetery, May, Brown County. FAMILY: Parents, Robert Slough (b. 1825, NC) and Mary E. A. Reynolds (b. 1826, AL); siblings, William L. (b. 1850, TN), Euphrasia (b. 1851, MS), Ellen Virginia (b. 1852, MS), George W. (b. 1855, MS), Robert A. (b. 1860, MS), Julia S. (b. 1865, MS); spouse, Nancy Elizabeth Ann "Bettie" May (b. 1860, MS), married Apr. 10, 1884, Brown County; children, Grover Cleveland (b. 1885, TX), Mary Rebecca "Mayme," Robert Pierce (b. 1889, OK), James Franklin (b. 1891, TX), Delia Lemon (b. 1892, TX), John Walter (b. 1893, TX), Bessie Lee (b. 1895, TX), twins (?) Nettie and Nathan (b. 1896, TX), Barney Gibbs (b. 1898, TX), William Jacob, Essie May (b. 1902, OK). *SR; A1b, e, f; A2b; A4b.*

SLOVER, MARION FRANKLIN. Born Apr. 1, 1870, Tarrant County, Texas. Ht. 5 ft. 8 ½ in., dark eyes, dark hair, dark complexion, married. Farmer, Whiteflat, Motley County, Texas. LOYALTY RANGER June 29, 1918–Feb. 1919. REMARKS: "Sheriff . . . and deputy many years, in various counties in Texas. . . ." including Randall County sheriff

Nov. 8, 1904–Nov. 3, 1908. Several sources cite birthplace as Parker County, Texas. Had been a stock farmer in Castro County, Texas. In 1930 was a farmer in Motley County. Died Feb. 27, 1941, Matador, Motley County, Texas; buried in Whiteflat Cemetery, Prairie Branch. FAMILY: Parents, William Alfred Slover (b. 1843, AR) and Louisa Paralee Shadle (b. 1844, TX); siblings, William Jackson (b. 1864, TX), Mary Josephine (b. 1866, TX), Charles Wesley (b. 1868, TX), James Samuel (b. 1872, TX), M. E. (b. 1874, TX), Leo Riley (b. 1876, TX), Ira D. (b. 1878, TX), Lillie Eva (b. 1883, TX), Rebecca Paralee (b. 1888, TX); spouse, Emma D. Cox (b. 1872, TX), married 1895, Matador; children, Ira Lee (b. 1896, TX), Leona May (b. 1898, TX), Mary Frances (b. 1899, TX), Mamie D. (b. 1902, TX), Paralee Virginia (b. 1903, TX), William Franklin (b. 1908, TX), Lillie Ellen (b. 1909, TX), Marion Gladys (b. 1911, TX), Woodrow Wilson (b. 1917, TX). *SR; A1b, d, e, f, g; 1503:429; A2b; A4a, b; B1.*

SLUDER, EDWIN ANTHONY. Born Dec. 12, 1876, Saint Louis, Saint Louis County, Missouri. Ht. 5 ft. 10 in., brown eyes, black hair, dark complexion, married. Traveling auditor, Houston, Harris County, Texas. SPECIAL RANGER July 24, 1917–Dec. 1917 (attached to Co. C). REMARKS: World War I Draft Registration document states Sluder is a salesman at army camps, living in Houston. FAMILY: Parents, Edwin Sluder (b. 1843, TN) and Cecile (b. 1849, MO); sister, Minnie (b. 1870, MO); spouse, Mary A. (b. 1885, MO), divorced by 1930; sons, Edwin (b. 1907, MO), Robert (b. 1912, TX). *SR; Sluder to Harley, Jan 2, 1918, AGC; A1b, f, g; A3a.*

SMILEY, SYLVANUS. Born Mar. 30, 1889, La Vernia, Wilson County, Texas. Ht. 5 ft. 11 in., gray eyes, brown hair, fair complexion. Law office clerk. REGULAR RANGER Oct. 7, 1911–Jan. 31, 1912 (private, Co. B). Discharged—reduction in force. REMARKS: In 1910 lived in Kenedy, Karnes County, Texas. Died May 27, 1912; buried in Concrete Cemetery, Guadalupe County, Texas. FAMILY: Parents, Peter Curran Smiley (b. 1832, MO) and Mary Pettis (b. 1852, TX); siblings, Elizabeth (b. 1882, TX), Thomas Brannon (b. 1886, TX). *SR; 471; SAE, Nov 2, 1911; LWT, Feb 4, 1912; 508: 66; A1e; A4b, g.*

SMITH, BLACKSTON L. Born Nov. 8, 1888, Junction, Kimble County, Texas. Ht. 6 ft. 4 in., gray eyes, black hair, light complexion. Stockman, Junction. SPECIAL RANGER Mar. 16, 1918–Jan. 15, 1919. REMARKS: Had been a deputy sheriff for 8 years. Died Feb. 16, 1976, Kimble County, Texas. FAMILY: Parents, John James Smith (b. 1834, IL) and Lenora Billingslea (b. 1855, TX); siblings, Walter W. (b. 1867, IL), Willie (b. 1880, TX), Lewis (b. 1883, TX), Rada "Pet" (b. 1889, TX), Hunter (b. 1892, TX), Jessie (b. 1897, TX); spouse, Nannie Lois McHugh (b. 1895, TX), married Dec. 25, 1919, Vernon, Wilbarger County, Texas; sons, Blackston L., Jr. (b. 1918, TX), James Edgar (b. 1925, TX). *SR; A1d, e, f, g; A2a, b; A3a; A4a, b; B1.*

SMITH, CHARLES D. Born May 9, 1895, Paola (Paoli, Garvin County?), Oklahoma. Ht. 5 ft. 8 ½ in., brown eyes, black hair, dark complexion, married. Mechanic, Littlefield, Lamb County, Texas. LOYALTY RANGER July 9, 1918–Feb. 1919. REMARKS: In June 1917 was a mechanic in Abernathy, Hale County, Texas. A Charles Smith, born May 9, 1895, died Jan. 31, 1973, Nacogdoches County, Texas. FAMILY: Spouse, Edith (b. 1902, IN), married about 1918. *SR; A1f; A2a, b; A3a.*

SMITH, CHARLES KENNETH. Born Oct. 5, 1894, Fort Davis, Jeff Davis County, Texas. Ht. 5 ft. 11 in., gray eyes, brown hair, fair complexion. Stockman, Fort Davis. SPECIAL RANGER May 1, 1917–Dec. 1917 (attached to Co. C). REMARKS: Belonged to a prominent Jeff Davis County family. Owned a half interest in a 35-section ranch; his brother was his partner. Died Mar. 14, 1990, Brewster County, Texas. FAMILY: Parents, Claude S. Smith (b. 1867, England) and Lou or Low (b. 1869, TX); siblings, Tyrrel Earnest (b. 1891, TX), Mabel L. (b. 1902, TX); spouse, Alteretta or Anteretta (b. 1901, TX), married about 1920; daughter, Mary A. (b. 1921, TX). *SR; Petition to Ferguson, Apr 17, 1917, AGC; Stewart to Hudspeth, Apr 18, May 1, 1917, AGC; Hudspeth to Ferguson, May 17, 1917, AGC; AG to Smith, May 31, 1917, AGC; AG to Hudspeth, May 31, 1917, AGC; A1e, f, g; A2a, b; A3a.*

SMITH, CLAUDE THOMAS. Born Apr. 22, 1878, Taylor, Williamson County, Texas. Ht. 6 ft., dark eyes, dark hair, dark complexion. Peace officer, enlisted in Potter County, Texas. REGULAR RANGER July 31, 1909–Aug. 16, 1910 (private, Co. B). Discharged/fired. REMARKS: Was involved in a controversy over searching a house in Amarillo, Potter County, during a bootlegging raid in Oct. 1909. Ranger Capt. Marvin Bailey fired him because he was disagreeable and because his earlier record was suspect. In 1910 was stationed in Val Verde County, Texas. In Jan. 1915 was an El Paso County, Texas, special deputy sheriff. In Sept. 1918 was a sergeant, city detectives, El Paso city police department. FAMILY: Parents, Joseph Meg Smith (b. 1853, TX) and Sarah L. (b. 1859, TX); siblings, Beaula (b. 1875, TX), Ed (b. 1876, TX), Lettie (b. 1879, TX), Lillian (b. 1884, TX), Georgia (b. 1886, TX), John Pumphrey (b. 1890, TX), Breen (b. 1897, TX), Eloise (b. 1899, TX). *SR; 471; A.W. Brown's affidavit, Feb 11, 1910, WC; AG to Bailey, Sept 8, 1910, AGC; Bailey to Newton, Aug 13, 1910, AGC; Bailey to Phelps, Aug 18 [?], 1910, AGC; Co. B payroll, Aug, 1910, AGC; AA, June 17, 1915; A1b, d, e, f; A3a.*

SMITH, DICK. Born Feb. 1881, Dublin, Erath County, Texas. Ht. 5 ft. 8 in., blue eyes, black hair, fair complexion, married. Special agent, St. Louis Southwestern Railroad, Waco, McLennan County, Texas. SPECIAL RANGER Jan. 24, 1918–Jan. 15, 1919. Special officer, MKT Railroad, Dallas, Dallas County, Texas. RAILROAD RANGER Aug. 14, 1922–Aug. 14, 1924 (Co. B). Discharged—WA expired. Special officer, MKT Railroad, De Leon, Comanche County, Texas. SPECIAL RANGER July 1, 1925–July 1, 1927. Discharged. Special officer, MKT Railroad, Waco. SPECIAL RANGER Nov. 7, 1927–Nov. 7, 1928; Dec. 5, 1928–Dec. 5, 1929. Discharged. REMARKS: In 1910 was city marshal, Italy, Ellis County, Texas. In Mar. 1919 and June 1920, was described as the "office deputy sheriff" of Hill County, Texas. In Aug. 1922, Smith stated he had been city marshal and deputy sheriff for 20 years. FAMILY: Spouse, Maude F. (b. 1885, TX), married about 1906; son, Jack Austin (b. 1910, TX). *SR; Campbell to Harley, Jan 1, 30, 1918, AGC; McDaniel to Hobby, June 10, 1920, AGC; Ranger John B. Wilmoth Service Record, AGC; A1e, f, g.*

SMITH, ED "EDDIE." Born Sept. 10, 1873, Mason, Mason County, Texas. Ht. 5 ft. 10 in., blue eyes, dark brown hair, fair complexion, married. Ranchman, Mason. SPECIAL RANGER Dec. 6, 1917–unknown (Jan. 15, 1919 ?). REMARKS: Was a large landowner and cattle raiser. LAW ENFORCEMENT RELATIVES: Ranger Henry Hoerster, uncle. FAMILY: Parents, Caleb C. Smith (b. 1844, GA) and Carolina Hoerster (b. 1852, TX); brother, Caleb Howard "Dick" (b. 1877, TX), Amos Western "Wes" (b. 1881, TX); spouse, Mary Amanda King (b. 1879, TX), married about 1894; daughters, Lidia (b. 1895, TX), Lucille (b. 1901, TX). *SR; Smith to Hutchings, Oct 20, 1917, AGC; Smith to Governor, Oct 20, 1917, AGC; AG to Smith, Dec 5, 1917, AGC; A1b, d, e, f; A3a; A4b.*

SMITH, EDWARD HUME. Born Nov. 1862, Pulaski, Giles County, Tennessee. Ht. 5 ft. 8 in., blue eyes, very light brown hair, fair complexion, married. Peace officer, Waco, McLennan County, Texas. REGULAR RANGER Jan. 19, 1915–Jan. 15, 1919 (captain, Co. C; in the interest of economy, was transferred to the Oyster, Fish & Game Warden's office, Austin, Travis County, Texas as a REGULAR RANGER without pay and issued a SPECIAL RANGER commission, Jan. 22, 1917. Was reinstated Dec. 20, 1917). Peace officer, Waco. RAILROAD RANGER July 26, 1922–Nov. 23, 1922 (Co. B). Discharged. REMARKS: In Jan. 1915 stated he had 15 years' experience as a peace officer. Caused a scandal in Austin on Labor Day 1915 when he became drunk and disorderly. In Jan. 1919 was a special agent, MKT Railroad, Waco. In Dec. 1922 was deputy constable, precinct 1, McLennan County. In 1930 was still a railway officer in Waco. Died Dec. 24, 1932, McLennan County, Texas. FAMILY: Spouse, Emma (b. 1868, AR), married about 1889. *SR; AG to Solar, Jan 7, 1915, AGC; [AG] to Ferguson, Sept 8, 1915, WC; Depositions, Sept 8, 9, 1915, WC; White to Hutchings, Jan 18, 1917, AGC; AG to White, Jan 19, 1917, AGC; Hendricks to Ferguson, Jan 19, 1917, AGC; E. A. Barnes Service Record, AGC; BDH, Apr 5, 1916; 463:56; A1d, f, g; A2b.*

SMITH, GEORGE RICKS. Born Nov. 5, 1877, Clark, Liberty County, Texas. Ht. 5 ft. 6 ½ in., brown eyes, dark hair, brunette complexion. Road supervisor, Clark. LOYALTY RANGER. Aug. 5, 1918–Feb. 1919. REMARKS: had been a dry goods salesman. In 1930 was a retail grocery merchant in Cleveland, Liberty County. A George R. Smith died Feb. 18, 1947, Liberty County, Texas. FAMILY: Parents, Thomas B. Smith (b. 1835, FL) and Charlotte A. (b. 1843, LA); siblings, James (b. 1870, TX), Hattie A. (b. 1872, TX), Colleta T. (b. 1880, TX); spouse, Mattie I. Holt (b. 1894, LA), married about 1925; daughter, Anna Jane (b. 1926, TX). *SR; A1b, d, f, g; A2b, e; A3a.*

SMITH, GILBERT PENDLETON. Born Nov. 28, 1874, Hopkins County, Texas. Tall, slender, married. Farmer and stockman, Sulphur Bluff, Hopkins County. LOYALTY RANGER June 18, 1918–Feb. 1919. REMARKS: World War I Draft Registration document notes "withered arm." In 1920 was a livestock dealer in Hopkins County. Died May 26, 1957, Hopkins County, Texas. FAMILY: Parents, James Henry Smith (b. 1833, KY) and Diadamia Hannah Pendleton (b. 1836, MO); siblings, Ellen S. (b. 1857, TX), Charles T. (b. 1860, TX), Henry J. (b. 1867, TX), John W. (b. 1869, TX), Ann E. (b. 1872, TX), Sam S. (b. 1877, TX); spouse #1, Nora (b. 1876, TX), married about 1905; children, Roger (b. 1906, TX), Dow (b. 1908, TX), Etoila (b. 1909, TX), Henry G. (b. 1911, TX), Lucile (b. 1914, TX); stepdaughter, Blanche Wright (b. 1901, TX); spouse #2, Callie (b. 1884, TX); step-sons, Billie Fanning (b. 1905, TX), James Fanning (b. 1914, TX). *SR; A1a, b, e, f, g; A2b; A3a; A4b.*

SMITH, HASTON CLAY "CLAY." Born Sept. 7, 1878, Ovilla, Ellis/Dallas County, Texas. Ht. 5 ft. 8 in., blue eyes, light hair, fair complexion, married. Assistant adjutant general, Austin, Travis County, Texas. SPECIAL RANGER Oct. 1, 1919–Dec. 31, 1919. REMARKS: Had been a clerk in a law office in Austin. As of Sept. 1918 was a soldier in the U.S. Army, lived in Manor, Travis County. In 1930 was an automobile sales manager in Austin. Died Aug. 19, 1949, Travis County, Texas. FAMILY: Parents, Peter Perkins Smith (b. 1856, AR) and Nancy Laura Collier (b. 1859, MO); siblings, Mary (b. 1883, TX), Dossie (b. 1887, TX), Lee Hammett (b. 1896, TX); spouse, Jennie Gertrude Lane (b. 1880, TX), married about 1909; children, Haston Clay, Jr. (b. 1909, TX), Lane Eppright (b. 1911, TX), Annie Laurie (b. 1913, TX), William Peter (b. 1916, TX), David Collier (b. 1920, TX). *SR; A1b, e, f, g; A2b; A4a, b.*

SMITH, HUGH. Born Oct. 20, 1874, Salado, Bell County, Texas. Ht. 5 ft. 10 ¾ in., gray eyes, brown hair, medium complexion, married. Sheriff, Bell County, Belton. SPECIAL RANGER Mar. 20, 1918–Jan. 15, 1919. REMARKS: In 1900 was a policeman in Temple, Bell County. In 1910 was Bell County justice of the peace. Bell County sheriff Nov. 3, 1914–Nov. 2, 1920. FAMILY: Parents, Henry C. Smith (b. 1840, AR) and Virginia B. (b. 1843, TX); siblings, Ella (b. 1870, TX), Lula L. (b. 1877, TX), Marion (b. 1880, TX); spouse, Eula (b. 1880, TX). *SR; 471; LWT, Dec 31, 1916; HC, July 31, 1915; Smith to Ferguson, Apr 19, 1917, AGC; Gray to Ferguson, May 22, 1917, AGC; 1503:42; A1b, d, e, f; A3a.*

SMITH, JAMES MARCUS. Born Jan. 19, 1883, Walker County, Texas. Medium height, medium build, blue eyes, dark hair. Stockman, Huntsville, Walker County. LOYALTY RANGER June 3, 1918–Feb. 1919. FAMILY: Parents, James Hansford Smith (b. 1855, TX) and Katie (b. 1857, TX); siblings, John M. (b. 1881, TX), Opel (b. 1884, TX), Cora (b. 1887, TX), Lilah (b. 1892, TX), Ida or A. Bell (b. 1894, TX), Boyce B. (b. 1897, TX), William Bradley "Willie" (b. 1899, TX). *SR; A1d, e; A3a.*

SMITH, JESSE LEE. Born Apr. 9, 1874, Stephenville, Erath County, Texas. Ht. 5 ft. 10 in., gray eyes, dark hair, dark complexion. Ranch hand, Rocksprings, Edwards County, Texas. REGULAR RANGER Mar. 1, 1921–Sept. 30, 1921 (private, Co. C). Discharged. REMARKS: Had been sheep and goat inspector for almost a year. Died May 5, 1939, Brackettville, Kinney County, Texas. FAMILY: Parents, Simon Kenton Smith (b. 1849, TN) and Mary Jane Orr (b. 1855, TX); siblings, Lucy (b. 1877, TX), Luther Oscar (b. 1879, TX), George Webster (b. 1881, TX), Lela Ann (b. 1883, TX), Houston Franklin (b. 1885, TX). *SR; 471; A1b, d; A2b; A3a; A4a, g.*

SMITH, MATT CURRY. Born Jan. 30, 1890, Santa Maria, Cameron County, Texas. Ht. 5 ft. 10 in., blue eyes, brown hair, light complexion. Stock raiser, Mercedes, Hidalgo County, Texas. SPECIAL RANGER Dec. 3, 1917–Oct. 1918. Resigned. REMARKS: Caesar Kleberg sent in Smith's application. In June 1917 had been a trader in Sinton, San Patricio County, Texas. Lived in Sinton in 1920. A Matt C. Smith died Mar. 6, 1938, Cameron County, Texas. FAMILY: Parents, A. N. Smith (b. 1847, MS) and Mary E. (b. 1852, IL); siblings, Sherman (b. 1872, TX), Martha E. (b. 1874, TX), Norma (b. 1876, TX), George W. (b. 1880, TX), Willis (b. 1882, TX), Carrie (b. 1887, TX). *SR; Kleberg to Woodul, Dec 5, 1917, AGC; A1b, d, f; A2b; A3a.*

SMITH, OLIN WILBORN. Born Aug. 6, 1886, Fort Worth, Tarrant County, Texas. Ht. 5 ft. 11 in., brown eyes, dark hair turning gray, dark complexion, divorced. Former police officer, El Paso, El Paso County, Texas. REGULAR RANGER May 10, 1916–Oct. 1916 (private, Co. B). Resigned. Special agent, MKT Railroad, Wichita Falls, Wichita County, Texas. SPECIAL RANGER July 1, 1925–July 1, 1927. Discharged. REMARKS: El Paso city detective, 1911–1915. As of

June 1917 was deputy sheriff in El Paso, El Paso County. Notation on 1925 Service Record: "Gets drunk." In 1930 was living in Tarrant County. An Olin W. Smith died Dec. 19, 1943, Tarrant County, Texas. FAMILY: Parents, Charles L. Smith (b. 1858, VA) and Lilia Riggle (b. 1866, TX); siblings, Carl B. (b. 1888, TX), Charlie L. (b. 1893, TX), Thelma (b. 1895, TX), Lelia May (b. 1899, TX); spouse, unknown (b. TX); daughters, Celia M. (b. 1911, TX), Edna L. (b. 1913, TX). *SR; 471; EPMT, July 21, 1911, Aug 6, 1914, Apr 14, 1915; U.S. Commissioner, El Paso, Nos. 1260, 1298, FRC-FW; Fox to Hutchings, Sept 10, 1916, WC; Alderete to Ferguson, Aug 28, 1916, WC; A1d, e, f, g; A2b; A3a.*

SMITH, RALPH ROY. Born Feb. 21, 1880, Wilson County, Texas. Tall, medium build, gray eyes, dark brown hair, married. Cattleman, San Antonio, Bexar County, Texas. SPECIAL RANGER Feb. 23, 1918–Jan. 15, 1919. REMARKS: On World War I Draft Registration document stated was a lawyer for the U.S. Treasury Department, living in San Antonio. In 1920 and 1930 was an attorney in Pleasanton, Atascosa County, Texas. Died Mar. 20, 1944, Jourdanton, Atascosa County. FAMILY: Parents, Alexander Frohoc Smith (b. 1855, MS) and Mary McGill Matthews (b. 1857, AR); siblings, Tipton Allison (b. 1878, TX), Aubrey Matthews (b. 1882, TX), Cole Fro (b. 1884, TX), Willie Earl (b. 1887, TX), Karon Mac (b. 1889, TX), Landon Both (b. 1892, TX); spouse, Florence Bowen (b. 1879, TX), children, Roy Royale (b. 1911, TX), Frohoc Bowen (b. 1912, TX), Willard Mac (b. 1914, TX). *SR; A1b, d, f, g; A2b; A3a; A4a, g.*

SMITH, RILEY ROBERT. Born Apr. 3, 1873, near Taylor, Williamson County, Texas. Ht. 5 ft. 7 in., gray eyes, brown hair, light complexion, married. Ranchman, Marfa, Presidio County, Texas. LOYALTY RANGER July 20, 1918–Mar. 6, 1919. Rancher, Marfa. SPECIAL RANGER Aug. 4, 1919–Dec. 31, 1919. WA expired. REMARKS: As of June 1918, had been a peace officer for nearly nine years. 1919 letterhead: "R.R. Smith, Live Stock, Ranch Culberson County Texas, Postal Address: Marfa, Tex." FAMILY: Parents, W. Thomas Smith (b. 1842, AL) and Alice (b. 1853, TX); siblings, Oscar (b. 1871, TX), Edgar R. (b. 1875, TX), Fannie (b. 1877, TX); spouse, Mary (b. 1881, TX), married about 1901. *SR; A1b, e, f; A3a.*

SMITH, SLEDGE HARLAN. Born May 2, 1870, Bullard, Smith County, Texas. Ht. 5 ft. 11 ½ in., brown eyes, light hair, light complexion, married. Farmer, Gresham, Smith County. LOYALTY RANGER June 7, 1918–Feb. 1919. REMARKS: Still farming in Smith County in 1930. Died Nov. 4, 1944, Smith County, Texas; buried in Oakwood Cemetery, Smith County. FAMILY: Parents, Edward William or Willis Smith (b. 1841, SC) and Johnnie Arcadia Robertson (b. 1848, AL); siblings, Stuart Robertson (b. 1868, TX), Hope (b. 1869, TX), Edward William (b. 1872, TX), Robert Ewing (b. 1875, TX), Lloyd Travis (b. 1878, TX), Charles Daniel (b. 1879, TX), Maurice Virgil (b. 1882, TX), Swanie Brock, Benjamin Goodman; spouse, Bettie Shelton (b. 1879, TX), married Jan. 7, 1897, Smith County; children, Talmadge, Hampson Gary (b. 1898, TX), Johnnie E. (b. 1900, TX), Tillman (b. 1903, TX), Sammie H. (b. 1906, TX), Maurice (b. 1908, TX), Mary (b. 1915, TX). *SR; A1a, b, e, f, g; A2b; A4b, g; B1.*

SMITH, THOMAS RICHARD "RICHARD." Born July 1888, Val Verde County, Texas. Ht. 5 ft. 11 ½ in., brown eyes, brown hair, dark complexion. Merchant, Comstock, Val Verde County. SPECIAL RANGER Dec. 3, 1917–unknown (Co. A Volunteers). REMARKS: Was retail grocery merchant in Val Verde County in 1930. Died Nov. 15, 1949, Val Verde County, Texas. FAMILY: Father, Charley R. Smith (b. 1851, West Indies); mother's maiden name probably Small (b. TX); siblings, Dora H. (b. 1891, TX), Nellie R. (b. 1894, TX); spouse, Ella G. (b. 1886, TX), married about 1907; sons, Richard, Jr. (b. 1919, TX), James F. (b. 1920, TX), Guy R. (b. 1924, TX). *SR; A1d, e, f, g; A2b.*

SMITH, WALTER. Born Dec. 1870, Salado, Bell County, Texas. Ht. 5 ft. 8 in., blue eyes, light hair, fair complexion, married. Ranchman, Mertzon, Irion County, Texas. LOYALTY RANGER June 7, 1918–Feb. 1919. REMARKS: Had been a stockman in Crockett County, Texas. In 1930 was a ranchman in San Angelo, Tom Green County, Texas. FAMILY: Parents, Bart Smith (b. 1844, TN) and Mary A. (b. 1851, TX); siblings, William F. (b. 1868, TX), Willis A. (b. 1873, TX), Alfred T. C. (b. 1875, TX), Jennie (b. 1877, TX), Jeff M. (b. 1879, TX), Lula C. (b. 1881, TX), Eddie G. (b. 1885, TX), Bennett (b. 1887, TX), Barton C. (b. 1889, TX), Edna E. (b. 1893, TX); spouse, Minnie Clebarm (b. 1875, TX), married Dec. 28, 1892, Irion County; children, Minnie Gray (b. 1898, TX), Octie (b. 1900, TX), Alline (b. 1904, TX), Walter, Jr. (b. 1911, TX), Howard (b. 1914, TX). *SR; A1a, d, e, f, g; A2e.*

SMITH, WILLIAM "AUSTRALIAN BILLY." (His name was actually Charles E. Mathews.) Born about 1872, Adelaide, Australia. Ht. 5 ft. 11 in., blue eyes, red hair, fair complexion, married. Chief city detective, El Paso, El Paso County, Texas. REGULAR RANGER Sept. 1, 1911–Aug. 1912 (captain, Co. C; transferred to Co. D, Oct 5, 1911). Discharged—reduction in force. REMARKS: Immigrated to the U.S. in 1888, became a naturalized citizen. Was a deputy U.S. marshal, New Mexico; El Paso policeman, 1899–1902; special officer, Rock Island Railroad, El Paso; chief city detective, El Paso, 1902–1910; private detective in El Paso for Mexican provisional president Francisco I. Madero, May, 1911; employee of El Paso Health Department, Sept. 1911. Was the Texas Ranger detective, 1911–1912. City detective, El Paso, 1913–1915; house detective, Hotel Paso del Norte, El Paso, 1915–1916. Was appointed sergeant of El Paso city detectives, Dec. 1919. FAMILY: Spouse #1, Annie B. (b. 1882, OH), married about 1898; children, Chas. Geo. W. (b. 1900, TX), Ellen (b. 1903, TX); spouse #2, Robin (probably Harper) (b. 1886, TX), married about 1907; son, Jack C. (b. 1908, TX). *SR; 471; EPMT, Sept 8, 1911, July 31, 1913, July 17, Sept 10, 1914, Jan 4, Apr 18, Aug 15, Sept 14, Oct 21, Nov 22, Dec 10, 1915, Jan 8, 1916, Feb 3, 1918, Dec 30, 1919; BDH, May 29, Dec 19, 1911; Frederick Guy report, Feb 1, 1915, 5BI; U.S. Commissioner, El Paso, No. 86, FRC-FW; Leyendecker to Hutchings, Sept 2, 1911, AGC; Glisson to Keeler, Sept 15, 1911, AGC; Smith to Hutchings, Oct 25, 1911, Jan 26, Mar 19, Apr 15, July 10, 23, Aug 1, 19, 1912, AGC; Colquitt to Hutchings, Jan 10, 13, Apr 19, 1912, AGC; Wilson to Colquitt, Jan 9, 1912, AGC; Smith to Colquitt, Jan 11, 1912, WC; AG to Colquitt, Jan 19, May 4, 1912, AGC; Smith to AG, Apr 20, 1914, AGC; Assistant AG to Smith, Aug 28, 1915, AGC; A1d, e, f.*

SMYTH, JOT PITTS. Born May 26, 1877, Grandview, Johnson County, Texas. Ht. 6 ft. 2 in., blue eyes, brown hair, light complexion, married. Brand inspector, Cattle Raisers' Association of Texas, Lubbock, Lubbock County, Texas. SPECIAL RANGER July 2, 1917–Jan. 15, 1919 (WA was reinstated Dec. 20, 1917). REMARKS: Was classified as a REGULAR RANGER without pay in Jan. 1918, to avoid the draft. In 1930 was a stock rancher in Lubbock. Died June 27, 1960, Palo Pinto County, Texas. FAMILY: Parents, Rev. Daniel Isaac Smyth (b. 1841, AL) and Keziah Pitts (b. 1843, MS); siblings, Ogden P., Dannie J. (b. 1869, MS), Ora K. (b. 1873, TX), Jerry Clyde (b. 1879, TX); spouse, M. E. (b. 1889, TX), married about 1915; sons, Jot, Jr. (b. 1914, TX), Jerry (b. 1926, TX). *SR; Acting AG to GC&SF Railroad, Jan 9, 1918, AGC; A1b, f, g; A2b; A3a; A4a, b.*

SNODY, WALTER FRANKLIN. Born Mar. 1872, Bedford County, Tennessee. Ht. 5 ft. 9 in., blue eyes, dark hair, fair complexion, married. Farmer and ginner, Benjamin, Knox County, Texas. LOYALTY RANGER June 1, 1918–Mar. 6, 1919. REMARKS: Had been a farmer and cotton ginner in Knox County at least since 1900. In 1930 was manager of a cotton gin in Benjamin. Died Nov. 23, 1963, Knox County, Texas. FAMILY: Parents, William Snody (b. 1840, TN) and Mary (b. 1850, FL); siblings, Robert L. (b. 1875, GA), Belle (b. 1877, TN), Cora E. (b. 1879, TN); spouse, Hattie E. (b. 1875, AL), married about 1897; children, William O. (b. 1900, TX), Roy D. (b. 1903, TX), Walter Burl (b. 1908, TX), Lyndal Eleard (b. 1912, TX). *SR; A1b, d, e, f, g; A2a, b; A4a.*

SNOWDEN, JACOB GREEN. Born Aug. 30, 1875, McMullen County, Texas. Tall, stout, gray eyes, dark hair, married. County and district clerk, McMullen County, Tilden. LOYALTY RANGER June 8, 1918–Feb. 1919. REMARKS: Had been a farmer and a butcher in McMullen County. In 1930 was a land abstractor in McMullen County. Died Apr. 21, 1966, Frio County, Texas. FAMILY: Spouse, Mary Amelia (b. 1877, TX), married about 1899; children, Allie May (b. 1899, TX), Louis M. (b. 1903, TX), Gladys (b. 1905, TX), Eula J. (b. 1907, TX), Joseph Green (b. 1909, TX), Doris A. (b. 1912, TX), Philip (b. 1914, TX), Mary E. (b. 1915, TX). *SR; A1d, e, f, g; A2a, b; A3a.*

SNYDER, GUSTAVE "GUS." Born June 1885, Cologne, Germany. Ht. 5 ft. 9 in., gray eyes, iron gray hair, fair complexion. Special agent, Southern Pacific Railroad, El Paso, El Paso County, Texas. REGULAR RANGER May 13, 1916–July 20, 1916. Resigned. REMARKS: Note length of service. Was shot and seriously wounded in line of duty. On enlistment form stated "Secret Service, Chinese and Canadian Government; official translator, Alberta legislature." *SR; 471; Fox to Hutchings, May 16, 1916, WC; AG to Fox, May 19, 1916, WC; AG to Hotel Dieu, June 12, 1916, AGC; EPMT, May 15, 16, 20,1916.*

SNYDER, HARRY P. Born June 1861, Sandusky, Erie County, Ohio. Ht. 5 ft. 8 in., gray eyes, gray hair, light complexion, married. Freight conductor, I&GN Railroad, San Antonio, Bexar County, Texas. SPECIAL RANGER July 31, 1916–unknown. Was a railroad conductor in San Antonio as early as 1900. Died Apr. 13, 1930, Bexar County, Texas. FAMILY: Spouse, Kansas (b. 1861, OH), married about 1890; adopted daughter, Susan S. (b. 1893, TX). SR; *A1d, e, g; A2b.*

SNYDER, THOMAS WHIPPLE "TOM." Born Oct. 12, 1873, Liberty Hill, Williamson County, Texas. Ht. 5 ft. 11 in., brown eyes, red hair, fair complexion, married. Ranchman, Marfa, Presidio County, Texas. SPECIAL RANGER Dec. 31, 1917–Jan. 15, 1919. REMARKS: Had been a livestock buyer in Presidio County. Died Sept. 20, 1953, El Paso County, Texas. FAMILY: Parents, Thomas Shelton Snyder (b. 1839, MS) and Lenora Ann Bryson (b. 1845, SC); siblings, Dudley Weatherholz (b. 1869, TX), Pearl (b. 1870, TX), Clarence, Myrtle (b. 1876, TX), Eula S. (b. 1878, TX), Lenora (b. 1879, TX), Ann, John Wesley; spouse, Susan Steele (b. 1875, TX), married about 1898; daughters, Luci Belle (b. 1902, TX), Penelope (b. 1905, TX). *SR; A1b, e, f; A2b; A3a; A4b; B1.*

SNYDER, VIRGIL LESLY. Born June 21, 1878, Nettleton, Caldwell County, Missouri. Ht. 6 ft., blue eyes, light brown hair, light complexion. Federal government agent, San Antonio, Bexar County, Texas. REGULAR RANGER Feb. 19, 1921–Mar. 14, 1921 (private, Emergency Co. No. 1). Resigned. REMARKS: Note length of service. Private detective, El Paso 1912–1913. On Sept. 10, 1918, became an agent of the federal Bureau of Investigation in San Antonio, working for C. E. Breniman. In 1930 was an oil producer in San Antonio. Died Sept. 9, 1945, Bexar County, Texas. FAMILY: Parents, Dexter McClure Snyder (b. 1844, IN) and Martha A. Tippet (b. 1840, KY); siblings, Addie B. (b. 1862, MO), Lillie M. (b. 1866, MO), Ella C. (b. 1868, MO), Clara A. (b. 1870, MO), Walter Franklin (b. 1872, MO), Martha V. (b. 1875, MO), James Albert (b. 1877, MO); spouse #1, Blanche A. Battey, married about 1901; spouse #2, Marie L. (b. 1878, OH), married about 1908; daughter, Virginia (b. 1912, UT). *SR; 471; A1b, f, g; A2b; A3a; A4b, g; B1.*

SOAPE, RALPH. Born Aug. 1, 1889, Rusk County, Texas. Ht. 5 ft. 7 in., brown eyes, light hair, light complexion, married. Secretary to the governor, Austin, Travis County, Texas. SPECIAL RANGER Nov. 7, 1918–Jan. 15, 1919. Secretary to the governor, Austin. SPECIAL RANGER Oct. 29, 1920–unknown. REMARKS: In June 1917 worked for the Henderson Telephone Company, Henderson, Rusk County. In 1930 was a marketing agent living in Alamo Heights, Bexar County, Texas. Died Oct. 5, 1967, Dallas County, Texas. FAMILY: Parents, Henderson E. Soape (b. 1856, TX) and Elizabeth "Lizzie" Williams (b. 1859, TX); brother, Frank (b. 1894, TX); spouse, Rena M. (b. 1893, TX), married about 1911. *SR; Townes to Soape, Nov 5, 1920, AGC; A1d, e, f, g; A2a, b; A3a; A4b.*

SOMERVILLE, CHARLES F. (probably **FIDELIS**) **"CHARLIE."** Born Jan. 1868, Wiseburg, West Virginia. Ht. 6 ft. 3 in., blue eyes, dark hair, fair complexion, married. Special agent, Fort Worth and Denver City Railroad, Wichita Falls, Wichita County, Texas. SPECIAL RANGER Jan. 2, 1917–Jan. 15, 1919. Special agent, Fort Worth and Denver City Railroad, Wichita Falls. RAILROAD RANGER July 3, 1923–July 3, 1925. Discharged. Special agent, Fort Worth and Denver City Railroad, Wichita Falls. SPECIAL RANGER July 2, 1925–July 2, 1927; Aug. 18, 1927–Aug. 18, 1928; Sept. 19, 1928–Sept. 18, 1929; Sept. 18, 1929–Sept. 18, 1930; Sept. 18, 1930–Sept. 18, 1931; Oct. 10, 1931–Aug. 20, 1932. Honorably discharged. REMARKS: (Last name frequently misspelled, often as "Summerville.") As of Aug. 1927 had been a special officer for the FW&DC Railroad for the last 12 years, holding SPECIAL RANGER commissions most of the time. Had been a boarding-house keeper in Wichita Falls in 1910. Died Apr. 8, 1938, Wichita County, Texas. FAMILY: Parents, Andrew Jackson Somerville (b. 1832, WV) and Sarah Ott (b. 1831, WV); siblings, Edwin (b. 1853, WV), James (b. 1854, WV), Henretta (b. 1855, WV), Mary (b. 1857, WV), David J. (b. 1860, WV), Orlie C. (b. 1863, WV); spouse #1, unknown (probably Elizabeth, b. MO); sons, Jackson Wayne (b. 1891, MO), Charles L. (b. 1894, MO); spouse #2, Cora (b. 1882, WV), married about 1900; spouse #3, Ada Freese (b. 1888, TX), married about 1909; daughter, Orilea (b. 1915, TX). *SR; A1a, b, d, e, f, g; A2b; A4b, g.*

SOUTHWORTH, JOHN. Born Apr. 1875, Argo, Missouri. Ht. 6 ft. 1 in., gray eyes, brown hair, light complexion. Stockman, Matador, Motley County, Texas. LOYALTY RANGER June 29, 1918–Feb. 1919. Stock raiser (brand inspector, Cattle Raisers' Association of Texas), Matador. SPECIAL RANGER June 16, 1919–Dec. 31, 1919. REMARKS: In 1918, "deputy sheriff." For many years had been range boss for the Matador Land & Cattle Co. A John Thomas Southworth died May 15, 1954, Garza County, Texas. FAMILY: Parents, William Southworth (b. 1850, MO) and Elizabeth (b. 1852, MO); siblings, Lee (b. 1872, MO), Frank (b. 1877, MO), Allen C. (b. 1880, MO), Alta (b. 1884, MO). *SR; 471; Moses & Rowe to Harley, June 7, 1919, AGC; A1b, d, e; A2b.*

SOWELL, ANDREW JACKSON. Born Feb. 19, 1887, Kingsbury, Guadalupe County, Texas. Ht. 5 ft. 11 in., brown eyes, brown hair, dark complexion. Deputy sheriff, enlisted in Karnes County, Texas. REGULAR RANGER Oct. 16, 1911–Jan. 31, 1912 (private, Co. B). Discharged—reduction in force. Police officer, San Antonio, Bexar County, Texas. REGULAR RANGER Dec. 18, 1917–Jan. 1918 (private, Co. G). Discharged. Special officer, GH&SA Railroad (Southern Pacific), Galveston, Galveston County, Texas. RAILROAD RANGER Oct. 31, 1923–Oct. 31, 1925. Discharged. Special officer, T&NO Railroad (Southern Pacific), Ennis, Ellis County, Texas. SPECIAL RANGER Nov. 17, 1925–Dec. 10, 1927; Dec. 10, 1927–Dec. 10, 1928; Dec. 29, 1928–Dec. 29, 1930; Feb. 18, 1930 (residence was now San Antonio)–Dec. 29, 1930; Feb. 10, 1931–Jan. 18, 1933; Jan. 23, 1933–Jan. 22, 1935; June 11, 1935–Aug. 10, 1935. Discharged. REMARKS: Died Apr. 18, 1966, Lavaca County, Texas. *SR; 471; 508: 66; A2a, b; A3a.*

SPANG, FRANK ARMITAGE. Born Mar. 21, 1880, Ludington, Mason County, Michigan. Ht. 5 ft. 10 ½ in., gray eyes, dark hair, dark complexion, married. Railroad conductor, San Antonio, Bexar County, Texas. SPECIAL RANGER July 26, 1916–Dec. 1917 (attached to Co. C). REMARKS: Had been a railroad brakeman in Taylor, Williamson County, Texas. As of Sept. 1918 was a railroad conductor for the I&GN Railroad in San Antonio. Still a railroad conductor in 1930. Died Apr. 29, 1947, Bexar County, Texas. FAMILY: Mother, Mary (b. 1855, Canada); sister, Mamie (b. 1882, TX); spouse #1, unknown, married about 1901; spouse #2, Sarah Mechling Blake (b. 1875, British Honduras), married Aug. 20, 1907; children, Claude F. (b. 1909, TX), Mary B. (b. 1912, TX). *SR; AG to Spang, July 27, 1916, AGC; A1d, e, f, g; A2b; A3a; A4b.*

SPANGLER, ROSS ALBERT. Born Apr. 24, 1893, Mapleton, Huntingdon County, Pennsylvania. Ht. 5 ft. 7 in., blue eyes, blond hair, light complexion, married. Sales manager, Austin, Travis County, Texas. SPECIAL RANGER Apr. 19, 1920–unknown. REMARKS: Registered for World War I Draft in Altoona, Blair County, Pennsylvania. In 1920 was an auto sales manager in Austin. In 1930 was an auto salesman in Los Angeles, Los Angeles County, California. Died Sept. 9, 1957, Santa Clara County, California. LAW ENFORCEMENT RELATIVES: Constable, Altoona, Ward 1 (1910) James Spangler, stepfather. FAMILY: Stepfather, James Spangler (b. 1865, PA) and Hannah E. Fisher (b. 1873, PA); spouse, Agnes (b. 1899, PA), married about 1919; daughter, Betty J. (b. 1922, PA). *SR; A1d, e, f, g; A2f; A3a.*

SPANN, THADDEUS THEODORE. Born Feb. 2, 1878, Frankfort, Franklin County, Kentucky. Ht. 5 ft. 9 ½ in., gray eyes, light hair, light complexion, married. Land agent, Abilene, Taylor County, Texas. SPECIAL RANGER Apr. 23, 1917–May 23, 1917. Placed on active duty. REGULAR RANGER May 24, 1917–Sept. 1, 1917 (private, Co. C). Resigned/fired. REMARKS: Governor Ferguson sent a "Confidential" letter to the AG, Apr. 23, 1917, ordering that Spann receive a commission. On Oct. 15, 1917, an Abilene attorney wrote confidentially to the AG withdrawing his endorsement of Spann: "Spann is not really the kind of man for a ranger or any other officer. He uses bad judgment in many cases in making arrests, and runs with bootleggers, gamblers, pimps and lewd women and drinks considerable whiskey himself." Spann sent the AG a petition supporting his application for reinstatement. In 1910 had been a theater proprietor in Abilene. As of Sept. 1918 worked for the Texas Electric Company, lived in Ballinger, Runnels County, Texas. In 1920 was a grocery merchant in Ballinger. Died June 21, 1933, Abilene, Taylor County, Texas. FAMILY: Parents, Andrew Jackson Spann (b. 1839, TN) and Delia or Delilah Ann Short (b. 1840, KY); siblings, Eugene Adolphus (b. 1863, KY), Ira Willis (b. 1866, KY), Dorothy E. (b. 1867, KY), Leona E. (b. 1869, KY), Rufus Gustavas (1871, KY), Emma (b. 1873, KY), Albert Lewis (b. 1876, KY), Lena Leoti (b. 1880, KY); spouse, Lela (b. 1883, TX), married about 1903. *SR; 471; Ferguson to Hutchings, Apr 23, 1917, AGC; Graham to AG, Oct 15, 1917, AGC; Spann to Harley, Oct 15, 1917, AGC; A1b, e, f; A2b; A3a; A4a; B1.*

SPEARS, WALTER TAYLOR. Born Apr. 15, 1877, San Angelo, Tom Green County, Texas. Ht. 5 ft. 11 in., brown eyes, brown hair, sandy complexion, married. L.S.S. [*sic*] inspector, Menard, Menard County, Texas. SPECIAL RANGER Jan. 21, 1918–Jan. 15, 1919. Peace officer, Yates oil field, Pecos County, Texas. SPECIAL RANGER June 20, 1927–June 20, 1928. Inspector, Sheep and Goat Raisers' Association (since June 20, 1927), San Angelo. SPECIAL RANGER July 7, 1928–July 7, 1929; July 17, 1929–July 17, 1930; July 17, 1930–July 17, 1931; July 23, 1931–Jan. 20, 1933; June 1, 1933–June 12, 1935. REMARKS: As of Jan. 1918 had been a peace officer for many years. In 1910 was a jailer for Tom Green County jail. In Sept. 1918 was a cattle inspector for the Texas Sanitary Commission in Menard. In June 1927 had been a city marshal for 2 years. LAW ENFORCEMENT RELATIVES: Tom Green County sheriff (Nov. 2, 1880–Nov. 4, 1884) James D. Spears, father. FAMILY: Father, James D. Spears (b. 1839, AL); brother, James C. (b. 1876, TX); spouse, Agnes (b. 1883, TX), married about 1911; daughters, Jimmie B. (b. 1912, TX), Marie (b. 1916, TX). *SR; 1503:493; A1b, d, e, g; A3a.*

SPEED, ROBERT EUSTIS. Born Dec. 7, 1878, Cuero, DeWitt County, Texas. Ht. 5 ft. 8 in., brown eyes, black hair, dark complexion, married as of Apr. 1914. Stockman, enlisted in Karnes County, Texas. REGULAR RANGER Oct. 31, 1911–sometime between Apr. 1 and May 13, 1914 (private, Co. B; reenlisted Oct. 31, 1913). Honorably discharged. Stockman, Marfa, Presidio County, Texas. REGULAR RANGER Mar. 16, 1921–Dec. 10, 1923 (private, Co. A; reenlisted Mar. 16, 1923). Resigned. REMARKS: Excellent evaluation in Apr. 1914. As of Sept. 1918 was deputy sheriff, employed by Presidio Mining Company, Shafter, Presidio County. In 1930 was constable in Shafter. Died Jan. 1, 1940, Presidio County, Texas. FAMILY: Parents, Eustis Houston Speed (b. 1848, MS) and Letitia (b. 1852, TX); brother, William Ray (b. 1877, TX); spouse, Ida (b. 1889, TX); sons, Eustis G. (b. 1915, TX), Robert J. (b. 1917, TX). *SR; 471; AG to General Manager, May 13, 1914, AGC; 508: 66; A1d, f, g; A2b; A3a; A4b.*

SPEED, W. ROBERT. No Service Record. No personal description. REGULAR RANGER Jan 1, 1914–sometime after Dec. 1, 1914 and prior to Feb. 5, 1915 (private, Co. B). *MR, Co. B, Jan–July 1914. 471; AGC; Sanders to Hutchings, July 24, Oct 20, Nov 24, 1914, WC; Sanders to Hutchings, Jan 15, 1915, AGC; AA, Apr 16, 1914; BDH, Aug 24, Oct 7, 1914.*

SPEED, WILLIAM B. Born Apr. 1871, Jackson, Hinds County, Mississippi. No physical description, married as of 1920. City marshal, Freeport, Brazoria County, Texas. SPECIAL RANGER Mar. 21, 1918–Jan. 15, 1919. REMARKS: Had been city marshal of Texas City, Galveston County, Texas. His state representative requested that he be commissioned as a SPECIAL RANGER to combat bootlegging. In 1920 was a real estate agent in Texas City. FAMILY: Spouse, Evelin (b. 1872, MS). *SR; Beason to Harley, Mar 19, 1918, AGC; Assistant AG to Speed, Mar 19, 1918, AGC; A1f.*

SPIVEY, AUSTIN. Born May 14, 1895, Indian Gap, Hamilton County, Texas. Ht. 6 ft. 1 ½ in., brown eyes, dark hair, fair complexion, married. Stockman, Brownwood, Brown County, Texas. REGULAR RANGER Dec. 22, 1917–Feb. 1, 1918. Resigned because of illness in family. REMARKS: Had been a deputy sheriff; was exempted by local draft board. In 1920 was a laborer in De Leon, Comanche County, Texas. Died June 4, 1972, Hamilton County, Texas. FAMILY: Parents, Elias Spivey (b. 1834, TN) and Mary A. (b. 1860, AL); siblings, Elias, Jr. (b. 1869, TX), Ephraim (b. 1872, TX), Ella (b. 1877, TX), Enoch (b. 1884, TX), Alice Pearl (b. 1886, TX), Anna M. (b. 1888, TX), Jefferson (b. 1890, TX); spouse, Drudie (b. 1895, TX); children, Iva N. (b. 1914, TX), Bernice (b. 1916, TX), Violet (b. 1919, TX). *SR; 471; Spivey to Harley, June 24, 1918, AGC; A1b, d, e, f; A2a, b; A3a; A4b.*

SPIVEY, WILLIAM E. Born Jan. 1868, Pike County, Alabama. Ht. 5 ft. 10 in., blue eyes, gray hair, light complexion, married. Quarantine officer, Brownsville, Cameron County, Texas. SPECIAL RANGER Feb. 7, 1918–Jan. 15, 1919. REMARKS: Had been county health officer, Bell County, Texas; state quarantine officer for the past 18 months. A William Elisha Spivey died Dec. 19, 1957, Cameron County, Texas. FAMILY: Spouse, Sophia L. (b. 1872, AR), married about 1890; children, Sophia A. (b. 1893, TX), Sylvia C. (b. 1896, TX), Lillie B. (b. 1898, TX), Leta (b. 1901, TX), William L. (b. 1904, TX). *SR; Collins to Harley, Feb 1, 1918, AGC; A1d, e, f; A2b.*

SPRAGUE, GEORGE W. Born Feb. 1871, Corpus Christi, Nueces County, Texas. Ht. 5 ft. 10 in., gray eyes, brown hair, dark complexion, married. Railroad agent, enlisted in Webb County, Texas. SPECIAL RANGER Sept. 26, 1918–Jan. 15, 1919. REMARKS: Had been a telegraph operator in Corpus Christi. Was chairman, Webb County draft board. In 1930 was a rancher in Laredo, Webb County. Died Oct. 7, 1934, Webb County, Texas. *SR; A1a, b, d, e, f, g; A2b.*

SPROLES, THOMAS ANDREW. Born Oct. 4, 1876, Lexington, Lee County, Texas. Ht. 5 ft. 11 in., gray eyes, brown hair, dark complexion, married. Deputy sheriff, Wallis, Austin County, Texas. SPECIAL RANGER Jan. 7, 1918–Jan. 15, 1919. REMARKS: Had been a peace officer for 16 years. In 1920 was a house detective in Houston, Harris County, Texas. Died Mar. 19, 1923, Harris County, Texas. FAMILY: Parents, Thomas Jefferson Sproles (b. 1849, MS) and Emily Josephine (b. 1859, TX); sister, Ella L. (b. 1879, TX); spouse, Camilla "Millie" (b. 1883, TX), married about 1901; children, Grace (b. 1904, TX), Bernice (b. 1905, TX). Thomas Arthur (b. 1907, TX), Opal (b. 1909, TX), Vaughn (b. 1915, TX). *SR; A1b, d, e, f, g; A2b; A3a.*

SPRUILL, ANDREW JACKSON. Born Apr. 23, 1879, near Prairie Lea, Caldwell County, Texas. Ht. 6 ft. 1 in., brown eyes, brown hair, fair complexion, married. Brand inspector, Cattle Raisers' Association of Texas, Laredo, Webb County, Texas. SPECIAL RANGER, Jan. 19, 1918–Sept. 9, 1918. Discharged and placed on active duty. Cattleman, Laredo. REGULAR RANGER Sept. 9, 1918–Dec. 8, 1919 (private, Co. I; reenlisted under the new law, June 20, 1919). Discharged. REMARKS: In Jan. 1918 was classified as a REGULAR RANGER without pay, to avoid the draft. In 1920 and 1930 was a farmer in Frio County, Texas. Died Dec. 15, 1931, Frio County, Texas. FAMILY: Parents, Andrew Spruill (b. 1843, AL) and Louisiana "Lou" (b. 1849, AL); siblings, Lula B. (b. 1868, MS), Rosana (b. 1873, MS), Walter (b. 1876, TX), James (b. 1881, TX), Agusta (b. 1887, TX); spouse #1, Vida; spouse #2, Bela or Eula (b. 1897, TX), married about 1920. *SR: 471; Acting AG to Moses & Rowe, Jan 12, 1918, AGC; A1b, d, f, g; A2b; A3a.*

STACY, THOMAS E. "TOM." Born Apr. 30, 1882, Welch, McDowell County, West Virginia. Ht. 6 ft. 2 ½ in., blue eyes, light hair, light complexion, married. District special agent, GH&SA Railroad (Southern Pacific), San Antonio, Bexar County, Texas. SPECIAL RANGER Nov. 26, 1917–Jan. 15, 1919 (attached to Co. C); Mar. 5, 1927–unknown (was killed). REMARKS: In Nov. 1917 already had a Bexar County deputy sheriff's commission but needed a Ranger commission to operate along the GH&SA's entire line. A Tom Stacey (note spelling) died Sept. 27, 1927, Bexar County, Texas. FAMILY: Spouse, Mabel (b. 1890, VA). *SR; Stacy to AG, Nov 19, 1917, AGC; Webster to Harley, Nov 22, 1917, AGC; Harley to Stacy, Nov 24, 1917, AGC; A1f; A2b; A3a.*

STAGG, WILLIAM ALLEN "ALLEN." Born May 1868, Stewartsville, De Kalb County, Missouri. Ht. 6 ft. 2 in., brown eyes, brown hair, dark complexion, married. Grain dealer, Vega, Oldham County, Texas. LOYALTY RANGER June 1, 1918–Feb. 1919. REMARKS: Oldham County sheriff Nov. 4, 1902–Nov. 3, 1908. In 1920 and 1930 was a land title abstractor in Vega. Died Mar. 9, 1955, Armstrong County, Texas. FAMILY: Parents, Esquire "Squire" Bunton Stagg (b. 1826, KY) and Sarah Martha Wylie (b. 1845, KY); sisters, Lucy E. (b. 1872, MO), Mary Belle (b. 1879, MO); spouse, Ollie B. (b. 1874, KY); son, Sam (b. 1909, TX). *SR; A1a, b, d, f, g; 1503:399; A2b; A4b.*

STALLWORTH, FRANCIS MARION "FRANK." Born Dec. 27, 1860, Wilcox County, Alabama. Ht. 6 ft., blue eyes, iron gray hair, dark complexion, married. Bookkeeper, Marlin, Falls County, Texas. SPECIAL RANGER Oct. 23, 1918–Jan. 15, 1919. REMARKS: Was Marlin city marshal, Nov. 1917; ex-city marshal, Marlin, Oct. 1918. Had been deputy county clerk, Falls County. Died May 16, 1922, in the collapse of a Brazos River bridge during a flood, Falls County, Texas; buried in Calvary Cemetery, Marlin. FAMILY: Parents, Nicholas "Major," "Nick" Stallworth (b. 1837, AL) and Lucy McFarlin Turk (b. 1838, AL); siblings, George (b. 1858, AL), Landreas (b. 1869), Dosh West (b. 1876, TX); spouse, Bellah Etheridge (b. 1873, TX), married Dec. 23, 1891; sons, George A. (b. 1893, TX), William A. (b. 1894, TX), Edgar A. (b. 1896, TX). *SR; Johnston to Stallworth, Oct 22, 1918, AGC; Kennedy to Gray, Nov 18, 1917, AGC; A1b, d, f; A2b; A4b.*

STANDARD, LEROY THOMAS "LEE." Born Apr. 30, 1868, Panola County, Texas. Ht. 5 ft. 11 in., blue eyes, dark hair, fair complexion, married. Farmer, Henderson,

Rusk County, Texas. LOYALTY RANGER June 11, 1918–Feb. 1919. REMARKS: Rusk County sheriff Nov. 3, 1896–Nov. 6, 1900. Also had been deputy sheriff. Died Mar. 29, 1956, Henderson, Rusk County, Texas; buried in Millville Cemetery, Henderson. LAW ENFORCEMENT RELATIVES: Rusk County deputy sheriff (1900) James Standard, brother; Rusk County deputy sheriff (1900) Edward Standard, brother. FAMILY: Parents, William Henry Standard (b. 1839, GA) and Mary Elizabeth Morris (b. 1839, AL); brothers, James Wallace (b. 1870, TX), Edward Lawler (b. 1873, TX), Amos Gaines (b. 1876, TX), Henry Morris (b. 1879, TX), James Bell (b. 1884, TX); spouse, Julia Ann Burt (b. 1868, TX), married Mar. 26, 1891, Rusk County; children, Mary Gladys (b. 1893, TX), Lillie Faye (b. 1894, TX), William Horace (b. 1897, TX), Martha (b. 1898, TX), Ned Bradford (b. 1905, TX), Kathleen Elizabeth (b. 1907, TX). *SR; A1b, d, e, f, g; 1503:445; A2b; A4a, b.*

STANFORD, JOSEPH W. Born Mar. 1887, Hillsboro, Hill County, Texas. Ht. 5 ft. 9 in., blue eyes, light brown hair, light complexion. Commercial salesman. REGULAR RANGER Oct. 4, 1911–Nov. 8, 1911 (private, Co. A; transferred to Co. C, Oct. 6, 1911). Resigned. REMARKS: Note length of service. In 1910 was a commercial grocery traveler living in Austin, Travis County, Texas. FAMILY: Parents, George A. Stanford (b. 1861, AR) and Mary W. Pruitt (b. 1862, AL); sisters, Maude E. (b. 1883, TX), Myrtle (b. 1886, TX). *SR; AG to Fox, Nov 10, 1911, AGC; Fox to Hutchings, Nov 12, 1911, AGC; A1e; A4b.*

STANLEY, JAMES E. Born Dec. 1857, near Austin, Travis County, Texas. Ht. 6 ft., blue eyes, iron gray hair, light complexion, married. Stock farmer, Wheeler, Wheeler County, Texas. LOYALTY RANGER June 6, 1918–Feb. 1919. REMARKS: Had lived in Lampasas County, Texas in 1900. In 1930 was a stock farmer in Lampasas County. Died Feb. 17, 1931, Lampasas County, Texas. FAMILY: Parents, Thomas Edward Stanley, Jr. (b. 1832, TN) and Emily Jane Berry (b. 1839, TN); siblings, Sarah Ann (b. 1859, TX), Mary E. (b. 1861, TX), Emily H. (b. 1864, TX), Lena P. (b. 1866, TX), Susan R. (b. 1869, TX), John H. (b. 1871), Laura F. (b. 1883); spouse #1, Samantha Ann Tennison (b. 1856, MO), married about 1877; children, Alice (b. 1878, TX), Emma E. (b. 1881, TX), Maude (b. 1882, TX), Jimmie A. (b. 1886, TX), Thomas Edward (b. 1888, TX), George L. (b. 1890, TX); spouse #2, Care G. (b. 1883, TX), married about 1925. *SR; A1aa, a, d, e, f, g; A2b; A4b.*

STANLEY, L. N. Born Feb. 1864, Horry County, South Carolina. Ht. 5 ft. 11 in., brown eyes, gray hair, dark complexion. Lawyer, Marlin, Falls County, Texas. SPECIAL RANGER June 15, 1918–Jan. 15, 1919. Lawyer, Marlin. SPECIAL RANGER Nov. 20, 1934–unknown. REMARKS: As of June 1918, "6 yrs. Fire Marshal of Marlin, carrying police authority." In 1870 census, first name listed as "Lutisous"; in 1930 census, first name listed as "Laurence." L. N. Stanley died Feb. 7, 1936, Falls County, Texas. FAMILY: Parents, Drizel E. Stanley (b. 1805, SC) and Susan Inman (b. 1837, SC); siblings, Richard Luther (b. 1856, SC), Harriett (b. 1859, SC), Drisel Needham (b. 1862, SC), James Lutsious (b. 1870, SC). *SR; A1a, d, e, f, g; A2b; A4b.*

STARK, PRESLEY J. Born June 6, 1874, Cleburne, Johnson County, Texas. Ht. 5 ft. 11 in., blue eyes, brown hair, light complexion, married. Druggist, Sweetwater, Nolan County, Texas. SPECIAL RANGER May 25, 1918–Jan. 15, 1919 (attached to Co. C). REMARKS: Had been a cook in Brownwood, Brown County, Texas. In 1910 was a butcher in Fisher County, Texas. After receiving his Ranger commission, worked for oil companies. In 1920 was a team contractor in Desdemona, Eastland County, Texas. Died Jan. 21, 1945, Sutton County, Texas. FAMILY: Parents, Presley Summerfield Stark (b. 1840, KY) and Martha Jane "Mattie" Combs (b. 1844, KY); siblings, Ennis (b. 1867, KY), Eva (b. 1869, KY), Stella (b. 1871, KY), Guy (b. 1872, KY), Pearl (b. 1878, TX), James (b. 1880, TX), Lily (b. 1883, TX); spouse, Eva Smith (b. 1876, KS), married May 1900; sons, Aubrey B. (b. 1901, TX), John Wayne (b. 1915, TX). *SR; A1b, d, e, f; A2b; A3a; A4a; B1, 2.*

STEDHAM, G. W. "BILL." Born Feb. 1882, Batesville, Zavala County, Texas. Ht. 5 ft. 11 in., blue eyes, light brown hair, light complexion. Ranchman. REGULAR RANGER June 16, 1916–Sept. 4, 1916 (private, Co. B). Resigned. *SR; 417.*

STEELE, CHARLES. Born June 23, 1886, Cleveland, Cuyahoga County, Ohio. Ht. 5 ft. 9 in., dark brown eyes, brown hair, dark complexion, married. Oil operator, San Antonio, Bexar County, Texas. REGULAR RANGER Oct. 26, 1920–Nov. 6, 1920 (private, Emergency Co. No. 1).

Discharged. REMARKS: Note length of service. Claimed to have held military commission in 1911—Madero's revolution in Mexico. World War I Draft Registration document stated "Cpl; Sgt; QM Sgt Infty; Regular Army; 1st Lt Vmt N.G." *SR; 471; Steele to Governor, May 14, 1916, AGC; A3a.*

STELFOX, CLARENCE HENRY. Born Dec. 17, 1882, Austin, Travis County, Texas. Ht. 5 ft. 10 in., brown eyes, black hair, fair complexion, married. Peace officer. REGULAR RANGER Aug. 29, 1917–Nov. 16, 1917 (private, Co. A). Resigned. Peace officer. REGULAR RANGER Jan. 3, 1918–Feb. 1, 1918 (private, Co. F). Discharged. REMARKS: In 1917, "Mr. Stelfox had his relations with the Ranger service severed by his Captain. . . ." Apparently resigned in 1918 because he owed a bank in Alice $40 and because of family matters. As of Sept. 1918 was employed by the U.S. Government in the Selective Service office in Austin. In 1920 was a house painter in Austin. In 1930 was doing odd jobs in Austin. Died Feb. 18, 1943, Travis County, Texas. FAMILY: Parents, John H. Stelfox (b. 1854, TX) and Evalyn S. (b. 1858, TX); spouse, Minnie Mabel (b. 1887, TX), married about 1905; children, Elsie S. (b. 1906, TX), Amos Eugene (b. 1908, TX), Henry (b. 1912, TX). *SR; 471; Sanders to Stelfox, Aug 26, 1917, AGC; Assistant AG to Bowman, Dec 29, 197, AGC; Sanders to Harley, Nov 16, 1917, AGC; Assistant AG to Clark, Feb 9, 1918, AGC; A1d, e, f, g; A2b; A3a.*

STEPHENSON, J. C. Born 1873, Hempstead, Waller County, Texas. Ht. 5 ft. 10 ½ in., blue eyes, light hair, fair complexion. Trainman, San Antonio, Bexar County, Texas. REGULAR RANGER Oct. 13, 1911–Nov. 23, 1911 (private, Co. A). Discharged/fired—went AWOL. *SR; 471; MR, Co. A , Nov 1911, RRM.*

STERLING, WILLIAM WARREN "BILL." Born Apr. 27, 1891, Belton, Bell County, Texas. Ht. 6 ft. 3 in., gray eyes, light hair, light complexion, married. Ranchman, Monte Christo, Hidalgo County, Texas. SPECIAL RANGER July 12, 1918–Jan. 15, 1919. Stockman, Laredo, Webb County, Texas. REGULAR RANGER Apr. 15, 1927–Jan. 22, 1931 (captain, Co. B; transferred to Co. D, May 1, 1927; reenlisted Apr. 15, 1929). REMARKS: Attended Texas A&M College 1906–1908. Army scout in South Texas, 1915. Was a 2nd lieutenant, 9th Texas Infantry regiment, 1917. In 1919 was in the cattle business—letterhead: "Sterling Brothers, Stockmen, W. W. Sterling, E. A. Sterling, Jr. Monte Christo, Hidalgo Co., Texas." Was a Webb County deputy sheriff and justice of the peace, 1922. In 1930 was a Ranger Captain, stationed in Brooks County, Texas. Was Adjutant General of Texas, Jan. 15, 1931–Jan. 15, 1933. In World War II was a lieutenant colonel, military intelligence officer for the Southern Land Frontier. After World War II managed Driscoll ranches in South Texas, was a ranch appraiser. His wife was Caesar Kleberg's cousin. Died Apr. 26, 1960, Corpus Christi, Nueces County, Texas. LAW ENFORCEMENT RELATIVES: Ranger Edward A. Sterling, Jr., brother. FAMILY: Parents, Edward Arthur Sterling (b. 1855, OH) and Mary Louise Chamberlain (b. 1868, GA); siblings, Jesse Louise (b. 1888, TX), Edward A., Jr. (b. 1894, TX), Minnie J. (b. 1899, TX); spouse, Zora Louise Eckhardt (b. 1895, TX), married July 4, 1919, Corpus Christi; daughters, Inez Isabel (b. 1922, TX), Sarah Ross (b. 1931, TX). *SR; 471; Sterling to AG, Oct 5, 1911, AGC; AG to Ransom, Oct 11, 1915, AGC; Ransom to Hutchings, Oct 14, 1915, AGC; Scout Report, Co. D, Oct, 1915, AGC; Sterling to Harley, June 6, 1918, AGC; AG to Sterling, June 10, 1918, AGC; 172:VI, 92; 1514; BDH, Nov 24, 1913, Apr 10, 11,22, 1914, Feb 24, Oct 2, 1915, Mar 16, 29, 30, 1916; Austin American, Aug 28, 1969; 522: 929; 463: 129–131, 176, 279; 464: 74, 76; 5: 299; autobiography: 319; A1d, g; A2b, e; A3a; A4a, b.*

STEVENS, CHARLES F. Born Mar. 1868, San Antonio, Bexar County, Texas. Ht. 5 ft. 10 in., brown eyes, black hair, ruddy complexion, married. Peace officer, San Antonio. REGULAR RANGER Nov. 27, 1917–Feb. 3, 1920 (captain, Co. G; reenlisted under the new law, June 20, 1919; transferred to Co. B, Feb. 3, 1920). Resigned because he refused to carry out what he considered an unlawful order from the AG regarding a boundary dispute with Oklahoma. REMARKS: As of June 1917, had been a peace officer for about 20 years: constable, 7 years; deputy constable, 5 years; chief deputy sheriff, 6 years—all in Bexar County; deputy U.S. marshal, Western District of Texas, 2 yrs. Became a federal Prohibition agent, San Antonio, Mar. 26, 1920. Resigned in 1922 to become supervisor in San Antonio of mounted Customs inspectors. Resigned to become Prohibition agent, Fort Worth, New Orleans, San Antonio. On Sept. 25, 1929, was assassinated, presumably by bootleggers; died in Bexar County, Texas. LAW ENFORCEMENT RELATIVES: Bexar County deputy sheriff (1880) Edward Stevens, father. FAMILY: Parents, Edward Stevens (b. 1828, VA) and Eliza (b. 1838, France); siblings, Edward (b. 1859, TX), Virginia (b. 1862, TX), Louisa (b. 1864, TX), Adeline or Adella (b. 1865, TX), Katherine (b. 1870, TX), Lizzie (b. 1872, TX), Olliva (b. 1874, TX), Ellick (b. 1876, TX); spouse, Ygnacia (b. 1860, TX), married about 1892; step-son, Alfonso Newton (b. 1888, TX). *SR; 471; Stevens to Hutchings, June 30, 1917, AGC; Rogers to Hutchings, July 14, 1917, AGC; Nolte to Harley, Oct 16, 1917, AGC; Slayden to AG, Oct 25, 1917, AGC; Stevens to Harley, Nov 3, Dec 27, 1917, AGC; AG to Stevens, Nov 30, 1917, AGC; Heywood to Hobby, Aug 28, 1918, WC; Hanson to AG, Jan 29, 1919, WC; Canales to Joint Investigation Committee, Feb 3, 1919, WC; Hobby to Harley, May 19, 1919, WC; Stevens to Hanson, June 11, 1919, AGC; Stevens to AG, Dec 1, 1919, AGC; Stevens to Hobby, Feb 3, 1920, AGC; Aldrich to Moore, Aug 8, 1920, AGC; 1: 1323; U.S. District Court, El Paso, No. 1307, FRC-FW; Stevens file, 137; SAE, Mar 5, 11, Sept 30, 1911, Jan 14, Feb 26, 1913, June 30, 1916; BDH, Sept 5, 1912; EPMT, Mar 14, 1913; AS, Nov 17, 28, Dec 1, 1910, Apr 3, 1911; HC, Jan 8, 1922; AA, Mar 13, June 5, 1919; 463: 53; A1a, b, d, e; A2b.*

STEWART, JOHN WILLIAM. Born Sept. 30, 1872, Gabriel Mills, Williamson County, Texas. Ht. 5 ft. 8 in., brown eyes, brown hair, red complexion, married. Constable, Sweetwater, Nolan County, Texas. REGULAR RANGER Apr. 11, 1918–Apr. 11, 1918 (private, Co. C). Honorably discharged. REMARKS: Was enlisted and honorably discharged the same day. Had been a deputy sheriff and constable for the past 7 or 8 years. In 1920 lived in Hylton, Nolan County. In 1930 was a farmer in San Angelo, Tom Green County, Texas. One source states died Jan. 30, 1946, Potter County, Texas. Other sources list a John William Stewart who died May 10, 1959, Tom Green County, Texas. (Note: See entry for Ranger William "Bill" Stewart.) FAMILY: Parents, William Jefferson Stewart (b. 1846, TN) and Sarah Catherine Perry (b. 1841, AL); siblings, Bolin Christopher (b. 1864, TX), Arminta Frances (b. 1867, TX), Luna (b. 1869, TX), Sarah Martha (b. 1870, TX); spouse, Iona Rose Looney (b. 1873, TX), married Apr. 19, 1891, Williamson County; children, Mattie Caroline (b. 1892, TX), Ola M. (b. 1894, TX), Joseph A. (b. 1896, TX), twins Bolin S. and Bill A. (b. 1902, TX), Ruben M. "Rube" (b. 1906, TX), George M. (b. 1909, TX), Clarence D. (b. 1913, TX). *SR; A1a, b, d, e, f, g; A2b; A4b.*

STEWART, WILLIAM "BILL." Born Sept. or Oct. 1872, Williamson County, Texas. Ht. 5 ft. 8 in., brown eyes, brown hair, ruddy complexion, married. Stock farmer and peace officer, Hylton, Nolan County, Texas. LOYALTY RANGER June 10, 1918–Jan. 13, 1919. REMARKS: As of Mar. 1919 had been a Nolan County peace officer for 8 years. Note: This man, Ranger William "Bill" Stewart, may well be the same man as Ranger John William Stewart, above. Compare similarities in physical and other descriptions of the two men. Also, there is no census or other documentation fitting the time/place descriptions specific to a William "Bill" Stewart. *SR.*

STILLWELL, WILLIAM P. Born Feb. 24, 1870, Live Oak County, Texas. Ht. 5 ft. 11 in., gray eyes, brown hair, light complexion, married. Stockman, enlisted in Brewster County, Texas. REGULAR RANGER Feb. 15, 1918–Apr. 3, 1918 (private, Co. F). Killed in action, Apr. 3, 1918, at Santa Elena, Brewster County, Texas on the Rio Grande. REMARKS: Foreman of Piedras Blancas Ranch, 1915. Buried in Alpine, Brewster County. FAMILY: Parents, John Stillwell (b. 1832, MS) and Emily Kay (b. 1839, TX); siblings, Elizabeth Cornelias (b. 1860, TX), Lela or Lola (b. 1864, Mexico), Alice L. (b. 1866, TX), John E. (b. 1868, TX), Joseph (b. 1872, TX), Nellie Darcus (b. 1874, TX), Robert Roy (b. 1878, TX), Charles Olin (b. 1881, TX); spouse, Meddie Bennett (b. 1876, TX), married June 5, 1897, Alpine; daughters, Bernice (b. 1902, TX), Willie Jack (b. 1904, TX). *SR; 471; Bates to Harley, Apr 3, 4, 6, 1918, AGC; Harley to Bates, Apr 3, 1918, AGC; Harley to Bates, Apr 15, 1918, RRM; AA, Apr 4,11, Aug 1, 1918; A1b, d, e; A2b; A4a; B1.*

STILWELL, DUDLEY VICTOR "BUD." Born June 23, 1891, Corpus Christi, Nueces County, Texas. Ht. 6 ft. 1 ½ in., brown eyes, brown hair, fair complexion. Ranchman, Kingsville, Kleberg County, Texas. SPECIAL RANGER Jan. 29, 1916–May 8, 1916. Placed on active duty. REGULAR RANGER May 9, 1916–June 30, 1916 (private, Co. D). Resigned. Ranchman, enlisted in Jim Hogg County, Texas. SPECIAL RANGER Dec. 21, 1917–June 1918. REMARKS: As of Jan. 1916, had served as deputy sheriff and constable.

In Jan. 1916 was a King Ranch employee. In 1917 worked for Tom T. East, Kingsville; this was Stilwell's mailing address. Died Oct. 28, 1918, Kleberg County, Texas. *SR; 471; Scarborough to Hutchings, Jan 29, 1916, AGC; AG to Scarborough, Jan 31, 1916, AGC; AG to Kleberg, Jan 13, 14, 1916, AGC; Kleberg to Hutchings, Jan 12, 1916, AGC; Hutchings to Kleberg, Jan 14, 1916, AGC; AG to Ferguson, Jan 21, 1916, AGC; Stilwell to AG, Feb 26, Apr 4, 1916, AGC; Scarborough to Hutchings, July 5, 1916, AGC; AG to East, Dec 6, 1917, AGC; Capt. Will Wright's report, Mar 7, 1918, WC; Assistant AG to East, June 3, 18, 1918, AGC; East to Woodul [June, 1918?], AGC; Kingsville Record, Sept 25, 1914, Apr 30, May 7, Sept 3, 1915; A2b; A3a.*

STINSON, JAMES P. Born June 1871, Rusk, Cherokee County, Texas. Ht. 5 ft. 11 in., blue eyes, brown hair, fair complexion, married. Attorney, Anson, Jones County, Texas. SPECIAL RANGER May 31, 1917–Dec. 1917 (attached to Co. C). REMARKS: In 1920 and 1930 was a lawyer in Abilene, Jones County, Texas. FAMILY: Parents, Tom C. Stinson (b. 1847, TN) and Nancy Ann Morris (b. 1849, AL); siblings, George A. (b. 1874, TX), Amy P. (b. 1879, TX), Joseph C. (b. 1881, TX), Lee (b. 1888, TX), Eula Maggie (b. 1890, TX); spouse, Leta Morgan (b. 1879, MO), married about 1904; daughters, Jimti (b. 1905, TX), Laura Jane (b. 1906, TX). *SR; Dodson to Ferguson, May 18, 1917, AGC; Cunningham to Ferguson, May 18, 197, AGC; A1b, e, f, g; A2b; A4b.*

STOCKTON, JAMES T. Born 1879, Hopkins, Nodaway County, Missouri. Ht. 5 ft. 10 ½ in., gray eyes, brown hair, fair complexion, married. Assistant Quartermaster General, Texas National Guard, Austin, Travis County, Texas. REGULAR RANGER Feb. 1, 1917–Sept. 1, 1917 (captain, Quartermaster of the Rangers). Resigned—was called into federal service as a Major, Quartermaster Corps. Colonel, Texas National Guard, Austin. SPECIAL RANGER Feb. 24, 1933–[Feb. 24, 1935 ?]. FAMILY: Spouse, Erma or Vance L. (b. 1888, AR). *SR; 471; A1f, g.*

STOGNER, WALTER EDWARD. (Listed in Ranger Service Records as STAGNER.) Born Feb. 22, 1879, Comanche County, Texas. Medium height, stout, blue eyes, light hair, married. City marshal, Lamesa, Dawson County, Texas. LOYALTY RANGER June 10, 1918–Feb. 1919. REMARKS: In 1920 and 1930 was a carpenter in Lamesa. Died Nov. 28, 1962, Lamesa, Dawson County, Texas. FAMILY: Parents, Thomas Lee Stogner (b. 1851, NC) and Rebeka Loney Dickerson (b. 1858, AL); siblings, Samantha (b. 1875, AR), Charley (b. 1877, TX), Dollie (b. 1884, TX); stepmother, Sarah Hines (b. 1868, AR); spouse, Minnie Mae McGee (b. 1884, TX), married Dec. 23, 1902, Comanche, Comanche County; children, Flora Loveless (b. 1904, TX), Talma Lorene (b. 1906, TX), Eunice Mae (b. 1910, TX), Charles Lee (b. 1912, TX), Norris Edward (b. 1915, TX), Walter Wallace (b. 1919, TX), Bettie Katrina (b. 1922, TX). *SR; A1b, d, f, g; A2b; A3a; A4a.*

STOKES, JOHN BUFORD. Born Dec. 16, 1865, Oxford, Calhoun County, Alabama. No physical description, married. Merchant, Wichita Falls, Wichita County, Texas. LOYALTY RANGER May 31, 1918–Feb. 1919. REMARKS: Had been manager of the water and light company in Wichita Falls. In 1920 was a real estate salesman in Wichita Falls. In 1930 was manager of the electric company in Wichita Falls. Died Aug. 8, 1950, Wichita County, Texas. FAMILY: Parents, William Lunsford Stokes (b. 1832, SC) and Frances Ann Letitia "Fannie" Gwin (b. 1845, SC); siblings, Timie (b. 1862, AL), Della (b. 1869, AL), Thomas Lunsford (b. 1871, AL), Pliney G. (b. 1874, AL); spouse, Lula G. Deamon (b. 1861, AL), married about 1887; children, Joe Buford (b. 1889, TX), Julia (b. 1895, TX), Zula H. (b. 1902, TX). *SR; A1b, e, f, g; A2b; A4b; B1.*

STONE, CLIFFORD LEMUEL. Born Dec. 18, 1882, Rusk County, Texas. Ht. 6 ft. 1 in., blue eyes, dark hair, light complexion. Peace officer, enlisted in Smith County, Texas. REGULAR RANGER May 5, 1909–unknown (private, Co. C). REMARKS: Rusk County sheriff Nov. 8, 1904–Nov. 3, 1908. Was a lawyer in Henderson, Rusk County. Had been a state representative from Henderson. As of Sept. 1918 was a district attorney living in Henderson. In 1920 was a Texas assistant attorney general in Henderson. In 1930 was "chief, gas utility division" living in Austin, Travis County, Texas. Died June 7, 1940, Rusk County, Texas. FAMILY: Parents, Wm. D. Stone (b. 1856, TX) and Martha J. "Pattie" (b. 1856, TX); siblings, Jessie (b. 1878, TX), Margie (b. 1883, TX), John Reagan (b. 1886, TX), Jeanette (b. 1890, TX), Emerson (b. 1894, TX); spouse, Nanette Wallace (b. 1892, TX), married about 1916; daughters, Mildred L. (b. 1918, TX), Jane (b. 1925, TX). *SR; Stone to York, Apr 2, 1914,*

AGC; Smith to Hutchings, Apr 16, 1914, AGC; 1503:445; A1b, d, e, f, g; A2b; A3a.

STONE JOHN W. Born Sept. 1867, Fisherville, Augusta County, Virginia. Ht. 5 ft. 10 in., brown eyes, brown hair, dark complexion, married. Real estate and oil, Wichita Falls, Wichita County, Texas. LOYALTY RANGER June 1, 1918–Mar. 6, 1919. REMARKS: Had been the chief train dispatcher in Wichita Falls. 1919 letterhead: "J. W. Stone, Real Estate and Insurance, Wichita Falls." In 1930 still a real estate agent in Wichita Falls. A J. W. Stone died Aug. 27, 1934, Wichita County, Texas. FAMILY: Parents, Henry F. Stone (b. 1829, VA) and Martha J. (b. 1842, VA); siblings, Henry E. (b. 1857, VA), Mary Ann (b. 1861, VA), Luella C. (b. 1869, VA), Adelia (b. 1871, VA), Benjamin F. (b. 1873, VA), Jas. Watson (b. 1874, VA); spouse, Florence C. (b. 1871, GA), married about 1891; children, Jerome S. (b. 1892, TX), Helen (b. 1897, TX), John W. (b. 1899, TX), Robert A. (b. 1904, TX). *SR; A1a, b, d, e, f, g; A2b, c.*

STONER, GEORGE OVERTON, JR. Born Sept. 5, 1889, Victoria, Victoria County, Texas. Ht. 5 ft. 4 ½ in., blue eyes, blond hair, light complexion. Brand inspector, Cattle Raisers' Association of Texas, Houston, Harris County, Texas. SPECIAL RANGER Aug. 4, 1919–Dec. 31, 1919; June 5, 1926–Feb. 1, 1927; Feb. 19, 1927–Feb. 19, 1928; Feb. 19, 1928–Feb. 2, 1929; Feb. 6, 1929–Jan. 13, 1932 (reenlisted Jan. 16, 1930, Jan. 13, 1931); Jan. 30, 1932–Jan. 18, 1933; June 7, 1935–Oct. 1935. REMARKS: Was a brand inspector for the Cattle Raisers' Association of Texas as early as Aug. 1911, at Victoria. He was commissioned as a SPECIAL RANGER in Aug. 1919 at the request of Moses & Rowe, the attorneys for the Cattle Raisers' Association. Died of cancer Aug. 30, 1972, Houston, Harris County, Texas; buried in Evergreen Cemetery, Victoria. FAMILY: Parents, George Overton Stoner (b. 1847, TN) and Zilpa Rose Summers (b. 1850, TX); siblings, Margaret M. (b. 1870), Nannie Ulalume (b. 1872), Tillitha Imogene (b. 1874, TX); Blanche Elizabeth (b. 1876, TX), Michael Lowery (b. 1878, TX), Zilpha Evelyn (b. 1880), Kate Carlisle (b. 1883, TX), Mame Victoria (b. 1886, TX), Victor Rose (b. 1893, TX); spouse, Dana May Daniel (b. 1899, OK). *SR; 471; EPMT, Aug 19, Dec 2, 1911, Aug 1, 1913; A1d, e; A2a, b; A3a; A4a, b; B1.*

STOOPS, HARMON CLETE "CLETE." Born Apr. 26, 1880, Lamar County, Texas. Ht. 5 ft. 9 in., blue eyes, brown hair, medium complexion, married. Merchant, Riviera, Kleberg County, Texas. SPECIAL RANGER May 14, 1918–Nov. 1918. WA was cancelled—he had moved out of Kleberg County. REMARKS: Had been elected constable, precinct 2, Kleberg County, in June 1913. As of Sept. 1918 was a machinist in Mission, Hidalgo County, Texas. In 1920 worked in a blacksmith shop in Mission. In 1930 was a citrus farmer in Hidalgo County. Died Dec. 22, 1950, Hidalgo County, Texas. FAMILY: Parents, Jas. A. Stoops (b. 1858, AR) and Lucy D. (b. 1862, TX); siblings, Charles W. (b. 1883, TX), William J. E. (b. 1888, TX), Gertrude M. (b. 1892, TX), Birdie L. (b. 1893, TX); spouse, Anna Nora (b. 1887, TX), married about 1906; children, E. Lucille (b. 1910, TX), Harmon C. (b. 1912, TX), Melrose (b. 1914, TX), Anita L. (b. 1922, TX). *SR; BDH, June 30, 1913; A1b, d, f, g; A2b; A3a.*

STOUDENMIER, C. SAMUEL. Born Feb. 1851, Aberfoil, Alabama. Ht. 6 ft., blue eyes, light hair, light complexion, married. Trader, Eagle Pass, Maverick County, Texas. SPECIAL RANGER Sept. 30, 1915–unknown (attached to Co. C). REMARKS: Had operated a livery stable and been the proprietor of a pool and billiard hall in Llano, Llano County, Texas. Still living in Llano County in 1920. LAW ENFORCEMENT RELATIVES: El Paso marshal (before 1882) Dallas Stoudenmier, brother. FAMILY: Parents, Lewis Stoudenmier (b. 1784, SC) and Elizabeth (b. 1809, NC); siblings, Abednago (b. 1827, AL), Meshak (b. 1829, AL), Morgan Green (b. 1831, AL), John (b. 1837, AL), Malania Alabama (b. 1839, AL), Virginia (b. 1841, AL), Dallas (b. 1841, AL), Samuel's twin, Elizabeth C. (b. 1851, AL); spouse #1, unknown; spouse #2, Anna Lou Brown (b. 1859, TX), married Feb. 23, 1882, Llano County; children, Alice E. (b. 1883, TX), Dallas P. (b. 1884, TX), Samuel W. (b. 1888, TX), Johnie M. (b. 1889, TX), Harry L. (b. 1901, TX). *SR; Linden to Ferguson, Sept 11, 1915, AGC; AG to Stoudenmier, Sept 21, 1915, AGC; Ferguson to Hutchings, Sept 21, 1915, AGC; A1aaa, aa, d, e, f; A2e; A4b.*

STOVALL, ELMER JOSEPH. Born Sept. 27, 1897, Terrell, Kaufman County, Texas. Ht. 5 ft. 6 in., blue eyes, brown hair, dark complexion. Soldier, Terrell. REGULAR RANGER Mar. 1, 1921–Sept. 8, 1921 (private, Co. C). Discharged. Rancher, Dallas, Dallas County, Texas. RAILROAD RANGER

July 30, 1922–Feb. 26, 1923. Discharged. REMARKS: Went into the army when he was 16; as of Mar. 1921 had served 6 yrs in U.S. Army, with General Pershing in Mexico and during World War I in Germany and France. In 1920 had been a private 1st class, a "horseshoer," stationed at Camp Marfa in Presidio County, Texas; in Mar. 1921 was stationed at Eagle Pass, Maverick County, Texas. Was charged with assault to murder for shooting a black allegedly attempting to escape. In 1930 was a U.S. Immigration inspector in Presidio, Presidio County; served 25 years in the Immigration and Naturalization Service. Was a railroad special officer in Big Spring, Howard County, Texas, then chief deputy sheriff for 2 years. Died Dec. 30, 1985, Tarrant County, Texas. FAMILY: Parents, Joseph Elam Stovall (b. 1868, TX) and Tibitha "Randy" Lindsey (b. 1870, TX); siblings, Minnie (b. 1888, TX), Frank J. (b. 1889, TX), Crowell (b. 1893, TX); spouse, Beatrice Alice Bebbe (b. 1904, TX), married about 1922; children, Charleen (b. 1924, TX), Dawn or Don Joe (b. 1930, TX). *SR; 471; LWT, Apr 3, 1921; A1d, f, g; A2a, b, e; A4a, b; B1.*

STRAIT, JOHN SAMUEL. Born Feb. 13, 1884, Yancey, Medina County, Texas. Ht. 5 ft. 9 in., gray eyes, brown hair, red complexion. Stockman, Big Wells, Dimmit County, Texas. SPECIAL RANGER May 1, 1918–Jan. 15, 1919. REMARKS: Apr. 1918 was a Dimmit County deputy sheriff; Sheriff Gardner requested a Special Ranger commission for him. On Service Record is "Discharged June 18"—crossed out. Died Oct. 21, 1964, Frio County, Texas. LAW ENFORCEMENT RELATIVES: Ranger Y. C. Strait, brother. FAMILY: Parents, John Joseph Strait (b. 1848, AL) and Martha Eudora "Mattie" Kilgore (b. 1851, TX); siblings, Jesse Byron (b. 1877, TX), twins Viola Belle and Ofelia Dell (b. 1878, TX), Alma Laura (b. 1881, TX), Yancey Clarence (b. 1886, TX); spouse, Winnifred Baugh (b. 1893, TX), married Aug. 6, 1918, Baugh Ranch; son, John Byron (b. 1922, TX). *SR; 471; Assistant AG to Gardner, Apr 25, 1918, AGC; A1b, d, e, f; A2a, b; A3a; A4a, b; B1, 2.*

STRAIT, YANCEY CLARENCE. Born Oct. 5, 1886, Medina County, Texas. Ht. 5 ft. 10 in., dark eyes, dark hair, dark complexion, married. Stockman, Big Wells, Dimmit County, Texas. SPECIAL RANGER May 29, 1918–Jan. 15, 1919. REMARKS: 1919 was a Dimmit County deputy sheriff. Died Dec. 30, 1972, Frio County, Texas; buried in Big Wells. LAW ENFORCEMENT RELATIVES: Ranger John S. Strait, brother. FAMILY: Parents, John Joseph Strait (b. 1848, AL) and Martha Eudora "Mattie" Kilgore (b. 1851, TX); siblings, Jesse Byron (b. 1877, TX), twins Viola Belle and Ofelia Dell (b. 1878, TX), Alma Laura (b. 1881, TX), John S. (b. 1884, TX); spouse, Marie Vesper (b. 1890, TX), married Jan. 28, 1914, San Antonio, Bexar County, Texas; children, Mattie Louise (b. 1915, TX), Bernice Marie (b. 1919, TX), Yancey Clarence (b. 1921, TX), Charles Vesper (b. 1924, TX), John Joseph (b. 1926, TX). *SR; 471; A1b, d, e, f; A2a, b, e; A3a; A4a, b; B1, 2.*

STUBBS, TARPLEY J. Born July 1875, Ashland, Clay County, Alabama. Ht 5 ft. 8 ½ in., gray eyes, brown hair, dark complexion, married. Merchant, Anson, Jones County, Texas. SPECIAL RANGER May 31, 1917–Dec. 1917 (attached to Co. C). Merchant, Anson. LOYALTY RANGER June 1, 1918–Feb. 1919. REMARKS: Had been a cowpuncher; in 1900 had been a stock raiser in Eddy County, New Mexico. Was endorsed by the Jones County sheriff. FAMILY: Parents, William M. Stubbs (b. 1834, GA) and Emily Banks or Gibson (b. 1836, GA); siblings, Eugenia (b. 1862, AL), William Fannie (b. 1865, AL), Enos Sherman (b. 1867, AL), Martin (b. 1868, AL), Raymond (b. 1869, AL), Ellen (b. 1872, AL), George Fernando (b. 1879, AL); spouse, unknown, married about 1907. *SR; Dodson to Ferguson, May 18, 1917, AGC; Cunningham to Ferguson, May 18, 1917, AGCl; A1a, b, d, e; A4a, b.*

STUCKLER, EDWARD P. Born Oct. 1862, San Antonio, Bexar County, Texas. Ht. 5 ft. 10 in., blue eyes, gray hair, fair complexion. Cowman, Saragosa, Reeves County, Texas. LOYALTY RANGER June 3, 1918–Mar. 6, 1919. REMARKS: Had been a Reeves County deputy sheriff, 1911. An Edward Peter Stuckler died Jan. 23, 1949, Pecos County, Texas. FAMILY: Parents, William Stuckler (b. 1829, Austria) and Antonia Kriticzka (b. 1839, Prussia); siblings, William (b. 1860, TX), Paul (b. 1864, TX), Frederick Adolph (b. 1866, TX), Arthur Maximilian (b. 1868, TX), Antonie Marie (b. 1871, TX), Anna Laura (b. 1873, TX), Mary Luisa (b. 1876, TX); spouse, unknown; son, Edward Paul (b. 1897, TX). *SR; SAE, Sept 3, 1911; EPMT, Nov 4, 1911; A1a, d; A2b; A3a, b; A4a, b.*

STURGIS, DAWES ELIOT. Born Nov. 1, 1876, New Bedford, Bristol County, Massachusetts. Ht. 5 ft. 7 ½ in., hazel eyes, black hair, dark complexion, married. Deputy sheriff, Houston, Harris County, Texas. LOYALTY RANGER June 27, 1918–Mar. 6, 1919. REMARKS: As of June 1918 had served as a deputy sheriff for 7 years. In 1910 and 1920 was a jewelry merchant in Houston. In 1930 was a Harris County tax assessor. Died Feb. 25, 1944, Harris County, Texas. FAMILY: Parents, Appleton Sturgis (b. 1843, MD) and Emily Lamb Eliot (b. 1851, MA); siblings, Elizabeth N. (b. 1872, MA), Russell (b. 1874, NY), Arthur B. (b. 1879, MA); spouse #1, Daisy (b. 1876, TX), married about 1903; children, Daisy E. (b. 1904, TX), Ellen K. (b. 1905, TX), Mary Frances (b. 1906, TX); spouse #2, Fannie A. Bryan (b. 1873, TX), married about 1913. *SR; A1b, e, f, g; A2b; A3a; A4b.*

SULLENGER, ROBERT GIDEON. Born May 4, 1873, Pilot Grove, Grayson County, Texas. Ht. 5 ft. 9 in., dark eyes, dark hair, dark complexion. Special agent, FW&DC Railroad, Amarillo, Potter County, Texas. SPECIAL RANGER Jan. 2, 1918–Jan. 15, 1919. Special officer, FW&DC Railroad, Amarillo. RAILROAD RANGER Nov. 18, 1922–Nov. 18, 1924. Discharged. Special officer, FW&DC Railroad, Amarillo. SPECIAL RANGER July 13, 1925–July 13, 1927; Aug. 18, 1927–Aug. 18, 1928; Sept. 13, 1928–Sept. 13, 1929; Sept. 16, 1929–Sept. 16, 1930; Sept. 16, 1930–Sept. 16, 1931; Sept. 23, 1931–Jan. 18, 1933; Feb. 15,1933–Dec. 4, 1934. REMARKS: As of Jan. 1918, had been a deputy sheriff and deputy constable for 7 years. Died Dec. 4, 1934, Potter County, Texas. FAMILY: Parents, Gabriel T. Sullenger (b. 1823, KY) and Louisa Jane Trout (b. 1832, GA); siblings, Mary A. (b. 1851, TX), Alice (b. 1854, TX), Henrietta (b. 1857, TX), Gustavus (b. 1861, TX), Ruben (b. 1865, TX), Walter William (b. 1866, TX), Richard (b. 1870, TX), Laura Ophelia (b. 1875, TX); spouse, Bertha Texas Nichols (b. 1881, TX), married about 1900; children, Jewell Serena (b. 1902, TX), Ruel Arthur (b. 1904, TX), Ruth Anita (b. 1915, TX). *SR; AG to Barnett, Dec 27, 1917, AGC; A1a, d, e, f, g; A2b; A3a; A4a.*

SULLIVAN, HENRY EDWARD. Born Jan. 14, 1886, San Patricio, San Patricio County, Texas. Ht. 6 ft., gray eyes, dark brown hair, dark complexion, married. Brand inspector, Cattle Raisers' Association of Texas, Kingsville, Kleberg County, Texas. SPECIAL RANGER July 1916–Dec. 1917 (?); Jan. 2, 1918–Jan. 15, 1919. REMARKS: In 1913–1914 was a brand inspector for the Cattle Raisers' Association, at Sinton, San Patricio County. In 1930 was a ranch foreman in San Patricio County. Died Mar. 8, 1965, San Patricio County, Texas. LAW ENFORCEMENT RELATIVES: Ranger J. P. Sullivan, brother. FAMILY: Parents, Joseph E. Sullivan (b. 1845, NJ) and Theodia or Theresa Holly (b. 1850, Austria); siblings, Joseph E., Jr. (b. 1873, TX), John Pius (b. 1878, TX), J. R. (b. 1880, TX), Rachel Amelia "Millie" (b. 1882, TX); spouse, Sarah Josephine McFall (b. 1887, TX), married Jan. 11, 1913, San Patricio County; children, Josephine (b. 1915, TX), Mildred (b. 1915, TX), Ada Catherine (b. 1917, TX), Henry E., Jr. (b. 1918, TX), J. C. (b. 1921, TX), Natalie (b. 1923, TX), Arlene (b. 1926, TX). *SR; Scarborough to Hutchings, July 14, 1916, AGC; AG to Scarborough, July 8, 17, 1916, AGC; EPMT, Aug 1, 1913; BDH, Aug 24, Oct 8, 1914; A1d, e, f, g; A2a, b, e; A3a; A4b; B1, 2.*

SULLIVAN, JOHN F. Born Dec. 31, 1892, Muldoon, Fayette County, Texas. Ht. 5 ft. 11 in., blue eyes, light brown hair, ruddy complexion. Storekeeper, Austin, Travis County, Texas. SPECIAL RANGER Feb. 1, 1917–unknown. REMARKS: "Lunatic Asylum Eng. Dept." As of June 1917 was sergeant 4th class, a mechanic at the state arsenal, Camp Mabry, Austin. *SR; A3a.*

SULLIVAN, JOHN PIUS. Born Feb. 9, 1878, San Patricio, San Patricio County, Texas. Medium height, slender, blue eyes, light brown hair, married. Stockman, Falfurrias, Brooks County, Texas. SPECIAL RANGER July 19, 1918–Jan. 15, 1919. REMARKS: Had lived in Starr County, Texas. In 1930 was a state tick inspector in Brooks County. LAW ENFORCEMENT RELATIVES: Ranger Henry E. Sullivan, brother. FAMILY: Parents, Joseph E. Sullivan (b. 1845, NJ) and Theodia or Theresa Holly (b. 1850, Austria); siblings, Joseph E., Jr. (b. 1873, TX), J. R. (b. 1880, TX), Rachel Amelia "Millie" (b. 1882, TX), Henry E. (b. 1886, TX); spouse, Hanna Elizabeth (b. 1881, TX), married about 1904; children, Margaret (b. 1905, TX), Francis (b. 1908, TX), John (b. 1911, TX), Bernard (b. 1917, TX). *SR; A1b, d, e, f, g; A3a; A4b.*

SULLIVAN, MONTEREY "MONTIE" "RAY." Born July 29, 1885, Luling, Caldwell County, Texas. Ht. 5 ft. 10 in., brown eyes, black hair, dark complexion. Farmer, Luling. REGULAR RANGER Sept. 28, 1915–Jan. 10, 1916 (private, Co. A). Resigned. REMARKS: In Sept. 1918 was a carpenter in Gonzales County, Texas. In 1930 was a farmer in San Saba County, Texas. Died Nov. 30, 1971, Blanco County, Texas. FAMILY: Father, "Ike" Sullivan (b. 1862, TX or MO); spouse, Bertha (b. 1890, TX), married about 1924. *SR; 471; BDH, Oct 11, 1915; A1e, g; A2a, b; A3a.*

SULLIVAN, MORGAN ELZA. Born June 30, 1874, Burnet, Burnet County, Texas. Ht. 5 ft. 8 in., brown eyes, dark hair, dark complexion, married. Deputy sheriff, Lometa, Lampasas County, Texas. SPECIAL RANGER July 3, 1918–Jan. 15, 1919. Barber, Lometa. RAILROAD RANGER Sept. 1, 1922–Nov. 6, 1922. Discharged. REMARKS: Had been an acting deputy sheriff and a night watchman. A Morgan E. Sullivan died June 10, 1938, Taylor County, Texas. FAMILY: Parents, Louis Sullivan (b. 1840, Texas) and Lydia (b. 1851, GA); sisters, Sonora (b. 1876, TX), Maude (b. 1879, TX); spouse, Alice Gertrude "Alla" Templeton (b. 1880, TX), married June 25, 1905, Llano County, Texas; children, James Louis (b. 1908, TX), Rhita Jeanette (b. 1910, TX), Dainty Bell (b. 1913, TX). *SR; A1b, f; A2b; A3a; A4b; B1, 2.*

SULZBACHER, LAURENCE I. Born Oct. 8, 1888, San Antonio, Bexar County, Texas. Ht. 5 ft. 4 ¾ in., brown eyes, brown hair, dark complexion. REGULAR RANGER Dec. 12, 1917–Jan. 1, 1918 (private, Co. G). Resigned. REMARKS: Note length of service. Clerk, 4 yrs. as stockman. Stated: "If drafted I will resign." In 1920 was a government filing clerk in San Antonio. In 1930 was a customs inspector in San Antonio. FAMILY: Parents, Nathan Sulzbacher (b. 1861, NY) and Sara Moke (b. 1861, TX); sisters, Hermine (b. 1893, TX), Valerie (b. 1894, TX), Aline (b. 1901, TX). *SR; 471; Stevens to Harley, Dec 13, 1917, AGC; AG to Stevens, Dec 14, 1917, AGC; A1e, f, g; A2b, h; A3a.*

SUMMERS, JAMES WILLIAM. Born June 18, 1875, Wilson, Tennessee. Medium height, medium build, blue eyes, brown hair, married. Farmer, Gatesville, Coryell County, Texas. LOYALTY RANGER June 3, 1918–Feb. 1919. REMARKS: Was still a farmer in Coryell County in 1930. A John William Summers died Mar. 29, 1960, Coryell County, Texas. FAMILY: Spouse, Sara Ollie Britain (b. 1877, TX), married about 1899. *SR; A1e, f, g; A2b; A3a.*

SUMRALL, ROBERT WILLIAM. Born Nov. 28, 1893, Ballinger, Runnels County, Texas. Ht. 6 ft., gray eyes, light brown hair, light complexion, married, as of Sept. 1931. Ranchman, Alpine, Brewster County, Texas. REGULAR RANGER Dec. 8, 1919–Dec. 31, 1928 (private, Co. E; transferred to Co. A, Feb. 15, 1921; reenlisted Dec. 8, 1921; reenlisted Dec. 8, 1923; reenlisted Dec. 8, 1925; reenlisted Dec. 8, 1927). Resigned. Peace officer, Presidio, Presidio County, Texas. REGULAR RANGER Sept. 1, 1931–Jan. 18, 1933. REMARKS: In 1930 worked in the county sheriff's office, Coleman County, Texas. A Robert W. Sumrall died Sept. 29, 1944, Tom Green County, Texas. FAMILY: Parents, James Vining Sumrall (b. 1864, TX) and Viola Ross (b. 1869, TX); siblings, Giles Arnold (b. 1887, TX), Calvin Edgar (b. 1889, TX), Thomas Hampton (b. 1891, TX), Naomi Ruth (b. 1895, TX), James Alvin (b. 1898, TX), Laura Dail (b. 1901, TX), Frank Ellis (b. 1904, TX), Melvin Riley (b. 1907, TX); spouse, Lula Vivian Holder (b. 1904, TX), married Jan. 30, 1927, Garden City, Glasscock County, Texas; children, Robert Kent (b. 1928, TX), Shirley (b. 1930, TX), Tex Holder (b. 1933, TX). *SR; 471; 319: 200; 470: 43; 488: 58; A1d, e, g; A2b, e; A3c; A4a, b; B1, 2.*

SUTTON, CLAUD R. Born Dec. 27, 1887, near Llano, Llano County, Texas. Ht. 6 ft. 1 in., gray eyes, brown hair, light complexion. Lawyer, Marfa, Presidio County, Texas. SPECIAL RANGER June 6, 1917–July 9, 1917. Resigned. REMARKS: Note length of service. Had been a public school teacher in Menard County, Texas. In 1930 was district judge in Presidio County. A Claude R. Sutton died Dec. 20, 1958, Dallas County, Texas. LAW ENFORCEMENT RELATIVES: Ranger J. F. Sutton, brother. FAMILY: Parents, Ambers Likens Sutton (b. 1857, AR) and Sarah Elizabeth Long (b. 1858, TX); siblings, Albert B. (b. 1875, TX), Silas Perry or Peter (b. 1878, TX), Maude Lee (b. 1885, TX), John Floyd (b. 1890, TX), Carl Noble (b. 1894, TX); spouse, Willie Colbert Mimms (b. 1897, MS), married about 1919; sons, Claud R., Jr. (b. 1920, TX), William Mimms (b. 1922, TX), Bruce Colbert (b. 1927, TX), Joseph Wilson (b. 1929, TX). *SR; A1d, e, f, g; A2b, e; A3a; A4a, b; B1.*

SUTTON, JOHN FLOYD. Born May 26, 1890, Kingsland, Llano County, Texas. Ht. 6 ft. 2 in., gray eyes, black hair, dark complexion, married. Lawyer, Alpine, Brewster County, Texas. LOYALTY RANGER June 4, 1918–Feb. 1919. REMARKS: In 1930 was an attorney in San Angelo, Tom Green County, Texas. Died Apr. 4, 1973, Tom Green County,

Texas. LAW ENFORCEMENT RELATIVES: Ranger C. R. Sutton, brother. FAMILY: Parents, Ambers Likens Sutton (b. 1857, AR) and Sarah Elizabeth Long (b. 1858, TX); siblings, Albert B. (b. 1875, TX), Silas Perry or Peter (b. 1878, TX), Maude Lee (b. 1885, TX), Claud R. (b. 1887, TX), Carl Noble (b. 1894, TX); spouse, Pauline Irene Elam (b. 1892, LA), married Dec. 26, 1916, Dallas, Texas; children, John F., Jr. (b. 1917, TX), Dorthy (b. 1924, TX). *SR; A1d, e, f, g; A2a, b; A3a; A4a, b; B1.*

SUTTON, MARTIN VALENTINE "VAL." Born Feb. 14, 1875, Karnes County, Texas. Tall, stout, blue eyes, brown hair, married. Stockman, Pearsall, Frio County, Texas. LOYALTY RANGER Aug. 3, 1918–Feb. 1919. REMARKS: Had been a farmer in Karnes County and Wilson County, Texas. In 1930 was a stock farmer in Pearsall. Died Aug. 23, 1949, Frio County, Texas. LAW ENFORCEMENT RELATIVES: Ranger Robert Bell Sutton, nephew. FAMILY: Parents, James E. Sutton (b. 1845, TX) and Martha Ann "Marthy" Dees (b. 1846, LA); siblings, John William "Johnny" (b. 1871, TX), James Joseph "Joe" (b. 1873, TX), Robert Cook "Robbie" (b. 1877, TX), Walter W. (b. 1880, TX), Jimmie Sells (b. 1883, TX), Lula Mae (b. 1886, TX); spouse, Lillian Grace Johnson (b. 1880, TX), married Oct. 27, 1901, Wilson County, Texas; children, Effie May (b. 1903, TX), Joyce (b. 1909, TX), Frankie (b. 1912, TX), Robbie (b. 1919, TX), R. H. (b. 1923, TX). *SR; A1b, d, e, f, g; A2b; A3a; A4b; B1.*

SUTTON, ROBERT BELL. Born Aug. 26, 1897, Stockdale, Wilson County, Texas. Ht. 5 ft. 11 in., blue eyes, dark hair, dark complexion. Cowboy, enlisted in La Salle County, Texas. REGULAR RANGER Aug. 1, 1918–Mar. 15 [?], 1920 (private, Co. K; reenlisted in Co. D under the new law, June 20, 1919). Resigned. REMARKS: As of Sept. 1918 was a Ranger stationed in Laredo, Webb County, Texas. Died Jan. 5, 1935, Webb County, Texas. LAW ENFORCEMENT RELATIVES: Ranger Martin V. Sutton, uncle. FAMILY: Parents, John William Sutton (b. 1871, TX) and Alice "Allie" Sells (b. 1873, TX); siblings, Eula B. (b. 1895, TX), Jonnie May (b. 1901, TX), William Herbert (b. 1903, TX), Alice E. (b. 1907, TX); stepmother, Lela (b. 1890, TX); sister, Martha Nell (b. 1919, TX). *SR; 471; A1d, e, f; A2b; A3a; B1.*

SWENY, GUY RICHARD. Born Dec. 27, 1882, Montezuma, Poweshiek County, Iowa. Short, medium build, red hair. Farmer and rancher, Spurlock, Sherman County, Texas. LOYALTY RANGER July 20, 1918–Feb. 1919. REMARKS: In 1920 and 1930 was a farmer and stock farmer in Sherman County. Died Mar. 2, 1971, Dumas, Moore County, Texas; buried in Lane Memorial Cemetery, Sunray, Moore County. FAMILY: Parents, Charles Henry Sweny (b. 1859, IA) and Flora Lenora or Leona Bernard (b. 1861, IA); siblings, Ralph B. (b. 1884, IA), Roy Milton (b. 1887, IA), Edythe P. (b. 1890, IA), Meritt (b. 1892, IA), George Dewey (b. 1895, IA), Ethel (b. 1900, IA), Ruth (b. 1902, IA); spouse, Mary Dortch (b. 1892, MO), married about 1921; children, Flora (b. 1923, TX), Billy (b. 1924, TX), Robert Meritt "Bobbie" (b. 1925, TX), Ruby Lea (b. 1927, TX), Jimmie (b. 1929, TX), Carol May (b. 1937, TX). *SR; A1d, e, f, g; A2a, b, e; A3a; B1, 2.*

SWIFT, JOHN BEAKLEY "BEAK." Born Sept. 2, 1883, Fairview, Wilson County, Texas. Ht. 5 ft. 11 in., gray eyes, brown hair, dark complexion, married. Policeman, enlisted in Travis County, Texas. SPECIAL RANGER June 5, 1916–unknown (attached to Co. B and Co. C). REMARKS: Was still attached to Co. B as of Feb. 1917. Later served as a policeman in San Antonio, Bexar County, Texas, for 5 years. In Nov. 1918, worked as a private detective in El Paso, Texas, for T. B. Cunningham. Died Sept. 15, 1959, Floresville, Wilson County; buried at Fairview. LAW ENFORCEMENT RELATIVES: Wilson County Deputy Sheriff Tom Swift, father; Wilson County Deputy Sheriff Will Swift, brother; FBI Agent Erby E. Swift, brother. FAMILY: Parents, Isaac Thomas "Tom" Swift (b. 1852, MO) and Margaret Elizabeth "Maggie" Carver (b. 1859, AR); siblings, Violet Alice (b. 1874, TX), William Thomas (b. 1877, TX), Clarissa Maude (b. 1879, TX), James Edwin (b. 1881, TX), Margaret Ruby (b. 1888, TX), Erby Erwin (b. 1891, TX), Elsie Pearl (b. 1893, TX), Eugenia Louise (b. 1897, TX), Maida (b. 1900, TX), Grady (b. 1904, TX); spouse #1, Ola May (b. 1888, TX), married about 1905; children, Roy J. (b. 1907, TX), Lela M. (b. 1909, TX); spouse #2, Neppie D. (b. 1896, MS), married about 1922. *SR; MR, Co. B, Feb 28, 1917, AGC; Cunningham to Harley, Nov 21, 1918, AGC; 1000: 2, 122–123; A1d, e, f, g; A2b; A4b, g; B1, 2.*

SWIFT, OSCAR GEORGE. Born Dec. 18, 1892, Cuero, DeWitt County, Texas. Ht. 5 ft. 11 in., brown eyes, light brown hair, fair complexion, married. Peace officer, Beaumont, Jefferson County, Texas. SPECIAL RANGER Oct. 5, 1918–Jan. 15, 1919. REMARKS: Was chief of guards, Lone Star Shipbuilding Co., Beaumont. In 1920 was a railroad detective in Houston, Harris County, Texas. An Oscar Swift died Aug. 12, 1948, Harris County, Texas. FAMILY: Parents, Oscar Albert Swift (b. 1863, TX) and Minnie D. Minot (b. 1861, TX); sisters, Katie Lee (b. 1889, TX), Dovie E. (b. 1891, TX), Mabel E. (b. 1897, TX); step-siblings, Minot Andrews (b. 1882, TX), Fannie D. Andrews (b. 1885, TX); spouse, Hada (b. 1891, IA); daughters, Hada M. (b. 1916, TX), Evelyn (b. 1917, TX). *SR; Crawford to Harley, Sept 26, 1918, AGC; A1d, f; A2b; A3a; B1.*

SYLER, ROBERT E. or H. Born Oct. 4, 1879, Muldoon, Fayette County, Texas. Ht. 5 ft. 6 in., blue eyes, dark brown hair, light complexion, married. Railroad brakeman, North Pleasanton, Atascosa County, Texas. SPECIAL RANGER Aug. 15, 1916–unknown. REMARKS: "farm and ranch work; stationary engine work; private in 1st Texas Volunteers during Spanish-American War." Had been a stationary engineer in an oil mill in Coleman, Coleman County, Texas. As of Sept. 1918 was a railroad brakeman in San Antonio, Bexar County, Texas. In 1920 was again a railroad brakeman in Pleasanton. Died Nov. 29, 1944; buried in Harmony Baptist Church Cemetery, Karnes County, Texas. FAMILY: Parents, Thomas Jefferson Syler (b. 1838, TN) and Nancy Caroline Chandler (b. 1841, MO); siblings, Elizabeth J. "Lizzie" (b. 1862, TX), Sarah F. (b. 1864, TX), John Wesley (b. 1868, TX), Willis F. (b. 1870, TX), Clement or Clemmones Alfred (b. 1874, TX), Florence E. (b. 1882, TX); spouse, Claudia Alminta Upton (b. 1880, TX), married June 22, 1904. *SR; A1b, e, f; A3a; A4a, b; B2.*

TABOR, HORACE JAMES. Born Feb. 1871, San Saba County, Texas. No physical description, married. Farmer, Chillicothe, Hardeman County, Texas. LOYALTY RANGER July 13, 1918–Mar. 1919. REMARKS: Had been a farmer in Wichita County, Texas. Died Dec. 19, 1959, Hardeman County, Texas. FAMILY: Parents, Theron M. Tabor (b. 1837, MO) and Carrie Purdy (b. 1845, GA); siblings, Lauro O. (b. 1869, AR), William P. (b. 1873, TX); spouse, Jo Lee "Josie" (b. 1877, TX), married about 1898; children, Carrie B. (b. 1899, TX), Larie W. (b. 1902, TX), Mary Gertrude (b. 1904, TX), Frank Powell (b. 1906, TX), Ida Lee (b. 1909, TX), Horace Joe (b. 1912, TX), Alice (b. 1914, TX), Emily F. (b. 1917, TX). *SR; A1d, e, g; A2b; A4b.*

TACKETT, LOUIS JACKSON. Born Dec. 30, 1880, Delta County, Texas. Ht. 5 ft. 9 ½ in., gray eyes, medium light hair, fair complexion, married. Chief trusty inspector, Austin, Travis County, Texas. SPECIAL RANGER May 3, 1919–Dec. 31, 1919. REMARKS: Had been a nurseryman in Parker County, Texas. In 1920 was an agricultural inspector in Austin. In 1930 was nursery man/floral in Fort Worth, Tarrant County, Texas. Died Sept. 28, 1954, Nolan County, Texas. FAMILY: Parents, John Wesley Tackett (b. 1849, AL) and Nancy Ann Bishop (b. 1849, MS); siblings, William Albert (b. 1871, MS), Louvenia Jane (b. 1873, MS), Nancy Caroline "Callie" (b. 1875, MS), Isaac Elisha (b. 1879, TX), Evan McGarvey "Mack" (b. 1886, TX), Laura (b. 1889, TX); spouse, Leuna E. Brazier (b. 1888, TN), married about 1909; children, Louis Edwin (b. 1909, TX), Laura Leuna (b. 1915, TX), Charles Albert (b. 1916, TX), Ombra Elizabeth (b. 1919, TX), Henry Alpheus (b. 1921, TX), Margaret Ruth (b. 1926, TX). *SR; A1b, e, f, g; A2b, e; A3a; A4a.*

TAGLE, ALBERTO P. Born Jan. 1864, Reynosa, Tamaulipas, Mexico. Ht. 5 ft. 8 in., dark eyes, black hair, dark complexion, married. Deputy sheriff, enlisted at Mercedes, Hidalgo County, Texas. REGULAR RANGER June 1, 1918–Aug. 1, 1918 (private, Co. G). Discharged/fired. REMARKS: Immigrated to the United States in 1875; became a naturalized citizen. As of May 1918, had been a deputy sheriff and "has also been in the employ of the Government for a good many years." On Aug. 1, 1918, Ranger Capt. Charles Stevens suspended Tagle and took away his commission for letting illegal voters vote at Hidalgo and for being against Governor Hobby. Still lived in Hidalgo County in 1930. Alberto Pressiliano [*sic*] Tagle died Dec. 26, 1940, Hidalgo County, Texas. FAMILY: Spouse, Jesusa M. (b. 1868, Mexico), married about 1890; sons, Uvaldo Lorenzo (b. 1891, TX), Alberto, Jr. (b. 1893, TX), Protacio (b. 1898, TX), Alfredo Ernesto (b. 1899, TX), Leoncio (b. 1902, TX), Guillermo (b. 1905, TX), Amadeo (b. 1907, TX), Frank (b. 1910, TX), Daniel (b. 1903, TX); adopted daughter, Maria Gomez (b. 1910, TX). *SR; 471; Stevens to Woodul, May 31, Aug 2, 1918, AGC; A1d, f, g; A2b; A3a.*

TALBOTT, ELLIOTT L. Born Oct. 13, 1884, Frenchtown, Upshur County, West Virginia. Ht. 5 ft. 6 in., blue eyes, light brown hair, light complexion, married. Barber, Big

Wells, Dimmit County, Texas. SPECIAL RANGER Dec. 27, 1917–unknown (Co. C Volunteers). REMARKS: As of Sept. 1918 was a SPECIAL RANGER in Carrizo Springs, Dimmit County. Elliott Lowell Talbott died June 23, 1930, Upshur County, West Virginia. FAMILY: Parents, Lloyd Talbott (b. 1856, WV) and Hester M. Jones (b. 1856, WV); brother, Henry Otis (b. 1877, WV); spouse, Minnie Merle Colerider (b. 1886, WV), married June 20, 1906, Upshur County; children, Virginia, Annie, Evelyn, Alice, Lowell Arthur (b. 1907, WV), Maurice Stanley (b. 1910, WV). *SR; A1d, f, g; A3a; A4a, b.*

TARDY, JOHN TAYLOR. Born Apr. 23, 1892, Martindale, Caldwell County, Texas. Ht. 6 ft., brown eyes, black hair, ruddy complexion. Peace officer, enlisted in Travis County, Texas. SPECIAL RANGER Oct. 2, 1920–Oct. 22, 1920. Discharged. REMARKS: Note length of service. Was also a peace officer in El Paso, El Paso County, Texas. FAMILY: Father, John D. Tardy (b. 1854, MS); siblings, Pina (b. 1882, TX), Allie Mae (b. 1884, TX), Joseph W. (b. 1885, TX), Van (b. 1888, TX). *SR; 471; A1d, e; A3a.*

TATE, FREDERICK W. "FRED." Born Aug. 1860, La Grange, Fayette County, Texas. Ht. 6 ft. 1 in., gray eyes, light brown hair, medium complexion, married. Policeman, Brownsville, Cameron County, Texas. SPECIAL RANGER Apr. 26, 1917–Dec. 1917 (attached to Co. C). REMARKS: Mounted Customs inspector, Brownsville, Rio Grande City, and Roma, 1906–Oct 1915. Resigned. Brownsville traffic cop, 1915–1917; mounted Customs inspector Jan. 1918–Aug. 1, 1918 when killed in line of duty near Brownsville by a Mexican smuggler. Date of death recorded in Texas Death Index, 1903–2000 is Aug. 31, 1918. LAW ENFORCEMENT RELATIVES: Ranger Tom R. Tate, son. FAMILY: Parents, Frederick Tate (b. 1825, AL) and Lucy A. Groom (b. 1831, AL); sisters, Alice (b. 1856, TX), Lucy (b. 1858, TX); spouse, Alice Routh Hopper (b. 1866, TX), married Dec. 7, 1887, Fayette County; children, Thomas R. (b. 1888, TX), William "Billy" (b. 1891, TX), Lucy (b. 1894, TX). *SR; BDH, Feb 2, 1911, Jan 8, 9, 11, May 11, Dec 12, 1912, Dec 16, 1913, July 7, 38, Nov 18, 1914, Jan 15, 29, 30, Feb 1, 19, Apr 23, July 3, Oct 2, Nov 1, 1915, Feb 21, Aug 25, Sept 11, 1916, Feb 26, June 16, Aug 28, 1917, Jan 9, May 7, Sept 2, 6, 9, 1918; Hanson to Harley, Aug 1, 1918, WC; 319: 348; 485: 178–179; A1aa, a, b, d, e; A2b; A4b; B1.*

TATE, THOMAS R. "TOM." Born Nov. 1, 1888, La Grange, Fayette County, Texas. Ht. 6 ft.1 in., blue eyes, brown hair, light complexion, married as of Jan. 1926. Peace officer, enlisted in San Benito, Cameron County, Texas. REGULAR RANGER Nov. 25, 1910–Sept. 11, 1911 (private, Co. B). Resigned. Cowboy (foreman, Norias Ranch), Armstrong, Kenedy County, Texas. SPECIAL RANGER Aug. 25, 1915–Feb. 6, 1919 (attached to Co. C). Appointment was suspended. Foreman, Norias Ranch. REGULAR RANGER Jan. 8, 1926–Feb. 1, 1927 (no Co. listed). Discharged. REMARKS: As of Nov. 1910, had served as a deputy sheriff and Customs inspector in Brownsville, Cameron County, on several occasions. Was a Cameron County deputy sheriff, 1912. Beginning in 1913, worked for the King Ranch. LAW ENFORCEMENT RELATIVES: Ranger Fred Tate, father. FAMILY: Parents, Fred W. Tate (b. 1860, TX) and Alice Routh Hopper (b. 1866, TX); siblings, William "Billy" (b. 1891, TX), Lucy (b. 1894, TX); spouse, Mabel Esta Waters (b. 1901, WI), married about 1923; children, Alice Marie (b. 1925, TX), Tommie Esther (b. 1926, TX), Fred E. (b. 1928, TX). *SR; 471; BDH, Dec 2, 1910, Oct 13, 1913, Mar 7, 1914, Sept 24, 1915, Mar 21, May 22, 1916, Mar 10, 1917; Tate to Hutchings, July 31, 1917, AGC; AG to Tate, Aug 1, 1917, AGC; 319: 155; 463: 57; A1d, e, f, g; A2e; A3a; A4b.*

TAYLOR, ALBERT. Born Sept. 28, 1879, Luling, Caldwell County, Texas. Ht. 6 ft. 1 in., brown eyes, black hair, light complexion, married. Bank cashier, Luling. LOYALTY RANGER June 17, 1918–Feb. 1919. REMARKS: Had worked for Western Union Telegraph Co. In Sept. 1918 was a cashier at Lipscomb Bank and Trust, Luling. In 1930 was a bank vice-president in Austin, Travis County, Texas. Died June 21, 1955, Travis County, Texas; buried in Luling City Cemetery. FAMILY: Parents, Albert Taylor (b. 1841, MS) and Mary Elizabeth Williams or Newton (b. 1846, MS); siblings, Jasper Newton (b. 1867, MS), Eli A. (b. 1868, MS), James E. (b. 1871, TX), Isaac (b. 1874, TX), Artie (b. 1877, TX); spouse, Sallie Essie Greer (b. 1880, MS), married July 20, 1902; sons, Albert Brice (b. 1905, TX), Harold Earl (b. 1910, TX), Jack Greer (b. 1914, TX). *SR; 429:18; A1b, e, f, g; A2b; A3a; A4b; B1, 2.*

TAYLOR, ARTHUR WINSTON. Born Sept. 28, 1888, San Antonio, Bexar County, Texas. Ht. 5 ft. 10 in., brown eyes, brown hair, ruddy complexion. Clerk, Austin, Travis

County, Texas. SPECIAL RANGER July 13, 1917–Aug. 15, 1917 (attached to Co. C). WA was revoked because he was no longer working for the state. REMARKS: In June 1917 was a motor mechanic for the U.S. government at Fort Sam Houston in San Antonio. Had been a private and a sergeant in the Texas National Guard. In 1930 was an engineering accountant in San Antonio. Died May 8, 1939, Bexar County, Texas. FAMILY: Parents, James McDowell Taylor (b. 1854, MO) and Hannah Bell Glass (b. 1856, KY); siblings, Shelby G. (b. 1883, TX), John M. (b. 1886, TX). *SR; AG to Gen. Manager, Nov 13, 1917, AGC; A1d, g; A2b; A3a; B1.*

TAYLOR, CLAUDE ANTONE. Born Apr. 5, 1874, Daviess County, Kentucky. Ht. 6 ft. 2 in., blue eyes, black hair, brunette complexion, married. Farmer and merchant, Anderson, Grimes County, Texas. LOYALTY RANGER June 5, 1918–Mar. 6, 1919. REMARKS: 1919 letterhead: "Taylor Mercantile Company, General Merchandise, North Zulch, Tex., C. A. Taylor, President." In 1920 was a grain and hay merchant in Anderson. A Claude Antone Taylor died Dec. 28, 1953, Travis County, Texas. FAMILY: Parents, Henry Taylor (b. 1829, KY) and Mary A. (b. 1840, TN); spouse, Clara G. (b. 1878, TX), married about 1897; children, Claud (b. 1899, TX), Clarence Emory (b. 1900, TX), Edith E. (b. 1906, TX), Mildred E. (b. 1909, TX), William D. (b. 1914, TX), Emma J. (b. 1915, TX), Marion M. (b. 1918, TX). *SR; A1d, e, f; A2b; A3a.*

TAYLOR, DREW KIRKSEY. Born Apr. 16, 1857, Livingston, Polk County, Texas. Ht. 5 ft. 8 in., brown eyes, brown hair, light complexion, married. REGULAR RANGER 1874–1878. Peace officer, Austin, Travis County, Texas. REGULAR RANGER Oct. 1, 1920–Apr. 8, 1921 (private, Co. B). Resigned. Peace officer, Brownwood, Brown County, Texas. SPECIAL RANGER Oct. 7, 1933–Oct. 6, 1935. REMARKS: Had been a stock raiser in Val Verde County, Texas. Died Jan. 31, 1942, Travis County, Texas; buried in Austin Memorial Cemetery, Austin. FAMILY: Parents, Martin Junius Taylor (b. 1832, AL) and Almiria or Elvira Kirksey (b. 1846, AL); siblings, Annie H. Hardeman (b. 1859, TX), married about 1881, Brown County, Texas. *SR; 471; A1aa, d, f; A2b; A4b, g.*

TAYLOR, ELMER JOSIAH. Born Feb. 19, 1882, Beeville, Bee County, Texas. Ht. 5 ft. 8 in., brown eyes, black hair, dark complexion, married. Stockman, Marathon, Brewster County, Texas. SPECIAL RANGER Feb. 22, 1918–Jan. 15, 1919. REMARKS: In 1930 was manager of a service station in Alpine, Brewster County. Brewster County sheriff Nov. 3, 1936–Jan. 1, 1941. Died Dec. 2, 1956, El Paso County, Texas. LAW ENFORCEMENT RELATIVES: Ranger Thomas Creed Taylor, brother; Ranger Josiah Taylor, grandfather; Ranger Creed Taylor, great-uncle; Ranger William Walter Taylor, distant cousin; Ranger William R. "Buck" Taylor, distant cousin. See Taylor Family, Tumlinson Family, Wright Family charts for additional information. FAMILY: Parents, James Oury Taylor (b. 1850, TX) and Sarah Rebecca Smith (b. 1855, TX); siblings, Lugana Jane (b. 1875, TX), Ida May (b. 1877, TX), Thomas C. (b. 1879, TX), Laura Rachel (b. 1880, TX), Myrtle Irene (b. 1885, TX), Rufus Owen (b. 1886, TX), Robert Eugene (b. 1888, TX), Fred Carlton (b. 1890, TX), Ann Elizabeth (b. 1893, TX), Lillian Lilabel (b. 1895, TX); spouse, Alva Estelle White (b. 1884, TX), married Jan. 17, 1912; daughters, Ida Louise (b. 1913, TX), Helen Rebecca (b. 1915, TX), Sarah Alva (b. 1922, TX). *SR; 1503:65; A1b, d, f, g; A2b; A3a; A4b; B1, 2.*

TAYLOR, JOSEPH ALEC "PINKIE." Born June 5, 1887, Yorktown, DeWitt County, Texas. Ht. 5 ft. 10 in., blue eyes, light hair, light complexion. Stockman, enlisted in Goliad County, Texas. REGULAR RANGER Apr. 1, 1914–Jan. 1915 (private, Co. B). Resigned to become a mounted Customs inspector as of Jan. 15, 1915. Was reappointed in Apr. 1915. Stockman, Brownsville, Cameron County, Texas. SPECIAL RANGER Nov. 28, 1916–unknown; Jan. 7, 1918–Jan. 15, 1919. REMARKS: Got his nickname because he flushed pink when angry. In Aug. 1915 was one of the defenders of the Norias Ranch against Mexican raiders. He retired from Customs to become a farmer near San Benito, Cameron County. He was murdered June 14, 1924, San Benito, Cameron County, Texas. LAW ENFORCEMENT RELATIVES: Ranger William R. "Buck" Taylor, uncle; Ranger William Alonzo Taylor, cousin. See Taylor Family, Tumlinson Family, Wright Family charts for additional relatives. FAMILY: Parents, Joseph Lee Taylor (b. 1867, TX) and Elizabeth Patton "Bettie" Webster (b. 1856, TX); siblings, Elizabeth Webster "Lizzie" (b. 1884, TX), Hayes Emily (b. 1889, TX), Carrie Lee (b. 1895, TX), William Shafer (b. 1900, TX); spouse, Angie E. Demaree (b. 1898, IL), married Sept. 15, 1917, San Benito; son, James Lee

(b. 1922, TX). *SR; 471; Gay, "Amazing," WC; Sanders to Hutchings, Jan 15, 1915, AGC; AG to Taylor, Nov 24, 29, 1916, AGC; Taylor to Hutchings, Nov 28, 1916, AGC; Taylor to Ferguson, Nov 22, 1916, AGC; Wroe to Hutchings, Nov 23, 1916, AGC; HC, Aug 3, 9, 1915; BDH, Jan 15, Apr 23, Aug 3, 9, 24, 1915, Dec 4, 5, 1916; 1: I, 1315–1318; 469: 62, 89 n. 64; 463: 581–59; 417: 586–587; 319: 33–35; A1d, e, f, g; A2e; A3a; A4b; B2.*

TAYLOR, MARION DEKALB. Born Aug. 29, 1873, Marion County, Texas. Tall, medium build, blue eyes, brown hair, married. Merchant, Smithland, Marion County. LOYALTY RANGER June 3, 1918–Jan. 15, 1919. REMARKS: In 1930 was a farmer in Marion County. Died Oct. 3, 1951, Marion County, Texas; buried in Oakwood Cemetery, Marion County. FAMILY: Parents, Fleming Moses Taylor (b. 1850, TX) and Virginia Galveston "Jennie" Campbell (b. 1851, MS); siblings, Frank, Elizabeth "Lizzie" (b. 1871, TX), A. Jay C. (b. 1877, TX), Irby (b. 1880, TX), Ennis M. (b. 1882, TX), John Hilary (b. 1884, TX), Paul (b. 1885, TX), Lois E. (b. 1889, TX), Richard Fleming (b. 1891, TX), William Haywood (b. 1894, TX); spouse, Susana Zarvonia Moseley (b. 1871, TX), married Nov. 1, 1899, Marion County; children, Bessie Grace (b. 1900, TX), Virginia Ruth (b. 1902, TX), Zarvonia Dixie (b. 1905, TX), Marion Douglas (b. 1911, TX). *SR; A1b, d, e, f, g; A2b; A3a; A4b.*

TAYLOR, MILTON ISAAC, JR. Born May 15, 1889, Friotown, Frio County, Texas. Ht. 5 ft. 11 in., dark eyes, black hair, tan complexion, married. Bank clerk, Pearsall, Frio County. LOYALTY RANGER July 1, 1918–Jan. 15, 1919. REMARKS: Had been a cowpuncher. In June 1917 was a bank clerk, Peoples Bank, Pearsall. In 1930 was Frio County deputy sheriff living in Pearsall. Died Feb. 24, 1936, Frio County, Texas. FAMILY: Parents, Isaac Milton Taylor (b. 1850, TX) and Amanda Jane Slaughter (b. 1862, TX); siblings, Lora (b. 1881, TX), William Benjamin (b. 1883, TX), Hugh Albert (b. 1885, TX), Amos George (b. 1887, TX), Chula Flora (b. 1891, TX), Lawrence (b. 1894, TX), Kate (b. 1895, TX), Dewey Hobson (b. 1898, TX), Amanda (b. 1903, TX); spouse, Ollie Peace (b. 1897, OK), married Mar. 10, 1915, Frio County; children, Howard S. (b. 1916, TX), Ollie Mae (b. 1919, TX), Lora Grace (b. 1925, TX), Florence (b. 1927, TX), Milton Isaac, Jr. (b. 1930, TX), Peggy Jean (b. 1934, TX). *SR; A1d, e, f, g; A2b, e; A3a; A4a, b; B2.*

TAYLOR, P. CALHOUN. Born Sept. 16, 1884, Cisco, Eastland County, Texas. Ht. 5 ft. 11 ½ in., brown eyes, dark brown hair, dark complexion. Attorney, Tulia, Swisher County, Texas. LOYALTY RANGER June 17, 1918–Jan. 15, 1919. FAMILY: Spouse, Prudence M. (b. 1890, TX), married by 1920. *SR; A1f; A3a.*

TAYLOR, ROBERT ANDREW. Born Nov. 13, 1875, Austin, Travis County, Texas. Ht. 5 ft. 10 in., blue eyes, black hair, fair complexion, married. Merchant, Crystal City, Zavala County, Texas. SPECIAL RANGER Aug. 11, 1916–Jan. 15, 1919 (commission was renewed on Jan. 10, 1918). REMARKS: Operated Taylor Hardware Co. in Crystal City, 1916. In 1916 was secretary of some kind of local citizens' protection committee. Governor Ferguson had authorized 10 Special Rangers for the Crystal City area. In 1930 was a farmer in Crystal City. Died Feb. 15, 1959, Zavala County, Texas. FAMILY: Parents, Gus Taylor (b. 1851, LA) and Jennie or Jane (b. 1853, TX); siblings, Lula (b. 1873, TX), Martha A. "Mattie" (b. 1878, TX), twins Willie and Lillie (b. 1881, TX), Gabriel A. (b. 1884, TX), Ernest R. (b. 1890, TX); spouse, Margaret "Maggie" Graham (b. 1887, TX), married about 1908; children, Pauline (b. 1910, TX), Robert A., Jr. (b. 1912, TX), Joe W. (b. 1915, TX). *SR; Taylor to AG, July 16, 1916, AGC; Hale to AG [Aug 1916], AGC; A1b, d, f, g; A2b; A3a.*

TAYLOR, STEPHEN LEE. Born Nov. 1871, Hopkins County, Texas. Ht. 5 ft. 9 in., brown eyes, black hair, dark complexion, married. Peace officer and merchant, Llano, Llano County, Texas. SPECIAL RANGER May 25, 1917–Jan. 15, 1919 (attached to Co. C; commission was renewed Jan. 7, 1918). REMARKS: Had been a deputy sheriff in several counties for more than 20 years. In 1910 was a telephone company electrician in Blanco County, Texas. Letterhead: Jan. 1919—"Taylor & Moss, Garage, Sub-Agents for Hudson and Cadillac Cars, Goodyear Casings—S. L. Taylor, G. T. Moss, Oxford Texas"; Apr. 1919—"Taylor & Moss Garage, Hye, Tex." Oxford is in Llano County; Hye is in Blanco County. In 1930 was a repair man in a garage in San Antonio, Bexar County, Texas. Died Aug. 5, 1942, Angelina County, Texas. FAMILY: Parents, Joseph Burnett Taylor (b. 1846, LA) and Mary Jane Hodges (b. 1853, TX); sisters, Norah M. (b. 1873, TX), Lola C. (b. 1875, TX), Pheba C. (b. 1878, TX), Zilpha (b. 1879, TX); spouse, Miranda A.

(b. 1873, TX), married about 1896; children, Nathan Earl (b. 1897, TX), Alma G. (b. 1901, TX). *SR; Taylor to Harley, Apr 1, 1919, AGC; A1b, e, f, g; A2b; B1.*

TAYLOR, THOMAS CARNEY "CREED." (Listed in census records and World War I Draft Registration document as Thomas Creed Taylor or simply Creed Taylor.) Born July 15, 1879, Beeville, Bee County, Texas. Ht. 5 ft. 8 in., gray eyes, black hair, dark complexion, married. REGULAR RANGER (private, Co. E, Frontier Battalion, 1899; private, Co. B, 1902–1904). Stockman, enlisted in Brewster County, Texas. SPECIAL RANGER Apr. 7, 1917–Dec. 1917. REMARKS: Kimble County, Texas, deputy sheriff, 1897; Kimble County sheriff Nov. 8, 1904–Nov. 6, 1906. Said he had served in the Rangers for 6 years. In 1910 was a pool hall manager in Brewster County. Had been a Customs agent; as of Sept. 1918 was a Customs inspector in Marathon, Brewster County. In 1919 was Customs chief in the Big Bend; in 1930 was in charge of the Customs office in Marfa, Presidio County, Texas. Died Nov. 5, 1961, Alpine, Brewster County, Texas. LAW ENFORCEMENT RELATIVES: Ranger Elmer Josiah Taylor, brother; Ranger Josiah Taylor, grandfather; Ranger Creed Taylor, great-uncle; Ranger William Walter Taylor, distant cousin; Ranger William R. "Buck" Taylor, distant cousin. See Taylor Family, Tumlinson Family, Wright Family charts for additional relatives. FAMILY: Parents, James Oury Taylor (b. 1850, TX) and Sarah Rebecca Smith (b. 1855, TX); siblings, Lugana Jane (b. 1875, TX), Ida May (b. 1877, TX), Laura Rachel (b. 1880, TX), Elmer Josiah (b. 1882, TX), Myrtle Irene (b. 1885, TX), Rufus Owen (b. 1886, TX), Robert Eugene (b. 1888, TX), Fred Carlton (b. 1890, TX), Ann Elizabeth (b. 1893, TX), Lillian Lilabel (b. 1895, TX); spouse, Blanche E. Norton (b. 1887, TX), married Oct. 14, 1903, El Paso County, Texas; children, Lila Irene (b. 1905, TX), Thomas Ownie (b. 1907, TX), Glenna Eileen (b. 1911, TX), Louis Edith (b. 1914, TX). *SR; 471; Taylor to Hutchings, Apr 7, 1917, AGC; AG to Taylor, Apr 18, 1917, AGC; 1503:307; 1: I, 1521–1526; SAE, Oct 19, 1911; AG to Barker, Mar 23, 1917, AGC; Wroe to AG, Mar 27, 1917, AGC; 469: 71–72, 76; 470: 23; 488: 60; 319: 375; A1b, d, e, f, g; A2b; A3a; A4a, b; B1, 2.*

TAYLOR, THOMAS JEFFERSON "TOM." Born June 19, 1881, Montgomery County, Texas. Tall, slender, blue eyes, dark brown hair, married. Merchant, Bertram, Burnet County, Texas. LOYALTY RANGER June 6, 1918–Feb. 1919. REMARKS: In 1920 was a banker in Burnet County. In 1930 was president of a private bank in Bertram. Died Sept. 3, 1937, Burnet County, Texas; buried in Bear Creek Cemetery, Burnet County. FAMILY: Parents, William Washington Taylor (b. 1847, TX) and Mary Elizabeth Field (b. 1851, TX); siblings, Virginia Agnes (b. 1871, TX), James (b. 1872, TX), William (b. 1874, TX), S. H. (b. 1876, TX), Mary Ellen (b. 1878, TX), Carrie E. (b. 1889, TX), Q. C. (b. 1893, TX); spouse, Elizabeth Maud "Lizzie" Vaughn (b. 1888, TX), married about 1905; sons, T. J., Jr. (b. 1905, TX), Stillman Vaughn (b. 1907, TX), Dayton Reed (b. 1920, TX). *SR; A1b, e, f, g; A2b; A3a; A4b; B1.*

TAYLOR, WILLIAM ALONZO. Born Mar. 2, 1897, Goliad, Goliad County, Texas. Ht. 5 ft. 10 in., brown eyes, brown hair, dark complexion. In Nov. 1917 he lived in Goliad, enlisted as REGULAR RANGER (private, Co. A). No Service Record exists for this enlistment; served only one week—on AG's order was dismissed because he wasn't yet 21 years old. Returned to Goliad. Several Goliad lawyers asked AG to make an exception in his case; AG refused. Ranchman. REGULAR RANGER Mar. 1, 1918–Feb. 1, 1919 (private, Co. A). REMARKS: Owned El Mesquite Ranch. Became a Jim Wells County, Texas, deputy sheriff, 1919; a mounted Customs inspector, at Hebbronville, Jim Wells County, 1922. In 1927, resigned to accept appointment as Jim Hogg County sheriff, serving from Nov. 6, 1928–Sept. 29, 1950. Died Sept. 29, 1950, Jim Hogg County, Texas. LAW ENFORCEMENT RELATIVES: Ranger William R. "Buck" Taylor, father; Ranger Joseph A. Taylor, cousin. See Taylor Family, Tumlinson Family, Wright Family charts for additional relatives. FAMILY: Parents, William Riley "Buck" Taylor (b. 1867, TX) and Bettye Davis (b. 1875, TX); siblings, Elizabeth Agnes "Bessie" (b. 1892, TX), Onie Tom (b. 1895, TX), Hazel Nell (b. 1899, TX), Joe Davis (b. 1903, TX), Serena Fay (b. 1909, TX), Doris Margaret (b. 1915, TX); spouse, Evelyn Briscoe. *SR; 471; Fowler & Fowler to Woodul, Nov 30, 1917, AGC; AG to Fowler & Fowler, Dec 7, 1917, AGC; Patton to Woodul, Jan 23, 1918, AGC; Tumlinson to Aldrich, Dec 15, 1919, July 21, 1920, AGC; 1503:288; 469: 60, 62, 67, 75, 89 n. 64; 470: 128; 485: 196; A1d, e, f, g; A2b; A3a; A4b.*

TAYLOR, WILLIAM EDGAR. Born Nov. 4, 1879, Frio, Frio County, Texas. Ht. 5 ft. 10 in., brown eyes, brown hair, fair complexion, married. Brand inspector, Panhandle & Southwestern Cattlemen's Association, Wheeler, Wheeler County, Texas. SPECIAL RANGER Jan. 27, 1918–Jan. 15, 1919. REMARKS: Had been a stock farmer. State Senator Claude Hudspeth requested a SPECIAL RANGER commission for him. In 1920 was a hog and cattle trader in Shamrock, Wheeler County. A "Willar Egar" Taylor died Dec. 15, 1948, Wheeler County, Texas. FAMILY: Parents, John Taylor (b. 1850, MS) and Malinda Parilee Loyd (b. 1853, AR); siblings, Walter E. (b. 1875, TX), Sarah Eva (b. 1877, TX), John (b. 1882, TX), Loyd (b. 1884, TX), Willis (b. 1886, TX), Lottie Lucille (b. 1888, OK), Malinda Wilmoth (b. 1891, OK), Lula (b. 1894, OK); spouse, Mary Ellen Wright (b. 1885, AL), married Mar. 2, 1903, Wheeler County; children, Margaret or Margery (b. 1904, TX) Alice Louise (b. 1906, TX), William Edgar (b. 1915, TX), Johnnie Marie (b. 1918, TX). *SR; Hudspeth to Harley, June 15, 1918, AGC; A1b, d, e, f; A2b; A3a; A4a; B2.*

TAYLOR, WILLIAM RILEY "BUCK." Born Nov. 26, 1867, Yorktown, DeWitt County, Texas. Ht. 5 ft. 9 in., brown eyes, brown hair, light complexion. Stockman, Goliad, Goliad County, Texas. SPECIAL RANGER July 18, 1917–Dec. 1917 (attached to Co. C). REMARKS: Goliad County sheriff Nov. 6, 1900–Nov. 4, 1902 and Nov. 8, 1904–Nov. 6, 1906. Kleberg County, Texas, deputy sheriff, 1914–1915. His father was a large rancher and landowner in Goliad County. Taylor applied unsuccessfully for a Ranger captaincy in 1914 and 1918. Died Jan. 15, 1920, Goliad County, Texas; buried in Glen Dale Cemetery, Goliad. LAW ENFORCEMENT RELATIVES: Ranger William Alonzo Taylor, son; Ranger Joseph A. Taylor, nephew; Ranger William Walter Taylor, cousin; Ranger Creed Taylor, great-uncle; Ranger Josiah Taylor, great-uncle. See Taylor Family, Tumlinson Family, Wright Family charts for additional relatives. FAMILY: Parents, Joseph Taylor (b. 1833, TX) and Elizabeth Ann Silcriggs (b. 1838, TX); siblings, John Milam (b. 1858, TX), Elizabeth M. (b. 1861, TX), Joseph Lee (b. 1867, TX), Thomas Carney (b. 1865, TX), Charles Leslie (b. 1869, TX), Serena A. (b. 1870, TX), Martha J. (b. 1873, TX), Henry David (b. 1875, TX), Arthur E. (b. 1877, TX), Hayes Walter (b. 1879, TX); spouse, Bettye Davis (b. 1875, TX), married Jan. 27, 1892, Junction, Kimble County, Texas; children, Elizabeth Agnes "Bessie" (b. 1892, TX), Onie Tom (b. 1895, TX), William Alonzo (b. 1897, TX), Hazel Nell (b. 1899, TX), Joe Davis (b. 1903, TX), Serena Fay (b. 1909, TX), Doris Margaret (b. 1915, TX). *SR; Kingsville Record, Oct 30, 1914, Jan 29, 1915; Taylor to AG, Mar 22, 1914, CP; Passmore and Lutenbacker to Ferguson, Apr 7, 1917, AGC; Thornton to Ferguson, Apr 7, 1917, AGC; Seeligson to Ferguson, Apr 7, 1917, AGC; AG to Thornton, Apr 11, 1917, AGAC; Davidson to Ferguson, Apr 12, 1917, AGC; Wroe to AG, Apr 13, 1917, AGC; 1503:208; Passmore to AG, Jan 7, 1918, AGC; 469: 75; A1a, b, d, e, f; A2b; A4b; B1.*

TAYLOR, WILLIAM WALTER. Born June 2, 1868, Yorktown, DeWitt County, Texas. Ht. 5 ft. 9 in., black hair, black eyes, dark complexion, married. Ranchman, enlisted in Kimble County, Texas. SPECIAL RANGER Feb. 18, 1918–unknown. REGULAR RANGER Aug. 16, 1918–Dec. 31, 1918 (captain, Co. F). Discharged—reduction in force. Peace officer, Junction, Kimble County. REGULAR RANGER June 8, 1925–June 30, 1928 (sergeant, Cos. B, C, A). Resigned. Peace officer, Junction. SPECIAL RANGER Feb. 7, 1931–Feb. 3, 1932; Feb. 3, 1932–Nov. 3, 1932. Placed on active duty. REGULAR RANGER Nov. 3, 1932–Sept. 7, 1933 (captain, unassigned). SPECIAL RANGER Sept. 7, 1933–Jan. 22, 1935 (captain, station: Junction). Discharged. REMARKS: His father was shot to death in 1868 by Bill Sutton; thus began the Taylor-Sutton Feud in South Texas. W. W. Taylor was Kimble County sheriff Nov. 8, 1898–Nov. 8, 1904 and Nov. 6, 1906–Nov. 8, 1910 and Nov. 2, 1920–Jan. 1, 1923. In 1930 was deputy sheriff, lived in Junction. Died Feb. 22, 1945, Kimble County, Texas; buried in Junction Cemetery. LAW ENFORCEMENT RELATIVES: Ranger William Riley Taylor, cousin; Ranger Creed Taylor, great-uncle; Ranger Josiah Taylor, great-uncle. See Taylor Family, Tumlinson Family, Wright Family charts for additional family. FAMILY: Parents, William P. Taylor (b. 1837, TX) and Mary Anderson (b. 1850, TX); spouse, Mattie Onie Davis (b. 1877, TX), married about 1894; children, Alexis M. (b. 1894, TX), Lela A. (b. 1898, TX), Darby Preston (b. 1901, TX), Carlos L. (b. 1905, TX), Lura B. (b. 1907, TX), W. Kalleta (b. 1912, TX), Lucile L. (b. 1915, TX). *SR; 471; Linden to Harley, Apr 12, 1918, AGC; Newton to Harley, Apr 12, 1918, AGC; Bee to Hobby, Apr 12, 1918, AGC; Schreiner to Hobby, Apr 13, 1918, AGC; Assistant AG to Taylor, Apr 15, 1918 AGC; Assistant AG to Bee, Apr 15, 1918, AGC; Harley to Taylor,*

Dec 27, 1918, WC; Taylor to Cope, Nov 15, 1920, AGC; 1503:307; 463: 34, 81–84, 126; 314: 106, 4230425; 469: 63, 65, 76; 1000: 17; A1d, e, g; A2b; A4a, b; B1.

TAYLOR, WOODWARD ORELL. Born Mar. 18, 1877, Robertson County, Texas. Ht. 5 ft. 9 in., brown eyes, black hair, dark complexion, divorced. Peace officer, Karnes City, Karnes County, Texas. REGULAR RANGER Sept. 28, 1920–unknown (private, Headquarters Co., Emergency Co. No. 1). REMARKS: Had been a farmer in Karnes County. In Aug. 1914 was a deputy sheriff in Kingsville, Kleberg County, Texas. In Sept. 1918 was a railroad machinist helper in Kingsville. In 1930 was an oil field machinist in Karnes City. FAMILY: Father, Alfred J. Taylor (b. 1859, MS); stepmother, Catherine (b. 1857, MS); step-sister, Bertie (b. 1892, TX); spouse, Almira Cornelia "Mide" Parker (b. 1881, TX), married about 1899. *SR; 471; BDH, Aug 24, 1914; A1d, e, f, g; A3a; A4b.*

TERRY, ALMER LAIN. Born June 8, 1882, Basin Spring, Grayson County, Texas. Ht. 5 ft. 11 in., blue eyes, brown hair, fair complexion. Stock farmer, White Deer, Hutchinson County, Texas. LOYALTY RANGER June 10, 1918–Feb. 1919. REMARKS: Died Apr. 1, 1927, Hutchinson County, Texas. FAMILY: Parents, Campbell Stanton Terry (b. 1857, TN) and Delaney Louisa Barefoot (b. 1863, TX); siblings, Bertha (b. 1880, TX), Hugh (b. 1885, TX), Rupert (b. 1887, TX), Myrtle or Merle (b. 1889, TX), Lottie or Lola (b. 1893, TX), Campbell (b. 1895, TX), twins Fay and Foy (b. 1901, TX), Patrick (b. 1903, TX). *SR; A1d, e, f; A2b; A3a; A4g; B1.*

TERRY, THOMAS PINKNEY "TOM." Born Feb. 5, 1889, Lampasas, Lampasas County, Texas. Ht. 5 ft. 10 ½ in., gray eyes, gray hair, ruddy complexion. Farmer, Lampasas. REGULAR RANGER May 25, 1916–June 14, 1916 (private, Co. D). Resigned. REMARKS: Because of mother's illness couldn't leave home, had to resign from Rangers. Still a farmer in Lampasas County in 1920. FAMILY: Parents, Benjamin Franklin Terry (b. 1849, TX) and Julia A. Higgins (b. 1849, GA); siblings, Robert Franklin (b. 1877, TX), Minnie (b. 1879, TX), Judy E. (b. 1880, TX), John J. (b. 1882, TX), Nancy Kate (b. 1883, TX), Jesse Alexander (b. 1886, TX). *SR; 471; Terry to Hutchings, June 12, 1916, AGC; A1d, e, f; A3a; A4a.*

TEVIS, REID. Born Apr. 1, 1877, Beaumont, Jefferson County, Texas. Ht. 5 ft. 11 in., gray eyes, dark brown hair, medium complexion, married. Chief of detectives, Beaumont. LOYALTY RANGER Aug. 1, 1918–Mar. 6, 1919. REMARKS: Had worked in a lumber yard in Beaumont. Died Apr. 15, 1925, Jefferson County, Texas; buried in Magnolia Cemetery, Beaumont. LAW ENFORCEMENT RELATIVES: Beaumont city policeman (1900) Randolph W. Tevis, father. FAMILY: Parents, Randolph W. Tevis (b. 1847, TX) and Susan Wingate (b. 1847, TX); siblings, George Washington (b. 1869, TX), Evaline (b. 1871, TX), Iva (b. 1873, TX), Ella (b. 1875, TX); spouse, Julia King (b. 1887, MO), married Apr 15, 1915; son, Lee Kisler (b. 1920, TX). *SR; LWT, Apr 14, 1918; A1b, d; A2b; A3a; A4a, b; B1, 2.*

TEVIS, ROBERT MILLER. Born Nov. 8, 1868, Galveston, Galveston County, Texas. Ht. 5 ft. 6 in., brown eyes, brown hair, dark complexion, married. Superintendent, Galveston. SPECIAL RANGER June 26, 1918–Jan. 15, 1919. REMARKS: According to U.S. census records, in 1900 was a patient in John Sealy Hospital, Galveston. In 1910 was a cemetery sexton in Galveston. In 1930 was "president" of a cemetery in Galveston. Died Oct. 24, 1930, Galveston, Galveston County, Texas; buried in Lakeview Cemetery, Galveston. FAMILY: Parents, Robert Miller Tevis (b. 1830, KY) and Martha Lucas "Mattie" Mayfield (b. 1835, KY); siblings, Sophia J. (b. 1858, TN), Frank (b. 1860, TX), Louisa or Elizabeth (b. 1862, TX), James (b. 1865, TX); spouse, Nan "Nannie" Furlow (b. 1879, TX), married Dec. 28, 1896, Fort Bend County, Texas; children, Maidie (b. 1897, TX), Robert Starley (b. 1900, TX), Nan. *SR; A1a, d, e, f; A4a, b; B2.*

THOMASON, WILLIAM. Born Feb. 6, 1897, San Antonio, Bexar County, Texas. Ht. 5 ft. 11 in., blue eyes, brown hair, fair complexion, married. Peace officer, San Antonio. REGULAR RANGER Mar. 1, 1921–Aug. 31, 1921 (private, Co. B). Discharged. REMARKS: In June 1917 was a chauffer for Merchants Transfer Company, San Antonio. In 1920 was deputy sheriff, Bexar County. FAMILY: Parents, William Algie Thomason (b. 1867, LA) and Elnora "Nora" Bass (b. 1867, TX); siblings, Bessie (b. 1893, TX); Rex (b. 1901, TX); step-brothers, August "Gus" Briggs (b. 1887, TX), Harold Briggs (b. 1888, TX); cousin/adopted sister, Carlie Bass (b. 1906, TX); spouse, unknown, married after 1920, divorced before 1930. *SR; 471; A1d, e, f, g; A3a.*

THOMPSON, CALEB MARSHALL. Born July 30, 1864, Copiah County, Mississippi. Ht. 5 ft. 10 in., blue eyes, light hair, light complexion, married. Farmer, banker, merchant, Devine, Medina County, Texas. SPECIAL RANGER Jan. 12, 1918–Jan. 15, 1919. REMARKS: President, Adams National Bank, Devine, Jan. 1919. Died Nov. 8, 1932, Charlotte, Atascosa County, Texas. FAMILY: Parents, William Oliver Thompson (b. 1837, SC) and Mary Ann Belinda Mullen (b. 1843, MS); siblings, William Becton (b. 1862, MS), Robert Stillman (b. 1866, MS), Mary Frances (b. 1868, MS), Wiley Mayes (b. 1869, MS), Florence Eveline (b. 1872, MS), Charles Oliver (b. 1874, MS), Henry Eugene (b. 1876, MS), Eliza Ann (b. 1878, TX), Minnie Dosia (b. 1881, TX); spouse, Elizabeth Lee "Lizzie" Redus (b. 1872, TX), married Sept. 1, 1895, Devine; children, Charles Marshall (b. 1897, TX), Carrol Redus (b. 1899, TX), Ethel Florence (b. 1901, TX), Gladys Ray (b. 1903, TX), George William (b. 1905, TX). *SR; A1a, b, d, e, f; A2b; A4a, b.*

THOMPSON, ELONZO "LONNIE." Born Dec. 24, 1895, Utopia, Uvalde County, Texas. Ht. 5 ft. 10 in., gray eyes, brown hair, dark complexion. Farmer, Utopia. SPECIAL RANGER Aug. 6, 1917–Dec. 1917 (attached to Co. C). REMARKS: Was also a farmer in Bandera County, Texas. Died Aug. 10, 1992, Atascosa County, Texas; buried in Vanderpool Cemetery, Bandera County. FAMILY: Parents, Robert Hamilton Thompson (b. 1849, AR) and Mary Elizabeth Cummings (b. 1868, TX); siblings, M. Annie (b. 1890, TX), Eunice or Margaret B. "Maggie" (b. 1892, TX), Hamilton (b. 1893, TX), Johnnie Albert (b. 1899, TX), Joseph Francis (b. 1900, TX), George Powell (b. 1904, TX), Lela (b. 1906, TX), Jewette R. (b. 1908, TX); spouse, Elizabeth Heideman (b. 1908), married Feb. 18, 1934; sons, Gary Elonzo (b. 1934, TX), David Francis (b. 1936, TX). *SR; A1e, f; A2a, b, e; A3a; A4a, b; B1.*

THOMPSON, GUY. Born Feb. 24, 1873, Beeville, Bee County, Texas. Ht. 5 ft. 8 in., blue eyes, light hair, red complexion, married. Ranchman, Rio Grande City, Starr County, Texas. SPECIAL RANGER May 11, 1918–Jan. 15, 1919. REMARKS: In 1930 was a manager for a mercantile company in Jim Hogg County, Texas. A Guy Thompson died Sept. 8, 1935, Jim Hogg County, Texas. LAW ENFORCEMENT RELATIVES: Ranger and Jim Hogg County sheriff (1912–1916) Oscar Thompson, brother. FAMILY: Parents, John C. Thompson (b. 1836, MS) and Mary E. Coke (b. 1846, AL); siblings, Mattie (b. 1866, TX), Oscar (b. 1868, TX), Edgar (b. 1872, TX), Minnie L. (b. 1876, TX), Roy (b. 1878, TX), Ola (b. 1881, TX), Lella (b. 1883, TX); spouse #1, Neta Van Buren Bodenhamer (b. 1876, TX), married Oct. 23, 1893, divorced by 1910; daughter, Audrey C. (b. 1895, TX); spouse #2, unknown, married before May 1918, divorced by 1930; son, Hardy (b. 1916, TX). *SR; A1b, d, e, f, g; A2b; A3a; A4a, b; B1, 2.*

THOMPSON, JAMES C. Born Jan. 1861, Amite County, Mississippi. Ht. 6 ft. 1 in., gray eyes, light hair, light complexion, married. Farmer and rancher, Devine, Medina County, Texas. SPECIAL RANGER Jan. 12, 1918–Jan. 15, 1919. REMARKS: A James C. Thompson died Dec. 27, 1945, Medina County, Texas. FAMILY: Parents, William Thompson (b. 1835, MS) and Elizabeth (b. 1835, MS); siblings, Eunice E. (b. 1858, MS), William F. (b. 1863, MS), Martha C. (b. 1866, TX), Nancy M. (b. 1868, TX), Ida May (b. 1874, TX); spouse, Abbie (b. 1872, TX), married about 1897; sons, Homer D. (b. 1898, TX), Lesley J. (b. 1902, TX), Wallace (b. 1906, TX). *SR; A1a, b, d, e, f; A2b.*

THOMPSON, OSCAR. Born Sept. 1868, Fairview, Wilson County, Texas. Ht. 5 ft. 11 in., brown hair, dark complexion, married. Ranchman, Hebbronville, Jim Hogg County, Texas. SPECIAL RANGER Jan. 30, 1918–Jan. 15, 1919. REMARKS: Had been a rancher in Duval County, Texas. Was first Jim Hogg County sheriff Aug. 11, 1913–May 1916. Resigned because he had large mercantile and ranching interests. In May 1918 organized an 18-man force of home guards in Jim Hogg County. Letterhead in 1919: "Oscar Thompson, Dealer in Standard and Eclipse Windmills and Mill Fixtures, Pipe and Casing, Hebbronville." In 1930 was retired, living in Hebbronville. An Oscar Thompson died Apr. 5, 1936, Jim Hogg County, Texas. LAW ENFORCEMENT RELATIVES: Ranger Guy Thompson, brother. FAMILY: Parents, John C. Thompson (b. 1836, MS) and Mary E. Coke (b. 1846, AL); siblings, Mattie (b. 1866, TX), Edgar (b. 1872, TX), Guy (b. 1873, TX), Minnie L. (b. 1876, TX), Roy (b. 1878, TX), Ola (b. 1881, TX), Lella (b. 1883, TX); spouse, Alice M. (b. 1876, ME), married about 1902; sons, Webster J. (b. 1903, TX), Oscar A. (b. 1905, TX). *SR; Thompson to Ferguson, Apr 30, 1917, AGC; 1503:288; A1a, b, d, e, f, g; A2b.*

THORNTON, ROBERT A. Born Mar. 1859, Christian County, Missouri. Ht. 5 ft. 11 ½ in., blue-gray eyes, dark hair, fair complexion, married. Stock farmer, Stowell, Chambers County, Texas. LOYALTY RANGER July 15, 1918–Feb. 1919. REMARKS: Had been a deputy U.S. marshal. Had been a farmer in Long Creek, Boone County, Arkansas. A Robert Andy Thornton died Feb. 2, 1935, Chambers County, Texas. FAMILY: Parents, Kinnion Mason Thornton (b. 1805, MO) and Jane Boatright (b. 1816, TN); siblings, Martha (b. 1831, TN), Mary A. (b. 1835, TN), Louisa L. (b. 1837, TN), Obadiah N. (b. 1839, TN), Sarah "Sally" (b. 1841, TN), Julia (b. 1843, TN), Rebecca (b. 1844, TN), Frances Caroline (b. 1847, TN), Kinnion (b. 1849, TN), Elender (b. 1852, TN), Margaret (b. 1854, MO), Emaline (b. 1857, MO); spouse #1, Jennie Shaver (b. 1866, MO), married about 1879; children, Archie (b. 1881, AR), Jackson (b. 1883, AR), Thomas (b. 1885, AR), Mattie (b. 1888, AT), May (b. 1889, AR); spouse #2, Ida (b. 1881, MO), married about 1906; son, Robert A., Jr. (b. 1908, TX). *SR; A1aaa, aa, a, d, e, f; A2b; A4a, b; B1.*

THORP, THOMAS DILLIE "TOM." Born Sept. 19, 1881, Sherwood, Irion County, Texas. Ht. 5 ft. 8 in., gray eyes, brown hair, light complexion. Ranchman, enlisted in Val Verde County, Texas. SPECIAL RANGER Aug. 4, 1917–Oct. 21, 1917 (attached to Co. C). Placed on active duty. REGULAR RANGER Oct. 22, 1917–Sept. 1918 (private, Co. E). Ranchman, Sonora, Sutton County, Texas. SPECIAL RANGER Sept. 5, 1918–Dec. 1918. Resigned. REMARKS: Prior to Aug. 1917 had worked as a deputy sheriff for the Sheep and Goat Raisers' Association. In Dec. 1918 the association returned his commission to the AG because Thorp had resigned as an inspector. In 1930 was a ranch manager in Sonora. Died Sept. 18, 1945, Tom Green County, Texas. FAMILY: Parents, Albert Jasper Thorp and Mary Elizabeth Longley (b. 1859, TX); siblings, Ira Oliver "Ollie" (b. 1880, TX), Verbae (b. 1883, TX), Edward (b. 1885, TX), Luther (b. 1886, TX), Ada E. (b. 1889, TX); stepfather, M. Benton (b. 1840, MO); step-brother, Charley Benton (b. 1872, TX); spouse, Mattie Vera Simmons (b. 1894, TX), married about 1918; children, Thomas B. (b. 1922, TX), Addie (b. 1925, TX). *SR; 471; Almond to Hutchings, Aug 4, 1917, AGC; AG to Barler, Nov 10, 1917, AGC; Moore to Harley, Dec 19, 1918, AGC; A1b, d, g; A2b, e; A3a; A4g.*

THRASHER, CHESTER. Born Mar. 14, 1877, Travis County, Texas. Ht. 5 ft. 9 in., gray eyes, gray hair, fair complexion, married. Farmer, Austin, Travis County. SPECIAL RANGER Aug. 21, 1918–unknown (WA was cancelled—was lost). Ranchman, Austin. SPECIAL RANGER May 23, 1919–Dec. 31, 1919. Oil man, Webberville, Travis County. RAILROAD RANGER Aug. 12, 1922–Dec. 1, 1922. Discharged. Farmer, Austin. SPECIAL RANGER Oct. 25, 1926–Feb. 1, 1927. Discharged, WA expired. REMARKS: Commission in 1926 was issued at request of Governor Ferguson. Died Dec. 29, 1937, Travis County, Texas. FAMILY: Parents, William B. Thrasher (b. 1850, AR) and Christian McKay (b. 1856, AR); sister, Alva (b. 1879, TX); spouse, Daisy Dean Davis (b. 1880, TX), married Mar. 12, 1901; daughters, Elizabeth (b. 1903, TX), Cordelia Alva (b. 1908, TX). *SR; A1b, e, f, g; A2b; A3a; B1.*

TIBBS, KENDRELL PENELTON. Born Oct. 16, 1872, Tuscaloosa County, Alabama. Medium height, medium build, brown eyes, brown hair, married. Farmer, Scroggins, Franklin County, Texas. LOYALTY RANGER July 5, 1918–Mar. 6, 1919. REMARKS: Living in Franklin County by 1900. In 1930 was a farmer and justice of the peace in Franklin County. Died Oct. 18, 1946, Franklin County, Texas. FAMILY: Parents, Andrew Jackson Tibbs (b. 1841, AL) and Louisa Herring (b. 1842, AL); siblings, Amanda Jennie (b. 1869, AL), Annie (b. 1871, AL), Nancy (b. 1875, AL), Lucandy (b. 1877, AL), Laura (b. 1878, AL), Hester (b. 1880, AL); spouse, Sarah L. (b. 1871, AL), married about 1896; children, Argus E. (b. 1897, TX), Virgie V. (b. 1898, TX), Gladis (b. 1900, TX), Grady (b. 1905, TX). *SR; A1b, d, e, f, g; A2b; A3a; A4b.*

TILLEY, GEORGE WILLIAM. Born Mar. 30, 1863, Searcy, White County, Arkansas. Ht. 5 ft. 10 in., dark eyes, gray hair, brunette complexion, married. Special state traffic officer for the state Highway Commission, Waco, McLennan County, Texas. SPECIAL RANGER Dec. 2, 1918–Jan. 15, 1919. REMARKS: McLennan County sheriff Nov. 8, 1904–Nov. 5, 1912. In 1920 was an oil land broker in Waco. In Jan. 1921 became acting state fire marshal. In 1930 was oil and gas supervisor for the Texas Railroad Commission in Olney, Young County, Texas. Died Feb. 27, 1937, Young County, Texas. FAMILY: Parents, George William Tilley (b. 1830, NC) and Sarah Ellen Morrow (b. 1830, NC);

siblings, Martha Ann (b. 1850, NC), Kate (b. 1851, NC), James Franklin (b. 1852, NC), Laura Fletcher (b. 1854, NC), Nancy E. (b. 1856, NC), John (b. 1859, AR), Mary E. (b. 1867, AR); spouse, Fidelia (b. 1872, TX), married about 1890; children, Cora (b. 1890, TX), Lydia (b. 1892, TX), Ruby (b. 1895, TX), John (b. 1898, TX), Ruth (b. 1903, TX), Monette (b. 1908, TX). *SR; SAE, Mar 23, 1913; BDH, Oct 15, 1913, Feb 9, 1916; Hancock to Harley, Nov 26, 1918, AGC; Johnston to Tilley, Nov 27, 1918, AGC; 1503:365; LWT, Sept 18, 1921; A1a, e, f, g; A2b; A4a, b.*

TIMBERLAKE, DELBERT. Born Sept. 12, 1882, Floresville, Wilson County, Texas. Ht. 5 ft. 9 in., light brown eyes, black hair, dark complexion. Cowboy. REGULAR RANGER July 27, 1905–ca. July, 1907 (private, Co. A). Stockman, Del Rio, Val Verde County, Texas. SPECIAL RANGER Mar. 9, 1916–May 3, 1916 (attached to Co. C). Resigned to become city marshal of Del Rio. Peace officer, Laredo, Webb County, Texas. REGULAR RANGER June 27, 1918–Oct. 11, 1918 (sergeant, Co. F). Killed in action Oct. 11, 1918, at Brownsville, Cameron County, Texas. REMARKS: In 1910 was an officer in the sheriff's office, Galveston, Galveston County, Texas; was a deputy sheriff in Galveston for 2 years. Was Del Rio city marshal for 18 months. Was buried in Uvalde, Uvalde County, Texas. FAMILY: Parents, Joseph or Josiah Sirus "Joe" Timberlake (b. 1860, AR) and Martha "Lula" Sammons (b. 1861, AR); siblings, Nettie (b. 1883, TX), G. Cleveland (b. 1885, TX), Sam Ellis (b. 1886, TX), Lena (b. 1888, TX), Ora (b. 1892, TX), Joe Edna (b. 1894, TX), Tomie (b. 1896, TX); spouse, Annie (b. 1886, Poland), married about 1909. *SR; 471; AG to Almond, Mar 7, 1916, AGC; Almond to Hutchings, Mar 9, May 31, 1916, AGC; Barler to Hutchings, Apr 9, 1916, WC; AG to Almond, May 27, 1916, AGC; Davenport to Birkhead, June 18, 1917, AGC; Hanson to Harley, Oct 15, 1918, WC; BDH, Apr 10, 1916; 1000: iii, 61; 319: 423–425; 463: 81–84; 469: 63; A1d, e; A3a; A4g; B2.*

TIMMONS, JOSEPH A. "JOE." Born June 27, 1887, Graham, Young County, Texas. Ht. 5 ft. 9 in., blue eyes, brown hair, dark complexion. Stock farmer, Graham. LOYALTY RANGER June 10, 1918–Feb. 1919. LAW ENFORCEMENT RELATIVES: Ranger R. H. Timmons, cousin. FAMILY: Parents, William Simpson Timmons, Jr. (b. 1854, GA) and Julia Bunea Vista Putnam or Putman (b. 1864, GA); siblings, Wallace (b. 1883, TX), Mary Vashti (b. 1885, TX), James Osgood (b. 1889, TX), Sarah L. (b. 1892, TX), Esther Annie (b. 1895, TX), William (b. 1897, TX), Littleton (b. 1899, TX), Inda Pearl (b. 1901, TX). *SR; A1d, e, f; A4a, b; B2.*

TIMMONS, RUFUS HERSCHEL. Born Sept. 7, 1882, Graham, Young County, Texas. Ht. 5 ft. 11 in., dark eyes, dark hair, dark complexion, married. Stock farmer, Meadow, Terry County, Texas. LOYALTY RANGER June 10, 1918–Feb. 1919. REMARKS: Died Aug. 25, 1938, Brownfield, Terry County, Texas; buried in Meadow Cemetery. LAW ENFORCEMENT RELATIVES: Ranger Joe Timmons, cousin. FAMILY: Parents, Ambrose Alexander Timmons (b. 1844, GA) and Mary Ellen Howard (b. 1854, KY); siblings, Wilburn Herman (b. 1874, TX), Hope Hull (b. 1876, TX), Ambrose Alexander (b. 1877, TX), Virgil (b. 1880), John Alexander (b. 1884, TX), Selena Susan (b. 1887, TX), William Howard (b. 1889, TX), Sallie (b. 1892, TX), Dollie (b. 1894); spouse, Lillie Pearl Pardue (b. 1880, MO), married Dec. 21, 1904; children, Mary Fay (b. 1906, TX), Malcolm Alexander (b. 1909, TX), Rufus Ray (b. 1914, TX). *SR; A1d, f, g; A2b; A3a; A4a, b; B1, 2.*

TIPPEN, WILLIAM WASHINGTON. Born July 31, 1888, San Saba County, Texas. Tall, medium build, blue eyes, light hair, married. Banker and deputy sheriff, Mullin, Mills County, Texas. LOYALTY RANGER June 6, 1918–Feb. 1919. REMARKS: As of June 1917 was cashier, First State Bank, Mullin. In 1930 was president of a bank in Lometa, Lampasas County, Texas. Died Nov. 17, 1957, Austin, Travis County, Texas. FAMILY: Parents, George Washington Tippen (b. 1862, GA) and Lydia "Liddy" Brown (b. 1868, TX); siblings, John Wiley (b. 1890, TX), Effie B. (b. 1892, TX), Nettie M. (b. 1896, TX), Ollie M. (b. 1899, TX), Della (b. 1905, TX), Ervin (b. 1909, TX); spouse, Ollie Mae William (b. 1894, TX), married about 1915; children, Norma Sue (b. 1917, TX), Forrest Wade (b. 1919, TX), William K. (b. 1923, TX). *SR; A1e, f, g; A2b; A3a; A4a, b.*

TISDALE, IRA. Born Jan. 10, 1875, Cleburne, Johnson County, Texas. Ht. 5 ft. 4 in., brown eyes, dark brown hair, dark complexion, married. Accountant, Houston, Harris County, Texas. LOYALTY RANGER June 26, 1918–Mar. 6, 1919. REMARKS: Had been a real estate company bookkeeper in Houston. In 1917 was bookkeeper for the Texas Bread Company, Houston. As of Sept. 1918 was accountant, Toyah Sulfur Company, Houston. In 1919 was connected with "Sulphur Securities Sales Company, Houston." In 1920 was a railroad land appraiser in Houston. Died Mar. 19, 1920, Houston, Harris County, Texas; buried in Holy Cross Cemetery, Houston. FAMILY: Parents, Clement Richard Tisdale (b. 1846, TX) and Martha Ann Gohlson (b. 1852, TX); siblings, Lillian (b. 1873, TX), Henry or Harry (b. 1876, TX), Charles Bascom (b. 1878, TX), Edwin Houston (b. 1881, TX), James F. (b. 1882), Josephine (b. 1885, TX), William C. (b. 1887, TX), Frances M. "Frankie" (b. 1888, TX), Mary Belle (b. 1891, TX); spouse #1, Edith (b. 1872, CA), married about 1900; spouse #2, Mary Elizabeth Ray (b. 1884, TX), married about 1908; children, Mary Elizabeth (b. 1909, TX), Ruth (b. 1913, TX), Ray Keith (b. 1919, TX). *SR; A1b, d, e, f, g; A3a; A4a, b; B1.*

TISDALE, ISAAC MEMMON. Born June 16, 1876, Texarkana, Miller County, Arkansas. Ht. 5 ft. 10 in., blue eyes, dark hair, fair complexion, married. Merchant, Broaddus, San Augustine County, Texas. LOYALTY RANGER July 17, 1918–Feb. 1919. REMARKS: Had been manager of a lumber mill in Angelina County, Texas. In 1920 was a retail grocery merchant in San Augustine County. Died Jan. 2, 1950, Galveston County, Texas. FAMILY: Parents, Joseph Tisdale (b. 1840, MS) and Catherine (b. 1847, MS); siblings, Frank (b. 1867, TX), Roxie Lula (b. 1869, MS), Laura (b. 1870, AR), Lissa (b. 1874, AR), Charley E. (b. 1878, AR), Margaret (b. 1879, AR), Ambrose (b. 1884, AR); spouse, Dora A. (b. 1888, TX), married about 1905; children, Hazel E. (b. 1907, TX), Elma (b. 1909, TX), Dale (b. 1912, TX). *SR; A1b, e, f; A2b; A3a; A4b.*

TITTLE, CHARLES TARLTON "CHARLIE." Born Oct. 3, 1865, Franklin County, Texas. No physical description, married. Merchant and farmer, Mount Vernon, Franklin County. LOYALTY RANGER July 2, 1918–Feb. 1919. REMARKS: Was a dry goods merchant in Mount Vernon. FAMILY: Parents, George W. Tittle (b. 1831, TN) and Louvicia Matilda Hammock (b. 1830, AL); siblings, Mary E. (b. 1856, TX), Hardy Willouby (b. 1859, TX), Robert W. (b. 1861), George Henry (b. 1870, TX); stepmother, Sarah Matilda Gibson (b. 1850, TX); brothers, Emerson W. (b. 1872, TX), Edward Lee (b. 1874, TX), Luther Walker (b. 1876, TX), Walter Lee (b. 1878, TX); spouse #1, Sarah Delilah Tillman (b. 1870, TX), married about 1887; children, George Ennis (b. 1888, TX), Vida (b. 1892, TX), Wynton Willouby (b. 1894, TX), Charlie Cecil (b. 1896, TX), Unita (b. 1905, TX); spouse #2, Truma W. Johnson (b. 1898, TX); stepdaughter, Robertha Johnson (b. 1915, TX). *SR; A1b, e, f; A3a; A4a, b, g.*

TOBIN, CHARLES EDWIN "EDDY." Born Apr. 18, 1877, Travis County, Texas. Ht. 6 ft., dark eyes, dark hair, dark complexion, married. Merchant, Austin, Travis County. SPECIAL RANGER Jan. 26, 1918–unknown. WA was lost. REMARKS: As of Sept. 1918 was a stationery merchant, Tobin Book Store, Austin. FAMILY: Parents, John J. Tobin (b. 1838, AL) and Ida (b. 1847, AR); brothers, David (b. 1871, TX), Donald (b. 1873, TX), James (b. 1874, TX), John H. (b. 1876, TX), Wallace (b. 1881, TX); spouse #1, Edith (b. 1882, TX), married about 1901; daughter, Ida (b. 1902, IL); spouse #2, Nell Burns (b. 1885, TX); children, Eleanor B. (b. 1909, SC), Ted D. (b. 1915, TX). *SR; 471; A1b, d, e, f; A3a.*

TONCRAY, ARTHUR C. Born Sept. 1867, Omen, Smith County, Texas. Ht. 5 ft. 10 in., blue eyes, black hair, dark complexion, married. Clerk, Troup, Smith County. LOYALTY RANGER June 5, 1918–Feb. 1919. REMARKS: Had been city marshal of Omen, deputy city marshal of Troup. In 1900 was a railroad section foreman in Comal County, Texas. In 1910 was assistant engineer for a pipeline company in Rusk County, Texas. In 1920 was a garage owner in Troup. In 1930 was an oil and gas salesman in Lone Oak, Hunt County, Texas. Died Apr. 22, 1953, Smith County, Texas. FAMILY: Parents, E. H. Toncray (b. 1834, VA) and A. M. (b. 1842, GA); spouse, Andie Conaway (b. 1880, TX), married Dec. 22, 1895, Smith County. *SR; A1b, d, e, f, g; A2b, e.*

TOWNSEND, HOWARD ASA. Born May 31, 1883, Columbus, Colorado County, Texas. Ht. 5 ft. 10 in., blue eyes, dark hair, light complexion, married. Attorney, Columbus. SPECIAL RANGER June 22, 1918–Sept. 1918. Discharged. REMARKS: Died Apr. 26, 1930, Bexar County, Texas; buried in Columbus Odd Fellows Cemetery. FAMILY: Parents, James Light Townsend (b. 1845, TX) and Margaret Alice Cummins (b. 1852, TN); siblings, Charles (b. 1869, TX), Lumpien Elma (b. 1870, TX), Elizabeth Rebecca "Lizzie" (b. 1874, TX), Margaret Lee "Maggie" (b. 1876, TX),

Howard (b. 1879, TX), Carrie Estelle (b. 1882, TX), James Light (b. 1886, TX); spouse, Gladys Guen Johnson (b. 1887, TX), married Sept. 13, 1913, Niagara Falls, New York; son, J. Howard (b. 1917, TX). *SR; A1b, e, f; A2b; A3a; A4a, b; B1.*

TOWNSEND, SETH T. Born Mar. 7, 1871, Tuxpan, Veracruz, Mexico. Ht. 5 ft. 8 in., brown eyes, gray hair, dark complexion, married. Deputy sheriff. REGULAR RANGER Oct. 9, 1911–Jan. 31, 1912 (private, Co. B). Discharged—reduction in force. REMARKS: In 1920 was a retired rancher in San Antonio, Bexar County, Texas. Died Feb. 20, 1922, Phoenix, Maricopa County, Arizona. FAMILY: Parents, John Thomas Windfield Townsend (b. 1830, FL) and Georgia Ann Harrison (b. 1839, TX); siblings, Claud (b. 1869, TX), Thomas (b. 1873, TX); stepmother, Caroline "Carrie" Stockway or Brockway (b. 1830, AL); spouse, Alina (b. 1876, MO); sons, Seth T. (b. 1901, TX), Eugene (b. 1909, TX). *SR; LWT, Feb 4, 1912; 508: 66; A1b, f; A4a, b, e; B1.*

TOWNSEND, WILLIAM THOMAS. Born June 11, 1886, McKinney, Collin County, Texas. Tall, slender, brown eyes, dark hair, married. Grain dealer, Happy, Swisher County, Texas. LOYALTY RANGER June 17, 1918–Mar. 6, 1919. REMARKS: Had been a public school teacher in Swisher County. As of June 1917 was manager and part owner, Townsend Grain Company, Happy. In 1930 was a grain buyer in Happy. Died Feb. 23, 1940, Randall County, Texas. FAMILY: Parents, George Lee Townsend (b. 1861, KY) and Carrie Callie or Eugene Addington (b. 1869, MS); siblings, Eddie Lee (b. 1888, TX), Edna Nora (b. 1891, TX), Lillie (b. 1892, TX), Horace Herschel (b. 1895, TX), Eula Odell (b. 1897, TX), Lonnie Dee (b. 1900, TX); spouse, Susie Belle Harding (b. 1890, TX), married May 17, 1908; children, Arnel Naomi (1909, TX), Carrie Marie (1912, TX), Dorothy Belle (b. 1913, TX), Emma Lorraine (b. 1918, TX), William Thomas (b. 1920, TX). *SR; A1b, e, f, g; A2b; A3a; A4a, b; B1.*

TRAVIS, EDMUNDS. Born Feb. 6, 1890, Jackson, Madison County, Tennessee. Ht. 5 ft. 9 in., brown eyes, dark hair, fair complexion, married. Editor, *Austin Statesman* newspaper, Austin, Travis County, Texas. SPECIAL RANGER June 5, 1918–Jan. 15, 1919. REMARKS: In 1930 was a newspaper editorial writer in Houston, Harris County, Texas. Died Sept. 27, 1971, Austin, Travis County, Texas; buried in Austin Memorial Park. FAMILY: Parents, James Ludson Stephen Travis (b. 1850, TN) and Sarah "Sallie" Edmunds (b. 1862, TN); brother, James Edward (b. 1896, TN); spouse #1, Virginia May (b. 1887, TX), married about 1909; daughter, Virginia (b. 1911, TX); spouse #2, Winifred May (b. 1898, TX), married Aug. 1913; son, Edmunds, Jr. (b. 1927, TX). *SR; 172:VI, 550; A1d, e, f, g; A2a, b; A3a; A4b.*

TRAVIS, MILTON THOMAS. Born May 10, 1873, Greenville, Muhlenberg County, Kentucky. Medium height, slender, blue eyes, light hair, married. Farmer, Cone, Crosby County, Texas. LOYALTY RANGER June 6, 1918–Feb. 1919. REMARKS: Died Sept. 14, 1944, Crosby County, Texas. FAMILY: Spouse, Elizabeth J. (b. 1879, MS), married about 1900; children, George M. (b. 1901, TX), Emma L. (b. 1903, TX), Milton T. (b. 1909, TX), Curtis E. (b. 1917, TX). *SR; A1e, f, g; A2b; A3a.*

TRIMBLE, LA FETRA ELISHA "LEE." Born Sept. 22, 1894, Globe, Gila County, Arizona. Ht. 5 ft. 10 in., blue eyes, black hair, dark complexion, married as of Jan. 1930. Cowboy, Marfa, Presidio County, Texas. REGULAR RANGER Oct. 2, 1918–Dec. 10, 1924 (private, Co. B; reenlisted in Co. A under the new law, June 20, 1919; promoted to sergeant, Sept. 1, 1921; reenlisted June 20, 1923; reduced to private, Nov. 1, 1924). Resigned. Peace officer, Marfa. SPECIAL RANGER Nov. 12, 1925–Feb. 1, 1927—WA expired. Peace officer, Brady, McCulloch County, Texas. SPECIAL RANGER Jan. 14, 1930–Jan. 14, 1931; Jan. 24, 1931–Jan. 20, 1932; Jan. 20, 1932–Jan. 20, 1933; Oct. 5, 1933–Oct. 4, 1935. REMARKS: In June 1917 lived in Snyder, Scurry County, Texas and worked for a lady in Polar, Kent County, Texas. On 1918 enlistment form—"This boy can't get in the Army because he has one eye gone." In 1930 worked for the livestock commission in Brady. In Oct. 1935 received his mail at Harper, Gillespie County, Texas, where he was working on the James River Ranch. Died July 14, 1985, Concho County, Texas. FAMILY: Parents, Lambeth Hopkins Trimble (b. 1848, GA) and Mary S. (b. 1861, TX); siblings, Alston Means (b. 1881, TX), Bertha (b. 1882, TX), Briena or Buena (b. 1885, TX), Elmor (b. 1887, TX); spouse, Cadelia (b. 1903, TX), married about 1928. *SR; 471; 470: 43; 140; A1d, f, g; A2b; A3a; A4a, b.*

TROLLINGER, HARRIS C. "HARRY." Born Feb. 1878, Shelbyville, Bedford County, Tennessee. Ht. 5 ft. 7 in., gray eyes, dark hair, dark complexion. Peace officer. REGULAR RANGER Oct. 30, 1911–Jan. 31, 1912 (private, Co. C). Discharged—reduction in force. Peace officer. REGULAR RANGER Apr. 1, 1915–June 13, 1915 (private, Co. B). Discharged/fired. Peace officer, enlisted in Hartley County, Texas. REGULAR RANGER Oct. 16, 1915–Mar. 1, 1918 (private, Co. B; reenlisted Dec 15, 1917 as sergeant, Co. B). Resigned/fired for drunkenness. REMARKS: Before becoming a Ranger had been a peace officer in Kaufman County, Texas. Was fired in June 1915 in the wake of the May 1915 ambush in which Rangers Eugene Hulen and Joe Sitter died and of which Trollinger was a survivor. He appealed to Governor Ferguson, who allowed his reenlistment, in Oct. 1915. In Nov. 1917, while drunk in El Paso, El Paso County, Texas, he tried to pick a fight with the district attorney on two occasions. In 1920 was a special officer for a coal company in El Paso. FAMILY: Parents, John A. Trollinger (b. 1853, TN) and Susan (b. 1852, TN); siblings, Allen (b. 1880, TN), Emma (b. 1882, TN), Andrew Lafayette (b. 1885, TX); stepmother, Sallie (b. 1877, TN). *SR; 471; BDH, Jan 31, 1912; 1: I, 1532–1535; Bates to Ferguson, June 9, 1915, WC; Baldwin to Hutchings, July 27, 1910 [sic—1915], AGC; AG to Fox, June 2, 3, 4, 1915, WC; McKay to Hutchings, June 2, 1915, WC; Hutchings to Fox, June 5, 1915, WC; EPMT, May 31, 1915; AA, May 27, 1915; MR, Co. B, June 1915, AGC; Ferguson to Hutchings, Sept 22, 25, 1915, AGC; AG to Ferguson, Sept 24, 1915, AGC; Trollinger to Ferguson, Sept 16, 1915, AGC; Fox to Hutchings, Sept 29, 1915, AGC; AG to Fox, Sept 30, 1915, AGC; AG to Fox, Nov 10, 1917, RRM; Fox to Harley, Feb 22, 1918, AGC; Fox to Woodul, Mar 2, 1918, AGC; Hudspeth to Hobby, May 31, 1918, AGC; Harley to Hudspeth, June 2, 1918, AGC; 422: 77; 488: 35–36; A1b, d, f; A3a.*

TUCKER, BENJAMIN F. Born Dec. 1870, Clay County, Georgia. Ht. 6 ft. ½ in., blue eyes, gray hair, light complexion, married. Lumberyard foreman, Lufkin, Angelina County, Texas. LOYALTY RANGER July 5, 1918–Feb. 1919. REMARKS: Had been a sawmill yard foreman in Valley, Oachita County, Arkansas. In 1930 lived in Houston, Harris County, Texas with one of his sons and his family. Another son, Hollis H. "Harry" Tucker, a professional baseball player, also lived there. FAMILY: Spouse, Ella Priscilla Brannen (b. 1872, AL), married about 1893; children, Claud Victor (b. 1894, TX), Bernard Farris (b. 1898, TX), Jannita (b. 1901, AR), Hollis H. "Harry" (b. 1906, AR). *SR; A1d, e, f, g; A3a.*

TUCKER, JAMES SUMMERVILLE. Born Oct. 25, 1854, Refugio County, Texas. No physical description, married. Grade contractor, Ochiltree, Ochiltree County, Texas. LOYALTY RANGER July 16, 1918–Feb. 1919. REMARKS: Had been a farmer in Duke, Greer County, Oklahoma. In 1920 was retired, living with a son in Ochiltree County. Died Apr. 12, 1927, Thoreau, McKinley County, New Mexico; buried in Gallup, McKinley County. FAMILY: Parents, Lemuel Tarleton Tucker (b. 1824, MD) and Mary Francis Duke (b. 1831, TX); siblings, Kate Jane (b. 1848, TX), Leonard Thomas (b. 1851, TX), William Henry (b. 1857, TX), Laura Elizabeth (b. 1858, TX), Sarah (b. 1859, TX), John (b. 1862, TX), Stephen Tarleton (b. 1866, TX), Mary Alice (b. 1871, TX); spouse, Francis Jane "Fannie" Stephenson (b. 1859, TX), married Jan. 15, 1879, Victoria County, Texas; children, Alice Estelle (b. 1879, TX), Pearl Elizabeth (b. 1881, TX), James Simms (b. 1884, TX), Stephen R. (b. 1886, TX), Louie Tarleton (b. 1888, TX), Lillie Franci (b. 1891, TX), Lauretta M. (b. 1893, TX), Dewitt Clinton (b. 1896, TX), Mary Lee (b. 1900, OK). *SR; A1a, b, d, f; A2e; A4a, b; B2.*

TULLIS, WILLIAM ANDREW. Born April 3, 1880, Oakville, Live Oak County, Texas. Ht. 5 ft. 9 in., dark eyes, dark hair, dark complexion, married. County treasurer, Oakville. LOYALTY RANGER June 13, 1918–Feb. 1919. REMARKS: In 1930 was manager, "Bridge Corp.," Mercedes, Hidalgo County, Texas. Died Apr. 25, 1956, Hidalgo County, Texas. FAMILY: Spouse, Frances A. (b. 1887, TX), married about 1906; children, Woodie (b. 1908, TX), Maude E. (b. 1914, TX). *SR; A1f, g; A2b; A3a.*

TULLY, THOMAS L. "TOM." Born Sept. 21, 1886, Pearsall, Frio County, Texas. Ht. 5 ft. 10 in., gray eyes, brown hair, medium complexion. Ranchman. REGULAR RANGER May 18, 1916–June 18, 1917 (private, Co. A). Resigned. REMARKS: In 1920 and 1930 was a house painter in Pearsall. Died Aug. 29, 1967, Frio County, Texas. FAMILY: Parents, Walker R. Tully (b. 1854, TX) and Anna E. Hester (b. 1859, TX); siblings, Jullie E. (b. 1882, TX), Walker Hester (b. 1884, TX), Henry S. (b. 1888, TX). *SR; 471; A1d, f, g; A2a, b; A3a; A4a.*

TUMLINSON, BENJAMIN THOMAS, JR. Born Nov. 17, 1893, Carrizo Springs, Dimmit County, Texas. Ht. 5 ft. 9 in., brown eyes, brown hair, light complexion. Stockman. REGULAR RANGER Sept. 8, 1917–Apr. 1, 1923 (private, Co. A; reenlisted in Co. K under the new law, June 20, 1919; reenlisted in Co. D, June 20, 1921). Resigned. REMARKS: Had lived in Sinton, San Patricio County, Texas. As of May 1917 was a stockraiser in Duval County, Texas. Died June 10, 1923, Nueces County, Texas. LAW ENFORCEMENT RELATIVES: Ranger Captain Peter F. Tumlinson, great-grandfather; Ranger Lott Tumlinson (Co. A, 1903–1904), uncle; Ranger Peter C. Tumlinson, uncle; Ranger Otho Dee Vivion, cousin; Customs Inspector Benjamin T. Tumlinson, father; sheriff (Dimmit County, 1880–1890, and La Salle County, Texas, 1892–1894) Joseph W. Tumlinson, grandfather. See Tumlinson Family, Taylor Family, Wright Family charts for additional relatives. FAMILY: Parents, Benjamin Thomas Tumlinson (b. 1869, TX) and Lavenia Vivion (b. 1869, TX); siblings, Mabel (b. 1889, TX), Alfred Wiley (b. 1891, TX), Jodie (b. 1897, TX), Ophelia (b. 1906, TX). *SR; Special Orders No. 21, Mar 10, 1919, WC; 172:VI, 587–588; 525:23, 24; LWT, July 20, 1913; 469: 60, 62, 63, 66–67, 74; 470: 35; A1d, e, f; A2b; A3a; A4a; B1, 2.*

TURMAN, JOHN CYRUS, JR. Born June 12, 1894, Uvalde, Uvalde County, Texas. Ht. 6 ft. 2 in., blue-gray eyes, light hair, light complexion. Stockman, Uvalde. SPECIAL RANGER June 7, 1917–Dec. 1917 (attached to Co. C). REMARKS: Recommended by John Nance Garner and Thomas A. Coleman. World War I Draft Registration document states Turman had attended Texas A and M College for three months; occupation listed as coal miner, Bear Grass Coal Company, Jewell, Texas. Died Aug. 19, 1952, Uvalde, Uvalde County, Texas. FAMILY: Parents, John Cyrus Turman (b. 1863, TX) and Lula Burford Woodley (b. 1867, TX); sisters, Beatrice (b. 1892, TX), Mildred (b. 1897, TX); spouse, Rose Shaw Franks; children, Betty Lou (b. 1932, TX), John Franks (b. 1938, TX). *SR; Coleman to Ferguson, June 1, 1917, AGC; AG to Turman, June 2, 1917, AGC; AG to Garner, June 2, 1917, AGCl; A1d, e, f; A2b, e; A3a; A4g.*

TURNER, HENRY A. Born Sept. 20, 1872, Saint Jacobs, Madison County, Illinois. Ht. 5 ft. 8 in., blue eyes, light hair, fair complexion, married. Cattleman, enlisted in Madison County, Texas. SPECIAL RANGER Jan. 15, 1917–Dec. 1917. REMARKS: Had been a merchant and a farmer. Had resided in Madison County, Texas for 33 years. January 1917 letterhead: "Turner-Herring Co., Inc., Merchants, Midway." In 1920 was a banker in Madisonville, Madison County. A Henry A. Turner died Nov. 14, 1952, Madison County, Texas. FAMILY: Parents, Richard Turner (b. 1849, England) and Melissa (b. 1853, IL); brother, William (b. 1875. IL); spouse, Pearl E. (b. 1878, TX), married about 1895; sons, Allie (b. 1896, TX), Harvey R. (b. 1900, TX). *SR; Wroe to AG, Jan 11, 1917, AC; AG to Longbotham, Jan 11, 1917, AGC; A1b, e, f; A2b; A3a.*

TURNER, JOSEPH WALLACE "JOE." Born May 3, 1884, Itasca, Hill County, Texas. Ht. 5 ft. 10 in., blue eyes, dark hair, ruddy complexion, married. Ranchman, Raymondville, Hidalgo County, Texas. SPECIAL RANGER Apr. 22, 1918–Jan. 15, 1919. REMARKS: Recommended by Caesar Kleberg, a King Ranch manager. As of Sept. 1918 was a ranchman at the La Coma ranch in Hidalgo County. Willacy County sheriff Aug. 13, 1921–Jan. 1, 1925 and Nov. 8, 1938–Jan. 1, 1941. FAMILY: Parents, Richard J. Turner (b. 1855, TX) and Mittie (b. 1860, TX); siblings, Angie E. (b. 1881, TX), Ora E. (b. 1882, TX), Frank Maynor (b. 1889, TX), Thomas Lee (b. 1894, TX), Monroe Phearson (b. 1898, TX); spouse, Paula (b. 1889, TX). *SR; 1503:543; A1d, f; A3a.*

TURNER, O. A. Born 1882, Burnet, Burnet County, Texas. Ht. 5 ft. 10 in., blue eyes, brown hair, fair complexion. Carpenter. REGULAR RANGER Nov. 9, 1915–Nov. 7, 1916 (private, Co. B). Resigned. *SR; 471.*

TURNER, WILLIAM L. "BILLY." Born Feb. 1857, Yellow Prairie, Burleson County, Texas. Ht. 5 ft. 9 in., blue eyes, light hair, light complexion, married. Real estate agent, Madisonville, Madison County, Texas. LOYALTY RANGER July 6, 1918–Mar. 6, 1919. FAMILY: Parents, William M. Turner (b. 1821, GA) and Louisa (b. 1831, GA); siblings, Ella D. (b. 1850, GA), James B. (b. 1855, GA), Annanora Willis (b. 1859, TX), Mary Ziporah (b. 1861, TX), Emery F. "Guy" (b. 1866, TX); spouse, Nora Mary Eddleman (b. 1863, GA), married about 1882, Bryan, Brazos County, Texas; children, Leah B. (b. 1890, TX), Nugent W. (b. 1892, TX), Evelyn Nora (b. 1901, TX), Walter E. (b. 1894, TX). *SR; A1aa, e, f; A4g; B2.*

UMSCHEID, MAXIMILIAN JOHN "MAX." Born Sept. 13, 1875, Bexar County, Texas. Medium height, medium build, blue eyes, black hair, married. Peace officer, enlisted in Travis County, Texas. SPECIAL RANGER Oct. 29, 1918–unknown. REMARKS: In 1910 was a saloon keeper in Austin, Travis County. As of Sept. 1918 was a peace officer and salesman for Austin Mercantile Co., Austin. Died May 17, 1928, Travis County, Texas. FAMILY: Parents, Felix Umscheid (b. 1827, Bavaria) and Johanna (b. 1834, Bavaria); siblings, Anna (b. 1858, TX), Ragina (b. 1860, TX), Margaretha (b. 1862, TX), Henry (b. 1864, TX), Mary (b. 1866, TX); spouse, Ida Mary (b. 1876, TX), married about 1896; children, Margaret M. (b. 1905, TX), Gertrude B. (b. 1906, TX), Henry M. (b. 1909, TX). *SR; A1a, d, e, f; A2b; A3a.*

USSERY, CHARLES CHESTERFIELD "CHARLEY." Born Oct. 1869, Valley View, Cooke County, Texas. Ht. 5 ft. 10 in., gray eyes, brown hair, fair complexion, married. Farmer, Valley View. LOYALTY RANGER June 4, 1918–Feb. 1919. REMARKS: In 1920 was a stock trader in Valley View. Died Mar. 2, 1930, Cooke County, Texas. FAMILY: Parents, Dr. Chester C. Ussery (b. 1837, MS) and Sarah A. B. (b. 1840, TX); siblings, Dr. William H. (b. 1858, TX), Keziah (b. 1860, TX), James (b. 1865, TX), Emmett T. (b. 1867, TX), Mary (b. 1869, TX), John R. (b. 1872, TX), Anna (b. 1875, TX); spouse #1, Susian "Susie" (b. 1872, TX), married about 1893; children, Julian (b. 1893, TX), Mattie Pearl (b. 1896, TX), Maude M. (b. 1903, TX); spouse #2, Bessie C. (b. 1881, TX), married about 1913. *SR; Ussery to AG, Jan 12, 1919, AGC; A1a, b, d, e, f, g; A2b; B1.*

VALLE VILLAREAL, CALIXTO. Born July 1870, Camargo, Tamaulipas, Mexico. Ht. 5 ft. 6 in., black eyes, black hair, married. Merchant, Rio Grande City, Starr County, Texas. SPECIAL RANGER Aug. 5, 1919–Dec. 31, 1919. REMARKS: Immigrated to the United States in 1890, became a naturalized citizen in 1906. Had been a stock rancher in Starr County. In May 1920 opened, with others, the First National Bank in Rio Grande City. In 1930 was a retail hardware merchant in Rio Grande City. Died May 18, 1962, Starr County, Texas. FAMILY: Parents, Gabriel Valle Rucio and Barbara Villareal Lopez; spouse, Herminia Longoria (b. 1877, Mexico), married about 1899; children, Herminia T. (b. 1899, Mexico), Gabriel Ruben (b. 1901, TX), Rachel (b. 1904, TX), Calixto (b. 1906, TX), Raul D. (b. 1912, TX), Rodolfo R. (b. 1913, TX). *SC; Edds to Aldrich, May 2, 1920, AGC; A1d, e, f, g; A2a, b; A4a.*

VAN CLEVE, JACK. Born about 1895, Picoso, Zavala County, Texas. Ht. 5 ft. 6 in., blue eyes, brown hair, medium complexion. Stockman. REGULAR RANGER May 16, 1916–Sept. 20, 1916 (private, Co. A). Resigned. Stockman, Cometa, Zavala County. SPECIAL RANGER May 24, 1917–unknown (attached to Co. C). REMARKS: Resigned as SPECIAL RANGER to join the Marine Corps. Was killed in action in France in May 1918; was awarded a Purple Heart and a Silver Star. LAW ENFORCEMENT RELATIVES: Ranger Jack Van Cleve, nephew. FAMILY: Parents, Alonzo or Alfonda Van Cleve (b. 1845, TX) and unknown Cunningham; siblings, Almer (b. 1882, TX), Alfonda or Alford (b. 1884, TX), Harvey (b. 1885, TX), Susan (b. 1886, TX), John (b. 1887, TX), Elnora (b. 1888, TX), Lillie (b. 1898, TX). *SR; 471; Gardner to Hutchings, Apr 25, 1917, AGC; AG to Gardner, May 18, 1917, AGC; 470: 144; A1d; A4g.*

VANDERGRIFT, WILLIAM EDWARD. Born Mar. 18, 1885, Smiley, Gonzales County, Texas. Ht. 6 ft. 4 in., brown eyes, dark hair, dark complexion. Ranchhand, Norias Ranch, Armstrong, Kenedy County, Texas. SPECIAL RANGER Sept. 16, 1916–unknown. WA was renewed Dec. 22, 1917, and Jan. 23 1919. REMARKS: Was commissioned at the request of Caesar Kleberg, a King Ranch manager. Was killed on Feb. 11, 1920, Cameron County, Texas. FAMILY: Parents, Edward Milton Vandergrift (b. 1859, TX) and Carrie Elizabeth (b. 1868, TX); siblings, twins Mamie and Susie (b. 1889, TX), Laleat (b. 1893, TX), Frank (b. 1904, TX). *SR; AG to Vandergrift , Sept 8, 1916; A1d, f, g; A2b; A3a.*

VANDER STUCKEN, ALFRED EMIL BURCHARD. Born Sept. 12, 1867, Fredericksburg, Gillespie County, Texas. Ht. 5 ft. 7 in., brown eyes, iron gray hair, dark complexion, married. Stockman and banker, San Antonio, Bexar County, Texas. SPECIAL RANGER Jan. 25, 1918–Jan. 15, 1919. REMARKS: Had been a miller and banker in Fredericksburg. 1919 letterhead: "Alfred Vander Stucken, Cattle Loans, Brady Building, San Antonio." Died Mar. 12, 1920, Bexar County, Texas. FAMILY: Parents, Felix Vander Stucken (b. 1833, Belgium) and Christine Schoenewolf

(b. 1842, Germany); sisters, Constance Sophie Adele (b. 1859, TX), Marie Elise Auguste (b. 1860, TX), Mathilde Franziska (b. 1863, TX), Anna Mathilde (b. 1866, TX), Olga (b. 1869, TX), Louisa (b. 1871, TX); spouse, Cornelia Lungkwitz (b. 1863, TX), married Oct. 19, 1889, Gillespie County; children, Dora (b. 1894, TX), Liesel (b. 1896, TX), Edgar (b. 1899, TX), Margarette (b. 1902, TX), Christine (b. 1905, TX). *SR; A1a, b, d, e, f, g; A2b; B1, 2.*

VAN HAESEN, H. M. Born Oct. 1867, Toledo, Lucas County, Ohio. Ht. 6 ft. ½ in., blue eyes, brown hair, dark complexion, married. Warehouse manager, El Campo, Wharton County, Texas. LOYALTY RANGER June 8, 1918–Mar. 6, 1919. REMARKS: 1919 letterhead: "Wharton County Warehouse Co., Rough Rice Storage, El Campo, Tex." A Harry Van Hoesen (note spelling; b. about 1869, OH) was a probation officer in Houston, Harris County, Texas in 1930. FAMILY: Spouse (of Harry Van Hoesen), Nora (b. 1883, IL), married about 1919. *SR; A1g.*

VANN, BISHOP LAFAYETTE. Born June 14, 1883, Kerrville, Kerr County, Texas. Ht. 5 ft. 10 ½ in., blue eyes, dark hair, fair complexion, married. Assistant manager gas company, Austin, Travis County, Texas. SPECIAL RANGER May 12, 1917–unknown. REMARKS: As of Sept. 1918 was a farmer and merchant in Manor, Travis County. In 1920 was a merchant in Pflugerville, Travis County. In 1930 was a dry goods salesman in Austin. Died June 28, 1958, Travis County, Texas. LAW ENFORCEMENT RELATIVES: Ranger John W. Vann, brother; Ranger Charles C. Vann, nephew. FAMILY: Parents, Wilson Wade Vann (b. 1836, TN) and Margaret Laduska Bishop (b. 1841, MO); siblings, John William (b. 1860, TX), Mary Ann (b. 1863, TX), Murray Wilson (b. 1864, TX), Josie Ellen (b. 1873, TX), Thomas S. (b. 1875, TX), Maggie Mae (b. 1877, TX), Allie (b. 1878, TX), Etta (b. 1879, TX), Edna Blanche (b. 1880, TX); spouse, Lomie Lee Gibson (b. 1880, TX), married about 1905; son, B. L., Jr. (b. 1909, TX). *SR; A1d, e, f, g; A2b; A3a; A4a, b; B2.*

VANN, CHARLES CALEB. Born Mar. 29, 1888, Kerrville, Kerr County, Texas. Ht. 5 ft. 9 in., gray eyes, brown hair, dark complexion. Peace officer, enlisted in Cameron County, Texas. REGULAR RANGER May 1, 1911–July 1911 (private, Co. B). Resigned. REMARKS: Before and after Ranger service was a Cameron County deputy sheriff. As of June 1917 was a saloon keeper in Kerrville. In 1920 was a stock trader in Kerrville. In 1930 was a ranch hand in Kerrville. Died Apr. 28, 1938, Kerr County, Texas. LAW ENFORCEMENT RELATIVES: Ranger John W. Vann, father; Ranger Bishop L. Vann, uncle. FAMILY: Parents, John William Vann (b. 1860, TX) and Julia Blanche Weston (b. 1863, TX); siblings, William Walter (b. 1881, TX), Amy (b. 1884, TX), Jesse Stewart (b. 1894, TX); spouse #1, Margaret (b. 1888, TX); spouse #2, Josephine B. (b. 1901, TX); stepdaughters, Margy Mayes (b. 1922, TX), Bessie M. Mayes (b. 1924, TX). *SR; 471; BDH, Feb 5, 1910, July 17, 24, Aug 4, 8, 25, 1911; MR, Co. B, May–July, 1911, AGC; AG to SA&AP Railroad, Aug 21, 1911, AGC; A1s, f, g; A2b; A3a; B1.*

VANN, JOHN WILLIAM. Born Mar. 19, 1860, La Grange, Fayette County, Texas. Ht. 5 ft. 10 in., blue eyes, black hair, dark complexion, married. Chief special agent, MKT Railroad, Smithville, Bastrop County, Texas. SPECIAL RANGER Dec. 2, 1916–Jan. 15, 1919 (attached to Co. C). WA was reinstated Jan. 3, 1918. REMARKS: Kerr County, Texas sheriff Nov. 8, 1892–resigned June 18, 1902. Was deputy U.S. marshal for ten years. Special agent, federal Bureau of Investigation, El Paso, El Paso County, Texas and San Antonio, Bexar County, Texas, 1911. Apr. 1913 became chief special agent, MKT Railroad with headquarters in Dallas, Dallas County, Texas. In Mar. 1913 a J. W. Vann was a constable in Dallas. In 1920 was a railroad special agent in San Antonio. In 1930 was a deputy U.S. marshal in San Antonio. A John William Vann died June 21, 1943, Bexar County, Texas. LAW ENFORCEMENT RELATIVES: Ranger Charles C. Vann, son; Ranger Bishop L. Vann, brother. FAMILY: Parents, Wilson Wade Vann (b. 1836, TN) and Margaret Laduska Bishop (b. 1841, MO); siblings, Mary Ann (b. 1863, TX), Murray Wilson (b. 1864, TX), Josie Ellen (b. 1873, TX), Thomas S. (b. 1875, TX), Maggie Mae (b. 1877, TX), Allie (b. 1878, TX), Etta (b. 1879, TX), Edna Blanche (b. 1880, TX), Bishop L. (b. 1883, TX); spouse #1, Julia Blanche Weston (b. 1863, TX), married Mar. 25, 1880, Kerr County; children, William Walter (b. 1881, TX), Amy (b. 1884, TX), Charles Caleb (b. 1888, TX), Jesse Stewart (b. 1894, TX); spouse #2, Maude A. (b. 1887, England), married before 1920, divorced by 1930. *SR; Vann to Ferguson, Nov 27, 1916, May 3, 1917, AGC; AG to Vann, Nov 29, 1916, AGC; Vann to AG, Dec 2, 1916, AGC; 1503:304; EPMT, Apr 12, 1913; SAE, Mar 13,1913; A1aa, d, f, g; A2b; A3a; A4a, b; B1, 2.*

V

Texas Ranger Captain Jefferson Eagle Vaughan. *Photo courtesy Texas Ranger Hall of Fame and Museum.*

VAUGHAN, JEFFERSON EAGLE. Born Apr. 6, 1882, Perry County, Arkansas. Ht. 6 ft. 1 ½ in., hazel eyes, brown hair, fair complexion. Cattle raiser, Alpine, Brewster County, Texas. REGULAR RANGER Aug. 12, 1912–Dec. 1914 (private, Co A). Resigned to become a mounted Customs inspector (1914–1915), at Valentine, Jeff Davis County, Texas. Ranchman. REGULAR RANGER Sept. 15, 1917–July 1, 1920 (private, Co. B; promoted to sergeant, Co. F, Jan. 1, 1918; transferred to Co. B as sergeant, Dec. 1918; transferred to Co. C; reduced to private, Jan. 1, 1919; reenlisted in Co. A under the new law, June 20, 1919). Resigned to run for sheriff of Presidio County. SPECIAL RANGER Dec. 20, 1926–Feb. 1, 1927. Discharged. Ranchman, Marfa, Presidio County. REGULAR RANGER Jan. 19, 1933–Jan. 24, 1935 (captain, Co. A). Discharged.

REMARKS: Vaughan was evidently unsure where he was born: 1912 enlistment—Perry County, Arkansas; 1917 enlistment—Kendalia, Kendall County, Texas; 1919 enlistment—Kendalia; 1926 enlistment Trickem, Brown County, Texas; 1933 enlistment—Kendalia. (Note: There is no Trickem in Brown County. There is a Trickham in Coleman County, Texas.) In 1900 and 1910 U.S. Census records, Arkansas is listed as his place of birth. In 1910 was a stock farmer in Erath County, Texas. In Aug. 1912, Ranger Capt. John Hughes described Vaughan as "an old time cowboy." In 1917 was a deputy game warden for the Game, Fish, and Oyster Commission. Sheriff, Presidio County, Nov. 2, 1920–Jan. 1, 1927. In 1926 was commissioned by order of Governor Ferguson. Was a rancher after retiring from the Rangers. Was one of the four Rangers to whom Zane Gray dedicated *The Lone Star Ranger*. Died Oct. 1, 1958, Presidio, Presidio County, Texas; buried at Stephenville, Erath County, Texas. FAMILY: Parents, John Joseph L. Vaughan (b. 1854, MO) and Mattie O. (b. 1860, MO); siblings, Lillie S. (b. 1884, AR), Irene (b. 1887, AR), Willie C. (b. 1890, AR), Bird B. (b. 1893, AR), Cora M. (b. 1888, AR), Joe (b. 1902, TX). *SR; 471; Hughes to AG, Aug 29, 1912, AGC; MR, Co. A, Aug–Dec 1912, AGC; AG to Gen. Manager, Nov 29, 1912, AGC; AG to Gen. Manager, Feb 11, 1913, AGC; Crotty to Hutchings, Mar 15, 1913, AGC; Vaughan to Hutchings, Mar 24, 1913, AGC; Wager to York, Mar 24, 1913, AGC; Hughes to AG, Apr 1, 1913, AGC; AG to Hughes, Sept 6, Dec 5, 1913, AGC; Hughes to AG, Oct 10, Nov 9, 1913, AGC; Crotty to Hutchings, Mar 3, 1914, AGC; Hughes to Crotty, Mar 14, 1914, AGC; MR, Co. A, June, July, Dec 1914, AGC; AG to Fox, Sept 24, 1917, AGC; Fox to Harley, Dec 13, 1917, AGC; Bates to Harley, Apr 6, 1918, RRM; Oxford to Harley, June 28, 1918, WC; Brelsford to Harley, June 29, 1918, WC; Anders to Vaughan, Dec 9, 1918, AGC; 1503:424; BDH, Apr 2, 1913; AA, Mar 27, 1913, June 18, 1914, Aug 28, 1919, July 29, 1920; EPMT, Aug 16, 1912, July 30, 1913, Dec 31, 1914, May 19, June 12, Aug 8, Oct 6, Dec 2, 1915; 484: 311–312, 378; 1503:424; 204:II, 165; A1d, e, f; A2b; A3a.*

Texas Ranger Bert Clinton Veale. *Photo courtesy Texas Ranger Hall of Fame and Museum.*

VAUGHAN, RUFUS G. Born Oct. 2, 1884, Clarksville, Montgomery County, Tennessee. Ht. 5 ft. 10 ½ in., blue eyes, brown hair, fair complexion, married. Peace officer. REGULAR RANGER July 1, 1916–Aug. 15, 1917 (private, Co. C). WA was revoked. REMARKS: May have been a lighthouse keeper for the U.S. government in Portland, Cumberland County, Maine in 1910. Began U.S. Army service in 1911; as of 1920 was an Army officer living in San Antonio, Bexar County, Texas. Was a U.S. Army major in World War I. Died June 26, 1967, Bexar County, Texas; buried in Ft. Sam Houston National Cemetery, San Antonio. *SR; 471; A1e, f; A2b; A3b.*

VEALE, BERTRAM CLINTON "BERT." Born Sept. 13, 1889, Caldwell, Burleson County, Texas. Ht. 6 ft. 1 ½ in., gray eyes, black hair, light complexion. Peace officer (convict guard); applied from Houston, Harris County, Texas. REGULAR RANGER July 31, 1915–Feb. 7, 1919 (private, Co. D). REMARKS: In 1910 lived in Fort Worth, Tarrant County, Texas. As of June 1917 was a deputy sheriff living in Goose Creek, Harris County, Texas. Was killed Feb. 17, 1919, by Ranger Capt. K. F. Cunningham in a drunken shooting scrape in Austin, Travis County, Texas. FAMILY: Parents, Thomas L. Veale (b. 1850, LA) and Christina M. (b. 1861, TN); siblings, Eulah (b. 1894, TX), Mittie L. (b. 1897, TX), Vell W. (b. 1902, TX). *SR; 471; Veale to Hulen, June 1, 1915, AGC; AG to Veale, June 4, 1915, AGC; LWT, Feb 9, 1919; 319: 45; 508: 67; A1d, e, f; A2b; A3a.*

VILLARREAL, ERNESTO CELADONIO. Born Mar. 3, 1891, Brownsville, Cameron County, Texas. Tall, slender, brown eyes, black hair. Quarantine guard, Rio Grande City, Starr County, Texas. SPECIAL RANGER Feb. 5, 1918–Jan. 15, 1919. REMARKS: Had been a Texas quarantine guard in Brownsville in 1917. World War I Draft Registration document states "Stomach trouble, heart trouble." In 1930 was a grocery store salesman in Brownsville. Died May 13, 1974, Cameron County, Texas. FAMILY: Spouse, Lidia H.

Gutierrez (b. 1897, Mexico), married about 1921; children, Ernesto, Jr. (b. 1929, TX), Antonio L. (b. 1931, TX), Lidia Lucila (b. 1937, TX); adopted daughter, Beatriz Xamora (b. 1917, TX). *SR; Collins to Harley, Feb 1, 1918, AGC; BDH, Jan 3, Mar 3, 1917; A1g; A2a, b, e; A3a.*

VINSON, THEODORE RICHARD. Born Mar. 19, 1883, Holland, Bell County, Texas. Ht. 6 ft. 1 ½ in., blue eyes, light hair, fair complexion. Peace officer. REGULAR RANGER Oct. 12, 1917–Feb. 1, 1919 (private, Co. D; transferred to Co. H, Jan. 1, 1918; transferred back to Co. D, Dec. 1, 1918). Resigned. Clerk, Austin, Travis County, Texas. SPECIAL RANGER Nov. 25, 1919–Dec. 31, 1919. REMARKS: In 1920 was a clerk at the state arsenal, Austin. In 1930 was a stock farmer in Borden County, Texas. Died Mar. 28, 1969, Travis County, Texas. FAMILY: Parents, Rufus G. or R. Vinson (b. 1844, TN) and L. Anna (b. 1845, AL); siblings, Mildred C. (b. 1869, TX), twins Nettie E. and Emily A. (b. 1874, TX), E. L. (b. 1875, TX), Wm. R. (b. 1878, TX); spouse, Frances S. Barker (b. 1898, TX), married about 1915; son, T. R., Jr. "Teddy" (b. 1919, TX). *SR; 471; AG to MKT Railway, Oct 12, 1917, AGC; AG to Orient Railway, Oct 12, 1917, AGC; AG to Gen. Manager, Nov 13, 1917, AGC; A1a, b, d, f, g; A2a, b; A3a.*

VIVION, OTHO DEE. (Note: Many sources spell last name "VIVIAN," particularly in more recent documents.) Born Oct. 19, 1893, Carrizo Springs, Dimmit County, Texas. Ht. 6 ft., blue eyes, brown hair, medium complexion. Cowboy, Carrizo Springs. REGULAR RANGER June 20, 1916–Feb. 1, 1919 (private, Co. A; transferred to Co. I, Dec. 21, 1917; reenlisted in Co. I, Aug. 20, 1918). Honorably discharged. Returned to duty, Feb. 1919–unknown. REMARKS: As of June 1917, Ranger duty station was Raymondville, Willacy County, Texas. In 1920 was a rancher in Carrizo Springs. Died Jan. 10, 1973, Carrizo Springs, Dimmit County, Texas; buried in Mount Hope Cemetery, Carrizo Springs. LAW ENFORCEMENT RELATIVES: Ranger Benjamin T. Tumlinson, cousin; Customs Inspector Benjamin T. Tumlinson, uncle. See Tumlinson Family, Taylor Family, Wright Family charts for additional relatives. FAMILY: Parents, Lloyd Edward Vivion (b. 1867, TX) and Mary Elizabeth "Mollie" English (b. 1875, TX); siblings, Leslie Elmo (b. 1892, TX), Gus Otto (b. 1895, TX), Lottie Mae (b. 1896, TX), Lexie Elmira (b. 1897, TX), Laura Lee (b. 1898, TX), Edward (b. 1900, TX); spouse, Singne Olivia Nordberg (b. 1905, MA), married Sept. 24, 1924, Cuba; sons, Otho Dee, Jr. (b. 1931, TX), Ernest Clarence (b. 1940, TX). *SR; 471; Sanders to Harley, Dec 11, 1917, AGC; AG to Sanders, Dec 21, 1917, AGC; SAE, June 23, 1916; A1d, f; A2a, b; A3a; A4a, b, g; B1, 2.*

WADE, JOHN L. Born Jan. 1886, Dallas, Dallas County, Texas. Ht. 5 ft. 7 in., brown eyes, brown hair, dark complexion, married. Deputy sheriff. REGULAR RANGER Dec. 22, 1917–Feb. 1918 (private, Co. L). Discharged/fired—went AWOL. *SR; 471; Davis to Harley, Feb 4, 1918, AGC; Davis to Woodul, Feb 8, 1918, AGC; Assistant AG to Davis, Feb 11, 1918, AGC.*

WALBRIDGE, JESSE MONROE. Born Dec. 7, 1876, Lampasas, Lampasas County, Texas. Ht. 6 ft. ½ in., blue eyes, light hair, light complexion, married. Stockman, enlisted in El Paso County, Texas. SPECIAL RANGER Mar. 23, 1918–May 7, 1919 (attached to Co. L). Discharged—was notified to send in his commission. REMARKS: Name spelled in various ways in various documents, *i.e.* Walldridge, Wallridge, Walbridge; Walbridge is the most frequent spelling. Had been captain of police and a deputy sheriff. Had lived in Socorro, El Paso County. In 1930 was a cattleman in Ysleta, El Paso County. Died May 14, 1954, El Paso County, Texas. FAMILY: Parents, Rufus J. Walbridge (b. 1839, VT) and Mary Jane Bible (b. 1851, TX); sisters, Ara Lee (b. 1868, TX), Ina (b. 1881, TX); spouse, Juanita Loewenstein (b. 1883, TX), married about 1913; children, Monroe Morris (b. 1914, TX), Mary Lee (b. 1919, TX). *SR; A1b, e, f, g; A2b; A3a; A4a, b, g.*

WALKER, CHARLES EUGENE. Born July 26, 1876, Jacksonville, Morgan County, Illinois. Ht. 5 ft. 10 ½ in., blue eyes, brown hair, fair complexion, married. Jeweler, Baird, Callahan County, Texas. SPECIAL RANGER May 29, 1917–Dec. 1917 (attached to Co. C). FAMILY: Parents, Charles H. Walker (b. 1846, NH) and Grace (b. 1852, MA); brother, Fred W. (b. 1873, IL); spouse, Eleanor M. Cox (b. 1878, IL), married about 1897. *SR; A1b, d, e; A3a.*

WALKER, GEORGE HENRY. Born July 1864, Louisiana. Ht. 5 ft. 11 in., brown eyes, dark hair, fair complexion. Theater manager, Austin, Travis County, Texas. SPECIAL RANGER June 29, 1918–Jan. 13, 1919. REMARKS: Died Jan. 13, 1919, Travis County, Texas. FAMILY: Parents, Daniel Walker (b. 1837, MD) and Mary Jane (b. 1838, MO); siblings, Louisa (b. 1853, LA), Nicolas (b. 1855, LA), Mary E. (b. 1859, LA), Daniel (b. 1867, LA), Joseph (b. 1869, LA), Josephine (b. 1873, LA), Frank (b. 1875, LA), Laura (b. 1877, TX); spouse, unknown, divorced by 1900; son, Earl (b. 1886, TX). *SR; A1a, b, d; A2b.*

WALKER, JAMES CLAYTON. Born Dec. 27, 1874, Center, Shelby County, Texas. Ht. 5 ft. 11 in., gray eyes, black hair, fair complexion, married. Merchant, Center. LOYALTY RANGER June 18, 1918–Feb. 1919. REMARKS: Died Apr. 3, 1955, Dawson County, Texas. FAMILY: Parents, Joseph Jasper Walker (b. 1851, TX) and Mary Adaline Lucas (b. 1853, TX); sisters, Lucienda Jane (b. 1872, TX), Nancy M. (b. 1877, TX); spouse, Emma Estelle Polley (b. 1873, TX), married June 20, 1900, Shelby County; son, Ernest McDowell (b. 1903, TX). *SR; 471; A1b, d, e; A2b; A3a; B1, 2.*

WALKER, JOHN FRANKLIN. Born Mar. 10, 1888, Weimar, Colorado County, Texas. Ht. 6 ft., gray eyes, brown hair, married. Lumberman and cattleman, Weimar. LOYALTY RANGER June 12, 1918–Feb. 1919. REMARKS: Died Dec. 19, 1953, Colorado County, Texas; buried in Weimer Masonic Cemetery. FAMILY: Parents, John Thomas Walker (b. 1859, TX) and Anne Elizabeth Mitchell (b. 1857, TN); siblings, Ollie (b. 1882, TX), George (b. 1883, TX), Una (b. 1885, TX), Leo (b. 1891, TX), Bettie (b. 1893, TX); spouse, Elizabeth (b. 1891, TX), married about 1910; daughters, Mary E. (b. 1914, TX), Jaynice (b. 1916, TX). *SR; A1d, e, f; A2b; A3a; D.*

WALKER, ROY MERVIN. Born June 20, 1890, Salem, Dent County, Missouri. Medium height, medium build, blue eyes, brown hair, married. Electrician, El Paso, El Paso County, Texas. LOYALTY RANGER June 4, 1918–Feb. 1919. REMARKS: As of Sept. 1917 was an electrician for "National Telegraphone Supply Company" in El Paso. In 1930 was an electrical engineer for the El Paso public utility company. Died Feb. 25, 1968, El Paso County, Texas. FAMILY: Parents, John Hiley Walker (b. 1860, MO) and Irena Jennie Barker (b. 1859, MO); siblings, Irvin Burr (b. 1888, MO), Wilbert Ray (b. 1892, MO), John Lee (b. 1894, MO), Jessie May (b. 1897, MO), Clarence Morris (b. 1899, MO), Charles O. (b. 1901, MO), Thelma (b. 1908, MO); spouse, Helen Caspary (b. 1895, TX), married about 1913; children, Ellen M. (b. 1915, TX), Clarence D. (b. 1921, TX), Dorothy L. (b. 1924, TX), Maribeth (b. 1929, TX), James Keith (b. 1938, TX). *SR; A1d, f, g; A2a, b; A3a; A4b; B1.*

WALKER, SAM THOMAS. Born Feb. 23, 1886, Milam County, Texas. Ht. 6 ft. 2 in., blue eyes, brown hair, light complexion. Peace officer. REGULAR RANGER Feb. 10, 1921–May 20, 1921 (private, Emergency Co. No. 2). Resigned. REMARKS: As of Sept. 1918 was a meat cutter for Swift & Co. in Fort Worth, Tarrant County, Texas. In 1930 was a tailor in Fort Worth. FAMILY: Parents, Wilbur F. Walker (b. 1850, GA) and Sallie E. (b. 1845, MS); siblings, David F. (b. 1875, TX), Daniel Andrew (b. 1878, TX), Ida (b. 1880, TX); spouse #1, Jessie (b. 1897, TX), married about 1913; children, Sam, Jr. (b. 1915, OK), Bobbie (b. 1916, TX), Vernon (b. 1918, TX); spouse #2, Marie (b. 1902, TX), married about 1929. *SR; 471; A1d, f, g; A3a.*

WALKER, WILLIAM LEONARD "LEONARD." Born Feb. 2, 1897, Ezzell, Lavaca County, Texas. Ht. 5 ft. 7 in., dark eyes, black hair, fair complexion. Clerk and farmer. REGULAR RANGER May 25, 1918–Jan. 15, 1919 (private, Co. A). Resigned. REMARKS: As of June 1918, Ranger station was Falfurrias, Brooks County, Texas. In 1920 was a bookkeeper in Goliad, Goliad County, Texas. Died Apr. 29, 1978, Nueces County, Texas. FAMILY: Parents, William L. Walker (b. 1873, TX) and Nettie Gabie (b. 1874, TX); siblings, James L. (b. 1895, TX), Earnest Byram (b. 1899, TX), Mattie L. (b. 1902, TX), Lester (b. 1906, TX), Oscar T. (b. 1908, TX), Clifton (b. 1915, TX); spouse, Birdie Ivy (b. 1904, TX), married Mar. 25, 1923, Glendale, Goliad County; son, William Leonard (b. 1928, TX). *SR; 471; 469: 60; A1d, e, f; A2a, b; A3a; B1.*

WALL, ALONZO EUGENE. Born May 26, 1879, Winston Salem, Forsyth County, North Carolina. Ht. 5 ft. 9 in., black eyes, black hair, dark complexion, married. Peace officer, Wichita Falls, Wichita County, Texas. REGULAR RANGER Sept. 28, 1920–Jan. 26, 1921 (private, Headquarters Co.). Discharged/fired. REMARKS: Ranger Capt. C. J. Blackwell fired him because Wall alleged Blackwell was protecting gamblers. As of Sept. 1918 was a cabinet maker for National Shipbuilding Co., Orange County, Texas. In 1930 was a steel construction foreman in Dallas, Dallas County, Texas. Died Oct. 17, 1932, Bowie County, Texas. FAMILY: Parents, Leander B. "Lee" Wall (b. 1855, NC) and Louisa J. "Lula" Shore (b. 1859, NC); siblings, Laura Lola (b. 1881, NC), Elmer Marshall (b. 1882, NC), Anna L. (b. 1884, NC), Ernest (b. 1887, NC), Eva Almire (b. 1889, NC), Paul Grady (b. 1891, NC), Mary or Mamie Ellen (b. 1895, NC), Eula Dell (b. 1898, NC), Lillian V. (b. 1901, NC); spouse, unknown, widower by 1930. *SR; 471; Aldrich to McFatter, Feb 1, 1921, AGC; Wall to Neff, Feb 16, 1921, AGC; Wall to Aldrich, Feb 10, 1921, AGC; A1b, e, f, g; A2b; A3a; A4a, b; B1.*

WALLACE, EDGAR MORTIMER "TED." Born Sept. 1, 1887, Sherman, Grayson County, Texas. Ht. 5 ft. 11 in., blue eyes, black hair, dark complexion, married. Farmer and stock raiser, Judkins, Ector County, Texas. LOYALTY RANGER June 8, 1918–Feb. 1919. REMARKS: Grew up in Fort Worth, Tarrant County, Texas. In 1920 was an insurance agent in Fort Worth. An E. M. Wallace died Sept. 29, 1944, Tarrant County, Texas. FAMILY: Parents, Edgar

J. Wallace (b. 1858, GA) and Helen S. "Nellie" Phillips (b. 1866, NY); spouse, Blanche C. Connell (b. 1890, TX); children, John Edgar (b. 1914, TX), Harriett Elizabeth (b. 1917, TX). *SR; A1d, e, f; A2b; A3a; A4b.*

WALLACE, WILLIAM HAYS. Born Oct. 23, 1882, Llano County, Texas. Medium height, medium build, gray eyes, light brown hair, married. Merchant, Llano. LOYALTY RANGER June 4, 1918–Mar. 1919. REMARKS: Vice president and general manager, Acme Dry Goods Co., Llano. Died, Aug. 21, 1957, Llano County, Texas. FAMILY: Parents, William C. Wallace (b. 1856, TX) and Ida P. (b. 1861, TX); siblings, Kittie (b. 1879, TX), Claude (b. 1885, TX), Frank W. (b. 1889, TX), Howard Gillespie (b. 1892, TX), Charles (b. 1895, TX), Ida Maud (b. 1897, TX); spouse, Elizabeth G. "Lizzie" (b. 1884, TX), married about 1909; sons, William H., Jr. (b. 1922, TX), Joseph T. (b. 1924, TX). *SR; A1d, e, f, g; A2b; A3a; B1.*

WALLEN, JAMES AUGUST. Born Aug. 20, 1877, Ezzell, Lavaca County, Texas. Ht. 5 ft. 10 in., brown eyes, dark hair, dark complexion, married. Ranch hand, Del Rio, Val Verde County, Texas. REGULAR RANGER May 28, 1916–June 11, 1918 (private, Co. C; transferred to Co. E, Sept. 1917; promoted to sergeant, Oct. 1, 1917). Resigned. REMARKS: Had been deputy sheriff, Val Verde County. Was enlisted by Sheriff John W. Almond of Val Verde County by authority of the Adjutant General's Department. As of Sept. 1918 was a mounted watchman for the Immigration Service in Del Rio. Died Mar. 6, 1923, Val Verde County, Texas. LAW ENFORCEMENT RELATIVES: Val Verde County Chief Deputy Sheriff Calvin Andrew Wallen, son. FAMILY: Parents, Calvin Wallen (b. 1847, TX) and Jennie (b. 1848, TX); spouse, Mary Elizabeth (b. 1881, TX), married about 1903, she died Aug. 1918; children, Calvin Andrew (b. 1904, TX), Carl Lewis (b. 1907, TX), Edmund Thomas (b. 1908, TX), Bertha (b. 1911, TX), Lauranna (b. 1915, TX), Michael Lloyd (b. 1917, TX). *SR; 471; Almond to Hutchings, May 31, 1916, AGC; AG to Almond, June 2, 27, 1916, AGC; Barler to Woodul, Dec 2, 1917, AGC; Barler to Harley, Oct 12, 1917, AGC; A1b, e, f, g; A2b, e; A3a; A4b.*

WALLING, WALTER ALFRED. Born Nov. 1865, Hill County, Texas. No physical description, married. Farmer, Colleyville, Cottle County, Texas. LOYALTY RANGER July 1, 1918–Feb. 1919. REMARKS: Had been a saloon keeper in Robertson County, Texas. In 1910 was a farmer in Childress County, Texas. Died June 21, 1928, Cottle County, Texas. FAMILY: Father, John Gaines Walling (b. 1843, TX); mother or stepmother, Matilda Bankston (b. 1846 or 1853, TX); siblings, Jefferson Pyne (b. 1867, TX), Laura S. (b. 1869, TX), Matthew T. (b. 1875, TX), A. Clementine (b. 1877, TX), W. P. (b. 1879, TX), Jessie Bell (b. 1886, TX); spouse, Ellen or Ella W. (b. 1867, TX), married about 1888; children, John Travis (b. 1896, TX), Terry or Allie G. (b. 1899, TX). *SR; A1a, b, d, e, f, g; A2b; A3a; A4a, b, g.*

WALLIS, HAYES MOORE. Born Feb. 18, 1891, Rocksprings, Edwards County, Texas. Ht. 6 ft., gray eyes, dark hair, dark complexion. Stockman, Brownsville, Cameron County, Texas. SPECIAL RANGER Sept. 5, 1918–Jan. 15, 1919. Stock raiser, Brownsville. REGULAR RANGER Mar. 21, 1921–May 31, 1922 (private, Co. D). Resigned. Stockman, San Antonio, Bexar County, Texas. REGULAR RANGER Dec. 1, 1922–Aug. 17, 1923 (private, Co. D). Resigned. Stockman, Yoakum, Lavaca County, Texas. RAILROAD RANGER July 30, 1922–Oct. 18, 1922 (Co. D—assigned to St. Louis, Brownsville & Mexico Railroad at Kingsville, Kleberg County, Texas). Discharged. Stockman and special agent, Gulf Coast Lines, Kingsville. SPECIAL RANGER Sept. 15, 1923–Sept. 15, 1925; Sept. 23, 1925–Jan. 26, 1928 (reenlisted Jan. 26, 1927); Jan. 17, 1928–Jan. 15, 1929; Jan. 15, 1929–Jan. 14, 1931 (reenlisted Jan. 14, 1930); Jan. 26, 1931–Jan. 26, 1932; Jan. 27, 1932–Jan. 18, 1933; Jan. 20, 1933–Jan. 19, 1935; May 30, 1935–Aug. 10, 1935. Discharged. REMARKS: Cameron County deputy sheriff, ca. 1916–1918. In Aug. 1918 worked for Army Corps of Intelligence Police at Brownsville. His superior requested a Special Ranger commission for him. Was a sergeant, but wore civilian clothes and used a Cameron County deputy sheriff's badge. In Nov. 1919, applied to join the Customs Service. In 1936, was appointed chief special agent for the Missouri Pacific Railroad. Died Sept. 13, 1957, Anderson County, Texas; was buried in Seguin, Guadalupe County, Texas. FAMILY: Parents, William Morgan Wallis (b. 1859, TX) and Alice Kibbe (b. 1869, TX); siblings, Viora Alice "Ora" (b. 1889, TX), Alma (b. 1893, TX), Lilly (b. 1894, TX), Claude Miller (b. 1895, TX), Willie Belle (b. 1897, TX), Charles "Charley" (b. 1898, TX), Taylor (b. 1899, TX), Nell (b. 1901, TX), Bess (b. 1903, TX), Leroy (b. 1905, TX), Pauline. *SR; 471; Wallis to Ferguson, Apr*

3, 1917, AGC; Brooks to John _____, Aug 13, 1918, AGC; Wallis to AG, Nov 7, 1919, AGC; 470: 125; photos: 470: 35, 43, 125; 319: 82–83; A1d, e, f; A2b; A3a; A4a, b.

WALTERS, GUY E. Born Mar. 9, 1882, Unionville, Putnam County, Missouri. Ht. 5 ft. 10 ½ in., brown eyes, brown hair, dark complexion, married. Special agent, AT&SF Railroad, Amarillo, Potter County, Texas. SPECIAL RANGER Dec. 29, 1917–Jan. 15, 1919. REMARKS: In 1930 was an automobile salesman in El Paso, El Paso County, Texas. FAMILY: Parents, Archibald W. Walters (b. 1849, WI) and Margarete (b. 1846, IN); siblings, Willie C. (b. 1868, MO), Ira D. (b. 1873, MO); spouse, Grace (b. 1883, IA). *SR; Hale to Harley, Dec 21, 1917, Jan 3, 1918, AGC; AG to Hale, Dec 26, 1917, AGC; A1b, d, e, f, g; A3a.*

WALTERS, OTHELLO EDWARD. Born Nov. 9, 1881, Van Buren, Crawford County, Arkansas. Ht. 5 ft. 10 ½ in., dark eyes, black hair, dark complexion, married. Farmer. REGULAR RANGER Aug. 5, 1918–Aug. 1918 (private, Co. G). Discharged. REMARKS: Note length of service. Had lived in Ellis County, Texas. As of Sept. 1918 was a farmer in Cameron County, Texas. In 1930 was still farming in Cameron County. FAMILY: Parents, John Harrison Walters (b. 1841, KY) and Christiana Pauline Baldwin (b. 1845, MO); siblings, John M. (b. 1874, MO), Jessie H. (b. 1887, AR); spouse, Dora Ann, married about 1900, divorced by 1930. *SR; 471; Stevens to Woodul, Aug 26, 1918, WC; A1d, g; A3a; A4g.*

WARE, ARTHUR H. Born July 11, 1894, Amarillo, Potter County, Texas. Ht. 5 ft. 9 ½ in., blue eyes, brown hair, fair complexion. Bookkeeper, Amarillo. SPECIAL RANGER July 5, 1917–Dec. 1917. REMARKS: As of May 1917 was a banker, Amarillo National Bank. In 1930 was a bank vice president in Amarillo. An Arthur Hooper Ware died Dec. 5, 1959, Potter County, Texas. FAMILY: Parents, Benjamin Taliaferro Ware (b. 1853, GA) and Mary (b. 1860, GA); siblings, Floride (b. 1883, TX), Charles F. (b. 1886, TX), Richard C. (b. 1888, CA); spouse, Margaret H. (b. 1901, KS), married about 1922; twin sons, Cornelius H. and Charles R. (b. 1925, TX). *SR; Ferguson to Hutchings, [June, 1917], AGC; A1e, f, g; A2b; A3a; A4b.*

WARE, GRAYDON LESLEY. Born Nov. 11, 1898, Valentine, Brewster County, Texas. Ht. 5 ft. 10 in., gray eyes, brown hair, medium complexion. Officer. REGULAR RANGER Mar. 25, 1918–unknown (private, Co. L). REMARKS: Grew up in El Paso, El Paso County, Texas. "Officer for R.R. some time." Entered military service, U.S. Army, was an army sergeant in World War I. In 1930 was a city detective in Baltimore, Maryland. Died July 13, 1964; buried in Fort Bliss National Cemetery, El Paso. LAW ENFORCEMENT RELATIVES: El Paso city policeman (1910) and El Paso county deputy sheriff (1920) James I. Ware, father. FAMILY: Parents, James Ira Ware (b. 1872, TX) and Ada Priddy (b. 1879, AL); siblings, Ira Cummings (b. 1897, TX), Bonnie Ada (b. 1901, TX), Roy (b. 1904, TX), John Alfred (b. 1907, TX), Ida (b. 1909, TX), Todd (b. 1913, TX), Dorothy (b. 1917, TX), Joe (b. 1918, TX); spouse, Carmelita Doughney (b. 1899, MD), married about 1921; some sources list another spouse, Virginia Wister. *SR; A1e, f, g; A2a; A3a, b; A4a, b, g; B1, 2.*

WARTENBACH, FRIEDRICH C. "FRITZ." Born Mar. 18, 1870, Mason, Mason County, Texas. Ht. 6 ft., dark eyes, black hair, dark complexion, married. Peace officer, Mason. LOYALTY RANGER July 15, 1918–Feb. 1919. REMARKS: Was constable, precinct 1, Mason County; had been for the past year. Had been a peace officer for 3 ½ years. Was raised as a cowboy. In 1920 was a livestock trader in Mason County. Died Dec. 7, 1965; buried in Gooch Cemetery. FAMILY: Parents, Charles or Carl Wartenbach (b. 1847, Prussia or TX) and Anna Metzger (b. 1852, TX); siblings, Wendlin (b. 1871, TX), Louis K. (b. 1873, TX), John (b. 1874, TX), Katherine "Katie" (b. 1876, TX), Will (b. 1878, TX), Edward (b. 1880, TX), Amalie (b. 1881, TX); spouse, Bertha Simon (b. 1871, TX), married July 23, 1891, Hilda Bethel Methodist Church, Hilda, Mason County; children, Oskar Johannes (b. 1892, TX), Josephine Anna "Josie" (b. 1896, TX), Charles John "Charlie" (b. 1896, TX), Ida Mae (b. 1907, TX). *SR; Petition to AG [Dec 1917], AGC; A1a, b, d, e, f; A4b, g; B1.*

WASSON, ALFRED LEE. Born Oct. 21, 1869, Santoas, Brazil. Ht. 5 ft. 10 in., blue eyes, dark hair, ruddy complexion, married. Stockman, Big Spring, Howard County, Texas. LOYALTY RANGER June 8, 1918–Mar. 6, 1919. REMARKS: A U.S. citizen; born in Brazil of American parents. Lived in Hill County, Texas as a youth. Had been a farmer in Borden County, Texas. In 1930 was a farmer in Howard County. Died July 30, 1959, Howard County, Texas. FAMILY: Parents, Columbus Lee Wasson (b. 1843, TX) and Harriett Ann Dyer (b. 1847, TX); brothers, Claude Loraine (b. 1871, Brazil), James Wiley (b. 1874, TX), Craven Adair (b. 1877, TX), Ira Elmo (b. 1879, TX); spouse, Martha Elizabeth Pallmeyer (b. 1873, TX), married about 1891; children, Cecil L. (b. 1891, TX), Velma (b. 1893, TX). *SR; A1b, d, f, g; A2b; A4b, g; B1, 2.*

WATKINS, THOMAS. Born 1867, England. Ht. 5 ft. 5 ½ in., blue eyes, light brown hair. Storekeeper, enlisted in Austin, Travis County, Texas. REGULAR RANGER Nov. 20, 1913–Nov. 20, 1915 (sergeant, Co. C). Storekeeper, Austin. SPECIAL RANGER May 22, 1916–Aug. 15, 1917 (attached to Co. C). WA was revoked. REMARKS: Immigrated to the U.S. in 1887, became a naturalized U.S citizen. In 1920 was quartermaster, Adjutant General's office, Austin. In 1930 was a railroad agent in Austin. FAMILY: Spouse, Pearl (b. 1891, TN), married about 1916; children, Elizabeth (b. 1918, TX), Thomas Loyd (b. 1919, TX). *SR; A1f, g.*

WATSON, J. A. Born July 1899, Hill County, Texas. Ht. 6 ft. 1 in., gray eyes, brown hair, fair complexion. Farmer, Osceola, Hill County. REGULAR RANGER Jan. 16, 1918–May 16, 1918 (private, Co. G). Resigned. Was placed on active duty Jan. 22, 1918. Resigned because he was homesick. *SR; Stevens to Woodul, May 16, 1918, AGC.*

WATTS, CARL JOSEPH. Born Sept. 7, 1887, Macdona, Bexar County, Texas. Medium height, slender, gray eyes, dark brown hair, married. Railroad station agent, Macdona. LOYALTY RANGER June 12, 1918–Mar. 6, 1919. REMARKS: In 1930 was a railroad station agent in Sabinal, Uvalde County, Texas. A Carl Joseph Watts died June 15, 1963, Val Verde County, Texas. FAMILY: Father, Carl W. Watts (b. 1866, TX); stepmother, Clara (b. 1868, TX); siblings, John (b. 1889, TX), Anna (b. 1891, TX), Eddie (b. 1896, TX), Frederick (b. 1897, TX), Levi (b. 1900, TX), Burdett (b. 1905, TX), Alfred (b. 1907, TX); spouse, Viola M. (b. 1898, TX), married about 1910; daughter, Floy M. (b. 1913, TX). *SR; A1d, e, f, g; A2b; A3a.*

WATTS, REUBEN VAIL. Born Aug. 19, 1856, Sumter County, Alabama. Ht. 6 ft. 2 in., blue eyes, auburn hair, light complexion, married. Salesman, Lufkin, Angelina County, Texas. LOYALTY RANGER July 4, 1918–Feb. 1919. REMARKS: Angelina County sheriff Nov. 8, 1904–Nov. 3, 1914 and Nov. 2, 1920–Jan. 1, 1925. Died Sept. 26, 1927, Angelina County, Texas. FAMILY: Parents, John R. Watts (b. 1811, GA) and Elizabeth Thornton "Betsy" Asbury (b. 1815, GA); siblings, William (b. 1835, GA), Jesse A. (b. 1837, GA), John S. (b. 1841, AL), Richard J. (b. 1845, AL), Tandy Key (b. 1846, AL), Vincent T. (b. 1848, AL), Martha E. (b. 1851, AL), Archibald C. (b. 1853, AL), Josiah C. (b. 1859, AL); spouse, Beulah (b. 1874, TX), married about 1889; children, Duncan (b. 1891, TX), Della (b. 1892, TX). *SR; Brazil to Hobby, Nov 29, 1920, AGC; 1503:4; A1aa, a, b, d, e, f; A2b; A4a, g.*

WATTS, WALTER P. Born Sept. 1863, De Kalb County, Alabama. No physical description, married. Showman, Memphis, Hall County, Texas. LOYALTY RANGER July 9, 1918–Feb. 1919. REMARKS: Had been a farmer in Johnson County, Texas. In 1920 was a house carpenter in Memphis. Walter Poge Watts died Aug. 6, 1950, Hall County, Texas. FAMILY: Parents, William Jacobus Watts (b. 1821, GA) and Georgia Ann Childers (b. 1841, AL); siblings, Viola or Vida J. (b. 1860, AL), Benjamin T. (b. 1865, AL), Warren W. (b. 1869, AL), Henry R. (b. 1871, AL), Daisey Belle (b. 1874, GA), Myrtle Ruth (b. 1877, GA); spouse, Amanda H. Yeager (b. 1871, TX), married about 1885; son, Gordon (b. 1889, TX). *SR; A1a, b, e, f, g; A2b; A4a, g; B1, 2.*

WAUGH, ANDREW M. Born Jan. 1870, Oswego, Oswego County, New York. Ht. 5 ft. 10 in., gray eyes, gray hair, fair complexion, married. Lawyer, Sugar Land, Fort Bend County, Texas. SPECIAL RANGER Jan. 21, 1918–Jan. 15, 1919. REMARKS: Was vice president and attorney, Sugar Land Railway Company. Had been a banker in Eagle Lake, Colorado County, Texas. In 1910 was a rice broker in Houston, Harris County, Texas. In 1920 was a railroad attorney in Houston. In 1930 had a law office in Houston. Died June 20, 1939, Harris County, Texas. FAMILY: Parents, Francis D. Waugh (b. 1839, NY) and Martha Miller (b. 1843, NY); spouse, Hattie E. Hahn (b. 1875, TX), married Sept. 16, 1895, Colorado County, Texas; daughters, Kathryn (b. 1899, TX), Martha M. (b. 1902, TX). *SR; A1a, b, d, e, f, g; A2b; B2.*

WAY, JAMES ROLLIE "ROLLIE." Born June 10, 1894, Creedmore, Travis County, Texas. Ht. 5 ft. 8 in., gray eyes, dark hair, fair complexion. Farmer, enlisted in La Salle

County, Texas. SPECIAL RANGER Nov. 6, 1916–unknown. REMARKS: Had been a farmer in Atascosa County, Texas. In 1930 was a farmer, lived in Jourdanton, Atascosa County. Died Oct. 18, 1964, Atascosa County, Texas; buried in Jourdanton Cemetery. FAMILY: Parents, James Sidney Way (b. 1863, AL) and Margaret "Maggie" Chamberlain (b. 1868, TX); sisters, Gena (b. 1896, TX), Opal (b. 1905, TX), Willie Spenser (b. 1908, TX); spouse, Johnye Henry (b. 1910), married June 10, 1931. *SR; A1e, f, g; A2b; A3a; A4b.*

WAY, WILLIAM WARD. Born Jan. 1867, Brazoria, Brazoria County, Texas. Ht. 6 ft., gray eyes, brown hair, fair complexion, married. Railroad special officer, Houston, Harris County, Texas. SPECIAL RANGER June 5, 1917–Dec. 1917 (attached to Co. C). REMARKS: Was a night watchman for the I&GN Railroad at Houston. In 1910 was a house carpenter in Houston. In 1930 was a detective, Houston police force. A William Way died June 21, 1934, Harris County, Texas. FAMILY: Parents, William Joseph Duvall Way (b. 1828, MS) and Annie Elizabeth Holt (b. 1842, LA); siblings, Ann Lucretia (b. 1867, TX), Marta (b. 1869, TX), Horace G. (b. 1873, TX), Gussie (b. 1879, TX); spouse, Lola Virginia Woodruff (b. 1878, MS), married Sept. 22, 1897, Brazoria; children, Albert Ransom (b. 1899, TX), Mazie D. (b. 1902, TX). *SR; Williamson to Hutchings, May 31, June 5, 1917, AGC; AG to Williamson, June 1, 1917, AGC; A1b, d, e, f, g; A2b; A4a, b; B1.*

WEASE, DAVID CARRELL "DAVE." Born July 14, 1885, Pearsall, Frio County, Texas. Ht. 6 ft., gray eyes, brown hair, light complexion. Ranchman, Marfa, Presidio County, Texas. SPECIAL RANGER Dec. 13, 1917–Jan. 15, 1919 (attached to Co. B). REMARKS: Had been a house carpenter in Brewster County, Texas. In 1920 was a farmer in Presidio County. In 1930 was a cattleman in Marfa. Died Nov. 24, 1968, Presidio County, Texas. FAMILY: Parents, Julian David Wease (b. 1854, MO) and Ellen Josephine Bell (b. 1862, TX); siblings, Annie Laura (b. 1883, TX), Bessie (b. 1887), Grover C. (b. 1888, TX), Susie Olive (b. 1893, TX), twins Charles and Carlos (b. 1895, TX), Julian D. (b. 1898, TX); spouse, Mary Lucille Hood (b. 1897, TX), married about 1927; children, David C. (b. 1928, TX), Mira Ann (b. 1930, TX). *SR; Fox to Woodul, Dec 13, 1917, AGC; A1d, e, f, g; A2a, b; A3a; A4b, g; B1.*

WEATHERALL, JAMES GRANDBERRY "JIMMIE." Born July 18, 1880, Linden, Cass County, Texas. Ht. 5 ft. 10 in., blue eyes, dark hair, fair complexion, married. Special agent, St. Louis Southwestern Railroad, Mount Pleasant, Titus County, Texas. SPECIAL RANGER Jan. 24, 1918–Jan. 15, 1919. Special officer, Palestine, Anderson County, Texas. RAILROAD RANGER Aug. 12, 1922–Oct. 15, 1923 (Co. A). Discharged. REMARKS: In 1910 was superintendent of the Cass County prison farm. As of Sept. 1918 was special agent for the Cotton Belt Railroad in Texarkana, Bowie County, Texas. In 1920 was a railroad detective in Texarkana. Died May 20, 1953, Tarrant County, Texas. FAMILY: Parents, Joseph Dickson "Joe" Weatherall (b. 1842, MS) and Mary Caroline Reed (b. 1850, AL); siblings, Carrie F. (b. 1877, TX), Joseph Dickson (b. 1881, TX), twins Era D. and Vera Virginia (b. 1888, TX); spouse, Minerva "Minnie" Pierce (b. 1890, TX), married Oct. 29, 1911, Cass County; children, James (b. 1912, TX), twins Mary L. and Joe Albert (b. 1917, TX). *SR; Campbell to Harley, Jan 1, 30, 1918, AGC; A1e, f; A2b; A3a; A4b, g; B1.*

WEATHERFORD, WILLIAM WALLACE. Born Apr. 19, 1885, Kyle, Hays County, Texas. Ht. 6 ft., gray eyes, brown hair, fair complexion, married. Stockman, enlisted in Presidio County, Texas. SPECIAL RANGER Jan. 29, 1918–Jan. 15, 1919. REMARKS: Had lived in Frio County, Texas. In 1920 was a stock buyer in Marfa, Presidio County. In 1930 was a cattleman in Marfa. Died Jan. 13, 1953, Austin, Travis County, Texas. FAMILY: Parents, William Campbell Weatherford (b. 1840, KY) and Patsy Fontaine "Pattie" Wallace (b. 1855, AR); siblings, Katie Lee (b. 1889, TX), John Pierce (b. 1892, TX), Archie Fontaine (b. 1893, TX); spouse, Emma Katurah Martin (b. 1878, MS), married June 27, 1906, Driftwood, Hays County; children, Hazel Elizabeth (b. 1907, TX), Wallace Campbell (b. 1908, TX), Emma Katurah (b. 1916, TX), William Burton (b. 1917, TX). *SR; A1d, e, f, g; A2b; A3a; A4a, b, g.*

WEAVER, CLAREMORE MCKELVEY "BUCK." Born June 26, 1897, Batesville, Independence County, Arkansas. Ht. 6 ft. 1 in., blue eyes, black hair, dark complexion. Peace officer, Paris, Lamar County, Texas. REGULAR RANGER Feb. 23, 1921–Aug. 31, 1921 (private, Co. B). Discharged. REMARKS: As of Aug. 1918 was a fireman in Wichita Falls, Wichita County, Texas; still a fireman in Wichita Falls in

1920. After leaving the Rangers he became engaged in bootlegging in Medina County, Texas, and was sentenced to serve one year in the state prison. "He is considered a bad character by this Department." In 1931 was apparently a Winkler County, Texas, deputy sheriff. Died Nov. 19, 1956, Van Zandt County, Texas; buried in Ebenezer Cemetery. FAMILY: Parents, M. M. "Mac" Weaver (b. 1871, TN) and Kate (b. 1878, AR); brothers, Ray (b. 1902, TX), Mortimer (b. 1912, TX); spouse (?), Gladys Wave Marshall. *SR; 471; A1e, f; A2b; A3a; B1, 2.*

WEAVER, SAMUEL HOUSTON "BUD." Born May 19, 1874, Bandera, Bandera County, Texas. Ht. 6 ft., brown eyes, brown hair, light complexion, widower. Stockman, enlisted in Kimble County, Texas. REGULAR RANGER Sept. 5, 1917–June 8, 1918 (private, Co. B). Discharged/fired for his role in the Porvenir massacre. Peace officer, Amarillo, Potter County, Texas. RAILROAD RANGER Aug. 18, 1922–Nov. 30, 1922 (Headquarters Co.). Discharged. REMARKS: One source states he was "A native of the Big Saline area in Kimble County." In 1920 was a mounted Customs inspector at Terlingua, Brewster County, Texas, in the Big Bend. Died Feb. 24, 1958, Kerr County, Texas; buried in his family's plot in the London Cemetery, London, Kimble County. FAMILY: Parents, Franklin Amasiah Weaver (b. 1846, AL) and Cassandra Gaffey (b. 1856, TX); sisters, Emily A. (b. 1872, TX), Edna (b. 1877, TX), Maggie (b. 1880, TX); spouse #1, Julia Wheat Caruthers (b. 1878, TX), married about 1899, she died in 1909; daughters, Fay (b. 1903, TX), Gladys (b. 1905, TX), Julia (b. 1909, TX); spouse #2, Elizabeth Jane Jackson (b. 1890, TX), married July 25, 1934, Mason County, Texas. *SR; 471; General Orders No. 5, June 4, 1918, AGC; 422: 87–89; AA, May 13, Dec 16, 1920; 1522; A1b, e; A2b; A3a; B1, 2.*

WEBB, BRITAIN RICE. Born Aug. 12, 1881, Breckenridge, Stephens County, Texas. Ht. 5 ft. 10 in., gray eyes, blond hair, light complexion, married. Automobile distributor, San Antonio, Bexar County, Texas. SPECIAL RANGER Nov. 15, 1918–Jan. 15, 1919. Investor, San Antonio. SPECIAL RANGER Feb. 25, 1933–Feb. 24, 1935. REMARKS: As of Sept. 1918 was an automobile dealer in San Antonio for the Buick Motor Company. Died Mar. 24, 1968, Mesa, Maricopa County, Arizona. FAMILY: Parents, Britain R. Webb (b. 1852, MS) and Lilly J. (b. 1862, AL); siblings, Minnie S. (b. 1885, TX), Bessie G. (b. 1887, TX), Sanford R. (b. 1890, TX); spouse, Minnie Bryant (b. 1886, KY), married June 10, 1909; daughters, Mary B. (b. 1911, TX), Katherine G. (b. 1913, TX). *SR; A1d, e, f, g; A2a; A3a; A4b.*

WEBB, DAVID CORNELIUS "JACK." Born Feb. 1, 1886, Fairview, Wilson County, Texas. Ht. 5 ft. 8 in., blue eyes, light brown hair, light complexion. Stockman. REGULAR RANGER Aug. 19, 1915–June 12, 1917 (private, Co. A). Resigned. Stockman, Carrizo Springs, Dimmit County, Texas. REGULAR RANGER Feb. 20, 1920–Aug. 12, 1923 (private, Co. D; promoted to sergeant, Aug. 1, 1922). Resigned. REMARKS: After serving 22 months in Co. A, resigned in 1917, enlisted in the Navy. Was discharged from Navy on Nov. 8, 1919. In 1923 became a mounted Customs inspector. Died June 20, 1932, of a heart attack, Carrizo Springs, Dimmit County, Texas. LAW ENFORCEMENT RELATIVES: Ranger Grover Cleveland Webb, brother; Ranger Lake T. Webb, brother; Ranger David Franklin Webb, grandfather; Ranger Herff Alexander Carnes, cousin; Ranger Quirl Bailey Carnes, cousin; Ranger John Eckford Gilliland, cousin-by-marriage; Wilson County sheriff (Dec. 31, 1917–Jan. 1, 1937) Alfred Burton Carnes, cousin. See Webb-Carnes Families Chart for additional relatives. FAMILY: Parents, Neil Alfred Webb (b. 1851, TX) and Mary Ada Smith (b. 1863, TX); siblings, Lula Belle (b. 1887, TX), Grover Cleveland (b. 1888, TX), James Alfred (b. 1891, TX), Gussie (b. 1892, TX), Lake Thomas (b. 1894, TX), Wesley (b. 1895, TX), Ola (b. 1896, TX), Dewey Hobson (b. 1898, TX), Fannie Lee (b. 1901, TX); stepmother, Susan Fannie Haws (b. 1874, TX); brother, Frank G. (b. 1906, TX). *SR; 471; Webb to Wright, Jan 13, 1920, AGC; 1000: iii, 5, 81–83; 319: 91, 412, 414–415; 470: 35, 43, 59–61, 62–64, 67, 89–90; 330: 41; 1503:547; A1d, e, f; A2b; A4a, b, g; B2.*

WEBB, GROVER CLEVELAND. Born June 3, 1888, Floresville, Wilson County, Texas. Ht. 5 ft. 10 in., blue eyes, brown hair, light complexion. Stockman. REGULAR RANGER Aug. 1, 1910–Sept. 30, 1910 (private, Co. A). Discharged—Co. A was disbanded. Stockman. REGULAR RANGER Jan. 19, 1914–Aug. 31, 1914 (private, Co. A). Discharged. REMARKS: One source says he was born in Fairview, Wilson County. Became a mounted Customs inspector in 1915, at Valentine, Jeff Davis County, Texas. As of June 1917 was a U.S. Customs inspector for the

Eagle Pass District, stationed at Marfa, Presidio County, Texas. Volunteered for the Army in World War I, served in the Corps of Intelligence Police in the Big Bend. After discharge, rejoined Customs Service. Served as mounted Customs inspector in charge and chief patrol inspector, El Paso, El Paso County, Texas. In 1938 became district superintendent of the Southwest Customs Patrol District (Brownsville to San Diego). In 1948, when the mounted Customs Service was discontinued, was transferred and promoted to assistant supervising Customs agent for the 10th Customs Agency District, El Paso (Texas, New Mexico, Arizona). On June 27, 1952, retired from Customs and moved to Kerrville, Kerr County, where he died July 17, 1964; buried in Garden Of Memories, Kerrville. LAW ENFORCEMENT RELATIVES: Ranger David Cornelius "Jack" Webb, brother; Ranger Lake T. Webb, brother; Ranger David Franklin Webb, grandfather; Ranger Herff Alexander Carnes, cousin; Ranger Quirl Bailey Carnes, cousin; Ranger John Eckford Gilliland, cousin-by-marriage; Wilson County sheriff (Dec. 31, 1917–Jan. 1, 1937) Alfred Burton Carnes, cousin. See Webb-Carnes Families Chart for additional relatives. FAMILY: Parents, Neil Alfred Webb (b. 1851, TX) and Mary Ada Smith (b. 1863, TX); siblings, David Cornelius "Jack" (b. 1886, TX), Lula Belle (b. 1887, TX), James Alfred (b. 1891, TX), Gussie (b. 1892, TX), Lake Thomas (b. 1894, TX), Wesley (b. 1895, TX), Ola (b. 1896, TX), Dewey Hobson (b. 1898, TX), Fannie Lee (b. 1901, TX); stepmother, Susan Fannie Haws (b. 1874, TX); brother, Frank G. (b. 1906, TX); spouse, Jessie M. (b. 1893, NM), married about 1920. *SR; 471; Edwards to Hughes, Apr 25, 1914, AGC; 1: I, 1526–1531; 470: 84–86, 88–89; 1000, iii, 83–86; EPMT, Apr 26, 29, 1914, Aug 8, 1915; 422: 87; 1503:547; A1d, e, f, g; A2b; A3a; A4a, b, g; B2.*

WEBB, JAMES RICHARD. Born Nov. 19, 1884, Waco, McLennan County, Texas. Medium height, medium build, gray eyes, black hair. Garage man, Albany, Shackleford County, Texas. LOYALTY RANGER June 13, 1918–Feb. 1919. REMARKS: In 1920 was a ranchman in Shackelford County. In 1930 was a farmer in Shackelford County. Died Dec. 5, 1953, Shackelford County, Texas. FAMILY: Parents, Sam Webb (b. 1855, TX) and Ella Downs (b. 1858, TX); Siblings, William Graham (b. 1879, TX), Sam, Jr. (b. 1880, TX), Minnie Beall (b. 1888, TX), Camille Downs (b. 1891, TX), Moselle (b. 1894, TX), Louise (b. 1897, TX); spouse, Margaret Gray McCarthy (b. 1903, TX), married about 1923. *SR; A1d, f, g; A2b; A3a; A4b, g.*

WEBSTER, CHARLES H. Born May 1869, Sterling, Whiteside County, Illinois. Ht. 5 ft. 8 ¼ in., blue eyes, sandy hair, sandy complexion. Peace officer. REGULAR RANGER Jan. 13, 1911–July 1913 (private, Co. D, which was redesignated as Co. A). Resigned. REMARKS: Had been a stagehand in El Paso, El Paso County, Texas, and later operated "a vaudeville or moving-picture show of some kind." As of Aug. 1915, was an El Paso County automobile inspector. FAMILY: Spouse, Emma (b. 1877, PA), divorced before 1920; children, Gladys (b. 1895, CO), Sherman (b. 1902, CO), Joe (b. 1906, CO), Frank (b. 1909, TX). *SR; 471; 403: 648; EPMT, Aug 11, 16, 1915; A1e, f.*

WEBSTER, JAMES STANISLAUS. Born April 19, 1882, Moncure, North Carolina. Ht. 5 ft. 11 ½ in., brown eyes, black hair, dark complexion, married. Chief special agent, Southern Pacific Railroad, Houston, Harris County, Texas. SPECIAL RANGER June 16, 1917–unknown (attached to Co. C). WA was renewed Dec. 22, 1917. Investigator, Houston. SPECIAL RANGER Apr. 6, 1932–Jan. 18, 1933. Discharged. REMARKS: In 1910 was a railroad detective in Lafayette, Lafayette Parish, Louisiana. As of June 1917 had been employed in the Special Service Department, Southern Pacific Railroad, for the past 9 years. As of Nov. 1917 was chief special agent for the GH&SA Railroad. A James S. Webster died Oct. 21, 1944, Harris County, Texas. FAMILY: Parents, James Webster (b. 1858, NC) and Amelie (b. 1858, France); siblings, Charles H. (b. 1884, NC), Fannie J. (b. 1886, NC), Daniel Edward (b. 1891, NC), Amelie Catheryn (b. 1894, NC); spouse, Nina (b. 1882, NC), married about 1908; son, Jerome Morgan (b. 1911, LA). *SR; Webster to Tallichet, June 11, 1917, AGC; Tallichet to Hutchings, June 12, 1917, AGC; AG to Tallichet, June 14, 1917, AGC; Stacy to AG, Nov 19, 1917, AGC; A1d, e, f, g; A2b; A3a.*

WEIR, THOMAS CALVIN. Born May 2, 1868, Georgetown, Williamson County, Texas. Ht. 6 ft., brown eyes, dark hair, dark complexion, married. Private detective (bounty hunter), Abilene, Taylor County, Texas. SPECIAL RANGER Aug. 26, 1916–May 23, 1917 (attached to Co. C). Transferred to active duty. REGULAR RANGER May 24,

1917–Jan. 1, 1918 (private, Co. D; transferred to Co. M, Jan. 1, 1918). Resigned. REMARKS: Before enlisting in the Rangers had taught public school in Abilene for 14 years; was also a county commissioner four years, justice of the peace four years, and Taylor County sheriff Nov. 3, 1908–Nov. 3, 1914. Letterhead Sept. 1916: "T. C. Weir, Land and Live Stock, Abilene." Died Sept. 4, 1941, Taylor County, Texas. FAMILY: Parents, Thomas Calvin Weir (b. 1828, TN) and Valinda Evaline Camp (b. 1838, AL); siblings, Sallie D. (b. 1859), Martha Rankin (b. 1861, TX), Charles M. (b. 1863, TX), Lucy Avis (b. 1867, TX), Fannie L. (b. 1871, TX), Horace M. (b. 1872, TX), James Neely (b. 1875, TX), Mary L. (b. 1877, TX), William Newton (b. 1879, TX); spouse #1, Josie Oden (b. 1869, OK or MO), married July 23, 1893; sons, Henry Grady (b. 1894, TX), R. M. (b. 1898, TX), James Gordon (b. 1907, TX); spouse #2, Pearle Kenshaw Smith (b. 1883, TX), married before 1920. *SR; 471; Cunningham to Ferguson, Aug 14,1916, AGC; Wroe to Hutchings, Aug 23, 1916, AGC; Weir to Hutchings, Sept 5, 1916, AGC; Hollis to Harley, Dec 2, 1917, AGC; AG to Cunningham, Jan 3, 1918, AGC; 1503:485; A1a, b, d, e, f; A2b; A4a, b, g.*

WELBORN, MOSES BOWEN "BOWEN." Born Feb. 10, 1881, Liberty, Anderson County, Texas. Ht. 6 ft. 2 ½ in., blue eyes, black hair, florid complexion, married. Farmer, Liberty. LOYALTY RANGER July 5, 1918–Feb. 1919. REMARKS: As of Sept. 1918 was a farmer in Montalba, Anderson County. In 1930 was a state penitentiary guard, Huntsville, Walker County, Texas. Died Jan. 23, 1943, Walker County, Texas; buried in Poyner Cemetery, Poyner, Henderson County, Texas. FAMILY: Parents, Edward Calhoun Welborn (b. 1831, SC) and Margaret Pendleton Kay (b. 1838, SC); siblings, Charles Kay (b. 1858, SC), Mary J. (b. 1860, MS), James Edward (b. 1862, MS), Eleanor Harriett (b. 1864, MS), Sarah Jane (b. 1866, MS), Joel E. (b. 1868, MS), Martha Charity (b. 1871, MS), Margaret Elizabeth (b. 1873, MS), Lucinda N. (b. 1875, MS), William Albert (b. 1878, TX); spouse, Mary Anna Scarborough (b. 1888, TX), married Oct. 6, 1915, Henderson County, Texas; daughters, Maggie Fern (b. 1917, TX), Edith Bowen (b. 1919, TX), Mary Louise (b. 1922, TX). *SR; A1d, e, f, g; A2b; A3a; A4a, b, g; B1.*

WELLBORN, CHARLES VERNON. Born Sept. 16, 1867, Crawford, Russell County, Alabama. Ht. 5 ft. 11 in., blue eyes, dark hair, fair complexion, married. Farmer, Garrison, Nacogdoches County, Texas; enlisted in Rusk County, Texas. LOYALTY RANGER June 8, 1918–Mar. 1918. REMARKS: Had been a farmer in Johnson County, Arkansas. Was a LOYALTY RANGER in Rusk County. Had been justice of the peace four years at Mount Enterprise, Rusk County. In 1930 was Rusk County deputy sheriff, lived in Henderson, Rusk County. Died Dec. 8, 1942, Rusk County, Texas. FAMILY: Parents, Marshall J. Wellborn (b. 1832, TN) and Eugenia Teresia Roquemore (b. 1845, AL); siblings, William (b. 1861, AL), Marshall Jasper (b. 1862, AL), Emma (b. 1866, AL), Francis (b. 1869, AL), Robert (b. 1873, AL), Tinie (b. 1876, AL), twins Lenas and Lelas (b. 1880, AL); spouse, Alice Emma Dora Davis (b. 1872, TN), married about 1888; children, Blanche M. (b. 1888, AR), Charles Floyd (b. 1889, AR), Earl C. (b. 1891, AR), Edna L. (b. 1892, AR), Elvie E. (b. 1894, AR), Harold (b. 1895, AR), Mary E. (b. 1896, AR), Leona E. (b. 1898, AR), Ora M. (b. 1900, AR), Paul C. (b. 1904, TX), Ewell V. (b. 1906, TX), Geoffie (b. 1908, TX), Gordon R. (b. 1913, TX). *SR; A1a, b, d, e, f, g; A4g.*

WELLS, MONROE MADISON. Born Mar. 30, 1886, Fredericksburg, Gillespie County, Texas. Ht. 6 ft., blue eyes, light hair, light complexion. Stockman, enlisted in Kerr County, Texas. REGULAR RANGER Dec. 21, 1917–Mar. 1, 1919 (private, Co. K). Resigned. REMARKS: Ranger station as of Sept. 1918 was Rio Grande City, Starr County, Texas. In 1930 was a stock farmer in Kerr County. Died Oct. 12, 1934, Kerr County, Texas. LAW ENFORCEMENT RELATIVES: Ranger Captain William L. Wright, cousin; Ranger Milam H. Wright, cousin; Ranger Wright Wells, cousin; Ranger Peter F. "Capt." Tumlinson, great-uncle; Ranger John Jackson "Capt." Tumlinson, great-uncle. See Tumlinson Family, Taylor Family, Wright Family charts for additional relatives. FAMILY: Parents, William W. (or Baker) Wells (b. 1840, AL) and Matilda (or Martha) Elizabeth Tumlinson (b. 1850, TX); siblings, Sarah Elizabeth "Bessie" (b. 1868, TX), Joseph Brockman (b. 1869, TX), James Bailey (b. 1871, TX), John William (b. 1873, TX), Rachel Ann (b. 1875, TX), Margaret Lee "Maggie" (b. 1877, TX), Allan Tumlinson (b. 1879, TX), Harry Harrison (b. 1881, TX), Rufus Leroy (b. 1883, TX); spouse, Josephine "Joe" Miller (b. 1877, TX), married about 1922. *SR; 471; A1d, e, f, g; A2b; A3a; A4a, b; B1.*

WELLS, WRIGHT C. Born 1868, Batesville, Panola County, Mississippi. Ht. 5 ft. 8 ½ in., brown eyes, black hair, dark complexion. Lineman, enlisted in Wilson County, Texas. REGULAR RANGER Dec. 25, 1917–Feb. 9, 1920 (private, Co. K; reenlisted under the new law in Co. D, June 20, 1919). Resigned—had asthma and couldn't stand the climate of Brownsville, Cameron County, Texas. Stockman, Teague, Freestone County, Texas. RAILROAD RANGER Aug. 5, 1922–Oct. 1, 1922. Discharged. REMARKS: Had been overseer for a road gang in Kenedy, Karnes County, Texas. LAW ENFORCEMENT RELATIVES: Ranger Monroe Madison Wells, cousin. See Tumlinson Family, Taylor Family, Wright Family charts for additional relatives. FAMILY: Parents, Madison Monroe Wells (b. 1837, AL) and Mary Frances "Fanny" Wright (b. 1841, MS); siblings, Florence Linsey (b. 1866, MS), Oliver Waters (b. 1869, MS), William (b. 1871, MS), Annie (b. 1874, MS), Ealia (b. 1879, MS). *SR; 471; Wells to Cope, Jan 15, 1920, AGC; A1a, b, e; A4a, b, g.*

WEST, IKE. Born Oct. 14, 1885, Sweet Home, Lavaca County, Texas. Ht. 5 ft. 9 in., brown eyes, brown hair, dark complexion. Ranchman, San Antonio, Bexar County, Texas. SPECIAL RANGER Jan. 10, 1919–Dec. 31, 1919 (?). REMARKS: Captain, Co. D, 9th Infantry, Texas National Guard. In 1918 was in the cattle and ranching business in Batesville, Zavala County, Texas; lived in San Antonio. Died Aug. 20, 1960, Bexar County, Texas. FAMILY: Parents, Solomon "Sol" West (b. 1857, TN) and Nannie B. King (b. 1860, TX); siblings, George W. (b. 1879, TX), Mary. *SR; A1b, e, f; A2b; A3a; A4a; B1.*

WEST, JESSE EUGENE "EUGENE." Born Apr. 7, 1884, Rancho, Gonzales County, Texas. Ht. 6 ft., blue eyes, light hair, red complexion, married. Ranch foreman, Cuevitas, Jim Hogg County, Texas. SPECIAL RANGER May 24, 1918–Jan. 15, 1919. REMARKS: Had been a cowboy in Wilson County, Texas. In 1920 was a stock rancher in Starr County, Texas. In 1930 was proprietor of a meat market in Hebbronville, Jim Hogg County. Died Jan. 11, 1953, Webb County, Texas. LAW ENFORCEMENT RELATIVES: Ranger Milton C. West, father; Ranger L. Earl West, brother; Ranger Milton H. West, brother; Ranger Paul M. West, brother. FAMILY: Parents, Milton Crockett West (b. 1851, TX) and Pauline Malvina Cocke (b. 1855, TX); siblings, Mamie E. (a ward, b. 1878, TX), Larkin Earl (b. 1878, TX), Frederick Autie (b. 1880, TX), Sarah Cornelia "Sallie" (b. 1882, TX), Florence Rebecca (b. 1885, TX), Milton Horace (b. 1888, TX), Paul Morce or Maurice (b. 1890, TX), Pauline (b. 1893, TX), Frank Conn (b. 1896, TX), Pauline Vida (b. 1901, TX); spouse, Sofia Guerra (b. 1896, TX), married about 1917; children, Alma (b. 1921, TX), Edna (b. 1923, TX), Estela (b. 1926, TX), George Crockett (b. 1927, TX). *SR; A1b, d, e, f, g; A2b; A3a; A4b, B2.*

WEST, LARKIN EARL "EARL." Born Sept. 16, 1878, Rancho, Gonzales County, Texas. Ht. 5 ft. 10 in., gray eyes, brown hair, dark complexion, married. Farmer, Mercedes, Hidalgo County, Texas. SPECIAL RANGER June 19, 1918–Jan. 15, 1919. REMARKS: Moved to Wilson County, Texas as a child. Had been a deputy sheriff in Wilson and Hidalgo Counties, and a Cameron County, Texas constable. Was wounded in the San Benito ambush, July 31, 1910. Later became a mounted Customs inspector. Was an Army scout near Brownsville, Cameron County, in 1917. Was chief of police in McAllen, Hidalgo County. Died Dec. 14, 1955, Travis County, Texas; buried in Edinburg, Hidalgo County. LAW ENFORCEMENT RELATIVES: Ranger Milton C. West, father; Ranger Jesse Eugene West, brother; Ranger Milton H. West, brother; Ranger Paul M. West, brother. FAMILY: Parents, Milton Crockett West (b. 1851, TX) and Pauline Malvina Cocke (b. 1855, TX); siblings, Mamie E. (a ward, b. 1878, TX), Frederick Autie (b. 1880, TX), Sarah Cornelia "Sallie" (b. 1882, TX), Jesse Eugene (b. 1884, TX), Florence Rebecca (b. 1885, TX), Milton Horace (b. 1888, TX), Paul Morce or Maurice (b. 1890, TX), Pauline (b. 1893, TX), Frank Conn (b. 1896, TX), Pauline Vida (b. 1901, TX); spouse, Helen Clara Treon (b. 1880, TX), married Oct. 25, 1911, Mercedes, Cameron County; children, Larkin Earl (b. 1915, TX), David L. (b. 1915, TX), Roland Paul (b. 1918, TX), Helen. *SR; 471; 1000: iii, 56; 485: 163; BDH, Aug 1–3, 1910, Mar 20, 1913; 470: 74–77; Jones, West & West to Colquitt, Mar 8, 1912, AGC; A1b, d, e, f; A2b; A3a; A4b; B2.*

WEST, MILTON CROCKETT. Born Dec. 27, 1851, Leesville, Gonzales County, Texas. No physical description, married. Cattle dealer, Mercedes, Hidalgo County, Texas. SPECIAL RANGER June 19, 1918–Jan. 15, 1919. REMARKS: Had been a farmer in Floresville, Wilson County, Texas. In 1920 was a hotel proprietor in Mercedes. Died Mar. 25,

1925, Mercedes, Hidalgo County, Texas; buried in Mercedes Cemetery. LAW ENFORCEMENT RELATIVES: Ranger L. Earl West, son; Ranger J. Eugene West, son; Ranger Milton H. West, son; Ranger Paul M. West, son. FAMILY: Parents, Larkin Nash West (b. 1824, LA) and Rebecca Martha Conn (b. 1830, MO); siblings, William Mortimer (b. 1855, TX), Eugene Beverly (b. 1857, TX), Florence Louise (b. 1860, TX), Walter Larkin (b. 1864, TX), Jefferson Claiborne (b. 1867, TX); spouse, Pauline Malvina Cocke (b. 1855, TX), married Dec. 3, 1875; children, Larkin Earl (b. 1878, TX), Frederick Autie (b. 1880, TX), Sarah Cornelia "Sallie" (b. 1882, TX), Jesse Eugene (b. 1884, TX), Florence Rebecca (b. 1885, TX), Milton Horace (b. 1888, TX); Paul Morce or Maurice (b. 1890, TX), Pauline (b. 1893, TX), Frank Conn (b. 1896, TX), Pauline Vida (b. 1901, TX); ward, Mamie E. Griffith (b. 1878, TX), listed as "daughter" in 1900 U.S. Census. *SR; 471; A1b, d, e, f; A4b; B1, 2.*

WEST, MILTON HORACE "LECHE." Born June 30, 1888, Gonzales, Gonzales County, Texas. Ht. 6 ft. 3 in., blue eyes, light hair, fair complexion, married, as of Aug. 1927. Farmer. REGULAR RANGER Nov. 1, 1911–Jan. 31, 1912 (private, Co. C). Discharged—reduction in force. Attorney, Brownsville, Cameron County, Texas. SPECIAL RANGER Aug. 6, 1927–Aug. 6, 1928; Aug. 11, 1928–Aug. 11, 1929. REMARKS: Moved to Wilson County, Texas when one year old. Father operated a dairy farm; he delivered milk—hence nickname "Leche" (Spanish for "milk"). Attended West Texas Military Academy, San Antonio, Bexar County, Texas. Was admitted to the bar in 1915. Opened a law practice in Brownsville in 1917. As of June 1917 was an attorney in Floresville, Wilson County. In 1922, was elected district attorney for the 28th Judicial District. Served in the Texas legislature 1929–1933, when he was elected to the U.S. congress from the 15th District, succeeding John Nance Garner. Was reelected until his death Oct. 28, 1948, Washington, D.C.; buried in Buena Vista Cemetery, Brownsville. LAW ENFORCEMENT RELATIVES: Ranger Milton C. West, father; Ranger Jesse Eugene West, brother; Ranger Paul M. West, brother; Ranger L. Earl West, brother. FAMILY: Parents, Milton Crockett West (b. 1851, TX) and Pauline Malvina Cocke (b. 1855, TX); siblings, Mamie E. (a ward, b. 1878, TX), Larkin Earl (b. 1878, TX), Frederick Autie (b. 1880, TX), Sarah Cornelia "Sallie" (b. 1882, TX), Jesse Eugene (b. 1884, TX), Florence Rebecca (b. 1885, TX), Paul Morce or Maurice (b. 1890, TX), Pauline (b. 1893, TX), Frank Conn (b. 1896, TX), Pauline Vida (b. 1901, TX); spouse, Mary Templeton Worley (b. 1892, TX), married Feb. 25, 1914, San Antonio; son, Milton Horace, Jr. (b. 1917, TX). *SR; 471; 521: 881; BDH, Jan 8, 9, 11, 12, 13, 15, 31, Apr 12, 1912; 1000: 50–53; A1d, e, f; A3a; A4b; B1, 2.*

WEST, PAUL MORCE OR MAURICE. Born Mar. 24, 1890, Rancho, Gonzales County, Texas. Ht. 6 ft. ½ in., brown eyes, brown hair, dark complexion. Farmer. REGULAR RANGER Aug. 14, 1915–Nov. 1915 (private, Co. D). Discharged. REMARKS: In 1920 was an office clerk in Mercedes, Hidalgo County. In 1930 was a road construction foreman in Mercedes. Died in Edinburg, Hidalgo County, Texas; buried in Edinburg Cemetery. LAW ENFORCEMENT RELATIVES: Ranger Milton Crockett West, father; Ranger L. Earl West, brother; Ranger J. Eugene West, brother; Ranger Milton H. West, brother. FAMILY: Parents, Milton Crockett West (b. 1851, TX) and Pauline Malvina Cocke (b. 1855, TX); siblings, Mamie E. (a ward, b. 1878, TX), Larkin Earl (b. 1878, TX), Frederick Autie (b. 1880, TX), Sarah Cornelia "Sallie" (b. 1882, TX), Jesse Eugene (b. 1884, TX), Florence Rebecca (b. 1885, TX), Milton Horace (b. 1888, TX); Pauline (b. 1893, TX), Frank Conn (b. 1896, TX), Pauline Vida (b. 1901, TX); spouse, Mabel Frazier (b. 1890, TX), married Dec. 22, 1920; sons, Paul M. West, Jr. (b. 1923, TX), Claiborne Olive "Clay" (b. 1925, TX). *SR; 471; Ransom to Hutchings, Nov 2, 1915, AGC; AG to Ransom, Nov 3, 1915, AGC; 1000: iii, 54–55; BDH, Oct 2, 1915; 319: 39; A1d, e, f, g; A2e; A3a; A4b; B2.*

WEST, RICHARD SUMPTER "SUMPTER." Born July 1861, Harris County, Texas. Ht. 6 ft., brown eyes, light hair, light complexion, widower. Farmer, Gay Hill, Washington County, Texas. LOYALTY RANGER June 17, 1918–Mar. 1919. REMARKS: Lived in Grimes County, Texas as a youth. In 1900 was a carpenter in Navasota, Grimes County. An R. S. West died Jan. 13, 1927, Washington County, Texas. FAMILY: Parents, Richard West (b. 1830, NC) and Estelle (b. 1847, AL); spouse, unknown, widower by 1900. *SR; A1a, b, d, f; A2b.*

WEST, WILLIAM R. Born July 1865, Kentucky. Ht. 5 ft. 7 in., blue eyes, light hair, light complexion, married. Merchant, Hamlin, Jones County, Texas. SPECIAL RANGER

June 2, 1917–Dec. 1917. REMARKS: Had been a farmer in Callahan County. In 1910 had been a weigher for a public scale in Stamford, Jones County. In 1920 was a retired merchant in Hamlin. FAMILY: Spouse, Fannie (b. 1875, TN), married about 1891; children, Cordelia (b. 1907, TX), William Taylor (b. 1910, TX), LaVerne (b. 1914, TX), Fred (b. 1916, TX). *SR; Dodson to Ferguson, May 18, 1917, AGC; Cunningham to Ferguson, May 18, 1917, AGC; A1d, e, f.*

WESTBROOK, LOUIS CARR. Born June 3, 1885, Lorena, McLennan County, Texas. Ht. 5 ft. 10 ½ in., brown eyes, brown hair, fair complexion, married. Farmer. REGULAR RANGER July 16, 1918–unknown. (private, Co. E). REMARKS: As of Sept. 1918 was a Ranger stationed in Maverick County, Texas. A Louis Westbrook died June 14, 1927, Tom Green County, Texas. FAMILY: Parents, Charles A. Westbrook (b. 1838, NC) and Mary Virginia Whitsill (b. 1842, AL); siblings, Alice (b. 1860, TX), Lorena (b. 1861, TX), Moses S. (b. 1863, TX), Joel W. (b. 1865, TX), Thaddeus C. (b. 1867, TX), Virginia W. "Jennie" (b. 1869, TX), Eva M. (b. 1873, TX), Charles A. (b. 1877, TX), Coke (b. 1878, TX), Lucille (b. 1880, TX), Hallie Henry (b. 1882, TX); spouse, Mildred (b. 1886, TX), married about 1908. *SR; 471; A1a, b, d, e; A2b; A3a; A4b.*

WESTON, AUGUSTUS G. Born Aug. 1866, Kerrville, Kerr County, Texas. Ht. 5 ft. 8 in., blue eyes, dark hair, light complexion, married. Merchant, Leakey, Real County, Texas. LOYALTY RANGER Aug. 29, 1918–Feb. 1919. REMARKS: Letterhead, Mar. 1919—"A. G. Weston, Dealer in General Merchandise, Leakey, Tex." Had been a saloon keeper in Kerrville. In 1910 was a dry goods and grocery merchant in Edwards County, Texas. In 1930 was a real estate salesman in Carrizo Springs, Dimmit County, Texas. Died Feb. 8, 1953, Uvalde County, Texas; buried in Leakey Floral Cemetery, Real County. FAMILY: Parents, M. Weston (b. 1832, AL) and Caroline (b. 1838, TX); brothers, Charles (b. 1860, TX), Creed (b. 1869, TX), Mac (b. 1872, TX); spouse, Cora Etta Crenshaw (b. 1873, TX), married Sept. 12, 1894, Kerr County; daughters, Valma C. (b. 1896, TX), Allie Zoe (b. 1914, TX), Blanche Ola (b. 1918, TX). *SR; A1aa, b, d, e, f, g; A2b, e; A4b; B1, 2.*

WHATLEY, GEORGE WADDELL. Born Feb. 26, 1869, Delhi, Richland Parish, Louisiana. Ht. 6 ft. 2 in., hazel eyes, gray hair, fair complexion, married. Planter, Calvert, Robertson County, Texas. LOYALTY RANGER June 1, 1918–Feb. 1919. REMARKS: In Dec. 1906 purchased 530 acres of land on the Brazos River in Robertson County; was a cotton plantation owner. Died May 29, 1941, Robertson County, Texas; buried in Calvert Cemetery. FAMILY: Parents, Walton Whatley (b. 1828, AL) and Sarah Margaret Young (b. 1842, LA or MS); siblings, Green Berry (b. 1856, MS), Tillman Hullum (b. 1857, MS), Tammy Jones (b. 1866, LA), Margie R. (b. 1871, LA), Forrest Claybourne (b. 1874, LA), Calvin Young (b. 1877), Ben P. (b. 1879), Martha Edwards "Eddie" (b. 1881, TX), Samuel Walton (b. 1885, TX); spouse, Ella Alafair Peel (b. 1871, TX), married Feb. 7, 1894, Hearne, Robertson County; children, Lewis Carr (b. 1895, TX), Margaret Alafair (b. 1898, TX), George Aldridge (b. 1902, TX). *SR; A1b, d, f, g; A2b; A3a, b, g.*

WHEAT, ROUTHWIN ALLEN. Born Oct. 15, 1880, Richmond, Fort Bend County, Texas. Ht. 5 ft. 7 in., blue eyes, dark hair, dark complexion, married. Deputy sheriff, Liberty, Liberty County, Texas. LOYALTY RANGER July 14, 1918–Feb. 1919. Deputy sheriff, Liberty. SPECIAL RANGER Sept. 23, 1933–Jan. 22, 1935; July 24, 1935–Oct. 1, 1935. Discharged. REMARKS: Had been an oil field fireman in Liberty. Sheriff, Liberty County, 1920–1924. Deputy sheriff, Jefferson County, Texas, 1925–1929. Worked for stockmen of Liberty, Jefferson, and Chambers Counties, 1930–1933. Special officer for E. W. Boyt Interests and Yount Lee Oil Interests, 1935. Died Oct. 27, 1952, Liberty County, Texas. FAMILY: Spouse #1, unknown, married about 1901; spouse #2, Kaleta or Coledia Pearl (b. 1881, TX), married about 1913; children, Thomas A. (b. 1914, TX), Hattie Ellen (b. 1916, TX). *SR; A1d, f, g; A2b; A3a.*

WHEATLEY, JEROME B. "ROME." Born July 1867, Waxahachie, Ellis County, Texas. Ht. 6 ft. 1 ½ in., gray eyes, brown hair, medium complexion, married. Peace officer. REGULAR RANGER Feb. 15, 1921–Jan. 16, 1933 (private, Co. B; transferred to Headquarters Co. Sept. 1, 1921; sergeant, Headquarters Co., Feb. 15, 1923; transferred to Co. C, Sept. 1, 1925; sergeant, Co. C, Feb. 15, 1927; sergeant, Headquarters Co., Feb. 15, 1929; promoted to captain of Co. C, May 18, 1932). Resigned. Peace officer, Austin, Travis County, Texas. REGULAR RANGER Feb. 5, 1935–Sept. 1, 1937 (private, Headquarters Co.; promoted to sergeant, May 1, 1937; promoted to captain, Sept. 1, 1937, transferred to Narcotics Division of Texas Department of Public Safety). REMARKS: Potter County, Texas sheriff Nov. 6, 1894–Nov. 8, 1898. Had been a drug store merchant in Clayton, Union County, New Mexico. In May 1917 was Amarillo, Potter County, police chief. In 1920 was a real estate agent in Amarillo. Retired from the Texas Department of Public Safety in 1940. Died Apr. 18, 1944, Austin, Travis County, Texas; buried in Oakwood Cemetery, Austin. FAMILY: Parents, Dr. Pierce Stokes Wheatley (b. 1820, TN) and Terry Adaline Reagor (b. 1828, AL); siblings, J. R. (b. 1846, TX), Hazeltine (b. 1849, TX), Blanche (b. 1859, TX), Lola P. (b. 1861, TX), Robert R. (b. 1863, TX), Joseph R. (b. 1864, TX), Ida O. (b. 1868, TX); spouse, Mattie (b. 1877, TN), married about 1900; daughter, Roma (b. 1910, NM). *SR; 319: 200, 264–265; 470: 43; 463: 142; 1503:418–419; A1b, e, f, g; A2b; A4a, b.*

WHEELER, JOEL ROBERT "BOB." Born July 14, 1877, Center, Shelby County, Texas. Ht. 6 ft. 2 in., blue eyes, dark hair, light complexion, married. Railroad watchman, San Antonio, Bexar County, Texas. SPECIAL RANGER Jan. 7, 1919–unknown. Special agent, I&GN Railroad, Taylor, Williamson County, Texas. RAILROAD RANGER Aug. 19, 1922–Aug. 19, 1924 (Co. A). Discharged—enlistment expired. Special agent, I&GN Railroad, Taylor. SPECIAL RANGER June 29, 1925–Feb. 8, 1927; Feb. 8, 1927–Feb. 8, 1928; Feb. 23, 1928–Jan. 25, 1929; Jan. 25, 1929–Jan. 23, 1930; Jan. 23, 1930–Jan. 23, 1931; Jan. 27, 1933–Jan. 22, 1935; May 29, 1935–Aug. 10, 1935. Discharged. REMARKS: Had been a farmer in Bandera County, Texas and Bexar County. In Sept. 1918 was a truck driver in San Antonio. As of Jan. 1919 had been a deputy sheriff and city policeman for about 10 years. Died Jan. 29, 1945, San Antonio, Bexar County, Texas. FAMILY: Parents, Joel Preston Wheeler (b. 1842, AL) and Laura Ann Irish (b. 1848, GA); siblings, Walter S. (b. 1868, TX), Laura Alice (b. 1871, TX), Benjamin M. (b. 1874, TX), Alpha Rodell (b. 1880, TX); Carl Foster (b. 1882, TX); spouse #1, Judith Caldonia "Callie" Freeman (b. 1875, AR), married Oct. 30, 1898, Shelby County; children, Elva (b. 1899, TX), Freeman E. (b. 1900, TX), Laura M. (b. 1901, TX), Callie L. (b. 1904, TX); spouse #2, Gladys Vera Kuykendall (b. 1894, TX), married June 23, 1913, San Antonio; children, Robert J. (b. 1915, TX), Gordon K. (b. 1916, TX), Joel Andrew (b. 1918, TX), Gladys Novelle (b. 1928, TX). *SR; 471; Johnston to Williamson, Jan 20, 1919, AGC; Williamson to Harley, Jan 224, 1919, AGC; A1b, d, e, f, g; A2b, e; A3a; A4a, b, g; B1, 2.*

WHISENANT, JOHN MILTON "MILTON." Born Aug. 17, 1869, Collin County, Texas. No physical description, married. Grain dealer, Allen, Collin County. LOYALTY RANGER June 4, 1918–Feb. 1919. REMARKS: Died July 18, 1935, Collin County, Texas; buried in Allen Cemetery, Allen. FAMILY: Parents, Robert Benton Whisenant (b. 1843, MO) and Harriet Coffey (b. 1844, KY); siblings, Mary Ann (b. 1866, TX), Virginia E. (b. 1871, TX), Maude Franklin (b. 1873), Elzer L. (b. 1875, TX), Sarah Frances (b. 1878), Forest B. (b. 1880, TX), Henry W. (b. 1882, TX), Antha Lee (b. 1886, TX); stepmother, Clara V. (b. 1861, TN); siblings, Maya (b. 1893, TX), Mary J. (b. 1896, TX), Robert B. (b. 1898, TX); spouse, Ola Stansell (b. 1884, TX), married Apr. 8, 1908; sons, Robert Winfield, John Milton (b. 1919, TX). *SR; A1a, b, d, e, f; A2b; A4a, b, g; B1.*

WHITE, ARTHUR GOFF "GOFF." Born Sept. 18, 1870, Decatur, Wise County, Texas. Ht. 6 ft., gray eyes, brown hair, light complexion. Stock hand. REGULAR RANGER Sept. 7, 1905–Mar. 17, 1910 (private, Co. C). Resigned to accept a better job as a Waller County, Texas deputy sheriff. REMARKS: Was indicted in 1913 in Trinity County, Texas for having killed a man there, allegedly by mistake, on Sept. 9, 1909, in line of duty. State refused to provide legal assistance. In May 1915, lived in Houston, Harris County, Texas. In 1920 lived in Austin, Travis County, Texas. Died Oct. 7, 1922, Tarrant County, Texas. FAMILY: Parents, James Denny White (b. 1831, IL) and Mary Perrin (b. 1840, KY); siblings, Emma Jane (b. 1858, TX), Frank Sprague (b. 1859, TX), James P. (b. 1864, TX), John Irving (b. 1867, TX), William Denny (b. 1868, TX), Mary May (b. 1875, TX), Evalena "Lena" (b. 1878, TX); spouse, Mary Bacon (b. 1880, TX), married about 1908; children, Mary Jane (b. 1913, TX), William K. or William Wayne (b. 1915, TX). *SR; 471; AS, Feb 16, Mar 16, 1910; AG to Hulen, Mar 17, May 16, 1910, AGC; White to AG, Apr 1, 1913, May 18, 1915, AGC; Hutchings to Colquitt, Apr 2, 1913, AGC; Colquitt to Hutchings, Apr 16, 1913, AGC; Rogers to Hutchings, May 12, 19, 30, 1913, AGC; AG to White, Apr 17, May 18, 19, June 15, Nov 1, 1915, AGC; White to Hutchings, May 14, June 3, 8, 25, Oct 30, 1915, AGC;*

Hutchings to Rogers, May 24, 1915, AGC; Paget to Hutchings, Oct 30, 1915, AGC; AG to Cain, June 19, 1915, AGC; A1b, d, e, f, g; A2b; A4a, b, g.

WHITE, BUCK. Born Sept. 1863, Pickens, Mississippi. Ht. 5 ft. 6 in., gray eyes, black hair, dark complexion, married. Farmer, Baird, Callahan County, Texas. SPECIAL RANGER May 30, 1917–Dec. 1917 (attached to Co. C). *SR.*

WHITE, JAMES WILLIAM "WILL." Born Aug. 1867, Tupelo, Lee County, Mississippi. Ht. 6 ft., gray eyes, auburn hair, light complexion, married. Grocery merchant, Cooper, Delta County, Texas. LOYALTY RANGER June 10, 1918–Feb. 1919. REMARKS: Resident of Delta County for the last 40 years. Died Mar. 4, 1933, Delta County, Texas. FAMILY: Parents, James Benjamin White (b. 1826, AL) and Rebecca A. Johnston (b. 1828, GA); siblings, Mary (b. 1853, MS), Benjamin F. (b. 1855, MS), Anna (b. 1858, MS), Ella (b. 1859, MS), Laura (b. 1861, MS), Ethel Joda (b. 1864, MS), John D. (b. 1869, MS); spouse #1, Mattie W. (b. 1869, TN), married about 1889; sons, Alvin O. (b. 1889, TX), Hollis A. (b. 1891, TX), Benjamin L. (b. 1893, TX); spouse #2, Myrtie (b. 1878, MS), married about 1901; sons, William J. (b. 1904, TX), Morris P. (b. 1906, TX), James Buren (b. 1908, TX). *SR; A1a, b, d, e, f, g; A2b; A4g.*

WHITE, JOHN DUDLEY. Born June 1879, Austin, Travis County, Texas. Ht. 5 ft. 10 in., brown eyes, brown hair, dark complexion. REGULAR RANGER 1905–1911. Resigned to join Houston, Harris County, Texas police department. Farmer, Travis County. REGULAR RANGER May 15, 1913–Nov. 3, 1913 (private, Co. A). Resigned to join Customs Service Nov. 4, 1913. Mounted Customs inspector, El Paso area, 1913–1916. Stock farmer, enlisted in Austin. REGULAR RANGER May 10, 1916–July 12, 1918 (private, Co. B; transferred to Co. C, Sept. 1, 1917; transferred to Co. D, Nov. 1917). Killed by Army deserters at Broaddus, San Augustine County, July 12, 1918. REMARKS: He and brother Thomas Bruce White attended Southwestern University, Georgetown, Texas, for two years while their father, R. Emmett White, was mayor of Austin, then went into the cattle business on their father's ranch at Oak Hill, Travis County. LAW ENFORCEMENT RELATIVES: Ranger James Campbell "Doc" White, brother; Ranger Thomas Bruce White, brother; Ranger John Dudley White, Jr., son; Travis County sheriff (ca. 1890–1902) R. Emmett White, father; Travis County Constable (precinct 3 as of Sept. 1918) and Travis County sheriff Coleman "Coley" White, brother; FBI agent Thomas Bruce White, Jr., nephew. FAMILY: Parents, Robert Emmett White (b. 1848, TN) and Margaret Campbell (TN); siblings, Thomas Bruce (b. 1881, TX), Coleman Crockett (b. 1883, TX), James Campbell (b. 1884, TX); spouse, Selma R. (b. 1880, TX), married about 1901; son, John Dudley, Jr. *SR; 471; White to Hutchings, Mar 16, 1913, Aug 16, 1915, Apr 17, 28, Dec 27, 1916, AGC; Hughes to AG, Nov 6, 1913, AGC; AG to White, Apr 27, 1916 AGC; Alderete to Ferguson, Aug 28, 1916, WC; Fox to Hutchings, Sept 10, 1916, WC; Hutchings to Ferguson, Dec 29, 1916, WC; AG to General Manager, Nov 13,1917, AGC; Anders to Harley, July 12, 1918, WC; L. B. Harvey's statements, July 13, 17, 1918, WC; Assistant AG to Glenn, July 18, 1918, AGC; Erby E. Swift report, July 25, 1918, WC; Hanson to Judge Advocate, Oct 3, 1918, WC; EPMT, Oct 15, 1913, Feb 17, Apr 26, 1914, Sept 24, 1915, Jan 29, Feb 1, 8–10, Apr 14, 1916; 479: 10, 12–13, 72–73; 319: 395; A1d, e; A3a; A4b, g.*

WHITE, JOSEPH F. "JOE." Born Apr. 1872, Ozark County, Missouri. Ht. 5 ft. 11 in., blue eyes, dark brown hair, light complexion, married. Bridge foreman, I&GN Railroad, enlisted in Bexar County, Texas. SPECIAL RANGER Jan. 11, 1918–Jan. 15, 1919. REMARKS: Eight years as bridge foreman on I&GN. Had been a railroad carpenter in Williamson County, Texas. In 1920 was "car man" living in Taylor, Williamson County. A Joseph F. White died July 22, 1922, Williamson County, Texas. FAMILY: Parents, John White (b. 1843, MO) and Pernita Hudson (b. 1843, IN); siblings, Sarah Jane (b. 1863, IN), William D. (b. 1866, MO), Pinkney (b. 1871), Eliza L. (b. 1873, MO), John (b. 1877, MO); spouse, Janie (b. 1872, Ireland), married about 1899; children, Bennie (b. 1902, TX), Gladys (b. 1906, TX). *SR; 471; A1b, d, e, f; A2b; A4a, b.*

WHITE, THOMAS BRUCE "TOM." Born Mar. 6, 1881, Oak Hill, Travis County, Texas. Ht. 6 ft. 3 in., blue eyes, auburn hair, fair complexion, married as of 1916. Ranchman. REGULAR RANGER Sept. 18, 1906–Apr. 1, 1909 (private, Co. A; Co. B, 1909). Resigned to become special agent for Santa Fe Railroad at Amarillo, Potter County, Texas. Special agent, GH&SA Railroad, San Antonio, Bexar County, Texas.

SPECIAL RANGER Apr. 15, 1916–1917. Special employee, federal Bureau of Investigation, El Paso, El Paso County, Texas. SPECIAL RANGER May 17, 1918–Jan. 14, 1919. REMARKS: After two years as student at Southwestern University, Georgetown, Texas, he and brother John Dudley White went into cattle business on father's ranch at Oak Hill. A year later he turned his part of the business over to Dudley and worked for a construction company in Oklahoma. For a time he lived in Los Angeles, California where he delivered furniture. Returned to Oak Hill, helped Dudley run the cattle business. At the suggestion of Ranger Capt. John R. Hughes he enlisted in the Rangers in 1906. After working as a special agent for the Santa Fe Railroad, he worked in the same capacity for the Southern Pacific at San Antonio and El Paso. Held a deputy sheriff's commission in Bexar County, 1916. From 1917 to 1927 was an FBI agent. In 1930 was warden, U.S. Penitentiary, Fort Leavenworth, Leavenworth County, Kansas. From 1932 to 1951 was the warden of La Tuna Federal Correctional Institution, Anthony, El Paso County, Texas. In 1951 retired at age 70. Died Dec. 21, 1971, El Paso County, Texas. LAW ENFORCEMENT RELATIVES: Ranger John Dudley White, brother; Ranger James Campbell "Doc" White, brother; Ranger John Dudley White, Jr., nephew; Travis County sheriff (ca. 1890–1902) R. Emmett White, father; Travis County Constable (precinct 3 as of Sept. 1918) and Travis County sheriff Coleman "Coley" White, brother; FBI agent Thomas Bruce White, Jr., son. FAMILY: Parents, Robert Emmett White (b. 1848, TN) and Margaret Campbell (TN); siblings, John Dudley (b. 1879, TX), Coleman Crockett (b. 1883, TX), James Campbell (b. 1884, TX); spouse, Bessie Lee Patterson (b. 1884, MS), married about 1910; sons, Thomas B., Jr. (b. 1914, TX), Robert E. (b. 1915, TX). *SR; 471; SAE, Dec 14, 1911; Watkins to Ferguson, Apr 6, 1916, AGC; AG to Watkins, Apr 10, 1916, AGC; Watkins to Hutchings, Apr 15, 1916, AGC; White to Hutchings, May 7, 1917, AGC; White to Davis, Dec 22, 1917, AGC; Acting AG to Jones, June 5, 1918, AGC; 479: 1–74, 117–134; 1000: 118; 319: 395; A1d, e, g; A2a, b; A3a; A4g.*

WHITEFIELD, BENJAMIN FRANKLIN "BEN." Born Sept. 15, 1875, Ellis County, Texas. Medium height, stout, brown eyes, gray hair, married. Merchant, Midland, Midland County, Texas. LOYALTY RANGER June 14, 1918–Mar. 1919. REMARKS: Letterhead, Mar. 1919: "Midland Mercantile Co., General Merchandise, B. F. Whitefield, Treasurer and one of Directors, Midland." Died Oct. 21, 1947, Midland, Midland County, Texas. FAMILY: Parents, George Washington Whitefield (b. 1838, TN) and Eliza C. Brack (b. 1847, MS); siblings, James Marshall (b. 1866, TX), Lucy Emiline (b. 1869, TX), John William (b. 1871, TX), Albert Sidney (b. 1881, TX), George Henry (b. 1883, TX), Charles Overton (b. 1887, TX); spouse, Ada Earle Wolcott (b. 1878, TX), married Oct. 3, 1900, Midland; children, Franklin Wolcott (b. 1902, TX), Inabeth Elizabeth (b. 1907, TX), Eulalia (b. 1913, TX). *SR; A1a, b, e, f; A2b; A3a; A4a.*

WHITEKER, BOSQUE MONROE. Born Jan. 27, 1876, Coryell County, Texas. Tall, medium build, blue eyes, dark brown hair, married. Real estate and abstractor, Haskell, Haskell County, Texas. LOYALTY RANGER June 1, 1918–Mar. 1919. REMARKS: Grew up in Bosque County, Texas. In 1930 was retired, lived in Haskell. Died July 23, 1951, Haskell County, Texas. FAMILY: Parents, James Wiley Whiteker (b. 1852, MS) and Mathilda Beatty (b. 1860, MO); siblings, Rosa Alice (b. 1878, TX), Mollie (b. 1880, TX), Lillie Ella (b. 1882, TX), Oscar W. (b. 1884, TX), Bessie Mae (b. 1888, TX), Jessie (b. 1890, TX), Ewing H. (b. 1894, TX), Della "Pearl" Truman (b. 1897, TX), Floyd Mansel (b. 1905, TX); spouse, Myrtle E. (b. 1884, TX), married about 1904; children, John Wylie (b. 1905, TX), Marjorie (b. 1907, TX), Bosque Monroe, Jr. (b. 1910, TX), Mary Emma (b. 1911, TX), Clarence (b. 1913, TX). *SR; A1b, d, e, f, g; A2b; A3a; A4b, g; B1.*

WHITFIELD, ROBERT WILKINS. Born Feb. 1, 1875, Nashville, Davidson County, Tennessee. Ht. 5 ft. 10 in., light brown eyes, brown hair, ruddy complexion, married. Brakeman, enlisted in San Antonio, Bexar County, Texas. SPECIAL RANGER Aug. 28, 1916–unknown. REMARKS: Was 1st sergeant, regiment of Tennessee Volunteers; honorably discharged. Was a cowboy for 4 years. As of Sept. 1918 was a brakeman for the I&GN Railway Company in San Antonio. Was still a railroad brakeman in San Antonio in 1930. A Robert W. Whitfield died Nov. 22, 1935, Bexar County, Texas. FAMILY: Spouse #1, Margaret (b. PA), married about 1907; son, Charles (b. 1908, TX); spouse #2, Ophelia (b. 1908, Mexico), married about 1929. *SR; AG to Whitfield, Aug 31,1916, AGC; A1f, g; A2b; A3a.*

WHITLEY, WILLIAM ELISHA. Born Dec. 22, 1878, Refugio, Refugio County, Texas. Ht. 5 ft. 8 in., blue eyes, brown hair, light complexion. Stockman. REGULAR RANGER July 5, 1909–Feb. 15, 1910 (private, Co. A). Resigned. REMARKS: Became a bartender in Harlingen, Cameron County, Texas. On Sept. 5, 1910, shot Francisco Balli. As of Oct. 1910 was a member of the Harlingen Democratic Club. Died Mar. 20, 1913, Jim Wells County, Texas; buried in Old Alice Cemetery, Alice, Jim Wells County. FAMILY: Parents, John Madison Whitley (b. 1849, TX) and Penelope Smith Rowland (b. 1849, AL); siblings, Eddie Sharp (b. 1871, TX), Ella Lilly (b. 1874, TX), Mary Delphia (b. 1875, TX), Alma Dora (b. 1876, TX), James Luin (b. 1880, TX), Katie L. (b. 1882, TX), twins Jessie and Georgia (b. 1885, TX). *SR; 471; MR, Co. A, Feb 1910, AGC; BDH, June 29, Sept 5–8, Oct 8, 26, 29, Nov 3, 1910; Johnson to Newton, Sept 5, 1910, WC; A1b; A4a, b; B2.*

WHITMAN, WILLIAM JAMES "WILLIE JIM." Born Sept. 5, 1882, Liberty Hill, Williamson County, Texas. Ht. 5 ft. 8 ½ in., blue eyes, brown hair, fair complexion, married. Ranchman, Santa Elena, Starr County, Texas. SPECIAL RANGER May 18, 1918–Jan. 15, 1919. REMARKS: Had been a farmer in Webb County. As of Sept. 1915 worked for Henry Edds in Starr County. In 1930 was farming in Duval County, Texas. A William James Whitman died Aug. 11, 1963, Jim Hogg County, Texas. FAMILY: Parents, Licander Monroe Whitman (b. 1853, AL) and Ella Frances Bragg (b. 1853, VA); siblings, Ethel (b. 1877, MS), Eddie (b. 1879, MS); spouse, Anna "Annie" Ashabranner (b. 1886, TX), married about 1905; children, Nora (b. 1908, TX), Nedith or Neta (b. 1910, TX), Vera (b. 1912, TX), Wilmer or Wilber (b. 1915, TX), Edie (b. 1918, TX), twins Henry and Henrietta (b. 1920, TX). *SR; 471; A1b, e, f, g; A2b; A3a; A4g.*

WHITTINGTON, ARTHUR GEORGE. Born Aug. 14, 1872, Rockdale, Milam County, Texas. Ht. 5 ft. 10 ½ in., gray eyes, gray hair, dark complexion, married. General manager, I&GN Railroad, Houston, Harris County, Texas. SPECIAL RANGER Nov. 7, 1916–Jan. 15, 1919 (attached to Co. C). REMARKS: Had been a railroad freight agent in Fort Worth, Tarrant County, Texas and a railroad superintendent in Mart, McLennan County, Texas. Died Dec. 23, 1953, Houston, Harris County, Texas; buried in Forest Park Cemetery, Houston. FAMILY: Parents, George Ross Whittington (b. 1842, MS) and Rachel Frances "Fannie" Scarborough (b. 1846, LA); siblings, Emma Gretchen (b. 1874, TX), James Oliver (b. 1876, TX), Bertie Frances (b. 1878, TX), Lawrence Hall (b. 1884, TX), Harris Diaz (b. 1887, TX), Monnie (b. 1890, TX); spouse, Lula Mae Cantrell (b. 1873, AR), married Nov. 26, 1893, Eastland County, Texas; sons, Marcus Kelly (b. 1894, TX), Arthur George (b. 1896, TX), Harmon (b. 1899, TX). *SR; A1b, d, e, f, g; A2b; A3a; A4a, b, g.*

WILDENTHAL, BERNARD, JR. Born Aug. 13, 1885, San Antonio, Bexar County, Texas. Ht. 5 ft. 9 in., blue eyes, light hair, light complexion, married. Deputy sheriff, Cotulla, La Salle County, Texas. LOYALTY RANGER June 14, 1918–Feb. 1919. REMARKS: In 1920 was a bank cashier in Cotulla. In 1930 was a farmer in Cotulla. Died Aug 15, 1957, Cotulla, La Salle County, Texas; buried in Old Cotulla Cemetery. FAMILY: Parents, Bernard Wildenthal (b. 1846, Germany) and Aissa Margaret Von Wadgymar (b. 1862, TN); siblings, Mary (b. 1882, TX), Arthur Thomas (b. 1883, TX), Carl (b. 1887, TX), Otto (b. 1891, TX), John (b. 1892, TX), Adele (b. 1894, TX), Herman Hobson (b. 1897, TX), Helen (b. 1899, TX), Bryan (b. 1904, TX); spouse #1, Charles Mabel Lake (b. 1889, TX), married about 1909; daughter, Mary Louise (b. 1917, TX); spouse #2, Annie F. Henkel (b. 1907). *SR; Cardwell to Strawn, July 11, 1918, AGC; A1d, e, f, g; A2b; A3a; A4b, g; B1.*

WILHITE, JACOB TALLEY "JAKE." (In Ranger Service Record listed as WILKITE.) Born Apr. 3, 1877, Travis County, Texas. Ht. 6 ft., gray eyes, light hair, fair complexion. Physician, Austin, Travis County. SPECIAL RANGER Mar. 28, 1918–unknown. REMARKS: Was a physician at the Pasteur Institute, Texas State Lunatic Asylum, Austin. Died Jan. 27, 1927, Travis County, Texas. FAMILY: Parents, James Wilhite (b. 1840, MO) and Malissa Frances "Fanny" Brandenburg (b. 1850, MO); siblings, Cora Elliott (b. 1872, TX), Sallie Pearl (b. 1877, TX), James Smith (b. 1878, TX), Willard Moses (b. 1882, TX), Walton Francis (b. 1886, TX). *SR; A1b, d, e, f; A2b; A3a; A4b.*

WILKINS, JOHN EDMUND. Born Oct. 16, 1876, Atascosa County, Texas. Ht. 6 ft., blue eyes, dark hair, light complexion. Ranchman. REGULAR RANGER May 23, 1916–Mar. 1918 (private, Co. C). Resigned to become a mounted

Immigration inspector at Eagle Pass, Maverick County, Texas. REMARKS: In Aug. 1919 applied for reenlistment in the Rangers; had been laid off from Immigration Service because of budget cuts. By 1920 was a Customs inspector in La Pryor, Zavala County, Texas. Died Dec. 1963. FAMILY: Parents, William Martin Wilkins (b. 1855, TX) and Mary Jane Gates (b. 1857, TX); siblings, James Dwight (b. 1872, TX); Nancy Agnes (b. 1874, TX), William Martin (b. 1876), Elizabeth Jane (b. 1878), Mary Lavanna (b. 1880, TX), Mason Kizar (b. 1882, TX), Thomas McDaniel (b. 1884, TX), Amos Herbert (b. 1886, TX), Drusilla Emmaline (b. 1888, TX), Martin (b. 1893, TX), Henry Grant (b. 1895, TX), Andy Armstrong (b. 1898, TX). *SR; 471; Wilkins to Aldrich, Aug 27, 1919, AGC; A1b, d, e, f; A2a; A3a; A4a, b, g; B1.*

WILLETT, FRANCIS M. "FRANK." Born Apr. 23, 1876, Sunset, Wise County, Texas. Ht. 5 ft. 9 in., blue eyes, brown hair, fair complexion, married. Farmer, enlisted in Callahan County, Texas. SPECIAL RANGER July 2, 1917–Dec. 1917 (attached to Co. C). REMARKS: In 1920 and 1930 was an electrician at the Swift & Co. packing plant in Fort Worth, Tarrant County, Texas. Died June 10, 1976, Tarrant County, Texas. FAMILY: Parents, John Russell Willett (b. 1850, TN) and Minerva Ann Wainscott (b. 1855, IA); siblings, James Andrew (b. 1874, TX), Thomas Calvin (b. 1878, TX), Martha Elizabeth (b. 1879, OK), John Russell (b. 1880, OK), Sarah Jane (b. 1882, OK), Richard Daniel (b. 1889, TX), Lena May (b. 1895, TX); spouse, Annie E. Thomas (b. 1880, TX), married about 1896; sons, John C. (b. 1905, TX), Hugh M. (b. 1914, TX). *SR; A1b, e, f, g; A2a, b; A3a; A4b; B2.*

WILLIAMS, BEN. Born Dec. 1860, Paris, France. Ht. 5 ft. 8 in., blue eyes, light hair, fair complexion, married. Special agent (private detective), El Paso, El Paso County, Texas. SPECIAL RANGER June 11, 1918–Jan. 15, 1919. WA was renewed Jan. 20, 1919–Dec. 31, 1919. REMARKS: Immigrated to the United States in 1872 or 1876. Ranger Service Record states took out naturalization papers in June 1893. 1920 U.S. Census records state naturalized in 1878. In 1900 was deputy sheriff, Las Cruces, Dona Ana County, New Mexico. In Jan. 1911 was chief special agent for Santa Fe Railroad in El Paso. As of Feb. 1916 was head of Ben Williams Detective Agency, El Paso. In May 1918 worked as special agent at El Paso for T. B. Cunningham, special agent for the Chino Copper Company. In 1920 and 1930 was chief of a detective agency in El Paso. FAMILY: Spouse #1, Caleta L. (b. 1879, NM), married about 1898; son, Beltram (b. 1899, NM); spouse #2, Blanche (b. 1886, TX); step-sons, George B. Binkley (b. 1906, TX), Howell Binkley (b. 1908, TX), Ralph Binkley (b. 1911, TX). *SR; EPMT, Jan 31, Feb 2, 1911, Feb 14, 1916; Brahan to Harley, May 16, 1918, AGC; Cunningham to Harley, June 10, 1918, AGC; A1d, f, g.*

WILLIAMS, CALEB THOMAS. Born Mar. 1862, Mount Pleasant, Lewis County, Tennessee. Ht. 5 ft. 8 in., blue eyes, gray hair, medium complexion, married. REGULAR RANGER Oct. 1917–Dec. 27, 1918 (private, Co. D). Was on detached duty; his salary was $50 a month. In late July 1918, was detailed to work under Army Lt. Popenoe, and the government paid his expenses. On Dec. 27, 1918 he resigned in Waco, McLennan County, Texas. Peace officer. REGULAR RANGER Oct. 23, 1920–Feb. 15, 1921 (private, Co. D). Discharged. Peace officer, Breckenridge, Stephens County, Texas. REGULAR RANGER Apr. 11, 1927–May 31, 1927 (private, Co. D, but was unattached). Discharged. Peace officer, Breckenridge. REGULAR RANGER June 21, 1928–Aug. 31, 1928 (unattached). Discharged. REMARKS: Apr. 1927 and June 1928 enlistments were at request of Governor Moody—for undercover duty. In 1910 was a constable in Johnson County, Texas. In 1920 was a traffic officer in Cleburne, Johnson County. In 1930 was a "city collector" in Breckenridge. Died Nov. 8, 1937, Stephens County, Texas. FAMILY: Parents, Sidney A. Williams (b. 1832, TN) and Mary Catherine Cooper (b. 1830, TN); siblings, Mary (b. 1856, TN), Ida (b. 1858, TN), Margaret (b. 1859, TN), George (b. 1864, TN), Benjamin (b. 1867, TN); spouse, Sarah E. "Sallie" (b. 1871, TN), married about 1891; daughters, Mary or May B. (b. 1893, TX), Jewel L. (b. 1898, TX). *SR; 471; AG to MKT Railroad, Oct 12, 1917, AGC; AG to Orient Railroad, Oct 12, 1917; AGC; AG to General Manager, Nov 13, 1917, AGC; Acting AG to FW&DC Railroad, Jan 11, 1918, AGC; [AG] to Huddleston, Apr 15, May 29, 1918, AGC; Acting AG to Williams, Aug 31, 1918, AGC; Popenoe to AG, Sept 2, 1918, AGC; Gross to Harley, Dec 27, 1918, AGC; A1a, e, f, g; A2b; A4g.*

WILLIAMS, ELVIN W. Born Jan. 27, 1884, Green, Karnes County, Texas. Ht. 6 ft., brown eyes, black hair, dark complexion, married. Stockman. REGULAR RANGER

Apr. 10, 1918–unknown (private, Co. I). REMARKS: As of Sept. 1918 was a Ranger stationed in Webb County, Texas. In 1920 was a Ranger living in Kenedy, Karnes County. Died Nov. 26, 1928, Karnes County, Texas. FAMILY: Parents, Andrew Williams (b. 1849, AL) and Salome (b. 1860, TX); siblings, Ezra Y. (b. 1885, TX), Luther A. (b. 1891, TX), Lea L. (b. 1899, TX); spouse, Blanche Monica (b. 1892, TX), married about 1917; children, Louise Helen (b. 1918, TX), Leona B. (b. 1921, TX), Alline L. (b. 1922, TX), Andrew B. (b. 1924, TX), Mary A. (b. 1926, TX). *SR; 471; A1d, f, g; A2b; A3a.*

WILLIAMS, HARRY FRANK. Born Jan. 3, 1892, San Antonio, Bexar County, Texas. Ht. 5 ft. 8 in., gray eyes, auburn hair, light complexion. Clerk, Austin, Travis County, Texas. SPECIAL RANGER Aug. 3, 1917–Dec. 1917 (attached to Co. C). REMARKS: As of June 1917 was a U.S. government clerk at Fort Sam Houston, San Antonio. In 1920 was a government clerk in San Antonio. Died May 9, 1963, Bexar County, Texas. FAMILY: Parents, Unknown Williams (b. IL) and Mary (b. 1872, TX); stepfather, Frank Knox (b. 1875, OH); siblings, Harry E. Knox (b. 1896, TX), Frank J. Knox (b. 1899, TX); spouse, Luciel (b. 1897, TX), married sometime before 1920. *SR; A1d, g; A2a, b; A3a.*

WILLIAMS, J. J. Born Mar. 1871, Beeville, Bee County, Texas. Ht. 5 ft. 10 in., brown eyes, graying brown hair, fair complexion. Ranchman, Singleton, Grimes County, Texas. LOYALTY RANGER June 17, 1918–Feb. 1919. *SR.*

WILLIAMS, ROBERT D. Born July 15, 1894, Baird, Callahan County, Texas. Ht. 5 ft. 9 in., brown eyes, dark hair, dark complexion. Ranchman, Putnam, Callahan County. SPECIAL RANGER May 30, 1917–Dec. 1917. REMARKS: In 1930 was a ranchman in Putnam. FAMILY: Parents, Robert D. Williams (b. 1860, TX) and Louie or Lovie M. (b. 1868, IL); brothers, J. N. (b. 1891, TX), Wesley Weems (b. 1897, TX), Everett Henry (b. 1899, TX), Lynn L. (b. 1902, TX), Nathaniel H. (b. 1905, TX), Louis A. (b. 1907, TX); spouse, Lucille (b. 1902, TX), married about 1927; daughter, Ellen L. (b. 1928, TX). *SR; A1d, e, f, g; A3a.*

WILLIAMS, THOMAS W. Born 1875, Courtney, Love County, Oklahoma. (Note: At time of his birth, was Chickasaw Nation, Indian Territory.) Ht. 5 ft. 7 in., black eyes, iron gray hair, dark complexion, married. Stockman, Nocona, Montague County, Texas. LOYALTY RANGER June 5, 1918–Mar. 1919. REMARKS: In 1910 and 1920 was a dry goods salesman in Nocona. In 1930 was a cattle dealer in Austin, Travis County, Texas. FAMILY: Parents, Lycurgus S. Williams (b. 1853, CA) and Nancy (b. 1855, TX); siblings, Robert (b. 1874, Chickasaw Nation), Mary Maggie (b. 1880, TX); spouse, Stella Clark (b. 1877, PA), married about 1897; children, Margaret (b. 1899, TX), T. W., Jr. (b. 1900, TX), James S. (b. 1902, TX). *SR; A1b, e, f, g; A4b.*

WILLIAMS, TURNER VAN or VANN "CHAPO." Born Jan. 18, 1884, Atascosa County, Texas. Ht. 5 ft. 4 in., gray eyes, brown hair, florid complexion. Ranchman. REGULAR RANGER Dec. 22, 1917–Jan. 1918 (private, Co. I). Resigned. REMARKS: Was still in Rangers as of Jan. 9, 1918. As of Sept. 1918 was a ranch employee in Dimmit County, Texas. Died June 26, 1959, Bexar County, Texas; buried in San Jose Cemetery, Bexar County. FAMILY: Parents, Daniel Turner Williams (b. 1855, AR) and Ann Elizabeth "Annie" Neill (b. 1860, TX); siblings, Eller (b. 1877, TX), Morgan (b. 1880, TX), Ethel (b. 1882, TX), Annie (b. 1887, TX), Johanna (b. 1890, TX), Wright Allen (b. 1897, TX), John M. (b. 1898, TX). *SR; 471; Acting AG to GC&SF Railroad, Jan 9, 1918, AGC; A1b, f; A2b; A3a; A4b.*

WILLIAMSON, CHARLES E. Born Mar. 1872, Rusk, Cherokee County, Texas. Ht. 5 ft. 7 in., brown eyes, black hair, ruddy complexion, married. Special watchman, I&GN Railroad, New Braunfels, Comal County, Texas. SPECIAL RANGER Sept. 18, 1917–Jan. 15, 1919 (attached to Co. C). Special agent, I&GN Railroad, Waco, McLennan County, Texas. RAILROAD RANGER Aug. 23, 1922–Aug. 23, 1924 (Co. A). Enlistment expired. Special agent, Gulf Coast Lines and I&GN Railroads, Waco. SPECIAL RANGER Sept. 15, 1926–Jan. 14, 1928 (reenlisted Jan. 25, 1927); Jan. 14, 1928–Jan. 11, 1929; Jan. 11, 1929–Jan. 11, 1930; Jan. 13, 1930–Jan. 13, 1931; Jan. 26, 1931–Jan. 18, 1933 (WA was extended to Jan. 20, 1933); Jan. 20, 1933–died, date unknown. REMARKS: A Charles Edward Williamson died Feb. 7, 1933, Brazos County, Texas. LAW ENFORCEMENT RELATIVES: Ranger Nathan Fuller Williamson, brother. FAMILY: Mother, Sallie D. Williamson (b. 1849, TX); brother, Nathan F. (b. 1875, TX); spouse, Rosa B. (b. 1872, TX), married about 1897; son, Fuller J. (b. 1898, TX). *SR; Williamson to Harley, July 12, 1918, AGC; A1b, d; A2b.*

WILLIAMSON, JAMES E. Born July 1872, McKinney, Collin County, Texas. Ht. 5 ft. 11 in., blue-gray eyes, light hair, light complexion, married. Conductor, I&GN Railroad, enlisted in Bexar County, Texas. SPECIAL RANGER June 11, 1917–Dec. 1917 (attached to Co. C). REMARKS: Grew up in San Marcos, Hays County, Texas. In 1920 was a railroad conductor in Austin, Travis County, Texas. In 1930 was living in San Antonio, Bexar County. FAMILY: Parents, John Roland Williamson (b. 1837, TN) and Caroline "Carrie" Farris (b. 1846, IA); siblings, Willie Lou (b. 1867, TX), Hugh J. (b. 1868, TX), Elizabeth F. "Lizzie" (b. 1870, TX), Jessie R. (b. 1874, TX), St. Elmo Ernest (b. 1875, TX), Berta Carrie (b. 1876, TX), Jannie (b. 1881, TX); spouse, Sallie Joe (b. 1887, TX), married about 1909; daughter, Sara Joe (b. 1924, TX). *SR; Jones to Hutchings, June 18, 1917, AGC; A1a, b, d, f, g; A2e; A4b.*

WILLIAMSON, NATHAN FULLER "FULLER." Born Oct. 15, 1875, Corsicana, Navarro County, Texas. Ht. 5 ft. 10 ¾ in., blue eyes, brown hair, dark complexion. Chief special agent, I&GN Railroad, Houston, Harris County, Texas. SPECIAL RANGER Sept. 5, 1916–Jan. 15, 1919 (was reinstated Dec. 27, 1917). Chief special agent, I&GN Railroad, Palestine, Anderson County, Texas. RAILROAD RANGER Aug. 10, 1922–Aug. 10, 1924 (Co. A). Chief special agent, I&GN Railroad, Houston. SPECIAL RANGER June 25, 1925–Jan. 18, 1929 (reenlisted Jan. 24, 1927); Jan. 18, 1929–Jan. 15, 1931 (reenlisted Jan. 15, 1930); Jan. 22, 1931–Jan. 22, 1932; Jan. 22, 1932–Jan. 18, 1933; Jan. 21, 1933–Jan. 20, 1935; May 28, 1935–Aug. 10, 1935. Discharged. REMARKS: Was raised in Waco, McLennan County, Texas. Had been a deputy sheriff in Waco under John W. Baker for 6 ½ years. Became a special agent for the I&GN Railroad on Feb. 1, 1915. From 1925 on resided in Houston. A Fuller Williamson died Apr. 5, 1936, Harris County, Texas. LAW ENFORCEMENT RELATIVES: Ranger Charles E. Williamson, brother. FAMILY: Mother, Sallie D. Williamson (b. 1849, TX); brother, Charles E. (b. 1872, TX); spouse #1, Leta J. (b. 1895, TX), married about 1918; spouse #2, "Mrs. N. F." (b. 1879, TX). *SR; Whittington to AG, Aug 30, ept 5, 1916 AGC; AG to Whittington, Sept 2, 1916, AGC; A1b, f, g; A2b; A3a.*

WILLIFORD, FRANK, JR. Born Sept. 27, 1886, Richmond, Fort Bend County, Texas. Ht. 5 ft. 10 ½ in., gray eyes, brown hair, light complexion, married. Attorney, Houston, Harris County, Texas. SPECIAL RANGER July 2, 1917–Dec. 1917 (attached to Co. C). REMARKS: Grew up in Houston. As of June 1917 was an assistant criminal district attorney for Harris County. In 1930 was an attorney in private practice in Houston. Died Mar. 17, 1954, Harris County, Texas; buried in Briscoe Cemetery, Fort Bend County. FAMILY: Parents, Frank Williford (b. 1855, MS or AL) and Louise Estes Hunter (b. 1867, TX); siblings, Sam, Henry, Etta, William (b. 1889, TX), Patrick Johnson (b. 1891, TX), Jennie (b. 1896, TX), Vola Hunter (b. 1896, TX), Luis Estes (b. 1901, TX), Mary Louise (b. 1904, TX); spouse, Susie Hibernia Briscoe (b. 1890, TX), married Dec. 19, 1911, Fulshear, Fort Bend County; children, Nora Louise (b. 1912, TX), Susie Hibernia (b. 1914, TX), Frank III (b. 1933, TX). *SR; A1d, e, f, g; A2b, e; A3a; A4a, b; B1.*

WILLIS, CHRISTOPHER COLUMBUS "CHRIS." Born Mar. 19, 1887, Kaleta, San Patricio County, Texas. Ht. 5 ft. 9 in., blue eyes, brown hair, fair complexion. Farmer and ranchman. REGULAR RANGER Sept. 25, 1915–Sept. 30, 1915 (private, Co. D). Resigned. Farmer, Odem, San Patricio County. LOYALTY RANGER June 5, 1918–Feb. 1919. Farmer, Odem. RAILROAD RANGER Aug. 26, 1922–Jan. 11, 1923. Discharged. REMARKS: Note length of service in 1915. As of June 1918 had been a San Patricio County deputy sheriff for 7 or 8 years. Still a farmer in San Patricio County in 1930. Died Oct. 22, 1965, San Patricio County, Texas. LAW ENFORCEMENT RELATIVES: Ranger Lon L. Willis, brother; San Patricio County deputy sheriff (killed at Odem, Sept. 1915) Tom Willis, brother. FAMILY: Parents, James Dee Willis (b. 1842, AR or TX) and Blanche E. (b. 1857, TX); siblings, James D., Jr. (b. 1875, TX), William G. "Bill" (b. 1877, TX), Thomas T. "Tom" (b. 1880, TX), Leroy (b. 1881, TX), Sallie (b. 1885, TX), Lawrence L. "Lon" (b. 1889, TX), Ruth (b. 1891, TX), Nellie (b. 1893, TX); spouse, Sallie M. (b. 1889, TX), married about 1920; step-son, Crawford Dillion (b. 1916, TX). *SR; 471; Scout Report, Co. D, Sept 1915, RRM; Ransom to Hutchings, Sept 24, 1915, AGC; 319: 15; A1d, e, f, g; A2b; A3a.*

WILLIS, CLYDE EDWARD. Born Mar. 21, 1888, Bell County, Texas. Ht. 5 ft. 9 in., blue eyes, light hair, light complexion, married. Stock farmer, Littlefield, Lamb County, Texas. LOYALTY RANGER July 6, 1918–Feb. 1919.

REMARKS: Had been a peace officer. Elsewhere on his enlistment form his birthplace is listed as Williamson County, Texas. His World War I Draft Registration form lists the town of Bartlett, Texas as his birthplace; Bartlett straddles the county line between Bell County and Williamson County. Grew up in Borden County, Texas. Died Sept. 28, 1960, Lamb County, Texas. FAMILY: Parents, William Henry Willis (b. 1860, TX) and Mary Elma Kelly (b. 1869, KY); siblings, Catie T. (b. 1886, TX), Guy E. (b. 1891, TX); spouse, Claire (b. 1893, TX); daughter, Marjory (b. 1918, TX). *SR; A1d, e, f; A2b; A3a; B1.*

WILLIS, FORREST DAY. Born Aug. 29, 1888, Austin County, Texas. Ht. 5 ft. 6 in., gray eyes, dark hair, dark complexion, married. Lumberyard manager, Riviera, Kleberg County, Texas. SPECIAL RANGER May 16, 1917–Dec. 1917 (attached to Co. C). REMARKS: Had been a farmer in Lavaca County, Texas. Forrest Day Willis died Mar. 3, 1959, Tom Green County, Texas. FAMILY: Parents, Joseph A "Joe" Willis (b. 1856, TX) and Nora (b. 1869, TX); siblings, Ora (b. 1886, TX), Leslie (b. 1891, TX), Cerula (b. 1893, TX), Nina (b. 1896, TX), Pauline (b. 1899, TX), Rog (b. 1902, TX); spouse, name unknown, married before June 1917; child, name unknown, born before June 1917. *SR; Scarborough to Ferguson, June 4, 1917, AGC; Scarborough to Hutchings, May 12, 1917, AC; AG to Scarborough, May 14, 1917, AGC; A1d, e; A2b; A3a.*

WILLIS, LON LAWRENCE. Born Feb. 3, 1889, Odem, San Patricio County, Texas. Ht. 5 ft. 9 in., blue eyes, black hair, dark complexion. Stockman, enlisted at Corpus Christi, Nueces County, Texas. REGULAR RANGER Nov. 1, 1912–Nov. 1, 1914 (private, Co. B). Enlistment expired. Reenlisted Feb. 1, 1915–Apr. 15, 1919 (private, Co. A; reenlisted Feb. 1, 1917; promoted to sergeant and transferred to Co. I, Jan. 1, 1918; promoted to captain of Co. M, Sept. 10, 1918; on Mar. 10, 1919, Co. M was disbanded. Willis was reduced to sergeant and transferred to Co. I). Resigned Apr. 15, 1919. Ranchman, Del Rio, Val Verde County, Texas. SPECIAL RANGER June 10, 1931–unknown. LAW ENFORCEMENT RELATIVES: Ranger Chris C. Willis, brother; San Patricio County deputy sheriff (killed at Odem, Sept. 1915) Tom Willis, brother. FAMILY: Parents, James Dee Willis (b. 1842, AR or TX) and Blanche E. (b. 1857, TX); siblings, James D., Jr. (b. 1875, TX), William G. "Bill" (b. 1877, TX), Thomas T. "Tom" (b. 1880, TX), Leroy (b. 1881, TX), Sallie (b. 1885, TX), Chris C. (b. 1887, TX), Ruth (b. 1891, TX), Nellie (b. 1893, TX); spouse, Ethel Galloway (b. 1888, TX); son Hussie (b. 1914, TX); step-son, George Meyer or Meier (b. 1909, TX). *SR; 471; Assistant Quartermaster to Sanders, Dec 8, 1913, AGC; Sanders to Hutchings, Feb 27, July 24, Nov 24, 1914, WC; Acting AG to Willis, July 23, 1918, AGC; LWT, Sept 29, 1918; Special Orders No. 21, Mar 10, 1919, WC; 319: 15, 16, 424–425; A1d, e, f; A2b; A3a; A4b.*

WILMOTH, JOHN BUFORD. Born Oct. 29, 1875, Cleburne, Johnson County, Texas. Ht. 6 ft. 1 in., gray eyes, dark brown hair, dark complexion, married. Deputy sheriff, Hillsboro, Hill County, Texas. LOYALTY RANGER June 8, 1918–Mar. 5, 1919. REMARKS: Had been a drayman for local freight in Hill County. As of Sept. 1918 was an "official cotton weigher" in Hillsboro. In 1930 was a building carpenter in Hillsboro. Died Nov. 22, 1944, Hill County, Texas. FAMILY: Parents, Dawson Wilmoth (b. 1832, TN) and Susannah (b. 1832, IL); siblings, twins Mary and Allen (b. 1856, AR), Sarah Adaline (b. 1857, AR), Fannie (b. 1868, AR); spouse, Dell Phoi Smith (b. 1880, TX), married about 1901; children, Tracy or Terry M. (b. 1903, TX), Lillian (b. 1905, TX), Althea O. (b. 1909, TX), Buford Crowder (b. 1911, TX), Beulavonne (b. 1915, TX). *SR; A1a, b, d, e, f, g; A2b; A3a; A4a.*

WILSON, EDGAR. Born Nov. 1870, Abbeville, Lafayette County, Mississippi. Ht. 5 ft. 11 ½ in., gray eyes, dark hair, fair complexion, married. Trainmaster, San Antonio, Bexar County, Texas. SPECIAL RANGER Feb. 13, 1918–Jan. 15, 1919. REMARKS: In 1920 was a railroad dispatcher in Houston, Harris County, Texas. Died Oct. 1, 1939, Silverton, Briscoe County, Texas. FAMILY: Parents, James Lewis Wilson (b. 1847, MS) and Harriet Jane Houston (b. 1852, MS); siblings, Alex (b. 1873, MS), Eula (b. 1875, TX), Marie (b. 1877, MS), Harriet "Hattie" (b. 1879, MS), Birdie (b. 1882), James Lewis (b. 1888, MS), George (b. 1895); spouse, Ray Louise Baker (b. 1875, TN), married about 1893; children, Jessica "Jessie" (b. 1893, MS), E. Vaughn (b. 1897, MS), Francis. *SR; A1b, d, f; A2b; A3a; A4a, g.*

WILSON, EDWARD MELVIN. Born Dec. 22, 1874, Rutherford, Gibson County, Tennessee. Ht. 5 ft. 7 ½ in., gray eyes, light hair, light complexion, married. Cotton merchant, Bartlett, Bell County, Texas. (Note: Bartlett straddles the county line between Bell County and Williamson County, Texas.) LOYALTY RANGER June 4, 1918–Feb. 1919. REMARKS: Had lived in Bartlett for the past 24 years. Had been a cotton weigher, a retail hardware merchant, a cotton buyer and banker in Bartlett. In 1930 was a cotton exporter in Bartlett. FAMILY: Parents, Robert W. Wilson (b. 1840, TN) and Eveline Keathley (b. 1845, TN); siblings, Hawthorne (b. 1867, TN), Martha (b. 1869, TN), Charles (b. 1872, TN); spouse #1, unknown; spouse #2, Ida Cornelia Watson (b. 1880, AR), married about 1905. *SR; A1b, d, e, f, g; A3a; A4b.*

WILSON, HILLSMAN DAVIS. Born Sept. 8, 1873, Bryan, Brazos County, Texas. Ht. 5 ft. 11 in., blue eyes, light hair, light complexion, married. Farmer, Bryan. LOYALTY RANGER June 7, 1918–Mar. 6, 1919. REMARKS: Brazos County deputy sheriff and constable. FAMILY: Spouse, Annie Lee Thomas (b. 1876, TX), married Nov. 20, 1895, Bryan; son, Hillsman Davis, Jr. (b. 1905, TX). *SR; A1d, e, f; A3a; A4a; B2.*

WILSON, MAPLE. Born July 8, 1891, Plainview, Hale County, Texas. Ht. 5 ft. 11 in., blue eyes, brown hair, light complexion. Farmer and stockman, Plainview. SPECIAL RANGER Aug. 6, 1917–Feb. 1918 (attached to Co. C; private, then sergeant in Co. B Volunteers). Discharged—Co. B Volunteers was disbanded. REMARKS: His father was the first sitting judge in the Texas Panhandle. In Dec. 1917 Maple Wilson owned a ranch in Bailey County, Texas. In 1930 was a farmer in Lubbock, Lubbock County, Texas. Died June 16, 1975, Lubbock County, Texas. FAMILY: Parents, Judge Lafayette Greenhill Wilson (b. 1861, MO) and Martha Frances (b. 1867, MO); sister, Ethel (b. 1893, TX); spouse, Joy (b. 1899, TX), married about 1919; children, Jane L. (b. 1920, TX), Lynn Gerald. *SR; Rawlings to Harley, Dec 6, 1917, AGC; AG to Walling, Dec 15, 1917, AGC; A1d, e, g; A2a, b, e, j; A4a.*

WILSON, THOMAS FRANKLIN. Born Feb. 19, 1897, Eagle Pass, Maverick County, Texas. Ht. 5 ft. 10 in., brown eyes, light brown hair, dark complexion. Quarantine guard, Eagle Pass. SPECIAL RANGER Feb. 4, 1918–Jan. 15, 1919. FAMILY: Parents, John (b. 1857, LA) and Rafaela D. "Ella" (b. 1874, TX); siblings, John Henry (b. 1890, TX), Nannie (b. 1892, TX), Willie James (b. 1894, TX), Albert Prowdy (b. 1900, TX), Alma (b. 1904, TX), Agnes (b. 1906, TX), Ella (b. 1909, TX). *SR; Collins to Harley, Feb 1, 1918, AGC; A1e, f; A3a.*

WILSON, WILLIAM BENNET. Born Feb. 1874, Angelina County, Texas. Ht. 5 ft. 10 ½ in, blue eyes, brown hair, fair complexion, widower. Peace officer, Huntington, Angelina County. SPECIAL RANGER Dec. 10, 1917–Jan. 24, 1918. Discharged. REMARKS: Had been a farmer in Angelina County. In 1920 was a house carpenter in Angelina County. In 1930 was a farmer in Angelina County. A W. B. Wilson died Dec. 16, 1935, Angelina County, Texas. Another source says he died in 1937 in Angelina County. FAMILY: Parents, Philip or Preston or Pleasant Reavis Wilson (b. 1828, GA) and Jane Lucinda Brown (b. 1839, TX); siblings, Hiram Reed (b. 1863, TX), Sam (b. 1864, TX), James (b. 1868, TX), Harriet (b. 1869, TX), Thomas L. (b. 1871, TX), Henry E. (b. 1875, TX), Eliza J. (b. 1876, TX), Beulah "Biddie" (b. 1878, TX); spouse #1, Annie Runnels (b. 1876, TX), married July 23, 1893, Angelina County; children, Beauford (b. 1894, TX), Ettie (b. 1896, TX), Fannell "Fannie" M. (b. 1898, TX), William M. (b. 1899, TX), L. B. or Cooper (b. 1902, TX), Erin (b. 1904, TX); spouse #2, Mattie L. Marshall (b. 1880, MS), married about 1916; son, Pascal (b. 1917, TX). *SR; Wilson to AG, Dec 28, 1919, AGC; A1d, e, f, g; A2b; A4a, b.*

WINDHAM, WILLIAM CLAUDE. Born July 6, 1880, Shelbyville, Shelby County, Texas. Ht. 5 ft. 8 ½ in., blue eyes, brown hair, blond complexion, married. Physician, Shelbyville. LOYALTY RANGER June 25, 1918–Mar. 6, 1919. REMARKS: 1919 letterhead—"Drs. Windham & Windham, Physicians and Surgeons, Shelbyville, W. C. Windham, J. H. Windham." In 1930 William C. Windham was a physician in general practice in Center, Shelby County. Died Apr. 2, 1972, Texas City, Galveston County, Texas. FAMILY: Parents, Rufus T. Windham (b. 1852, TX) and Jane A. (b. 1859, TX); siblings, John Henry (b. 1882, TX), Hassie E. (b. 1885, TX), Nevada (b. 1887, TX), Levi D. (b. 1889, TX), Len Burk (b. 1893, TX), Isabella (b. 1895, TX); spouse, Zoe V. (b. 1892, TX), married about 1916; daughters, Billie B. (b. 1917, TX), Mariann (b. 1919, TX), Lucy V. (b. 1921, TX). *SR; A1d, e, g; A2a, b; A3a.*

WINFREE, EDWIN HAMILTON. Born Oct. 28, 1868, Chambers County, Texas. Ht. 5 ft. 10 in., gray eyes, brown hair, blond complexion, married. Hotel proprietor, Mont Belvieu, Chambers County. LOYALTY RANGER July 18, 1918–Feb. 1919. REMARKS: Served three years as deputy sheriff. In 1920 was both a hotel keeper and owned his own farm in Chambers County. Died Mar. 6, 1926, Chambers County, Texas. FAMILY: Parents, Zachary Taylor Winfree (b. 1847, TX) and Mary Catherine Fisher (b. 1850, TX); siblings, Kinsey or Kinney M. (b. 1872, TX), Sarah E. (b. 1874, TX), Ernest W. (b. 1878, TX); spouse, Mary Elizabeth "Lizzie" Hunt (b. 1869, IN), married about 1890; children, Leticia (b. 1890, TX), Ethel L. (b. 1893, TX), Guy H. (b. 1896, TX), Emma Elmira (b. 1898, TX), Edwina (b. 1912, TX). *SR; A1a, b, d, e, f; A2b, e; A4a, b, g.*

WINN, PETER BAYLOR, JR. Born Nov. 25, 1891, Campbellton, Atascosa County, Texas. Ht. 5 ft. 9 in., black eyes, black hair, dark complexion. Peace officer, Laredo, Webb County, Texas. REGULAR RANGER Mar. 14, 1921–Aug. 31, 1921. Discharged—reduction in force. REMARKS: Had been a deputy sheriff. In 1920 was a stock farmer in Atascosa County. Died Jan. 1977, Chandler, Lincoln County, Oklahoma. LAW ENFORCEMENT RELATIVES: Ranger Peter F. Tumlinson, great-uncle; sheriff (Dimmit County, Nov. 2, 1880–Nov. 4, 1890; La Salle County, Nov. 8, 1892–Jan. 1893) Joseph W. "Sheriff Joe" Tumlinson, great-uncle. See Tumlinson Family, Taylor Family, Wright Family charts for additional relatives. FAMILY: Parents, Peter Baylor Winn (b. 1862, TX) and Idella de la Garza (b. 1864, TX); siblings, Emma (b. 1889, TX), John Sullivan (b. 1890, TX), William Charles (b. 1893, TX), James Calvin (b. 1894, TX), Wesley Wilson (b. 1896, TX), Virginia (b. 1899, TX), Della Mae (b. 1902, TX), George Buford (b. 1904, TX), Arie (b. 1906, TX). *SR; 471;1503:160, 320; A1d, e, f; A2a; A4a, b, g; B1.*

WINTERS, HOWARD "MACK." Born Aug. 24, 1876, Caldwell County, Texas. Ht. 5 ft. 7 in., black eyes, black hair, dark complexion, married. Stock farmer, Moon, Frio County, Texas. LOYALTY RANGER July 1, 1918–Mar. 6, 1919. REMARKS: Had been a Frio County deputy sheriff for several years. In 1930 was a real estate agent in San Antonio, Bexar County, Texas. Died June 1, 1959, Bexar County, Texas. FAMILY; Parents, Benjamin Franklin Winters (b. 1849, TX) and Elizabeth Josephine Jenkins (b. 1854, TX); siblings, Ella E. (b. 1872, TX), Dora C. (b. 1875, TX), Virginia (b. 1879, TX), Hartford (b. 1884, TX), William Franklin (b. 1886, TX), Edgar Calmes (b. 1888, TX), Johanie (b. 1891, TX), Tom (b. 1896, TX), Joe (b. 1898, TX); spouse, Emma Outlaw (b. 1879, TX), married Sept. 30, 1895, Bexar County; children, Zelma E. (b. 1898, TX), Howard Field (b. 1901, TX). *SR; A1b, d, e, f, g; A2b; A3a; A4b, g; B1.*

WISBEY, ERNEST EDWARD. Born Oct. 2, 1866, Cambridge, England. Ht. 5 ft. 7 in., blue eyes, light hair, fair complexion, married. Special agent (private detective), El Paso, El Paso County, Texas. SPECIAL RANGER June 11, 1918–Jan. 15, 1919. REMARKS: Immigrated to the U.S. with his family in 1879; in 1880 they lived in Houston, Harris County, Texas. He became a naturalized U.S. citizen. His father served in the Texas legislature from Harris County in the early 1890s. In 1918 Ernest Wisbey worked as a special agent in El Paso for T. B. Cunningham, the special agent for the Chino Copper Company. In 1920 Wisbey did clerical work for the Chino Copper Company, El Paso. In 1930 was an oil lease salesman living in Houston. Died Dec. 15, 1937, Harris County, Texas. FAMILY: Parents, Alfred Wisbey (b. 1840, England) and Dora Jane Adams (b. 1842, England); siblings, Adelaide Dora (b. 1863, England), Alfred Lewis (b. 1864, England), John M. (b. 1869, England); spouse unknown, married about 1915, divorced by 1920. *SR; Brahan to Harley, May 16, 1918, AGC; Cunningham to Harley, June 10, 1918, AGC; A1b, f, g; A2b; A4a; B2.*

WOELBER, ALBERT HENRY. Born July 8, 1885, Honey Grove, Fannin County, Texas. Ht. 6 ft. 1 in., gray eyes, brown hair, fair complexion, married as of Dec. 1917. Peace officer. REGULAR RANGER Nov. 12, 1915–Mar. 10, 1919 (private, Co. B; reenlisted Dec. 15, 1917; promoted to sergeant, Mar. 1, 1918). Honorably discharged—Co. B was disbanded. REMARKS: In 1919 was a clerk in Army Wagon Company No. 4 at Camp Alberts, Marfa, Presidio County, Texas. In 1930–1931 was a deputy U.S. marshal in El Paso, El Paso County, Texas. An Albert Henry "Weelber" died Apr. 11, 1936, El Paso County, Texas. FAMILY: Spouse, Mary Elizabeth Walker (b. 1897, TX), married about 1917; children, William Walker (b. 1921, TX), Emma Gene (b. 1924, TX). *SR; 471; Special Orders No. 21, Mar 10, 1919, WC; Petition to Harley, Mar 14, 1919, AGC; Scullin to Singleton, Mar 17, 1919, AGC; Singleton to Carlton, Mar 20, 1919, AGC; AA, Jan 3, Dec 5, 1918; 422: 87; V. L. Snyder report, Aug 18, 1919, 23BI; A1g; A2b, e; A3a; A4g.*

WOFFORD, DANIEL WEBSTER. Born Feb. 4, 1868, Runge, Karnes County, Texas. Ht. 6 ft. 3 in., blue eyes, brown hair, fair complexion, married. Farmer, Runge. LOYALTY RANGER June 4, 1918–Mar. 6, 1919. REMARKS: Died Jan. 26, 1953, Karnes County, Texas; buried in Runge. FAMILY: Parents, John A. Wofford, Jr. (b. 1841, MS) and Nancy Taylor (b. 1842, MS); siblings, Lou Martha (b. 1863, TX), Araminta (b. 1866, TX), Mattie (b. 1872, TX), Ardela (b. 1874, TX), Martin (b. 1876, TX), Olly (b. 1878, TX); spouse, Eugenia K. Kelly (b. 1875, TX), married about 1895; children, Ida (b. 1896, TX), Houston Powell (b. 1897, TX), Alonzo (b. 1900, TX), Mamie (b. 1902, TX), Albert Y. (b. 1905, TX). *SR; A1b, d, e, f, g; A2b; A4a, b, g; B1.*

WOFFORD, WILLIAM FILMORE. Born Oct. 13, 1880, Lampasas, Lampasas County, Texas. Ht. 5 ft. 10 ½ in., gray eyes, auburn hair, light complexion, married. Well driller, Stratford, Sherman County, Texas. LOYALTY RANGER June 6, 1918–Feb. 1919. REMARKS: Had been a deputy sheriff for about 6 years. Had been a farmer in Sherman County. In 1920 was an oil well driller in Wichita County. In 1930 was a hotel manager in Electra, Wichita County. FAMILY: Parents, William Henry Wofford (b. 1849, KY) and Nannie C. Brown (b. 1851, TN); siblings, James Thomas (b. 1878, TN), Martha Joseph (b. 1879, KY), Nannie Elizabeth (b. 1882, TX), Henry Allen (b. 1885, TX), Emily Ethelina (b. 1886, TX), Joseph M. (b. 1890, TX); spouse, Marcye Prentiss (b. 1884, TX), married Sept. 30, 1903; children, Raymond Henry (b. 1905, TX), Nannie Leatrice (b. 1906, AZ). *SR; A1b, e, f, g; A3a; A4b.*

WOLF, CARL MANN or MANNING. Born July 8, 1891, Burnet, Burnet County, Texas. Ht. 6 ft., gray eyes, black hair, fair complexion, married. Ranchman, Junction, Kimble County, Texas. SPECIAL RANGER June 21, 1918–Jan. 15, 1919. REMARKS: Still a stockman in Kimble County in 1930. Died May 1982, Anchorage, Alaska. LAW ENFORCEMENT RELATIVES: Ranger O. P. Wolfe, uncle. FAMILY: Parents, Newman Kellis Wolf (b. 1859, TX) and Fanny Bradley (b. 1862, CA); siblings, Edgar L. "Coots" (b. 1879, TX), Thomas Hopkins (b. 1880), Harriet (b. 1881, TX), Clara Dale (b. 1883), Ida Blanche (b. 1885), Florence (b. 1887); spouse, Willie V. (b. 1897, TX), married about 1913. *SR; A1b, f, g; A2a; A3a; A4b; B1.*

WOLFE, OTHA PASCAL "PACK." Born Aug. 10, 1857, Burnet, Burnet County, Texas. Ht. 6 ft., blue eyes, red hair, blond complexion, married. Stock raiser, Snyder, Scurry County, Texas. SPECIAL RANGER June 11, 1917–unknown (attached to Co. C). Farmer and city marshal, Snyder. LOYALTY RANGER May 31, 1918–Feb. 1919. REMARKS: As of June 1917 had been city marshal of Snyder for 8 years; had been a deputy sheriff for 25 years. Died Sept. 4, 1927, Taylor County, Texas. Note: In some resources his surname is spelled "Wolfe," in others, "Wolf," and still others, "Woolf." LAW ENFORCEMENT RELATIVES: Ranger Carl M. Wolf, nephew. FAMILY: Parents, Thomas Hopkins Wolf (b. 1818, TN) and Clarissa "Clara" O'Hair (b. 1830, IL); siblings, Emily Elizabeth, Monroe (b. 1849, TX), A. Madison (b. 1852, TX), Newman Kellis (b. 1859, TX), Joseph C. (b. 1862, TX), William Henry (b. 1865, TX), Texana Eleanor "Texellen" (b. 1867, TX), Olley A. "Babe" (b. 1871, TX); spouse, Mary Olivia "Mollie" Sims (b. 1861, TX), married Nov. 11, 1877, Burnet County; children, Mike (b. 1878, TX), William Monroe (b. 1881, TX), Leona Pearl (b. 1883, TX), Bessie (b. 1884, TX), twins Garland and Tom Gordon (b. 1887, TX), Ruby (b. 1888, TX), Joe Carneth (b. 1892, TX). *SR; Merrill to Ferguson, Dec 20, 1916, June 6, 1917, AGC; A1aa, a, b, e, f; A2b; A3a; A4b; B1.*

WOOD, CARL BURNARD. Born Apr. 7, 1889, San Saba, San Saba County, Texas. Ht. 6 ft. 2 ½ in., gray eyes, brown hair, medium complexion. Farmer. REGULAR RANGER Nov. 16, 1910–Dec. 3, 1910 (private, Co. C). Discharged. REMARKS: Note length of service. FAMILY: Parents, Warren David Crockett Wood (b. 1861, TX) and Polly Anna "Annie" Harkey (b. 1864, TX); siblings, Lennie A. (b. 1881, TX), Rosa M. (b. 1883, TX), Mamie B. (b. 1887, TX), Emory R. (b. 1895, TX), Gladys Verna (b. 1900, TX), Harris (b. 1904, TX); spouse, Mattie Forrest Harris (b. 1895, OK), married Oct. 5, 1915; daughter, Vynomma B. (b. 1917, TX). *SR; MR, Co. C, Nov–Dec, 1910, AGC; A1d, e, f; A2e, A3a; A4b, g; B1.*

WOOD, DANIEL WASHINGTON. Born July 14, 1867, Smith County, Texas. Ht. 5 ft. 9 ½ in., blue eyes, light hair, light complexion, married. Land abstracter, Longview, Gregg County, Texas. LOYALTY RANGER June 7, 1918–July 23, 1919. WA was cancelled. REMARKS: As of June 1918 claimed about 20 years acting peace officer together with being timekeeper and superintendent of public works.

For the past 9 years had been principally in the abstract business. Died Dec. 9, 1925, Longview, Gregg County, Texas; buried in Grace Hill Cemetery, Longview. FAMILY: Parents, Moses Wood (b. 1831, AL) and Margaret Ann Hoffman (b. 1828, AL); siblings, Albert Louis (b. 1865, AR), Moses Cullin (b. 1869, TX), James Daniel (b. 1872, TX); spouse, Maude Watkins (b. 1879, TX), married Oct. 25, 1897, Gregg County; children, Christine (b. 1899, TX), Royce Mellersh (b. 1901, TX), Lewis Van Allen (b. 1905, TX). *SR; A1b, e, f; A4a, b; B1.*

WOOD, FRED T. Born Oct. 1884, Abilene, Taylor County, Texas. Ht. 5 ft. 11 in., gray eyes, brown hair, light complexion, married. Commercial secretary, Abilene. SPECIAL RANGER June 18, 1917–Dec. 1917 (attached to Co. C). *SR; Register to Ferguson, May 18, 1917, AGC; Cunningham to Ferguson, May 18, 1917, AGC.*

WOOD, JAMES GILLAM. Born Apr. 17, 1880, Azucena, Louisiana. Ht. 5 ft. 9 ½ in., brown eyes, dark brown hair, dark complexion, married. Railroad special agent, enlisted in Robertson County, Texas. SPECIAL RANGER May 15, 1918–Jan. 15, 1919. Special officer, Saint Louis San Francisco (Frisco) Railroad, Fort Worth, Tarrant County, Texas. RAILROAD RANGER Sept. 4, 1922–Nov. 10, 1922. Discharged—good record. Special officer, Frisco Lines, Fort Worth. SPECIAL RANGER Mar. 3, 1927–Mar. 3, 1928; June 1, 1928–June 1, 1929; June 1, 1929–May 31, 1930; May 31, 1930–May 31, 1931. Discharged. Special officer, Frisco Railroad, Sherman, Grayson County, Texas. SPECIAL RANGER June 20, 1931–Jan. 18, 1933. WA was honorably cancelled. REMARKS: Had been a special agent for the Southern Pacific Railroad in Beaumont, Jefferson County, Texas. In 1920 was a railroad special agent living in Del Rio, Val Verde County, Texas. In 1930 was a railroad detective in Fort Worth. Died Jan. 10, 1967, Tarrant County, Texas. FAMILY: Parents, Alexander Wood (b. 1845, MS) and Ollie J. (b. 1859, MS); siblings, Eva (b. 1883, MS), Jefferson (b. 1892, LA), Augustus J. (b. 1894, LA), Robert (b. 1897, LA); spouse, Frances Treagle (b. 1884, TX), married about 1912. *SR; A1d, f, g; A2a, b; A3a.*

WOOD, SAMUEL MOHON or MAHAN. Born Oct. 7, 1877, Williamson County, Texas. Ht. 5 ft. 9 in., blue eyes, light hair, fair complexion, married. Printer, Austin, Travis County, Texas. SPECIAL RANGER Oct. 3, 1918–Jan. 15, 1919. REMARKS: As a youth lived in Robertson County, Texas. In 1900 worked as a "compositor" in Marlin, Falls County, Texas. In 1910 was a newspaper printer in Beaumont, Jefferson County, Texas. As of Sept. 1918 worked for the *Austin American* newspaper. FAMILY: Parents, H. R. Wood (b. 1853, CT) and Ada M. (b. 1857, NE); siblings, Henry E. (b. 1874, IA), Annie M. (b. 1876, IA), Mary F. (b. 1880, TX); spouse, Lillian (b. 1879, MS), married about 1901; children, Ruthie May (b. 1902, TX), Mable L. (b. 1903, TX), Robert S. (b. 1906, TX). *SR; A1b, d, e; A3a.*

WOODLAND, BEN HAYS. Born July 21, 1881, Caldwell County, Texas. Ht. 5 ft. 11 in., blue eyes, black hair, dark complexion. Clerk. REGULAR RANGER Apr. 16, 1918–Mar. 10, 1919 (private, Co. M). Honorably discharged—Co. M was disbanded. Peace officer, Lockhart, Caldwell County. REGULAR RANGER Oct. 1, 1919–Jan. 31, 1920 (private, Co. A). Resigned. Farmer, Lockhart. RAILROAD RANGER July 27, 1922–Dec. 26, 1922. Discharged. REMARKS: Before enlisting in the Rangers had been a peace officer in Caldwell County; also guarded convicts on road work there for one year. Had lived in Asherton, Big Wells, Crystal City, Dentonio, and Alice for short periods of time. As of Sept. 1918 was a Ranger stationed in Del Rio, Val Verde County, Texas, serving under Capt. L. L. Willis. In 1920 was a Ranger in Marfa, Presidio County, Texas. Died June 28, 1966, Caldwell County, Texas; buried in Lockhart City Cemetery. FAMILY: Parents, Alexander Archcillas Wood (b. 1851, LA or CA) and Harriet Eveline Sites (b. 1860, TX); siblings, Thomas B. (b. 1883, TX), Oliver W. (b. 1886, TX), Lucinda V. (b. 1889, TX), David Crockett (b. 1892, TX), Kyle A. (b. 1894, TX), Travis (b. 1897, TX), twins Mary E. and James B. (b. 1904, TX). *SR; 471; Special Orders No. 21, Mar 10, 1919, WC; Richards to Harley, Jan 2, 1918, AGC; Hanson to Col. Smith, Assistant AG, Feb 9, 1920, WC; 1: I, 1536–1537; 429:47; A1d, e, f; A2a, b; A3a; A4b.*

WOODLEY, MARO BASCOM. Born July 26, 1883, Fayette County, Texas. Medium height, medium build, brown eyes, light hair, married. Stockman, Sabinal, Uvalde County, Texas. LOYALTY RANGER May 30, 1918–Feb. 1919. REMARKS: In 1930 was a bookkeeper for a wholesale grocer. Died Apr. 8, 1956, Uvalde County, Texas. FAMILY:

Parents, Henry B. Woodley (b. 1852, TX) and Alice C. (b. 1861, TX); siblings, Oscar (b. 1882, TX), Thomas Mac (b. 1889, TX), Glenn (b. 1891, TX), Kenneth (b. 1892, TX), Alice (b. 1897, TX); spouse, Sallie Mangum (b. 1886, AL), married about 1909; children, Helen (b. 1913, TX), Jack A. (b. 1916, TX), S. Jean (b. 1918, TX), Nell (b. 1921, TX). *SR; A1b, d, e, f, g; A2b; A3a.*

WOODS, ALVA. Born Sept. 1891, Lowry, Scurry County, Texas. Ht. 6 ft., blue eyes, dark hair, red complexion. Cowpuncher. REGULAR RANGER May 13, 1916–July 9, 1916 (private, Co. B—crossed out and Co. C written in). Resigned. REMARKS: Note length of service. *SR; 471.*

WOODS, HENRY. Born Dec. 24, 1892, Matador, Motley County, Texas. Ht. 5 ft. 9 in., blue eyes, light brown hair, light complexion, married. Ranch foreman, Hebbronville, Jim Hogg County, Texas. SPECIAL RANGER Mar. 9, 1918–Jan. 15, 1919. REMARKS: Was foreman of Wilbur P. Allen's Jesus Maria Ranch, 20 miles southeast of Hebbronville. In 1930 was a dairy farmer in Jim Hogg County. FAMILY: Spouse, Verna Lee "Vernie" Meeks (b. 1896, TX), married about 1913; daughters, Josephine (b. 1917, TX), Gladys (b. 1919, TX), Golden Effie (b. 1922, TX). *SR; LWT, Feb 17, Mar 3, 1918; A1f, g; A2e; A3a; A4b.*

WOODS, JOHN DAVID. Born Feb. 13, 1878, Breckenridge, Stephens County, Texas. Ht. 6 ft., gray eyes, brown hair, dark complexion, married. Brand inspector, Cattle Raisers' Association of Texas, Dalhart, Dallam County, Texas. SPECIAL RANGER July 2, 1917–Sept. 13, 1918 (attached to Co. C). Discharged. Patrolman, Texas and Pacific Railroad, Dalhart. RAILROAD RANGER June 19, 1923–July 11, 1923. Discharged. REMARKS: Was reclassified in 1918 as a REGULAR RANGER without pay, to avoid the draft. Was a brand inspector at Dalhart as early as 1913. In Sept. 1918 no longer worked for the Cattle Raisers' Association, so his Ranger commission was revoked. In 1930 was a farmer in Howard County, Texas. FAMILY : Spouse, Bessie Hopkins (b. 1884, TX), married about 1905; sons, Clyde D. (b. 1907, TX), James B. (b. 1913, TX). *SR; EPMT, Aug 1, 1913; Moses & Rowe to Harley, Oct 9, 20, Sept 13, 1918, AGC; Moses to AG, Oct 22, 1917, AGC; Acting AG to GC&SF Railroad, Jan 9, 1918, AGC; Acting AG to FW&DC Railroad, Jan 11, 1918, AGC; A1e, f, g; A3a.*

WOODWORTH, WILLIAM W. Born Jan. 1871, Quincy, Lewis County, Kentucky. Ht. 5 ft. 8 in., gray eyes, light brown hair, light complexion, married as of July 1919. Contractor, Houston, Harris County, Texas. SPECIAL RANGER Nov. 1, 1917–Dec. 1917 (attached to Co. C); July 17, 1919–Dec. 1919 (WA issued at Governor Hobby's request). Oil business, San Antonio, Bexar County, Texas. SPECIAL RANGER May 17, 1921–unknown. REMARKS: Said he had been a (Special) Ranger during Hobby and Neff administrations, and had been a deputy sheriff in numerous counties. Had been a clerk in New Orleans, Orleans Parish, Louisiana. In 1910 was an oil tank builder in Houston. In 1930 was an oil prospector in San Antonio. A William W. Woodworth died Dec. 26, 1941, Jim Wells County, Texas. FAMILY: Parents, John W. Woodworth (b. 1844, OH) and Hannah E. (b. 1847, OH); siblings, Frederick C. (b. 1872, KY), Anna (b. 1875, KY); spouse #1, Sallie (b. 1876, KY), married about 1893; daughter, Bertha (b. 1894, KY); spouse #2, Yrene (b. 1896, TX), married about 1920; daughter (?), Rosa (b. 1912, TX). *SR; A1a, b, d, e, f, g; A2b; A4a, b.*

WORD, THOMAS STUTSMAN. Born May 1870, Dallas, Dallas County, Texas. Ht. 6 ft. 1 5/8 in., black eyes, black hair, dark complexion, married. Watchman, I&GN Railroad, Palestine, Anderson County, Texas. SPECIAL RANGER Aug. 15, 1917–Dec. 1917 (attached to Co. C). REMARKS: Grew up in Palestine. Had been a farmer and an insurance agent in Palestine. Justice of the peace, 3 years 9 months; Anderson County deputy sheriff, 6 months. In 1920 was an oil field fireman in Palestine. In 1930 was a retail grocer in Burkburnett, Wichita County, Texas. FAMILY: Parents, John J. "Jack" Word (b. 1844, MS) and Katie B. (b. 1850, OH); siblings, Ethelena (b. 1883, TX), Jettie (b. 1888, TX), John (b. 1890, TX); spouse, Daisy Stuart (b. 1876, MO), married July 27, 1893, Anderson County; children, Catherine C. (b. 1895, TX), Dorothy Linda (b. 1897, TX), Eolina L. (b. 1903, TX), Daisy M. (b. 1904, TX), Terrance S. (b. 1905, TX). *SR; Williamson to Hutchings, Aug 9, 1917, AGC; AG to Williamson, Aug 10, 1917, AGC; A1a, b, d, e, f, g; B1.*

WORSHAM, JOE BOONE. Born Sept. 21, 1894, Austin, Travis County, Texas. Ht. 5 ft. 10 in., blue eyes, dark brown hair, fair complexion. Farmer, El Paso, El Paso County, Texas. SPECIAL RANGER June 16, 1917–unknown (attached to Co. C). REMARKS: Grew up in El Paso County.

As of June 1917 was farming in Clint, El Paso County. AG sent Worsham's enlistment papers through state Senator C. B. Hudspeth, who wanted to keep him out of the Army. In 1920 was a fuel and grain merchant in El Paso. In 1930 was a farmer in El Paso. Died May 25, 1945, El Paso County, Texas. FAMILY: Parents, Dr. Ben H. Worsham (b. 1864, TX) and Margaret "Maggie" Boone (b. 1873, TN); spouse, Genevieve Lorey Pattison (also used stepfather's name: Bannell), married about 1921; sons, Joe Bannell (b. 1922, TX), James Pattison (b. 1926, TX). *SR; Hudspeth to Hutchings, June 13, 1917, AGC; AG to Hudspeth, June 13, 1917, AGC; Worsham to Hutchings, June 1917, AGC; A1e, f, g; A2b, e; A3a; A4b.*

WREN, JOHN KILLIAN. Born July 1, 1875, Hays County, Texas. Ht. 5 ft. 11 in., brown eyes, dark brown hair, dark complexion, married. Government employee (federal Bureau of Investigation agent), El Paso, El Paso County, Texas. SPECIAL RANGER May 16, 1918–Jan. 15, 1919. REMARKS: Had been a stockman in Hays County. Was an El Paso County deputy sheriff, 1914–1916. As of Feb. 1920, was still a BI agent. In 1930 was an agent of the U.S. Department of Justice in El Paso. Died Apr. 13, 1939, El Paso County, Texas. LAW ENFORCEMENT RELATIVES: Hays County Sheriff (1880) James A. Wren, father. FAMILY: Parents, James A. Wren (b. 1832, VA) and Matilda Dockery (b. 1851, TX); spouse #1, Jennie Blair or Bernard Edmonston (b. 1884, TX), married Dec. 22, 1902, Hays County; children, Joe F. (b. 1905, TX), Elizabeth (b. 1907, TX); spouse #2, Louise or Lucy K. (b. 1887, NM or AZ); children, John Gus (b. 1918, TX), Mathilda Loise "Mattie" (b. 1923, TX). *SR; EPMT, July 25, 1914, Jan 2, Nov 9, 1915, Mar 5, 1916; U.S. Commissioner, El Paso, No. 393, FRC-FW; A1b, d, e, f, g; A2b, e; A3a; A4g; B1.*

WREN, WILLIAM RODOLIPHIS. Born July 1853, Mount Carmel, Smith County, Texas. Ht. 6 ft. 2 in., light brown eyes, graying black hair, dark complexion, married. Farmer, Snyder, Scurry County, Texas. LOYALTY RANGER May 31, 1918–Mar. 6, 1919. REMARKS: Lampasas County, Texas sheriff Nov. 8, 1892–Nov. 3, 1896. One source listed his occupation as "Sheriff and minister." In 1930 lived in Snyder, retired. Died May 21, 1936, Scurry County, Texas; buried in Snyder Cemetery. LAW ENFORCEMENT RELATIVES: Ranger Nicholas Wren, father. FAMILY: Parents, Nicholas Wren (b. 1807, KY) and Mariah D. Johnson (b. 1820, AL); brother, George Mason (b. 1855, TX); spouse, Sarah Elizabeth "Lizzie" Higgins (b. 1858, TN), married about 1878; children, Josie L. (b. 1878, TX), Nicholas (b. 1880, TX), Mary Frances (b. 1883, TX), Horace Lyman (b. 1884, TX), William Randall (b. 1886, TX), Alberto Leon (b. 1888, TX), George Robert (b. 1890, TX), Byron L'Acee (b. 1893, TX). *SR; 471; 1503:319; A1aaa, b, d, e, g; A2b; A4b, g; B1.*

WRIGHT, CHARLES HAYS. Born Feb. 25, 1894, Sutherland Springs, Wilson County, Texas. Ht. 6 ft. 1 in., blue eyes, dark hair, fair complexion. Laborer, enlisted in Wilson County. REGULAR RANGER May 11, 1916–Nov. 30, 1916 (private, Co. A). Resigned to enlist in the Army. REMARKS: Served overseas in World War I with the 131st Field Artillery, 36th Division. After his discharge became a mounted Customs inspector. Served until his death on June 27, 1938, at Eagle Pass, Maverick County, Texas; buried in Floresville, Wilson County. LAW ENFORCEMENT RELATIVES: Ranger Capt. William Lee Wright, father; Ranger Emanuel Avant "Dogie" Wright, brother; Ranger Milam H. Wright, uncle; Sheriff of Karnes County, Texas (Sept. 8, 1860–Nov. 16, 1861) and Ranger L. B. Wright, grandfather; Ranger Sanford Brown, grandfather; Ranger Charles Brown, uncle; descendant of Ranger Capt. Peter F. Tumlinson and Ranger Capt. John J. Tumlinson. See Wright Family, Taylor Family, Tumlinson Family charts for additional relatives. FAMILY: Parents, William Lee Wright (b. 1868, TX) and Mary Ann "Mollie" Brown; siblings, Maurice (b. 1895, TX), Zora Belle (b. 1899, TX), Emanuel A. "Dogie" (b. 1901, TX), William, Jr. (b. 1905, TX), Tom (b. 1915, TX). *SR; 471; Wright to Hobby, Apr 28, 1919, AGC; Houston to Hobby, Apr 28, 1919, AGC; Fore to Hobby, Apr 27, 1919, AGC; Dewees to Whom, Apr 1, 1919, AGC; SAE, May 13, 1916; 1000: iii, 73–74; 469: 62, 64, 67, 77, 89 n. 64; 485: 210 ff; 470: 114; 1503: 295, 160, 321; A1d, e; A2b; A3a; B1.*

WRIGHT, EARL RAY. Born Sept. 6, 1892, Banquette, Nueces County, Texas. Ht. 5 ft. 9 in., dark eyes, brown hair, dark complexion. Stockman. REGULAR RANGER Sept. 1, 1917–Apr. 20, 1919 (private, Co. A; transferred to Co. K because Co. A was disbanded Mar. 10, 1919). Resigned. REMARKS: Had been a grocery store clerk in Nueces County. At the time he filed his World War I Draft

Registration form, was a stockman in both Nueces and Jim Hogg Counties, living in Robstown, Nueces County. Had no prior experience as a peace officer when enlisted in Rangers. Spoke Spanish, knew the border. In June 1919 lived at Concepcion, Duval County, Texas. In 1930 an Earl Wright (born about 1893) was Nueces County assessor, living in Corpus Christi. An Earl R. Wright died Aug. 22, 1947, Nueces County, Texas. LAW ENFORCEMENT RELATIVES: Ranger James B. Wright, cousin; Nueces County sheriff (Nov. 4, 1902–Nov. 7, 1916) Mike B. Wright, distant cousin. See Wright Family, Taylor Family, Tumlinson Family charts for additional relatives. FAMILY: Parents, William Woodson Wright (b. 1866, TX) and Emma Lenora Bitterman (b. 1866, TX); siblings, Mabel Clare (b. 1887, TX), Ghaskye (b. 1889, TX), Harry Lee (b. 1891, TX), W. Cotton (b. 1894, TX), William Woodson, Jr. (b. 1898, TX), Pearl Anais (b. 1900, TX), twins Fred B. and Emma Lee (b. 1902, TX), Hannah L. (b. 1903, TX). *SR; 471; Wright to Aldrich, June 28, 1919, AGC; Sanders to Hutchings, Sept 19, 1917, AGC; Sanders to Harley, Dec 11, 1917, AGC; Special Orders No. 21, Mar 10, 1919, WC; 1503:395; A1d, e, g; A2b; A3a; A4b.*

WRIGHT, EMANUEL AVANT "DOGIE." Born Apr. 25, 1901, Laredo, Webb County, Texas. Ht. 5 ft. 7 in., gray eyes, light brown hair, light complexion. No occupation or residence listed. REGULAR RANGER June 10, 1918–Oct. 1918 (private, Co. K). Resigned because of illness. Student, Floresville, Wilson County, Texas. REGULAR RANGER Mar. 25, 1921–Aug. 31, 1921 (private, Co. C; transferred to Co. A, Aug. 1, 1921). Discharged—reduction in force. REMARKS: In 1918 served for 4 months in the Rangers at age 17 under his father, Capt. W. L. Wright. In 1920–1921 was a deputy U.S. marshal at Laredo. Served in the Border Patrol at El Paso, El Paso County, Texas, beginning Sept. 18, 1924. Was appointed senior patrol officer at Sierra Blanca, Hudspeth County, Texas, 1926. Was appointed assistant chief, El Paso District, 1938. Was transferred to Tucson, Pima County, Arizona as assistant chief, Tucson District, 1940. In 1946 was transferred to Sierra Blanca. Retired in 1951. Hudspeth County sheriff Nov. 4, 1952–Jan. 1, 1957, and Nov. 8, 1960–Jan. 1, 1969, when he retired. As of 1977 lived in Sierra Blanca. Died Dec. 19, 1989, Hudspeth County, Texas. LAW ENFORCEMENT RELATIVES: Ranger Capt. William Lee Wright, father; Ranger Charles H. Wright, brother; Ranger Milam H. Wright, uncle; sheriff of Karnes County, Texas (Sept. 8, 1860–Nov. 16, 1861) and Ranger L. B. Wright, grandfather; Ranger Sanford Brown, grandfather; Ranger Charles Brown, uncle; descendant of Ranger Capt. Peter F. Tumlinson and Ranger Capt. John J. Tumlinson. See Wright Family, Taylor Family, Tumlinson Family charts for additional relatives. FAMILY: Parents, William Lee Wright (b. 1868, TX) and Mary Ann "Mollie" Brown; siblings, Charles H. (b. 1894, TX), Maurice (b.1895, TX), Zora Belle (b. 1899, TX), William, Jr. (b. 1905, TX), Tom (b. 1915, TX); spouse, Mabel Beulah Love (b. 1908, TX), married July 21, 1928 at Sierra Blanca; daughters, Ellen Frances (b. 1931, TX), Zorabelle (b. 1935, TX). *SR; 471; 1000: iii, 6, 74–75; 469: 34, 67, 69, 70, 71, 77; 470: 115–116; 330: 33, 42, 46, 69–70; 1503:17, 160, 270, 307, 321, 547; his papers are at the Center for American History, the University of Texas at Austin; A1e, g, A2a, b, e; B1.*

WRIGHT, EUGENE CLARK. Born Feb. 4, 1895, Lockhart, Caldwell County, Texas. Ht. 5 ft. 10 in., gray eyes, brown hair, fair complexion. Stockman, Falfurrias, Brooks County, Texas. SPECIAL RANGER May 19, 1917–Dec. 1917. REMARKS: Lived in Karnes County, Texas and Hidalgo County, Texas as a youth. In 1930 was a tick inspector in Brooks County. Died June 15, 1966, Falfurrias, Brooks County, Texas. LAW ENFORCEMENT RELATIVES: Ranger Thomas Rowan Wright, distant cousin; Ranger Little Berry Wright (not his father), distant cousin; Ranger Captain William Lee Wright, distant cousin; Ranger Milam H. Wright, distant cousin; Nueces County sheriff (Nov. 4, 1902–Nov. 7, 1916) Mike B. Wright, distant cousin. See Wright Family, Taylor Family, Tumlinson Family charts for additional relatives. FAMILY: Parents, Little Berry Wright (b. 1854, MS) and Luella Stockwell Gunn (b. 1864, IL); siblings, Nettie (b. 1886, TX), Cleveland L. (b. 1888, TX), Clara (b. 1890, TX), Mary Linn (b. 1896, TX), William P. "Willie" (b. 1899, TX), Earl (b. 1904, TX); spouse, Lela Elizabeth Hensley (b. 1895, TX), married May 21, 1917, Brooks County; children, Claudie (b. 1919, TX), Nell (b. 1921, TX), Jean (b. 1922, TX), Margaret (b. 1924, TX), Mike (b. 1926, TX), Birdie Louise (b. 1929, TX), Olene (b. 1933, TX). *SR; AG to Wright, May 16, 1917, AGC; 1503:395; A1d, e, f, g; A2a, e; A3a; A4g; B2.*

WRIGHT, HOWELL J. Born May 23, 1895, Willow City, Gillespie County, Texas. Ht. 5 ft. 11 in., brown eyes, black hair, light complexion, married. Stockman, Junction, Kimble County, Texas. SPECIAL RANGER Feb. 18, 1918–Jan. 15, 1919. REMARKS: Had lived in Kerr County, Texas. Died July 6, 1971, Gillespie County, Texas; buried in Junction Cemetery. FAMILY: Parents, Dr. Robert H. Preston Wright (b. 1871, TX) and Beatrice E. "Lizzie" Walters (b. 1875, TX); siblings, Blanche Fay (b. 1896, TX), Reba (b. 1897, TX), Willie B. (b. 1898, TX), Doris (b. 1904, TX), Margarite (b. 1908, TX), Carlton (b. 1915, TX); spouse, Dora "DoDo" Ragland (b. 1895, TX), married about 1913 in Junction; children, Maxine (b. 1916, TX), Joyce (b. 1919, TX), Preston H. (b. 1922, TX), Gwendolyn (b. 1923, TX). *SR; A1d, e, f, g; A2a, b; A3a; A4b, g; B2.*

WRIGHT, JAMES BAILEY. Born Sept. 14, 1880, Banquette, Nueces County, Texas. Ht. 5 ft. 11 in., brown eyes, light hair, fair complexion, married. Bookkeeper, Kingsville, Kleberg County, Texas. SPECIAL RANGER June 20, 1918–Dec. 31, 1919 (WA was renewed Jan 23, 1919). REMARKS: Had been a stenographer and store manager in Nueces County. As of Sept. 1918 was a bookkeeper for Mrs. Henrietta King in Kingsville; also was a livestock farmer. In 1920 was a stockman in Kleberg County. Died July 14, 1927, Kleberg County, Texas. LAW ENFORCEMENT RELATIVES: Ranger Earl Ray Wright, cousin; Nueces County sheriff (Nov. 4, 1902–Nov. 7, 1916) Mike B. Wright, distant cousin. See Wright Family, Taylor Family, Tumlinson Family charts for additional relatives. FAMILY: Parents, Cotten Cullen Wright (b. 1859, TX) and Ada Thomas Clark (b. 1862, TX); siblings, Oscar N. (b. 1879, TX), Thomas Hines (b. 1882, TX), C. C., Jr. (b. 1884, TX), Laura M. (b. 1889, TX), Philip S. (b. 1896, TX); spouse, Myrtle Hall (b. 1889, TX), married about 1907; children, Walton (b. 1911, TX), Virginia (b. 1915, TX). *SR; 471; 1503:395; A1b, d, e, f; A2b; A3a; A4a, b; B2.*

WRIGHT, MILAM HARPER. Born May 1878, Yorktown, DeWitt County, Texas. Ht. 5 ft. 8 in., gray eyes, light brown hair, dark complexion. REGULAR RANGER 1898–1901 (Frontier Battalion). REGULAR RANGER Dec. 27, 1904–unknown (private, Co. D). Peace officer. REGULAR RANGER July 29, 1905–Jan. 1910 (private, Co. D). Resigned to accept a more lucrative position as deputy sheriff in Del Rio, Val Verde County, Texas. REGULAR RANGER Mar. 20, 1911–July 15, 1912 (private, Co. A; promoted to sergeant, Aug. 1911). Discharged. REMARKS: In May 1911 was a secret agent of the Mexican government on the border under future Ranger Captain William M. Hanson. In 1912 became a mounted Customs inspector until 1928 when he resigned and became a rancher in Chihuahua, Mexico. In 1930 was a farmer in Sierra Blanca, Hudspeth County, Texas. Hudspeth County sheriff Nov. 8, 1932–Feb. 12, 1938 when he died. Buried in Evergreen Cemetery, El Paso, El Paso County, Texas. LAW ENFORCEMENT RELATIVES: Sheriff of Karnes County, Texas (Sept. 8, 1860–Nov. 16, 1861) and Ranger L. B. Wright, father; Ranger Capt. William L. Wright, brother; Ranger Charles H. Wright, nephew; Ranger Emanuel A. Wright, nephew; Ranger Capt. Peter F. Tumlinson, great-uncle; Ranger Capt. John J. Tumlinson, great-uncle; Ranger Monroe Madison Wells, cousin. See Wright Family, Taylor Family, Tumlinson Family charts for additional relatives. FAMILY: Parents, Leander "Little" Berry Wright (b. 1830, AL) and Ann Elizabeth Tumlinson (b. 1842, TX); siblings, Aurelia E. (b. 1862, TX), Zora Lee (b. 1864, TX), William L. (b. 1868, TX), Mary H. (b. 1872, TX), Joseph T. (b. 1875, TX); spouse, unknown, married about 1903. *SR; 471; AG to Everman, Jan 3, 1910, AGC; Assistant Quartermaster to Hughes, Mar 27, 1911, AGC; AG to Colquitt, Jan 19, 1912, AGC; MR, Co. A, July, 1912, CP; Ellsworth to Secretary of State, May 11, 1911, 812.00/1779, RDS; EPMT, June 24, Sept 1, 1911; EPH, Jan 25, 1912; 469: 58, 59, 61, 76, 89 n. 64; 1000: iii, 71–73, 116, 118; 319: 340, 359; 470: 113; 1503: 160, 270, 321; A1b, d, e, g; A2b.*

WRIGHT, THOMAS ROWAN. Born Apr. 5, 1875, Caldwell County, Texas. Ht. 5 ft. 6 in., dark eyes, dark hair, dark complexion, married. Watchman, Austin, Travis County, Texas. REGULAR RANGER Aug. 1, 1920–Feb. 23, 1921 (private, Co. C). Discharged. REMARKS: Grew up in Gonzales County, Texas. Had been a depot agent in Uvalde, Uvalde County, Texas. As of Sept. 1918 was a clerk at the Texas state capital. Was enlisted in the Rangers by order of Governor Hobby. In 1930 he was a manufacturer of poultry medications in Austin. Died Apr. 1, 1957, Travis County, Texas. LAW ENFORCEMENT RELATIVES: Ranger Captain William Lee Wright, distant cousin; Rangers Little Berry Wright (not his father), Eugene Clark Wright, Milam H. Wright, distant cousins; Nueces County sheriff (Nov. 4, 1902–Nov. 7, 1916) Mike B. Wright, distant cousin. See

Wright Family, Taylor Family, Tumlinson Family charts for additional relatives. FAMILY: Father, Littleberry Wright (b. 1842, AL); sister, Cora O. (b. 1877, TX); spouse, Zillah Bunting (b. 1877, TX), married Nov. 5, 1894, Gonzales County; children, Ray Bunting (b. 1895, TX), Lefford Autry (b. 1897, TX), Margaret Marie (b. 1900, TX), Knox Elroy (b. 1903, TX), Alice Lee (b. 1906), Lilla Lorene (b. 1910, TX). *SR; 471; 1503:395; A1b, d, e, f, g; A2b; A3a; A4b.*

WRIGHT, WILLIAM JAY "JAY." Born Oct. 14, 1874, Colorado County, Texas. Medium height, medium build, brown eyes, brown hair, married. Farmer, Alleyton, Colorado County. LOYALTY RANGER June 14, 1918–Mar. 6, 1919. REMARKS: On enlistment form residence was changed to Eagle Lake. Was still a farmer in Colorado County in 1930. Died Dec. 15, 1944; buried in Eagle Lake Masonic Cemetery, Colorado County. FAMILY: Parents, Timothy or Tennessee C. Wright (b. 1833, NC) and Mary Elizabeth Alley (b. 1844, TX); siblings, Laura Ann (b. 1856, TX), Lula (b. 1866, TX), Alley (b. 1869, TX), Annie (b. 1872, TX), Timothy (b. 1873, TX); spouse, Mary Bessie Wilson (b. 1873, TX), married Jan. 23, 1895; daughter, Mary Beth (b. 1896, TX). *SR; A1a, b, d, e, f, g; A3a; A4b; D.*

Texas Ranger Captain William L. Wright was perhaps the greatest of the Ranger captains of the decade. This is a little known photo of Wright who preferred to be photographed with his hat on. *Photo courtesy "Dogie" Wright Collection, Dolph Briscoe Center for American History, University of Texas at Austin.*

WRIGHT, WILLIAM LEE. Born Feb. 19, 1868, Yorktown, DeWitt County, Texas. Ht. 5 ft. 10 in., gray eyes, gray hair, fair complexion, married. REGULAR RANGER Jan. 1, 1899–Sept. 1, 1902 (private, Co. E, Frontier Battalion; one year as first lieutenant). Resigned. Sheriff, Floresville, Wilson County, Texas. REGULAR RANGER Jan. 1, 1918–Apr. 1, 1925 (captain, Co. K; reenlisted under the new law as captain, Co. D, June 20, 1919). Resigned. Peace officer, Robstown, Nueces County, Texas. REGULAR RANGER May 15, 1927–Jan. 18, 1933 (captain, Co. A). Discharged. Peace officer, Kenedy, Karnes County, Texas. REGULAR RANGER Feb. 14, 1935–1939 (private, Co. D). Resigned. REMARKS: Two sources (319:397 and 470:107–109) state that he was born in Caldwell County, Texas, and moved to DeWitt County as a child. He was a cowboy in DeWitt County; was a Wilson County deputy sheriff, 1892–1898. In 1900 was a Ranger stationed in La Salle County, Texas. Wilson County sheriff Nov. 4, 1902–Dec. 31, 1917. Died Mar 7, 1942, Floresville, Wilson County, Texas. LAW ENFORCEMENT RELATIVES: Sheriff of Karnes County, Texas (Sept. 8, 1860–Nov. 16, 1861) and Ranger L. B. Wright, father; Ranger Milam H. Wright, brother; Ranger Charles Hays Wright, son; Ranger Emanuel Avant Wright, son; Ranger Sanford Brown, father-in-law; Ranger Charles Brown, brother-in-law; Ranger Capt. Peter F. Tumlinson, great-uncle; Ranger Capt. John J. Tumlinson, great-uncle; Ranger Monroe Madison Wells, cousin. See Wright Family, Taylor Family, Tumlinson Family charts for additional relatives. FAMILY: Parents, Leander "Little" Berry Wright (b. 1830, AL) and Ann Elizabeth Tumlinson (b. 1842, TX); siblings, Aurelia E. (b. 1862, TX), Zora Lee (b. 1864, TX), Mary H. (b. 1872, TX), Joseph T. (b. 1875, TX), Milam H. (b. 1878, TX); spouse, Mary Ann "Mollie" Brown (b. 1871, TX), married about 1893; children, Charles H. (b. 1894, TX), Maurice (b. 1895, TX), Zora Belle (b. 1899, TX), Emanuel

Captain William L. Wright preferred photographs on his horse. *Photo courtesy Texas State Library.*

"Dogie" (b. 1901, TX), William, Jr. (b. 1905, TX), Tom (b. 1915, TX). *SR; 471; McDonald to Hutchings, Dec 12, 1916, AGC; Hanson to Harley, Feb 8, 1918, RRM; 172:VI, 1093; BDH, Aug 2, 5, 1910; LWT, Feb 5, 1911; 1000: iii, 35, 68, 71; 319: 82–83, 91, 200, 397–399, 408–416, 507; 469: 57–59, 64–69, 76; 470: 22–26, 35–41, 43, 46, 53, 56–57, 107–112; 485: 221ff, 226; 1503: 160, 295, 321, 546–547; 1505; A1a, b, d, e, f, g; A2b; A4b.*

WUERSCHMIDT, PAUL GEORGE. Born Dec. 14, 1885, Mitchell, South Dakota. Ht. 5 ft. 9 in., blue eyes, brown hair, light complexion, married. Mechanic, El Paso, El Paso County, Texas. SPECIAL RANGER Apr. 22, 1918–Jan. 15, 1919 (attached to Co. L; station—Ysleta). REMARKS: As a youth had lived in Nebraska. By 1910 was in El Paso County, worked as a grocery store clerk. In 1914 was a deputy constable at Ysleta, El Paso County. By Apr. 1918 had been an El Paso County deputy sheriff for many years. As of Sept. 1918 was a steam fitter for the GH&SA Railroad, lived in Ysleta. In Apr. 1919 held an El Paso County deputy sheriff commission and was a truck driver for the U.S. Reclamation Service at Ysleta. In 1930 was a plumbing and electrical contractor in El Paso County. Died Jan. 16, 1944, El Paso County, Texas. FAMILY: Parents, Rev. Christian Wuerschmidt (b. 1850, Germany) and Anna M. (b. 1852, Germany); siblings, Elfrieda G. (b. 1887, SD), Marcus Augustus (b. 1890, SD); spouse #1, unknown, married about 1908; spouse #2, Ella Mary or Mary Ellen McClure (b. 1897, TX), married about 1917; children, Mary E. (b. 1918, TX), Paul George (b. 1919, TX), William Thomas (b. 1928, TX). *SR; EPMT, Apr 24, 26, 29, 1914; Davis to Harley, Apr 21, 1919, AGC; A1d, e, f, g; A2b, e; A3a, b.*

WYNN, FRED CHARLEY. No Service Record. Born Aug. 7, 1885. Medium height, stout, blue eyes, brown hair. REGULAR RANGER Nov. 1909–apparently until Oct. 1914 (private, Co. B; promoted to sergeant, Jan. 12, 1910; demoted to private as of Mar. 1910). REMARKS: On Jan. 12, 1910 was promoted to sergeant to succeed Ranger Roscoe Redus, who was dismissed the same day. In 1916 he became a Cameron County deputy sheriff and jailer until at least Apr. 1918. Died Apr. 18, 1957, Cameron County, Texas. *471; EPMT, Nov 19, 1909; Thorne to Newton, Jan 13, 1910, AGC; Ross to Newton, Jan 12, 1910, AGC; AG to Ross, Mar 4, 1910, AGC; AG to Bailey, Jan 18, Sept 8, 1910, AGC; Assistant AG to Rodgers, Dec 9, 1910, AGC; BDH, Aug 17, 1911, Oct 7, 1914, Aug 7, 12, 22, 1916, Jan 1, Feb 26, Aug 1, 1917, Apr 10, 1918; A2b; A3a.*

YAEGER, WILLIAM HENRY. Born Feb. 21, 1887, Cotulla, La Salle County, Texas. Ht. 5 ft. 10 ½ in., gray eyes, brown hair, light complexion, married. Ranchman, Hebbronville, Jim Hogg County, Texas. SPECIAL RANGER May 6, 1918–Feb. 3, 1919. REMARKS: In 1930 was a rancher in Laredo, Webb County, Texas. Died Sept. 26, 1962, Victoria County, Texas. FAMILY: Parents, Heinrich Carl Yaeger (b. 1850, GA) and Florence Mary Waugh (b. 1864, TX); siblings, May Theresa (b. 1884, TX), Louis (b. 1889, TX), Lawrence (b. 1892), Robert Royal (b. 1894); spouse, Mary Adeline Small (b. 1892, PA), married Aug. 11, 1913, San Antonio, Bexar County, Texas; children, Carl Henry (b. 1914, TX), William Henry, Jr. (b. 1915, TX), Joseph O'Brien (b. 1917, TX), Loretta Margaret (b. 1921, TX). *SR; A1d, e, g; A2b; A3a; A4a.*

YARBROUGH, JOHN SWANSON. Born Mar. 12, 1867, near Tilden, McMullen County, Texas. Ht. 5 ft. 10 in., brown eyes, red hair, red complexion, married. Cowboy, Asherton, Dimmit County, Texas, enlisted in Maverick County, Texas. SPECIAL RANGER Dec. 27, 1917–Oct. 5, 1918 (private, Co. C Volunteers; station—Indio Ranch). REMARKS: On Oct. 5, 1918, Ranger Capt. E. Buck, commanding Co. C Volunteers, notified AG to cancel Yarbrough's commission, as he was no longer a Ranger. On Oct. 11, 1918, AG noted that he had no record of Yarbrough ever having been a Ranger. In 1930 was a cattleman living in LaSalle County, Texas. Died July 17, 1940, Cotulla, LaSalle County, Texas; buried in Old Cotulla Cemetery in an unmarked grave. FAMILY: Parents, Lorenzo Dow Yarbrough (b. 1840, TX) and Nancy Parilee White (b. 1847, TX); siblings, William Clinton, Selitha Y. (b. 1864, TX), Betty Ann (b. 1869, TX), Anthony Headley (b. 1873, TX), Nancy Parilee (b. 1877, TX), Lidia Martha (b. 1878, TX), Jonathan David (b. 1880, TX), Alevia (b. 1882, TX), Lorenzo Skid (b. 1885, TX); spouse, Jane Louise Crawford (b. 1867, TN), married May 14, 1891, Carrizo Springs, Dimmit County; children, William Dowe (b. 1892, TX), Mary Jane (b. 1893, TX), Edward Jackson (b. 1895, TX), Sidney (b. 1897, TX), Nannie (b. 1899, TX), Johnnie (b. 1900, TX). *SR; Buck to Harley, Oct 5, 1918, AGC; A1d, e, g; A2b; A3a; A4a, b, g; B2.*

YATES, OLEN WILLIAM. Born Oct. 9, 1881, Palo Pinto, Palo Pinto County, Texas. Ht. 5 ft. 9 in., gray eyes, brown hair, light complexion, married. Abstracter of land titles, Anson, Jones County, Texas. SPECIAL RANGER May 31, 1917–Dec. 1917 (private, attached to Co. C). REMARKS: In 1930 was an insurance manager in Las Vegas, Clark County, Nevada. Died Mar. 22, 1938, Loma Linda, San Bernardino County, California. FAMILY: Parents, William Yates (b. 1850, AR) and Harriet Elizabeth Crowley (b. 1850, MS); sisters, Martha "Mattie" (b. 1883, TX), twins Marie and Nannie (b. 1885, TX), Elizabeth (b. 1889, TX), Alma (b. 1891, TX); spouse, Willie or Billie Warren (b. 1880, TX), married June 1, 1910. *SR; Dodson to Ferguson, May 18, 1917, AGC; Cunningham to Ferguson, May 18, 1917, AGC; A1d, e, g; A4a, b, g; B1, 2.*

YATES, WILLIAM J. Born Apr. 1870, Charlotte, Mecklenburg County, North Carolina. Ht. 6 ft., blue eyes, light hair, light complexion, married. Wax manufacturer, Alpine, Brewster County, Texas. SPECIAL RANGER Mar. 7, 1918–Jan. 15, 1919. REMARKS: Had been the editor of the *Alpine Avalanche* newspaper. Had been a Brewster County deputy sheriff for 10 years. Had been the constable, precinct 1, Brewster County, 1914–1918. In 1930 was agent for the Magnolia Company, Marfa, Presidio County, Texas. FAMILY: Parents, William J. Yates (b. 1829, NC) and Sarah S. "Sallie" (b. 1836, NC); siblings, Lizzie (b. 1858, NC), Clara (b. 1859, NC), Sallie S. (b. 1860, NC), Laura E. (b. 1861, NC), Ada P. "Addie" (b. 1865, NC), Mary W. (b. 1867, NC), Bettie G. (b. 1868, NC), David S. (b. 1877, NC); spouse, Jennie M. (b. 1875, TX), married about 1897. *SR; AA, Nov 16, 1916, May 24, 1917, May 16, 1918; A1a, b, e, g.*

YEARY, EARL R. Born Dec. 1880, Helena, Karnes County, Texas. Ht. 5 ft. 8 in., gray eyes, black hair, dark complexion. REGULAR RANGER 1903–1904 (private, Co. D). Farmer. REGULAR RANGER Oct. 7, 1911–ca. Jan. 5, 1912 (private, Co. B). Resigned. REMARKS: In 1910 was a farm laborer, living with a cousin in McLennan County, Texas. Died in 1912. FAMILY: Parents, John Marion Yeary (b. 1837, AR) and Nancy Jane Crain (b. 1838, TX); siblings, Walter C. (b. 1865, TX), John C. (b. 1867, TX), James B. (b. 1873, TX), David F. (b. 1876, TX). *SR; 471; AG to Sanders, Jan 2, 1912, AGC; AG to General Manager, Jan 8, 1912, AGC; 508:66; A1b, d, e; A3a, b, g; B1.*

YEATES, JOHN C. Born Feb. 1859, England. Ht. 5 ft. 11 in., blue eyes, sandy hair, light complexion, married. Stockman, San Antonio, Bexar County, Texas. SPECIAL RANGER Jan. 24, 1918–Jan. 15, 1919. REMARKS: Immigrated to the United States in 1881; was a naturalized U.S. citizen. Had served as a deputy sheriff for 20 years. Had been a SPECIAL RANGER for 4 years (attached to Co. D). In 1910 was a pawn shop proprietor in San Antonio. In Jan. 1919 was a San Antonio city detective. FAMILY: Spouse, Susanah "Susie" Hutchison (b. 1878, TX), married about 1897; children, Charles Fred (b. 1898, TX), Myrtle (b. 1901, TX), Lester (b. 1904, TX), Bertha (b. 1907, TX), Raymond (b. 1908, TX), Theo (b. 1912, TX). *SR; Yeates to Ferguson, Apr 15, 1917, AGC; Anderson to Ferguson, Apr 15, 1917, AGC; Murchison to Hobby, Oct 29, 1917, AGC; A1d, e, g.*

YELVINGTON, HENRY BLAKELY. Born Nov. 1886, La Vernia, Wilson County, Texas. Ht. 5 ft. 5 in., brown eyes, black hair, fair complexion, married. Operator, San Antonio, Bexar County, Texas. SPECIAL RANGER Nov. 27, 1917–Aug. 25, 1919. Commission expired. Newspaperman, McAllen, Hidalgo County, Texas. SPECIAL RANGER Aug. 1919–Jan. 1, 1920. Commission expired. Newspaperman, Laredo, Webb County, Texas. SPECIAL RANGER Dec. 8, 1927–Dec. 8, 1928; Jan. 16, 1929–Jan. 16, 1930. Oil operator and newspaper man, San Antonio. SPECIAL RANGER Feb. 7, 1930–Jan. 1, 1931. Minister, San Antonio. SPECIAL RANGER Mar. 13, 1931–Mar. 13, 1932. Commission expired. REMARKS: Had been a correspondent in Mexico for the *New York World* and other publications. In 1910 was a newspaper reporter living in Fayette County, Texas. In Feb. 1911 operated a 50-acre truck farm near Laredo with Dr. J. E. Jones. In Aug. 1911 joined the Immigration Service at Hidalgo, Hidalgo County, as a mounted inspector for the next 3 years. Was a special deputy sheriff in several counties. Was an informant for the federal Bureau of Investigation. Was an operative for the Thiel Detective Agency at Laredo. In Feb. 1919 was evidently a reporter for the *San Antonio Express*. A Henry B. Yelvington died Feb. 28, 1944, Hays County, Texas. FAMILY: Parents, Alvaro Leonard Yelvington (b. 1850, MS) and Mary Fullerton Legette (b. 1854, SC); siblings, Jeannie (b. 1878, TX), Jesse L. (b. 1892, TX), Alvaro L. (b. 1909, TX); spouse, Annie Pauline Moore (b. 1892, TX), married about 1910; children, Henry W. (b. 1912, TX), Armand J. (b. 1914, TX), Thomas M. (b. 1916, TX), Legette (b. 1918, TX), Lavarro (b. 1923, TX), Mary Jo (b. 1927, TX). *SR; LWT, Feb 19,1911; BDH, Aug 1, 1911, May 13, 1912; 508: 59; Yelvington to Harley, Feb 8, 1919, AGC; A1b, e, f, g; A2b, e; A4g; B2.*

YOLTON, FRANK LOUIS. Born May 23, 1881, Kahoka, Clark County, Missouri. Ht. 6 ft. ½ in., brown eyes, black hair, medium complexion, married. Special agent, GH&SA Railroad, Galveston, Galveston County, Texas. SPECIAL RANGER Apr. 16, 1917–Dec. 22, 1917. WA was renewed Jan. 1918–Jan. 15, 1919. Assistant chief special agent, Southern Pacific (T&NO) Railroad, Houston, Harris County, Texas. SPECIAL RANGER Dec. 7, 1923–Dec. 7, 1925; Jan. 4, 1926–Feb. 1, 1927; Feb. 4, 1927–Feb. 4, 1928; Feb. 15, 1928–Feb. 15, 1929; July 6, 1929–July 6, 1930; Nov. 6, 1930–Nov. 6, 1931; Mar. 15, 1932–Jan. 18, 1933;

Jan. 28, 1933–Mar. 14, 1934; June 11, 1935–Aug. 10, 1935. Discharged. REMARKS: Died Mar. 24, 1959, Harris County, Texas. FAMILY: Spouse #1, Alvina Diedrich (b. 1874, WI), married about 1902, divorced before 1920; children, Raymond (b. 1905, WI), Leslie (b. 1907, WI), Naomi (b. 1915, WI); spouse #2, Eva B. (b. 1885, IA). *SR; Buckner to Ferguson, Apr 10, 1917, AGC; AG to Buckner, Apr 13, 1917, AGC; Wroe to AG, Apr 13, 1917, AGC; AG to Parker, Jan 3, 1918, AGC; A1f, g; A2b; A3a; A4b.*

YOUNG, JAMES WILEY. Born Nov. 11, 1873, Bastrop, Bastrop County, Texas. Ht. 5 ft. 6 in, black eyes, black hair, dark complexion. Lawyer, Crockett, Houston County, Texas. LOYALTY RANGER June 5, 1918–Mar. 6, 1919. REMARKS: A J. W. Young died Aug. 9, 1941, Houston County, Texas. FAMILY: Parents, Mark Hutchins Young (b. 1839, AL or TN) and Mary Catherine Douglas (b. 1849, AL or MO); siblings, Jessie Bell (b. 1870, TX), Hallie (b. 1876, TX), Joseph Kleber (b. 1879, TX), Mary S. (b. 1881), Mark Hutchings (b. 1886), Ellen Norval (b. 1889); spouse, Hattie (b. 1877, TX), married by Sept. 1918; stepdaughter, Leita Cunyus (b. 1900, TX). *SR; A1b, d, e, f; A2b; A3a; A4b.*

YOUNG, MATTIE CURTIS. Born July 18, 1886, Moffat, Bell County, Texas. Ht. 5 ft. 11 in., blue eyes, light hair, fair complexion. Peace officer. REGULAR RANGER Sept. 1, 1917–Oct. 1, 1918 (private, Co. C, transferred to Co. D, Sept. 1, 1917). Was discharged for disobeying orders—had returned to Austin, Travis County, Texas from Baird, Callahan County, Texas without permission. REMARKS: As a youth had lived in Blevins, Falls County, Texas. FAMILY: Parents, Joseph C. Young (b. 1860, VA) and Isabell Alford (b. 1861, TX); siblings, Aline (b. 1880, TX), Luther (b. 1881, TX), Mary Virginia (b. 1884, TX), Frank (b. 1888, TX), Joseph D. (b. 1890, TX), Claborne S. (b. 1895, TX), Fannie or Minnie B. (b. 1897, TX), Clarence H. (b. 1898, TX); spouse, Annie, married by Sept. 1918. *SR; 471; Johnston to Cardwell, Oct 2, 1918, AGC; A1b, d; A3a; A4b.*

YOUNG, THOMAS PIERCE. Born Sept. 6, 1887, Albuquerque, Bernalillo County, New Mexico. Ht. 5 ft. 8 ½ in., gray eyes, brown hair, light complexion, married. Cowboy, Austin, Travis County, Texas. REGULAR RANGER Mar. 10, 1921–Aug. 31, 1921 (private, Emergency Co. No. 1). Resigned. REMARKS: As a youth lived in McLennan County, Texas. In 1920 was a barber in Austin. In 1930 was a farmer in Willacy County, Texas. Died Nov. 11, 1931, McAllen, Hidalgo County, Texas. FAMILY: Parents, John Calvin Lafett Young (b. 1858, MS) and Martha Ann "Mattie" Wyatt (b. 1868, TX); siblings, Grover Alberta "Berty" (b. 1885, TX), Joseph Bruno (b. 1886, TX), Edwin Earl (b. 1889, TX), John William (b. 1891, TX), Vida Ann (b. 1895, TX), Samuel Wyatt (b. 1897, TX), Clarence B. (b. 1893, TX), Robert Sherrell (b. 1899, TX), Mable Frances (b. 1901, TX); spouse, Dora Frances Burrier (b. 1890, TX), married Oct. 8, 1911, Gillespie County, Texas; children, Price Pierce (b. 1912, TX), John C. "Johnny" (b. 1915, TX), Dorothy (b. 1917, TX). *SR; 471; A1d, e, f, g; A2b; A3a; A4a, b; B2.*

YOUNG, WILLIAM EARLY "EARL." Born Nov. 4, 1883, La Grange, Fayette County, Texas. Ht. 6 ft. 1 in., brown eyes, dark hair, dark complexion, married. Cowboy, Marathon, Brewster County, Texas. REGULAR RANGER Nov. 1, 1919–May 15, 1927 (private, Co. E; transferred to Co. A, Feb. 15, 1921; reenlisted in Co. A, Nov. 1, 1923, Nov. 1, 1925). Discharged. Peace officer, Marathon. REGULAR RANGER July 1, 1928–Jan. 18, 1933 (private, Co. A). Discharged. REMARKS: As a youth had lived in San Antonio, Bexar County, Texas. Died Sept. 29, 1965, Brewster County, Texas. FAMILY: Parents, Dr. Franklin Early Young (b. 1854, TX) and Mary Louise Carter (b. 1858, VA); siblings, Genevieve (b. 1885, TX), Flint Carter (b. 1889, TX), Louise Franklin (b. 1893, TX); spouse, Martha Lula Moore (b. 1884, TX), married Dec. 28, 1911, Fayette County; daughters, Mary Elizabeth (b. 1913, TX), Katherine Earline (b. 1915, TX), Virginia (b. 1917, TX). *SR; 471; 470: 43; 310:200; A1d, f, g; A2b; A3a; A4b.*

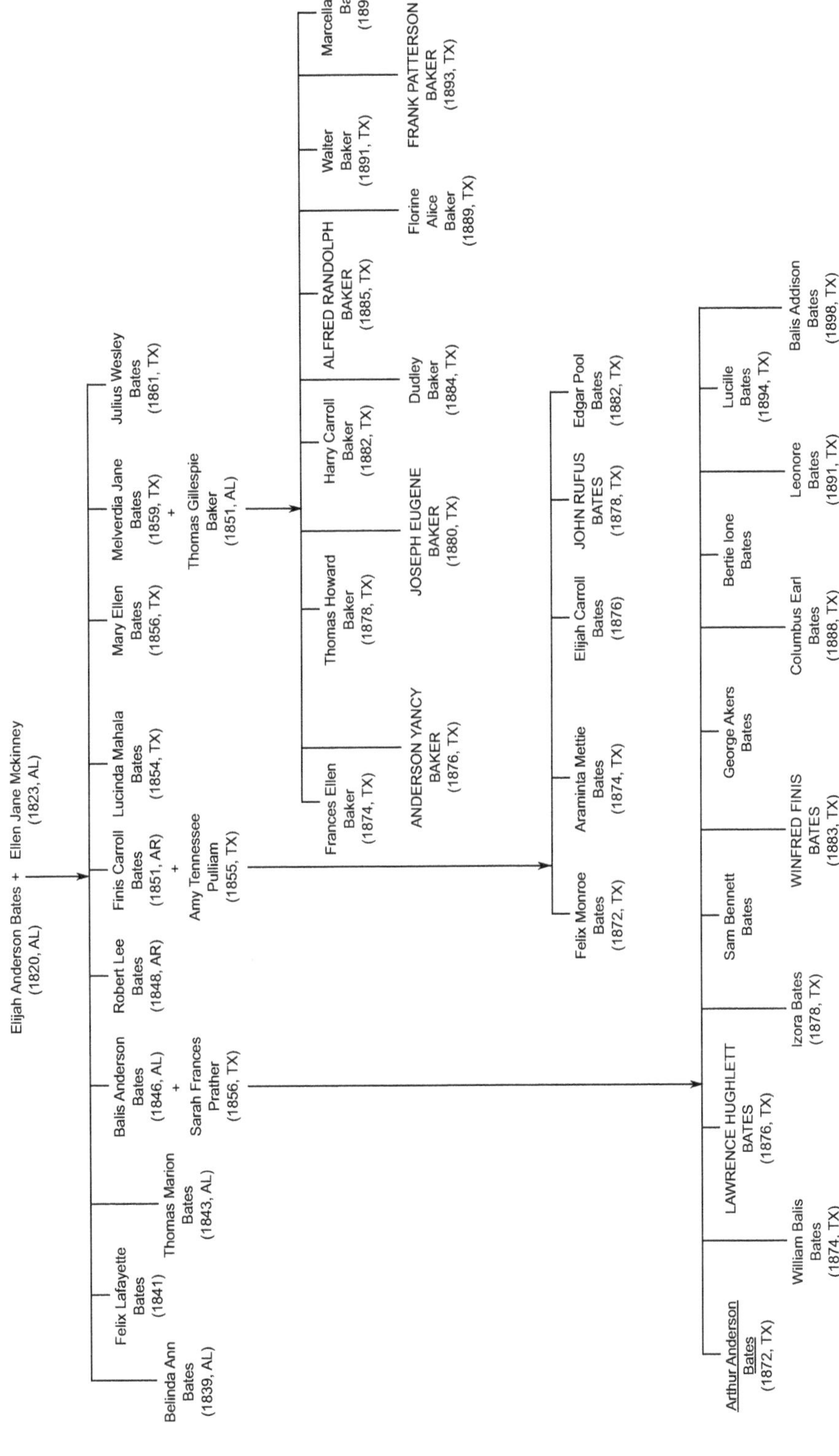
BATES-BAKER FAMILIES
Elijah Anderson Bates + Ellen Jane Mckinney
(1820, AL) (1823, AL)
Belinda Ann Bates (1839, AL)
Felix Lafayette Bates (1841)
Thomas Marion Bates (1843, AL)
Balis Anderson Bates (1846, AL) + Sarah Frances Prather (1856, TX)
Robert Lee Bates (1848, AR)
Finis Carroll Bates (1851, AR) + Amy Tennessee Pulliam (1855, TX)
Lucinda Mahala Bates (1854, TX)
Mary Ellen Bates (1856, TX)
Melverdia Jane Bates (1859, TX) + Thomas Gillespie Baker (1851, AL)
Julius Wesley Bates (1861, TX)
Frances Ellen Baker (1874, TX)
ANDERSON YANCY BAKER (1876, TX)
Thomas Howard Baker (1878, TX)
JOSEPH EUGENE BAKER (1880, TX)
Harry Carroll Baker (1882, TX)
Dudley Baker (1884, TX)
ALFRED RANDOLPH BAKER (1885, TX)
Florine Alice Baker (1889, TX)
Walter Baker (1891, TX)
FRANK PATTERSON BAKER (1893, TX)
Marcella Cornelia Baker (1896, TX)
Felix Monroe Bates (1872, TX)
Araminta Mettie Bates (1874, TX)
Elijah Carroll Bates (1876)
JOHN RUFUS BATES (1878, TX)
Edgar Pool Bates (1882, TX)
Arthur Anderson Bates (1872, TX)
William Balis Bates (1874, TX)
LAWRENCE HUGHLETT BATES (1876, TX)
Izora Bates (1878, TX)
Sam Bennett Bates
WINFRED FINIS BATES (1883, TX)
George Akers Bates
Columbus Earl Bates (1888, TX)
Bertie Ione Bates
Leonore Bates (1891, TX)
Lucille Bates (1894, TX)
Balis Addison Bates (1898, TX)
Note: Names of Rangers are capitalized and those of other types of peace officers are underlined.
The years under the names are birth dates.

WEBB-CARNES FAMILIES

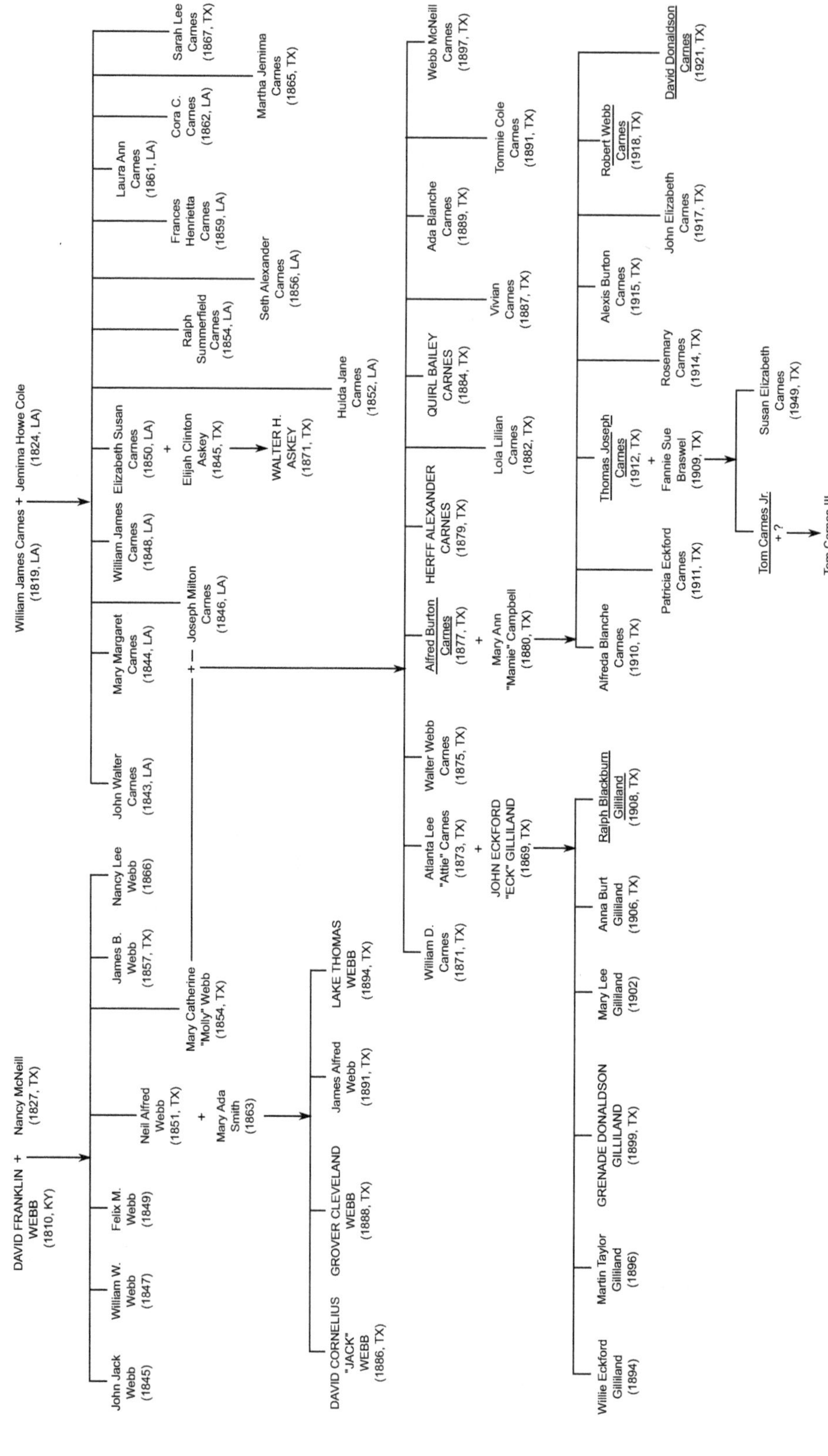

Note: Names of Rangers are capitalized and those of other types of peace officers are underlined.
The years under the names are birth dates.

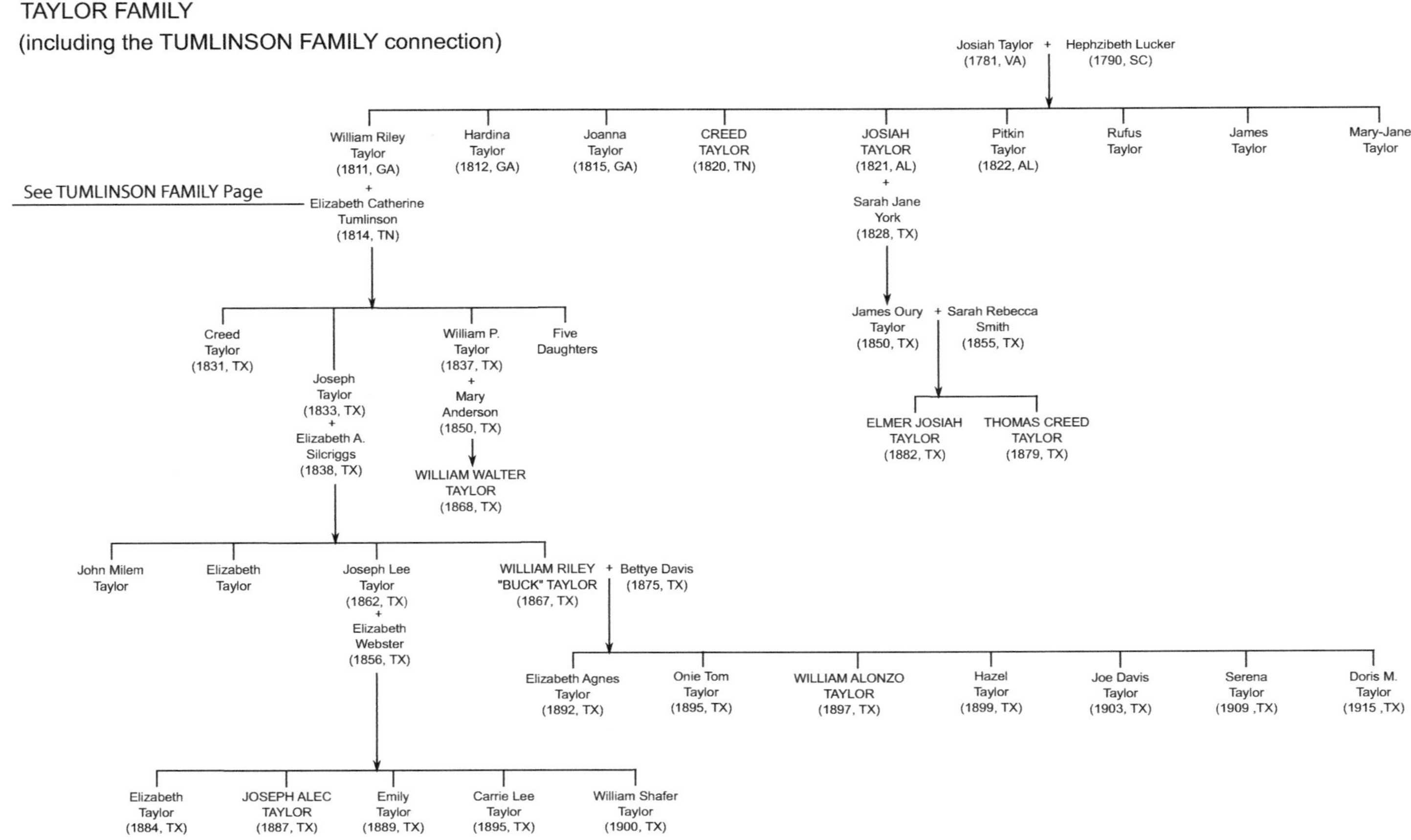

Note: Names of Rangers are capitalized and those of other types of peace officers are underlined.
The years under the names are birth dates.

TUMLINSON FAMILY
(including the WRIGHT FAMILY and TAYLOR FAMILY connections)

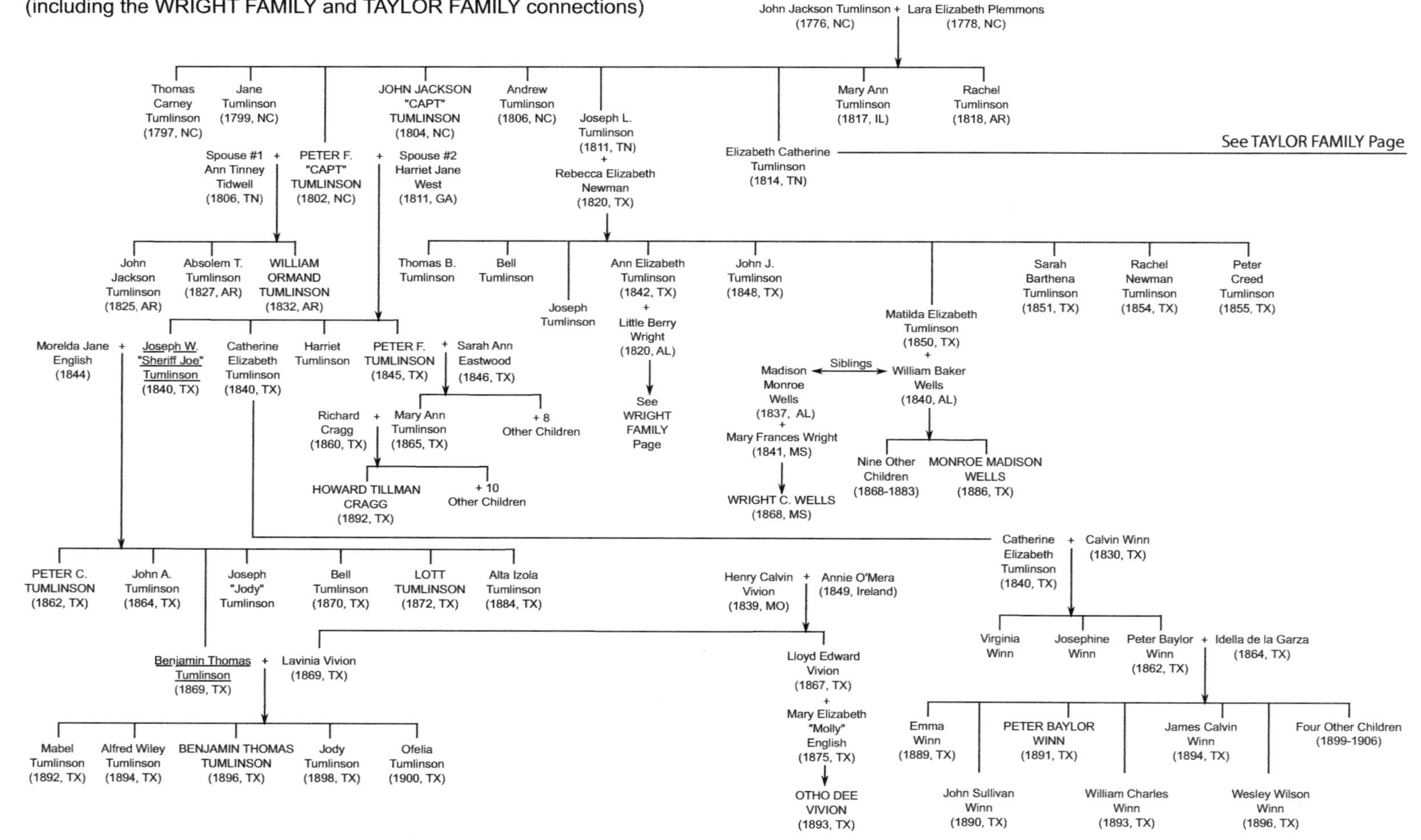

Note: Names of Rangers are capitalized and those of other types of peace officers are underlined.
The years under the names are birth dates.

WRIGHT FAMILY
(including the TAYLOR-TUMLINSON families connection)

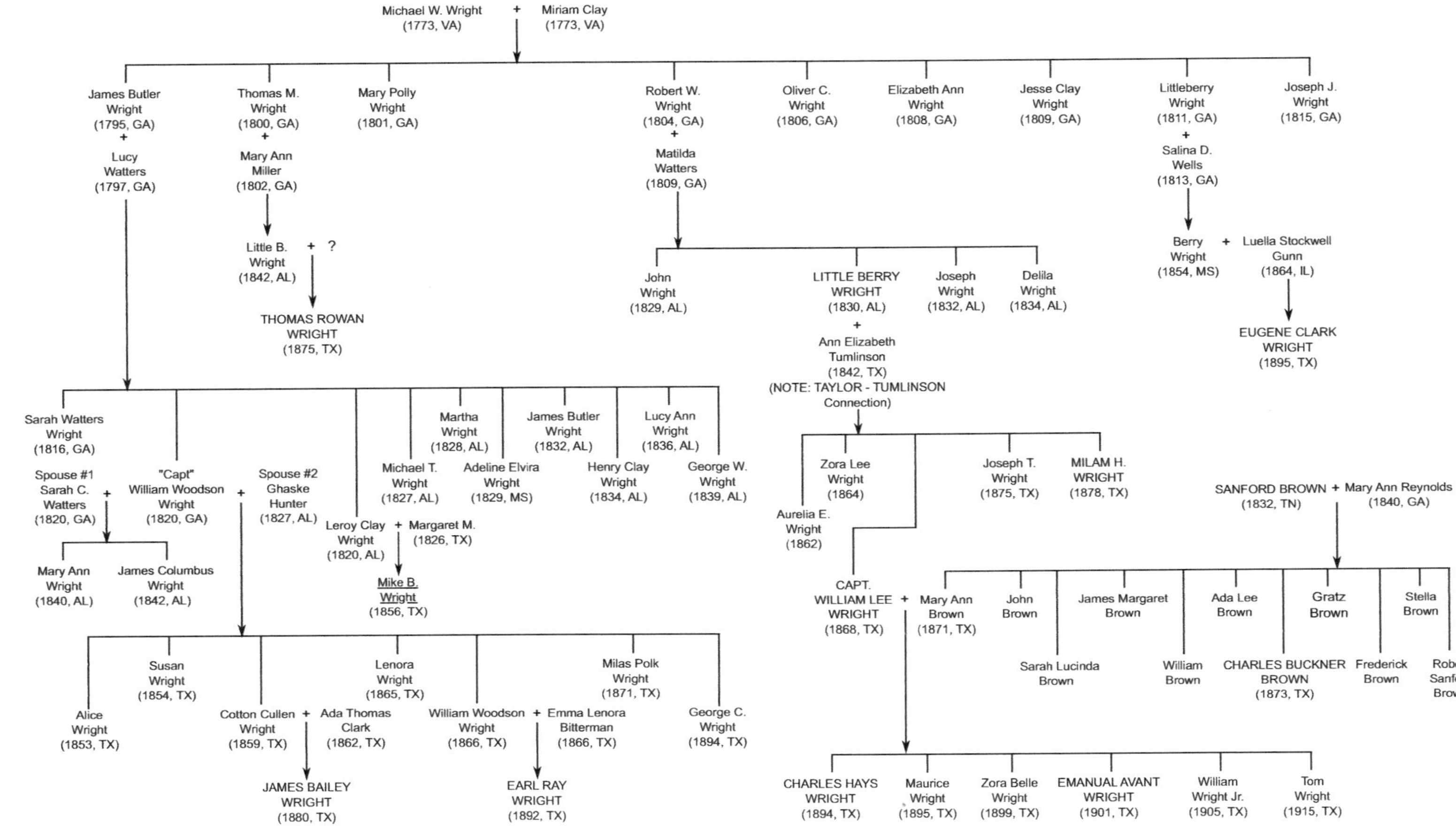

Note: Names of Rangers are capitalized and those of other types of peace officers are underlined.
The years under the names are birth dates.

ABBREVIATIONS

AA	*Austin American* and *Austin American-Statesman* newspaper
AG	Adjutant General
AGC	Adjutant General's Correspondence, Archives and Information Services Division, Texas State Library, Austin, Texas
BDH	*Brownsville Daily Herald* newspaper
BI	federal Bureau of Investigation (renamed Federal Bureau of Investigation in 1935). Records of the Federal Bureau of Investigation—Old Mex 232, microcopy, no number, Record Group 65, National Archives and Records Service, Washington, D.C.
CO	Company
CP	Governor Oscar B. Colquitt Papers, Archives and Information Services Division, Texas State Library, Austin, Texas
DPS	Department of Public Safety, Austin, Texas
EPH	*El Paso Herald* and *El Paso Herald-Post* newspaper
EPMT	*El Paso Morning Times* newspaper
FR	Department of State. *Papers Relating to the Foreign Relations of the United States.* Washington, D.C.: Government Printing Office
FRC-FW	Federal Records Center, Fort Worth, Texas
HC	*Houston Chronicle* newspaper
LWT	*Laredo Weekly Times* newspaper
MR	Monthly Return, Texas State Ranger Force, Archives and Information Services Division, Texas State Library, Austin, Texas
RDS	Records of the Department of State, Decimal Files, Internal Affairs of Mexico, 1910–1929. National Archives Microfilm Publication, Microcopy no. 274. National Archives and Records Service, Washington, D.C.
RRM	Ranger Records, Texas National Guard Archive, Camp Mabry, Austin, Texas
SR	Service Record, Texas State Ranger Force, Archives and Information Services Division, Texas State Library, Austin, Texas
WC	Walter Prescott Webb Collection, Center for American History, University of Texas at Austin
WA	Warrant of Authority

BIBLIOGRAPHY

1 United States. Senate. Committee on Foreign Relations. *Investigation of Mexican Affairs.* 66th Cong., 2nd sess, 2 vols. Washington, D.C.: Government Printing Office, 1919–1920.

5 Marvin, George. "The Quick and the Dead on the Border." *World's Work.* XXXIII (Jan. 1917): 295–302.

8 Marvin, George. "Bandits and the Borderland." *World's Work.* XXXII (Oct. 1916): 656–63.

36 Perkins, Clifford Alan. *Border Patrol: With the U.S. Immigration Service On the Mexican Boundary 1910–54.* El Paso: Texas Western Press, 1978.

51 Rausch, George. "The Exile and Death of Victoriano Huerta." *Hispanic American Historical Review.* XLII, no. 2 (May 1962): 133–51.

100 Webb, Walter Prescott. *The Texas Rangers: A Century of Frontier Defense.* 2nd ed. Austin: University of Texas Press, 1965.

114 *Las Cruces Sun-News*, Las Cruces, NM, Apr. 3–4, 1951.

137 National Personnel Records Center: Civilian Personnel Records, National Archives and Records Administration, St. Louis, Missouri.

140 *San Antonio Express-News*, Aug. 29, 1981.

142 Webb, Walter P. "Oil Town Cleaned Up." *The State Trooper*, Vol. 8, No. 4 (Dec. 1926): 11–12.

154 Sowell, A. J. *History of Fort Bend County: Containing Biographical Sketches of Many Noted Characters.* Houston: W. H. Coyle & Co., 1904.

168 Stephens, Robert W. *Lone Wolf: The Story of Texas Ranger Captain M. T. Gonzaullas.* Dallas: Taylor Publishing Co., 1979.

172 *The New Handbook of Texas.* 6 vols. Austin: Texas State Historical Association, 1996.

204 Thompson, Cecilia. *History of Marfa and Presidio County, Texas, 1535–1946.* 2 vols. Austin: Nortex Press, 1985.

236 Braddy, Haldeen. *Mexico and the Old Southwest: People—Palaver—Places.* Port Washington, N.Y.: Kennikat Press, 1971.

240 *Memorial and Biographical History of McLennan, Falls, Bell and Coryell Counties, Texas.* Chicago: Lewis Publishing Co., 1893.

319 Sterling, William Warren. *Trails and Trials of a Texas Ranger.* Norman: University of Oklahoma Press, 1959.

320 United States. *Annual Report of the Attorney General of the United States for the Year 1918.* Washington, D.C.: Government Printing Office, 1918.

321 United States. *Annual Report of the Attorney General of the United States for the Year 1919.* Washington, D.C.: Government Printing Office, 1919.

322 United States. *Annual Report of the Attorney General of the United States for the Year 1920.* Washington, D.C.: Government Printing Office, 1920.

330 Myers, John. *The Border Wardens.* Englewood Cliffs, N.J.: Prentice-Hall, 1971.

333 Stephens, Robert W. *Texas Ranger Indian War Pensions.* Quanah, TX: Nortex Press, 1975.

403 United States. Senate. *Revolutions in Mexico.* 62nd Cong., 2nd sess. Washington, D.C.: Government Printing Office, 1913.

406 Casey, Robert J. *The Texas Border and Some Borderliners.* New York: Bobbs-Merrill Co., 1950.

416 Clendenen, Clarence C. *Blood on the Border: The United States Army and the Mexican Irregulars*. London: Macmillan Co., 1969.

417 Lea, Tom. *The King Ranch*, II, Boston: Little, Brown & Co., 1957.

421 Rausch, George J., Jr. "Victoriano Huerta: a Political Biography." Ph.D. dissertation, University of Illinois, 1960.

422 Smithers, W. D. "Bandit Raids in the Big Bend Country." *Sul Ross State College Bulletin.* XLIII, no. 3 (Sept 1963): 75–105.

424 Stambaugh, J. Lee and Lillian J. Stambaugh. *The Lower Rio Grande Valley of Texas*. San Antonio: Naylor Co., 1954.

425 Pierce, Frank C. *A Brief History of the Lower Rio Grande Valley*. Menasha, Wisconsin: George Banta Publishing Co., 1917.

428 *Corpus Christi Caller*, July 6, 7, 1925.

429 Appling, Arnolia, Marjorie Fairchild & Vivian Gray, comps. *Caldwell County Texas Cemetery Records*. n.p., 1981.

461 Wilkinson, J.B. *Laredo and the Rio Grande Frontier*. Austin: Jenkins Publishing Co., 1975.

463 Frost, Gordon H. and John H. Jenkins. *I'm Frank Hamer: The Life of a Texas Peace Officer*. Austin: Pemberton Press, 1968.

464 Gilliland, Maude T. *Rincon (Remote Dwelling Place): A Story of Life on a South Texas Ranch at the Turn of the Century*. Brownsville: Springman-King Co., 1964.

468 Paine, Albert Bigelow. *Captain Bill McDonald, Texas Ranger: A Story of Frontier Reform*. New York: J. J. Little & Ives Co., 1909.

469 Kilgore, D. E. *A Ranger Legacy: 150 Years of Service to Texas*. Austin: Madrona Press, 1973.

470 Gilliland, Maude T. *Horsebackers of the Brush Country: A Story of the Texas Rangers and Mexican Liquor Smugglers*. [Brownsville]: Springman-King Co., 1968.

471 Vertical Files, Texas Ranger Hall of Fame & Museum, Waco, Texas.

472 Martin, Jack. *Border Boss: Captain John R. Hughes, Texas Ranger*. Austin: State House Press, 1990.

479 Adams, Verdon R. *Tom White: The Life of a Lawman*. El Paso: Texas Western Press, 1972.

480 Sims, Orland L. *Gun-toters I Have Known*. Austin: Encino Press, 1967.

484 Raht, Carlysle Graham. *The Romance of Davis Mountains and Big Bend Country*. 2nd ed. Odessa, Texas: The Rahtbooks Co., 1963.

485 Peavey, John R. *Echoes From the Rio Grande*. n.p., 1963.

488 Smithers, W. D. *Chronicles of the Big Bend: A Photographic Memoir of Life on the Border*. Austin: Madrona Press, 1976.

496 Johnson, David Nathan. "Exiles and Intrigue: Francisco I. Madero and the Mexican Revolutionary Junta in San Antonio, 1910–1911." M.A. thesis, Trinity University, 1975.

497 Hatley, Allen G. *Texas Constables: A Frontier Heritage*. Lubbock: Texas Tech University Press, 1999.

499 Barnhill, John H. "The Punitive Expedition Against Pancho Villa: The Forced Motorization of the American Army." *Military History of Texas and the Southwest*. XIV, no. 3: 135–45.

504 Trow, Clifford Wayne. "Senator Albert B. Fall and Mexican Affairs, 1912–1921." Ph.D. dissertation, University of Colorado, 1966.

508 Rascoe, Jesse Ed. *The Treasure Album of Pancho Villa*. Toyahvale, Tex.: Frontier Book Co., 1962.

520 Webb, Walter Prescott, ed. *The Handbook of Texas*. vol. 1 (2 vols.). Austin: Texas State Historical Association, 1952.

522 Branda, Eldon Stephen, ed. *The Handbook of Texas: A Supplement*. Vol III. Austin: Texas State Historical Association, 1976.

525 Ingmire, Frances T. *Texas Rangers: Frontier Battalion, Minute Men, Commanding Officers, 1847–1900*. 6 vols. St. Louis, Mo.: Ingmire Publications, 1982.

530 Interview with Art Robertson, Jr., Nov. 29, 2004, Las Cruces, N.M.

552 Duncan, Virginia. "The Life of Captain Roy W. Aldrich." M.A. thesis, Sul Ross State Teachers College, 1942.

553 Cook, Christabel Hargett. *Salmon and Related Families*. Phoenix: Apex Printing Corp., 1983.

840 Nieman, Robert, "20th Century Shining Star: Frank Hamer," *Texas Ranger Dispatch Magazine*, No. 11 (Summer 2003).

841 Parsons, Chuck, "The Border Boss: John R. Hughes," *Texas Ranger Dispatch Magazine*, No. 10, Spring 2003.

842 Young, Lee, "'Go When You Get Ready,'" *Texas Ranger Dispatch Magazine*, No. 9, Winter 2002.

843 Young, Lee, "One-Armed Miller," *Texas Ranger Dispatch Magazine*, No. 8, Fall 2002.

844 Stephens, Bob, "Capt. Manuel Trazazas Gonzaullas," *Texas Ranger Dispatch Magazine*, No. 7, Summer 2002.

901 Vertical Files, The Haley Memorial Library and History Center, Midland, Texas.

1000 Gilliland, Maude T., comp. *Wilson County Texas Rangers, 1837–1977*. Brownsville: Springman-King Co., 1977.

1020 Pettey, Weston A. "The Seminole Incident and Tom Ross." *West Texas Historical Association Year Book*. 56 (1980): 133–42.

1021 Theoharis, Athan G. ed., with Tony G. Poveda, Susan Rosenfeld, and Richard Gid Powers. *The FBI: A Comprehensive Reference Guide*. New York: Checkmark Books, 2000.

1500 De la Garza, Beatrice. *A Law for the Lion: A Tale of Crime and Injustice in the Borderlands*. Austin: University of Texas Press, 2003.

1501 Alexander, Bob. *Fearless Dave Allison, Border Lawman: A Transitional Lawman on a Transitional Frontier*. Silver City, NM: High-Lonesome Books, 2003.

1502 Malsch, Brownson. *Captain M.T. Gonzaullas, Lone Wolf: The Only Texas Ranger Captain of Spanish Descent*. Austin: Shoal Creek Publishers, 1980.

1503 Tise, Sammy. *Texas County Sheriffs*. Albuquerque: Oakwood Printing, 1989.

1504 Goodrich, Pat Hill. *Captain Ransom, Texas Ranger: An American Hero (1874–1918)*. Nappanee, Ind.: Evangel Publishing House, 2007.

1505 Coffey, Jim. "Will Wright: Ranger and Prohibition," *Texas Ranger Dispatch Magazine*, No. 19, Winter 2006.

1506 "20th Century Shining Star: Harrison Hamer," *Texas Ranger Dispatch Magazine*, No. 17, Summer 2005.

1507 Spellman, Paul N. *Captain John H. Rogers, Texas Ranger*. Denton: University of North Texas Press, 2003.

1508 Rozeff, Norman, "The Harlingen Connection," Harlingen Historical Preservation Sociey (July 2203) *http://www.cameroncountyhistoricalcommission.org/Harlingen%20History.htm*

1509 Parsons, Chuck and Donaly E. Brice. *Texas Ranger N. O. Reynolds the Intrepid*. Honolulu: Talei Publishers, 2005.

1510 Gwynne, S. C. "The Next Frontier," *Texas Monthly*, August, 2007, pp 110–24, 178–81, 193–96.

1511 Parsons, Chuck. "George P. Durham: A Shining Star," *Texas Ranger Dispatch Magazine*, No. 22, Spring 2007, pp. 16–22.

1512 "Rangers Bob Goss and M. T. 'Lone Wolf' Gonzaullas," *Texas Ranger Dispatch*, No. 21, Dec. 2006, p. 1.

1514 "20th Century Shining Star: William Warren Sterling," *Texas Ranger Dispatch Magazine*, No. 15, Winter 2004.

1515 Stroud, David V., "Ranger Chapman's 1907 Winchester," *Texas Ranger Dispatch Magazine*, No. 13, Spring 2004.

1516 Whittington, Mike, "Hughes and Aten Solve the Williamson Family Murder," *Texas Ranger Dispatch Magazine*, No. 12, Winter 2003.

1517 Nieman, Robert, "The Hamers: Bud, Bobbie, & Harrison, Texas Ranger Descendants," interview Sept. 23, 2000. Texas Ranger Hall of Fame and Museum, Waco, Texas.

1518 Coffey, Jim and John T. Barnett, "Graham Barnett: Legend in the Big Bend," *Journal of Big Bend Studies*, 19 (2007): 97–124.

1519 Alexander, Bob. *Lawmen, Outlaws, and S. O. B.s: Gunfighters of the Old Southwest*. Vol. II. Silver City, NM: High-Lonesome Books, 2007.

1520 Brice, Donaly E. "John Jesse Sanders: Lawman and Texas Ranger," *The Plum Creek Almanac*. Luling, TX: The Genealogical and Historical Society of Caldwell County, (Spring 2008): 45–50.

1521 Letter from Steven A. Henrich's granddaughter, Jean Middlebrooks Shroyer of Marble Falls, Texas, to Louis R. Sadler, Nov. 3, 2005.

1522 Wyatt, Frederica, "Texas Ranger Crosses Dedicated," *The Junction Eagle* [Junction, TX], Feb. 4, 2006.

1523 Skelton, Bart, "A Border Lawman's Legacy—September 2004." *Guns & Ammo*. *http://www.gunsandammomag.com/gun_columns/border/db0409/*

A Genealogy, Family Trees and Family History Records online—*http://www.ancestry.com/*

1 Census records

aaa 1850

aa 1860

a 1870

b 1880

c 1890 fragment

d 1900

e 1910

f 1920

g 1930

h 1890 Veterans Schedules

i 1881 England Census

2 Birth, marriage, death records

a Social Security Death Index

b Texas Death Index, 1903–2000

c Texas Marriage Collection, 1814–1909 and 1966–2002

d Texas Marriages 1814–1900

e Texas Birth Index 1903–1997

f California Death Index 1940–1997

g England and Wales Free BMD Birth Index 1837–1983

h California Birth Index 1905–1995

i Ohio Deaths 1908–1944 and 1958–2002

j Tennessee State Marriages 1780–2002

k Alabama Marriage Collection, 1800–1964

1 N.C. Death Certificates 1909–1975

3 Military Records

a WWI Draft Registration Cards, 1917–1918

b U.S. Veterans Cemeteries Ca. 1800–2004

c WWI Civilian Draft Registration Cards

4 Trees and Community

a One World Tree

b Ancestry World Tree

c Family Data Collection—Individual Records

d Family Data Collection—Births

e Family Data Collection—Deaths

f Family Data Collection—Marriages

g Public Member Trees

5 Directories and Membership Lists

a City Directories

6 Immigration and Emigration

a U.S. Passport Applications, 1795–1925

B Family Search Internet Genealogy Service, The Church of Jesus Christ of Latter Day Saints—*http://www.familysearch.org/* FamilySearch.org data used by permission. Copyright © 2008 by Intellectual Reserve, Inc.

1 International Genealogical Index—North America (IGI Individual Records)

2 Ancestral File, Pedigree Resource File (Individual Record)

C Index to Texas Death Records, Bureau of Vital Statistics, Texas State Department of Health, Texas State Library, Austin, Texas.

D Nesbitt Memorial Library, Columbus, Texas—*http://www.columbustexas.net/library*

www.ingramcontent.com/pod-product-compliance
Lightning Source LLC
Chambersburg PA
CBHW050405110426
42812CB00006BA/1810
9780826347480